William Taubman received his undergraduate degree from Harvard and his Ph.D from Columbia. He is the Bertrand Snell Professor of Political Science at Amherst College, where he has taught for over thirty years. His previous books include *Nikita Khrushchev* (a collection of essays co-edited with Sergei Khrushchev and Abbott Gleason), *Moscow Spring* (written with Jane Taubman), and *Stalin's American Policy*. He chairs the Advisory Committee of the Cold War International History Project at the Woodrow Wilson International Center for Scholars in Washington, and is an Associate of the Davis Center for Russian and Eurasian Studies at Harvard University. He has held fellowships from the Wilson Center, the National Endowment for the Humanities, and the Harriman Institute at Columbia University. He lives with his wife, a professor of Russian, in Amherst, Massachusetts.

KHRUSHCHEV

THE MAN AND HIS ERA

WILLIAM TAUBMAN

First published in the United States by W. W. Norton & Co. in 2003
First published in Great Britain by The Free Press in 2003
An imprint of Simon & Schuster UK Ltd
A Viacom company
This edition published in 2004

1 3 5 7 9 10 8 6 4 2

Simon & Schuster UK Ltd
Africa House
64–78 Kingsway
London WC2B 6AH

www.simonsays.co.uk

Simon & Schuster Australia
Sydney

A CIP catalogue for this book is available
from the British Library.

ISBN: 0-7432-3166-X

Design by Brooke Koven
Printed and bound in Great Britain by
The Bath Press, Bath

To the memory of my parents,

NORA AND HOWARD TAUBMAN

CONTENTS

Note on Russian and Ukrainian Usage

There are several systems of transliteration of the Russian language. Throughout the text of this book I have used transliterations that will be most familiar or most accessible to the reader and most likely to capture the sound of Russian. However, in the Notes and Bibliography, when I cite specific Russian-language material, I employ the Library of Congress transliteration system, which is often used in library catalogs. So, for example, although Oleg Troyanovsky, one of Khrushchev's aides, appears as such in the text, when I refer to his Russian-language memoir, I spell his name Troianovskii.

During almost the entire period covered in this book, Ukraine was part of the Russian Empire and later of the Soviet Union. In that time Russian versions of Ukrainian personal and place-names were used in official, and often in informal, discourse. For that reason, and to avoid confusing readers, I use those Russian versions. However, for books and articles published, and interviews conducted, when Ukraine was an independent state, Ukrainian place-names are used. In the Index, Ukrainian public figures are identified by both Russian and Ukrainian versions of their names.

PREFACE

Ask many Westerners, and not a few Russians, and they're likely to recall Nikita Khrushchev as a crude, ill-educated clown who banged his shoe at the United Nations.[1] But the short, thick-set man with small, piercing eyes, protruding ears, and apparently unquenchable energy wasn't a Soviet joke even though he figures in so many of them. Rather, he was a complex man whose story combines triumph and tragedy for his country as well as himself.

Complicit in Stalinist crimes, Khrushchev attempted to de-Stalinize the Soviet Union. His daring but bumbling attempt to reform communism began the long, erratic process of putting a human face (initially his own) on an inhumane system. Not only did he help prepare the way for Mikhail Gorbachev and Boris Yeltsin a quarter of a century later, but Khrushchev's failure to set a stable and prosperous new course for his country anticipated the setbacks that would thwart their attempts at reform.

I saw Khrushchev for the first and only time in September 1959. Just before returning to college for my sophomore year, I caught a glimpse of him as his limousine drove through New York's Central Park during his tumultuous tour of the United States. In 1964, while on a Russian language-study tour of the USSR, I descended into a coal mine in Donetsk, Ukraine, where Khrushchev had worked as a young man. By the time I spent the academic year 1965–1966 as an exchange student at Moscow State University, he was out of power and in official disgrace. My student friends were grateful to Khrushchev for unmasking Stalin's crimes but ashamed that a man they regarded as a boor had been their country's leader. They reserved both a special affection and special disdain for Khrushchev, a combination that I can't help feeling myself as I finish writing his biography.[2]

In the early 1980s, after writing the book *Stalin's American Policy*,[3] I began to examine Khrushchev's American policy. Yet I soon found his personality more fascinating than his foreign policy, so I opted for a biography instead. If I had delivered the manuscript in 1989 as originally promised, the result would have been very different from this book.

During his time as Communist party leader, Khrushchev was remarkably loquacious. His speeches on agriculture alone fill eight volumes;[4] he seemed to give long interviews every other week. After his ouster from power in 1964, he was the first Soviet leader to publish his memoirs. But his public utterances were carefully edited and sanitized before being printed, and as initially published in English in 1970 and 1974, his memoirs did not include some of the most revealing passages he had dictated, material that he and his family declined to transfer to the West.[5] In the mid-1980s Soviet party archives were still off-limits, and most Western documents from Khrushchev's reign had not yet been declassified. As late as 1988, when I spent five months in Moscow on the academic exchange program, I thought I couldn't admit that my subject was Khrushchev (instead I called it "the origins of U.S.-Soviet détente") lest I alarm the Soviet authorities, although in retrospect, I think I was probably more cautious than they were. I managed to interview just a handful of people who had connections with Khrushchev; it was only at the very end of my stay that I arranged to telephone, but not actually to meet, Khrushchev's son Sergei.

By 1991 the situation had changed radically. Khrushchev-era memoirs had begun to appear (including books by Sergei and by Nikita Khrushchev's son-in-law Aleksei Adzhubei, the former editor of the government newspaper *Izvestia*); a third volume of Khrushchev's memoirs (containing material he had held back in 1970) was published in the United States; and an edition of his recollections, prepared by Sergei Khrushchev, started coming out in the history journal *Voprosy istorii*.[6] Asked by an American publisher to translate and edit Sergei Khrushchev's and Adzhubei's books, I used the opportunity to pepper them with questions, getting answers that I hope enriched their books, but that certainly have mine.[7]

With the fall of the USSR, long-closed Soviet archives finally opened, erratically and not necessarily permanently, but at least for a while. The Presidential Archive (formerly the Politburo Archive), which contains particularly sensitive material on Soviet leaders, and the KGB archives remain closed to all but a favored few, but key party depositories became accessible, not only in Moscow but throughout the former Soviet Union. Fortunately, some of these turned out to contain carbon copies of documents that the secretive Soviets thought had been preserved in the Politburo Archive alone.

Over the next ten years I worked off and on in archives in Moscow, Kiev, and Donetsk and interviewed Khrushchev family members, Kremlin colleagues, subordinates who worked for and against him, and people who knew him long before he succeeded Stalin in 1953. With the help of Sergei Khrushchev, I traveled to Nikita Khrushchev's birthplace in Kalinovka and visited his adolescent haunts in eastern Ukraine. Since the Soviet era was only just over, some former officials I wished to see were still reluctant to talk to an American, while archivists were unsure what they could safely show. In that sense, my efforts to track people down, to get them to see me and to talk candidly, and to unearth long-hidden documents involved as much detective work as it did traditional academic research.

My next challenge became how to organize and interpret all this material. Until the fall of the USSR, and especially during the Gorbachev era, the key questions about Khrushchev concerned his reforms: why and how he attempted them and why they largely miscarried. Since 1991, however, Khrushchev's career has assumed a larger meaning. For taken in its entirety, his life holds a mirror to the Soviet age as a whole. Revolution, civil war, collectivization and industrialization, terror, world war, cold war, late Stalinism, post-Stalinism—Khrushchev took part in them all. What attracted so many men and women to revolution and communism? What kept them loyal after the terrible bloodletting began? What led at least some of them to break with their own past and try to reform the regime? Finally, what frustrated and defeated them, bringing on a long era of stagnation followed by the fall of the Soviet Union itself? Khrushchev's biography can provide at least some of the answers.

Even as I broadened my focus to give equal time to all periods of his life, I narrowed it so as to concentrate on his character. In some ways Khrushchev was the archetypical Soviet man, but he was also unique. Countless workers and peasants rose through the ranks after the revolution, but he climbed to the very top. While most of his Kremlin colleagues became impersonal cogs in the Stalinist machine, he somehow retained his humanity. All of Stalin's men worked overtime to please him, but Khrushchev was preternaturally hyperactive, endlessly prone to palaver with everyone from collective farm milkmaids to heads of state. His most important foreign and domestic policies were also exceptional, ranging from his denouncing of Stalin to secretly installing missiles in Cuba to suddenly removing those rockets so as to end the nuclear confrontation that his own reckless gamble had provoked.

This pattern leaped out at me from the historical record. Seeking to understand its psychological as well as political roots, I consulted theories of personality[8] and asked several psychologists and psychiatrists to serve as sounding boards for my notions. Not being a psychologist myself, however, I have for the most part eschewed technical terms, seeking instead to portray Khrushchev's character in ordinary language.

The truism that historical documents don't speak for themselves but have to be interpreted applies particularly to Soviet documents prepared with an eye on what the leader wanted and on the consequences if he didn't get it. I have relied heavily on such documents but have interpreted them in the light of other sources. Post-Soviet Russians who write memoirs or are interviewed long after the fact are now remarkably free to tell the truth, but only as they remember or choose to remember it. Many of them have long-standing scores to settle, which they do with more relish than regard for facts. In that sense documents provide a useful corrective to memories, which in turn check them.

Khrushchev kept no diary and didn't write many letters. He was too busy to do so, it wasn't safe to put one's inner thoughts on paper in Stalin's time, and given his somewhat shaky hold on Russian grammar and spelling, he preferred to dictate to a stenographer than to write. In any case, whatever private papers he had accumulated were confiscated by the KGB after his death and have not been released since. In the absence of a personal archive, Khrushchev's memoirs take on particular importance, but they also present special problems. He was mostly alone when he dictated them into a tape recorder, long after the events in question, with no access to documents or archives and with one eye on the omnipresent KGB. He had a prodigious memory, but also a deep need to justify himself to future generations. I have tried to distinguish what is factual in Khrushchev's memoirs from the way he wished to see himself and be seen by others. Yet I have also learned a lot from what I have come to think of as Khrushchev's myth of himself.

The full Russian version of Khrushchev's memoirs edited by his son covers more ground than the three English-language volumes. But occasionally the English volumes contain revealing passages not found in the Russian edition.[9] Verbatim tapes and transcripts of his memoirs, which I've also examined, bring one even closer to Khrushchev, but in their rambling, disjointed form, they can be difficult to follow.[10] I considered quoting from these transcripts instead of the edited versions, but that not only would be a trial for readers, but would betray Khrushchev himself, who supervised his son's and others' editing while he lived and surely wanted it to be continued after his death. Khrushchev in the flesh spoke in considerably less polished fashion, as the reader will see from verbatim examples of his speech quoted in this book. But as far as I can tell, the published Russian and English versions of his memoirs are true to the text that he dictated, haltingly but with fierce determination, at the very end of his life.

WT

Amherst, Massachusetts

February 2002

INTRODUCTION

In Stalin's last years Soviet officials shunned gatherings at Western embassies; at most, a couple of low-level Soviet diplomats would show up, stand around stiffly and formally, and leave as soon as they could. Under Khrushchev on the other hand, especially in the mid-1950s, Soviet leaders frequently mixed with Western diplomats and journalists, who crowded around them at diplomatic receptions. Khrushchev himself regularly attended such gatherings, circulating freely among the guests, bantering with correspondents, telling jokes, even sending an occasional message to foreign leaders through correspondents from their countries.[1]

One evening in November 1957 he seemed in what witnesses described as "a particularly buoyant and garrulous mood," and with good reason: A few months earlier he had thwarted an attempted Kremlin coup against him; more recently he had fired the top Soviet military man, Marshal Georgy Zhukov, who had become too powerful and popular for his own good. With guests milling around him, Khrushchev recounted a story by the Ukrainian writer Volodymyr Vinnichenko that he said he had read when he was young.[2]

"Once upon a time," Khrushchev said, "there were three men in a prison: a social democrat, an anarchist and a humble little Jew—a half-educated fellow named Pinya. They decided to elect a cell leader to watch over distribution of food, tea and tobacco. The anarchist, a big burly fellow, was against such a lawful process as electing authority. To show his contempt for law and order, he proposed that the semi-educated Jew, Pinya, be elected. They elected Pinya.

"Things went well, and they decided to escape. But they realized that the first man to go through the tunnel would be shot at by the guard. They all turned to the big brave anarchist, but he was afraid to go. Suddenly poor little Pinya drew himself up and said, 'Comrades, you elected me by democratic process as your leader. Therefore, I will go first.'

"The moral of the story is that no matter how humble a man's beginning, he achieves the stature of the office to which he is elected.

"That little Pinya—that's me."

According to a Central Intelligence Agency "personality sketch" prepared for President Kennedy prior to the Vienna summit in 1961, the story the Soviet leader told revealed "consciousness of his humble origin," his "sense of personal accomplishment," plus his "confidence that his vigor, initiative and capacity are equal to his station."[3] Or was he really so confident? Did the story not imply that because of his humble origin, and despite his vigor, initiative, and accomplishments, Khrushchev was far from certain of his capacities? To appreciate that possibility, consider the rest of the Vinnichenko story.

The title, "Talisman," suggests that Pinya's transformation is nothing short of incredible. For Pinya is not just an ordinary underdog; he is the saddest of sad sacks. When he worked as an apprentice for a tinsmith, his boss beat him about the head with a soldering iron, while other tormentors smeared his sore lips with salt and forced him to eat out of a dog's dish. All these he endured silently, telling himself, "Some people are bigger, richer and more powerful, and some are smaller, poorer and weaker, but you, Pinya, are the smallest, poorest and weakest of all."

To his fellow prisoners' mockery, Pinya responds with sadly obsequious smiles. The idea of electing him as their leader is the biggest joke of all. "He wasn't suited for the job, he didn't know anything, he was only an ill-educated worker." But overnight Pinya proves himself efficient, responsible, decisive and bold. "Without question," says Vinnichenko's narrator, "what happened was a miracle, the kind that occurs in fairy tales when the hero, a lousy, beaten-down, spat-upon Vanya-the-Fool suddenly obtains a talisman from somewhere and turns into a famous hero and heir to the imperial throne." If Khrushchev really saw himself as Pinya (as a poor little Jew, no less, in a land in which anti-Semitism ran deep), his doubts about himself were more profound than he ever admitted. Moreover, the end of Pinya's story foreshadows Khrushchev's own fate. By insisting on being first through the tunnel, Pinya ensures his own martyrdom. While he grabs the sentry's rifle and sinks his teeth into the guard's leg, his fellow prisoners escape. Before Pinya himself can get away, three other guards approach and club him to death.[4]

Like Pinya, Khrushchev rose from the humblest of backgrounds to unimaginable heights. Not only did he reach Stalin's inner circle and survive nearly two decades there, but he also bested Kremlin rivals who seemed far more likely than he to succeed Stalin. Khrushchev tried bravely to humanize and modernize the Soviet system. Having served Stalin loyally for nearly three decades, he unmasked him and helped release and rehabilitate millions of his victims. Whereas Stalin was largely responsible for triggering the cold war, Khrushchev tried awkwardly to improve relations with the West. He also attempted to revitalize areas of Soviet life—agriculture, industry, and culture among others—that had languished under Stalinism.

All this deserves to be recognized. But Khrushchev's miraculous rise was itself deeply tainted by his complicity in Stalin's crimes. His de-Stalinization was erratically implemented and largely reversed by his successors. He himself crushed the Hungarian Revolution of 1956 and arrested many who dared challenge him at home. Moreover, although he held several summits with Western leaders and coauthored the partial nuclear test ban of 1963, he also provoked the Berlin and Cuban crises and escalated the arms race he had set out to diminish. Not to mention his nonstop reorganizing of party and state, his erratic interference in the economy, his addiction to stultifying collectivism in agriculture, and his tumultuous love-hate relationship with the intelligentsia, all of which helped bring on the coup that ousted him in October 1964.

To be sure, not all of Khrushchev's troubles were of his own making. Although the Stalinist system cried out for change, as even Khrushchev's most Stalinist colleagues recognized, it also stubbornly resisted reform. His role as Communist party leader required him to pronounce on multiple matters of which he knew little or nothing. But too often Khrushchev made a bad situation even worse. His "secret speech" denouncing Stalin sparked bloody upheavals in Eastern Europe. He alienated almost everyone, including his own allies and supporters. Toward the very end, his behavior was almost surreal: stubbornly persistent in futile policies, seemingly blind to his disintegrating political base, recklessly unresponsive to the growing conspiracy against him.

Behavior like this demands attention to Khrushchev's psyche, attention of the sort paid by some twenty American psychiatrists and psychologists at the behest of the United States Central Intelligence Agency in

1960. According to an account of the study that the CIA would rather not have seen published, specialists took note of Khrushchev's "depressions and vulnerability to alcohol" but focused on his "hypomanic" character.[5] A standard psychology manual defines "hypomania" as a "syndrome that is similar to, but not as severe as that described by the term 'mania.'" As with full-fledged mania accompanied by its bipolar opposite depression, hypomania is commonly associated with "lability of mood, with rapid shifts to anger or depression."[6]

Psychoanalyst Nancy McWilliams's listing of hypomanic characteristics describes Khrushchev almost perfectly: "Elated, energetic, self-promoting, witty and grandiose . . . Overtly cheerful, highly social, given to idealization of others, work-addicted, flirtatious and articulate while covertly . . . guilty about aggression toward others, incapable of being alone . . . corruptible and lacking a systematic approach in cognitive style . . . Grand schemes, racing thoughts, extended freedom from ordinary physical requirements such as food and sleep. . . . constantly 'up'—until exhaustion eventually sets in."[7] Khrushchev's wife, Nina Petrovna Khrushcheva, put it more simply to U. S. Ambassador Llewellyn Thompson's wife, Jane, as the Soviet delegation flew toward the United States in September 1959: "He's either all the way up or all the way down."[8]

Ups and downs, pauper to Soviet prince, both Stalinist and de-Stalinizer, brutal and decent in turn—Khrushchev is a study in unresolved contrasts, and in pathos. As the result of his miraculous rise, the man whom artist Ernst Neizvestny called "the most uncultured man I've ever met" found himself in over his head.[9] He played the role of Pinya to get to the top; although no one could survive in Stalin's court without being a master Machiavellian, it was safer to resemble Vanya-the-Fool. However, the reason that Khrushchev performed that part so brilliantly is that it was not just a role but a reality. In the end he hoped that his accomplishments outweighed his failings, that Pinya-like, he had freed his fellow prisoners from their Stalinist chains and set them on a path to a humane Soviet society. In fact, he began the process that destroyed the Soviet regime, while at the same time undermining himself. "After I die," he said toward the very end of his life, "they will place my actions on a scale—on one side evil, on the other side good. I hope the good will outweigh the bad."[10] Whether it does is for the reader to judge.

KHRUSHCHEV

CHAPTER ONE

The Fall: October 1964

Midway between Gagra and Sukhumi, in the Abkhaz region of Georgia, a particularly scenic slice of land juts out into the Black Sea. On a Cape Pitsunda promontory rising perhaps three hundred feet, with tall Caucasian mountains in the background, stands a forest of trees that have the appearance of yellow pine, but whose needles are more like cedar. Behind a stucco wall and a massive iron gate, in the midst of spacious, carefully tended grounds, are three magnificent villas connected by paths that zigzag among the trees, one of them a slatted three-foot-wide boardwalk stretching more than a half mile along a low wall that borders the gravel beach. Several blue-and-white canvas-covered cabanas were scattered along the boardwalk in the fall of 1964. One of them was reserved for guests who liked to sleep next to the water; the others were used as dressing rooms. A few hundred feet from the house stood a seaside platform with wicker chairs where guests were often served fresh fruits under a large umbrella.[1]

The villas were built in the early 1950s on Khrushchev's order.[2] One was assigned to him and his family; the other two were occupied on a Soviet-style "time-sharing" basis by other top Soviet leaders. Khrushchev's was a large white stucco two-story building with airy ground-floor rooms open to the sea and with white draperies and tasteful furniture built of what looked like bleached teakwood. On the second floor, a long balcony extended the length of the house. Attached to the house were a small indoor gymnasium fitted with a badminton net and other fitness equipment, an immense swimming pool whose glass enclosure rolled back to reveal an unobstructed view of the sea, and a large veranda a stone's throw from the shore. Opening onto the veranda through French doors was a smallish study with mahogany-paneled walls, a curved sofa and several leather-upholstered chairs tastefully centered on a large oriental rug, and a large mahogany desk in the corner covered with a battery of telephones. One of these phones, a special KGB-controlled high-frequency line, connected Soviet party and government offices (and their occupants' residences and dachas) around the country. There were extensions in Khrushchev's second-floor bedroom and office, in aides' offices at the villa, and by the pool. It was the high-frequency phone that rang on the evening of October 12, 1964.

That autumn Khrushchev seemed at the peak of his power. In fact, he was on the verge of disaster. Three years after a new party program had pledged Communist abundance by 1980, food shortages had spread throughout the land. Party officials resented the loss of privileges and the job insecurity he had made their lot. For the military, deep cuts in troop strength and conventional weapons were the last straw. The liberal intelligentsia had lost faith, and rank-and-file workers and peasants too had turned against him.

Faced with this grim situation, Khrushchev had talked vaguely of retiring, but he couldn't bring himself to act. Instead he was hatching plans for further reforms. Some ideas—such as a new constitution that would limit the terms of Soviet leaders (except of course for certain indispensable ones like him) and perhaps even provide for multiple candidates in legislative elections—were ahead of his time. Others took his penchant for reorganization to what his colleagues regarded as ridiculous extremes. His latest brainstorm for energizing Soviet agriculture was to create nine centralized agencies in Moscow, each responsible for a particular crop nationwide. In standard Soviet parlance, each "main administration" would be known by an abbreviation such as *Glavzerno* (MainGrain), *Glavmyaso* (MainMeat), *Glavsakhar* (MainSugar), etc. Besides anticipating that this latest inspiration would fail, leaving them to pick up the pieces, his Kremlin colleagues joked about which benighted bureaucrat would have the honor of heading up MainGoose or MainSheep.[3]

By the summer of 1964 Khrushchev badly needed a vacation. Instead he undertook a hectic two-and-a-half-week trip to Egypt that accomplished little, a three-week Scandinavian journey consisting mostly of sightseeing, a tour of the Soviet farm belt that provided scant cause for satisfaction, and a visit to the Tyura-Tam missile test site (later called Baikonur) in Kazakhstan in the company of generals who could no longer stand their commander in chief. Only in early October did he allow himself to take a vacation.

Khrushchev liked to tell visitors that he came to Pitsunda to think as well as to rest. "There are some things that can be done right only if you take the time they require," he told visiting American magazine editor Norman Cousins in April 1963. "A chicken has to sit quietly for a certain time if she expects to lay an egg. If I have something to hatch, I have to take the time to do it right."[4]

All too often Khrushchev hadn't taken the time to do things right. Instead of thinking things through, he could rarely sit still, even on vacation. He preferred visiting neighboring farms or sanatoriums, filling his days with meetings with Soviet officials or foreign leaders and guests. In October 1964 he did concentrate on his work, attending to incoming ambassadorial and intelligence telegrams and planning for a November Central Committee plenum at which, he had threatened his Kremlin colleagues, he might replace some of them with leaders more energetic and effective than they were.[5] In between working sessions, he took long walks by the sea several times a day.

It was during his evening walk on October 12, in the company of Anastas Mikoyan, the Armenian Communist who had been a Kremlin fixture since Lenin's time and was now Khrushchev's chief ally in the ruling party Presidium, that the high-frequency phone rang. The two men were halfway down the boardwalk, followed closely by a bodyguard, when another security officer ran up. Leonid Brezhnev, the number two man in the Kremlin, was calling from Moscow. After turning back to the house, Khrushchev and Mikoyan entered the study, where Khrushchev picked up the phone. According to Brezhnev, the Presidium wanted to hold a special meeting the next day in the capital.

"Why?" Khrushchev demanded. "On what issue?"

"On agriculture and some others," Brezhnev explained.

"Decide things without me!" Khrushchev ordered curtly.

"We can't decide without you," Brezhnev replied. "Members have already gathered. We are asking you to come."

"I'm on vacation. What could be so urgent? I'll be back in two weeks, and we'll discuss it then." After a pause Khrushchev continued. "I don't understand any of this. What do you mean you all got together? We'll be discussing agricultural questions at the November plenum. There'll be plenty of time to talk about everything!"

Brezhnev insisted. Finally, Khrushchev agreed to return to Moscow the next day if a plane could be prepared on short notice. After instructing a security man to contact his personal pilot, and other aides to move up the next day's luncheon with the visiting French minister of state Gaston Palevsky, Khrushchev and Mikoyan returned to the path by the beach.

They walked in silence until Khrushchev spoke. "You know, Anastas, they haven't got any urgent agricultural problems. I think the call is connected with what Sergei was telling us."[6]

KHRUSHCHEV'S SON Sergei worked as a control systems engineer for Soviet missile designer Vladimir Chelomei. What Sergei had been telling his father and Mikoyan was that their colleagues in the Presidium were conspiring against Khrushchev.

Sergei learned of the plot in September 1964 from the chief bodyguard of Nikolai Ignatov, a high party official who was a central figure in the conspiracy. Trying to sound a warning, the security man had called the Khrushchev residence, reached Sergei when his father was at the Kazakhstan test site, and then recounted what he knew of the conspiracy when the two met for a secret rendezvous in the woods outside Moscow.

Earlier that summer Khrushchev's daughter Rada, married to Aleksei Adzhubei, Central Committee member and the editor of the government newspaper *Izvestia*, received a phone call from a woman with "important information." When Rada declined to see her, the woman blurted out that she knew of a plot to oust Khrushchev. Told by Rada to inform the KGB, the woman objected, "How can I call them if the KGB chairman himself is present at the meetings? That's why I wanted to talk to you."

Because the KGB chief Vladimir Semichastny was a friend of Rada's husband, she didn't take the tip seriously. Khrushchev had taught all his children not to "poke your noses" into politics. So she politely asked her caller not to call again.

Another tip reached Rada from the former business manager of the Central Committee. This time she consulted with a trusted family friend, who thought her informer was hypersuspicious by nature. So Rada ignored this warning too.

A third signal arrived from Soviet Georgia, where Adzhubei lieutenant Melor Sturua's brother, a high-ranking party official, deduced what was up from a hint by Georgian party leader Vasily Mzhavanadze. Devi Sturua told his story to Adzhubei. But Adzhubei too never informed Khrushchev.[7]

It took Sergei a week to tell him after his father returned to Moscow from Kazakhstan; he broke the family taboo during a Sunday morning walk at the Khrushchev dacha near the Moscow River. Showing no emotion, Khrushchev heard him out in silence and then said, "You've done the right thing." He asked Sergei to repeat the names of Presidium members allegedly involved in the plot, thought for a moment, and then snorted, "No, it's incredible. Brezhnev, [Nikolai] Podgorny, [Aleksandr] Shelepin—they're completely different types. It can't be. Ignatov—that's possible. He's very dissatisfied, and he's not a good man anyway. But what can he have in common with the others?"

Turning back to the dacha, Khrushchev cautioned Sergei not to tell anyone else about his meeting with Ignatov's bodyguard. But the very next day at work Khrushchev himself alerted one of the plotters. "Evidently what you told me is nonsense," he told his son that same evening. "I was leaving the Council of Ministers with Mikoyan and Podgorny, and I summarized your story in a couple of words. Podgorny simply laughed at me. 'How can you think such a thing, Nikita Sergeyevich?' Those were his actual words."[8]

Sergei found his father's behavior "strange, illogical and inexplicable." What had he achieved by telling Podgorny? "Did he expect to evoke a confession? He had been guilty of naiveté at times in the past, but never in a situation like this."[9]

"Strange, illogical and inexplicable" is putting it mildly. Those scheming to oust Khrushchev lived in fear as much as hope. Brezhnev himself was particularly apprehensive. At the Kazakhstan test range, he groveled before Khrushchev, running after the boss's fedora when it blew away in the wind, beating a younger man to it, and carefully brushing away dirt and dust before returning it to Khrushchev's head.[10] More than once in September, Brezhnev called the KGB chief Semichastny, who was on vacation in the south, telling him to prepare to launch the coup, only to phone back almost immediately reversing his previous order.[11] One morning in early October, Brezhnev asked Moscow party boss Nikolai Yegorychev to drop by Brezhnev's Kutuzovsky Prospekt residence on his way to work. Pale and shaking, Brezhnev led him into a corner room.

"Kolya," stammered Brezhnev, "Khrushchev knows everything. All is lost. He'll shoot us all."

Brezhnev was sniffling and almost "broke into tears." Yegorychev tried to calm him, but Brezhnev refused to be reassured. "You don't know Khrushchev, you don't know Khrushchev," he kept repeating.[12]

Apparently Brezhnev didn't either. For even after being informed of the plot, Khrushchev did nothing to resist it. Shortly after he reached Pitsunda, one of the coconspirators, Krasnodar Province party boss Georgy Vorobyov, arrived for a visit. Khrushchev asked Vorobyov about his alleged conversations with Ignatov, Vorobyov denied them, and Khrushchev left it at that.

"It turns out nothing of the sort happened," Khrushchev told Sergei, who arrived in Pitsunda shortly afterward. "[Vorobyov] assured us that the information from that man—I've forgotten his name—was sheer fantasy. He [Vorobyov] spent the whole day here. Brought a couple of turkeys as a present, fine looking ones too. Drop by the kitchen and have a look."[13]

Khrushchev wasn't as oblivious as he seemed. Several days later he telephoned Presidium member Dmitri Polyansky, demanded to know what was going on behind his back in Moscow, and threatened to fly back himself to find out. To Polyansky's reply that Presidium members would be glad to see him, Khrushchev replied sarcastically, "So you'll be pleased, will you?" But this only prompted the plotters to act more quickly.[14]

Brezhnev and company feared Khrushchev's erratic behavior might be a trick, that he wouldn't return to Moscow after all. Brezhnev called Semichastny on and off all evening on October 12, demanding further information. Only toward midnight did Semichastny assure him that Khrushchev's plane was being readied.[15] Even then he feared an unpleasant surprise. After all, Semichastny later remarked, the old man "had crushed the likes of Malenkov and Molotov—all of them. As the saying goes, nature and his mama provided him with everything he needed: firmness of will, quick-wittedness and capacity for fast, careful thinking. When I went to brief him, I had to be prepared for anything. With Lyonia [Brezhnev] I could do it with my eyes closed. All I had to do was tell a couple of jokes and that was it."[16]

Yet that same evening in Pitsunda, an hour after Brezhnev's call, Sergei found his father standing alone in the villa dining room, sipping mineral water and looking "tired and distraught." Before his son could say anything, Khrushchev snapped, "Don't pester me!" and walked slowly toward his bedroom. "Good night," he muttered without turning around.[17]

The next morning dawned bright and warm with the sun breaking through a thin fog and the gardens between the house and sea bursting with flowers. After breakfast Khrushchev conferred on the veranda about the day's schedule and read through the most urgent telegrams that had arrived overnight. Presently the French delegation headed by Minister of State Palevsky appeared on the long, winding driveway leading up to the front door. Khrushchev rose slowly, donned his jacket, and moved to meet them. Usually he introduced such guests to his family before getting down to business; this time he didn't even glance at Sergei. Often visitors ended up staying for hours; this time they were gone after thirty minutes.

During the light lunch that followed—vegetable soup and boiled perch—Khrushchev and Mikoyan ate in silence. Then it was time to go. As usual, the woman who managed the dacha presented Khrushchev with a farewell bouquet of autumn flowers. Khrushchev had just settled himself in the front seat of his oversize ZIL limousine when a barrel-chested general, the commander of the Transcaucasian Military District, rushed up to the car. Since the heads of the Georgian party and government were in Moscow to take part in the planned coup, the general had been assigned to accompany the republic's honored guest to the airport. It was his job to see that Khrushchev got there in time to be overthrown.

At the Adler airport, Khrushchev's longtime personal pilot, General Nikolai Tsybin, who had flown his boss safely through World War II and around the world as Soviet leader, was waiting by the plane. Khrushchev and Mikoyan entered the rear cabin, in which passenger seats had been replaced by a sofa, two easy chairs, and a table. This was the leader's domain; staff members traveled in the forward cabin. But in the air, as on vacation, Khrushchev didn't like to be alone. If he wasn't bent over papers surrounded by aides and stenographers, he usually invited some of them back just to talk. This time, however, only he and Mikoyan sat in the rear. "Leave the two of us alone," Khrushchev ordered gruffly; when a stewardess tried to serve Armenian cognac, mineral water, and hors d'oeuvres, she too was swiftly shooed away.

Moscow in mid-October is often gray with cold rain, but the sun was shining brightly on the thirteenth, when Khrushchev's jetliner touched down smoothly at Vnukovo-2, the airport south of the city reserved for official arrivals and departures, and taxied toward the glass-enclosed government pavilion. Ordinarily the leader's top party and government colleagues were lined up waiting to welcome him home. Although he loved being met, Khrushchev usually grumped at them for leaving their desks, adding good-naturedly, "Do you think I don't know the way without you?" This time, however, the tarmac was empty except for three figures approaching in the distance. By the time the stairway was rolled up to the plane's door, the KGB chief Semichastny, accompanied by the head of the Soviet equivalent of the U.S. Secret Service, and an official of the USSR Supreme Soviet were at the bottom of it.

Khrushchev was the first to descend the stairs.

"Glad you've arrived safely, Nikita Sergeyevich," said the round-faced forty-year-old Semichastny, who owed his remarkably rapid rise to Khrushchev. Khrushchev had made him a high official of the Ukrainian Young Communist League at the age of twenty-two in 1946; in 1961, when he was all of thirty-seven, Semichastny had taken charge of the Soviet secret police. While his benefactor was still at Pitsunda, Semichastny had sent Khrushchev's longtime chief bodyguard packing, and the moment Khrushchev reached the Kremlin, a fresh set of security guards took control of his Moscow residence and dacha.[18]

Back at Vnukovo-2, Semichastny shook hands with Khrushchev but averted his eyes as he did so. "They've all gathered at the Kremlin," he said. "They're waiting for you."[19]

"Let's go, Anastas," Khrushchev muttered to Mikoyan. The pavilion was empty except for security men posted at the four corners. Outside the door on the other side stood Khrushchev's massive ZIL-111 limousine, and behind it several other black cars: Mikoyan's ZIL and Semichastny's only slightly less imposing Chaika limousine, several Volga sedans for lesser lights in Khrushchev's entourage, plus security cars.

Khrushchev and Mikoyan got into one car. His bodyguard slammed the rear door shut and leaped into the front seat. With Semichastny following the Khrushchev security car in his own, the procession raced down the eight-lane Leninsky Prospekt toward the center of the city with policemen stopping traffic along the way. Past the inner ring road, left onto Dimitrov Street, across the Moscow River, and sharply right up a short incline into the Kremlin through the Borovitsky Gate.

THE PRESIDIUM'S meeting room on the second floor of the old tsarist Senate building was two doors down the hall from Khrushchev's office. When late-arriving members entered the room shortly before 4:00 P.M. on October 13, they found Khrushchev in his usual chairman's seat at the end of a long, rectangular green baize-covered table, with other Presidium members and candidate members and Central Committee secretaries, seated around the other three sides. With a few exceptions, all present were Khrushchev protégés, promoted by him to high office, and veterans of past battles in which they had backed him against his enemies. Yet none of them, except for Mikoyan, was about to say a word in his defense.

Looking sunburned but hardly refreshed from his aborted vacation, Khrushchev opened the meeting.[20] Called on to explain why the special session had been summoned, the burly, beetle-browed Brezhnev launched into a searing indictment of his former patron. Two years earlier, when Khrushchev divided the party into industrial and agricultural wings so as to guide the economy better, Brezhnev had led the chorus of praise. Now he charged that Khrushchev's reform "contradicted Lenin's teaching" and "sowed disorganization" in both industry and agriculture.

Khrushchev had been treating his colleagues "rudely," Brezhnev continued. He had gotten into the habit of "making decisions over lunch," had "ignored others' opinions," and frequently seemed to be distracted, virtually "in a state of depression." In the midst of preparations for the coming November Central Committee plenum, he had disappeared on vacation, so that his Presidium colleagues "knew nothing about them." As usual, Khrushchev was acting "unilaterally, ignoring the Presidium."

"Your behavior," said Brezhnev to his boss, "is incomprehensible." That was why Khrushchev's colleagues had called him back from Pitsunda. The subject of the meeting was not agriculture, Brezhnev declared, but Khrushchev himself.

Briefly and haltingly Khrushchev began to defend himself. He had long served the party and people. Even now he had responded to the Presidium's sudden summons to return to Moscow. He admitted he had made mistakes, but he considered the people around him his friends.

"You have no friends here," Gennady Voronov shouted.

"Why are you doing this?" Khrushchev demanded, his voice rising. "Why?"

"Wait a minute," someone shouted. "You listen to us for a change."

Pyotr Shelest, short, broad-shouldered, and completely bald, but with thick, bushy eyebrows, began politely. "We have respected you and learned much from you," he said, but "you have become a changed person." Khrushchev had turned Central Committee plenums into mass meetings at which "no one can speak frankly." His pledge to overtake America in agricultural output, made in 1957 without his consulting his Presidium colleagues, had turned from an embarrassment into a disaster. Khrushchev was "unpredictable, arbitrary, and unrestrained."

Next to speak was the thickset, bespectacled Voronov. "It's become impossible to get anything done in the Presidium," he said. "Instead of the Stalin cult, we have the cult of Khrushchev." Although Voronov was the Presidium's expert on agriculture, Khrushchev monopolized policy making in that area, proclaiming "truths" (such as "cucumbers need to be salted," "fertilizers increase output," and "bees pollinate buckwheat") that "any peasant already knew." During the last three and half years Voronov hadn't been able to express his opinion without being "shouted at and insulted." He declared: "It's time to send Comrade Khrushchev into retirement."

Next was Aleksandr Shelepin's turn. Forty-six years old, darkly handsome, and openly ambitious, Iron Shurik (as he was known to his friends) owed his spectacular rise to Khrushchev, from Young Communist League leader to Central Committee official to KGB chief in 1959 to Central Committee secretary. He was clearly a long-term threat to Brezhnev, but the two men put mutual suspicions aside to smash their former benefactor. Shelepin accused Khrushchev of being "coarse, demonic, and infected with inordinate conceit"; he was also "hasty, erratic, and inclined to intrigues." The "rudeness" of which Lenin had once accused Stalin "applies fully to you." Khrushchev had become "Bonapartist" in his use of "crude threats" and had surrounded himself with "sycophants." In an act of crass favoritism, he had written off millions in debt incurred by a collective farm in his home village of Kalinovka. Shelepin accused him of bringing the USSR to the brink of war in the 1956 Suez crisis, of mishandling the Berlin crisis, and of "juggling the fate of the world" in Cuba.

Andrei Kirilenko stressed Khrushchev's isolation. It had become impossible to get an audience or even to consult with him about your work. Khrushchev hadn't telephoned Kirilenko for almost three years! Instead he spent his time berating people, calling them fatheads, and dismissing them with curses like "Why don't you look up your own ass?"

Khrushchev blamed his own mistakes on party leaders of constituent Soviet republics, charged Byelorussian party boss Kirill Mazurov. As a result of the Khrushchev cult, there was no genuine discussion at party conclaves. The same fawning and flattering had led to discord in the international Communist movement.

Leonid Yefremov, Khrushchev's first deputy for the Russian Republic, charged him with making foreign policy "in ad hoc fashion," either "over lunch" or "in the course of reading telegrams."[21] Because Mikhail Suslov had been appointed a Central Committee secretary by Stalin in 1947, he was less beholden to Khrushchev than were the others. The tall, ascetic Suslov looked, sounded, and *was* more conservative (i.e., Stalinist) than the impulsive, explosive Khrushchev, yet the two had been allies in the past. "Nikita Sergeyevich," Suslov said, "you don't even understand how far you've allowed this to go. . . . You don't listen to anyone. You say party officials have hindered agricultural development—when it's you who's messed up everything. . . . You listen too much to members of your family, especially to Adzhubei. You take family members abroad with you. As a result of your foreign trips, we end up arguing with foreign friends. Our press is too full of 'Khrushchev this, Khrushchev that,' and there are too many pictures of you. We must put an end to this."[22]

By the time the trade union chief Viktor Grishin complained that Khrushchev hadn't given him an audience for four years, it was evening. Although several speakers remained to be heard from, the plotters felt confident enough now to adjourn until the next morning, but not enough to stop worrying about a last-gasp Khrushchev surprise. After he had left the room, everyone swore not to take any calls from him lest he try to recruit allies for a counteroffensive. Later Brezhnev called Semichastny to ask where Khrushchev's car had headed after the meeting. To his apartment? To his dacha?

"I've got everything ready," Semichastny told him, "here, there, everywhere. We've anticipated everything."

"What if he phones? What if he calls?"

"He's got no place to call. The whole communications system is in my hands!"[23]

Khrushchev's limousine dropped him at the gate of his Lenin Hills residence around eight. He set off along the path by the fifteen-foot-high yellow stone wall that hid the house from nearby Vorobyovsky Avenue. Sergei Khrushchev, who had found his own way back from Vnukovo-2 and had been waiting in suspense all afternoon and evening, walked beside him.

"Everything happened just the way you said it would," said the elder Khrushchev, looking exhausted and upset. "Don't ask any questions. I'm tired, and I have to think." After trudging two times around the house, Khrushchev entered it and climbed the stairs to his second-floor bedroom. His only request was that tea be brought to him there. No one dared disturb him. Nina Petrovna Khrushcheva was on vacation in Karlovy Vary, Czechoslovakia, accompanied, ironically, by Brezhnev's wife, Viktoria.

Later that same evening Khrushchev phoned Mikoyan. "I'm old and tired," he said. "Let them cope by themselves. I've done the main thing. Could anyone have dreamed of telling Stalin that he didn't suit us anymore and suggesting he retire? Not even a wet spot would have remained where we had been standing. Now everything is different. The fear is gone, and we can talk as equals. That's my contribution. I won't put up a fight."[24]

IF KHRUSHCHEV'S PHONE was bugged by the KGB, as he and his family assumed, his words to Mikoyan ended the suspense. Yet the next day's Presidium meeting wasn't anticlimactic, at least not for Khrushchev. Even in the best of times he couldn't abide criticism; now, at the lowest point in his career, he had to endure a barrage of it.

Dmitri Polyansky renewed the assault when the Presidium reconvened at 10:00 A.M. "You used to behave yourself. Now, you're a changed man. . . . Stalin himself behaved more modestly than you do, Nikita Sergeyevich. . . . You've been reviling Stalin to the point of indecency. . . . You're suffering from megalomania, and the illness is incurable." Just in case Mikoyan still thought of defending his friend, Polyansky revealed Khrushchev had mocked Mikoyan too, calling him "nothing but slush" and "a persistent fly."[25]

Mikoyan was next. He too criticized Khrushchev's errors, including his "explosiveness," "irritability," and reliance on yes-men. However, he partially defended Khrushchev's Suez and Berlin policies and reminded his colleagues that they all had approved sending missiles to Cuba. He favored letting Khrushchev stay on as prime minister, while stepping down as party leader. To strip him of both jobs would be "a great gift to the Chinese and Mao Zedong, not to mention that Khrushchev's achievements are part of our legacy, which we mustn't lose."

Even this limited defense produced an explosion of protest. Shelepin bolted from his seat to the head of the table. Yuri Andropov, Pyotr Demichev, and others joined in. The dour-looking deputy premier, Aleksei Kosygin, rejected any "half measures."

"You're an honest man," Kosygin said to Khrushchev. "But you've set yourself up in opposition to the Presidium. You don't pay attention to anyone, you don't hear anyone out, you interrupt everyone. . . . You love ovations. . . . You're constantly involved with intrigues—putting down one man, toying with another."

Khrushchev had made Nikolai Podgorny a rival heir to Brezhnev, but Podgorny too had been in on the plot from the start. Khrushchev had blasted Stalin for incompetence in military matters, Podgorny now recalled, but "you yourself, Nikita Sergeyevich, don't comprehend them. Military men say that you don't understand how things stand with the defense of our country." Still, since the world might look askance if Khrushchev were summarily dumped, it would be better if he himself "asked to be relieved of his posts."

After Brezhnev had summed up, adding that Khrushchev once referred to his fellow Central Committee secretaries as "male dogs peeing on curbstones," he too demanded that Khrushchev "voluntarily" retire. Noting that Central Committee members were already gathering in the Kremlin's nearby Sverdlovsk Hall, Brezhnev proposed that "debate" be ended and the motion to oust Khrushchev put to a vote. All present voted in favor. Mikoyan dropped his objection.[26]

His fate decided, Khrushchev spoke for the last time. He was, Yefremov recalls, in a state of "profound nervous agitation." Shelest describes him as "crushed, isolated, powerless." Tears welled in his eyes.

"All of you spoke a lot about my negative characteristics and actions," he said, "but you also mentioned my positive qualities, and I thank you for that. I'm happy for the Presidium, for its maturity; a grain of my work too helped to create that maturity."

Khrushchev asked his colleagues to "forgive me my rudeness. . . . A lot of what you described I don't remember, but I admit that I manifested weakness, and then it became a habit, and my high position turned my head. I'm accused of combining the posts of first secretary of the Central Committee and chairman of the Council of Ministers. Well, I tried not to take both, but you yourselves gave them to me, and I made the mistake of agreeing. It's a mistake to combine them. I made an error in not raising this issue at the Twenty-second Congress. I could already see and understand that the load was too great for me."

His eyes filled with tears again. "These aren't tears of self-pity. The battle with Stalin's cult of personality was a big one, and I made a small contribution. You've already decided everything. I'll do what's best for the party.

"I understand that my role doesn't exist anymore, but if I were you, I wouldn't dismiss me entirely. I don't intend to speak at the plenum. I'm not going to ask for mercy. The issue is decided. As I told Mikoyan, I'm not going to resist. I'm not about to smear you; after all, you and I hold the same views. I'm upset, but I'm also glad that the party has gotten to the point that it can rein in even its first secretary. You call this a cult? You smeared me all over with shit, and I say, 'You're right.' You call that a cult?

"I've been thinking for a long time that it's time for me to go. But it's hard to let go. I myself could see that I wasn't coping with my responsibilities, that I wasn't meeting with any of you. I cut myself off from you. You've really let me have it for doing so, but no more than I suffered over this myself.

"I never played dice or pool [as so many of his colleagues did]. I was always working. I thank you for the opportunity you've given me to retire. I ask you to write me a suitable statement, and I'll sign it. I'm ready to do anything in the interests of the party. I've been a party member for forty-six years, so please understand me! I thought that maybe you'd think it possible to create some sort of honorary position for me, but I'm not asking you to do so. As for where I'll live, decide that yourselves. If you insist, I'll leave Moscow and go wherever you want."[27]

After Khrushchev finished, the Presidium unanimously granted his "request" to retire "in connection with his advanced age and deterioration of his health." Later the same day Brezhnev opened the Central Committee plenum, held in the Kremlin's blue and white Sverdlovsk Hall, with a brief summary of the indictment, after which Suslov detailed all the main charges. His speech was punctuated by shouts and insults directed at Khrushchev from the floor: "Exclude him from the party! . . .Turn him over to a court!" Throughout these Stalinist outbursts, Khrushchev sat silently to one side, his eyes often closed, his head sometimes in his hands. In conclusion, Suslov read a statement by Khrushchev citing age and health as reasons why "I can no longer carry out my responsibilities."[28]

When Suslov was through, no discussion was allowed. Two Central Committee members from Ukraine who might have resisted were denied admission to the hall and soon afterward were relieved of their posts.[29] The vote to adopt the resolution was unanimous. Likewise, votes to select Brezhnev as party first secretary and Kosygin as prime minister. With that, Brezhnev declared the plenum adjourned.[30]

After the Presidium session ended, Khrushchev returned to his office, where his longtime foreign policy aide, Oleg Troyanovsky, found him looking "exhausted and overwhelmed." "My political career is over," Khrushchev said. "The main thing now is to get through this with dignity."[31] Just before the plenum Troyanovsky had glimpsed Khrushchev walking through a small Kremlin square, hatless (which was unusual for him) despite a sharp chill in the air. Afterward, when Khrushchev returned to his residence, he thrust his black briefcase into his son's hands and sighed. "It's over," he said. "I'm retired."

That evening Mikoyan arrived with a message from Khrushchev's successors. Over tea in the dining room, Mikoyan told him, "Your present dacha and city residence are yours for life." In fact, both were shortly taken away.

"Good," replied Khrushchev distractedly.

"You will have bodyguards and a domestic staff, but new personnel will be assigned." Actually, the new guards enforced a kind of house arrest rather than protecting Khrushchev.

Khrushchev grunted.

"Your pension will be set at five hundred rubles a month, and you'll have a car. It was suggested that you remain a deputy of the Supreme Soviet, although a final decision on that hasn't been taken. [Khrushchev did not remain a deputy.] I also suggested setting up the post of consultant to the Presidium for you, but that was rejected."[32]

"There was no need to," Khrushchev replied. "They'd never agree to that. Why would they want me around after everything that's happened? Of course, it would be nice to have something to do. I don't know how I'll be able to live in retirement, doing nothing. But it was a mistake to propose that. Thanks anyway. It's good to know you have a friend at your side."[33]

As the two men parted in the paved square in front of the house, Mikoyan embraced Khrushchev and kissed him. Then, with Khrushchev watching, his only friend in the leadership walked to the gate. Whether because Mikoyan feared for his own career or because he too had been insulted and alienated by Khrushchev and no longer considered him a friend, Khrushchev never saw him again.

CHAPTER TWO

Kalinovka's Own: 1894–1908

KHRUSHCHEV WAS born on April 15, 1894, in the southern Russian village of Kalinovka.[1] His parents, Sergei Nikanorovich Khrushchev and Aksinia Ivanovna Khrushcheva, were poor peasants, as were the godparents who attended his christening in the village's Archangel Church. Nikita Khrushchev lived in Kalinovka until 1908, when his family moved to the mining town of Yuzovka in eastern Ukraine. Khrushchev devoted to the first fourteen years of his life only a handful of the several thousand pages of memoirs he dictated during the last five years of his life. "He declared at the very start," recalls his son, "that he was not going to describe his life beginning with childhood. He couldn't stand chronological narratives; they depressed him."[2] But he dedicated more of his memoirs to his life near the Yuzovka mines, and throughout his career he described his father not as a peasant but as a miner or a worker. Some of this selective emphasis was political—the leader of a workers' state needed a proletarian past—but not all. For there were plenty of things about life in Kalinovka that its leading native son preferred to ignore or forget.[3]

TO GET TO Kalinovka from Moscow nowadays, you take an overnight train to Kursk, a provincial capital of one million about sixty miles from the Ukrainian border. From there you drive west for about two hours along decrepit, potholed roads to Dmitrievka, turn south to Khomutovka (the district center of six thousand people whose name is derived from *khomut* [horse's collar]), and then southwest to Kalinovka just down the road.[4]

In late June the broad meadows around Khrushchev's village look green and lush, not as rich as the nearby Russian and Ukrainian black earth zone but much more so than farther north near Moscow. To judge by the look of the land, the villages nestled among the green fields should be prosperous. Yet a century after Khrushchev's birth the only reliable way to reach most of them in the spring, when the annual thaw turns unpaved roads to mud, is by jeep. In all the other villages in the area the main streets are rutted dirt roads, the peasant houses wooden and mostly ramshackle. But not in Nikita Khrushchev's hometown.

Kalinovka's main street is paved, as is the main road to it from Khomutovka. The asphalt was first laid down when Khrushchev was in office, the same time that an astonishing ensemble of buildings in Kalinovka's central square were constructed: a neoclassical four-columned "palace of culture," said to have replaced the church in which Khrushchev was christened; the campus of an agricultural college that was moved from Kursk to Kalinovka; and a five-story school dormitory, also used to house visitors who came from around the country and the world to contemplate Kalinovka's remarkable progress under Khrushchev's benevolent tutelage. Across the road from the square lies a large artificial lake, while on the other side, along the road from Khomutovka, is a row of neat red-brick houses. These wouldn't look out of place in Britain, but in 1991 they were still home to peasants of a collective farm that, until 1964, was named Khrushchev's Native Land.

A short walk from the square (past the palace of culture, along the edge of the lake, down a road next to which goats are grazing) leads to an older part of town, where a tombstonelike slab identifies the place where "Nikita Khrushchev spent his childhood." The house where he was born has long since been torn down, but the adobe-walled cottage that stands on the site is neat, clean, and ready for inspection. The peasant woman who lives there proudly displays a large portrait of Khrushchev in a corner of the parlor where, in the year of his birth, an icon would have hung.

In 1894 Kalinovka was a far cry from the model town into which Khrushchev transformed it. With the abolition of serfdom in 1861, some land came into the possession of the peasants who worked it, but even for better-off peasants, the end of serfdom brought formal liberation but no real prosperity. A grave flaw with the emancipation was that too little land was given to the newly freed serfs, and too much payment was demanded for it. Agricultural productivity failed to keep pace with rapid population growth. Add the tsarist government's increasing commitment to industrialization, plus the combination of rising land costs and falling grain prices, and the result was a crisis that swept across the countryside toward the end of the nineteenth century. By 1900 most Russian peasants could earn only about a quarter of their livelihoods by farming; to make up the rest, they had to hire themselves out to landlords or rich peasants as laborers or to till leased land as sharecroppers, in effect reverting to semiserf status.[5]

According to a Russian account of peasant life published in 1888, "all peasants, the rich as well as the poor, live, with very few exceptions, in the same narrow peasant's izba [hut], these homesteads [consisting of] a square of fifteen to twenty feet in length and width. In this space, divided into one or two rooms, both children and grown-ups are all huddled together. The quantity of air afforded for respiration is so puzzlingly small that our hygienists are forced to admit the osmosis-like action of the walls as the only hypothesis which accounts for the fact that these people are not literally suffocated."[6]

An early-twentieth-century report added these details: "Cottages having no chimneys are still very common. . . . Almost all have thatched roofs which often leak, and in the winter the walls are generally covered with dung to keep the place warm. A peasant family . . . sleep[s] in two tiers—on benches and on bunks—behind the stove. . . . Bath houses are practically non-existent. . . . They almost never use soap. . . . Skin diseases . . . syphilis . . . epidemics, under-nourishment. . . . Such foodstuffs as meat, meal, bacon and vegetable oils appear on the family table only on rare occasions, perhaps two or three times a year. The normal fare consists of bread, *kvas* [a kind of nonalcoholic beverage brewed from bread] and often cabbage and onions, to which fresh vegetables may be added in autumn."[7]

Two years before Khrushchev was born, Kalinovka had 1,197 residents, 588 men and 609 women. There were 156 peasant huts in the village, with an average of about 8 persons living in each.[8] In the middle of the nineteenth century, most izbas in the village of Viriatino in nearby Tambov Province were smoke huts, dark, smoke-blackened hovels that residents often shared with their animals during the winter months. But by the 1880s only two or three smoke huts remained in Viriatino.[9] As for work, according to an 1880 account, "all those who have written about Russian village life—nay, all who have ever spent a few holiday months in a Russian village—know that it is difficult to conceive of more exhausting work than that which is performed by the peasants. . . ."[10] Beginning at age six or seven, village boys fetched water and wood and tagged along with their fathers to work in fields. At eight or nine they tended cattle or sheep, and by thirteen they worked alongside their fathers from dawn to dusk.[11] Khrushchev started working almost as soon as he could walk. Soon he was tending calves and sheep, and later cows, on the nearby estate where his father worked.[12] We have no photograph of Nikita as a boy, but it is not hard to imagine an energetic towhead, wearing only a long peasant shirt until age six or seven, then rough, crude trousers home-sewn out of flax or wool.[13] He recalled going barefoot as a boy from spring until late fall. "Every villager dreamed of owning a pair of boots. We children were lucky if we had a decent pair of shoes. We wiped our noses on our sleeves and kept our trousers up with a piece of string."[14]

For a boy like Nikita, who was healthy and spent a lot of time in the open air, this existence seemed tolerable. But later he spoke of the poor peasant's way of life as shameful and desperately in need of change. Shepherds like him were "the lowest of the low in the village," he recalled.[15] The "shoes" Khrushchev wore in Kalinovka were bast slippers called *lapty*, made by weaving narrow strips of linden tree bark. Too light to offer protection in rain or snow, which was just when they were needed most, *lapty* symbolized peasant poverty. Much later, as leader of the Soviet Union, Khrushchev repeatedly insisted that he and his country had outgrown *lapty* and could no longer be pushed around. How ironic that in pounding his brown shoe at the United Nations in the fall of 1960, he only strengthened his image around the world as a crude, ignorant, peasant muzhik.

If work in Kalinovka did little to refine the sensibilities, neither did organized amusements such as fist-fighting competitions. Until the turn of the century these took place during holidays like Christmas, Epiphany, and Shrove Tuesday. In Viriatino, "two teams, each representing half the village, faced each other on the meadow near the church. They fought in street clothes. It was strictly against the rules to use anything but fists; whoever broke that rule was eliminated from the competition. . . . Not only adult men but adolescents took part. Youngsters started the fight; adults would join in later. Each fighter selected a partner [i.e., opponent] equal to himself in age and size; old men, for example, would fight one another. Some needed a few drinks to bolster their courage. The whole village turned out to watch."[16]

Education wasn't a high priority in the life of Russian peasants like the Khrushchevs. In 1881 only 46 of the 922 adults in Viriatino were literate. The number of pupils in village schools increased toward the end of the century, but boys attended primary school for only two or three years. Parents took their sons out of school as soon as they were "barely able to read and write." One villager recalled his father's announcing one spring: "Take the books back to school. We're going to plow."[17]

Schools came in two varieties, Orthodox Church parochial schools and schools run by zemstvos, local government agencies formed during the Great Reforms of the 1860s.[18] Nikita Khrushchev apparently attended both sorts for a total of about two years.[19] Of the two, state schools were somewhat better. In Viriatino the state school "did not satisfy the most basic educational or even sanitary requirements," while in the two-grade church school, instruction was "even worse."[20] The curriculum in both included elementary reading, writing, and arithmetic, as well as religion taught by the local priest, but according to a 1913 study of another province, "the majority of pupils attained only basic literacy—the ability to read but not always to write." Instruction was not only rigidly organized but often deliberately uninspiring. Teachers "must not be carried away with a desire to share with children all the knowledge they have about a given subject," said a 1887 directive from the Viriatino district office.[21]

KHRUSHCHEV'S MATERNAL grandfather was among the poorest of the poor. "He could neither read nor write," Khrushchev recalled. "He had a bath two times in all his years—once when he was christened as a baby, again when the neighbors prepared him for his burial."[22] When he "got out of the army, where he served twenty-five years," according to Khrushchev, his grandfather "settled down to a peasant's life."[23] But his cow gave "only enough milk to whiten the soup" and so hide the fact there were no potatoes in it.[24] Khrushchev's grandfather had three daughters; Aksinia, or Ksenia, for short, was to become Khrushchev's mother. She was sent to live with her older sister, Aleksandra, in the village of Tishkino, where she earned her living scrubbing floors for a landowner.

Khrushchev's paternal grandfather, on the other hand, was more prosperous. Nikanor Khrushchev, born in 1852, was the son of a peasant who fled serfdom in 1816.[25] Nikanor served in the army with Ksenia's father. Yet, when Nikanor's son Sergei married Ksenia and brought her back to Kalinovka, Nikita Khrushchev's recollection was that, "no sooner did they get there than his father made him leave. According to the custom of the day, the father drove the eldest son out of the house when he was married, not giving him any land or gifts for his marriage. My mother and father left and settled elsewhere, but they lived in poverty."[26]

Contrary to Khrushchev's recollection, no such custom actually existed in peasant Russia. Sons and daughters-in-law usually lived with their parents, contributing their wages to the commonweal, except when severe generational conflicts resulted in "premortem" divisions of households. These divisions "occurred either on the patriarch's or his son's initiative as a result of irreconcilable dissension between father and son." Only in such cases did a father oust his son "with little or no property, or [did] an independent-minded son [choose] to leave his father's household without first seeking permission, thus risking not only his father's displeasure but disinheritance."[27]

In this sense alone, then, Nikita Khrushchev's father could be said to have been a victim of custom. Moreover, Nikanor Khrushchev threw Sergei out not once but twice. Having no land and few prospects, Sergei Khrushchev left his family and migrated 275 miles southeast to Yuzovka in the Donbas (the Donets Basin). There, according to his son, Nikita, Sergei Khrushchev "first worked as a common laborer on the railroad. He sorted railroad ties, leveled embankments, drove stakes, and dug drainage ditches. When that seasonal job ended, he worked in a brick factory. He mixed the clay and laid bricks until he had gained enough experience to be allowed to work the kiln. This work, too, was seasonal, and he left."[28]

While in Yuzovka, Nikita Khrushchev's father earned enough money to support his family and apparently to win back his father's respect. Sergei and his family must have resumed living in Nikanor Khrushchev's house because according to Nikita Khrushchev, eventually "my father's money ran out and my grandfather chased us out of the house again. We ended up in a clay hut with a dirt floor and tiny windows. My grandfather was fond of me. At night he let me sleep above the stove in his log cabin. My father went to the next village to work as a farmhand for the landowner. My mother went too. She was now a laundress and sewed clothes for the other peasant women."[29]

Deprived for a second time of a relatively comfortable existence, Ksenia Khrushcheva never let her husband forget it. Nikita Khrushchev recalled how his parents built their own hut and how his mother "overstrained herself in the course of this work, with the result that she had a hernia for the rest of her life."[30] Ksenia Khrushcheva's own version was that she built the hut herself while her husband was away in Yuzovka. "The miner's life swallowed up my husband," she complained. "He [eventually] tore us away from the village and took us to the Uspensky mine."[31]

As if owning no land were not bad enough, Sergei and Ksenia Khrushchev had no horse. In Viriatino, ownership of a horse was a prime social indicator. Nearly half its 252 households owned two or three horses each, 71 owned one horse each, and only the 28 poorest households had none at all.[32] "He who has a horse is a man," went a village saying; "he who doesn't wears a harness himself."[33] Recalled Khrushchev: "My father . . . worked in the mines in the winter in the hope that he would some day earn enough money to buy a horse, so that he could raise enough potatoes and cabbage to feed his family. He never got the horse."[34]

According to Khrushchev, his parents pursued this hope even after the whole family had moved to Yuzovka in 1908. His father worked in the mines, his mother took in washing, and he himself crawled into huge sooty boilers to clean them. But "both my father and my mother, but particularly my mother, dreamed of the day when they could return to the village, to a little house, a horse, and a piece of land."[35]

When the dream was postponed, Ksenia Khrushcheva blamed her husband. According to Khrushchev's daughter-in-law, Liuba Sizykh, who first met her in the late 1930s, Ksenia almost never referred to her recently deceased husband, and when she did, it was "disrespectfully," as if "she considered him a fool." Khrushchev's mother, a broad-faced, stern-looking woman with long hair combed straight back, was "powerful," but her husband was "weak," said Sizykh. "Ksenia was not only smart but wise too. If she'd had any education at all, she would have really been something!"[36] Nina Ivanovna Kukharchuk, a niece who lived with the Khrushchev family from 1939 to 1949, recalled Ksenia as "a determined person. She could even be sharp with Nina Petrovna [Khrushchev's wife]." As for Khrushchev's father, who had died before Nina Ivanovna joined the family, "nobody talked about him."[37]

A very old woman encountered in Kalinovka in 1991 remembered Nikita Khrushchev's parents. "His mother was a strong-willed woman, a real battler. She was a bold one, she was, in the way she treated people. His father—he was much softer, goodhearted, but she—she was hard, and tough."[38] Listening to the old woman, Nikita Khrushchev's son Sergei nodded in agreement. "That's the way they were described to us," he said. "He was soft, and she had him under her thumb."

Nikita resented it when his father pulled him out of school to work in the fields. "After a year or two of school, I had learnt to count up to thirty and my father decided that was enough of schooling. He said that all I needed was to be able to count money, and I would never have more than thirty rubles to count anyway."[39] Later in Yuzovka, Sergei Khrushchev arranged for his son to apprentice with a shoemaker. "My father said that being a shoemaker was a good deal: 'You've always got a roof over your head and money in your pocket because everyone wears boots, and everyone wants good boots.'" When Nikita rejected shoemaking, his father had another scheme: "to make me a store clerk." Sergei Khrushchev "liked how polite the clerks in the company store were to workers, always trying to please them and offering them the best goods." But his son would have none of that either. "I categorically refused. I even told my father that if he was going to force me to become a clerk, I would leave home."[40]

Sensing his grandfather's and his mother's contempt for his father, Nikita resented Sergei's advice all the more. Given his own poverty, Sergei Khrushchev's wish for his son was ambitious, but not nearly as challenging as Nikita's hopes for himself. One source of his ambition must have been the favored treatment he received from his grandfather. Then there were the hopes Ksenia Khrushcheva invested in her son. Nikita had a sister, Irina, who was two years younger than he, but he was the apple of his mother's eye. Liuba Sizykh recollected that Ksenia seemed to "worship" him, often referring to him as "my son, the tsar," and boasting, "I always knew someday he'd become a great man."[41]

As a Moscow party bigwig in the early 1930s, Nikita Khrushchev brought his parents to live in his family's large apartment. According to Rada Adzhubei, her grandparents had no special liking for city life. They moved to Moscow, said Aleksei Adzhubei, because "their son had preserved the traditional Russian respect for and attachment to his parents, and they, in their turn, knew that Nikita was a good son who had invited them out of a pure heart."

But Adzhubei himself admitted to being puzzled about Khrushchev's real attitude toward his father.[42] Once in Moscow, Sergei Khrushchev was frequently ill, and he died in a special tuberculosis hospital in 1938. He was buried in a nearby cemetery, but Rada didn't remember Khrushchev's visiting his father's grave before the family moved to Kiev the same year, nor did she recall his ever mentioning the old man after they returned to live in Moscow in 1949. So silent was Khrushchev about his father that to this day Rada doesn't know the site of her grandfather's grave.[43]

Khrushchev family members deny that this neglect signaled filial disrespect. Communists were militantly unsentimental, they say, and had too much worldly work to do to spend their time visiting graves. But that didn't prevent Khrushchev from frequently visiting his mother's grave in Kiev.[44]

"A man who has been the indisputable favorite of his mother," wrote Sigmund Freud, "keeps for life the feeling of a conqueror, that confidence of success that often induces real success."[45] The pursuit of political power, added Harold Lasswell, is often spurred by a mother who has married "beneath" her potential and is determined to "vindicate" herself through "the vicarious triumphs of her children."[46] But a man whose father has been a disappointment knows all too well what it means to fail and to be despised for doing so by his wife. That made it all the more important for Khrushchev to outdo his father, yet such success risked evoking guilt at succeeding where his father did not. In that sense, Khrushchev's dream of power and glory and his ambivalence toward both were legacies of his childhood.[47]

In addition to his mother, young Nikita was inspired by a teacher in the Kalinovka state school. In contrast with his parochial school teacher, who "hit the children hard on the forehead and the hands with a ruler" and "made us learn by rote,"[48] Lydia Mikhailovna Shevchenko was an atheist and a village rebel. "She never went to church," Khrushchev recalled. "For this the peasants of the village never forgave her. Although they had great respect for her, the fact that she did not attend church made them feel something was wrong with her.

"I first saw banned [political] books at Lydia's house," Khrushchev continued. "Once I called on her and she introduced me to her brother, who was visiting from the city and lying in bed. 'This is the boy I told you about. He is asking me for forbidden pamphlets,' she said. Her brother smiled and replied, 'Give him these. Perhaps he'll make some sense of them, and then when he grows up he'll remember.' "[49]

The theme of the first encounter with banned books is a classic trope of Russian revolutionary memoirs. Obviously, Lydia Shevchenko's brother (if brother he really was, rather than someone whose presence in her bed would have been awkward to explain otherwise) was prescient. But Khrushchev basked even more in the notion that he was just plain smart: "I was very quick at math. I could quickly grasp any problem they threw at me and solve it in my head. I often stood in for Lydia Mikhailovna when she had to go into the city or run her own errands. . . . When I finished school, only four years in all, Lydia said, 'Nikita, you should study further. Don't stay here in the village; go to the city. A person like you must study. You should become educated.' These words struck a chord deep inside me, but my father's money had run out and my grandfather chased us out of the house again."[50]

In 1960, by which time Lydia Shevchenko's star student had achieved far more than even she could have anticipated, he mentioned her in a Moscow speech. Eager Khrushchev aides tracked her down and brought her to Moscow, where she told a conference on education that she had never seen a village as poor as Kalinovka had been. Khrushchev's granddaughter Yulia tells this story to show how sycophantic assistants made more of his former teacher than she had ever meant to Khrushchev himself. But an extraordinary incident that occurred ten years later, on the very day before Khrushchev died, suggests otherwise.

Nikita and Nina Khrushchev were visiting the Adzhubeis at their dacha outside Moscow in September 1971. The family went for a walk in the woods after lunch, but Khrushchev didn't feel good and sat down to rest on the folding stool he always carried with him. After the others walked on into the woods, Khrushchev began speaking to Aleksei Adzhubei in a calm, gentle tone that was unusual for him. "When I was a small boy, I was watching over some cows in the woods once—it was an autumn day like today—when I met an old woman in a little clearing. She stared directly at me for a long time. I was struck dumb. Then I heard her say something strange: 'Little boy, a great future awaits you. . . . '"[51]

That night Khrushchev felt even worse. Shortly thereafter he had a massive heart attack, from which he never recovered.

"What was Khrushchev trying to say?" asked Adzhubei about his father-in-law's Kalinovka vision. Clearly, the vision was some sort of reworking of the sense Khrushchev got from his mother and from his teacher that he was meant for far greater things than his father had ever achieved or had dreamed of for his son.

KHRUSHCHEV'S MOTHER instilled in him a sense of rectitude and responsibility, a conscience that carried with it the capacity for guilt and shame. "My mother was very religious," recalled Khrushchev, "likewise her father—my grandfather. . . . I remember being taught to kneel and pray in front of the icons with the grown-ups in church."[52] When Khrushchev thought back to his childhood, he could "vividly remember the saints on the icons against the wall of our wooden hut."[53] He even claimed, in a speech given in France in March 1960, to have been a "model pupil" in religion.[54]

Unlike most of his peers, Khrushchev later shunned tobacco and alcohol—until Stalin forced him to drink and the strain of World War II drove him to cigarettes. These twin abstinences reflected his mother's influence. His father's inept way of teaching restraint was to promise his son a gold watch that he couldn't afford to buy him if Nikita promised not to smoke.[55]

Khrushchev's idealism also reflected his religious training. Given the harsh conditions of life in Kalinovka and Yuzovka, it is not surprising that he eventually embraced the revolution. Communism itself is a secular religion, which, in Khrushchev's understanding of it, boiled down to believing in a better life for ordinary men and women. Yet the Communist party not only required compromises but demanded that he trample on his moral code. That was one reason why he eventually turned against Stalin and Stalinism. Not immediately, not until he had made his career, not until he had saved his own life while helping deprive countless others of theirs, not until Stalin was safely in his grave, but rebel he finally did.

The notion that an abiding, or at least residual, religious sense played any role in Khrushchev's belated and partial repentance seems ludicrous. He seemed to pride himself on his scorn for religious obscurantism. He eventually proved a fiercer scourge of religion than Stalin was.[56] Yet his close assistant for more than a quarter century, Andrei Shevchenko, insisted that Khrushchev secretly feared God. Witness the fact that when they first visited Kiev after Stalin's death, "Khrushchev placed a cross at his mother's grave, knelt before it, and made the sign of the cross"[57]

If Khrushchev's attitude toward religion was contradictory, so was his feeling for the land. Once he became party leader, he insisted on being treated as the party's reigning expert on agriculture. He was constantly traipsing around cornfields, barking out instructions to farmers and agronomists. Khrushchev's speech was as pungent as the earth, filled with tangy proverbs that enabled him to communicate with peasants better than any other Soviet leader could. At his state dachas Khrushchev's gardeners raised various crops, experimental and otherwise, and after he left office, he devoted endless hours to tending a large garden.

Khrushchev genuinely loved the land, and he wanted to help peasants improve their lives. But early in his career, when he filled out job and study questionnaires, and later in his speeches and writings, he identified himself as a worker, not as a peasant. Far from requesting agricultural assignments, he tried to avoid them and acquiesced only when Stalin insisted. Khrushchev's memoirs are filled with nasty and demeaning descriptions of peasants. He was forever advising them to give up their primitive ways and embrace a modern form of rural life. He kept returning to Kalinovka, sometimes as often as twice a year, but rather than revel in the world he had known, he relished the fact that he had transformed it. Nowhere else could he find so respectful an audience, but when his former neighbors resisted his nostrums, Khrushchev lost his temper and raged at them. The only way Shevchenko could explain this ironic reaction was to say that his boss, despite having grown up in Kalinovka, had no sense of "peasant psychology."

Khrushchev's impatience with peasants reflected his Marxist-Leninist creed. Bolsheviks viewed peasants as dangerous reactionaries, as prisoners of what Marx called "the idiocy of rural life."[58] Lenin and his followers pledged to "eliminate the distinction between city and countryside." One could argue that Khrushchev's determination to transform his own former way of life was ideological rather than personal. But why had that ideology appealed to him in the first place? It was because, like so many Russian peasants who fled to the cities in the twentieth century, he had felt that "idiocy" on his own neck and wanted to leave it as far behind as he could, because also like them, he had a naive faith in education and culture that contrasted sharply with the jaded views of longtime urbanities.[59] Khrushchev broke off a promising political career not once but twice to resume his education. He befriended leading lights of the cultural and scientific intelligentsia and frequently attended the theater, opera, and ballet. He came to think of himself as an expert not only on agriculture but on almost everything else under the sun. All this was built into the role of the all-knowing Communist leader, but it also buttressed Khrushchev's self-image. He wanted to transform not only the countryside but himself. Yet no matter how hard he tried, even the self-made Khrushchev couldn't undo what Kalinovka had made of him.

CHAPTER THREE

Making It as a Metalworker: 1908–1917

AT SOME POINT in 1908 Khrushchev's grandfather took him 30 miles in a horse-drawn cart to the railroad station nearest to Kalinovka and sent him off on a 250-mile journey, requiring two changes of train, to Yuzovka, 550 miles southeast of Kiev in the Donbas. When no one met him at the station, the fourteen-year-old Nikita, who had previously been in Yuzovka with his father, found his way to the mine where his father worked.[1] Sometime later his mother and sister joined them. They shared two tiny rooms with another family, in a one-story barrackslike structure near the Uspensky mine at the edge of the steppe.

The train that carried Khrushchev to Yuzovka transported him from a backward village into the chaotic new world of the Industrial Revolution. The name of the town, pronounced with the accent on the first syllable, sounds Russian enough. In fact, Yuzovka, which was founded in 1869, was named after John Hughes, a Welshman. (The city was renamed Stalino in 1924 and then changed in 1961 to Donetsk, the name it still bears. Ukraine, in which Yuzovka was located, was part of the Russian Empire.) Hughes's firm, the New Russia Company, had contracted with the tsarist government to build an ironworks and to manufacture railroad rails.[2] Hughes brought from Britain some seventy engineers and technicians, for whom he built brick and wood houses. In 1956 Khrushchev's "first and most lasting impression of England" was the "long stretches of little red-brick houses [which] stuck in my memory because they reminded me so much of houses I had seen in my boyhood. . . . I remember that during the summertime in the Donbas, you could only see the windows of these houses because the ivy covered the rest."[3]

John Hughes's British technicians and Russian and Ukrainian workers erected a vast industrial complex, including mines, blast furnaces, rolling mills, metalworking factories, and repair and other workshops. In due course, railroad spurs extended to several mines in and around the town. By 1904 the population of Yuzovka and environs had climbed to forty thousand; by 1914 it had reached seventy thousand. The Donbas is an area the size of Vermont; in 1913 its mines produced 87 percent of Russia's coal.[4]

Industrial development far outstripped the growth of housing and services. Not, to be sure, for the British and other Western Europeans who owned or operated mines and mills. They lived in the "English colony," with neat houses, treelined streets, electricity, and a central water system. But the rest of the landscape was bleak. "Mud, stench and violence," was the way a revolutionary described it on the eve of World War I.[5] According to another witness, "the ground was black; so were the roads. Not a tree was to be seen near the mine, not even a bush; no pond, or even a stream. And beyond the mine, as far as the eye could see, only the monotonous, sunburned steppe."[6]

Living and working conditions in Yuzovka were the stuff of which anticapitalist tracts were made. "It seemed to me," Khrushchev recalled in 1958, "that Karl Marx had actually been at the mines," that "he had based his laws on what he observed of our lives."[7] The wretched workers' settlements in and around Yuzovka were derisively known as Shanghais and Dogsvilles; two, in particular, were called Bitch and Croak.[8] In 1910 residents hauled water from twenty-seven hand pumps scattered around town; the only pump house served the foreigners. Teeming barracks housed fifty to sixty men in each dormitory room. Besides the rows of plank beds in these barracks, there was no furniture, only a rope overhead on which to dry clothing and foot cloths (which served as socks). Miners neither wore special work clothes underground nor washed anything more than their faces before returning to their barracks. Each bed was home to two men, who took turns sleeping and working in the mines.[9]

Khrushchev's father, Sergei, had lived in quarters like this during the winters he spent away from Kalinovka. His bunk mates were seasonal workers from nearby villages. In Yuzovka's mines and mills they were transformed from peasants into first-generation proletarians, a process for which not just capitalists but Marxists as well could work up considerable abstract enthusiasm. In fact, it was appalling. As late as 1920, when Nikita Khrushchev returned to another mine after the Russian civil war, he found the miners "misused the latrine so badly that you had to enter it on stilts if you didn't want to track filth home to your own apartment at the end of the workday. I remember I was once sent somewhere to install some mining equipment and found the miners living in a barracks with double-deck bunks. It wasn't unusual for the men in the upper decks simply to urinate over the side."[10]

The primitive habits Khrushchev encountered in Yuzovka were bred by brutalizing conditions of labor. The workday stretched up to fourteen hours. Miners crawled through dark underground shafts dragging their picks and worked the entire shift lying down or crouching in waterlogged tunnels only three to four feet high. In the deeper shafts, where the temperature soared to thirty to thirty-five degrees (centigrade), they toiled naked in what they called Adam's costume.[11]

Average pay for such work was a paltry one to one and half rubles a day.[12] Often miners were paid with coupons redeemable for high-priced, low-quality goods at the company store. In 1908, 274 men died from a gas explosion; another 118 died in 1912. There were 157 doctors in the whole Donbas region, and only 18 doctors, 23 doctor's assistants, and 5 nurses for 100,000 people in Yuzovka in 1916. Fierce epidemics swept through with frightening regularity: Cholera killed 313 in Yuzovka alone in 1892; typhoid and dysentery took 400 in 1896. During a 1910 cholera outbreak, Khrushchev recalled, "when the miners got sick, they were taken off to the cholera barracks from which no one returned. A rumor started to circulate among the miners that the doctors were poisoning their patients. Witnesses were found who claimed they had seen someone throw powder in the well."[13]

Many of Yuzovka's residents took refuge in drink and crime. In 1908 the town boasted no fewer than thirty-three wine and liquor shops. From these it was a short step to mayhem. The writer Konstantin Paustovsky, who spent a year in Yuzovka, witnessed fights that spread until "the whole street joined in. Men came out with leaded whips and knuckle dusters, noses were broken and blood flowed." In 1912 a visiting journalist described Yuzovka this way: "All the dregs of mining industry life gather here. Everything dark, evil and criminal—thieves, hooligans, all such are drawn here."[14]

IT HAS BEEN said that one effect of World War I on Europe was the "brutalization" of public life.[15] In the Donbas at the turn of the century, life was already brutal enough. If the miners sometimes seemed primitive and irrational, the bosses' fierce exploitation was largely to blame. Minimal pay was reduced by an elaborate system of fines and by bribes demanded by the police as well as foremen. When workers struck, demanding, among other things, more "respectable" treatment, they were subjected to further humiliation in the form of public flogging.[16]

Strikes were rare during Yuzovka's early decades. Isolated socially and spatially by the nature of their work, and ground down by inhuman working conditions, miners endured long periods of passivity, punctuated by violent explosions that quickly degenerated into mindless riots and pogroms. The cholera riots of 1902 and 1910 fitted this pattern. So did the strikes of 1905, which turned into looting and savagery against Jews.

Revolutionary groups made little headway in Yuzovka. The Social Democrats, forerunners of the Communists, attracted few followers. When they bitterly split into extremist Bolshevik and more moderate Menshevik wings in 1902, there was so little comprehension of the split in Yuzovka that the two groups remained united there until May 1917.

When the Revolution of 1905 broke out, Yuzovka Social Democrats were too weak to capitalize on it. In 1913 only about four hundred of thirty thousand workers in the area considered themselves Bolsheviks. The massacre at the Lena River goldfield in Siberia (in which tsarist police killed striking miners) triggered a strike in Yuzovka on April 16, 1912, but 1914 was a year of relative prosperity with mines and factories all working full blast.

When World War I began in the summer of 1914, a large crowd gathered in Yuzovka and listened approvingly to patriotic speeches. But by 1916 the war's initial popularity had dissipated under the impact of horrendous losses at the front and declining living standards at home. Then the tsar's abdication in February 1917 sparked bloody conflict between workers and bosses that was to deepen as revolution gave way to a savage civil war. In hindsight it is too easy to say that this outcome was inevitable. That would ignore a countertendency, visible in Yuzovka as elsewhere in the Russian Empire, that might have eventually rendered public life less violent and brutal if the First World War had not intervened.

"In the 1870's," reported a history of the town, "poverty and hardship might have been seen as the natural lot of the vast majority. By 1913, the migrant miner was the neglected fringe of a society that was making visible progress both economically and socially. Six hundred workers of the

New Russia Co. owned their own homes. . . ."[17] In 1897 only 31 percent of Donbas miners could read simple sentences, and in 1921 only 40 percent. As late as 1922 more than two-thirds of miners never read newspapers or books.[18] But the number of schools was growing, as was the availability of libraries and reading rooms, theater and music, and adult education. In 1900 Yuzovka's amenities included a brick Orthodox church with an attached parochial school, two primary schools (one Russian, the other English), a pharmacy, a bookstore, a printing shop, five photographers, and a notary public. By 1913 there were three private high schools, one trade school, and five libraries with books on loan, plus summer concerts and a circus in an outdoor amphitheater. In the summer of 1917, 56 percent of Yuzovka's children between the ages of seven and thirteen were in school, a goodly portion of them from working-class families. Besides the New Russia Company's ten schools, there were two church schools, an Armenian-Gregorian school, Jewish schools for men and women, a higher municipal school, a commercial or vocational school, and two private women's *gimnazii* (high schools).[19]

These institutions set a higher benchmark to which a young man like Khrushchev could aspire. By succeeding economically, one could rise into the more sophisticated working class that was emerging, not so much in the mines as in the factories that surrounded them. This new class represented a kind of labor aristocracy that enjoyed higher wages and employment security, as well as better diet, housing, and education. An even smaller number of workers, approximately 10 percent of them (or about six hundred in all), underwent a process of embourgeoisement that included obtaining property and beginning to act like property owners.[20]

In 1881 there were only 434 mining engineers in the whole Russian Empire, of whom only 127 were employed by private enterprise as opposed to government ministries and other offices. A mid-1890s survey of the Donbas listed (apart from 137 foreign personnel) 80 mining engineers and 67 technicians and technologists, along with 150 foremen, 1,150 gang bosses and senior workers in the mines, and 400 shop bosses and foremen in the factories.[21] It wasn't easy to climb into these categories, but those who showed energy, initiative, and what factory authorities viewed as a responsible attitude could hope to go far.

Those who made it might have eventually constituted the "missing middle class" whose absence partially accounted for the empire's economic backwardness and political violence. Other ambitious proletarians might someday have become part of a democratic workers' movement committed to constructive modernization. Instead they found themselves trapped between a decaying tsarist regime that refused to allow them to form trade unions and the Bolsheviks who eventually seized power in their name but against their long-term interests.

THIS WAS THE world Khrushchev entered in 1908 and inhabited until 1917. In all likelihood he thoroughly enjoyed it. Khrushchev's early biographer Edward Crankshaw didn't think so. Kalinovka had been rough, he wrote, but "the long hours in the fields were mitigated by the deep satisfactions of country life. The boy had no boots, but at least he could feel the hot sand of the dirt roads and the spongy grass of the pastures between his toes. He could fish . . . ; he could drink in the sounds and smells of the broad, ever fluid Russian plain." Kalinovka had "the glow of life," but Khrushchev's rough adolescence in Yuzovka had "no redeeming feature."[22]

No redeeming feature, that is, except a boy's awakening to a world humming with energy and activity and to his own powers in it. When Nikita arrived in Yuzovka, he was fourteen; in 1917 he turned twenty-three. During these years he found not just a job but a dream, and he also found a wife to share it with.[23]

Khrushchev's parents' view was closer to Crankshaw's. They sent their son back to Kalinovka at times of strikes and other turmoil. But their effort to shield him from Yuzovka probably heightened his fascination with it. At first he worked as he had in Kalinovka, tending cows, sheep, and gardens for a local landowner. Then he joined other youths cleaning out mine boilers, a job that required him to crawl inside and chip away at the slag with an iron bar before scrambling out covered with soot and ash.[24] Before long he was an apprentice in the boiler shop, but by this time he "dreamed of becoming a fitter." Offered the choice of apprenticing to a lathe operator or a fitter, he chose the latter, and "after brief training, I was given my vise and tools and began to work in the shops. Thus, I became a worker at the age of fifteen."[25]

A fitter is to metals what a carpenter is to wood. Khrushchev said that when asked at the time why he chose to become one, he replied, "A lathe operator makes only single parts, while a fitter assembles all the parts and breathes life into the whole machine so that it begins to work."[26] In his first years in Yuzovka he built a bicycle out of scrap metal; later, with the help of a makeshift motor, he turned it into a "motorcycle" on which he roared around town.

Khrushchev became an apprentice to a Jewish fitter named Yakov Kutikov at the Bosse and Genefeld Engineering Works and Iron Foundry located near the mines in what is now called the old town, a dark area of narrow, cobbled streets downhill from newer post–World War II Donetsk with its parks, squares, broad streets, and tall buildings. The German-owned Bosse and Genefeld was one of the first plants in the Donbas to repair complicated mining equipment—elevators, boilers, winches, pumps, trolley trucks—while also manufacturing simpler devices used in nearby mines. Khrushchev worked at the plant from six in the morning until six at night, with a half hour for breakfast and an hour for lunch, and received twenty-five kopecks a day for his labor. Before building his bicycle, he had to walk several miles to work.[27]

The routine was rough, but it was overshadowed by his growing sense of excitement. A 1910 photograph shows a group of Bosse and Genefeld workers wearing what appear to be dark, padded work jackets and warm hats. Most of them are grizzled veterans of the workplace. The youngest by far, but standing in the middle of the first row with an eager-to-please look on his round, shining face, is the pug-nosed, splay-lipped apprentice Nikita Khrushchev.[28]

Nikita wasn't alone in his enthusiasm. According to a study of young St. Petersburg workers of the same period, "those who entered an apprenticeship were more likely than others to find themselves inducted into the adult sub-culture of the factory or shop and to develop, albeit gradually and tenuously, a new self-image that corresponded to their growing skill. . . ."[29]

A young Moscow worker conveyed his growing sense of mastery and control this way: "After a year's experience at the workbench, I already knew how to draw and could design a pattern if it wasn't very complex. My confidence in my own powers was growing stronger. . . . I was becoming bolder and more definite in my opinions. The authority of my 'elders' was beginning to lose its effect on me. I already had a critical attitude toward everyday, conventional morality."[30]

In a passage that Fyodor Gladkov, the socialist realist author of *Cement*, could have written, this same worker recalled being "gripped by the poetry of the large metal factory, with its mighty metallic roar, the puffing of its steam-driven machines, its columns of high pipes, its rising clouds of black smoke, which sullied the clear blue sky. . . . I had the feeling of merging with the factory, with its stern poetry of labor, a poetry that was growing dearer and closer to me than the quiet, lazy poetry of our drowsy village life."[31]

Khrushchev derived an even headier feeling from the fact that the labor force was highly stratified, with metalworkers like him near the top. Factory workers were paid much better than miners, and a listing of New Russia Company factory wages shows fitters with the third-highest wages of the top ten categories.[32] Construction workers, for example, were much lower down, with the result, Khrushchev remembered, that "people who built houses weren't even considered professional tradesmen. They were usually just peasants who knew how to slap bricks and mortar together."[33]

He further distanced himself from his peasant past by embarking on an active social life. He stayed for days at a time at the home of Misha and Ilya Kosenko, brothers who worked as apprentices along with him. Eighty-one years later Ilya's daughter Olga still lived in the small clay-walled house built in 1910. The street Nikita took to visit the Kosenkos may have looked worse in 1991 than it did in 1910: A ditch with a stream in it, and with grass growing alongside, runs down the middle of the road; other adobe-walled houses from Khrushchev's time sit behind broken-down fences; passersby pick their way amid the rocks and ruts and around piles of garbage. Back in 1910, the future still seemed bright to the fresh-faced towhead who sometimes arrived at the Kosenkos on his homemade motorcycle, alerting the whole neighborhood to his arrival by its raucous roar.

Khrushchev was "the life of the parties" that gathered at the Kosenko house. He loved to joke and make people laugh. But behind his cheerful efforts to ingratiate himself was a sense that he had to work hard to do so. Nikita was already known as something of a ladies' man, but if he had any amorous designs on the Kosenko brothers' three sisters, he didn't succeed. They regarded him as a *katsap* (a not altogether friendly Ukrainian term for Russians) and found the "red-headed ragamuffin" too short and unattractive, and perhaps also too poor, to evoke any romantic interest.[34]

Romance aside, Khrushchev had his first brushes with politics. One evening at the Kosenkos', he and his friends decided that cleaning boilers was worse than hard labor; when they complained to the boss, they were fired.[35] About the same time, Khrushchev was beginning to read radical newspapers that were handed out at the gates to workshops and mines. By May 1912 he had graduated to gathering donations for the families of murdered Lena goldfield strikers, a suspicious fact duly noted by the province police.[36] When they passed the word to Bosse and Genefeld authorities, he was again fired. With some difficulty, he signed on at mine no. 31 in nearby Rutchenkovo, where he repaired underground equipment. There he is said to have distributed Social Democratic newspapers and helped organize political study groups. In 1914 he moved again, to a machine repair shop that, since it served ten different pits, enabled him further to expand his growing circle of acquaintances.[37]

Everywhere he worked, Khrushchev was an unusually visible figure. According to a flattering Soviet account, "his work constantly kept him among other workers, and his warm, happy-go-lucky character attracted their affection." Before each shift the miners waiting for the elevator "made the perfect audience for Khrushchev. With a remarkably engaging storyteller like him around, they were never bored."[38] Khrushchev himself added that "the workers said that I spoke well, and therefore they chose me as their spokesman before the owner when they wanted to obtain some improvement or benefit. They often sent me with ultimatums because they said I had the courage to stand up to the owner."[39]

EVEN IF KHRUSHCHEV'S recollections are accurate, they still constitute retrospective mythmaking. For although he was a budding political activist, he was equally, if not more, devoted to making it as a metalworker, to courting and marrying an educated and attractive woman from a fairly prosperous family, to fathering children, and to earning enough money to live in an apartment that was large and luxurious by the standards of the day.

Not that these political and personal aims were necessarily contradictory. If and when a new order arrived in Russia, it would by definition be more open than the old to talent and ambition of the sort Khrushchev possessed. Meantime, until that new day dawned, he applied himself to making it under the old regime.

While he was still living with his parents, Nikita started spending more and more time at the home of Ivan Pisarev, who ran the main elevator at the Rutchenkovo mine. According to a Soviet account, Pisarev was also a political soul mate, and the Pisarev apartment "became a safe place for the kind of sharp and significant conversations that couldn't take place near the elevator."[40] But Khrushchev was at least as attracted by a social milieu that was new for him and into which he aspired to rise.

The fact that the name Pisarev derives from the Russian verb for "to write" suggests that the family's forebears were literate peasants who prepared letters and documents for their fellow villagers. Ivan Pisarev was indeed literate (although largely self-taught) and hence a member of the "working-class intelligentsia." Besides running the mine elevator, he made shoes for his family and extra money repairing shoes for others. He owned two cows and several pigs and was well enough off that his wife did not have to work. The Pisarevs were acquainted with French and Germans who worked in the mine administration and at least once visited the home of a family with a governess.[41]

Ivan Pisarev is remembered by a granddaughter as a powerful personality. His wife was a warm, even-tempered, intelligent woman who was unusually cultivated even though she lacked a formal education. But the main attraction for Khrushchev was the fact that the Pisarevs had five daughters. Yefrosinia was born in 1896, followed by Marusia in 1901, Vera in 1903, Anna in 1905, and Agafia in 1908. Although the girls resembled one another physically, they had quite different characters. Red-haired with freckles and extremely good-looking, Yefrosinia was "soft and feminine," in contrast with Anna, who became one of the first Young Communist activists in the Donbas and later attended the Moscow Aviation Institute. As the eldest, Yefrosinia helped raise her sisters. All five daughters completed the local *gimnaziia.*

One can understand why the ambitious, upwardly mobile Khrushchev was attracted by this family, but what did they see in him?[42] Pisarev family lore has it that Nikita was charming and outgoing, especially when there was music and dancing. Anna Pisareva recalled him as "thin, wiry and handy," a young man who "could do everything," who "repaired his house together with his father," and who was always "neatly dressed." When Khrushchev began to court Yefrosinia, known as Frosia in the family, he showed special respect to her father.

Anna Pisareva described her sister as "very beautiful, with a good figure and a pale face." Anna remembered Khrushchev as so serious-minded that he preferred the company of his elders to that of people his own age. Yet he also had a lively, roguish air about him. He raced around the settlement giving local boys a ride on his homemade motorcycle, and "once he was supporting himself, he bought a camera, a watch and a [new] bicycle. At the time, all these things were marvels. He was stubborn, sometimes very silent. When he got angry his face would redden. We'd ask him, 'Why are you angry?' He'd keep silent. Later he'd say, 'I'm not angry.' We'd say, 'But it's all over your face, so don't try to hide it.' At that point, he'd burst out laughing. He didn't drink and he was a member of the temperance society. He didn't smoke either."[43]

In an informal moment during his 1961 summit meeting with President John F. Kennedy in Vienna, Khrushchev recalled his annoyance as a young man when people took him for younger than he was and his feeling relieved when his hair started to turn gray at age twenty-two.[44] The fact that he not only didn't drink or smoke but even joined the temperance society confirms he demanded much of himself and of others. That he tried and failed to conceal his anger suggests he couldn't always live up to the standards he set.

In 1914, Nikita Khrushchev married Yefrosinia Pisareva. Their daughter, Yulia Nikitichna Khrushcheva, was born the next year, and two years after that, three days after the Bolshevik Revolution, on November 10, their son, Leonid, arrived. As a skilled metalworker Nikita Khrushchev was exempt from military service in World War I. With his good job came high pay and valuable privileges. Years later he proudly told his son-in-law that he had earned thirty gold rubles a month, or two or three times as much as an ordinary worker.[45] "I got married in 1914 when I was twenty years old," Khrushchev reported in his memoirs. "Because I had a highly skilled job, I got an apartment right away. The apartment had a sitting room, kitchen, bedroom, and dining room. Years later, after the Revolution, it was painful for me to remember that as a worker under capitalism I'd had much better living conditions than my fellow workers now living under Soviet power."[46]

When Khrushchev encountered Governor Nelson Rockefeller in New York City in 1959, Rockefeller needled him by saying that half a million Russians had emigrated to New York at the turn of the century seeking freedom and opportunity. "Don't give me that stuff," Khrushchev replied. "They only came to get higher wages. I was almost one of them. I gave very serious consideration to coming."[47]

Even if Khrushchev had emigrated (in which case, Rockefeller told him, "You would have been the head of one of our biggest unions by now"), he could hardly have looked more prosperous than he did in photographs taken around 1916: slim, trim, and positively dashing in a jacket and tie or an attractive Ukrainian shirt. One extraordinary snapshot shows him in what looks like a dinner jacket and bow tie, his wife standing demurely by his side, the very image of a Yuzovka yuppie, a far cry from the fat little man in the ill-fitting suit who waddled onto the world stage some forty years later.

Khrushchev was friendly with an older, intellectually more advanced miner named Pantelei Makhinia who aspired to become a foreman. According to a Soviet account, Pantelei's "tiny closet of a room was filled with books; they covered the tables, the floor, his trunk, everything."[48] Here the young men and their friends supposedly talked for hours about life and politics, with Nikita struggling through his first political pamphlets, including *The Communist Manifesto.* Makhinia wrote poems, which he read aloud from a blue notebook. Nikita responded with a beginner's version of literary criticism.

One poem that Nikita parsed in Pantelei's room merits quotation in full, both because it inspired Khrushchev at the time and because he read it nearly fifty years later to instruct a gathering of writers in "the tasks of literature" under socialism:

When I read a book
I like it to kindle the true flame of feeling,
So that, amidst our busy lives,
It will burn and burn, a constant flare
To ignite the impulses, the forces of men's heart,
So that we can fight against darkness till our death,
So that our lives do not pass in vain.
For it is my duty, brothers,
To leave behind at least one fragment of honest labor,
So that in the black, sepulchral shades,
Conscience will not nag.[49]

"Terrific, absolutely terrific, Pantelei," said Nikita. "Perhaps not quite as smooth as it should be, but powerfully spoken."[50]

IF THE RUSSIAN Revolution had not intervened, the path Khrushchev chose for himself before 1917 would probably have led to a career as an engineer or industrial manager. It is clear from things he said and did later in life that this was, and in some ways remained, his dream. He encouraged both his son Sergei and his grandson Yuri to become engineers, and in following his advice, they understood that they were fulfilling his dream as well as their own.[51] Of all of Khrushchev's children, Sergei, son of his second wife, Nina, was clearly his favorite: He did well in school and became not just an engineer but a rocket scientist. Nikita Khrushchev's granddaughter, Yulia Leonidovna Khrushcheva, who was raised as his daughter, is a charming, urbane woman who has worked in Moscow as the literary adviser to the Vakhtangov Theater. Khrushchev encouraged her to become an agronomist. When she proposed studying international relations instead, he grumbled, "What kind of work is that? You'll end up translating the nonsense politicians speak."

"For him," said Yulia, "a 'real job' was director of a factory or a collective farm." She remembered taking arithmetic problems that she and a school friend couldn't solve to her grandfather. "He listened to us calmly, grinned, and then solved the problems instantly," she said, "even though his mind must have been filled with affairs of state." Khrushchev's daughter Rada, who became a biologist, chose what he regarded as a more acceptable profession. "But it wasn't the best of all," according to Yulia. "That would have been to be an engineer."[52]

Khrushchev's dream of becoming an engineer himself was not impossible. Even before 1917 the ranks of engineers and managers weren't entirely closed to ambitious proletarians. After 1917 it was certainly doable. But there was one big distraction, the revolution itself. In 1914 Khrushchev seemed to be settling down to a life that revolved around his job and his family. But as the war's destructive effects were felt in Yuzovka, and strike activity flared in response, he could not resist getting ever more involved.

In March 1915 a big strike broke out at the Rutchenkovo mine. It began in Khrushchev's workshop, and he is said to have been one of three main leaders. When the workers gathered to demand higher wages and better working conditions, Khrushchev reportedly delivered a "fiery speech."[53] Later the same year a man from another mine came looking for him. "I've heard that you are an activist," said Khrushchev's visitor. "We need a very trustworthy man who has good handwriting and is very literate. Do you know of anyone?"

"The next day," Khrushchev's account continued, "I sent my coworker over and he copied down in his best handwriting the resolution of the Zimmerwald Conference. The copy was run off and distributed to the workers and miners in the Donbas."[54]

Neither the Zimmerwald Conference of European socialists, held in Switzerland in September 1915, nor its resolution, which called for peace as a prelude for world revolution, is the point of this story. The point was that "in the mining region I was widely considered an activist worker and was trusted." Another implication is that Khrushchev wished he could have done the whole job himself, wished, that is, that not only he were "very trustworthy" and "very literate," but that he had had "good handwriting." Why else would such seemingly prosaic details be emphasized in a story about the rise of revolution in the Donbas?

In 1916, as demonstrations against the war spread, Khrushchev helped organize new strikes by Rutchenkovo miners.[55] In February 1917 word of the tsar's abdication reached Yuzovka in the form of a telegram to railroad workers. "I remember with what joy we read that telegram," Khrushchev wrote five years later in a local newspaper. On Sunday, his first day off, he rushed into town, where he attended the biggest demonstration he had ever seen. "We were so sure of victory that we weren't even afraid of the policemen who were standing right there."[56]

How can one call the revolution, which launched Khrushchev on a career that lifted him to the summit of world power, a distraction? The reason is that, strange as it sounds, he might have made a better manager or engineer than a political leader. Although his native gifts sustained him during his rise to the top, they failed him once he was there. Yet they surely would have sufficed had he pursued his original dream of becoming an industrial engineer. Along the way he would have received the higher education he craved and felt more confident, less driven to play the very role he was determined to transcend, that of a simple peasant muzhik whom even a paranoid like Stalin could trust.

Khrushchev's political role was thrust on him by events, both before the revolution and after. But it offered an alternative path toward his dream. Making it as a metalworker, or even a trained engineer, was the slow road to glory. Political power was more immediately satisfying, even though ultimately more treacherous.

Khrushchev recalled early in Yuzovka, before he had any contact with Bolsheviks, his arguing with coworkers about the question " 'What would you rather have, power or education?' Opinions were split, and the arguments were heated. One of my comrades, who eventually became a prominent Bolshevik, and I both said that we would rather have power, of course. With power, we would take control of the schools. The universities and high schools would be in our hands and we could then easily obtain an education. If we had only education, it would still not mean that we had power."[57]

This story underlines Khrushchev's aspiration to become an educated man. It presents power as a means to education and self-development but forgets that education itself grants a kind of power, the kind that comes with knowledge and self-knowledge. Khrushchev's tragedy was that the path of power ultimately made demands upon him that he couldn't meet, and others he shouldn't have, with the result that in his desperate search for respect he ended up lacking respect for himself. Asked at the very end of his life what he regretted, he mentioned the fact that "I had no education and not enough culture. To govern a country like Russia, you have to have the equivalent of two academies of sciences in your head. But all I had was four classes in a church school and then, instead of high school, just a smattering of higher education. So I acted inconsistently; I kept rushing about this way and that. I offended many good people. . . . I shouted and swore . . . at the intelligentsia, which actually supported my anti-Stalinist policies. They supported me, and look how I treated them in return."[58]

CHAPTER FOUR

To Be or Not to Be an Apparatchik: 1918–1929

BETWEEN FEBRUARY 1917, when the tsar abdicated in Petrograd, and 1929, when Khrushchev left the Donbas for Moscow, Russia and its Soviet successor state endured a succession of terrible ordeals. On top of world war and revolution came civil war and famine. In the Donbas, where Reds, Whites, Blacks (anarchists), and Greens (peasant armies) clashed, the struggle was so furious that power changed hands at least twenty times.[1] Reconstruction commenced in 1921, but before the wounds could heal, the Bolsheviks began a violent campaign to collectivize agriculture and industrialize the country. In the late twenties, having smashed capitalists, landowners, and priests, and repressed Ukrainian nationalists and such non-Communist parties as Mensheviks and Socialist Revolutionaries, the Bolsheviks were purging their own ranks.

Ironically, these were the years when Khrushchev convinced himself that a new world in which peace and justice would reign was aborning. It was to the "time and atmosphere" of that period, he recollected in retirement, that he "always dreamed of returning." Asked why he had "raised [his] hand against Stalin" after the dictator's death, Khrushchev replied, "Because I wasn't a man of the thirties." Instead he considered himself a product of the early postrevolutionary period when, he recalled, "I became a Communist," when "the scales fell from my eyes."[2]

In February 1917, Khrushchev was a minor figure on the periphery of a vast upheaval. Eleven years later he was a high-level party apparatchik in the Soviet Ukraine. But it took him awhile to choose revolutionary politics over mere metalworking. He didn't join the Bolshevik party until late in 1918, more than a year after it had seized power. When the civil war ended, he took a job as the deputy director of a mine. Not once but twice during this period he resumed his schooling in hope of becoming an engineer or a factory manager, yet each time he was again "distracted" by his budding political career.

If Khrushchev hesitated to commit himself to a career in the Communist apparatus, it was partly because the party's prospects were uncertain, but also because he sensed his own limitations. He remembered feeling unsure of himself at almost every step up the ladder. He resisted promotions so as to remain in familiar places surrounded by respectful colleagues and friends. Some of this was the natural nervousness of the neophyte. But not all.

Khrushchev compensated for his flaws by making the most of his gifts: his remarkable capacity for hard work, his seemingly straightforward, hail-comrade-well-met personality. But another quality helps explain his rise: the very fact that he was unsure of himself and of his chances to succeed. Particularly in the bloody thirties, but in the tumultuous twenties as well, the Bolshevik party was filled with ambitious careerists. If Khrushchev projected a becoming modesty, his bosses must have been surprised. The question, then and now, is whether his seeming simplicity and decency were genuine or contrived. The answer is that they were real but that he also manipulated them with stunning success. For Khrushchev proved to be no slouch as an intriguer. That side of him is almost totally obscured in his own account of the 1920s and only dimly visible in surviving documents of the time, but it too was real.

EVEN BEFORE the Bolsheviks seized power in October 1917, the fall of the Romanovs transformed Khrushchev's world.[3] The new Provisional Government in Petrograd reigned but did not rule, especially in the southern reaches of the empire. With conservative and liberal parties discredited along with the monarchy, such minimal order as existed in the Donbas was kept by elected soviets (councils) of workers' deputies. Often, however, near anarchy prevailed. What Yuzovka mineowners called workers' excesses included the introduction of a de facto eight-hour workday. But there were real excesses too: seizures or wrecking of bosses' flats, beatings, summary arrests, and kangaroo courts.

For the moment the Bolsheviks were almost as unpopular as the hated *burzhui*, the pejorative term for the bourgeoisie. The miners' imperial patriotism led them to lynch several antiwar Bolsheviks in Yuzovka. After a July 1917 uprising against the Provisional Government in Petrograd (following which Lenin went into hiding and Trotsky was arrested), Bolsheviks were even more vulnerable in the Donbas. When Lenin seized power in Petrograd, the Yuzovka soviet passed a Menshevik-sponsored resolution condemning the Bolshevik coup. Only by forcing out their rivals did the Bolsheviks eventually obtain an unreliable majority in the Yuzovka soviet. "To save the Bolsheviks," comments a careful historian, "it would take a civil war."[4]

Khrushchev quickly found his footing in the confusion of 1917, but not on the Bolshevik side. When deputies to the Rutchenkovo soviet were chosen, he was among them; on May 29, 1917, he was "unanimously" elected chairman. In August he joined a political-military group defending the revolution at Rutchenkovo, and December found him chairing the Council of Mining and Metalworkers' Unions, which linked workers at eight mines and factories in the Yuzovka area. During this same period Stalin's future henchman Lazar Kaganovich led the Bolsheviks in Yuzovka. A Soviet account insists Khrushchev too was already a Bolshevik at heart. But he was not yet a member of the party.[5]

"He was no revolutionary," said Vyacheslav Molotov nearly seven decades later. "It was only in 1918 that he joined the party. That's how active he was! By that time plenty of simple workers had joined. Yet this is the kind of man who later became the leader of our party! It's absurd! Absurd!"[6]

Although Molotov's contempt could be dismissed as sour grapes, Khrushchev himself was extremely defensive on this score. "I was known as something of an activist, but I did not become a party member until 1918," he said in retirement. "When people asked me why I did not join earlier I explained that in those days joining the party was not the same as it is now. No one campaigned or tried to convince you to join. There were many different movements and groups, and it was difficult to keep them all straight. When the revolution took place I decided on my position immediately."[7]

As self-justifications go, this one is particularly inept. That no one pressured him to join is hardly the excuse of a committed, self-motivated revolutionary. The difficulty Khrushchev had distinguishing among competing groups contradicts his assertion that he "intuitively sided with the Bolsheviks."[8] Also, his claim that he determined his ideological position immediately after October 1917 is just plain false. In fact, Khrushchev probably felt closer to the Mensheviks, with their emphasis on economic improvement, than to the Bolsheviks, who sought political power at any cost. After all, the Mensheviks' main constituency was better-off workers with something to lose, and Khrushchev was one of them. As long as the moderates were in control, he had plenty to gain. Only after the Bolsheviks took control and seemed the most likely to beat back attempts at counterrevolution did Khrushchev come down on their side.

IF THE REVOLUTION sparked disorder, the civil war that followed proved much worse, particularly in the Donbas, where a third of the miners perished. South of the Donbas a powerful White Army forced the Reds to retreat. In December 1917, Cossack contingents under General Kaledin murdered twenty workers in Yasinovka and threw their bodies into cesspools and dung heaps. In nearby Makeyevka, Cossacks gouged out eyes, cut throats, and hurled other miners alive down mine shafts. In response, workers' detachments known as Red Guards arrested White officers, mine managers, and Cossacks, shot them on the spot, and left their bodies in the streets.[9]

As Kaledin's troops moved toward Yuzovka, creating a flood of refugees as they went, they met resistance from Red forces sent from Petrograd. At several points in the struggle, Kaledin's forces clashed with a battalion of Rutchenkovo Red Guards said to have been led by Ivan Danilov and Nikita Khrushchev.[10]

By February 1918 Kaledin had been defeated.[11] By April another anti-Bolshevik force, the Central Rada in Kiev, which had declared itself the government of an independent Ukraine, had been toppled. Now the Bolsheviks faced a more dangerous enemy, the powerful German Army, which was still at war with Russia and the Entente.[12] As German and Austrian troops approached Yuzovka, the Bolsheviks fled, leaving the town briefly in the hands of anarchists. The Germans and their Ukrainian partner, Hetman Pavlo Skoropadsky, restored the mines' former managers, who took fierce revenge on politically suspect workers. In one town the Germans shot forty-five miners to death on the day they arrived. Before long most of the miners who hadn't left with the Bolsheviks or joined the Red Army or fled south to escape famine returned to their villages.[13]

Khrushchev was among those who fled.[14] When next heard from, he was back in the countryside, where yet another round of violence was erupting in 1918.[15] Although viscerally suspicious of the peasantry, the

Bolsheviks had promised them land (as well as peace and bread) to obtain their support. Yet when land was redistributed, it was taken not only from landlords and the church but from better-off peasants, and in the spring of 1918 the Bolsheviks were confiscating grain to feed city dwellers and the new Red Army. When peasants resisted, armed detachments seized the grain by force, triggering famine on top of the death and destruction of war.

Khrushchev headed the Committee of the Poor in Kalinovka. In theory, villagers were divided into rich (kulaks), middle, and poor peasants. In fact, the distinctions weren't so clear. Nonetheless, the Bolsheviks set out to exploit this "class rivalry" by pitting neighbor against neighbor.[16] One can't be sure how bloody the fratricide became in Khrushchev's village. One can assume he played a part in fomenting it.

Sometime in late 1918 or early 1919, Khrushchev was mobilized into the Red Army. By this time White forces, the Germans having left Ukraine when the armistice was signed in November 1918, were savaging Yuzovka. General S. V. Denisov ordered one of every ten workers arrested to be hanged; hundreds of corpses were left dangling for days in the streets. In response, the Reds shot engineers and technicians suspected of collaborating with the Whites. Skoropadsky's police and Nestor Makhno's anarchist followers butchered their foes too, while Jews were the targets of bloody pogroms from all sides.[17]

Farther south, where Khrushchev was now stationed with the Reds' Ninth Army, the fighting was even more barbaric. Although Commissar of War Leon Trotsky had barred executing prisoners, "wounded or captured [White] officers were not only finished off and shot but tortured in every possible way. Officers had nails driven into their shoulders according to the number of stars on the epaulets; medals were carved on their chests and stripes on the legs. Genitals were cut off and stuffed in their mouths."[18]

White General Anton Denikin's forces retook the whole Kuban region and the northern Caucasus, capturing fifty thousand prisoners. By midsummer 1919 the Red Army in southern Russia seemed on the verge of a rout. White forces captured Kharkov, Yekaterinoslav (later called Dnepropetrovsk) and Tsaritsyn (later Stalingrad and then Volgograd). Kursk fell to a coup de main by a White armored train on September 20. But then the tide turned. The same flaws that prevented Denikin from moving on Moscow—shortage of troops, poor organization, and lack of mass appeal—led to drastic reverses. The end for his Volunteer Army came in May 1920. The civil war as a whole ended when White General Pyotr Wrangel's troops were evacuated from the Crimea in November.

Khrushchev's Ninth Army apparently had a mixed record. According to one account, it "repeatedly ran away" from action.[19] Still, it managed to march 620 miles from the upper reaches of the Don to the shore of the Black Sea, and as it did, Khrushchev rose from head of a small party cell to battalion political commissar to instructor in the Ninth Army's Political Department.

The institution of the political commissar was introduced in April 1918 as Red forces came to rely less on committed worker activists and more on politically unreliable peasants. The commissar's role was to promote combat readiness, high troop morale, and good relations with the civilian population, partly by raising the cultural level of the troops. As revolutionaries the Bolsheviks took these goals seriously. The task of "agitational, propaganda and enlightenment work" included teaching illiterate recruits how to read and write, publishing pamphlets and newspapers, staging plays, establishing libraries, and maintaining Red Army clubs.[20]

Yet the commissars who enlightened their comrades were barely more educated than their men. In January 1919, Stalin and Feliks Dzerzhinsky, head of the security police, demanded a purge of commissars, explaining that the word itself had become "a term of abuse." A Red Army brigade commander who defected in 1919 considered only 5 percent of the commissars "idealistic Communists," with the rest consisting of careerist workers, backward peasants, and "the dregs of the other classes, mostly youngsters and failures, and of course, almost a majority of Jews." Yet the same defector had to admit that for all their faults, the commissars were "amazingly hard-working, supervising commanders and agitating among the men" and that their role in maintaining "class antagonism among the mass of soldiers" was "enormous."[21]

Khrushchev's account of his own activities is equally contradictory. He claimed a heroic frontline role: "We took the offensive and marched right through a hail of enemy bullets. . . . We . . . drove the White-Guardist bands into the sea."[22] But for much of the time he was in a construction battalion not an infantry unit; he spent at least two months taking a training course for political instructors; and many of his later "war stories" had more to do with his own and his troops' cultural backwardness than their military exploits.

"We weren't gentlemen in the old-fashioned sense," he recalled. When he and his men were billeted for two days on the estate of former gentry, "it became impossible even to enter the bathroom. Why? Because the people in our group didn't know how to use it properly. Instead of sitting on the toilet seat so that people could use it after them, they perched liked eagles on top of the toilet and mucked the place up terribly. And after we'd put the bathroom out of commission, we set to work on the park [grounds and gardens] nearby. After a week or so, the park was so disgusting it was impossible for anyone to walk there."[23]

On another occasion, he was housed with a family of intelligentsia. His hostess had graduated from a school for daughters of the nobility in St. Petersburg, and other family members included a jurist, an engineer, a teacher, and a musician. Khrushchev recalled the lady of the house's saying "very bravely to me, 'Now that you Communists have seized power, you'll trample our culture into the dirt. You can't possibly appreciate a fragile art like the ballet.' She was right. We didn't know the first thing about ballet. When we saw postcards of ballerinas, we thought they were simply photographs of women wearing indecent costumes."[24] Yet while Khrushchev admitted that he and his men were "uncouth, uneducated workers," he insisted that they "wanted to receive an education, we wanted to learn how to govern a state and to construct a new society." He told his hostess, "Just you wait, we will have everything including ballet."[25]

The fact that Khrushchev retold *these* war stories says a lot. The cultural gulf between him and the old intelligentsia was on his mind not only during the civil war but decades later, when he dictated his memoirs. The ostensible point of describing his comrades' toilet habits was that he and they had long since been transformed. But if so, why bring it up at all? Khrushchev anticipated just such an objection. "Well, my answer," he replied, "is that such conditions persisted for a long time. It took decades for people to advance from their primitive habits."[26]

After the civil war ended in 1921 with the Donbas in ruins, construction battalions were renamed labor brigades. "So, you're a miner?" a division headquarters clerk asked Khrushchev. "Good. You are just what we need at the moment—a [labor brigade] commissar!"

Khrushchev resisted the assignment. "The clerk and I swore at each other. 'Who do you think you are?' I shouted. 'And who do you think you are?' he replied."[27] The words actually exchanged were almost certainly more pungent than that. But Khrushchev's status was still lowly enough that, as he puts it, "I ended up going."

With the war over, the Red Army lost its favored position. Weakened by undernourishment, soldiers could not fight off epidemics of typhus and scurvy.[28] "Living and working conditions were terrible," Khrushchev later said. "There were no uniforms and no changes of clothes. The men went unwashed and unshaven and were overworked. There was not enough food."[29] Khrushchev himself was reduced to depending on a peasant family, to living again in the back of a peasant hut. He survived on scraps from the family's table. Only in 1922 did a friend, who had become the director of the Rutchenkovo mine, come to his rescue by making him assistant director for political affairs. In the meantime disaster had struck his family.

When Khrushchev fled Yuzovka for Kalinovka in 1918, he took his wife and two children with him, and he left them there with his parents when he joined the Red Army. Parted for the first time from her parents and sisters, Yefrosinia was at the mercy of her strong-minded mother-in-law. Although protected from the worst of the war, she must have feared it would claim her husband's life. Ironically, it was she whom war, or rather the hunger and disease that went with it, claimed. She fell ill with typhus, and by the time Khrushchev, who wasn't far away on the southern front, could return home, she died.[30]

"Her death was a great sadness to me," Khrushchev said laconically but poignantly in his memoirs. The story Kalinovka residents tell is that he arrived there the day after she died. His parents had planned a funeral service in the village church, to be followed by burial in the cemetery. But Khrushchev arranged to have the coffin passed by hand over the fence, rather than through the church, whose back door led into the cemetery. What he was trying to do, Nina Petrovna Khrushcheva explained to her children after their father died, was to avoid offending religious relatives while not violating his atheistic Communist principles. "This was typical of his future behavior," Nina Petrovna commented, "unexpected, sometimes shocking, and always out of the ordinary. At the time, the villagers all condemned Father. To this day they still shake their heads disapprovingly when they remember what happened."[31] His parents' reaction must have been considerably stronger than that.

THE YUZOVKA to which Khrushchev returned in 1922 was shattered. Coal production had ceased. Everything from food and housing to dynamite and fuses for the mines was in short supply. Mineowners and operators had fled; so had many miners. Hyperinflation added to the town's miseries: In February 1922 a thirty-six-pound bag of flour cost two million rubles, while a pound of meat of ominously uncertain origin cost thirty-seven thousand rubles.[32]

Pestilence struck as the civil war ended. Typhus and cholera spread quickly, while crop failures produced widespread starvation. In the country as a whole, deaths from famine in 1921 and 1922 exceeded the combined total of casualties in the world war and civil war.[33] In the spring of 1922 approximately 38 percent of the Yuzovka district population was going hungry, and some four hundred thousand children were starving in the Donbas as a whole.[34] Father Neveu, an Assumptionist priest who lived through the famine in Makeyevka, saw scenes "reminiscent of Flavius Josephus' description of the siege of Jerusalem. Mothers kill their children and then commit suicide to put an end to their suffering. Everywhere we see people with haggard complexions and swollen bodies, people who can hardly drag themselves around, and who are driven to eating dead cats, dogs and horses."[35]

In Shakhty, a man bought and ate cooked meat from an old woman whose house was subsequently searched; in it were found "two barrels containing parts of children's bodies, sorted and salted, and scalped heads." A crowd that gathered at the house beat the woman and her husband to death.[36]

In 1921, at Lenin's insistence, the regime adopted the New Economic Policy (NEP), which replaced forced requisitioning of grain with a tax in kind, and allowed peasants to dispose of their surpluses on the open market. Although the NEP eased conditions in the country at large, its effects were not immediately felt in the Donbas, where hunger drove thousands from the mines in search of food, and the resulting shortage of coal prevented trainloads of supplies from reaching the area. Moscow dispatched 150 top managers to the Donbas, drafted all males between eighteen and forty-six and all miners up to the age of fifty to work in the pits, and mobilized tens of thousands of civilians who arrived from around the country.[37] But in Yuzovka itself the Bolsheviks were still few in number and extremely unpopular.[38]

Despite their weakness, or perhaps because of it, Donbas Bolsheviks showed no mercy to their "class enemies." So-called revolutionary tribunals meted out death and long prison sentences to "counterrevolutionaries." Viewing Donbas miners as "pyschologically smashed," with "their proletarian consciousness, not very high to begin with, now completely crushed," the party imposed harsh discipline to get them to work.[39] The result was the triggering of widespread labor unrest, with strikes continuing through the twenties.[40]

It was only natural under these conditions that dissent spread within the Bolsheviks' ranks. In May 1922 Lenin suffered his first stroke, after which, except for a few months, he was a complete invalid until his death on January 21, 1924. Meanwhile a split developed between Stalin, Grigory Zinoviev, and Lev Kamenev, on the one hand, and Trotsky, on the other. For the moment Stalin and his allies championed an indefinite continuation of the NEP, whereas Trotsky warned that core socialist values, such as the priority of industrialization and of the proletariat over the peasantry, were being jeopardized. Trotsky also raised the issue of "intraparty democracy," charging that a dictatorship of Stalin's faction had taken over the party. In October 1923 the Politburo in Moscow received a declaration, signed by forty-six high-ranking Bolsheviks, criticizing the "inadequacy of the party leadership" and the "completely intolerable" regime within the party.[41]

Two years later Stalin defeated Trotsky politically. Two years after that, in 1927, Stalin sent him into exile. But in the early twenties Trotsky and other dissidents were still very popular in the Donbas. Consequently, although the Declaration of the Forty-six was condemned by the party Central Committee in Moscow, and the Yuzovka party committee voted to back the Kremlin, twelve Yuzovka committee members (out of seventy-nine) voted to support it, the highest pro-Trotsky total in the Donbas.[42]

This was the situation to which Khrushchev returned in 1922. His stint at the Rutchenkovo mine lasted only a few months, but it established the energetic, hands-on style of leadership he was to exhibit from then on. Working without blueprints (the owners had taken them when they fled), he and his men "took the ovens to pieces so that we could find out what the production of coke by-products involved and how to get it going. We had no engineers then to service the machines. Many of the engineers who had stayed behind in the Donbas were opposed to us."[43] Khrushchev donned his old miner's outfit and descended underground to inspect machinery. He met nonstop with fellow managers and party and trade union officials; he inspected workers' barracks and requisitioned desperately needed food.[44]

In contrast with other Bolsheviks, who had soured on seemingly "declassed" workers, Khrushchev felt genuine sympathy for his former brothers at the bench. "Here we'd overthrown the monarchy and the bourgeoisie, we'd won our freedom, but people were living worse than before. No wonder some asked, 'What kind of freedom is this? You promised us paradise; maybe we'll reach paradise after death, but we'd like to have a taste of it here on earth. We're not making any extravagant demands. Just give us a corner to live in.' "[45]

But while restive miners "gave it to [me] good and hot," Khrushchev recalled, "even though they knew [me] inside out since I worked with them in the mines before the revolution," he gave back as good as he got. "Hold up your hands and let us see them," he shouted at those he regarded as "hostile elements." "Those are not the hands of a miner. Those are the hands of a shopkeeper."[46]

So successful was Khrushchev as Rutchenkovo deputy director that he was soon named to head the nearby Pastukhov mine. But instead of accepting the appointment, he applied to a workers' training program that had just opened in what was to become the Donetsk Mining Technical College (*tekhnikum*). When his Yuzovka party superiors resisted, he appealed to the director of mines for the Donbas, who had also applied for the program: "You're an educated man, you've finished high school, and now you've applied to study at the mining institute. But you won't let me go. I don't think that's right. Why won't you let me go? I've finished only four years of school . . . , but you won't let me continue my education."[47]

Khrushchev's thirst for education wasn't unique. The Bolsheviks were supposed to become a cultural as well as political vanguard; party members would be required not only to "work productively" but to "rest culturally." That meant cleanliness and decent table manners; reading a Russian classic and seeing a ballet would be even better.[48] Why, then, did Khrushchev's bosses resist his request? Was it because he was such a good administrator that they couldn't spare him? Or was it because they couldn't imagine a year or two of study lifting the crude Khrushchev's level anyway? In the end, however, they relented, and he enrolled.

The *tekhnikum*'s mandate was to turn into engineers its initial class of 208 students, most of them with at least partial secondary education, ten years in the mines, and party or Communist Youth League membership. The workers' training program (*rabfak*) that Khrushchev entered had more modest aims. After two to three years of study, which would in effect take the place of high school, its graduates would be eligible to enter the first year of the *tekhnikum*. On the *rabfak* application he filled out on August 24, 1922, Khrushchev listed his reason for enrolling: "to obtain technical knowledge necessary for more productive work in industry."[49]

The Yuzovka *rabfak* was part of a larger educational movement. As in the case of American affirmative action, the movement tried to channel disadvantaged groups toward higher education. According to a Western history, the effort "involved a temporary lowering of academic standards; and it was accomplished by a series of governmental actions which were resisted by the educational institutions involved and resented by middle-class parents."[50]

Rabfak entrance requirements were as low as could be imagined: Entrants in 1924 were to have "a firm command of the four arithmetical functions using whole numbers; to be able to express their thoughts adequately in written and spoken form; and to possess general political education to the level of elementary programs of political literacy."[51] When it came to political literacy, Khrushchev must have been first in his class. But although he is described in a Soviet account as not just "diligent" but "distinguished by profound learning,"[52] one of his teachers remembered otherwise. According to her, the future leader of the USSR and the world Communist movement "could barely hold a pencil in his calloused hands" when he arrived. Obviously lacking in self-confidence, he tried especially hard to please. She recalled his struggling to grasp a point in grammar and, when he at last understood it, smiling and shouting, "I got it." Yet, despite his efforts, she thought he remained "a poor pupil."[53]

One reason was that he was preoccupied by his political obligations. Early on he was appointed party secretary not just of the *rabfak* but of the whole *tekhnikum.* That made him responsible for the political health of the institution and (along with its director) for the physical condition of the place. The building, which had held a high school of commerce before the revolution, looks imposing in pre-1917 photographs, as it still did in 1991. But when the *tekhnikum* first opened its doors, it was lucky if it had doors to open. Most students lived, thirty or forty to a large room, in broken-down barracks that had once housed the dreaded Cossacks.[54] As party leader Khrushchev had the "privilege" of sharing a small corner room with only three other students.

The first students had to repair the building before their studies could start. At Khrushchev's urging, they foraged for rusty machinery and spent weeks repairing it, and they erected makeshift workshops, laboratories, and an electricity-generating station.[55] Since suitable textbooks were lacking, Khrushchev proposed printing their own on an improvised press in the cellar. He "kept popping in on us," the chief typographer recalled, "checking on what was going on, and giving us instructions."[56] When the party cell put out a newspaper, Khrushchev oversaw its planning and layout. As party leader he was responsible for the ideological purity of the paper, but he seemed just as interested in how it got put out. His multiple duties demanded peripatetic activity, but it was also as if Khrushchev's idea of getting an education were doing what he had always done—rushing around, meeting people, and coping with emergencies—in a new, more academic setting, as if having worked so hard for a chance to educate himself, he now found reasons to avoid doing so.

In September 1924 Khrushchev was a member of the commission that granted diplomas to the first fifteen graduates of the *tekhnikum.* But he himself never received one. Although he claimed to have finished the *rabfak,* that isn't certain either.[57] Even if he did, the low quality of its curriculum, and the limited amount of time he devoted to his studies, ensured that his educational level wasn't elevated significantly.

Party Secretary Khrushchev rode political herd on students and faculty alike. If that responsibility seems daunting for a mere *rabfak* enrollee, he had extra authority that came from other, more important party assignments. In December 1923 he represented his party cell at the fourth conference of the Yuzovka regional party committee; that same month he joined the committee itself, becoming one of forty party and government officials who constituted the local Bolshevik elite. In this capacity Khrushchev became a familiar figure at Yuzovka mines, factories, and educational institutions. After almost single-handedly bringing a strike at one mine to a halt, he was appointed to the Yuzovka party committee's inner circle, its bureau.[58]

Responsible positions like these were reserved for the ideologically reliable. It is all too easy to imagine Khrushchev's falling for Stalin's simplified, primer-level Marxism during these years.[59] In fact, however, he briefly joined Trotskyite oppositionists in rejecting the Stalinist line, a grave political error that later placed his career, and even his life, at risk.

"In 1923," Khrushchev said in his memoirs, "when I was studying at the workers' training program, I was guilty of Trotskyite wavering. . . . I was distracted by Kharechko, who was a rather well-known Trotskyite. . . . I didn't stop to analyze various tendencies in the . . . party; all I knew was this was a man who had fought for the people before the revolution, fought for workers and peasants."[60]

Trofim Kharechko was a prominent Bolshevik who had signed the Declaration of Forty-six.[61] Since the issue of internal party democracy (or rather the lack thereof) was hotly contested, Khrushchev must have known what he was doing. He certainly couldn't admit that while Stalin lived, however, and he never did afterward either.

WHEN KHRUSHCHEV returned to Yuzovka in 1922, he was frequently seen in the company of young women, hardly surprising for a vigorous twenty-seven-year-old who had been away at war for four years. What hasn't been known until now is that he met and married a young woman of about seventeen fresh out of the *gimnazium.* Marusia, whose last name isn't known, had been going out with a young man whom her father didn't admire and had had a daughter by him. Marusia's father knew Khrushchev from the mine, considered him a good man, and convinced his daughter to marry him instead.

Preoccupied with her child, Marusia was apparently unwilling or unable to cope with Khrushchev's children, who had by now joined him from Kalinovka. Yulia was seven and Lyonia five; raised by doting grandparents, both were a handful. Khrushchev's mother criticized Marusia for neglecting her stepchildren, and she apparently convinced him to leave his new wife. Some of his friends in Yuzovka considered Marusia an opportunist. She is said to have forever regretted losing Khrushchev. He continued to help her out, especially when her daughter became ill and later died before she turned twenty.[62]

The brief marriage does more than fill a gap in Khrushchev's personal history in the twenties. It constitutes a second guilty secret (Khrushchev's Trotskyism was the first) that tormented him later on. This, according to Sergei Khrushchev, may be what his father and mother, Khrushchev's third wife, Nina Petrovna, used to have angry arguments about, arguments that they tried to hide from their children. This may also be one reason that Nikita Sergeyevich and Nina Petrovna never officially registered their marriage until after his ouster in the late 1960s.[63]

Abandoning Marusia is a striking private example of a pattern that marked Khrushchev's public life: his willingness to violate his own moral injunctions, at the price of a deep sense of guilt. According to his children, Khrushchev set strict rules for his family. The relatively few times they saw him very angry was when they violated these rules. One rule was that his children must lead productive lives. He was distressed when they seemed idle. He was upset when their schoolwork was less than excellent, especially when teachers complained about their behavior. He prided himself on being highly organized and efficient (even though one couldn't tell that from some of his helter-skelter policies) and insisted that they be likewise.

Another Khrushchev maxim was that drinking to excess was despicable. A glass or two was all right (although never, ever before driving), but according to his adopted daughter, Yulia, Khrushchev "couldn't stand drunkards; he positively hated them. He insisted over and over that a man must know his limits, and he despised people who did not."[64]

A third rule had to do with immorality and divorce. Khrushchev was outraged when his son Leonid turned out to be a playboy, and when Leonid's illegitimate son, Yuri, at first seemed a chip off the same block. Khrushchev was scandalized when his other children contemplated or, worse yet, embarked upon divorce. According to Yulia, Khrushchev's first principle was that "when you marry someone, you commit yourself for life. For him, there was no greater tragedy than a marital rupture or divorce." Since Yulia herself has had several husbands, and Sergei Khrushchev has been divorced twice, Nikita Khrushchev had plenty of cause for concern. One of his children preserved an unhappy marriage for nearly two decades rather than cross the old man.

Soon after leaving Marusia, Khrushchev met Nina Petrovna Kukharchuk. Though six years younger than he, she was more highly educated and even more of a Communist puritan than he was, perfectly suited, that is, to become both his tutor and his conscience.

Nina Petrovna's parents were peasants too, she later noted, but her mother had received a dowry consisting of "several hectares [1 hectare equals 2.47 acres] of land, several oak trees in the forest, a trunkful of clothes, and a bed." Her father's family "had three-quarters of a hectare free and clear, an old log hut, and a little garden with plum trees and one cherry tree."[65] Nina Petrovna was born on April 14, 1900, in the village of Vasiliev in the province of Kholm (or Chelm, as it is known in the stories of Sholem Aleichem) in the Ukrainian part of the kingdom of Poland, which was itself part of the Russian Empire. Like most children in her village, Nina Petrovna spoke Ukrainian, but was forced to use Russian in school—at pain of a rap across the palm (called getting a paw) when she made a mistake. Ethnically Ukrainian, she spoke the language far better than her husband, the future Communist party boss of Kiev.

Like Khrushchev, his future wife caught the eye of a primary school teacher who told her father that she should study in the city. In 1912 he "put me, a sack of potatoes, and a chunk of a hog on a cart and drove us to Lublin, where his brother was a conductor on freight trains." After a year in a Lublin school and another in Kholm (to which her uncle moved), Nina Petrovna was home on vacation in Vasiliev when war broke out in August 1914. When the Austrian Army rampaged through the village, abducting women and girls as they went, her mother saved her by pretending Nina had typhus. When Russian forces recaptured the village and ordered its evacuation, Nina's mother and her two children became refugees. They eventually encountered Nina's father and then tagged along with Pyotr Kukharchuk's military unit. The unit's commander gave Kukharchuk a letter to the bishop of Kholm, who arranged for Nina to study at an exclusive girls' school, which had been evacuated from Kholm to Odessa. "The school didn't admit the children of peasants," Nina Petrovna later recalled. "Only specially selected daughters of priests and officials studied there. I ended up there because of the wartime circumstances I've described."

After graduating in 1919, Nina Petrovna briefly worked in the school office, writing out diplomas and copying documents. She joined the Communist party in 1920, and that summer, as the Red Army drove toward Warsaw intent on conquering Poland, she worked as a party propagandist in Ukrainian villages near the front. When the Communist party of western Ukraine was formed, Nina Petrovna headed its women's section. After the Red Army had been forced to retreat from Poland, she was sent to Moscow for six months of study at the recently formed Sverdlov Communist University. Her next assignment, in the Donbas, was to help carry out purges (still nonviolent in the twenties) of careerists and other scoundrels who had attached themselves to the party during the civil war. Next, she was to teach "the history of the revolutionary movement and political economy" at a province party school, but before she could begin, she caught typhus and almost died. After she recovered, she worked briefly at a teacher-training program at Taganrog. She arrived in Yuzovka in the autumn of 1922 to teach political economy in the district party school.

The future Mrs. Khrushchev also served as a party propagandist at the Rutchenkovo mine, where she taught the miners "basic political literacy" and gave lectures on politics at their club. Khrushchev attended her lectures at the mine and at the Yuzovka *tekhnikum.* In that narrow sense, and in a larger sense too, she was his teacher. In accordance with the traditional patriarchal pattern, he appeared to be the boss of their household. "He was the head of the family," according to Sergei Khrushchev. "No one ever talked back to him—not because they feared he would shout but because it just never came into our head that we could do so. But real power in the family was exercised by Mama. She ran the house; she checked up on how we studied; she tried to bring us up so that we didn't go around thinking we were the children of powerful people and could do whatever we wanted. I know now that my teachers in school wanted to give me straight As and that they gave me lower grades only because Mama went to school and convinced them to be a bit stricter with me. After all, if that's what she wanted, they were ready to oblige."[66]

Nina Petrovna's image, like her husband's, has been shaped by her physical appearance in her later years. Short and plump and with a round peasant face, she resembled a Russian matryoshka doll or tea cozy. She seemed as calm and steady as her husband was mercurial. But Nina Petrovna was far more strict and severe than the outside world understood. Yulia described the woman who reared her as "an iron lady." If the Khrushchev home was filled with books, and their lives were replete with attendance at opera and theater, that was partly her doing. She insisted all her children study English and arranged for music lessons as well.

Khrushchev's attraction to Nina Kukharchuk was as revealing as his choice of Yefrosinia Pisareva. Both represented the higher level of culture and the stricter moral standards to which he aspired, but of which he repeatedly fell short.

In July 1925, Khrushchev was appointed party boss of the Petrovo-Marinsky District near Stalino (formerly Yuzovka). He remained there until the end of 1926. The district included four Petrovka mines and the farmland of Marinka and seven surrounding villages. It covered four hundred square miles (roughly half the size of Rhode Island), with a population divided between seventeen thousand peasants and twenty thousand miners. Khrushchev lived on the border between the two parts of his realm in a little house with a bin for potatoes to which his neighbors had access when they had extras to store. Nina Petrovna worked in Petrovka as a party propagandist, and (since agitators were paid by Moscow while district bosses were paid locally) she earned considerably more than her husband.[67]

Compared with the years before and afterward, life was relatively good in 1925 and1926. Coal production had been largely restored, and the NEP had stabilized the countryside. Stalin's ally Nikolai Bukharin was urging the peasants to "enrich themselves" as a way of getting agriculture back on its feet. But that clashed with the Bolshevik antipathy to kulaks (well-off peasants), who did particularly well on Ukraine's rich soil. Moreover, with working conditions around the mines still abysmal, strikes continued apace.

As district boss Khrushchev relied on a pitifully small cadre of fellow party members: When he arrived, there were only 715 in the whole district, nine-tenths of them in Petrovka, where the district party office was located. By the end of 1925 party membership had crept up to only 1,108.[68] By now many local party officials had put on "bourgeois airs" and were completely corrupt. On top of that, the battle in the Bolshevik leadership was intensifying. Having defeated Trotsky in 1923 and1924, Stalin clashed with his own allies Zinoviev and Kamenev in 1925. They then joined Trotsky in a united opposition in 1926.

Khrushchev threw himself into finding housing for restless miners, rustling up clothing and food, and in general badgering and dragooning them into line. Even when they were "angry and shouting," one of them recalled forty years later, "he soon would have them laughing." But there were also "times when he could be very rude and strong. A miner who would not work . . . he would fire at once."[69] A former party colleague particularly remembered Khrushchev's "personal modesty," for example, the way he would work alongside other Communists doing "volunteer" labor on Sundays.[70]

At least for the time being, the party was competing peacefully with kulaks and middlemen. "We were supposed to [beat] them at their own game," Khrushchev recalled. "We tried hard to underprice the NEPmen in state cooperatives and also to offer higher quality and better service. But we didn't have much success. Merchants who were in business for themselves could put up better displays of their products and give their customers more personal attention. Private stores catered to housewives, who like to have choice when they shop; they like to browse around and examine everything carefully."[71]

These recollections reveal one of Khrushchev's virtues, his capacity to see clearly what clashed with his ideological preconceptions. But dealing with ornery peasants brought to the surface one of his vices, his irritation at people and incidents that reminded him of his own peasant past. "You must forget all the old ways," he once instructed a group of gawking peasants who had gathered around a new tractor. We "walked behind it," one of his audience recalled, and marveled at its "strength," but "it gave off a peculiar smell." The peasants shook their heads. "Grain will never grow again," they said. "The machine is poisoning the land." Khrushchev berated the peasants: "Old ways will never build a new society."[72]

Transport and communication were primitive; the railroad didn't reach Khrushchev's district, and motor vehicles were few. Yet he was constantly on the move. In the winter "I used to pay calls on villages. I would get into a sledge—at the time, we had sledges instead of motorcars—and wrap myself up in a sheepskin coat, and the frost would not bite me." The rest of the year he got around in a horse-drawn gig. "If you sit around in your office," he later said, "you won't understand what's going on, you won't develop any wisdom."[73]

Although his position as a district party boss was modest, Khrushchev's first steps onto the larger political stage came during these years. In late 1925 he represented his district at the Ninth Ukrainian Party Congress. Shortly thereafter he was one of several delegates from Stalino to the Fourteenth USSR Party Congress in Moscow. He was a nonvoting delegate, but being chosen at all "was for me a great joy."[74]

Khrushchev behaved on his first trip to Moscow like a quintessential provincial. He and his Stalino buddies spent as much time relishing one another's awed reactions to the capital as they did appreciating the big town itself. He tried to take a streetcar to the Kremlin but ended up on the wrong side of town. His failure was all the more galling because he wanted to beat his fellow delegates there and grab the center seat in the very first row, no less. He had a chance to get it because the Ukrainian delegation was assigned to the central section, with the Stalino group given the first rows in recognition of its proletarian composition and its key position in the Ukrainian party.

No longer trusting streetcars, Khrushchev set out early each morning on foot, planning his route ("so as to get to the Kremlin without making any more mistakes") and running most of the way to Vladimir Hall, where the congress met. "Here I was, as they say, only a few feet from the leaders of our state and Party! I could see them in the flesh!" Stalin especially made a powerful impression, not only with his speeches but in an incident involving the Kremlin photographer. The Stalino delegation had asked to be photographed with Stalin, and when word came that the great man was willing, the group gathered in Catherine Hall during a recess.

"Stalin came in," Khrushchev remembered. "We asked if he would sit in the middle and we all took places around him. The photographer, Petrov . . . had worked for many years in the Kremlin. Well, as you would expect, Petrov began to tell everyone what to do, who should turn his head this way or that, where we should look. Well, suddenly, Stalin came out with a remark that everyone could hear: 'Comrade Petrov loves to order people around. He orders people around even though that's now prohibited here. No more ordering people around!' It seemed to us that Stalin was a really democratic person, that his joking remark to Petrov was not really a joke, but an organic reflection, so to speak, of the essence of the man."[75]

The Fourteenth Congress was a milestone in Stalin's rout of the Zinoviev-Kamenev opposition. It included the shouting down of speakers, including Lenin's widow, Nadezhda Krupskaya. The Ukrainian delegation outdid itself in baying and heckling, with the Stalino party boss Konstantin

Moiseyenko in full cry. It would defy natural law if a person of Khrushchev's volubility did not join the chorus, but he was too junior to have his contribution recorded in the official proceedings.

Ukrainian party conclaves were another matter, however. In October 1926 the First Ukrainian Party Conference opened the same day that six opposition leaders (Trotsky, Zinoviev, Kamenev, Georgy Piatakov, and two others) issued a declaration of submission in an effort to preserve at least some influence in the party. Despite that, an oppositionist named Golubenko continued to demand greater intraparty democracy, criticized the Ukrainian party leader Lazar Kaganovich, and defended the opposition.

"In Stalino," retorted Khrushchev, "I'm happy to say we don't have the luxury of listening to comrades like Golubenko." His speech was "intentional slander." Khrushchev was certain Golubenko "hasn't said everything he thinks." The opposition leaders' declaration was "insincere" and a "maneuver." Only if the opposition came clean in deeds as well as words could their errors be forgiven. Otherwise, "we must demand that the highest party organs apply the most repressive measures against incorrigible oppositionists, unconditionally and regardless of their former merits or positions."[76]

This speech was more Stalinist than Stalin himself. For while Stalin had temporarily accepted the opposition's submission for tactical reasons, Khrushchev did not. The "most repressive measures" that Khrushchev called for were not yet what they were to become a decade later. But his aggressive speech, with its sarcastic tone and its unsubstantiated accusations, was the sort that soon demanded that oppositionists be put to death.[77]

BY THE MID-1920S Lazar Kaganovich was one of Stalin's main liegemen. Born to a Jewish family in Kiev Province in 1893 and apprenticed to a shoemaker because he was too poor to afford an education, he had joined the Bolsheviks in 1911. Khrushchev first encountered him in 1917 in Yuzovka. "I knew him not as Kaganovich, but as Zhirovich. I trusted and respected him one-hundred percent."[78] "Actually"—Khrushchev corrected himself at another point in his memoirs—"when I first met Kaganovich his last name was not Kaganovich, but Kantorovich."[79] In yet a third rendition Khrushchev remembered him as Kosherovich.[80] Perhaps all Jewish names sounded the same to him. But if Khrushchev confused the names, he knew very well that Kaganovich had become the

Ukrainian party boss in 1925 and that the quickest way to rise through party ranks was on his coattails.[81]

Kaganovich probably helped arrange Khrushchev's December 1926 promotion to be the head of the Organization Department of the Stalino party committee and the deputy leader of the Stalino party organization. The Organization Department was the heart of the party apparatus, charged with organizing and supervising the party's professional apparatchiks, as well as keeping track of rank-and-file party members. As deputy party leader Khrushchev helped his boss, Moiseyenko, supervise the local economy; he chastised local oppositionists (for example, chairing a meeting that called on Trotsky and Zinoviev to disband their faction); he even signed death sentences for those accused of having been on the wrong side in the civil war.[82]

Then, a mere nine months later, Khrushchev helped arrange Moiseyenko's ouster. First, he informed his Stalino colleagues that the Ukrainian party leadership had decided to recall Moiseyenko. Next, he revealed that he himself had taken part in the Ukrainian Politburo's discussion of the case.[83] The Kaganovich connection must have helped; likewise, Khrushchev's friendship with Stanislav Kossior, who soon replaced Kaganovich as Ukrainian party leader. The two may have met when Kossior headed the Ninth Army's Political Department during the civil war. Newsreel coverage of the Fifteenth Party Congress, which took place in Moscow in October 1927, shows Khrushchev sitting next to Kossior in the middle of the Ukrainian delegation. Khrushchev looks like a young naval cadet in a dark suit and dark shirt, with his hair trimmed short and a broad grin on his face. When he turns and speaks to the short, bald tunic-clad Kossior, it is clear that the two enjoy each other's company.

Moiseyenko was charged with corruption and dissipation, including "systematic drinking bouts" in which top party and government leaders took part.[84] Khrushchev's protemperance Puritanism helped turn him against his boss. Forty years later he still felt self-righteous: Moiseyenko had a "powerful petty-bourgeois streak in him. . . . Therefore we had to remove him. This caused an uproar that reached all the way up to the Central Committee of the Ukrainian party, which sent a commission to investigate. It looked into our disagreements, recognized that our arguments were well-founded, and fired him."[85]

But there was more to it than that. According to Kaganovich, Moiseyenko wouldn't let Khrushchev forget his flirtation with Trotskyism.[86] Perhaps that's because in his brief Trotskyite phase, Khrushchev had criticized Moiseyenko's "violations of intraparty democracy."[87] In addition,

Khrushchev must have hoped to replace Moiseyenko. If so, he was disappointed. Instead the Ukrainian Politburo appointed V. A. Stroganov, whom, not surprisingly, Khrushchev didn't think much of either: He turned out to be "shallow," and "he loved to drink and engage in intrigues."

Before long, Stroganov's underlings began bringing important issues to Khrushchev instead of to him. "For me," Khrushchev later said, "this was understandable, but it completely diminished his role. They came to me because from childhood I had grown up in Yuzovka . . . and had a wide circle of friends. . . . So I was pretty well acquainted with industrial questions . . . which were central for us in those days. A leader who didn't know about those things was considered, to put it crudely, an idiot. And that's exactly what happened to Stroganov, although he wasn't stupid. He, too, perished, the poor guy. I was sorry then and am sorry now. He didn't deserve to be arrested and shot."[88]

Khrushchev depicted himself as an innocent bystander in Stroganov's undoing. He claimed he left Stalino so as to give the poor man a chance "to get his roots down."[89] But the story of Khrushchev's departure for Kharkov in March 1928, and his moves in rapid succession from there to Kiev and Moscow, raise the same questions about his motives as do his relations with his Stalino superiors.

AS TOLD BY Khrushchev, Kaganovich summoned him to Kharkov (then serving as the Ukrainian capital) early in 1928 and proposed making him head of the Ukrainian Central Committee's Organization Department. "We need to proletarianize the apparat," Khrushchev said Kaganovich told him.

"I think you're right," Khrushchev said he replied, "but I wouldn't want that proletarianization to come at my expense. I very much want to stay in Stalino, where I'm tied in with everything and everyone. It would be very difficult for me to move; it would be a whole new situation which I don't know, and I don't think I could get used to it." If he did transfer to Kharkov, he expected coworkers there to "greet me badly" because they were jealous of Stalino, where "we are workers, we are miners, metalworkers, and chemical workers, where we are the salt of the earth, or rather, so to speak, the salt of the party." If he had to leave Stalino, then let it be to Lugansk, where he knew and liked the regional party boss and could serve as secretary of another district like Petrovo-Marinsky.[90]

According to Khrushchev, he hesitated long and hard before he accepted Kaganovich's offer with the condition that he "be sent to another region at the first opportunity. Which region? 'It's all the same to me,'" Khrushchev told Kaganovich, "except it would be preferable if it were an industrial area, because I don't know agriculture very well, I never have spent much time in an agricultural area . . . ."[91]

Never spent much time in an agricultural area? What about the first fourteen years of his life? Wouldn't Lugansk be a step backward in his career? How could Khrushchev even think of turning down Kaganovich? Is Khrushchev's recollection a smoke screen designed to obscure naked ambition, or does it reflect genuine insecurity, or both? Kaganovich later insisted that Khrushchev begged him to arrange the transfer to Kharkov (he had come there several times unannounced and expected to be fed from the Central Committee canteen before continuing his pleading), though he granted that Khrushchev seemed uncertain about whether he could cope with new responsibilities in the Central Committee apparatus.[92]

"As I had expected"—Khrushchev's account continued—"I didn't like my job in Kharkov. It was all office work; everything had to be handled on paper, real life wasn't visible at all. But I'm a man of the earth, a man of concrete affairs, of coal, mainly, and metal and chemicals, and to a certain degree, of agriculture. . . . So I developed good relations in Kharkov with the coal and steel people. . . . Still, everything fell apart for me. I was living on a diet of paperwork, and it didn't agree with my stomach. It turned me off from the very start."[93]

According to Khrushchev, he pressed Kaganovich for another transfer; Kaganovich soon suggested a slot in Kiev, and he left that same evening: "For the first time in my life, I found myself in Kiev. What a city! . . . At that time, Yuzovka wasn't even considered a city, it was just a small town. Well, Kiev made a powerful impression on me. As soon as I got off the train, I picked up my suitcase and headed down to the bank of the Dnieper. I'd heard and read so much about it, but I just wanted to see such a powerful river with my own eyes."[94]

But he had forebodings about Kiev too. As in Kharkov, there "weren't enough workers in the Kiev party organization." On the other hand, the nationalist-minded intelligentsia, grouped around the (Ukrainian) Academy of Sciences, was active in the city, as were certain Trotskyite elements. In addition, Khrushchev later said, "the attitude toward Russians wasn't particularly favorable, so it was difficult for them to work there. I assumed nationalists would consider me a hopeless *rusak* [derogatory term for a Russian], and that it would be hard for me there too."[95]

Once again Khrushchev's modesty wasn't entirely false. Kiev, with its fabled history, its magnificent churches, and its great green parks sweeping down to the broad Dnieper, was a symbol of Ukraine, a fact that created problems for Stalin's men. Earlier in the decade they had supported a policy of "indigenization" which fostered Ukrainian language and culture within the overall framework of Soviet rule. By the end of the twenties they were increasingly alarmed by Ukrainian nationalism, especially when it seemed to infect otherwise loyal Communists,[96] and also by non-Communists who had agreed to work for the Soviet regime. In March 1928 the Soviet press announced the arrest of more than fifty Donbas engineers and technicians charged with "wrecking" activities (such as intentional flooding of mines and sabotage of equipment) and "economic counterrevolution." Between May and July the so-called Shakhty trial (after the Donbas mining town of the same name) was held in Moscow, after which at least four of the defendants were executed.[97]

These circumstances help explain Khrushchev's concerns about Kiev. He characterized his knowledge of Ukrainian as "poor" in a *rabfak* questionnaire filled out in 1922.[98] Back in Stalino in the Russian-dominated eastern Ukraine, he didn't need to speak Ukrainian, and he could get by in Russian in Kiev as well. But his combination of minimal Ukrainian and limited formal education was to lower his standing with the local intelligentsia.

Kiev turned out better than Khrushchev expected, partly because its party leader, Nikolai Demchenko, concentrated his efforts on the intelligentsia, leaving workers and peasants to Khrushchev. Still, he missed the Donbas. Once unemployed workers, egged on by assorted opponents of the Bolshevik regime, demonstrated at city hall. When Khrushchev offered them jobs, they took heart—until he revealed the jobs were in the Donbas. "There they were; they had been unemployed for a year or even two, but they were prepared to remain on the street rather than go to the Donbas. 'The Donbas is the provinces,' one of them said. . . . Well, talk like that infuriated me, because I lost my childhood there. For me, the Donbas, Yuzovka—this was my element. I had grown up in it, I had gotten used to it, I missed it."[99]

Although Khrushchev spent the rest of 1928 and early 1929 in Kiev, he devoted much of his time to trying to move to Moscow. "In 1929, I would already turn 35 years," he later said. "It was the last year I could think of entering an institution of higher education. All I had ever finished was the *rabfak*, and ever since then I had felt this pull toward getting a higher education. So I set out to try to arrange for them to send me back to school."[100]

Khrushchev's party colleagues were skeptical. Some assumed he wanted to get away from Kossior and follow Kaganovich to Moscow. Others assumed Demchenko was Khrushchev's bête noire. Khrushchev assured his colleagues that he and Demchenko were "on the very best of terms." He also explained to Kossior, "in basic human terms, that I was thirty-five years old. 'You must understand me. . . . I want to enroll in the Industrial Academy in Moscow. I want to become a metallurgist.' Kossior was understanding. He heard me out and agreed."[101]

From Stalino to Kharkov to Kiev to Moscow, all in a year and a half. However, Khrushchev's motives and machinations are still not clear. Where there was smoke (the ouster of Moiseyenko, strained relations with Stroganov, his Kiev colleagues' assumption that he was at odds with Demchenko and Kossior, the Kaganovich connection), there was probably fire. Despite his seeming modesty and straightforwardness, Khrushchev was already scheming with the best (or worst) of them. But if his Kiev colleagues assumed his craving for culture was mere manipulation, that revealed more of their preoccupations than his own. They couldn't believe his desire to educate himself was genuine; he couldn't conceive of himself without an added measure of learning.

The Khrushchev family lived on the seventh floor of a party-owned apartment house on Olginskaya Street midway between Kiev's main avenue, Kreshchatik, and the long, broad park that parallels the Dnieper. Their apartment was luxurious by the standards of the time. Besides a small kitchen and bath, there were five rooms. Nikita and Nina used one as their bedroom, in which Khrushchev also worked; although a second room was designated as a study, he never used it. A third room served as both dining room and bedroom for Yulia and Lyonia; even though two more rooms were available, the Khrushchevs couldn't imagine the children having their own room, let alone separate rooms for each of them. Instead the remaining two rooms were given over to Nina Petrovna's friend Vera Gostinskaya and her five-year old daughter.[102]

Nina Petrovna met Gostinskaya in 1926, when the two women were studying to be teachers (Nina Petrovna of political economy, Gostinskaya of history) at the Krupskaya Pedagogical Institute in Moscow. Both were originally from the same part of Poland, and they quickly became close friends. After graduation in 1928, both were sent to Kiev (Nina Petrovna to lecture at the Kiev party school, Gostinskaya to prepare teachers for local Polish-language schools), where Khrushchev was already ensconced.

(During Nina Petrovna's absence between 1926 and 1928 the Khrushchev children were once again cared for in Stalino by their grandparents.) When Gostinskaya decided to return to Moscow rather than live in her tiny dormitory room, the Khrushchevs invited her to occupy their two "spare rooms."

By this time Yulia and Lyonia were thirteen and eleven years old respectively. They were often sick after so many years in the polluted Donbas, and to make matters worse, they didn't get along very well. Lyonia, Vera Gostinskaya recalled, was "a terrible little hooligan." One day he took a gun his father kept in a closet, gathered a group of neighborhood boys, and led them away to parts unknown, leaving Nina Petrovna to spend the whole night trying to explain to anxious parents what had happened.

Nina Petrovna was soon spending more time at home than at the party school, especially after giving birth to Rada on April 4, 1929. (Another daughter, Nadia, born in 1927, died when she was three months old.[103]) Khrushchev was rarely home, and when he was, he was almost always working—except for two or three months, according to Gostinskaya, when he became so seriously ill that a doctor had to be summoned from Germany. ("Until then," she recalled, Khrushchev was "a handsome young fellow. After that grippe, and some complications that came with it, he began to change physically and lost his good looks.") After every Central Committee plenum, Khrushchev made the rounds of factories and other enterprises, explaining and expounding the party line. Before doing so, he invited Gostinskaya, a devout Communist who had joined the Polish party in 1920 at the age of fifteen, to join him at a table in the apartment, reading through the plenum transcripts and deciding what to say about them to the workers. "He loved to do everything collectively," she remembered.

It wasn't that Khrushchev was unable to parse the plenums himself. On the contrary, although he was self-educated in Marxism and Leninism, Gostinskaya regarded him not just as highly intelligent (in fact "much smarter" than his wife) but as "highly cultured." She and Nina Petrovna "never felt he was beneath us, although we had a higher education. Perhaps he understood less than we did about the precise sciences, but as far as politics was concerned he was highly educated himself. He was an extraordinarily interesting man."

When he wasn't working, Khrushchev loved to go to the theater and opera, where he sat in the party leadership box. He also enjoyed socializing with his boss Demchenko and his wife (whom Gostinskaya regarded as a particularly intelligent woman) and with Iona Yakir, who commanded the Ukrainian military district. The Demchenkos lived on the same floor as the Khrushchevs, Yakir had an apartment in the same building, and both men often dropped by to chat or play chess, sessions Khrushchev must have remembered all too well when both were executed as "enemies of the people" less than a decade later.

Gostinskaya also recalled the first time Khrushchev mentioned his move to Moscow. "If I don't go," he said, "they'll make me first secretary in some sort of Shepetovka [a rural district in the Donbas] where I'll have to understand agriculture. But I don't know a thing about agriculture."

"He dreamed of being a factory director," Gostinskaya added. "He said, 'I'll go to Moscow, I'll try to get in the Industrial Academy, and if I do, I'll make a good factory manager. A good director I can be. But as a party secretary in a rural district I'll be awful!' "[104]

CHAPTER FIVE

Stalin's Pet: 1929–1937

LOCATED BEYOND THE Garden Ring Road in a prerevolutionary villa where the tsars had a summer residence, Moscow's Stalin Industrial Academy was a flagship institution of the new socialist society. By 1929, the Bolsheviks were purging the remaining "bourgeois specialists" whom they had drafted to serve the revolution in the years after 1917. To replace them, the party was recruiting former proletarians into universities and other schools.[1] The Industrial Academy's mission was to turn cadres with previous management experience (in the party, government, trade unions, or Communist Youth League) into socialist executives. Only one hundred new students, selected from all parts of the country, were admitted in 1929. After completing a three-year course of study, graduates were to direct large factories and industrial trusts and government economic agencies.[2]

Despite their importance to the regime, Industrial Academy students were a trial for their teachers. "When you try to offer higher mathematics to someone who's had only three winters of schooling in his whole life," said a former instructor, "there are bound to be difficulties. And the same goes when you ask a nearly forty-year old man with a job and a family to sit still in class like an eight-year-old. They tried, but it was tough."[3]

In September 1929 Khrushchev enrolled in the academy. Nina Petrovna and their children remained in Kiev until the next summer, when they joined him in the capital. Khrushchev was thirty-five years old.

He had excelled in the Ukrainian party apparatus and had a powerful patron, Kaganovich, in the Kremlin. Still, according to his own account, he was greeted at the academy with disdain. "The comrades there said that I didn't suit them and recommended that I take courses on Marxism-Leninism at the Central Committee instead." They said Khrushchev lacked sufficient experience in a high-level economic job. After all, he was told, "this is an academic institution for training administrators and factory directors."[4]

Even in 1929, when courses in Marxism-Leninism evoked more respect than they did in later, ideologically desiccated decades, this suggestion was clearly condescending. It was a commentary on Khrushchev's lack of education but also on his Stalinist loyalties; when he arrived, many in the academy had doubts about Stalin, and they probably cited Khrushchev's inexperience as an excuse to turn him away. It took Kaganovich to get him in, after Khrushchev promised that if an exception were made to admit him, he would work hard to "catch up."[5] Less than ten years later the same Khrushchev, now one of the fifteen most important men in the country, left Moscow to become party boss of Ukraine, but he never finished the academy.

Between 1929 and 1938 Khrushchev's career rocketed upward: May 1930, head of the Industrial Academy's party cell; January 1931, party of the Bauman District, in which the academy was located, followed six months later by the same job in Krasnopresnensky, the capital's largest and most important borough; January 1932, number two man in the Moscow party organization itself; January 1934, Moscow city party boss and member of the party Central Committee; early 1935, party chief of Moscow province too, a region about the size of England and Wales with a population of eleven million people.[6] Even in an era of extraordinary upward mobility, Khrushchev's was stunning. Yet during the same decade in which he reached the heights, his country experienced nothing short of a holocaust.

The human cost of collectivizing agriculture was incalculable. Stalin himself later told Winston Churchill that the "great bulk" of ten million kulaks were "wiped out."[7] Many died during the great famine of 1932–1933, a terrible man-made disaster visited on the countryside (particularly but not exclusively in Ukraine) as the result of collectivization.[8] Horrors on such a scale shook the resolve of party leaders, not just those like Nikolai Bukharin, who warned in advance against coerced collectivization, but even some who supported Stalin against the Bukharinist "right opposition." In response to these doubts, exaggerated in his own paranoid imagination, Stalin released a wave of terror that eventually swept over the higher reaches of the party, the government, the military, and the intelligentsia. By the time the wave subsided somewhat in 1939, it had destroyed countless more victims, most of them accused of fantastic crimes that they had never dreamed of, let alone committed.[9]

Khrushchev not only survived but prospered. Not that he initiated or controlled the carnage. It was Stalin along with his closest associates—Vyacheslav Molotov, Lazar Kaganovich, and Kliment Voroshilov—who launched it and secret police chiefs Genrikh Yagoda, Nikolai Yezhov, and Lavrenty Beria, who operated the machinery of repression. Khrushchev wasn't a member of Stalin's inner circle until the very end of the decade. But he too bore a terrible responsibility. Even as sympathetic a biographer as Roy Medvedev can find no sign that Khrushchev "ever opposed Stalin's measures or made any effort to protect officials of the Moscow party and soviet from reprisals."[10] At the height of the terror Khrushchev gave violent, bloodcurdling speeches rousing "the masses" to join in the witch-hunt. As Moscow party boss he personally approved the arrests of many of his own colleagues and their dispatch into what he later called the meat grinder.

What explains Khrushchev's behavior? Can anything at all be said in his defense? Like many others, Khrushchev thought he was building a new socialist society, a glorious end that justified even the harshest means. If he was too busy, or too blind, to see what was happening around him or what loomed later on, he wasn't alone. Stalin concealed his intentions and alternated periods of retreat with new increments of repression. Until 1935 or perhaps 1936, it was possible for someone like Khrushchev to believe in Stalin. After that it was too late not to. He and others like him were trapped. The cost of resistance was death. The only way to save your skin, and your family, was to kowtow to the great leader, the *vozhd*.

This is the sort of defense Khrushchev might have mounted. What is remarkable is that he never did so, at least not in any detail. Instead, both while he was in power and in his memoirs, he practiced deception and self-deception. He never fully owned up to his complicity. He insisted he believed in Stalin and in the guilt of Stalin's imagined enemies. He denied he understood what was going on until after Stalin's death. Yet, read carefully in the context of his life, his memoirs belie these denials.[11]

Khrushchev had powerful political reasons not to come clean. To go beyond his famous attack on Stalin in 1956 and admit his own guilt would have undermined the whole Soviet regime, let alone his own position. In addition, he felt a personal guilt so profound that he couldn't bear to admit it, even to himself. Even beyond all this, there was another reason for his loyal service to Stalin and his silence about it afterward: While the thirties were the worst of times for many of his compatriots, they were the best of times for him.

After his discouraging reception at the Industrial Academy, what a heady feeling it must have been to rise so high so fast, to come to know Stalin himself, to sit by the great man's side in the Kremlin and at family dinners at his dacha, to think that the leader of USSR and of world communism regarded him with respect and even affection as a young man of special promise. Disappointed as he was in his own father, is it too much to say that Stalin seemed like a father figure to Khrushchev, one he insisted on idealizing despite increasingly powerful evidence of his flaws? "Stalin liked me," Khrushchev later insisted. "It would be stupid and sentimental to talk about this man loving anyone, but there's no doubt that he held me in great respect."[12] He declared: "Stalin treated me better than the others. Several Politburo members virtually considered me his pet [*liubimchik*]."[13]

If Khrushchev still cherished that memory in retirement, how much sweeter it must have been when he was just starting out! In this sense, his complicity in great crimes was rooted in more than belief in the cause, or hope for advancement, or fear of prison or death. It was tied to nothing less than his own sense of self-worth, to his growing feeling of dignity, to the invigorating, intoxicating conviction that Stalin, a man he came almost to worship, admired him in return.

WHEN KHRUSHCHEV moved to Moscow, the USSR was beginning a new "revolution from above." The gradualist New Economic Policy, which had brought a modicum of peace and prosperity to the nation, was scrapped. Trotsky, Zinoviev, and Kamenev, leaders of what Stalin labeled the "left opposition," had long favored faster industrialization to build a base for socialism. Stalin and Bukharin had insisted that accommodating the countryside was essential to Bolshevik survival in what was still an overwhelmingly peasant country. After the winter of 1927–1928, however, when peasants demanding better terms of trade withheld grain, Stalin decided to drive them onto collective farms that the state could control. As late as 1928 nearly 99 percent of the land remained uncollectivized. The first five-year plan, adopted in April 1929, envisaged collectivizing only 17.5 percent by 1933. Even that much coercion seemed the height of folly to Bukharin. But Bukharin's "right opposition" (including Premier Aleksei Rykov, trade union chief Mikhail Tomsky, and Moscow party boss Nikolai Uglanov) was defeated in April 1929 and forced to recant seven months later. Thereupon, in January 1930, Stalin ordered the *complete* collectivization of the country's most important regions by the fall of that year and then almost immediately upped the ante by demanding the bulk of the peasantry be collectivized by the start of spring sowing in 1930.[14]

What followed was all-out war against the peasantry, including forced expropriation, deportation of millions to Siberia, peasant protests ranging from arson to armed rebellions, and the famine that followed. The full picture was not visible in Moscow, even though the capital suffered food shortages and was inundated by rural refugees. But any Russian with connections in the countryside sensed what was going on, especially those like Khrushchev with roots in southern Russia and Ukraine where the famine was the worst.[15]

Khrushchev recollected a spring 1930 trip to a collective farm near Samara, where he encountered starving peasants who "moved as slowly as flies in autumn." Until then, he asserted, he'd had "no idea things were this bad. At the Industrial Academy we'd been living under the illusion . . . that everything was fine in the countryside." He heard from Ukrainian friends about peasant uprisings put down by the Red Army, which then tried to harvest sugar beets, a delicate crop that the soldiers were sure to ruin. Yet in almost the same breath Khrushchev contended, "It wasn't until many years later that I realized the scale of the starvation and repression which accompanied collectivization as it was carried out under Stalin."[16]

Desperate conditions in the countryside compelled Stalin to write an article in March 1930 blaming local officials' "dizziness from success." In a speech thirty-four years later, Khrushchev sneeringly asked, "What kind of dizziness was this in 1930? It was dizziness from hunger, not success. There was nothing to eat. I lived in Moscow at that time, comrades, and we all knew what we were dizzy from."[17] Yet at the time, he insisted in his memoirs, he considered Stalin's article a "masterpiece," even if he was "bothered by the thought: if everything has been going as well on the collective farms as Stalin has been telling us up to now, then what's the reason for [Stalin's article] all of a sudden?"

Two years later, Khrushchev later said, he was horrified to learn that "famine had broken out in Ukraine. I couldn't believe it. I'd left in 1929, only three years before. . . . Food had been plentiful and cheap. Yet now, we were told, people were starving. It was incredible." But having admitted this much, the memoirist reversed his field: "It wasn't until many years later" (when he heard of a train loaded with corpses that had pulled into Kiev) that "I found out how bad things had really been in Ukraine in the early thirties."[18]

Accompanying collectivization was all-out, forced-draft industrialization. The first five-year plan focused on iron and steel, the sinews of defense as well as industry. The targets for industrialization were impossible to fulfill yet were repeatedly raised. For workers in Moscow, real wages dropped by half between 1928 and 1932. Draconian new laws banned free movement of labor, ended unemployment relief (on the ground that there could be no unemployment under socialism), and punished violations of labor discipline with sanctions ranging up to death for theft of state property. Severe shortages of food and housing provoked frequent strikes in the capital and elsewhere.[19]

All this turmoil sparked new voices of doubt. Rank-and-file Communists complained to Stalin that his "dizziness from success" article had blamed everyone except the top party leadership.[20] In August 1932, the former Moscow district boss Mikhail Riutin accused Stalin of ruining the country and urged that he and his clique "be removed by force . . . as soon as possible." Interpreting this as a call for his assassination, Stalin demanded its author be executed, but members of the Politburo, including Sergei Kirov, apparently objected.[21]

It sounds like an oxymoron, but if these protests actually occurred, they suggest that "moderate Stalinism" was possible, that some Bolsheviks who had backed using force and violence up to 1929 now tried to draw the line. That may be why Stalin retreated again. At the Seventeenth Party Congress in 1934, he declared that with no more "anti-Leninist groupings" to be "finished off," there was now "nothing to prove and, it seems, nobody to beat."[22] In the meantime he pursued his war against "double dealers masked as Bolsheviks" by ousting from the party one out of six Communists in Moscow, Leningrad, and several other regions.[23]

Some of Stalin's top lieutenants apparently tried to convince him that his leadership was so undisputed, and his genius so widely recognized, that he could afford to be generous with former critics and foes.[24] He knew better. All the speakers at the Seventeenth Congress praised his name, but just before elections to the Politburo and Secretariat, a delegation of Central Committee members reportedly approached Kirov and urged him to stand as an alternative to Stalin as general secretary. According to Khrushchev, Kirov told Stalin about the approach, to which the *vozhd* replied simply, "Thank you, Comrade Kirov."[25]

Doubts about Stalin were also reflected in balloting for the Central Committee. The ballots contained a single slate of nominees; the way to express dissent was to cross off those to whom one was opposed. Candidates with the fewest votes against them were celebrated as the most popular party leaders. The voting was supposed to be secret, according to Khrushchev, but Kaganovich secretly "instructed us, the relative newcomers to Moscow, on how we should treat the candidates' ballot." Kaganovich wanted to ensure that "Stalin did not receive fewer votes than . . . any other Politburo members, if there happened to be any votes against Stalin."[26]

Khrushchev claimed afterward to have been upset by Kaganovich's behavior. He also found striking the way Stalin himself voted: "Very demonstratively, in front of everyone, he took the ballots without even glancing at them, went up to the box and dropped them in." What Khrushchev did not know at the time, what he says he found out only after Stalin's death, was that the number of votes against Stalin was not a handful, as announced at the time, but more like 160 or even 260.[27]

The fact that so many delegates out of a total of 1,225 had voted against him convinced Stalin that treason was rife. Subsequently 1,108 of the congress delegates were arrested for counterrevolutionary crimes and liquidated. Some 70 percent of the 71 full and 68 candidate members of the Central Committee elected at the congress were also destroyed as "enemies of the people" before the decade was out.[28]

Yet February 1934 was the very moment when Khrushchev leapfrogged over candidate member status to become a full member of the Central Committee. As he himself explained later, "Stalin was a clever man. He understood who might have cast the votes against him at the Seventeenth Party Congress. Only the cadres from Lenin's time could have voted against him. He could not possibly believe that Khrushchev, or the likes of Khrushchev—young cadres, who rose through the ranks under Stalin and deified him, hanging on his every word—would vote against him."[29]

It wasn't just naive deification that won him advancement, however; it was concrete everyday service to Stalin's cause.

THE INDUSTRIAL ACADEMY was a stronghold of anti-Stalin sentiment in the fall of 1929. It was "teeming with rightists," Khrushchev insisted, "and they'd gotten control of the party cell." The old guard, former plant directors and trade union leaders ostensibly at the academy for advanced training, "supported the rightists Rykov, Bukharin and Uglanov, against Stalin. . . ."[30]

Having gained entry to the academy, Khrushchev helped purge its rightists. He had personal as well as political reasons for doing so. Those who had condescended to him were "unstable and undesirable elements," as he later called them, "people who for one reason or another had abandoned their party, trade union, or managerial duties and had settled into cozy niches." According to Khrushchev, they were wasting the opportunity they had tried to deny him: "They did nothing but loaf. We had two days off a week—Sunday and another day we were supposed to use for 'assimilating' what we had learned that week. Well, I used to notice how these good-for-nothings would leave the dormitory early in the morning and not come back until late at night. I don't know what they did all day, but it's a sure thing they weren't 'assimilating' their studies. Most of them hadn't come to the academy to study at all; they had come because it was a good place to lie low and wait for the political storm to blow over."[31]

In contrast with these "good-for-nothings," Khrushchev declared he wanted to read but had no time to do so, both then and later in his career.

> I remember Molotov once asked me, "Comrade Khrushchev, do you have much time to read?"
>
> "Very little," I replied.
>
> "It's the same with me. My job never lets up. Much as I'd like to sit down and read a book, and much as I know I should, I never have a chance."
>
> I knew what he meant. Ever since I'd returned from the army in 1922, I'd been too busy to read. I was an active party member. . . . My life wasn't my own. If someone did have a chance to appreciate literature, he was likely to be reproached for shirking his civic and party duties. I remember Stalin once put it very well: "So this is how it's turned out! The Trotskyites and the rightists have been rewarded for their activities with the privilege of higher education! The Central Committee doesn't have confidence in them so it removes them from the party posts, and they rush straight into our

scientific and technical institutes. And meanwhile, the people who've stood firmly for the General Line and done the day-to-day practical work of the party never have an opportunity to advance their education and their professional training."[32]

These recollections blend respect for learning with a bitter, anti-intellectual envy. The combination would be poignant if it weren't so deadly. Stalin cleverly connected his own cause with the yearnings and resentments of young men like Khrushchev. Yet Khrushchev's insistence that he was too busy to read must itself be "read" carefully. Embarrassed by his humble origins and uncertain of his ability to overcome them, he may well have welcomed, at a level of which he was not himself aware, the fact that he was "too busy" for more intellectual pursuits. First at the Yuzovka *rabfak* and now at the Industrial Academy, he threw himself into a ceaseless round of political activity that reflected his restless nature, but it may also have been a way both of compensating for his sense of inadequacy and of protecting himself against the possibility of failure in his studies.

Among required subjects at the academy was a foreign language; students were supposed to learn enough (about two to three hundred words) to read a simplified text. Perhaps influenced by Nina Petrovna, Khrushchev chose English. His teacher, Ada Federolf-Shkodina, remembered taking an article from an English magazine, abridging it so as to remove the most demanding passages, translating the remaining difficult words on the blackboard, and asking her students to read the text aloud. Khrushchev, she said, had been too busy politicking to learn the Latin alphabet and soon stopped attending class altogether. Yet when the course ended, the academy director expected him to receive a top grade of five, or at the very least a three. Federolf-Shkodina refused to agree (on the ground that Khrushchev "hadn't learned a thing" in her class) and suggested instead that the English course simply be left off his transcript, an omission no one in party circles was likely to notice.

"There are much more important things for me than English," Khrushchev once told her.[33] But his course on ancient history wasn't one of them, she recalled. He did better at more technical subjects (in contrast with students who seemed convinced that a diameter was something to be weighed). But his most notable accomplishment was that he talked more than anyone in class and was often at the core of clumps of students who gathered in the hallways.

"That's where I saw him most often," said Federolf-Shkodina. "He loved to joke around, and he was terrific at telling stories. He was really very clever. He had a kind of peasant wit, the kind you find in people who have no education, and instead have to discover everything and resolve everything for themselves. He always seemed to be surrounded in the hallways by party people who flattered him to his face while laughing at him behind his back. Many of them came from province capitals, whereas he was a miner from a village and seemed so plain."[34]

Much later, according to his son-in-law, Khrushchev "would put aside a book, become lost in thought and return to the past as if talking to himself. He regretted he hadn't graduated from the Industrial Academy, and in general that he hadn't had much luck with his studies. The problem was that his other obligations were always taking him away from his classes."[35]

That was how he explained it to himself. Whether he convinced himself is another matter. Back in the thirties, however, he had plenty of other satisfactions. In contrast with rank-and-file students, he had a room of his own in a dorm (where the Ural Hotel was later located) at 40 Pokrovka (later Chernyshevskaya) Street. After Nina Petrovna joined him with the children, she recalled, "We had two rooms at opposite ends of the corridor. We slept in one with little Rada, and in the other were Yulia, Lyonia, and Matryosha—a nanny N. S. had engaged on our arrival."[36]

The academy itself was on Novaya Basmannaya Street, a direct tram ride from the dormitory. But Khrushchev insisted on walking. "I never took the streetcar," he said, perhaps still smarting from his initial encounter with public transport or maybe so as to avoid getting crushed in overcrowded trams by the very "masses" from whose ranks he was proud to be rising.[37]

BECAUSE OF ITS Moscow location and high-priority mission, the academy got special attention from the Kremlin. *Pravda* published academy party cell resolutions as models for educational institutions around the country. In April 1930, Stalin gave a speech at the academy urging its leaders to step up their campaign against rightists.[38] The subject of academy politics even came up in correspondence between Stalin and Molotov: On October 7, 1929, Stalin wrote, "I have read the transcript of the Industrial Academy's party cell. The matter will have to be put on the agenda of the Central Committee plenum."[39] On top of that, Stalin's young wife, Nadezhda Alliluyeva, was a student in the academy's textile section, and their correspondence too is full of references to her studies there.[40]

For a young man on the make like Khrushchev, all this high-level attention was a godsend. "My role there stood out clearly," he recalled, "and it was all visible in the Central Committee. That's how my name rose to the surface as an active party member, as someone who led a group of Communists in the struggle against Uglanovites, Rykovites, Zinovievites, and Trotskyites in the Industrial Academy."[41]

That struggle was just heating up in the fall of 1929. On September 4 a student named Vorobyov confessed at a party cell meeting that he had supported Bukharin and named others who shared his views. Later that month the party cell, along with the Bauman District party bureau, condemned what it called "the antiparty work of the rightists" and asked higher authorities to take action. (It was this transcript to which Stalin referred in his October 7 letter to Molotov.) On November 4, when the Bauman District party boss, A. P. Shirin, demanded that the academy cell redouble its vigilance, his warning was seconded by one Nikita Khrushchev, whose maiden appearance in the protocols of the academy party organization was marked by a particularly nasty tone: "The rightists created an atmosphere of treason around Vorobyov. But all the cell did was pass a 'wise' resolution excluding Vorobyov from the academy. All the other [rightists] remain!!! It's time to elect a [party] bureau that won't permit any false rumors concerning political matters."[42]

Obviously such a bureau should have included Khrushchev. For the moment, however, Stalinist justice did not triumph. Instead Khrushchev's candidacy was turned aside not once but several times. Of course he blamed renegade "rightists" and "leftists" of all sorts, but typically, he claimed not even to "remember" exactly what the differences were between them. "Rightists, oppositionists, right-leftists, deviationists—these people were all moving in basically the same political direction and our group was against them."[43]

Rightists in the academy were encouraged by Stalin's "dizziness from success" article and by the ouster, in the spring of 1930, of the hard-line Moscow party chief Karl Bauman, who was made a scapegoat for Stalinist excesses. They even managed to elect their own kind to the district party conference in May. On May 25, Bauman District party officials alerted Kaganovich and *Pravda* to rightist machinations at the academy. That same evening the phone rang in Khrushchev's dormitory, and someone asked for him.

"I didn't have many acquaintances in Moscow, and I couldn't imagine who would be calling me," he said later, indicating how wrapped up he was in the political cocoon of the academy. The call was from Lev Mekhlis, an especially sleazy arch-Stalinist who had once been the great man's political secretary, now edited *Pravda,* and later kept his master reliably informed about "enemies of the people" in the Red Army. According to Khrushchev, Mekhlis dispatched a car to bring him to *Pravda*'s offices. There he was asked to sign a letter purportedly written at the academy and attacking rightists there for rigging the election of district conference delegates. Khrushchev said he hesitated since he "didn't have anything to do with drafting the letter" and didn't "even know who the author is" but then signed. "The next day *Pravda* carried the letter in its correspondence column. It was like a clap of thunder out of a clear blue sky. The Academy was thrown into turmoil. Classes were suspended, and the party group organizers called a meeting at which all the Academy delegates to the Bauman District conference were recalled. . . . I was made chairman of the meeting and was put on the new delegation."[44]

The episode was a test. Whether or not Khrushchev actually hesitated before signing (or conveniently recalled doing so long afterward), he passed it. Academy party cell leader A. Levochkin condemned *Pravda*'s pronunciamento as an "absolute falsehood" that "blackens our political line." Two days later Khrushchev succeeded Levochkin as academy party leader.[45]

Under Khrushchev's leadership, party cell meetings rarely discussed educational matters. Instead, they were devoted to reprimanding alleged rightists and kicking them out of the academy and the party itself. Admissions of guilt were browbeaten out of the accused. Khrushchev gave credence to rumors and slander, but not to painfully heartfelt denials bravely offered in self-defense. Years later he maintained that these tactics (in contrast with the blood purges that followed) were based on "discussion and voting in party bodies."[46] Still, the tone of these meetings wasn't far from the witch-hunts to come.

On June 11, 1930, one Iu. P. Berzin, formerly the party leader of a district near Moscow, admitted that he used to think it "wrong to exclude Bukharin . . . from the Central Committee." Now he confessed he had been "deeply in error." At first Khrushchev seemed satisfied with this admission, but not after Berzin committed the cardinal sin of counterattacking Khrushchev: "In answer to the statement made public by Comrade Khrushchev, to the effect that I supposedly have been conducting factional activity at the garment factory, and that my brother is a former white officer with whom I maintain contact, I categorically deny these charges and I declare that they are an insolent lie."[47]

Khrushchev's accusation *was* outrageous, even though guilt by association, which became deadly a few years later, still wasn't fatal. Moreover, he devalued the very confession he had forced from Berzin by adding, "It should be emphasized that we obtained that admission only under great pressure."[48]

Khrushchev accused another student, Mukhitdinov, of spreading counterrevolutionary rumors, insulting party and government leaders, having been fired from a factory for hooliganism and excluded from Sverdlov University for Trotskyism, plus several other sins—all based on hearsay by one of Mukhitdinov's classmates.[49] Like Berzin, Mukhitidinov had the temerity to protest: "Khrushchev has slandered and libeled me. The statement about attacks on Comrade Stalin is an insolent lie." Other party cell members rushed to defend their new chief; one of the them condemned Mukhitdinov for daring to "demand proof of his own guilt." As for Khrushchev, several days later he branded Mukhitdinov "a rightist opportunist whose disagreements with the party began with collectivization . . . and finished with spreading counterrevolutionary rumors about [peasant] unrest in the northern Caucasus." According to Khrushchev, Mukhitdinov had attacked both "the Central Committee and the leader of our party, Comrade Stalin," for which he must forthwith "be excluded from the party and the Academy as an incorrigible deviationist."[50]

Khrushchev's persistence in pursuing "deviationists" soon earned him panegyrics at party cell meetings. The only mistake he made, reminiscent of 1927 in Ukraine, was to be somewhat more Stalinist than Stalin himself, who was still feigning moderation with occasional concessions to his enemies. On November 20, 1930, the Khrushchev-led party bureau condemned Bukharin's admission of mistakes. On November 22, *Pravda* assessed Bukharin's statement more positively. In the confusion that followed, the academy party bureau met again to consider a revised statement personally drafted by Khrushchev: "The evaluation of Comrade Bukharin's statement contained in the resolution passed at the last meeting was incorrect, and this constitutes an ultraleft political error. This meeting hereby retracts that assessment."[51]

Despite such errors, Khrushchev felt vindicated. "As the Academy began to play the leading role in the struggle against the opposition," he recollected later, "my name became even better known to the Moscow Party organization and to the Central Committee." It became so well known that he soon replaced the Bauman District party boss, the man "who only a year before had opposed my candidacy to the Sixteenth Party Congress. Shirin was politically immature. I'm sure he had his own reasons for voting against me in 1930, but all that was over and done with. My future as a party worker now looked very bright."[52]

The Sixteenth Congress had taken place in June–July 1930. Since he wasn't an official delegate, Khrushchev had to make do with a Central Committee guest pass.[53] But once he became Bauman party leader, Khrushchev imagined Stalin himself was watching his progress.

What convinced him of this was the presence of Nadezhda Alliluyeva at the Industrial Academy. By all accounts, Stalin's wife was as modest and gracious as Stalin was neither. Dark-eyed, dark-haired, and twenty-two years younger than her husband, she was born in 1901, the daughter of a Georgian metalworker who met Stalin in the prerevolutionary underground. The year 1917 found the Alliluyev family in Petrograd; Lenin took refuge with them there for a time. Nadezhda joined the party the same year Khrushchev did, in 1918, when she was seventeen. After working briefly in Lenin's secretariat, she was sent to Tsaritsyn, where Stalin was political commissar at that civil war front. There they courted and married. After the war she worked for a *Pravda*-sponsored magazine titled *Revoliutsiia i Kultura* (revolution and culture). In 1929, having borne two children, Vasily and Svetlana, she enrolled in the textile section of the Industrial Academy, studying chemistry and specializing in artificial fibers.

Stalin's wife didn't advertise who she was, but once he became party cell leader, Khrushchev found out.[54] He admired the way she "never abused her connection with Stalin," never "took advantage of the privileges available to her as Stalin's wife," never "traveled between the Academy and the Kremlin by car, but always by streetcar."[55]

Alliluyeva worked as a party group organizer and as such coordinated her efforts with Khrushchev. He often thought: "When she gets home she will tell Stalin about my words, and what will he say?" Later, after becoming Kaganovich's deputy, Khrushchev was invited to Stalin's dacha for dinner, where his host surprised him by recalling details of Khrushchev's activities at the academy.

"I didn't respond," Khrushchev said later. "I remained silent: I didn't know whether to rejoice or to hunker down like a hedgehog. I thought to myself: 'How does he know all this?' But then I saw that he was smiling. That's when I realized that Nadezhda Sergeyevna had probably been informing him in detail about life in our party organization and presenting my role as its secretary in a positive light."[56]

Later still, after the terror had taken so many while sparing Khrushchev, he thought again of Alliluyeva:

> I stayed alive while most of my contemporaries, my classmates at the Academy, my friends with whom I had worked in the party organization, lost their heads as enemies of the people. I've often asked myself, how was I spared? The fact that I am truly devoted to the party has always been beyond doubt. But those comrades who perished were also devoted to the party. . . . Why did I escape the fate they suffered? I think part of the answer is that Nadya's reports helped to determine Stalin's attitude toward me. I call it my lucky lottery ticket. I drew a lucky lottery ticket when it happened that Stalin observed my activities through Nadezhda Sergeyevna. It was because of her that Stalin trusted me. In later years he sometimes attacked and insulted me, sometimes made rude remarks about me; but he always got over it, and right up until the last day of his life he liked me.[57]

At times in his memoirs Khrushchev sounded infatuated with Alliluyeva. "What a beautiful, blooming woman she was!" he mused.[58] That would be particularly understandable in the light of her terrible demise. On the fifteenth anniversary of the revolution in 1932, Stalin and his wife reportedly quarreled at a Kremlin party. Stalin is said to have cursed her and thrown a lighted cigarette in her face, and later that night, after learning her husband was sleeping with another woman at his dacha outside Moscow, she shot herself.[59]

Could the sensitive Alliluyeva have so admired the rough-and-ready Khrushchev? The opposite scenario is just as likely. If, as has been reported, Stalin's wife was horrified by some of Stalin's policies, she probably regretted Khrushchev's hounding of academy rightists. If, in addition, she complained to her husband, it is just possible that it was this condemnation, rather than her endorsement of Khrushchev, that recommended him to Stalin.[60]

On the other hand, Khrushchev had ulterior motives for attributing his survival and success to Alliluyeva. For one thing, that reduced the need to credit Kaganovich.[61] For another, the notion of a "lucky lottery ticket" reduced his own responsibility for his rise into Stalin's inner circle, while confirming his self-image as a miracle man who ended up higher than anyone expected. The very thought that Nadya sang his praises to her husband made Khrushchev's heart swell with pride. "I felt like Pinya, the hero of the story by Vinnichenko."[62]

In 1930 Moscow was divided into ten districts. Bauman, the smallest, extended eastward from the center, while Krasnopresnensky, one of the largest and most important, stretched westward. Under the centralized Soviet regime, district governments had little power compared with that of the municipality as a whole. But district party leaders oversaw everything in their realms from economic plan fulfillment to the purging of rightists in their ranks. Concentrating Khrushchev's mind further in his new job were the facts that the first five-year plan's targets were virtually impossible to meet, that district party bosses were blamed for nonfulfillment, and that a chaotic overlapping of his authority with that of other officials limited his ability to do his job.

Such a thankless position suited Khrushchev perfectly. The enormity of the challenge ensured that successes would seem triumphs, while the unstructured bureaucratic environment allowed him to interfere in anything and everything, putting a premium on his energy and drive. Moreover, he applied his skills as a master purger on a larger scale. "Facts relating to right-opportunist theory and practice" were unearthed at People's Commissariats of Railroads and of Trade, the All-Union Oil Trust, and the Center for Collective Farms. Bauman party authorities annulled party cell elections at the Russian Federation's State Planning Commission on the grounds of "political near-sightedness and suppression of self-criticism," dispersed party bureaus at the Nitrogen Institute and the Moscow Furs Trust, and demanded a new party bureau be elected at the "Young Guard" Publishing House on the ground that the old one had "not reacted to the publication of ideologically hostile books."[63]

Nor did Khrushchev forget his grudge against old-guard academy rightists. "When instructions on the [academy] party purge were being worked out," he told the Bauman party conference in January 1931, "they said that it was being directed against the best part of the party, and that people who would be left would be one hundred percent lackeys." In return, he charged them with trying to "crawl into the swamp, and to remain in the swamp, while awaiting a more favorable moment."[64]

Settling scores with academy enemies was all too easy. Khrushchev's economic stewardship wasn't nearly as successful. The Bauman District failed to rank near the top in plan fulfillment, partly because many of its light and food industry enterprises were neglected during all-out industrialization. But the less than stellar results didn't derail the Khrushchev express.

Next stop: Krasnopresnensky, hallowed in Bolshevik lore as "the district of the revolution," where a historic clash between workers and police had taken place in 1905. Its leader was regarded as preeminent among district party secretaries.[65] Khrushchev was asked to say a few words at the city party bureau meeting that chose him to be that leader.

"Kaganovich conducted the meeting," recalled E. G. Goreva, who headed the Moscow party's Women's Department at the time. "Khrushchev was asked briefly to summarize his biography. Either because he was greatly agitated or for some other reason, Nikita Sergeyevich stammered and frequently mispronounced words. 'Can it really be that they couldn't find a minimally literate person for Krasnopresnensky?' I said quietly to the person sitting next to me at the table. I saw that the chairman was shaking his finger at me, apparently indicating that I shouldn't be conversing. But I was wrong. After the meeting was over, and Khrushchev's candidacy confirmed, Kaganovich called me over. 'I heard everything,' he said to me extremely severely. 'If you want to hold on to your job, you'd better watch your tongue.'"[66]

This was not Khrushchev's only awkward debut. His first formal address as Krasnopresnensky party boss was so long that he had to request special dispensation from the delegates to finish it; he overemphasized economic matters so much as to seem guilty of mere "technocratism"; and most embarrassing, he declared that it was only when Kaganovich had become Moscow party chief in 1930 that "all the excesses and distortions" had been overcome and "the true line adopted." Apparently it had slipped Khrushchev's mind that Kaganovich's predecessor had been none other than Stalin's closest comrade-in-arms Vyacheslav Molotov, now serving as head of government of the USSR.[67]

Both episodes show Khrushchev's real limitations. But he did well enough in his new post to justify his promotion. His new district was more diverse economically than Bauman. District party bureau meetings were devoted to such issues as management of industry and construction, provision of raw materials to factories, and food supply. Khrushchev mobilized the whole district to fulfill the plan and to recruit new party members. He organized some twelve thousand workers into 2,250 "shock brigades," which worked according to the so-called *progressivka,* a system that provided minimal pay until a certain level of output was achieved, and then bonus pay for reaching constantly escalating targets.

For Khrushchev and his colleagues, there were "no fortresses that Bolsheviks couldn't storm." Even a Russian historian generally hostile to Khrushchev is impressed by his Krasnopresnensky record. Although Khrushchev's report to a district party conference in January 1932 contained the usual invective against deviationists of all stripes, for the most part it was "the report of a conscientious economic expert who knew of what he spoke."[68]

ALTHOUGH BAUMAN and Krasnopresnensky were steps up the ladder, Khrushchev's appointment as Kaganovich's deputy was the real turning point. Since the latter held three top posts (Moscow province party leader, Stalin's deputy in the Central Committee, and city party boss), Khrushchev was in effect running Moscow. Moreover, given its importance, the capital's party and governmental authorities got special attention from Stalin himself, symbolized by the location of Moscow party headquarters just two doors away from the Central Committee Secretariat on Staraya Ploshchad' (Old Square).

From then on, the notion that Stalin was watching Khrushchev wasn't a fantasy. At the same time, having finally to abandon his schooling left Khrushchev feeling particularly insecure: "Much as I appreciated the honor and responsibility that went with this promotion, I was sorry to have to leave the Industrial Academy without graduating. Taking the job on the Moscow city committee meant giving up my hopes of ever completing my higher education. Furthermore, as I confided to Kaganovich, I was apprehensive about the difficulties I was sure to encounter in the city apparatus. But I proved up to the challenge. . . ."[69]

"Khrushchev's rapid rise astonishes me," a Moscow official confided to his diary. "He was a poor student at the Industrial Academy. Now he's second secretary along with Kaganovich. Yet he's amazingly dull-witted and a flatterer of the first rank."[70]

Dull-witted Khrushchev was not. Still, the challenge he now faced must have seemed almost overwhelming. New industries were building flagship factories in the capital while older enterprises retooled and expanded. A vast military-scientific-industrial complex was forming in and around the city. Inundated with new construction projects (one hundred new factories came on line in 1931 while three hundred were rebuilt during the first five-year plan), Moscow was further swamped by migration from the countryside: 411,000 new residents (an increase of 15 percent) in 1931; 528,000, or nearly 1,500 a day, in 1932; and a total of 1.5 million, or a 70 percent rise, between 1928 and 1933.

The model socialist metropolis was supposed to expand according to a preconceived blueprint. But although a Master Plan for the Reconstruction of the City of Moscow was promulgated in 1935, growth was actually chaotic. Housing and social services lagged badly behind industrial development, partly because more old housing was demolished than new apartments built during the first five-year plan.

Central to the new socialist showcase were high-profile projects such as the new Metro and the mammoth Moscow–Volga canal. To make way for all the new construction, older landmarks were razed en masse. They included great churches like the Cathedral of Christ the Savior, the triumphal gates on the road to Leningrad, the sixteenth-century brick wall around the Kitaigorod section of the city, and the seventeenth-century Sukharev Tower at the junction of Sretenka and Sadovoye Kol'tso.[71]

A German writer who visited Moscow in the summer of 1934 described it this way:

> The streets had been excavated; there were long, muddy trenches floored with dirty planks; heaps of soil lay everywhere. The whole city was in a mess, and heavily loaded trucks were busy shifting the accumulated debris. Everywhere one saw long fences around the Metro stations that were under construction; everywhere scaffolding shrouded half-built skyscrapers and houses. In every quarter of the city the earth shook with the ringing of hammers, the banging, bumping and screeching of single-bucket excavators, concrete mixers and machines that turned out mortar. Thousands of men worked day and night with almost fanatical diligence. Packed trams rumbled along the streets. There were only a few cars to be seen, of all makes and vintages. The streets were full of one-horse carriages, their boxes occupied by surly drivers. In the center of the city there were some large, very up-to-date trolley buses.[72]

This was the capital of which Khrushchev suddenly took charge. It became clear during his first presentation to the Politburo that he was understandably nervous. Moscow's working class, allegedly the apple of Stalin's eye, was going hungry in 1932, and with his legendary concern for their welfare, the great man "suggested the idea of raising rabbits for food." Naturally Khrushchev was "all for this plan and worked zealously to carry out his instructions. Almost every factory, plant and workshop started raising rabbits to help stock its own kitchen. Then we began pushing a plan to raise mushrooms in cellars and ditches around Moscow. Some establishments contributed their share, but every mass movement had its bad elements and some factory directors didn't support the cause. We ran into more trouble when it came to distributing ration cards.

There were never enough cards, and a certain amount of swindling was inevitable."

Kaganovich assigned Khrushchev to report to the Politburo on what he was doing to rectify the situation. "This assignment worried me," Khrushchev remembered later. "I'd go so far as to say I was really frightened by the prospect of delivering a speech to our most prestigious body; Stalin would be there judging my report."

The report didn't go well. His strategy of saying what his bosses wanted to hear—that he had successfully streamlined the ration card system—wasn't entirely misguided; Stalin often credited news that was too good to be true. But rabbits and ration cards were matters on which he could stand the truth, and he knew enough about Moscow life to know Khrushchev wasn't telling it.

"Stop bragging, Comrade Khrushchev," grumbled Stalin. "There are still many thieves left—very many—don't think you've caught them all." One can imagine the chuckles and smiles exchanged among Politburo members. Stalin was having fun at Khrushchev's expense, but in a benevolent way that reassured rather than humiliated the nervous rapporteur. "Stalin's remark was made in a fatherly tone and it didn't upset me at all. He was right. I had convinced myself that we had rounded up all the ration card swindlers, and I was astounded that Stalin—who hardly ever left the confines of the Kremlin—was so all-seeing that he probably knew exactly how many thieves were still at large! This raised Stalin all the more in my eyes."[73]

Khrushchev overcame his shortcomings by relying on his skills. "I had to make up in diligence what I lacked in experience," he said later.[74] Or, as Ernst Kolman, who worked for Khrushchev at the time, later put it, he "made up (not always successfully) for gaps in education and cultural development with intuition, improvisation, boldness and great natural gifts."[75]

In theory, party officials like Khrushchev were supposed to be general overseers; in fact, they exercised day-to-day supervision of their domains. They weren't just administrators but Soviet-style politician/managers. Khrushchev wasn't a specialist on industry and construction, but he knew enough to understand the experts who worked for him. Moscow party protocols from the summer of 1933 overflow with the most mundane of matters, ranging from industry to transportation and housing to vacations for secretariat staff.[76] According to Khrushchev, "It was a period of feverish activity, and stupendous progress was made in a short time. . . . The huge task of overseeing all this was largely mine because Kaganovich was up to his ears in work outside the Moscow Party organization. In addition to putting up new buildings, there was a lot to be done in the way of modernizing the most basic metropolitan services. Moscow's sewage and water drainage systems were long out of date, and there were no water mains in the city. Most of the streets were cobblestone, and some were completely unpaved. Much of the city's transport was still horsedrawn. It's incredible to look back on it all now, but things were really that primitive."[77]

Ernst Kolman became deputy head of the Moscow party Science Department in 1936. Although it didn't have a single professional staff person, the department supervised hundreds of scientific and research institutes. "One needed absolutely encyclopedic knowledge which none of us had or could have had," Kolman recalled. "As everyone did at that time, we worked not only day but night, until dawn, in fact, not with great results, but probably even doing harm." It surely didn't help that those two paragons of science and culture, Kaganovich and Khrushchev, were in overall charge of Moscow intellectual life. Yet Kolman remembered both kindly, at least from this period: "Both men boiled over with energy and cheerfulness. They were very different people whom many things had brought together. Kaganovich particularly had a simply superhuman capacity for work. . . . Kaganovich was inclined to try to systematize and even to theorize. Khrushchev tended to be overly practical and technical. I remember how Khrushchev and I visited the Polytechnical Museum and its exhibit of the newest Soviet inventions. He was like a child; he was enraptured by the 'talking paper,' that is, by a kind of tape recorder tape on which we both spoke a few words and on which my wife, Katia, sang a little song."

Neither Khrushchev nor Kaganovich "was yet spoiled by power," according to Kolman. "Both were simple and straightforward in a comradely sort of way, and both were accessible, especially Nikita Sergeyevich, that 'wide-open Russian soul,' who wasn't ashamed to keep learning, to ask me, his subordinate, for explanations of scientific wisdom that was beyond him. But even Kaganovich, who was drier in personal contacts, was not yet as stern as he would become; he was almost soft, and of course did not allow himself the tricks, the shouting, and the cursing for which he later became infamous in imitation of Stalin."

Once Kolman mentioned a reference by Lenin to the underground gasification of coal. Typical of his penchant for supertechnical deus ex machina solutions to economic problems, Khrushchev "caught fire with the idea. He decided to send me to the Donbas to acquaint myself with the best work on gasification, so as to put it into practice in the Moscow region. Although I protested, suggesting instead that a specialist in the field be sent to look into it, he insisted." So Kolman set off, taking his wife with him, did his research both above- and belowground, and returned with a report on Donbas gasification processes that was, he later wrote, "not especially comforting." Undeterred by this warning (another characteristic reaction), Khrushchev ordered the same processes put into effect near Moscow.

On another occasion Kolman accompanied Khrushchev and two high-ranking military officers to a top secret facility near the town of Mozhaisk. There, deep in a forest, and defended by a small army of guards, was "a wooden shed, about thirty to forty meters long, without windows, but brightly lighted." At one end of the shed was a bulky scientific apparatus of some sort; at the other was a cage holding a large rat. When the inventor of the apparatus pressed a lever, "the poor rat keeled over, extended its little feet in the air, and gave up the ghost. The inventor explained to us in not very articulate fashion that some sort of ray or beam into the heart of the animal had done the job. In answer to Nikita Sergeyevich's passionate questions, he admitted that increasing the ray's radius to three or four kilometers would require ten thousand times as much energy, and that consequently it was not yet usable for military purposes."[78]

More than likely, added Kolman, the show in the shed was a trick, with the rat actually being electrocuted. As the Soviet leader, Khrushchev later proved himself unusually resistant to military procurement requests, but he couldn't resist high-tech weapons. His susceptibility to such schemes was the other side of what became a nasty anti-intellectualism. Both reflected his love-hate relationship with the higher education that he insisted eluded him but that, in a sense, he himself eluded.

Of all the construction projects Khrushchev superintended, the biggest and most important was the Moscow Metro, a classic Stalinist project built in a quintessentially Stalinist way. What's more, having met and mastered this impossible challenge and having been lavishly rewarded for doing so, Khrushchev was forever wedded to the techniques that worked miracles on the Metro but proved less successful later on.

The Metro was to be the best and most expensive on earth—not because the people of Moscow really needed it (if their welfare had been the aim, surface transport would have been more cost-efficient, leaving funds for underdeveloped housing and services) but because it served larger state purposes. In wartime, its unprecedentedly deep tunnels and stations could double as bomb shelters. In the meantime it would show the world that socialism really was the wave of the future. For that demonstration no price tag was too high; not the 350 million rubles spent in 1934 alone (compared with the 300 million per year devoted to consumer goods nationwide during the first five-year plan); nor the endless tons of marble, bronze, and other expensive materials (some of it surely confiscated from churches) poured into stations decorated with sculptures, stained glass, and mosaics.[79]

Although the work had started in 1931, Metro construction began in earnest after Khrushchev took the reins in Moscow, with the first subway line slated to enter operation on November 7, 1934, the anniversary of the revolution. Khrushchev's experience in the Yuzovka mines helped him see the wisdom of closed-tunnel, as opposed to open-trench, construction.[80] But "when we started building," he said later, "we had only the vaguest idea of what the job would entail. We were very unsophisticated. We thought of a subway as something almost supernatural. I think it's probably easier to contemplate space flights today than it was for us to contemplate the construction of the Moscow Metro in the early 1930's."[81]

Despite his ignorance (or perhaps because of it), Khrushchev took mind-numbing risks to get the job done. He and Moscow Mayor Nikolai Bulganin drove the more than seventy thousand workers mercilessly, demanding that they work forty-eight hours without respite and ignoring engineers' warnings that tunnels or the buildings above them would collapse. Terrible accidents occurred, including underground fires and floods, only to be portrayed in fevered accounts of the project as instances of heroism in service to the great cause.[82]

Khrushchev drove himself as hard as his crews. "Even though I kept my formal job at the City Committee," he recalled, "I gave eighty percent of my time to the Metro. I went to and from the Moscow Committee through the shafts. In the morning I climbed down a shaft near where I lived and came up out of a shaft near the Party office building. It would be hard for me to describe how strenuous a working day we put in. We slept as little as possible so that we could give all our time to the cause."

The Metro didn't make the November 1934 deadline. But on May 1, 1935, when the first trains rumbled from Sokolniki to Park Kultury and from Komintern Street (later Kalininskaya) to Kiev Station, Khrushchev was aboard, sharing the glory with Kaganovich, after whom the Metro was named. Wrote a Metro engineer: "In the life of man there are especially memorable days. On days like this, he suddenly begins to understand in a new way all the simple things which he thought he knew all about long ago. On days like this he becomes inspired with love for things and phenomena which he had taken for granted. Just such a day was the day when Comrade Khrushchev talked to me."[83]

Khrushchev was awarded the coveted Order of Lenin for his role in the Metro construction, a Moscow factory that made precision electrical devices was given his name, and it was now that he added the Moscow Province first secretaryship to his city portfolio. How gratifying was all this recognition? "The Order of Lenin had been established in 1930," Khrushchev remembered. "I believe I was the 110th person to be so honored. So in five years only 110 people in all had been awarded the Order of Lenin. That says something about how highly it was regarded. I think that was as it should have been: the more honor and value attached to the award, the better. Later, the Order of Lenin began to be used more widely, and it diminished in significance."[84]

Compare Khrushchev's insecurity in 1932 to the sense of power and authority captured in 1935 newsreel footage. One sequence shows him inspecting a new Moscow River bridge leading to the Kiev Metro station. Khrushchev arrives in a big black limousine with a suite of functionaries. Wearing a long, dark, well-tailored overcoat and workman's cap (and followed closely by an NKVD bodyguard), he waves at the assembled workers, grins broadly, and then shakes hands all around. Since his arrival coincides with the customary *perekur* (smoking break), everyone in the picture has a cigarette hanging from his fingers or lips—except for the self-denying Khrushchev. He walks resolutely across the bridge, barking out orders left and right, and then gets into his black limousine and drives off, followed by several other black cars.

Before he departs, the camera zooms in on his eyes. They are piercingly bright and penetrating, fully concentrated on the task at hand. Those same eyes struck a boyhood friend of Sergei Khrushchev's when he first met Sergei's father in the 1950s. The friend was stunned by the contrast between Khrushchev's unimpressive figure and the burning intensity of his eyes. "All you had to do to understand how Khrushchev could have become so powerful was to look in his eyes."[85]

ANOTHER 1935 NEWSREEL shows Khrushchev visiting Moscow Nursery School no. 12, which also bore his name. Everything is neatly in place, with the children dressed up and sipping tea, when Khrushchev and his entourage arrive. He and all his men are wearing white smocks, his over a dark suit, the others' over what appear to be NKVD uniforms. Khrushchev examines a small chair, turning it over in his hands to see how it was built, and then a tiny child's shoe. The kindly city father's face breaks into an infectious smile as he waves good-bye. The grin is equally winning at the electric lamp factory, where Khrushchev is seen addressing an audience of party activists. Wearing a Stalin-style tunic and constantly gesticulating with both hands like an orchestra conductor, he seems completely at ease before the public. Throughout the speech he engages in informal exchanges with his listeners, obviously enjoying the repartee.

Not everything went so smoothly. As early as the mid-thirties Khrushchev's tendency to decide too quickly and to take things to extremes got him into trouble. His campaign to spur Stakhanovite workers to overfulfill their norms brought a rebuff from higher authorities, who condemned such "blind chasing after records."[86] In 1934 Khrushchev got a message to call a phone number he recognized as Stalin's apartment. The *vozhd* wanted to talk about public toilets. "Apparently people hunt around desperately and can't find anywhere to relieve themselves," Stalin remarked. "This won't do. It puts citizens in an awkward position. Talk this matter over with Bulganin and do something to improve these conditions."[87]

Khrushchev wasn't the prime mover in tearing down old Moscow neighborhoods, but he didn't resist either. "We're cutting down trees," he told a 1937 Central Committee plenum, "so as to rebuild Moscow, so that it will be a real capital and not a village, so as to finish with the view that Moscow is just a big village."[88]

"Some Bolsheviks shed tears," he said at a 1937 city party conference. "'Look at what you're pulling down!' they say. I'd say that . . . when they shed a tear like this, they resemble the heroes of *The Cherry Orchard*. . . . We can't subordinate the interests of the whole city to those of people living on a tiny piece of land."[89]

Stalin encouraged his Moscow underlings' contempt for the old, but when complaints reached him, he blamed them anyway. One day the noted aircraft designer Aleksandr S. Yakovlev lingered for some small talk after his business with Stalin was done. Stalin asked what Muscovites were saying, and since he seemed to be in a good mood, Yakovlev dared to say that people blamed the wholesale destruction of Moscow greenery on the fact that the *vozhd* "didn't like trees." Stalin replied by blaming Khrushchev and Bulganin, to whom he had once pointed out some unsightly shrubbery. "I told them . . . that greenery of that sort wasn't needed. But

Khrushchev and Bulganin interpreted what I'd said in their own way and proceeded according to the old proverb 'Force a fool to pray, and he'll break his forehead on the ground.'"

"Isn't that so, Molotov?" the boss asked his prime minister, who was standing nearby. "Whatever they do, we get blamed for everything."[90]

AFTER THE Seventeenth Party Congress in 1934, at which Khrushchev made a speech praising "our leader of genius Comrade Stalin" and attributing "the principled, ideological-based solidarity of the Moscow party organization to the skillful day-in, day-out leadership of Lazar Moiseyevich Kaganovich,"[91] it wasn't long before the dictator began settling accounts with those who had dared oppose him. On December 1, 1934, Kirov was assassinated in Leningrad.[92] Afterward Stalin authorized a decree, apparently without consulting the full Politburo, that sped up cases allegedly involving terrorist acts, and he demanded that resulting death sentences be carried out "immediately."[93] On the basis of this order, dozens of cases of "counterrevolutionary crimes" having nothing to do with Kirov's murder were quickly decided, with death sentences carried out at once.[94] In January 1935 a secret Central Committee letter called on party organizations to expel oppositionists of all stripes hidden within the party. A wave of arrests followed, later known in the prison camps as the Kirov flood. Several tens of thousands (mostly former aristocrats, merchants, and civil servants and their families, but also workers and peasants) were deported from Leningrad, a smaller number from Moscow.[95] An intraparty purge carried out in the capital in 1935 resulted in the expulsion of 7.5 percent of those whose cases were examined, many of them former oppositionists, but others rank-and-file Communists.[96]

In January 1935, Zinoviev, Kamenev, and seventeen others were tried in Moscow, charged with constituting a Moscow Center involved in Kirov's assassination. For the time being they were sentenced to five- to ten-year prison terms. The period between July 1935 and August 1936 turned out to be a calm before the storm. A new Soviet constitution, written largely by Bukharin and containing all manner of democratic freedoms and rights, was promulgated; Bukharin himself thought parts of the new charter might actually be implemented. Meanwhile, however, Stalin was secretly preparing a new trial of Zinoviev, Kamenev, and other members of an alleged Trotskyite-Zinovievite Center, this time on the basis of forced confessions of their having plotted to murder Stalin as well as Kirov.

The new trial began on August 19, 1936, in the blue and white former Nobles' Club ballroom now known as October Hall in Trade Union House. The chief prosecutor Andrei Vyshinsky demanded that "these dogs gone mad should be shot—every one of them." Of course they were, despite Stalin's personal promise to Zinoviev and Kamenev, instrumental in producing their confessions, that their lives, as well as those of their families and supporters, would be spared.[97]

Before, during, and after the trial, Khrushchev served as one of the most voluble cheerleaders for the Stalinist line. He exhorted Moscow party workers to "educate the masses in hatred for the enemy, hatred for the counterrevolutionary Trotskyite-Zinovievites, hatred for the rightist deviationist heretics, and love for the party of Bolsheviks, love for our boss and teacher Comrade Stalin."[98] Three days before the trial's end, he demanded death for Zinoviev and Kamenev: "Everybody who rejoices in the successes achieved in our country, the victories of our party led by the great Stalin, will find only one word suitable for the mercenary, fascist dogs of the Trotskyite-Zinovievite gang. That word is execution."[99]

In January 1937 another show trial got under way.[100] This time Khrushchev called for blood in a speech to some two hundred thousand Muscovites gathered in frigid cold on Red Square: "The Trotskyite clique was nothing but a gang of spies and mercenary murderers, diversionist wreckers, and agents of German and Japanese fascism. The stench of carrion rises from the vile, base Trotskyite degenerates." The vilest crime of "Judas-Trotsky and his band" was to have raised "their evil-doing hand against Comrade Stalin . . . the beacon of all that is good and progressive in humanity. Stalin is our banner! Stalin is our will! Stalin is our victory!"[101]

Before Stalin could try and then execute Bukharin and Rykov, whom Zinoviev and Kamenev had been forced to implicate, the two men had to be expelled from the Central Committee. Although Bukharin and Rykov were shouted down when they tried to defend themselves at a February 1937 Central Committee plenum, a thirty-six-member commission formed to decide their fate found itself divided, with some favoring a trial followed by shooting (so much for even the sham independence of judges), but with others preferring lesser penalties.[102] Khrushchev's only set speech at the plenum concerned a more innocuous agenda item, party preparations for the upcoming elections.[103] Of those who interrupted Bukharin, Khrushchev was one of the more restrained,[104] and he voted to try Bukharin and Rykov but without preordaining a death sentence.[105]

The pace of the purges now quickened. Next to be crushed was the Red Army officer corps, including gifted generals like Marshal Mikhail

Tukhachevsky, who was sorely missed when Hitler attacked the Soviet Union. Khrushchev vouched for Deputy People's Commissar of the Army and Navy Jan Gamarnik before his election to the Moscow party committee. Seven days later, when *Pravda* revealed Gamarnik was a "Trotskyite degenerate," Khrushchev declared his election proved "that the enemy foully disguises himself and carries out his subversive activity deep underground. . . . "[106]

Squads of Stalin's henchmen descended on the provinces. Only in Andrei Zhdanov's Leningrad, Beria's Caucasus, and Khrushchev's Moscow were the first secretaries trusted to superintend the purge.[107] Obscene as it was to foment mass hatred against former Kremlin colleagues, it was worse to encourage rank-and-file party members, crazed with fear, to denounce one another. Yet that was precisely what Khrushchev did. "This is not an open struggle," he warned delegates to the Moscow city party conference in May 1937, "where bullets come flying from the enemy's side. This is a struggle with the man who sits next to you, who hails our successes and our party's achievements, while at the same time squeezing the revolver in his pocket, choosing the moment to put a bullet into you the way they did into Sergei Mironovich Kirov." The way to handle such a traitor was "to smash him in the snout"[108] and then relish the thought of his confessing "under the weight of unimpeachable evidence exposed by the NKVD."[109]

"These scoundrels must be destroyed," Khrushchev thundered in August 1937. "In destroying one, two, or ten of them, we are doing the work of millions. That's why our hand must not tremble, why we must march across the corpses of the enemy toward the good of the people."[110]

KHRUSHCHEV ASSISTED in the arrest and liquidation of his own colleagues and friends. Of 38 top officials of Moscow city and province party organizations, only 3 survived. Of 146 party secretaries of other cities and districts in the Moscow region, 136 were, to use the post-Stalin euphemism, "repressed." Of 63 people elected to the Moscow city party committee in May 1937, 45 presumably perished. Of 64 on the province party committee, 46 disappeared.[111]

Two of Khrushchev's personal assistants, Rabinovich and Finkel, were arrested. So was Semyon Korytny, who had first worked with Khrushchev in Kiev. A man named Margolin had assisted Khrushchev in Kiev, studied with him at the Industrial Academy, replaced him as Bauman party boss, and served as his deputy in the Moscow city organization. "In short,"

Khrushchev said in his memoirs, "almost everyone who worked along with me was arrested."[112]

The purge process required that Khrushchev approve these arrests. The party boss of each region had to authorize the seizure and sentencing of his subordinates, and along with the local NKVD chief and local procurator, he served on so-called troikas, which had the authority to impose the death penalty without any appeal. At first, the NKVD needed prior consent to arrest party members in their jurisdiction; later, apparently, the police chief initialed the sentences before they were carried out, with his colleagues approving afterward.[113]

In some cases, Khrushchev had a more direct role. On June 27, 1937, the Politburo set a quota of 35,000 "enemies" to be seized in Moscow and Moscow Province, of whom some 5,000 were to be shot. Khrushchev himself asked that 2,000 former kulaks who were now living in Moscow be liquidated in partial fulfillment of this total.[114] On July 10, 1937, he reported to Stalin that some 41,305 "criminal and kulak elements" had been arrested in Moscow Province and city. In the same document, he himself relegated 8,500 to the "first category" of enemies deserving the death penalty.[115]

According to a historian who interviewed survivors, Khrushchev did little or nothing to help save his friends and colleagues.[116] He did help Rykov's twenty-one-year-old daughter, Natalia, find a job as a teacher, although later, after Khrushchev departed for Ukraine in 1938, she was arrested and spent eighteen years in the gulag.[117] Moreover, although he asked Ernst Kolman to resign when Kolman's brother-in-law was arrested, he found new work for Kolman too. But Khrushchev could not or would not prevent even his closest and most trusted associates from being arrested and shot.[118]

MOLOTOV, KAGANOVICH, and Voroshilov signed hundreds of long death lists at Stalin's behest, scrawling curses next to the names of the condemned to curry favor with their boss.[119] Let us suppose, in the absence of conclusive evidence to the contrary, that Khrushchev signed fewer lists and without the curses.[120] The secret police chiefs Yezhov and Beria knew the killing grounds throughout Moscow: the execution cellar of the Supreme Court's Military Collegium across Dzerzhinsky Square from Lubyanka; Vagan'kovskoe Cemetery in Krasnopresnensky District, where weeping prisoners dug their own graves before alcohol-soused guards dispatched them; the NKVD's state farm at Kommunarka, south of the city, where dogs prowled the grounds with body parts in their jaws; the municipal crematorium at Donskoi Monastery, where the ashes of thousands ended up in a great pit covered over by asphalt.[121] Let us also suppose that although he was asked to inspect Moscow's prisons, these killing fields were beyond Khrushchev's ken. Nonetheless, his record is damning enough, even though his memoirs attempt to obscure it.

Khrushchev admitted he caught "an occasional accidental glimpse" of the terror's inner workings. During the May 1937 Moscow party conference he nominated a respected military commissar to the party committee. The candidate had just received thunderous applause when "I suddenly got a message from the NKVD: 'Do everything you can to bring that man down. He's not to be trusted. He's connected with enemies of the people and will be arrested.' We obeyed and defeated his nomination, but it was a distressing experience for all the delegates. The very next night that commissar was arrested."[122]

Another time, a similar NKVD order came too late to defeat the candidacy of veteran Bolshevik Yemelyan Yaroslavsky, even though Khrushchev tried manfully to do so. "The order was very hard on me," Khrushchev insisted, and even harder was a letter from someone he respected blaming him for his treatment of Yaroslavsky. "I couldn't explain to her that I had just been following orders."[123]

When "a list was put together of people who should be exiled from the city," Khrushchev later said, he didn't "know where these people were sent. I never asked. We always followed the rule that if you weren't told something, that meant it didn't concern you; it was the State's business, and the less you knew about it the better."[124]

At another party conference, where delegates tried desperately to save their own skins by trading accusations of wrecking and treason, Khrushchev read through a draft resolution. "It was awful," he later commented, "full of denunciations of enemies of the people. It demanded that we keep sharpening the knives so as to take vengeance on what we now know were imaginary enemies. I didn't like the resolution, but I was in a difficult spot. What was I to do?" At the time, according to his memoirs, "we didn't know that those who were arrested were destroyed; we thought they were simply put in prison where they served out their terms."[125]

As a candidate member of the Politburo, Khrushchev was entitled to receive all documents considered by it. Instead, he insisted, "I received only those materials that Stalin directed to my personal attention. More often than not they had to do with 'enemies of the people': their testimony, a whole pile of so-called confessions." Khrushchev claimed he had no doubt about their veracity. After all, "Stalin himself had sent them to me."[126]

The best test of what Khrushchev knew and when he knew it involves the arrest of his closest friends. It was one thing to believe that distant figures like Zinoviev and Kamenev were traitors, but Iona Yakir and Semyon Korytny? General Yakir had been his friend in Kiev. They kept in contact when Khrushchev moved to Moscow because Yakir's sister was married to Khrushchev's colleague Korytny. "Whenever Yakir would visit the city, he would drop in on his sister," Khrushchev recalled. "We would all go out to Korytny's dacha."[127]

During the civil war Yakir personally executed several White Army commanders.[128] He condoned collectivization and famine in Ukraine. But when the police started seizing his close associates, Yakir insisted on visiting them in jail, and he went so far as to question their guilt to Voroshilov and Stalin.[129] That added his own name to the roster of the doomed.

By May 1937, with the ring tightening around his fellow officers, and Marshal Tukhachevsky himself about to confess to high treason, Yakir must have been nearly crazed with fear. It is conceivable that he concealed it from his friend Nikita as they strolled the grounds of a Moscow dacha complex; even close friends didn't confide in each other during such terrible times. Then suddenly, a day or two later, according to Khrushchev, "Yakir was a traitor, Yakir an enemy of the people. Previously Stalin had greatly respected Yakir. But suddenly Yakir and his whole group were enemies of the people?" Yet, said Khrushchev, "at the time it still didn't occur to us that they could be victims of slander. . . . At the time none of this gave rise to any doubt."

The next day Khrushchev scrawled his assent across the top of Stalin's note asking Central Committee members to approve excluding Yakir from the party and turning his case over to the NKVD: "I vote for the Politburo's proposal. N. Khrushchev."[130] If in the end he really convinced himself Yakir was guilty, he did so to save his own skin. "I was disturbed," he later said. "First of all, I pitied him. But secondly, they might drag me into it, saying that several hours before his arrest, Yakir had been at Khrushchev's, that he had spent the night there, that they had been walking around and talking about something."[131]

As for Korytny, he broke under the strain, suffered a heart attack, and was admitted to a hospital. The same night Khrushchev visited him there the police took Kortyny away. As for this case too, Khrushchev maintained, "I managed to come up with an explanation. Although I considered Korytny the most honest and irreproachable of men, after all, Yakir had turned out to be a 'turncoat, a traitor and a fascist agent,' and Kortyny was Yakir's closest friend. . . . So it was possible that I had been mistaken and had trusted him in vain."[132]

Khrushchev's adopted daughter, Yulia, cites the Korytny case as proof that he knew many were innocent.[133] Khrushchev himself came close to admitting as much in the case of his assistants Rabinovich and Finkel: "I couldn't even imagine that these two, whom I knew so well, could really be 'enemies of the people.' But there were 'factual materials' [presumably signed confessions] incriminating all of them, and I had no possibility of refuting it." In Margolin's case, he dropped his guard altogether for a brief moment: "I simply couldn't conceive that Margolin was an enemy of the people."[134]

At another point in his memoirs Khrushchev said of the men he branded as traitors, "It would be advantageous to me now to say, 'In the depths of my soul I sympathized with them.' But no, on the contrary, I not only didn't sympathize with them in my soul, deep down I was angry and indignant with them because we were convinced then that Stalin could not be mistaken."[135]

But to say he sympathized with alleged traitors would *not* have been advantageous. For to do so would imply that he knowingly condemned the innocent. What *was* advantageous was not only to insist that he believed in their guilt but to half convince himself that he did. The discrepancies in Khrushchev's account are so sharp that a previous biographer contends it is "impossible to accept [his] unsupported word for anything at all."[136] In fact, Khrushchev's stunning blend of deception and self-deception is not so much an obstacle to understanding as itself the main point to be understood.

By 1937, Communists of all ranks were being denounced, arrested, and tortured into incriminating their colleagues. With so many of his subordinates being worked over by NKVD interrogators, Khrushchev must have assumed he could be next. During a party conference at which even top leaders had to be "reelected," Malenkov's civil war record suddenly struck delegates as suspicious. It took Khrushchev's vigorous defense to save him, but on the eve of the conference, Khrushchev confessed his 1923 dalliance with Trotskyism to Kaganovich.

Kaganovich blanched (knowing that any Khrushchev sins were a stain on his own record) and urged him to take the matter up with Stalin himself. Receiving Khrushchev in his office, Stalin calmly advised him not to mention the episode at the party conference. But Molotov, who was with him, thought it better for Khrushchev to own up in public, and Stalin nodded. "Yes," said Stalin, "better to tell what happened, because if you don't then, they'll all be able to pester you; they'll bombard you with questions—and us with reports."

How lucky could Khrushchev get! Suddenly the deadly torrent of denunciations was reduced to "pestering" and "reports." Reassured in advance by the one who really counted, Khrushchev informed the conference of his transgression, adding that Comrades Stalin, Molotov, Kaganovich, and other Politburo members "know about my mistake" but that he considered it necessary that "our Moscow party organization should know as well." No wonder his "confession" produced applause and immediate reelection to the party committee, an outcome that "further strengthened my trust in Stalin, my confidence that those who were arrested were in fact enemies of the people."[137]

However, what Stalin gave he also could take away. During a stroll around the closed Kremlin grounds, he informed Khrushchev that the recently arrested Post and Telegraph Commissar Nikolai Antipov had incriminated him. Stalin looked Khrushchev in the eye and waited for him to respond. "Accidentally, I think, my eyes gave him no cause to conclude I was linked to Antipov. If he had gotten the impression that somehow my eyes 'gave me away,' then right then and there you would have had a new enemy of the people."[138]

Defending oneself was permissible, but not anyone else. Refusing to sign death warrants would have meant a swift end to Khrushchev and his family. As Molotov said later, when asked if Khrushchev had signed death lists, "Of course he did. Otherwise he wouldn't have been moved up. Any intelligent man could see that."[139]

Lesser-known officials fled Moscow and managed to disappear into the countryside. Tomsky, Gamarnik, and others committed suicide when faced with arrest. Sergo Ordzhonikidze was the only top leader who apparently killed himself (after years of loyal service, to be sure) rather than do Stalin's bidding. But Khrushchev had too much to live for. By 1937 he was omnipresent in the life of the capital. In 1935 he made sixty-four speeches at meetings and conferences; in 1936, at least ninety-five.[140] During a December 5, 1936, parade through Red Square, demonstrators celebrating the new Stalin constitution carried his portrait along with those of other top party leaders.

Contemporary newsreels register Khrushchev's progress and his evident enjoyment of it. At a funeral in Novodevichy Cemetery, the camera catches him whispering to Bulganin and grinning at his own joke. The two of them are young and vigorous, overflowing with energy, relishing life. At another funeral Khrushchev stands next to more senior leaders: Stalin in his signature tunic, his cold, hypnotic eyes surveying the scene; Molotov almost dandyish in a tailored suit and tie, with his neatly trimmed mustache, closely cropped hair, and pince-nez; Khrushchev in a white turtleneck, his thick lower lip turned out, his long nose not yet bulbous, his eyes, like dark coals, continually darting in Stalin's direction.[141]

Even in his public speeches, Khrushchev projected informality, warmth, and a direct engagement with his audience. On one occasion recorded on film he modestly apologizes for the heat in the hall, genially accepts a reproach from an old woman in the first row, and then flashes a shy but sly grin as if to say, "What can you do?" His oddly high-pitched, somewhat nasal, singsong voice doesn't fit his full, round face, but his right arm and fist pound the air punctuating his Stalin-style cadences. "If I may speak about myself," Khrushchev said in his memoirs, "I was considered a pretty good orator. I would speak without a text and even without an outline." He was nervous when once asked to follow Kirov, who was known as a splendid speaker. But afterward Kaganovich congratulated him: "Remarkable, you spoke brilliantly. Stalin noticed too. He said, 'It's very hard to follow Kirov, but Khrushchev did a good job.' "[142]

Khrushchev had a bad case of Stalin worship; he particularly admired qualities that he was trying to cultivate in himself. From the beginning he esteemed Stalin's "clearness of mind and the conciseness of his formulations." Later, as he watched Stalin close up, "my admiration for him continued to grow. I was spellbound by the patience and sympathy for others that he showed at Politburo meetings in the mid thirties."[143]

These encomiums too could be part of Khrushchev's retrospective smoke screen of deception and self-deception. But they have the ring of truth. Stalin possessed formidable energy and inflexible will. His way of reducing complicated Marxist-Leninist matters to seemingly straightforward syllogisms appealed to the likes of Khrushchev. Cleverly concealing his overweening ego, Stalin managed to seem sincere and straightforward. Many years later, even after Khrushchev had denounced his former master, it struck one of his closest aides that more than anything else, Khrushchev "envied Stalin."[144]

As Kaganovich's deputy Khrushchev made at least two appearances in Stalin's Kremlin office as early as the fall of 1932 (one lasting thirty-five minutes, the other forty), while the dictator's office log records four visits (ranging from half an hour to two and half hours) between April 1 and May 18, 1934.[145] Khrushchev also observed his idol at Politburo meetings that Central Committee members were privileged to attend, but most of all, he treasured informal sessions with the *vozhd.* "Sometimes Stalin would instruct someone to call up Bulganin and myself and have us join him at the theater. We always concentrated hard on what he was saying and then tried to do exactly as he had advised us."[146] Even better were invitations to Stalin's dacha on weekends: "Stalin would always seat Bulganin and me next to him and pay close attention to us during the meal. He was fond of saying, 'Well, how's it going, City Fathers?'"

This was heaven itself! "Worshiping him as I did, I couldn't get used to being with him in relaxed surroundings: Here he was . . . laughing and joking like the rest of us! After a while I began to admire him not only as a political leader who had no equal, but simply as another human being."[147]

Stalin seemed almost to reciprocate. In December 1937 he spoke briefly at a Moscow conference that Khrushchev chaired. "Comrades," he said, "I must admit that I didn't intend to address you. But our respected Nikita Sergeyevich just about dragged me over here to the meeting. 'Come on,' he says to me. 'Give a good speech.'" Stalin's words conveyed a kind of affection. As recounted by him, Khrushchev had used the familiar second-person singular in pressing him to "give a good speech." That Khrushchev actually felt free to address Stalin so informally seems doubtful. That Stalin felt warmly toward him had now been demonstrated for all to see.[148]

WHY SHOULDN'T Stalin have liked Khrushchev? Besides rendering loyal service and idolizing him, Khrushchev had strengths and weaknesses that complemented Stalin's. Stalin didn't like making speeches, but Khrushchev was never happier than when on display. If Stalin was gloomy and unsociable, Khrushchev was friendly and approachable. Except for vacations in the Caucasus, Stalin rarely left Moscow, while Khrushchev couldn't sit still. Until he got too popular for his own good, Kirov, who appeared "open and uncomplicated," was particularly close to Stalin.[149] Likewise, the seemingly guileless, straightforward Khrushchev.

Physically Stalin was unimpressive. Only about five feet six inches tall,[150] he wore elevator shoes and stood atop a wooden platform on public occasions. His face was pockmarked; his teeth were uneven, his left arm and shoulder forever stiff from a childhood accident. His torso was too short, and his arms were too long. "It even makes him miserable," said Bukharin of Stalin, "that he cannot convince everyone, including himself, that he is a taller man than anybody else."[151] It helped that Khrushchev was just five feet one inch.

Intellectually too Stalin fell short of his own ideal. What he had learned in a religious seminary was no match for Lenin's and Trotsky's erudition. He built a vast library, read and underlined extensively, engaged a philosopher as his private tutor, authored (if that is the word for a process to which others doubtlessly contributed) abstruse treatises on subjects ranging from economics to linguistics, and in effect served as Soviet censor in chief. But still, said Bukharin, Stalin was "eaten up by the vain desire to become a well-known theoretician. He feels it is the only thing he lacks."[152] Most of Stalin's henchmen (Molotov, Mikoyan, and Zhdanov excepted) were primitives even by Stalinist standards (Voroshilov went to work as a herdsboy at the age of eight), but Khrushchev probably was the least threatening of all.

Two other Khrushchev traits were invaluable. His garrulousness was golden to a connoisseur of silence like Stalin; Khrushchev could be trusted to betray any incipient disloyalty. In addition, Khrushchev genuinely liked his Kremlin cronies and hoped they liked him. He praised Kaganovich as "a man who got things done. If the Central Committee put an axe in his hands, he would chop up a storm; unfortunately he often chopped down the healthy trees along with the rotten ones. But the chips really flew—you couldn't take that away from him."[153] He was also "a friend of Malenkov's. We'd worked together on the Moscow Committee." Moreover, Khrushchev had "always liked Yagoda," who headed the NKVD "meat grinder" until 1936. But he "certainly had no objections to Yezhov," who had been his Central Committee supervisor when Khrushchev served as Industrial Academy party cell leader.[154]

After Yezhov took over as secret police chief, Khrushchev said later, "a literal slaughter began, and masses of people became caught up in the meat-grinder." Still, he regarded Yezhov as a "diligent and reliable" man.[155] Eventually, Stalin liquidated Yezhov (who, like Yagoda before him, knew too much and made a good scapegoat) and replaced him with Beria, whose crimes eventually ranged from mass murder to serial rape. But in the thirties, according to his memoirs, Khrushchev was "on good terms with Beria."[156]

The list of people Khrushchev liked includes Stalin's bloodiest butchers. Were a Nuremberg type of prosecution ever posthumously to indict the Stalin era's leading criminals, it would arraign Khrushchev's friends. Not everyone he liked was unsavory. Nor, apparently, did he like absolutely everyone he met. Still, the fact that he liked so many and that he admitted as much even when he was out of power and could only incriminate himself by so doing underscores how important to him and his self-image was his liking people and being liked in return. He conceived himself to be, and compared with his Kremlin cronies, he actually was, a nice guy. There seems no better way to say it.[157]

Another newsreel shows Khrushchev standing slightly behind Yezhov and Politburo member Andrei Andreyev at a party conclave. As Yezhov and Andreyev try to chat, Khrushchev keeps leaning forward, grinning, joking, and relishing their grins in return. In a revealing sequence shot during a Red Square parade, party leaders stand atop the Lenin Mausoleum. At one point Khrushchev, bearing some sort of news, approaches Stalin and Kaganovich from behind. As they watch the parade while listening to him, their stony faces show no emotion. He, on the other hand, is cheerful self-abasement personified, his eager-to-please face wreathed in an ingratiating smile as he jabbers animatedly to the back of their heads.

THE MIXED IMAGE of Khrushchev that the camera caught—on the one hand, outgoing and exuberant, on the other, tense and insecure—emerges as well from what is known of his private life. As a rising Kremlin star he was living the good life Soviet style. Yet he was also under incredible strain stemming not only from his visible public role but from domestic pressures hidden from public view.

By 1934 Khrushchev and his family had moved into the massive new Government House on the Moscow River later made famous in Yuri Trifonov's novel *The House on the Embankment.* Completed in 1931 as a residence for Moscow's upper party and state elite (with the exception of the still-higher circle that lived in the Kremlin itself), Government House was a massive eleven-story structure consisting of several attached buildings grouped around separate courtyards. Twenty-five separate entrances led to a total of 506 multiroom apartments, all (according to one who lived there) "luxuriously but tastelessly appointed with government-issue furniture."[158] Services provided to tenants were equally fantastical for the time: central heating and gas, around-the-clock hot water, a telephone in each apartment at a time when ordinary Muscovites waited years for one, two elevators in each entryway (one a service elevator located near each apartment's kitchen), stores, a hairdresser, a clinic, a cafeteria, even a movie house. The security police were omnipresent as well, supposedly protecting VIPs such as Marshal Tukhachevsky, Georgy Dimitrov, head of the Comintern, and assorted relatives of Stalin, Kaganovich, and others, but of course spying on them as well.

In an era when most Muscovites were crammed into communal apartments, with several families sharing single kitchens and bathrooms, the Khrushchevs had a spacious five-room flat. By Soviet standards it was more than comfortable, even though at times it had to accommodate as many as five children (Rada, Sergei, born on July 6, 1935, and Yelena, July 17, 1937, as well as Yulia and Lyonia from Khrushchev's first marriage), Khrushchev's parents, and bodyguards who occupied one room.[159] Khrushchev also had a chauffeured car, yet he later insisted he lived modestly: "Nowadays, unfortunately, a lot of that spirit of idealism and self-sacrifice has gone out of the party; many of the attitudes that seem all too prevalent today have a touch of bourgeois pettiness about them. Back when I helped run the city of Moscow, no one would have permitted himself so much as a single thought about having his own dacha. After all, we were Communists! We always went around in plain work clothes. None of us ever wore suits. Our uniform was a field shirt with an open collar or a white peasant smock. Stalin set a good example in this regard."[160]

As a member of the *nachal'stvo* (bosses), Khrushchev got not only a high salary but goods and services money couldn't buy. Some privileges, such as his car, were open secrets, but restricted stores and cafeterias, special resorts, and a monthly "sealed envelope" with money over and above one's formal salary were hidden. Khrushchev conceded that he and his colleagues "used to gorge ourselves on sandwiches, sausages, sour cream, and sweet tea between working sessions at the Kremlin" but insisted that "we often didn't have enough to eat at home."[161] Moscow coworker Ernst Kolman recalled "hearty breakfasts brought to the [Moscow party committee] office free of charge by a waitress with a red kerchief in her hair," as well as elegant lunches in the Kremlin cafeteria, "the best restaurant in town." The same cafeteria offered high-quality dishes "to go" for holidays. Kolman also remembered meeting Khrushchev at "one-day" resorts, not far from the city, to which Moscow party officials could retreat with their families on holidays. The accommodations were cozy, said Kolman, and the food was "fit for a king." No rabbits here, or ration cards either: "The table groaned under the weight of wines and all manner of treats; everyone was free to eat as much as he wished."[162]

The Ogaryovo estate, where Khrushchev (and Boris Yeltsin in his turn) later had their state dachas, had formerly belonged to a tsarist governor-general. The main building was now reserved for city party and government leaders. The Khrushchevs had two rooms on the second floor of another house, which previously had been occupied by princely retainers. Bulganin and his family were downstairs. Nearby were Moscow colleagues, including the doomed Semyon Korytny.[163] Maria Sorokina worked her way up from maid to deputy director of the dacha used by the Khrushchevs. Her son, Dima, was a pal of Khrushchev's son Lyonia in the early thirties. Sorokina's photo album includes pictures of Dima and Lyonia sunning themselves on chaise longues, swimming and rowing in the Moscow River, and playing tennis.[164]

Beneath this comfortable surface, however, life was more complicated. Khrushchev's father helped out by going to special stores to pick up extra food, which he lugged home on his back, and by carrying Rada to the kindergarten on the eleventh floor of Government House when the elevator wasn't working. Khrushchev's father struck Dima Sorokin as the archetypal peasant muzhik, puffing away on foul-smelling, peasant-grown tobacco stuffed into a homemade wrapper. In response to his son's complaints, the old man grumbled that he could always go back to Kalinovka, where "I can smoke without getting in anyone's way."

One day Nikita Khrushchev's mother told him his father was angry at him because Khrushchev had not "paid his debt." Khrushchev had promised his father a new pair of boots and then forgotten his promise. Khrushchev later told this story laughingly, but it reveals the humiliating extent to which the father had become dependent on his son.[165]

From a position of dominance in the family, Khrushchev's mother had been likewise reduced to dependence, often sitting alone in her room or gossiping with other oldsters in the courtyard as she had with Kalinovka neighbors. Wherever Ksenia Ivanovna planted herself on a stool she carried with her, other babushkas soon gathered. Khrushchev didn't approve of these gabfests, which, as his wife later put it, "could have cost you your life in the thirties." But, said Nina Petrovna, his mother "wouldn't listen to him."[166] When Ksenia Ivanovna demanded that Rada obey her because she was older and wiser, the little girl asked, "Wiser than Stalin?" Her grandmother replied, "Of course I am."[167]

Another issue between Khrushchev and his mother, and between him and his wife as well, was Lyonia's behavior. Lyonia didn't get along with his sister Yulia. He abused his access to special party-provided food and clothing by giving it away to his friends. He once drove a motorcycle down the stairs of an official state residence. His doting grandmother forgave him these and other trespasses, while his stepmother bit her tongue. It was Khrushchev's job to tame Lyonia, but he was surprisingly irresolute. Instead of punishing him, he blamed Lyonia's friends. Lyonia and Dima Sorokin wanted to go to flying school together, but Khrushchev vetoed the plan. Dima was a "bad influence" on Lyonia, Khrushchev said. Let Dima find another occupation.[168]

The task of disciplining Lyonia was complicated psychologically because his most serious transgressions echoed Khrushchev's own. By 1937, when he was only twenty, Lyonia had lived with and abandoned not one but two women, both of them Jewish, leaving at least one of them with a child. In 1935 he got Esther Naumovna Ettinger pregnant. According to her son, Yuri Leonidovich Khrushchev, a career air force officer and test pilot, Ettinger was a technical designer who met Lyonia at a summer camp outside Moscow. The two didn't remain together long, but that wasn't for lack of insisting by Nikita Khrushchev. Apparently, the elder Khrushchev was so outraged by his son's behavior (with its eerie echoes of his own in 1922) that he practically evicted him from the household.[169]

Lyonia's second woman was Rozalie Mikhailovna Treivas, a pretty, blond, blue-eyed actress whose uncle Boris had worked for Khrushchev in the Bauman District and then become a ranking Komsomol official. Khrushchev later said that Treivas was "an intelligent, capable, decent man" but also that Kaganovich "took me aside and warned me that Treivas . . . had once signed a declaration in support of Trotsky." Naturally, Treivas was arrested, after which Khrushchev caught sight of him while inspecting NKVD prisons on Stalin's order. Treivas "didn't escape the meat-grinder when the butchery began in 1937," lamented Khrushchev in his memoirs.[170] But however much he sympathized with Treivas, he was horrified to discover his son's involvement with Treivas's niece. Even worse, Lyonia actually married her on November 11, 1937. When finally introduced to Roza, Khrushchev exploded and tore the marriage certificate in half. After that the two newlyweds lived with a friend until January 1938, when Lyonia accompanied his family to Kiev, abandoning Roza for good.[171]

The large Khrushchev household required careful management. But Khrushchev himself avoided not only its daily care and feeding but also regular intercourse with it. His work was all-consuming. Even when he had time for himself, on weekends at the dacha outside Moscow, he often preferred to spend it with colleagues and friends. When he did see his children, he was full of life and cheer, singing songs, reading poems, and taking them cross-country skiing. Still, "Father never had any time for us," Rada recalled.[172] Nina Petrovna ran the household, but until 1935 she also worked overtime at Moscow's electric lamp factory, where she organized and directed a party school on the premises and served as head of "agitation and propaganda" for the plant's party committee.

Nina Petrovna's work was apparently fulfilling. "I carried out my part of the first five-year plan in two and a half years and received a certificate of honor from the plant authorities," she recalled. "I met a wide circle of people as well—party activists, writers, Old Bolsheviks, collective farmers whose kolkhozy came under the plant's patronage. . . . I regard those years as the most active of my political, and in general, of my public life." But her schedule was exhausting. The plant had some three thousand workers laboring on three shifts. Nina Petrovna left for work at eight in the morning and returned at ten at night "at the earliest." Since the six-day workweek followed a staggered schedule, "I never had a free day at the same time as N. S., who had a fixed day off." Nina Petrovna told of how "annoyed" she was when theater excursions were arranged for her comrades at work, and she couldn't go along because she worked on Sundays. As for "all the cultural activities in which N. S. participated," they were "unavailable to me. . . ."

Nina Petrovna tried to keep her connection to Khrushchev secret. She used her maiden name and traveled to work by tram, rather than official car, a trip that took "at least an hour" each way. One day the plant's party secretary called Khrushchev late at night, and when Nina Petrovna picked up the phone, he asked curtly to whom he was speaking. "Kukharchuk," she replied automatically. "'And what are you doing in Comrade Khrushchev's apartment?' he asked. He was quite surprised that I turned out to be Khrushchev's wife."

The strain intensified when the children got sick. When Rada came down with scarlet fever, "we put her in the hospital next to the plant, and every evening I hurried over to see how she was doing. I had to look through the window of the ward [because Soviet hospitals were so fearful about diseases transmitted by outside visitors]. I saw them give her a bowl of kasha and big spoon, and how the nurse then went off to gossip with her friends. Rada was little. . . . I could see her standing there crying, with her feet in a bowl of kasha, but the nurse didn't come and there was no way for me to help. We signed a waiver and took the child out of the hospital ahead of schedule. With a lot of special care we managed to nurse her back to health."

Nina Petrovna quit her job when Sergei was born and then worked as a manager of the All-Union Council of Engineering-Technical Societies until Yelena arrived. After the family moved to Kiev in 1938, "the only work I did was an occasional assignment from the district party committee. I taught party history . . . and English in evening courses. The three children were small and often ill."[173] Once she stopped working regularly, Rada recalled, Nina Petrovna was "less irritable." Having been particularly strict with Rada ("It was very difficult to ask for anything, practically impossible"), Nina Petrovna eased up and "even spoiled" Sergei and Yelena.[174]

According to Rada, Nina Petrovna "never expressed any regret about breaking off her personal career, at least not in the children's presence."[175] But she wasn't the type to complain. Only at the very end of her life, living mostly alone after her husband's death, did she lament to a housekeeper, "I never really had a chance to experience life."

Some of her burden was self-induced. But her strain surely added to her husband's. Whether Khrushchev dared share with her his deepest hopes and fears during the most dreadful passage in Russian history remains unclear. In front of their children at least, Nikita and Nina Khrushchev never talked politics, never criticized Stalin, of course, but never praised him either.

CHAPTER SIX

Stalin's Viceroy: 1938–1941

"WE WANT TO send you to Ukraine to head the party organization there. Kossior doesn't seem able to manage. We'll transfer him to Moscow to be First Deputy of the Council of People's Commissars and Chairman of the Central Control Commission."

This was how Stalin announced Khrushchev's promotion late in 1937. Here are Khrushchev's own words about his reaction:

> I was reluctant to accept it for three reasons. First, I liked Kossior and was uncomfortable about taking his place. I'd known him when he succeeded Kaganovich as First Secretary of the Ukrainian Central Committee in 1929. . . . Second, I doubted I was experienced or qualified . . . ; I thought the cap of the Ukrainian First Secretary was simply too big for my head. Finally, the nationality question entered into my thinking. It's true, I'd already worked in Ukraine and had always gotten along well with Ukrainian Communists and non-party members alike. Nevertheless, as a Russian, I still felt some awkwardness among Ukrainians. Even though I understand the Ukrainian language, I'd never mastered it to the extent that I could make speeches in it. I explained all these drawbacks to Stalin, and told him that I was afraid the Ukrainians, particularly the intelligentsia, might be very cool to me: "It hardly makes sense to send me, a Russian, to Ukraine," I told him.

> "Kossior's not a Russian, is he? He's a Pole. Why should a Russian have a harder time with the Ukrainians than a Pole?"
>
> "Kossior may be a Pole," I conceded, "but he can give speeches in Ukrainian. Moreover, Kossior is much more experienced than I am."
>
> "No more argument. You're going to Ukraine."
>
> "Very well. I'll try to do everything I can to justify your confidence in me and put the Ukrainian party back on its feet." I was still worried that I wouldn't be able to manage the assignment, but I won't deny I was flattered that the Central Committee would entrust me with such a high post.

Not only was Khrushchev assigned the top spot in Ukraine (although on an "acting" basis only for the time being), but Stalin insisted he head the Kiev city and regional party committees as well.

> I told him it was impossible for me to hold so many positions at once, but he was insistent.
>
> "You can manage," he said. "Just select whom you want to help you when you get there. "[1]

Given his abundant ambition, wouldn't Khrushchev have leaped at the chance to lead the territory in which he had lived and worked for so many years? But his self-doubt was real too, as was the benefit of emphasizing it to Stalin. Not to mention (which he couldn't, of course) the danger that he might be next in the lengthening line of Ukrainian leaders whose heads rolled in the purge.

Khrushchev left Moscow for Kiev in January 1938. In the decade that followed, he was often in the capital for Politburo and other meetings. But it was only in late 1949 that he returned for good as a newly appointed secretary of the Central Committee. By that time he had grown more independent from Stalin and more disillusioned with him too. Still, during the same period he served Stalin ever more effectively. More than anything else, it was the war that changed Khrushchev. But the process began in Ukraine in the three years before Hitler attacked the USSR in 1941.

The key to Khrushchev's partial emancipation, and to his more efficient service, was his distance from Moscow. No one in Stalin's orbit, not even his viceroy in Ukraine, was anywhere near autonomous. But Kiev was far enough from the center to allow for what the Soviets called localism.

Khrushchev believed he knew Ukraine better than the Kremlin did. He not only resented having to go through the men around Stalin to get to the boss but began to see through Stalin himself.

Distance gave Khrushchev the chance to hone his own style and skills. He was "one of kind," recalled Vasily Kostenko, a Communist Youth League (Komsomol) official who worked for him in Kiev. He "knew concretely how things worked." He "knew how to talk to people. He sensed which people he could joke with and which people, like me, were too young to know how to take jokes from someone like him." He was "fearless," a "great man to have as a boss."[2]

Upon returning to Kiev, Khrushchev quickly learned more about the collectivization and the famine and the terror that had been raging in Ukraine. On a visit to the Petrovo-Marinsky District he had headed in 1925, he explicitly asked about peasants he had befriended, including kulaks with whom he had been on good terms. "He was afraid they had been 'dekulakized,'" recollected Zakhar Glukhov, who held Khrushchev's former post in 1938. "Khrushchev was the kind of man you could talk to candidly. He had a friend, a man called Gomlia from whom he'd been inseparable, a man whom he greatly respected and who told him everything that had occurred."[3]

By the time Khrushchev reached Kiev, purges had swept through Ukrainian institutions of every kind. The party had been largely demolished, with so many arrested that its Central Committee couldn't convene a quorum. Several teachers at the Stalino metallurgical institute whom he "greatly respected" had been arrested. One of them whom he encountered there was "a shadow of his former self. 'How are you doing?' I asked him. He looked dismal and uncommunicative. He mumbled that things were bad, that he had been arrested. Others told me later that he had been beaten terribly and his health had been ruined. It wasn't long before he died."[4]

Encounters like this help explain extraordinary incidents in which Khrushchev confessed doubt and disillusionment to old friends. Yet the same Khrushchev presided over the purges, which apparently accelerated after his arrival. In 1938 alone, 106,119 people are said to have been arrested; between 1938 and 1940 the total was 165,565. According to Molotov, hardly objective but extremely well informed, Khrushchev "sent 54,000 people to the next world as a member of the [Ukrainian] troika." Khrushchev's speeches dripped venom, and at least one case has come to light in which he scrawled, "Arrest," across the top of a document that doomed a high official of the Ukrainian Komsomol.[5]

As in Moscow, belief in the Soviet system still inspired him. Master of a domain roughly equal in size to France, he convinced himself he was contributing to its welfare by taking under his wing with his usual energy and determination agriculture, industry, and culture; by conquering western Ukrainian lands and uniting them with the rest of Soviet Ukraine; by trying to ameliorate, within strict limits and in circumscribed ways, the very terror that he himself superintended. But he served his own interest too. The Khrushchev household now consisted of his five children plus several other relatives who joined it in Kiev. All of them, even those who had lived the good life in Moscow, enjoyed privileges they could hardly have imagined. Fear for himself and his family also drove Khrushchev. His purged Kiev predecessors had lost everything; even their wives and children had perished. Yet at the same time, no matter how contradictory it seems, he was having a wonderful time. No longer up-and-coming, he had fully arrived; he was enjoying Stalin's ever-warmer approbation; he was gaining confidence from his own successes as well as the failures of others, including those of Stalin.

APART FROM Russia itself, Ukraine was by far the most important part of the USSR. Yet it, or at least some of its citizens, particularly in the intelligentsia, were susceptible to nationalist yearnings that clashed with both Marxist internationalism and Stalin's drive for totalitarian control. After several centuries of Kievan rule, during which the civilization inhabiting Ukraine controlled its own destiny and loomed large in the life of its Eastern European neighbors, the area came under control of others, first the Mongols, then Lithuania, Poland, and Russia. From the late eighteenth to the early twentieth century, Ukrainian lands were divided between the Russian and Hapsburg empires with some 80 percent of the population subjects of the former. National consciousness gained ground during the late nineteenth century, and the collapse of the Russian empire in World War I offered a chance for Ukrainian independence. The Bolsheviks received only 10 percent of the vote in Ukrainian elections to the 1917 Constituent Assembly (peasant-based Socialist Revolutionary parties got 75 percent), and nationalist regimes of various hues briefly seized power between 1917 and 1920. But it was Lenin's party that prevailed.[6]

In an effort to hold Ukraine, and in keeping with his theoretical rejection of Russian chauvinism, Lenin accepted nationalist-minded colleagues as leaders of the Ukrainian Communist party, men like Panas Lyubchenko and Grigory Grinko, who later perished in the Great Purge.

Other leading Ukrainian Communists, such as Nikolai Skrypnik, opposed the December 1922 agreement that formally established the USSR, with Ukraine as a theoretically autonomous but actually subordinate Soviet republic. Once the union was created over Ukrainian objections, Skrypnik and Ukrainian Prime Minister Vlas Chubar resisted efforts by Moscow-based all-union agencies to take control of Ukrainian economic life.

Ukrainian "national Communists" lost out on the form the USSR was to take, but for the time being they were allowed, even encouraged by Moscow, to foster Ukrainianization of cultural life. Ukrainianization was part of a larger effort to legitimize Bolshevik rule in non-Russian areas by clothing communism in local languages and cultures. It meant appointing Ukrainians to high party and state posts, establishing Ukrainian as the official language in state institutions, promoting the use of Ukrainian in schools, and fostering Ukrainian literature, art, and historiography.

Stalin had doubts about Ukrainianization from the beginning. Witness his appointment of Lazar Kaganovich as Ukrainian party leader in 1925. By 1928 Kaganovich had so antagonized people like Grinko and Chubar that they complained to Stalin, who replaced Kaganovich with Kossior.[7]

Ironically, Kaganovich's recall marked the beginning of the end of Ukrainian national communism. Non-Communist Ukrainian nationalists, still influential in 1930, were the target of trials in the spring of that year. Tensions rose higher when Stalin's terror-famine reached its climax in the spring of 1933.[8] By now even Stalinist Communists, who had loyally carried out his dreadful decrees, were full of doubt. That was why Stalin dispatched Pavel Postyshev to Kiev with a mandate to replace disloyal Ukrainian Communists with reliable Russians from outside Ukraine.[9] Skrypnik, who was viciously attacked in the party press in the summer of 1933, committed suicide in July. His supporters in the intelligentsia were "unmasked" as members of an alleged "Ukrainian Military Organization" in several trials that followed.[10]

As in Moscow, a pause ensued before the 1937 storm. In the beginning of that year Postyshev himself came under attack when his supporters were expelled from the Kiev party organization. Next, Stalin revealed that a woman named Nikolayenko, "a rank-and-file member of the party . . . an ordinary 'little person,'" had been exposing "Trotskyite wreckers" in Kiev only to be "shunned [by the Kiev party organization] like a bothersome fly." Moscow had launched an investigation, Stalin continued. "It was revealed that the Nikolayenko was right, while the party organization was wrong."[11]

In March 1937 the Ukrainian Central Committee dropped Postyshev from his post. For the time being, Kossior hung on by leading the attack on his fallen deputy. Lyubchenko survived until August, when the Ukrainian Central Committee voted to expel him from the party and authorized his arrest.[12] Just a few weeks earlier Khrushchev had given Lyubchenko, Kossior, and Postyshev a guided tour of Moscow in Stalin's car. "The relationship among us couldn't have been better or more full of party camaraderie," Khrushchev remembered.[13] But late on the afternoon of August 30, Lyubchenko shot his wife and himself, and on the same day, Grinko, by then the USSR people's commissar of finance, was arrested in Moscow. Kossior, whom Khrushchev was to replace as Ukrainian party leader, was temporarily appointed a deputy all-union premier along with his former Kiev colleague Chubar. Then Kossior was arrested at the end of April 1938 (the only "announcement" being the fact that Kiev Radio stopped describing itself as Radio Kossior), while Chubar was removed from his post in June, sent to work in the Urals, and later arrested there. Both Kossior and Chubar were tried in February 1939. Along with Postyshev, they were shot on February 26, 1939, after having been tortured into confessing. Kossior's surviving brothers (two others having previously committed suicide and been shot respectively) were executed too, as was his wife, Yelizaveta. Postyshev's eldest son was also shot, his other children were dispatched to the camps, and his wife was tortured and later reportedly shot. Chubar's wife was also killed.[14]

ALL THIS was a tough act to follow. Khrushchev's way of protecting himself from his predecessors' fate was to outdo them in carrying out Stalin's orders. It was "only after the faithful Stalinist Nikita Sergeyevich Khrushchev arrived in Ukraine [that] the smashing of enemies of the people began in earnest," claimed the Ukrainian NKVD chief Aleksandr Uspensky.[15] It was in his interest of course to flatter Khrushchev; on the contrary, said Khrushchev's defenders, the terror eased after he took over in Kiev. The precise pace of the purge is uncertain, but the broad outline is clear. All members but one of the Ukrainian party Politburo, Orgburo, and Secretariat were arrested. The entire Ukrainian government was replaced, as were party leaders and their deputies in all twelve Ukrainian provinces and virtually all Red Army corps and division commanders. Of eighty-six Central Committee members elected in June 1938, only three remained from a year before, while half of all party members in Kiev, and up to 63 percent in one district, were denounced. Only after June 1938 did the purge pace seem to ease. In 1939 "only" twelve thousand are reported to have been arrested, in 1940 about forty thousand.[16]

Khrushchev ordered that his speeches at Ukrainian party congresses and Central Committee plenums not be included in the stenographic records normally compiled on such occasions; instead his remarks were preserved in a special, secret archive of the party apparatus. Before returning to Moscow in December 1949, he directed that this special material (a list of which filled fifty-two pages) be transferred there too. If the fate of these documents suggests Khrushchev had something to hide, surviving excerpts from these speeches suggest why.[17]

"We must conduct the battle with enemies, provocateurs, and slanderers decisively," he announced at the Fourteenth Ukrainian Party Congress in June 1938. "The struggle is still being carried out too weakly. . . . We must . . . mercilessly smash spies and traitors. And we shall smash them and finish them off."[18] The following March in Moscow he boasted about having extirpated "vermin" during his first year in Ukraine.[19]

Khrushchev signed numerous arrest warrants for party and Komsomol functionaries. He never admitted as much, but his future Ukrainian Communist Youth League chief so testified,[20] and Khrushchev's memoirs provided indirect confirmation: " . . . even leaders as highly placed as I (at that time I was already a Politburo member) were completely in thrall to documents presented by NKVD personnel who determined the fate of this or that party member or nonparty member."[21] "In thrall" almost certainly means that Khrushchev was approving NKVD lists.

Stepan Ivanovich Usenko was on one of them. Usenko was a twenty-nine-year-old official who was arrested on November 14, 1938, per an NKVD order of the previous day. Charged with having led a "counterrevolutionary right-Trotskyite organization," he at first denied any guilt but eventually was coerced into confessing. Despite sending a seven-page handwritten letter to Khrushchev in which he admitted his guilt but begged for mercy on the grounds that he was young and would repent, Usenko was shot on March 7, 1939. Khrushchev was allegedly the target of an assassination plot masterminded by Usenko. He was also the author of a signature, scrawled Stalin-style in large, rolling letters across the top of a November 13 report summarizing the "evidence" against Usenko: "Arrest him! N. Khrushchev, 18/XI/38."[22]

By the time Khrushchev presided over the Ukrainian terror, his doubts about the purges had ripened into anger. During his first return trip to Stalino in April 1938 he paid a visit to the Kosenko house. His childhood friend Ilya Kosenko, who still lived there, had taken a path very different from Khrushchev's. Khrushchev's parents had praised the devout Ilya, who sang in the church choir, as a model for their son, and they had also greatly admired Ilya's sister, Liusha. After the revolution Khrushchev had convinced Ilya to join the Bolsheviks, but when the party recruited him for "dekulakization," Kosenko quit its ranks. When his daughter Olga later asked how he managed to survive the terror that claimed so many Bolsheviks, Kosenko answered, "Because I turned in my party card, that's how!"[23]

Ilya Kosenko was tending the garden behind his house in April 1938 when seven black limousines roared up and disgorged a small army of security men, who lined up in two rows on either side of the cottage gate. Khrushchev emerged from one car and caught sight of young Olga: "Are you the daughter? Go call your father."

"Father, you better go, they've come to arrest you," Olga shouted.

Ilya Kosenko's hands shook, his daughter recalls, until he recognized his old friend. Khrushchev entered the cottage, followed by several of his aides and bodyguards.

"So, tell me how you've been," asked Khrushchev.

"What's there to tell?" Kosenko replied.

"How's life for you? What's new?"

"There's not much to tell you," Olga remembered her father whispering. "If you were alone, I'd have a lot more to say. This way you'll drive off, and what will happen to me? You won't even find out."

Two years later Khrushchev returned to the Kosenko house. This time his only bodyguard remained by the door.

"Stop playing the fool," said Khrushchev to Kosenko after a while. "Join the party, and I'll bring you to Kiev with your family. It's time to get the kids some real education."

"But no one got you and me educated," Kosenko replied. "They'll do it themselves too. As for me, I'm not leaving my house, and I won't join the party the way it is now. To join that party is to join shit. You've destroyed the real party, the one you joined back then, the one that included Yakir, Tukhachevsky, and Kirov."

Close as the two friends had been, Kosenko was taking an awful risk.

But Khrushchev answered in kind: "Don't blame me for all that. I'm not involved in that. When I can, I'll settle with that 'Mudakshvili' in full. I don't forgive him any of them—not Kirov, not Yakir, not Tukhachevsky, not the simplest worker or peasant."

Stalin's real Georgian name was Dzhugashvili. Khrushchev altered it by playing on one of the many Russian words for "prick," *mudak.* Olga, twelve at the time, later asked her father what their guest had been talking about.

"You mean you heard it all?" he exclaimed. "Get this straight, if you mention a word of this conversation to even one person, they'll shoot both him [Khrushchev] and me."[24]

Granted, Khrushchev was justifying himself to an old friend. Still, the fact that he sought out Kosenko and explained himself in this way is stunning.

Pyotr Kovalenko was another old friend who had known Khrushchev in the twenties. Later he had been arrested and imprisoned but then released. In the summer of 1939 Khrushchev received Kovalenko in his Kiev office, asked him about his imprisonment, and pressed him to describe beatings he had endured during his interrogation. When Kovalenko finished, Khrushchev seemed shaken.

"Pyotr!" he exclaimed. "Do you think I understand what's going on in this country? Do you think I understand why I'm sitting in this office as Ukrainian first secretary rather than in a cell at Lubyanka? Do you think I can be sure that they won't drag me out of here tomorrow and throw me in prison? Nonetheless we must work, we must do everything possible, everything in our power, for the happiness of the people."[25]

KHRUSHCHEV'S CONVERSATION with Kovalenko took place at the Ukrainian Central Committee, where the walls surely had ears. The last part of his remarks provided some protection, but even the first part wasn't as daring as it seemed. For by 1939 even Stalin was admitting that innocent people were being arrested, if only because "enemies of the people" had penetrated the secret police and were using their power to destroy loyal party officials.[26]

"Now and then," recalled Khrushchev, Stalin "would assess arrests soberly and several times he even condemned them in face-to-face conversations with me."[27] But often it seemed as if a kind of madness had overtaken everything and everyone, including Stalin. "Party organs were reduced to nothing," according to Khrushchev. "The leadership was paralyzed. No one could be appointed to a high post without approval of the NKVD . . . , but even NKVD approval offered no guarantees. Sometimes someone would be approved, and several days later he would turn up behind bars. . . . But then it turned out that the person who denounced him had himself been denounced. All this created . . . a vicious circle by which the leadership in effect put itself on the road to self-extermination."[28]

By reducing the purge process to a species of madness, Khrushchev distanced himself from it. If madness it was, that explained how good men could turn bad. Yezhov, who had struck Khrushchev as a "simple man, a former Petersburg worker" when they first met in 1929, "lost his humanity entirely."[29] Other NKVD officials, who "were not necessarily cruel men," had turned into "automatons . . . guided by one thought only: 'If I don't do this to others, then others will do it to me; better I do it than have it done to me.'"[30]

Khrushchev refused to concede that he followed the same path. But his story of the Ukrainian NKVD chief Uspensky reveals how intimately Khrushchev was involved in a purge process that was as surreal as it was macabre. When Khrushchev arrived in Kiev, Uspensky "was literally cramming the Central Committee full of memoranda about enemies of the people." Yet one day Stalin phoned Khrushchev, mentioned unspecified "evidence against Uspensky which leaves us with no doubts as to his guilt," and asked, "'Can you take care of arresting him yourselves?'

"'Of course we can, if those are your instructions.'

"'Then arrest him.'"

Khrushchev, it seems, had misheard the name and thought the intended victim was someone else. But even if the wrong man had been nabbed, Khrushchev added, no great injustice would have been done since "it so happened that there was also incriminating evidence against him." Khrushchev finally grasped the correct name, and he was about to order Uspensky's arrest when Stalin called back with a change in plans. Instead of arresting Uspensky in Kiev, they would summon him to Moscow and collar him along the way. Why Stalin thought Uspensky would fall for a trick that had been used many times isn't clear. Actually, he didn't. He left a fake suicide note saying he would throw himself in the Dnieper, but all police divers found there was a drowned pig. Alas, poor Uspensky, in the end he got what he deserved. After he spent five months on the lam, "they caught him somewhere," Khrushchev said later, "and he was shot."[31]

They almost caught Khrushchev himself soon after he arrived in Kiev.

The man he had brought with him from Moscow to be Ukrainian minister of trade, a man Khrushchev "trusted and respected," was arrested. The fact that Lukashov was soon released was reassuring but not what he told Khrushchev about his interrogation. He had been "beaten mercilessly and tortured" in an effort to get him to incriminate Khrushchev. The accusation—that Khrushchev had sent him abroad to establish links with counterrevolutionary groups—was ludicrous (his actual mission, Khrushchev said, was to purchase onion seeds and other vegetables), but no more so than countless others that had been deadly to those denounced. According to Khrushchev, his friend "refused to confess and was released—a rare thing." Equally rare, Khrushchev decided to tell Stalin about the whole episode.

"'Yes,'" the boss replied, "'I know what you mean; there are these kinds of perversions. They're gathering evidence against me, too.'"[32]

By boldly raising the subject himself, Khrushchev proved he had nothing to hide from Stalin, who took even small signs of nervousness as indications of guilt.[33] If nothing else proved to Khrushchev that innocent people were being arrested, surely the accusation against himself should have. The way he resisted was playing up the danger that unjustified arrests were being used by enemies to subvert the Stalinist regime.

Khrushchev did just this at the Fourteenth Ukrainian Party Congress, at which he said: "Comrades, we must unmask and relentlessly destroy all enemies of the people. But we must not allow a single honest Bolshevik to be harmed. We must conduct a struggle against slanderers." One slanderer, Khrushchev added, had complained to province party authorities, "I've worn myself out in the battle with enemies, and therefore request a stay at a resort [Laughter in the hall]."[34] At the Fifteenth Congress in 1940, Khrushchev repeated the warning: Slanderers were still "prowling dark alleys doing their dirty work. It doesn't take much brains to do it. They write names down in a notebook and proceed alphabetically. Let's see, they say, what letter am I up to? They have all the letters covered, you see [Laughter in the hall]."[35]

Words like these hardly compensate for the way Khrushchev fanned the flames of fear.[36] But he also cited deeds with which he tried to slow the conflagration, such as balking at NKVD evidence incriminating his deputy in the Kiev party organization and demanding to interview the prisoner—too late, it turned out, since the man confirmed his previous confession, but in time to save another suspect in a related case: "My conscience tormented me about him. I kept insisting that he was beyond reproach and had been unjustly accused."[37]

This particular claim of conscience may be suspect, but few of Khrushchev's colleagues had any conscience left at all. Whether or not this one is true, he convinced himself that he was protecting the defenseless. That helps explain how he could play his part in the horror without feeling entirely compromised by it.

WHEN STALIN first assigned Khrushchev to Ukraine he noted his protege's "weakness for cities and industry" and warned him "not to spend all of your time in the Donbas" at the expense of "your agricultural responsibilities." Khrushchev wrote: "I heeded his warning, although it wasn't easy to resist the temptations of my first loves, mining and industry. . . . I tried to learn everything I could about farming. I spent a lot of time traveling around Ukraine, visiting farms and villages, talking to agronomists and managers."[38]

One of the first things he did was to look for an assistant who could devote full time to agriculture. He chose Andrei Shevchenko from the Institute of Agriculture in Kiev. After the twenty-eight-year-old Shevchenko proved himself by working nonstop for a week, he was hired. Khrushchev had already concluded that the agricultural planning system needed changing, Shevchenko recalled: fewer orders from above, more decisions to be made by collective farms. But before trying to convince Moscow, Khrushchev dispatched Shevchenko to try the idea out on peasants themselves.

"Don't drive up in a car," Khrushchev told him. "Arrive on foot so the peasants can see that you're their sort of man. You don't smoke, do you? Well, take tobacco anyway because almost all peasants smoke, and you'll need to win them over so as to get them to open up. Don't raise any bureaucratic issues. Give them a chance to think. Once you've done that, ask them how they'd react if they had to draw up their own plan instead of getting one from Stalin. Take your time, and see if you can get them to plan."

Shevchenko returned to Kiev with a scheme for reform. Khrushchev worked on it for several days and then took it to Moscow. With Shevchenko in tow, he presented his idea to Stalin, who at first dismissed it: "If we do it your way, they won't grow any beets. Raising beets is labor-intensive and doesn't pay very well, so they won't plant it. All they'll grow is oats." When Khrushchev contended that the peasants could be trusted, Stalin retorted that Khrushchev was "talking nonsense," that without force and discipline, things would "fall apart." In the end Stalin authorized certain changes only in Ukraine: Collective farms would be allowed to prepare their own plans for certain crops (rye, oats, barley, and millet); plans for all the rest would continue to come down from on high. "If there's not enough rye, we'll put someone in prison," Stalin grumbled. "If they don't plant it, you'll be responsible."

Khrushchev formed a special committee to promote cattle raising and commissioned playwright Aleksandr Korneichuk to write a play about a farsighted collective farm chairman. In addition, Khrushchev tried to restructure incentives so that farmers who worked harder and produced more would be better paid, a notion that anticipated reforms he pressed for after Stalin's death.[39] If he began pushing them twenty-five years earlier, that was partly because, unlike other top Soviet leaders, he spent enough time in the countryside to know its real condition.

One day in 1940 he returned to the Petrovo-Marinsky District, where he had been party leader in 1925. His successor, Zakhar Glukhov, expected a huge suite of officials and bodyguards, but Khrushchev had only one aide and a driver with him. Unfortunately, the first person he laid eyes on was a drunken collective farm chairman. But after at first reacting angrily, Khrushchev inquired sympathetically about the terrible working conditions that drove men to drink. It was during this visit that he asked whether kulaks he had known in the twenties had "escaped alive." Khrushchev impressed Glukhov as "simple and direct. After talking to him for about five minutes, you felt as if you had known him your whole life and could speak to him about anything."[40]

The Stalino *tekhnikum* where he had been party secretary got a whirlwind visit in April 1938. Most students were in class when he arrived, but they rushed into the hall, applauding his arrival. Khrushchev feigned annoyance, chiding the rector for allowing studies to be interrupted, but agreed to address students and teachers jammed into the auditorium. As usual, he spoke without a text and quickly established rapport with his audience. What students had most on their mind, one of them recollected, was the wave of repression that had carried away so many teachers. Khrushchev warned instead about the danger of Nazi Germany and called for vigilance against internal enemies, but he did so in a distinctively informal way, and he closed by apologizing, with a broad grin, for interrupting classes.[41] Khrushchev's performance typified the way he put his personal stamp on meetings of all sorts, even Central Committee plenums. Rather than listen to others, he made himself the main attraction by interrupting speakers (sometimes before they could begin their remarks), instructing, cajoling, needling, and berating them.[42]

The 1939 Ukrainian harvest reportedly exceeded that of 1938 by 21.5 percent, while production in the coal mines of the Donbas grew, and new factories came on-line.[43] Whatever his actual contribution to these gains, Khrushchev took credit for them in Kiev and Moscow, as he did in his memoirs for solving a mystery involving automobile tires. As befitted a "man of the people," Khrushchev "respected and trusted" his chauffeur, Aleksandr Zhuravlev, known to the Khrushchev children as Uncle Sasha. Khrushchev treated Uncle Sasha's complaint that Soviet tires wore out too quickly as if it had been delivered by the Academy of Sciences; he even informed Stalin, although the boss "never liked to hear anyone criticize something that was Soviet-made."

Stalin's revenge (he didn't like getting bad news) was to assign Khrushchev to rectify the situation. Khrushchev's response was another display of not entirely false modesty: "I'm absolutely unfamiliar with the rubber industry and tire manufacturing." Later he recalled: "I was a bit worried. I didn't know how much time it would take, and I didn't know if I would be able to cope with the problem."

The rest of the story is also predictable. He inspected the best tire factory the Soviets had (equipped, not coincidentally, with American machinery), saw firsthand how tires were made, asked probing questions, and diagnosed the problem: In their haste to overfulfill production norms, workers were violating assembly instructions by eliminating one or two layers of rubber cording. This discovery was especially sweet because it turned out that Kaganovich had suggested the change while on a previous inspection tour and because of Stalin's reaction when Khrushchev delivered the news. Although "terribly irritated," the master pronounced his blessing: "I agree with you. Give us your recommendations and we will approve them."

"I've told this story," Khrushchev concluded, "to illustrate how Stalin was sometimes capable of a conscientious and statesmanly approach to problems. He was a jealous lord and master of the state, and he fought against bureaucracy and corruption and defects of all kinds. He was a great man, a great organizer and a leader, but he was also a despot."[44]

ALTHOUGH KHRUSHCHEV worried that Ukrainian intellectuals might prove hostile to him, they were at his mercy. Desperate to stay alive and, if possible, to maintain positions of power, many flattered and fawned shamelessly. Eager to be respected by men and women of culture, as well as to show Stalin who was in charge in Kiev, Khrushchev was the perfect mark.

By 1938 the Bolsheviks' initial policy of Ukrainianization had been replaced by its opposite, Russification. Ukrainian history was purified by emphasizing "historical and fraternal ties between the Ukrainian and Russian peoples." The Russian language was reemphasized in schools, and the Ukrainian language was enriched with terms like *piatisotnitsa* (a heroic female farm worker who harvested at least five hundred centners of sugar beets from one hectare) and purged of words for the very pieces of peasant apparel, such as bast shoes (*postoli*) and rope belt (*ochkur*), that Khrushchev had worn in Kalinovka.[45]

Khrushchev conducted Russification with a vengeance. In 1938 he lashed out at "Polish-German agents and bourgeois nationalists" who "did everything they could to exterminate the Russian language in Ukraine" and at "bastards who did everything to toss out Russian from Ukrainian schools."[46] Yet he also made overtures to Ukrainian intellectuals who were in political trouble. He arranged for a terminally ill composer to be awarded a high medal and then personally presented the award in the sick man's apartment. According to his future Komsomol chief Kostenko, Khrushchev's gesture was taken by the intelligentsia as a "sign of benevolence, especially against the background of what was then going on."[47]

Within weeks of his arrival in Kiev in January 1938, Khrushchev began to cultivate well-known writers. Maksym Ryl'ski, born in 1895, was perhaps the best of a distinctly nonproletarian group of neoclassicist poets formed in 1917. In 1925 Ryl'ski condemned Communist literary strictures as useful only for "those without any talent," and in 1931 he was attacked as one of a group of "rightists" who "display in their works motifs of nationalist voluntarism" and "idealize kulaks and the bourgeoisie." In 1931 Ryl'ski was arrested and spent half a year in prison, after which he renounced his past and was readmitted to the ranks of loyalist writers.[48] The fact that Ryl'ski outlived Stalin apparently owes a lot to Khrushchev. With Ryl'ski's rearrest imminent in 1938, Khrushchev reminded the NKVD chief Uspensky that the poet had written verses praising Stalin that became the words of a popular song. "Yet you want to arrest him? No one will understand it if you do."[49]

Two other Ukrainian poets whom Khrushchev befriended were Pavlo Tychyna, who had been a symbolist, and Mykola Bazhan, a neoromantic. Both had joined proletarian writers' groups after the revolution but had resisted Bolshevik attempts to organize the "literary front." Tychyna was attacked in 1927 for "peddling a nationalist opiate under the banner of proletarian literature," and Bazhan's work was condemned in 1934 for "not measuring up to the demands of the working class." By the early thirties such warnings had become all too ominous. Mykola Khvyl'ovyi, a Communist writer who had tried to defend Ukrainian culture against Russian centralist controls, committed suicide in 1933. Tychyna recanted in that same year; Bazhan, in 1934. Both turned to eulogizing Stalin and were lavishly rewarded for their efforts, Tychyna becoming a leader of the Ukrainian Union of Soviet Writers, Bazhan later representing the Ukrainian Soviet Socialist Republic at the United Nations after the war.[50]

Bazhan wasn't as close to Khrushchev as Ryl'ski was. Yet his widow, Nina, a physician, recalls getting to know not only Khrushchev but Nina Petrovna, who brought her children in for medical treatment, and Khrushchev's daughter by his first wife, who worked as a laboratory assistant at the Institute of Physiology. Signs of how well the Bazhans lived under Khrushchev's benevolent tutelage are still plentiful in their elegantly furnished six-room apartment and in family photo albums that include pictures of the poet hobnobbing with Khrushchev and other Ukrainian leaders.[51]

Tychyna and Bazhan are said to have "experienced moral torture" as they sold out to Stalinism.[52] Not so, apparently, the playwright Korneichuk, whom Khrushchev also befriended. Pro-Soviet from the start, Korneichuk was rewarded with prizes, a leading role in the Writers' Union, and an appointment as Ukrainian "foreign minister" after the war. Although he denounced fellow writers to the NKVD, even Korneichuk got into trouble when Stalin disliked the libretto he and his wife, Wanda Wasilewska, wrote for a new opera, *Bogdan Khmelnitsky*, about the leader of a Ukrainian uprising against the Poles in 1648. But Khrushchev remained the Korneichuks' friend and protector.

The filmmaker Aleksandr Dovzhenko was devoted to the revolution but had his own unorthodox vision of it. His most famous film, *Earth* (1930), portrayed collectivization in a positive light, but not positive enough for Stalinist critics who condemned it as "counterrevolutionary" and "defeatist." Dovzhenko's next film, *Ivan*, about the effect of industrialization on a single Dneprostroi construction worker, was removed from circulation amid accusations of fascism and pantheism, while its director was dismissed from the Kiev film studio.[53]

Afraid, as he put it to a friend, that "I'll be arrested and eaten alive," Dovzhenko appealed directly to Stalin himself, who had once praised *Arsenal*, an earlier Dovzhenko film about the revolution and civil war. Miraculously, the dictator received him warmly less than twenty-four hours later, introduced him to Molotov, Voroshilov, and Kirov "as if he had known me well for a long time," and encouraged Dovzhenko to work on his next film, *Aerograd* (in which heroic Soviet border troops guard a newly built "Air City" from infiltration by hostile Japanese spies and saboteurs), thus beginning a twenty-year role as the filmmaker's personal censor and adviser, on the model of Nicholas I and Aleksandr Pushkin.[54]

Stalin's patronage brought Dovzhenko a coveted Order of Lenin.[55] No wonder Khrushchev valued his acquaintance with Dovzhenko, whom he first met in Moscow in 1934, and took a particular interest in the film about the late Red Army commander Mykola Shchors that Dovzhenko, advised by Shchors's former deputy Ivan Dubovoi, was shooting in Kiev in 1938. Both Dovzhenko and Khrushchev were shocked when Dubovoi was suddenly arrested and shot, having "confessed" to murdering his commander. Still, Khrushchev remained close to the director, becoming even more friendly when Dovzhenko made a documentary film, *Liberation*, glorifying the Soviet occupation of western Ukraine that Khrushchev led in 1939.[56]

EVEN MORE than poets and filmmakers, Khrushchev was attracted to scientists and engineers, practical intellectuals who were less intimidating to him than artists and writers and more likely to provide practical payoffs for the economy. His account of his first meeting with academician Yevgeny Paton is full of nostalgia for his own road not taken.

"When he came in to see me I found him to be a thick-set man with gray hair, already well along in years, with a face like a lion's and bright piercing eyes. He greeted me and immediately produced a lump of metal from his pocket. . . . 'Look at this, Comrade Khrushchev, look what our institute can do! This is a piece of bar iron ten millimeters thick, and look how well we've been able to weld it!'

"I examined the joint closely. As a metalworker myself, I'd had occasions to inspect welded joints. Here was a seam as smooth as if the bar had been cast in a single piece.

"'That's an example of fusion welding,' said Paton."

Khrushchev had never heard the term before. Paton explained how he made portable fusion welders for ships and bridges. "I was literally enchanted by Academician Paton," said Khrushchev. "All my life I've been fascinated with metalworking. . . . I knew that Academician Paton was a man after my own heart. I decided then and there to see that his invention received the attention it deserved."

On Khrushchev's recommendation, fusion welding was applied in industry and then to the production of tanks. Paton pleaded with his patron to be admitted to the Communist party, despite "an old-fashioned tsarist upbringing" and "not sympathizing with the October Revolution." Khrushchev recalled being "deeply moved" and forwarded the petition to Stalin, who "was obviously very moved, too, although he rarely showed his emotion. He said simply, 'So Paton has decided he wants to join the party. I see no reason why he shouldn't.'"[57]

How easily Khrushchev could be beguiled by a charismatic scientist promising miracles! How sentimental he could be when his benevolent image of himself was confirmed! Khrushchev had an appalling ability, during Stalin's lifetime and after, to separate the horrors carried out by the party from the great cause it supposedly served. No matter how much blood flowed in the name of socialism, tears came to his eyes when someone like Paton declared himself converted.

Trofim Lysenko too won Khrushchev's heart. Born into a peasant family, the "barefoot scientist" (as he was called in a 1927 *Pravda* article that helped launch his career) professed to have solved problems that plagued Soviet agriculture: how to enrich soil without fertilizers or minerals; how to protect wheat by "vernalizing" it—i.e., by soaking and chilling the seed before planting it—and how to cross-breed wheat (rather than plant the pure varieties recommended by specialists) by having peasants march through fields using scissors and tweezers to open up self-pollinating spikelets to wind-driven cross-pollination.[58] Lysenko also claimed to have disproved the genetic theory of inheritance and (contra Darwin) to have altered the basic nature of plants and animals by changing environmental conditions.

Lysenko mastered the art of self-advertisement and denounced rival scientists. After he warned a 1935 congress of collective farm shock workers that "a class enemy is always a class enemy whether he is a scientist or not," Stalin, in attendance with other members of the government, shouted, "Bravo, Comrade Lysenko, bravo!"[59] Lysenko's main rival, the renowned geneticist Nikolai Vavilov, was arrested in 1940 and sent to the gulag, where he perished from illness and malnutrition. It was also in 1940 that Khrushchev supported Lysenko's latest scheme, a proposal to mobilize chickens to exterminate the weevil ruining sugar beets in Ukraine. Lysenko said that his plan had been criticized by other specialists but added that "the clear and correct intervention made by Nikita Sergeyevich" convinced him that his critics had been in error.[60]

Khrushchev hailed Lysenko in July 1939 as "a first-rate man who heads a whole school of first-rate people."[61] Lysenko's pseudoscience fitted the

Bolshevik ethos. Recognizing few socioeconomic or even physical limits on their ambitions, Stalin and his colleagues hailed crackpot claims masquerading as scientific truths. Even reputable Soviet scientists, desperately trying to escape persecution for "opposing progress," were endorsing Lysenko in 1939.[62] Khrushchev's support for Lysenko was not a quirk of character. But one reason he liked the barefoot scientist was that he could respect Lysenko without envying his erudition.[63]

NOT LONG after Khrushchev arrived in Kiev, Molotov suggested making him deputy head of the Soviet government in Moscow. Khrushchev declined the invitation (which couldn't have been that serious if Stalin didn't insist on it), citing the need to remain at his Ukrainian post. Another reason, surely, was that in Kiev he was the subject of a cult in his own right.[64]

A brief biography published when he was appointed Ukrainian leader described him this way: a man of "highest principles, of selfless dedication to the party of Lenin and Stalin, a man who knows how to finish whatever he starts no matter what the obstacles, a man of Bolshevik straightforwardness, sensitivity and exceptional modesty—all these are characteristic features of this Stalinist."[65] *Pravda Ukrainy* conveyed the "limitless joy" with which Khrushchev's constituents learned of his decision to represent them in the rubber-stamp USSR Supreme Soviet in Moscow. According to Khrushchev's party deputy Demian Korotchenko, it took "that best son of our people, that brilliant Bolshevik, that miner from Donetsk, Nikita Sergeyevich Khrushchev," finally to smash Trotskyite-Bukharinist enemies and their Ukrainian nationalist confederates.[66] Korotchenko was a classic yes-man. He was "always silent at [Ukrainian Politburo] meetings," Vasily Kostenko recalled. "Silence was his trump card. He would wait until Nikita Sergeyevich made some sort of proposal, and then say, 'Yes, yes of course, that's exactly right.'"[67]

Khrushchev's face and figure (still relatively lean and trim) were all over the Ukrainian press: jaunty and smiling, with his worker's cap set at a rakish angle as he reviewed a physical fitness parade; wearing an embroidered Ukrainian shirt at a Ukrainian Supreme Soviet meeting; huddled with Stalin and Zhdanov in a cozy group portrait. A photo of him surrounded by delegates to the Fourteenth Ukrainian Party Congress, just as his Stalino delegation had posed with Stalin a decade before, must have been particularly satisfying to him.[68]

A painting of Khrushchev talking to Molotov while Stalin looks on benevolently dominated Ukrainian newspaper front pages on December 23, 1939. On May 12, 1940, another nearly full-page painting depicted Stalin instructing Khrushchev, who listens intently with notebook and pencil at the ready. Three days later Khrushchev is seen addressing the Fifteenth Ukrainian Party Congress, the kind of display reserved for Stalin alone in *Pravda* and *Izvestia* but bestowed upon Khrushchev in the Ukrainian press.

Artificial adulation was standard for Soviet leaders of Khrushchev's rank, but he took particular delight in it. In one sequence captured on film, he is receiving the Order of the Red Banner in the Kremlin in 1939. The camera shows him walking across a carpeted floor to accept the award from Kalinin, shaking hands with the Soviet head of state, and then delivering a brief speech of acceptance. When the film is viewed one frame at a time, it is clear that his eyes are fixed, like those of a hungry cat on its supper, on the award that Kalinin holds in his hands. As the treasure is handed over, the two men shake hands vigorously, and Khrushchev's face breaks into a radiant smile. For a moment his eyes close in silent reverence. After a deep breath, he strides briskly to the podium and begins to speak, jaw firmly set, right fist punching the air.

A second scene took place during the Eighteenth Party Congress in March 1939, an occasion for which the whole Khrushchev family came up from Kiev, spent a few days in their Moscow apartment, and attended the theater in the evening. The film shows the entire Politburo entering a room where they are to be photographed with rank-and-file delegates. As the leaders file through the door, Khrushchev is several men removed from Stalin, but by the time they seat themselves in the front row of chairs, he has somehow managed to end up next to the *vozhd.* Neither Molotov nor Kaganovich, whom Khrushchev has practically shoved aside, seems to mind, while Stalin, a dark look on his face, seems preoccupied with other things. Khrushchev starts to grin triumphantly, then glances around nervously to make sure no one is offended. Poking Molotov and Kaganovich with his elbow in friendly fashion, he gazes around the room savoring the moment, and then breaks into an exultant smile.

THE YEAR 1939 brought another set of misdeeds in which Khrushchev played a leading part: the Soviet occupation of western Ukraine and western Byelorussia that followed Hitler's attack on Poland in September 1939. If anything, Khrushchev's role was more odious than in the terror itself, for he went to his death convinced that the conquest of western

Ukraine, complete with the arrest and deportation of hundreds of thousands of people, was a triumph for socialism and for him.

Hitler's all too obvious designs on Eastern Europe and the USSR added to the tension of the late 1930s. Like many Communists, Khrushchev counted on Stalin to resist Hitler's evil plans. Yet in August 1939, when Stalin signed his famous nonaggression pact with Hitler, Khrushchev welcomed the deal. Hitler was thirsting to take on the Red Army, Khrushchev later recollected; the British and French "rubbed their hands in delight at the idea of lying low while Hitler's rampage took its toll of our blood"; the USSR desperately needed to buy time and territory. But apart from its realpolitik merits, the Nazi-Soviet Pact had another virtue in Khrushchev's eyes: the fact that he himself was present when Stalin's cronies celebrated its signing.[69]

Khrushchev wasn't involved in the diplomatic maneuvering. But he happened to spend the second half of August 1939 in Moscow, superintending preparation of the Ukrainian pavilion at the All-Union Agricultural Exhibition. He learned about the German foreign minister's unexpected climactic visit the day before Joachim von Ribbentrop arrived. Stalin enjoyed springing the news on his unsuspecting aide. He "smiled and watched me closely to see what sort of impression the news would make. At first I was dumbfounded. I stared back at him, thinking he was joking. Then I said, 'Why should Ribbentrop want to see us? Is he defecting to our side, or what?' "[70]

After a dumb question like that, it's no wonder Khrushchev's presence wasn't required the next day, August 23, at the negotiations themselves. Khrushchev intended to go hunting with Malenkov, Bulganin, and Voroshilov. He had taken up hunting a few years before near Moscow, but this would be his first outing at the Moscow military district reserve near Zavidovo. "Go right ahead," said Stalin. "There'll be nothing for you to do around here tomorrow."

Three decades later Khrushchev still cherished the memory of the next day's camaraderie. The lights of peace were going out all over Europe, but for Khrushchev, the day and evening were bathed in a warm, mawkish glow. "There were some other marshals and generals at the preserve, too, and we all went on the hunt together. It was a wonderful day. The weather was warm, and the hunt was a great success—for me particularly. Please don't misunderstand me: I'm not one to brag about my skill as a hunter, but that day I was able to bag one duck more than Voroshilov. I mention this only because the press had already begun to build up Voroshilov as our number one marksman."

When the hunters returned, Khrushchev knew Stalin would call them to dinner, so "I brought my ducks along to share with the other Politburo members that evening. I told Stalin about the hunt, and he boasted jokingly about our successes of the day. He was in a very good mood and was joking a lot himself."[71]

The Nazi-Soviet Pact had fateful consequences: It included a secret protocol authorizing the two dictators to carve up Poland and other parts of Eastern Europe between them. When the Nazis attacked Poland on September 1, quickly crushing weak Polish resistance, thousands of Polish troops and other refugees fled eastward. When Soviet troops marched west into Poland on September 17, Khrushchev accompanied his dear friend Semyon Timoshenko, head of the Kiev special military district. Khrushchev's ostensible mission was to protect his fellow Slavs in western Ukraine. His actual task was to conquer and Sovietize, to expropriate and collectivize, to organize new party and state institutions and make sure they opted "voluntarily" to join the Union of Soviet Socialist Republics.[72] Poles and Ukrainians each constituted about one-third of the western Ukrainian population, with the rest split between Jews and Byelorussians. During the eighteenth century Poland had been partitioned among Russia, Prussia, and Austria. After World War I, when Poland regained its independence, Warsaw had reconquered western Ukraine from the Bolsheviks. Polish administration of the area was a disaster for non-Polish national minorities, exceeded only by the damage done to non-Ukrainians, and many Ukrainians as well, by the Soviet administration that Khrushchev directed.

"The only possible point of dispute" about the pre-1939 Polish administration, writes historian Jan Gross, is "the extent of official discrimination [by Poles against other ethnic groups], never its existence." This "sorry record of successive Polish administrations" helps explain the initially friendly reception that Soviet troops received in 1939. Crowds turned out, sometimes spontaneously, waving red or yellow-and-blue Ukrainian banners.[73] But Poles weren't the only ones who had no use for Soviet Russia. Neither did Ukrainian nationalists, who dreamed of an independent state including the already Sovietized eastern Ukraine. Nor did landowners, capitalists, and priests. Yet Moscow aimed not only to incorporate the area into the USSR as quickly as possible but to make the whole process seem democratic.

Two sets of elections were conducted during the first six months of occupation, in October 1939 and March 1940. Each was preceded by a vast effort to mobilize the population through meetings, marches, and demonstrations. A train left Kiev for Lvov on October 15, carrying a traveling museum, a portable movie theater, cars full of journalists, and a dance ensemble. "Suddenly," according to a eyewitness account, "cities and countryside swarmed with throngs of propagandists—mostly Red Army or NKVD lieutenants. All in leather coats or jackets."[74]

Many voters were paid to participate while others thought they were voting for independence rather than incorporation into the USSR. When sloppily selected candidates muffed their campaign speech lines, NKVD handlers hustled them off the stage or, in one case, read the speech anyway, insisting that the candidate in question had a sore throat. On election day, "superintendents began pounding on apartment doors at 4:00 or 4:30 [A.M.] urging sleepy residents to get it over with, and returned every hour until midday, when they were replaced by militiamen who then began to check on inhabitants."[75]

Despite these preparations, Soviet authorities still had to falsify the voting so as to produce western Ukrainian and western Byelorussian national assemblies that would vote unanimously to join the USSR. Meanwhile the NKVD disbanded Ukrainian educational and religious institutions and arrested leading intellectuals. All told, about one and a quarter million people (including Jews, Ukrainians, and Byelorussians as well as Poles), or nearly 10 percent of the total population, were deported from western Ukraine and Byelorussia to the Soviet interior. Approximately half a million were imprisoned during the twenty-one months of Soviet rule between 1939 and 1941, including about 10 percent of all adult males. Some fifty thousand were executed or tortured in prison, while three hundred thousand more perished during deportation or in exile.[76]

So dreadful seemed their fate under the Soviets that many Jews who fled Poland when the Nazis invaded now sought to return to German-occupied Poland. According to Gross, Soviet occupation was "less oppressive in its atmosphere and style" than the German variety, if only because the Soviets were initially "somewhat awed, insecure and intimidated" (in contrast with the Germans with their *Übermensch* arrogance) and because "Soviet personnel arriving in West Ukraine and West Byelorussia had experienced the same hardships (and were likely to experience them again at any time) to which the population of the newly liberated territories was being subjected." But for many in western Ukraine there was little, if anything, to choose between Soviet and German totalitarianism.[77]

KHRUSHCHEV'S ROLE in the events just described was pivotal. With Stalin looking over his shoulder, the stakes were high and time was short. Lvov, the largest city in western Ukraine, wasn't captured until September 22. Yet as early as October 26 and 27 "elected" national assemblies of western Ukraine and Byelorussia met and empowered their representatives to request incorporation into the Soviet Union. The USSR Supreme Soviet approved their requests on November 1, prompting this expression of gratitude to Stalin: "From the kingdom of darkness and boundless suffering which the nation of Western Ukraine bore for six hundred long years, we find ourselves in the fairy land of true happiness of the people, and of true freedom."[78]

In two short months Khrushchev had pulled off another miracle. The Soviet press covered the joyful jamboree in detail, with Khrushchev the star of the show. Informed, in a town close to the line between Soviet and German troops, that a local bystander was a metalworker, Khrushchev rejoiced, "Well, what do you know? I'm a metalworker too," prompting "cries of delight and applause" from the crowd.[79] A newsreel showed Khrushchev and Timoshenko greeting ecstatic villagers, the tall Timoshenko towering over Khrushchev, who is proudly wearing a military tunic with a wide belt and a military cap. As he addresses a cheering crowd, Khrushchev doffs his cap, grins boyishly as the applause rolls in, and then stands relaxed, with thumbs tucked into his belt, while Timoshenko speaks. Afterward the dignitaries stand around talking, all except Khrushchev puffing on cigarettes. As they walk toward a small fleet of black cars, accompanied by security guards, Timoshenko deferentially steps aside so that Khrushchev can settle himself first into their automobile.

Dovzhenko's film *Liberation* is Leni Riefenstahl–like in its depiction of a festive triumph of good over evil. The treacherous bourgeoisie, who once lorded it over workers and peasants, are forced to sweep the streets. A Polish landowner, a crippled old woman, is dragged from her farm. Captured Polish soldiers straggle by on their way to oblivion. Monks vote for Soviet power while peasants dance in celebration. Throughout it all, Khrushchev appears and reappears, blessing the proceedings, joining in hosannas for Stalin, basking in what is portrayed as a wave of popular adoration.

Khrushchev did mitigate certain features of the repression. Although Stalin had disbanded the Polish and western Ukrainian Communist parties in 1938, Khrushchev used former members as volunteer organizers of the 1939 elections. He restrained the pace of collectivization and dekulakization, for which occupying forces had little time anyway before the Nazi attack in June 1941.[80] But he liked virtually everything else about the occupation. He welcomed the uniting of western and eastern Ukraine.[81] He hailed the extension and strengthening of the USSR's western border. When peasants on newly formed collective farms sang the "Internationale," he feared they wouldn't know the words. "But just imagine," he exclaimed, "they sang it through to the end beautifully." The trouble with Polish intellectuals, according to Khrushchev, was that they didn't see what Soviet culture had to offer. "Brought up in a bourgeois culture on bourgeois ideas . . . , they neither understood nor accepted Marxist-Leninist teachings, they couldn't imagine that their culture would actually be enriched by the annexation of their lands to the Soviet Union."[82]

Khrushchev relished tutoring people who misunderstood their own interests, especially lower-level officials as unsophisticated as he had once been. One time he dropped in on a Lvov functionary who was recertifying former city officials, most of them Poles, for jobs in the new municipal administration. There were "two revolvers sticking conspicuously out of his overcoat," Khrushchev said later. "It looked as if the only reason he didn't have a cannon slung over his shoulder was that it would have been too heavy. The people sitting around waiting to talk to him were obviously scared of him." Khrushchev lectured the man on some not so fine points of Communist manners: "You're making a terrible impression on these people; you're going to give a bad name to yourself and to our party. What are you going to do if a terrorist comes charging in here and tries to kill you? He'll be able to shoot you with one of your own pistols! From now on, if you want to carry a revolver, make sure that the butt isn't sticking out of your coat like that."[83]

By now Khrushchev was throwing his weight around in higher circles too. The NKVD sent two agents to western Ukraine (one of them, William Fisher, aka Colonel Rudolf Abel, was arrested by the FBI in 1957 and called the highest-ranking Soviet spy ever caught in the United States) to recruit German residents allowed by the Nazi-Soviet Pact's secret protocol to return to German-occupied territory. When one agent disappeared, Khrushchev berated Beria for sending incompetents to Ukraine. According to Pavel Sudoplatov, who was sitting in Beria's office at the time, "the high-frequency telephone line made it possible to hear his angry voice across the desk." When Sudoplatov himself got on the line, Khrushchev "didn't bother to listen . . . cut me short . . . and then . . . hung up on me."[84]

On September 23, 1939, in a village close to Lvov, Khrushchev shook his fists and cursed NKVD generals for the behavior of their forces. On the one hand, they were lazy: "You call this work? You haven't carried out a single execution!" On the other hand, they were lording it over party leaders like him: "What weasels you are! We know very well how your agents are trying to crush the party leadership under your heels." Reporting on this exchange to Beria in Moscow, the Ukrainian NKVD chief Ivan Serov characterized Khrushchev as an "arrogant man who isn't averse to playing the democrat; he just loves it when the people around him flatter him. . . ." The real lesson of the incident, however, is the extraordinary two-sidedness of Khrushchev, simultaneously demanding that police shoot more people and give him more space.[85]

While Khrushchev was hectoring and lecturing, he was indeed lapping up flattery from sycophants like Aleksandr Korneichuk and his Polish wife to be, writer Wanda Wasilewska. Wasilewska had fled eastward from occupied Warsaw, arriving in time to help Soviet authorities round up her fellow Poles in western Ukraine. "I had heard about a writer," Khrushchev recalled, "whose voice carried a great deal of weight among Polish intellectuals. She and I became fast friends. She was a good person, very smart and very honest." He added: "She came from a distinguished Polish family. She was the daughter of a minister in Piłsudski's government. It was even rumored that she was Piłsudski's god-daughter. . . ." There was something naughtily nice about Khrushchev's image of Wasilewska fleeing on foot from Warsaw "dressed like a peasant in a sheepskin coat and plain black boots."[86] Eventually he arranged for her to be appointed deputy prime minister of Ukraine.

Khrushchev's rosy recollection culminates in his description of assemblies that voted to unite western Ukraine with the rest of the Soviet Union. When Ukrainian delegates gathered in Lvov, he "didn't hear a single speech expressing even the slightest doubt that Soviet power should be established in the Western Ukraine. One by one, movingly and joyfully, the speakers all said that it was their fondest dream to be accepted into the Ukrainian Soviet Republic." When the USSR Supreme Soviet accepted the western Ukrainian request, it gave Khrushchev "great joy and pride" because "I had organized and supervised the Sovietization of the Western Ukraine." He noted: "I won't hide it, this was a happy time for me. . . . At the same time," he added with breathtaking ingenuousness, "we were still conducting arrests. It was our view that these arrests served to strengthen the Soviet state and clear the road for the building of socialism on Marxist-Leninist principles."[87]

GETTING TO EXPAND his circle of powerful friends and acquaintances was another dividend of Khrushchev's Ukrainian viceroyalty. While the Red Army was "liberating" Bessarabia from Romanian occupation in 1940, Khrushchev and Marshal Timoshenko flew deep behind Romanian lines to visit Timoshenko's native village of Furmanka. Timoshenko was a former cavalry officer of peasant stock who, according to Mikoyan, "probably never read a book."[88] Whether or not his and Khrushchev's bold foray had any military purpose, it certainly was fun. Khrushchev savored a bearded peasant with a foul mouth and no use for Romanian officers. "I hadn't heard such choice, unrepeatable Russian cursing for a long time," he recalled, not to mention the evening's feast with Timoshenko's relatives that Khrushchev found still going on the next morning. "I asked whether the marshal had gotten up or was still asleep and was told he hadn't gone to bed yet."[89]

Khrushchev particularly admired the tough, hard-driving Georgy Zhukov, who took over in Kiev when Timoshenko was made defense commissar in 1940. He loved the way the tank commander Dmitri Pavlov "practically flew across swamps and sands" at a testing ground near Kharkov in 1940. But when Pavlov got out of his tank and started talking, the increasingly self-assured Khrushchev found him "undeveloped" and with "a limited horizon."[90] Mikhail Kirponos, who later took Zhukov's place, "didn't have the necessary experience to direct such a huge number of troops." As for Lev Mekhlis, with whom Khrushchev had been "on very good terms" since his Industrial Academy days, he now considered Mekhlis "a nitwit."[91]

Khrushchev's best friends in the Kremlin were Malenkov and Bulganin. Malenkov shared Khrushchev's avid interest in hunting. Bulganin dared quip that there was no need to read *Pravda* editorials because they were empty and predictable.[92] Although this was an era of relatively good feeling among Stalin's lieutenants, mutual envy and irritation were growing, and Khrushchev wasn't exempt. At a February 1939 Central Committee plenum, he remembered, "everybody had something critical to say about everybody else." He himself escaped criticism until he was suddenly accused of encouraging "everyone in the Moscow organization [to call] me Nikita Sergeyevich.[93]

Being known by his first name and patronymic was part of Khrushchev's earthy, populist style. As he saw it, his Kremlin colleagues were too removed from the the people. Voroshilov was "much more interested in showing off his impressive military bearing at public celebrations than he was in supervising arms procurement and organizing troop deployments." Instead of preparing the armed forces for battle, he "just smiled for the photographers and strutted about in the front of the movie cameras." He also "made quite a name for himself as a connoisseur and critic of opera. I remember once in my presence the name of some opera singer came up, and Voroshilov's wife, letting her eyes drop, remarked, 'Kliment Efremovich doesn't hold a particularly high opinion of her.'"[94]

Khrushchev too cultivated artists and writers, not to mention strutting around in front of Dovzhenko's movie cameras. But what he treasured most were invitations to Stalin's dacha on his trips to Moscow in 1938 and 1939. " . . . it was always pleasant to meet, to listen, to hear the news he recounted, to report to him directly. He would always have something encouraging to say, or would he would explain this or that situation. . . . I always looked forward to it."[95] He added: "It was always easier to exchange opinions with him candidly if we were alone."[96] Yet after a while, seeing Stalin close up began to disillusion him.

Khrushchev had no doubt the 1939–1940 war with Finland was justified by "our desire to protect ourselves." Nor did he blanch when "we lost as many as a million lives." What troubled him were the "strategic miscalculations on our side." The day the war started he was in Moscow. Stalin "didn't even feel the need to call a meeting. He was sure all we had to do was fire a few artillery rounds and the Finns would capitulate. Instead, they rejected our terms and resisted."[97]

As Soviet soldiers died, their supreme leader and his defense commissar quarreled. Stalin "jumped up in a white-hot rage and started to berate Voroshilov" for failures in Finland. Voroshilov "leapt up, turned red, hurled Stalin's accusations back into his face," and even "picked up a platter with a roast suckling pig on it and smashed it on the table."[98] Even the pleasure of seeing Voroshilov sacked didn't banish the bad taste in Khrushchev's mouth.

Moscow's lack of preparation for war with Germany wasn't fully clear until Hitler attacked on June 22, 1941. But even before then, Khrushchev insisted, he sensed that Stalin's seeming overconfidence was the product of fear. Khrushchev glimpsed that fear when the Germans occupied Paris in 1940. Stalin "nervously swore at the English and French governments for allowing their forces to be routed." Another clue was the way he surrounded himself with people late at night at his dacha as if he "needed a lot of company to banish the thoughts that were disturbing him." Before 1940–1941, according to Khrushchev, he was free to drink or not at

Stalin's dacha; when he declined, Stalin didn't object, and that "pleased me very much." That winter, however, Stalin "started drinking more and compelling others to do so. He literally made drunkards out of people!" Egged on by Beria, who seemed intent on loosening his colleagues' tongues, Stalin detained his lieutenants until dawn, supposedly transacting business but actually "doing nothing, just sitting there at these dinners, which became disgusting, which undermined your health, which clouded your mind and made head and your whole body ache." Anyone besides Stalin who declined to drink was subject to a "fine," in the form of another glass or perhaps several of them. "This was a joke," Khrushchev said, "but the person who was forced to drink paid with his health. All this stemmed from Stalin's mental condition."[99]

NOT THE LEAST attraction of Kiev was that Khrushchev could control his own style of life there. His family lived in an elegant villa (which had belonged to a sugar factory owner before the revolution) with its ornate entrance framed by a row of tall trees, a stately central staircase just inside the front door, a grand piano in the dining room, and a large garden in back protected by a high green wall.[100]

Even more magnificent was the Khrushchev dacha about two hundred feet above the west bank of the Dnieper thirty miles from Kiev. Formerly a monastery had stood on the spot. Now the Khrushchevs lived in a large brick building while his lieutenants, Mikhail Burmistenko and Leonid Korniets, occupied two others nearby. Called Mezhgorie (between the mountains), the compound commanded a majestic view of the river and the small islands that dot its expanse. Faded photographs in Khrushchev family albums show a broad stone terrace looking out over land that slopes down to a sandy beach. Aleksei Adzhubei, who first visited Mezhgorie after the war, remembered cherry, apple, and pear trees surrounding the house. Rada Adzhubei recalled a steady stream of guests, including artists from the Kiev Opera.[101]

Both the Kiev villa and the Dnieper dacha came with large staffs of servants—bodyguards, cooks, chauffeurs. Nina Petrovna first heard about all these at a rare reception for party and government leaders and their wives that Stalin threw when she was still in Moscow. She sat across from the wife of Stanislav Kossior; their conversation focused on kitchen utensils. When Nina Petrovna asked what to take with her to Kiev, Kossior's wife was astonished. It turned out, recollected Nina Petrovna, that "there was a cook with utensils the number and like of which I'd never seen. The dining room was similarly equipped. We set up housekeeping with things supplied by the government: furniture, dishes, beds—all state issue. Food was brought from a warehouse; you had to pay the account once a month."[102]

Although he was now based in Kiev, Khrushchev received a Moscow pied-a-terre even grander than his former Government House apartment. Granovsky Street is a quietly elegant lane just two blocks from the Kremlin. Khrushchev's new apartment house was a massive five-story structure with a large inner courtyard graced by several tall trees. His new flat boasted three bedrooms for the children, one for their parents, two guest rooms, a kitchen, a combination living room–dining room, an office for Khrushchev, and one large bathroom. Across the hall in 1940 lived Bulganin and his family. Malenkov's apartment was directly beneath Khrushchev's on the fourth floor. Khrushchev stayed on Granovsky Street during his periodic visits from Kiev and later from the wartime front.[103]

Materially speaking, the Khrushchev family could hardly have been more comfortable. But family tensions moved with them to Kiev and even increased. Some reflected the sheer size of the extended Khrushchev clan. Khrushchev's father had died of tuberculosis in 1938, but his mother lived on. Nina Petrovna Khrushcheva's parents moved in after she had plucked them out of what was to become Nazi-occupied Poland in September 1939,[104] as did her niece and nephew, Nina and Vasya, whom she also rescued from her native village. Of course there were also the Khrushchevs' children, Rada, who was nine in 1938, Sergei, age three, and Yelena, one, plus Nikita Khrushchev's children by his first marriage, Yulia, twenty-three when the family moved to Kiev, and Lyonia, twenty-one, who divided his time between Moscow and Kiev.

Directing a household this large and unwieldy wasn't easy. Khrushchev was consumed by his work, and the younger children were often sick. In the spring of 1941 Sergei came down with tuberculosis of the hip, which settled in his legs. For the next two years he was tightly bandaged in a prone position to a plaster cast that covered most of his lower body; only one foot, his arms, and the upper part of his chest were left free. The same spring Yulia too contracted TB, requiring an operation on her lungs.[105]

Nina Petrovna was a meticulous housekeeper and a strict disciplinarian. According to Rada, her mother believed it "her party duty to look after her family properly, and she imposed party order on the family." She kept "a tight hold" on her husband's salary (even though all household needs were provided by the state), maintained particularly close track of the liquor, "never threw anything away" (to the point that "after her death we found piles of old dresses and jumpers that had been sewn and often repaired"), and monitored her children's schoolwork, especially Rada's. "She had strict party principles, and I suffered from them," Rada recalled. "We always had a difficult relationship, even though we loved each other."[106]

Once, before he got sick, when little Sergei threw a crust of bread on the floor, his mother slapped his face hard, while her husband, who happened to be home that day, dragged Sergei off his chair and shoved him under the table, shouting "Pick it up!" Sergei's mortal sin was to waste bread that peasants had worked hard to provide. Lyonia's was to defy his stepmother directly by smoking, by taking things without asking and failing to put them back. Lyonia "didn't accept Nina Petrovna as a mother," said Liuba Sizykh, whom Lyonia met and married in 1938. Khrushchev's mother, Ksenia, openly sided with her dear grandson. On top of that there were strains between Lyonia and his sister Yulia, who had long ago alienated him by tattling on him to Nina Petrovna. When Lyonia and his wife, Liuba, had a daughter in 1940 and Liuba wanted to call the child Yulia, Lyonia vetoed the name lest his sister think she was being honored. Instead they planned to call the baby Yolanda, after a film star friend of theirs, but when Ksenia Khrushcheva landed on Liuba for giving her great-grandchild a name that was neither Russian nor Christian, the young parents settled for Yulia after all.[107]

Liuba was a lot like the brash, precocious young man she married. Her father, a bank worker, who was Orthodox and deeply religious, broke off relations with her when she became a Young Communist activist. If they hadn't quarreled then, she noted, they would have later when she took up flying, although her aerial exploits eventually brought about a reconciliation when they were widely publicized in the press.

Pictures of Liuba in her photo albums show a beautiful, vivacious young woman. Dressed in her pilot's outfit, she caught the eye of the dashing Lyonia Khrushchev, who had taken up flying in Moscow and now worked as an instructor at an air club in Kiev. He was tall and handsome, he drove her home the day they met, and the next day he presented her with a flowering lilac branch. After that they were rarely apart. "He was the most charming man I ever met," said Liuba. In one picture from her album, she is laughingly thumbing her nose at the camera held by Lyonia. Photos of him range from a pensive Lyonia in a dark suit and tie to a brooding Lyonia in a worker's cap like his father's to a smirking Lyonia in a military uniform.[108]

Attractive as Liuba was, and appealing as her Young Communist League activism must have been to her future parents-in-law, there was a blot on her record. She was denounced by a "friend" who spotted a copy of Trotsky's *Lessons of October* in her room. Expelled from the Komsomol, she was reinstated two months later (for the moment such transgressions weren't held against young people her age), but even a whiff of Trotskyism was dangerous in Khrushchev's family.

It is not clear how much Nikita Khrushchev knew about Liuba's past when he first asked to meet her. Khrushchev told his son to bring Liuba to the Kiev house late in the evening and to "wait for me." When he arrived home just before midnight, Khrushchev sat down at the table with Lyonia, Liuba, and Lyonia's sister, Yulia. Nina Petrovna wasn't invited. Reflecting the tension between her and Lyonia, he introduced Liuba to his father but not to his stepmother. Nina Petrovna entered the room, snatched a dish from a sideboard, and departed without greeting Liuba, leaving Khrushchev to press food on his guests while teasing Lyonia about letting himself be outdone by a female flier.

This first meeting was followed by invitations to the theater and later to Mezhgorie. Liuba became especially friendly with Khrushchev's mother, Ksenia. After Lyonia and Liuba were married in 1938, they lived in the Khrushchevs' Moscow apartment, where they and some friends had a spirited 1939 New Year's Eve party that Lyonia captured on film. One photo shows six people lounging on a sofa and the floor in front of it. Two of the women and one of the men look relatively sober, but one of the men appears to be guzzling vodka from a bottle, another seems completely soused, and Liuba herself is reclining in the center of the group with a bottle of champagne in her hand and a loopy grin on her face. The revellers weren't actually drunk, Liuba later insisted; the photo was staged as a joke. But Nikita Khrushchev didn't get it. Whether fearful that it would compromise him, or out of an excess of Communist puritanism, he was appalled.

"Liuba," he exploded, "what kind of behavior is this? How could you behave in such a way? You're a Komsomolka [Communist Youth League member], aren't you? This is a disgrace! You should be ashamed of yourself!" But his rage didn't last long; she remembered later cozy chats with him at the kitchen tables in Kiev and Moscow. Likewise, she said, Khrushchev couldn't stay mad at his son.

Decades later Liuba kept coming back to another family incident. Khrushche, Lyonia, Liuba, and Tolya, Liuba's son by a orevious marriage, had arrived in Moscow from Kiev in Khrushchev's private railcar. He wanted the limousine that met him to wait 20 minutes for them, too, but for security reasons his NKVD bodyguards insisted he depart. When Lyonia and Liuba arrived later at Khrushchev's residence, they found him screaming at his bodyguard: "Where are my children? Why don't I have a right to wait for them? Why do you surround me with all these restrictions?"

CHAPTER SEVEN

Khrushchev at War: 1941–1944

TWO DAYS BEFORE the Nazis attacked, Khrushchev was in Moscow. He had been "literally wasting away" there, he recalled, but couldn't get Stalin's permission to return to Kiev. He wanted to be at his post. What was the point of lingering at Stalin's "liquid luncheons and dinners," which were "already simply disgusting to me"?

"Stay on," Stalin kept insisting. "Why are you bursting to get away? Stay here awhile."[1]

Finally, the *vozhd* relented, and Khrushchev arrived in Kiev on Saturday morning, June 21, 1941. Having gone directly to his office from the train station, he didn't get home until evening. An hour or so later, around 10:00 P.M., he was called back to the Central Committee, where an intelligence aide showed him a document indicating the Germans were likely to strike within days or even hours. Almost immediately word came from Ternopol in western Ukraine: According to a German defector, the attack was to start at 3:00 the next morning. Khrushchev spent the night in his office. A little after 3:00, with first light breaking in the eastern sky, he learned the German assault had begun. An hour later German planes began bombing the Kiev airport.

Khrushchev knew Soviet defenses weren't ready. His old friend Defense Commissar Timoshenko had inspected the westernmost military districts and found serious shortcomings at all levels. Zhukov, who succeeded Timoshenko as Kiev military district commander, had led the

"Blues" (the German side) to a decisive victory over the "Reds" in December 1940 war games. Even if Khrushchev wasn't privy to most military secrets, Timoshenko and Zhukov must have shared some of their concerns with him. In an April 1941 report to Stalin, Khrushchev noted disturbingly slow progress in constructing "fortified districts" and offered some one hundred thousand workers to finish the job by June 1, 1941.[2]

Despite all this, Khrushchev remained confident the Red Army would triumph. The full extent of Soviet unpreparedness became clear only after June 22. The purges had demolished the officer corps, not just leading marshals and generals, but all military district commanders, 90 percent of district chiefs of staff and deputies, 80 percent of corps and divisional commanders, and 90 percent of staff officers and chiefs of staff. The USSR had a numerical advantage over Germany in certain tanks and planes, but all-out defense modernization had come too late; combat and staff training was oriented toward offensive operations; frontier zone troops were concentrated on vulnerable front lines; armored units were ineffectively organized and inexperienced in mass maneuvers; and ordnance and supply depots were too close to the border.[3] On top of all this, Khrushchev recalled, "we were woefully lacking in rifles and machine guns. . . . I couldn't imagine we'd be unprepared in such an elementary respect."[4]

Stalin had ignored multiple warnings: an April 1941 report from Churchill that the Germans were massing troops; a May 22 report from the Berlin embassy that the German attack was scheduled for June 15; a London embassy cable warning that Hitler would strike no later than "the middle of June." With war only a few hours away, Stalin told Zhukov that the conflict "might still be settled by peaceful means," muttering, "I think Hitler is trying to provoke us. He surely hasn't decided to make war."[5]

The more ominous the warnings, the greater Stalin's stake in ignoring them. That was why the first order Khrushchev and his colleagues received after the German attack was not to return fire and why a directive that arrived midmorning on June 22, when the battle was already raging, ordered Soviet planes not to fly more than sixty to ninety miles into enemy territory and troops not to cross the border "until receipt of special orders."[6]

That afternoon Stalin's Directive No. 3 commanded his forces to counterattack, smash the enemy, and advance into his territory. But "we still don't know exactly where the enemy is striking and in what strength," Zhukov objected to Deputy Chief of the General Staff Nikolai Vatutin. "Wouldn't it be better to find out what is actually going on at the front by tomorrow morning and then adopt the requisite decision?"

"I think you are right," Vatutin replied, "but the thing is settled."[7]

Several hours later Zhukov and Khrushchev were in Ternopol; Zhukov had flown to Kiev, where the two men embarked on a long, dangerous car ride to western Ukraine. Stalin had been awakened that morning at three twenty-five. The Politburo had assembled at dawn in the Kremlin. By the end of the day some twelve hundred Soviet aircraft were destroyed, giving the Germans total air supremacy, while Nazi forces penetrated deep into Soviet territory. Bad as that was, it took several more days for the whole truth to sink in: Soviet forces on the western front were surrounded or shattered; German troops had total freedom of action.[8] Only the southwestern front, where Khrushchev was to serve as chief political officer, held its ground for a while. But with German tanks racing eastward at a rate of 125 miles a week, Kiev was under threat by the middle of July.

TWENTY-SEVEN MILLION Soviet citizens perished in the conflict they called the Great Patriotic War,[9] an inconceivable number that includes soldiers and civilians. Those who survived faced unimaginable horrors, not only from Nazi invaders but from Soviet secret police, who arrested skilled military officers even as the war was beginning, uprooted and exiled whole peoples whom Stalin distrusted, and imprisoned and exterminated former Soviet prisoners of war whose only "crime" was to have been captured by the Germans.

Paradoxically, however, for many who survived, the war years were the best of their lives as well as the worst, a time they remembered with nostalgia as time passed. After all the fantastical "enemies of the people," at last the nation faced an all-too-real foe. With the important exception of people in western Ukraine and other borderlands, who at first greeted German troops as liberators, Soviet citizens pulled together against a common enemy. Stalin put Communist ideology aside, rallying Russians in the name of nationalism and even religion. People dared to talk more freely and to hope for a better life after the war.[10]

In his 1956 secret speech, Khrushchev mocked Stalin for planning complex war operations "on a globe."[11] In fact, Stalin was a gifted grand strategist and a master at mobilizing the country for total war, but he was out of his depth in planning and managing large-scale campaigns and remarkably ignorant of military tactics. Determined to prevail as quickly as possible and utterly indifferent to the cost, he conducted the war in a way that maximized casualties on the Soviet side.[12] Yet he emerged from the war stronger than ever: the architect of victory, the symbol of the nation, the occupier of half of Europe.

The war changed Khrushchev. From June 22 on he was in the thick of the fight, retreating with the Red Army from Kiev to Stalingrad, then tramping back to resume his duties as Ukrainian party leader. Thousands died before his eyes, from simple soldiers mowed down in ill-advised battles to generals who committed suicide in his presence, guilty of nothing except defending their country and indeed Stalin himself. That was why Khrushchev felt free not only to lament unnecessary losses but to try to prevent them.

Khrushchev served as chief political commissar (although that term itself was no longer used after 1941) on a series of crucial fronts. Military councils of which he was a member consisted of the front commander, the chief of staff for the area, and the top political officer. The latter's responsibility was equal to the commander's; no order could be issued without his signature. Actually, many commanders wanted only formal equality, preferring that their commissars concentrate on keeping up morale and lobbying with the Kremlin for supplies and reinforcements. However, Khrushchev wanted a voice in operational matters, and as a member of the ruling Politburo he got it.

He became a kind of middleman between his military colleagues and authorities in Moscow. Stalin used him to keep commanders on a tight leash. They used him to try to influence Stalin. Moscow couldn't provide enough troops and equipment for all fronts. Armies in the field couldn't meet Moscow's exacting expectations. Ultimately, of course, Khrushchev was answerable to Stalin, but he came to identify with the commanders at his side. This sort of localism (as the Soviets called it) had characterized Khrushchev in Kiev. But the generals around him had their own special perspective: Some even dared grumble to him that soldiers wouldn't die for land that they didn't actually own.[13] Khrushchev rejected that, of course, but not the commanders' contempt for Moscow's ruinous strategic mistakes.

Of all Khrushchev's Politburo colleagues, only Zhdanov and Bulganin had a roughly equivalent role as political commissars, but they weren't very good at it.[14] The rest were active and important in Moscow but not in the field. Malenkov ran the party apparatus for Stalin; he visited the front several times, especially at Stalingrad, but according to historian Dmitri Volkogonov, "because he was utterly lacking in military competence he left no trace whatsoever on the military sphere."[15] Molotov was the deputy chairman of the State Defense Committee, which supervised the overall war effort along with the Headquarters of the Supreme Commander in Chief (Stavka), the General Staff of the Soviet Armed Forces, and the People's Commissariat of Defense. Beria and Voroshilov and later Kaganovich, Mikoyan, and Nikolai Voznesensky, an up-and-coming young economic planner, were also State Defense Committee members, with the right to attend Stavka meetings.

Khrushchev envied his Moscow colleagues and resented it when they arrived on inspection trips, sniffing out disloyalty and malfeasance and ordering him and his generals around. He came to see them, as did others who observed them in Stalin's presence, as ciphers. "When I went to the Kremlin," said former Transport chief Ivan Kovalev, "Molotov, Beria and Malenkov would usually be in Stalin's office. I used to feel they were in the way. They never asked questions, but just sat there and listened, sometimes jotting down a note. Stalin would be busy issuing instructions, talking on the phone, signing papers . . . and those three would just go on sitting there. . . ."[16]

The war traumatized Khrushchev: It drove him to smoke and to drink; it commanded more attention in his memoirs than almost any other subject, but he couldn't bring himself to read others' war memoirs in retirement.[17] Yet the same war added several more medals to his collection. In 1942 a Moscow ceremony commemorating the twenty-fifth anniversary of the Soviet Ukraine paid tribute to him in absentia as "the leader of the Bolsheviks in the Army who are fighting the enemy." On February 12, 1943, he was named a lieutenant general. He wore the uniform to the end of the war, even after returning to civilian duties in Kiev. In 1943 he was awarded the Order of Suvorov, Second Class, and the Order of Kutuzov, First Class. A contemporary newsreel captures his exultation: standing at attention, his face solemn as the medals are prepared, then radiant as his is presented.

These medals reflect Khrushchev's role in triumphs at Stalingrad and Kursk. But he was also involved in disasters at Kiev and Kharkov in which hundreds of thousands of soldiers died unnecessarily. Although not primarily responsible for either these victories or defeats, he contributed to both. Volkogonov's judgment, that "as a military mind, Khrushchev was an absolute zero," may be unfair, but a revealing 1930 document prefigures his shortcomings both in wartime and afterwards. The senior officer of the reserve unit in which he served as a political commissar deemed Khrushchev's overall record, especially his "tactical preparation," to be merely "satisfactory." His "approach to evaluating situations and to taking decisions is *not systematic* [emphasis added]."[18]

Khrushchev later claimed to have "argued with Stalin many times [during the war]. Even though he could have blasted me with fire and water, I doggedly tried to persuade him of my point of view. Sometimes, I succeeded."[19] This may even be true. Stalin once complained to two wartime interlocutors, "What can I tell you? No matter what I say, you'll reply, 'Yes, Comrade Stalin,' 'Of course, Comrade Stalin,' 'You've made a wise decision, Comrade Stalin.' Only Zhukov sometimes argues with me."[20] Zhukov and Molotov did indeed argue with Stalin, and Khrushchev probably did too, if only to win his respect. But Khrushchev also spent plenty of time currying favor, bombarding the boss with reports as ingratiating as they were informative, maneuvering to get himself into the great man's presence, and basking in Stalin's praise whenever he could wangle it.

EXCEPT FOR RARE reunions with his wife and daughter Rada, who met him in Moscow, Khrushchev never saw his family between July 1941 and late 1943.[21] Yet during that time the Khrushchev family experienced three personal calamities that must have affected his morale. Nina Petrovna tried not to burden her husband with troubles, but these couldn't be concealed, either because Khrushchev was officially informed or because his wife's strain must have shown no matter how hard she tried to hide it. What happened to his family must have shaken Khrushchev all the more because it was linked, through the fateful figure of his son Lyonia, with his own shaky sense of himself.

Khrushchev's family fled Kiev on July 2, 1941. After several weeks in Moscow, they moved on to Kuibyshev, a middle-size city on the Volga south of Kazan, to which much of the Soviet government and the diplomatic corps was evacuated. The Khrushchev entourage included Nina Petrovna, her three young children, and her niece and nephew, Nina and Vasya. Six-year-old Sergei traveled on a stretcher. He did not walk again (on crutches and in a special corset) until late 1942; until then he spent his time in bed or being moved around in a carriage, requiring attention that, according to a relative who wishes to remain nameless, "spoiled him rotten." Khrushchev's sister, Irina Sergeyevna, and her two daughters, Rona and Irma, also traveled with Nina Petrovna, as did his mother, Ksenia. They were joined in Moscow by Lyonia Khrushchev's wife, Liuba, and her two children, one-and-half-year-old-Yulia (who developed dysentery upon arrival in Kuibyshev) and Tolya, now seven. Nina Petrovna's parents eventually joined them in Kuibyshev, as did Vitya Pisarev, a nephew of Khrushchev's first wife, and Zina Bondarchuk, the daughter of Nina Petrovna's cousin, in Moscow in 1944. All told, at least fifteen relatives were in Nina Khrushcheva's care during the worst of the war.[22]

Until Germany attacked, Lyonia and Liuba had been living in Khrushchev's Moscow apartment, ordering food from the Kremlin canteen, frequently attending the theater, and employing a nanny. Lyonia, who had joined the military in 1939, was training as a bomber pilot at Podolsk outside Moscow; he often invited pilot friends to stay the night in the apartment, as they did—yet another sign of the Red Army's low state of readiness—on June 21. When Irina Sergeyevna's husband called from Kiev the next morning to say German planes were bombing the city, Lyonia and his friends rushed back to their base.

Kuibyshev was an oasis, but getting there wasn't easy. The writer Ilya Ehrenburg remembered a five-day journey from Moscow in an overcrowded suburban railway coach, but also that "the diplomats traveled in a sleeper, and another car was occupied by members of the Comintern."[23] The Khrushchev family had to wait two or three hours at the Moscow station, but their special car felt, Liuba said, "like home on the rails."

Kuibyshev had a claustrophobic quality with so many refugees crowded into it, but according to the novelist Vasily Grossman, "there was something strangely attractive in the coming together of the weighty apparatus of the State with the bohemianism of the evacuation." As the temporary Soviet capital, Kuibyshev housed not only government and newspaper offices and the diplomatic corps, but writers, impresarios, and the Bolshoi Ballet. Grossman wrote:

> All these thousands of people lived in cramped little rooms and hotels, and yet carried on with their usual activities. People's commissars and the heads of important enterprises planned the economy and gave orders to their subordinates; extraordinary and plenipotentiary ambassadors drove in luxury cars to receptions with architects of Soviet foreign policy; [Galina] Ulanova, [Sergei] Lemeshev and [Maksim] Mikhailov delighted audiences at the ballet and the opera; Mr. [Henry] Shapiro, of the United Press Agency, asked . . . awkward questions at press conferences; writers wrote radio broadcasts or articles for national and foreign newspapers. But the everyday life of these people from Moscow was quite

> transformed. [The British ambassador's wife, Lady Cripps] ate supper in a hotel restaurant in exchange for a meal-coupon, wrapped up the left-over bread and sugar-lumps in a newspaper and carried them up to her room; representatives of international news agencies pushed their way through crowds of wounded at the market, discussed the quality of home-grown tobacco and rolled sample cigarettes—or else stood and waited, shifting their weight from foot to foot, in the queue for the baths; writers famous for their hospitality discussed world politics and the fate of literature over a glass of home-distilled vodka and a ration of black bread.[24]

Along with relatives of Malenkov, Voroshilov, Bulganin, and Semyon Budyonny, the Khrushchevs at first lived in a special Kremlin-East apartment complex that occupied a whole city block by the bank of the Volga. The Khrushchev family got a seven-room apartment, as well as a separate three-room flat, for Liuba and her children and for Khrushchev's sister, Irina Sergeyevna, and hers. Later Nina Petrovna and her immediate family shared a large dacha with the Malenkovs at the Volga military district sanatorium. Nearby was a large stone house with an elaborate network of underground rooms and passages, which had been prepared for Stalin in the event Moscow fell. The Malenkov family fled eastward to Sverdlovsk as Germans approached Stalingrad, but Nina Petrovna, too exhausted to retreat farther, refused to leave.

In a time of hardship and danger, the Khrushchev household was a safe harbor. Relatives craved invitations to join it and resented it when they were left out. Nina Petrovna took in her niece and nephew, but not their parents, her own brother and sister-in-law. She accepted Khrushchev's sister only when the war left her no choice. According to Liuba, Nina Petrovna looked down on Irina Sergeyevna, a peasant woman who seemed out of place in the now-elite Khrushchev family, and Irina Sergeyevna disliked Nina Petrovna. Added Irina Sergeyevna's daughter, Rona Kobiak: "Nikita Sergeyevich hardly acknowledged my mother's existence. I can't forgive either him or Nina Petrovna. My mother died prematurely because of the way they treated her."[25]

The Soviet literary critic Sara Babyonysheva, who met Irina Sergeyevna in Kuibyshev, remembered a talkative dark-complexioned woman of medium height who was full of complaints. Khrushchev had urged his sister to arrange piano lessons for her daughter and had offered a hundred rubles a month to pay for them. "He doesn't know anything about life,"

Khrushchev's sister griped. "He doesn't even know that you can't buy bread at the market for that amount. But why should he know how people live? Everything they want is delivered to them at home, and all we get is the crumbs. . . . Just look at her mug," Irina Sergeyevna said sneeringly of her sister-in-law. "How unattractive! And take a look at her legs. They're this fat," she said, spreading her hands wide apart.[26]

Ksenia Khrushcheva's attitude toward Nina Petrovna was equally negative. By this time, Khrushchev's mother was spending a lot of time in the hospital. Although still a formidable woman, she clung fiercely to Liuba, moving in with her and Irina Sergeyevna when they occupied a separate apartment of their own, talking endlessly of her son but hardly ever of her late husband, whom she referred to as a "fool." Nina Petrovna's niece, Nina Kukharchuk, who used to bring meals to Khrushchev's mother, remembered her muttering bitterly, "Can it be that I'm going to die out here in the sticks? Why did you want to worm your way into this nest?"

At first, young Sergei and his plaster cast had to be hauled up and down four flights of stairs. "Seryozha would lick his food to see if he liked it and would reject what he didn't want," a family member said. He was Nina Petrovna's biggest burden, but he wasn't the only one. One day Liuba took baby Yulia for a walk. "Yulochka had to poo," Liuba recalls, "and since I didn't have anything else with me, I ripped off a piece of *Pravda* and wiped her with it. When I got home with the paper torn, Nina Petrovna really lit into me: How could I do such a thing! How crude and uncultured I was! I answered back impertinently."

In Kuibyshev, as in Kiev, the sharpest family tension revolved around Lyonia. Until the war his school and work record was uneven at best. After finishing seven years of schooling, plus a brief stint at a factory-based vocational school, he had taken up metalworking, his father's first love, in 1933. Next he tried flying, not at a prestigous Moscow academy, where sons of the elite enrolled, but at a civil aviation school in Balashov between Voronezh and Saratov. From there he transferred in 1937 to another school in Ulianovsk, after which he served as a flying instructor at the Moscow and Kiev air clubs. Lyonia joined the Young Communist League and became a Komsomol organizer, but he was officially reprimanded for "drunkenness and lack of discipline" in Balashov and later for nonpayment of dues. Khrushchev's son never joined the Communist party. Despite all this, he was commissioned as a junior lieutenant with the 134th Air Bomber Group in July 1939.[27]

The diploma Lyonia received from the Engels Military Aviation Academy on May 21, 1940, raved about his skills as a pilot. In the first month and a half of the war he flew twenty-seven missions, most without cover. A July 16, 1941, report recommended him for an Order of the Red Banner, describing him as a "courageous, fearless pilot" who emerged from a July 6 dogfight with his plane riddled with bullets, but who quickly returned to battle in place of fallen comrades.[28]

Even if Lyonia was "a pilot from God" (his widow's description), as Khrushchev's son he got special treatment and praise. A January 9, 1942, military report characterized him as a "fine, experienced pilot who can be called a good son of his father."[29] The press featured several accounts of his exploits, one of them, in *Pravda,* accompanied by a photo of the dashing pilot grinning at the camera.[30] When his son was recommended for the Order of the Red Banner, Khrushchev sent him a telegram: "I am glad for you and for your fighting comrades. Atta boy! I congratulate you on your success in battle. Keep beating up those German bastards, smash them day and night. Your father, N. Khrushchev." It was about this time that Khrushchev reportedly said, "Our boys are fighting brilliantly. I forgive Lyonia for everything."[31]

On July 26, 1941, Lyonia's plane was hit by German fighters; he had to crash-land and broke his leg so badly that the bone protruded through his torn boot. From then until at least March 1942 he was hospitalized. Although his injury left him with one leg slightly shorter than the other (a contemporary newsreel shows him limping along with a cane next to his father when they met in 1942), he was scheduled to return to active duty. In the meantime a scandal intervened, one the family considered so shameful that they didn't speak of it for decades.

Lyonia was injured near Moscow (according to a family friend, a field hospital doctor wanted to amputate until Lyonia threatened him with a pistol)[32] but was hospitalized in Kuibyshev, where his family lived. That of course was a special privilege. But Lyonia suffered as much from enforced idleness as from his wound. As soon as he could get around on crutches, he began to hang out with Ruben Ibárruri (son of Dolores Ibárruri, the famous Spanish Civil War firebrand known as La Pasionaria), who was also recovering there.

A prewar snapshot in Liuba's scrapbook shows a grinning Lyonia, wearing a leather coat, with a cigarette dangling from his lips, jauntily holding what looks like a small pistol (or prehaps a pistol-shaped cigarette lighter) to Ibárruri's head. Several times Liuba had witnessed Lyonia shoot bottles and wine glasses off friends' noggins, a trick he had perfected in Moscow. In response to a drunken naval officer's dare in Kuibyshev, he shot the neck off a bottle on his first try, but when the sailor insisted the bottle be completely destroyed, Lyonia fired again, hitting the sailor in the face and killing him.[33]

Lyonia was court-martialed, but instead of being sentenced to a penal battalion, he was allowed to undertake new training as a fighter pilot.[34] He passed his flight tests in November 1942 with a grade of "good" (compared with the "excellent" he had received in bomber training), but his commanders at first kept him out of combat for which he didn't seem fully prepared. When they relented, First Air Force Commander General Ivan Khudiakov later wrote to Nikita Khrushchev, "your son attacked the foe boldly and pursued him relentlessly, and afterwards literally exulted, recounting all the details of the battle."[35]

About noon on March 11, 1943, Lieutenant Khrushchev and eight other pilots took off over Kaluga Province southwest of Moscow, their mission to protect advancing Soviet troops against German bombers. When German fighters appeared, the Soviet planes broke into three groups, with Lyonia and a Lieutenant Zamorin chasing two enemy aircraft back over German-occupied territory. Zamorin shot down one, while Khrushchev flew off to his right, protecting Zamorin's tail. When the other German plane targeted Khrushchev. Zamorin saw Lyonia turn and dive at steep angle. He reported that Khrushchev had gone into a protective spin, but Lyonia failed to return to base.

"We organized a careful search from the air and dispatched partisans on the ground," General Khudiakov wrote to Nikita Khrushchev, "but without results. For the next month we held out hope . . . , but circumstances and the passage of time compel a sorrowful conclusion—that your son, Senior Lieutenant Leonid Nikitich Khrushchev, died the death of the brave in battle with the German invaders."

"Leonid, who was a pilot, died in battle," Khrushchev said in his memoirs. "It was war, and many good men died as they do in every war."[36] This is one of only two references to Lyonia in the more than two thousand pages of Khrushchev's recollections. A picture of his son later hung in the family living room, but Khrushchev rarely mentioned him. No full search was made in the area where Lyonia's plane went down, even after the territory was retaken by Soviet troops. Only in 1960 was an exhaustive inquiry undertaken, but it failed definitively to establish Lyonia's fate.

That fate has been grist for nasty rumors: One has it Lyonia survived his crash, was captured by Germans, and then cooperated with them until Stalin ordered him seized by Soviet commandos and executed. Nikita

Khrushchev allegedly begged for his son's life, but Stalin refused to pardon him. According to those spreading this rumor, it explains why Khrushchev turned against Stalin.[37] Molotov later insisted that Khrushchev's son "was a kind of traitor," that "Stalin didn't want to pardon him," and that Khrushchev's "bitterness at Stalin . . . led him to do anything he could to blacken Stalin's name."[38] As if Khrushchev had no other reason to denounce Stalin! If the Germans had captured Lyonia, surely they would have trumpeted that fact as they did when Stalin's son, Yakov, fell into their hands. Researchers have found no sign of Lyonia in German interrogations of Soviet prisoners.[39] Also, Lieutenant Zamorin later confessed that he had covered up the fact that he saw Lyonia's plane disintegrate, presumably so as to avoid any seeming responsibility for the death of a Politburo's member's son.[40]

Why then did Khrushchev react so minimally to his son's death? Perhaps it was too painful to bear. Or perhaps it was his son's life, with all its trespasses, that he couldn't bring himself to think about.

THE FATE of Lyonia's widow and her son compounded his tragedy. At the time he was killed, Liuba was enrolled in the Institute of Foreign Languages, which had been evacuated from Moscow to Stavropol on the Volga, some forty miles downstream from Kuibyshev. When she got the bad news, the Volga was still frozen; since a riverboat was the main transport to Kuibyshev, she and a friend walked all the way there, and a day later she and Nina Petrovna flew to Moscow to meet Khrushchev.

Vera Chernetskaya, the daughter of a Soviet composer and conductor and the wife of a Frenchman who worked in the French consulate in Kuibyshev, had persuaded Liuba to study French. Chernetskaya and her husband lived in a hotel where Lyonia and Liuba often befriended Soviet artists and musicians. Socializing with foreigners (not to mention marrying one) was dangerous, even during the war, when Russians and Westerners were thrown together and restrictions on contacts relaxed. After Lyonia returned to the front, Liuba dared accompany a French military attaché (whom she described as "an amazingly attractive man") to the theater.[41]

At first Liuba left her children in Kuibyshev, Tolya with Irina Sergeyevna, Yulia with Nina Petrovna. One blisteringly hot day in June 1943 (so hot that Tolya remembers not being able to walk on the asphalt), she picked up her son, took a steamer down to Stavropol, and walked several miles to the former sanatorium in the forest where the institute had been relocated. Tolya lived with Liuba's French teacher while she stayed in a dorm.

A short while later Liuba was arrested. She believed the chief of the Khrushchevs' security detail, whom she and Lyonia had ignored, denounced her. Two other NKVD agents took her by train to Moscow; after confiscating her belongings, including a treasured watch Lyonia had given her, they dumped her in a Lubyanka prison cell with two other prisoners she assumed were stool pigeons. At first she assumed a mistake had been made, but not after being interrogated by Viktor Abakumov himself, the deputy chief of the NKVD and head of SMERSH, the counterespionage agency known as Death to Spies.[42]

Like his master Beria, Abakumov was capable of personally torturing prisoners. Liuba learned later that he had knocked out the teeth of one of Vera Chernetskaya's relatives. With Liuba, however, the tall, broad-shouldered, dark-haired Abakumov was friendly, even flirtatious. Sitting in a huge Lubyanka office with his legs crossed and a smile on his sensuous face, he didn't accuse her of anything. "He didn't say I was a spy," Liuba remembered, "just that I had gone to the theater with the military attaché who had given me a piece of paper." Liuba refused to talk "because I had nothing to say." Abakumov told her tauntingly, "Perhaps you won't speak, but you could if you wanted to." He threatened to transfer her to Lefortovo Prison. "It's horrible there," he warned her, "not as nice as our place. It's filled with rats, and you'll lose your teeth there." When Liuba refused to confess to crimes of which she hadn't even been accused, another interrogator cursed and threatened to beat her. In the end she was deprived of all but minimal sleep for nearly eight months (like all the prisoners on the Lubyanka "conveyor belt"), then tossed into solitary confinement for two months in Butyrka Prison in Moscow, and finally sentenced to five years in a Mordovia labor camp.

Liuba worked on a logging crew in the camp until she collapsed and was sent to what passed for a camp clinic. After recovering, she served as a medical orderly and nurse until she fell ill again, losing most of the sight in one eye, ceasing to menstruate, and dropping in weight to around seventy pounds. At one point, lying on a plank bed in a delirium, she imagined she was riding a swan and heard Nikita Khrushchev's voice crying, "Liuba must be freed!" Later she received an anonymous package containing a pair of boots, a pea jacket, a winter cap with earflaps, and other clothing. She suspected Khrushchev's sister sent it since Irina

Sergeyevna dispatched several other packages to her, whereas Nikita and Nina Khrushchev did not.

Released from the camps in 1948, Liuba spent five years of exile in Kazakhstan, where she found geological work and continually fended off pressure to work as a police informer. She stayed on in Karaganda after Khrushchev succeeded Stalin, partly as a result of what had happened when she visited Moscow in 1954. Khrushchev had refused to let her see Yulia, now fourteen years old, whom Nina and Nikita Khrushchev had adopted and who thought of them as her parents. Nina Petrovna apparently wanted to allow a mother-daughter reunion, and sometime later, when Yulia was filling out a university entrance form, she revealed the truth to her.[43] In 1956, when Khrushchev was out of town, Nina Petrovna arranged for Liuba to see Yulia. "You're the very image of Lyonia!" Liuba cried. Nina Petrovna urged her to stay on, but Liuba declined, thinking she wasn't really wanted. In later years, especially after he was ousted from power, Khrushchev talked with his daughter-in-law, but he never asked his family about her, and he saw her in person only once between 1943 and his death in 1971.

Khrushchev might have feared he'd lose Yulia. Liuba also suspected he believed the espionage accusations against her. "They must have told him some very bad things about Liuba," Yulia said. She added that neither Nikita nor Nina Khrushchev ever hugged her as warmly as Liuba did in 1956. In fact, they never hugged her at all. "Nina Petrovna was just like that. She was cold, and she didn't teach me how to be warm."

LIUBA WASN'T the only relative of a Politburo member whom Stalin arrested. Molotov's wife, Kalinin's wife, Kaganovich's brother, Mikoyan's sons: None of their powerful relatives could protect them. Khrushchev wasn't to blame for not rescuing Liuba from prison. But why did he hold a grudge? Rather than alleged espionage, it may have been her imprudent style of life, like Lyonia's, that grated on him. Although Liuba's son, Tolya, who was nine years old in 1943, wasn't Lyonia's boy, he might as well have been.

"I was the sort who couldn't concentrate on anything," Tolya recalled. "I was always in motion, always needing something. When Lyonia arrived, he had this wonderful helmet with him, and I took it; I wore it when I went ice skating. I once grabbed on to a car, and it pulled me down the frozen street. Lyonia didn't mind, but Mama got mad. Lyonia had a box of revolvers and cartridges. It was locked, but I managed to open it when

Mama and Lyonia were at the theater, and I took out a pistol to play with my friend, the son of Khrushchev's chauffeur, who lived in the basement of our building. I put in a cartridge clip, and he insisted on shooting. The bullet missed me, but it broke a window, and the room filled with smoke. We were so scared we hid under a blanket in case anyone came, and the next day, when Lyonia asked me about it, I denied it and then confessed. Lyonia made me stand in a corner but then let me go. One time I threw a bottle out of the window, and it just missed Vyshinsky, who was walking through the courtyard."

A direct hit on Stalin's favorite purge trial prosecutor might have brought Tolya glory in the hereafter. But not trying to strangle a dog with a silk scarf given to him by Irina Sergeyevna. To make matters worse, the dog managed to escape with the present. The tall, clumsy Tolya was teased so mercilessly by first-grade schoolmates that Liuba hired a governess, an old woman who combined tsarist-era culture with preternatural strictness. Nikita Khrushchev's mother adored Tolya,[44] but the Malenkovs complained about him. Nina Kukharchuk recalled Tolya urinating in the sink and Nina Petrovna crying, "He will ruin the girls!" Once Liuba and her children moved into a separate apartment, Tolya hardly ever saw the other Khrushchevs. "I felt as if I had fallen out of the family," he commented.

All Tolya was told when his mother was arrested was that she had "left." That morning an institute functionary walked him to Stavropol and placed him in an orphanage. God-awful in peacetime, Soviet orphanages were far worse in war. No one said anything about Liuba or about his sister and other relatives in Kuibyshev. "They have thrown me away," Tolya thought. A month later he fled the orphanage, sneaked onto a steamer to Kuibyshev, and arrived at Irina Sergeyevna's apartment lice-ridden and covered with a rash. His former governess applied medications from the special Kremlin clinic. But Nina Petrovna soon dumped him in another orphanage, telling him only that his mother had gone to Moscow on business.

Nina Petrovna gave Tolya two sausages. Orphanage food was so bad (no more than three hundred grams of bread per day) that children were reduced to chewing buttons made of cow's horns and hooves, which they warmed on the stove. For a while the director summoned Tolya to secret sausage-eating sessions, which his own two children watched drooling; it made Tolya feel so uncomfortable that he gave the rest of the sausage to them.

Children of Tolya's age attended a separate school. That gave him the chance to escape again. He stole some pastries at the railway station and was seen begging at the town marketplace. He fled back to Kuibyshev in February 1944, only to find the Khrushchevs had departed for Moscow. To get money for a railway ticket, Tolya stole a dinner service set that he tried to sell, but he was caught and returned to the orphanage. After he attempted several more escapes, the orphanage got rid of him by sending him to a naval cadet school in Leningrad.

The rest of Tolya's story is even more appalling. The cadet school physical examination discovered a heart problem, so Tolya was sent instead to a Kronstadt naval base paint shop, whose underage workers breathed poisonous fumes and ate wallpaper paste to supplement meager rations. Trying to flee to Moscow, Tolya traipsed across the ice of the Gulf of Finland at night and boarded a train before being caught and sent to an orphanage in Pskov. After he escaped that one too, and from another one in Vologda, he finally reached Moscow, where after being nabbed again at the Kursk Station, he headed for Ukraine. In Kiev he "lived" in a railroad station ventilation shaft until he was caught and dispatched to a correctional colony from which he escaped three times. Finally, fearing arrest and imprisonment, he found a steady job, and then, in 1952, he joined the army.

Tolya managed to track down his half sister, Yulia, in Moscow in 1955. She was now an elegant, privileged young woman, while he considered himself a poor, awkward creature whose shoelaces kept unraveling. So Tolya returned to Kiev, where his mother finally found him. Did he ever again try to contact the Khrushchev family? Tolya was asked. "No," he replied bitterly. "I forgot all about them. I didn't want anything to do with them. They didn't interest me at all. They didn't exist for me. They gave me away to the orphanage."

Whether Nikita Khrushchev knew of Tolya's fate is unclear. Whether he would have helped him if he had known is even more uncertain.

SOON AFTER Hitler attacked, when the full extent of the catastrophe became clear, Stalin's nerves cracked. "Lenin left us a great legacy, and we, his heirs, have fucked it all up," he snarled to Molotov and Beria. For several days Stalin brooded alone in his dacha. When his colleagues arrived on June 29, hoping to convince him to return to his post, he looked as if he expected to be arrested. Later in July Khrushchev saw him at supreme headquarters, deep underground in the Kirov Metro station: "The man sat there devastated and couldn't say anything, not even any words of encouragement which I needed. . . . What I saw before me was a leader who was morally crushed. He was sitting on a couch. His face was empty . . . he was at a complete loss and didn't know what to do."[45]

While Stalin struggled to regain his confidence, Khrushchev and his colleagues fought to save Kiev. The abortive defense and eventual fall of the city, along with the appalling Soviet losses that accompanied it, constituted the first major crisis of the war for Khrushchev.

On July 29, Chief of Staff Zhukov spread maps on a long, green cloth–covered table in Stalin's large wood-paneled Kremlin office. Zhukov advised Stalin that the Germans were likely to delay their assault on Moscow and strike first at the "weakest and most dangerous sector" on the central and southwestern fronts. If that happened, Zhukov continued with great trepidation, his recommendation was to "abandon Kiev."

"How could you even think of giving up Kiev to the enemy?" Stalin exploded.[46]

"If you think the chief of staff can talk nothing but sheer nonsense," Zhukov said he retorted, "then he has no business here." Stalin sent him packing and decreed that Kiev be held.[47] On September 10, with a massive German tank wedge driving deep into the Southwest Army Group, Major General Vasily Tupikov concluded that "if we delay the withdrawal, a catastrophe is inevitable."[48] But Stalin forbade a retreat. Tupikov warned of "catastrophe" in "a matter of couple of days." But all that produced was the charge that he was a "panic-monger" and a demand that Stalin's orders be executed.

Timoshenko was so alarmed on September 15 that he issued a verbal order, with Khrushchev's concurrence, to withdraw *without* Stalin's permission. But when Southwest Army Group Commander Mikhail Kirponos feared to act and cabled Stalin again, he received a contradictory command: "to abandon Kiev, but under no conditions pull out from the encirclement."[49]

Twenty-four hours later Kiev fell. Kirponos, Tupikov, and Khrushchev's former deputy Ukrainian party chief Mikhail Burmistenko, who was their main political officer, were killed. The Germans boasted of taking 655,000 prisoners; according to the Russians, only 150,541 men out of 677,085 fought their way out of the trap. At the point when Khrushchev's command had no choice but to evacuate Kiev, he got a telegram from Stalin "unjustly accusing me of cowardice and threatening to take action against me. He accused me of intending to surrender Kiev. This was a filthy lie."[50] But instead of arresting Khrushchev, Stalin ignored him on his next trip to Moscow, leaving it to his deputy head of government Nikolai Voznesensky to administer a tongue lashing.[51]

This experience seared itself into Khrushchev's memory. But according to Zhukov, Khrushchev *was* largely at fault. When Zhukov tried to argue for a withdrawal in August, Stalin "told me that he had just consulted once again with Khrushchev, who had convinced him that under no circumstances should Kiev be abandoned."[52]

Zhukov's testimony is suspect; after all, Khrushchev fired and disgraced him in 1957. But it's likely Khrushchev did initially swear that Kiev could be defended, so as to avoid saying what the *vozhd* didn't want to hear. Stalin's underlings' servility led him astray; if later on they tried desperately to change his mind, he refused to do so and blamed them to boot. That may explain why Khrushchev didn't stand up to Stalin, but not his later denial that he failed to do so.

THE CATASTROPHIC Kharkov counteroffensive of May 1942 fits the same pattern. During the autumn of 1941 Moscow itself was threatened; on November 28, German troops encircling the city were less than twenty miles from the Kremlin. But a Soviet counteroffensive turned them back.[53] "We can't sit here on the defensive with our hands folded," Stalin complained at a State Defense Committee meeting in March 1942. "We must launch several preemptive attacks on a broad front. . . ."[54] Stalin overrode General Staff opposition to a winter offensive, but by March 1942 it had stalled. Zhukov's successor as chief of staff, the elderly former tsarist colonel Boris Shaposhnikov, urged a "provisional strategic defensive" for the early summer of 1942. But the southwestern sector, commanded by Timoshenko, with Ivan Bagramian as chief of staff and Khrushchev as political officer, had bigger ideas.

Timoshenko and Khrushchev wanted to destroy the German Army Group South so that Soviet forces could hold a line extending from Gomel in Byelorussia through Kiev down to Nikolayev on the Black Sea. They proposed that ninety-two Soviet divisions take on sixty-four German divisions, far short of the decisive superiority needed to ensure victory. Bagramian had doubts, but since Khrushchev and Timoshenko seemed sure Moscow would buy the proposal, he kept them to himself.[55]

The General Staff too opposed the proposal. But after Timoshenko, Khrushchev, and Bagramian made their case, Stalin approved a limited version designed to retake only the Kharkov region, and invited them to dinner.[56]

With the politicking over, the pace of preparations picked up. Timoshenko commanded 640,000 men, 1,200 tanks, 13,000 guns and mortars, and 926 planes. Early in May, he, Khrushchev, and Bagramian visited frontline troops, stopping in a village where Khrushchev's Red Army unit had defeated White forces in 1919. None of them suspected that the Germans had deduced that a Kharkov attack was coming and were preparing to spring a giant trap.[57]

The Soviet offensive opened on May 12. The southwest command initially reported that its troops had penetrated German lines both north and south of Kharkov. Another report on May 15 oozed even more optimism. So delighted was Stalin, wrote Vice Chief of Staff Aleksandr Vasilevsky, that he "sharply reproached the General Staff at whose insistence he had almost called off an operation that was now developing so successfully."[58]

Two days later, however, the situation was deteriorating drastically. Timoshenko's troops had created a bulge in the Barvenkovo area, leaving their flanks exposed. At 3:00 A.M. on May 17, German units assaulted the southern flank, and by noon they had punched ten miles into positions held by the Soviet Ninth Army. With other German forces crashing down from the north in a giant pincers movement, Soviet troops were in danger of being cut off.[59]

Vasilevsky urged that the offensive be halted, but after talking to Timoshenko, Stalin refused.[60] That same day Timoshenko and Khrushchev found time to send Stalin a two-page report, titled "Successful Attack by Southwestern Forces in the Kharkov Theater: What We Have Captured," on war booty seized between May 12 and May 16.[61]

On May 18 the southwest command had decided to halt the offensive, but Moscow countermanded the order. Khrushchev was getting ready to go to sleep when Bagramian brought the bad news at 3:00 A.M. "I implore you: speak to Comrade Stalin personally," Bagramian begged. "Our only chance is that you can talk him into reversing his decision. . . ."

When Khrushchev called supreme headquarters, Vasilevsky answered the phone. "Aleksandr Mikhailovich," Khrushchev recalled saying, "as a military man who has studied maps and who understands enemy strategy, you know the situation in greater detail than Comrade Stalin does. Please . . . explain to Comrade Stalin what will happen if we continue this operation."

"Stalin's now at the nearby Dacha," said Vasilevsky.

"Then go talk to him there. . . . Take a map and show him how our decision to call off the offensive is the only rational thing to do."

"No, Comrade Khrushchev. Comrade Stalin has already made up his mind. He has already issued his orders."

Khrushchev hung up, then called back and tried again, but Vasilevsky wouldn't budge. His only hope now was to speak to Stalin himself. "This was a very dangerous moment for me," Khrushchev later said. "I knew Stalin by now considered himself a great military strategist." Malenkov answered when Khrushchev telephoned Stalin's dacha. "Stalin must have been there," Khrushchev recalled. "I knew the layout of the dacha very well, I knew exactly where everyone would be sitting and how many steps it would take Stalin to reach the telephone." But Stalin wouldn't talk to him. "Comrade Stalin knows you didn't get the Front commander's approval for your decision to halt the offensive," Malenkov said when he returned to the phone. "He knows that calling off the operation was your idea, and your idea alone, and he's against it." When Khrushchev hung up, Bagramian, who was standing next to him, "burst into tears. His nerves cracked. He foresaw what was going to happen. He was weeping for our army."[62]

Khrushchev's account is devastating. But is it accurate? By May 18 Stalin was worried, according to Zhukov. But Timoshenko was still downplaying the danger, and Khrushchev "supported Timoshenko." Khrushchev's insistence that he warned Stalin doesn't "correspond to reality," Zhukov wrote later. "I can testify to this because I personally was present when Stalin spoke to Khrushchev over the high-frequency phone."[63]

The Soviet *Military Historical Journal* cites three messages from Khrushchev to Stalin (two dispatched by him and Timoshenko at 5:30 P.M. on May 17 and at 12:30 A.M. on May 19, plus a personal message sent at 2:00 A.M. on the nineteenth), and not one calls for a halt in the offensive.[64] But Khrushchev insisted he telephoned instead of writing (the journal had no access to telephone transcripts), and Bagramian and Vasilevsky, although they published their memoirs after he had become a nonperson, partially supported his account. Bagramian said Timoshenko urged Stalin to continue the offensive and remembered assuming that Khrushchev was trying to call it off. Vasilevsky recalled Khrushchev's calling him on the eighteenth, reporting that Stalin had "rejected their proposal for an immediate halt to the offensive, and asking me to convey their request once again to the Supreme Commander." Vasilevsky also confirmed Khrushchev's recollection that "a conversation with the Supreme Commander was conducted through G. M. Malenkov, and that this conversation confirmed the order that the offensive be continued."[65]

The truth is that all parties were to blame for the Kharkov debacle: Khrushchev and colleagues, for overselling their idea and then blaming Stalin; Stalin, for accepting the plan and then refusing to reconsider; and the General Staff, for not daring to protest in time. Whatever the cause, the troops paid the price: 267,000 men lost, including more than 200,000 captured.[66] In addition, recollected Vasilevsky, it was their victory at Kharkov that enabled the Germans to break through toward Stalingrad and the Caucasus.[67]

Khrushchev paid a lesser price that, as usual, Stalin doled out slowly and painfully. After demoting Bagramian and Timoshenko, he dissolved the southwest sector altogether and summoned Khrushchev to Moscow. "I was very depressed," Khrushchev later noted. "We had lost many, many thousands of men. More than that, we had lost the hope we had been living by. . . . To make matters worse, it looked as if I were going to have to take the blame for it personally." For Stalin "would stop at nothing to avoid taking the responsibility for something that had gone wrong. As I flew toward Moscow I . . . put myself in the hands of fate. I was ready for anything, including arrest."

Stalin toyed with his intended victim for several days. Were the Germans lying when they claimed capture of more than two hundred thousand men? "No, Comrade Stalin," Khrushchev answered. During World War I a tsarist general was hanged, Stalin continued, when his army fell into German hands. "I remember this event well, Comrade Stalin," replied Khrushchev.

Khrushchev endured the suspense (the two dined together several times) with seeming good cheer. Stalin mixed veiled threats with practical questions about how to defend the Donbas. The longer Khrushchev stayed, "the more wearisome and painful became the process of waiting to see what would happen to me. I doubted very much that Stalin would forgive the defeat. He still must have wanted to find a scapegoat. Here was a chance to demonstrate his implacable toughness and dedication. . . . I knew exactly how Stalin would formulate his revenge. He was a master at this sort of thing."

To Khrushchev's immense relief, he was allowed to return to the front. But the royal pardon might be a trap; Khrushchev knew of "many cases when Stalin would reassure people by letting them leave his office with good news, and then have them picked up and taken somewhere other than the place they expected. But nothing happened to me during the night after I left his office, and the next morning I flew back to the front."[68]

Stalin's fury did not abate. Later that summer, in the presence of several commanders, he picked with a match at tobacco in his famous pipe and then tapped the pipe on Khrushchev's bald pate, covering it with ashes. "That's in accordance with Roman tradition," Stalin explained to his stunned audience. "When a Roman commander lost a battle, he lit a bonfire, sat down in front of it, and poured ashes on his own head. In those days, that was considered the greatest disgrace a commander could endure."[69]

Unlike Bagramian and Timoshenko, Khrushchev wasn't even demoted but appointed instead to the Stalingrad front's Military Council. But he was humbled ("I'm not competent enough in strictly military matters," he replied when asked to lobby for more resources in Moscow, "so it will be hard for me to persuade supreme headquarters"),[70] and the pain endured. "Many years later," he said in retirement, "this issue is still weighing on me. I think about it constantly. It was a landmark in my life, a painful landmark."[71] According to his daughter, Rada, "He agonized over it to the end of his days."[72] If only his Kharkov warnings had been heeded! If only the bolder Zhukov had been in Vasilevsky's place![73] Nowhere did Khrushchev admit to his own responsibility.[74]

IN 1942 Hitler's plan was to conquer the southern reaches of the Soviet Union, including the vital oil fields of the Caucasus, before turning north toward Moscow. The capital understood, Zhukov recalled, that if Stalingrad fell, the Germans "would be able to cut off the south of the country from the center. We might also lose the Volga, the country's most important waterway. . . ."[75]

Khrushchev was at Stalingrad when the German assault began in August and throughout the awful months that followed. "Each building in Stalingrad became its own battle-ground," the military historian John Erickson writes, "with fortresses fashioned out of factories, railway stations, separate streets or small squares and finally single walls." The giant Stalingrad tractor factory became the site of savage nighttime engagements that littered its workshops with corpses. After these battles, maimed Soviet soldiers crawled to the banks of the Volga, where, if they were lucky, boats ferried them to the other side in the midst of a fiery German bombardment. At one point in late October the territory controlled by the Soviets on the west bank shrank to a thousand yards.[76] By November, however, the Red Army was preparing the surprise counteroffensive that broke the back of the Wehrmacht.

Khrushchev's role was to mediate between the generals in Stalingrad and supreme headquarters in Moscow. Stalin consulted him before appointing or firing commanders like Andrei Yeremenko and Vasily

Chuikov. Prior to the Soviet counterattack, he shuttled from front to front, checking on troop readiness and morale, personally interrogating German prisoners, recruiting some of them for propaganda, and preventing others (or so he insisted) from being executed or otherwise abused by their Soviet captors.[77]

Khrushchev was almost killed when German planes bombed his command post. He was south of the city when German Messerschmitts attacked Soviet bombers heading for the front. Their planes in flames, several Soviet pilots bailed out, only to be fired on by Soviet infantry who mistook them for Germans. Khrushchev remembered how one pilot screamed, "'I'm one of you! I'm one of you!' Then there was a burst of machine-gun fire, and it was all over."[78]

Thousands of German corpses were dug out of the frozen ground, stacked in layers alternating with railway ties, and set afire. "I didn't go back a second time," Khrushchev recalled. "Napoleon or someone once said that burning enemy corpses smell good. Well, speaking for myself, I don't agree."[79]

The filmmaker Dovzhenko, who was traveling with Khrushchev, described a scene the two of them witnessed: "An airplane was lying in the road, still burning: not more than half an hour had elapsed since it crashed. Near the airplane lay the pilot—legless, charred, with a white skull, armless. Naked white bones protruded from his shoulders. The co-pilot had been tossed out and lay at a distance. His head was shattered. The pink brain, hemispheres separated, lay in the stubble and large green flies crawled over it. I looked at the pilot's face, which had been covered with a cloth. A dark, bloody hole gaped in his forehead. That was where his brain had come out."[80]

Perhaps Khrushchev thought of Lyonia. Scenes like this soured him forever on war. Still, he kept his balance. General Rodion Malinovsky's widow, who ran a mess hall for officers at one of the fronts, recalled a moment when German bombs were crashing ever closer, and she huddled in a corner expecting to die. In walked Khrushchev grinning broadly. "What's so awful?" he asked brightly.[81]

In contrast with Kiev and Kharkov, Khrushchev's role at Stalingrad was unambiguously positive. Yet he was touchy about how his contribution compared with others' and especially about how Stalin perceived it. He later chided Zhukov and Vasilevsky for claiming to have proposed the decisive Stalingrad counteroffensive: "Zhukov visited Stalingrad only once. He stayed with us awhile and never appeared there again. He arrived when the decision to launch the operation had already been taken."[82] The main thing, Khrushchev insisted, was to celebrate "the victory of our people," not to argue over who achieved it,[83] but as usual, he violated his own rule. He didn't claim sole authorship of the Stalingrad counteroffensive, but he certainly took credit for a large part of it.[84]

Zhukov was no more modest than Khrushchev, but his account is more convincing. By October 6, when Khrushchev and Yeremenko proposed a counteroffensive, the Supreme Command and the General Staff had already opted for one. The reason Khrushchev didn't know that, according to Zhukov, was that "the Supreme Commander had warned me to keep the draft plan for a big counter-offensive a strict secret."[85]

Khrushchev wanted to be part of the action in Moscow as well—precisely because he *wasn't* as influential as he later portrayed himself to be. Several times he asked Vasilevsky to get Stalin to invite him. "Why don't you call him yourself?" Vasilevsky asked. But "Khrushchev found excuses not to and insisted that I do the calling: 'It's easier for you to call. He's already summoned you.' "

"What's with him?" Stalin asked when Vasilevsky gave in and interceded on Khrushchev's behalf. "Why does he want to come to Moscow? Why is that necessary?" Stalin finally agreed, "All right. Take him with you. Let him fly up."[86]

Khrushchev resented those who saw more of Stalin than he did, especially when they swooped down on his own domain. Part of the problem was the built-in conflict between supreme headquarters and field commands: Stalin couldn't understand the dilemmas of local commanders, yet his emissaries insisted on limiting local initiative. There was also ego and envy involved, as well as fear that Stalin's fantasies would focus on Khrushchev's "disloyalty" if he weren't in the great man's presence as often as possible.

"Whenever the situation was looking gravest," Khrushchev said later, "Malenkov would fly in with Vasilevsky, [Nikolai] Voronov, [Aleksandr] Novikov or some other representative of the General Staff. Frankly, I was never very pleased to see them. . . . These celebrities always chose the wrong time to make a personal appearance, and they weren't very popular at our command post when they showed up. It was so crowded you could hardly move."[87]

Khrushchev was particularly irritated when Malenkov and Vasilevsky went off in a corner to confer. "Always at the most critical moment, I sensed that Stalin was paying especially keen attention to me and that he had sent Malenkov to keep an eye on me. I would notice Vasilevsky and Malenkov whispering together. Malenkov would have to return to

Moscow and report to Stalin about why the battle was going so badly, and naturally he wanted to avoid any personal responsibility for what was happening. In his whispered talks with Vasilevsky, Malenkov was preparing to denounce someone, and I knew I was the obvious choice. He didn't know anything about military matters, but he was more than competent when it came to intriguing."[88] About the only useful legacy Malenkov left in Stalingrad, Khrushchev contended, was "a luxurious toilet—although, to tell the truth, it only remained in mint condition until the emissaries departed and then it became impossible to enter."[89]

Khrushchev denied that he craved access to Stalin—but he contradicted his own point. If he kept mentioning such sessions in his memoirs, he wrote, that was because "after all, I was a member of military councils at the front, and of the Politburo, and Stalin knew me well, and reckoned with me. . . ."[90]

As the war progressed, Khrushchev warmed toward Stalin again, partly because the boss seemed to be warming toward him. As Soviet fortunes improved, and with them Stalin's mood, it became positively "pleasant" to report to him, Khrushchev recollected.[91] Throughout the war his field reports seem designed to please or amuse Stalin. Two June 1942 dispatches contain excerpts from a dead German officer's diary and compared the American M-3 tank unfavorably with Soviet tanks.[92] Not to mention Khrushchev's story of a hot exchange between a general and colonel that ceased abruptly when the general barked, "Comrade Colonel, do not forget yourself!" He remembered, "Stalin really liked this one. Many years later, he would smile and say, 'Comrade Colonel, do not forget yourself!' What he meant, of course, was that a junior personage must subordinate himself to a senior. . . ."[93]

No matter how hard he tried, however, Khrushchev couldn't entirely satisfy his master. In March 1943, Zhukov recalled, Stalin telephoned Khrushchev on the Voronezh front and "sharply berated him" for the "failure to take action against the enemy's counterblows. During the same conversation he reminded Khrushchev of all his errors on the southwestern front during the summer battles of 1942."[94] Another source confirmed that "when Golikov and Khrushchev lost control of their men on the Voronezh Front at Belgorod, Zhukov virtually took over command. . . ."[95]

In July 1943 the biggest tank battle in history took place at Kursk, pitting nearly four thousand Soviet tanks against some three thousand German tanks and assault guns.[96] Khrushchev naturally remembered Kursk from his own vantage point, but his emphasis on his own role was almost certainly exaggerated.[97] He claimed that an SS defector informed him that the Germans were preparing to attack the next day and that he called Moscow to alert the high command: "Stalin listened calmly as I explained the situation. He wasn't rude or impatient as he had sometimes been in the past. This pleased me."[98] Khrushchev said that Stalin asked him to recommend a response and that he answered as follows: "Our defensive positions are solid, and we'll make the enemy pay in blood when he tries to break through. Even though we're still waiting for the reinforcements, we'll be able to hold our ground. It takes fewer forces to defend than it does to attack."

Whether Khrushchev dared instruct Stalin on such basics or only remembered it that way, the recollection triggered a moment of embarrassed self-awareness: "Whenever I say Stalin called me, I'm not claiming he didn't call the commander as well. I don't want people thinking, 'There goes Khrushchev, building himself up again, all the time saying, "I, I, I."' No, my esteemed friends, I'm not trying to build myself up. I'm just trying to tell you what happened as I saw it. . . . Even if [Stalin] did sometimes make me a scapegoat . . . he still had great confidence in me. He often called and asked my opinion. He did so when I was in Stalingrad and in the South, and he did so here at the Kursk Salient."[99]

DMITRI SUKHANOV first met Khrushchev in 1940. At Stalingrad, Khrushchev struck him as "an intriguer," a man who "loved to criticize others but couldn't take criticism himself," a person who "liked to be surrounded by flatterers" and "loved his privileges. He had his own cook with him at the front; he loved to eat (Stalin liked that) and he drank his share too. When he was a member of the Military Council, he had his own special bodyguards, right there at the front."[100]

Sukhanov too had reason to hate Khrushchev (a longtime aide to Malenkov, he was arrested after his patron's fall), but his testimony isn't entirely untrustworthy. That Khrushchev had his own cook and bodyguards isn't surprising, nor that a man who expended so much energy liked to eat well. But a friendlier witness who spent a lot of time with Khrushchev during the war, the filmmaker Dovzhenko, shared the impression that he surrounded himself with shallow and superficial aides.[101]

In early 1943, when Khrushchev was already selecting party and government cadres to run the postwar Ukraine, he summoned Communist Youth League official Vasily Kostenko to a command post in a forest. His "small, bright eyes felt as if they were drilling into me," Kostenko recalled.

"I tried not to say too much, mostly answering yes and no while he did the talking. He loved to talk; he'd get carried away. It was a normal, democratic conversation." But although Khrushchev "seemed simple and unsophisticated, he didn't like or permit familiarity, and he liked it and accepted it when certain people bowed down before him."

It turned out Khrushchev wanted Kostenko to head the Ukrainian Komsomol. Asked if he knew his predecessors as Komsomol leaders, Kostenko thought: "What kind of question is that? After all, almost every Komsomol secretary had been wiped out, at least one of them after N. S. [Khrushchev] himself arrived in Kiev."

Kostenko answered that he knew them. "Which ones?" Khrushchev wanted to know. Kostenko answered "Twelve." Khrushchev demanded, "Give me a list of them."

"That request really shook me up," Kostenko said. "Why did he want it? But I typed it up and brought it in."

"Drive over to the NKVD office [in the next town]," Khrushchev ordered, "and give them this list in my name. Let them find out through Beria's office which of the people on the list are still alive."

Kostenko did as he was told. When he picked up the list two months later, he found a minus sign in red pencil next to every name. "No one was left alive," he recalled. He took the list back to Khrushchev and found him alone in his office. "I told him that I had the list and that no one on it was still alive. He stood up, walked over to the window, looked out, and then paced around the room. He turned to me and said, 'They destroyed people for no reason.'"[102]

Later in 1943 Khrushchev's aide Pavel Gapochka sent another list of forty-eight Ukrainian intellectuals—historians, artists, writers, musicians, linguists, and physicists—to the Ukrainian NKVD chief Sergei Savchenko. Savchenko was to find out which ones "could be returned to Ukraine to take part in scientific or cultural work." Of forty-six people on whom the NKVD claimed to have data, twenty-six had been sentenced to "the highest measure of punishment" (with "the sentence duly implemented") and sixteen more had been imprisoned with "no further information about location available at this time."[103]

No record of Khrushchev's reaction exists. But his preparation of the two lists has several implications: It confirms that he didn't know the full extent of the terror; it belies his claim to have discovered the truth only in the 1950s; it shows that even at the height of the war, culture and the men and women who created it were on Khrushchev's mind. He took time out during the conflict to respond to letters and petitions of all sorts from Ukrainian intellectuals.[104] He made sure the poet Tychyna was admitted to the party;[105] he invited Dovzhenko, who was in good odor again by this time, to travel with him at the front.[106]

Khrushchev appreciated the propaganda uses of photography and film and made sure he got his share of personal exposure on both. His assistant Gapochka also served as his unofficial photographer, constantly "shooting" Khrushchev throughout the war. Dovzhenko submitted cinematic plans to Khrushchev and received advice in return. Several days before the Kharkov disaster, Khrushchev found time to instruct his pupil on some not so fine points of Marxism and national consciousness, stressing his love for Ukraine but worrying that Ukrainians had "forgotten Marxism and history."[107]

He proposed that "a historical document be compiled about the liberation of Ukraine from the Nazi yoke. Make the document solemn, meaningful, and beautiful so that the people will remember it for ages to come, so that it will be reprinted in anthologies, and memorized and quoted." What a "beautiful, brilliant thought on the part of N. S.," Dovzhenko confided to his diary. "Must become involved in this work. Length: 15–20 pages, maybe less. Must prepare myself for this work. Need statements by poets, writers, and composers. Here N. S. also raised the question of a Ukrainian anthem."[108]

In the summer of 1943 Dovzhenko presented his patron with a scenario for a film to be titled *Ukraine in Flames*: "I read the scenario to N. S. until two o'clock in the morning in the village. After I had finished, we had a rather long and pleasant conversation. N. S. liked the scenario very much, and he expressed the view that it ought to be published as a separate book, in both Russian and Ukrainian. So that people can read about it, so that they learn that it wasn't so easy."[109]

The image of Khrushchev's blessing a movie scenario in the predawn darkness is priceless, but the consequences for Dovzhenko were not. Khrushchev gave his permission to publish the scenario "immediately and in its entirety."[110] But Stalin didn't like it. "To put it mildly," he told the Politburo in January 1944, "this work revises Leninism. . . . Dovzhenko's scenario contains the crudest sort of anti-Leninist mistakes. It is an open attack against the policy of the party. Anyone who reads Dovzhenko's 'Ukraine in Flames' can see that it is precisely that sort of attack."[111]

Anyone except for Khrushchev. Perhaps his strong feelings for Ukraine's wartime suffering blinded him to the scenario's "errors": the fact that it focused on ordinary villagers and mentioned Stalin only four times; the paucity of non-Ukrainian characters; the veiled references to the way Soviet rule had rendered Ukraine vulnerable to Hitler's attack. Obviously, Khrushchev missed what Dovzhenko regarded as the point of his script: "We were wrong to give up the whole of Ukraine to that damn Hitler, and we liberate Ukraine badly. We, the liberators . . . are to some extent guilty . . . toward the liberated. Yet we look down on them and think they're guilty toward us."[112] No wonder Khrushchev refused to see Dovzhenko on December 31, 1943, and that on January 3, 1944, their meeting went badly. Dovzhenko confided to his diary: "It seemed as if he wasn't N. S. and I wasn't myself," as if he were "a cold, merciless atheist and judge" and Dovzhenko "a guilty amoral criminal and enemy of the people." Khrushchev had said: "We'll come back to a consideration of your work yet. We won't just leave it as it is." Dovzhenko's diary continued: "Lord, give me strength. Send me the wisdom to forgive good N. S. who showed himself to be small in stature, for he is a weak person."[113]

At Stalin's behest, Khrushchev supervised Dovzhenko's punishment, signing the order that led to his dismissal as artistic director of the Kiev film studio. The filmmaker's fall signaled Stalin's shift from using Ukrainian nationalism against the Germans to attacking it again as bourgeois and reactionary. But behind the scenes Khrushchev tried to limit the anti-Dovzhenko campaign, if only to prevent it from incriminating himself.[114] He admitted to Stalin that he had read *Ukraine in Flames*, but claimed that "three fourths of my attention had been taken up by the enemy attack, and I hadn't been able to concentrate on the text of Dovzhenko's work. I explained this to Stalin. He said I was trying to weasel out of my responsibility for what had happened. . . ."[115]

Stalin was right. Khrushchev was prevaricating. After Stalin died, he saw to it that Dovzhenko was "rehabilitated."[116]

KHRUSHCHEV ADMIRED military officers who were brave, tireless, conscientious, and incorruptible. He despised those who were crude and uncultured, or dandified and pretentious, especially those who bragged and drank to excess. In short, the qualities he did or didn't like in others were those he valued or resisted in himself.

He felt a special kinship for Rodion Malinovsky, who later became his defense minister. Malinovsky's origins were even humbler than Khrushchev's, but he too had managed to transcend them. "I don't think his mother was married," Khrushchev recalled. "In any case, he'd never known his father. He was raised by his aunt. . . ."[117] It's not easy to imagine

Khrushchev and the granite-faced Malinovsky reminiscing about their mothers. Khrushchev also remembered Malinovsky with "tears streaming down his face" at news that a friend and fellow officer had committed suicide. It was a suicide note, on which "Long Live Lenin!" was written just above the signature, that got Malinovsky into trouble with Stalin. Because the note didn't say, "Long Live Stalin!," the dictator assigned Khrushchev "to spy on Malinovsky every hour of the day. I had to watch him even when he went to bed to see if he closed his eyes and went to sleep." After Stalin died, Khrushchev revealed his role—only to learn that Malinovsky "had known all along why I was following him around and taking quarters next to his." Fortunately, added Khrushchev, Malinovsky had "understood the awkwardness of my position and hadn't held it against me. He had known that as long as he did an honest and competent job, I wouldn't interfere with him and I would give a good report on him to Stalin."

A prudent thing to say to a man who was now Malinovsky's boss! But apart from revealing Malinovsky's adroitness, the story confirms three things about Khrushchev: He resented Stalin's instructions ("I didn't like having to [spy on Malinovsky] one bit"); he followed them anyway; and twenty-five years later he still basked in the thought that it was his influence on Stalin that saved the day. "I don't know what actually saved Malinovsky. . . . Perhaps it had something to do with my own intervention on his behalf that Malinovsky was spared. After all, my influence with Stalin was not inconsiderable."[118]

Andrei Grechko, who worked closely with Khrushchev in Kiev after the war and commanded Warsaw Pact forces beginning in 1960, arrived at Khrushchev's command post before the operation to liberate Kiev. "I remember the sun was setting," Khrushchev observed later. "It was a warm evening, though autumn was already setting in. We had come outdoors with our burkas thrown back over our shoulders. Grechko drove up and reported directly to me. I had known him a long time and respected him very much, so I allowed myself to joke about his incredible height: 'Comrade Grechko, please stand back a bit so I can look you in the eye.' He laughed."[119]

Khrushchev loved being the down-to-earth comrade to whom the brave Grechko conveyed his news, the boon companion of stouthearted men who deferred to him. "I'm not without certain human weaknesses, including pride," Khrushchev admitted, "and I'm certainly pleased to have been a member of the Military Council. . . ."[120] Even Vasilevsky, whom Khrushchev later forced into retirement, conceded that Khrushchev was "energetic, brave and constantly with the troops. He never sat around in offices or at headquarters, but kept trying to see and talk to people, and I must admit those people liked him."

Once, as Vasilevsky and Khrushchev drove across the steppe near the Volga, they stopped to eat in an abandoned lean-to near the road. Not far away stood an elderly couple. "The man was bearded and sullen-looking," Vasilevsky recalled, and when Khrushchev greeted them and asked, "How's life?" the man grunted. "What do you mean, how's life? What kind of life is this?"

It turned out the man had been a collective farm chairman near the Black Sea, and he had once met and talked with "Mikita." The Ukrainian party leader was now wearing an ordinary-looking overcoat, a cap without a general's insignia, and no other sign that he was in fact Khrushchev. "Don't you recognize this man?" Vasilevsky asked.

"No, I don't."

"Come on! Take a close look!"

The old man stared and then cried out (referring to Khrushchev in the second-person familiar form), "Is it really you, Mikita? Are you here too?"

"Khrushchev couldn't have been more delighted," Vasilevsky concluded. "He began to embrace the old man, who embraced him back no less enthusiastically. After that, of course, Khrushchev invited him to join us for breakfast."[121]

RECROSSING THE DNIEPER would have been costly under any circumstances, but Stalin insisted that Kiev fall no later than November 5 or 6, in time for the twenty-sixth anniversary of the revolution on November 7, 1943.[122] Soviet troops and tanks forded the river not far from Khrushchev's dacha at Mezhgorie.[123] On liberation day, several U.S.-provided lend-lease jeeps carried the top brass into the shattered city, Zhukov and his bodyguards in the first one, Khrushchev with Dovzhenko, behind them. "I can't express the emotion which overwhelmed me as I drove along the road to Kiev," Khrushchev explained later. "It was an old familiar one we used to take to and from our dacha before the war. We passed through the suburbs and came to the Kreshchatik. . . ." Across from the Central Department Store, he greeted a short, bearded old man who "threw himself on my shoulder and kissed me on both cheeks. I was very touched." A photograph taken that morning shows Khrushchev comforting a tearful woman, himself weeping as he embraces her.[124]

Later the cortege drove up to the Shevchenko monument to which Khrushchev bowed his head in respect. Kiev University, which the Germans had torched before leaving, was still burning. "The barbarians themselves should be burned!" Khrushchev shouted to Zhukov.[125] Mixed with anger was elation: "It was a special joy for me. After all, I had to 'answer' for Ukraine, I was the Central Committee secretary of its Communist party, and I'd spent my childhood and youth there. . . ."[126]

The final victory over Hitler was even more satisfying.[127] But Khrushchev's joy had an ironic effect. The fact that so many fought and died for the Soviet system deepened his faith in socialism. The elation of victory further buttressed his creed. Khrushchev even remembered to think of Stalin. After Kiev was retaken, he sent a note to the *vozhd* "because I simply wanted to make Stalin happy for a while."[128] After the German capitulation, he telephoned his congratulations, only to receive a rebuke in return. "What [Stalin] wanted to get across," Khrushchev recalled, "was that I was taking up his valuable time. What he said froze me to the ground. How could he react that way? I felt very bad and cursed myself out: why had I phoned him? After all, I knew his character and couldn't have expected any good to come of it. I knew that he would want to show me that the past was past and he was now thinking about great new deeds."[129]

CHAPTER EIGHT

Ukrainian Viceroy Again: 1944–1949

Seventeen hundred towns and townships destroyed, seventy thousand villages and hamlets burned to the ground, thirty-two thousand factories blown up or rendered unusable, fifty-two thousand miles of railway track demolished, one hundred thousand collective and state farms laid waste. As the result of the war, Stalin's economic administrator, Nikolai Voznesensky, informed him in January 1946, the USSR lost 30 percent of its national wealth.[1]

Ukraine's share of the losses was proportionately even more staggering: about 5.3 million, or 1 in every 6 inhabitants, killed; an additional 2.3 million shipped to forced labor in Germany; more than seven hundred cities and towns and twenty-eight thousand villages in ruins; sixteen thousand industrial enterprises and twenty-eight thousand collective farms completely or partially destroyed; 40 percent of the national wealth gone.[2]

Statistics, even as stunning as these, fail to convey the pain and suffering. They also obscure the sense of hope that sustained many throughout the war, hope that their terrible sacrifices would lead to a better life, that the regime would come to trust those who had saved it from destruction, that terror and intolerance would subside, that collective farms, which had disintegrated during the war, would not be reimposed. For many, the writer Boris Pasternak recalled, the war seemed "an omen of deliverance, a purifying storm." He wrote: "So many sacrifices cannot result in nothing," and "a presage of freedom was in the air." Andrei Sakharov remembered: "We all believed—or at least hoped—that the postwar world would be decent and humane. How could it be otherwise?"[3] All too easily it turned out.

Khrushchev too hoped for change. Not, of course, for liberalization or Westernization; he was committed to reimposing party control, to rebuilding collective farms, to crushing nationalist guerrillas in western Ukraine. What he did not want was a return to what he regarded as "excesses" of the prewar period, to the famine of the early thirties, to the persecution of Ukrainian intellectuals he had taken under his wing.

In his own way, Khrushchev loved Ukraine and the Ukrainian people, and he believed that "the Ukrainian people regarded me favorably."[4] He had seen their suffering close up during the war and was determined to help them recover. His version of Ukrainian patriotism was overlaid with Communist internationalism and pursued within strict Soviet limits, but it was real. He was prepared to stand up to Stalin on occasion, yet the same Khrushchev led a savage war against nationalist partisans in western Ukraine. Though he helped rebuild the economy, the very system he re-created contributed to renewed famine. He lobbied Stalin to stop Ukrainian starvation, but that led the *vozhd* to demote him as Ukrainian party leader.

The immediate postwar period combined tragedy and farce. The western Ukrainian civil war featured barbarism by both sides as well as madcap dissembling by officials trying to avoid getting killed. The 1946 famine led to cannibalism in the countryside but also to a reprise of Khrushchev's contradictory role in the doomed Kharkov offensive of 1942. Stalin credited the Russian people in particular for his victory over Hitler. "Any other people," he declared in a May 1945 victory toast, "might have said to its government: you have not fulfilled our expectations, away with you, we shall conclude a peace with Germany and bring us rest."[5] Stalin had deported whole peoples, such as the Crimean Tatars, the Kalmyks, Balkars, Chechens, and Ingush, whom he accused of collaborating with the Nazis. "The Ukrainians avoided meeting this fate," Khrushchev said in his 1956 secret speech, "only because there were too many of them and there was no place to which to deport them. Otherwise he would have deported them also."[6]

Khrushchev's distinctive character played a supporting role in this postwar surrealism. When it came to crushing nationalist guerrillas or collectivizing western Ukrainian agriculture, he promised far more than even he could deliver. When his broken promises threatened his self-esteem as well as his political position, he bullied and browbeat his subordinates and took comfort in an absurd cult of his own personality.

In early 1947 Stalin fired Khrushchev as the Ukrainian party leader (while allowing him to remain head of the Ukrainian government) and dispatched Lazar Kaganovich from Moscow to replace him. In short order, Khrushchev disappeared from public view, fell gravely ill, and nearly died. Behold, another miracle! By the fall of 1947 he had regained his health, and Stalin reappointed him party chief. Moreover, 1948 and 1949, among the worst years in Soviet history, proved perhaps the most satisfying of Khrushchev's career.

THE RED ARMY liberated Lvov in July 1944, soon reached the frontier established as part of Stalin's 1939 deal with Hitler, and raced on toward Germany and Berlin. The new border incorporated western Ukraine in the USSR, but it had yet to be accepted as permanent by the rest of the world.

By late 1944 Khrushchev's mission was Ukrainian reconstruction. But he couldn't resist engaging in what amounted to military tourism. When Mikoyan visited Kiev, Khrushchev took him on a tour of nearby battlefields. Khrushchev kept dropping by the front so as "to spend some time with my military comrades, to listen to them, to have a look at German territory . . . , to look in German eyes and read on their faces how . . . the war that Hitler had unleashed against us tasted to them."[7] Even in Kiev, he followed the war's progress on the phone. One day a jubilant Zhukov telephoned and said, "Soon I'll have that slimy beast Hitler locked up in a cage. And when I send him to Moscow, I'll ship him by way of Kiev so you can have a look at him."[8]

As western Ukrainian territory was reconquered in the summer of 1944, 750,000 men were conscripted. All men between nineteen and fifty, regardless of the state of their health, were given inferior arms and sent into battle after only eight days of training. To hear Khrushchev tell it, "the recruits from the liberated areas understood their duty and didn't need to be preached at about their obligation to join the ranks of the Soviet Army . . . ." Actually, many resisted the draft or deserted as soon as they could, influenced by nationalist partisans, who now launched all-out war against the re-Sovietization of Ukraine.[9]

Those left to rebuild the Ukrainian economy were, besides miners, engineers, and skilled workers exempted from military service, "old men, invalids, those unfit for military service, and particularly the women."

Khrushchev swore that all these, "including many young girls, worked willingly. Their zeal was understandable. For one thing, patriotism drew many of them to the cause." His only hint that the whole effort wasn't a picnic was his acknowledgment that people were drawn to industrial labor because "there was more food in the cities than in the villages."[10] Khrushchev himself reassumed direct control of the Ukrainian party apparatus in 1943. In February 1944 he was named head of the Ukrainian government as well, the only Soviet leader other than Stalin to combine those two top posts.

Although he served Stalin faithfully, Khrushchev resisted what he could safely condemn as errors of lower-level officials rather than as essential features of the Soviet system. Soviet citizens who had remained in German-occupied territory, and soldiers taken prisoner by the Germans, were suspect in Stalin's eyes and subject to severe punishment. Khrushchev asserted he protected such people ("It was we after all who abandoned all of Ukraine, so that those who stayed behind have a right to accuse us of leaving and forsaking them"[11]), and available evidence supports his claim. At an April 1944 meeting of party personnel specialists, he called those who stayed behind "our people" and warned his listeners not to "smear" them.[12] That same spring he again sought out his old Yuzovka friend Ilya Kosenko. Kosenko wasn't there when he arrived, but when his daughter Olga overheard an aide tell Khrushchev that Kosenko had survived the war in occupied territory, she blurted out, "Then why have you come to visit him if it was wrong to remain under the Germans? He wasn't using his skills for them; he was cleaning toilets. Otherwise, they would have put a noose around his neck." Khrushchev patted her head and exclaimed, "Well done! What a good daughter you are! One who knows how to defend her father!"[13]

In a long letter to Stalin in July 1944, Khrushchev described meeting former Soviet POWs. All of them, he reported, had feared to flee lest the Germans kill them or, as the Germans had warned them, lest they be shot or hanged by the Soviets themselves. "We must unmask the German lie that we ourselves will arrest and execute such people," Khrushchev advised Stalin. "We should spread around leaflets urging Russians, Ukrainians and Byelorussians to scatter into the woods."[14] Leaflets or not, former prisoners of war *were* arrested and sent to Soviet prison camps. But by portraying the alleged practice as a German lie, Khrushchev was lobbying cautiously against it.

He was more open and direct at a Ukrainian Central Committee plenum a year later. The security police had arrested a civilian in Odessa

Province who paraded around in a military uniform trying to nominate Marshal Zhukov to the Supreme Soviet. Khrushchev chastised the Odessa Province party chief: "Why not have party members deal with it? Why did the NKVD have to get involved? Maybe it was just the man's mood, or perhaps he is psychologically disturbed . . . . I don't see this as an anti-Soviet act. [Laughter in the hall.] But you call in [police] organs that are designed for other matters. That sort of behavior will discredit . . . our system. That's no way to act. It's going to be awkward now when I meet with Zhukov. He'll ask me why we arrested someone who was supporting his candidacy, and whether it's some sort of joke, this being Odessa and all. Well, it's actually stupidity pretending to be vigilance, that's what it is."

At the same plenum the Chernovtsy Province propaganda chief crowed about disciplining a peasant woman who dared ask why there was no kerosene or salt for sale in her "great and all-powerful" country. "What you should do," Khrushchev interjected, "is tell her when there *will* be kerosene and salt. It's not right that you didn't tell her. If I were she, I would have asked you the same question. . . . You may not need kerosene because you have electricity, but they do." When the same official labeled another "hostile" peasant a "kulak," Khrushchev blasted him again: "So he's a kulak, is he? Did you check to make sure? I know what's going on: You don't check, but you repeat it anyway. What you're doing is primitively classifying people as if this were a political game."[15]

THE PARTY and government rebuilding Ukraine needed rebuilding themselves. Already depleted by terror, official ranks were further reduced by the war. By late 1946, Khrushchev reported, 38 percent of district party secretaries, 64 percent of local soviet chairmen, and more than 60 percent of machine tractor station directors had been replaced, usually by outsiders sent from Russia or into western Ukraine from the east. Organizing, energizing, and inspiring these new cadres were Khrushchev's métier; accompanied by a large retinue of officials, he rushed from one Ukrainian province to another in 1944 and 1945. The USSR depended on Donbas coal, but sentiment too accounted for his presence in Stalino on his fiftieth birthday. He descended into a mine where he had worked as a young man; a newsreel shows him in a miner's outfit, lighting the lamp on his helmet and smiling broadly. He appealed to former fellow townsmen to supplement food supplies by raising rabbits and chickens, catching fish, and expanding vegetable gardening. When local leaders expressed skepticism, he pointed at a nearby wetland. "Here's a little swamp which is empty. Water from the mines flows by here toward the steppe without being used. Do you realize what remarkable cabbage could be grown right here? And what terrific tomatoes over there?"[16]

Petrovo-Marinsky, where he had been party secretary in 1925 and 1926, was also graced by his presence in 1944. Although the district center was in ruins, local officials had put the reopening of factories and mines first. Khrushchev corrected them: "Before that, you must feed people and provide them with water and only then work on the factories." The local party chief Glukhov's only means of transportation was a broken-down truck, so Khrushchev commandeered a car in Kiev. "Can you imagine," Glukhov marveled decades later, "he took it upon himself to send it? Without even being asked."[17]

Kalinovka too, just across the border in Russia, got a visit, but only after Stalin shamed Khrushchev into going. According to Khrushchev's close aide Andrei Shevchenko, Stalin teasingly asked Khrushchev where he was from.

"From Kalinovka," Khrushchev answered.

"Where's that?" Stalin asked.

"In Kursk Province," replied Khrushchev.

"When's the last time you were there?

"Not for a long time," Khrushchev said.

"Well, that doesn't do you any honor," Stalin said.[18]

Of some 800 men who had left Kalinovka for the front, only 276 returned. There were no draft animals left, no electricity, no machinery. "All we had for light was torches," a resident recalled forty-five years later. "We scraped the bark off birches, and in the evening we wove bast shoes by the light of the fire. That's how bad it was."

"He came right out to the fields where we were using cows to plow," a wizened old woman remembered. "He drove up and talked with us. We wanted to show him some hospitality, but we had nothing to offer. I remember we went looking for something in Fedosia Lavrentievna's house. But Nikita Sergeyevich ended up providing *us* with food: watermelons, braised chicken, hot tea."

"We were threshing grain next to our hut when he came up," added a grizzled old man. "My grandmother brought up a chair and said, 'Sit down. You're our tsar.' 'No, I'm not,' he joked, 'I'm the tsarevich.'"[19]

According to Shevchenko, who accompanied his boss to Kalinovka, the peasants desperately needed horses. At Khrushchev's request, his old friend General Grechko sent fifty large German cart horses which needed to be fed lots of grain. When Khrushchev returned the next year, he found the horses dying off. "They were eating up everything we had," the peasants explained.

"What did you want"—Khrushchev lit into them—"that they not eat at all? How can you behave this way after I sent you horses?"

Frustrated and chagrined, he ordered Shevchenko to find an enlightened collective farm chairman for Kalinovka. Several appointees proved unsatisfactory, but after assorted adventures, including a night in a peasant hut during which a calf started chewing on one candidate's hair, Shevchenko finally found a good one. Although Khrushchev continued to provide assistance, it kept falling victim to the "backward" thinking he was trying so hard to overcome. When a cousin living in Kalinovka later asked for help in building a new house, Khrushchev pulled out five hundred rubles he had earned as a Supreme Soviet deputy; Shevchenko had to explain to him that a house cost far more than that. The cousin's old hut was a shambles, but when Shevchenko offered her a flat in a planned apartment house, she demanded to know where she'd keep her pig. Shevchenko explained that the collective farm would provide what she needed, but she turned down her cousin's offer.

Khrushchev was livid. Shevchenko recalled telling him, "You don't entirely understand the peasant's psychology." Khrushchev growled: "Go to hell. What do you mean she needs a little land? Lenin decreed there would be no individual farming, but you're wallowing in the idea of personal property and can't tear yourself out of it."[20]

Like the good Marxist he wanted to be, Khrushchev believed in reducing the difference between town and country so all could live equally well. Such a "paradise" was farther off than ever in 1944 and 1945, but he kept it in mind. He dreamed of surrounding Kiev with a huge garden zone. "He wanted to plow up and cultivate a million acres between the Dnieper and the Irpen' rivers," Shevchenko recollected. "He wanted to plant vegetables for Kiev, especially Ukrainian ones like huge pumpkins and early radishes. Taking his cue from gas pipelines, he proposed building pipes to pump milk from five hundred thousand cows in the zone into the city. The milk would arrive at so-called transfer bases, from which it would be delivered fresh and steamy to beautiful new stores. Khrushchev set up a commission and ordered it to figure how many pipes, roads, and houses would be needed. He appointed as chief agronomist an awful, vile woman with no professional training, and he didn't inform Stalin about the project. But Stalin must have heard rumors, perhaps from Kaganovich, because he called it off, saying it was a matter for the distant future and accusing Khrushchev of being 'an agronomist with fantasies.' "[21]

KHRUSHCHEV ALSO had fantasies about expanding Ukrainian territory. The area west of the Carpathian Mountains, the Transcarpathian Ukraine, had belonged to Czechoslovakia before the war. Khrushchev reconnoitered the region incognito in the fall of 1944, sounding out popular attitudes about unification with Ukraine and plotting with local Communists to bring it about. He advised Stalin that the populace "greatly aspired" to join the Soviet Ukraine and recommended it be "helped" to do so. In due course, Khrushchev recalled proudly, "Transcarpathia became a province of the Soviet Ukraine." He didn't mention complaints about "forced Ukrainianization" that reached Moscow two years later, leading the Central Committee to adopt a special resolution ordering Khrushchev to rectify the situation.[22]

Khrushchev also tried to grab Polish territory (the Kholm region), which, as he put it to Stalin, "historically belonged to Ukraine and was part of the Russian state." He proposed immediately organizing "our Soviet administration so that later, when it's advantageous to do so, we can declare that these regions are joining Soviet Ukraine and the USSR." Knowing Stalin's allergy to Ukrainian nationalism, Khrushchev justified the annexation as a way to "straighten the frontier." So as not to alienate the Poles, Stalin rejected Khrushchev's suggestion and ordered instead that hundreds of thousands of Ukrainians in the area be "voluntarily" resettled from Poland into Ukraine itself.[23]

A decade before Khrushchev extracted the Crimea from Russia and benevolently presented it to Ukraine (thus ensuring trouble between the two after the collapse of the USSR in 1991), he tried to pull off the same trick in 1944. What gave him an opening was the Crimea's need for Ukrainian peasants to replace the Crimean Tatars Stalin had forcibly exiled from the area. When he was in Moscow, he told a Ukrainian colleague later that year, he said "Ukraine is in ruins, but everybody wants something from it. Now what if it received the Crimea in return?"[24]

Although he failed to annex the Crimea, other efforts bore fruit: By October 1945 coal output had reached 40 percent of prewar levels, while land under cultivation had risen to 71 percent of what it had been in 1941.[25] These figures don't seem impressive, but considering the extent of wartime destruction, they were. In February 1945 Khrushchev received the Order of the Fatherland, First Degree, for "successful fulfillment of grain procurement in 1944," and in May, the Order of Suvorov, First Class, for organizing and directing the Ukrainian partisan movement. Meantime, on his fiftieth birthday in April 1944, yet another coveted Order of Lenin was bestowed upon him.

Beginning in the early 1930s, the Soviet press published obsequious telegrams to Stalin from workers and collective farmers, lengthy discussions of his utterances, and photos, drawings, and paintings of the great man. Khrushchev was similarly glorified when the Ukrainian press resumed publishing in early 1944. When thirteen prominent Ukrainian poets wrote "To the Great Stalin from the Ukrainian People," an ode allegedly signed by 9,316,973 Ukrainian citizens, two quatrains were reserved for Khrushchev:

Kiev is free, will remain so for ages,
Our land, our Mother, salutes it with cheer,
Khrushchev and Vatutin, brave and courageous,
Led forward the armies who fought without fear.

We're united and solid, and no one will dare,
To touch our young land which is clean as first love,
As fresh and as young with his silver-grey hair,
Is Stalin's companion, Nikita Khrushchev.[26]

Five years later, an opulent leather-bound book issued in Kiev, also titled *To the Great Stalin*, included the following stanzas:

We are the great foundation
That is the summit's base,
On the ancient Kiev elevation
I see Khrushchev's fine face.

And if my eyes look higher,
I see our Lenin, the foreseer,
The truth and power that inspire,
And Stalin's glorious name I hear.[27]

The greatest outpouring came on Khrushchev's fiftieth birthday in 1944: a huge front-page portrait of him in a military uniform bedecked with medals, another large painting of Khrushchev with his mustachioed master, plus a series of fulsome reminiscences by leading Ukrainian writers and artists. "I will allow myself to say it," Maksym Ryl'ski's tribute began. "I love this man with a really personal sort of love. . . . Our dear Nikita Sergeyevich" was a "great Leninist," a "glorious Stalinist," a man of "matchless will, brilliant mind, and warmhearted sincerity." Ryl'ski's pièce de résistance was the way he transformed qualities Khrushchev obviously lacked into scintillating virtues. Sensing that the mercurial Khrushchev pined for some of Stalin's stony gravitas, Ryl'ski described him as a man who "never hurries with an answer, for such haste is utterly alien to him. When Comrade Khrushchev is silent, he is not just reflecting, he forces his interlocutor to reflect as well. And often, even before Nikita Sergeyevich starts to speak, his interlocutor begins to understand better the issue asked about in the first place, to see it in a completely new light, to see that perhaps the issue didn't need to be raised at all, or rather needed to be posed in an entirely different way."[28]

Birthday well-wishers ranged from rank-and-file Communists to General Bagramian and Khrushchev's Ukrainian party deputy Korotchenko.[29] Khrushchev claimed he hated flattery. "As far as honors and birthdays were concerned," his daughter Rada recalled, "his attitude was quite calm. There was no celebrating." According to Nina Petrovna's niece Nina Kukharchuk, "He didn't like bootlickers. He didn't like spending time with them." Kostenko insisted "There were no bombastic speeches in his presence. He always behaved simply; he was always just himself. When a small-minded man like Shelest [Pyotr Shelest later became Ukrainian party chief] came to town, he would be greeted with bread and salt by young women in national costumes. It was ridiculous. When Khrushchev flew in, he'd get right down to business. So that I don't agree there was some sort of cult of Khrushchev. Of course, there was a bit of petty groveling, but Khrushchev didn't encourage it."[30]

Khrushchev didn't have to encourage it; he got it anyway. He might complain about toadying, but he didn't put a stop to it. His efforts to limit the fawning amounted to a vain effort to contain his own craving for it.

ALTHOUGH HIS KIEV villa had burned to the ground during the war, Khrushchev's new official residence proved even more luxurious. It was the former estate of a prerevolutionary pharmaceutical manufacturer on Osievskaya Street (later called Herzen Street), a safe distance from the city center. The main house was a massive one-story structure with several wings and verandas, its stone walls ornately decorated with friezes. Khrushchev moved in early in 1944; his family came down from Moscow for his birthday in April and joined him for good in September. Nikita Sergeyevich and Nina Petrovna had a large bedroom on one side, and his mother had her own on the other, with the rest of the family spread out in between.[31]

Khrushchev turned the vast grounds into a combination of formal gardens, experimental farm, and zoo. A portion of the park was elaborately landscaped with ponds, paths, bridges, and statues. Where a narrow path dipped down toward a picturesque lake, a statue of a lion guarded the way. Besides the children, who roamed the grounds, there was a goat, two dogs (German shorthairs given to Khrushchev as "war booty" by Soviet generals), and a tame fox that followed him around like a pet but also ate the ducks that belonged to Nina Petrovna's mother, Yekaterina Grigorievna. In another part of the grounds, Khrushchev grew peach trees to see if they could adapt to Kiev's climate.

When he wasn't working, Khrushchev found time to take his children cross-country skiing and on walks in the woods. Photographs show him and Nina Petrovna hugging granddaughter Yulia near a corner of the estate on a bright winter day, Khrushchev and Rada reclining on the grass (he in a formal suit and light-colored fedora) at a Mezhgorie picnic, and Khrushchev holding eight-year-old Yelena's hand as they and a group of officers inspect captured German trophies in Moscow's Gorky Park. But he still crowded his weekends with colleagues—Central Committee secretaries, deputy heads of government, and military officers—whom he invited to his dacha. Besides swimming in the Dnieper, where a dam created a shallow lake, and where motorboats were available on order from Kiev, the company sometimes clambered into an inflatable rubber boat lifted from one of the American bombers that Stalin had allowed to land at Poltava during the war. Knowing Khrushchev's fascination with technology, the military sent along detailed instructions for the dinghy. Because it looked incapable of holding the six people for which it was configured, he set sail with two large colleagues at bow and stern, their equally broad-beamed wives at port and starboard with lilacs in their arms and nervous looks on their faces, and himself in command at the oars, wearing his lieutenant general's uniform and a beatific smile.

In the autumn the company repaired to nearby collective farms to "admire the harvest," as Khrushchev put it. Afterward, at raucous dinners at the dacha, he recounted his impressions so vividly and amusingly that the children would break into peals of laughter. His favorite pastime was hunting. Sometimes he and his guests would spread out in a line and march through the woods, hoping to scare out a hare or a fox. When the hunters got tired, children and bodyguards assumed the role of beaters, trying to chase animals toward the firing line. On other occasions Khrushchev retreated alone to a hunting lodge midway between Kiev and Poltava that was originally meant for overachieving workers. He got up early, dressed in a protective service jacket with large pockets, riding breeches, and a cloth cap, and set out in a boat with a guide who helped him reload two rifles. Especially in the beginning, when wildlife wasn't used to danger, an hour and a half on the water netted him as many as fifty ducks. Several of them were delivered to the hunting lodge kitchen; the rest were sent back to the Kiev Government House cafeteria, where diners were told, "Today it's Nikita Sergeyevich's treat." Khrushchev loved to "joke with the hunting lodge staff and occasionally to curse like a trooper."[32]

The year the war ended must have seemed especially sweet. Yet, even then, according to several family members, using virtually the same words, there was "no great warmth" in the Khrushchev household. Nina Petrovna's niece, Nina Kukharchuk, was too afraid to ask either elder Khrushchev for anything. Granddaughter Yulia confirms the distance between the generations. Lively and voluble as he was in public, Khrushchev could be taciturn and moody at home, and he was inept at expressing his feelings. When Nina Petrovna's nephew, Vasya, was killed just before the war ended, Khrushchev tried to comfort the young man's father. After a long silence he blurted out, "Come on, I'll give you a gun from my collection."

Yulia remembered Nina Petrovna's setting up a New Year's tree and inviting friends over, taking the children to the theater and the cinema, and reading aloud to them. But mostly she was strict and severe. In addition to their studies in school, she insisted the children be tutored in English at home. Even pleasures were regimented, whether swimming lessons in the Dnieper or learning to ski and to skate. Leonid's death and Liuba's arrest weren't mentioned. Liuba was still in prison; her son Tolya's whereabouts were presumably unknown. Leonid's illegitimate son, Yuri, and his mother had been evacuated to Barnaul in the Altai region of Siberia, and they had no contact with the Khrushchevs after they returned to Moscow in 1943. "It wasn't our place to contact them," Yuri recalled; it was only in the summer of 1947 that the Khrushchevs got in touch with them. Much later, in 1963, Khrushchev cited Yuri and his Jewish mother to refute a charge of anti-Semitism in a conversation with visiting American editor Norman Cousins: "I'm the grandfather of a Jewish boy. My son married a Jewish girl. They had a child. Then my son went off to war and was killed. The mother and child became part of my family. I brought the child up as my own. You see how preposterous it is to say that I'm anti-Semitic?"[33]

Yuri was *not* raised as a member of the Khrushchev family, but he did pay them an occasional visit. A student at the Suvorov Military Academy in Moscow, he was on summer vacation in 1947 when an officer appeared at his door. Two days later he was flown to Kiev on a military plane. Nina Petrovna met him at the dacha, introduced him to Rada, Yelena, and Yulia and asked him to guess which one was his half sister and which his aunts. Yuri spent the summer at Mezhgorie, but the reunion was bittersweet. His looks and his "difficult" character reminded Nina Petrovna of Lyonia and Tolya. She "didn't hesitate to express her dissatisfaction with me," Yuri said, "especially with my interest in riding motorcycles and horses." His first day at the dacha Yura took a motorboat out on the Dnieper without permission and had to be rescued by Khrushchev's security men. He got his black military shoes so muddy that he had to fly back to Moscow wearing girls' bedroom slippers. No wonder Nina Petrovna kept telling him, "Be careful," "Be more serious," "Think before you act." In a Freudian slip that helps explain why he didn't treat his grandson like his own son, Khrushchev once shouted at Yura, "Lyonia, cut it out!"[34]

MARSHALL MACDUFFIE was an American who headed the United Nations Relief and Rehabilitation Administration (UNRRA) to Ukraine just after the war. If he didn't get to know Khrushchev as well as later Western emissaries like U.S. Ambassador Llewellyn Thompson, it wasn't for lack of interest on Khrushchev's part. MacDuffie's first meeting with him took place in a modern government building on a hill overlooking the Dnieper. Khrushchev's office was very large, McDuffie later wrote, but "I never felt there was anything elaborate about it other than its size, and other than the double leather doors through which we entered the room. The other notable thing was that in the corner of the room was a series of plaster casts which had to do with building material for some of the new construction then going on in the Ukraine."

Double leather doors were standard for Soviet high officialdom, and so was the lack of decoration. But the office's occupant was anything but. Khrushchev's English interpreter was "all bespangled in one of those new blue uniforms which had just been given to the Ukrainian foreign office, with epaulets, and very proud of himself." Khrushchev himself, with his pug nose, "loving cup ears," and "smiling eyes," kept staring at his guest "curiously as though he was looking at a bug on the rocks." Another occasion, a banquet with high Ukrainian officials in a lavishly appointed mansion, was formal, with stilted toasts to peace and friendship, but the genial host was not. Khrushchev pointed to his deputy premier in charge of agriculture, Vasily Starchenko, who was even shorter and wider than he ("Mr. Five by Seven not Mr. Five by Five," MacDuffie later remarked), and joked: "I must be a little crazy. I sent *him* to the United States to ask for *food* for Ukraine."

Khrushchev showed off in other ways. When a visiting UNRRA official timidly expressed the hope of meeting Stalin, Khrushchev bounded into another room and returned a few minutes later saying, "I just spoke to Comrade Stalin on the phone. He'll see you tomorrow at two P.M."[35] Nor, in contrast with other Soviet leaders, did he conceal his fascination with the United States. On the UNRRA mission's last day in Ukraine, he gave another lavish dinner and then took his guests to his Mezhgorie dacha. To their surprise, he kept them sitting on the veranda until almost three in the morning, plying them with questions about life in America: where they lived, what they earned, what they planned to do after returning to the States.[36]

Milovan Djilas, the future Yugoslav dissident, was one of Tito's top associates when he and his boss stopped in Kiev in the spring of 1945. Khrushchev's "unrestrained garrulity" struck the Yugoslavs, but so did his "naturally simple and unaffected behavior and manner of speaking"; his sense of humor was not "predominantly intellectual, and as such, cynical," like Stalin's, but "typically folksy and thus often crude"; his ideological clichés, unlike his Kremlin colleagues', reflected "both real ignorance and Marxist maxims learned by rote, yet even these he presented with conviction and frankness."

Khrushchev "was the only one among the Soviet leaders," Djilas wrote later, " who delved into the daily life of the Communist rank and file and the citizenry." His "extraordinarily practical sense" was visible at a meeting with economic administrators: "Unlike Yugoslav ministers, his commissars were excellently acquainted with such matters and, what was more important, they realistically gauged possibilities." In comparison with Moscow, Djilas sensed "a certain freshness" in Kiev, thanks not only to the city's beauty but also to its party leader's "limitless vigor and practicality."

Besides his real skills, however, Khrushchev's shortcomings were also on display. He had been "constantly improving himself," Djilas noted, gleaning wisdom "from his lively and many-sided activities." But "his knowledge of some rare fact and his ignorance of some elementary truths" were equally astonishing. Khrushchev's memory struck Djilas as "excellent, and he expresses himself vividly and graphically." But he ate the way he spoke (while "Stalin and his entourage gave the impression of gourmandism," Khrushchev "practically bolted down impressive quantities of food"), and Djilas observed that Khrushchev drank "even more" than Stalin did.

Despite Khrushchev's primitiveness, Djilas thought that "he suffers less than any other Communist autodidact and unfinished scholar from a feeling of inferiority," that he did not feel "the need to hide his personal ignorance and weaknesses behind an external brilliance and generalizations." But it would have been hopeless for Khrushchev to feign brilliance. What he hid behind instead was his extroverted style and his self-proclaimed special relationship with Stalin. "Whenever there was talk of Stalin," Djilas remembered, Khrushchev "spoke of him with respect and stressed their closeness."[37]

The Organization of Ukrainian Nationalists (OUN), established in 1929, gained new adherents when the USSR occupied and began Sovietizing western Ukraine in 1939. Khrushchev briefly tried to win over the nationalists, but the NKVD soon turned to arresting, imprisoning, and deporting them. To Ukrainians thus persecuted, Nazi invaders at first seemed saviors. The OUN faction led by Stepan Bandera proclaimed a short-lived independent Ukrainian state in Lvov on June 30, 1941, and launched an armed uprising to which the retreating Soviets responded with great brutality. Unwilling to evacuate their prisoners, the NKVD massacred ten to fifteen thousand of them, summarily shooting many and burning others alive inside abandoned prisons.[38]

The Nazi response to Ukrainian nationalism was equally brutal. Many Ukrainian nationalists resembled right-wing, anti-Semitic nationalists in other European countries whom Hitler had encouraged. But to the Nazis, Ukrainians were only slightly less subhuman than Jews. Some Ukrainians assisted the Nazis in exterminating Jews, but many others fought against them, if not in the Red Army, then in the Ukrainian Insurgent Army (UPA), which, after merging with underground units of the OUN's Bandera faction, numbered as many as 150,000 to 200,000 by 1944.[39] When the victorious Soviets returned in 1944, most of the UPA turned their guns against them.

Two other postwar challenges faced Khrushchev. One was the Ukrainian Greek Catholic Church, a primary bearer of the idea of Ukrainian identity, whose adherents had numbered as many as three million before the war.[40] Between 1939 and 1941 the Communists moved to limit its influence (by imposing discriminatory taxes, disseminating antireligious propaganda, and collecting or fabricating incriminating evidence against the church hierarchy), but given the precarious international situation and the church's strong popular base, Khrushchev proceeded cautiously. In 1944 he still had reason for caution, especially until the Western allies accepted Soviet control over western Ukraine as part of the end-of-war settlement. The task of crushing the Greek Catholic Church still lay ahead.[41]

Khrushchev's second challenge was to collectivize western Ukrainian agriculture. Before the war only about 13 percent of peasant households and 15 percent of arable land were collectivized. Now it was time to finish the job, especially since collective farms made it easier to blockade food supplies to nationalist partisans. But collectivization further alienated western Ukrainian peasants, who resisted with the help of armed partisans.[42]

All told, the western Ukrainian situation was daunting. Yet that was not what Stalin wanted to hear, nor did Khrushchev fully realize what he was up against. In January 1944, having toured several newly liberated provinces, he informed Stalin that the general mood was "very good and Soviet" and that he found "no sign of large [nationalist] formations." Three months later he wrote Stalin that "reports of actions by Ukrainian-German nationalist bands are greatly exaggerated" and that although OUN leaders were trying intimidation tactics, "we now have everything we need to smash them." By November 1944 the guerrillas' mood was "bad," according to Khrushchev, with many of them "on the brink of disintegration." In January 1945 the Ukrainian Politburo resolved "to use the winter months to complete [their] rout and liquidation." And in February, it set March 15, 1945, as the date for the "final liquidation" of nationalist bands in western Ukraine.[43]

In fact, Ukrainian partisans weren't finally defeated until the early 1950s.[44] When the Red Army arrived, nearly every western Ukrainian peasant household had dug shelters concealing weapons, ammunition, food, and clothing; between 1945 and 1946 Soviet forces claimed to have unearthed 28,969 rebel hideouts in western Ukraine. Although they shifted in 1944 and 1945 from open warfare using large heavily armed detachments to ambushes by small units, nationalist guerrillas continued to hold their own. As late as February 1947 "remnants" of partisan forces were holding off nearly 70,000 crack troops, plus 63,000 local militia organized in special battalions.[45]

Savagery characterized both sides. According to Soviet data, the nationalist underground carried out 14,500 acts of sabotage and terrorism that killed more than thirty thousand Communist officials and local inhabitants.[46] OUN instructions authorized "liquidating counter-agents [as well as their family members, both adults and children] with all available methods (execution by firing squad, hanging, quartering with notes left on their chests: 'For collaborating with the NKVD')". Atrocities carried out by partisans in 1944 included stripping corpses, hog-tying arms and legs and slicing faces to pieces, gouging out eyes, and castrating and beheading bodies.[47]

Between February 1944 and May 1946 the Soviet military and police reported killing 110,825 "bandits" and arresting 250,676 more. As many 600,000 may have been arrested in western Ukraine between 1944 and 1952, with about a third of that number executed and the other two-thirds imprisoned or exiled.[48] Black operations units known as *spetsgruppy* sometimes posed as nationalist partisans. In one incident, fake nationalists got a family to admit they were nationalist sympathizers and then arrested them for collaborating with "bandits." On another occasion a black operations unit beat a seventeen-year-old peasant girl, serially raped her, hung her upside down from a tree, and shoved a stick up her vagina.[49]

Distrustful of western Ukrainians, the Soviets imported easterners to man western party and police agencies. Pressed to produce results, yet fearing for their own lives, many officials inflated reports of "spies" recruited and "bandits" destroyed, took refuge in drink, and suffered nervous breakdowns.[50] Khrushchev's role in the mayhem was to supervise security police who bore the brunt of the struggle, but his hands-on style kept him closely and cruelly involved. In a November 1944 letter to Stalin he proposed that partisans be "sentenced to death" by NKVD tribunals, "not to be shot but to be hanged," after public trials. He urged setting up troikas of province officials (the same institution that had wreaked such havoc in the thirties) with the right to pass death sentences that would be "immediately carried out."[51]

Khrushchev spurred local officials on with biting humor and calls for blood. He mocked one official for being "so scared that his hair stands on end even though he's bald." Others, he grumbled in November 1944, would be sorry to see the rebels destroyed since then they would have no one to blame for their failures.[52] "Find the family members of those who are helping [the resistance] and arrest them," he exhorted his men in 1945. "We won't be respected if we don't take harsh measures. We must arrest even the most unimportant ones. Some must be tried, others simply hanged, the rest deported. For one of ours, we will take a hundred of them. . . . [You] haven't used enough violence! When you seize a village where [they] killed two women, you must destroy the entire village."[53] Five months later he demanded: "Why haven't you killed bandits? . . . You haven't done anything. . . . While you're figuring out who's a bandit, they're getting ready to attack. . . . You say they stole ninety cows; how fast can cows go, three or four kilometers a day? Yet you still can't find them? Even with a plane? Even peasants with sticks could catch them. . . . I myself used to be able to walk sixty kilometers a day."[54]

Many western Ukrainian towns and villages were blockaded in 1946 by military and police units supported by 300 "extermination detachments."[55] At first Khrushchev used the Greek Catholic Church to encourage partisans to accept a series of amnesty offers. But when the church proved unable or unwilling to help, he began arresting its leaders (Metropolitan Iosyf Slipyi eventually spent eighteen years in gulag prisons and camps) and then arranged the "voluntary" dissolution of the church, and its "reunion" with the state-dominated Russian Orthodox Church in March 1946.[56] The Greek Catholic archpriest Havryil Kostel'nyk, who supported this merger, became disillusioned when repression of the clergy continued. He was assassinated in 1948 by a killer who was himself gunned down from a nearby escape car.

Soviet sponsorship of this assassination hasn't been documented.[57] But Khrushchev's role in the October 1947 slaying of Bishop Teodor Romzha, who resisted NKVD intimidation tactics in Transcarpathian Ukraine, has been. Romzha was returning from a village where he had consecrated a new church when his horse-drawn coach was rammed by a military truck that was closely followed by a car. Occupants of the car attacked Romzha with iron bars. Taken to a hospital (after an approaching post office truck scared off his assailants), the bishop was operated on but then injected with fatal poison in an act witnessed by a Greek Catholic nun who worked in the hospital.[58] Khrushchev had asked Stalin to sanction the assassination and then appealed for help when the first attempt was botched. Before leaving for the region, Ukrainian Police Chief Savchenko and MGB toxicological expert Maironovsky were received by Khrushchev, who gave them specific orders and wished them success. Two days later, after receiving final authorization from Khrushchev, Maironovsky gave an ampule of curare poison to a local MGB "nurse" who administered the fatal injection.[59]

Khrushchev didn't admit any of this, of course. In fact, he didn't say much at all in his memoirs about his role in the western Ukrainian bloodbath.[60] Whatever guilt he felt was not about his role in crushing nationalist resistance. He couldn't conceive of the USSR without Ukraine or of Ukraine without its western regions. Nationalist guerrillas had relied first on German patrons and then on Western intelligence agencies.[61] On top of that, guerrillas tortured to death Nina Petrovna's uncle Anton and his daughter and assassinated Khrushchev's close friend General Vatutin.[62] Not to mention an attempt on Khrushchev's own life, which barely misfired in May 1945.[63] For all these reasons the guilt Khrushchev felt had less to do with the brutality of the civil war and more with the fact that he wasn't winning it fast enough.

In September 1944 the Central Committee in Moscow chastised Communists in Kiev for "major and serious deficiencies" in restoring order and indoctrinating the populace in western Ukraine.[64] As late as 1949, when Sudoplatov was in Lvov investigating the murder of a Ukrainian writer, Yaroslav Galan, who had attacked Vatican and Greek Catholic Church officials for collaborating with the Germans, he encountered Khrushchev "in a bad mood, fearing Stalin's rage for his inability to stamp out the resistance of the armed Ukrainian nationalists."[65] Determined to finish off the guerrillas, Khrushchev readily resorted to any and all means.

NATIONALISM IN western Ukraine wasn't the only thing souring Khrushchev's mood by 1946. So were difficulties facing the USSR abroad and economic and political dangers at home. In the summer of 1945 Stalin hoped to dominate Eastern Europe, exert influence over Western Europe, and extend Soviet leverage into the Middle East and Asia, all while preserving good relations with the West.[66] By 1946 East-West tensions were rising, and Washington's 1947 offer of Marshall Plan aid to Eastern Europe seemed to threaten Moscow's control over the region. The onset of the cold war meant the USSR would have to rely on its own resources, but would they suffice? There was starvation in the provinces, while armed resistance continued in the Baltics as well as western Ukraine. Instead of girding for renewed sacrifice, many Soviet citizens still hoped for an easing of police state controls.[67]

Stalin's response was to launch a new crackdown, singling out the restive intelligentsia for particularly malign attention. The *Zhdanovshchina*, as the campaign of vilification and repression led by Andrei Zhdanov became known, excommunicated writers like Anna Akhmatova and

Mikhail Zoshchenko and soon extended first into the theater, music, history, and philosophy, and later into biology and philology.[68] Meanwhile Stalin was deteriorating physically and mentally. Zhukov was shocked when he saw him in March 1945. "From the way he looked, talked and moved you could tell he was extremely fatigued. After four years of war he was utterly overworked. He had worked too hard, and slept too little all that time. . . . All this was bound to tell on his health and nervous system."[69]

In the fall of 1945 the sixty-five-year-old Stalin took a lengthy vacation by the Black Sea. According to his daughter, he "fell ill, and was quite sick for many months." In the summer of 1946 he traveled south by car, stopping in towns "to see for himself how people were living. What he saw was havoc wrought by the war on every side." Visiting her father for three weeks in Sochi in August 1947, Svetlana found "he had aged" even more. "He wanted peace and quiet. Rather, he didn't know just what he wanted." In the evening he viewed upbeat prewar musical comedies like *Volga-Volga*; afterward he ate and drank late into the night.[70]

Milovan Djilas, who spent an evening at Stalin's Moscow dacha in early 1948, was struck by "conspicuous signs of his senility." Although Stalin had always eaten with gusto, he "now exhibited gluttony, as though he feared there would not be enough of the desired food left for him. . . . It was incomprehensible how much he had changed in two or three years." The man Djilas remembered as "lively, quick-witted," and with "a pointed sense of humor," now "laughed at inanities and shallow jokes," guffawing with "an exaggerated, immoderate mirth" at a record on which "the coloratura warbling of a singer was accompanied by the yowling and barking of dogs."

Stalin was still "stubborn, sharp and suspicious whenever anyone disagreed with him," Djilas added, so his colleagues "paid court to him, avoiding any expression of opinion before he expressed his, and then hastening to agree with him."[71] The positive side of Stalin's deterioration was that it reduced his role in day-to-day administration, allowing his underlings occasionally to ignore his irrational demands. But he was more vindictive than ever when things went wrong, more determined to find someone to blame.

Unfortunately for Khrushchev, a great deal went wrong in Ukraine. He admitted in 1946 that "the preparation, selection and assignment of leadership cadres has [*sic*] been carried out in an unsatisfactory manner in the Central Committee and province committees . . . ."[72] But this admission was deemed unsatisfactory. Ukrainian Communists were censured for underestimating "the significance of ideological work," for allowing newspapers, magazines, and books to contain "ideological blunders and distortions [and] attempts to revive bourgeois nationalist concepts."[73]

The mood of intellectuals wasn't good; as overheard by ubiquitous police informers, many complained not only about each other but about Stalin himself.[74] During the war Khrushchev used Ukrainian national sentiment to appeal to the intelligentsia. But once the *Zhdanovshchina* began, he attacked anything that smacked of nationalism, including books and writers he had previously supported. In the summer of 1946 the Ukrainian Central Committee criticized the Ukrainian Writers' Union and its chairman, Maksym Ryl'ski, for tolerating "tendencies alien to Soviet literature." A few days later Ryl'ski was assailed for thinking he had "a right to make ideological mistakes."[75] Khrushchev later recalled having "great difficulty in fending off criticism of such a deserving writer as Maksym Ryl'ski. . . ."[76] The only way he could protect his old friend, and himself as well, was to take on the job of attacking him.[77]

Meanwhile Ukrainian economic conditions were worsening. The autumn of 1945 was too dry, and the following winter too harsh. After another dry spring, a full-fledged drought descended on the region. Khrushchev recalled that "severe climatic conditions, combined with the poor mechanization of our agriculture, made [a poor harvest] inevitable. We were short of tractors, horses, and oxen. . . . Men were coming back from the war ready to work, but no one fitted into his old place. After a long time away, some men were no longer qualified for skilled farm labor, and others had never been qualified in the first place."[78]

All this was true, but the harsh system of state quotas forced farms to surrender the bulk of the harvest, despite a yield even lower than in 1944 and 1945.[79] Instead of reducing mandatory deliveries, the state actually *raised* them in July 1946, partly to supply Communist allies in Eastern Europe.[80] "We were supposed to supply the state first and ourselves second," Khrushchev commented later. The Ukrainian quota was established "arbitrarily, although it was dressed up in the press with supporting scientific data. It had been calculated not on the basis of how much we really could produce, but on the basis of how much the state could beat out of us. The quota system was really a system of extortion. I saw that the year was threatened with catastrophe. It was difficult to predict how it would end."[81]

The quotas were ruinous, but Khrushchev was partly responsible for setting them too high in the first place.[82] As in Kiev and Kharkov during the war, he led Stalin to expect too much and tried too late to save the situation. According to Stalin's housekeeper, "some party leaders who later rose very high came to see him in the south [in the summer of 1946] and reported on agricultural conditions in Ukraine. They brought watermelons so huge you couldn't put your arms around them. They brought fruit and vegetables and golden sheaves of grain, the point being to show off how rich Ukraine was. Meanwhile, the chauffeur of one of the leaders, whose name was Nikita Khrushchev, told the servants there was a famine in Ukraine, that there was nothing to eat in the countryside, and that peasant women were using cows for plowing."[83]

Khrushchev tried to expiate his own sin, his determination to do so reinforced by "heartrending" letters from collective farmers. "Well, Comrade Khrushchev," wrote one farm chairman, "we've delivered our quota to the state; we've given everything away, and we have nothing left for us. We are sure the state and the party won't forget us and that they will come to our aid." Khrushchev commented: "He obviously thought the peasants' fate depended on me. After all, I was the chairman of the Council of People's Commissars of the Ukraine and first secretary of the Ukrainian Central Committee. He supposed that since I was head of the Ukrainian state, I wouldn't forget the peasants." But no matter how much Khrushchev wanted to help, "there was nothing I could do once the grain had been turned over to the state delivery points. It was no longer in my power to dispose of it. I myself was forced to beg that the grain we needed be left for us."[84]

Even in this painful recollection Khrushchev pronounced his titles trippingly on the tongue. Yet by now he was defending the people against his own government. On a trip to his old district, Petrovo-Marinsky, he was shocked to learn there was no grain left after compulsory deliveries, only seed that the state was also demanding. "We're not Gypsies," the district party secretary remembered Khrushchev's saying. "We have to sow."[85]

"Soon I was receiving letters and official reports about deaths from starvation," Khrushchev later wrote. "Then the cannibalism started. I received a report that a human head and the soles of feet had been found under a little bridge near Vasilovo, a town outside Kiev. Apparently, the corpse had been eaten."

Aleksei I. Kirichenko, the Odessa party chief, checked on how farmers were surviving the winter. He described the following scene to Khrushchev: "The woman had the corpse of her own child on the table and she was cutting it up. She was chattering away while she worked, 'We've eaten Manechka [Little Maria]. Now we'll salt down Vanechka [Little Ivan]. This will keep us for some time.'" Khrushchev noted: "As I retell this story, my thoughts go back to that period. I can see that horrible scene vividly in my mind. There was nothing I could do."

On top of his wartime experience, this fresh encounter with unnecessary suffering ("necessary" suffering was an entirely different matter to which he had long been inured) prompted him to take new risks. Khrushchev later insisted he had told Stalin the unvarnished truth: "In the past I had sometimes succeeded in breaking through the bureaucratic resistance . . . . Sometimes, if I was able to present carefully selected material with logically constructed conclusions, the facts would speak for themselves and Stalin would support me."[86] But not this time. After calling Stalin about the famine, "I put down the receiver and thought, That's it. Stalin hadn't said anything. All I heard was his heavy breathing." Another time, Stalin snarled, "'You're being soft-bellied. They're deceiving you. They're counting on your sentimentality when they report things like that. They're trying to force you to give them all your reserves.' It was as if he thought I had given in to local Ukrainian influence, as if I had become a nationalist who didn't deserve to be trusted."[87]

Documents in the archives confirm Khrushchev's courage. In an October 15, 1946, letter to Stalin, he asked that grain delivery quotas be reduced. Around December 1 he described an "extremely tense situation," and on December 17, he pleaded for emergency aid.[88] But Khrushchev also resorted to a ploy that reduced his risk. He proposed ration cards that would guarantee the farm population a bare minimum of food, but not to Stalin himself. "All official documents were addressed to Stalin," Khrushchev explained, "but he never set eyes on most of them, just as many government decrees he'd never seen appeared over his signature." Stalin wasn't supposed to see Khrushchev's proposal either, but "thanks to Malenkov and Beria, this request of mine went straight to [Stalin in] Sochi."

Whether or not it was Malenkov and Beria's doing, Khrushchev was in trouble: "Stalin sent me the rudest, most insulting telegram. I was a suspicious element, he said; I was writing memoranda to prove that Ukraine was unable to take care of itself, and I was requesting an outrageous quantity of ration cards for feeding people. I can't express how murderously this telegram depressed me. I clearly saw the whole tragedy; it wasn't hanging over me personally, but over the whole Ukrainian people. Famine was now inevitable; Stalin's response dashed our last hopes that it could be avoided."

Once again Khrushchev trekked to Moscow to be dressed down by his master. "I was prepared for anything," he recollected, "even to be counted an enemy of the people. All it took was a instant; all you did was blink and the door would open and you'd find yourself in Lubyanka."[89] Although he rejected the ration cards, Stalin ended up giving Ukraine limited assistance, including food products, seed, and money to organize free soup kitchens.[90] But the dictator's annoyance with his top advisers on agriculture led him to call a rare meeting of the Central Committee in Moscow in February 1947.

"Who should deliver the General Report?" Khrushchev recalled Stalin's asking. "Malenkov? He's in charge of agricultural matters, but what kind of report can he deliver? He doesn't know the first thing about agriculture. He doesn't even know agricultural terminology."[91] Stalin's next candidate was Khrushchev, but "I was simply terrified by this instruction," he insisted. "I could deliver a report on Ukraine," he told Stalin. "I've been concerned with Ukraine for some years now, and I know more or less what the situation is there. But I don't know anything about agriculture in the Russian Federation, and I haven't the slightest idea about Siberia. I've never even been in Central Asia. I've never seen cotton, and I don't know how it grows."

Stalin persisted, but Khrushchev did too: "No, Comrade Stalin, I ask you to please release me from this. I don't want to mislead the Central Committee, nor do I want to put myself in a stupid position by trying to make a report on subjects which I don't understand."

By now Khrushchev's routine was familiar. But whereas earlier his humility had been real, or at least partly so, he was now almost entirely dissembling. Even if he hadn't been to Central Asia, he could have gotten help in preparing his speech. But the invitation to speak was a trap, a way to force him either to declare his differences with Stalin (and face the consequences) or to bury them once and for all.

Luckily for Khrushchev, Stalin relented and recruited another speaker. But when Stalin asked him what he thought of Andrei Andreyev's report, Khrushchev couldn't resist criticizing it. "First you refuse to deliver the report yourself," Stalin snapped, "and now you're criticizing it."

Khrushchev was protecting himself, since Andreyev had criticized his stewardship of Ukrainian agriculture. But he was probably also tired of playing the fool. He claims to have pressed hard on two issues: the need to set seed aside for sowing before delivering grain to the state and the danger of planting spring wheat according to rigid, compulsory quotas. That may exaggerate his resistance to Stalin. But what then occurred confirms that his defiance was real. "The next thing that happened," Khrushchev reported, "is that Stalin suddenly raised the question of what sort of help I should be given in the Ukraine."[92]

In March 1947 the Ukrainian Central Committee decided "to strengthen party and state work" by separating the posts of party and government leader, which Khrushchev had combined in his own person. It elected Kaganovich party leader while removing Khrushchev as head of the Kiev Province and city party committees.

Khrushchev's speech to the Central Committee was uncharacteristically subdued. Instead of peppering his address with jokes and proverbs and hectoring other speakers, he engaged in "self-criticism," admitting "vast errors in party and state leadership of agriculture, errors that are all too visible in the Ukraine."[93] Until then Khrushchev had been a ubiquitous presence throughout the republic. Beginning in May, his name vanished from the press. Many of Stalin's victims had followed this route: demotion, limbo, arrest, liquidation.

When Khrushchev later said he'd been sick, his illness seemed political. In fact, he caught a cold that turned into pneumonia. Rada Adzhubei remembered her father "at death's door; if it hadn't been for Kaganovich, he might not have survived." Kaganovich summoned a physician from Moscow to treat Khrushchev with penicillin, an act that took courage since Stalin frowned on Western antibiotics.[94] But the penicillin didn't bring immediate relief. Khrushchev's son remembered two professors of medicine "shaking their heads in distress" as they emerged from his father's bedroom. Sergei could still see "Father's motionless gray face on the pillow, the hoarse whistle of his breathing, and his uncomprehending look."[95]

After Khrushchev recovered, doctors insisted he rest by the sea. At first he sat on a Latvian beach in an overcoat while his children braved the chilly water. But before long he was duck hunting at nearby lakes. In mid-August he flew to Kaliningrad (the former German Königsberg, which the Soviets seized after the war) to see how German scientists had made fabrics out of brown coal, and by early autumn he was back in Kiev in time for the start of the school year.

This was Khrushchev's first "vacation" since before the war. It was a miracle that he hadn't broken under the strain long before 1947. Even so, his collapse seems partly psychosomatic. The prospect of political oblivion was too much to bear. When Stalin first offered Kaganovich's "help," Khrushchev said later, he welcomed the change, and once

Kaganovich arrived, "everyone went to his post and proceeded with his duties."[96] Nor did Rada notice any "change in his behavior in the family. We all knew Kaganovich quite well . . . . When he arrived in Kiev, we retained dacha number one at Mezhgorie, and he took dacha number two opposite ours. We were friendly with his children, with whom we often watched movies. The Kaganoviches often visited us at our house and we dropped in on them. He and Nikita Sergeyevich took long walks and drove to work together. So that at the family level, at least, the change did not feel like a tragedy."[97]

Khrushchev was too proud to reveal his humiliation. In addition, he felt threatened, especially when Kaganovich made "bourgeois nationalism" his main target. Kaganovich not only stepped up the campaign against nationalist "deviationists" (making it seem Khrushchev hadn't done enough) but attacked people with whom Khrushchev had been associated. "A Jew himself, Kaganovich was against the Jews!" Khrushchev sneered, especially "against the Jews who happened to be on friendly terms with me."[98] Kaganovich also went after Ryl'ski and Dovzhenko.[99]

Kaganovich condemned industrial and agricultural shortfalls as manifestations of "Ukrainian bourgeois nationalism." He began preparing a Central Committee plenum, scheduled for the winter of 1947–1948, on "The Struggle against Nationalism as the Main Danger Facing the Ukrainian Communist Party."[100] As these storm clouds gathered, Khrushchev was still nursing his wounds, paying a nostalgic visit to Petrovo-Marinsky accompanied by Rada, showing his daughter, or so it seemed to the district party leader Glukhov, "just how much the wonderful people of the district valued him."[101] But before long he was undermining his former mentor. Khrushchev claimed that Kaganovich "was grinding out a steady stream of political complaints against everybody in sight" and that many of them "found their way" to Stalin.

"One day Stalin called me," Khrushchev recalled, "and said, 'Why isn't your signature on these memoranda of Kaganovich's?' "

"Comrade Stalin, these memoranda aren't government business, they're party business: therefore, my signature isn't required." Khrushchev's comment implied that his demotion had been a mistake that needed rectifying. But Stalin apparently already knew that.

"Not so," he said. "I've told Kaganovich that I won't accept any more of his memoranda unless they're cosigned by you."

Kaganovich's Kiev days were numbered. "You won't succeed in getting me to quarrel with the Ukrainian people," Stalin warned him in December 1947.[102] Remembered Khrushchev: "The stream of official complaints from Kaganovich soon dried up because he knew that he could never get me to sign them. That was certainly a welcome development in itself, but the most important thing about this story is that it shows that Stalin's trust in me had been restored. I took his telephone call as a signal that I had been returned to good standing as a member of the Politburo. My morale improved immeasurably."[103]

It improved even more when Kaganovich was called back to Moscow and on December 26, when the Ukrainian Central Committee reappointed Khrushchev party leader (while appointing his yes-man Korotchenko to head the Ukrainian government). Especially after Kaganovich tried and failed to oust Khrushchev in 1957, Nikita Sergeyevich and his disciples portrayed Kaganovich's behavior in Kiev in 1947 as monstrous.[104] But if Kaganovich was an inveterate Stalinist, so was Khrushchev, as his resumption of the Ukrainian party leadership confirmed. Actually, Khrushchev had reason to be grateful to Kaganovich in 1947; not only did he help Khrushchev when he was ill, but his excesses made Khrushchev look good in comparison. As a Jew, Kaganovich couldn't have replaced Khrushchev permanently as Ukrainian leader. If Stalin had really wanted to finish off Khrushchev, he would have sent someone else. As irritated as he was with Khrushchev, Stalin was trying to help him.

KHRUSHCHEV'S LAST two years in Ukraine were his best years yet. Although sporadic fighting continued in the west, the 1947 harvest exceeded planned targets, a trend continued in 1948. By mid-1949 collectivization had incorporated 60 percent of peasant households. Pursuing his dream of "eliminating contradictions between town and countryside" Khrushchev set out to amalgamate collective farms into agro-cities complete with municipal services and other amenities. In a hurry as usual, he spoke of "transforming all our villages in the very near future." In fact, he created only one demonstration agro-city in the Cherkassy District before leaving Kiev, but he presented it to Stalin as a seventieth birthday present in December 1949.[105]

The vitality that had drained out of Khrushchev's speeches in 1947 returned. He was greeted at the Sixteenth Ukrainian Party Congress in January 1949 by a prolonged standing ovation and shouts of "Glory to Comrade Khrushchev." His 1948 and 1949 letters to Stalin, many of them covering such relatively minor matters as whether Ukraine should receive a delegation of Polish peasants, numbered in the hundreds.[106] In 1948 he and other Ukrainian leaders each received the Order of Lenin commemorating with the thirtieth anniversary of the Ukrainian Soviet Socialist Republic. On the tenth anniversary of the Soviet occupation of western Ukraine in October 1949, a huge painting of Stalin and Khrushchev standing before a portrait of Lenin led the main Ukrainian papers. Although the artist didn't realize it, he had portrayed the line of leadership succession.

In the summer of 1949 the Khrushchev family vacationed at the huge tsarist palace at Livadia near Yalta, where Stalin had met Roosevelt and Churchill four years previously. The Khrushchevs stayed in a large outbuilding while Stalin's daughter, Svetlana, and her second husband, Yuri Zhdanov, occupied the palace proper. According to Aleksei Adzhubei, there was no contact between the families: "Vacations of high-ranking families took place in seclusion. Absolute comfort, complete solitude, beaches segregated from the public, high fences patrolled continuously by security men with dogs, and—boredom. Even a trip to Yalta, say to a concert or restaurant, was practically impossible. Like the old, the young were supposed to rest."[107]

Boredom or not, the invitation was a sign of Stalin's regard. No wonder Khrushchev's recollection of the time glows with satisfaction: "My last year in the Ukraine was 1949 . . . [it] was also our best year. Our agricultural successes elevated the stature of the Ukraine and the prestige of the Ukrainian leadership in the eyes of the whole country. I look back on that period with warm memories. Stalin more than once instructed me to deliver reports on agricultural topics such as livestock raising in the Ukraine, and on his instructions my reports were reprinted in *Pravda* as examples for others to follow. But far be it from me to take all the credit. I myself am a Russian and wouldn't want to slight the Russian people, but I must attribute our success . . . to the Ukrainian people themselves."[108]

If all was well for Khrushchev, the same can't be said for Ukrainians. The USSR Supreme Soviet passed a decree in February 1948 "On the Expulsion from the Ukrainian SSR of Individuals Maliciously Shirking Labor Activity in Agriculture and Leading an Antisocial Parasitic Way of Life." The decree allowed collective farm assemblies to exile those who didn't work diligently. Khrushchev had proposed the edict in a long letter to Stalin to which he appended a similar tsarist-era law as a model. As could have been predicted, implementation of the decree involved what even Soviet procurators viewed as excesses: Among those exiled were old people too sick or infirm to work, disabled war veterans, whole families expelled to punish one "parasite," and people sent away to settle personal scores. Khrushchev condemned such excesses in another long letter to

Stalin, but for his boss's delectation described collective farm meetings he had attended where peasants denounced one another using "language that would make a Turkish sultan blush." Khrushchev even recommended that similar laws be adopted in other Soviet republics, promising that "universal application of the decree would accelerate the strengthening of labor discipline and in turn guarantee timely carrying out of agricultural tasks, achievement of bountiful harvests, an increase in the productivity of animal husbandry, and the more rapid growth of the whole collective farm economy."[109]

Between February 1948 and June 1950, 11,991 "parasites" were reportedly exiled from Ukraine, while thousands of others were threatened with a similar fate.[110] Other Stalinist excesses of 1948 and 1949 owed less to Khrushchev's personal initiative. They included the continuing assault on "bourgeois nationalism"; Stalin's new campaign against "cosmopolitanism," of which Jews and Westernized intellectuals were the main targets; and the dictator's support of Lysenko, whose 1948 pogrom against geneticists and other scientists was faithfully carried out in Ukraine.[111] Khrushchev's loyal support for all this and much more merited the next step in his remarkable rise: his promotion to Stalin's inner circle in Moscow.

CHAPTER NINE

The Heir Nonapparent: 1949–1953

Rada Khrushcheva entered Moscow State University in 1947 to study journalism. There she met and fell in love with a fellow student, Aleksei Adzhubei, whose mother is remembered by Stalin's daughter, Svetlana, as "the best dressmaker in Moscow," a woman "who dressed all the ladies in the 'top ten' families. She was really a talented person, and good deal of her artistic sense and energy had been passed on to her beloved only son."[1]

Having demonstrated her seriousness with a straight A high school record, Rada was allowed by her parents to live in their Granovsky Street apartment. A housekeeper employed by the security police looked after the place, and Malenkov's wife, who lived one floor below, kept an eye on Rada at her mother's request. Mrs. Malenkov "wasn't very enthusiastic to learn about her ward's suitor," Adzhubei recalled, "and even tried to prevent our romance." She told Rada, "You're only twenty," but Khrushchev's daughter brooked no interference in her affairs.[2]

Adzhubei's mother made dresses for Beria's wife, who asked her ominously, "Why did Alyosha get mixed up with the Khrushchevs?"[3] But like his intended, Adzhubei persevered. Khrushchev first met Adzhubei in the spring of 1949 at his dacha outside Moscow. "Khrushchev barely spoke a few words to me and asked no questions. It was as though he had no interest in the young man who wanted his daughter's hand. I think

Nikita Sergeyevich was as embarrassed as I was and simply didn't know what ought to be said in such a situation."

Nina Petrovna invited Adzhubei to Kiev that summer; he spent an idyllic time swimming, fishing, and sunbathing near the Mezhgorie dacha. At the end of his stay Rada's mother announced that the pair could proceed to get married. But Rada's parents did not attend the Moscow wedding. "The idea of a wedding ceremony was absolutely alien to the Khrushchevs," Adzhubei recollected. A sole member of Khrushchev's security detail accompanied the couple to the district registry office on August 31, 1949, and only a small company of friends headed out to Abramtsevo for a wedding feast in a meadow in the woods.[4]

The newlyweds took up residence on Granovsky Street. Furnished in austere Stalinist fashion without carpets or decorations, the apartment felt particularly "hollow and empty," since the larger family still lived in Kiev and since Khrushchev came to Moscow infrequently and paid no attention to his surroundings when he did.

Several weeks after their marriage the newlyweds were studying for exams when they heard voices on the landing. It was Khrushchev, with the Ukrainian playwright Aleksandr Korneichuk and his wife, Wanda Wasilewska, in tow. Rada disappeared into the kitchen to help the maid; the company sat down for tea. Khrushchev had come from seeing Stalin and on his way home had picked up Korneichuk and Wasilewska at their Moscow hotel. Khrushchev announced he was being named Moscow party leader. At this point, Wasilewska burst into tears. "You'll be sorely missed in Ukraine, Nikita Sergeyevich."[5]

Korneichuk and Wasilewska owed much to Khrushchev's patronage.[6] Yet after his ouster in 1964 the Khrushchev family never heard from Korneichuk again (not even a brief expression of sympathy when Nikita Sergeyevich died), and if Wasilewska herself hadn't died in July 1964, she would undoubtedly have behaved the same way. That was the way of the Soviet world, according to Adzhubei. "You ate and drank with somebody whose favor you cultivated; you hunted, fished, asked advice, rushed to help, but then came the moment when you claimed not even to know him. Your very bones trembled lest someone remember that you too, brother, were his friend." But Khrushchev's craving for the respect of the intelligentsia made him especially vulnerable. That evening, remembered Adzhubei, "it was obvious that Khrushchev had to talk to someone," and clearly his daughter and son-in-law wouldn't suffice.[7] How much more satisfying to have Wasilewska weep at his departure! Nearly twenty years later Khrushchev still relished the scene: "'How can you go? How can you leave the Ukraine?' [Wasilewska] wailed. Here was a Polish woman bewailing the departure of a Russian from Ukraine! That sounds odd. But I respected her and she returned the same sort of respect. I don't hide this, because even though that may seem vain on my part, it's a pleasant memory for me, of course."[8]

Khrushchev was clearly nervous that evening. "In the midst of the conversation," Adzhubei recalled, "he would suddenly lapse into thought, withdraw into himself, and then ask, 'What were we talking about?' He asked his guests not to hurry off even though it was long after midnight. He didn't want to be alone."[9] Khrushchev himself confirmed Adzhubei's impression. He had been speaking at a rally in Lvov when Malenkov called and told him to catch a plane to Moscow the next morning. "I was ready for anything," Khrushchev later said. "I didn't know what my status would be when I returned to Ukraine—or even if I would return at all."[10]

But Stalin greeted him warmly: "How long are you going to stay down there in Ukraine? You've already turned into an Ukrainian agronomist. It's time for you to return to Moscow." Khrushchev would resume his former Moscow party posts and became one of four Central Committee secretaries besides Stalin, while retaining his membership (one of eleven) on the party's ruling Politburo. "Of course, I thanked him for that trust," Khrushchev remembered. "I said I'd return with pleasure because I'd been pleased with my work in the capital eleven years before. . . ."[11]

In the past Khrushchev had felt or feigned uncertainty at moments like this, and he had plenty of reason to do so again. Stalin was more paranoid than ever. Nikolai Voznesensky and Aleksei Kuznetsov, two younger Politburo members whom Stalin had spoken of as possible political heirs, were arrested in 1949 and were to be shot a year later.[12] Molotov, Mikoyan, and Voroshilov were also in danger. Malenkov and Beria seemed invulnerable; indeed, Stalin's reason for summoning Khrushchev from Kiev was probably to balance and limit their power. But that gave them reason to undermine him, and he later claimed (not entirely ingenuously, it turns out) that he feared and hated them both. Beria comes across in Khrushchev's memoirs as evil incarnate; Malenkov "was a typical office clerk and paper-pusher. Such men can be the most dangerous of all if given power. They'll freeze and kill anything that's alive if it oversteps its prescribed boundaries."[13]

Although the Kremlin was a viper's nest, Khrushchev didn't try to ride out Stalin's last years in Kiev. He had no choice, of course, once the *vozhd* summoned him to Moscow, but other calculations counted as well. The only way to avoid losing the Kremlin duel to the death that marked Stalin's last years was to win, and the place to prevail was on the spot in Moscow, especially since Stalin's summons demonstrated his continuing support. "Despite everything," Khrushchev insisted, "Stalin regarded me highly. If he hadn't, if he distrusted me, he could easily have made short work of me. . . . I'd even say he regarded me with a kind of respect. So that each time, after being rude or spiteful to me, he would express his good will."[14]

Of Khrushchev's Kremlin colleagues, Beria was particularly dangerous. But like all of Stalin's men, he had weaknesses, and by now Khrushchev himself had important strengths, particularly a reputation that led potential rivals to underestimate him. In their eyes he seemed the same peasant turned court jester who had left for Kiev eleven years before. In fact, he had become far more self-assured, and he had gained more confidence by the time Stalin died. By then Malenkov looked like Stalin's heir apparent. The fact that Molotov, Mikoyan, and Voroshilov managed comebacks after Stalin's death made Khrushchev seem an even darker horse. No one realized that between 1949 and 1953 he began to think of himself as Stalin's successor.[15]

STALIN'S LAST THREE YEARS were the bleakest of all, not just for his country but for himself and his lieutenants. Far fewer people perished between 1950 and 1953 than in the thirties or during the war. But the hope that had coexisted with the suffering had also dimmed.[16] By 1950 the revolution had degenerated into a miasma of Russia-first chauvinism, while a new burst of bloodletting settled scores within the ruling elite.

Reportedly Stalin suffered a small stroke in 1945 and another in 1947. Between 1947 and 1951 his annual Black Sea vacations stretched from late August until early December.[17] The arteriosclerosis that was to kill him in 1953 was already having an effect. "As he had gotten older," Svetlana Alliluyeva remembered, "my father had begun feeling lonely. He was so isolated from everyone by this time, so elevated, that he seemed to be living in a vacuum. He hadn't a soul he could talk to. . . . He was bitter, as bitter as he could be against the whole world. He saw enemies everywhere. It had reached the point of being pathological, of persecution mania, and it was all the result of being lonely and desolate."[18]

Stalin drastically cut back on formal party meetings during his last years, conducting business instead in bizarre all-night movable feasts.

Although party congresses were supposed to be convened every few years, none was held between 1939 and 1952. Central Committee plenums too were rare, and the Politburo as a whole hardly met.[19] Vast swaths of policy were delegated to six- or seven-man Politburo commissions (named sextets and septets), but they didn't meet either. Instead, Stalin would summon his inner circle (Beria, Malenkov, Khrushchev, and Bulganin) to watch movies in the Kremlin, after which they would repair to his dacha to eat, drink, and talk until dawn.

Stalin selected the movies, many of them American, for screening with an obsolete projector.[20] "He liked cowboy movies especially," Khrushchev said later. "He used to curse them and give them a proper ideological evaluation and then immediately order new ones." Since the prints were "captured trophies" purloined from the West, they lacked subtitles. Cinematography chief Ivan Bolshakov would "translate" them aloud from a variety of languages he didn't know. "He had been told the plot in advance," Khrushchev explained. "He would take pains to memorize it. . . . In many of the scenes, Bolshakov . . . would just explain what anyone could see was happening on the screen: 'Now he's leaving the room . . . Now he's walking across the street.' Beria would then chime in and give Bolshakov some help: 'Look! He's started running! Now he's running!' "[21]

History doesn't record if Beria's interjections produced the same effect on Bolshakov that Stalin's did on a Soviet film director who was present when his film was viewed. The idea was to give the man the leader's critical comments directly. "This will be beneficial for the directors and for their work," was the way Stalin put it. But when this director overheard Stalin whisper that a document his secretary brought him was "rubbish," he feared that the rubbish in question was his film and proceeded to soil his pants and collapse.[22]

Sometimes the films cut too close to the bone. This was especially true of an historical epic about a deranged pirate captain who systematically went about liquidating his crew until he himself was eliminated. However, what followed the cinema, what Khrushchev called the *kormlenie* (feeding), was even worse. "Well," Stalin would suggest, "let's go get something to eat." According to Khrushchev's account, "The rest of us weren't hungry. By now it was usually one or two in the morning. It was time to go to bed, and the next day we had to work." Not only that, but "there was always a risk that if you didn't take a nap [during lunch hour], you might get sleepy at the table; and those who got sleepy at Stalin's table could come to a bad end." But "everyone would say, yes, he was hungry too."[23]

At this point the weary company piled into several cars (Beria and Malenkov in Stalin's copycat version of an armor-plated Packard, and Khrushchev with Bulganin) and raced through dark and deserted streets to Stalin's dacha in Kuntsevo, just off the high road to Mozhaisk. Stalin chose a different route each time to thwart would-be assassins, informing his chauffeurs and bodyguards just before leaving the Kremlin. Painted a dark green camouflage, the dacha was surrounded by a vast expanse of asphalt to facilitate detection of intruders, by woods filled with land mines and patrolled by crack security troops, and by a high fence and barricades. The main house itself had been built in 1934 to replace an earlier dacha in Zubalovo that Stalin had abandoned after his wife's suicide. According to his daughter, the new place was a "wonderful, airy, modern, one-story dacha set in a garden, among woods and flowers." But the restless dictator, who rarely remained seated at meetings, instead pacing up and down puffing on his pipe, had his dacha "rebuilt over and over again." According to Alliluyeva, ". . . the same thing happened to all his houses. He would go south to one of his vacation retreats, and by the time he went back the next summer the place would have been built all over again."

Stalin added a second floor to the Kuntsevo dacha in 1948 but used it only once for a reception for a visiting Chinese delegation. He received Politburo colleagues and international visitors in a large dining room–living room with wood-paneled walls, a long table and heavy chairs, and a great soft rug and fireplace—"all the luxury my father wanted," said Alliluyeva. As described by Djilas, it was a "spacious and unadorned, though tasteful, dining room," with half the long table "covered with all kinds of food on warmed heavy silver platters as well as beverages and plates and other utensils. Everyone served himself and sat where he wished around the free half of the table. Stalin never sat at the head, but he always sat in the same chair—the first to the left of the head of the table."[24]

Beyond the dining room, through a nearly invisible door in the wall, was Stalin's bedroom, containing a bed, two small dressers, and a sink. But he often slept in his library, another small chamber whose many shelves and cupboards were filled with books and papers. It was in this study, on a sofa by the wall, that Stalin lay dying in March 1953.[25] During late-night gatherings before then, his guests felt as if they were. These were "frightful . . . , interminable, agonizing dinners," Khrushchev complained. Since Stalin feared his food might be poisoned, each guest (except Beria, who brought his own) sampled dishes before the boss did.

Stalin would say, "Look, here are the giblets, Nikita. Have you tried them yet?" The faithful Khrushchev would reply, "Oh, I forgot." Khrushchev "could see that he would like to take some himself but was afraid. I would try them and only then would he start to eat them himself."[26]

After Stalin's guests had drunk themselves into a stupor, his daughter recalled, their "personal bodyguards would step in, each 'custodian' dragging away his drunken 'charge.'"[27] Molotov said that Voroshilov, Bulganin, and Beria (who didn't like to get drunk but did so to please his master) got particularly soused, as did Khrushchev "later."[28] Khrushchev insisted he and others asked waitresses to pour them "colored water instead of wine," but Stalin "fumed with anger and raised a terrible uproar." According to Mikoyan, Stalin wanted to "loosen our tongues" so as to find out "who was thinking what." Khrushchev thought Stalin "found it entertaining to watch the people around him get themselves into embarrassing and even disgraceful situations. For some reason he found the humiliation of others very amusing."[29] Khrushchev imagined that someday the *vozhd* would go so far as to "take down his pants, relieve himself at the table, and then tell us that was in the interests of Russia."[30]

The formerly pro-temperance Khrushchev was particularly embarrassed to be hung over the next morning: "It was shameful to be met at the airport by someone who would see, when you started talking to him, that you were in that condition. It was disgraceful."[31] Not to mention the practical jokes: tomatoes left on chairs so that "when the victim sat on it there would be loud roars of laughter"; a spoonful of salt in a glass of wine or vodka mixed with the wine. Stalin's assistant, Aleksandr Poskrebyshev, described by Sergo Beria as a "narrow-shouldered dwarf" who "resembled a monkey," was regularly the butt of such jokes; often, wrote Alliuyeva, he had to be "carried home dead drunk, after having lain some time in the bathroom."[32] Khrushchev was also a favorite target, particularly of Beria. One night Beria scrawled the word "prick" on a piece of paper and pinned it to the back of Khrushchev's overcoat. Khrushchev donned the garment without noticing and was preparing to leave when the company burst into guffaws. According to an aide, "Khrushchev was proud and touchy, and the incident still stung years later."[33]

Then there was the dancing. The Polish Communist leader Jakob Berman recalled dancing with Molotov in the late 1940s. Didn't he mean Mrs. Molotov? Berman was asked. "No, she wasn't there; she was in a labor camp. I danced with Molotov—I think it was a waltz. . . . I don't know the faintest thing about dancing, so I just moved my feet in rhythm. Molotov led." This was a "good opportunity," Berman added, "to whisper to each other things that couldn't be said out loud."[34] But Khrushchev was less pleased to perform the traditional Ukrainian gopak: "I had to squat down on my haunches and kick out my heels, which frankly wasn't very easy for me. But I did it and I tried to keep a pleasant expression on my face. As I later told Anastas Ivanovich Mikoyan, 'When Stalin says dance, a wise man dances.'"[35]

A wise man also listened to Stalin's long-winded stories. One of them concerned a hunt during his prerevolutionary exile in Siberia. According to Khrushchev, who probably heightened Stalin's own hyperbole, the boss claimed to have skied eight miles into the forest, spotted twenty-four partridges in a tree, killed twelve of them with twelve shots, skied back to town for more ammunition (while the remaining birds kindly waited for him to return), and then bagged the other twelve and dragged them home. "After dinner," Khrushchev said later, "while we were washing up before leaving, we were literally spitting with scorn in the bathroom. Beria said: 'Listen, how could a man from the Caucasus, who never had much chance to ski, travel a distance like that? He's lying!' Of course, he was lying. None of us had any doubt about that."[36]

Awful as these sessions were, it was better to be there than not, better to be humiliated than annihilated. The same went for accompanying Stalin on vacation. Once Khrushchev and other leaders summering by the Black Sea were summoned to Borzhomi, where Stalin was staying. Since the big house had previously been a museum, "there were no bedrooms, and we used to sleep all crowded together. It was awful. We depended on Stalin for everything. We were on an entirely different schedule from his. In the morning we would be up and have taken a walk, and Stalin would still be sleeping. Then he would get up and the day would officially begin." Nights were devoted to hazing of the sort inflicted on the brutal Hungarian Communist dictator, Mátyás Rákosi. Rákosi had intruded on Stalin's vacation and compounded his sin by complaining about the drunkenness around him. In response, Stalin pumped so much wine into the Hungarian that Khrushchev feared he would drop dead then and there. After Rákosi departed the next morning, Khrushchev remembered, "Stalin was in a good mood all day and joked, 'You see what sort of a state I got him into?'"[37]

Worse than collective vacationing, Khrushchev insisted, was the "great honor" Stalin paid him of dragging him along on solo holidays. "I clearly would have preferred not to go," Khrushchev insisted, "but to have said so would have been absolutely unthinkable. I always went along and suffered. I once spent a whole month on vacation with him. He put me right next door to him. It was sheer torture. I had to spend all my time with him, sitting over endless meals. Whenever I was offered up in sacrifice, Beria used to cheer me up by saying, 'Look at it this way: someone had to suffer; it might as well be you.' "[38]

If Beria believed that, he wasn't Beria. What greater boon for a clever courtier than to have the king to himself for days and weeks at a time! Khrushchev admitted that "putting up with the ordeal had its rewards and advantages, too. Conversations were always going on which you could use profitably, and from which you could draw useful conclusions for your own purposes."[39]

Although he knew Stalin's dark nature, Khrushchev still admired his mind and thought he could learn from him. "We no longer looked on him as we had when 'enemies of the people' were first being unmasked, when it seemed he could see through iron and stone. . . . But after smashing Hitler's forces, he still had an aura of glory and genius about him." The consequences of Stalin's actions were sometimes odious to Khrushchev, but "he remained a Marxist" who "did everything in his power for the victory of the working class. . . . I have to give him his due," Khrushchev said. "Until the day of his death he could dictate and compose quickly and clearly. His formulations were short and easy to understand. This was his great gift, and it gave him great power; you can't minimize it or take it away from him. Everyone who knew Stalin admired this gift and was therefore proud to work with him. . . . Especially when he was sober and in sound mind, he gave the people around him good advice and instruction. I'll say it straight: I valued him highly and strongly respected him."[40]

As a judgment on one of history's greatest villains, this is a moral travesty, but it helped Khrushchev keep his balance in a power struggle that was ever more perilous. Stalin's suspicions were sharpening, but his declining memory allowed room to maneuver. Just when they were most needed, allies and friends were particularly distrusted, while enemies who couldn't be eliminated had to be appeased.[41]

Molotov had proved his loyalty again and again.[42] His capacity for endless hard work was legendary; not only did he sign thousands of death sentences for "enemies of the people," but decades later he still justified the arrests of their wives and children: "They had to be isolated to some extent. Otherwise, of course, they would have spread all sorts of complaints and demoralization."[43] Nevertheless, in March 1949 Molotov was replaced as foreign minister by the purge trial prosecutor Andrei Vyshinsky, a month after Molotov's wife, Polina Zhemchuzhina, was arrested. Zhemchuzhina had risen from deputy commissar of food industry to commissar of fish industry to head of the state perfume trust. According to Svetlana Alliluyeva, she was "the first lady of Moscow, hostess at diplomatic receptions at her own dacha and in other official residences. . . . Our own dull government apartment in the Kremlin," Stalin's daughter wrote, "could not compare with the Molotovs'. . . ."[44]

Molotov's wife was charged with stealing documents, promiscuity and debauchery (two officials in her ministry "confessed" to sexual relations with her), and Zionism. She was sentenced to five years in a Siberian prison camp.[45] Zhemchuzhina was Jewish, but apart from having a sister in Palestine and a brother in America, her only brush with Zionism was on direct orders from Stalin himself: As a former member of the wartime Jewish Anti-Fascist Committee she had been assigned to cultivate the first Israeli ambassador to Moscow, Golda Meir, in 1948. It wasn't Molotov who suffered because of his wife, he later said, but she because of him. "They were looking for a way to get at me, and tried to do so through her."[46]

"It suddenly came into Stalin's head that Molotov was an agent of American imperialism," Khrushchev remembered. "It seemed that when Molotov was in the United States he traveled from Washington to New York by train. Stalin reasoned that if Molotov traveled by train, then he must have had his own private railway car. And if he had his own private railway car, then where did he get the money? Hence, Molotov must have sold himself to the Americans."[47]

Klim Voroshilov's military career never recovered from his blunders during the Finnish war and the defense of Leningrad. He fancied himself a patron of the arts, but the film director Mikhail Romm got the impression that Voroshilov wasn't so much in charge of culture as "attached" to it. "I feel I am getting older and more stupid," he confessed to Romm.[48] But even a pretentious fathead like Voroshilov (who rode around his estate in a white flannel suit on horses received from his vassals and insisted on making political speeches even at intimate family dinners)[49] struck Stalin as a Western spy. "How did Voroshilov worm his way into the Politburo?" he suddenly asked in the middle of a late-night dacha dinner.[50]

Kaganovich had been tainted ever since his older brother, Mikhail, who was fired as commissar of the aircraft industry and dropped from the Central Committee for alleged Nazi links, shot himself. Refusing to defend his brother didn't ensure Kaganovich's safety. As a sycophant par excellence, a ruthless mobilizer of men and machines, and a Jew Stalin could point to in his highest councils, he was useful. But by 1952 he too had been excluded from the inner circle.

Mikoyan was a more sympathetic figure. Alliluyeva credits Mikoyan and his wife, Ashken ("a quiet, attractive woman, an excellent housewife"), with fostering a "democratic attitude and a simplicity of relationship" in their family.[51] Like all of Stalin's men, Mikoyan carried out even the most awful orders, but his life too hung by a thread in 1952. At a Central Committee plenum after the Nineteenth Congress in October, Stalin attacked Molotov and Mikoyan mercilessly. According to the writer Konstantin Simonov, who was present, Stalin "pitched into Molotov, accusing him of cowardice and defeatism. . . . Then he turned on Mikoyan, and his words became angrier and ruder still. There was a terrible silence in the hall. The faces of all the Politburo members were rigid, petrified. They were wondering whom he would attack next. Molotov and Mikoyan were deathly pale."[52]

Khrushchev says that he, Malenkov, and Beria tried to "soften Stalin's attitude" toward Molotov and Mikoyan. When Stalin barred them from dacha soirees, Khrushchev and friends quietly informed them of the schedule so they could try to attend anyway. But after awhile it was "useless to persist. It wouldn't do Molotov and Mikoyan any good, and it might jeopardize our position in Stalin's eyes. . . . I'm convinced that if Stalin had lived much longer, Molotov and Mikoyan would have met a disastrous end."[53]

IF THE OLD GUARD was doomed, who would replace them? After the war two factions of somewhat younger leaders jockeyed for position. Beria and Malenkov headed one while a second, known as the Leningrad faction, included Zhdanov, Voznesensky, and Kuznetsov.[54] On paper, Malenkov and Beria looked unbeatable. Both had held key posts in Moscow since 1939 (Malenkov in charge of party personnel, Beria heading the secret police), both had served on the State Defense Committee and as Stalin's deputies on the Council of Ministers after the war, and both became full Politburo members in 1946.[55] But both had flaws that offered openings to their rivals.

Although he possessed great power, Malenkov was unprepossessing, at least in the eyes of his colleagues. According to Molotov, Malenkov was "a good implementer, a 'telephone man,' as we used to call him. He was always on the phone; he knew how to find things out, how to get through—that, he could do." He was "active, lively, and sociable. And he kept his mouth shut on the big issues. But he never headed even one party organization, in contrast with Khrushchev, who did so both in Moscow and Ukraine."[56]

Andrei Malenkov portrays his father as an "enlightened technocrat" with wide-ranging intellectual interests and no taste for bloody intrigues. Malenkov's longtime aide Dmitri Sukhanov insisted his boss was "free from many ideological dogmas." But even if these qualities were real (and that is hardly guaranteed), they could be liabilities. Alliluyeva regarded Malenkov as "clearly the most reasonable and sagacious member of the Politburo," but his Kremlin peers perceived him as weak. Malenkov and Andrei Zhdanov resembled each other: Zhdanov's son (whom Alliluyeva later married) was a chemist; Malenkov's children, she wrote, "were brought up like any other children in an intellectual milieu." But, she added, Zhdanov regarded Malenkov with contempt, constantly referring to him as "'Malanya,' on account of his round womanish face—Malanya or Malashka, being a common name among Russian peasant women."[57]

Beria, to put it mildly, wasn't weak. He was smart, calculating, and entirely cynical. He had a territorial base in the Caucasus, the secret police at his fingertips, and Stalin himself seemingly under his thumb. "I speak advisedly," wrote Alliluyeva, of Beria's "influence on my father and not the other way around. Beria was more treacherous, more practiced in perfidy and cunning, more insolent and single-minded than my father. In a word, he was a stronger character."

Like Stalin's daughter, his lieutenants later used Beria as a scapegoat. Actually, Stalin, not Beria, was the primary engine of the terror, but Beria too was a monster. True, the terror eased after he replaced Yezhov in 1939, but he personally tortured prisoners in his NKVD office. True, he had an impressive family. Nina Teimurazovna, a beautiful woman trained as a chemist, "played the part of wife and hostess, although she had long since ceased being either," said Alliluyeva, and their only son, Sergo, "knew German and English, and became one of the first missile engineers in the country. . . . He was gentle-mannered and agreeable like his mother."[58] However, Beria himself was a marauding rapist.

"Ordinary" womanizing was a favorite game in Stalin's court. Besides Poskrebyshev and Stalin's chief bodyguard, Nikolai Vlasik, active players included the elderly, wispy-bearded Soviet president Mikhail Kalinin (whether before or after his wife was arrested is not clear), and Bulganin. The latter consorted with a well-known singer who lived in his Granovsky Street apartment house, and he once introduced another mistress as his wife.[59] As for Beria, he cruised Moscow streets in his limousine, spotted young women and girls to be delivered to his Kachalov Street town house, plied them with wine containing a sleeping potion, and then raped them.[60]

Milovan Djilas described Beria as "somewhat plump, greenish pale, and with soft, damp hands. With his square-cut mouth, and bulging eyes behind his pince-nez, he suddenly reminded me of Vujkovic, the chief of the Belgrade Royal Police who specialized in torturing Communists."[61] Even Stalin was apparently afraid of him; he once called his daughter at Nina Teimurazovna's house, cursing and shouting, "Come back at once! I don't trust Beria!"[62] "Stalin realized," wrote Khrushchev, "that if Beria could eliminate anyone at whom Stalin pointed his finger, then Beria could also eliminate someone of his own choosing. . . . Stalin feared that he would be the first person Beria might choose. Naturally Stalin never told anyone about this, but I could sense it nonetheless."[63]

Evil genius though he was, Beria had fatal flaws. A brief 1918 stint as a spy in an anti-Bolshevik Azerbaijani government could be, and later was, portrayed as treason. His transparent ambition alarmed his colleagues. Beria "was arrogant about everything," said Khrushchev. "Nothing could be decided without him. . . . [I]f you made a report to Stalin in Beria's presence and if you hadn't cleared it with him beforehand, he would be sure to tear down your report in Stalin's eyes with all sorts of questions and contradictions."[64]

Beria's defects gave an advantage to Zhdanov. In 1934 Zhdanov had replaced the murdered Kirov as head of the Leningrad party organization, second only to Moscow's in prestige and importance. In 1939 he became a full Politburo member, six years before Malenkov and Beria. Like Khrushchev, Zhdanov was left off the State Defense Committee; instead he was given the thankless task of overseeing Leningrad's defense. At war's end he was sent away to Finland, where he represented the USSR on the Allied Control Commission in Helsinki. But his endless loyalty and submissiveness, and his workaholic perfectionism, helped restore him to Stalin's favor.

Zhdanov had intellectual pretensions; the same man who laid waste to Russian literature and music played the piano. He was also adroit enough to outdo Malenkov and Beria, at least for a while. In 1946 Malenkov was dropped from the Central Committee Secretariat, while Beria had lost direct control over the police ministries.[65] Zhdanov's number two man in Leningrad, Kuznetsov, replaced Malenkov as Central Committee secretary in charge of personnel, while Voznesensky replaced a Malenkov protégé as head of the State Planning Commission and became a full Politburo member in 1947.[66]

Kuznetsov and Voznesensky were ambitious and hard-driving, but better educated than their elders and with less blood on their hands. For a while Stalin let Voznesensky chair sessions of the government in his absence, and he mentioned him as a future head of government and Kuznetsov as a potential party general secretary.[67] But if Stalin elevated Zhdanov because Malenkov and Beria got too powerful, he could and did do the reverse. Zhdanov's ill health didn't help his cause (by 1948 he was obese, pasty-faced, asthmatic, and often drunk), and Beria apparently convinced Stalin to rehabilitate Malenkov.[68] Zhdanov died in August 1948 under circumstances that remain less than clear, and after Malenkov visited Leningrad in early 1949, Kuznetsov, Voznesensky and other top Leningrad leaders were accused of factionalism, Russian nationalism, and assorted other sins. Kuznetsov was arrested (in Malenkov's office, no less), in August 1949, Vozensensky in October. The day Kuznetsov was relieved of his post, his family was celebrating his daughter's engagement to Anastas Mikoyan's son, Sergo. Kaganovich warned Sergo's father: "Are you allowing this wedding? Have you lost your mind? Don't you understand that Kuznetsov is doomed?" He was right. In September 1950 Politburo members, including Khrushchev, signed death sentences for Kuznetsov, Voznesensky, and several others. Several weeks later they were secretly "tried" and convicted; immediately afterwards, executioners placed white shrouds over their heads, carried them out of the courtroom feet first, and shot them. Kuznetsov's wife was also arrested and sent to the camps, as were Voznesensky's brother, who was the rector of the Leningrad State University, and his sister, Maria.[69]

The gruesome denouement of the Leningrad affair left Beria and Malenkov in charge. Malenkov's assignment to give the main report at the Nineteenth Congress in October 1952 seemed to anoint him as Stalin's chosen successor. Beria's standing was shakier, however. In late 1951 Stalin ordered the arrest of officials in Mingrelia, the region of Georgia from which Beria came, and personally instructed the new police chief, Semyon Ignatiev, not to forget "the big Mingrelian." Beria parried the blow by rushing to Georgia and arresting his own clansmen, but he had no such answer to the "Doctors' plot" affair. Stalin credited wild charges that Kremlin physicians were plotting assassinations, and *Pravda* announced that Beria's state security organs "did not uncover in good time the wrecking terrorist organization among doctors."[70] Asked many years later if Stalin really needed the doctors' plot to bring down Beria, Molotov replied, "No, not really. But it would have been needed to convince others. Without it they would have kept quiet, but they wouldn't have believed."[71]

Kremlin doctors, most of them Jews, were arrested in January 1953. Mikoyan feared a return to the terror of the late thirties. If, as rumors had it, thousands of Jews had been exiled to the Far East, the new wave of terror might have brought down the entire top leadership, including Beria, Malenkov, and Khrushchev.[72]

KHRUSHCHEV'S ROLE in all this infighting isn't clear. He denied he knew "all the details" about the arrests of Kuznetsov and Voznesensky: "Stalin never discussed the Leningrad affair with me." But he did know that Beria and Malenkov had been plotting against their rivals since 1946. Stalin wavered in his determination to finish off Voznesensky, according to Khrushchev, but Beria and Malenkov kept pressing him. Khrushchev admitted he signed "the investigatory materials" when the Leningrad dossier was passed around the Politburo, but when Stalin asked him to investigate a similar affair in Moscow, again according to Khrushchev, he prevented "the sickness" from spreading to the capital.[73]

"Things aren't going very well," Stalin told Khrushchev in December 1949. "Plots have been uncovered. . . . So far we've exposed a conspiracy in Leningrad, and Moscow too is teeming with anti-party elements. We want to make the city a bastion for the Central Committee." He handed Khrushchev a lengthy document listing the party chief Grigory Popov and other Moscow officials as conspirators. Khrushchev said he "put the document in my safe and decided not to mention it again unless Stalin brought the subject up himself. I felt the longer I let the matter rest, the better."

Ignoring Stalin's instructions was daring enough. When the boss mentioned the issue again, Khrushchev claimed to have told him the document was in error. "It would have been easy enough," Khrushchev maintained, "for me to have improved my own position and to have won Stalin's confidence simply by supporting the fabricated charges. . . . All I would have had to do was say: 'Yes, Comrade Stalin, this looks serious. We'd better investigate.' . . . Popov and all the others . . . would have confessed, of course, and we would have had a conspiracy trial in Moscow every bit as disgraceful as the one in Leningrad. And I would have gotten credit. . . ." To save Popov, Khrushchev says he arranged for him to be transferred out of Moscow, so that when the forgetful dictator occasionally remembered to ask menacingly, "Where's that Popov, anyway?" the answer could be "He's in Kuibyshev."[74]

After the Nineteenth Congress, Stalin suddenly replaced the Politburo with an expanded twenty-five-man Presidium consisting of younger leaders, his apparent aim being to prepare a final purge of the old guard. "Once again I didn't understand," Khrushchev insisted. "How could this be?" He claimed he was equally horrified by the arrest of the Kremlin doctors; he was sure they were innocent and condemned himself for not saying so: "I reproach myself for this. We should have been more decisive; we shouldn't have allowed such a mad campaign. . . . I blame myself for not seeing things through to the end."[75]

Was he as innocent as he claimed? Like Pavel Sudoplatov, two well-informed historians aren't so sure, and Molotov repeatedly insisted Khrushchev was part of a troika with Malenkov and Beria during Stalin's last years.[76] But if he was closer to Malenkov and Beria than he let on, his return to Moscow in 1949 must have strained their ties. Khrushchev carried out his own purge of the Moscow party organization and certain state ministries, removing Malenkov's allies in the process.[77] When Ignatiev became secret police chief in 1951, several men who had worked with Khrushchev popped up as his deputies, while other Khrushchev protégés gained key Central Committee positions. Malenkov and Khrushchev denied to each other that either had helped Stalin select the new twenty-five-man Presidium. But if Malenkov later told his son he'd gotten several of his men appointed, was Khrushchev's denial any more sincere? If Khrushchev didn't nominate members of the new Presidium, how did his men in Ukraine get appointed to it? Also, if Khrushchev was undermining Beria, could he conceivably have encouraged Stalin to pursue the doctors' plot too?[78]

All this is speculation. In truth, Khrushchev seems to have protected those he could, like an energetic young Moscow party official who disappeared and then suddenly reappeared as the director of an aviation plant, and like a popular Komsomol leader, Nikolai Sizov. When Komsomol activists dared demand that charges against Sizov be made public, Khrushchev called them to a meeting. Instead of dressing them down, he regaled his audience with stories about his youth and talk of Moscow's economic situation. Then, having won them over, he coldly announced they would have no say in Sizov's fate: "That's the way it is, young comrades. There's a lot to do. Party decisions must be obeyed—and that means you and the Komsomol." By the time Khrushchev left the hall, the would-be protest had lost its momentum. However, while appearing to abandon Sizov, Khrushchev actually saved him; he was fired as Komsomol secretary but stayed out of harm's way at the advanced party school. "In this way," recalled Adzhubei, "it was sometimes possible to help an individual ward off a still more powerful blow."[79]

About the same time, Khrushchev's former Ukrainian Komsomol chief Kostenko was offered a job in the Central Committee apparatus in

Moscow. "Don't quote me," whispered Khrushchev when his protégé asked for advice. "Don't take it! Don't come here!" Kostenko rode out Stalin's last year in a provincial job.[80]

Whatever Khrushchev's precise role in Stalin's last years, the game he was playing required him simultaneously to befriend Malenkov and Beria and to betray them. He remembered being "friends" with Malenkov when they worked together in the thirties. He stayed at Malenkov's dacha during wartime visits to Moscow, and he often dropped in on the Malenkovs when he was in town from Kiev. Khrushchev and Malenkov went hunting together, and beginning in 1950, their families went on mushroom-picking expeditions, followed by dinners at each other's dachas. Khrushchev even recruited the Malenkovs for evening strolls, which he had made a habit of in Kiev but which were new to Stalin's courtiers in Moscow. Followed by their wives and children (trailed in turn by nervous bodyguards), the two men walked down Granovsky Sreet, turned right on Kalinin Prospekt, continued along the Mokhavaya, turned right on Gorky Street, and then headed home. Sometimes the group even took the long way home via the Aleksandrovsky Garden alongside the Kremlin wall.[81]

Asked who her father's "friends" were between 1949 and 1953, Rada Adzhubei answered coolly: "It's a complex question. It's hard to say. From the thirties on, we had been friends with the Malenkov and Bulganin families, and here in Moscow, where we lived in the same apartment house, we often got together. But although we saw a lot of each other in the postwar period, I couldn't really call it friendship."[82]

Stalin didn't encourage friendships among his lieutenants. But personal strains also intervened. Malenkov's son, Andrei, reported that Khrushchev was the only colleague with whom his father socialized. The two men called each other Nikita and Yegor and celebrated each other's birthdays, and their children constantly visited each other's Granovsky Street apartments. But although Nina Petrovna was "an intelligent woman," Andrei said, and her husband was "the liveliest" of Malenkov's colleagues, Khrushchev was "incredibly crude." "My parents were of gentry origin," Malenkov explained, "they had graduated from a *gimnazium,* they had higher education, and they often had academics and professors as guests. Khrushchev was completely uncouth, had a shockingly coarse sense of humor, and obviously didn't read and didn't know literature."[83]

Malenkov was too smart to display his disdain, but Khrushchev was too shrewd not to sense it. Malenkov "showed a certain amount of condescension toward me during the war," Khrushchev later noted, "especially when Stalin displayed his dissatisfaction toward me."[84] If the two of them did not have a falling-out, that was because neither could afford not to cultivate the other. In that sense, both men wore masks, as each did with Beria and he did with them.

Khrushchev had plenty of reason to fear Beria. According to Adzhubei, Beria's operatives tried to raid Khrushchev's Moscow party office in 1951, threatening the aide on duty with dire consequences if he didn't let them "check the security of Khrushchev's safe and telephone." When his refusal produced a volley of curses but no further consequences, Khrushchev's aide concluded that Beria had decided not to pick a fight with Khrushchev.[85]

After Adzhubei and Rada Khrushcheva were married, state security reported that the young couple had been "chattering" about the "good life" the Khrushchev family led. Khrushchev blamed Adzhubei (correctly, said Sergei Khrushchev many years later); Adzhubei and Rada suspected university friends who had visited them at the family dacha. Nikita Khrushchev later told Adzhubei that the denunciation had been "specially arranged" to compromise the Khrushchev family.

One summer vacation in the Caucasus Beria took Khrushchev up to a high mountain pass overlooking the Black Sea. "What a vista, Nikita! Let's build houses for ourselves here. We'll breathe the mountain air and live to be a hundred like the old people in this valley." When Beria proposed resettling people who lived on the spot, Khrushchev smelled a "provocation," just as he did when Beria tried "to drag me into anti-Stalinist talk and then denounce me to Stalin."[86]

Despite Beria's machinations or, rather, because of them, Khrushchev was loath to offend or alienate him. According to Molotov, "Malenkov, Beria and Khrushchev were a core group, a 'trinity.'"[87] When Adzhubei worked late at *Komsomolskaya pravda,* the newspaper that took him on after journalism school, he often rode home with his father-in-law. Sometimes, obviously by prearrangement, Khrushchev's car rendezvoused on the dark road with Beria's; Adzhubei then traded places with Beria so that he and Khrushchev could talk. When the two cars drove up to the gates of Khrushchev's dacha, said Adzhubei, "Nikita Sergeyevich got out and shook Beria's hand for a long time. Then he stood there, hat in hand, until Beria's car was out of sight. Khrushchev understood very well that the duty officer at the gate would surely inform his bosses as to the deference with which he saw Beria off."[88]

Beginning in 1939, according to Khrushchev, Beria started warning him that Malenkov had been too close to the fallen police chief Yezhov. A decade or so later Beria confided to Khrushchev, "Listen, Malenkov is weak-willed; he's a goat who might suddenly jump if he's not held on to. That's why I . . . go around with him. On the other hand, he's Russian and a cultured man who can come in handy when needed." That gave Khrushchev an opening. "I'm amazed that you don't realize what Beria's attitude toward you is," Khrushchev whispered to Malenkov when they were at Stalin's Sochi dacha. "Don't you see it? Do you think he respects you? I think he's mocking you." After a long pause Malenkov replied, "Yes, I see it, but what can I do?" Khrushchev replied, "I'd just like to be sure you understand. It's true you can't do anything now. But there'll be a chance later."[89]

Stalin's men played games within games, and Khrushchev was getting good at them. One of Beria's ploys was to surround Stalin with Georgian servants. Each time Khrushchev encountered the Georgian chef whom Beria had made a major general, the man wore more ribbons and medals. Once Stalin caught Khrushchev staring at the ribbons, and the two exchanged looks. "He knew what I was thinking, and I knew what he was thinking, but neither of us said anything," Khrushchev recalled.[90] Another time, at a late-night dinner at Stalin's dacha at which Beria served as *tamada* (master of the revels), Khrushchev declined to sing a solo. "I refused, and Stalin looked at me and Beria, waiting to see how it would come out. Beria saw I wouldn't give in and left me alone, sensing that Stalin liked my stubbornness."[91]

What is so striking about these vignettes is Khrushchev's ability to "read" Stalin and Beria and to read them reading him. Even more important was his capacity to conceal his growing mastery behind a convincing image of himself as a crude and limited man.

KHRUSHCHEV'S DECIDEDLY mixed record as Moscow party leader helped do the convincing. While his post-1949 accomplishments in industry and agriculture won him points with Stalin, his failures ensured that his rivals would continue to underestimate him.

Khrushchev attacked Moscow's housing crisis with energy and imagination. Most residents lived in communal apartments, often with two families to a single room, while tens of thousands made do in barracks. Although the city's population had grown by a million in ten years, the total amount of housing barely exceeded the 1940 level.[92] Khrushchev revolutionized housing by using prefabricated reinforced concrete.[93] Metro construction also leaped ahead, but so did the heedless destruction of historical sites (including the old Kitaigorod wall along the Moscow River bank) to which he had shown so little sensitivity in the thirties.[94]

Soviet agricultural output in 1950 still fell far short of pre-1913 levels. Instead of pouring resources into the countryside, the regime continued to pump them out. Payments for mandatory deliveries were so low that peasants sold their output for much less than the cost of production, while the price of industrial goods, such as trucks and tractors, rose several times. Many peasants in effect worked without pay under a new sort of serfdom; the only way to survive was to concentrate on their small individual plots, yet taxes on these were continually raised. Lacking internal passports, peasants could not escape to the city.[95]

The Moscow region, whose soil compared poorly with the southern black earth zone, had been particularly neglected. As soon as he was settled in the capital, Khrushchev sent his aide Andrei Shevchenko on an inspection tour. The small, decrepit collective farms Shevchenko visited bore grandiose names like Death to Capitalism, but had no machinery, no electricity, and few, if any, males of working age. When the lone teacher in a broken-down one-room schoolhouse offered Shevchenko some soup, he picked out some ratty-looking threads and tossed them away. "But that's meat," the teacher protested.

Soon afterward Khrushchev and Shevchenko descended on an out-of-the-way kolkhoz. They found no one in the chairman's ramshackle office, and the chairman's keys were on a table. "He up and left," someone said. "Just chucked it. We're too poor." Khrushchev summoned the local schoolteacher, gave him the keys, and appointed him chairman on the spot. When Khrushchev returned to Moscow, Stalin rebuked him for "rattling around the countryside."[96]

Khrushchev's agricultural innovations included expanding livestock and poultry farms, consolidating small fields, and adopting land improvement schemes. Promoting the planting of Central Asian melons and Jerusalem artichokes turned out to be less helpful.[97] When peasants refused to change and new managers proved incompetent, he took their failures as a personal affront. "It used to drive me crazy to see how unsophisticated our farmers were," Khrushchev said later. When authorities delivered fertilizer, "more often than not the peasants let it rot next to the railroad station. For two or three years the stuff would sit there in a huge pile, serving as a perfect slide for the kids in the winter."[98] In 1950 he dropped in on an institute near Moscow that specialized in potatoes. When the director reported her experimental fields yielded only half of what nearby farms obtained, Khrushchev exploded. "Poor thing, she hadn't expected such a reaction. Tears came to her eyes, and she sobbed, 'We've been looking forward to your visit with such pleasure, and now you come here and say such unpleasant things to us.' I don't think anybody had ever before told her truthfully what a miserable job her institute was doing."[99]

At an April 1950 meeting with farmers and agronomists, Khrushchev stayed mad the whole day. Provoked by a string of hapless orators, he shouted out edicts ("Investigate and punish him!"; "Exclude him from the party!"; "Take him to court for a formalistic approach to his work!"), plus a barrage of personal attacks: "You're lying!" "Go to hell!"[100] When a local official not only complained about the failure of officials to clean up manure from an infected herd but dared blame Khrushchev, he at first brushed aside the criticism: "Comrade Director, this isn't central to our meeting. If we stick to the issue of infected manure, we'll end up sitting on a pile of it ourselves." When his critic refused to subside, Khrushchev raged at him for nearly an hour.[101] Brutal bullying of subordinates was standard under Stalinism, but Khrushchev had once been more tolerant. It wasn't that power corrupted him; rather, it allowed him to express openly the sensitivity to slight that had been there all along.

While eruptions like this didn't get Khrushchev into trouble, his championing of agro-cities did. By the summer of 1949 the Kremlin was pressing for the amalgamation of small collective farms into larger kolkhozy. The ostensible reason was to boost efficiency; the real aim was to reach peasants who evaded state controls in isolated farms far from district centers.[102] For Khrushchev, who had begun amalgamating farms in Ukraine, the campaign gave him a chance to grab the national spotlight. Since Moscow Province farms were especially small, the case for consolidating them seemed strong. But as usual, Khrushchev overdid it. In March 1950 he called for resettling collective farmers from "small and badly laid-out villages" to "new villages [with] good living and cultural conditions," including "comfortable, high-quality housing"—all in "the very near future." Peasants who failed to work a minimum number of days for the collective would have their individual plots taken away. Even Stalin was cautious about plots that raised nearly half the nation's livestock. To Khrushchev, however, his proposal needed no special justification: "Just take them away, and put up a fence, and that's that."[103]

He outlined his vision of an urbanized countryside in a January 18, 1951, speech: settlements into which smaller villages would be merged; communities with "a school, hospital, maternity home, club, farm studies center and other public buildings collective farms need," with "water mains, power lines, street lights, and sidewalks," with "apartment houses" taking the place of "individual huts," with the small plots adjacent to houses limited in size, and with the remainder of these individual allotments moved to special areas outside the settlement.[104] A *Pravda* correspondent who attended this meeting asked for a copy of the speech. Sensing danger, Shevchenko urged his boss not to hand it over in a hurry. But Khrushchev wanted attention, and he got it: His speech took up two full pages of *Pravda* on March 4. Unfortunately, Stalin didn't like what he read. He called *Pravda* to tell it so, and the next day the following abrupt announcement appeared in the paper: "Through an oversight of the editorial office in printing Comrade N. S. Khrushchev's article on 'Building and Improvements in Collective Farms' in yesterday's *Pravda*, an editorial note was omitted in which it was pointed out that Comrade N. S. Khrushchev's article was published [only] as material for discussion. This statement is to correct the error."[105]

The next day Khrushchev dispatched a craven apology to Stalin: "You were absolutely correct to point out my mistakes. . . . After you did so, I tried to think about the issue more deeply. . . . My crude error . . . has inflicted harm on the party. . . . If only I had consulted with the Central Committee. . . . I ask you, Comrade Stalin, to help me correct my crude mistake and thus, as far as possible, reduce the damage I have done to the party."[106] That wasn't enough. Stalin appointed a commission, chaired by Malenkov, "to work Khrushchev over a bit more soundly." The commission prepared an eighteen-page secret letter, to be distributed to party organizations around the country, which accused Khrushchev of "endangering the whole collective farm system." The draft was discussed at a Moscow party plenum in April. Two Beria disciples, the Armenian and Azerbaijani party chiefs, lambasted Khrushchev in the press. Malenkov continued the drumbeat at the Nineteenth Party Congress in October 1952, when he criticized "certain of our leading officials" who proposed that "collective farmers' homes be pulled down" and "'agro-cities' [be] built on new sites."[107]

Khrushchev tried to conceal his chagrin: On leaving a meeting at which Stalin had chastised him, he grumbled to Minister of Agriculture Ivan Benediktov, "He knows a lot; it's easy to lead, but when you try concretely to—" but then insisted he was referring to himself.[108] Khrushchev's aides could see he was devastated. "He suffered terribly, he thought it was the end, and that they'd remove him," recalled Shevchenko. "It was terrible," said Pyotr Demichev. "He was on edge. He stopped sleeping. He aged ten years before our eyes."

Yet this too passed. Stalin condemned Khrushchev's plan as "harebrained scheming, pure and simple," "ultraleft racing ahead," and "petty bourgeois hotheadedness," but he still had a warm spot in what passed for his heart for "my little Marx." Having read a draft of the Malenkov commission report, he told Molotov, "Make it a little softer." Shortly afterward he walked over to Khrushchev, gently tapped his pipe against Khrushchev's forehead, and said, jokingly, "It's hollow."[109]

Khrushchev's landing was remarkably light, but the pain lingered. Shortly after he became head of the Soviet government in early 1958, adding that post to his Communist party leadership, the Politburo's April 1951 resolution condemning his mistake was repealed.[110] According to Adzhubei, it wasn't Khrushchev himself but his "toadying minions" who rescinded the 1951 decree. If so, those minions knew their master well.[111]

WHEN STALIN finally got around to calling the Nineteenth Party Congress in late 1952, he didn't feel up to delivering the main report. Malenkov would give it instead, he announced, while Khrushchev would speak on party statutes. His assignment made him "nervous," said Khrushchev later. "I knew that when I submitted a draft of the report, I could expect the others to attack it—especially Beria, who would pull Malenkov along with him. And that's exactly what happened." Beria's attack wasn't political; it was stylistic. He insisted Khrushchev's draft was "too long." The trouble, Khrushchev admitted, was that he had "padded" his text with "supporting examples," following Zhdanov's 1939 example. "I don't know how necessary they were, but I figured that because that particular style of report had already been approved, I would follow it."[112] Like an insecure schoolboy, he had imitated an older pupil in hopes of impressing the teacher. Then he conveniently fell ill after giving his report. "I couldn't leave home when my report was being discussed at the Congress. I had to stay in bed for a few days."[113]

Khrushchev devoted a great deal of time to filling the cultural gap about which he was so sensitive—except that instead of sampling a wide variety of what artistic Moscow had to offer, he kept returning to what he already knew. His favorite troupe was the staid Moscow Art Theater, "even though," Adzhubei remembered, "he had seen almost every play many times." He particularly liked A. N. Ostrovsky's witty plays about everyday life, and he saw Ostrovsky's *The Passionate Heart* at least ten times. "He even remembered to bring along a handkerchief," Adzhubei says, "since he anticipated the pleasure of having to wipe away tears of delight."[114]

Actually, insists Khrushchev, the petty tyrant who is the main character in *The Passionate Heart* reminded him of Stalin. The bored merchant "kept asking his retainer, 'Well, what shall we do today?' And the retainer kept trying to dream things up. They would end up playing robbers or occupying themselves with all sorts of other escapades. Just like this merchant, Stalin kept asking us, 'Well, what are we going to do today?' He wasn't capable anymore of doing anything serious."[115]

Khrushchev agreed to see any opera at the Bolshoi, and when the Kiev Opera came to town on tour, he invited its lead singers to his dacha. There, Adzhubei recalled, his father-in-law "would sing (if you can call it that) Russian and Ukrainian folk songs along with the artists. What it amounted to was a sort of musical competition as to who could recall more obscure folk songs. Khrushchev had no voice at all—his mother, Ksenia Ivanovna, also loved to sing, or rather, 'shout' a song, as they did in the villages—but he would passionately declaim opening lines as if they were a kind of recitative. The Ukrainian singers almost always recognized the words of even the most 'forgotten' refrains and sang along in full voice."

Khrushchev loved the circus too, but not the ballet unless Galina Ulanova or some other well-known dancer was performing. He lapped up documentary films, especially newsreels on science, construction, and agriculture. When interesting people or technical innovations were shown on the screen, he would order his aides to get more information about them. "Alas," Adzhubei added, "not everything that appeared on the screen existed in real life. What was called movie-fake greatly irritated Khrushchev, who took lying as a personal insult. He never watched films about himself."

Once he succeeded Stalin, Khrushchev made pronouncements on all aspects of cultural life. In the early fifties, however, Adzhubei reported, "he didn't consider himself a judge of theater, cinema, or literature. True, in the car [on the way back to the dacha] he would drop a comment such as 'That was nonsense.' But nothing more than that." According to his son-in-law: "Khrushchev's love for the theater and music shouldn't be understood as some sort of effort at adult self-education," since "he didn't talk about or analyze what he saw." This was just his way of "exercising his feelings and the way he relaxed." But Adzhubei himself admitted that "Khrushchev thirsted greedily for culture and knowledge."[116]

His colleagues weren't impressed. "Khrushchev wasn't stupid," Molotov recalled, "but he was a man of meager culture. . . . Khrushchev reminded me of a fishmonger, a petty fishmonger, or a man who sold cattle. . . . He was a shoemaker in matters of theory. . . . He was a very primitive man."[117] But Khrushchev exploited his colleagues' condescension. He was a "cunning secretive man," Adzhubei confirmed, "who in Stalin's presence played the role of a simple slogger."[118]

On top of everything else, the sheer physical strain was nearly overwhelming. "He had breakfast around 11:00 A.M." Adzhubei remembered, "came home for lunch during the day when the family was away, napped for a few hours, and in the early evening went back to Moscow party headquarters." After all-night soirees at Stalin's dacha Khrushchev returned home around dawn, but no matter how late he got back, he forced himself to walk a brisk kilometer or two around the grounds. On weekends too he awaited Stalin's summons, having to decide in the meantime whether to risk arriving at Stalin's feast with a full stomach, or to hold off on eating while waiting for the call that didn't always come.[119]

"The atmosphere was heavy," Rada Adzhubei remembered. "It was as if there weren't enough air to breathe."[120] The Khrushchev family was "a world of silence," Alksei Adzubei recalled, in which it was "unthinkable" to talk "openly about anything."[121] Nina Petrovna's rule was: "Don't ask unnecessary questions! Don't stick your nose into conversations where you don't belong!" When Khrushchev's bodyguard called to say that he'd be detained at Stalin's dacha, his son-in-law wrote later, "Nina Petrovna gave no sign of anything; she knew how to keep herself under iron control, but of course she worried. In Moscow she lived under constant stress.[122] Khrushchev's wife led a party history discussion group for apartment house service personnel at Granovsky Street. She socialized solely with Valeria Malenkova and Yelena Bulganina and saw other Kremlin wives only at huge ceremonial gatherings, like the holiday parades at Red Square, to which all households were invited.[123]

The Khrushchev children leaped to attention when Khrushchev wanted it. The eldest, Rada, and her husband (who had once aspired to be an actor) had the duty of accompanying him to the theater. "I do not misspeak," said Adzhubei, "it was a duty. One didn't refuse Nikita Sergeyevich's invitation even when it interfered with our personal plans." He added: "There was little real warmth and sensitivity in the family. It was lacking even among the children, and once they grew up they scattered far away from each other."[124] In the children's presence, Nina Petrovna referred to her husband as Nikita Sergeyevich, or Father, or N. S. Khrushchev addressed his son-in-law as Comrade Adzhubei, although out of earshot he occasionally asked his daughter about Alyosha. Family secrets were guarded as closely as political ones, partly because they *were* political. Not until many years later did Adzhubei learn that Leonid Khrushchev's widow, Liuba, had been arrested and exiled.[125]

The household's daily routine was strictly regimented: "Breakfast for the children going to school, lunch, dinner, hours for homework—everything worked like clockwork with no violations of the schedule." If the children "weren't subject to constant checking and monitoring," that was partly because they "were all careful and responsible where their studies were concerned, taking their lead from their mother's punctiliousness."[126]

Privileges and perquisites surrounded the family, but Nina Petrovna kept them at a distance. She and her husband never gave the Adzhubeis any money and insisted that they make it through the university on student stipends. It was Adzhubei's mother, the dressmaker, who helped the young couple until he landed a job (not without the help from his father-in-law's name) on the prestigious newspaper *Komsomolskaya pravda.*[127] When Adzhubei was invited to visit Austria with a delegation of journalists, Khrushchev looked very unhappy. "Be careful that everything's in order, and if something goes wrong, act appropriately!" he told his son-in-law. "Of course," Adzhubei observed, "Khrushchev knew that Beria's department would have its eye on me at all times."[128]

DESPITE EVERYTHING, Stalin's last years had golden moments for Khrushchev. One of them was Stalin's birthday, December 21, 1949. As usual, the great man feigned indifference, telling Malenkov, "Don't even think of presenting me with another Star [Hero of the Soviet Union medal]!"[129] But his acolytes knew enough to plan a lavish jubilee. During the months before the great day, tributes filled the nation's newspapers. On December 21 a portrait of Stalin's face was projected on a huge balloon suspended over the Kremlin, while throughout the land citizens, followed by floats celebrating the "Greatest Genius of All Times and Nations," paraded through cities and towns.

The climax came that evening in the Bolshoi Theater. On the flower- and banner-bedecked stage in front of a mammoth portrait of Stalin sat leaders of the USSR and world communism: Mao Zedong, Palmiro Togliatti, Walter Ulbricht, Dolores Ibárruri, Mátyás Rákosi, and others. The rest of the hall was filled with specially invited, carefully screened, and hierarchically seated guests. "The Beria family came in first," Adzhubei later wrote, "then the Malenkovs and the Molotovs. The young people sat alongside their seniors. As soon as this or that family neared the first row of seats, the stalwart lads [bodyguards] who had occupied the seats for their masters stood up. In the Khrushchev family, only Nina Petrovna had the right to sit in one of the first rows next to the Malenkovs." Adzhubei and his wife occupied less prestigious seats in the amphitheater.[130]

The speeches lasted for hours. Khrushchev's ended this way: "Glory to our dear father, our wise teacher, to the brilliant leader of the party of the Soviet people and of the workers of the entire world, Comrade Stalin!"[131] Most of the orators sounded alike, recalled Adzhubei, except for Ibárruri, the fiery La Pasionaria of Spanish Civil War fame, who "threw words out into the audience with the kind of power and enthusiasm that only religious fanatics can muster when they're about to be burned at the stake." When she began to speak, Stalin shifted his pose and lifted his head a little.

Adzhubei was surprised by "how small and frail Stalin looked" and by "a huge bald spot [that] glistened on the head of this small, even pitiful little man." To Dmitri Goriunov, a young journalist seated in the balcony, the *vozhd* looked like "an insect" on the stage below.[132] But to the top Soviet leaders nervously surveying the scene for signs of one another's status, the most important symbol was the seating arrangement. The day before, Stalin had agreed to suspend his rule of sitting "modestly" in the second row onstage. Instead he was in the first row with Mao to his right and Khrushchev to his left. Although Khrushchev's seat of honor reflected his role as Moscow party chief and hence official host for the evening, it was still a coup. But on this occasion too Khrushchev knew his limits. Noticing that the cornucopia of flowers had almost hidden Stalin's face, Adzhubei whispered to his wife, "Why doesn't Nikita Sergeyevich move them aside?" Rada replied, "Because Stalin hasn't asked him to."[133]

ON MAY DAY 1952, as crowds of citizens formed columns, preparing to parade through Red Square in the bright spring sunshine, Stalin and his lieutenants gathered inside the Kremlin. Film taken that day shows Stalin shaking hands all around, while his men bow slightly in return. What distinguishes Khrushchev on this occasion is that almost nothing does. No longer does he stand out as a junior member in a distinctive worker's cap or a Ukrainian shirt. Like all the others, except Stalin and Malenkov who are dressed in military-style tunics, he is wearing a light-colored business suit and a homburg. He is now, as he put it in his memoirs, a "full citizen" of the top leadership.[134] The only throwback in the scene is that he is the only one to salute Stalin as well as bow to him, a gesture, whether intentional or not, that reminds the boss and the others that he still knows his place.

ON NEW YEAR'S EVE 1953 at Stalin's dacha, he grabs his reluctant daughter by the hair with his fist and drags her onto the dance floor. Yet as sorry as Khrushchev felt for Svetlana, whose face turned red while tears welled in her eyes, his account of the evening is bathed with a bright, nostalgic glow: "We were all in a state of great elation. A new year! We could count to our credit one more year of victories and successes! There were tables spread with hors d'oeuvres. We had a huge dinner and a great deal to drink. Stalin was in high spirits and was therefore drinking a lot and urging everyone else to do the same."

When Stalin put Russian and Georgian folk music on the record player, "we all listened and started singing along with the records." When he put on dance music, "we started to dance. . . . I dance like a cow on ice. But I joined in nonetheless." Even Stalin, who usually stood rooted by the record player, joined in. "He shuffled around with his arms spread out. It was evident that he had never danced before.

"I would say that the general mood of the party was good," Khrushchev continued. He even explained away Stalin's loutish treatment of Svetlana. "He behaved so brutishly not because he wanted to cause Svetlanka pain. No, his behavior toward her was really an expression of affection, but in a perverse, brutish form that was peculiar to him."[135]

The same could be said of Stalin's regard for Khrushchev.

CHAPTER TEN

Almost Triumphant: 1953–1955

KHRUSHCHEV GOT THE NEWS late on March 1 at his dacha. He had spent the previous night, Saturday, February 28, 1953, with Stalin and the inner circle in the usual way: a movie at the Kremlin, followed by a late dinner at the Kuntsevo dacha. Stalin's guests departed at four o'clock in the morning, Beria and Malenkov sharing a car and Khrushchev and Bulganin leaving separately. Stalin had been in high spirits, Khrushchev recalled: "He was joking boisterously, jabbing me playfully in the stomach with his finger, and calling me 'Mikita,' with a Ukrainian accent, as he always did when he was in a good mood."[1]

Although Sunday was a day off, Khrushchev expected another summons. When the call didn't come, he finally got ready for bed. That same morning Stalin's guards and servants had expected him to rise between 10:00 and 12:00 o'clock. They noticed a light go on in his semidarkened room and waited for him to ring for food. When no call followed, they assumed he was drinking tea from a thermos by his bed. No further sign of life was observed for the rest of the afternoon. But although guards were stationed just a few steps down a corridor, they had strict orders not to enter unless ordered to do so. Sentries outside the house noticed a light in Stalin's quarters at about 6:30 P.M., but still no call came. Finally, at 10:00 or 11:00, the guards used the arrival of the evening "mail" as an excuse to send in a maid, who found Stalin lying on the floor. His hand was raised slightly. His pants were wet with urine. A copy of *Pravda* and a bottle of mineral water were nearby. When he tried to speak, all that emerged was a buzzing sound. His watch had stopped at 6:30 P.M. Apparently he had risen from his bed only to fall victim to a massive stroke.[2]

The guards lifted Stalin and placed him on a sofa. Later they moved him to another couch in the dining room. Meanwhile, they telephoned Minister of State Security Ignatiev, who, fearing to take responsibility, told them to call Malenkov and Beria. Malenkov said it would take some time to find Beria, who was apparently spending the night in a special villa in the company of his latest mistress. Finally, Beria telephoned. "Don't tell anyone about Comrade Stalin's illness," he ordered.[3]

Soon Beria and Malenkov arrived. Malenkov took off his shoes, which squeaked on the shiny parquet floor, tucked them under his arm, and tiptoed toward the dining room. As he and Beria stood by, Stalin started snoring loudly. By now it was about eight hours since his stroke, but instead of summoning medical help, Beria, who looked as if he had been drinking, berated the guards. "Can't you see Comrade Stalin is sleeping soundly? Get out of here, all of you, and don't disturb his sleep!"[4] According to Khrushchev, he too was present at this fateful moment, but the guards said he didn't arrive until seven in the morning, when Beria and Malenkov returned with other leaders and Kremlin doctors. This was not something Khrushchev was likely to have misremembered. Either the guards had it in for the man who later denounced their boss, or Khrushchev convinced himself such a crucial turn of events couldn't have occurred without him.[5]

By the time doctors arrived, Stalin had been ill for twelve hours. This delay can hardly be explained, as Khrushchev did, by saying it would have been "embarrassing" for Stalin to be seen in such an "unseemly" situation.[6] On March 3, as Stalin lay slowly dying, his wayward son Vasily screamed at Beria and the others, "You bastards, you murdered my father!"[7] Beria himself later told Molotov, "I did away with him, I saved all of you."[8] At least one Stalin biographer has imagined how Beria did it.[9] But while Beria and Malenkov may have delayed mobilizing medical assistance so as to hasten Stalin's departure, it is also possible that they were afraid to summon help. By the beginning of 1953 Stalin had fainted several times, and his blood pressure was rising. But although he stopped smoking, he didn't give up steam baths, which further raised his pressure (partly because Beria urged him not to), and he distrusted doctors until the very end.[10] So if help had arrived immediately, and if Stalin had recovered, Beria and Malenkov might not have.[11]

When doctors finally did arrive, they were obviously terrified. The primary physician's hands twitched as he opened the dictator's shirt. "You're a doctor," Beria growled, "take hold of it the way you're supposed to." Other specialists, who crowded into the room along with Politburo members, tried not to get too close. A dentist who removed Stalin's false teeth dropped them on the floor. Leeches were applied, and Stalin's lungs X-rayed, but an artificial respirator, attended by jittery technicians, stood by unused. Every medical measure required prior approval by Politburo members, who were of course incompetent to decide what to do.[12]

Stalin lingered three more days in a mostly comatose state. During this interval two members of the leadership remained by his side at all times: Beria and Malenkov during the day, Khrushchev and Bulganin at night, with Kaganovich and Voroshilov filling in. According to Molotov, Beria seemed to be in charge. He and Malenkov often stood off to one side; sometimes Khrushchev joined them, but mostly he kept a deferential distance in the doorway, while lesser leaders remained in the adjoining chamber. Beria didn't hide his hatred when Stalin was clearly unconscious but rushed up to kiss his hand when the patient came to. "That's the real Beria for you," Khrushchev remarked in his memoirs, "treacherous even in relation to Stalin whom he pretended to worship."[13] Was it better to half believe in Stalin, as Khrushchev still did?

On March 3 doctors characterized Stalin's condition as so grave that death was inevitable. By the time he died on March 5, Beria, Malenkov, Khrushchev, and Bulganin had huddled several times with Molotov, Kaganovich, Mikoyan, and Voroshilov. Malenkov chaired the meetings, and he and Beria suggested the new leadership lineup. Malenkov would succeed Stalin as chairman of the Council of Ministers. Beria, Molotov, Bulganin, and Kaganovich (in that order) would be first deputies. Beria would regain control over the Ministry of Internal Affairs, which would be reattached to the Ministry of State Security. Khrushchev would step down as Moscow party leader to concentrate on his role as one of eight Central Committee secretaries. The party Presidium, which Stalin had expanded in October 1952, would be reduced from twenty-five to ten full members, all but two of them veterans of Stalin's old guard.

So far Stalin's heirs seemed to be united. But one night, as they stood vigil, Khrushchev warned Bulganin that Beria wanted the top police post "for the purpose of destroying us, and he will do it, too, if we let him. Therefore, no matter what happens, we can't let him do it, absolutely no matter what!" Bulganin said he agreed, but they needed Malenkov's support. Yet, Khrushchev later said, "Malenkov had always thought it was profitable to play up to Beria, even though he knew Beria pushed him around and mocked him." Moreover, "now that Stalin was dead, Malenkov was sure to 'come in handy' for Beria's plans, as Beria had once told me he would."[14]

On the evening of March 5 the leaders called a joint meeting (for which there was no sanction in recently adopted party rules) of the Central Committee, the Council of Ministers, and the Supreme Soviet's Presidium. With Stalin still clinging to life, they dropped him as head of government (while continuing to list him as a member of the party Presidium). Khrushchev chaired the meeting, but Malenkov and Beria commanded it; the *Literaturnaya gazeta* editor and Central Committee member Konstantin Simonov could see and feel their predominance. Malenkov spoke first and then introduced Beria. Beria nominated Malenkov to head the Soviet government. Returning to the podium (which required squeezing past Beria, stomach to fat stomach on the narrow stairs), Malenkov designated Beria to head the police. Simonov sensed in all the leaders, except the immobile, stone-faced Molotov, "a suppressed feeling of relief that they tried not to show openly. . . ." But Malenkov and Beria spoke with a special energy and vitality.[15]

Having divided the spoils, Stalin's men raced back to Kuntsevo to witness his death agony. "His face altered and became dark," his daughter recalled. "His lips turned black and his features unrecognizable. . . . He literally choked to death as we watched. At what seemed like the very last moment he suddenly opened his eyes and cast a glance over everyone in the room. It was a terrible glance, insane or perhaps angry and full of the fear of death. . . . He suddenly lifted his hand as though he were pointing to something above and bringing down a curse on us all. . . . The next moment, after a final effort, the spirit wrenched itself free of the flesh."

At the same moment, Alliluyeva said, Beria darted out of the room. "The silence of the room . . . was shattered by the sound of his loud voice, the ring of triumph unconcealed, as he shouted [to his driver], 'Khrustalyov! My car!'"[16] Khrushchev recalled: "Beria was radiant." He "was sure that the moment he had long been waiting for had finally arrived. There was no power on earth that could hold him back now. Nothing could get in his way. Now he could do whatever he saw fit."[17]

Khrushchev grieved over Stalin's death, partly out of fear for an uncertain future but also because he "was attached to Stalin." When Alliluyeva started to cry, he later said, "I couldn't control myself. I started to weep, too, and I wept sincerely over Stalin's death." Alliluyeva remembered seeing Khrushchev, along with Voroshilov, Kaganovich, Malenkov and Bulganin, in tears. Dmitri Shepilov, then the editor of *Pravda*, attended a morning meeting on March 5 at which funeral arrangements were discussed. He remembered Beria and Malenkov "obviously in an excited state, constantly interrupting their colleagues and speaking more often than the others. Beria simply blossomed. Khrushchev said very little, clearly still in a state of shock." At the funeral in the Hall of Columns, Shepilov noticed that Khrushchev's "eyes were red and that from time to time he wiped away the tears that flowed down his cheeks."[18]

Even in Stalin's prison camps, many of his victims wept. Simonov, who knew more about Stalin's crimes than he later let on, recollected sitting down on March 5 to compose a poem about Stalin for *Literaturnaya gazeta.* He had written two lines when, "suddenly and to my surprise, I burst out weeping. I could pretend it didn't happen . . . , but I probably can't convey the extent of the shock unless I admit it. I didn't cry from grief, or from pity for one who had died; my tears weren't sentimental, they were from shock."[19]

For Khrushchev, Stalin's death was a decidedly mixed blessing, just as his patronage had been. Stalin had been a benefactor who threatened to destroy him, both mentor and tormentor in turn. His death freed Khrushchev from physical fear and psychological dependence. But it also exposed him to deadly new dangers—first from his Kremlin colleagues, later from himself, and all the while from the terrible legacy that Stalin's heirs faced and that eventually defeated them all.

DURING STALIN'S last months, Khrushchev was second or third in the Kremlin hierarchy, depending on whether Beria still ranked higher or was actually about to be purged. When the new party Presidium was chosen, Khrushchev was listed fifth, behind Malenkov, Beria, Molotov, and Voroshilov. Malenkov was the heir apparent, Beria the power behind the throne. Molotov, who had been Stalin's close collaborator longer than anyone else, also seemed a contender. The fact that these three gave the funeral orations in Red Square suggested that they formed a ruling triumvirate. Virtually no one in the USSR or abroad imagined that Khrushchev had a chance of besting them all.[20]

Two and half years later Beria had been arrested and executed, Malenkov demoted, and Molotov subjected to withering criticism. Despite falling from grace, Malenkov and Molotov retained seats on the Presidium, but by then, if not before, Khrushchev was the boss. In August 1954 he led a Soviet delegation to Beijing. Although Bulganin, who replaced Malenkov as prime minister, was theoretically the main Soviet spokesman at the four-power Geneva summit in the summer of 1955, Western leaders realized that Khrushchev was their primary interlocutor.

If Khrushchev foresaw his own triumph, he was the only one who did. In that sense, his victory was the greatest of all the miracles that marked his astonishing rise. Yet the way he pulled it off was utterly predictable. Like Stalin in the twenties, he identified his cause with that of the Communist apparatus, manipulated the party machine against his rivals, wielded domestic and foreign policies for political purposes, and made and betrayed allies—first Beria, then Malenkov, finally Molotov.

The real puzzle is not how Khrushchev did it but why his colleagues allowed him to. The answer is that they still underestimated him. Even before 1953 Khrushchev had been no slouch at dissembling. Yet until then he had largely hidden his skill. Between 1953 and 1955, for the first time, Khrushchev's Machiavellian side was almost fully visible—not only in circumstantial evidence but in his memoirs, in which he proudly guided us step by step through his betrayal of Beria. Having revealed that much, he could hardly deny that he practiced the same skills before then and afterwards but he did. Only Beria was evil enough in Khrushchev's rendition to justify conspiring against him. It was quite another thing to betray Malenkov and Molotov, particularly since one of Khrushchev's gravest charges against them was that they betrayed him. The story of their rout must therefore be pieced together on the basis of incomplete evidence. So too must the plot against Beria. For despite his unprecedented candor, Khrushchev didn't tell the whole story of that intrigue either, concealing his initial partnership with Beria after Stalin's death, just as he hid his alliance with Beria and Malenkov in the last years of the dictator's life.

IN THEIR FIRST public pronouncements after Stalin's death, his successors put a brave face on his legacy. In his funeral oration Beria hailed the "unity" of the country's leadership and warned enemies counting on "disorder and confusion" in Soviet ranks that no one would "catch us unawares." The official death announcement predicted reassuringly that the Soviet people would rally around the new leadership.[21]

In actuality, Stalin's men knew they were in trouble, but their troubles went deeper than they knew. Prisoners still languishing in labor camps on January 1, 1953, numbered almost two and one-half million, of whom more than half a million were listed (arbitrarily in a society in which so much was a crime) as "political" prisoners.[22] Should they be released and the dead be rehabilitated? How could they not be? Yet the cost of doing so could be devastating. If the imprisoned were innocent, those who had imprisoned them were guilty. Stalin's successors soon began releasing "nonpolitical" prisoners, and they executed the former police chiefs Beria and Abakumov in 1953 and 1954, as well as the former heads of the "special investigative unit on important crimes." But these steps, accompanied by the destruction of incriminating documents, were intended more to protect Stalin's successors than to avenge his and their victims.[23] When rebellions broke out in the labor camps, they were smashed by the military: in May 1953 in Norilsk, where more than a thousand died and two thousand were injured; in Vorkuta that summer; in early 1954 in Kengir, Kazakhstan, where inmates took over the camp for forty days before they were crushed by tanks and planes.[24]

All sectors of the population, the party elite and the intelligentsia in particular, had been terrorized. Giving the elite a sense of security was now an obvious priority, especially for Khrushchev, whose political base was the party apparatus. The intelligentsia, with its capacity to ask incriminating questions and ultimately to indict the whole Stalinist system, posed a special problem. In due course what Ilya Ehrenburg called the thaw began. But as Khrushchev later admitted, "We were scared—really scared. We were afraid the thaw might unleash a flood, which we wouldn't be able to control and which would drown us."[25]

Stalin's supercentralized command economy had produced miracles of heavy industrial growth and postwar reconstruction (at horrendous human and environmental costs that no one mentioned, let alone calculated) but had left other areas starved or stunted. Consumer goods were in perpetually short supply, and so was housing. Malenkov pronounced the country's grain problem finally solved in 1952, but it could hardly have been worse. Overall harvests were smaller than before World War I, and the number of livestock was lower than in 1928 or even, in some places, 1916. Individual plots produced much of the nation's milk, meat, and vegetables, yet the state limited their size and virtually taxed them out of existence.[26]

Soviet relations with the outside world were also at a dead end in 1953. During and immediately after the war, Stalin played his hand adroitly, maintaining what was useful to him in the wartime Grand Alliance while consolidating gains in Eastern Europe. But by 1953 the West was mobilizing itself against him, and even friends and neutrals had been alienated. Except for Yugoslavia, Moscow's control over Eastern Europe seemed absolute, but economic conditions were deteriorating and anti-Soviet rage was building. As for China, its maximum leader paid Stalin public obeisance but nursed resentments that soon boiled over. Altogether, according to Oleg Troyanovsky, who soon became Khrushchev's chief foreign policy assistant, Stalin's legacy "was appalling. The international situation had become so tense that another turn of the screw might have led to disaster."[27]

Stalin counted heavily on military might. To Western eyes, his conventional forces seemed massive enough to overrun Western Europe. The Soviets confounded expectations by exploding their first atomic bomb in 1949 and their first thermonuclear device in 1953. Yet the USSR was far weaker than it seemed. The USSR's only long-range bomber, the Tu-4, which was a copy of the U.S. B-29, couldn't reach the United States except on a one-way suicide mission. An American advisory committee warned in mid-1953 that one hundred Soviet atomic bombs could be dropped on the United States, producing thirteen million casualties and incinerating up to one-third of America's industrial potential. But according to Khrushchev, the Tu-4 was "already outdated by the time it went into production," and several models of another bomber, which entered service in 1956 and 1957, crashed during test flights. When one airplane designer assured the Kremlin leadership that his plane could land in Mexico after bombing the United States, Khrushchev replied, "What do you think Mexico is—our mother-in-law? You think we can simply go calling any time we want?"[28]

Stalin began an urgent effort to develop intercontinental missiles, but an operational ICBM was still years away. To make matters worse, Khrushchev and his colleagues felt like "technological ignoramuses" when it came to rockets. When the missile designer Sergei Korolyov briefed the Presidium on his plans, the former Kalinovka shepherd and his associates "gawked at what he showed us as if we were a bunch of sheep seeing a gate for the first time. When he showed us one of his rockets, we thought it looked like nothing but a huge cigar-shaped tube and we didn't believe it could fly. . . . We were like peasants in a marketplace. We walked around and around the rocket, touching it, tapping it to see if it was sturdy enough—we did everything but lick it to see how it tasted."[29]

The Americans had superior air power, and they flaunted it. "We were surrounded by American air bases," Khrushchev remembered. "Our country was literally a great big target range for American bombers operating from airfields in Norway, Germany, Italy, South Korea and Japan." During the early postwar years American planes continually overflew Soviet territory. Some of them were high-level reconnaissance flights;

some probed Soviet radar and air defenses; still others delivered agents and supplies to agents. Although a substantial number of low-flying planes were shot down, with pilots killed or perhaps captured, the psychological impact on Stalin's associates was devastating. "The United States was conducting an arrogant and aggressive policy toward us," said Khrushchev, "never missing a chance to demonstrate its superiority. The Americans . . . kept sending planes deep into our territory, sometimes as far as Kiev."[30]

On top of all this, a struggle to succeed Stalin loomed. His successors pledged themselves to collective leadership, but they knew only but one-man rule, and no way to achieve it except to fight for the top spot. Domestic and foreign policies were weapons in the struggle; all contenders played double and triple games. This made for a terrible international liability. The capitalists "knew we were in a complicated and difficult situation after Stalin's death," Khrushchev said later, "that the leadership that Stalin left behind was no good because it was composed of people who had too many differences among them."[31]

It is obvious in retrospect that far-reaching reform was necessary. But even in the late 1980s, after the Soviet system had had thirty-two more years to demonstrate its bankruptcy, change came painfully. Could it have gone more easily in the 1950s when the economic system still produced rapid growth and many people wanted to humanize communism, not abandon it? Not when Stalin's successors were men raised and trained by his own hand.

AFTER FOUR DAYS of mourning, in which thousands filed by his bier in the Hall of Columns, and a terrible crush on nearby Pushkin Street in which at least a hundred were trampled to death, Stalin's funeral was held in Red Square on a cold gray March 9.[32] When Molotov, Malenkov, and Beria addressed the throng from atop the now Lenin-Stalin Mausoleum, all in heavy overcoats and fur hats, except for Beria, whose broad-brimmed black hat hung low over his famous pince-nez, their breaths were visible in the cold air. Only Molotov conveyed what Simonov described as a sense of "love and bitter grief that carried over with a kind of shudder into the voice of this rock-hard man." Malenkov's and Beria's speeches "lacked any pity or agitation or feeling of loss," projecting instead the sense that "these were men who had come to power and who were delighted that they had."[33] As chairman of the occasion Khrushchev stood off to the left, looking uncharacteristically dark and somber.

Having replaced Stalin as prime minister, Malenkov now chaired Presidium meetings, as had been the custom since Lenin's time. In addition, two of his protégés, Mikhail Pervukhin and Maksim Saburov, joined the Presidium while another ally, Nikolai Shatalin, served on the Central Committee Secretariat. Apparently prompted by colleagues' fear that he had too much power, Malenkov stepped down as senior Central Committee secretary on March 14. However, his partner, Beria, not only controlled the police but ran the country's nuclear and missile programs, and he had confiscated enough material from Stalin's personal files to blackmail or destroy his associates.[34]

Despite his unrivaled seniority, Molotov seemed content to be foreign minister. Khrushchev became the senior Central Committee secretary on March 14, but the party's writ seemed reduced to propaganda and ideology, with political and economic matters left to Malenkov and Beria. As senior secretary Khrushchev should have nominated Malenkov as prime minister at a Supreme Soviet session on March 15, but Beria usurped his role. Although the senior secretary had long signed Politburo meeting protocols, now they were approved collectively by the Presidium of the Central Committee.[35]

Konstantin Simonov concluded from signs like these that Beria viewed Khrushchev as a "second-rater." Molotov thought likewise, according to Pyotr Demichev, Khrushchev's assistant between 1950 and 1953. Anastas Mikoyan's son, Sergo, a historian, suggested that Malenkov and Beria sought a return to the pre-Stalin pattern in which Central Committee secretaries performed technical rather than political functions and viewed Khrushchev as suited by his talents (or rather lack of same) for that much-diminished role.[36]

With power and authority distributed for the time being, new domestic and foreign policies followed. All leaders formally approved the changes (and some probably even believed in them), but Beria, even more than Malenkov, was the prime mover. Beria was not a closet liberal; he played the role of reformer just *because* he was drenched in blood. The way to improve his reputation and taint that of others was to incriminate Stalin, whose orders all of them had carried out. As police chief, Beria knew how bad the Soviet situation really was. Unparalleled in his cynicism, he didn't let ideology stand in his way. Had he prevailed, he would almost certainly have exterminated his colleagues, if only to prevent them from liquidating him. In the meantime, however, his burst of reforms rivaled Khrushchev's and in some ways even Gorbachev's thirty five years later.[37]

On the day of Stalin's funeral, which also happened to be Molotov's birthday, Beria personally delivered Polina Zhemchuzhina from a labor camp to her husband, doubtless with an eye on a future alliance with the foreign minister.[38] Between March 10 and 13 he ordered state security groups to reexamine falsified cases, including the doctors' plot, and to report their findings "to me." On March 17 he proposed transferring a large part of the MVD's industrial and construction empire to ordinary economic ministries, and three days later he suggested halting construction projects carried out with forced labor. On March 26 he informed the Presidium that 2,526,401 political and nonpolitical prisoners (including 438,788 women, 35,505 of them with children and 62,886 pregnant) were then in prisons and labor camps; lamented that imprisonment "placed the condemned, their relatives, and others close to them in an extremely difficult situation that often destroyed their families and negatively affected the rest of their lives"; and proposed a mass amnesty that eventually released 1,181,264 nonpoliticals serving terms of five years or less. On March 28 Beria urged transferring corrective labor camps from the MVD to the Ministry of Justice. On April 2 he informed Malenkov that the famous Jewish actor Solomon Mikhoels had been murdered in 1948 on Stalin's orders. Two days later Beria announced publicly that the doctors' plot case had been fabricated. The same day he ordered an end to "cruel beatings of those arrested, round-the-clock handcuffing with arms behind their backs which sometimes lasted several months, long periods of sleep deprivation, leaving prisoners naked in isolation cells, etc."[39]

Several days after the imprisoned doctors were released, Central Committee members were invited to examine case documents. According to Simonov, who spent three or four long sessions scrutinizing them, they established Stalin's personal involvement, including his demand that prisoners be tortured to extract confessions. The fact that the documents came from the MVD suggested that it was Beria's personal idea to display them.[40]

The Georgian Mikhail Chiaureli's sycophantic films about Stalin had earned him a role as the dictator's drinking companion. Since Beria had been part of the same company, the filmmaker naturally showed Beria a scenario glorifying his former master. "Forget about that son of a bitch!" Beria swore as he flung down the manuscript. "Stalin was a scoundrel, a savage, a tyrant! He held us all in fear, the bloodsucker. And the people too. That's where all his power came from. Fortunately we're now rid of him. Let the snake rot in hell!"[41]

Beria also targeted Stalin's practice of Russifying non-Russian Soviet republics. In a series of memorandums to the Presidium, he condemned the predominance of Russians and the Russian language in high places in Byelorussia, Lithuania, Estonia, and, ominously for Khrushchev, western Ukraine. Beria's MVD chief in Kiev, Pavel Meshik, stunned the Ukrainian Central Committee by addressing it in Ukrainian. Meshik tried to compromise Khrushchev's protégé, Lvov internal affairs chief Timofei Strokach, by ordering him to collect dirt on local party officials. When Strokach reported the request to another colleague of Khrushchev's, the Lvov party boss Zinovy Serdiuk, Beria reportedly erupted. "You don't understand anything. Why did you . . . tell Serdiuk? We'll run you out of the organs, arrest and let you rot in the camps. We'll beat you to a pulp and turn you into camp dust."[42]

In foreign policy too, Beria broke with ideological and political orthodoxy. Among papers later confiscated from his safe was a secret letter to Tito's top aide Aleksandr Ranković, not authorized by the Presidium, proposing a "fundamental improvement" in Soviet-Yugoslav relations, and a "confidential meeting" to arrange it.[43] When East German leaders were summoned to Moscow on June 2, and Hungarians arrived eleven days later, Soviet leaders took turns berating them for following orders that Moscow had imposed on them, but it was Beria who shouted at the Hungarian Communist boss Mátyás Rákosi, "How could it be acceptable that in Hungary, a country with 9,500,000 inhabitants, 1,500,000 were persecuted? . . . Even Comrade Stalin made a mistake [when] he directly gave orders for the questioning of those arrested. . . . A person who's beaten will make the kind of confession that interrogating agents want, will admit that he is an English or American spy or whatever we want. But we will never learn the truth this way. This way, innocent people may be sentenced. There is law, and everyone must respect it."[44]

East Germany was a particularly sensitive case. As a result of the Ulbricht regime's forced draft industrialization, coerced collectivization, and harsh antireligious campaign, nearly half a million had fled westward during the past two years. The German Democratic Republic faced what Malenkov later called "the danger of an internal catastrophe." Beria's remarkable response was to think of abandoning East German communism entirely, allowing reunification of neutral Germany in return for substantial Western compensation. When the Kremlin leadership took up the German question on May 27, 1953, Beria exclaimed, "The GDR? What does it amount to, this GDR? It's not even a real state. It's only kept in being by Soviet troops, even if we do call it the German Democratic Republic." In the course of the discussion, Molotov recommended against the "forced" socialization of East Germany, whereupon Beria moved to delete the word "forced" from the instruction. Wouldn't that mean an end to socialism itself? Molotov asked. Why did Beria propose that? "Because," Beria was said to have replied, "all we need is a peaceful Germany; whether it is socialist or not isn't important to us."[45]

Taken together, Beria's moves add up a stunning first "hundred days" (no offense to FDR intended). Although some of his initiatives belied his reputation for shrewdness (especially his defending non-Russian nationalities against Russian chauvinism in a country still dominated by Russians), he at first overwhelmed his competitors. The sheer number of his maneuvers, many of them in fields outside his formal ken, indicated contempt for his peers. In one memo to Khrushchev, Beria didn't "request" that his recommendations be "examined" but demanded that they be "affirmed." He was overheard berating Malenkov, Khrushchev, and Bulganin on the telephone. In the early going after Stalin's death, Beria's colleagues seemed to deserve his disdain. Yet his offensive alerted them to the danger, while giving them ammunition to use against him.[46]

Khrushchev claimed that he saw through Beria from the start and moved against him as soon as he could. "With Stalin's body not yet cold," he told the Central Committee after Beria's arrest, "we couldn't raise this issue. Otherwise, the comrades could have said, 'He's using Stalin's death to create a split and disarray in the Party leadership.' . . . we would have looked like fools, big fools in fact!"[47] However, Khrushchev in fact not only sided with Beria but might have kept doing so if Beria hadn't turned against him.

Immediately after Stalin's death, Khrushchev seemed as close to Beria and Malenkov as they did to each other. According to Molotov, Khrushchev was part of an initial troika with the other two.[48] Molotov was biased, of course, but Khrushchev virtually confirmed his account: Beria "didn't waver in his obviously friendly connections with Malenkov, but suddenly he began to establish equally friendly relations with me. Beria and Malenkov started including me in their strolls around the Kremlin grounds. Naturally, I didn't resist or object, but my opinion of Beria didn't change. . . . I understood that his friendly behavior toward me was a trick."[49]

Speaking to the Central Committee after Beria's arrest in June 1953, Khrushchev sounded defensive: "Some people have said, 'How can this be? Malenkov went around arm in arm with Beria. . . . ' Others were probably told Khrushchev hung around with them, too. [Laughter] And this is correct. They did, and I did, too. . . . Beria wasn't such an easy person to see through and unmask. . . . His attitude toward me particularly changed after Stalin's death. If I didn't call him on any given day, he would call me and ask, 'Why haven't you called?' 'I didn't have time,' I'd reply, 'too busy.' So he'd say, 'You should call more often.'" During the same conversations, Beria "let loose poison against [Malenkov and Molotov], while letting me know, stressing it, that I was better than they. I later told them about it."[50]

At the same time that Beria, Malenkov, and Khrushchev became practically inseparable, they were already undercutting one another. "We've got complete chaos in the ministry [of Internal Affairs]," a middle-ranking official told a writer friend of his. "Beria gives an order, and Malenkov phones from the Kremlin, cancels Beria's order, and gives one of his own."[51] In April 1952 Khrushchev apparently helped Beria dump from the Central Committee secretariat the Malenkov ally Semyon Ignatiev, who had headed the security police during the doctors' plot affair.[52] But Beria couldn't have been pleased when, presumably with Malenkov's support, the Khrushchev protégé Aleksei Kirichenko became the new Ukrainian party leader.

It wasn't deep policy disagreements that provoked the eventual Khrushchev-Beria split. Khrushchev was appalled by Beria's apparent willingness to "hand over 18 million East Germans to American imperialist rule," but that in itself didn't justify the risk of conspiring against him. Khrushchev later charged Beria with driving "a wedge between ethnic groups." However, he not only supported Beria's nationality reforms at the time but borrowed wholesale from them in his own similar reports on Latvia and Estonia. Khrushchev took Kaganovich's arm during the preparations for Stalin's funeral and asked, "Lazar, how are we going to live and work without Stalin?" In addition, he initially endorsed a proposal to rename the Komsomol in Stalin's memory. But Khrushchev also joined Beria in chipping away at Stalin's reputation: The morning after a *Literaturnaya gazeta* editorial called on writers to praise Stalin's name, Khrushchev threatened to fire its editor, Konstantin Simonov.[53]

"When Beria was in the saddle," recalled the former Khrushchev aide Pyotr Demichev, "Nikita Sergeyevich of course tried to get along with him, although he hated and feared him. Beria sensed that Khrushchev couldn't be ignored, so he treated him carefully."[54] What finally turned Khrushchev against Beria was fear that Beria would get him if he didn't get Beria first.

Khrushchev and Malenkov each claimed he led the coup against Beria.[55] Molotov, who hated them both, and Mikoyan, who got along with both, confirmed Khrushchev's account.[56] Khrushchev's request for help against Beria put Malenkov in a double bind: If Beria caught on, he could destroy them; if Beria were defeated, Malenkov would lose Beria's support and be forever tainted by their alliance. So Khrushchev began with a more modest suggestion: to prove Beria mortal by blocking some of the proposals with which he was swamping the Presidium. "The trouble is," he told Malenkov, "you never give anyone a chance to speak at our Presidium sessions. As soon as Beria introduces a motion, you always jump in immediately to support him. . . . Give the rest of us a chance to express ourselves for once and you'll see what happens. Control yourself. Don't be so jumpy. . . . You and I put the agenda together, so let's include for discussion some matters on which we believe Beria is mistaken. Then we'll oppose him."[57]

Exactly when this minuet started isn't clear. But it apparently produced resistance to Beria's proposals to reduce sentences that could be imposed by MVD special boards to a maximum of ten years ("What that meant," Khrushchev told the July 1953 plenum, "was that he could sentence people to ten years and then sentence them again for ten more. That's the way he turned people into camp dust").[58] It also shaped the Presidium's discussion of the German question. Molotov led the opposition to Beria's plans for East Germany. Considering Khrushchev a Beria ally, he was pleasantly surprised to have his support. The straitlaced foreign minister was so grateful he proposed that henceforth he and Khrushchev address each other as *ty*, in the familiar second-person singular, instead of *vy*. After the meeting on Germany, Khrushchev remembered, "Beria's external behavior toward me didn't change. But I understood that this was a barbarous Asian trap—Asian in the sense that a person thinks one way and speaks another. I understood that Beria was playing a double game with me, reassuring me while awaiting the moment to make short work of me as soon as he could."[59]

At some point in mid-June, just days before Beria was arrested on June 26, Khrushchev moved from resisting Beria to arranging his demise.[60] "When Beria realized the other Presidium members were overriding him . . . , he put on a tremendous show of self-importance, trying to demonstrate his superiority in every way he could. We were going through a very dangerous period. I felt it was time to force the situation to a confrontation."[61]

Beria gave Khrushchev an opening by trying to enlist him in a plot against Malenkov. That allowed Khrushchev to convince Malenkov that he had no alternative but to take Beria down first.[62] Once Malenkov agreed, the next step was to recruit their colleagues. Bulganin would be easy, but approaching the others was dangerous. If any one of them alerted Beria, the game would be over. Even if no one did inform him, Beria's eavesdropping equipment might pick up signs of the plot.

Khrushchev approached Voroshilov. But the minute he stepped inside the latter's Supreme Soviet office (using their common membership on a government commission as the excuse for his visit) Voroshilov began "singing Beria's praises: 'What a remarkable man we have in Lavrenty Pavlovich, Comrade Khrushchev! What a remarkable man!'" The best response Khrushchev could muster was a lame "Maybe not. Maybe you overestimate him," followed by a few words on the ostensible purpose of his visit and a quick departure. Khrushchev's reading of the scene was acute: "I thought perhaps Voroshilov had spoken as he did because he thought he was being overheard and that he'd said it for 'Beria's ears.' On the other hand, maybe it was because he considered me Beria's ally." If Khrushchev had carried out his mission, Voroshilov "would have been unable to agree with me simply out of pride. He couldn't have come straight over to my position after having just praised Beria as soon as I came through the door."[63]

Voroshilov was more available than he seemed. When Malenkov hinted at the conspiracy, Voroshilov rushed to cover up nearby telephones, whispered his assent, and then, weeping, embraced and kissed him.[64]

Khrushchev invited Kaganovich to his office. His mind wonderfully concentrated by the danger, the usually loquacious Nikita Sergeyevich even let Kaganovich go on at length about a just-completed inspection tour of Siberian sawmills. "I didn't try to interrupt him although I had other things than sawmills on my mind. I showed proper courtesy and tact and waited for him to get tired of talking. When he finished his report, I said, 'What you've told me is all very well. Now I want to tell you about what's going on here.' I told him what the circumstances were and what conclusions we had reached."

"Who is we?" the sly old Kaganovich wanted to know. Informed that Khrushchev and Malenkov already had a majority, Kaganovich immediately joined it. "I'm with you, too. Of course, I'm with you. I was just asking." Recalled Khrushchev, "I knew what he was thinking, and he knew what I was thinking."[65]

Khrushchev also knew what Molotov would be thinking. Since

"Molotov had personally been a victim of Beria's hypocrisy," and Khrushchev had "heard him call Beria's activities by their proper names to Beria's face," he immediately leveled with him. Molotov too asked where Malenkov stood but then quickly agreed, proposing that Beria not simply be ousted from all his posts but that "more extreme measures" be taken.[66]

The hardest of all to suborn was Mikoyan. The plotters left him for last because, as Khrushchev later put it, "Everyone knew that Mikoyan was on the best of terms with Beria. They were always together and always following each other around." Since the same could be said of Malenkov and indeed of Khrushchev himself, the real reason lay elsewhere. According to Mikoyan's son, Sergo, it was probably an ethnic stereotype: Khrushchev assumed two Transcaucasians could not help being allies. So he didn't confide in Mikoyan until the morning of the coup. Mikoyan stopped by Khrushchev's dacha on his way to the Kremlin, and the two men spent several hours in the garden, keeping security guards at a safe distance. A guest in the morning was unusual, Sergei Khrushchev recalled. So were the "intent expressions" on the two men's faces when they finally walked toward Khrushchev's car, an armored vehicle that Khrushchev was using for the first time since Stalin's death. During their long talk Khrushchev's sole proposal was that Beria be dropped as security chief and appointed minister of industry instead, a suggestion Mikoyan accepted. Only at the meeting itself did Khrushchev spring on Mikoyan the idea of arresting Beria.[67]

THE EVENING BEFORE the blow that ended Beria's bid for power and launched Khrushchev's, the two men and Malenkov rode home from work together as usual, Beria dropping his colleagues off at Granovsky Street and then continuing on his way. When Beria bade them good-bye, Khrushchev recalled at a Central Committee plenum a week later, "I thought, you scoundrel, this is our last handshake. Tomorrow at two o'clock we'll shake you up pretty good. [Laughter] We won't shake your hand, but we'll shake your tail a bit."[68]

But Beria was confident too. A day or two earlier he had warned his colleagues he was watching them. After Beria dropped them at Granovsky Street, Khrushchev, Malenkov, and Bulganin stopped to chat, at which point Khrushchev and Bulganin decided in view of the summer's heat to drive out to their dachas. Neither man informed Beria, but the next day, in Malenkov's office, Beria pointed to Khrushchev and Bulganin and said, "They tricked us. They went up to their apartments but then left for their dachas instead." Khrushchev treated Beria's remark as a joke, saying, "How do you know so much? Do you have spies or something?" But coming two days before the trap was sprung, Beria's "joke" wasn't funny.[69]

Beria's confidence wasn't groundless. Two MVD divisions were stationed in Moscow, Kremlin guard troops were under his command, and the Moscow Military District commander, Colonel General Pavel Artemev, was a former NKVD officer. Beria's rivals had access to other forces, but mobilizing them before he was arrested would have alerted him to the danger. Troops and tanks from the Taman' Division (which later supported Boris Yeltsin and Gorbachev during the abortive August 1991 putsch) did enter Moscow and move toward Red Square, but only as Beria was being detained in the Kremlin. "Who actually is going to arrest him?" Khrushchev asked at the time. "Our own security details are subordinate to him."[70] The conspirators would have to spirit armed men into the Kremlin, grab Beria, and change the Kremlin guards, all before his forces discovered what was happening.

Khrushchev's plan was to call a meeting of the Presidium of the Council of Ministers, rather than that of the party, so as not to arouse Beria's suspicion. At some point in the meeting Malenkov would suggest switching to party business and then propose dismissing Beria from all his posts. At that moment, Beria would be seized. However, "the Presidium bodyguard . . . would be sitting in the next room during the session," Khrushchev later said, "and Beria could easily order them to arrest us all and hold us in isolation."[71]

The plotters therefore arranged for Colonel General Artemev to be out of town on maneuvers, while the Kremlin commandant was suddenly called away. At about 9:00 A.M. on June 26 Khrushchev telephoned his wartime friend Kirill Moskalenko, the chief of Moscow air defense forces, and told him to gather a few trusted men and wait for a summons to the Kremlin to discuss air defense readiness. Moskalenko was to be sure to bring "cigars" with him.

"Do you understand me?" Khrushchev asked.

"I understood," Moskalenko recalled. "Cigars meant weapons." Since weapons weren't allowed into the Kremlin, Moskalenko and his men hid them in briefcases and under their jackets in a government car, provided by Bulganin, that guards hesitated to search. Meanwhile Malenkov and Bulganin recruited Marshal Zhukov and four others (including Leonid Brezhnev, then the party's number two man in charge of the military), who entered the Kremlin in Zhukov's car.

Once inside, both groups of officers were escorted into a room that had formerly belonged to Stalin's secretary Poskrebyshev. By this time the soldiers knew their mission in general terms; a short while later Khrushchev, Malenkov, Molotov, and Bulganin explained the details. Upon a signal from Malenkov's aide Sukhanov, who was sitting in an outer office, they were to enter the Presidium meeting room and arrest Beria. He, who was late as usual for the meeting, still hadn't arrived. When he walked in, he was dressed casually, not wearing a necktie but carrying a briefcase. Fifteen or so of his guards and assistants were outside in a reception area. Zhukov recalled being warned that Beria knew jujitsu.[72]

The meeting began about noon and lasted about two hours. Malenkov apparently made the case against Beria, seconded by others.[73] Khrushchev, who spoke especially sharply, according to Mikoyan, charged that Beria had once worked for British intelligence and that since Stalin's death he had been trying to "undermine socialism" and "legalize arbitrary rule." Beria was "no Communist," said Khrushchev. "He is a careerist who has wormed his way into the party for self-seeking reasons. His arrogance is intolerable. No honest Communist would ever behave the way he does. . . ."

At first Beria didn't realize the seriousness of the situation. "What's with you?" he demanded. "Are you looking for a flea in my pants?" Later he admitted to "mistakes" but asked not to be expelled from the party. As Malenkov began summing up, he pressed a button summoning the military men in the next room and declared, "As chairman of the Council of Ministers of the USSR, I request that you take Beria into custody pending an investigation of charges made against him." When Zhukov shouted, "Hands up!" Beria reached for his briefcase on a nearby windowsill. Fearing the case contained a gun, Khrushchev seized Beria's arm.[74]

Moskalenko, Zhukov, and the other officers hustled Beria into an adjacent waiting room. There they removed his belt and cut the buttons off his pants to retard his movements. Pending the arrest of his top associates, and the neutralizing of troops loyal to him, he and his fate had to be hidden. He kept asking to go to the toilet, probably hoping somehow to get word to his guards, but no one came to his rescue. Many hours later (during which Sukhanov provided sandwiches to Beria's high-level guards), under the cover of what passes for darkness in late June, Moskalenko shoved Beria into a car sent from air defense headquarters, covered him with a carpet, and drove quickly to a heavily protected guardhouse, from which he was moved to Moskalenko's underground bunker on Kommissariat Lane near the Moscow River embankment the next day. Late on the evening of June 26 Khrushchev returned to his dacha looking tired. "Today Beria has been arrested," he told his wife and son. "It seems that he is an enemy of the people and a foreign spy."[75]

Thus ended what Khrushchev was to regard as one of his finest hours. In fact, the last-minute coup could easily have been smashed if Beria hadn't been sure it would never take place. The most likely reason for his overconfidence is that he considered his colleagues inept. But there is a more Machiavellian possibility that at least ought to be considered—namely, a double conspiracy by Khrushchev and Beria that ended in a stunning Khrushchev double cross.

According to Malenkov's son, Andrei, and his former aide Sukhanov, Malenkov feared just such a scenario, and that was why he recruited Zhukov to carry out the arrest along with Moskalenko. Malenkov later insisted that Beria remained seemingly calm and confident throughout much of the June 26 Presidium meeting and that a satisfied smirk played across his face when Khrushchev left to consult officers concealed in the next room. The same smirk allegedly returned when Moskalenko and his men entered with the guns drawn. It was only when Beria caught sight of Zhukov and heard him shout that he was under arrest that he collapsed, so stunned by the unexpected turn of events that "despite all his resourcefulness, quick-wittedness and determination to fight to the end, he didn't cry out, throw himself on Zhukov, or take any other action."[76]

Obviously this account is self-serving. But it might explain why Beria was caught totally off guard. Secret police channels must have picked up hints of the plot, the information, for example, that Presidium colleagues had suddenly started appearing at Khrushchev's dacha in the middle of the day. To be sure, they headed off toward the river so as not to be overheard, but other conversations took place in offices and apartments. It's conceivable that Beria's agents were incompetent, that they lacked the time to play back and transcribe what their bugs recorded, or that Khrushchev's man in Beria's entourage, Ivan Serov, made sure Beria never got the word.[77] But it's also possible that signs reaching Beria failed to alarm him because he assumed they were part of a plan to lull *others'* vigilance.

If so, Beria expected the June 26 meeting to end with Malenkov's arrest. "What's going on, Nikita?" he cried, seizing Khrushchev by the arm and staring into his face, as the real trap was sprung. "What are you mumbling about?"[78] Such a plot within a plot sounds too devious for Khrushchev. That one can imagine it at all confirms how far the seemingly guileless Nikita Sergeyevich had come.

IN CLASSIC Stalinist fashion, the victors of June 26 accused Beria of being "an enemy of the people" and arrested his wife and son as well as his MVD associates. The interrogation of Beria and his henchmen that began in early July was headed by Moskalenko and Roman Rudenko, who had been Khrushchev's chief prosecutor in Ukraine and was now the USSR procurator-general. Fearing that he would incriminate them, Beria's Presidium colleagues listened to his secret December 1953 trial on closed-circuit radio. But Beria's only chance to survive was to flatter, not finger, them; until he was denied pen and paper, he begged forgiveness of all of them, writing with particular warmth to "Dear Georgy." Malenkov "got agitated when he read these notes," Khrushchev recalled, as if "afraid that the Beria affair would turn against him. But we replied that all we were discussing *now* was Beria [emphasis added]."[79]

Early in December Khrushchev told Rudenko, "It's time to finish it." On December 18 a six-day trial of Beria and six accomplices began in accordance with Stalinist procedures: no counsel in the courtroom; no appeals allowed; sentences to be carried out immediately. The special judicial panel, consisting of Moskalenko and several high party and state officials, had no constitutional standing. Formal charges included treason, terrorism, and counterrevolution. As much as anything else, Beria's former colleagues were interested in the long list of women, including well-known actresses and others from prominent families, whom he had raped.[80]

Following Presidium directives that dictated the verdict in advance, the special judicial panel declared Beria and his men guilty on all counts and sentenced them to be shot in the same bunker in which the trial was held. After the sentence was pronounced, guards removed Beria's prison shirt, leaving him in a white undershirt, tied his hands behind his back, and attached the rope to a hook hammered into a wooden board designed to shield witnesses from ricocheting bullets. When Beria tried to speak, Rudenko ordered him gagged with a towel. Beria wasn't dispatched by an ordinary executioner but by a three-star general, A. Batitsky. At the very last minute, witnesses saw one of Beria's eyes protruding wildly just above the bandage across his face. Batitsky fired directly into Beria's forehead. Immediately afterward the corpse was incinerated at the Donskoi crematorium.[81]

The verdict and its immediate implementation were announced on December 24. A week earlier the Soviet press had printed a brief summary of the main charges. Of course, the Central Committee hadn't waited for the trial; its members had met in July to condemn Beria and begin using him as a scapegoat, blaming him for the worst of Stalinism while leaving Stalin's reputation intact and cleansing their own hands in the bargain. Malenkov, who led off the plenum, was the most guarded, as if trying to prevent the torrent of accusations against Beria from drowning him. Kaganovich too was cautious, Molotov focused on foreign policy, and Mikoyan was also restrained. The most fiery speech of all, vivid and personal in tone and obviously calculated to shape the succession struggle, was Khrushchev's. His indictment stressed the thirties, when his Kremlin colleagues had been closer to the terror than he had been. Since it was too soon to attack Malenkov directly, he merely hinted how close the latter had been to Beria. Trying delicately to defend himself, Malenkov implied that Stalin himself was responsible for what happened on his watch. But Khrushchev dominated the plenum. Konstantin Simonov was struck by the "passionate satisfaction" with which he recounted Beria's capture. "You could tell from his account," recalled Simonov, "that it was Khrushchev himself who had played the main role . . . that he had initiated the action, that he had turned out to be more penetrating, more talented, more energetic, and more decisive than the others."[82]

IN THE SPRING and summer of 1953 Rada Adzhubei and Sergei Khrushchev spent a lot of time at their father's dacha, a huge two-story pseudo-Gothic palace that had once belonged to Nicholas II's uncle and the governor-general of Moscow Grand Duke Sergei Aleksandrovich and that now boasted a bomb shelter in the basement. As soon as the weather allowed, Nikita Khrushchev fled his Granovsky Street apartment, whose windows opened only onto a courtyard. He loved flowering apple and cherry trees, lilac and rose bushes, and long walks down to the Moscow River. Rada didn't see much of her father, who left early for work and returned late, but she well remembered his reaction to the Beria denouement: "He understood perfectly that either this would be the end for him, or it would be a great victory. Every other issue hung in the balance."[83]

Once victory was his, Aleksei Adzhubei recalled, "Khrushchev changed, even externally. He became more self-assured, more dynamic." His very "manner of speaking had changed: he sounded much more independent. . . . " Others recognized the shift and reacted accordingly. Khrushchev's security detail behaved "more insolently." Presidium colleagues deferred to him; when the leadership traveled en masse, his automobile was the first to arrive and depart.[84]

It was in July 1953, Adzhubei thought, that Khrushchev decided "his hour had come," a moment he was to relive again and again, embellishing the story each time he told it. Several years later Khrushchev emerged from the Black Sea in baggy swim trunks, plopped down on the beach near his Crimean dacha, and began boasting to aides about how he had bested Beria. During the November 1960 world conference of Communist parties, an emotional Khrushchev shocked Soviet and foreign guests by describing how Malenkov "went white" at the climactic moment and had to be "kicked under the table" and how Beria "was all green and shat in his pants." What made Khrushchev's victory all the sweeter, according to Konstantin Simonov, was that Beria considered him "a fat, clumsy, red-mugged fool whom he, Beria, past master of intrigue, could wrap around his finger." No wonder Khrushchev ended his November 1960 rendition by retelling Vinnichenko's short story and comparing himself yet again with "the shoemaker, Pinya."[85]

Despite Khrushchev's role in Beria's demise, Malenkov and others still underestimated him. If they promoted him from ordinary Central Committee secretary to first secretary in September 1953, a move that allowed him to mobilize the party machinery on his own behalf, it was because they counted on him to know his place. According to agriculture minister Benediktov, Khrushchev's colleagues viewed him as "king for a day." That his promotion was listed as the eleventh or twelfth item on the Central Committee plenum's agenda suggests how little his peers thought of it.[86]

So much for their acumen! In the months to come Malenkov came to rue his mistake. But was his clash with Khrushchev inevitable? Malenkov was no superman, but he had strengths that complemented Khrushchev's. Khrushchev was impulsive; Malenkov was steadier. Khrushchev craved the limelight; Malenkov might have settled for a lesser role. They had certain aims in common (especially in agricultural and foreign policy), and they were as close personally as any Presidium members could be.

Sergei Khrushchev described the relationship as an "alliance," not a "friendship." But Nina Petrovna "had a high opinion" of Malenkov's wife, the Adzhubeis were friendly with Malenkov's daughter and her husband, who were architects, and Sergei himself was close to Malenkov's scientist sons, Andrei and Yegor. After Stalin died, Malenkov proposed that both families move into new houses to be built on the Lenin Hills. In the meantime both took up residence in adjoining downtown villas on Yeropkinsky and Pomerantsev lanes. Both were turn-of-the-century mansions (Malenkov's with ornate tiles inlaid above the front door and along the roof and elaborate filigreed ironwork atop the front gate), and each had a large courtyard (Khrushchev's with a garden and a sunken pool with fountain and terrace, Malenkov's even grander with a covered patio supported by four Greek columns). Protected from prying eyes by long, high walls, and with an unobtrusive door connecting their gardens, the two families saw a lot of each other. Malenkov even decided to build a new dacha at Novo-Ogaryovo near Khrushchev's—"so he could always drop in and ask for advice," according to Sergei Khrushchev. But just after he moved in, Malenkov was moved out of the Presidium forever, leaving his new dacha to be used for negotiations with foreign delegations and for talks among Gorbachev, Yeltsin, and other republic leaders thirty years later.[87]

What explains the intense antipathy between Khrushchev and Malenkov? Kremlin political culture bred mutual suspicions, but personal animosity sharpened them. Malenkov couldn't abide Khrushchev's being number one. Khrushchev couldn't resist humiliating Malenkov. To make matters worse, their Kremlin colleagues quickly chose sides. "It was common knowledge that Molotov, Kaganovich and other members of the Presidium hated Malenkov," wrote Malenkov's former son-in-law, Vladimir Shamberg. They were all too ready to back Khrushchev, whom they would soon come to hate even more.[88]

After Beria's arrest, Malenkov expanded his base in the central state apparatus by appointing several of his supporters as deputy premiers. He broadened his popularity by raising the standard of living—retail prices were cut; annual state bond sales, theoretically voluntary but actually mandatory, were reduced—and he proposed agricultural reforms. His men even spread rumors that he was Lenin's nephew (Malenkov's mother's family name was Ulianova), while he cultivated academician Gleb Krzhizhanovsky, who had been Lenin's close friend and collaborator and was married to Malenkov's wife's aunt.[89]

However, Khrushchev had greater advantages. As party leader he gained from the party's enhanced authority after Stalin's death. He expanded his leverage by appointing local party bosses, who took seats on the Central Committee.[90] Malenkov was intellectually and culturally sophisticated, but he came across as colorless. Khrushchev, on the contrary, seemed an open, down-to-earth activist prepared to take on any challenge. Gennady Voronov, the party boss of the Chita region, was delighted with a "straightforward" man who "restored Leninist norms of party life." Ivan Benediktov, who was to turn against Khrushchev, relished his "keen native wit and resourcefulness, his peasant cunning and gumption, his ability to take the initiative and to win over people of all sorts. . . ." Aleksandr Shelepin later heard from Presidium elders how "democratically Khrushchev behaved" during those years, "how carefully he listened to his comrades' opinions and how respectfully he treated them, how he used to spend Sundays with them at state dachas outside Moscow, and how they used to decide matters of all sorts while lunching together every day in the Kremlin."[91] Even Molotov admitted that "Khrushchev traveled to the provinces a lot, to collective and state farms, and you can't fault him for this. This was precisely his positive quality. He was everywhere—stables, boilers, etc. He met with simple workers and peasants more than Lenin or Stalin did. There's no denying that. People were at ease with him; they treated him as one of their own."[92]

Besides energy and enthusiasm, Khrushchev possessed incriminating information confiscated from Beria's secret files. Malenkov managed to snatch testimony against himself extracted from Yezhov before the latter's execution, but not, apparently, "evidence" that he had plotted to assassinate Kaganovich.[93] Khrushchev denied he ever read such documents, but his new KGB chief, Ivan Serov, surely must have.[94]

Malenkov's agricultural reform proposals were the centerpiece of his program. In August 1953 he proposed a reduction in taxes, an increase in procurement prices paid by the state for obligatory collective farm deliveries, and encouragement of individual peasant plots, which produced so much of the nation's vegetables and milk. So popular were these changes in villages throughout the country that a saying coined at the time is still remembered: "Malenkov came by, and we ate some blini."[95]

Malenkov also reached out to the intelligentsia. It was on his initiative, his son insisted, that impressionist paintings long hidden in museum basements appeared on display. Malenkov also asked leading economists to suggest broader economic reforms and leading scientists to prepare a report on pure and applied science; the latter condemned the charlatan biologist, Lysenko, whom Khrushchev supported until the bitter end.[96]

For both Malenkov and Khrushchev, a prime obstacle to domestic reform was the Stalinist image of the outside world. If capitalist states were irredeemably hostile, and a new world war was inevitable, then the USSR could hardly afford to reduce its military might or slacken its domestic vigilance. Malenkov undermined these axioms when he insisted there were "no contested issues in U.S.-Soviet relations that cannot be resolved by peaceful means" and warned that a nuclear war could destroy not just capitalism but "world civilization."[97]

Khrushchev had never been an "ideologue," but he attacked

Malenkov's heresies, just as he did Malenkov's championing of the state bureaucracy at the expense of the party apparatus. In November 1953 Malenkov chastised high-level party officials for corruption and threatened to remove government agencies from their control. His speech was greeted by "the silence of the grave" as "incomprehension blended with confusion, confusion with fear, and fear with indignation." At that point Khrushchev's voice rang out: "All that is, of course, true, Georgy Maksimilianovich. But, still, the apparat is our foundation." At that the hall exploded with enthusiastic applause.[98]

Khrushchev's post-Beria program also centered on agriculture. According to Molotov, Khrushchev "was supposed to announce the new policy" and "was indignant" when Malenkov stole the mantle of reformer with his August speech. What Khrushchev "could neither forget nor forgive," added Mikoyan, was that Malenkov "got the credit." So Khrushchev tried to steal it back at the September Central Committee plenum.[99] In a more open society the decision-making process might have included widespread consultations, legislative hearings, and parliamentary debate. Here two Khrushchev aides, two *Pravda* editors, and one agricultural specialist met day and night behind closed doors at the Central Committee headquarters on Old Square, trying to discover how deep the agricultural crisis actually was, demanding accurate figures from the Central Statistical Administration, and getting inflated statistics instead from officials who assumed their bosses wanted good news, not bad.[100]

Despite the agency's best efforts, the extent of the disaster was clear. Khrushchev's willingness to spell it out at the plenum won him the reputation of a leader prepared to look unflattering facts in the face. Moreover, the same facts gave the lie to Malenkov's 1952 boast that the grain situation had been "solved." Four months later, when Khrushchev addressed an even more brutally frank memo to his Presidium colleagues, he cited Malenkov's 1952 claim in the very first sentence, although without, for the moment, naming Malenkov himself.[101]

Khrushchev's reform proposals incorporated and extended Malenkov's: higher procurement prices, reduced taxes, strengthened individual plots. All these made eminent sense, but not, in the long run, to Khrushchev himself. Although practical enough to see what needed doing, and bold enough to do it, he was ideologically opposed to the very principle that underlay his own recommendations—namely, that peasants should be freer to move away from collectivism.[102]

His September speech made him the regime's leading spokesman on agriculture. Other leaders might blame bad harvests on bad weather and on the nation's past troubles, but he almost never did. As he put it with characteristic candor in a 1955 speech, "Comrades, this is already the 38th year of Soviet power. That's not a short amount of time. That means we should be ashamed to keep blaming Nicholas II. [Laughter in the hall.] The man's been dead for a long time." Khrushchev told another gathering: "The people put it to us this way: Will there be meat to eat, or not? Will there be milk, or not? Will there be decent pairs of pants? This isn't ideology, of course, but what good does it do if everyone is ideologically correct but goes around without trousers? [Laughter. Applause.]"[103]

The reforms Malenkov suggested and Khrushchev endorsed involved land already under cultivation; as such they would take too long to boost output. So Khrushchev's next proposal, a dramatic innovation uniquely his own, called for a crash program to develop the so-called Virgin Lands of Kazakhstan and western Siberia.[104] Kazakh party leaders he consulted were against the idea; they feared traditionally Kazakh lands would end up in the hands of Russian and Ukrainian farmers, but they didn't dare say so in 1953. Instead they played down the potential yields. "Kazakhstan is for sheep, not for grain. The Virgin Lands mustn't be developed," said Kazakh party leader Rakhmizhan Shayakhmetov. "But couldn't we plow up at least fifty thousand hectares?" Khrushchev asked his aide Andrei Shevchenko. "My relatives wrote me that a hundred thousand could be developed."[105]

Khrushchev trusted his relatives (who lived in northern Kazakhstan) more than his Kazakh party chief, in whose resistance he detected "the virus of nationalism." So he promptly replaced Shayakhmetov with a Ukrainian, Panteleimon Ponomarenko, and Shayakhmetov's deputy with Leonid Brezhnev, and he sent Shevchenko to Kazakhstan and Siberia to investigate. When Shevchenko returned two months later, Khrushchev was sick in bed with a high temperature. Nina Petrovna warned Shevchenko not to "do him in," but Khrushchev insisted on hearing him out, after which he ordered him to draw up a formal proposal that Khrushchev signed, almost unchanged, and sent to the Presidium.

The memo promised quick results (no fewer than 13 million hectares would be developed in the next two years, 2.3 million in 1954 alone)[106] by ideologically pure means. Instead of bribing peasants with "individual material incentives," it beckoned idealistic youths to a great socialist adventure. The Soviet system was good at mobilizing vast numbers of people and machines, and so, he liked to think, was he himself. The Virgin Lands campaign cast him in the role he loved: proclaiming a crisis, recruiting men and women brave enough to face it, inspiring them with his own selfless zeal, and basking in triumph as news of their victories flowed in.

During the spring and summer of 1954, three hundred thousand Komsomol "volunteers" headed east on special trains, some from rural areas, but many with little or no preparation for the hardships, ranging from high summer heat to bitter cold, that awaited them. While the volunteers built tent cities for themselves, Khrushchev commandeered tens of thousands of tractors and combines. Deprived of their fair share of such equipment, older, non-Virgin Lands fell even farther behind, increasing the country's stake on Khrushchev's great gamble.[107] He didn't take the risk alone; most of his colleagues supported him, even after he called for doubling the amount of new land to be cultivated. Within a few years his campaign turned into an agricultural and ecological disaster. In the meantime he was displaying the leadership that Malenkov lacked.

Khrushchev opened up the Kremlin in reality as well as figuratively. Under Stalin the medieval fortress had been closed to all but the highest party elite. Since the 1920s such selected leaders as Molotov, Kaganovich, Mikoyan, and Voroshilov had lived within its walls. A few months before Stalin's death, Sergei Khrushchev and some of his classmates managed to get a look inside, after Kremlin guards ran lengthy security checks on all of them. Then, in 1954, a New Year's Eve Youth Ball was held in the Kremlin at Khrushchev's suggestion, after which he opened the grounds to visitors in general. Brushing aside Voroshilov's complaint that he'd no longer be able to walk near his home, Khrushchev took to strolling among Russian tourists, mostly unrecognized because few could imagine that the party leader would dare mingle with ordinary people.[108]

OPENING THE KREMLIN had great public resonance. Blackmailing Malenkov proceeded in secret. By the spring of 1954 several USSR Supreme Court commissions were beginning to scrutinize past political trials, as were young jurists freshly assigned to the chief military procurator's office. When Khrushchev allowed the 1949 Leningrad affair to be probed, he knew that the investigation would point in Malenkov's direction. In April 1954 the Supreme Court rehabilitated Kuznetsov, Voznesensky, and others, and shortly thereafter their party memberships were posthumously restored. Khrushchev journeyed to Leningrad in early May to brief party stalwarts. If he blamed the secret police and didn't mention Malenkov's name, that was because he didn't need to; the message had already been conveyed when Malenkov's protégé Vasily Andrianov, who had become Leningrad party leader in 1949, was fired. The trial and execution of the former MGB chief Abakumov, which followed in Leningrad in December 1954, further underlined the danger facing Malenkov. In effect, according to a Russian historian, Khrushchev had surrounded Malenkov with "a leaden coat of mail that crushed Malenkov's will," depriving him of the ability not only to fight back but even to carry out his regular governmental responsibilities.[109]

Khrushchev's progress was obvious to Communist officials who read the tea leaves. By the end of 1953 his approval was required for all major decisions. Until February 1954 Malenkov occupied the seat of honor when the Presidium gathered for ceremonial occasions in the Great Kremlin Palace; after that Khrushchev did. On April 26, 1954, it wasn't the prime minister but the party leader who summarized the budget for the Supreme Soviet. Beginning in June, Malenkov's name ceased appearing at the top of Presidium membership lists, thenceforth published in alphabetical order. In November the Presidium Chancellery, headed by Malenkov's longtime aide Sukhanov, was replaced by a General Department controlled by Khrushchev. That left the entire Central Committee apparatus, with its tentacles reaching into every sphere of life, in his hands. In the meantime, in March 1954, his man Ivan Serov took charge of the KGB.[110]

By the spring of 1954 Khrushchev had not only Bulganin's backing but that of Molotov, Kaganovich, Voroshilov, and Mikoyan. During August and September, while vacationing in the Crimea with Mikoyan and Bulganin, Khrushchev called in party bosses of the country's key regions, including Leningrad's Frol Kozlov, Moscow's Yekaterina Furtseva, Ukraine's Aleksei Kirichenko, and others and won their allegiance as well.[111] That same summer, if the avowedly anti-Khrushchevian Albanian Communist leader Enver Hoxha can be believed, Khrushchev argued at length in Malenkov's presence that the most authoritative man in any Communist country must head the party, not the government. According to Hoxha, Malenkov sat "motionless, his whole body sagging, his face an ashen hue."[112]

That fall, leaving Malenkov behind, Khrushchev led a delegation to China to celebrate the People's Republic's fifth anniversary. He conducted both party and government business with Mao Zedong and Zhou Enlai. On the way home Khrushchev met with local party leaders in the Far East and Siberia. All this further buttressed his position, but it was plenty strong to begin with if he was willing to leave Moscow for an extended length of time.

By now personal relations between Khrushchev and Malenkov had deteriorated badly. After years of their addressing each other as equals, Khrushchev had begun to "instruct" Malenkov in a tone that left even Nina Petrovna and Sergei Khrushchev uncomfortable. Malenkov at first seemed to accept Khrushchev's condescension (more than appears to have been the case for Mrs. Malenkov), but before long he could barely conceal his dislike. Khrushchev even began to complain about Malenkov at home, especially about his lack of initiative, but as Sergei Khrushchev admitted, "if Malenkov had shown any initiative, Father would have been even more displeased." During their 1954 Crimean vacation the two men clashed about Khrushchev's idea of using construction crews that had rebuilt Kiev after the war to erect sanatoriums in the Crimea. When Malenkov objected that the country couldn't afford that, Khrushchev's aide Andrei Shevchenko remembered, "they really got into it, even using foul language. Let's put it this way: Each mentioned the other's mother."[113]

The split came into the open in early 1955, first at a Central Committee plenum in late January and then, publicly, at a February Supreme Soviet session that demoted Malenkov from prime minister to minister of electrification. At the plenum Khrushchev accused Malenkov of being Beria's "right hand." Molotov chimed in: "Lavrenty and Georgy, Georgy and Lavrenty, they were always together, drinking, riding in the same car, at each other's dachas." The plenum's draft resolution charged Malenkov with "moral responsibility" for the Leningrad affair, as well as for other cases "fabricated by Beria and Abakumov." As Stalin lay dying, the resolution continued, Malenkov "eased Beria's way toward power." It wasn't until the very last minute that Malenkov opposed Beria, nor did he "subject his own closeness to Beria over a long period of time to decisive criticism at the July [1953] plenum."

During his brief time at the top, Malenkov was guilty of two major heresies. His declared preference for light industry (and by extension consumer goods) at the expense of heavy industry, Khrushchev now declared, "was designed to win him cheap popularity. It was the speech of a real opportunist, not the speech of a leader." "Why did he join the party," Molotov demanded to know, "if he doesn't know whether he's following a Communist or a capitalist course?" Given Malenkov's "theoretically and politically incorrect" formulation, the Central Committee resolution intoned, it was no wonder that "some pseudo-economists" had begun to voice "clearly anti-Marxist, anti-Leninist, and right-opportunist views on the core questions of the Soviet economy."

Malenkov's warning that a nuclear war could destroy civilization had "confused the comrades," Khrushchev said. "The devil knows what sort of nonsense this is," added Molotov. More than century ago Marx had foretold the end of capitalism, so anyone who said that nuclear war threatened civilization "didn't have his head on his shoulders, but at the other end of the body [Laughter]."

Khrushchev blamed Malenkov for backing Beria's plan to sell out East Germany. Kaganovich charged that Malenkov stood for "capitulationism, social democratism, Menshevism" and "political cowardice" and cited one of Stalin's favorite aphorisms against him: "A man may be physically brave but a political coward."[114]

In Stalin's time, accusations like these would have presaged Malenkov's arrest and liquidation. Instead he was permitted to remain in the party Presidium, nursing his grievances and planning his revenge.[115] One reason for Khrushchev's restraint was that he too had been close to Beria and would soon be adopting the very views for which Malenkov was condemned. Another was that Malenkov's animus against Molotov and Kaganovich could prove useful when Khrushchev attacked his next targets.[116]

FOR AT LEAST a while the alliance between Khrushchev and Molotov held firm. Some of the awe Khrushchev felt for Stalin's oldest associate remained. Early after Stalin's death, he had kept clear of Molotov's foreign policy bailiwick, and when he didn't, the two men seemed to work together without strain.[117] When Malenkov was dropped as prime minister, Molotov proposed that Khrushchev replace him.[118] Yet even before then Molotov was starting to snipe at Khrushchev on important domestic and foreign issues, while the two men increasingly grated on each other's nerves.

"There wasn't a single big issue on which Molotov didn't pose objections," Khrushchev told the July 1955 Central Committee plenum at which their clash was revealed. "Why? I think it all stems from his absolute isolation from life."[119] Molotov objected when Khrushchev proposed developing thirteen million hectares of Virgin Lands, objected again when Khrushchev added two million more, and protested all the more fiercely when the total was raised to twenty-eight to thirty million. Khrushchev's plan wasn't just "premature," Molotov remarked later; it was "absurd."[120] Molotov favored investing in long-cultivated areas, but that required "both a highly advanced farm labor force and enormous material resources," and Khrushchev recalled "we had neither."[121] There was truth on both sides of this issue, but for Khrushchev it was "clear and doesn't require any proof." In case anyone had any doubts, Khrushchev told the July 1955 plenum, Molotov's previous record showed he "knows practically nothing about agriculture." In all the years Molotov had been living at his dacha, Khrushchev added, "he didn't once visit the collective farm next door," whereas he himself, Khrushchev reminded his audience, did so all the time.[122] "Khrushchev was so carried away" by his Virgin Lands scheme, Molotov responded much later, "that he was like a runaway horse" or like "a cattle dealer, a small-time cattle dealer. Without doubt, a man of little culture. A cattle trader. A man who sells livestock."[123]

Housing construction was another bone of contention. Stalin's architectural taste had run toward monstrous wedding cake skyscrapers. "We've won the war and are recognized the world over as the glorious victors," Khrushchev remembered Stalin's saying. "What will happen if [visitors] walk around Moscow and find no skyscrapers? They will make unfavorable comparisons with capitalist cities." Khrushchev preferred the mass production of inexpensive, prefabricated apartment houses—only five stories (so as to eliminate the need for expensive elevators) and no balconies either. When Molotov reported popular dissatisfaction over housing conditions, Khrushchev recalled, "you'd have thought he'd been born only yesterday. He acted as though he'd just learned that people were living in overcrowded, vermin-infested, intolerable conditions, often two families to a room."[124]

Khrushchev also started interfering in Soviet diplomacy, especially in relations with other Communist countries since these involved party-to-party as well as state-to-state links. Having previously joined Beria and Malenkov in pressing reforms on Eastern European parties, he traveled to Warsaw and Prague in 1954. However, his gravest challenge to Molotov was to propose rapprochement with Tito's Yugoslavia. He did so partly to correct what he regarded as one of Stalin's greatest errors but also as a way of undermining Molotov.

When Moscow drummed Tito out of the Communist camp in 1948 (ironically for being more Stalinist than Stalin himself), Molotov had been a primary architect of the split. After Stalin's death, Molotov approved the reestablishment of diplomatic relations with Belgrade, but no more than that. Yugoslavia was "no socialist country," he insisted. To welcome Tito back into the fold would encourage Yugoslav-style "revisionism" in the rest of Eastern Europe; the way to hold the Soviet bloc together was not to appease Tito but to demonstrate Soviet strength. By virtue of their constant repetition, these Stalinist formulas had a hold over Khrushchev himself. "We'd made up the story about all the terrible things the Yugoslavs were doing, and we'd heard the story so often that we started to believe it ourselves."[125]

Would that Khrushchev had seen so clearly through other myths he himself had propagated! Nor could he simply brush aside the party line on Yugoslavia. In February 1954 the Presidium ordered the Foreign Ministry to improve relations with Belgrade. But Molotov continued to depict Yugoslavia as a fascist state. At this point Khrushchev proposed a commission to decide what sort of social system Yugoslavia really had, and its report declared Yugoslavia socialist after all. When that opened the way to direct contact with Tito, Molotov demanded the Yugoslavs come to Moscow for talks. Only after Khrushchev insisted that the Yugoslavs couldn't "come begging with their hats in their hands" did his colleagues agree to send a delegation, headed by Khrushchev, and Molotov-less, to Belgrade in late May 1955.[126]

Although the visit produced a substantial thaw in relations with Tito,[127] Molotov refused to retreat. That gave Khrushchev the chance, which he doubtless was seeking anyway, to mount an assault at the July 1955 plenum. His opening remarks were relatively restrained. But when Molotov accused him of "saying anything that happens to come into his head," Khrushchev blurted out something that wasn't officially admitted by Moscow until thirty-five years later. As an example of how Molotov's foreign policy mobilized the world against the USSR, Khrushchev pointed to Korea. "We began the Korean War. Everyone knows we did," he exclaimed. "Everyone but our own people," Mikoyan reminded him in a passage that was removed from even the secret printed transcript of the plenum.[128]

Molotov's complaint that the Presidium decided Yugoslav issues in his absence prompted this profound exchange. Khrushchev: "We told you before you left." Molotov: "What I said is a fact." Khrushchev: "What we're saying is a fact." The question of whether Molotov deviated from the party line triggered this colloquy: Khrushchev: "You were against." Molotov: "No. I expressed my opinion." Khrushchev: "You didn't agree with us." Molotov: "I expressed my point of view." Khrushchev (flashing the biting humor that was a strong source of his appeal): "All the soldiers are out of step, it turns out. Only Molotov is in step."

All other Presidium members, even Malenkov, who was appeasing Khrushchev and paying back Molotov at the same time, joined in the bombardment.[129] Kaganovich, known for matchless fawning on Stalin, now kowtowed to Khrushchev: "Comrade Khrushchev carries out his work . . . intensively, steadfastly, actively, and enterprisingly, as befits a Leninist Bolshevik and Central Committee first secretary."[130] After defending himself vigorously, Molotov finally recanted: "I consider that the Presidium has correctly pointed out the error of my position on the Yugoslav question. . . . I shall work honestly and actively to correct my mistake."[131] That provoked a long tirade from Khrushchev: "For thirty-four years he sat in the Politburo, and then for ten years he talks nonsense." If you intend to keep this up, Khrushchev continued, foreshadowing his own fate nine years later, "then why don't you retire, we'll give you a good pension, we'll respect you, but don't interfere with our work." Yes, he admitted, "the biggest clashes in the Presidium" had been between Molotov and him, but "I've given him no cause to attack me." Molotov was "the aggressor," because he "aspired to the role of grandee in the Presidium, and I didn't go along with that."

Khrushchev's concluding speech got even more petty. Molotov had wanted to present the East Germans with twenty to twenty-five Soviet-made buses. "Not out of general party considerations," complained Khrushchev, but so as to get a grand welcome when he visited East Berlin. Molotov's wife allegedly received U. S. Ambassador Charles Bohlen and his wife. "That's incorrect, even scandalous," Khrushchev charged. "We members of the Presidium don't receive foreign correspondents without the Presidium's permission, and here a minister's wife opens a private diplomatic shop and receives anyone who strikes her fancy. You're the minister of foreign affairs, but your wife isn't your deputy! . . . I have to tell you, Vyacheslav Mikhailovich, that she does you a disservice, your wife." The same Mrs. Molotov had accompanied her husband to Berlin and had tagged along to Geneva too, Khrushchev complained—several years before Nina Petrovna's presence on overseas trips was added to the long list of transgressions for which he was ousted.[132]

When the plenum ended, Molotov was still foreign minister and a member of the Presidium. With the Twentieth Party Congress scheduled the next winter, when demonstrating party unity would be important, it was not time for a radical purge.[133] Khrushchev even said something nice at the plenum: "I will extend every effort to work in friendly fashion with Comrade Molotov, so that his knowledge and experience may be more fully used to multiply the strength of our party."[134] But although the appearance of peace was preserved, Molotov, like Malenkov, never forgave Khrushchev, held every error he made against him, and took advantage of the first opportunity to get even.

CHAPTER ELEVEN

From the Secret Speech to the Hungarian Revolution: 1956

THE TWENTIETH CONGRESS of the Soviet Communist party convened on February 14, 1956, at 10:00 A.M. in the Great Kremlin Palace. Some 1,355 voting and 81 nonvoting delegates "represented" 6.8 million full and 620,000 candidate members of the CPSU. In attendance were emissaries from fifty-five Communist and workers' parties, including the leaders of all Eastern European Communist countries except Yugoslavia. As the first congress since Stalin's death (and the first to be held on schedule since 1939), the gathering presumably was to clarify the post-Stalin party line, including the posthumous status of Stalin himself, as well as the relative standing of his successors in the formally collective leadership. Both the seventy-fifth anniversary of Stalin's birth in December 1954 and the second anniversary of his death in March 1955 had been marked by expansive tributes in the press. But without explanation, *Pravda* had barely noted his seventy-sixth birthday in December 1955.[1]

When delegates first entered the hall, they saw a large statue of Lenin in its usual place of honor. But there wasn't even a picture of Stalin. Khrushchev's first words were: "In the period between the Nineteenth and Twentieth congresses, we have lost distinguished leaders of the Communist movement—Joseph Vissarionovich Stalin, Klement Gottwald and Kyuchi Tokuda. I ask everyone to honor their memory by standing."[2] Gottwald had been the Czech Communist leader; Tokuda, the Japanese Communist party's general secretary, had died in 1953. After a few seconds of silence, Italian delegate Vittorio Vidali recalled, "we looked at one another in surprise. Why? Who was Tokuda? What a strange tribute this was, made in such a hurry; it was almost as if he were afraid of the dead or ashamed to mention them."[3]

The main business of the congress was the Central Committee's report on domestic and foreign policy, delivered by Khrushchev, and Premier Bulganin's report on the sixth five-year plan. These were followed, as usual, by "discussion," consisting of set speeches by Soviet and other delegates. Both reports, especially their long sections on the economy, were mostly unexceptionable. But Khrushchev's contained several hints that Stalin's strange bedfellows in the opening tribute hadn't been accidental. The Central Committee, he declared, had "resolutely condemned the cult of the individual as alien to the spirit of Marxism-Leninism." At another point he lashed out at "an atmosphere of lawlessness and arbitrariness." The reference couldn't be to "anyone but Stalin," Vidali thought. But the Brazilian delegate seated next to him assured him that Khrushchev's target was Beria.[4]

The foreign policy section of Khrushchev's speech also broke significantly with Stalinist dogma (a new world war was *not* "fatalistically inevitable"; different countries could take *different* roads to socialism; even a peaceful, *nonrevolutionary* path to socialism was possible), but without mentioning Stalin's name. Anastas Mikoyan was slightly more explicit in his speech to the congress: " . . . for about twenty years we actually had no collective leadership; instead the cult of the individual flourished. . . . "[5] But delegates burst into applause at a favorable reference to Stalin in a letter from Mao Zedong and leaped to their feet cheering when the French Communist leader Maurice Thorez praised Stalin's name.[6]

After ten days of sessions, the congress was slated to end on February 25. Foreign delegates and guests were packing their bags that morning when Soviet delegates arrived for an unscheduled secret session. When Khrushchev and other Presidium members took their seats on the stage, they looked "red-faced and excited," recalled the Central Committee cultural specialist Igor Chernoutsan, who was seated down front and took detailed notes. Khrushchev talked for nearly four hours with one intermission. The heart of his speech was a devastating attack on Stalin. He was guilty of "a grave abuse of power." During his reign "mass arrests and deportation of thousands and thousands of people, and executions without trial or normal investigation, created insecurity, fear and even desperation." Stalinist charges of counter-revolutionary crimes had been "absurd, wild, and contrary to common sense." Innocent people confessed to crimes "because of physical methods of pressure, torture, reducing them to unconsciousness, depriving them of judgment, taking away their human dignity." For all this Stalin was personally responsible; he "personally called in the interrogator, gave him instructions, and told him which methods to use, methods that were simple—to beat, beat and, once again, beat."[7] Khrushchev cited "honest and innocent Communists" who had been tortured and killed, despite their recanting their forced confessions and begging Stalin for mercy. He assailed Stalin for incompetent wartime leadership, for his "monstrous" deportation of whole Caucasian peoples, for the "mania for greatness" that led him to boast, "I'll shake my little finger—and there will be no more Tito," for "nauseatingly false" adulation and self-adulation, and for the wholesale ruination of agriculture by a man who "never went anywhere, never met with workers and collective farmers" and knew the country "only from films that dressed up and prettified the situation in the countryside."[8]

Despite all this and more, Khrushchev's indictment was neither complete nor unalloyed. The Stalin he depicted had been a paragon until the mid-thirties. Although the Trotskyite and Bukharinist oppositions hadn't deserved "physical annihilation," they had been "ideological and political enemies." Khrushchev's sympathy was reserved for Stalin's *Communist* victims, many of whom died with non-Communist blood still on their hands. Khrushchev not only spared Lenin and the Soviet regime itself but glorified them. Stalin betrayed Lenin, he insisted, as Lenin himself had warned he might in documents that Khrushchev had distributed to congress delegates.[9]

Khrushchev pledged to return the country to Leninism. In the meantime he defended himself and Stalin's other heirs. "Where were the members of the Politburo?" he asked. "Why didn't they come out against the cult of personality in time? Why are they acting only now?" His lame answer, the same one contained in his later memoirs, was that Politburo members "viewed these matters differently at different times," that they hadn't known what Stalin was doing in their name, and that once they did know, it was too late to resist. Khrushchev quoted what Bulganin once said to him when the two were driving home from Stalin's dacha: "Sometimes when you go to Stalin's, he invites you as a friend. But while you're sitting with him, you don't know where they'll take you afterward: home or to prison." In his last years, Khrushchev told the congress, Stalin "apparently had plans to finish off the old members of the Politburo," to "destroy them so as to hide the shameful acts about which we are now reporting."[10]

He ended with a plea: "This subject must not go beyond the borders of the party, let alone into the press. That's why we are talking about this at a closed session of the Congress. . . . we must not provide ammunition for our enemies, we mustn't bare our injuries to them. I assume congress delegates will understand this correctly and evaluate it accordingly."[11]

Many in the audience were unreconstructed Stalinists; those who had denounced former colleagues and clambered over their corpses suddenly feared for their own heads. Others, who had secretly hated Stalin, couldn't believe his successor was joining their ranks. As the KGB chief-to-be Vladimir Semichastny remembered it, the speech was at first met with "a deathly silence; you could hear a bug fly by." When the noise started, it was a tense, muffled hum. Zakhar Glukhov, Khrushchev's successor in Petrovo-Marinsky near Donetsk, felt "anxious and joyous at the same time" and marveled at how Khrushchev "could have brought himself to say such things before such an audience." Dmitri Goriunov, the chief editor of *Komsomolskaya pravda,* took five nitroglycerin pills for a weak heart. "We didn't look each other in the eye as we came down from the balcony," recalled Aleksandr Yakovlev, then a minor functionary for the Central Committee Propaganda Department and later Gorbachev's partner in perestroika, "whether from shame or shock or from the simple unexpectedness of it, I don't know." As the delegates left the hall, all Yakovlev heard them muttering was "*Da-a, da-a, da-a,*" as if compressing all the intense, conflicting emotions they felt in the single, safe word, "yes."[12]

Khrushchev spoke with "agitation and emotion," Chernoutsan remembered, his speech peppered with explosive asides—"the most interesting things he said," according to Yakovlev—that never made it into the official transcript that found its way to the West in 1956 and wasn't published in the USSR until 1989. His hatred for Stalin was particularly visible when he held him accountable for the disastrous Kiev and Kharkov defeats in 1941 and 1942. "It burst forth," according to Chernoutsan, "when he cried out in fury, 'He was a coward. He panicked. Not once during the whole war did he dare go to the front.' "[13]

While Khrushchev raged on, his Presidium colleagues sat stony-faced. Reportedly Khrushchev taunted Molotov, Malenkov, Kaganovich, and Voroshilov, demanding that they explain their behavior under Stalin, but none of them uttered a word either during or after the speech.[14] At one point Khrushchev snarled at Voroshilov (using the familiar second-person singular in Russian), "Hey, you, Klim, cut out the lying. You should have done it long ago." By this time, Chernoutsan wrote, "Voroshilov's face had reddened to the roots of his gray hair." Still, Khrushchev pressed his attack: "You're old and decrepit by now. Can't you find the courage and conscience to tell the truth about what you saw with your own eyes?"[15]

During the intermission, Chernoutsan and Konstantin Simonov stood smoking in the corridor. "We already knew a lot," Chernoutsan later wrote, "but we still were stunned by the way the truth caved in on us. But was it the whole truth? And how to distinguish the real social tragedy from the accusations that the speaker was angrily flinging this way and that?"[16] Fyodor Burlatsky, then a young party operative, did not attend the congress. He was waiting at the party journal *Kommunist* when his boss, Sergei Mezentsev, returned from the Kremlin looking "white as snow—or more gray than white, like the color of salt marshes." Burlatsky asked: "Well, what was it like, Sergei Pavlovich?" Mezentsev "did not reply; his lips did not even move, as if his tongue had got stuck between his teeth." After a lengthy pause Burlatsky asked if the party had kicked out someone or elected someone it shouldn't have. Or was it, he added jokingly, that it had decided to close down the journal?

"The journal? . . . It's not the journal. . . . The things that were said . . . God knows what we're supposed to think . . . what will happen next . . . what should we do?" Mezentsev couldn't reveal what happened at the closed session. "They stipulated that there should be no leaks. Otherwise our enemies will use it to chop us down at the roots."

Four years later Burlatsky heard Khrushchev describe the secret speech to a group of foreign Communist leaders. As he spoke, Khrushchev waved a glass in the air, "spilling brandy on the white tablecloth and frightening those next to him without being aware of it himself." Only later "did he carefully place the glass on the table, thus releasing his right hand which was absolutely essential to add conviction to his words." Why had he given that speech at the Twentieth Congress? The answer required telling a story he read in school: "There were these political prisoners in jail under tsarism—Socialist Revolutionaries, Mensheviks and Bolsheviks. Among them was an old shoemaker named Pinya. . . .

"And that's what I did at the Twentieth Congress," Khrushchev continued. "Since I was chosen to be First [Secretary], I had to—like the shoemaker Pinya. I was obliged to tell the truth about the past, whatever the risks to me."[17]

KHRUSHCHEV'S SPEECH denouncing Stalin was the bravest and most reckless thing he ever did. The Soviet regime never fully recovered, and neither did he. Before he spoke, Malenkov and Molotov seemed defeated politically. Just to make sure, he had stacked the congress with his supporters and strengthened his position in the Central Committee. He was now first among supposed equals, perfectly positioned eventually to expel his rivals from the party. Instead, his rivals came close to removing him; fifteen months after the secret speech, a majority of Presidium colleagues voted to oust him as party leader. Under the rules of the game as played until then (the Presidium decides; the Central Committee rubber stamps), Khrushchev should have been finished. But with his back to the wall, he triumphed in a marathon eleven-day showdown. So dramatic was the duel, so decisive seemed the victory, that the main point seems to be the way that he won. In fact, the real question is how he almost managed to lose.

Part of the answer is the logic of power in the Kremlin: Khrushchev's rivals were bound to try to get him before he got them. The lesson, as Kremlinologist Robert Conquest puts it, is that "the leading figure in a 'collective leadership' is in constant danger unless he crushes his enemies in the Presidium completely and assures himself of a solid and devoted majority."[18] Another answer is that Stalin's legacy was so combustible that there was no way to defuse it without the convulsions that shook Eastern Europe in the fall of 1956, undermining Khrushchev's authority in the process. But it was his secret speech that triggered those upheavals. Did he fail to foresee the consequences? Did he act impulsively? Was he seeking to buttress his power or to assuage what was left of his conscience?

BERIA'S ARREST, investigation, and trial widened the circle of those aware of Stalin-era crimes. A forty-eight-page indictment of Beria was shown to local party leaders and educators. After Beria was executed, requests poured in for reconsideration of high-level purges, requests that were sent, on Khrushchev's insistence, first to the procurator, the KGB, and the Party Control Commission and then to the Presidium for final decision.[19]

By the end of 1955 thousands of political prisoners had returned home, bringing stories of what went on behind the barbed wire. Yet the gulag system was still functioning, the most infamous show trials of the thirties hadn't been reexamined, and labor camps and colonies still held 781,630 inmates, and prisons contained 159,250 more. Until September 1955 requests for information about relatives who had never returned received a standard answer: "Sentenced to ten years' deprivation of freedom without right of correspondence, with present whereabouts unknown." In 1955 the sister of General Jan Gamarnik, who committed suicide when faced with arrest in 1937, had been in prison and exile for seventeen years. She appealed for release directly to Khrushchev, whom she had known in the Kiev party organization, and he saw the letter, but the Central Committee rejected her request on grounds that the sister of an "enemy of the people" must serve her entire sentence.[20]

Deported peoples had begun to trickle back to their homelands, even before being given permission to do so. Letters inundated the Central Committee; many of them were addressed to Khrushchev and asked about the Stalinist past.[21] Those who had suffered sought some sort of reckoning; party and state officials themselves hoped to prevent a return to arbitrary terror. Add alterations in Stalin's domestic and foreign policies, especially the ballyhooed embrace of his archenemy Tito, and it is hard to see how the Kremlin could *not* have at least partly reassessed Stalin. But millions were still in thrall to his memory, and thousands of informers, interrogators, jailers, and executioners feared revenge and retribution. Even Khrushchev's most Stalinist colleagues favored at least some de-Stalinization, if only to prevent their own power struggles from being resolved by violent means. Still, all feared their complicity could be used against them.

Khrushchev took the lead in gathering information, pressing for reconsideration of cases, and releasing prisoners. He had a naive faith that socialism, once purified of its Stalinist stain, would command ever more loyalty from its beneficiaries. But his secret speech was also an act of repentance, a way of reclaiming his identity as a decent man by telling the truth. On the night before he delivered it, he later recalled, he could "hear the voices of comrades who perished."[22]

Khrushchev's account of his motives contains the same mix of deception and self-deception that mars his recollections of the thirties. As late as 1955 he was only "beginning to doubt whether all the arrests and convictions had been justified from the standpoint of judicial norms." Evidence gathered that year by a Presidium commission "came as a complete surprise" to him, he recalled. "Even in death Stalin commanded an almost unassailable authority, and it still hadn't occurred to me that he had been capable of abusing his power."[23] In actuality, the only news that may have truly surprised him was the extraordinary scale of the repressions, the fact that the great purge trials weren't partly but totally falsified, and, perhaps, particularly gruesome accounts of torture during interrogations.[24]

What Khrushchev was feeling in 1955 was a kind of manic ambivalence, his consciousness streaming wildly from self-justification to guilt to pride, which is captured in his memoirs: "I had mourned for Stalin as the only real force for our solidarity. . . . Of course doubts had crept into my mind, as they would into any man's. . . . But Stalin, this was Stalin! . . . I had no idea that this man was capable in principle of consciously abusing his power. . . . If he were alive now and we were voting on the question of his responsibility, I'd favor bringing him to trial." But "we ourselves were constrained by our activities under Stalin's leadership; we couldn't free ourselves from his pressure even after he died, couldn't imagine that all the executions were . . . pure crimes. . . . We had no right not to know," but "we were told not to stick our noses into things. . . . There are different degrees of responsibility. As for me I'm prepared to bear my share of responsibility. . . . Even in the life of people who have committed crimes, there comes a moment when they can admit it, and when they do so, it will bring them leniency if not exculpation. . . . I've always stood, and stand now, for veracity, for absolute veracity before the party. . . . Even after the Beria trial, we gave the party and the people incorrect explanations; we did everything to shield Stalin, although we were shielding a criminal, a murderer. . . . I first felt the falseness of that position when we arrived in Yugoslavia, talked with Tito and the others. When we blamed Beria, they laughed and made ironic remarks."[25]

Since thirteen years had elapsed between the Eighteenth and Nineteenth party congresses, Khrushchev was determined to convene the Twentieth on time in early 1956. He informed the Presidium as much on April 7, 1955, and it agreed the next day, followed by the Central Committee on July 12, 1955. In the fall of 1955 the security police stepped up its reexamination of cases dating back to 1936–1939. About the same time, USSR Procurator-General Rudenko reported to Khrushchev that "from a juridical point of view, there was no basis" for the mass arrests of the late thirties, "let alone the executions."[26]

During this same period Khrushchev had several long conversations with old comrades who had just returned from the camps. He had known Aleksei Snegov in Ukraine in the late twenties; alas, Snegov had also known Beria and enough about Beria's machinations to get himself arrested in 1937. Somehow Snegov survived sixteen years beyond the Arctic Circle, and after Stalin's death he managed to smuggle a letter to Khrushchev out of his labor camp. Khrushchev summoned Snegov, used him as a witness against Beria, got him released for good, and used him to speed release of others by appointing him a high official of the whole gulag system. Khrushchev considered having Snegov and other former political prisoners speak at the Twentieth Congress and ended up incorporating material Snegov sent him in his own secret speech, all at a time when camp returnees were still so suspect that police sometimes forced them to leave Moscow.[27]

Mikoyan later recollected he pressed Khrushchev to denounce Stalin, saying, "There has to be a report on what had happened, if not to the party as a whole, then to delegates to the first congress after Stalin's death. If we don't do that at this congress, and someone else does it sometime before the next congress, then everyone would have a legal right to hold us fully responsible for the crimes that had occurred." According to Mikoyan's son, Sergo, it was Snegov who first told Khrushchev, "Either you tell them at the upcoming congress, or you'll find yourself under investigation." Anastas Mikoyan complained that Khrushchev took all the credit in his memoirs, refusing "to share the glory with anyone else."[28]

Whatever advice Khrushchev received, it was he who acted: he who insisted on the speech and he who delivered it. In October 1955 he suggested informing congress delegates of what was known about Stalin's crimes. On December 31 he proposed a commission to look into Stalin's activities. "Whom will that benefit?" Molotov demanded. "What will that give us? Why stir up the past?" Kaganovich objected: "Stalin personifies the multiple victories of the Soviet people. Examining possible mistakes by Lenin's successor will raise doubts about the correctness of our whole course. People will even say to us, 'Where were you? Who gave you the right to judge the dead?' "[29]

The squabble that day centered on the purges of the late thirties, particularly of those of delegates to the Seventeenth Party Congress in 1934. Khrushchev promised that the commission would focus on "violations of socialist legality" for which Beria was primarily responsible and would be chaired by seeming arch-Stalinist Pyotr Pospelov. Pospelov had edited *Pravda* from 1940 to 1949, directed preparation of the second edition of Stalin's *Brief Biography* (of which seven million copies were printed in 1951 alone), and, Khrushchev recalled, had sobbed so hard when Stalin died that Beria had to shake him, saying, "What's the matter with you? Cut it out!" "We thought Pospelov would be a good choice as chairman of the commission," Khrushchev explained, "because this would create a sense of confidence" in its report. That Pospelov was capable of drafting long, mind-numbing documents in one sitting was also in his favor.[30]

Khrushchev ordered commission members to pay particular attention to executed party officials, including his predecessors in Ukraine, Pavel Postyshev and Stanislav Kossior. The commission pored over purge case files for more than a month. Meanwhile, on February 1, 1956, the Presidium called in the former deputy head of "specially important investigations" for the NKVD Boris Rodos, who had personally beaten "confessions" out of Kossior, Vlas Chubar, and Aleksandr Kosarev. Rodos was "a good-for-nothing with the brain of a chicken," Khrushchev soon told the Twentieth Congress, "a moral degenerate" who "determined the fate of well-known party officials." But Rodos told the Presidium he had acted on orders not just from from Beria but directly from Stalin as well.[31]

Rodos's answers to Presidium questions sparked a hot exchange among its members. "Will we have the courage to tell the truth?" asked Khrushchev. "If these are facts," exclaimed Saburov, "can we really call this communism? This is unforgivable." Malenkov favored informing the congress. Bulganin and Pervukhin agreed. Molotov objected, supported by Voroshilov and Kaganovich.[32]

Several days later the Pospelov commission delivered a seventy-page report along with copies of Stalin's orders unleashing the Great Purge. Between 1935 and 1940, the report said, of the 1,920,635 persons arrested for anti-Soviet activity, 688,503 had been shot. All alleged plots and conspiracies had been fabricated; Stalin had personally sanctioned the torture that produced the confessions. Politburo members besides Stalin had seen copies of interrogation protocols and knew about the torture. "The facts were so horrifying," Mikoyan later recalled, "that in certain very difficult passages Pospelov's voice shook, and once he broke down and sobbed."[33]

After Pospelov finished, Khrushchev declared, "Stalin's bankruptcy as a leader is revealed. What sort of leader is it who destroys everyone? We've got to have the courage to tell the truth." Any such report, Molotov countered, must insist that "Stalin was Lenin's great successor." After all, "the party lived and worked under Stalin's leadership for thirty years, industrializing the country, gaining victory in the war, and emerging from it as a great power." Whether in a spasm of guilt (he mentioned his purged brother Mikhail) or to please Khrushchev, Kaganovich chided Molotov: "You can't deceive history. Facts can't be thrown out. Khrushchev's proposal for a report is correct. . . . We bear responsibility, but the situation was such that we couldn't object." Still, he added, congress delegates should be informed in such a way that "we don't unleash anarchy."

Kaganovich changed his mind in the course of the debate. In the end he, Voroshilov, and Molotov opposed Khrushchev, but they were outvoted. Malenkov: "You can't explain the slaughter of cadres by citing a struggle against enemies." Averky Aristov: "To say, 'We didn't know,' would be unworthy of members of the Politburo." Shepilov: "We must tell the party; otherwise they will never forgive us." Khrushchev tried to minimize the differences by saying that he didn't see any major ones and that "the congress must be told the truth," but "without relish."[34]

On February 13, the day before the congress convened, the Presidium decided Khrushchev would speak to a closed session. Later the same day he conveyed the recommendation to the Central Committee: " . . . we haven't been posing the issue of the cult of personality the way it ought to be posed. . . . Congress delegates need to know more than they can learn from the press. Otherwise they won't feel in command of their own party. They need more factual material to understand the turnabout that has occurred. I think members of the Central Committee will agree." Needless to say, they at least seemed to do so.[35]

Once Khrushchev's speech was authorized, the text became the subject of complicated maneuvering in which Khrushchev's tactic was to shape the speech himself and spring the final version on the Presidium at the eleventh hour.[36] On February 15 he asked Pospelov and Aristov to prepare a draft. Pospelov hastily churned out a thirty-seven-page text (of which a pencil-written version remains in the archives) and delivered it to Khrushchev on February 18. In contrast with the speech Khrushchev actually delivered, Pospelov's is shorter (covering just the late thirties) and both duller and sharper at the same time. Pospelov's draft lacks the biting personal stories Khrushchev told but includes statistics Khrushchev left out, such as the 383 lists containing 44,465 names of party, state, and other personnel whose executions Stalin personally authorized during 1937 and 1938 alone.[37]

On February 19, Khrushchev dictated additional material to his stenographer, including passages marked by particular passion and anger. Besides lambasting Stalin for his conduct of the war, for postwar purges like the Leningrad affair and the doctors' plot, and for ruining agriculture, he awkwardly tried to explain why he and his colleagues had been helpless to restrain the "tyrant": "He used us"; "Anyone who objected . . . was doomed . . . to immediate destruction"; "He tried to drill through us with his eyes; . . . he'd say, 'Why are your eyes darting about today?' or 'Why are you looking away?' "[38]

Four days before dictating these lines, Khrushchev had recruited Shepilov, Pospelov's successor as *Pravda*'s editor, who had become a Central Committee secretary in July 1955, to prepare yet another version. Unusually well educated, a Moscow University graduate with a stint at the Institute of Red Professors on his résumé, Shepilov was unique among Khrushchev's protégés. He had just finished addressing the congress on February 15 and was sitting among other dignitaries on the right side of the stage when Khrushchev approached. The two men had previously discussed Stalin; Khrushchev had talked openly and "with hatred" about Stalinist repression. After they drove from the Kremlin to Central Committee headquarters on Old Square, Shepilov asked Khrushchev what he should write. "You and I have talked it over," Khrushchev answered. "Now it's time to act." When Khrushchev delivered the speech on February 25, Shepilov recognized his own paragraphs sprinkled throughout, but someone had reshuffled them. If that had been Khrushchev himself, Shepilov later speculated, "he must have dictated it, since Nikita Sergeyevich himself never wrote things out; he had problems with spelling as he himself knew quite well. I once saw an instruction of his on a document in which he misspelled the word *oznakomitsia* [for your information] as *aznakomitsa*."[39]

On or about February 20, someone constructed yet another draft from the Pospelov–Aristov and Shepilov versions, plus Khrushchev's dictations. By that time Mikoyan, Saburov, and other allies had proposed passages on foreign relations and the wartime repression of non-Russian nationalities, additions that must have particularly appealed to Khrushchev because they concerned the period during and after the war when he was farthest from Stalin's inner circle. On February 23, with two days to go before the closed congress session, a penultimate version was circulated to Presidium members. One copy preserved in the archives has marginal comments written in several colors of pencil. After the description of party official Robert Eikhe's torture and last desperate appeal to Stalin, someone wrote of Stalin, "That's our dear father!" Another comment coined the phrase "we mustn't bare our injuries," which Khrushchev added to his warning in the final text: "This musn't go beyond the borders of the party, let alone into the press."[40]

On February 22, Khrushchev had received a letter from Vasily Andrianov, the former Leningrad party boss who helped stage the infamous Leningrad affair, offering to recount that bloody episode during the congress's closed session, "just as I did in my memorandum to you and in the audience you granted me." Two days later, Khrushchev's Stalingrad comrade General Yeremenko offered to reveal how Stalin's orders almost led to the fall of the city.[41] At ten that same evening Khrushchev called in his aides, Grigory Shuisky and Pyotr Demichev, dictated additional passages to a stenographer, who reportedly broke into tears in the middle of one of them, and ordered the final text brought to him the next morning, February 25.[42]

ON THE FORTIETH anniversary of the secret speech, at a conference he organized to pay tribute to the Twentieth Party Congress, Mikhail Gorbachev marveled at the "huge political risk" Khrushchev took, at his "political courage," at the way he showed himself to be "a moral man after all" by "beginning the process of unmasking Stalin's crimes."[43] Even apart from the secret speech, the first congress after Stalin's death was "a test" for Khrushchev, and he thought he passed it. After taking a whole day to deliver the Central Committee's general report, he "returned home dead tired, but extremely pleased," Sergei Khrushchev recalled. His father was "simply beaming. To be the one delivering the general report to a congress was the highest honor imaginable."[44]

The congress also strengthened Khrushchev's power position. Four Khrushchev supporters (Georgy Zhukov, Leonid Brezhnev, Yekaterina Furtseva, and Nuriddin Mukhitdinov) became Presidium candidate members, Brezhnev and Furtseva joined the Secretariat too, and the Central Committee got a massive infusion of new members, many of them local party leaders who owed their positions to Khrushchev.[45] Asked later why he hadn't rebutted Khrushchev on floor of the congress, Molotov replied, "The party wasn't ready for that; they simply would have chucked us out." By early 1956, "I was already entirely off to one side, and not just in the ministry [of Foreign Affairs]. People tried to keep away from me. The only reports I got were at formal sessions [of the Presidium]."[46]

Popularity wasn't as important as power in the Soviet system, but that too was coming Khrushchev's way, especially in intelligentsia circles. "I like him ever so much!" gushed Andrei Sakharov in 1956. "After all, he so differs from Stalin!"[47] Likewise, more material comforts of the sort he wanted to disdain but never rejected, including a new residence into which he and his family moved in late 1955.[48] The new villa was one of five built on the Lenin Hills west of downtown Moscow, across the Moscow River from the Luzhniki sports complex, where the land juts up toward a broad plateau on which Moscow State University's Stalinist skyscrapers stand. Protected by tall yellow and white fences and numerous guards, the Khrushchev residence sat on a large plot that had a magnificent view of Moscow to the east, with several walks and driveways (on one of which the family sometimes played tennis without a net) leading to a fountain on the western side and with more paths twisting among birches, pines, and rowan trees above the river. The house is a massive two-story affair with a large entrance hall with marble columns, a large living room with an inlaid wooden floor and a dazzling Czech chandelier, and an equally imposing dining room seating ten people on either side of a long table. On the second floor are several bedrooms, a combination billiards and film-screening room, and a wood-paneled study that Khrushchev ignored, preferring to work and receive visitors at the dining room table.[49]

When the Khrushchevs first moved to the Lenin Hills, the Mikoyans lived next door, the Kaganoviches and Bulganins nearby. With their spacious downtown apartments and grand dachas in the countryside, Molotov and Voroshilov had little cause to envy Khrushchev's housing. But his senior colleagues had plenty of other reasons to resent him and plenty of opportunity to act on that feeling as the unforeseen consequences of his secret speech unfolded.

THE SPEECH didn't stay secret for long. That was just fine with Khrushchev.[50] "I very much doubt that Father wanted to keep it secret," said Sergei Khrushchev. "On the contrary! His own words provide confirmation of the opposite—that he wanted to bring his report to the people. Otherwise all his efforts would have been meaningless. The secrecy of the sessions was only a formal concession on his part. . . ."[51]

By March 1 Khrushchev had sent the Presidium an edited copy that, "if there arise no objections to the text, will be distributed to party organizations."[52] Four days later the Presidium approved sending the speech, in a small red-covered booklet on which the warning "Top Secret" had been reduced to "Not for the Press," to party committees around the country, which were to "acquaint all Communists and Komsomol members, and also nonparty activists including workers, white-collar personnel, and collective farmers" with its contents.[53] All told, up to seven million party and eighteen million Komsomol members had the speech read to them in the weeks that followed, in factories and government agencies, on farms and in institutes, even, as it turned out, in high schools.[54]

Eastern European Communist leaders attending the congress got to hear the speech during the night of February 25–26, read very slowly by Soviet emissaries to allow them to take notes. The East German delegation was stunned, but its leader, Walter Ulbricht, seemed quickly to recover; asked the next morning what an associate should say to East Germans studying at the CPSU party school, he replied cynically, "You can just tell them that Stalin is no longer considered a classic." Actually, Ulbricht was more shaken than he appeared; he tried to conceal the speech from his own people until the Western press published reports that filtered back into East Germany.[55]

The Poles weren't so careful. Their Politburo let Central Committee members and key party activists peruse the Russian text in a special room at party headquarters. Less than a month later an official translation was distributed to all party cells in Poland. Initially some three thousand numbered copies were printed, but printers took it upon themselves to run off an extra fifteen thousand. Khrushchev "let us know that it was possible his speech would be published," recalled Edward Morawski, the Polish party propaganda chief who supervised its distribution. "We understood it was also necessary for us to print and distribute the speech. Many people in the leadership were against it, although that didn't surprise me. A person had to go to [party] meetings, answer questions; he felt like a criminal."[56]

One of the Polish copies reached the CIA, delivered in early April by Israeli intelligence, which got hold of it in Warsaw. In late May the U.S. State Department released a copy to the *New York Times*, which published it on June 4, 1956.[57] Soviet authorities neither confirmed nor denied its authenticity. Asked about it by Western reporters, Khrushchev jokingly referred them to the director of central intelligence Allen Dulles.[58] Back in the USSR, the speech's widespread distribution mocked its formal secrecy, but it still wasn't officially public. Since Stalin wasn't formally discredited, his portraits were still omnipresent. When the new Yugoslav ambassador, Veljko Mićunović, stopped at the Lvov and Kiev airports in late March, he noticed "enormous portraits of Stalin in very bright colors and in gold wherever it was possible to gild them . . . as though the Twentieth Congress of the CPSU had never taken place and Khrushchev's secret speech had never been pronounced."

The same never-never land extended into the Kremlin itself. Khrushchev received Mićunović for four hours (instead of the scheduled fifteen minutes), much of it devoted to a lengthy diatribe against the late dictator, whose portrait still hung in his own outer office. If Stalin was still there, Mićunović asked himself in his diary, "what is happening in the rest of the Soviet Union? If Khrushchev is not yet able to get rid of Stalin from his office in Moscow, how can he be removed from Russia?"

Hardly any of the other Soviet leaders on whom Mićunović paid courtesy calls mentioned Stalin at all. Molotov avoided sensitive subjects altogether, not even "hinting that we had been involved for ten years in an ideological and political war which Molotov himself had started. . . ." Voroshilov, still the nominal head of state despite what Khrushchev had described to Mićunović as his "decrepitude," limited himself to diplomatic niceties. Kaganovich sounded totally unreconstructed. Of all the Russians Mićunović and his staff talked to between March 27 and April 18, not one "has spoken of the condemnation of Stalin with a sense of personal satisfaction or with the conviction that it was necessary to act in this way (apart, of course, from Khrushchev and Bulganin)."[59]

Open publication of the speech could have encouraged a fuller break with the Stalinist past. A total blackout, on the other hand, might have prevented the turmoil that soon followed. Khrushchev who wanted more publicity, and others who wanted less, compromised on a middle road. But Khrushchev was still torn. "He was a man who had risen to the top on the Stalinist wave," said his daughter Rada. "His heroism was in the fact that he could overcome this in himself. . . . But on many things he thought Stalin was right because he himself thought like Stalin."[60] Immediately after the speech, according to Aleksei Adzhubei, "Khrushchev sensed the blow had been too powerful. For the time being, he continued denouncing Stalin's tyranny, disclosing new facts about the bloody terror in speeches. . . . But increasingly he sought to limit the boundaries of critical analysis, lest it end up polarizing society. . . ."[61]

"Now those who were arrested will return," said the poet Anna Akhmatova in March 1956, "and two Russias will look each other in the eye: the one that sent people to the camps and the one that was sent away."[62] At numerous meetings at which the speech was read and discussed, criticism of Stalin rippled way beyond Khrushchev's. Anti-Stalinists homed in on precisely the sore spots Khrushchev had avoided: Why had it taken so long to speak of Stalin's crimes? Weren't current Presidium members accomplices? What about Khrushchev himself? Why had he kept silent for so long and attacked Stalin only after his death? Why hadn't Khrushchev grieved for Stalin's *non*-Communist victims? Wasn't the Soviet system itself at fault?

Some meetings passed or tried to pass resolutions on issues that weren't debated again in public until the late 1980s: the need for real rights and freedoms and for multiparty elections to guarantee them. A Moscow University meeting turned into a madhouse when local party bosses tried to oust non-Communists who crowded in to hear Khrushchev's report. At the Academy of Sciences Thermo-Technical Laboratory, applause greeted a junior fellow's remark that "power belongs to a heap of scoundrels. Our party is shot through with the spirit of slavery." When the chair tried to cut off discussion, nearly half those present flouted party discipline and voted to continue it. Either because he didn't get Khrushchev's message or because he did, the procurator of the Kabardian Autonomous Soviet Socialist Republic in the Caucasus dared to inform party activists of the number of people arrested and executed there in late 1937, to describe the torture used to extract confessions, and to name those responsible. In Siberia a young Komsomol functionary who read Khrushchev's speech aloud to students had no idea what to say when he was finished, nor did the local party propaganda boss, to whom he appealed, leaving the students to seek edification from their physical education instructor.[63]

In April the KGB reported portraits and busts of Stalin torn down or defaced, that Communists at one meeting had tried to declare Stalin "an enemy of the people" and at another had demanded his body be removed from the Lenin-Stalin Mausoleum. But those who defended Stalin were even more numerous, as a young Komsomol official named Mikhail Gorbachev found out when he reported on the Twentieth Congress in a rural district near Stavropol in southern Russia. When his party boss warned him, "The people don't understand; they don't accept it," Gorbachev assumed he meant party apparatchiks rather than simple citizens. But two weeks of daily meetings set him straight. Younger and better-educated people, especially those who had been or knew Stalin's victims, seemed pleased with Khrushchev's speech. A second group "refused to believe . . . or rejected his assessment," and a third kept asking, "What for? What is the point of washing one's dirty linen in public?" The most ironic reaction came from ordinary citizens who hailed Stalin for "punishing" (i.e., purging) the party and police officials who had oppressed them. "They paid for our tears!" said Gorbachev's listeners. "And this," he recalled, "in a region that had gone through the bloody carnage of the terrible 1930's."[64]

No region had shed more of its blood than Stalin's native Georgia, but none remained more loyal to his memory. On the third anniversary of his death Georgians gathered in the streets of Tbilisi and several other cities. What began as peaceful tribute to Stalin turned into four days of protests against Khrushchev's secret speech. More than sixty thousand people carried flowers to the Stalin monument in Tbilisi, while hundreds of others with portraits of Stalin careered around the city in trucks and commandeered buses, trams, and trolleys. "Glory to the Great Stalin!" "Down with Khrushchev!" "Molotov for Prime Minister!" "Molotov to Head the CPSU!" Some demonstrators even demanded Georgia secede from the USSR. When they marched on the radio station, troops and tanks moved in. In two clashes alone, one of them at the Stalin monument, fifteen were killed and fifty-four were wounded; five of them died subsequently. In the end at least twenty demonstrators were killed, sixty wounded, and many arrested and imprisoned. When the trouble first started, Sergei Khrushchev remembered, his father hoped the young demonstrators would "kick up a row and then calm down." But in the end "we intervened very sharply," Khrushchev told Yugoslav Ambassador Mićunović. "A few" had been killed or wounded, he said; others had repented and were promising to behave. From now on, Khrushchev added, "We won't be caught off guard."[65]

The Presidium responded to the tumultuous party meeting at the Thermo-Technical Laboratory by sending a resolution to Communists around the country. It condemned "hostile outbursts," disbanded the laboratory's party cell, purged all its members, and allowed back into the party "only those who are genuinely capable of carrying out the party's general line. . . . "[66] *Pravda* lambasted unnamed Communists guilty of "slanderous fabrications," "antiparty assertions," and "nonparty statements" and demanded an end to "excessive liberalism" toward "antiparty slanderers." On April 7 the party newspaper reprinted an editorial from the Chinese press calling upon Communists to study and to treasure Stalin's works and "historical inheritance." Khrushchev's retreat climaxed on June 30, when a Central Committee resolution in effect rewrote his secret speech as his Stalinist colleagues would have preferred he had given it: with a dry, impersonal tone, blaming Stalin for, at most, "serious errors," rejecting any attempt "to find the source of this cult in the nature of the Soviet social system," and with high praise for the "Leninist core of leaders" who "set a course of resolute struggle against the personality cult . . . immediately after Stalin's death."[67]

None of these epistles halted the rehabilitation of rank-and-file Stalinist victims; indeed the pace quickened from the roughly seven thousand who had been rehabilitated before the congress to several hundred thousand afterward. Release of prisoners continued as well with the help of nearly a hundred USSR Supreme Soviet commissions that traveled to labor camps to "examine the basis for sentences of those accused of carrying out crimes of a political character."[68] But when it came to more famous victims, Khrushchev drew back. A commission appointed in 1955 to reexamine the purge of Marshal Tukhachevsky and other generals finished its work, with their rehabilitation announced in January 1957. But another commission on the trials of Zinoviev, Kamenev, and Bukharin, among others, chaired by Molotov, of all people, and with Kaganovich and Voroshilov among its members, squabbled for several months and then reported "no basis" for reexamining these cases since the defendants had "led an anti-Soviet fight against the construction of socialism in the USSR."[69] In July 1957, after the attempted coup against Khrushchev failed, he promised to return to these cases, but he never did, lest he discredit foreign Communist leaders who had hailed the purge verdicts, as he himself had done.[70]

Khrushchev wanted to keep de-Stalinization going, although at a more measured pace. But when Molotov insisted on the June 30 Central Committee statement, he had to accept it. Two months before that, the Yugoslav envoy Mićunović got a glimpse of tensions among Soviet leaders at a May Day luncheon. After reviewing the parade from the Lenin-Stalin Mausoleum, Soviet leaders and foreign guests repaired to a lavish feast. As host Khrushchev improvised twelve to fifteen toasts in the course of the meal. Then he launched into a harsh condemnation of Stalin, interlaced with references to Molotov and Voroshilov. He was ostensibly defending his colleagues (Molotov was an honest Communist; Voroshilov was certainly not the British agent Stalin had accused him of being), but the effect was to link them with the late dictator. After Bulganin urged him to stick to Stalin, Khrushchev explained why he had given his secret speech—because, according to Mićunović, "he [Khrushchev] was already an old man, and might depart at any moment" and because "before he departs this world, everyone has to give an account of what he had done and how he did it."

Moved by Khrushchev's obvious emotion, the ambassadors applauded, making the reaction of his colleagues all the more remarkable. Bulganin and Mikoyan alone seemed to approve. Molotov, Malenkov, and Kaganovich "remained passive throughout." Mićunović was particularly struck by Molotov, who was closest to him at the table: "At times it seemed to me that Khrushchev was touching him on the raw." It was clear that as people, Presidium members "simply cannot stand each other any longer." Molotov and Malenkov could hardly bear "the relish and ebullience with which Khrushchev played the role of master and host."[71]

In June, Khrushchev mounted a counteroffensive against his critics. On June 1, the day Yugoslav President Tito arrived in the USSR for a twenty-three-day visit, Molotov was forced to yield the Foreign Ministry, over which he had presided since 1939 (except for a four-year break in Stalin's last years), to Khrushchev's disciple Shepilov. Several days later Kaganovich stepped down as the chairman of the State Committee on Wages. Although both men remained on the Presidium, their demotions signaled that Khrushchev had weathered the storm. His talks with Tito looked like a triumph, from the two leaders' impromptu visit to a Gorky Street ice-cream store (where it turned out neither leader had a kopeck in his pocket) to a gala dinner at which Soviet leaders, including Molotov, took turns condemning Stalin's treatment of Yugoslavia to a trip to Stalingrad and the Black Sea on which Khrushchev personally accompanied Tito.[72] In fact, however, the Yugoslavs rebuffed Khrushchev's pressure to draw even closer to Moscow, and five days after Tito left Moscow, workers in the Polish city of Poznań launched a massive strike demanding "Bread and Freedom," which ended only after thousands of Polish army and security troops killed at least fifty-three and wounded many hundreds more.[73] Five months after that Hungary rose in a far fiercer revolt.

THE DEEPER ROOTS of Eastern European unrest had to do with long-standing Polish and Hungarian resentment of Russian rule and especially with the forced imposition of Stalinism after World War II. In neither country would the Communists have come to power in truly free elections. The Polish Communist leadership, headed by Bolesław Bierut, toned down the worst of Stalinism, including forced collectivization of agriculture, and resisted physical liquidation of the purged Communist leader Władysław Gomułka. Hungary's Mátyás Rákosi, on the other hand, emulated Stalin up to and including the show trial and execution of the deposed Stalinist leader László Rajk.

After Stalin died, Soviet insistence on reform undermined the Polish and Hungarian regimes. The fact that the Warsaw leadership remained intact gave it time to adjust to the new era. Moscow allowed Rákosi to remain in control but insisted he accept the reform-minded Imre Nagy as prime minister. Rákosi conspired to oust Nagy, and finally succeeded in 1955 by taking advantage of Malenkov's fall in Moscow. Accused, like Malenkov, of "right-wing deviationism," Nagy was ousted as head of government and expelled from the party, leaving Hungary a tinderbox into which Khrushchev's speech threw a lighted match.[74]

Having first met leading Communists in both countries in 1945 and visited Poland several times after the war, Khrushchev knew Poland and

Hungary fairly well, and he assumed what was good for the USSR was good for its allies. During a 1955 visit to Warsaw, he tried to persuade Poles to shift four million acres to corn. "I'm telling you," recalled Stefan Staszewski who was a deputy minister of agriculture, "utter despair descended" on the Polish Politburo. It didn't help that Khrushchev buttressed his case by citing his grandmother's success raising corn; the Poles might have reservations about his advice, he told agronomists and farmers, but "all of you also have grandmothers." When a Polish agronomist complained that she and her colleagues were being treated as if they knew nothing, Khrushchev burst out at Staszewski, who was translating for him: "So, do you hear that? You hear what they're saying? That's the Poles for you: they always think they know everything better than we do!"[75]

Khrushchev had failed to consult Eastern European leaders before giving his secret speech. As he later admitted, the speech was "especially painfully received in Poland and Hungary." The Polish leader Bierut was in the Kremlin hospital with pneumonia when a copy of the speech reached him. He had a heart attack when he read it, and he died on March 12. (Interestingly enough, Khrushchev himself took ill about the same time. "Only I was tough and he was weak," Khrushchev later told Staszewski.)[76] The speech "was like being hit over the head with a hammer," recalled Beirut's successor, Edward Ochab. Polish party meetings at which it was read erupted into anti-Soviet and anti-Russian protests.[77]

Khrushchev's courtship of Tito, with whom Rákosi had long been at odds, undermined the Hungarian leader even before the Twentieth Congress, and the secret speech nearly finished him. Although Khrushchev later admitted it was "a great mistake" to "rely on that idiot Rákosi," Moscow allowed him to hang on until the summer. The ferment encouraged by Khrushchev's speech crystallized in June in a tumultuous meeting of the Petőfi Circle, an intellectual forum Rákosi had set up in March for party youth but that turned into a center of opposition to him; the June 27 session, which Soviet leaders later described as "an ideological Poznań [the site of the bloody Polish clashes in June], without the gunshots," exploded in condemnation of Stalinism.[78] When the Soviet Presidium met on July 12, members blamed both Poznań and Petőfi on "subversive imperialist activity" designed to "divide [the socialist countries] and destroy them one by one." It took an urgent trip to Budapest the next day by Mikoyan, who recommended that Rákosi be dumped, before the Kremlin authorized replacing him with Ernö Gerö, who proved no more capable of holding Hungary together.[79]

For the next four months, unrest in Poland and Hungary consumed Khrushchev and his colleagues. The stakes were high and getting higher. At times there seemed no good way out. Letting events take their own course risked the collapse of communism, but occupying Poland or Hungary would discredit it. Khrushchev's Kremlin rivals blamed him for the mess. He sought desperately to resolve the twin crises brought on by de-Stalinization while continuing de-Stalinization itself. If he failed, his own position would be at risk.

Polish turbulence had required Khrushchev's presence as early as March 1956. He traveled to Warsaw for Bierut's funeral and remained while the Polish Central Committee picked Bierut's successor. "We'd assumed," recalled Staszewski, "that the first secretary of a great party didn't have too much time on his hands." However, Khrushchev not only outstayed his welcome but rambled on in a way that astounded the Poles, trying to explain why he had unleashed de-Stalinization, conversing not so much with his audience as with himself, reaching for moral terms but grasping political clichés, contradicting himself constantly because the circle of his relationship with Stalin couldn't be squared.

"We freed thousands, tens of thousands, we rehabilitated our friends," he said proudly at the beginning. "And what could we say to them then? We couldn't look them in the eye and say nothing happened. . . . We decided to read the whole speech to Komsomol members, eighteen million warmhearted young people; if they don't know everything, then they won't understand us, they won't understand us. And also to gatherings of workers, not just party members, so that nonparty members will feel that we trust them. . . . That's why there's now a colossal rise in solidarity around the Central Committee. . . . That's why as a result of our work, comrades, and I'm absolutely sure of it, in fact I answer with my own head for it, we will achieve an unprecedented closing of ranks within our own party, and of the people around our party.

"It was a tragedy," Khrushchev said of Stalin. "If you ask, comrades, how we now evaluate Stalin, who Stalin was, what was Stalin, was he an enemy of the party and the working class, then the answer is no, and that's what the tragedy is, comrades. This wasn't an enemy, this was a really cruel man who was convinced that all his cruelty, injustice, and abuses, everything he did, was in the interests of the party." Or was he? Suddenly, Khrushchev threw up his hands. "I don't know, the devil knows how to explain why so many perished.

"What would you have done, comrades," Khrushchev suddenly asked his audience, "if they had sent you signed confessions? What would you have said after reading them? You would have been indignant. You would have said this is an enemy of the people. [Voice in the hall: No!] No? No, comrades? You say you wouldn't have? I'm not offended. Because you say this in 1956 after my report. As the saying goes, the fool becomes smart afterwards." For if he had defended Stalin's victims while Stalin was still alive, "they would have declared me an enemy. . . . If you didn't drink and eat with [Stalin], that meant you were his enemy. If he hadn't been so entrenched, we would have thrown him out, we would have said, little pigeon [*golubchik*], listen, you can't be a drunkard, you've got to work, we're responsible before the people. Why didn't we act sooner? I have a little grandson, comrades, and he's always asking me why this, and why that. Well, there were circumstances which we couldn't ignore. . . . "

Back to Stalin again: "Was he more stupid than we were? No. Smarter than we were? As a Marxist he was stronger. We have to give him his due, comrades, but Stalin was ill, he abused his power." Still, "he wanted to serve society with all his heart and soul. I'm absolutely convinced of that. The whole question has to do with the ways and means. And that's a separate question. How to tie all this together? It's a hard question. It's very hard. Everyone must recook it in his own mind. . . . We're now recounting the negative side of history. But, comrades, Stalin—I wish I could describe the warm side, his concern for people. This was a person, a revolutionary. But he had a mania, a persecution mania, you understand. That's why he didn't stop at anything, even at executing his own relatives."[80]

Khrushchev spoke for several hours. Afterward, hoping that he would depart, the Poles called a two-hour recess. When he didn't leave, they served tea. In answer to a question on Stalin's treatment of Jews, Khrushchev suddenly praised the secret Soviet quota on Jews in high places. Not only was this subject taboo, recalled Staszewski, but Khrushchev "started talking about it in a way which almost made us fall off our chairs." He blurted out: "We have two percent, which means that ministries, universities, everything, is made up of two percent Jews. You should know that. I'm not an anti-Semite, indeed we have this minister who's a Jew . . . and we respect him, but you have to know the limits." At this point, economic planner Hilary Minc, who was Jewish, said to Staszewski "in a terrified whisper, 'Stop it, for God's sake stop talking to him, he doesn't understand anything! Stop!' "[81]

Khrushchev failed to see how his audience, "little pigeons" as he called them at one point, regarded him. He prided himself on his ability to read faces and minds, but he was lecturing, not listening, not gleaning what he needed to know to hold the empire together, but sharpening the strains tearing it apart.

After the Poznań revolt in June, Polish Communists began to get desperate. By October, they were moving to name Gomułka, only recently released from jail, as their chief, and to drop the Soviet marshal Konstantin Rokossovsky, whom Moscow had imposed on them, as their defense minister. Gomułka seemed to be rising "on the anti-Soviet wave," Khrushchev recalled. "Poland might break away from us at any moment." With "no time to lose," he demanded to be invited to Warsaw.[82] The Poles refused, but Khrushchev's delegation, including Molotov, Kaganovich, Mikoyan, and Zhukov, as well as the Warsaw Pact commander Marshal Ivan Konev and eleven other Soviet generals in dress uniforms, flew in anyway at 7:00 A.M. on October 19. The presence of Molotov and Kaganovich showed how profoundly the crisis had undermined Khrushchev's authority. The scene at the airport, he admitted, was "very stormy." According to the Poles, that understated the case.

Knowing his own explosiveness, Khrushchev had asked Mikoyan to present the Soviet case, but as soon as he got off the plane and noticed Rokossovsky being ostracized by the other Poles, he erupted. "He began demonstratively to shake his fist at us from a distance," the Polish party chief Ochab recollected. When he got closer, Khrushchev "started brandishing his fist under my nose." He shouted: "We know who's the enemy of the Soviet Union here! Ochab's treasonous activity has been detected. This number won't pass." Gomułka told his colleagues later that morning: "It was beyond comprehension. The entire conversation was carried out in a loud tone, so that everyone at the airport, even the chauffeurs, heard it."[83]

Khrushchev was still "shouting" when he reached the Belvedere Palace, where the Soviet delegation had to wait for two hours while the Polish Central Committee convened in a nearby hall. The Poles' reluctance to receive him, he said, had been like "spitting in our faces." After the Soviet-Polish talks (if that is the word for them) resumed,[84] Soviet troops began moving toward Warsaw. The Poles countered by mobilizing internal security forces of their own. Gomułka was so tense, Khrushchev later said, that "foam appeared on his lips," but he managed to pronounce words that won Khrushchev over: "Comrade Khrushchev, I ask you to halt Soviet troop movements. You may think it's only you who need friendship with the Polish people. But as a Pole and a Communist, I swear that Poland needs Russian friendship more than Russians need Polish friendship. Don't we understand that without you we won't be able to exist as an independent state? Everything will be in order here, but don't allow Soviet troops into Warsaw, or it will become virtually impossible to control events."[85]

After visibly vacillating, Khrushchev ordered Soviet troop movements halted. On the flight back to Moscow, he calmed down and even recalled the proverb "The next morning is wiser than the evening before." Mikoyan, who was even more relieved, was relaxing in a hot bath that same night at home when the KGB chief Serov arrived and asked him to report immediately to Khrushchev's residence next door. The Presidium wasn't supposed to meet until the next day, but a rump session was under way in front of Khrushchev's door when Mikoyan, who had demonstratively taken his time, walked up. "We've decided our troops should enter Warsaw tomorrow morning after all," Khrushchev informed him. Mikoyan objected, but he was the only one to do so. Molotov supported Khrushchev with special vigor. Bulganin and Zhukov, who was to direct the operation, were silent. Mikoyan managed to delay a final decision until the full Presidium met the next day, by which point Khrushchev had changed his mind again. This time he counseled "patience" to his colleagues, recommending that they "refrain from armed interference," and two days later he urged another meeting, including Eastern European leaders as well as Presidium colleagues, to "avoid nervousness and haste." He said: "Finding a reason for conflict now would be easy," whereas "finding a way out to put an end to such a conflict would be very hard."[86]

In the end Khrushchev exercised prudent restraint. But that shouldn't obscure the ignorance he exhibited, the primitive pressure he employed, his desperate, indecisive searching for a solution, and his good fortune that Gomułka proved both more pliable than Khrushchev originally feared and more capable of pacifying his fellow Poles.

IF THE KREMLIN had replaced Rákosi with Nagy, Hungary too might have found its way to a more moderate kind of communism. Nagy wasn't as canny as Gomułka, but he was more popular than Gerö, who practiced Rákosism without Rákosi and compounded the situation by going on vacation for much of September and October, returning just before Budapest exploded on October 23. That day a huge demonstration organized by students hailed Gomułka's ascendance in Poland and demanded similar reforms in Hungary, including appointment of Nagy as prime minister. Splitting into several groups, several hundred thousand demonstrators marched to Parliament to hear Nagy speak, to the radio station to insist on the broadcast of their demands, and to the Stalin statue, which they proceeded to tear down. Other rallies in other Hungarian cities called on the government to resign. Late in the evening Hungarian security forces fired on unarmed demonstrators outside the radio station. In the clash that followed, rebels quickly overwhelmed Hungarian police.[87]

That same evening in Moscow all the Presidium members except Mikoyan favored sending Soviet troops to Budapest. "Hungary is coming apart," cried Molotov. "The government is being overthrown," Kaganovich wailed. "It's not the same as Poland," Zhukov said. "Troops must be sent." Mikoyan proposed letting the Hungarians "restore order on their own," with the help of Nagy, who had now joined the government. "What are we losing? If we bring in troops, we'll spoil things for ourselves. We should try political measures and only then send troops." With his rivals in full cry, and his own fears rising, Khrushchev too supported armed intervention but tried to cushion the blow by agreeing with Mikoyan that Nagy should be co-opted and by sending Mikoyan and Suslov to monitor the situation on the ground.[88]

Early on October 24 thousands of Soviet troops and tanks entered Budapest. But instead of pacifying the city, they deepened the crisis. When armored vehicles were surrounded by Molotov cocktail–wielding youths, Hungarian security forces offered little support, and some went over to the rebels. By midafternoon at least twenty-five protesters had been killed, and more than two hundred injured. Mikoyan and Suslov reported "further panic among senior Hungarian officials."[89]

Kremlin leaders met again on October 26 and 28. By then Gerö had been replaced as party leader by János Kádár, and a new government including pre-Communist–era politicians had been formed, but resistance to Soviet troops was continuing. Molotov: "Things are going badly. The situation has deteriorated and is moving toward capitulation." Voroshilov: "Comrades Mikoyan and Suslov are . . . poorly informed. . . . American secret services are more active there than Comrades Suslov and Mikoyan report." Bulganin and Zhukov defended Mikoyan, but then leveled their own criticism. Khrushchev sounded confused and panicky: "We have a lot to answer for. We must face facts. Will we have a government that is with us, or one that isn't with us and will ask us to pull the troops out? What then? . . . There is no firm leadership there, either in the party or the government. The uprising has spread into the provinces. Their troops may go over to the rebels." But despite everything, there was "no alternative" to supporting the suspect government currently in power.[90]

By October 30 hundreds of Hungarian civilians and Soviet soldiers had died. The situation seemed more dire than ever, yet the Presidium in Moscow decided to accept it. "We should withdraw our troops from Budapest," said Zhukov, "and from all of Hungary if that's demanded. There's a military-political lesson for us in this." Furtseva added: "We must search for other sorts of relations with the people's democracies." Said Saburov: "It's impossible to lead against the will of the people," as if the Bolsheviks hadn't been doing just that for forty years. Even Molotov and Kaganovich appeared to agree. "We are unanimous," Khrushchev proclaimed. "There are two paths, a military path, one of occupation, and a peaceful path—the withdrawal of troops, negotiations." Incredible as it looks in retrospect, the Soviet leadership had opted to acquiesce in the loss of Hungary.[91]

But only for a few hours. That same day the Soviet government issued a declaration admitting that Moscow had committed "egregious mistakes" and "violations of the principle of equality in relations with socialist countries," and pledging to "observe the full sovereignty of each socialist state." If that had been proclaimed several months earlier, and if Nagy had been in a position to cite it to the more extreme critics of the Communist regime, the Hungarian Revolution might have been stillborn. But by October 30 events were careening out of control, with Nagy becoming ever more radical in a vain effort to master them. Reacting to an earlier incident in which Hungarian security forces fired on a Parliament Square crowd, killing at least a hundred demonstrators, an angry mob attacked Budapest party headquarters, grabbed security police, whose regulation light-colored shoes gave them away, and lynched them from lampposts in scenes featured on Soviet newsreels a few hours later. Several Hungarian army tanks sent to party headquarters defected. That same day Nagy called upon Hungary to leave the Warsaw Pact, and opened talks with Mikoyan and Suslov about a withdrawal of all Soviet troops from Hungary.

Khrushchev arrived at his Lenin Hills residence very late on October 30–31. "I couldn't sleep," he recalled. "Budapest was like a nail in my head." All week the pressure had been building. On October 23 he had looked "preoccupied but not grim," his son remembered. Two days later, during their usual walk around the grounds, he was "silent and answered questions reluctantly." Only long afterward did he talk about how, "unable to make up his mind," he had "vacillated" throughout the crisis.[92] Apart from losing Hungary, he agonized about rebellion spreading to its neighbors. Student demonstrations in Romania had led Bucharest authorities to close their border with Hungary. Czechoslovakia and East Germany seemed vulnerable as well. The Soviet bloc threatened to crumble. "What is there left for us to do?" Khrushchev asked Tito three days later. "If we let things take their course, the West would say we are either stupid or weak, and that's one and the same thing. We cannot possibly permit it, either as Communists or internationalists, or as the Soviet state. We would have capitalists on the frontier of the Soviet Union." Stalin had warned of a disaster under his successors. Now, Khrushchev told Tito (as paraphrased by Mićunović), people would say that "when Stalin was in command everybody obeyed and there were no big shocks, but that now, ever since *they* had come to power [and here Khrushchev used a coarse word to describe the present Soviet leaders], Russia had suffered defeat and the loss of Hungary. And this was happening at a time when the present Soviet leaders were condemning Stalin."[93]

"Present Soviet leaders"? It wasn't "they" who merited the "coarse word" (if only Mićunović hadn't been so diplomatic) but Khrushchev. It wasn't just his country that the West might think "weak and stupid" but Khrushchev himself. Beginning on October 23, when a senior delegation headed by Liu Shaoqi arrived in Moscow, Khrushchev had heeded Chinese counsel. As late as October 30, Mao urged that "the working class of Hungary" be allowed to "regain control of the situation and put down the uprising on its own." But that very night, after the Chinese ambassador in Budapest reported the lynching of Hungarian secret policemen, Mao changed his mind and passed the word to Moscow.

That Khrushchev needed advice from Mao confirms his crisis of confidence. With or without Chinese sanction (the issue of when and how Khrushchev learned of Mao's change of position remains unclear), Khrushchev reversed his stance on October 31.[94] "We must . . . not pull troops out of Budapest," he told the Presidium. "We must take the initiative and restore order in Hungary. If we leave Hungary, that will encourage the Americans, English and French, the imperialists. They will perceive it as weakness and go on the offensive. . . . Our party won't understand our behavior. To Egypt they [the imperialists] will add Hungary. We have no other choice."[95]

Several days earlier, with the British and French embroiled in a seemingly endless dispute with Egyptian President Gamal Abdel Nasser, Khrushchev cited their plight as reason to let Hungarian events take their own course: "The English and French are making trouble for themselves in Egypt. We shouldn't get caught in the same company." By October 31, however, with British and French troops landing at Suez and reportedly sweeping all before them, and with Moscow assuming (mistakenly it turned out) that the Americans would back them, Khrushchev had another reason to crush Hungary after all.[96]

Orders went out from Moscow on October 31 to prepare armed action several days later. Yet even then Khrushchev's agonizing wasn't over. When Mikoyan returned from Budapest late that night, he called Khrushchev, who had just fallen asleep for the first time in two days. Mikoyan warned that military intervention would be a "terrible mistake" and begged that it be called off "lest we undermine the reputation of our state and our party." Khrushchev insisted it was "too late to change anything." The next morning before dawn, with Khrushchev preparing to join Molotov and Malenkov on a trip to brief Eastern European leaders, Mikoyan came over from his adjacent residence on the Lenin Hills. As the two men walked along a path by the house, the gates from the street clanged open and Khrushchev's massive ZIS-110 limousine rolled up the driveway. "Do you think it's any easier for me?" Khrushchev asked. "We have to act. We have no other course."

"If blood is shed, I don't know what I'll do with myself," Mikoyan shouted.

"That would be the height of stupidity, Anastas," Khrushchev replied, edging toward his waiting car. "You're a reasonable person. Think it over, take all the factors into account and you'll see we've made the right decision. Even if there is bloodshed, it will spare us bloodshed later on. Think it over and you'll understand."[97]

Khrushchev thought his closest colleague was hinting at suicide. (In fact, Mikoyan later insisted, he was threatening to resign.) At the next morning's Presidium session, with Khrushchev absent, Mikoyan pleaded for ten to fifteen more days, or three at the very least, to let the Hungarians try to stabilize the situation. János Kádár, Nagy's erstwhile partner whom the Soviets spirited out of Budapest, himself warned that the use of force would "hurt the socialist countries" and cause "the morale of [Hungarian] Communists to be reduced to zero."[98]

Kádár changed his mind. Mikoyan lost out. Together with Malenkov and Molotov, Khrushchev informed the Poles at Brest near the Polish-Soviet border on November 1. From there he and Malenkov flew to Bucharest to brief the Romanians and Czechs, to Sofia to edify the Bulgarians, and on to inform Tito on the Adriatic island of Brioni, a trip that perfectly mirrored Khrushchev's state of mind. Khrushchev and Malenkov traveled incognito (if that was possible) in a two-engine Ilyushin 14. When they took off for Yugoslavia, according to Khrushchev, "the weather couldn't have been worse. We had to fly through the mountains at night in a fierce thunderstorm. Lightning was flashing all around us. I didn't sleep a wink. I had flown a great deal, especially during the war, but I'd never flown in conditions this bad."

Khrushchev and Malenkov landed at the Pula airport and transferred to a boat to Brioni. "Malenkov was pale as a corpse," Khrushchev recalled. "He gets carsick on a good road. We had just landed after the roughest flight imaginable, and now we were heading out into a choppy sea in a small launch. Malenkov lay down in the boat and shut his eyes."[99]

Ambassador Mićunović was waiting on the landing with Tito. "It was pitch dark outside, you couldn't see your hand in front of your face, there was a howling gale," he remembered. "Khrushchev and Malenkov looked very exhausted, especially Malenkov who could scarcely stand up. The Russians kissed us on both cheeks." Four days later Mićunović could still feel "Malenkov's fat round face, into which my nose sank as if into a half-inflated balloon as I was drawn into a cold and quite unexpected embrace."

The talks that began a half hour later at 7:00 P.M. lasted until dawn, the fourth night in a row Khrushchev hardly slept. He wasn't begging for Tito's support (which he eventually got anyway); whatever the Yugoslav reaction, Soviet troops would again march into Budapest the next morning. But the fact that he talked so long, in what Mićunović described as a great state of agitation, showed how besieged he felt.

After the talks ended, there was a long, awkward silence. Khrushchev and Malenkov left for Moscow by plane from Pula on the morning of November 3. Flying conditions, according to Mićunović, were still "exceptionally bad."[100] Two days later Soviet tanks and troops crushed the Hungarian Revolution at a cost of some twenty thousand Hungarian and fifteen hundred Soviet casualties.

CHAPTER TWELVE

The Jaws of Victory: 1956–1957

KHRUSHCHEV LURCHED from surrender to bloodbath in Hungary. The whole terrible sequence confirmed that he and his colleagues were in over the heads, just as Stalin had predicted they would be. Khrushchev put a good face on the awful outcome. "The whole thing had been crushed in a single day," Mićunović remembered his saying on November 7. "There had been practically no resistance. Kádár was a very good Communist and he would now extend and strengthen the government."[1] But Khrushchev's cheerfulness on the anniversary of the revolution (wearing a dark suit with two gold stars, he received Mićunović shortly before a gala reception in the Kremlin's St. George Hall) was forced. He was sour and depressed. The Hungarian crisis had deepened his self-doubts. After the initial shock, he redoubled his efforts to consolidate his power. But his actions had a wild, self-destructive quality about them that, instead of strengthening his position, brought on the nearly successful coup against him in the summer of 1957.

Khrushchev's bile showed through at a Presidium meeting the day Soviet troops moved to crush the Hungarian insurrection. When Molotov criticized the new Kádár leadership for condemning the old Rákosi regime, Khrushchev snapped, "I don't understand Comrade Molotov. He keeps coming out with the most harmful ideas." Two days later he lashed out at Kaganovich: "Comrade Kaganovich, when will you get it right and stop your toadying?"[2] On November 12 the Soviet leader seemed "a very

Khrushchev's tough-minded mother, Ksenia Ivanovna Khrushcheva. (copy of a picture in the collection of Liuba Sizykh)

Khrushchev's elementary school teacher, Lidia Shevchenko, who encouraged him to dream dreams of glory. (copy of a picture in an exhibit in Kalinovka)

Industrial area of Yuzovka at the turn of the nineteenth century. (copy of a picture in an exhibit in Donetsk)

Scene of Yuzovka about 1900. (copy of picture in Donetsk exhibit)

House of Ilya Kosenko in Yuzovka/Stalino/Donetsk where Khrushchev visited as a youth and as party leader of Ukraine. (photo by author)

Efrosinia Pisareva, first wife of Khrushchev, mother of Yulia and Leonid. (courtesy of MN Publishing House)

Khrushchev and his wife, Efrosinia Pisareva, looking remarkably up-and-coming in Yuzovka, about 1916. (copy of picture in Liuba Sizykh collection)

Khrushchev (center, wearing black Caucasian fur hat) as political commissar during Russian Civil War, 1920. (courtesy of MN Publishing House)

1939 New Year's Eve celebration of Leonid Khrushchev and Liuba Sizykh (center, holding champagne bottle) and friends at Nikita Khrushchev's Granovsky Street apartment in Moscow. Leonid took the picture, which outraged Nikita Khrushchev when he saw it. (copy of picture in Liuba Sizykh collection)

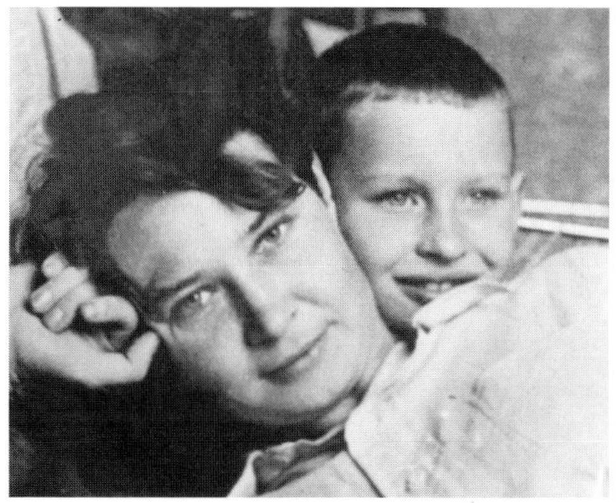

Leonid Khrushchev's wife, Liuba Sizykh, with her son, Tolya, by a previous marriage, about 1941. (copy of picture in Liuba Sizykh collection)

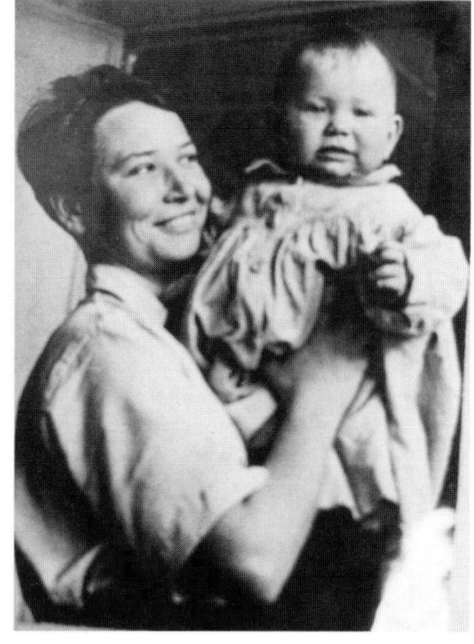

Yulia Khrushcheva, daughter of Leonid Khrushchev and Liuba Sizykh, in her mother's arms, about 1941. (copy of picture in Liuba Sizykh colllection)

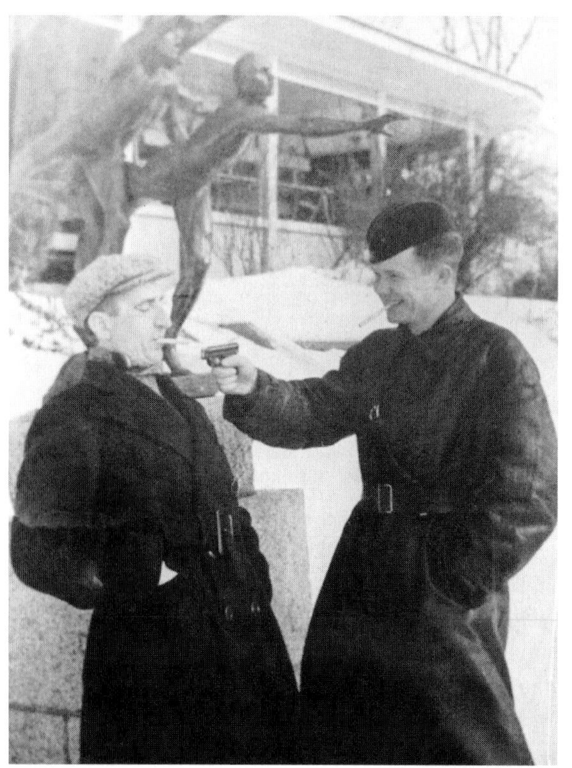

Leonid Khrushchev playfully threatening Ruben Ibarurri with a pistol-shaped cigarette lighter, Kuibyshev, 1942. Leonid later accidentally killed a fellow officer while attempting to shoot a bottle off his head. (copy of picture in Liuba Sizykh collection)

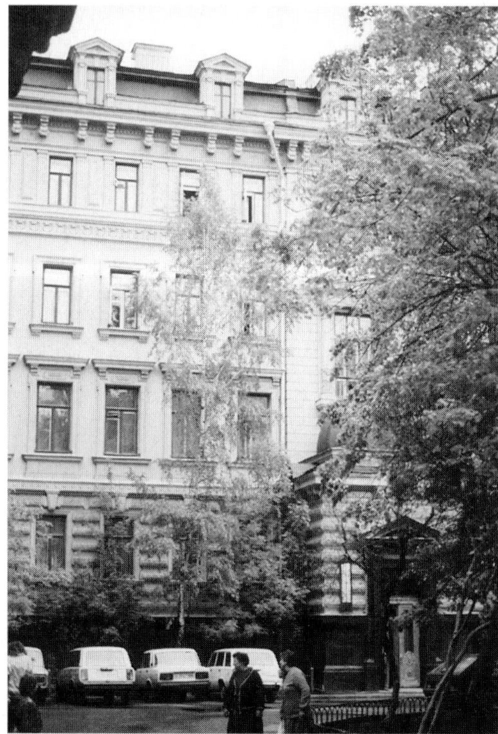

Courtyard view of Granovsky Street apartment house in Moscow where Nikita Khrushchev had an apartment on the top floor beginning in 1939. (photo by author)

Khrushchev (first row, fifth from left) was deputy director at Rutchenkovo mine, Yuzovka, 1922. (courtesy of MN Publishing House)

Khrushchev (first row, third from left) in Yuzovka, 1923. (courtesy of MN Publishing House)

Khrushchev (center) was party cell leader at the Stalino *rabfak* in 1924. (courtesy of MN Publishing House)

Khrushchev with his daughter Yulia and son Leonid, Stalino, 1924. (courtesy of MN Publishing House)

Khrushchev and his new wife, Nina Petrovna Kukharchuk, Stalino, 1924. (courtesy of MN Publishing House)

Nikita Sergeyevich and Nina Petrovna with Yulia, Rada, and Leonid, Kiev, April 4, 1929. (from collection of Sergei Khrushchev)

Putting up plaques honoring outstanding collective farms, including one (third from top on left) which bears his name, Moscow, 1936. (from Sergei Khrushchev collection)

First secretary of Moscow city party committee, 1936. (courtesy of MN Publishing House)

Inspecting a potato harvesting machine in Moscow Province, 1936. (courtesy of MN Publishing House)

Khrushchev with his hero, Stalin, and Sergo Ordzhonikidze (center) by the wall of the Great Kremlin Palace in the early 1930s. (courtesy of MN Publishing House)

With Stalin by the Lenin Mausoleum in Red Square in the early 1930s. (courtesy of MN Publishing House)

Party leader of Ukraine, 1938. (courtesy of MN Publishing House)

Khrushchev dacha at Mezhgorie, outside Kiev, 1938. (Sergei Khrushchev collection)

With other Ukrainian leaders, Kiev, May 1941 (left to right: NKVD chief, Ivan Serov; head of government, Leonid Korniets; head of the Supreme Soviet, M. S. Grechukha; Central Committee secretary, Demian Korotchenko; deputy party leader, Mikhail Burmistenko; deputy head of government, K. S. Karavaev; Stalino Province party leader, K. Z. Litvin). (courtesy of MN Publishing House)

With daughter, Yulia, at Mezhgorie, 1938. (Sergei Khrushchev collection)

Leonid Khrushchev, about 1939. (copy of picture in Liuba Sizykh collection)

Lunching in the shadow of a haystack, and thereby demonstrating his earthy populism, Kherson Province, Ukraine, summer 1940. (Sergei Khrushchev collection)

Leonid Khrushchev after graduating from the Zhukovsky Military Aviation Academy, Moscow, 1940. (courtesy of MN Publishing House)

Inspecting tank forces on the Voronezh front, April 26, 1942. (courtesy of MN Publishing House)

At test of antitank mines, May 1943. (courtesy of MN Publishing House)

With troops at the Battle of Kursk, July 1943. (Sergei Khrushchev collection)

Comforting a resident of Kiev after the city's liberation, November 6, 1943. (courtesy of MN Publishing House)

With Generals Kirill Moskalenko (right) and Aleksei Yepishev in Western Ukraine, 1944. (courtesy of MN Publishing House)

Nina Petrovna Khrushcheva in the Khrushchevs' Moscow apartment with daughters Yelena (left) and Rada after return from wartime evacuation in Kuibyshev, 1943. (courtesy of MN Publishing House)

Outside Kiev after the war.
(courtesy of MN Publishing House)

In a rubber raft (obtained from an American bomber based on Ukrainian soil during the war) on the Dnieper at Mezhgorie dacha outside Kiev. With Khrushchev are his associates M. Grechukha (left) and Vasily Starchenko and their wives. Of the rotund Starchenko, Khrushchev joked, “I must be a little crazy [to send] him to the United States to ask for food for Ukraine.” (Sergei Khrushchev collection)

With his former mentor, Lazar Kaganovich (center), who briefly replaced Khrushchev as Ukrainian party leader in 1947, and Dmitry Manuilsky at Mezhgorie outside Kiev, May 1, 1947. (Sergei Khrushchev collection)

Villa in Kiev where Khrushchev family lived after the war. (photo by author)

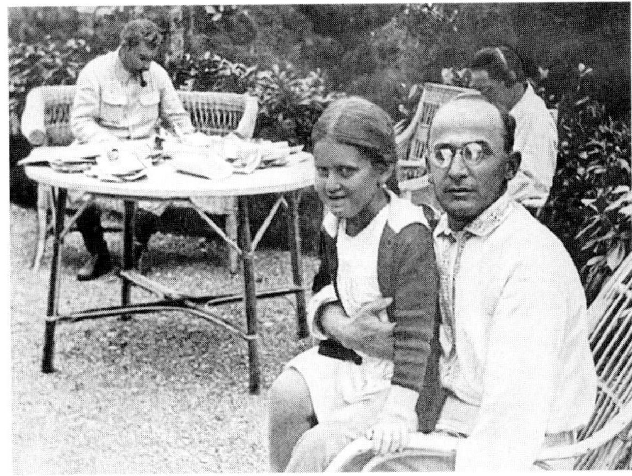

Stalin, secret police chief Lavrenty Beria, and Stalin's daughter, Svetlana, at Stalin's dacha. (courtesy of MN Publishing House)

Stalin with Beria, Georgy Malenkov, Panteleimon Ponomarenko, and Kaganovich in the Kremlin about 1952. (courtesy of MN Publishing House)

Following funeral cortege at Stalin's funeral (first row, left to right: Vyacheslav Molotov, Nikolai Bulganin, Kaganovich, Klimenty Voroshilov, Malenkov, Zhou Enlai, Beria, Khrushchev. Anastas Mikoyon is seen in the second row between Beria and Khrushchev. (courtesy of MN Publishing House)

Speaking to the Twentieth Party Congress in February 1956. (courtesy of MN Publishing House)

With Kaganovich (center) and Bulganin, outside Moscow, 1956. (Sergei Khrushchev collection)

With USSR Defense Minister Marshal Georgy Zhukov, whom Khrushchev ousted unceremoniously a year later, in the Great Kremlin Palace, 1956. (courtesy MN Publishing House)

Khrushchev's daughter Rada (left) and his granddaughter, Yulia, whom he and Nina Petrovna adopted, in the 1950s. (copy of picture in Liuba Sizykh collection)

worried man in great difficulties." When Mićunović mentioned the Twentieth Congress to him, Khrushchev muttered, "There are some people among us who think that the new decisions are responsible for everything bad that has happened."

What was to have been a brief visit to Khrushchev's office on December 12 turned into a three-hour harangue. Mićunović had never seen him in "such a state" before. Khrushchev's reaction to a speech by Tito aide Edvard Kardelj reflected the chill that had come over Soviet-Yugoslav relations since the Hungarian intervention, but what infuriated Khrushchev most was that Kardelj seemed to be mocking him when he "poked fun at the policy of maize [corn] and potatoes." More than a month later Khrushchev was still fuming at what he said must have been a personal attack because "everyone knew how interested Khrushchev was in agriculture."[3]

In November, Molotov was named minister of state control (in charge of seeing that government decrees were enforced), not as important as foreign minister, but a sign he was making a comeback. Khrushchev changed his tone on Stalin too. At a massive New Year's Eve reception for the diplomatic corps and the Soviet elite, he startled his audience by declaring that he and his colleagues all were Stalinists in their uncompromising fight against the class enemy. Three weeks later, before eight hundred guests at a Chinese Embassy reception, he declared that being a Communist was "inseparable from being a Stalinist," so that even though "mistakes" had been made in the struggle against the enemies of Marxism-Leninism, "may God grant that every Communist will be able to fight for the interests of the working class as Stalin fought." Communism's enemies had tried to exploit his criticism of Stalin's shortcomings to undermine the Soviet regime. But "nothing will come of this, gentlemen, any more than you will be able to see your ears without a mirror."[4]

The new line on Stalin was a tactical retreat, but it also reflected Khrushchev's inner doubts. His appearances before Komsomol gatherings were invariably pep rallies celebrating this or that success of communism. But on November 8 he mocked Mikoyan, ostensibly for doubting the Virgin Lands campaign would succeed, but probably, subliminally, for supporting the same de-Stalinization and soft line on Hungary that had gotten Khrushchev into such trouble.[5] At the Chinese Embassy reception, Khrushchev mentioned his own advanced age, as he did at several other low points later in his career.[6]

On top of everything else, the Polish and Hungarian crises sparked Soviet unrest, building on that which had followed the Twentieth Congress. On October 25, at the USSR Ministry of Internal Affairs Club no less, students from the Moscow State Historical Archive Institute toasted Polish and Hungarian developments and the "impending fourth Russian revolution." Moscow State University students openly challenged official lecturers who tried to justify the invasion. Illegally mimeographed journals circulated in Leningrad. During the November 7 holiday parade in Yaroslavl, high school students marching by the regional party leadership's reviewing stand unfurled a huge poster calling for withdrawal from Hungary. About this time young Vladimir Bukovsky (later a leading Brezhnev-era dissident) joined a Dostoevskian "secret society" whose activity consisted of recruiting new members, none of whom were supposed to know one another, for unspecified actions that never took place.[7]

Established intellectuals were also incensed. According to a KGB informer's report, the leading physicist Lev Landau railed against official justifications of the Hungarian intervention: "How can you believe that? Are we supposed to believe butchers? They are butchers after all, vile butchers." Biologist Aleksandr Liubishchev attributed the Hungarian revolt to Khrushchev's anti-Stalin speech: "He did much more than all the propaganda of 'Voice of America' and 'Radio Liberty.'" When the Moscow party leader Yekaterina Furtseva tried to calm an unruly meeting at the Moscow Geology Prospecting Institute, the majority voted not to let her interrupt. When she finally got a chance to speak, she tried conciliation ("You want to know more about events in Hungary? You're quite right. We made a mistake in printing too little information") and seemed even to support demands for disbanding the bureaucracy-encrusted Komsomol. But once she left the hall the most active protesters were reprimanded or arrested.[8]

In Sevastapol someone slashed fourteen portraits of national leaders on the wall of a bread factory. A worker defaced Khrushchev's portrait in Serpukhov. In a December 5 report to Khrushchev, the Leningrad party leader Frol Kozlov cited a factory worker's warning that if the standard of living didn't rise, "the same thing that happened in Hungary could happen here." According to another official report, a thirty-one-year-old Yaroslavl automotive designer (and party member) characterized the party line as "'Shut up or we'll arrest you.'" He asked: "Haven't we learned the lessons of Hungary?" To clinch his point, he quoted a colleague who had visited France: "There they think it's better to die than to live the way we do here."[9]

Such protesters were few and isolated. Still, their alienation caused near panic at the top. On December 19 the Central Committee approved a secret letter to all party organs prepared by a commission headed by

Brezhnev.[10] Referring to "hostile rabble," it called for the "dictatorship of the proletariat" to be "merciless" so as to "cut off their criminal actions."[11] But the letter itself ignited a further uproar when it was discussed in party cells. In early 1957 several hundred protesters were sentenced to terms ranging up to seven years in prison camps. During the first three months of that year, the Russian Republic Supreme Court received thirty-two cases of "counterrevolutionary crimes," while over the next six weeks it processed ninety-six more, many appealed by local prosecutors charging that lower courts had treated culprits too leniently. "Counterrevolutionary criminals" included a schoolboy who had carried an "anti-Soviet poster," a student who had "openly made anti-Soviet pronouncements" in a lecture hall, and a worker who had pasted an "anti-Soviet" leaflet on a fence. All were sentenced under the infamous Article 58 of the Stalinist Criminal Code. So were people who wrote anonymously to newspapers, not realizing their letters would be forwarded to the KGB. All this shortly before Khrushchev boasted to the world that there were no more political prisoners in the USSR.[12]

Khrushchev also got some good news. He regarded the outcome of the Suez crisis (about which more in chapter 13) as a triumph for his foreign policy. The Virgin Lands came through with a record harvest just when he needed it most.[13] On the other hand, the newly inaugurated sixth five-year plan's overly expansive targets had to be revised in December 1956 at a Central Committee plenum that hardly mentioned Khrushchev's name and that dropped his protégé Shepilov from the Central Committee Secretariat.[14] Little wonder that Khrushchev embarked on a nonstop tour of agricultural regions, awarding medals to province party leaders ("I don't think there has ever been such a mass distribution of medals and orders," Mićunović wrote in his diary on January 14, 1957), reminding them that he, not Malenkov or Molotov, was their man, acting like an American politician campaigning for office, as in fact, in the aftermath of 1956, he was.[15]

KHRUSHCHEV'S JANUARY barnstorming launched a counteroffensive that included a radical restructuring of industrial management, a national campaign to overtake American agriculture, and a new overture to the artistic intelligentsia. Designed to demonstrate his capacity for dynamic, decisive leadership, it served instead to undermine his position.

In February, Khrushchev proposed to abolish most national economic ministries and replace them with regional economic councils.[16]

Even when the economy was smaller and simpler, it hadn't been easy for Moscow-based ministries to direct diverse enterprises scattered across eleven time zones. In addition, a more decentralized system of industrial administration was more likely to survive nuclear war. But Khrushchev's reform was also political: The local party leaders who would dominate regional councils were his prime Central Committee constituency, whereas the ministers and planners likely to be exiled to the provinces (a fate almost worse than death in the Moscow-centric Soviet Union) were allies of his critics.

Khrushchev's scheme had defenders, some of whom still praise it.[17] But although central ministries had favored their own narrow needs at the expense of local areas in which their plants happened to be located, the new system fostered localism and lost sight of all-Union interests. If the issue had been economic change alone, Khrushchev might have moved gradually, but because the reform was political, and because he was incapable of containing himself anyway, he brooked no delay. He did allow a limited "national discussion" in the press before the new law was adopted on May 10. But considering the drastic nature of the change (creating the 105 councils, including one for virtually every province and region, was roughly equivalent to replacing American states with a new set of territorial-administrative entities), the transformation occurred almost overnight.

Molotov and Kaganovich, among others, objected. Molotov insisted the plan "wasn't properly prepared." Kaganovich said later: "Khrushchev spoiled an idea that wasn't bad. It would have been useful if [he] hadn't aspired to stamp his 'Eureka!' all over it."[18] When Frol Kozlov presented the reform plan to Leningrad party activists, he encountered a blizzard of questions: What would happen to employees of soon-to-be-abolished ministries? What would become of ministry-built housing and communal services?[19] Enterprise directors and economists criticized specific features of the reform, but not, heaven forbid, the whole scheme. Before long, critics were using Khrushchev's own favorite rhetorical devices—anecdotes and proverbs—against him. "There once was man named Trishka," went one story picked up by Yugoslav Embassy officials, "who had a fine caftan but who started altering it to make it even better and went on doing so until his caftan was completely ruined."[20] After the anti-Khrushchev coup failed, Presidium member Furtseva condemned criticism of economic regionalization as "effrontery." She did *not* add that when the regional council "epic" (as Shepilov later called it) began, she herself was aghast. "I am an economist," recalled Shepilov, "and I understood that decentralization was necessary. But it had to be done in a well-considered way." Shepilov remembered Furtseva's asking, "'What shall we do? They're appointing people we've never heard of to head these councils. All the decisions are impulsive and not thought through.'"[21]

On May 22, in Leningrad, Khrushchev pledged the USSR would overtake the United States in per capita output of meat, butter, and milk in a few short years. It was an article of Bolshevik faith that socialism could accomplish in a few decades what had taken capitalist countries several centuries. Since the USSR had collectivized and industrialized almost overnight, why should meat and milk pose a problem? But whereas traditional Bolshevik boasting constituted a generalized sort of bravado, Khrushchev made a concrete pledge that proved impossible to fulfill.

Recent agricultural successes encouraged him: Since 1953, output of meat had grown by 162 percent, milk by 105, and grain production by 189 percent. (But why should that growth necessarily continue, as Khrushchev assumed it would? Even if it did, the United States wouldn't be standing still.) After a forty-day trip to the American Midwest, Soviet Agriculture Minister Vladimir Matskevich confirmed Khrushchev's conviction that American agricultural abundance was the result not of capitalism but of large farms, enterprising farmers, and widespread planting of corn. American mockery of Soviet agricultural pretensions was a further goad. "How our enemies crowed" in 1953, Khrushchev told his Leningrad audience; now it was time to challenge the United States itself, "before whom everyone goes on tiptoes lest it be offended."[22]

Previously Khrushchev had talked at most of catching America in "a few years" or "a short time." Actually in Leningrad too, he began cautiously. To match the Americans, the USSR would have to increase its 1956 meat output 3.2 times, he said, without specifying how long that would take. Then, suddenly, he couldn't contain himself: If Soviet farmers set their mind to it, "we shall be able by 1960 to catch up with the United States in per capita meat output."

A prognostication like that should have had the whole Presidium behind it. Instead Khrushchev spoke out on his own. He had been warned by his own economists, he himself gleefully admitted: "I asked the economists to find out when we would be able to catch up with the United States in the foodstuffs I've mentioned. I will let you in on a secret: they gave me a piece of paper; they had signed it; they had even put their seal on it. It says on this piece of paper: If we can step up the output of meat 3.2 times, we can catch up with the United States by 1975! [Laughter] Excuse me, comrade economists, if I have hit a sore spot."

The economists were "arithmetically" correct, Khrushchev contended, but they failed to understand what the Soviet people were capable of. "Sometimes man can exceed his own strength by making a sudden spurt. Let our opponents ponder what the working class can perform." Let the skeptics contemplate Kalinovka. If the majority of farms matched his own village's extraordinary pace, "we will successfully solve the task we have set for ourselves."

His critics pounced on this latest piece of impulsiveness. "He came up to us afterward," Kaganovich recalled, "with the self-satisfied smile of a man who had invented a great idea." When Presidium members cited statistics giving the lie to his claims, Khrushchev "got mad, raising his little fist threateningly, but he couldn't refute Gosplan's figures."[23] According to then-Khrushchev ally Aleksei Kosygin, "Molotov spent a long time gathering materials to show that no one—not the party, not the people, not the agricultural leadership, not the peasantry—that no one was in a position to overtake the United States in output of meat."[24] But instead of retreating, Khrushchev broadcast his promise in a widely publicized interview with CBS Television. Informed that American specialists considered the prediction unrealistic, Khrushchev conceded only that it might take until 1961, instead of 1960, to outdo the United States. If so, he joked, "we shall not be very upset, and our people will not bear a grudge against the Central Committee of the Communist party and the government."[25]

By the time of its collapse in 1991 the Soviet Union was still far from fulfilling Khrushchev's pledge.

LITERATURE WAS hardly the most important matter on the Presidium's agenda, but given their determination to control intellectual life, Soviet leaders paid particular attention to culture. What has been called the thaw began slowly after Stalin's death but picked up momentum after the Twentieth Congress. After the long night of late Stalinism, with its pogrom against great artists like poet Anna Akhmatova and composer Sergei Prokofiev, recalled veteran critic Maya Turovskaya, "the coming of Khrushchev and the Twentieth Congress felt like a great holiday of the soul."[26] Ilya Ehrenburg's novel *The Thaw,* among others, included biting criticism of the ruling elite. Reproaches directed at hidebound officials weren't new, but whereas such functionaries had previously been depicted as remnants of a presocialist age, they now personified the Soviet system. The authorities at first seemed to encourage the critics but then moved to regain control by attacking authors and firing their editors.[27] Khrushchev's role in the initial skirmishing was restrained: Still consolidating his authority, he apparently hesitated to inject himself into cultural matters. He had been both patron and scourge of the arts in Ukraine, and the same role awaited him in Moscow. But he remained ill at ease with artists and writers, particularly at large gatherings, where, while he was laying down the law to them, they were judging him. Given his insistence on ideological discipline, which artists and writers naturally resisted, there was bound to be tension. What they didn't realize was that their recalcitrance challenged not only the party line but his own self-esteem. That's why clashes with the "cultural intelligentsia" provoked him into swirls of angry rhetoric, simultaneously offensive and defensive, lashing out at his audience in a violent, disconnected way that circled back and undermined him.

Khrushchev's attack on Stalin at the Twentieth Congress inspired liberal writers. Among fresh new works that appeared in 1956 was *Not by Bread Alone*, a novel by Vladimir Dudintsev about an idealistic engineer who is thwarted by mindless, heartless bureaucrats. November 1956 saw the appearance of *Literaturnaya Moskva*, a literary almanac of prose, poetry, plays, criticism, and social commentary. A poem by Margarita Aliger, one of its editors, mocked the official image of "the new Soviet man." Yevgeny Yevtushenko's long poem "Zima Station" registered the shocking impact of de-Stalinization on the younger generation.[28]

Party cultural potentates tried to call a halt, but for the first time in decades, writers refused to kowtow. At a March 1957 meeting of the Moscow writers' association several of them, including Dudintsev and Aliger, dared exhibit what the authorities labeled "intolerance of criticism."[29] Although Khrushchev was tacking back toward Stalinism, he hesitated to join in the literary crackdown. After all, his speech had won him support by the intelligentsia at a time when he was under attack by Stalinists. Yet with unruly, freethinking writers as supporters, he didn't need opponents. So he joined the fray in May.

When party leaders met with them on May 13, 1957, Writers' Union board members weren't sure what to expect, but there was some "hope," Veniamin Kaverin recalled, that "Khrushchev would support the 'liberal' tendency in literature." The meeting lasted all day, itself testimony to the deadly seriousness with which the party took "cultural construction." Khrushchev spoke last, for nearly two hours. The prepared part of his remarks was predictable: Certain writers had "one-sidedly and incorrectly understood the essence of party criticism of Stalin's personality cult," interpreting it as "indiscriminate rejection of the positive role of J. V. Stalin in the life of our party and country"; Dudintsev's novel, despite "powerfully written pages," was "false at its base"; *Literaturnaya Moskva* contained "ideologically fallacious" work. But the ad-libbed section of his sermon was, according to Kaverin, "incoherent" in the extreme: "He began by declaring there were many of us and only one of him, that we had written many books that he hadn't read because if he started to read them, he would have been 'thrown out of the Central Committee.' In the middle of his speech, out popped some woman, not a Russian, he said, who had once swindled him in Kiev. Right behind her came a broadside against Hungary, to which he added that he'd ordered Zhukov to finish off the rebels in three days, but Zhukov took only two. It was at this point, I think, that he landed on the 'Petőfi Circle,' comparing it to certain writers who were trying 'to knock the legs out from under Soviet literature.'"

During this tirade Marietta Shaginian, an elderly writer of Armenian heritage who had moved from writing erotic symbolist verse before the revolution to Stalinist best sellers afterward, approached the podium with hearing aid in hand. Since her appearance detracted from the solemnity of the occasion, Khrushchev was annoyed, even more so when she asked in a loud voice why there was no meat in Armenia. "What do you mean there's no meat?" he shouted. "No meat? Why right here in the hall there's. . . . " At this point Khrushchev pointed to a bulky, obviously well-fed Armenian functionary. But Shaginian wouldn't subside. Several days later Khrushchev was heard to refer to her as "that Armenian sausage."[30]

Khrushchev's listeners were appalled by his behavior, but they might well have been sorry for him too. He was out of his depth on occasions like this. He was also being manipulated by conservative writers and cultural bureaucrats with reputations and perks to lose if literary liberals went unpunished. Their best weapon was to play on Khrushchev's taste (or lack thereof) to rile him against their foes. If they did so in a way that made him look bad, so much the better. Mikoyan tried hard to explain that "Dudintsev's novel was only confirming Khrushchev's own pronouncements, but it didn't help. Khrushchev considered the novel slanderous, and it was hopeless to try to talk him out of it."[31]

Literaturnaya Moskva was a huge two-volume affair. The fact that Khrushchev denounced it to the chairman of the Moscow Writers' Union as "a filthy and harmful *brochure* [emphasis added]" showed, said his aide Igor Chernoutsan, that Nikita Sergeyevich had "never laid eyes" on the almanac. According to the playwright Nikolai Pogodin, the culprit was Khrushchev's dear friend and sycophant from Kiev Aleksandr Korneichuk, who was furious that his work had been attacked as "conflictless and superficial" and denounced the almanac in return. Korneichuk "never forgets or forgives such things," Pogodin told Chernoutsan. "The only thing he forgot to say in egging on Khrushchev was that the 'brochure' was several hundred pages long, and no one managed to correct this false impression."[32]

Khrushchev half realized he was the target of disinformation. In the case of *Literaturnaya Moskva,* he half apologized to Chernoutsan. "I suppose I offended you," he said. "Why didn't you tell me that 'brochure' was two volumes? But anyway, all this is just a trifle. Let's figure out how we can cheer up all these literary types. Why don't we get the Moscow writers and artists together next Sunday at the dacha? Let them stroll around a bit, and catch some fish, and then let's fill them with food under a clear sunny sky. Go ahead and give the necessary instructions."[33]

As conceived by Khrushchev, the gala outing outside Moscow in May was a Chekhovian picnic in the company of the Kremlin leadership. The three hundred or so guests "went boating," said Adzhubei, "while in the shady glades, tables laden with a lot more than just cold drinks awaited them. Lunch was served under tents. The scent of grass and delicious food—everything should have led to a pleasant discussion, but sharp words ensued. Many well-known writers, actors, musicians and artists spoke. Everyone had his own pain, and the more this pain splashed out, the more irritable Khrushchev became."[34]

Several accounts portrayed him as tipsy, but he may have been emotional rather than inebriated. He tried to be evenhanded; he even criticized old-style socialist realist "varnishers." But he also blasted *Literaturnaya Moskva* again and then the offending poet, Margarita Aliger. "You're nothing but an ideological saboteur!" Khrushchev shouted. "You're just a remnant of the capitalist West!"

"What are you saying, Nikita Sergeyevich?" the fragile, diminutive Aliger replied. "I am a Communist, a member of the party. . . ."

"You're lying." Khrushchev cut her off. "I have no faith in Communists like you."

In the middle of this exchange a sudden squall sprang up. The weight of the heavy rain nearly collapsed the tent; although security men kept the leaders from getting wet, many of the guests were soaked. But when the thunder and lightning ended, Khrushchev raged on. By now even Molotov looked upset. Mikoyan whispered something to Khrushchev, trying to calm him down. Meanwhile, struck dumb, Aliger left the tent, shunned by everyone except the writer Valentin Ovechkin.[35]

Chernoutsan named as villains of this surreal piece Korneichuk, Leonid Sobolev, who was soon to head the particularly reactionary Russian Republic Writers' Union, and Nikolai Gribachev, another old guard writer, whom Khrushchev regarded as an expert on aesthetics. Whoever egged him on, Khrushchev's behavior provided ammunition for his Kremlin critics. It wasn't because Molotov admired Aliger that he charged Khrushchev with boorishly threatening to "grind [her] into dust." He was more genuinely upset that Khrushchev "proclaimed to all and sundry that he had disagreements with me. I was particularly displeased with this because it was a nonparty gathering he was speaking to."[36] Kaganovich and Malenkov also used the incident against him. "His speech wasn't transcribed," Kaganovich recalled. "If it had been, no stenographer would have been able to follow it." It was partly the alcohol, Kaganovich claimed, that accounted for "this matchless masterpiece of oratorical art."[37] According to Mikoyan, the already high tension in the Presidium "became simply unbearable after the meeting with the writers."[38]

KHRUSHCHEV'S BULLYING of writers certainly didn't trigger the June coup attempt, but it didn't help his cause either. He later dismissed criticism of his conduct as "just an excuse" for restoring Stalinism. But while three of the conspirators (Molotov, Kaganovich, and Voroshilov) were indeed inveterate Stalinists, five others were less so (Malenkov, Saburov, Pervukhin, Bulganin, and Shepilov), and even Khrushchev's supporters came close to forsaking him in part because of his unpredictable, explosive behavior.

Molotov's role was no surprise. As he said, he had "consistently opposed" Khrushchev since 1954, especially after their open clash in July 1955, and more stridently in 1956 and 1957. Dubbed by Khrushchev the "ideological leader" of the conspiracy, Molotov had resisted Khrushchev's initiatives in many fields, but especially the de-Stalinization campaign that threatened both his creed and his neck.[39]

Kaganovich—the "knife sharpener" of the group, according to Khrushchev—had particular reason to loathe his former protégé, who now lorded it over him. But he and Molotov were also "two opposites," their former Politburo colleague Andrei Andreyev recalled. "Molotov can't stand Kaganovich; all through their joint work in the Central Committee they've hated each other." As for Malenkov—the main "organizer" of the putsch, Khrushchev said—he had no use for Molotov either, even before the latter joined Khrushchev in deposing him in January 1955. "And Kaganovich has always been terribly dissatisfied with Malenkov," said Andreyev, "constantly suspicious that Malenkov was about to sweep him away."[40] Malenkov had been more supportive of Khrushchev's policies than either Molotov or Kaganovich, but he believed he had no choice but to act. "If we don't remove them, they'll remove us," he reportedly told Saburov. The fact that Khrushchev was talking of expanding the Presidium the next autumn seemed to foreshadow a purge. That led Malenkov to urge action on Molotov and Kaganovich.[41]

Voroshilov wasn't really a player. Although still the head of state, he was a figurehead and not taken seriously; he was capable, or so Khrushchev said, of insulting the shah while receiving the new Iranian ambassador's diplomatic credentials. "We had our own tsars," he allegedly told the envoy, "we had Nicholas II, whom the people threw out, and we do just fine without them."[42] Besides the blood on his hands, what rendered him recruitable was the way Khrushchev mocked him. "He lands on comrades who don't agree with him," Voroshilov griped later. Shepilov recalled Voroshilov as one of the first to complain to him about Khrushchev. "Little pigeon," Voroshilov said to Shepilov, "the man insults absolutely everyone!"[43]

Bulganin was no genius either. "The post of Prime Minister of the Soviet Union is not intended for an idiot," Khrushchev told Mićunović with a sneer after the coup failed.[44] With his trim mustache and goatee, Bulganin had "an intellectual look and a gentle pleasant manner," recalled the opera star Galina Vishnevskaya; she should have known because he pursued her shamelessly on innumerable occasions, including a birthday party for him at which the assembled leaders talked "loudly and imperiously," drank "hard," "flattered Bulganin, calling him 'our intellectual' over and over because they knew he liked that," and reminisced about the thirties as if they had been a golden age.[45] Besides being a brazen womanizer and habitual imbiber, Bulganin kept getting off gaffes that mortified Khrushchev. He equated Gandhi and Lenin at a Calcutta reception in 1955. "I trembled with anger," Khrushchev remembered. Bulgarin called Tito a Leninist prematurely in 1956. "We condemned him for that," said Khrushchev; "he took it like a thorn in the heart." In touchy Finland, which remembered its war with the USSR all too well, Bulganin remarked that a farmstead he was visiting would make a perfect military observation post. "I almost died," Khrushchev told the Central Committee. "'Listen,' I said, 'what are you saying?' He tells me

I'm a civilian and he's a military man. 'What kind of military man are you?' I say. 'You've got to think before you speak. As the saying goes, in the hanged man's home don't mention the rope.'"[46]

Khrushchev had made Bulganin the head of government, partly, no doubt, so as to shine in comparison. Bulganin resented Khrushchev's mockery but didn't dare object. He'd been no friend of the coup plotters (or so he claimed afterward) but grew closer to them as his gorge rose. By joining them, he made the putsch possible. After all, he headed the Soviet government, the post Lenin and Stalin both had held, and his office had resources and information (including intelligence on Khrushchev's activities) that facilitated the conspiracy. "If Bulganin hadn't joined," Khrushchev said afterward, "Saburov and Pervukhin wouldn't have either."[47]

Saburov and Pervukhin had never been close to Khrushchev, and as central industrial administrators they were threatened when he opted for economic regionalization. According to Pervukhin, he was first recruited on May 20, the day after the stormy picnic with writers and artists; what particularly won him over was having the grievances of so many others recounted to him.[48] Saburov was warmed up more gradually. In early May, Bulganin complained that the KGB chief Serov was spying on Presidium members. About the same time that Malenkov warned Saburov that Khrushchev was out to get him, he began to call Saburov by his first name. But it was not until the actual showdown began that, as Khrushchev told Saburov at the postcoup attempt plenum, "the devil pulled you in."[49]

Chernoutsan described Shepilov as "civilized, sensitive, and courteous."[50] Shepilov himself boasted that he had memorized nearly a dozen operas and could sing them all, "including choral, female and orchestral parts, rhythmically, precisely and without mistakes."[51] By promoting Shepilov to ever-higher office (from *Pravda* editor to Central Committee secretary, Presidium candidate member, and foreign minister in turn), Khrushchev signaled his respect for intellectual refinement. But Shepilov's sophistication also reminded Khrushchev of how far he himself fell short. Sensing that, Shepilov was careful; according to Chernoutsan, he tried "to avoid independent literary judgments so as to please Khrushchev." At lunch with Tito in 1955, Khrushchev several times asked Shepilov to confirm an incident he had just described. "Shepilov would remove the table napkin," Mićunović recalled, "stand up from the table, and as though he were reporting officially, would reply: 'Just so, Nikita Sergeyevich!' and sit down again. I found such behavior on Shepilov's part most unusual, as I did Khrushchev's in tolerating it."[52]

This relationship was not only special (Shepilov was the first veritable intellectual Khrushchev had taken under his wing) but close. The two worked together in the Central Committee Secretariat as well as the Presidium, and Shepilov and his family spent at least one Sunday at the Khrushchev dacha. If, as seems possible, Khrushchev was cultivating a potential political heir, it was all the more devastating when Shepilov betrayed him. After that Khrushchev never again trusted the sort of sophisticated alter ego whom he more than ever needed. "What a rotten role 'Academician' Shepilov played," Khrushchev snapped at the post-coup plenum. "Every man has some sort of weakness, and mine was supporting Shepilov's advancement."[53]

According to Shepilov, he "fell in love" with Khrushchev's simple, democratic nature. But by 1957 he was recording in a notebook both Khrushchev's complaints about colleagues and theirs about him. "All sorts of vile and indecent things" was how Khrushchev artlessly described what he had told Shepilov "confidentially." After the coup attempt failed, the Khrushchev ally Averky Aristov called Shepilov "a political prostitute": "You should have seen with what cynicism and sarcasm he spoke at the Presidium, with what self-importance: like a professor, like a very important person, he slandered people without limit, without conscience."[54] After the coup was launched on June 18, Shepilov read from his notebook to show Khrushchev what even his apparent allies thought of him. Shepilov was "one of those loathsome people who remember everything everyone says, no matter where, and then pulls it out and uses it," said the Leningrad party chief Frol Kozlov.[55] "Do you know what he said?" Khrushchev later asked an Egyptian journalist with whom he was on close terms. "He said that when I met the President of Finland I was scratching my armpits as if they had been invaded by an army of fleas. . . . "[56]

After the plot failed, endless official condemnations of it listed the main conspirators as Malenkov, Molotov, Kaganovich, and "Shepilov who joined them" (*primknuvshii k nim Shepilov*), a sobriquet that wags said gave him the longest first name and patronymic combination in the country. Shepilov apparently joined them at the last minute, after Kaganovich, whose dacha was nearby, invited him for several walks in the woods and assured him that an anti-Khrushchev majority was at hand.[57] Once he did join, he zeroed in on his former patron's vulnerable psyche. "It all goes back to the fact that Khrushchev was deeply uneducated," Shepilov recalled many years later, "even though he had a good head on his shoulders. Instead of knowledge and argumentation, his formula was, 'I smell things out.' And that's completely impermissible for a leader, especially of such a great state." Or as Shepilov put it on another occasion, "Someone who's illiterate can't govern a country."[58]

"You've become 'the expert' on everything—from agriculture to science to culture," Shepilov chided Khrushchev once the plot was sprung. How many years of education did Shepilov have? Khrushchev demanded. Shepilov had graduated from high school, spent four years at the university, and three more at the Institute of the Red Professors.

"And I," snapped Khrushchev, "I studied for all of two winters, for which my father paid the priest two poods of potatoes."

"If so, then why do you pretend to be all-knowing?"

At this point, Shepilov recollected, "Khrushchev said he had never expected to hear anything like that from me and that he regarded my remarks as treason."[59]

SO MUCH FOR the gang of eight (seven of them constituting a majority of the Presidium's full members) who soon launched the putsch. Like Shepilov, Marshal Georgy Zhukov was only a candidate member, but he'd been instrumental in arresting Beria and would be so again in Khrushchev's 1957 victory. Of all the attacks on the conspirators after their plot failed, Zhukov's was by far the fiercest. Perhaps that's because he himself had secretly been one of Khrushchev's sharpest critics. Back in May 1956, at a Kremlin reception for visiting Western air force officers, a seemingly tipsy Khrushchev laid into Britain and France as second-rate states. "Zhukov and other Soviet dignitaries were disgusted," American Ambassador Charles Bohlen later wrote, "and said openly that the remarks were out of place." After Khrushchev was ushered off the stage, Zhukov told Bohlen: "You should not pay attention to that; it's the way things are done around here."[60]

Knowing Zhukov's attitude, Malenkov tried to recruit him. "It's time to finish with Khrushchev," Bulganin said to him.[61] Shepilov had known Zhukov since 1941 and said he regarded him as his closest friend in the leadership. About the only thing they disagreed about, during the period when Shepilov was "entranced" by Khrushchev's "simplicity and accessibility," was Khrushchev. "In the spring of 1957," Shepilov insisted, "Zhukov once said in passing that we ought to get together and talk. Khrushchev, he said, had seized so much power that nothing remained of collective leadership. We talked while taking a walk outside; dachas, apartments, cars—they were all bugged and everybody knew it."[62]

Shepilov incriminated the Khrushchev protégée Yekaterina Furtseva too, as did Pervukhin at the postplot plenum.[63] Furtseva practically confirmed the accusation when she charged Shepilov with "repeating conversations [presumably including her own] that were one on one, in exaggerated form so as to set people against one another."[64] If so, Khrushchev's opponents nearly corralled three of five Presidium candidate members (Zhukov and Furtseva as well as Shepilov) to go along with their full-member majority. If the balance had shifted that far, Khrushchev would almost certainly have lost Suslov, who before and afterward proved himself an inveterate Stalinist, leaving Mikoyan as his only defender. Except that Mikoyan himself may have been teetering too. Pervukhin's testimony to that effect is of course questionable, but Khrushchev suspected as much. He later told Mićunović that Mikoyan had reserved his final position until he knew the final outcome and that "if events had taken the opposite course it was not impossible" that Mikoyan's speech at the Central Committee "would have been adapted to suit such a turn of events."[65]

Mikoyan did in fact have doubts about Khrushchev—he "went to extremes," got "carried away," and roared ahead "like a tank"—but he also considered Khrushchev "an unpolished diamond," who "quickly grasped and learned," who was "persistent in pursuit of his aims" and "courageous." What led Mikoyan to back Khrushchev in 1957, he recalled, was that "Molotov, Kaganovich, and to some extent Voroshilov were unhappy that Stalin had been unmasked. If they had prevailed, the process of de-Stalinizing the party and society would have been slowed."[66]

The group that nearly overthrew Khrushchev mimicked his tactics against Beria. After the big three (Molotov, Malenkov, and Kaganovich) stopped quarreling among themselves, they began resisting minor Khrushchev initiatives. On June 10, with Khrushchev and Bulganin in Finland, they attacked his proposal for buying paper industry machinery in Austria. Five days later, after they prevailed on another trade matter, Khrushchev reportedly blew up but failed to carry the day.[67]

Khrushchev's rivals were no pikers; they had been through the wars and won most of them. If they were to win this one too, then woe to those who had refused to march with them. Fear was a persuasive recruiter, but they also counted on obedience to party rules—not the formal rules according to which the Central Committee elected the Presidium and its first secretary, but the Politburo's practice of appointing its own leader, leaving the Central Committee to rubber-stamp the result. Once Khrushchev's rivals had a majority in the Presidium, the Central Committee would presumably follow along. Molotov and Malenkov expected

Khrushchev to concede, just as they had in 1955, even though he controlled the party apparatus, plus the KGB and the armed forces, through Serov and Zhukov respectively.

The trap was to be sprung on June 18. To lull their intended victim, the plotters called a meeting of the Council of Ministers' presidium, of which most party leaders were members but Khrushchev wasn't, ostensibly to discuss a trip to Leningrad that the leadership was planning later that month.[68] Once in session, the meeting was to be declared a session of the party Presidium itself. Since this trick too had been used against Beria, how could Khrushchev have missed it? Did he not see what was coming? Is it possible that he actually provoked his rivals into a showdown that he was bound to win?

In February 1957 the Yaroslavl Province party committee reported rumors that "Comrade Khrushchev will be named minister of agriculture with Comrade Malenkov becoming party first secretary." Loose talk in a Moscow ministry about "changes in highest-level party and government bodies in the nearest future" also reached the Central Committee.[69] Surely the KGB must have picked up echoes of the conspiracy. When his critics stopped quarreling and started outvoting him, didn't that sound the alarm? Didn't what happened at his son's wedding do likewise?

Sergei Khrushchev got married on June 16 with the entire party leadership in attendance. His father couldn't "resist boasting" about the upcoming event, Sergei recalled, and once he mentioned it, Russian custom demanded that his Presidium colleagues "honor the ceremony by their presence." To Nina Petrovna's chagrin, the dacha's large dining room couldn't accommodate the crowd, which even included a few relatives and friends of the married couple, so tables were set up on the veranda. Sergei was struck by the Malenkovs' behavior: They arrived late, looked grim, and in contrast with lavish past gifts—a set of drawing instruments in a polished wooden box when he entered the university and magnificent magnifying glasses later on—presented him with a cheap alarm clock with a picture of an elephant on its face. Nikita Khrushchev could be excused for missing this clue, but not others. When he needled Bulganin (toward the end of a well-lubricated speech that was largely devoted to praising his own mother), the prime minister "reacted with fury. He simply exploded. He started to shout that he wouldn't let anyone shut him up and order him around, and that all that was soon going to end." As soon as the wedding meal was over, Zhukov recalled, Molotov, Malenkov, Kaganovich, and Bulganin demonstratively got up and drove off to Malenkov's dacha.[70]

Former aide and ally Pyotr Demichev insisted Khrushchev knew the coup was coming. "Who told him is hard to say, but he must have felt it. As early as May 1, when party activists gathered at a dacha outside the city, and Bulganin was the formal host, the anti-Khrushchev mood was obvious. Khrushchev had to have detected it; after all, he was a sensitive man."[71] Was he? The last thing he let himself believe was that the power and glory he craved were about to be taken from him.

KHRUSHCHEV WAS LUNCHING at his Lenin Hills residence when Bulganin summoned him to the Council of Ministers' meeting on June 18. At first he resisted attending (just as he did when Brezhnev called him at Pitsunda in October 1964), saying the Leningrad trip had already been decided on, but late in the afternoon he arrived at the Kremlin. Eight of eleven full members of the Presidium were present. Khrushchev's protégé Aleksei Kirichenko was addressing a Ukrainian Central Committee meeting in Kiev; he had just finished when he was told to fly back to Moscow immediately. Saburov was in Warsaw; he feigned family reasons for departing forthwith. Suslov, who was on holiday outside Moscow, also returned at once. Of seven candidate members, Shepilov, Brezhnev, Furtseva, and Nikolai Shvernik were there. After an hour Zhukov arrived from the Solnechnogorsk District outside the capital; Kozlov and Mukhitdinov, much later from Leningrad and Uzbekistan respectively. Absent also, because the meeting began as a Council of Ministers' session, were the Central Committee secretaries Nikolai Belyaev and Pospelov and the secretary Aristov, who was ill.[72]

Malenkov, speaking first, proposed that the meeting address Khrushchev's behavior. To encourage candor, he demanded that Bulganin, not Khrushchev, chair the session. (The pedantic Molotov later added that Khrushchev should never have been chairing Presidium meetings in the first place since Lenin, Rykov, Molotov himself, and Stalin all had chaired the Politburo as heads of the government.[73]) One can imagine Khrushchev's reaction when Zhukov arrived: Malenkov was still shaking, while at the same time pounding the green felt-covered table with such force as to make Zhukov's glass jump. But Khrushchev and Mikoyan, the only two to oppose Malenkov's motion, were voted down.

With Bulganin in the chair, itself a de facto demotion for Khrushchev, his foes launched into a scathing indictment. Malenkov recounted "error after error." Voroshilov called Khrushchev "unbearable" and demanded his removal as party leader. Kaganovich linked Khrushchev's insistence on reexamining thirties' show trials with his dalliance with Trotskyism in 1923. "Others' cows may moo, but yours should stay silent," snapped Kaganovich, prompting Khrushchev to sputter, "What are you hinting at? I won't take it anymore." Molotov joined the assault. Bulganin and Pervukhin piled on. According to Kaganovich, Mikoyan tried to restrain Khrushchev and partly succeeded. Although Khrushchev rejected most accusations, he accepted a few and even promised to correct his mistakes. Stalling, he and Mikoyan demanded delay until all full and candidate members and all Central Committee secretaries were present. They got the meeting adjourned until the next day. However, Khrushchev was reeling.[74] When he arrived that evening at a Bulgarian Embassy reception, he looked "preoccupied, even depressed." Usually ebullient on such occasions, this time he was "gloomy and silent."[75] That same evening, the Ukrainian party chief Kirichenko prepared his boss for seemingly certain defeat: "So you'll live in Ukraine. You'll have a home and a dacha." Khrushchev aide Andrei Shevchenko recalled, "He was shaking, he was distraught."[76] Others found him weeping.[77] Zhukov later wrote that Khrushchev begged him to "save" the day, promising that if he did so, "I will never forget you."[78]

He wasn't without supporters. Despite his Stalinist proclivities, Suslov, apparently convinced by Mikoyan that Khrushchev would prevail in the end, was one of them.[79] Besides Zhukov, Khrushchev protégés like Kirichenko, Brezhnev, and Furtseva also backed their patron. When Saburov returned from Warsaw at two that morning, Mikoyan immediately phoned him, and the two men met the next morning. Still, Saburov joined the enemy camp.[80] Khrushchev phoned Bulganin: "Come to your senses, my friend. Get back on the right track. . . . They've pulled you into this group for their own reasons. . . . Leave them alone." He wasn't the only one calling. "Nikolai," Malenkov told Bulganin, "hold yourself together! Be a man! Don't give in!"[81] For the moment Bulganin didn't.

When Khrushchev and Bulganin entered the Presidium meeting room on the nineteenth, both men grabbed for the chairman's seat, creating a standoff resolved in Bulganin's favor by a seven to four vote of full members. Counting Presidium candidate members plus Central Committee secretaries, Khrushchev had an overall majority of thirteen to seven, but only full members could vote. Malenkov and his allies continued the first day's blitzkrieg and received a counterbarrage in return. Kaganovich sneered at Khrushchev for "knocking about the whole country" on all manner of misspent missions. Candidate member Shvernik called the rebels an "antiparty group," the kind of label that had doomed "deviationists" in the thirties. How could a majority in the party's ruling body be an "antiparty" grouping? Kaganovich demanded. At one point in the struggle, when Kaganovich slammed Brezhnev and other junior colleagues for daring defy their elders, Brezhnev fainted and sank slowly to the floor, to be carried out by guards and revived by doctors in the a nearby room.[82]

The anti-Khrushchev majority held firm throughout the day. His enemies still held the upper hand when they huddled in Bulganin's office after the Presidium adjourned, but Bulganin looked grim at a Yugoslav Embassy reception later that evening; never had Mićunović found him "in such a bad mood so lacking in courtesy and ready for a quarrel," while Khrushchev seemed "almost his usual self," trying "to be in as good a mood as possible although he did not always succeed."[83] Bulganin's problem was that not to win outright was to lose, that the longer the battle continued, the more time Khrushchev and Mikoyan had to pressure wavering rebels and to mobilize the Central Committee, to which the Presidium was theoretically responsible.

Frantic maneuvering took place on both sides that night. Mikoyan and Zhukov pressed Bulganin, Pervukhin, and Saburov to jump ship before it sank. Khrushchev aides drafted a letter from twenty Central Committee members demanding a Central Committee plenum. With the help of the KGB and the military, Khrushchev loyalists prepared to ferry Central Committee members to Moscow. A special plane was sent for the Orenburg party boss Gennady Voronov. Mukhitdinov was inspecting sheep raising in Uzbekistan's Fergana Valley when he got the call. It took a massive emergency airlift to deliver to the Kremlin Central Committee members who were spread out across the country. It was like a "crash campaign to bring in the harvest," Khrushchev's aide Shevchenko recalled. It was "a factional, Trotskyite act," Kaganovich later insisted, "whereas we strictly observed party norms in hope of preserving unity."[84] Kaganovich, of course, had smashed party norms in the thirties, but when Khrushchev didn't observe them either, his adversaries had no backup plan and little support outside the Presidium itself. After all, Khrushchev had appointed many of the local party officials who constituted the bulk of the Central Committee.

By June 20 the "antiparty group" was in retreat. Dropping their demand that Khrushchev step down as party leader, they proposed instead that there be no party first secretary at all. By late afternoon, 87 Central Committee members had gathered in Moscow; together with Presidium members and Central Committee secretaries, they constituted

107 out of 130 full members. At 6:00 P.M., 20 of them brought to the Presidium meeting room a petition that 57 had signed. Khrushchev, of course, favored receiving them. His adversaries exploded with frustration and rage. "It was a like bomb going off," Zhukov later said. The fact that the delegation was headed by Marshals Konev and Moskalenko, along with the Gorky Province party boss Níkolai Ignatov, provoked protests against being "surrounded by tanks," but then it had a "calming" effect. After an hour's wrangling the Presidium sent a subgroup out to meet the delegation. In the corridor Voroshilov poked his finger in Aleksandr Shelepin's chest and shouted, "Are we supposed to give an explanation to *you*, boy? First you'd better learn to wear long pants!" But Voroshilov's cause was almost lost. Before adjourning, the Presidium agreed to convene a Central Committee plenum the following afternoon.[85]

THE PLENUM that began on June 22 at 2:00 P.M. didn't end until June 28. However, Khrushchev's rivals were vanquished from the start. Some fought back, at least in the beginning, but most quickly submitted. By the end of the marathon session only Molotov refused to vote for his own final defeat. In that sense the assembly was anticlimactic. But because Khrushchev used the issue of Stalin's crimes to demolish his foes, it was one of the most extraordinary plenums in Soviet history. In comparison, Khrushchev's 1956 secret speech only scratched the surface. This time speakers cited the number of those murdered and named those who were guilty. Molotov, Malenkov, and Kaganovich mostly tried to save themselves, but their sniping provoked Khrushchev to a fury.

Contrary to party rules, the Presidium minority (i.e., the pro-Khrushchev members) prepared the agenda without even informing the majority.[86] There was no majority report at all; Khrushchev's opponents were allowed only individual speeches, with the most stubborn of them, Molotov, left for last after his allies had conceded defeat. Khrushchev himself opened the plenum. Suslov delivered a general indictment of "the antiparty group." But it was left to Zhukov to level the gravest charges—clearly by prearrangement, probably because as a World War II hero he was the most popular member of the Presidium—but with a force and intensity that surprised even his allies.[87]

He named Malenkov, Kaganovich, and Molotov as the "main culprits" in the "arrests and executions of party and state cadres." Between February 27, 1938, and November 12, 1938, he revealed, Stalin, Molotov, and Kaganovich personally authorized 38,679 executions. On one day alone,

November 12, 1938, Stalin and Molotov dispatched 3,167 people "like cattle to slaughter." The death lists they signed were a shambles with names listed inaccurately, some of them several times. Wives of "enemies of the people" also got "a bullet in the head." General Yakir (Khrushchev's former friend) had begged Stalin for mercy, Zhukov explained. "Scoundrel and prostitute," Stalin had scrawled on Yakir's appeal. "A perfect description," had added Molotov. "Blackguard, bastard, prick," Kaganovich had chimed in. "Only one punishment for him: death!" Malenkov's guilt was even greater, Zhukov went on, because he was supposed to be supervising the NKVD. "If only the people had known that these leaders' hands were dripping with blood, they would have greeted them not with applause but with stones." And not just these leaders. "Others too," Zhukov declared, "former members of the Politburo, were guilty. I assume, comrades, that you know whom I'm talking about. But you also know that these comrades have earned the trust of the Central Committee and of the whole party with their honest work and their straightforwardness. I'm sure that for that, as well as for their candid confessions, we will continue to recognize them as leaders. [Stormy applause]."[88] Khrushchev was the subject of these last lines: Zhukov first accused him and then in effect pardoned him. Khrushchev must have been stunned—and frightened as well.

Accused of masterminding the 1949 Leningrad affair, Malenkov denied any role in it. "That's untrue!" Khrushchev shouted. "Only you are completely pure, Comrade Khrushchev," Malenkov retorted sarcastically. "The whole Politburo signed" the death warrants, Kaganovich insisted, and province party chiefs (of whom Khrushchev was one) served on the death-dealing troikas. "Who set up the troika system?" Khrushchev countered. "Didn't you sign death warrants in Ukraine?" Kaganovich demanded. "Come on, now," Khrushchev replied. "Were judicial organs and security police really taking party orders? I myself was labeled a Polish spy." Kaganovich shot back: "Me, too." "I defended hundreds of thousands. . . . Didn't you sign too, Comrade Zhukov, as division commander?" Zhukov: "I didn't send a single person to be executed." Khrushchev: "We all gave our approval. I voted against Yakir and slandered him, many times, as a traitor. I believed the charges against him, that he was our enemy and had abused our trust; I assumed you [Kaganovich] had checked into those charges. You were a member of the Politburo back then. You should have known."[89]

Apart from these sharp exchanges, Malenkov and Kaganovich offered little resistance. Deprived of their leadership, Bulganin prostrated himself, and Saburov and Pervukhin did too. Only Molotov was defiant, despite being interrupted by catcalls and curses. There had been no plot and certainly no "antiparty group," he claimed, just an accumulation of justified grievances. Khrushchev himself was at fault: in his insistence on monopolizing all issues, his treating others as "pawns" and browbeating them into silence, his dismissal of colleagues as "mindless old men," "loafers," and "careerists." What united diverse colleagues against Khrushchev was his "arrogance," Molotov continued. Although he "keeps calling for modesty, he lacks it himself. [Noise in the hall.] When we chose him as first secretary, I thought he'd remain the same person he'd been before that, but it hasn't turned out that way, and it gets worse all the time."

As Molotov plowed on, Zhukov reminded him of his complicity in Stalin's crimes. "I accept that responsibility," Molotov replied, "as do other members of the Politburo." Who authorized torture to produce false confessions? Khrushchev demanded. "All Politburo members," Molotov insisted. "But you were the second-in-command after Stalin," said Khrushchev, "so you bear the main responsibility, and right after you, Kaganovich." Molotov replied, "But I raised more objections to Stalin than any of you did, more than you did, Comrade Khrushchev."[90]

Shepilov urged the plenum to address criticisms of Khrushchev instead of just punishing his critics. Later Khrushchev described Shepilov's speech as "disgusting" and informed Mićunović that Shepilov had been given "an especially bitter reception."[91] Mikoyan was the only Khrushchev ally who credited some of the charges: Khrushchev was indeed "hotheaded, hasty, and too sharp-tongued," but his cutting remarks "came from the heart, not any intrigues," and his critics "used isolated shortcomings to obtain their political aims." He defended Khrushchev against accusations including drunkenness at diplomatic receptions (Khrushchev drank "no more than others," said Mikoyan) and entertaining the Finnish president in an undignified 3:00 A.M. sauna (Khrushchev had no need to wash himself, Mikoyan said, but was merely showing respect for his Finnish host). Lesser Khrushchev allies defended his record under Stalin. Aristov quoted Molotov's and Kaganovich's calls for blood in 1937, but not Khrushchev's. "Comrade Khrushchev never proposed that a single person be arrested or shot," said Aristov. When Frol Kozlov brought up the Leningrad affair, Khrushchev shouted at Malenkov: "Your hands are covered with blood, Malenkov; your conscience isn't clean; you're a vile person."[92]

Finally, after six days of speeches, including a final round of self-abasement by Khrushchev's opponents, he himself summed up the proceedings. Kaganovich had roared like "an African lion" on June 18 but was now a "beaten cat." Bulganin had ended up on "a pile of manure." Pervukhin, once "wavering personified," now "squirmed like a fish on a hot griddle." As for "academician" Shepilov, he "sure knows how to express himself, like an artist." He "looks in a book and sees a shnook. He doesn't understand the simplest things, but he wants to instruct others. . . . And you call yourselves politicians?" Khrushchev sneered at all of them. "No, they're just pathetic schemers." The only opponent he still respected at all, he said, was Molotov.

Yet "Molotov was closest of all to Stalin," Khrushchev himself admitted. "He was the number two man." When Khrushchev quoted a Molotov panegyric on Stalin's sixtieth birthday in 1939, Molotov broke in: "Why don't you recount your own speeches?" Who forced Molotov to scrawl curses on death warrants? Khrushchev retorted. "Stalin didn't dictate those to you. You wanted to please Stalin, to show him how vigilant you were. You sent innocent people to death with taunts and a smirk. The mothers, wives, and children who remained alive shed a sea of tears. Many relatives now ask to see photographs of husbands and fathers whose pictures they had to destroy. . . . How can you look them in the eye?"

How could Khrushchev himself? What made him purer than his colleagues? That he had signed fewer death warrants? That he had done so without a smirk? No one truly recanted, but his outnumbered rivals came closer than he did. Malenkov finally professed "shame" and "guilt" for his role in the Leningrad affair and said he was "prepared to bear the responsibility" for it. Molotov said he had never denied his "political responsiblity for the errors of mistakes" of 1937. ("Not mistakes, but crimes," someone shouted.) Kaganovich too called his responsibility "political." Zhukov added: "And criminal."[93] Khrushchev's own lips pronounced the terrible numbers—in 1937 and 1938 alone there were arrests of more than 1.5 million, of whom 681,692 were shot—but not his own complicity. Yes, he had "called for popular anger" against his friends Yakir and Korytny, but he had believed they were enemies. "I understand the suffering of these people. I believe that those who were guilty in these affairs must answer for them. If only Stalin hadn't had two evil geniuses, Beria and Malenkov, at his side, a lot could have been prevented."

THE JUNE 1957 plenum was the closest Stalin's henchmen ever came to a day of reckoning. But it was certainly no Nuremberg Trial. The prosecutors themselves were guilty. Zhukov's speech barely approximated the arraignment that all of them, Khrushchev included, so richly deserved. No formal charges were leveled, no real evidence was presented, no defense was mounted—except in the course of cursing one another—and no transcript was made available for nearly four decades. Initially, the Central Committee's public announcement contained a short paragraph about "mass repressions" of the thirties, but that was too strong and was cut. A motion from the floor to publish the incriminating documents Zhukov had cited was ignored. Although Khrushchev's rivals were publicly denounced and lost their high posts, they remained in the party. The sins of Bulganin, Voroshilov, Pervukhin, and Saburov weren't even publicized lest Khrushchev be revealed to have been in the minority.

Although Khrushchev recounted his great victory again and again over the years, it wasn't the triumph it seemed. Aleksei Kosygin, who replaced Khrushchev as prime minister in 1964, later explained he had backed him in 1957 because if Molotov had won, "blood would have flowed again."[94] But the conspirators who seemed capable of renewing the terror couldn't even carry out a coup.[95] At one point during the showdown Khrushchev shouted, "Why do you all keep on about Stalin this, Stalin that? All of us taken together aren't worth Stalin's shit."[96]

By belittling himself as well as his rivals, Khrushchev revealed his own continuing dependence on Stalin. Instead of finishing off the *vozhd*, now that his own rivals were routed, Khrushchev began resurrecting him. On July 14, 1957, Mićunović wrote in his diary: "It looks as though the same thing is happening now as happened after the speech about Stalin at the Twentieth Congress. It is as though the people here are afraid of their own anti-Stalinist decisions. Khrushchev . . . talks as the members of the 'anti-Party group' used to talk."

Perhaps, it occurred to Mićunović, Khrushchev sought "to win over supporters of Molotov in the Soviet Union and the 'camp' and in this way . . . 'preserve the unity' of the party and the country."[97] One reason Khrushchev had denounced Stalin at the Twentieth Congress was to dissociate socialism from the evil Stalin committed in its name. But the tumultuous events of 1956 and 1957 had taught him that socialism could unravel, and his own authority with it, if Stalin were totally discredited.

CHAPTER THIRTEEN

The Wider World: 1917–1957

Even before Khrushchev defeated the "antiparty group," thus eliminating his last apparent domestic opposition, he had begun to direct Soviet foreign relations. Stalin ventured abroad only twice during his nearly thirty-year reign, to the Tehran and Potsdam conferences during the war. By June 1957 Khrushchev had visited Eastern Europe several times, led a Soviet party and government delegation to China in 1954, met with leaders of the United States, Britain, and France in Geneva in July 1955, barnstormed through India, Burma, and Afghanistan later that year, and toured Great Britain in April 1956. These trips were meant to revitalize Soviet foreign policy, partly by improving relations with allies, adversaries, and neutral countries alike. Applying the same distinctive style he exhibited at home—engaging on several fronts simultaneously, underwhelming and then overwhelming his interlocutors, and taking bold risks—he seemed at first to succeed. But by 1957 his new approach was in trouble, partly because of resistance from the outside world but also because of the same characteristics, personal as well as political, that got him into trouble at home. Khrushchev's diplomacy wasn't the main target of the "antiparty group," but it too was held against him in the June 1957 showdown.

As he consolidated his hold on the Kremlin, the world stage beckoned to Khrushchev. The outside world posed both mortal threats and irresistible opportunities to a superpower-on-the-make. Khrushchev wasn't the first leader to whom foreign affairs offered escape from intractable internal problems or the first to be frustrated by other countries' national interests. But the Soviet Union had particular handicaps. Marxist-Leninist ideology heightened enmity with adversaries while leading Moscow to take friends for granted. The size and apparent strength that allowed the USSR to bully and intimidate also provoked opposition. The fact that Khrushchev and his colleagues were accustomed to obedience from subjects and satellites made it difficult to deal with statesmen not subject to their will. That same authoritarianism also precluded the sort of domestic debate that sometimes, but not always, saves democracies from self-inflicted wounds.

If these were among the forces that eventually thwarted Khrushchev, he knew precious little about them at the start. For the first fifty years of his life he had little exposure to the outside world and almost none to the great powers. After Stalin's death he at first remained on the sidelines; he was ignorant and ill equipped, and he knew it. But it was only a matter of time until he swallowed whole the formerly forbidden fruit, representing his country abroad, basking in the glory of global statesmanship, hobnobbing with the great, the near great, and the merely swollen.[1]

BEFORE AND JUST after the Bolshevik Revolution Khrushchev crossed paths with a few foreigners, encounters that fitted neatly into his crude but comprehensive view of the world. That world was riven, he assumed, by a fierce class struggle: The foreign owners of the Yuzovka mines represented "capitalist exploiters"; non-Russian laborers were the "workers of the world" whom Marx called upon to unite. The mines were "like an international labor camp," he recalled, in which all peoples were "equal in that they were equally oppressed by the yoke of capital."[2]

"I've had contact with Poles ever since my childhood," Khrushchev noted in his memoirs. Former Czech prisoners of the Austro-Hungarian Army, who supported the Bolsheviks in the civil war, taught him that Slavic brotherhood reinforced class solidarity.[3] Bulgarians stood out in his memory as "wonderful vegetable growers," as well as brother Slavs. He hailed soldiers of Chinese origin in the fledgling Red Army as "absolutely fearless in battle" and mocked their accent: "You give food, gun will work. You no give food, gun won't work."[4] Russian miners gawked at a German engineer who "couldn't even speak their language," and they couldn't understand a German Communist any better, but the fact that he was Marxist "was enough for them to welcome him with an outpouring of fraternal warmth."[5]

The twenties were the high point of Communist internationalism. Stalin appointed a Jew (Kaganovich) and then a Pole (Kossior) as Ukrainian party leader. "Nationality wasn't an issue with us," Khrushchev insisted. "Kossior didn't conceal the fact that he was a Pole. He didn't have to; no one cared what nationality he was. What mattered was whether he was a good Communist or not."[6]

In the early thirties Khrushchev encountered foreign Communists in Moscow, for example, when he hosted a reception and luncheon for delegates to the Seventh Congress of the Communist International in 1935. Klement Gottwald, who became Czechoslovakia's prime minister in 1946 and president in 1948, was "really sloshed" at the luncheon, but he was "under control," Khrushchev reported, "out of respect" for the Moscow party organization. Gottwald's wife, who was "also tipsy," was wearing a gold ring and gold earrings, while Khrushchev and his colleagues "lived like monks in those days, as far as clothes and other things went. To our way of thinking, she looked like an extravagant woman who had fallen under petit bourgeois influence."[7]

Khrushchev often asked Wang Ming, China's representative to the Comintern, to address workers in Moscow factories, and Wang Ming "never refused." Khrushchev was aware of other Chinese leaders such as Zhu De and Liu Shaoqi, but "as for Mao Zedong [who had been elected to the Comintern's Executive Committee at this Seventh Congress], I'd never heard of him."[8]

The first time Khrushchev stepped onto foreign soil was when the Red Army invaded Poland in 1939. After the war he made several trips abroad, mostly to Poland, and at least one to Germany, Austria, and Czechoslovakia. But this last trip was political tourism. Traveling incognito as "General Petrenko," he glimpsed West Berlin out the window of a Soviet military staff car, but saw more of Vienna—factories, laundries, the Schönbrunn Palace (whose park with fountains particularly "delighted" him), the Vienna woods, the American occupation zone, even Scottish riflemen wearing kilts.[9]

Khrushchev met quite a few foreign leaders after the war, but mostly at social rather than diplomatic occasions. As party boss of Ukraine he was involved in postwar negotiations with the Poles. Since Poland's new pro-Communist army fought on Ukrainian territory, Khrushchev got to know (and of course like) its leading generals. When tensions arose between Polish recruits and Ukrainians and the Poles complained to

Stalin, Khrushchev proudly took part in a high-level meeting to address the problem. But its successful resolution loomed only slightly larger in his memory than the sumptuous supper at which it was settled: "We discussed the problem . . . over a very respectable dinner with drinks and so on; it was a meal fit for so important a group."[10]

After a provisional Polish government was set up by the Red Army in Lublin, Khrushchev shuttled back and forth from Kiev to assist it. In addition, "Stalin was always summoning me to listen to the Poles' requests and complaints because he didn't want to be bothered himself." Khrushchev's role at these meetings—to reject Polish petitions Stalin didn't want to accept—provided an excuse for Stalin to mock his protégé's inexperience in foreign affairs. " 'Here's Khrushchev,' " Stalin would say. " 'Let him decide. You two know each other, and I'm sure you can work out an agreement between you.' Then he'd just sit there listening, waiting to see how I'd handle the job of turning down whatever request the Polish comrade had made."[11]

Khrushchev wasn't directly involved in Polish punitive operations against anti-Communists, but he wasn't offended by them either. For "sooner or later Poland would be a socialist country and our ally. Many of us felt, myself included, that someday Poland would be part of one great country or socialist commonwealth of nations," a project that Stalin quickly nixed lest an expanded USSR end up swallowing more than it could digest and alarming erstwhile Western allies in the process.[12]

Khrushchev oversaw the rebuilding of Warsaw's water, electric, and sewage systems in 1945. While there, he squeezed in an overnight excursion to Lodz for "an uproarious visit with [General Michal] Rola-Zimierski, who was full of good spirits and joking all through the meal."[13] He met and took his usual liking to future Polish leader Władisław Gomułka, as he had during the war to Tito and German Communist Walter Ulbricht. In 1948 Stalin telephoned him from Yalta, where he was vacationing with Gottwald: "Gottwald is here and he says he can't live another day without you." Khrushchev dropped everything and flew down for an endless round of drinking and boasting interspersed with pressure on Gottwald to find traitors hidden inside the Czech Communist party.[14] Khrushchev met Bulgarian leaders in Yalta that same year and Romanian leader Petru Groza at Stalin's Sochi dacha in 1951. He encountered North Korean leader Kim Il Sung in Moscow and Ho Chi Minh, who was so in awe of Stalin (or at least pretended to be) that he asked the great man to autograph a copy of a Soviet magazine, only to have the suspicious dictator order the magazine purloined back because, according to Khrushchev, "he was worried about how Ho might use it."[15]

Khrushchev had much less exposure to the non-Communist camp, but he treasured what he had and thirsted for more. Charles de Gaulle spent eight days in Moscow in December 1945, jousting with Stalin over whether to recognize the would-be Communist government in Poland in return for a Franco-Soviet treaty on which Paris set great store. According to de Gaulle, he got what he wanted in the end (the treaty without recognition of the so-called Lublin Committee) by breaking off a lavish feast and threatening to return home without any agreement at all. He later quoted Stalin as complimenting him (at the 4:00 A.M. treaty signing): "You have played well! Well done! I like dealing with someone who knows what he wants, even if he doesn't share my views."[16] Khrushchev attended only the ceremonial occasions but was fascinated by the powerful, inscrutable foreigner: "Throughout the signing ceremony, de Gaulle behaved with great pride and dignity. You could see he wasn't bowing his head to anybody. He walked straight and tall, like a man who had swallowed a stick. He struck me as being rather aloof and austere."[17]

By the summer of 1944 Stalin and Molotov had been negotiating with Americans for years. Khrushchev had met American miners in Yuzovka in 1922 and American Communists in Moscow, but the first American leader he glimpsed was visiting General Eisenhower, whom Stalin invited to review a Red Square victory parade from atop the Lenin Mausoleum in June 1945. Khrushchev barely exchanged words with the man who became first his partner and then his nemesis a decade later.

For the most part Stalin kept foreign policy to himself, helped only by Molotov (as foreign minister), Zhdanov (on Communist bloc affairs), Vyshinsky (after he succeeded Molotov), and Mikoyan, who undertook special overseas assignments. "The rest of us were just errand boys," Khrushchev recalled, "and Stalin would snarl threateningly at anyone who overstepped the mark."[18] Since the Central Committee and Politburo rarely convened after the war, and the Council of Ministers "had ceased to exist except as a list of names," Khrushchev was reduced to scavenging for information.[19] He wasn't sure whether Stalin "seriously intended to create a socialist state" in East Germany, he had to guess why Moscow blockaded Berlin in 1948 since "Stalin never actually discussed issues like this with anyone," and he also didn't know the full story of the Soviet-Yugoslav split: "I was working in Ukraine at the time and wasn't involved in foreign affairs; I was isolated from them and didn't receive the relevant documents."

When the Czech Communist leader Rudolf Slansky was denounced as a traitor in 1951, Khrushchev was given only "'background material,' that is, information that Stalin sent around to all the Politburo members with his decisions already attached." Yet he didn't remember "having any doubts about it at the time. I had no opinion of my own." All he knew about Sino-Soviet relations was "what I was supposed to know." But that was a lot compared with what he knew about the West. "Only Molotov had personal experience in that area, only he had [extensive] contacts with capitalist representatives." Khrushchev didn't dare show much interest in defense policy (since Stalin might suspect anyone who did of being "a foreign agent who had been recruited by the imperialists"), and he later claimed that he didn't see any documents concerning the North Korean invasion of South Korea; all he saw were battle reports that Mao Zedong transmitted to Stalin.[20]

Some of these disclaimers, especially about Eastern European purges, are reminiscent of Khrushchev's self-proclaimed "ignorance" of the terror at home. His exposure to the outside was probably somewhat more extensive than he let on. What it didn't do was equip him to conduct Soviet foreign policy after Stalin died.

IN FOREIGN AFFAIRS, as in domestic, Khrushchev was Stalin's pupil; his first premise was that the Soviet cause was just. He was aware, for example, that many Poles weren't exactly pro-Soviet or pro-Russian, especially after the Nazi-Soviet Pact of 1939. He knew the Polish elections of 1945 were rigged, but so what? "The Polish people didn't stage any resistance against their newly-elected officials. If they had voted for Stanisław Mikołajczyk but got Gomułka instead, they didn't do anything about it—which meant, to my mind at least, that they lacked deep, consciously determined political convictions."[21] Actually, there was plenty of anti-Communist resistance in Poland, but if it could be readily put down, then by Khrushchev's lights it wasn't important.

Romania had the smallest and weakest of all Eastern European Communist parties; the bulk of it arrived in postwar Bucharest in railroad baggage cars with Soviet officials who browbeat King Michael into fleeing the country. In Khrushchev's simplistic version, "the King acknowledged that the Communist party enjoyed wide support among the Romanian people," so eventually he "boarded a train and left. Thus the monarchy came to an end, and the red banner of socialism was lifted over Romania."[22]

Khrushchev hoped socialism would triumph in Western Europe too.

He was convinced "Germany would stage a revolution" after the war. "[A]ll of us thought it would happen because we wanted it so much," and he wished the same for France and Italy. Whether Stalin himself shared these hopes isn't so clear, since a Communist France and Italy wouldn't have been as easy for him to control as Romania and Bulgaria.[23]

Khrushchev was convinced that the USSR was in danger. Hadn't the West intervened against Bolshevism in the Russian civil war? Hadn't the United States waited sixteen years to recognize Soviet Russia? Hadn't the Anglo-Americans tried to "bleed us dry so that they would come in at the last stages [of the war] and determine the fate of the world"? When the war was over, the Americans "wanted to drive us into bankruptcy." Thank goodness the Soviet Union had broken "the ring of capitalist encirclement." That there were now many socialist countries in Europe and Asia "was a consoling and inspiring thought for all Communists who had been fighting with such dedication for socialism and justice."[24]

According to Marxism-Leninism, economic imperatives dictated capitalist foreign policies. Characteristically, however, Khrushchev concentrated on the personalities of the Western leaders. Winston Churchill was "an arsonist and a militarist." Harry Truman was "an aggressive man and a fool." Dean Acheson was "a "political half-wit." But Khrushchev also gave credit where he thought it was due, or rather where Stalin said it was.[25] He respected Roosevelt ("who always treated us with understanding") because Stalin did. "Stalin had no respect for Truman at all," reported Khrushchev. "He considered him worthless." Khrushchev heard Stalin say that "if it hadn't been for Eisenhower, we wouldn't have succeeded in capturing Berlin." Later, when Khrushchev himself negotiated with Eisenhower, he "kept in mind Stalin's words about him. Stalin could never be accused of liking someone without reason, particularly a class enemy."[26]

LIKE MANY OTHER students, Khrushchev needed to believe that he could outdo his teacher, especially since Stalin mocked his associates, and Khrushchev in particular, as diplomatic incompetents. Time and again Stalin warned that when he was gone, the imperialists would strangle his successors "like kittens," or "partridges," or "baby calves." His view wasn't so different from that of Maksim Litvinov, who, upon being replaced as foreign commissar by Molotov in 1939, dismissed Stalin's men as "the half-wit Molotov, the careerists Kaganovich, Mikoyan, Beria, the short-sighted Malenkov, Khrushchev the fool. . . . "[27] Stalin once asked his henchmen before dismissing all but the bumbling Bulganin as a possible heir: "Who shall we appoint to head the government after me?" Beria was Georgian, Kaganovich a Jew, Molotov too old, Malenkov and Voroshilov were too weak. And Khrushchev? "No," Stalin said, "he's a worker. We need more of an intellectual."[28]

In contrast with Stalin, Khrushchev asserted, he would have candidly admitted the extent of wartime American aid to the USSR. Stalin blockaded Berlin in 1948 "without gauging our possibilities realistically. He didn't think it through properly."[29] Khrushchev backed North Korea's invasion of the South: "No real Communist would have tried to dissuade Kim Il Sung. . . . To have done so would have contradicted the Communist view of the world." When the North Koreans "liberated" Seoul, "we were all delighted and again wished Kim Il Sung every success." What Khrushchev regretted was that Stalin didn't support Kim enough and that he was prepared to abandon Kim altogether after the Americans entered the war. But Stalin, who was ready to cut his losses in timely fashion, was probably right, and Khrushchev wrong.[30] This episode echoed another in June 1945, when the USSR had been preparing to enter the war against Japan. Should the Red Army invade Hokkaido, an effort that Zhukov estimated would require four full-strength armies? Molotov warned that Moscow's Western allies would see this as a flagrant violation of the Yalta Agreement. Zhukov labeled it an adventure. The only member of the Politburo who favored it was Khrushchev. Stalin didn't take his advice.[31]

Khrushchev worried most of all about the danger of war. The Americans had an overwhelming superiority in air power and nuclear weapons. The Soviet Union was "literally a great big target range for American bombers operating from airfields in Norway, Germany, Italy, South Korea and Japan." He hailed Stalin's all-out effort to develop nuclear weapons but swore "Stalin trembled with fear" at the prospect of an American attack. "How he quivered! He was afraid of war." Once he took power, Khrushchev determined not only to seem fearless but to strike fear into his Western opponents. The result was to bring nuclear war closer than it had ever been under Stalin.[32]

BERIA AND MALENKOV were the first to try to repair the damage Stalin had left behind, Beria by cutting losses from foreign commitments, possibly even including any to East Germany, Malenkov by adopting a more conciliatory tone toward the West.[33] Even Molotov, described by a former aide as so rigid as to "repeat literally the same hidebound formula over and over in negotiations, like a record player,"[34] actually "loosened up a bit," according to American Ambassador Charles Bohlen. Bohlen and his boss, John Foster Dulles, both respected Molotov's skill. British Ambassador Sir William Hayter found him "a little ridiculous with his stammer and his pince-nez," but so "formidable," nonetheless, that when he stepped down as foreign minister in June 1956, "most of the ambassadors in Moscow regretted his departure; we felt that in dealing with him we were dealing with the real thing." Molotov's inflexibility was such (and the shape of his head sufficiently square) that Stalin referred to him as the blockhead. But Molotov too favored reducing tensions with the West.[35] "Neither confrontations nor major concessions" seemed Molotov's rule of thumb.

Once Beria was gone, and Malenkov came under fire from Khrushchev, Molotov conducted Soviet diplomacy. Typical of his stewardship was the four-power foreign ministers' conference of January–February 1954 in Berlin. All major issues were on the table, but none moved an inch. According to the American delegate C. D. Jackson, Molotov turned out to be remarkably "winning," with a sense of humor that "even in translation had a really entertaining edge," whereas his deputy and eventual successor, Andrei Gromyko, perhaps taking up the slack, looked like "death warmed over."[36] Dulles too was in an innovative mood, employing a Russian-speaking lip-reader to scrutinize the Soviet delegation.[37] But when it came to substance, there wasn't any. Dulles assured Molotov with a straight face that a unified pro-West Germany wouldn't threaten Soviet security. Molotov generously suggested that the West scrap both the proposed European Defense Community and NATO.

Khrushchev combined qualities of all three of his rivals. He was bold like Beria, but within ideological limits at which Beria sneered; he was wary of war, like Malenkov, but addicted to bluster and bluff; like Molotov, he was a true believer, but as mercurial as Molotov was disciplined and phlegmatic.[38] In 1953 Khrushchev's focus was still on domestic and Communist bloc matters, not general foreign policy. According to Georgy Kornienko, who worked for the Foreign Ministry's Committee for Information, which prepared intelligence reports for the party leadership, Presidium members returned these materials after reading and marking them up in the margins. "It was easy to tell who had read them carefully," Kornienko said later. "Khrushchev's copies came back without any sign that he had read or studied them or that in fact he had even opened the cover. It was only in 1954 that he began to focus on foreign policy. I remember that when our delegation was getting ready to go to Geneva for the conference on Korea and Indochina in the spring of 1954, Khrushchev's name was mentioned several times as someone who had said this or that about what we hoped to accomplish."[39]

In the meantime, Khrushchev encountered more Westerners and for the most part left them unimpressed. Marshall MacDuffie, the American UNRRA representative who had first met him in Ukraine after the war, found him physically unchanged in October 1953—"the same hard physique, round animated face, and lively humorous features"—but better dressed in an expensive blue serge suit, a starched white shirt, and cuff links set with red stones. Khrushchev's large Kremlin office, a thirty-by-fifty-foot wood-paneled room, with two maps and a picture of Stalin as a young man, bespoke his power. His manner was "relaxed and fairly reasonable," yet during translations "he fiddled impatiently with a pencil as if he wasn't used to such blank spots in his life," and he showed what seemed "a shocking rigidity in his thinking about the West—an apparent willingness to swallow the propaganda he himself has helped to create."[40]

Britons who met Khrushchev in 1954 were even less swayed, perhaps because they put higher stock in the sort of breeding he so conspicuously lacked. In August a Labor party delegation including Clement Attlee and Aneurin Bevan passed through Moscow on its way to China. Prime Minister Malenkov gave a dinner at his dacha, and the next evening, when Ambassador Hayter invited the party leader Khrushchev, as the closest Soviet counterpart to leading Laborites, to dine at the embassy, Malenkov, Molotov, Mikoyan, and others showed up as well. Malenkov seemed "easily the most intelligent and quickest to grasp what was being said"; he said "no more than he wants to say"; he was "an extremely agreeable neighbor at the table"; he was abstemious when it came to liquor (more so than Khrushchev); he had "a pleasant, musical voice and spoke well-educated Russian"; he even recommended quietly that British diplomat-translator Cecil Parrott read the novels of Leonid Andreyev, then condemned as decadent. Khrushchev, by contrast, struck Hayter as "rumbustious, impetuous, loquacious, free-wheeling, alarmingly ignorant of foreign affairs." He "spoke in short sentences, in an emphatic voice and with great conviction. . . . Grinning good-naturedly," he often "stumbled in his choice of words" and "said the wrong thing," which his translator, Oleg Troyanovsky, discreetly corrected. He seemed "incapable of grasping Bevan's line of thought," which Malenkov had to explain to him in "words of one syllable." Given to "interrupting," he seemed more eager to talk than to listen and understand. He was "quick but not intelligent," Hayter summed up, "like a little bull who if aimed the right way would charge along and be certain to arrive with a crash at his objective, knocking down anything that was in his way." Convinced that Malenkov was in charge, no one in the British delegation wanted to be bothered with Khrushchev.

Hayter's first reports to London compared Khrushchev with "the typical peasant as he appears in the classical Russian novels of the nineteenth century, sly, shrewd, suspicious, cautious under the appearance of abandon, fundamentally contemptuous of the *barin*, the master." He also compared him with the British trade union leader Ernest Bevin, both born on the land and with almost no education, both "awkward colleagues and good bosses," but with one key difference: Whereas Bevin was "a magnanimous man, assured and self-confident, Khrushchev's shoulder retained its chip, even when he was the head of one of the greatest powers in history. . . . " Hayter later admitted that once Khrushchev "applied his powerful intelligence and encyclopedic memory to foreign affairs, he mastered them completely."[41] But U.S. Ambassador Bohlen shared his initial negative impression. Malenkov "spoke the best Russian of any Soviet leader I have heard"; his "speeches were well constructed and logical in their development"; he seemed "a man with a more Western-oriented mind." With Khrushchev and the others, "there was no meeting point, no common language." As far as Bohlen could tell, Khrushchev "wasn't especially bright."[42]

To OUTSIDE OBSERVERS, Sino-Soviet relations seemed in fine shape in 1953. Communism had triumphed in China, the Chinese Communist party had cast its lot with Moscow (rather than attempt to reach some sort of accommodation with the United States), and Chinese troops had fought UN forces to a standstill in Korea. Actually, ties between Moscow and Beijing weren't as good as they appeared. Stalin had doubted Communist prospects during Mao's long march to power and at times had even hindered them—partly to fulfill formal obligations to his wartime ally Chiang Kai-shek, partly to appease the United States, perhaps in fear that a huge Communist ally would prove hard to handle. Even after Mao's victory Stalin treated him cavalierly. On his first pilgrimage to Moscow in December 1949, Mao cooled his heels for nearly two and half months before receiving less support and cooperation than he had hoped to obtain.[43] The Korean War itself was a source of Sino-Soviet strain, especially when Stalin refused to back North Korea to the hilt and pressured the Chinese to save Kim Il Sung from defeat by the Americans.[44]

Although Khrushchev sat between Stalin and Mao at Stalin's seventieth birthday celebration in December 1949, he played no role in their talks. But he heard a lot about Mao and about Stalin's handling of him. "What sort of man is Mao?" Stalin asked more than once during late-night gatherings of his inner circle. "He's got some sort of odd, peasant-like views; it's as if he's afraid of the workers and therefore isolated his armies from people who live in cities." Stalin mocked Mao as "caveman Marxist," and after Mao's visit to Moscow, Stalin "never expressed any delight in him and never even spoke of him favorably." Khrushchev thought Stalin's effort to extract one-sided trade concessions from the Chinese was "a mistake," and while Mao was in Moscow, "I saw how Stalin treated him with a false politeness; you could feel his arrogance in relation to Mao. Mao wasn't stupid, and he immediately understood and was irritated, but he didn't show his dissatisfaction. . . . "[45]

Nor of course did Khrushchev. But after 1953 he resolved to manage Mao better than Stalin had. That Stalin had nearly ruined relations with the Chinese gave Khrushchev a chance to outdo his former master. If Mao's "peasant" Marxism was as primitive as Stalin maintained, Khrushchev could play the benevolent tutor. It was all the more devastating when, instead of expressing gratitude and respect, Mao started condescending to Khrushchev, not just denying him the satisfaction of surpassing Stalin but returning Khrushchev to his former role of an upstart mortified by a new master.

For a while, however, things went well. Between 1953 and 1956 Moscow agreed to build, or aid in the construction of, 205 factories and plants valued at about $2 billion, with $727 million financed with Soviet credits, all at a time when the Russians themselves suffered shortages. In October 1954 the Soviets agreed to send a small corps of experts; by 1957 at least twenty-five hundred were tutoring the Chinese in everything from construction to atomic energy. In April 1955 the USSR promised to help Beijing develop nuclear technology for peaceful purposes. During these same years, about ten thousand Chinese students studied in the Soviet Union, while another seventeen thousand were trained by Soviet teachers in China.[46]

Besides helping economically, Moscow provided diplomatic and military support. Stalin's successors helped bring the Korean War to an end, sponsored Beijing's participation in the 1954 Geneva Conference on Indochina and Korea, and urged its inclusion in talks on European issues. The Soviets backed Chinese shelling of the offshore islands of Jinmen (Quemoy) and Mazu (Matsu) in late 1954. Chinese representatives attended the founding meeting of the Warsaw Pact in 1955, were informed before Khrushchev normalized relations with Tito, and Mao was consulted frequently and at length during the Eastern European upheavals of late 1956. Soviet military advisers helped the Chinese master Soviet-made weapons, and in 1957 Moscow even agreed to provide Beijing with a sample nuclear bomb.[47]

All this largesse added up to what historian William Kirby called "the greatest transfer of technology in world history." According to Mao's former Russian interpreter Yan Mingfu, Khrushchev "greatly improved the situation Stalin left behind," and Mao "appreciated" it.[48] But even these "good years" sowed seeds of future discord. Khrushchev's recollection of his 1954 visit to China is full of bile. He generously offered to return Port Arthur and Dairen to China. But instead of being grateful, Mao objected (citing the need for Soviet protection against the Americans), then agreed reluctantly, and finally asked Khrushchev to leave Soviet heavy artillery behind in Port Arthur. "We wouldn't have minded obliging," Khrushchev said later, "if the Chinese had been willing to pay for the guns, but Zhou Enlai asked us to hand them over free." Khrushchev also reacted badly to the atmosphere in Mao's court, which he describes as "typically Oriental. Everyone was unbelievably courteous and ingratiating, but I saw through their hypocrisy." To make matters worse, Khrushchev was "never sure what Mao meant. . . . I believed in him and he was playing with me. . . . I remember that when I came back from China in 1954, I told my comrades, 'Conflict with China is inevitable.'"[49]

Khrushchev's memory almost certainly failed him in this case; surely he was transposing later outrage onto his first trip to China. But the Chinese did engage in a bravura blend of begging and bargaining, and Khrushchev characteristically overdid his generosity. Before his trip Chinese negotiators requested a vast amount yet refused to put the request in writing. Later, in the absence of written evidence to the contrary, Zhou Enlai got Khrushchev to fulfill obligations that Moscow had not in fact undertaken. Khrushchev was determined to have a triumph in Beijing, but his strategy created doubts at home.

Mikoyan was in charge of the prejourney talks with the Chinese; his point man was K. I. Koval, vice minister of external trade. According to Koval, "Khrushchev took this decision [to give the Chinese everything they wanted] on foreign policy grounds only, without any sense at all of the scale of promised aid or of the problems and difficulties involved." Koval objected that the Soviet heavy machine-building industry couldn't provide what the Chinese wanted, but "each time I spoke, Khrushchev seemed more irritated. . . . " The first secretary "didn't know how to hear out arguments opposed to his own, and he couldn't stand those who tried to make them." Khrushchev "incinerated me with a withering glance. It was clear that he had forever put me on the list of his opponents." Mikoyan got Khrushchev to delay delivery of some plants until after 1960. But even so, when the aid package reached the Presidium, Voroshilov objected. Khrushchev threatened to call off the trip if he had to go "empty-handed." He berated Voroshilov, got him to change his mind, and then, after his colleagues had left, asked Koval suspiciously if he hadn't talked Voroshilov into his negative vote.[50] The fact that Khrushchev expended so much political and economic capital to help China meant he expected a lot in return. When he didn't get it, his disappointment was all the greater.

Cultural misunderstandings didn't help either. The Chinese outdid themselves in hospitality, escorting the Soviets on an extended tour of the country. Treated to a fabled Cantonese dish, "Fight of the Dragon and the Tiger," with the dramatis personae a snake and a cat respectively, most of the Soviets, including Khrushchev, refused even to taste it, and the two women in the party, Yekaterina Furtseva and Yadgar Nasredinova, burst into tears. Even tea drinking became a kind of torture. "During meetings, they kept serving tea," Khrushchev recalls. "As soon as you finished one cup they'd bring you another. If you didn't manage to finish, they'd take away the cup and produce a fresh one, again and again." The result was that delegation members couldn't sleep at night until a Soviet doctor told them to cut down on caffeine. But although "we weren't used to this sort of ceremony," Khrushchev added, "we engaged in it out of respect for our hosts."[51]

The years 1956 and 1957 seemed the best yet in Sino-Soviet relations. "Relations were at their closest," Yan Mingfu recalled forty years later. "This was the peak of the friendship," added former Soviet Central Committee official, Lev Deliusin. But beneath the surface the ground was beginning to shift. Khrushchev neither consulted the Chinese in advance about his secret speech, nor invited their delegation at the Twentieth Congress to hear it. Mao had grievances against Stalin, but he wasn't about to undermine the cult of his own personality by smashing Stalin's. Khrushchev "made a mess" of things, Mao told party colleagues on March 17, 1956. "He's just handing the sword to others, helping the tigers harm us," Mao grumbled to his personal physician, Dr. Li Zhisui. Stalin should have been "criticized but not killed," interpreter Li Yueren remembered Mao's saying. "Mao decided Khrushchev wasn't mature enough to lead such a big country," said Yan Mingfu. "Mao never forgave Khrushchev for attacking Stalin," concluded Dr. Li.[52]

For the time being, however, the Chinese not only needed Soviet help themselves but were convinced the whole Communist camp did. So Mao set out to "assist" Khrushchev. Chinese editorials insisted that despite "serious mistakes," Stalin must be respected as a "great Marxist-Leninist." Beijing instructed Chinese students in the USSR to attend Soviet study circles on the results of the Twentieth Congress and even consulted Moscow about whether to display Stalin's portrait on May Day 1956. Since Stalin's picture didn't grace Red Square that day, the Chinese were probably instructed to abstain. But the Chinese deployed giant Stalin portraits in Tiananmen Square anyway.[53]

The Polish and Hungarian crises of 1956 confirmed Mao's view of Khrushchev's limitations. So did the way the Soviet leader relied on Chinese support that autumn and to rebuild the bloc afterward. Whether Mao's advice to crush the Hungarian rebellion arrived before or after Khrushchev decided to do so, the Chinese were in effect coaching the Soviets, a reversal of roles the touchy Khrushchev could hardly accept for long.[54]

By the end of 1956 Mao had concluded Khrushchev had botched the entire Stalin issue. People like Khrushchev "do not adhere to Marxism-Leninism," he implied in a speech that fall, "they do not take an analytical approach to things, and they lack revolutionary morality." In January 1957 he described Soviet leaders as "blinded by lust for gain," so that "the best way to deal with them is to give them a tongue lashing."[55] That same month Premier Zhou Enlai traveled to Eastern Europe and the USSR to survey the damage. When Khrushchev publicly reversed himself at the Chinese Embassy reception and called Stalin a "true Marxist-Leninist," Lev Deliusin, who was covering the event for *Pravda*, was standing nearby. Deliusin assumed that Khrushchev, who had been drinking heavily, had misspoken, and he was shocked to be ordered to quote him in print.[56] The journalist deduced that the leadership was using a Khrushchev slip to mend fences with the Chinese. Nor was Zhou impressed. Soviet leaders, he said on his return to Beijing, "often fail to overcome subjectivity, narrow-mindedness and emotion." They concentrate on "specific and isolated events rather than anticipating situations thoroughly from different angles." Being "extremely conceited . . . lacking farsightedness and knowing little of the ways of the world, some of their leaders have hardly improved themselves even with the several rebuffs they have met in the past year." Yet "they appear to lack confidence, suffer from inner fears, and thus tend to employ the tactics of bluffing or threats in handling foreign affairs or relations with brotherly parties."

As a summary of Khrushchev's flaws, this could hardly be improved upon. Zhou also homed in on guilty secrets Khrushchev failed to address in his secret speech and avoided again in private conversations. "He made no self-criticism," reported Zhou, who had needled Khrushchev by asking how Stalin's successors could "decline to assume any responsibility." Khrushchev had replied that "had they not been afraid of getting killed, they could have at least done more to restrict the growth of Stalin's mistakes." But "before getting out of the car at the [Moscow] airport, Khrushchev explained to me that they could not conduct the same kind of self-criticism as we do: should they do so, their current leadership would be in trouble."[57]

Opposition from Molotov, Malenkov, and Kaganovich increased Khrushchev's need for Chinese support. The Chinese ambassador to Moscow Liu Xiao thought the Soviet leader was particularly attentive to Chinese wishes in early 1957. When Voroshilov was showered with high-level hospitality in China, Khrushchev was jealous; at least that was what Voroshilov told his hosts. Nor were Chinese leaders pleased with Khrushchev's June 1957 triumph over the "antiparty group." How could a founder of the party like Molotov conceivably head an "antiparty group"? Peng Dehuai asked the Soviet emissary who delivered the news. "Why did you put it that way?" he asked. "Couldn't you think of something wiser?"[58]

Despite his doubts about Khrushchev, Mao backed the winner in Moscow. In the fall of 1957 he made his second and last trip to the USSR to celebrate the fortieth anniversary of the revolution with other Communist parties. Before long he replaced the Soviet model of development and challenged Soviet foreign policy too, but for the moment he still lavished praise on Khrushchev, or so it seemed. According to Mao, the June 1957 Kremlin showdown had been "between two lines: one erroneous and one relatively correct."[59] If that sounds like faint praise, what Mao's interpreter rendered into Russian was apparently even fainter. According to Yugoslav Ambassador Mićunović, the translator mentioned something about "two different groups," of which one "tendency led by Khrushchev won the day." As for "[W]hat exactly Mao said, nobody except the Chinese knew." But Mikoyan knew enough, or thought he did, to "rise demonstratively from his seat with an expression on his face which was anything but friendly."[60]

If Mikoyan detected double entendres, what did Khrushchev think of this? "Lenin once said that there is not a single person in the world who has not made mistakes," Mao declared. "I have made many mistakes and these mistakes have been beneficial to me and taught me a lesson. . . . a Chinese proverb says that with all its beauty the lotus needs the green of its leaves to set it off. You, comrade Khrushchev, even though you are a beautiful lotus, you too need leaves to set you off. I, Mao Zedong, while not a beautiful lotus, also need leaves to set me off. Still another Chinese proverb says three cobblers with their wits combined equal Zhuge Liang, the master mind. This corresponds to comrade Khrushchev's slogan—collective leadership."[61]

Was that a compliment or wasn't it? Also, how were Mao's musings on war to be taken? "If worse came to worst [in a nuclear war] and half of mankind died," Mao told the November conference, "the other half would remain, while imperialism would be razed to the ground and the world would become socialist." If the West invaded the Soviet Union, he advised Khrushchev, Soviet forces ought not fight back but should retreat to the Urals for up to three years, by which time the Chinese could rescue them. "I looked at him closely," Khrushchev later said. "I couldn't tell from his face whether he was joking or not."[62]

Mao's personal conduct in Moscow sent a clearer message. In sharp contrast with Stalin, Khrushchev showered Mao with attention and hospitality. He put his guest up in an opulent palace that once belonged to Catherine the Great; provided him with an endless supply of fruits, chocolates, cigarettes, and drinks; dropped in on him every morning to make sure he was well; and accompanied him to political gatherings and cultural events. He couldn't have been more "friendly and respectful," recalled Mao's physician. Yet Mao practically oozed dissatisfaction and disrespect in return. The huge soft bed in Catherine's bedchamber didn't suit him, so he slept on the floor on a blanket and sheets. The flush toilet in the adjoining bathroom didn't please him either; he used his own chamber pot instead. Although the Soviets assigned him two Russian chefs, Mao accepted only Hunanese dishes prepared by his personal cook. Taken to see *Swan Lake* at the Bolshoi, he rejected Khrushchev's special box, insisted on sitting with "the masses" (who weren't there anyway, especially in the first three rows usually filled with KGB agents, who cleared out so that Mao could settle himself in the orchestra), and then demanded to leave almost immediately, as if, said Dr. Li, "he was deliberately refusing to appreciate Russian culture." In private conversations with Chinese colleagues (which the KGB must have overheard and reported), Mao overflowed with "private barbs" against his host. Khrushchev's very efforts to make up for Stalin's 1949 mistreatment of Mao turned out to be strikes against him. "Look how differently they're treating us now," Mao remarked disdainfully. "Even in this Communist land, they know who is powerful and who is weak. What snobs!"

Mao's message got through to lower-level officials on both sides. He treated Khrushchev like "an obsequious, uncouth fool," recalled Lev Deliusin. Khrushchev just didn't understand Mao, remembered Li Yueran. "He didn't understand that Mao was a great leader to whom you didn't just say whatever came out of your mouth."[63]

KHRUSHCHEV'S JOURNEY to Belgrade in May 1955 carried higher risks than his trip to Beijing. His new formula for the Soviet bloc was to tolerate a modicum of diversity and domestic autonomy, to emphasize ideological and political bonds and reinforce economic and military ties, and to weave all this together with his own direct, personal involvement.[64] But Eastern European Stalinists obstructed his scheme, as did his own assumptions. Although Khrushchev admitted that Stalin exploited the Eastern Europeans, he bridled when they failed to concede the CPSU's "leading role": "Even though we were often clumsy in our relationship with other socialist countries . . . we never used this friendship to pursue any selfish goals." But this very attitude of his, as self-righteous as it was inaccurate, was part of the problem, as was his sense of Russian superiority. Poles who didn't appreciate Soviet aid and perpetually clamored for more were ingrates. All the socialist countries, Khrushchev remarked toward the end of his life, "look on the Soviet Union as one big feeding trough. I know because I've dealt with them all."[65] Add his crude bullying tactics, which were all the more transparent because other Communist leaders used them on one another and on their own peoples, and it is clear why reconstituting the Soviet camp on a more voluntary basis proved so difficult.

When the Stalinist purges were exported to Eastern Europe in the late forties, the worst that could be said of "traitors" like Hungary's Lászlo Rajk and Czechoslovakia's Rudolf Slansky was that they were Titoist spies. The Western powers had seized on the Soviet-Yugoslav split to establish economic and even military ties to Tito. If Yugoslavia could now be reincorporated into "the socialist commonwealth," the future looked bright. Going to Belgrade in May 1955 took courage, and Khrushchev's Yugoslav trip seemed crowned with success. Soviet and Yugoslav leaders solemnly pledged "respect for the sovereignty, independence, integrity and equality of states in their relations with each other and in relations with other states." Tito later told his colleagues: "Only Khrushchev could have done this. Molotov, Malenkov, Voroshilov—none of them would have changed anything."[66]

But this first encounter established a pattern that was to plague Khrushchev. Tito was eager for reconciliation, but on his own terms. His aim was to reform the camp, not to buttress it; to preserve Yugoslav independence, including ties with the West, not to restrict it. Having broken with Stalin before Khrushchev did, Tito was proud and touchy. Khrushchev needed far-reaching Yugoslav concessions to prove he was right to conciliate Tito, while Tito was determined to postpone close party-to-party ties until Stalinism was dead and buried in the USSR.

The strain showed at the Belgrade airport when Khrushchev arrived. After a polite welcome from Tito, Khrushchev stepped to the microphone. His speech had been carefully crafted and vetted by the Presidium. It blamed Beria, not Stalin, for past trespasses against Belgrade. After Khrushchev finished, Tito interrupted the interpreter. "No need to translate, everyone here understands Russian," he said, and stalked off, waving his Soviet guests to waiting cars. In later years Khrushchev loved to cite the incident to show you couldn't get away with blaming Beria for Stalin's sins. But at the time he was deeply chagrined. Since far from all Yugoslavs knew Russian, Tito was in effect snubbing his guest. Those back in Moscow who opposed the trip were "quite powerful," Khrushchev said later, "and the cold reception in Belgrade could be taken as a hostile act and set us back."[67]

This first embarrassment was followed by others. Although Tito and his senior ministers arrived at a lavish White Palace reception in dinner jackets, with their wives in full evening regalia, Khrushchev and company wore baggy summer suits. During the Soviet delegation's tour of the country, its reception was noticeably restrained. Tito reduced Khrushchev to a quivering wreck by racing him about the Adriatic in a high-powered motorboat. Khrushchev got stupefyingly drunk at a Soviet Embassy reception. At dinner with Tito and his wife afterward, as Mikoyan was pronouncing toast after toast, and Bulganin tried to keep the conversation going, Khrushchev kept trying to kiss everyone, particularly Tito, to whom he kept cooing, "Iosya, quit being angry! What a thin-skinned one you are! Drink up and let bygones be bygones."[68]

Khrushchev did better on occasions that didn't demand diplomatic finesse. At a factory in Zagreb he sat down at a round table to examine blueprints, observed by, among others, Edward Crankshaw, then correspondent for the *Observer*. "He was a man transformed, no longer the public clown, no longer the bullying demagogue, no longer the man showing off. . . . His whole immense vitality was concentrated on the job at hand." The job was to understand the details of concrete construction and to disabuse the Yugoslavs of their notion that workers' councils, rather than factory managers and state agencies, could best direct the economy, and "all this was done very quietly but with an authority which was absolute." In this situation, wrote Crankshaw, Khrushchev "had become, without emphasis, without raising his voice, the born and unquestioned master." It was as if "all the energies, all the vitality of everybody in that room were being drained from each individual and absorbed into this small figure who knew just what he wanted and was going to get it with perfect economy of effort. . . ."[69]

Getting Tito to rejoin the Soviet bloc was another matter. Khrushchev intensified his courtship during the rest of 1955 and the first half of 1956. His boldest moves of course came at the Twentieth Congress. His approval of multiple paths to socialism included Yugoslavia's. His pressure on Rákosi and other Eastern European Stalinists to warm up to Tito and the formal April 1956 disbanding of the Cominform, which had been used a club to beat Belgrade, also impressed Belgrade. When Tito traveled to the USSR in June 1956, military bands and an artillery salute greeted him at the border; large crowds waited at railroad stations in Moldavia, Ukraine, and Moscow; nearly a million lined the streets of Leningrad; and enthusiastic throngs in Stalingrad got out of control, almost crushing Tito and Khrushchev. The Soviet leaders were on their best behavior. At a Yugoslav Embassy dinner, even Molotov competed with others "to see who could condemn Stalin's policy toward Yugoslavia in the sharpest terms."[70]

The actual negotiations were more difficult. Intergovernmental issues were manageable: The Soviets neither chided Tito on his Western ties nor pressed him to recognize East Germany. Extension of Soviet credits would depend on Yugoslav "cooperation," but Khrushchev didn't rub that in. Still, getting Tito to sign on to ideological unity proved impossible. Denied a full and complete reconciliation, Khrushchev tried to convey the image of one in a joint appearance with Tito before ten thousand people at the Dinamo sports stadium. In fact, reported Mićunović, the Russians were "really disappointed. They invested a great deal in this visit, but their investments have not paid off."[71]

Khrushchev's disappointment deepened over the next four months. Instead of reinforcing Communist unity, the uppity Yugoslavs accelerated its unraveling. Shortly after the Polish city of Poznań erupted in strikes, Mićunović found Khrushchev looking grim at a Kremlin reception. Tito had censored Khrushchev's Dinamo stadium speech before publishing it in Belgrade, Khrushchev complained. He and his colleagues had "treated Tito with the utmost sincerity," and in return the Yugoslavs had "broken agreements in the crudest way." Khrushchev seemed beside himself with anger. He was not going to "let anyone play around" with the Soviet leadership.[72]

Mićunović hadn't even known about what he regarded as a "technical slip" by the Yugoslav press. But the Soviet Presidium had compared copies of *Pravda* and the Yugoslav paper *Borba* line by line. Once he cooled down, Khrushchev said it wasn't he but his colleagues who wanted this quarrel. However, the incident was a sign of things to come. Tito wasn't just defending his brand of national communism; he was offering it for export, especially to Poland and Hungary. Yet if Khrushchev had second thoughts about Tito, he had to prove to the Presidium that his first thoughts were correct. So he tried to pressure the Yugoslav leader by showing him a "secret" film of a Soviet hydrogen bomb explosion and showering his aides with blandishments and bribes. Everywhere the Yugoslavs went in the USSR, both that summer and in September, when Tito was invited to "vacation" in the Crimea with Khrushchev, they found listening devices in their bedrooms. Being plied with vodka was also standard, even though, while under the influence, Bulganin insulted the Yugoslavs most undiplomatically. But the pièce de résistance in the Crimea was the way Ernö Gerö, the warmed-over Hungarian Stalinist who had replaced Rákosi but was soon to be replaced himself by Imre Nagy, suddenly materialized without any warning to the Yugoslavs. Khrushchev's obvious aim was to get the Yugoslavs to bless the new Hungarian party leader, if only by announcing a meeting between the two men to which Tito hadn't agreed in advance.[73]

Despite Soviet bullying, Tito invited Gerö to Belgrade and gave him a royal welcome. But it was too late to ward off the Hungarian revolt, and afterward the Yugoslavs misbehaved again. They gave Nagy asylum in the Yugoslav Embassy in Budapest on November 4. (On November 22, he left with a Soviet promise of safe passage, but the Soviets nonetheless detained him, imprisoned him in Romania, and eventually executed him.) Then, in a November 11 speech in the town of Pula, Tito tried to distance himself from the Soviet intervention in Hungary.[74] Mićunović hadn't read Tito's speech when he arrived at a Kremlin reception where Khrushchev's reaction made the previous July's cold shoulder look like a warm embrace. Without a word of greeting, he dragged Mićunović into an empty room, where, with Molotov and Bulganin standing beside him, he berated the Yugoslav ambassador for nearly an hour. Realizing toward the end that the scene was visible to other guests, Khrushchev led Mićunović into a less public room for another hour of recriminations. Bulganin joined in the bashing, while Molotov remained mostly silent with an "I-told-you-so" look on his face. Yet when the storm was over, Khrushchev insisted on driving Ambassador and Mrs. Mićunović (who had been left to her own devices the entire time) back to their embassy. The ambassador's wife got out when Khrushchev's limousine stopped in narrow Khlebnyi Lane, but Khrushchev wasn't finished with her husband. It was long past midnight, with the temperature about ten below, when Khrushchev suddenly changed his tone: Ever since 1954 he had invested his own personal prestige in improving relations with Yugoslavia. Now he would have to join his colleagues in attacking Yugoslavia publicly, triggering further conflict between Moscow and Belgrade. "If only you had seen the written report I made following the talks in Yugoslavia and in the Crimea, and knew how I expected relations between us to improve," he said gloomily.

This, Mićunović wrote in his diary, "was the strangest conversation I have had so far with Khrushchev." The Soviet leader was a good actor, capable of feigning rage as well as friendship, and that night he doubtless played up the hurt he felt. But the hurt was real, as was his anger when the Yugoslavs descended to what he regarded as personal mockery. Arriving in December for a short Kremlin conversation that turned into another three-hour marathon, Mićunović "found Khrushchev in such a state as I have never seen him before, not even after Tito's Pula speech. . . . Khrushchev knew [Yugoslav Vice-President Edvard] Kardelj was thinking of him when he 'poked fun at the policy of maize and potatoes.'" Two months later Khrushchev was still steaming. A week after that the Soviet leader invited Mićunović to sit next to him at a concert and whispered a fierce protest against a "disgusting" caricature of himself and Bulganin that had appeared in the Belgrade paper *Politika*. When Khrushchev handed over the offending paper "like a sort of *corpus delecti*," the Yugoslav ambassador pointed out that the bald man standing next to Bulganin wasn't Khrushchev but Eisenhower.[75]

Khrushchev was always sensitive to slight, but his discomfort increased when his policies weren't going well. Alas, Soviet-Yugoslav relations never regained the warmth of the summer of 1956. To be sure, Poland and Hungary remained in the Soviet camp, and Yugoslavia's star soon faded in both the East and the West. But if Khrushchev had won a victory, it was pyrrhic. Tito was more determined than ever to promote the Yugoslav model. Khrushchev tried to cordon off the infection by launching a campaign against Yugoslav "revisionism." The very fact that he had to do so, after having wooed the Yugoslavs so long and so ardently, was itself a kind of defeat.[76]

CHINA AND YUGOSLAVIA could challenge the USSR. The United States could destroy it. By 1954, if not sooner, Khrushchev was paying close attention to East-West relations. His son detected he was "noticeably nervous" during the January 1954 Berlin foreign ministers' conference. "He began to return home late and spent a lot of time on the telephone" with Molotov. According to a Molotov aide, Khrushchev wasn't happy with the foreign minister's "sluggishness and lack of initiative"; he continually groused about them to colleagues, often in a somewhat "lubricated condition" after diplomatic receptions. Needing Molotov's support against Malenkov, Khrushchev didn't confront him directly until early 1955.[77] In the meantime he took the lead on defense policy, trying to reduce the defense burden on the Soviet economy, but without lowering the nation's guard, instead even raising it. The solution, he thought, was to rely on nuclear weapons.

When Stalin died, his crash program to develop atomic weapons had been under way for eight years.[78] U.S. intelligence estimated in 1952 that the USSR could have as many as 200 bombs by mid-1953. In fact, Moscow had no more than 120 bombs in mid-1953, and as late as 1956 it had no planes that could bomb the United States and return home.[79] However, a substantial buildup of nuclear weapons would increase defense spending rather than reduce it. Khrushchev's solution to this dilemma was bluff. His core axiom was that nuclear weapons were so destructive they would never be employed; when he first learned "all the facts about nuclear power," he remarked, "I couldn't sleep for several days. Then I became convinced we could never possibly use these weapons, and . . . I was able to sleep again."[80] This allowed him to threaten nuclear war without, he thought, actually risking it, while at the same time cutting back conventional weapons like surface ships and bombers. Eisenhower's "New Look" strategy likewise threatened "massive retaliation" rather than a conventional response to Soviet "aggression." But the Americans had far more nuclear weapons and the planes to deliver them. Instead of bombers, Khrushchev opted for missiles. The most likely ICBM, Sergei Korolyov's 270-ton one-and-half stage Semyorka (R-7), had yet to be flight-tested in the winter of 1956, but Khrushchev was already "using" it in his first jousts with Western statesmen.[81]

The centerpiece of Khrushchev's new diplomacy was a campaign for what a later era labeled detente. As he saw it, reducing tensions could undermine Western resistance to Communist gains, tempt capitalists to increase East-West trade, and project a more friendly image in the Third World. Stalin and Molotov had welcomed "breathing spells" too, but Khrushchev preferred an indefinite period of "peaceful coexistence." Not that he was forsaking the Bolsheviks' revolutionary mission. Rather, by pursuing it in the Third World, which Stalin and Molotov had mostly ignored, he would outdo them in yet another realm. By barnstorming abroad, by smothering foreign statesmen with personal attention, by breaking through distrust with his own energy and tenacity, he would woo the West while at the same time undermining it. Stalin would have been appalled. An aide once heard Molotov complain that naiveté in foreign policy was "tantamount to a crime."[82] But that sort of contempt only whetted Khrushchev's appetite to succeed.

The Kremlin now gave lavish banquets for diplomats, followed by gala concerts in St. George Hall. An August 1955 garden party created what British diplomat Cecil Parrott described as "an atmosphere of enchantment" at Semyonovskoye, sixty miles southeast of Moscow, with rowboats on several ponds, hammocks strung between tall trees, and a magnificent feast with a military band playing. Khrushchev wore his trademark Ukrainian shirt under a light tropical suit. Parrott wouldn't have been surprised to see the tall ascetic Suslov "turn into a white rabbit, take out several watches from his pocket, and disappear down a hole." The scene reminded him of "a Shakespearean fairyland, through which Bulganin seemed to move, now like Prospero, now like the Duke in the Forest of Arden."

Other gatherings, however, misfired. It took only the sight of Zhou Enlai in Khrushchev's company in July 1954 to alter Ambassador Hayter's view of the balance of power, or rather, of culture, between the USSR and its Chinese "satellite." Zhou showed up his hosts by speaking "excellent, fluent English, not one word of which was comprehensible to his Russian hearers." After drinking liberally at an open-air party following the June 1956 Tushino air show, Hayter remembered, Khrushchev "insulted literally every country in the world." Bulganin tried to intervene; Molotov pursed his lips; Kaganovich whispered, "All this is very unnecessary." Finally several colleagues put a stop to the proceedings by going around and saying good-bye while Khrushchev was still talking.[83]

Khrushchev's first major East-West initiative concerned Austria. Like Germany, Austria had been occupied after the war. But not much would be lost, Khrushchev thought, if Soviet troops pulled out in return for a treaty under which the Austrians, like the Swiss, would proclaim their neutrality. Austrian negotiations had been stalled for years, and Molotov, who had been conducting them, regarded Khrushchev as an interloper. Khrushchev himself was at first reluctant to advance his own position. Lacking "much experience in international contacts," he felt like "Dun'ka getting ready to go to Europe"—that is, like the simple, illiterate country woman in Konstantin Trenyov's play *Liubov' Yarovaya,* whose very name conveys disdain.[84] But that didn't deter him for long.

Julius Raab, the Austrian chancellor, was the first Western leader with whom Khrushchev actually negotiated. "You know, Mr. Raab," he recalled saying, "this is the first time in my life I've sat next to a real capitalist." By achieving the Austrian State Treaty, which was signed in May 1955, Khrushchev "passed a test demonstrating that we could conduct complex negotiations and conclude them successfully." In the end, he boasted, "Dun'ka had done well in Europe; we proved we could orient ourselves in foreign affairs without Stalin's instructions. In effect, we had exchanged our kids' shorts for adult trousers. Our effective debut was recognized not only in the USSR but abroad. . . . We could feel our own strength."[85]

KHRUSHCHEV'S NEXT TEST was the Geneva summit of July 1955. Summits were still four-power gatherings in the 1950s, and London and Paris were eager to attend. But the United States was the primary player in Soviet eyes, and it played hard to get. Dulles was more flexible than he seemed (more alert to fissures in the Soviet bloc and more eager to lower cold war tensions), but he assumed a summit would prove fruitless. Eisenhower, however, like Khrushchev, liked to take the measure of "the other fellow's mind," to gauge what he called "the personal equations" of his counterparts, to win the day through the force of his own personality.[86] On the eve of the summit Dulles confided to a friend that he was "terribly worried." Eisenhower "likes things to be right and pleasant between people" and "tires when an unpleasantness is dragged out indefinitely." Dulles feared Ike would take a tactical smile as "a sign of inner warmth" and accept a promise at "face value."[87]

One reason Khrushchev and Eisenhower put personal contacts ahead of substantive agreements was that the latter seemed beyond reach. The German question, and the related issue of European security, offered no room for compromise: The West insisted on unifying Germany through free elections; the Soviets were determined to keep Germany divided. Eisenhower's most dramatic move at Geneva, his Open

Skies proposal for observation flights over each other's military installations, struck Khrushchev as legalized espionage.[88] Bohlen called Geneva "one of the most disappointing and discouraging of all the summit meetings." Hayter says he spent most of the session rereading *War and Peace*, and Anatoly Dobrynin, later Soviet ambassador to Washington but then a junior diplomat, remembered the following "highlight": In response to Eisenhower's denial that NATO was "an aggressive bloc," Khrushchev demanded to know why the USSR wasn't allowed to join it. "'Have you applied?' Eisenhower asked, surprised. 'Several months ago,' Khrushchev replied. Eisenhower was obviously at a loss."[89]

With prospects for actual agreements so dim, the real test for Khrushchev became how he would conduct himself. "Would we be able to represent our country competently? Would we approach the meeting soberly, without unrealistic hopes, and would we be able to keep the other side from intimidating us?" On July 4, before departing Moscow, he stridently denied that the Soviet delegation was going to Geneva "on its knees," with "its legs broken." But could he handle threats to his own self-esteem? "He was morbidly suspicious," according to his son, "that he would not be shown the formal tokens of respect called for by protocol." He "kept referring indirectly to this painful subject." What to wear, how to address people, what utensils to use at official dinners? Since Bulganin hadn't been out of the country much either, Khrushchev was reduced to asking Molotov for advice on etiquette. Should they wear white tie and tails as suggested by the Foreign Ministry? "No, they'll have to take us as we are," he grumbled to his family. "We won't play up to them. If they want to talk with workers, they had better get used to us."[90]

Actually, Khrushchev's first worry was that he might not even get to go. He desperately wanted to, his son recalled; "he simply couldn't bear to miss the first meeting of heads of great powers to be held since he became the nation's leader." But Premier Bulganin was to lead the Soviet delegation, and since Khrushchev lacked any formal government position, his presence could be awkward. Many years later he was still ruminating about it: "I'm still not sure whether or not it was proper for me to attend the Geneva meeting; but it's too late to worry about that now, and I won't deny I was very anxious to have a chance to meet the representatives of the USA, England, and France and to join the solution of international problems."[91]

Humiliations began at the airport. Western delegations arrived in four-engine planes, the Soviets in a two-engine affair. "Their planes were certainly more impressive than ours," Khrushchev later admitted, "and the comparison was somewhat embarrassing." Somewhat? "Until the day he died," said his son, "he never forgot how humiliated he felt when the delegation's two-engine Il-14 landed. It looked like an insect" next to the Western airliners. When Bulganin stepped forward to review the Swiss honor guard, a hulking protocol officer blocked Khrushchev's path "with his back up against my nose. I wasn't permitted to join in that part of the ceremony, so the Swiss government very rudely had that man stand in front of me!"[92]

The very room in which the conference was held, the League of Nations Council Chamber at the Palais des Nations, was daunting. A large four-sided table dominated the room, with two rows of chairs for the main delegates and banked seats behind them for aides. Sepia murals depicting scenes from antiquity decorated the walls, and a huge picture window opened onto Lake Geneva with rolling meadows and mountains beyond. Each delegation had five chairs at the table. Eisenhower sat in the middle with Dulles at his right hand. To their right was Bulganin with Khrushchev and Marshal Zhukov on one side, Molotov and Gromyko on the other. The urbane Anthony Eden anchored the British front benchers, while the French were led by Prime Minister Edgar Faure and Foreign Minister Antoine Pinay.[93]

Not only did Khrushchev have to negotiate with these imposing statesmen, but he had to make small talk too. Eisenhower suggested a happy hour after each plenary session so as to dissolve tensions in martinis. On one such occasion he introduced Khrushchev to Nelson Rockefeller, an adviser to the American delegation. Surprised to see Rockefeller "was dressed fairly democratically," Khrushchev playfully poked his first American millionaire in the ribs with his fist. "So this is Mr. Rockefeller, himself!" he said. Doubtless he was relieved when the down-to-earth Rockefeller "took this as a joke and did the same thing to me."[94] The urbane Gromyko was also capable of coarseness. When he was informed that servants at the American villa were Filipinos, the dour diplomat replied, "I can never tell any of the Orientals apart."[95]

Bulganin did most of the talking for the Soviets at formal sessions, sometimes sounding, according to an American present, like "the chairman of a large charity organization delivering his annual report." But Khrushchev didn't hesitate to interrupt, and he dominated the dinners that the delegations exchanged. Eden described him as "butting into conversations" and "taking the play away from his comrades." At the American villa Khrushchev mocked Bulganin's fondness for alcohol. Bulganin was the nominal host at a Russian lunch, but according to Assistant

Secretary of State Livingston T. Merchant, "Khrushchev dominated the board by his loquacity and equally by his extraordinary table manners." Before dinner on another occasion, "Mr. Khrushchev waxed eloquent on the unusual success they had in crossing zebras with cows. He said the stripes were still quite apparent, but that the animal had the complete appearance of a cow, including horns."[96]

If the relatively informal Americans were struck by Khrushchev's boorishness, the more cultivated Europeans were appalled. "Khrushchev is a mystery," confided Harold Macmillan to his diary on July 22. "How can this fat, vulgar man, with his pig eyes and his ceaseless flow of talk, really be the head—the aspirant Tsar—of all these millions of people and this vast country?" Antoine Pinay marveled at "this little man with his fat paws."[97] Macmillan almost pitied the poor Russians who so obviously wanted "to be liked—even loved."[98]

Compared with the fraternizing, the actual negotiating was easy: The Soviets wouldn't budge from prior positions on Germany and disarmament, and they brooked no interference in their Eastern European sphere of influence. Not only did Khrushchev refuse to bow down to the imperialists, but he concluded they might yet bow down to him. During dinner at the American villa Eisenhower insisted passionately on the "futility of war in the nuclear age," saying that any nation that used nuclear weapons risked destroying itself since such a major conflict was likely to incinerate the Northern Hemisphere. Assistant Secretary Merchant later hailed this as turning point: "The most important result of the summit was to remove from the minds of the Soviet leaders any fear that the United States would attack Russia. The President, by his character and sincerity, convinced them of that [thus removing] the genuinely dangerous risk of Soviet action based on a miscalculation of our own intentions." But the real effect was almost the opposite. Khrushchev left Geneva "encouraged, realizing now that our enemies probably feared us as much as we feared them." That prompted him to practice nuclear bluster and bluff so as to play on American fears.[99]

Another impression reinforced Khrushchev's confidence. The fact that Eisenhower relied heavily on Dulles during negotiations, that Dulles kept passing him notes, which Eisenhower "read conscientiously like a schoolboy," left Khrushchev feeling "sorry for him. That was no way for him to behave in front of the other delegations. The President of the United States lost face." After Geneva, Khrushchev told a Presidium meeting, "I cannot judge how good Eisenhower is as a president. It is for the American people to decide that. But as a father and grandfather I would gladly entrust my kids to him at school or a kindergarten." Dobrynin later wrote that this showed Khrushchev trusted Eisenhower, "as one war veteran would trust another," not to allow a war between the two countries. But the same trust made it safer for Khrushchev to threaten war in a crisis.[100]

The trip to Geneva paid other dividends. Khrushchev himself didn't go shopping, but he sent his chief of security to find out how much Swiss watches cost. He had acquired one in Yuzovka before the revolution and remembered it, according to his son, "with veneration." Since such watches were now inexpensive, he ordered self-winding ones for his family, prompting everyone else in his delegation to do likewise. He also bought a Swiss Army knife, which he used for slicing mushrooms and peeling apples until the day he died.[101]

According to his son-in-law, Khrushchev returned from Geneva looking "satisfied, even joyful." As he put it, he had shown that he could "worthily represent" his country.[102]

IF IT HAD been up to Khrushchev, he would have been on a plane to Washington immediately after Geneva. Khrushchev and Bulganin had actually asked to be invited, Eisenhower told several members of Congress. "They would come fast. They want to be in the public eye." Eisenhower's instinct had been to say, "Good, come on over." But Dulles "thought I had been impulsive enough," so the president had merely assured Bulganin he would study the suggestion.[103]

A postsummit foreign ministers' meeting in October 1955 agreed on nothing, not even banal generalities to be used as a basis for further empty discussion. On his return, Dulles announced that the cold war continued apace. Khrushchev's response registered intense irritation. "We had very little, perhaps just microscopic success as a result of the Geneva meetings," he said on November 24. He claimed to be "ready to wait; as the saying goes, the wind is not blowing in our faces." But a mere two days later he impatiently spoke of letting atomic bombs "act on the nerves of those who would like to unleash war," adding, "We must mobilize everything necessary to force aggressive circles of a number of countries to speak less about war and more about contacts . . . and the elimination of international tensions."[104]

Stymied for the moment in his wooing of Washington, Khrushchev branched out toward Bonn. The Western powers had by now ended their occupation of West Germany and admitted the Federal Republic to

NATO, but Bonn's allies feared Moscow would somehow lure it away from the West. That was why the news that Chancellor Konrad Adenauer was going to Moscow caused a sensation. His talks there in September 1955 produced relatively little (the Soviets agreed to release German war prisoners still held in the USSR; Adenauer acquiesced, but not permanently, in the existence of two Germanys), but Khrushchev was pleased. "We broke through the isolation which had surrounded us, and that was a setback for the Americans."[105]

October found Khrushchev and Bulganin on a lengthy tour of India, Burma, and Afghanistan. Stalin had kept his eye on the Middle East, but his hands off it, for fear that Britain wouldn't stand for Soviet interference. Like the rest of the less developed world, India "didn't especially interest" Stalin, Khrushchev recalled. But with European colonialism collapsing and the United States trying to pick up the pieces, Khrushchev rushed in with flags flying. Molotov characterized this new offensive as "adventurism," Khrushchev later told Egyptian President Nasser. Khrushchev had replied, "Offense is the best form of defense. I said we needed a new, active diplomacy because the impossibility of nuclear war meant that the struggle between us and the capitalists was taking on new forms. I told them, 'I'm not an adventurer, but we must aid national liberation movements. . . .' "[106]

The Khrushchev-Bulganin Asian tour lasted nearly two months, taking the two men thousands of miles by plane, train, and car. Millions turned out to see and hear them. They visited cultural and industrial sites, and Khrushchev rode on an elephant. ("An elephant riding an elephant," Molotov later grumbled.) Bulganin started out as chief spokesman but didn't remain so for long. Khrushchev's constant patter ranged from the political to the technical to the deliberately comic, while Soviet performing artists traveling with the delegation entertained along the way. Khrushchev's speeches, especially one in which he compared British imperialism with Hitler's, annoyed them to no end, but the addresses also turned off local hosts trying to preserve their neutrality. Whether the results of the trip matched its unprecedented scope and duration wasn't clear.[107]

Other new departures from this same period included Moscow's abandoning its long-standing insistence on immediate, unenforced disarmament, announcing a unilateral troop cut of 640,000, and returning air and naval bases on Finland's Porkkala Peninsula even though its fifty-year lease still had forty-two to go.[108] Letters from Bulganin, including one proposing a treaty of friendship and cooperation, elicited an Eisenhower response that amounted to "Don't call me, I'll call you." In March, Bulganin took Bohlen aside in the Kremlin and offered a "heart-to-heart" talk with him or Khrushchev anytime Bohlen wanted one. This was precisely what Bohlen had been angling for, but "unfortunately, Dulles never authorized me to take up the offer." One reason for Dulles's resistance was Khrushchev's secret speech itself. If, as Dulles concluded, America's hard line had forced the Soviets to contemplate reform, now was the time to keep up the pressure. Not the least of that pressure was the first U-2 spy flight that soared over Moscow and Leningrad on July 4, 1956, the very day Khrushchev and his colleagues graced the American Embassy's Independence Day party with their presence.[109]

LACKING AN INVITATION to the United States, Khrushchev opted for a tryout on the road in Britain, to which Eden had invited him and Bulganin the year before.[110] "Not counting Geneva," recalled Khrushchev in his memoirs, "this was my first official trip abroad."[111] Not so, of course, but the slip confirms his sense that the really meaningful part of the world was the West. In civilized, sophisticated Britain, Khrushchev wanted to appear not just the confident leader of a powerful nation but a person of dignity and refinement.

"Father was nervous," Sergei Khrushchev wrote later. "He was particularly worried about making a fool of himself." What if the British tried to embarrass his delegation? What if the Soviet Foreign Ministry botched preparations for the trip? "Worried about making a mistake," Khrushchev dispatched Malenkov to London as a guinea pig and was reassured when he got a respectful reception. If only Khrushchev could arrive on a new four-engine Tu-104. It was "one of the first jet passenger planes in the world," he crowed, "and we wanted our hosts to know about it." Malenkov was allowed to risk his life on the Tu-104, but the plane's designer didn't trust it to carry Khrushchev and Bulganin; instead they sailed to England on an advanced battle cruiser, celebrating Khrushchev's sixty-second birthday en route. Khrushchev did arrange for the new jet to deliver his mail to him in London and was particularly pleased that "the Queen had seen the plane in the air as it flew over her palace on its way to land." When she had the grace to mention seeing it, "we thanked her and agreed that, yes, it was an excellent plane—very modern, undoubtedly the best in the world."[112]

Khrushchev had other worries. To make sure Bulganin didn't misspeak, he scrutinized his speeches, which were typed on small sheets of paper that fitted in the prime minister's jacket pocket. Why was the delegation staying at Claridge's, the poshest hotel in London, rather than a special villa, as was the Soviet custom? Was that some sort of snub? Khrushchev rejected the tailcoat normally worn when one was received by the queen but agreed to have a black suit custom-made at the last minute. When the British Secret Service bugged Khrushchev's room at Claridge's, reported MI5 counterintelligence official Peter Wright, it overheard no national security secrets—just "long monologues addressed to his valet on the subject of his attire. He was an extraordinarily vain man. He stood in front of the mirror preening himself for hours at a time, and fussing with his hair parting."[113]

Khrushchev hardly had any hair. Family members swear he didn't care how he looked. But if there was any place he wanted to shine, it was in the company of the elegant Eden and his associates. Khrushchev repeatedly described himself to his British hosts as "a simple man," but he "explicitly said he was anxious that his hosts should form a good impression of him." He tried hard to restrain himself; disclaiming expert knowledge, he let delegation members speak on their specialties. But whenever basic policy was involved, he shoved aside Bulganin, who formally headed the delegation. After the delegation returned home, Molotov chided Khrushchev for "doing all the answering." Khrushchev later said: "I won't play at false modesty. Bulganin knew his own limits and that he couldn't answer certain questions. He just wasn't up to it." British observers noticed that "Khrushchev often teased Bulganin, but Bulganin never teased Khrushchev."[114]

According to British officials, Khrushchev stated his views "clearly and effectively," knew his subjects and spoke "without notes or briefs," and reduced complex problems to "large simple outlines." Even when he was speaking plainly and bluntly, his "earthy confident sense of humor kept breaking through." According to Soviet diplomat/interpreter Oleg Troyanovsky, "He behaved almost like a gentleman." But not quite. At a monument to Prince Albert, Khrushchev's English guide explained that Victoria's prince consort had performed no state duties and served only as the queen's spouse. "And what did he do during the daytime?" Khrushchev inquired mischievously.[115]

Apropos of spouses, Mrs. Eden may not have divined that the predawn knock on her bedroom door at Chequers (the prime minister's country house) was the Soviet party leader in search of his prime minister ("Bulganin and I had a good laugh over this incident," Khrushchev recalled, "but we decided not to mention it to our hosts"), but she couldn't help remarking that Khrushchev's idea of dinner table repartee was to declare that Soviet missiles "could easily reach your island and quite a bit farther," a comment that he later admitted was "a little bit rude." Queen Elizabeth was spared such braggadocio and made a good impression in return. She was wearing "a plain white dress," Khrushchev remembered. She looked "like the sort of young woman you'd be likely to meet walking along Gorky Street on a balmy Sunday afternoon." She was "completely unpretentious, completely without haughtiness." She might be the queen of England, "but in our eyes she was first and foremost the wife of her husband and mother of her children."[116]

Despite being on his best behavior, Khrushchev let himself be irritated and provoked. After being booed by bystanders, he asked Hayter to explain "the oo oo noise" he had heard. Hayter hesitated but admitted it meant disapproval.[117] After that Khrushchev spent the rest of that day's car trip saying "boo boo" over and over again. A luncheon encounter with Labor party leader Hugh Gaitskell went off all right even though Gaitskell came away thinking Khrushchev looked like "a rather agreeable pig." But a dinner did not when the fiery Laborite George Brown cracked a series of jokes implying that Sergei Khrushchev, who was traveling with his father, dared not disagree with his old man. Perhaps because that challenged Khrushchev's image of himself as a loving father, itself a way of compensating for having been a rebellious son, Khrushchev launched into a lengthy speech delivered, recalled Gaitskell, with "vehemence, even brutality." R. H. S. Crossman added, "I will never forget" Khrushchev's "couldn't-care-less suggestion that we should join with the Russians because, if not, they would swat us off the face of the earth like a dirty old black beetle."

Not just Brown but Bevan too interrupted Khrushchev, at one point demanding to know the fate of fellow socialists whom the Communists had liquidated. "If you want to help the enemies of the working class," Khrushchev shouted, "you must find another agent to do it." When Brown raised his glass in hope they could part as friends, Khrushchev barked, "Not with me," and stomped out of the room. The next day he refused to shake hands with Brown, a step that led Bevan to grumble in a loud voice, "He's impossible. It's time he grew up." It was not translated for Khrushchev as he departed.[118]

This sort of antagonism between rival left-wing parties was hardly unprecedented. But Khrushchev hadn't been subjected to it for quite some time. "I haven't met people like you for thirty years," he had shouted at Brown. If he was offended by Brown's "rudeness," that was partly because it echoed his own. As for Eden, he naturally relished the whole episode. "The thing that men of Mr. Khrushchev's temperament and background cannot endure," he noted shrewdly, "is anything in the nature of intellectual patronage."[119]

Eden found Khrushchev and Bulganin "perfectly capable of upholding their end of the discussion of any subject" and viewed their performance "with respect." In his dealing with Eden himself, Khrushchev was unfailingly polite (even when the two sides clashed on the Middle East, with Khrushchev seeking to poach on Britain's preserve and Eden warning him away), but also revealingly self-deprecating: As the Soviet delegation took their seats at the Downing Street negotiating table, Khrushchev said, "See how well trained we are; we file in like horses into their stalls."[120]

ALTHOUGH THE "B and K" tour (as the British tabloids tagged it) produced few, if any, substantive results, it kept Khrushchev's diplomatic offensive moving forward. But that too was soon to change. In public at least, Khrushchev blamed the West for the Eastern European convulsion. Behind the Polish troubles "stood the United States spurred on by Dulles," he told Mićunović in July 1956. "He alleges," Mićunović noted on October 25, "that the West is seeking a revision of the results of World War II, has started in Hungary, and will then go on to crush each socialist state in Europe one by one."[121]

The Eastern European upheavals did indeed raise hopes in Washington. The Soviet withdrawal from Hungary, announced on October 31, seemed "the dawn of a new day" to Eisenhower. If carried out, it would constitute "the greatest forward stride toward justice, trust and understanding among nations in our generation."[122] U.S. efforts to "liberate" Poland and Hungary included Radio Free Europe broadcasts that seemed to encourage an uprising. But none of them amounted to the all-out subversion that Khrushchev assumed.[123] Not once during the Hungarian crisis did Eisenhower consider direct aid to the rebels, for fear of transforming a regional crisis into a global war. The only way to help the Hungarians, Eisenhower and Dulles concluded, was to assure the nervous Russians that the United States would not get involved.[124]

Blaming the West, rather than Moscow's own errors, had many advantages, among them the satisfaction of foiling "imperialist plans." One result of Hungary, Khrushchev told Mićunović, was to show the West that the Soviets were "strong and resolute," whereas "the West was weak and divided." He continued: "There was now going to be a resumption of the cold war, but that wasn't a bad thing for the Soviet Union," a conclusion strengthened by the results of the Suez crisis, which occurred at the same time.[125]

By the summer of 1956 the Soviets had taken Egypt under their wing. Moscow had provided Cairo with Czech arms, and shortly after Nasser nationalized the canal, Khrushchev told Ambassador Hayter, "A war of Egypt against Britain would be a sacred war, and if my son came to me, and asked me if he ought to volunteer to fight against Britain, I would tell him he most certainly should do so." The Kremlin tried to avert a conflict, but Israel attacked Egypt, with British and French support, on October 29. When Syrian President Shukri al-Kuwatly arrived in Moscow on October 30, begging for Soviet help, Khrushchev replied, "But what can we do?" He turned to Marshal Zhukov, who had spread a map of the Middle East on the table, and asked, "Are we supposed to send our armies through Turkey and Iran, then into Syria and Iraq, and on into Israel so as to eventually attack British and French forces?" Folding up the map, Khrushchev muttered, "We'll see what we can do."[126]

The answer he came up with was atomic blackmail. "What situation would Britain find itself in," asked Bulganin in a November 5 letter to Eden, "if she were attacked by stronger states possessing all kinds of modern destructive weapons?" To Eisenhower, who had disassociated himself from Britain and France and was trying to arrange a cease-fire, Bulganin proposed that the United States and the USSR act jointly to end the fighting. Khrushchev drafted Bulganin's threatening letters and begrudged him the world attention they received. He also dreamed up the idea of joint Soviet-American action (which he later said Molotov opposed) and insisted the idea worked exactly as planned. When the Americans rejected it, they gave the lie to their claim of standing for peace and justice and nonaggression. Exulted Khrushchev: "We had unmasked them!"[127]

He claimed even more for his rocket rattling. The cease-fire agreed to on November 6, he told Mićunović, "was the direct result" of Soviet warnings issued two days earlier. "Father was extraordinarily proud of his victory," Sergei Khrushchev recalled. The lesson he learned and applied in later crises was both that nuclear weapons were all-powerful and that he didn't need many of them.[128]

In fact, it was American rather than Soviet pressure that forced Egypt's attackers to cease and desist. Soviet threats were issued only *after* the outcome was no longer in doubt. But although that was clear to the Egyptians, it wasn't to Khrushchev: "I've been told that when [French

Premier] Guy Mollet received our note, he ran to the telephone in his pajamas and called Eden. I don't know if this story is true, but whether or not he had his trousers on doesn't change the fact that twenty-four hours after the delivery of our note the aggression was halted." As for the Americans, Khrushchev went on, they ended up helping their allies "the way the rope helps the man who is being hanged." Dulles used to boast about his brinksmanship, Khrushchev told Egyptian journalist Mohamed Heikal several years later, but when "we dispatched an ultimatum to London and Paris, Dulles was the one whose nerves broke." Those "with the strongest nerves will be the winner," Khrushchev concluded. "That is the most important consideration in the power struggle of our time. The people with the weak nerves will go to the wall."[129]

CHAPTER FOURTEEN

Alone at the Top: 1957–1960

WHEN MARSHAL GEORGY ZHUKOV flew from Moscow to Sevastopol on October 4, 1957, to board a Soviet cruiser that would take him on an official visit to Yugoslavia and Albania, he had no notion that three weeks later he would be fired and disgraced. On the contrary, he was at the height of his authority, with his tenure as defense minister and Presidium member seemingly assured for as long as Khrushchev remained party leader.

The two men had known each other since the late 1930s, and the war had brought them closer together. Khrushchev was impressed by Zhukov's "mind, military knowledge and strong character" and sympathized with him when Stalin, alarmed by some of the same qualities, demoted the nation's leading war hero and exiled him to Odessa after the war.[1] Khrushchev was instrumental in returning Zhukov to Moscow after Stalin's death and in naming him defense minister in 1955 and a candidate member of the Presidium in 1956. The promotions rewarded Zhukov for his role in arresting Beria. After helping to trounce the "antiparty group" in June 1957, Zhukov also became a full member of the Presidium. On his sixtieth birthday in late 1956 he received medals and tributes usually reserved for the top party leader.[2] In July 1957 he swept into Leningrad like a conquering hero, riding slowly down Nevsky Prospekt in an open ZIS limousine to the cheers of tens of thousands.[3] That summer Zhukov was a frequent guest at the Khrushchev dacha, where the two men took long strolls in the woods and meadows, and in August he was invited to visit Khrushchev in the Crimea.[4]

Khrushchev had good reason to keep the nation's most powerful military man by his side. "You're depriving yourself of your best friend," Zhukov warned when he telephoned Khrushchev in late October to plead for his political life.[5] But instead of cementing his alliance with Zhukov, Khrushchev secretly prepared his demise. One reason he invited Zhukov to the Crimea was to keep an eye on him.[6] As soon as Zhukov sailed for the Balkans, Khrushchev flew to Kiev for what he later called "a political hunting party" with other leading generals, to make certain they would back a move to oust their chief.[7] On October 19 the Presidium passed a resolution condemning Zhukov. Five days later he learned what was afoot in Moscow, called his old friend the KGB chief Ivan Serov, and raced home to try to save his career. But like Khrushchev himself seven years later, he was whisked directly from the airport to a Presidium session that informed him he was through. At a Central Committee plenum two days later, not a single word was said in his defense. The decision to oust Zhukov was "very painful," Khrushchev recalled, "but it had to be done."[8]

The most serious charge against Zhukov was that he was preparing to seize power with the help of a secret commando unit based near Moscow; the Moscow party chief Furtseva later described the unit as a "school of saboteurs." It was to forestall any move by Zhukov's special forces, according to Sergei Khrushchev, that Khrushchev moved so suddenly and so decisively.[9] Zhukov was also said to have undercut party controls over the military by barring political officers from criticizing military commanders and by trying to place Interior Ministry and KGB border troops under his command. A third charge (one that made the others seem more credible) was that Zhukov was fostering his own cult of personality. He allegedly insisted on restaging and reshooting documentary footage of the World War II victory parade because the white horse he had been riding in 1945 had stumbled.[10] Khrushchev told the October plenum that Zhukov had forced naval officers attending a reception to don dark pea jackets so that he, dressed in a white uniform, could stand out "like a white seagull." According to Marshal Rokossovsky at the October 1957 plenum, "It wasn't just that he was rude during the war. His way of commanding was literally obscene; we heard nothing but continuous cursing and swearing mixed with threats to shoot people."[11] Marshal Moskalenko denounced Zhukov's "vanity, egoism, limitless arrogance, and narcissism." Marshal Malinovsky blasted his "stubbornness, despotism, ambition, and search for self-glorification." Marshal Bagramian chimed in: "He's simply a sick man. Self-aggrandizement is in his blood."[12]

With friends and colleagues like these, Zhukov needed no enemies.[13] Many of their accusations were exaggerated; some were probably flat-out untrue. It is impossible in retrospect to establish their credibility, but Khrushchev apparently believed them. When Khrushchev visited East Germany in August 1957, the commander of Soviet troops there, Andrei Grechko, prepared to meet the arriving Soviet delegation. But Zhukov ordered him to remain in the field where military maneuvers were under way, and Grechko complained to Khrushchev.[14] "One may respect me personally or not," Khrushchev told the Central Committee in October, "but when the defense minister says it's not necessary to meet the first secretary, that is undermining ties between army and party, whether the first secretary's name is Khrushchev, Ivanov, or Petrov, whoever he is. That is vileness. Comrades, I'm not defending myself, I'm defending the party."[15]

It wasn't just Shepilov who contended that Zhukov had initially supported Khrushchev's ouster. Bulganin made the same charge, and Saburov did too.[16] At one point during the June 1957 crisis, when Khrushchev's rivals complained he was preparing to use tanks against them, Zhukov reportedly snapped that the tanks would move "only on his order." Khrushchev quoted these words approvingly at the June 1957 plenum, adding that they reflected a "strictly party-line view." But his approval was dropped from the edited plenum transcript, and in October Mikoyan quoted Zhukov's very words against him.[17] If Zhukov's militant anti-Stalinism at the June plenum was intended to win back Khrushchev's trust, it backfired badly. It was one thing to indict the likes of Molotov, Malenkov, and Kaganovich, but another to imply that Khrushchev himself had been Stalin's accomplice and then, as if Zhukov himself were the conscience of the revolution, to forgive him.[18]

That same summer several members of the leadership celebrated Central Committee Secretary Andrei Kirilenko's birthday at his Black Sea dacha. With June's factional fight behind them, and with food and wine in abundance, Aristov got out his harmonica, and out-of-tune singing began. Toasts were plentiful, and although all began in praise of Kirilenko, they ended up hailing Khrushchev, who insisted on orating at great length. Zhukov remembered asking that others be given a chance to speak, prompting Khrushchev to retort: "What are you saying—that I can't say anything if you don't want to listen?" After an obligatory nod to Kirilenko, Zhukov reportedly directed his own toast to Ivan Serov, adding, "Don't forget, Ivan Aleksandrovich, the KGB is the eyes and ears of the army!" Instantly Khrushchev leaped to his feet to contradict Zhukov: "Remember, Comrade Serov, that the KGB is the eyes and ears of the party."[19]

All these transgressions, whether real or imagined by Khrushchev, are sufficient to explain Zhukov's fall. They loomed even larger because the failed putsch of the "anti-party group" had left Khrushchev feeling particularly vulnerable. His main speech to the October 1957 plenum was remarkably defensive—about his secret speech, his promise to overtake American agriculture, his industrial reorganization, his relations with the intelligentsia, his conduct of foreign policy. At that moment the debt that he owed Zhukov for helping thwart the coup was the last thing he needed. Khrushchev's speech also depicted Zhukov as a self-made man with a barely controlled ego.[20] When they first met, their common background made for understanding and friendship. Once Khrushchev began to distrust Zhukov, he needed only look at himself to gauge how far the marshal might go to satisfy his ambition.

THE ROUT OF Molotov, Malenkov, and Kaganovich in June 1957, followed by the sacking of Zhukov four months later, left Khrushchev as the USSR's undisputed leader. The Twenty-first Party Congress in early 1959 celebrated "Nikita Sergeyevich Khrushchev personally," as many of the delegates put it. Theoretically the Presidium was exercising collective leadership, but one couldn't tell that from speeches to the congress. "We all listened with profound excitement to Nikita Sergeyevich Khrushchev's remarkable report," said Yekaterina Furtseva. Aleksei Kirichenko hailed Khrushchev's "outstanding activity, Leninist firmness, devotion to principle, initiative . . . and enormous organizational work." Aleksandr Shelepin lauded his leader's "steadfast staunchness of spirit, personal courage, and firm faith in the strength of the party." These three were particularly loyal retainers (at least for the time being), but more independent-minded party elders, like Suslov and Kosygin, were only slightly less fawning.[21] Thirty-five years later Nikolai Yegorychev, who became Moscow party boss in 1962, explained: "You have to understand that the Presidium hadn't changed much from Stalin's time. Anyone who dared come out against Khrushchev would have to leave the Presidium; everyone understood this perfectly. Could anyone say directly to Khrushchev, 'You're wrong'? No one would have dared."[22]

In other ways too Khrushchev was triumphant. The grain harvest of 1958 was 30 percent higher than 1957 and almost 70 percent above the

1949–1953 average, with much of the success due to Khrushchev's Virgin Lands program.[23] Rapid economic growth convinced not only Khrushchev but many Westerners that the USSR could soon outstrip the United States.[24] *Sputnik*, the world's first artificial earth satellite, was launched in October 1957, with the first rocket to the moon following in 1959. That same year Khrushchev's peace offensive was crowned with a grand tour of the United States, the first ever by a Soviet leader, with a long-sought four-power summit scheduled for May 1960.

In these and other ways the years between 1957 and 1960 were Khrushchev's best yet. At the same time he began to change for the worse. Witnesses differ on when it happened, but not on what occurred. Those who eventually turned against him had self-serving reasons for alleging Khrushchev's metamorphosis: It explains how they could loyally follow the "the good Khrushchev" during the early fifties and then betray "the bad Khrushchev" in 1964. But others, including family members who are his most ardent defenders, confirm the pattern.

According to Presidium colleague Gennady Voronov, who was so close to Khrushchev that the 1964 plotters waited until the last minute to inform him of the planned coup, "Khrushchev in 1956 and Khrushchev in 1964 were very different people; in some ways they didn't resemble each other at all. His innately democratic approach, which couldn't but win you over when you first met him, gradually gave way to estrangement, to an attempt to close himself off in a narrow inner circle of people, some of whom indulged him in his worst tendencies."[25]

"After pushing aside the 'antiparty group,'" former Agriculture Minister Benediktov recalled, Khrushchev "literally began to change before our very eyes. His democratic approach began to give way to an authoritarian manner . . . ." The defeat of his rivals "gave him freedom of action," said Aleksandr Shelepin. He "began to display arrogance, to insist on the infallibility of his own judgments, and to exaggerate successes which had been achieved." According to Mikoyan, "After 1957," Khrushchev "got conceited," as if feeling that "he didn't have to reckon with anyone, that everyone would just agree with him."[26]

Georgy Kornienko was in the Soviet Embassy in Washington in 1959. From observing Khrushchev there, and from Moscow contacts, including Foreign Minister Gromyko (whose deputy he later became), Kornienko got the impression that the Khrushchev era "divides neatly into two periods, before and after 1958." After 1958 Khrushchev stopped listening and surrounded himself with "yes-men."[27] Oleg Troyanovsky, who served as Khrushchev's English interpreter beginning in 1954 and became his foreign policy assistant in 1958, dates "the start of the transformation" to 1957, when the last visible opposition to Khrushchev disappeared.[28] Rada Adzhubei recalled how her father's judgments about literature and art got ever more "peremptory. It was as if whatever he pronounced was the truth, although he didn't have the right to such judgments because he didn't understand what was at issue." In addition, Khrushchev's "attitudes toward people got harsher," not so much within the family but reflected even there. "At an earlier stage, he would hear you out even if you were telling him something that included criticism. But at a certain stage, he said, 'That's enough! Don't tell me that sort of thing. I'm sick and tired of it. I don't want to hear it.' He wanted to distance himself from anything unpleasant. When did these changes occur? Toward the end of the 1950s, I think."[29]

Alone at the top, Khrushchev was too dominant for his own good. Yet at the same time, paradoxically, he seemed defenseless against his own weaknesses and against entrenched bureaucratic resistance. No longer constrained by powerful critics like Molotov, he was free to pronounce on subjects of which he knew nothing, to consult or not as he pleased, to establish high policy on impulse, and to act out the self-condemnation that giving in to such temptations provoked. As paramount leader he sat astride mammoth bureaucracies whose tentacles reached into all corners of Soviet society. But these had parochial interests of their own, and his personal staff was remarkably small. In contrast with Stalin's personal secretariat, through which the *vozhd* manipulated the secret police as well as the party and state, Khrushchev's consisted of four assistants (Troyanovsky for foreign policy, Shevchenko for agriculture, Vladimir Lebedev on culture and ideology, and Grigory Shuisky in charge of general affairs), plus a handful of clerks and stenographers. In addition, a "Press Group," consisting of Adzhubei, *Pravda* editor Pavel Satiukov, TASS general director Dmitri Goriunov, Central Committee official Leonid Ilychev, and Foreign Ministry press aide Mikhail Kharlamov, shaped Khrushchev's speeches, not so much writing them as editing what he dictated and then scrambling to render presentable the words he actually spoke when he invariably strayed from his text. Although Khrushchev's staff became an informal center of power, often jousting with other agencies, it could hardly control the vast party-state system.[30] Party and government functionaries didn't dare criticize Khrushchev publicly, but in a sense they didn't have to. No longer terrorized by Stalinist purges, they distorted information on which he depended, delayed implementing his decisions (or ignored them altogether), or carried them out so zealously as unintentionally to turn them into parodies of what he intended. The party apparat in particular, having backed Khrushchev in June 1957, now expected his support and was determined to get it.

During the fall of 1958, when a group of high party officials visited the Khrushchev dacha near Moscow, the Presidium member Nikolai Ignatov, who had helped rout the "antiparty group," fell into conversation with Sergei Khrushchev. Ignatov talked about "how they wouldn't let Father be insulted." Sergei was "amazed by the patronizing tone about Father."[31]

Earlier that summer Yugoslav Ambassador Mićunović detected "spontaneous signs of displeasure and hostility" toward Khrushchev. Mićunović's sources said there was "no organized opposition, but there were spontaneous outbursts of discontent" because of his "continual surprises" and "changes of line." After decades in which Stalin spoke hardly at all, Khrushchev talked so much that "people found it impossible to follow him even if they wanted to."[32]

In early 1958, when Nikolai Bulganin stepped down as prime minister, the next to last (except for Voroshilov) "antiparty" plotter to lose his formal position, Khrushchev himself replaced him. In 1964, when his colleagues condemned this as self-aggrandizement, Khrushchev insisted they had made him take both jobs. But he admitted in his memoirs to having "criticized Stalin for allowing a single person to have [both] posts" and in that sense conceded that "my acceptance of [the premiership] represented a certain weakness on my part—a bug of some sort which was gnawing away at me and undermining my powers of resistance."[33]

Not bad as self-knowledge goes, but too little and too late.

AFTER THWARTING the coup against him, Khrushchev moved to settle accounts with his rivals. Their ouster from top party and government posts wasn't surprising. Their exile to minor jobs in the provinces compared favorably with the fate of Stalin's victims. But the personal wounds they had inflicted demanded special vengeance. Malenkov was convinced that Khrushchev hated him.[34] According to Shepilov, Khrushchev proved himself a "spiteful, unforgiving man."[35] Even if Khrushchev did not want to plague them, his underlings assumed that he did. But since far less important matters routinely reached the leader's desk, it is virtually certain that Khrushchev himself micromanaged his challengers' humiliation.

Molotov, of all people, got off easiest, perhaps because despite everything, Khrushchev still respected him. Like the other losers, Molotov feared arrest. Instead he was hastily forced out of his Moscow residence and dacha and exiled to Outer Mongolia as Soviet ambassador, forced to abandon, he later complained, a large library of books that were subsequently ruined by a flood in the Foreign Ministry basement.[36] With little else to do in Ulan Bator, Molotov peppered the Central Committee in Moscow with criticism of Khrushchev. He twice telephoned Suslov to gripe that Khrushchev was ruining relations with China, and in May 1959 he proposed founding a new "Confederation of Socialist States" to save the day.[37] In a letter to the Party Control Commission, he challenged Khrushchev's remark to U.S. Vice President Nixon that Molotov had opposed signing the Austrian State Treaty in 1955: "I protest N. S. Khrushchev's attempt to depict me, a Communist, as a virtual advocate of war against the 'West,' and I must declare that his statement constitutes slander similar to the sorts of poisonous attacks which the Mensheviks directed against the Bolsheviks."[38] Early in 1960 Molotov sent an article commemorating Lenin's ninetieth birthday (April 22) to several Soviet newspapers. It wasn't published, of course, and only one editor bothered to reply, but by recalling his personal conversations with Lenin (whom Khrushchev had never met), Molotov underlined his claim to represent the true faith.[39]

As a political offensive, Molotov's missives were pretty puny, but Khrushchev was stung. The Party Control Commission compiled a long report refuting Molotov's Austrian account.[40] The Soviet delegation to a Mongolian party congress treated Molotov with breathtaking contempt: He was allowed neither to greet the delegation when it arrived, nor to attend its meetings with the Mongolian government; he was banned from attending the congress (where the delegation chief, Nikolai Ignatov, lambasted him), and he was denied a seat at a gala reception (he had to remain standing the whole time). "There were similar scenes every day," recalled Yugoslav Ambassador Mićunović, who attended the congress. Mićunović was certainly no fan of Molotov's, but "there are many other ways this situation could have been handled," he wrote in his diary, "any of which would have been better in my opinion for the Soviet Union and Khrushchev than the one they used."[41]

Mićunović called on Molotov and found him depressed at being surrounded by nomads and yaks. "Even the foreign minister is a veterinarian here," Molotov grumbled. Although Molotov was almost entirely isolated from the world, Ignatov was concerned enough to eavesdrop on his encounter with Mićunović from a nearby room and then crudely comment, when he next saw the Yugoslav, that his conversation with Molotov had been "strained," not natural and spontaneous like Mićunović's talks with Khrushchev.[42]

In 1960 Molotov was transferred to Vienna as the Soviet representative to the International Atomic Energy Agency, apparently to get him away from the Chinese, who felt an increasing kinship with his anti-Khrushchev stance. On the eve of the Twenty-second Party Congress in October 1961, Molotov dispatched a detailed critique of the new party program on which Khrushchev prided himself. After that, he and other "antiparty" veterans were subjected to fierce new attacks and expelled from the party.[43]

Malenkov was sent to northern Kazakhstan in 1957 to direct a hydroelectric station near Ust-Kamenogorsk. He and his family were given ten days to evacuate their Lenin Hills villa and suburban dacha, with their former servants and bodyguards turned overseers specifically barred from lending a hand; like Molotov, Malenkov claimed he had to abandon a large library. He and his wife were removed from the train twenty-five miles west of Ust-Kamenogorsk (lest he receive a warm greeting there) and driven directly to the tiny settlement of Albaketka, where they lived in a small dark house until the summer of 1958. At that point, as a reward for being elected a delegate to a provincial party conference, Khrushchev dumped him even deeper into exile in the town of Ekibastuz, where police observed his every move, shadowed his children when they came to visit, and even stole his party card and then accused him of losing it so as to threaten him with expulsion from the party. At one point Malenkov was called back to Moscow to face Party Control Commission charges concerning his role in Stalin's terror. Several times during his interrogation he was convinced he heard Khrushchev angrily denouncing him in a nearby room.[44]

Two days after the June 1957 plenum, Kaganovich phoned Khrushchev to plead for his life: "I have known you for many years. I beg you not to allow them to deal with me as they dealt with people under Stalin." Khrushchev is alleged to have taunted his former mentor, saying, "We'll think about it."[45] Kaganovich was dispatched to manage the Urals potash works in Solikamsk in Perm Province. Before being expelled from the party in 1962, he was returned to Moscow and retired on an ordinary pension.

Shepilov was sent to Central Asia, where he directed the Kirghizia Institute of Economics. When he was named a delegate to the Kirghiz Republic party conference in 1959, Khrushchev aide Leonid Ilychev rushed to Frunze to chastize local authorities for "ingratiating themselves with Shepilov" and to demote him. Shepilov's wife had remained in their Moscow apartment, where they had lived since the thirties. When Shepilov learned the apartment was being emptied in 1959, he left a hospital where he was awaiting surgery and rushed to Moscow. There he found his several thousand books (Stalin had ordered that virtually all books published in the USSR be provided to his Politburo colleagues, apparently in the hope that they would help monitor their ideological orthodoxy) strewn on the landing and stairs outside his door. "I don't know anything," said Mikoyan when Shepilov appealed to him for help. "You didn't call me," he added. Shepilov thought of hanging himself with the cords used for book packing. His wife appealed to Nina Petrovna Khrushcheva. With or without her assistance, they were allowed to stay in Moscow in a two-room apartment that opened onto a dark courtyard where a large exhaust pipe from a food-processing plant ended just outside their window. Shepilov was expelled from the USSR Academy of Sciences in 1959 (thereby losing still more perquisites and privileges) and from the party in 1962.[46]

The increasingly feeble Voroshilov remained titular head of state until 1960 and a member of the Supreme Soviet's Presidium after that. Mikhail Pervukhin headed the State Committee on Foreign Economic Relations until 1958, when he was shipped to East Germany as Soviet ambassador; his deputy until 1958, Maksim Saburov, was assigned to direct a heavy machine-building plant near Kuibyshev. As for Bulganin, who was demoted to the State Bank and later to the Stavropol Economic Council, he was "a fool," Khrushchev later said. "He always was and always will be," and "the post of prime minister of the Soviet Union wasn't intended for an idiot."[47]

One other key participant in the June 1957 struggle was eased out of office in late 1958. Ivan Serov, whom Sergo Mikoyan remembered as "short, balding, always joking," seemingly "a nice man," had a particularly sordid past: He had helped organize the Katyn Forest massacre of Polish officers, had helped Stalinize Ukraine and the Baltics, had deported the Crimean Tatars and other "lesser" peoples, had pacified Soviet-occupied East Germany, and had been Beria's MVD first deputy in Stalin's last years. Just because he had so much blood on his hands, he had served Khrushchev faithfully as KGB chief. When Mikoyan urged dropping Serov, Khrushchev at first defended him ("He wasn't zealous; he acted moderately"), but then agreed to replace him with Aleksandr Shelepin. "It was as if," Adzhubei remarked, "he was burning his bridges to those on whom he had depended. He wanted to be his own man and he was driving away everyone he'd had to rely on when he was clearing his path to power."[48]

ONCE KHRUSHCHEV became his own man, agriculture became perhaps his top priority. At times he sounded like a born-again free-marketeer. "Excuse me for talking to you sharply," he told a gathering of state farm workers, "but if a capitalist farmer used eight kilos of grain to produce one kilo of meat, he'd have to go around without pants. But around here a state farm director who behaves like that—his pants are just fine. Why? Because he doesn't have to answer for his own mess; no one even holds it against him."[49] Still, the same Khrushchev was convinced that capitalism as a whole was calamitous: "After all, a man makes a fortune there by ruining another." Under capitalism big farmers regarded manpower "as a source of profit. If a worker loses his health, if he can't produce maximum profit, the capitalist throws him out. It is different in our country."[50]

Khrushchev had defended collective farmers' individual plots and their right to own livestock in September 1953: "Only people who do not understand the policy of the party see any danger to the socialist system in the presence of individually owned productive livestock . . . ." Yet he himself saw just such a danger. In nearly the next sentence he insisted that "communal animal husbandry is the main way" and that "communal output" would soon reach such heights that collective farmers would no longer want or need their own animals.[51]

The alternative to material incentives was mobilization and exhortation. Khrushchev's joy was all the greater when his native village led the way. Kalinovka "chose" to build a communal cowshed and turn over half the cows in town to the collective farm. Of course, he added, "anyone who doesn't want to sell his cattle doesn't have to do so." But, not surprisingly, shortly after he left town, "all the collective farms decided to sell all their cows to the kolkhoz, and they did just that, after a period of careful preparation, of course."[52] Just in case other farms didn't get the message, a series of laws and decrees tightened limitations on the very individual peasant plots that he had once seemed to encourage.[53]

Attracted by the forbidden fruit of market-style motivation, as well as by miraculous quick fixes of technology and organization, Khrushchev was fascinated by the country that led the world in both. Back in the 1940s he had pressed for adoption of the American square cluster method of planting corn and potatoes—that is, along wires or ropes with knots tied in them at regular intervals where machines were to drop seeds into the furrows. The virtue of this method was that it allowed mechanized weeding. The scheme turned out to be too complicated,[54] but Khrushchev kept pursuing American know-how. At the height of the cold war, when not many Americans dared to provide it, his main American supplier turned out to be the shrewd, earthy Iowa farmer Roswell Garst, who was as interested in easing East-West war tensions as in selling hybrid corn seed.

After a February 1955 Khrushchev speech calling for an Iowa-style corn belt in Russia, the *Des Moines Register* invited him to "get the lowdown on raising high quality cattle, hogs, sheep and chickens." A Russian delegation, headed by Deputy Minister of Agriculture Vladimir Matskevich, visited Iowa that summer. Garst caught up with the group in Jefferson and spirited Matskevich away to his twenty-six-hundred-acre farm in Coon Rapids. The deputy minister spent the day inspecting Garst's hybrid seed corn plant, learning about drought-resistant hybrids and grain sorghums, and hearing about what the American called ways to "jack up" production.[55] Matskevich credited some U.S. successes to Americans' native enterprise and favorable climate and to their good luck in avoiding war and serfdom. But others reflected institutions and practices the Soviet Union could borrow, such as large-scale, specialized farms and agricultural extension services around the country. Matskevich kept a diary and reported personally to Khrushchev: "That which the Americans have taken decades to achieve we can manage to do in just a few years."[56]

Garst was perfectly suited to be Khrushchev's guru. Both men loved to gab, sprinkling their conversation with jokes and proverbs. Khrushchev relished Garst's cantankerousness, especially when it justified his own, such as when the American bawled out Soviet farmers for sowing corn without simultaneously fertilizing the soil. When Garst traveled to the USSR in the fall of 1955, Khrushchev received him at his dacha near Yalta. The nearly twenty-four hours Garst spent there revealed Khrushchev at his relaxed, unaffected best. Garst asked how the Russians could know so little about American agriculture when they had managed to steal the atomic bomb in three weeks. "It took us only two weeks," Khrushchev corrected him. "You locked up the atomic bomb, so we had to steal it. When you offered us information about agriculture for nothing, we thought that might be what it was worth." A magnificent three-hour dinner would have been even more lubricated by fine Georgian wine if Nina Khrushcheva hadn't unobtrusively limited her husband's consumption. The focus of the talks, during which Khrushchev was joined by Mikoyan, Matskevich and others, was corn. In the end, the Soviets ordered five thousand tons of American hybrid seeds.[57]

Aware of the difficulties of growing corn in the USSR, Garst pulled out a map showing the most promising areas in the southern part of the country. In a pamphlet the Russians translated and distributed widely, he stressed other necessary preconditions—hybrid seed, fertilization, irrigation, mechanization—plus use of insecticides and herbicides. The Soviet Union lacked many of these, but once Khrushchev opted for corn, there was no stopping him.

"Corn has been raised in Kursk Province gardens since ancient times," Khrushchev reported in his memoirs. "My grandmother fed me stewed corn, which was considered a delicacy." Although corn was grown in Ukraine, Khrushchev had realized its full potential ("as a basic silage crop which had no equal when it came to fodder units") when he returned to Moscow in 1949.[58] Typically, his conversion came when he tried out an American variety at his dacha and then ordered more planted at a collective farm next door. The kolkhoz chairman "demonstrated how tall the corn was by riding through the field on horseback—you couldn't even see the top of his head until he came to the road." Even before Garst arrived, Khrushchev was a "champion of corn." Before long, his crusade turned into an irrational obsession.

Khrushchev and his defenders contend he wasn't responsible for the overplanting of corn. Under the Soviet system, he said in his memoirs, "people overreact in implementing the recommendation of the man who holds a high post; and a new measure which starts out as an improvement goes too far." Officials who wanted to play up to him "acted like a bunch of toadies. They insisted on planting corn on a large scale without properly preparing the peasants first." As a result, "corn was discredited as a silage crop—and so was I as the one who had advocated the introduction of corn in the first place."[59]

Khrushchev did indeed caution against corn mania. He ridiculed zealots who "would have us plant corn over the whole planet." He insisted that party officials "look before you leap."[60] He warned on another occasion: "Forcible methods will get us nowhere. We've got to organize people, select suitable soil, prepare the right seeds, do the sowing on time, and then carefully oversee the growing."[61] He even laughed at his own weakness for corn. During a speech in Smolensk Province, he lugged a nine-foot-tall cornstalk from Moscow up to the lectern to illustrate his remarks.[62] At a Latvian kolkhoz, he guessed some in the hall were "probably sitting there thinking, 'Will Khrushchev say something about corn or won't he?' I must admit, I was asking myself the same thing: should I or shouldn't I?" Of course he did, rebuking his audience for not planting more corn.[63]

It wasn't local zealots but Khrushchev himself who insisted, "We must raise corn in Yakutia [in Siberia] and perhaps in Chukotka [near the Bering Strait]. Do potatoes grow there? They do. So I think corn will too."[64] If corn wasn't producing sufficient yields, "there is but one cause—a lack of concern for its cultivation." Had the Central Committee made a mistake in recommending corn be grown throughout the entire Soviet Union? "No, comrades, it was not a mistake." The facts proved convincingly, Khrushchev added, "that corn can produce high yields in all areas of our country, that corn is unequaled by any other crop."[65]

He hailed corn as "the queen of the fields."[66] He proclaimed that "corn and only corn" would enable him to keep his promises.[67] "What will it take to overtake the United States meat and dairy production? It will take learning to raise corn for silage everywhere—that's the task we must set for the Soviet Union."[68] The fact that he had to keep repeating himself indicated he was encountering resistance. "I want to say some unpleasant things," he told a gathering of Moscow Province farmers in January 1958. "The truth is I've been telling you all about it for eight years, but not much has come of it. What I have in mind, comrades, is corn."[69]

Khrushchev once brought five sacks of corn seed to Warsaw. "For the sake of peace and quiet," Staszewski recalled, the Poles designated 1 million acres for corn in the plan but actually cultivated only 150,000. Staszewski was reminded of a Stalin-era incident that Khrushchev once recounted to him. Moscow's chief agronomist dared say that Khrushchev knew nothing about agriculture. "Can you believe it?" Khrushchev asked Staszewski. "*I* didn't understand anything about agriculture? He actually claimed I didn't understand it! He actually said that. Well, of course I could have done anything I wanted with him, I could have destroyed him, I could have arranged it so that, you know, he would disappear from the face of the earth. But I didn't. Instead I said to him: get out, out of Moscow, and don't ever let me see your face around here again. That was all, and he went off to Siberia."[70]

Thanks largely to Khrushchev, disappearances from the face of the earth were no longer an option in the late 1950s. Instead Khrushchev chastised cadres that couldn't or wouldn't perform. The issue, he insisted, was "people, it's who happens to be the kolkhoz chairman, and who heads its various brigades and work teams."[71] When "people come to know their own strength, they create miracles."[72] They were not like bureaucrats, who "sit around their offices and juggle with figures" instead of dealing "with people face to face."[73] Scientists with fancy pedigrees were even worse. "Only a bad manager tries to do business without science, without knowledge, relying only on what his grandfather told him," Khrushchev admitted.[74] But woe to district party officials who didn't know how much time it took a chicken to hatch an egg, who reminded Khrushchev of the "pointy-headed intellectual who turns up his nose at veal, saying, 'Foo, it smells like cow,' without realizing where calves come from," whereas "we working people, we who rose from the ranks of workers, collective farms and labor intelligentsia, we can never think that rural work is dirty work."[75]

The very model of the modern district official fitted Khrushchev's idealized image of himself. "I didn't get to know agriculture right away," he told an April 1957 gathering of district party functionaries. "I rode around to collective and state farms, I listened to people, I acquainted myself with the best examples and informed others about them, and I read up on the specialized literature. That's how my knowledge accumulated and multiplied."[76] When rural party officials failed to deliver, Khrushchev shouted, "Give me the most difficult district, the one where you tried but couldn't resolve the problem. Give that one to me. I hereby declare, with all honest people as my witness, that we will send out cadres, I myself will go out there (if the Central Committee sends me); I'll pledge in writing right here at this meeting that we'll not only fulfill, but overfulfill, the plans . . . ."[77]

The notion that people with the "right stuff" could accomplish miracles was a trap. They got the credit when things went well. But when failures occurred, as they were bound to in a system with insolvency built into it, the same people took the blame, and so did their Kremlin patron. Take, for example, Khrushchev's abolition of the so-called machine tractor station (MTS for short) and the sale of its equipment to collective farms in 1958. As the name implies, the MTSs were rural agencies that supplied collective farms with agricultural machinery and people to run it. They were set up in the late 1920s and early 1930s, when the kolkhozy were too weak and disorganized to manage their own equipment. Ideologically, collective farms were a "lesser" form of property (since theoretically they belonged to the collective rather than the state as a whole); hence it would not do to have them own part of the "means of production." Politically, the new collective farms, into which so many peasants were dragooned, were unreliable. So the MTS also served as a party (and police) stronghold in the countryside. Over the years, at least some of the collective farms had strengthened themselves sufficiently to take control of their own machinery. But far from all were ready for the reform Khrushchev now forced on them.

He used the Russian proverb "With seven nannies, the child loses an eye" to justify the change. But with him in charge it took only one nanny. He gave collective farms more responsibilities, but not the resources to carry them out. When he first suggested abolishing the MTS, he recalled, Molotov, who was still in the leadership, "blew his stack at the idea. He ranted and raved about how we were resorting to 'anti-Marxist measures' and 'destroying our socialist achievements.' What nonsense! Hadn't we had enough stupid slogans about agriculture? I don't think you can find a single person with common sense about agriculture and economics who would consider our decision incorrect."[78]

At the time Khrushchev took Molotov's opposition into account. Even with Molotov in Mongolian exile in late 1957, Khrushchev asked defensively whether "it wasn't time to think of transferring *some* MTS machinery to the collective farms [emphasis added]." When he raised the matter for formal discussion, he urged implementation over two to three years or even longer, adding, "In this matter, one mustn't hurry."[79] But by the end of 1958 more than 80 percent of all farms had bought former MTS machinery.[80]

The consequences were devastating. After paying for their new machinery, even better-off farms couldn't afford other needed investments. Meanwhile, they made less efficient use of their new equipment than the MTS had. MTS workers had been a kind of elite. Since those who transferred to the kolkhozy suffered a drop in status and income, many fled to the cities. The result, according to Roy Medvedev, was that "farm production suffered irreparable damage."[81]

Of course local officials, trying to please their master, overdid this reform too. But when reports from the field claimed the change was proceeding smoothly, Khrushchev's underlings were telling him what he wanted to hear. In that sense, lower-level officials knew him better than he knew himself. One of them was Aleksei Larionov, Ryazan party boss, whose madcap efforts to exceed Khrushchev's unreal expectations ended in tragedy for himself while staining Khrushchev's reputation.

Larionov's story (let's title it "Dead Cows" on the model of Gogol's "Dead Souls") begins in late 1958, when overall Soviet grain production rose substantially, but meat output by only 5 percent.[82] Larionov couldn't resist promising to triple Ryazan meat production in 1959. Khrushchev's aide, Andrei Shevchenko, remembered warning his boss that the pledge was "impossible," to which Khrushchev reacted by slamming down the phone and looking sulky and angry the next time they met.[83] Newspaper editors also resisted publishing Larionov's pledge, but Khrushchev insisted, he recalled a year later: "The Ryazan people have made promises, and they will fulfill them. I know Comrade Larionov as a serious, thoughtful man. He would never take the step of making an unrealistic pledge, of showing off, and then spitting up . . . . He would not do that."[84] But he did.

Pravda hailed Larionov's promise on January 7, 1959. Khrushchev did so at the Twenty-first Party Congress later that month and then headed out to Ryazan, southeast of Moscow, to award the province the Order of Lenin. "I like people with gusto who know how to show their worth," he told his audience.[85] That October, in a speech omitted from a compilation of his orations published four years later, Khrushchev congratulated the province and goaded it to do even more. At the rate things were going, "it won't take long to catch up with America in meat production, and, as they say, 'Grab God by the beard.' [Stir in the hall, applause]"[86] A month later: "One can, of course, run away from one's promises, just as the gypsies used to do. But the people of Ryazan do not intend to run away. They have made a pledge and they are keeping it. This is wonderful, comrades! [Stormy applause]."[87]

Khrushchev made Larionov a Hero of Socialist Labor in December 1959. At the same Central Committee plenum, Larionov hailed Khrushchev for introducing corn, with its "incalculable benefits," to the country. Khrushchev chided the Ukrainian party chief Podgorny for letting Larionov "get the jump on you," and the Byelorussian leader Mazurov for letting Ryazan "show you the beetle's mother" (i.e., what the score actually was).[88] Meanwhile, back on Ryazan collective and state farms, virtually all cattle, including dairy cows and breeding animals, were being slaughtered, while cows and pigs on individual plots were being commandeered for public herds. When even these extraordinary measures didn't suffice, Ryazan "procurement agents" fanned out to other provinces, buying up cattle as far away as the Urals. Since those provinces too had meat targets to fulfill, they set up police roadblocks, which Ryazan operatives circumvented by smuggling cattle by night along little-used roads. The desperate Larionov levied taxes payable in meat, not just on farms and farmers but on schools and other institutions. In response, people bought meat at state stores and delivered it to collection stations, which in turn sold it back to the state.

In the end, Ryazan Province delivered 30,000 tons of meat to the state, a mere one-sixth of the 180,000 it had promised. Larionov's cover-up lasted until a special Central Committee investigative team arrived and confirmed the awful truth. At that point Larionov shot himself to death in his party committee office.[89]

"HOW CAN WE not rejoice, comrades," Khrushchev asked in 1958, "at the gigantic achievements of our industry? . . . What other state has ever built on such a scale? There never has been such a country. Only for our country and its remarkable people—a people of fighters, a people of pioneers—are such things possible. [Stormy applause]."[90] Exactly how rapidly the Soviet economy grew in these years isn't entirely clear, but it was fast enough to elate Khrushchev.[91] Even more satisfying was the great breakthrough in science and technology represented by the successful launching of the first *Sputnik* on October 4, 1957. Khrushchev was in Kiev, meeting with civilian and military officials in the Marinsky Palace, when the news arrived. His face was "shining," according to his son, as he reported it to the gathering. "The Americans have proclaimed to the whole world that they are preparing to launch a satellite of the earth. Theirs is only the size of an orange. We, on the other hand, have kept quiet, but now have a satellite circling the planet. And not a little one, but one that weighs eighty kilos."[92] In January 1958 he chortled that the USSR had "outstripped the leading capitalist country—the United States—in the field of scientific and technical progress." He added in April, "It is the United States which is now intent on catching up with the Soviet Union. . . ."[93]

Sputnik stunned the world and particularly the Americans. But Khrushchev's euphoria was more fragile than it seemed. When the United States managed to launch a satellite only a thirtieth of *Sputnik*'s weight, Yugoslav Ambassador Mićunović found Khrushchev "moody and depressed," whereas he "simply beamed" after further Soviet launchings which, his son recalled, were like "balm" for his soul."[94] In August 1957 Khrushchev had announced the USSR had intercontinental rockets capable of reaching "any part of the globe." Some Americans hadn't believed him, he told *New York Times* correspondent James Reston in October, but "now only technologically ignorant people can doubt this."[95]

Of course Khrushchev was bluffing. The Semyorka rocket that lifted Sputnik into orbit wasn't an operational weapon. To supply it with all too flammable fuel, a factory would have to be built at every launch site. To guide the Semyorka to its destination, radio guidance points would have to be placed "every 500 kilometers [300 miles] along the way." Morever, each launch site cost half a billion rubles, far more than Khrushchev was prepared to pay. As he later admitted, the new weapon "represented only a symbolic counterthreat to the United States." It wasn't until the 1960s that the first Soviet ICBMs, a grand total of four them, actually became operational.[96]

Even empty nuclear threats could pay big dividends, Khrushchev thought. But his own military wasn't convinced—not just because they knew Khrushchev was bluffing, but also because he cited mostly imaginary missiles as a justification for cutting back conventional weapons of all sorts.[97]

Planned long-range bombers were among the first to go, with aircraft factories converted to making missiles or passenger planes. Work slowed on fighter planes too. Military air bases, such as Sheremetyevo outside Moscow and Brovari near Kiev, became civilian airfields. Artillery also took a hit, as did the navy, which Khrushchev described to Vice President Nixon as "fodder for sharks."[98] Not submarines, of course, especially those to be equipped with nuclear missiles, but surface ships were vulnerable to American attack. "The Americans had a mighty carrier fleet," Khrushchev recalled in his memoirs, and he "felt a nagging desire to have some in our own navy, but we couldn't afford to build them." Troop transports weren't necessary for a peace-loving socialist country (or so Khrushchev said) and would soon be "replaced by air transports anyway."

Several Soviet battle cruisers had just been built at great cost. Khrushchev thought of mothballing them, but that would have been too expensive. After "long and painful deliberation" about converting cruisers to fishing vessels, passenger ships, or floating hotels, Khrushchev "gave up and accepted the fact that we had no choice but to destroy those 'boxes,' as we were now calling them." Later he agreed to start selling off destroyers and coast guard cutters. As a concession to the navy he finished building four cruisers, even though they were "good solely as showpieces, and very expensive showpieces at that." His naval commanders "thought they looked beautiful and liked to show them off to foreigners. An officer likes to hear all the young sailors greet his command with a loud cheer."[99]

Between 1955 and 1957 the USSR unilaterally reduced Soviet troop strength by more than 2 million men. In January 1958 another 300,000 were cut, and in January 1960 Khrushchev announced a further reduction of 1.2 million troops, including 250,000 officers.[100] What particularly galled the military was that, with no preparations made for housing and employing thousands of former officers, many were in effect dumped in the street. Before long grumbling could be heard in almost all branches of the armed services. In the spring of 1960 a naval captain visiting the young diplomat Arkady Shevchenko described how fellow officers "had wept as they watched nearly completed cruisers and destroyers at the docks in Leningrad being cut up for scrap on Khrushchev's orders."[101] According to Sergei Khrushchev, his father was accused of "ignorance, of short-sightedness, of wreaking criminal havoc in the army and of disarming it in the face of the enemy." Sergei characterized the opposition as "muffled" but said his father "knew about these moods but held firmly to his course. His view was that if you gave the military free rein they would ruin the whole country and then declare, 'You've still given us too few resources.'"[102]

By about 1958, according to Sergei Khrushchev, his father had decided "he knew more than the top military commanders who would be using the new technology if and when war broke out."[103] With issues large and small passed to the top for decision, it was no wonder Khrushchev's head swelled. One didn't have to be a rocket scientist (although many of his most determined lobbyists actually were) to see that flattering him paid. Still, on some occasions Khrushchev deserved to be praised. As in the United States, first-generation Soviet missiles were to be launched from aboveground sites, leaving them vulnerable to enemy preemptive strikes. Khrushchev came up with the idea of placing them in protective underground silos. He was vacationing in the Crimea in the summer of 1958; nearby was the Nizhnaya Oreanda resort sanatorium where top officials—ministers, party leaders, and scientists, including the father of the Semyorka rocket, Sergei Korolyov—were staying. Searching for companionship and conversation, Khrushchev often visited the sanatorium. As soon as he walked in, all the guests would gather around. It was here that he informed Korolyov of his brainstorm. The designer objected that silo-based rockets would burn up in the white hot gases emitted by their own engines, but Khrushchev countered that if a missile were placed in a steel cylinder, the gases could dissipate in the space between the cylinder and the wall of the shaft.

Recounting this episode in his memoirs, Khrushchev made much of yielding to the experts: "I realized I had no right to force the idea down their throats. I assumed these people knew their own professions, so I let the matter drop."[104] But when Korolyov turned down his idea, Khrushchev looked for others who wouldn't. He invited Vladimir Barmin, who designed the launching pads for Korolyov's rockets, and Mikhail Yangel, an archrival of Korolyov's, to his spacious white stone residence by the sea, but they weren't impressed either. Sergei Khrushchev, who was present, felt sorry for his father. But sometime later he came across a reference in an American technical journal to a new method for protecting missiles: in cylinders located in underground silos. When Khrushchev saw the drawing that accompanied the article, he "rejoiced like a child," and his errant scientists soon got a lecture on the need to keep up with technical journals. When the first Soviet missile was actually launched from a silo in September 1959, Khrushchev took the success as a "personal triumph."[105]

Meanwhile, in September 1958, Khrushchev decided to acquaint his top military men, along with party and government officials with military-related responsibilities, with the wonders of modern weaponry. The gathering took place at Kapustin Yar, the country's main missile test site, sixty miles southeast of Stalingrad. As a series of rockets was launched, with the results announced over a loudspeaker, Khrushchev "was smiling broadly. He was simply in raptures over what he had seen."[106]

After the show the most important guests (including the Presidium members Kirichenko and Brezhnev, Defense Minister Malinovsky, and Marshal Sokolovsky) gathered in a specially equipped railroad car near the test site where Khrushchev delivered an impromptu sermon. "Father had already decided," remarked Sergei, who was seated at the edge of the group. "He had no doubt that the next war, if and when it came, would be a missile war." Animatedly and at length, barely pausing to breathe or to sip tea from his cup, he insisted on discarding out-of-date weapons and centering the armed forces on missiles. As he spoke, his listeners "were guardedly, stubbornly silent. All you could hear was the sound of their spoons as they stirred their cups. . . . The more Father talked on, the more fixedly Malinovsky stared at the table, breathing loudly through his nose. When Father's long drawn-out monologue came to an end, no one objected but no one supported him either. Sensing the painful silence that had descended over the table, Father added, 'Of course, all this must be calculated and thought through, with decisions made only afterwards.' "[107] But formal approval of his ideas quickly followed.[108]

THROUGHOUT HIS CAREER Khrushchev cultivated both the respect of the intelligentsia and the image of a man of the people. After consolidating his power in 1957, he reached out to both constituencies, seeking their favor but not necessarily obtaining it.

Stalin's legacy included a dreadful housing crisis. There was massive overcrowding, armies of young workers living in dormitories, multiple families crowded into communal apartments with each occupying one room and all sharing a single kitchen and bathroom. The shortage dated back to before 1917 but was compounded by the forced draft industrialization and urbanization of the 1930s, the destruction of the war, and Stalin's insistence on hoarding resources to strengthen the state. Under Khrushchev, the annual rate of housing construction nearly doubled. Between 1956 and 1965 about 108 million people moved into new apartments. In his haste to provide Soviet citizens with what had so long been denied them, Khrushchev encouraged rapid, assembly-line construction of standardized five-story apartment houses built out of prefabricated materials. Many of the new complexes welcomed occupants before they were actually completed and were still unsafe. Millions were grateful, but it was not long before the buildings became known as *krushchoby*, a word combining Khrushchev's name and *trushchoba*, the Russian word for "slum." In Khrushchev's eyes, the new houses were a stopgap quick fix (not unlike his Virgin Lands campaign), to be replaced in twenty years or so by new and better buildings. Nine-story houses began to go up in the early 1960s, but the *khrushchoby* were still around, crumbling but still inhabited, when the USSR collapsed in 1991, and many still serve into the twenty-first century.[109]

Like housing, Soviet education badly needed reform. The Bolsheviks had initially tried to combine academic and vocational training, but under Stalin, schools had turned into training grounds for the new Soviet elite—to the point that fees were charged for the last years of secondary schooling. Khrushchev not only abolished the fees but in 1958 proposed adding a year to the ten-year program, to be partly devoted to learning a manual trade at a local factory or farm, while at the same time favoring admission of working-class children to universities. "The fact that young people are being cut off from life," he told the Presidium in a November 1958 memorandum, "the fact that they are being brought up not to respect physical labor, is shameful and we can no longer tolerate it." Not surprisingly, such sentiments met widespread resistance from factory directors loath to take on restless teenagers in addition to their other burdens, intelligentsia families fearful that the reform would limit their children's prospects, and educational administrators opposed to diluting academic standards. As a result, Khrushchev's proposals were never fully implemented and were reversed after his ouster.[110]

The post-Stalin cultural thaw was gathering momentum. During the

World Youth Festival in Moscow in 1957, thousands of young people from around the world flooded the city, singing and dancing late into the night to the beat of African drums, Scottish bagpipes, and jazz bands, cheering open-air poetry readings, and carousing along gaily decorated streets on which masses of young Muscovites turned out to meet the foreign guests. Previous Communist youth festivals (in Bucharest in 1953 and Warsaw in 1955) had been rigidly controlled propaganda affairs. Khrushchev hoped the 1957 jamboree would impress the world with Moscow's new openness. It did, but the Soviet young people who turned out were even more impressed with Western popular culture.[111]

Jazz and rock and roll, formerly suspect or even banned, were beginning to be heard over the Voice of America, then recorded and played back, or performed by fledgling amateurs, in Soviet apartments. "See ya later, alligator," Soviet kids began saying to each other (courtesy of Bill Haley and the Comets), some of them turning into *stilyagi,* who wore tight suits and short skirts, and later, *shtatniki,* zoot-suited "Americans" who favored big bands, and *bitniki* in jeans and sweaters, who preferred rock music. Meanwhile, another new genre, "composer's songs," many of them apolitical ballads about personal loneliness sung by bards such as Bulat Okudzhava, spread on tape from hand to hand.[112]

New journals, such as *Yunost* (Youth), *Molodaia gvardiia* (Young Guard), and *Nash sovremennik* (Our Contemporary), appeared or were reestablished. Popular literature like detective, adventure, and science fiction stories took on new life. Films by new filmmakers treated old themes, such as the civil war (*The Forty-first* by Grigory Chukrai) and World War II (*The Cranes Are Flying* by Mikhail Kalatozov and *Ballad of a Soldier* by Chukrai), in new ways, or took up new themes like private, domestic life (Lev Kulidzhanov's *The House I Live In*). Resistance to such innovations was inevitably mounted by conservative cultural watchdogs, but the battle in which Khrushchev got most directly involved concerned literature.

Literature had long been the conscience of the Russian nation, a kind of "second government" (the phrase is Solzhenitsyn's). The Communists demanded that art glorify positive heroes of the revolution. For a leader who sought to renovate the Soviet system, reform-minded writers and artists were a natural constituency. But liberal intellectuals wanted to move farther and faster than Khrushchev did, while conservatives exploited his old-fashioned taste to turn him against the liberals. Balancing both sides in Soviet culture wars would have been difficult even for a more sophisticated leader, but for Khrushchev, it proved impossible. He had little or no time to continue his self-education by attending the theater or reading books. The best he could do was ask family members to read aloud to him on weekends. "Let my eyes rest and yours do the work," he would say. He had no knowledge of disputed literary works until cultural "advisers" with axes to grind brought them to his attention, nor would he have necessarily understood them had he been able to read them himself.[113]

After Khrushchev slammed liberal writers at the infamous Semyonovskoye picnic in the spring of 1957, published extracts from his remarks tied him even more closely to conservatives.[114] Then in July Khrushchev had two private meetings with Aleksandr Tvardovsky, the liberal poet and editor whose peasant background resembled his own. Back in 1954 Khrushchev had acquiesced in Tvardovsky's being dismissed as editor of the journal *Novyi mir* (New World). Now he struck Tvardovsky as patient, tolerant, and balanced. Khrushchev listened politely as the editor outlined "the needs and troubles of literature" and condemned its "bureaucratization." He invited Tvardovsky back for another conversation, on July 31, that lasted two and half hours. Tvardovsky defended Margarita Aliger and Vladimir Dudintsev, whom Khrushchev had berated in May, and urged patience in dealing with literary matters. "That's interesting," Khrushchev kept saying, "everything you're saying is interesting and must be studied."[115] He even agreed to receive Aliger and Dudintsev, but Writers' Union conservatives prevented the meeting. His discussion with Tvardovsky touched on *War and Peace* and Sholokhov's *Virgin Soil Upturned,* with Khrushchev eager to show he had read them. Malenkov seemed cultured, he informed Tvardovsky, but he was actually a "worm." Khrushchev began to recount how Stalin liquidated his own relatives but stopped; that "would be too much for the ears of a poet."

As Tvardovsky departed, a Central Committee cultural watchdog cooed, "Don't you realize that they're more interested in you here than in any other writer in the country, that they say you're our number one poet?" Tvardovsky thought Khrushchev's face "wasn't as fat or stupid-looking as it seemed in photos, but was more that of an old man, dried out, but enlivened by interior understanding, thoughtfulness and cunning. This was the first time it struck me that he was old, yet in [literary] matters as naive as a child." Khrushchev had told him, "Better a work that's bad, as long as it's ours," than "a work of talent that isn't ours."[116]

Although conservatives still controlled the Writers' Union and most of the literary journals, Tvardovsky was reappointed editor of *Novyi mir* later that spring. Moderation and restraint seemed Khrushchev's new hallmark, yet he allowed it to be marred by the Pasternak affair in October 1958. The great poet Boris Pasternak transgressed ideological limits not with political broadsides, but with mostly apolitical poetry and prose.[117] His novel *Doctor Zhivago* didn't so much attack the revolution as affirm other values personified in the novel's nonheroic hero, Yuri Zhivago. Assuming his novel would be published first in the USSR, Pasternak gave it to the Italian Communist publisher Giangiacomo Feltrinelli. But when *Novyi mir*, still edited by Konstantin Simonov, refused to publish it, Feltrinelli went ahead with the translation over Pasternak's pro forma protests. Compounding the felony, Pasternak was awarded the Nobel Prize for Literature on October 23, 1958.

A fierce campaign against Pasternak quickly followed. A *Literaturnaya gazeta* editorial labeled him a "Judas." *Pravda* called the novel "low-grade reactionary hackwork." The Writers' Union expelled him, and a meeting of Moscow writers demanded "the traitor Boris Pasternak" be deprived of his citizenship. In the meantime, the head of the Komsomol, Vladimir Semichastny, addressing an audience of fourteen thousand including Khrushchev, compared Pasternak unfavorably with a pig that "never makes a mess where it eats and sleeps," adding that "this internal emigrant" should "become a real emigrant and go to his capitalist paradise."[118]

In despair, Pasternak at first proposed double suicide to his longtime mistress, Olga Ivinskaya, but then appealed to Khrushchev. Having previously declined the Nobel Prize, he now begged to be allowed to remain in his homeland. Soon after that the campaign died down. Khrushchev later admitted he had never read the offending novel; rather, recalled his son, he had received "several typewritten pages of quotations plucked out of *Doctor Zhivago* to prove its anti-Soviet character." It was on this basis, said Sergei, that his father sanctioned the anti-Pasternak campaign, but it was also Khrushchev who said, "Enough. He's admitted his mistakes. Stop it."[119] Khrushchev insisted in his memoirs that he agonized over *Doctor Zhivago*, came close to authorizing its publication, and later regretted not doing so.[120] But according to Semichastny, it was Khrushchev who ordered him to "work over" Pasternak, dictated the reference to pig shit, and said the Soviet government wouldn't stand in Pasternak's way if he "so wanted to breathe the air of freedom that he would abandon his motherland." When Khrushchev dictated this last phrase, recollected Semichastny, "I said, 'Nikita Sergeyevich, I can't say that in the name of the government.'" Khrushchev allegedly replied, "'You say it and we'll applaud. Everyone will understand.' And that's exactly what happened."[121]

Once the Pasternak affair was over, Khrushchev tried to reestablish the liberal-conservative balance. He fired the ultraorthodox editor of *Literaturnaya gazeta,* Vsevolod Kochetov, who had penned the first anti-Pasternak editorial and addressed the Third Writers' Congress in May 1959. But once again his own ignorance and insecurity confounded his plans. He asked the Central Committee official Igor Chernoutsan and the moderate writer Boris Polevoi to prepare a draft speech, supervised by his reform-minded personal aide Vladimir Lebedev. But when he reached the lectern, Khrushchev abandoned his text, saying that his "lads" had written a pretty good speech, but that after thinking about it all night, he had decided to speak not from a text but "for himself." What followed, Chernoutsan remembered, was "something unimaginable," a wild, disconnected lurching from topic to topic instead of an address.

Khrushchev began with Pantelei Makhinia, his poet friend from Yuzovka days, reading lines (about the need "to fight the world of darkness 'til the grave") that he had critiqued to its author nearly fifty years before. Next he told of setting free a petty criminal from whom he had received a poignant letter. (Several days after being released, reported Chernoutsan, the man committed a murder.) Khrushchev praised writers as soldiers, exhorting them to attack the "submachine gunners" who challenged party positions. Then he compared errant, unorthodox intellectuals to "criminals" whom Feliks Dzerzhinsky, founder of the Soviet secret police, had managed to "reform." Before that less than reassuring analogy could sink in, Khrushchev launched another one: "I am recognized as a champion of corn raising. I want to give you an example of how corn is grown in normal, and in hot-house, conditions, and to cite a certain analogy with the education of young writers [Animation in the hall. Applause]."[122]

Khrushchev reminded the critic Sara Babyonysheva, who was present in the hall, of a "village idiot," the sort of eccentric [*chudak*] who appears in the short stories of the "village prose" writer Vasily Shukshin, the kind of "phenomenal autodidact who has learned a little about a lot and insists on impressing the world with his knowledge."[123] During a break in the action the writer Vladimir Tendryakov rushed up to his friend Chernoutsan and whispered, "Listen, the guy's simply a dolt, that's all there is to it." Chernoutsan replied, "You're wrong, Volodya. He's a man of talent and energy, but improvised speeches aren't his best genre, and he doesn't do well with them."[124]

Khrushchev seemed painfully aware of the impression he was making and half apologized for it. "Unfortunately, I've read few books . . . not because I have no urge, no wish to read. I probably read as much as you do, but what I read is ambassadors' communications and foreign ministers' notes." Unfortunately, some books "put you to sleep. You want to finish the book because some comrades who have read the book have talked about it and you want to form your own opinion. But it is hard reading and so your eyes close." He asked the audience to forgive him for "oversimplifying" and for the "crude comparisons" in his remarks. "If I have said something in the wrong way, forgive me. I confess that I was very agitated and worried. At first, I thought of speaking from a prepared text. But you know how I am—I don't like to read, I like to talk." And "when you are going to speak without a text, you don't sleep well. You wake up and begin to think how best to formulate this or that point, and you begin to argue with yourself. Speaking without a text is a very tall order for a speaker." So "if you noticed slips, do not judge me too harshly."[125]

The spectacle of the party leader begging forgiveness from the very writers he had chastised so harshly is almost poignant. (Of course, before Khrushchev could leave the rostrum, his longtime friend/sycophant Korneichuk jumped up and shouted that the speaker had "illuminated the path ahead" and "opened new vistas" for Soviet literature.) But if improvised speeches were so difficult, why did Khrushchev insist on giving them, especially to sophisticated audiences that were likely to be particularly critical? He apparently hoped to impress them with his homespun, down-to-earth delivery. Yet extemporizing may also have attracted him just *because* it was so difficult, because it provided an excuse for the poor impression he would leave no matter what he did.

Whatever his motivation, both warring camps exploited his insecurity. Conservatives played on his hostility to modernist works that he couldn't understand. Liberals massaged the anti-Stalinist side of his ego. What they had to do, Tvardovsky joked to his colleagues in early 1960, was "to use one cult [Khrushchev's] to fight another [Stalin's]."[126] A good case in point was an anti-Stalinist chapter ("The Way It Was") from Tvardovsky's long poem *Distance beyond Distance.* After the censor vetoed it, Tvardovsky took his case to Khrushchev. Lebedev recommended presenting his boss with the chapter on Khrushchev's birthday, April 17, 1960. "Let me put it to you this way," Lebedev told Tvardovsky. "He's a person. He'll be immensely pleased (forgive me if I seem to flatter you) to receive a gift from the great poet of our time."

And so he was, especially when Tvardovsky expressed "respect and appreciation" and best wishes for "dear Nikita Sergeyevich's good health, and many more years of an active life devoted to the well-being and happiness of your own people and of all working people of the whole world."[127] Lebedev approved this language, arranged for the chapter to be delivered to Khrushchev, who was resting in the south after a strenuous trip to France, and late that same night called Tvardovsky with the good news: "He read it with pleasure. He liked it, he liked it; he liked it a lot, and he thanks you for thinking of him. Of course, I never doubted this would happen, but it gives me joy to live through this with you."[128]

The chapter Khrushchev approved appeared, in *Pravda* no less, on April 29 and May 1. The poem as a whole was brought out in record time three months later.[129] But the battle wasn't over, neither between the two cultural camps nor between the two sides of Khrushchev's conflicted nature.

KHRUSHCHEV'S ISOLATION at the top was also visible in his dealings with Communist allies/adversaries. By October 1958, when departing Yugoslav Ambassador Mićunović paid a farewell visit to Pitsunda, a new Soviet-Yugoslav quarrel had broken out. Tito refused to attend the November 1957 meeting of Communist party leaders, and Belgrade restated its heretical principles in a new party program in March 1958. Khrushchev boycotted the Yugoslav party congress called to ratify the new program, authorized a lengthy refutation of it in the Soviet press, and unilaterally suspended a major line of credit to Yugoslavia. Then, having compared Belgrade's betrayal with "the treachery" of Imre Nagy, Khrushchev approved the execution of Nagy, who had been held in prison since November 1956, on June 17, 1958.

Yet as he and Mićunović talked in Pitsunda, on a veranda overlooking the sea and in the water itself, where the corpulent Khrushchev bobbed up and down in a cork life belt, the Soviet leader seemed much better disposed toward Belgrade. Out of the Kremlin cauldron, alone with his guest except during a family lunch, Khrushchev seemed systematically misinformed about Yugoslavia's transgressions, either by anti-Tito underlings or by those telling him what they assumed he wanted to hear. Three times he cited cases of Yugoslav maltreatment of Soviet citizens; three times Mićunović refuted the charges. Retreating, Khrushchev said that the three cases were "not so important in themselves; what was more important was the 'bad blood' which was being introduced into our relations day after day." When Mićunović rebutted other anti-Yugoslav reports in the Soviet press, Khrushchev sighed: "You think it's all being done on Khrushchev's instructions, but I don't know anything about it. There are many things I hear about only after they've happened."

Before flying out the next morning, Mićunović spent the night at a nearby villa (Beria's former residence). There he encountered seven or eight top Soviet officials, waiting to see Khrushchev, who had been cooling their heels all day. Only one of them, Central Committee Secretary Leonid Ilychev, deigned to speak to him, muttering that Mićunović had "ruined their working day." The contrast between their behavior and Khrushchev's could not have been clearer. Obviously, Mićunović concluded, Khrushchev's bureaucracy was systematically misinforming him. But what made the mix so explosive was Khrushchev's doubts about his own pro-Yugoslav policy. The Stalinism Khrushchev was appeasing didn't just surround him; it was in his own head.[130]

As late as the fall of 1957 prospects for Sino-Soviet relations seemed promising: Mao backed Moscow's bloc leadership at the November meeting of Communist leaders in Moscow, and Khrushchev agreed to provide Beijing with a sample nuclear weapon and to help the Chinese develop missiles as well.[131] But the situation changed in the summer of 1958.[132] By then Mao had dropped his Let a Hundred Flowers Bloom campaign and launched the Great Leap Forward instead. Eventually the Great Leap triggered the worst famine in Chinese history. In the meantime it challenged the Soviet claim to be leading the way to communism.

Just when Mao wanted to increase Chinese "self-reliance," Khrushchev proposed a new form of military dependence. The Soviet Navy was planning to station new submarines in the Pacific Ocean. But maintaining reliable communication with them from Soviet territory would be difficult and prohibitively expensive. Longwave radio stations on the Chinese coast, which Moscow suggested building, could serve not only Soviet subs but a joint Soviet-Chinese submarine fleet that Moscow also proposed. "We fully expected the Chinese to cooperate with us when we asked for a radio station on their territory," Khrushchev recalled.[133] Instead, when Soviet Ambassador Pavel Yudin met with Mao on July 22, 1958, the Chinese leader condemned not only these two proposals but Soviet chauvinism in general and Khrushchev in particular.

Mao apparently saw the longwave radio stations as a way to obtain Soviet military bases in China and the joint fleet as a substitute for helping Beijing build its own. If Moscow wanted "joint ownership and operation," he told Ambassador Yudin sarcastically, then let there be joint ownership of "our army, navy, air force, industry, agriculture, culture, education." The USSR could have "all of China's more than ten thousand kilometers of coastline," while Beijing maintained "only a guerrilla force." The Soviet proposals showed that "some Russians look down upon the Chinese people." For too long there had been no "brotherly relations" between the Soviet and Chinese parties, just relations between "father and son or between cats and mice." Khrushchev's latest proposals reminded Mao of "Stalin's positions." Khrushchev had "criticized Stalin's [policy], but now adopts the same policies Stalin did."[134]

Yudin talked with Mao for two days. At the end of the first session on July 21, Mao shouted, "Go home, you can't explain things clearly. Go back and tell Khrushchev to come here. Let him tell me directly exactly what he wants."[135] Yudin sent a coded message to Moscow. "Out of the blue," according to Khrushchev, Yudin described "all sorts of incredible things he had heard from Mao Tse-tung."[136] When Yudin repeated his arguments to Mao the next day, the Chinese leader snapped, "You've still missed the point. I asked you what exactly do you want. You are not good enough. Tell Khrushchev to come here. You tell him I have invited him to come here immediately. I want to talk to him."[137]

Khrushchev dropped everything and rushed to Beijing. He thought the Chinese had misunderstood Yudin, that all it would take to clear the air would be to explain the situation himself.[138] Instead he found himself the target of new round of Maoist condescension and humiliation. His reception at the airport was cool. The top Chinese leaders (Liu Shaoqi, Zhou Enlai, and Deng Xiaoping as well as Mao) were there, but according to a Chinese witness, there was "no red carpet, no honor guards, no hugs."[139] The first day's talk, at a villa in the Chinese leadership compound, Zhongnanhai, began calmly.[140] Mao declared that Sino-Soviet cooperation was assured for ten thousand years. In that case, Khrushchev replied, "we can meet again in 9,999 years to agree on cooperation for another 10,000 years." The two leaders confessed that neither had been able to sleep as the result of the seeming disagreement over the joint submarine fleet. Khrushchev explained the Soviet proposal at great length, emphasizing the purity of Moscow's intentions. Mao smoked throughout, despite Khrushchev's aversion to cigarettes, and mocked his guest for rambling on in disorganized fashion. "You've talked a long time but have still not gotten to the point," said Mao, waving his hand dismissively.

Shocked and embarrassed, Khrushchev is said to have mumbled, "Yes, don't worry, I will continue." But when he insisted "a common fleet" was necessary to contend with America's Seventh Fleet, Mao "banged his large hands against the sofa, and stood up angrily. His face turned red and his breath turned heavy. He used his finger to point impolitely at Khrushchev's nose: 'I asked you what a common fleet is. You still didn't answer me.'"

By this time Khrushchev's lips were pursed and white with strain, while his small, intense eyes flared with anger. He swallowed hard and spread out his arms. "I don't understand why you are acting like this," he said. "We came here just to discuss things together." Mao retorted: "What does it mean to 'discuss things together'? Do we still have our sovereignty or don't we?"[141]

Struggling to stay calm, shrugging his shoulders and blinking his eyes, Khrushchev asked for permission to refuel Soviet submarines at Chinese ports while offering China access to Soviet Arctic ports. "We aren't interested," replied Mao, looking at Khrushchev as if (recollected a Chinese witness) the Soviet leader "were a kid trying to do a trick in front of an adult." When Khrushchev's face turned red with anger, Mao seemed positively pleased. "We don't want to use your Murmansk, and we don't want you to come to our country either." Then followed a further lesson, as if to a particularly dense student: "The British, Japanese, and other foreigners who stayed in our country for a long time have already been driven away by us, Comrade Khrushchev. I'll repeat it again. We do not want anyone to use our land to achieve their own purposes anymore."[142]

The next day was more relaxed. How could it not be? Mao said the clouds had lifted, but this time he put his guest on the defensive in more subtle fashion. Khrushchev found Mao waiting for him at his residence in a bathrobe and slippers. With no advance warning he invited Khrushchev to swim in an outdoor pool. Khrushchev at first spluttered about in the shallow area, then relied on a life ring tossed to him by Chinese aides. Mao watched Khrushchev's clumsy efforts with obvious relish and then dived into the deep end and swam back and forth, using several different strokes. For his next trick, Mao floated and treaded water while interpreters scrambled around the edge of the pool, trying to keep pace with the leaders' conversation.[143] According to Mao's physician, Dr. Li, "the chairman was deliberately playing the role of emperor, treating Khrushchev like a barbarian come to pay tribute. It was a way, Mao told me on the way back to Beidaihe, of 'sticking a needle up his ass.'"[144]

Khrushchev claimed in his memoirs that he wasn't upset: "Of course, I couldn't compete with Mao in the pool. . . . I'm ready to take my hat off to Mao when it comes to swimming."[145] But in 1962 he revealed to an audience of artists and writers how he really felt: "He's a prizewinning swimmer, and I'm a miner. Between us, I basically flop around when I swim; I'm not very good at it. But he swims around, showing off, all the while expounding his political views. The interpreter is translating, and I can't answer as I should. It was Mao's way of putting himself in an advantageous position. Well, I got sick of it. All the while I was swimming, I was thinking the hell with you. So I crawled out, sat on the edge, and dangled my legs in the pool. Now I was on top and he was swimming below. . . . But all the time he keeps talking to me about their communes."[146]

The Soviet delegation went home thinking the worst was over. Instead Mao began bombarding the offshore islands of Jinmen and Mazu on August 23 without giving Moscow advance warning.[147] The bombardment triggered an international crisis. The Americans mounted a massive show of force in the Taiwan Strait, including more than two hundred planes capable of delivering nuclear weapons. If a Sino-American war had broken out, the Soviet Union could probably have been drawn in. However, Moscow had no choice but to declare its resolute support for Beijing, which the Americans took as confirmation that Khrushchev was behind whatever Mao was up to.[148]

On September 4, Secretary of State Dulles threatened war to defend the offshore islands. The next day Soviet Foreign Minister Gromyko scurried to Beijing. According to Gromyko, Mao boasted that if the United States bombed China with nuclear weapons, Chinese forces would retreat deep into the interior, luring American troops after them. Once the Americans were in the heartland, Mao said, the Soviets should hit them "with everything you've got." Gromyko remembered he was "flabbergasted" by the suggestion and politely turned it down.[149]

One reason Mao provoked the crisis was to derail Khrushchev's pursuit of détente with Washington. According to Dr. Li, he wanted "to demonstrate to both Khrushchev and Eisenhower that he could not be controlled, and to undermine Khrushchev in his quest for peace." Or as Mao himself put it to his physician, "the islands are two batons that keep Eisenhower and Khrushchev dancing, scurrying this way and that. Don't you see how wonderful they are?"[150]

After the Taiwan Strait crisis died down (as it began to do as early as September 6, when Zhou Enlai called for Sino-American talks in Warsaw to be resumed), Sino-Soviet relations stabilized for several months. But by the summer of 1959 a much larger explosion was building.[151] Just before a crucial July 1959 meeting of Chinese leaders to reassess the Great Leap, Khrushchev openly criticized the new Chinese communes. Soon Mao attacked Peng Dehuai, who had close ties to Moscow, as a traitor allied with Khrushchev. When Chinese and Indian troops clashed on the border between the two countries, Moscow adopted a neutral stance. On August 20, 1959, the Soviets informed Beijing that they would not provide the Chinese with an atomic bomb prototype after all.[152]

In late September, immediately upon his return from a tumultuous two-week trip to the United States, Khrushchev flew to Beijing for the tenth anniversary of the Chinese Revolution. According to Ambassador-designate to China Stepan Chervonenko, who was part of a large Soviet delegation, Khrushchev seemed optimistic. But his late arrival on the second day of anniversary celebrations didn't bode well, and his reception at the airport was worse than in 1958: no honor guard, no Chinese speeches, not even a microphone for the speech Khrushchev insisted on giving, complete with accolades for Eisenhower that were sure to rile Mao.[153]

The talks that followed made Khrushchev's 1958 visit seem warm and fuzzy by comparison.[154] The United States was China's mortal enemy. But according to the Chinese interpreter Li Yueren, Khrushchev described his American visit "with shining eyes and with a tone and expression that implied he had discovered a new continent: 'This time I traveled to America and saw it in person. They are really rich. Rich indeed.'" Khrushchev asked the Chinese to consider releasing five American pilots who had parachuted into northern China during the Korean War and were now languishing in Chinese prisons. Obviously irritated, Mao refused to do so.

Khrushchev chided the Chinese for "offending" Nehru (the land at issue between Beijing and New Delhi was "just a frozen waste where nobody lives," he said), for babying the Dalai Lama (who would be "better off if he were in his grave"),[155] and for not consulting Moscow before shelling the offshore islands ("We don't know what your policy will be from one day to the next"). Marshal Chen Yi's response ("Do you mean to accuse us on behalf of Chiang Kaishek and the American imperialists?") provoked Khrushchev to a fury. His face turning bright red, he shouted at Chen, "You may be a marshal in the army, and I a lieutenant general. But I am the first secretary of the CPSU, and you are offending me."

"You are the general secretary, all right," Chen shot back. "But when you are right I listen to you, and when you are wrong I will certainly refute you."

Khrushchev complained that he and his delegation were outnumbered: "There are three of us here and nine of you, and you all keep repeating the same thing."

Mao smiled, according to his interpreter, and began speaking slowly and in a low voice: "I have listened to you for a long time. You have accused us of quite a lot. You say we . . . did not unite with Nehru, that we shouldn't have shelled Jinmen, that the Great Leap was wrong, that we brag about ourselves as orthodox Marxists. Therefore I have an accusation for you, too: that you are guilty of 'time-serving.' "

Later, when Chen Yi repeated that charge, Khrushchev blew up. "If you consider us time-servers," he shouted at Chen, "then don't give me your hand, and I won't take it."

"I'm not afraid of your anger," answered Chen.

"Don't you dare spit on us from your marshal's height," Khrushchev retorted. "You don't have enough spit."

Outside the formal talks (if that is the term for the Sino-Soviet slugfest) things went no better. Trying to restore a friendly atmosphere, Khrushchev talked too long at a banquet for five thousand guests in the Great Hall of the People. After he had counseled the Chinese not to test the firmness of "the American imperialists," Mao declined to speak and assigned Zhou Enlai to give the Chinese response.[156] Alone with Soviet colleagues in what he must have known was a bugged reception room, Khrushchev ridiculed his Chinese hosts, rhyming their names with Russian obscenities, referring to Mao as "old galoshes," a term that is colloquial for condoms in Chinese as well as in Russian.[157]

The visit was supposed to last seven days. It collapsed after three. "What happened?" the former Soviet Central Committee official Lev Deliusin remembered Khrushchev's exclaiming. "I can't figure it out."[158] His aides didn't say so, according to Chervonenko, but they mostly blamed him. Those aides themselves were guilty of not alerting him to Mao's sensitivities, but Deliusin insisted the worst of the dispute could have been prevented if Khrushchev had shown more "patience and understanding." Not surprisingly, Mao's former aides agreed. Khrushchev was "smart and quick," said interpreter Li Yueren, but "not in the same class as Mao." "Mao saw himself as a bullfighter," added Yan Mingfu, and "Khrushchev as the bull."[159]

The bull looked "terribly depressed" when he departed for home, leaving most of the Soviet delegation to follow later. Instead of flying directly to Moscow, Khrushchev stopped in the Soviet Far East for rest and recreation on a two-day cruise. As he boarded a Soviet destroyer in Vladivostok Harbor, the ship's chief political officer was shocked at the sight. Khrushchev wasn't "the same man we were used to seeing on television, not physically or emotionally. We were used to seeing a vibrant, energetic man with a sense of humor. When he arrived on board he was dispirited, indifferent, glum." His mood wasn't improved by a dreary hunting excursion on a nearby island on which tame deer politely emerged from the woods and waited to be shot. "That's not hunting, that's murder," Khrushchev growled, before quickly calling it off. Nor would it have cheered him to know how many officers on board hated him for the meat cleaver cuts he was taking out of the navy budget. For much of the time he remained out of sight in his cabin.[160]

Just back from talks with American and Chinese leaders that were to shape the world for years to come, surrounded by obsequious flunkies, yet alone with thoughts that left him deeply despondent: That too was what supreme power meant to Khrushchev.

CHAPTER FIFTEEN

The Berlin Crisis and the American Trip: 1958–1959

BIG, LAVISH "FRIENDSHIP MEETINGS" were frequent during Khrushchev's time. When visiting Communist dignitaries came to town, thousands of Soviet "toilers" were herded into large Moscow halls to welcome them to socialism's homeland. On November 10, 1958, Khrushchev welcomed Władysław Gomułka and other Polish Communist leaders at the Sports Palace. Two months before, the East German government had demanded that the Western powers sign a peace treaty recognizing East Germany and thus ratifying the division of Europe. West Germany had counterproposed that the two Germanys be reunified through free elections. Since neither proposal was novel, and since Moscow and Washington backed their respective German allies, nothing new was expected from Khrushchev on November 10. Instead he dropped this bombshell: "The time has obviously arrived for the signatories of the Potsdam Agreement to . . . create a normal situation in the capital of the German Democratic Republic. The Soviet Union, for its part, would hand over to the sovereign German Democratic Republic the functions in Berlin that are still exercised by Soviet agencies. . . . Let the United States, France and Britain themselves . . . reach agreement with [the GDR] if they are interested in any questions concerning Berlin. As for the Soviet Union, we shall sacredly honor our obligations as an ally of the German Democratic Republic. . . . "[1]

Translation into plain language: If the West didn't recognize East Germany, Moscow would give Walter Ulbricht control over access to Berlin, thus abrogating Western rights established in the postwar Potsdam accords. If the Western powers tried forcibly to prevent East Germany from carrying out its new duties, Moscow would fight to defend its ally.

Khrushchev's remarks prompted urgent consultations in Western capitals. U.S. Ambassador to the USSR Llewellyn Thompson, who knew Khrushchev better than most, concluded he was trying to force a summit meeting to obtain Western recognition of East Germany and a ban on nuclear arms for West Germany. But Thompson and his fellow Western envoys were "baffled" by how Khrushchev expected to pull this off and speculated that "he may have so misjudged [the] Western reaction that he thinks he can get away with it." Back in Washington, President Eisenhower covered his edginess with bravado. His instinct, he told Acting Secretary of State Christian Herter, was "to make a very simple statement to the effect that if the Russians want war over the Berlin issue, they can have it." For the time being, however, his administration kept its mouth shut so as to avoid seeming nervous.[2]

Khrushchev dropped a second bombshell on November 27 at his first-ever formal press conference. At four o'clock that afternoon he entered the oval mahogany-paneled chamber of the Council of Ministers in the Kremlin. Since it was Thanksgiving Day, American correspondents, who were summoned at the last minute, left their turkey dinners on the table. "We have made many moves to ease tensions," declared Khrushchev, looking sunburned and sounding "emotional and emphatic." But the Western powers wanted to "perpetuate the tension not to eliminate it." West Berlin had become "a sort of malignant tumor." Therefore, the Soviet Union had "decided to do some surgery," as explained in a twenty-eight-page diplomatic note handed to Western ambassadors that morning. The note included an ultimatum: Either the Western powers signed a German peace treaty and agreed to turn West Berlin into a demilitarized "free city" within six months, or the Soviets would turn control of access over to East Germany.[3]

Eisenhower got this news in Augusta, Georgia, where he was spending Thanksgiving with his family. If West Berlin were surrendered under Soviet pressure, he told his son, "then no one in the world could have any confidence in any pledge we make." If efforts to defend West Berlin led to war, "we are not going to be betting white chips, building up gradually. Khrushchev should know that when we decide to act, our whole stack will be in the pot." Yet several days later he unhappily described the need to defend Berlin, located deep inside East Germany, as an "instance in which our political posture requires us to assume military positions that are wholly illogical" and the American position on Berlin as a "can of worms."[4]

Khrushchev's Berlin ultimatum began a long standoff that didn't end until after the Cuban missile crisis four years later. In remarkably short order his pressure tactics produced a long-coveted invitation to visit the United States, followed by Western agreement to a full-fledged summit conference in May 1960. But strategically Khrushchev's whole approach was fatally flawed. The German concessions he demanded proved impossible for the West to provide. His threat to sign a separate peace treaty within six months was as dangerous for the East as for the West. His attempt to force the West to yield clashed with his campaign to reduce East-West tensions.

Khrushchev had plenty of reasons to act. East Germany was lagging behind West Germany's economic miracle; many skilled workers and professionals were fleeing to the West through Berlin. West Berlin was also a source of ideological infection and political subversion, and potentially a base for nuclear weapons. Several times that fall the East German leader Walter Ulbricht complained that Moscow wasn't doing enough to keep nuclear weapons out of West German Chancellor Konrad Adenauer's hands.[5] But Khrushchev neither thought through his plan nor fully consulted with others who might have.

Khrushchev later told visiting American Senator Hubert Humphrey that he had "given many months of thought to the Berlin situation." Doubtless that was why he saw no need for advice from his aides and associates. According to Mikoyan, Khrushchev did not clear his November 10 speech with his colleagues at all, although this was the "grossest violation of party discipline." Mikoyan said he objected and requested that Gromyko present the Foreign Ministry's views, whereupon Gromyko mumbled something incoherent. According to one of his former aides, Gromyko "was afraid of Khrushchev to a degree that was indecent," even when Khrushhcev's "tirades" occurred over the telephone rather than in person. In this case, Gromyko already knew his advice wasn't wanted. Earlier that fall he had brought draft language concerning Berlin to Khrushchev's office. The foreign minister had donned his glasses and begun to read from a memorandum when Khrushchev cut him off rudely: "Wait a minute. You listen to what I'll now dictate to a stenographer. If that coincides with what you've got written down, fine. If not, throw yours in the wastebasket." At this point, recalled the Gromyko assistant Andrei Aleksandrov-Agentov, Khrushchev "began to dictate (carelessly and even chaotically as always, but with the meaning sufficiently clear nonetheless) about how West Berlin would be proclaimed a 'free city.'"[6]

According to Oleg Troyanovsky, who had recently become Khrushchev's chief foreign policy assistant, Moscow's November 27 memorandum was vetted by the Presidium and contained minor corrections suggested by its members, but by then Khrushchev's colleagues didn't dare challenge his views. Troyanovsky had doubts about where Khrushchev wanted to come out and what steps would take him there. He feared his boss would "show [him] the door," but Khrushchev listened carefully and then cited Lenin's 1917 injunction, itself borrowed from Napoleon, to "engage in battle and then see what happens."[7] Sergei Khrushchev too wondered whether the Americans would yield and if they didn't, what then? "Father laughed at my fears, and said that no one would start a war over Berlin." What if the West still rejected Soviet terms when the six-month ultimatum ran out? "Father gave me no clear answer. He intended to act in accord with circumstances and depending on our partners' reactions. He hoped to give them a good scare, and thereby extract their agreement to negotiate." What if negotiations didn't work? Sergei asked. "Then we'll try something else," his father answered with a tone of irritation in his voice. "Something will always turn up."[8]

By 1958 nearly five years had passed since Stalin's successors set out to ease cold war tensions. As Khrushchev saw it, he had opened the USSR up to Western influence despite the risks for his regime; he had jettisoned the Stalinist notion that another world war was inevitable; he had made deep unilateral cuts in Soviet armed forces and moved toward Western positions on disarmament; he had pulled Soviet troops out of Austria and Finland; he had encouraged reform in Eastern Europe; he had pleaded for a four-power summit or at least an informal invitation to the United States.

And what had he received in return? According to no less than Ambassador Llewellyn Thompson, who said he was summarizing Khrushchev's view but was partly reflecting his own, virtually nothing. "We have refused these overtures," he cabled Washington in March 1959, "or made their acceptance subject to conditions he as a Communist considers impossible. We are in the process of rearming Germany and strengthening our bases surrounding Soviet territory. Our proposals for settling the German problem would in his opinion end in dissolution of the Communist bloc and threaten the regime in the Soviet Union itself. He has offered a European settlement based on the status quo while we engage in economic competition. This we have also rejected and he has therefore determined to nail it down without our consent."[9]

After a pause following the Soviet crackdown on Hungary and the Suez crisis in 1956, Khrushchev's courtship of the West had resumed in 1957. In response to upbeat letters from Premier Bulganin that spring, Dulles remarked in June that it was as if the Soviets "had hired a letter writing bureau." As "the world's greatest expert on negotiating with the Russians," he added in December, he could attest that "one can't rely on the Soviets to live up to their promises."[10] Disarmament talks in London adjourned in September. Exchanges on Germany (the West was committed to reunification even though no Western power was in a hurry for it, with the Russians trying to ratify the status quo) didn't look promising.

Despite this bleak pattern or, rather, just because of it, Khrushchev gave no fewer than eight interviews to Western journalists between May and December 1957 in which he combined occasional rocket rattling with appeals for summit-level talks. "There are no problems between our countries on which we could not agree," he informed the *New York Times* managing editor Turner Catledge on May 13. If matters were left to Dulles and Gromyko, "they wouldn't come to an agreement in a hundred years." When asked if he would like to visit the United States, Khrushchev tried not to appear too eager. "I cannot go as a tourist," and there was "no reason for me to go there now as a statesman," but of course a meeting with Eisenhower would be useful because "I greatly respect President Eisenhower and I have told this to him personally."[11] By November Khrushchev's tone had become more urgent. The more high-level talks were "resisted and opposed," he told UPI correspondent Henry Shapiro on November 14, "the worse it will be for peace."[12]

The clearest signal of Khrushchev's interest in U.S.-Soviet détente came at an extraordinary New Year's Eve 1958 dinner in the Kremlin's vast St. George Hall. The lavish affair for a thousand guests began at 11:00 P.M. and didn't end until nearly 7:00 A.M. In contrast with the previous year, when the Soviet leader's New Year's greeting had been so hostile that NATO ambassadors walked out of a smaller reception, the atmosphere this time was friendly and festive. Khrushchev toasted the wartime Grand Alliance for the first time in years, singled out the United States for special approbation, and ended up praising Eisenhower, the only foreign leader he mentioned by name. "Khrushchev did not even mention the socialist camp," noted Yugoslav Ambassador Mićunović.

Ambassador Thompson and his wife, Jane, were seated at one of many long tables that radiated out from the Presidium's head table. If Khrushchev acted up again, Thompson told his wife, she should simply follow him out of the hall. Since her Russian wasn't up to following Khrushchev's speech, all she knew was that in the middle of it, her husband got up and started walking. Looking grim, she followed, only to discover his destination wasn't the door but the head table, where smiling broadly, he clinked glasses with Khrushchev and the entire Kremlin leadership.[13]

Three weeks later, a Soviet secret agent masquerading as a junior embassy officer in Washington asked an American with government connections, "What if Mr. Khrushchev were to come here, to Washington, for some informal talks with Mr. Eisenhower? Would your government permit that?"

"You mean just on a visit, no conference staffs, or agenda, or anything else?" the American asked.

"Exactly!" Yuri Gvozdev replied. "Mr. Churchill and many other heads of government have come here for informal talks with the President. . . . Mr. Khrushchev would like to come here on that basis."

How did Gvozdev know? he was asked. "I know!" he replied. "I can tell you our government is seeking the means to secure an invitation. To Mr. Khrushchev it is very important."[14]

Khrushchev's pursuit of a summit during the first half of 1958 was punctuated by outbursts that reflected frustration at Washington's nonresponsiveness, plus concern that his virtual begging might be seen as a sign of weakness. The same day Gvozdev solicited an invitation, Khrushchev threw a temper tantrum in Minsk. By then Bulganin had written two letters to Eisenhower proposing a summit (as well as a nuclear test moratorium, a ban on nuclear weapons in Germany, and a series of cultural exchanges). In reply, Eisenhower insisted any talks begin in regular diplomatic channels, while Dulles characterized the Soviet proposals as "Mr. Khrushchev's lullaby."[15]

"What do Eisenhower and Dulles want?" Khrushchev thundered in Minsk. "Apparently they want to meet and talk over the liquidation of the socialist system in the Soviet Union. . . ." Well, Hitler had tried that and failed, and the same fate would await the Americans.[16] In March Khrushchev fished publicly for an American invitation: "For us the distance between Moscow and Washington is not so terrible. We can have breakfast at home, lunch on the plane, and dinner in the USA."[17]

In May Khrushchev fumed that the Western powers were displaying "the mobility of a snail."[18] Then events got in the way. The execution of Imre Nagy sparked Western protest demonstrations to which the Soviets replied with "spontaneous" counterrallies.[19] In July a military coup killed pro-Western King Faisal II of Iraq, prompting Washington and London to land troops in Lebanon and Jordan, to which Khrushchev responded by threatening force in defense of the "Iraqi revolution." According to Sergei Khrushchev, his father was nervous at first but was soon in his element: "In the heat of battle, Father felt like a fish in the sea." Khrushchev told Egyptian President Nasser, who arrived in Moscow in the midst of the crisis: "The situation is highly dangerous, and I think the people with the strongest nerves will be the winners." Khrushchev seemed to love what he called "a game that is being played at very high speed, in which everyone has to act quickly without being able to judge what the other players are going to do. It is like playing chess in the dark."[20]

Even in the midst of this game, however, he tried to squeeze in a summit. On July 19, 1958, he proposed an immediate meeting of the heads of governments of the Big Four plus India. In response to a British counterproposal, he agreed to meet under the aegis of the UN Security Council, on which the hated Chiang Kai-shek still occupied China's permanent seat. The would-be elevation of India to a great power, plus the further legitimization of Nationalist China at Mao's expense, was an extraordinary gaffe. Fortunately for Khrushchev, the Americans rebuffed the whole idea. But the episode left a bad taste, as Adlai Stevenson discovered when he was received by Khrushchev in August. When Stevenson innocently brought up the subject of a Security Council summit, Khrushchev, who had just returned from China, snapped, "We do not intend to sit at the table with Chiang Kaishek. . . . No one will drive us into the stable . . . with Chiang Kaishek. We don't like the smell."[21]

The Taiwan Strait crisis of the fall of 1958 further delayed East-West talks. Khrushchev first warned that the USSR would treat any attack upon China as an attack on itself and then, when the crisis was almost over, sent such an abusive missive to Eisenhower that the president returned it as unacceptable. But the Soviet leader was still determined to force a summit, partly, he told Mićunović on October 8, because the Soviet Union had "a special need for peace for the next fifteen or twenty years," after which "no one will be able to go to war even if he wants to" and partly because "any relaxation in Europe would . . . weaken the system of American domination in vast areas around the world, and weaken American military alliances and their military bases, and that would in turn produce political problems" in the United States.[22]

Two days earlier Eric Johnston, president of the Motion Picture Association of America, who had good connections in Washington and had once been President Roosevelt's emissary to Stalin, spent the afternoon with the Khrushchev family at Pitsunda. The visit would have lasted even longer (Khrushchev invited him to have dinner, stay the night, and go grouse hunting the next day), but Johnston had to return to Moscow. Several times that afternoon Khrushchev repeated that he'd like to see Eisenhower: "You know, I really like that man. At the Geneva conference he took me to the bar after every meeting and we had a drink together. I hope his health is good. I'd like to sit down and have another talk with him."[23]

Khrushchev's Berlin ultimatum was a way of getting Eisenhower to the table. By the fall of 1958, Troyanovsky recalled, there had been "no breakthrough" in relations with the West, and "the situation was getting even worse." West Germany was "being drawn ever deeper into the Western alliance; the arms race was gathering steam and spreading into outer space; disarmament negotiations were getting nowhere with defense spending weighing more heavily on the economy; East Germany was isolated and under pressure as before; the Soviet Union was being surrounded by American military bases; new military blocs were being set up in Asia and the Middle East." In addition, trouble was brewing in Sino-Soviet relations, and Troyanovsky remembered "voices saying ever more distinctly that if the Soviet Union had to choose between the West and China, preference should be given to the latter."

The prospect of West Germany's getting nuclear weapons was the last straw, according to Troyanovsky. "If that happened without any Kremlin opposition, it was obvious that Khrushchev's prestige would plummet." Troyanovsky also suspected that his boss was still trying to prove that Molotov and the others were wrong and that he, not they, belonged on top.[24]

Apart from not knowing where exactly he was going or how he was going to get there, Khrushchev misjudged the obstacles in his way. Although he worried that wily eighty-two-year-old West German Chancellor Adenauer might "put a spoke in the wheels," he underestimated the man he called "that old fogey."[25] Compared with East Germany, West Germany was thriving, but with West Berlin deep inside Ulbricht's realm and with full NATO backing uncertain, Adenauer felt vulnerable. His aim was to integrate West Germany into Western Europe, but that could risk losing the chance to reunify Germany as a whole. Adenauer bitterly opposed the sort of Western recognition of East Germany that Khrushchev was seeking. The German chancellor's stubbornness and rigidity drove Eisenhower (and later Kennedy) to distraction, but in view of West Germany's importance, for the most part Washington followed Adenauer's lead.

De Gaulle feared a Western withdrawal from Berlin would mean the neutralization of Germany and eventually a Soviet-German alliance. The French president's over-riding goal, as always, was to restore France to the status of a world power, and for that he needed Adenauer's active support. De Gaulle also understood Khrushchev better than any of his Western colleagues; he sensed the Soviet leader was bluffing and would pull back to avoid an armed clash. Hence de Gaulle proved even more adamant than Adenauer as the crisis took its course.

Khrushchev's best hope in the Western camp was Britain. For all sorts of reasons, ranging from Prime Minister Macmillan's fear that Khrushchev might be a megalomaniac to the widespread British view that whether Russians or East Germans stamped Berlin access documents wasn't worth a nuclear holocaust to the Conservative party's electoral needs in an upcoming campaign, the British were willing to recognize East Germany and work out new access arrangements for Berlin. However, London soon found itself isolated within the Western camp.[26]

As Eisenhower saw it, giving in to Khrushchev could destabilize West Germany, destroy the Western alliance, and isolate the United States. Yet he was almost as disturbed as Khrushchev by the international stalemate and almost as anxious for a breakthrough. Eisenhower was dismayed at the nuclear danger, which he graphically described in his diary after a January 1956 air force briefing on the likely initial stages of a nuclear war. The briefing imagined two scenarios. In one, the United States received virtually no warning of a Soviet atomic attack; in the other, the country had a month to prepare. In the first case the United States would experience "total economic collapse," with some 65 percent of the population needing medical help and "in most instances no opportunity whatsoever to get it," while the damage to the USSR would be three times greater. This, Eisenhower wrote, was "appalling," and there would be "no significant difference in the losses we would take" in the second scenario. The only way to reduce losses would be to launch a surprise attack, but that "would be against our traditions" and out of the question unless Congress secretly declared war, and that "would appear to be impossible."[27]

In retrospect, this briefing greatly exaggerated the losses Moscow was in a position to inflict in 1956. Just as Khrushchev hoped, the USSR's nuclear potential was playing on the president's nerves even before it became a reality. To Dulles, Soviet foreign policy seemed an open book, specifically, Stalin's *Problems of Leninism,* copies of which lay on his desk and at his bedside. But Eisenhower kept hoping Moscow might surprise him. When Khrushchev defeated his rivals in 1957, Dulles "was not happy about it because Khrushchev is undependable and erratic," whereas Eisenhower hoped the Soviet leader "might try friendship."[28]

By early 1958 Eisenhower's frustration was building. The United States was losing the propaganda battle and, at worst, the chance for peace. On February 9 he confessed to Dulles that he was beginning to feel "desperate." He thought of inviting Khrushchev to the United States for a "fact-finding mission," but Dulles objected: "Nobody would believe it; you would be having a summit meeting without any preparation which is what we have said we will not have." Eisenhower thought instead of inviting Presidium members who did not hold government posts; that way there would be no negotiations; "just show them around the country." But Dulles cited laws "against Communists coming" without approval of the attorney general and the secretary of state. Then there was the president's idea of placing as many as ten thousand Soviet students in American colleges. That would look like "a maneuver," objected Dulles; besides, "we probably could not handle that many students." Eisenhower had to agree, but he was "looking for anything that would break the impasse."[29]

One final hindrance in Khrushchev's path was his own East German ally. Ulbricht was as ornery as Adenauer. He wanted Western recognition, of course, but in the first instance he wanted Berlin. For him West Berlin was the prize, whereas for Khrushchev it was a lever to break the international deadlock.[30] Ulbricht demanded not only action but stepped-up Soviet aid. Khrushchev was willing to help. Indeed Moscow had been helping, but the Soviet economy was itself strained. When the crisis began, East Germany enjoyed special access to Western markets through special inter-German trade arrangements. The loss of that status, which would presumably follow if Khrushchev carried through on his threats, would harm not only Ulbricht's regime but Khrushchev's too, not to mention the increased military spending that would be required—just when Khrushchev was trying to reduce Soviet troop levels—if the crisis persisted.

If the West held its ground, leaving Khrushchev to sign a separate treaty with Ulbricht, Western recognition of East Germany would have eluded him. If he then turned access to Berlin over to East Germany, Ulbricht could determine whether there would be war or peace. Because Western leaders couldn't be sure Khrushchev was bluffing, they set out to prove they weren't, by staging troop movements and preparing to force their way into Berlin. Even if shooting broke out, or if East Germans rose in rebellion as they had in 1953, Khrushchev assumed that war could be avoided. But what if it could not? For all these reasons, his overall strategy (if in fact it deserves the name) was bizarre from the start.[31] Yet for more than a year it worked.

THE INITIAL Western reaction to Khrushchev's Berlin ultimatum was cautious. Neither Britain nor France was prepared to countenance even a limited use of force, especially before a good-faith effort at negotiation. Eisenhower and Dulles were prepared to treat East German border controllers as mere Soviet agents, but they retreated in the face of West German objections. The question of where and when armed force might be used required extensive Allied consultation. In the meantime, as Eisenhower put it on December 11, "Our main task should be to reach Khrushchev, ascertain what he wants. . . ."[32]

Senator Hubert H. Humphrey made a valiant attempt to find out during an extraordinary eight-hour conversation with the Soviet leader on December 1, 1958, a session during which, according to Troyanovsky, Khrushchev was equally intent on discerning what Eisenhower and Dulles were thinking.[33] Two more ebullient (not to say manic) interlocutors can hardly be imagined. Their meeting, as described by Humphrey in notes dictated the next day, may have been the most effervescent in the history of the cold war. Humphrey was stunned when the interview he requested was scheduled on one hour's notice at 3:00 P.M. At 4:30 he figured his time was up, but Khrushchev insisted he stay. Sitting across a long table from each other in the premier's high-ceilinged Kremlin office, with only Troyanovsky present, the two men talked until 7:00, when Khrushchev ordered that food be brought in. After dinner Khrushchev summoned Mikoyan, and the three continued sparring until 11:00 at night.

When it was finally over, the irrepressible Humphrey could barely contain his delight. First of all, he had survived. "I'm the only living American that's gone to the men's room three times in one day in the Kremlin," he joked afterward. What's more, he was snowed by his host. "This guy has a great sense of humor, and he's very clever, very clever. Believe me, you're not dealing with a nonentity. This boy was born early and leaves late, believe me." Especially when it came to the United States: "What this guy has been reading up on [the political situation in New York, California, and Minnesota, including the election of what Khrushchev called 'the new McCarthy,' i.e., Representative Eugene McCarthy]

—I wish I had." At one point, Humphrey's host "tore off on a whole long lecture like I wish I could remember [because it would have been] the best speech I could ever make in my life on antiracialism. Boy, he really gave me a talk on that. . . . We really got along just fine. I liked him like nobody's business."

History does not record if Humphrey's admiration was reciprocated. But the senator admitted that the meeting wasn't all sweetness and light. It was deadly serious and at times even frightening. During the discussions, Khrushchev imparted a little secret "no American has heard of": that the Soviets had just exploded a five-megaton hydrogen bomb. They also had a new rocket that traveled so far (9,000 miles) that there was no place to test it. Smiling slyly, Khrushchev asked Humphrey what his native city was, then got up from the table, approached a large wall map of the United States, and drew a circle around Minneapolis with a fat blue pencil. "That's so I don't forget to order them to spare the city when the rockets fly," Khrushchev said.

Humphrey apologized that he wouldn't be able to reciprocate and spare Moscow.

The Soviet leader returned twenty times or more to Berlin, referring to it as "a thorn," "a cancer," a "bone in my throat," omitting only to call it (as he did in 1962) "the testicles of the West."[34] He told Humphrey, "We mean business." Soviet troops in Eastern Europe were "not there to play cards." Khrushchev pounded the table. He didn't raise his voice but leaned forward, his small eyes flashing, his finger jabbing, his voice firm and staccato.

Humphrey replied in kind. When his host referred to American economic troubles, Humphrey "told him, by God, he didn't know what he was talking about." He warned, referring to the 1960 election, "Wait till my crowd gets in. You've had it easy. We'll run you right out of Gorky Park." According to Humphrey, Khrushchev "loved" this sort of repartee, but when warned not to threaten Berlin, Khrushchev took that as a threat to him and repeated several times with great emotion, "Don't threaten me!"

The Russian seemed to be keeping a list of "every [American] general who ever said a bad word about him," especially those who talked about what the United States would do, when, where, and with how many casualties, if war came. "Every time you say something like this," Khrushchev explained, "I must respond." Aware that his retorts could be counterproductive, he said he'd thought of putting a stop to unnecessarily belligerent exchanges. Perhaps that explained the remarkable non-fit between his medium and his message, even between parts of the message itself. Menacing words were followed by entreaties. If only the Berlin question could be solved, then "everything will be better." If the West were unhappy with Soviet proposals, "then give us a counterproposal. We are prepared to accept anything reasonable. What do you suggest?"

He "badly wants a summit and badly wants to be invited to the U.S.," Humphrey later told high administration officials. The Soviet leader didn't say so in so many words, but his small talk was transparent: He loved to travel; he had really enjoyed England; Mikoyan, whom Khrushchev teased constantly, had been in America and had learned a lot there. "Imagine how much I would know if I ever go there," Khrushchev added.

He struck his guest as "a man who is insecure, who thinks [we] are rich and big and . . . keep picking on [him]," a man who is "defensive in an offensive way, insecure in a superconfident way," who "has to pretend that he is secure," and in the process "demonstrates his insecurity by overstatement." Khrushchev's two favorite words, Humphrey reported, were "stupid" and "fool." Several times the Russian repeated that there should be "no room for fools in modern government," fools like the "antiparty group," for instance. "'They thought they had me beat,' he said, and just bristled up, you know, and he sparkled when he talked about this. He was just, you know, Boy, this is my meat. 'You know what I did,' he says. 'I just summoned the Central Committee, and I was so persuasive, Senator, that when I got through, even the seven [who had originally voted against him] voted for me.'"

Khrushchev's deepest fear seemed to be that he was being played for a fool by the Americans. Humphrey urged the administration to study Khrushchev's personality carefully, to expose the impressions of all who had met the Soviet leader "not to a diplomat but to a psychiatrist." Yet the same qualities that demanded a shrink offered a golden opportunity: "This is a man who is very much up our line. . . . Just the sort of man with whom a man like Ike could do business."

EVEN AS he set out to bully Eisenhower, Khrushchev offered reassurance lest the president overreact. Gvozdev passed a new message to Vice President Nixon: "Don't worry about Berlin. There's not going to be any war over Berlin." A month later, in December, he relayed word that Khrushchev was "very interested" in a Nixon visit to the Soviet Union and would "bid very high for it in terms of constructive proposals on Berlin."

The administration's response, quietly passed through Gvozdev, was that Nixon would come if there ensued "a period of relative quiet" on the Berlin front.[35]

The two months that followed Khrushchev's ultimatum produced nothing he could call progress. "One third of the time until expiration of the deadline had passed," Sergei Khrushchev recalled, "and nothing had changed. Father grew nervous." As Troyanovsky saw it, his boss was "trapped, and wasn't sure what to do." Theoretically he could use negotiations as an excuse for extending the deadline. But no talks seemed likely under the shadow of his threats.[36] The trick was to convince Eisenhower to talk without removing those threats; for that delicate task neither Soviet Ambassador Mikhail Menshikov nor Foreign Minister Gromyko would do. Instead Khrushchev asked his longtime Kremlin colleague, the shrewd Armenian Anastas Mikoyan, to go to Washington to ease the tensions triggered by his own actions. "You started it, so you go!" Mikoyan remembered replying sharply. "Besides, no one is inviting me." "No, I can't go," Khrushchev said. "I'm the top man. You go as the personal guest of Menshikov."[37]

Besides Washington, Mikoyan's early January trip included New York (where he met with top business leaders), Chicago (where demonstrators threw eggs at him), Los Angeles (where protesters carried an open coffin with a sign saying, FOR MIKOYAN), plus multiple press conferences at which questions were anything but polite. "Imagine how Khrushchev would have reacted!" recalled Troyanovsky, who accompanied both men on their American journeys. "But Mikoyan had his own style—irony, sarcasm, humor or just calm refutation."[38]

In his talks with Eisenhower, Dulles, and Nixon, Mikoyan tried to lower the international temperature. He practically begged them to understand how much the Soviet Union had changed since Stalin's death; he assured them Moscow did not want to undermine the West in Berlin; he denied that the new Soviet proposals were an ultimatum or a threat. What the Kremlin wanted, he insisted, was negotiations, yet "it had met nothing new from the United States."[39]

Mikoyan brought back mixed news from America. The big businessmen he met, such as Averell Harriman and John J. McCloy, were remarkably sober-minded. Dulles hinted free elections weren't the only way to unify Germany, and Eisenhower seemed receptive to a foreign ministers' meeting. But the president rejected a summit and didn't move an inch on Berlin itself. According to Sergei Khrushchev, this outcome "not only disappointed Father, it left him somewhat vulnerable." But he "recounted Mikoyan's stories about his meetings in the US with a smile. The Americans would agree to sit down at the negotiating table."[40]

KHRUSHCHEV'S NEXT HOPE was Harold Macmillan. The British prime minister feared a drift toward war. So he invited himself to Moscow by taking up the long-standing invitation that Khrushchev and Bulganin had issued to his predecessor when they toured England in 1956.

This was not the way Washington liked to do business. Eisenhower and Dulles worried that the Brits were "going soft." Although Macmillan later insisted the Americans had "complete confidence" in his mission, what Dulles actually said was that if the prime minister went to Moscow, he would be speaking only for himself.[41]

Khrushchev laid on all the warmth Moscow could muster in the middle of winter. When Macmillan deplaned from the Queen's Flight on February 21, wearing the same black winter coat and white astrakhan hat he had sported as a junior envoy in Finland in 1940, Khrushchev was there to greet him.[42] Following a lavish state dinner in the Kremlin, the two leaders departed for Semyonovskoye, where they drove through the snow in a horse-drawn troika, shot clay pigeons, and then, huddled together in a large wicker basket, went skidding down an icy slope. Khrushchev relished demonstrating his earthy goodwill. The urbane Macmillan later noted that his basket ride "was regarded by some with amusement and others with astonishment. It marked, in the opinion of experts, a high degree of intimacy."[43]

Khrushchev lapped up Macmillan's praise of his war record, accepting the compliments "with beaming, almost Pickwickian smiles."[44] When the PM defended Western rights in Berlin and rejected an early summit, Khrushchev erupted. If the West didn't understand the Soviet government's position, he warned during a well-lubricated luncheon, "the conversation would become a conversation between dead people." When the usually unflappable Macmillan answered in kind, saying, "If you try to threaten us in any way, you will create a Third World War," Khrushchev leaped to his feet, shouting, "You have insulted me!"[45]

He insulted Macmillan in turn. The Soviet leader had looked forward to escorting Macmillan to Kiev; for days, recalled Sergei Khrushchev, "he had been describing all the wonders of Kievan hospitality, the beauty of the Dnieper River." Now, suddenly, he couldn't go because his tooth hurt. "I've got the most terrible toothache," Khrushchev complained, "and a prime minister without teeth [is] no use." But that didn't keep him from receiving an Iraqi delegation that same afternoon. British tabloids christened this "The Toothache Insult," with one of them characterizing the prime minister's whole journey as a "monumental flop."[46]

Macmillan was shaken. After huddling with his foreign secretary, Selwyn Lloyd, in the frigid garden outside his dacha ("You must imagine," Macmillan wrote later, "two middle-aged, not to say elderly politicians clothed in fur coats, fur hats, and above all the inevitable but essential galoshes, tramping up and down with their advisers and engaged in long and earnest discussion—*sotto voce*—about a situation which if not immediately dangerous, threatened to become ridiculous."), Macmillan conveyed to Khrushchev two key points that he had carefully memorized, and of which he hoped "Mr. Khrushchev will take careful note. The first is that the German situation is full of danger and could develop into something tragic for us all. The second is that it must surely be possible to avoid this by sensible and cooperative work."[47]

Macmillan's account continued: "There followed a pause during which Gromyko and Mikoyan looked at each other and at their boss." No wonder! What the prime minister had so solemnly proclaimed was identical with the message Khrushchev had been dramatizing in his every speech. If that was the line that Macmillan took home from Moscow, then from the Soviet point of view, his trip was helpful after all.

One other result of the visit was that Khrushchev dropped his May 27 Berlin deadline. If the West didn't like May 27, he said with seeming insouciance, let it name any other date in June or July: "There is no time limit."[48] If the West wouldn't accept a summit, how about a foreign ministers' meeting to begin at the end of April and to last no more than two or three months? Since such a meeting would be in session on May 27, the deadline would have been automatically extended.

The British were transfixed by Khrushchev's behavior. He had "completely dominated his colleagues," except for Mikoyan, who was "clearly in a class by himself as the second personage of the regime," while they "watched him with wary subservience." Khrushchev "spoke without a note, made no notes, and hardly ever consulted his colleagues." He had a "remarkable grasp of detail" but "did not always find it easy to follow complicated or subtle logical argument." He showed "a certain hostility to intellectual refinement" and was "remarkably emotional" in his reactions. He showed "an acute consciousness of power," along with "an inferiority complex that still goes very deep. . . . Extremely sensitive to any imagined slight," he even bristled when Macmillan and Lloyd were so impolite as to whisper to each other while the interpreter was translating Khrushchev's words to them into English.[49]

The sophisticated, diplomatic Troyanovsky was "amazed" at how "aggressively and provocatively" Khrushchev treated his guest. After bullying Macmillan at one session, Khrushchev boasted to Troyanovsky that he had "fucked [the prime minister] with a telephone pole," adding apologetically, "You're an intellectual. You must be shocked."[50]

Khrushchev thought "he himself had retreated" after his "bluff" had been called. "Deep in his heart," according to his son, he knew he had lost, although he tried hard to convince himself and his associates that he had won.[51]

THE FOREIGN MINISTERS convened in Geneva on May 11. That same day Khrushchev struck a euphoric note in a speech in Ukraine: "A meeting of heads of state will take place." Macmillan was in favor, chortled Khrushchev, Eisenhower was "inclining" that way, and so was de Gaulle. The Soviet Union's international position was "better than ever before."[52]

By mid-June, however, the foreign ministers were deadlocked. The Western powers were prepared to break Berlin out of their "package" (that still called for German unification via free elections) and to alter their role in Berlin (by reducing garrisons and negotiating a new access agreement), but they wouldn't yield their basic rights or formally recognize East Germany. The Soviets might accept an interim agreement that would preserve Western rights in Berlin while the two Germanys negotiated, but Gromyko wouldn't promise that those rights would remain if agreement were reached, meaning, in effect, that the threat to annul Western rights would hang in the air as the talks proceeded.

Even before May 11 Eisenhower had established progress at the foreign ministers' level as a precondition for a summit. He hadn't defined progress exactly, but what had been achieved in Geneva wasn't it. That being the case, why didn't Khrushchev offer a better deal? The fact that East German observers were included in the Geneva conference (after an excruciating debate about the shape of the table at which they and West German observers would sit) constituted a kind of de facto recognition. Moreover, Ulbricht regarded the foreign ministers' meeting as an achievement, whereas (he told Khrushchev in March) an overall German settlement would take years, perhaps even decades. It was Khrushchev, not Ulbricht, who was in a hurry for a summit.[53] If so, why not grant that

Western rights would *not* lapse if there were no overall settlement within a year or two?

Khrushchev may have been tempted to do so. According to Secretary of State Herter, the Soviet negotiating position seemed flexible until June 7, when it suddenly hardened. Having threatened to establish a new Berlin regime so as to obtain a new German treaty, Khrushchev couldn't accept an outcome offering neither. In that sense, his tactics had now trapped him. But the trap still smelled like an opportunity. The international situation was not at an impasse, he declared on June 7. If an agreement weren't reached by the foreign ministers, it would probably be reached at a summit conference, which would be all the more needed if and when the ministers failed. If the summit too failed to produce progress, then "world public opinion" would demand yet another try. "If necessary, " Khrushchev added generously later that month, "I shall be glad to meet more than once with heads of government of the Western powers."[54]

In the meantime Khrushchev had to settle for Averell Harriman, whom he received on June 23 for another marathon conversation. This one began at one o'clock in the Kremlin. Harriman thought his host, who was wearing a baggy gray suit with two medals on his left breast and one on his right, a gray and red polka dot tie, and large red cuff links, looked "tired."[55] But after an hour and a half, the meeting adjourned to the guest dacha at Novo-Ogaryovo, where it continued until 10:30 P.M., when Khrushchev stood in the door for fifteen minutes to make sure he got the last word.

Khrushchev wasn't nearly as serene as his public tone indicated. Harriman's wealthy, patrician credentials seemed to intimidate him, and Khrushchev reacted with a defensiveness that encompassed current colleagues and former rivals. "I was a miner," Mikoyan's father was "a plumber," and Kozlov, although "not as crude as we are," had been "a homeless waif." Malenkov was "a shit—a yellow chicken," Khrushchev informed Harriman, and Beria was "also shit"; only Molotov was worthy of respect. Kirichenko seemed the current heir apparent, but Khrushchev warned Harriman not to bet on Kirichenko's prospects. "I am very jealous of my prerogatives," Khrushchev announced candidly, "and while I live I will run the party. If you are trying to bury me, you are engaged in wishful thinking."

"But your word is law in the Presidium, isn't it?" Harriman asked.

"Yes," replied Khrushchev, "but there's no law one can't get around."

The same sort of touchiness carried over to foreign relations. "Don't think the Soviet Union still wears bast shoes as it did when the tsar sold Alaska to you. We are ready to fight." The USSR wants "your friendship, but not from weakness. If you try to speak to us from strength, we will answer with the same."

As usual, Khrushchev's defensiveness took the form of an offensive. One bomb would be "sufficient" for Bonn; three to five would do for France, Britain, Spain, and Italy. In case Harriman had any doubt, just compare the size of rocket payloads: U.S. missiles could carry a warhead of only 22 pounds whereas Soviet rockets carried 2860 pounds.

To his credit, Harriman talked back to Khrushchev. The latter's threats were "appallingly dangerous." He trusted Mr. Gromyko would be more amenable when the foreign ministers met again on July 13. Gromyko would reflect the views of the Soviet government, snapped Khrushchev. If not, he would be "fired and replaced." After that came another round of threats: West Germany could be destroyed in "ten minutes." One bomb could take care of "Bonn and the Ruhr and that is all of Germany. Paris is all of France; London is all of England. You have surrounded us with bases but our rockets can destroy them. If you start a war, we may die but the rockets will fly automatically.

"You may tell anyone you want," Khrushchev continued, "that we will never accept Adenauer as a representative of Germany. He is a zero. If Adenauer pulls down his pants and you look at him from behind you can see Germany is divided. If you look at him from the front, you can see Germany will not stand."

Still later: "We are determined to liquidate your rights in Western Berlin. What good does it do you to have eleven thousand troops in Berlin? If it came to war, we would swallow them in one gulp. . . . Your generals talk of tanks and guns defending your Berlin position. They would burn."

On paper Khrushchev's tirades look Hitlerian. Yet according to Harriman's account, the Soviet leader was "most genial throughout the evening, smiling incessantly, proposing toasts frequently—chiefly in cognac, which he drank liberally—and constantly flattering [Harriman] as a great capitalist." Still, he was threatening war. Another Soviet leader might have feared an American overreaction—Stalin himself had carefully avoided the sort of bluster that was his successor's stock-in-trade—but Khrushchev knew (or thought he did) how far he could push Eisenhower.

By the time Eisenhower held a press conference on July 8, there had been public reports on the Khrushchev-Harriman meeting. Asked about his reaction to Khrushchev's demeanor, the president replied coolly, "Well, I don't think anything about it at all. I don't believe that responsible people should indulge in anything that can be even remotely ultimatums or threats. That is not the way to reach peaceful solutions."[56]

The president's equanimity was deceptive. In fact, he had blown hot and cold as evidence of Khrushchev's erratic behavior accumulated. When Macmillan pleaded for high-level talks, Eisenhower refused to "be dragooned to a summit meeting." But "as the world is going now," he complained to advisers on April 7, "there seems no hope for the future unless we can make some progress in negotiation (it is already four years since the Geneva meeting)."[57]

Eisenhower puzzled over what manner of man he was dealing with. "Did you read that [Khrushchev] speech?" the president had asked reporters at a February 1959 press conference. "Some of the language he used to describe us as a nation . . .!" Asked how he explained Khrushchev's behavior during Macmillan's visit, Eisenhower said this was the sort of question to which he had been "trying to get an answer for a long time."[58]

The president prided himself on his ability to gauge people at close range. On the eve of Mikoyan's visit, he hoped they would "try to get behind each other's facial expressions and to see what we are really thinking. Is there an honest and peaceful motive behind all these things? Are both of us really so sick of the burden we have to carry in the armament field that we want to find . . . a way out of this dilemma?"[59] In March he thought of meeting with Khrushchev "to save the situation." Soon afterward the president ordered the State Department to prepare a "very secret" study of the possibility of inviting Khrushchev to the United States. In mid-June, with the Geneva talks stalled, Eisenhower told his personal secretary Ann Whitman that the only "other idea he had was to ask Mr. K. over here to see the president alone." By the time the foreign ministers reconvened in Geneva a month later, the president had approved a plan for inviting Khrushchev to the United States, a visit he hoped would "break the logjam" at the foreign ministers' conference.

Eisenhower's plan conditioned an invitation on concrete progress at Geneva. Undersecretary of State Robert Murphy was to convey this qualified message to Kozlov, who had been in New York to open an exhibition of Soviet art and technology and was catching a return flight on July 13. Murphy was to say that if the Geneva negotiations went well, the two leaders could hold informal talks in the United States, with a tour of the country to follow if Khrushchev so wished. Instead Murphy transmitted an "unqualified" invitation, as Eisenhower learned when Khrushchev accepted it on July 21. The president was "extremely disturbed," in fact, "staggered," he told Murphy on July 22. Now he would have go through with a meeting he "despised," with no clear idea of "just what purpose" a meeting with Khrushchev would serve.[60]

The story of this snafu is hard to believe; indeed some historians do not believe it.[61] Khrushchev himself was flabbergasted. He had been angling for an invitation for months without success. He had told a delegation of American governors in July that he was available for a trip to the United States and would like the president to come to the USSR.[62] But by then, according to Sergei Khrushchev, his father had given up hope and as a result had grown "sad."[63]

That was the situation on the weekend morning in July, when Kozlov returned from New York. Khrushchev was at his dacha by the Moscow River when Kozlov called and drove right over. "I couldn't believe my eyes," Khrushchev said later. "We had no reason to expect such an invitation—not then, or ever for that matter. Our relations had been extremely strained. Yet here was Eisenhower, President of the United States, inviting Khrushchev, the Chairman of the Council of Ministers of the Soviet Union and Secretary of the Central Committee, to head a government delegation on a friendly visit. . . . What did it mean? A shift of some kind?"[64]

Khrushchev received the stunning news "with immense satisfaction," his son remembered, "even I would say, with joy. He took it as a sign that the United States had finally accepted our socialist state. He had become the first Soviet leader ever to be invited to the United States on an official visit." It seemed just the "breakthrough" he had been waiting for, according to Troyanovsky, "a concrete result of the Berlin pressure he had been exerting on the Western powers."[65]

NOT SURPRISINGLY, when the foreign ministers reconvened on July 13, their talks went nowhere. Although Khrushchev's visit to the United States wasn't announced until August, Geneva was now a sideshow with Washington to be the main event. Meanwhile Vice President Nixon's visit to the USSR, from July 23 to August 2, previewed the coming attraction.

The two men were very different: Khrushchev open and ebullient, Nixon constricted and constrained. Yet both were extraordinarily sensitive to slight and determined to show they couldn't be intimidated. As Nixon flew toward Moscow, his thoughts were on "how I should conduct myself in my meeting with Khrushchev." Although he expected to be bullied, he was reluctant to answer "threat with threat and boast with boast." Still, he was "keyed up and ready for battle. . . . "[66]

The first Nixon-Khrushchev conversation was a verbal slugfest. A few days earlier the U.S. Congress had passed the Captive Nations Resolution, condemning Soviet domination of other Communist countries. The resolution was routine, having been adopted every year since 1950, but to Khrushchev, it seemed designed to soften him up for Nixon's arrival.

"This resolution stinks," he announced at his first meeting with Nixon in the Kremlin. "It stinks like fresh horse shit, and nothing smells worse than that." Nixon replied with expletives undeleted: "I am afraid the Chairman is mistaken. There is something that smells worse than horse shit, and that is pig shit."[67]

After a start like that, the talks could only get better—but not by much. Khrushchev crowed that while Nixon was a lawyer and he a mere miner, he could still outargue him. He boasted of his rockets' power and accuracy, confided "secrets" (e.g., that the USSR had purloined U.S. operational war plans) never before revealed to anyone, except perhaps a previous week's visitor, threatened to destroy Germany, Britain, and France on the first day of a war, and then denied he was menacing anyone.[68]

When the two men visited the American exhibition in Sokolniki Park (which Nixon was to open, as Kozlov had the Soviet exhibition in New York), the clash continued. The exhibition's display of American superiority—inside a seventy-eight-foot high geodesic dome a huge screen displayed slides of American cities, highways, supermarkets, and college campuses, accompanied by music and a Russian-language sound track—was massively subversive of Soviet claims to be outdoing the United States.[69] An RCA television studio equipped with color TV cameras and monitors particularly provoked Khrushchev. Dressed in his trademark panama hat and baggy light gray suit, he bragged that the Soviet Union soon would catch up with the United States and "wave bye-bye" (at this point Khrushchev waved a limp wrist and guffawed) as it moved on. Still irked by the Captive Nations Resolution, he embraced a Soviet workman standing nearby: "Does this man look like a slave laborer? With men of such spirit, how can we lose?"[70]

As host at the exhibition Nixon initially forbore to reply. Yet Khrushchev's attack shook him "right to my toes," especially since, with a little more than a year to go before the next presidential election (for which Nixon had by no means clinched the Republican nomination), it would be shown on television to millions of American voters. Sweating profusely as he emerged from the TV studio, Nixon found himself in a six-room model ranch house's "Miracle Kitchen," which became famous after the debate that now ensued. Khrushchev took the kitchen too, with its gleaming appliances, as a rebuke and insisted his country had plenty of similar machines. Soon he and the vice president were "going at it toe-to-toe" (as Nixon put it), with each man poking his finger in the other's face.[71]

After this exchange the mercurial Khrushchev turned on the charm, inviting Nixon's party (which included Eisenhower's brother Dr. Milton Eisenhower, whom the president sent along to prepare a report parallel to Nixon's) to top off its toasts at a Kremlin luncheon by flinging its champagne glasses into the fireplace. Midway through a dinner at the American ambassador's residence, in the midst of praising the beauty of the Russian countryside, Khrushchev impulsively proposed that the Americans drive out to his dacha right then and there, rather than the next morning, as planned. When he did go the next day, Nixon found the dacha "as luxurious an estate as I have ever visited, with a mansion larger than the White House surrounded by neatly kept grounds and gardens, and with a marble staircase descending to the banks of the Moscow River." During a two-hour ride on the river, for which Khrushchev's outfit included an embroidered Ukrainian shirt and open-toed sandals but that Nixon sweated out in his business suit, the twenty-five-foot motor launch stopped at least eight times near bathers, so Khrushchev could ask, "Are you captives? Are you slaves?" Having obtained the proper answer, *nyet, nyet,* he poked Nixon in the ribs: "See how our slaves live!"

Khrushchev bragged again about Soviet military prowess during a not-so-leisurely five-hour lunch. Nixon counterattacked. "It was cold steel between us all afternoon," he gloated afterward. The voluble Khrushchev displayed what Nixon called "a repertoire of gestures that a conductor of a brass band would envy": a "quick flip of the hand to ward off a statement as he would a fly"; an impatient glance skyward "if he felt he had heard enough of an argument to anticipate the rest"; arms outstretched with hands cupped "as if they held self-evident truths for all to witness"; both hands waving in unison when angry, "as if exhorting his band to play louder."[72]

All these were soon to be deployed on American soil. In the meantime America's allies had to be soothed. The announcement of Khrushchev's upcoming visit, made at joint press conferences in Moscow and Washington on August 3, caused deep dismay. The ever-distrustful Adenauer feared an eleventh-hour betrayal. De Gaulle suspected a Soviet-

American deal that would leave out the French. Having rebuffed Macmillan's proposals for high-level talks, Eisenhower had now stolen the show himself. The president "has caused me great annoyance—alarm—and even anger," the British prime minister complained. "It is not (as some of my colleagues seem to feel) the result of American bad faith, but rather of their stupidity, naivete and incompetence. . . . Everyone will assume that the two Great Powers—Russia and U.S.A.—are going to fix up a deal over our heads and behind our backs."[73]

Eisenhower offered to meet his allies at a "Western summit" before Khrushchev arrived in the States. When de Gaulle rejected that, lest the president seem to be anointed "spokesman" for all of them, Eisenhower visited each capital in turn. But his talks only reinforced his sense of how little room there was for maneuver. What he heard in Europe persuaded the president to try to delay any resolution of the German and Berlin problems for several years, by agreement with the Soviets if possible, by Western stalling if necessary.

He tried to lower expectations. He hoped only "to melt a bit of the ice that seems to freeze relations with the Soviets," he said at the August 3 press conference. On September 10, he stipulated two conditions for a formal four-power summit: Western rights in Berlin would have to be respected, and there must be "some clear Soviet indication, no matter how given, that serious negotiations would bring about real promise of reducing the causes of world tension."[74]

In fact, these conditions marked a retreat from previous American insistence on real progress *before* a summit, rather than *at* one. What's more, as Khrushchev's arrival approached, Eisenhower's hopes rose that he might achieve a personal, if not a political, breakthrough by discovering at long last "whether this man personally was ready or had any intention" of probing for peace. Whatever else happened, Eisenhower said in August, Khrushchev would see " a free people living and working," and that "lesson" might "have some effect."[75]

FOR KHRUSHCHEV, the coming journey was "his hour of glory," recalled son-in-law Aleksei Adzhubei, "a recognition of his personal services" that at the same time "bestowed honor on his country." According to Sergei Khrushchev, he "was excited, and he kept ramming this into his listeners: 'Who would have guessed, twenty years ago, that the most powerful capitalist country in the world would invite a Communist to visit? This is incredible. Today they *have* to take us into account. It's our strength that led to this—they have to recognize our existence and our power. Who would have thought that the capitalists would invite me, a worker? Look what we've achieved in these years.' "[76]

But the trip would also be another test. Khrushchev feared, said his son, that American " 'capitalists and aristocrats' viewed him, a former worker, as inferior, and condescended to sit down with him at the same table only because of extreme necessity."[77] As a result, he would have to be at his very best: to speak carefully, negotiate shrewdly, and conduct himself with poise and dignity.

All this put a premium on the painstaking preparations that preceded his departure. On the beach by the Black Sea, under linen awnings that protected them from the hot sun, Khrushchev and Gromyko and their aides pored over materials prepared by the Foreign Ministry and the KGB, trying to anticipate all contingencies. Meanwhile, speechwriters drafted remarks for all occasions: arrivals and departures, breakfasts and luncheons, before businesspeople and journalists. Later, in Moscow, another brain trust gathered at nine o'clock each morning in Khrushchev's Kremlin office to review the texts once again, only to have him cast them aside when he addressed American audiences.[78]

Framing a negotiating strategy was particularly important. "When it came to these issues," remarked Sergei Khrushchev, "Father himself had to decide." But what he lacked in solicitude for others' opinions, he made up in agonizing. "Father thought about the upcoming negotiations constantly, whether sunning himself on the beach or floating in the sea in his inflated inner tube, but most of all during his evening strolls along the so-called 'tsar's path.' "[79]

After returning from these walks, Khrushchev would summon stenographers and begin to dictate his ideas. He would show the Americans that "we will not allow anyone to push us around or to sit on our necks." But he also wanted to get beyond minimally peaceful coexistence to resolve difficult questions. This combination of far-reaching aims and a touchy emphasis on standing his ground was typical of Khrushchev. So was what his son called his "carping, suspicious" approach to protocol aspects of the visit. Soviet Ambassador Menshikov, already known in Washington as "a man of limited talents and vast suspicions," outdid himself in demanding an itinerary that would allow his boss to shine.[80] But Khrushchev was still afraid of being snubbed and humiliated.

His pre-visit nightmares began with the arrival ceremony itself. Although he headed both the Soviet government and the Communist party, parity with Eisenhower required that he be received as chief of state. Even after having been assured that he would be, Khrushchev worried about being denied the proper level of protocol, which "would have inflicted moral damage." Just to be sure, he passed a warning through Menshikov (who if he had any sense didn't deliver it) that the welcome that awaited Eisenhower in Moscow on his reciprocal visit would be no better than that which Khrushchev got in Washington.[81]

Then there was the specter of Camp David, which was included in an American-drafted itinerary that Gromyko brought from Moscow to Pitsunda. "*K-e-mp-David?*" Khrushchev asked suspiciously. "What's that?" All Gromyko could offer was a translation: "Camp David."[82] Khrushchev demanded: "What sort of camp is it?" Why hold talks there rather than in the capital itself? Only after inquiries were made in Washington was Khrushchev reliably informed that Camp David was the president's dacha in Maryland.

Years later Khrushchev cited this confusion to show how ill informed the two sides were about each other, but it revealed more than that. Was Camp David "a place they put people they don't trust," he had wondered, "where they put people in some sort of quarantine, where the president would travel alone to meet with me?" Was it like Prinkipo Island in the Sea of Marmora near Istanbul, where a Soviet delegation had been invited to meet with Western representatives in 1919, a place, Khrushchev remembered hearing, where "stray dogs were sent to die"?[83]

All sorts of other arrangements were cause for concern: Who should accompany Khrushchev to America? How should they travel? What time should they arrive? Certain members of the delegation, such as Gromyko, were obvious choices, but Khrushchev wanted to take a leading writer to lend cultural weight to the delegation. On literary grounds, his choice was Mikhail Sholokhov, author of *And Quiet Flows the Don*, but Sholokhov was too much of a tippler. Khrushchev had hesitated to let him travel abroad before (as was the party leader's prerogative in the Soviet regime), for fear "he'd lose his wits and stumble about, perhaps inflicting physical injury on himself, and moral injury on his country." But after Sholokhov managed to remain on his feet in Britain and Scandinavia, he was included on the trip.[84]

Should Khrushchev take his family? Precedent was against it. "Stalin was very suspicious of anyone who took his wife on a trip with him," Khrushchev recalled. Presidium members themselves had considered it "unbusiness-like—and a petty-bourgeois luxury—to travel with our wives." Yet Mikoyan, who had been to America, was in favor, partly because he thought Nina Petrovna would have a calming influence on her explosive husband. What Mikoyan actually said, recalled Khrushchev, was "that it might make a better impression on the general public abroad if I took Nina Petrovna and some members of my family." Since Ambassador and Mrs. Thompson agreed, Khrushchev took not only his wife, but his children, Yulia (by his first wife), Rada, Sergei, Yelena, and his son Leonid's daughter, Yulia, whom he and Nina Petrovna had raised as their own.

What plane should he take? An Ilyushin 18 jet would require embarrassing stops for re-fueling. The new Tupolev 114 could reach Washington nonstop, but its maiden long-distance flight had occurred only in May, after which microscopic cracks had been found in the engine. Despite objections from Presidium colleagues, Minister of Defense Malinovsky, and his own longtime personal pilot, Khrushchev insisted on taking the new plane. Remembering the Tu-104's triumphal appearance in London in April 1956 (even though it was just bringing him and Bulganin their mail), he imagined an even greater sensation in Washington. Khrushchev forced the reluctant Kozlov to fly the new plane to Washington earlier that summer, and by God, the Americans didn't have a ramp high enough for it. "Look at us! See what we can do," Khrushchev exulted when he heard about Kozlov's landing. "Let them see what we can do!" Little did he know, because no one dared tell him, that one reason the plane was so high off the ground was to keep its engines from ingesting stones, dirt, or other debris on unkempt Soviet runways. All he knew was that Tupolev's creation was the tallest plane in the world.[85]

Tupolev himself blessed the undertaking; he even sent his son along as a sign of his confidence in the plane. Any CIA operative who guessed why Alyosha Tupolev was on board deserved an award for acumen; still, Khrushchev took no chances. "We didn't publicize the fact that Tupolev's son was with us," he later recalled, for "to do so would have meant giving explanations, and these might have been damaging to our image."[86]

Arriving on time was equally important. "We carefully calculated how long the flight from Moscow to Washington would take. A special ceremony was planned for us on our arrival, and we couldn't afford to be late, nor did we want to land too early. We could always circle a few times over Washington in order not to arrive before the scheduled time, but if we were late it would be a blow to our prestige."[87]

Most of Khrushchev's nervous anticipation was hidden from view. On the eve of the great voyage he tried to seem statesmanlike and dignified. But twice at the August 3 press conference he flared up. When a reporter cited Adenauer's remark that Khrushchev would now see how strong the United States was, he denied his "legs would bend" in America and called the West German Chancellor "sick" and "senile." Would Eisenhower be invited to see a Soviet missile site on his return visit in June? Khrushchev took that to mean, Would he try to frighten Ike with Soviet might? "You want to give our meeting a bad taste," he snapped. If he were to do that to Eisenhower, the president would have every right to say, "What did you invite me for, to intimidate me?"

At the end of the press conference Khrushchev asked reporters' "indulgence" if he had committed "any slips of the tongue." What he had wanted to say was that "we are going to America with an open mind and pure heart." If, therefore, "any of my statements today may be construed in a different spirit, please ask me to clarify . . . for I do not want aggressive forces to be able to use anything I have said here to intensify 'the cold war.' "[88]

Khrushchev's tension peaked on September 15. The big plane lifted off the runway at 7:00 A.M. Twelve hours later Eisenhower would be waiting at Andrews Air Force Base outside Washington. Besides Khrushchev and his party, a platoon of jet engine specialists were seated in a specially cordoned-off corner of the main cabin. With the help of a special apparatus, which resembled a cross between a stethoscope and a heart monitoring machine, they were checking the pulse of the jet engines. Red flashes would signal trouble; green ones meant all was well.[89]

Down below there was also anxiety. The KGB had wanted Soviet cruisers and destroyers to be posted along the route in case the plane went down, but Khrushchev vetoed the scheme as too expensive and unlikely to be of any help anyway. Soviet security settled instead for freighters, tankers, and fishing boats strung out along the flight path from Iceland to New York.[90]

"I had a lot on my mind when we took off from Moscow and headed West," Khrushchev later said. "All sorts of thoughts went through my head as I looked out the window at the ocean below." Pride was one of them: "From a ravaged, backward, illiterate Russia we had transformed ourselves into a Russia whose accomplishments had stunned the world." Yet "I'll admit that I was worried. I felt as if I were about to undergo an important test." Part of the challenge would be his face-off with the president, whom he was meeting "man to man" for the first time.[91] Beyond that, there was America. He'd "already passed the test in India, in Burma and in England. But this was America! Not that we considered American culture to be on a higher plane than English culture, but American power was of decisive significance. Therefore, our task would be to represent our country with dignity and understanding of our partner's position. If a disagreement arose, as undoubtedly it would, we had to express our point of view without raising our voice . . . without letting ourselves be humiliated or saying more than was necessary in diplomatic negotiations."

What made the situation even "more complicated" was the fact that "Stalin [had] kept trying to convince us that we . . . were no good, that we wouldn't be able to stand up to the imperialists, that the first time we came into personal contact with them we wouldn't be able to defend our interests, and they would simply smash us." As the plane raced toward Washington, "Stalin's words sounded in my head. They didn't depress me. On the contrary, they helped me mobilize my forces to prepare myself morally and psychologically for the meeting. . . . In the midst of these thoughts I was informed that we were approaching the United States. We had begun to circle and were about to land. In a few minutes we'd be face to face with America. . . . Now I'd be able to see it with my own eyes, to touch it with my own fingers. All this put me on my guard, and my nerves were strained with excitement."[92]

THE WEATHER in Washington was hot; the sky above Andrews Air Force Base was cloudless. Flags of both countries fluttered in a slight breeze while the fifty-six-piece military band's shiny instruments sparkled in the bright sun. Despite his best efforts, Khrushchev had arrived an hour late. The president of the United States, together with his secretary of state, the chairman of the Joint Chiefs of Staff, the permanent representative to the United Nations, and other officials, had had to wait in the heat. Whether or not *they* were impressed by the mighty plane that at last soared into view, Adzhubei and the other Khrushchev aides and speechwriters who later chronicled the trip in *Face to Face with America* certainly were: "He arrived in a powerful swept-winged colossus that had no equal anywhere," that was "carried across the ocean not only by its mighty engines . . . but by the solicitous and considerate strength of millions of Soviet toilers, of all progressive people on earth, by their indomitable and passionate desire for peace."[93]

The Americans had prepared a stunning ceremony, complete with red carpet, anthems, and a twenty-one gun salute. Khrushchev was "terribly impressed. Everything was shining and glittering. We didn't do such things in our country; we always did things in a proletarian way, which sometimes, I'm afraid, meant they were done a bit carelessly." He was also moved: "It was a very solemn moment, and it made me immensely proud; it even shook me up a bit. Not because they were welcoming me in this way, but because that's the way they were meeting a representative of a great socialist country."[94]

Khrushchev's dark medal-bedecked suit was elegantly tailored. He was surprised to find Eisenhower in civilian dress rather than a military uniform. Expecting the president to try to intimidate him from the start, Khrushchev had prepared a ploy of his own. Several days earlier Moscow had launched a rocket to the moon. Khrushchev wanted to rub in Soviet space superiority by presenting Eisenhower with a replica of the pennant that arrived on the moon the day before he did in Washington. He had nearly salivated at the thought of doing so in front of television cameras at Andrews Air Force Base. Only after Troyanovsky and other aides objected did he agree to tender the president the polished wooden box in the Oval Office. According to official American minutes of the occasion, "the President accepted the souvenir with interest and appreciation." Actually Eisenhower was appalled by Khrushchev's crudity but tried not to show his anger. "After all," he told his son later, "this fellow *might* have been sincere."[95]

After the airport ceremony Khrushchev and his wife squeezed into the back seat of an open limousine with the president and headed down the fifteen-mile parkway toward Washington. Except for a few who smiled and waved, most people lining the route were stone-faced and strangely silent. Khrushchev later claimed a special car had driven the route a few minutes before with a sign reading NO APPLAUSE—NO WELCOME TO KHRUSHCHEV. Eisenhower's aide Andrew Goodpaster suspected the Russians put the car up to it themselves to embarrass the president. According to *Pravda*, "such a sea of people had not been seen in the streets of the city since the end of World War Two. . . . Millions of Americans know and believe that the leader of the great Soviet power came here with an open heart and the most noble intentions. . . ."[96]

Thus began what the trip's Soviet chroniclers called "the thirteen days that stirred the world," a "triumphant journey" that had "no precedent in history."[97] In many ways Khrushchev's trip *was* a success: his very presence in the citadel of capitalism; the way many ordinary Americans received him; "progress" enough on Berlin to justify the president's endorsing the summit Khrushchev had so long been seeking. But the glass was also half empty. The progress in Berlin was more image than substance. Khrushchev's personal failings undermined his diplomacy. From his being unsure if he would measure up, it was a short step to his assuming his hosts were showing him up, and in the process of putting the Americans in their place, he overreacted as usual.

Khrushchev's aides tried to "explain American pluralism" to him, telling him that "any hostility he encountered was the work of a minority and that the majority of Americans . . .. sympathized with him. . . . "[98] But they too were sure that unfriendly questioning was orchestrated. "He felt this wasn't proper," recalled Troyanovsky, "After all, he was a head of state, and it wasn't right for people to start rebutting him whether before or after he spoke. This sort of thing got him really angry. This was perhaps another case of his inferiority complex acting up when he felt that not only he but the country he represented was being insulted."[99]

Of course the Soviet leader was also a good actor. At least one American diplomat assigned to accompany him came away convinced that his outbursts were designed to put Eisenhower on the defensive.[100] But Khrushchev's amour propre was also at stake. He was resolved "not to be amazed by the grandeur of America, not to appear an envious provincial." That required him to rein in his natural curiosity, even though every evening he asked other members of the delegation, such as his minister of education, Vyacheslav Yeliutin, and the chairman of the Dnepropetrovsk regional economic council Nikolai Tikhonov, to report impressions they'd gathered that day.[101]

The result of trying to control both his temper and his curiosity, wrote Adzhubei later, was that "Khrushchev was always on guard," and his aides were even more "nervous and worried." Every morning they scrutinized newspapers, looking for positive coverage they could report to the boss, as well as slights they could blame on the other side. (Khrushchev family members who could read English also inspected local newspapers. At one point Mrs. Khrushchev mistook an unflattering picture of an overweight woman for one of herself and took offense. "If I'd known there would be pictures like these," she complained to Jane Thompson, "I wouldn't have come."[102]) Aides were relieved when "Nikita Sergeyevich's ability to act naturally under all circumstances came to his aid," even at mammoth official receptions and dinner parties attended by dignitaries in white tie and tails and in evening gowns. But Adzhubei also stole nervous glances at Khrushchev's table manners, "afraid that he wouldn't be able to handle all the many spoons, forks and other utensils arrayed in front and beside his plate."[103]

At first, Khrushchev did a creditable job of containing himself. When the president took him up in a helicopter to display thousands of "decent, fine comfortable homes" and had the pilot hover low over rush-hour traffic, Khrushchev pretended not to be impressed, nor did he reveal how appalled he was by all the automobiles "jamming up the highway." At a formal state dinner—to which Americans wore formal dress while the Soviets appeared in business suits and what Mamie Eisenhower called street dresses, and at which guests dined on traditional American roast turkey with cranberry sauce to the accompaniment of "Zip-A-Dee-Doo-Dah," "Over the Rainbow," and "The Battle Hymn of the Republic" played by Fred Waring and the Pennsylvanians—Khrushchev's formal toast mixed modesty ("I don't pretend I have too profound a knowledge of history") with his usual braggadocio ("It is true that you are richer than we are at present. But tomorrow we will be as rich as you are. The next day? Even richer! But is there anything wrong with this?").[104]

At a U.S. Department of Agriculture research center in Beltsville, Maryland, the next morning, when hundreds of journalists waited at the main entrance and researchers in white smocks hung out of every window, the distinguished guest complimented his hosts on their "very good cows," while reminding them, "without wishing to belittle your successes," that "in the course of three years the average milk yield per cow in our country has risen by 600 liters."[105]

Khrushchev's speech at the National Press Club that day was notable for its upbeat and constructive tone and for his obvious concern not to misspeak: "If I should happen to make a slip, ask me to repeat what I said . . . because I don't want misunderstood words to clash with what I meant to say and what I strive for."[106] All the more galling, then, that the first questioner asked about Khrushchev's role in Stalin's terror: Was it true that Khrushchev had once turned aside an anonymous question about his role by asking the questioner to stand up and then saying, when no one did, "You see, there's your answer." The question stung all the more because the audience laughed. Khrushchev's eyes narrowed, his face turned red, and he replied with considerable heat. But he was also determined not to be provoked: "You apparently want to place me in an embarrassing position, and are laughing beforehand. The Russians say, 'He who laughs last laughs best.' . . . I will only add that a lie, however long its legs, can never keep pace with the truth."[107]

Another apparent "provocation" (as Khrushchev saw it) harked back to a famous phrase he had uttered in November 1956, in the heat of anger about the Hungarian and Suez crises. At a Polish Embassy reception in honor of Gomułka, Khrushchev had directed his wrath at Western diplomats: "Whether you like it or not, history is on our side. We will bury you."[108] The context, a reference to the Soviet idea of peaceful coexistence, suggested that he was referring to victory in economic and political competition, but many in the West took the remark literally. "If you didn't say it," a National Press Club questioner remarked, "you could deny it, and if you did say it, could you please explain what you meant?" Khrushchev deflected the challenge with a joke: "My life would be too short to bury every one of you if this were to occur to me."[109] But another question on Soviet intervention in Hungary ignited his anger. "The so-called Hungarian question," he snarled, "has stuck like a dead rat in the throat of some people—they are disgusted with it and yet cannot spit it out." According to Soviet chroniclers, this "straight talk won over the audience with that natural combination of theoretical depth and down-to-earth simplicity which is known in the West as the 'Khrushchev style.'"[110]

After several more Washington events—a visit to the city's monuments, a meeting with the Senate Foreign Relations Committee (including an encounter with John F. Kennedy), and a reception and dinner at the Soviet Embassy—the Khrushchev party left on a special 8:22 A.M. train for New York, which Khrushchev found to be "a huge, noisy city with an enormous number of neon signs and automobiles, and hence vast quantities of exhaust fumes that were choking people."[111] After depositing his wife and daughters at the Waldorf-Astoria Hotel, Khrushchev dined with sixteen hundred civic leaders at the Hotel Commodore. His aides interpreted speeches by Mayor Robert F. Wagner and by U.S. Ambassador to the UN Henry Cabot Lodge, official host throughout the tour, as more "provocations."[112] But Khrushchev coolly explained he had "not been converted to your capitalist faith" since, as the Russian proverb has it, "every snipe praises its own bog."[113]

Later that afternoon Averell Harriman invited to his East Eighty-first Street town house thirty men each of whom owned or controlled assets of a hundred million or more. John J. McCloy, the unofficial chairman of the eastern establishment, was there. So were John D. Rockefeller III, Dean Rusk of the Rockefeller Foundation, David Sarnoff of RCA, and the heads of Metropolitan Life, Cities Service, and the First Boston Corporation. Compared with these titans, the guest of honor looked oddly out of place. The Harvard economist John Kenneth Galbraith, whose assets fell far short but who had wangled an invitation from his old friend Averell, later described a "very shapeless man in a rather shapeless suit with a very large pink head and very short legs" sitting beneath the large Picasso that hung over the fireplace.[114]

To Khrushchev, Harriman's guests "looked like typical capitalists, right out of the posters painted during our Civil War—only they didn't have the pigs' snouts our artists always gave them." Khrushchev liked cocktails American-style: "Instead of making us sit at a table in an assigned place, Harriman had us moving around freely, talking to people we were interested in." He didn't like the "tobacco smoke [that] hung in the room like a cloud," through which "people kept coming up to me to exchange a few words, obviously trying to sound me out and see what kind of man I was."[115]

As a change of pace from his other appearances, Harriman offered Khrushchev the chance to ask questions instead of answering them. But that clashed with Khrushchev's determination not to seem too interested; besides, it would give the assembled dignitaries the opportunity to "instruct" him. When it turned out that he couldn't lecture them and that they weren't willing to press Washington for increased trade with the USSR, he brusquely excused himself and returned to the Waldorf, where another group of businessmen was giving a dinner in his honor.

Nearly two thousand attended the Economic Club of New York affair in the Grand Ballroom, with extra tables set up on the balcony of the nearby billiard hall. Khrushchev's speech in praise of trade and peaceful coexistence was mild enough, but the first questioner, *Look* magazine's publisher Gardner Cowles, challenged him to explain how peaceful coexistence squared with Soviet insistence on the inevitable triumph of communism. Khrushchev was instructing Cowles on fine points of the Marxist dialectic when someone in the balcony shouted, "That doesn't answer the question." When Khrushchev ducked a question about why Soviet citizens couldn't read American newspapers or listen to the Voice of America, shouts of "Answer the question!" rang out.

"They were acting like a bunch of tomcats on a fence," Khrushchev later recalled. "If you don't want to listen, all right," he responded at the time. "I am an old sparrow and you cannot muddle me with your cries. If there is no desire to listen to me, I can go. I did not come to the USA to beg. I represent the great Soviet state."[116]

The next day's schedule included a car trip to FDR's home at Hyde Park, a visit to the Empire State Building, a talk with Governor Nelson Rockefeller, plus an appearance at the United Nations. On the way to Hyde Park, Khrushchev seemed to be brooding. He was "of two minds" about his Economic Club appearance, he told Lodge: His speech had been a success, but the evening as a whole had not been.[117]

ON SEPTEMBER 19, the Khrushchev party rose before dawn in New York in order to see Harlem on the way to the airport and to arrive in Los Angeles before lunch. The long, hot day (the weather in L.A. was "smoldering and Sahara-like," Lodge recalled) ended with a Khrushchev speech that began at nearly midnight. By that time he was frazzled and on edge.

The Soviet delegation was welcomed at the airport by the mayor and a group of dignitaries. Deputy Mayor Victor Carter, a Russian émigré who was assigned to accompany Khrushchev, spoke Russian "poorly—with a thick Jewish accent," Khrushchev later said. Since Carter had grown up in Rostov, where only a rich Jew would have been allowed to live before 1917, his father must have been a wealthy merchant, one whom the Red Army (in whose ranks Khrushchev had fought in Rostov) had "failed to take care of during the Revolution," Khrushchev told Lodge.[118]

Lunch at Twentieth Century–Fox studio's Café de Paris brought out the cream of Hollywood society, including Kirk Douglas, Frank Sinatra, Gary Cooper, and Elizabeth Taylor. Ronald Reagan boycotted the lunch. Marilyn Monroe, asked to wear her "tightest, sexiest dress" and leave her husband, Arthur Miller, at home, later told her maid, "I could tell Khrushchev liked me. He smiled more when he was introduced to me than for anybody else. . . ."[119]

Fox paid for the luncheon to save U.S. taxpayer money.[120] That left Spyros Skouras, the Greek-born self-made movie mogul, in charge, and he was bent on teaching his guest a thing or two about the American dream by recounting his rags-to-riches rise. "In a word," *Face to Face with America* reported afterward, "his speech followed the same plan concocted by someone else and somewhere else—to outargue Khrushchev at all costs." When Khrushchev spoke after lunch, Lodge recalled, "the heat from the floodlights, added to the weather and the low ceiling, made the place almost unbearable."[121] Nonetheless, he was determined to top Skouras's story. "I began working when I learned to walk. Till the age of fifteen I tended calves, then sheep, and then the landlord's cows. . . . Then I worked at a factory owned by Germans, and later in coal pits owned by Frenchmen . . . and now I am Prime Minister of the great Soviet state."

"We knew that," someone shouted.

"What if you did?" Khrushchev yelled back. "I'm not ashamed of my past."

Flaunting his humble origins before Hollywood glitterati must have been as painful as it was satisfying. He had meant to make "a very short and unemotional speech," he told his audience, but "I cannot be silent when someone treads on my pet corn, even if he does so after putting a pad on it."[122]

He didn't like being denied Disneyland either. He'd been told he couldn't go because the Los Angeles Police Department couldn't guarantee his safety without emptying the whole park. The fact that Soviet security people approved the cancellation didn't soften the blow. Why couldn't he go? Had cholera broken out? Had Disneyland "been seized by bandits who might destroy me"? It was at this point that Frank Sinatra whispered to David Niven, Nina Khrushcheva's neighbor at the table, "Screw the cops! Tell the old broad you and I'll take 'em down this afternoon."[123]

From a mezzanine overlooking Fox Sound Stage 8, the Khrushchevs watched Sinatra, Shirley MacLaine, and Maurice Chevalier filming *Can-Can.* Descending from the perch to mingle with the dancers, Khrushchev at first grinned but then tried to look subdued. KTLA television cameras recorded him posing happily with female dancers on either side of him. But he scolded photographers who shouted at the dancers to raise their skirts: "In the Soviet Union, we are in the habit of admiring the faces of the actors rather than their backsides."[124] The next day, at a stormy confrontation with labor leaders in San Francisco, Khrushchev stood up, turned his back to them, flipped up his coat, and mimicked the *Can-Can.* "This is what you call freedom—freedom for the girls to show their backsides. To us it's pornography. It's capitalism that makes the girls that way."[125]

In his memoirs Khrushchev asked: "What kind of man would ask a girl to do something like that? He just wanted to get a juicy picture of a girl in that sort of outfit next to Khrushchev. I still have those pictures somewhere."[126] If he still had those pictures, maybe he wasn't so outraged after all. State Department interpreter Alexander Akalovsky, who stood right behind Khrushchev on the sound stage, thought the Soviet leader "thoroughly enjoyed it."[127]

With Disneyland off limits, Khrushchev's hosts killed time by, as he put it, "driving practically aimlessly around the Los Angeles suburbs for two hours" in a closed armored Cadillac. Even Lodge agreed: "The interminable afternoon dragged on."[128] At one point the car passed a woman dressed in black with a black flag in one hand and a sign reading DEATH TO KHRUSHCHEV, THE BUTCHER OF HUNGARY.

"If Eisenhower wanted to have me insulted," said Khrushchev angrily, "why did he invite me to come to the United States in the first place?"

Did Khrushchev really think the president had arranged for this protest? Lodge objected.

"In the Soviet Union she wouldn't be there unless I had given the order," was Khrushchev's self-incriminating reply.

Ever more irritated, he insisted that nothing he had seen impressed him since he had known all about the United States before coming. One reason he was so well informed, he told Lodge, was that his intelligence services regularly provided him with confidential messages from Eisenhower to other world leaders. Lodge "probably didn't know" about a letter Eisenhower sent to Nehru on the Sino-Indian border dispute. If so, Khrushchev could "supply him with a copy." In fact, he got too many American reports "sent out by Mr. Allen Dulles." He "would rather read good novels."[129]

That evening the Ambassador Hotel ballroom was packed with prominent Angelenos. Khrushchev later admitted that the tables were "beautifully decorated and gently lit" and that "the meal was delicious and lavishly served: no cabbage soup for these people." On his right sat a middle-aged woman who seemed "very rich; she had to possess huge amounts of capital—otherwise she wouldn't have been there." She treated him "civilly," he recalled, but "she obviously considered us exotic. I could imagine her thinking to herself: 'How exciting! Here's a real Russian bear! In Russia, bears actually roam the streets. This one has come to our country and is sitting right here beside me.' "

The scene reminded Khrushchev of a fair he had attended in Yuzovka at age fourteen. For fifty kopecks he had seen an elephant and even pulled its tail. Now he was the elephant, and the woman was wondering, "What does he look like? Does he know how to sit at a table in polite society and properly hold a knife and fork, or will he lap up his food off his plate?"[130]

Khrushchev was already fuming when Mayor Norris Poulson "welcomed" him by recalling Khrushchev's infamous phrase "We will bury you." The mayor warned: "You can't bury us, Mr. Khrushchev, so don't try. If challenged we shall fight to the death."[131]

"I was furious," Khrushchev remembered. "I couldn't pretend I didn't know what he was really saying, so I decided to deal him a counterblow then and there publicly."[132] He began by saying, "You know that I have come here with good intentions, but some of you would like to reduce the matter to a joke." Perhaps some viewed him and his delegation "as poor relations begging for peace." Perhaps he'd been invited so as "to give him a 'going over,' to show him the strength and might of the United States, so that his knees would bend a bit." If so, he was ready to go home right then and there. All it would take would be about ten hours by plane.[133]

As Khrushchev ranted on, a horrified hush fell over the room. His threat seemed all too real. Later, in the hotel's huge presidential suite, Khrushchev took off his suit jacket, gathered his family and aides around him, and lambasted the reception he had received. "He didn't stint on colorful phrases," recalled his son. "At times his voice rose to a scream; his fury seemed to have no limits." Finally, he stood up, wiped the sweat from his forehead, and instructed Gromyko to "tell Lodge everything I just said."

By now it was nearly 1:00 A.M. Lodge was dictating his diurnal telegram to Eisenhower recounting the day's doings, when Gromyko barged in, looking disheveled, with the long underwear he wore in spite of the heat sticking out where his shoes and trousers met. The circumspect foreign minister apparently did not transmit his master's message verbatim.[134]

Afterward Khrushchev portrayed his eruption as a charade: "I was in full control of my nerves: I was giving vent to my indignation for the ears of the American accompanying us. I was sure that there were eavesdropping devices in our room and that Mr. Lodge . . . was sitting in front of a speaker with an interpreter and listening to our whole conversation."[135]

What seemed "the explosion of a very emotional man" was actually "calm calculation," Sergei Khrushchev contended. But if so, why did Lidia Gromyko leap up as her husband headed for Lodge's room to implore him, "Andryusha, be more polite with him," and then run off to get a tranquilizer for Khrushchev. Why was Khrushchev's daughter Rada "frightened" too?[136]

Certainly there was calculation, but also real rage, not only at Americans' disrespect but at himself for earning it. After all, it was his ill-conceived "We will bury you" that they kept throwing in his face. What they were doing, Adzhubei confirmed later, was "harping on his blunder—that was how he understood what was happening in Los Angeles."[137]

Khrushchev's outburst had a positive effect, not at the L.A. train station the next morning, where no one from the city administration showed up to bid him farewell, but on the train trip up the coast to San Francisco, which couldn't have been nicer. "We've decided to manage the trip as if you were a Presidential candidate," Lodge told Khrushchev. When the train pulled into Santa Barbara and San Luis Obispo, the "candidate" kissed babies, bowed to ladies, pinned hammer and sickle pins on men, and beamed as large crowds applauded him. "The plain people of America like me," he exclaimed to Lodge. "It's just those bastards around Eisenhower that don't." When his train passed in plain view of Atlas rockets of the Strategic Air Command's First Missile Division at Vandenberg

Air Force Base, just the sort of provocative sight that could have inflamed him again, Khrushchev cheerfully refused to look, telling journalists "confidentially" that "we have more of these bases than you have and, besides, they're much better equipped."[138]

Los Angeles Mayor Poulson was but a dim, malodorous memory by the time the campaign train reached the Golden Gate. "He tried to let a fart and instead shit in his pants," the Soviet premier remarked to special presidential representative Lodge as they took a boat ride in the bay.[139]

San Francisco Mayor George Christopher was as welcoming as Poulson was not.[140] Other events on his schedule, including a tour of a San Jose IBM plant and a civic dinner, went off just as smoothly even though the IBM chief Thomas Watson, in accord with advice received from Washington, tried not to smile at Khrushchev's jokes. Khrushchev relaxed enough to reveal his amazement—not at IBM's computers, which he boasted the Soviet Union had plenty of, but at shiny Formica tabletops in the plant's self-service cafeteria that rendered tablecloths, forever dirty and spotted in Soviet restaurants, unnecessary. "You brush off the crumbs, wipe it with a cloth and everything's clean," he said.[141]

The only event that didn't go swimmingly in San Francisco was the meeting with United Automobile Workers president Walter Reuther and other trade union leaders. When Khrushchev charged the United States with exploiting other countries, he was informed that he himself exploited East German workers. "Do you have credentials to speak for the workers of the world?" asked Reuther. "Do you have credentials to poke your nose in East Germany?" retorted Khrushchev.

With the participants angrily interrupting each other, the discussion hopped from topic to topic. "How can you open your mouth like that and represent the workers?" Khrushchev yelled at the longshoremen's union chief Joseph Curran. "Do you want a discussion, or is this a bazaar?"

"Is he afraid of my questions?" Reuther demanded.

"I'm not afraid of the devil, and you're a man," answered Khrushchev with a swagger.[142]

Many years later Reuther still rankled Khrushchev. "Here was a man who had betrayed the class struggle," he wrote. His struggle was for "an extra nickel or dime," not for "the victory of the working class." As for the head of a brewery workers' union who had been at the San Francisco session, an "old fool" who had gold watches on both wrists and "just sat there the whole meeting drinking beer and eating everything within reach," he "had completely lost his wits, and I don't think his craziness had anything to do with his age. I think he'd probably been a piece of crap as a young man, too."[143]

This shoot-out outdid even Los Angeles. Yet jousting with trade union rivals was child's play for Khrushchev. The fact that the meeting was private (although the Americans later distributed its transcript) allowed him to let off steam without worrying about the public reaction. The deeper irony of the event, which was visible in the way it failed to faze him, was that the "treachery" of American trade unionists was easier for him to take than the contempt of high-and-mighty capitalists.

FROM SAN FRANCISCO it was on to Iowa for a visit to Roswell Garst's farm, where Khrushchev's host ended up throwing heads of corn at a mob of reporters who tried to pursue the Soviet leader across a field. From there he went to Pittsburgh and then back to Washington on September 24 for the Camp David talks that would determine if the trip was a diplomatic success.

The two leaders helicoptered out to Maryland on Friday afternoon, September 25. Eisenhower, who had a cold, felt "lousy." Khrushchev, who had slept poorly the night before, relished the cool Catoctin Mountain air. After a roast beef and red snapper dinner, Eisenhower showed movies of the North Pole taken from the U.S. nuclear submarine *Nautilus*—not quite as crude as Khrushchev's showing films of a nuclear explosion to Tito, but pretty crass nonetheless. Both men retired at midnight.

The next morning Khrushchev rose early, donned an embroidered Ukrainian shirt and trousers, and set off down a forest path with Gromyko to discuss tactics without being overheard by what he assumed were American microphones. At breakfast with Eisenhower in the Aspen Lodge at 8:15 A.M., the Soviet leader rattled on about wartime adventures, hardly touching his eggs, steak, hotcakes, and grits. Afterward he complained to John Eisenhower about his kidney and other ailments.[144]

At 9:20 A.M. the two leaders and their top aides sat down to discuss Berlin and Germany. Khrushchev declared that the main problem wasn't Berlin. Nor did the United States need to recognize East Germany formally. All it had to do was sign a peace treaty with West Germany, while the USSR did so with both Germanys. Eisenhower seemed to reply in kind: the United States would not mind if Moscow signed a treaty with the East Germans as long as that "did not thereby alter our position in Berlin." But Khrushchev called that "an impossible condition." All he could guarantee was that West Berlin would "remain peaceful and prosperous" as a "free city." In the meantime an interim agreement could "take the edge off the Berlin question so that there would be no injury to U.S. prestige."

Khrushchev reminded Eisenhower of the reforms under way in Moscow. Speaking quietly but intently, he listed his government's disagreement with "many things done by Stalin," its ouster of Molotov and other conservatives, its curbing of the police and closing of concentration camps. As a result of all this, he had come to the United States with broad public support "to improve relations between our countries and with you personally." For too long, talks on key issues like disarmament had been "frozen." The American attitude toward the Soviets on Germany had been "high-handed." It was to break through these barriers that the Soviet government had set its Berlin time limit.

This was the truth as Khrushchev understood it. With his own prestige on the line, it was a kind of *cri de coeur.* Eisenhower's response was to suggest a half hour adjournment. Khrushchev invited the president to take a walk. Eisenhower declined. It was "not a very good day outside," he said; besides, he needed to consult his doctor.[145]

A little later, at a bridge table on the corner of the terrace, Eisenhower presented a short paper suggesting "permanent consultative machinery" (including regular foreign ministers' meetings and summits) to address not just Germany and Berlin, but a whole range of other issues. The precondition for such meetings was that "no unilateral action will be taken at any time that would vitiate the operation of this process of peaceful negotiation."[146]

Khrushchev was dismayed. Eisenhower's proposal meant "nothing would happen except that the foreign ministers would pull out their old papers and restate their old positions," with the result that "solutions of problems would be put off for ten or fifteen years or even indefinitely." The president was demanding the Soviets not sign a German peace treaty. Now it was Washington that was imposing "an ultimatum."

Khrushchev's reaction was understandable but also petulant. Just because he needed "progress" on Berlin didn't mean that Eisenhower had to provide it. After all, the president said, if he ever accepted a time limit after which the United States would have to withdraw from Berlin, he "would have to resign." For "such a proposition would never be accepted by the American people."

Neither man raised his voice, but both looked grim. Trying to ease the tension at lunch, Nixon asked whether Khrushchev preferred hunting birds and big game with a rifle or a shotgun. The vice president didn't know what he was talking about, Khrushchev snapped; big game obviously required rifles while shotguns were used for birds. Nor did Gromyko, whom Khrushchev accused of "buying" the ducks he pretended to bag when they went hunting. When Gromyko objected that his wife had seen him shoot the ducks, Khrushchev announced he didn't trust Mrs. Gromyko either.[147]

Eisenhower tried to deflect the conversation. After complaining that the telephone kept ringing when he was on vacation, he asked whether Khrushchev's did too. At this point Khrushchev "became almost violent, stating that telephones were even installed on the beach when he went swimming, and that he could assure us that soon they in the USSR would have more and better telephones than we have and that then we would cut off our telephones since we are always afraid of comparisons."[148]

Khrushchev seemed about to burst. Eisenhower, recalled White House science adviser George Kistiakowsky, "was intensely angry and just managed to control himself." Gromyko and his aides seemed "totally frozen."[149]

After lunch the president took a nap. When he reappeared around four o'clock, he found Khrushchev pacing the grounds. The president invited him to pay a brief visit to his Gettysburg farm. As the presidential helicopter took off for the short flight, "everybody was very much depressed," Kistiakowsky later wrote. "There was a general feeling that the meeting will end in a nearly complete failure and hence may actually worsen rather than improve relations."[150]

Gettysburg helped. Khrushchev admired Eisenhower's house ("a rich man's house but not a millionaire's"), his cattle (one of which the president asked him "right then and there" to accept as a gift), and his grandchildren (whom Khrushchev kindly invited to visit the USSR with their grandfather). When the two men arrived back at Camp David at six-thirty for cocktails and supper, Khrushchev seemed "considerably more relaxed."[151]

After breakfast the next morning he erupted again. Undersecretary of State Douglas Dillon assured him that items that Moscow seemed interested in importing (including equipment for manufacturing shoes) were not strategic commodities and hence were readily available. Khrushchev retorted that he had not come to the United States "to learn to make shoes or sausage." The Soviet people knew quite well how to make them, "perhaps even better than the Americans." If Mr. Dillon doubted that, let him look at Khrushchev's shoes and see for himself.[152]

At ten-fifteen the president and the chairman sat down again with their aides. After the conversation touched on nuclear war (Khrushchev said he wasn't afraid of it; Eisenhower said he was and thought everyone should be), the Soviet leader mentioned China. Instead of probing for Sino-Soviet differences, Eisenhower repeated the standard American indictment of Beijing, leaving Khrushchev no choice but to defend his ally, after which the president said U.S. and Soviet views on China were so divergent there was "no point in discussing the question in detail." The only result of this exchange was a Khrushchev comment that soon got him into trouble with Mao: that although he knew nothing about five Americans the Chinese were holding prisoner, he might when he was in Beijing "ask the Chinese leadership about the question."[153]

What happened to Berlin and Germany? It turned out the two leaders reached an agreement. Khrushchev withdrew his ultimatum, while Eisenhower promised that current Berlin arrangements would not be maintained indefinitely. As Eisenhower summed it up, the United States was "not trying to perpetuate the situation in Berlin, while Mr. Khrushchev had agreed not to force the Western powers out of Berlin."[154] In addition, the president now agreed to attend a full four-power conference. For months he had refused to do so without prior diplomatic progress. Now he declared that "a situation where he would not have to act under duress could be regarded as progress."[155]

No sooner had the two leaders settled on this than they disagreed over a joint communiqué. Eisenhower suggested doing without one since the talks had been advertised as informal. Khrushchev insisted on demonstrating what he had accomplished. After lunch Khrushchev demanded that his main concession, the elimination of a fixed time limit for talks on Berlin, be dropped from the draft text. Although he confirmed that he had "agreed substantively" to this point, he feared that including it in the communiqué would lead to "difficult and embarrassing interpretations," especially by Adenauer, who wanted to spin out talks for as much as eight years and would now claim "a great victory."[156]

Now it was Eisenhower's turn to explode: "This ends the whole affair. I will go neither to a summit nor to Russia."[157] Since the president insisted, Khrushchev offered a compromise: Eisenhower could state orally that there would be no fixed time limit on Berlin talks, and he (Khrushchev) would not deny it. Reluctantly the president agreed.

By now the two leaders were behind schedule. They hurried back to Washington in the president's limousine, shook hands on the steps of Blair House, and assured each other that they looked forward to meeting in Moscow the next spring. That evening Khrushchev addressed Americans on television, praising them as an "amiable and kindhearted people," commending their president, who had referred to him as "my friend," as a man who "sincerely desires an improvement of relations between our countries," and closing in heavily accented English: "Gootbye! Goot-luck! Friends!"

That same evening the Khrushchev party took off for home.

Not to deny that his ultimatum had been at least temporarily lifted: That was all Khrushchev agreed to at Camp David. No wonder Eisenhower looked to him "like a man who had fallen through a hole in the ice and been dragged from the river with freezing water still dripping off him."[158] But what had Khrushchev achieved? Eisenhower's acceptance of four-power talks neither committed his allies to attend nor ensured an accord at the summit. For the moment, however, Khrushchev was elated by his success.[159] In fact, "success" is a mild term for how he portrayed it back home. He not only allowed his propaganda machine to spread a fantastic picture of what he had accomplished and what lay ahead, but came to believe it himself.

His grueling American trip was just ending. An equally exhausting trip to China lay just ahead. Yet instead of resting from his labors as his Tu-114 headed for Moscow, he summoned two stenographers and set to work. His flight was due to arrive at 3:00 P.M. Moscow time; an hour later he was to report on his trip to thousands gathered in the Luzhniki sports stadium.

The whole Presidium was at Vnukovo Airport to greet him. So, it seemed, was almost the whole party and government apparat, along with the diplomatic corps. Children presented him and his family with flowers. Tens of thousands lined Leninsky and Lomonosovsky Prospekts and waved at the motorcade from the windows of high-rise apartment houses. "I saw pride shining on Khrushchev's face," Adzhubei recalled. "He refused even to stop at home" before he "set off for the rally."[160]

Thousands more waited at the stadium. After the Soviet national anthem and a greeting by the Moscow party leader, representatives of the masses added their welcome: an automotive machine tool adjuster ("Nikita Sergeyevich is crushing the ice of the cold war with the strength of an ice breaker"), a female team leader from a collective farm ("The clouds of the cold war are dispersing; life and work have become more cheerful"), an academician, and a student "on behalf of Soviet youth."[161]

Khrushchev's speech, interrupted fifty times by applause, promised a new era of peace. Eisenhower had "displayed wise statesmanship" and "courage and determination." The president enjoyed "the absolute confidence of his people" (a notion radically at odds with the official Communist view of American politics). Of course Eisenhower and Khrushchev could not "clear away all the accretions of the cold war in one sitting." "Evil forces" in America still needed to be "roasted like devils in a frying pan." But the president "sincerely wishes to see the end of the cold war" and "is prepared to exert his efforts and his will to bring about agreement between our countries."

This sort of talk was a serious political error; it raised expectations that could not be fulfilled. But it was rooted in Khrushchev's psychological state. So "euphoric" was he over his American trip, according to his son, that he thought he could resolve any contradictions with China in conversations with Mao.[162]

Even the disastrous China trip that followed didn't derail Khrushchev; on the contrary, it increased his stake in showing that his personal diplomacy could bear fruit. The most dramatic expression of his confidence was his January announcement that Soviet armed forces would be reduced by a million more men. He predicted that the question of West Berlin also would be settled "on an agreed basis." In February the Warsaw Pact's Political Consultative Committee declared the world had entered "a phase of negotiation" to settle "major, disputed international issues."[163]

If the audience for such pronouncements were only foreign, they could be written off as propaganda. But similar hype was heard at home, especially as preparations for Eisenhower's return visit began. The Eisenhowers were to arrive on June 10 and to spend a week visiting Moscow, Leningrad, Kiev, and Irkutsk; from there they would take a boat trip down the Angara River before leaving for Tokyo on June 19.

Khrushchev personally supervised the arrangements. Although he was notorious for stinting on funding for new government buildings and new dachas for the elite, he quickly approved construction of a series of luxurious villas in places the president was to visit. One of them, a hunting lodge on a wooded bluff over Lake Baikal, was still called the Eisenhower dacha years later. Determined to match the hospitality he had received at Camp David, Khrushchev agonized over whether to host the Eisenhowers at his own dacha outside Moscow, or at the state guesthouse at Novo-Ogaryovo. The former corresponded more closely to Camp David since he lived there, but he wasn't sure there were enough bathrooms.

Since the Union of Soviet Socialist Republics had no golf course, Khrushchev had one built for his guest. When Eisenhower asked to use his own plane within the Soviet Union, Khrushchev overrode the objections of the military. The KGB feared the plane would take secret photographs of Soviet bridges, highways, and railroads—and they were right. High-resolution cameras were soon being built into the belly of Air Force One in a secret hangar at Andrews Air Force Base.[164]

Although not all preparations for the Eisenhower visit were made public, the Soviet people got the message. Whole neighborhoods in Moscow and Leningrad got face-lifts (streets repaved, facades repainted, etc.). So did a small village in the hinterland through which an American diplomat happened to travel. The village wasn't anywhere near the presidential itinerary, but it was spruced up anyway just in case the president decided to drop in. "You know," said a local official, "when that president of yours gets here, we will give him a welcome the likes of which no Soviet leader has ever had."[165]

For decades Muscovites hadn't dared telephone Americans for fear their lines were tapped. Now Americans suddenly got calls from Soviet friends proposing that they get together. Moreover, all this genuine enthusiasm could only be expected to swell into a tremendous pro-American crescendo once Eisenhower arrived. Soviet ideological watchdogs were alarmed. The image of the United States as the "class enemy," carefully cultivated for forty years, was proving hollow. A massive, spontaneous, public ideological defection was in effect taking place.

Khrushchev was worried too, his son recalled. "All his hopes were now linked with the upcoming summit and even more with President Eisenhower's visit to the Soviet Union." Since he was laying the foundation for a new era, "it was particularly important not to stumble at the start of the process when everyone's nerves were on edge. One false move, one wrongly understood step, and all his labors would go up in smoke."[166]

CHAPTER SIXTEEN

From the U-2 to the UN Shoe: April–September 1960

ALONG WITH THE November 7 anniversary of the Bolshevik Revolution, May Day was the most important Soviet holiday of the year. The entire Kremlin leadership assembled atop the Lenin Mausoleum in Red Square to review a mammoth parade. Lesser officials and diplomats stood to either side of the reddish brown marble mausoleum on rows of white-painted stands. After tanks, artillery, and missile launchers roared across the cobblestones, thousands of citizens in festive spring attire walked across the square, carrying banners hailing peace and communism and waving at their leaders. From a distance they looked like an undifferentiated throng; actually, groups from factories and other enterprises marched in prearranged columns mustered on the streets outside the square. Although the regime's purpose was to project popular support for itself, for many of the marchers their May Day pass-by was mostly a good time.

May 1, 1960, dawned bright and sunny. Khrushchev was asleep in his Lenin Hills residence at about 6:00 A.M. when the secure Kremlin phone on a small bedside table rang. Defense Minister Malinovsky reported that an American U-2 spy flight had crossed the USSR's southern border with Pakistan and was heading into the Soviet heartland.

Khrushchev looked grim when he came down for breakfast. He sat silently, tapping the side of his glass of tea with a spoon. His family knew better than to ask what was wrong; if he wanted to tell them, he would.

After downing his tea, he walked outside to his limousine. The family had expected to accompany him to Red Square, where, as was the custom since Stalin's day, they had tickets to the stands to the left of the mausoleum. This time they would have to get there on their own. Khrushchev was hurrying to an emergency meeting of the Presidium in the Kremlin. Beyond the high walls that separated the Khrushchev compound from Vorobyovsky Avenue, loudspeakers were already booming out revolutionary songs.

"They've flown over us, again, in the same area," Khrushchev grunted to his son, who followed him out to the car.

"Will we shoot it down?" Sergei asked.

"That's a stupid question," snapped his father. Malinovsky had sworn that interceptors and antiaircraft missiles were at the ready, but the planes were too few, and the missiles' capabilities limited. "It all depends on what happens, on whether it stumbles on our batteries, on whether we hit it or miss." Where was the plane now? Sergei asked. Near Tyura-Tam, replied Khrushchev, "but where it will turn next, who knows?" He climbed into his car and drove off.[1]

This was not the first American overflight of Soviet territory. Starting in 1946, aerial reconnaissance flights approached Soviet borders, and some strayed into Soviet airspace. Beginning in 1952, secret American and British flights had brazenly soared past the Urals into Siberia and photographed cities like Murmansk in the far north, Vladivostok in the far east, and Stalingrad.[2] The first U-2 flight took off from Wiesbaden, West Germany, on July 4, 1956, soared across Poland and Byelorussia, and passed over Moscow twice before turning north to Leningrad and exiting over the Baltic. Six more U-2 flights covered central Russia and Ukraine that same week. After a pause, flights resumed in November 1956 and the summer of 1957 and continued irregularly after that.

Eisenhower, who personally approved every U-2 flight, realized the gravity of what he was doing. Nothing would make him "request authority to declare war more quickly than violation of our air space by Soviet aircraft," he once admitted.[3] Yet he felt compelled to monitor Soviet missile building (which Democratic party critics charged had created a "missile gap" in Moscow's favor) so as to avoid a potential surprise attack; Soviet interceptors and antiaircraft missiles seemed unable to reach the high-flying U-2s, let alone shoot them down; and furthermore, after lodging several protests in 1956 and 1958, the Soviets had stopped complaining about the flights, as if they had become reconciled to them.

Despite these reassuring developments, the president allowed no flights for seven months after Khrushchev's American trip. Eisenhower was worried about derailing the upcoming summit, especially if in the meantime Moscow developed the capacity to shoot down the intruders. But U.S. intelligence pressed for more flights, installed new engines allowing U-2s to fly even higher and new devices to foil Soviet radar, and pointed out that Khrushchev had not uttered a word of complaint either at Camp David or since. That persuaded the president to authorize yet another flight on April 9, 1960.

Far from being reconciled to American intrusions, Khrushchev was obsessed by them. If he had stopped protesting and held his tongue at Camp David, that was to avoid humiliation. He kept harping on the situation in conversations with his son. So outraged was he that it seemed to Sergei that his father actually hoped another intruder would appear so that he could shoot it down. "The way to teach smart alecks a lesson," Khrushchev said, "is with a fist. Our fist will look impressive enough. Just let them poke their nose in here again."[4]

Khrushchev was in the Crimea on April 9, 1960, meeting at his dacha with Soviet military and industrial officials, when a U-2 took off from Peshawar in Pakistan and headed west over the USSR. It sailed over the supersecret nuclear test site near Semipalatinsk, the air defense missile test range near Sary Shagan on Lake Balhkash, and the ballistic missile test site at Tyura-Tam, later world-famous as Baikonur, in Kazakhstan. Soviet aircraft and anti-aircraft crews scrambled urgently, but a MiG-19 that couldn't have come close to the U-2 anyway crashed near Semipalatinsk, T-3 interceptors couldn't get Moscow's permission to use the secret Semipalatinsk airfield until the trespasser was gone, Sary Shagan had no antiaircraft missiles ready for launching, and two Tyura-Tam T-3s, one without its own rockets but with a MIG-19 missile jerry-rigged to its wing at the last minute, couldn't reach their target.[5]

After Khrushchev's Crimea guests departed, he and Sergei walked in gloomy silence along the seashore. Asked how the American plane could get away, Khrushchev replied with a curse. He had no choice, he said, but to swallow this "bitter pill." Another protest would only confirm the imperialists' assumption that "the weak complain against the strong; the strong pay no attention and continue their insolent action."[6]

Khrushchev couldn't figure out who had authorized this latest flight. Surely not his "friend" Eisenhower; surely not just before the summit in Paris on May 16. Allen Dulles must have done it to rub in American superiority on the eve of the meeting. All the more reason to read the riot act to the Soviet military, sternly ordering Malinovsky to make sure the next intruder was shot down and directing that several generals and other officers be severely punished.[7]

However, not only had Eisenhower authorized the April 9 incursion, but he had also approved another one for later the same month. Dulles and Richard Bissell, who ran the U-2 program at the CIA, wanted fresh photos of Tyura-Tam, a look at military-industrial sites near Sverdlovsk, and some shots of Plesetsk, about six hundred miles north of Moscow, where the first operational Soviet ICBMs were reportedly being readied for deployment. If those missiles weren't photographed in the next three months, the sun's angle in the northern latitudes would preclude another chance for an entire year. Once again Eisenhower hesitated, but then he reluctantly authorized another flight no later than April 25, and when bad weather intervened, he extended the cutoff date to May 1. The flight that took place on May Day was the most daring yet. Until then a U-2 had never flown more than halfway across the USSR. The new mission, called Operation Grandslam, was to take off from Pakistan, fly over Tyura-Tam, turn north to Sverdlovsk and northwest to Plesetsk, and then land in Bodø, Norway.[8]

By the time Khrushchev's limousine raced from the Lenin Hills to the Kremlin, the command post of Soviet air defense forces had gone into a panic. Not just Malinovsky but Khrushchev himself had called to deliver a warning: A further failure to bring down the American spy plane, after all the money the state had spent to destroy them, would be a disgrace. Yet on a high holiday when the Soviet military was in a low state of readiness, all signs pointed to just such a disaster.

As Francis Gary Powers's plane neared Sverdlovsk, the air defense command dispatched a lone high-altitude interceptor that just happened to be at the nearby Koltsovo air base en route to somewhere else. The T-3's pilot, Captain Igor Mentyukov, had been waiting at a local bus stop in his parade uniform when a car roared up and raced him back to the base. He had neither his high-altitude flight suit nor his oxygen mask handy, and his plane was unarmed at the time. At an altitude of twelve miles he would have no air to breathe; nonetheless, he was ordered to find the U-2 and to ram it. Fortunately for Mentyukov he never got close enough to lay eyes on Powers and instead returned safely to base.[9]

Senior Lieutenant Sergei Safronov wasn't so lucky. His MIG-19 was shot down by a rocket meant for Powers. By that time Powers's plane itself had been hit or, rather, broken apart by a missile that detonated just behind it. But when large pieces of the U-2 made it look on Soviet radar screens as if his flight were continuing, the additional missiles that were fired claimed Safronov instead.[10]

Although the CIA was certain no pilot could endure the destruction of a U-2, Powers parachuted safely to earth and landed on a state farm. He was helped to his feet by a baffled Soviet peasant and soon found himself in the hands of the KGB. His capture and confession would have devastating consequences for both Khrushchev and Eisenhower, but it would be days before the president learned Powers's fate, and when Khrushchev got the news, he was elated. By that time, midmorning in Moscow, he was reviewing the Red Square parade (with its banners proclaiming DEMAND THE IMMEDIATE SIGNING OF A GERMAN PEACE TREATY! and MORE FERTILIZER FOR AGRICULTURE!) when Marshal Sergei Biryuzov, commander of Soviet air defense forces, pushed through the leaders atop the mausoleum and approached Khrushchev. The fact that Biryuzov wasn't wearing his dress uniform alerted watching diplomats that something special had occurred. The microphone in front of Khrushchev didn't pick up their whole conversation, but the whole square heard Khrushchev exclaim, "Well done!"[11]

When he arrived home that evening, according to his son, Khrushchev was "extraordinarily pleased. At long last he felt himself avenged," but his vengeance was far from complete. His next move would be to trap the Americans by not revealing that he had the plane and its pilot, by waiting for Washington to invent some sort of cover story, and then unmasking it. That way, recalled Sergei, he would get back at his tormentors for "all the years of humiliation."[12]

Khrushchev still assumed Eisenhower wasn't responsible, that rogue elements in the military and the CIA were. Ordinarily that would have been extremely disturbing, but for the moment it reassured him. For if spying was spying but diplomacy was another matter, as Khrushchev told his son, then the long-awaited Paris summit could open as scheduled. Even Air Marshal Konstantin Vershinin's visit to Washington, slated to begin on May 14, could proceed as planned. Khrushchev figured that when he sprang his trap and revealed Powers's fate, the chagrined Eisenhower would apologize and even sit still for a show trial of the captured American pilot.[13]

His plan was too clever by half, and he became its main victim. In fact, as he admitted to a visiting American in 1969, the U-2 was the beginning of the end. Dr. A. McGehee Harvey came to Moscow to treat Khrushchev's daughter Yelena, who was suffering from collagenitis. During a dinner at Khrushchev's house (itself not easy to arrange since Khrushchev then lived under virtual house arrest), Dr. Harvey asked why his host had fallen from power. "Things were going well until one thing happened," Khrushchev answered. "From the time Gary Powers was shot down in a U-2 over the Soviet Union, I was no longer in full control." After that, "those who felt that America had imperialist intentions and that military strength was the most important thing had the evidence they needed, and when the U-2 incident occurred, I no longer had the ability to overcome that feeling."[14]

Not the whole truth and nothing but the truth. But revealing nonetheless.

THE FULL IMPACT and consequences of the U-2 disaster can't be understood without tracking the East-West diplomacy that preceded and immediately followed it. As far as the Western powers were concerned, any hopes generated by Khrushchev's American trip didn't last long. But it wasn't until April 1960 that Khrushchev himself began to despair.

Eisenhower tried to carry out the promise he made at Camp David. As summarized by Ambassador Thompson in January 1960, "at Camp David we undertook in effect to secure agreement of our allies to further effort to solve the specific problem of Berlin."[15] Initially Eisenhower sought a summit in December 1959. The president "was in something of a hurry," Macmillan later recalled, but de Gaulle and Adenauer were not. The French president detected no progress resulting from Khrushchev's American trip that would justify haste, and he had his own agenda to accomplish before any four-power talks. Intent on parity with his Western partners, de Gaulle wanted to explode France's first atomic bomb, to have Khrushchev tour France as he had the United States, and to hold a Western "presummit" before the real thing. If that meant a delay until the spring, so much the better since, as de Gaulle saw it, a summit would amount to "a chorus of mutual assurances of good will and of effusive statements on both sides, alternating with criticism addressed to the regimes of others and presentations of reasons which each has for fearing no one."[16]

Adenauer was even less eager for a conference he would not even get to attend. Any agreement that altered West Berlin's status would mean a capitulation to Khrushchev's demands. So obstructionist was the West German chancellor that by March, Eisenhower, who briefly considered countenancing "some sort of free city" in West Berlin with either a United

Nations or a four-power guarantee to replace the Allies' juridical rights, was complaining that Adenauer was "showing real signs of senility."[17] But although Eisenhower complained to Macmillan that he was "disgusted by the delay," he was "not disposed to argue any more." That confirmed Macmillan's sense that "only Khrushchev and I were genuine supporters of an effective summit meeting."[18] But even his enthusiasm had limits. When de Gaulle told Macmillan in December 1959 that he regarded Khrushchev's upcoming French visit with "considerable distaste," the best the prime minister could muster was his view that Khrushchev had become "rather less tiresome and that was one advantage of seeing him."[19]

The result of allied jockeying was that the Western negotiating position on Berlin reverted to where it had been before Khrushchev's American tour. Prospects for a limited nuclear test ban agreement seemed somewhat better; although differences remained on the number of onsite inspections, the makeup of control commissions, and peaceful explosions, Macmillan thought "all the [test ban] omens were good." By April he believed the world was "on the eve of a great step forward."[20] But de Gaulle expected "few positive results from the Paris meeting."[21]

In the afterglow of his American trip, Khrushchev considered a summit agreement on Berlin almost a sure thing and a test ban accord also likely.[22] That helps explain why he devised another radical reduction in Soviet armed forces, by another 1.2 million troops, including 250,000 officers. The memorandum he sent to the Presidium on December 8 was bursting with optimism and enthusiasm. "We now have a broad range of rockets and in such quantity that we can virtually shatter the world," boasted Khrushchev, when the USSR had but four barely workable intercontinental missiles near Plesetsk in northern Russia. While "some comrades" might object to what looked like unilateral disarmament, Khrushchev assumed the Western powers were trapped; if they did not follow the Soviet example, they would be "sucking from their budgets, depleting national economies," and "thereby contributing to the advantages of our system." Khrushchev was so sanguine that he foresaw a day when the Red Army could move toward a militia-based force built on the "territorial principle with citizens recruited to serve without leaving their industries."

Khrushchev claimed to be proceeding deliberately. "Perhaps I cannot foresee everything," he remarked modestly. Nonetheless, he expected the cuts to be adopted "at the end of January or in February," and they were: The Presidium assented on December 14, two weeks after that the Central Committee plenum offered its blessing, and in mid-January

Khrushchev presented the deepest cuts in Soviet armed forces since 1924 to the Supreme Soviet for its rubber-stamp approval.[23] Neither the Warsaw Treaty Organization nor the frontline German Democratic Republic was consulted at all. Khrushchev confided to Ambassador Thompson that "he had been obliged to use all of his authority to persuade the Soviet military, but that they now agreed with him."[24]

Thompson had another glimpse of Khrushchev's euphoria on New Year's Eve. Again Soviet high society gathered with diplomats in the Kremlin, where a huge New Year's tree towered over tables groaning with food and drink. The toasts didn't end until nearly 2:00 A.M., and couples were still dancing when Khrushchev swept Ambassador and Mrs. Thompson, the French ambassador and his wife, and Italian Communist Luigi Longo into a smaller room boasting a fountain filled with colored plastic rocks. He tried to corral the British and German ambassadors too, but for some reason they had gone home to sleep, so he settled for Mikoyan and Kozlov instead. While an alcoholic haze settled over the company, Khrushchev announced (as Thompson's dispatch the next day put it) that "he was exceedingly pleased by his trip to the US and that President Eisenhower had simply overwhelmed him with his personality," adding that "if only the President could serve another term he was sure our problems could be solved." After "repeatedly and solemnly" proclaiming that war would be suicide because of the "awful nature of modern weapons," Khrushchev boasted he had thirty such bombs earmarked for France and about fifty for Britain. How many did he have for the United States? Jane Thompson asked. That, he replied, was a secret. Khrushchev warned again that if the upcoming summit produced no German agreement, he would sign a separate treaty with East Germany that would end Western rights in Berlin. Kozlov and Thompson tried several times to break up the party. They finally succeeded just before 6:00 A.M.[25]

That same evening Khrushchev issued an extraordinary invitation to the Thompsons: that they and their children, and Thompson's deputy Boris Klosson and his, spend the next weekend at the Khrushchev dacha. Long black limousines took the two families out on Friday evening; upon their arrival KGB security men pulled the children on sleds along snow-covered paths. Khrushchev arrived the next morning, wearing a fur hat with flaps pulled down over his ears. The day's revels included riding Arabian horses at a nearby stable ("Be sure to pick gentle ones," the Americans' genial host instructed a stable hand), followed by a long, informal luncheon at which Mikoyan served as toastmaster, Gromyko seemed more lighthearted than Klosson had ever seen him, Mrs. Gromyko assured the Americans they'd have plenty of time to eat since Khrushchev would "talk forever," and Aleksei Adzhubei put records on the phonograph. "If only Stalin could see us here with the American ambassador," said Mikoyan, "he would turn over in his grave."[26]

Khrushchev was still upbeat when Henry Cabot Lodge came calling in early February. The Soviet leader sent word to Eisenhower that he would be free to travel "anywhere in the USSR," even to secret military bases, that he hoped the president's grandchildren would accompany him, and that the president's reception would be so friendly that there would be no need for security precautions. When Lodge regretted Khrushchev's visit to Los Angeles hadn't gone "just right," his host brushed off the episode, saying that as time passed, he was "more and more delighted with his visit."[27]

Despite his seeming optimism, Khrushchev must have picked up signs that the summit might not meet expectations. If he was increasingly torn between hope and concern, that could account for his frenetic whirl of activity during the next three months. It was as if he couldn't wait for the summit, yet didn't want to think about it either, as if he were determined to have no time to rejoice prematurely or to despair. "It was as if the dam burst," Sergei Khrushchev remembered, inundating his father with international visits and meetings of all sorts. "Father spun this way and that," Sergei said, switching metaphors, "like a squirrel in a cage."[28]

Shortly after seeing Lodge, Khrushchev set out for Asia (accompanied by Sergei, daughters Rada and Yulia, and granddaughter Yulia). He arrived in India on February 11, Burma on February 16, Indonesia, February 18, and Afghanistan on March 2, and returned to Moscow on March 5. The tour confirmed the USSR's budding bond with developing countries, but considering that he had visited three of the four countries five years earlier and that his schedule was more crowded with rallies and receptions than with serious talks, its main payoff was probably the personal adulation he received at each stop, plus the chance to engage in Khrushchev's patented brand of populist sightseeing. Nearly a decade later he "vividly" recalled a mammoth Calcutta rally at which "an enormous quantity of doves" was released: "Night was falling. One of the doves landed on my arm. People started making jokes, and the photographers naturally couldn't resist taking pictures. I'd been speaking out in favor of peace in all the countries I'd visited, so people remarked that here was a dove who knew where to perch." In Indonesia "we were greeted by huge crowds and with much pomp, in a manner appropriate to our rank."[29]

At India's Bhilai iron and steel plant, which had been built with

Soviet support, the minister of industry welcomed Khrushchev as a man who "has a profound understanding of metallurgy." Without missing a beat, the honorary engineer advised his audience to "substitute reinforced concrete for metal structures in construction" and instructed his listeners on how to process slag: "You have to take the slag hot, without cooling it, keep it at the required temperature and not waste fuel heating it, and immediately convert it into the finished product." He also found time to note that housing construction at the plant reflected "primitive work" and "a peasant psychology." Instead of catering to every "peasant individualist" who wanted "a separate house," the Indians should build four- and five-story apartment houses, as he was doing in the USSR—the very sort, one can't help adding, that the Soviet peasants were rejecting, even in his native Kalinovka.[30]

Khrushchev's sightseeing included bare-breasted village women in Indonesia; he later noted they lacked "Helene Kuragina's lovely figure and voluptuous breasts," about which he'd read in *War and Peace.* An Indonesian fruit called a durian, which when opened emitted "the foulest, most repulsive smell—an odor like rotten meat," made a striking impression on Khrushchev's unsuspecting Presidium colleagues, to whom he asked his security guards to ship several cartons by air.[31]

Toward the end of his trip, when a Western correspondent confronted him with rumors that a secret Khrushchev-Eisenhower meeting would occur before the summit, Khrushchev mock seriously confessed: "I must admit that, yes, such a meeting between President Eisenhower and me took place yesterday. He was in Indonesia and I had a long talk with him. It was a very friendly talk. He took off for Washington today."[32]

Both these episodes had a deeper meaning: foul-smelling fruit for colleagues he disdained; just the sort of tête-à-tête with Ike that he wished had taken place. There were other pranks too. As their plane crossed the equator, Khrushchev watched grinning while his associates cavorted in the aisle in makeshift costumes devised by Adzhubei for his father-in-law: the usually dour Gromyko disguised in black and red as the devil; the head of the Committee on Economic Ties with Foreign Countries in a false beard; Adzhubei himself wearing a goofy paper hat.[33]

An hour after returning to Moscow, Khrushchev reported on his trip to fifteen thousand Muscovites at the Luzhniki sports stadium. Ten days later he was off again to France for another week and a half, meaning that all told, he was away from Moscow for almost all of February and March.

FRANCE OF COURSE was not Burma. De Gaulle was one of the Big Four, and he was causing trouble for his allies as well as for the Soviets. If Khrushchev could get him to join Eisenhower and Macmillan in endorsing a summit agreement on Germany, then Adenauer would be isolated.[34] In addition, de Gaulle was fascinating personally as well as politically. "Something in de Gaulle's personality charmed Khrushchev," his son-in-law remembered. Adzhubei guessed that "something" was de Gaulle's "firmness of will."[35] But Khrushchev also zeroed in on other qualities. Echoing Stalin's opinion, he considered de Gaulle "one of the most intelligent statesmen in the world, at least among bourgeois leaders." He also liked de Gaulle's "self-confidence and air of authority." The French leader passed the "doesn't consult with his foreign minister" test that Eisenhower had flunked at Geneva. The tall, dignified Frenchman was also "incredibly calm and unhurried," traits that "bothered" the hot-blooded, restless Khrushchev.[36]

Given his respect for de Gaulle, Khrushchev wouldn't have been entirely pleased to know how he struck his host. With the exception of "one somewhat violent speech," de Gaulle later told Macmillan, "Mr. Khrushchev had been very pleasant." He was "proud and somewhat self-conscious in that he watched the effect that his words had," but they didn't always produce the effect he sought. He was a "cunning, intelligent, self-made man," but although he knew the fundamentals under discussion very well, he was "not always meticulous in detail," and "he had a set piece formula for each question which he continually repeated."[37]

Khrushchev stuck to set pieces because de Gaulle did anything but. "I couldn't figure out exactly what he had in mind," Khrushchev recalled later. "He dropped some hints, but I couldn't tell exactly where they were leading." De Gaulle shared Khrushchev's view that Germany could conceivably become a threat ("If it does," he promised, "then we will be with you"), and he certainly was no champion of German reunification. But the way to reach a German agreement, he insisted, was to lower the very tensions Khrushchev's Berlin pressure had raised. If a real European power balance could be achieved, de Gaulle continued, using words that must have made Khrushchev's mouth water, "then we won't even need the United States." But according to de Gaulle, such a balance required that West Germany be firmly anchored in the Western camp, and that was something Khrushchev was trying to prevent. De Gaulle made Khrushchev's diplomacy sound downright dumb. He chided the Soviet leader as if he were an errant child, saying, "Your anxious tone on the German question can only amaze me." Khrushchev did have a point—that prospects for a German agreement were nil until he upped the ante on Berlin—but that didn't mean his Berlin pressure would produce a German treaty in the end.[38]

Besides the talks with de Gaulle, which touched on subjects like disarmament and Africa as well as Germany, the trip was notable for seeing and being seen. Fortunately the official welcome was grand, in both Paris and the provinces. When he heard he was to be hosted by local prefects who, among other duties, supervised the police, Khrushchev was "somewhat offended." He "didn't like the idea of traveling under the wing of the French police. I thought our delegation was being discriminated against in some way." It took the French Communist leader Maurice Thorez to reassure him that "President de Gaulle ordered his [prefects] to receive only the most honored guests."[39]

Khrushchev boasted that the USSR would soon overtake the West, but—*pace* his experience in America—there was no more talk of "burying" the competition. He was impressed by the beauty of Paris and by the Louvre, which reminded him of the thirties, when he tried to swallow the Hermitage whole in a day: "After a whole day of moving as quickly as I could from room to room, I was so exhausted that I couldn't walk; I just collapsed on a bench to rest—and that was when I was young and strong!"[40] But making propaganda and getting edified could provide only so much satisfaction, and occasionally frustration set in. In Reims, Minister of State Louis Jacquinot referred to past invaders of France, hesitated to identify the culprits, and told Khrushchev to be patient when he demanded the Germans be named. "Sometimes I regret that I had no chance to go to a school of diplomacy," Khrushchev retorted, but as a former miner he preferred to speak "sharply, as is the case among workingmen, without resorting to smooth phrases and expressions with hidden meanings." Unlike his suave hosts, he would "call things by their right names." Also, "I want to tell you that I have patience. I have strong nerves. I can be patient and I am being patient."[41] In an impromptu press conference on the train from Lille to Rouen, Khrushchev scolded CBS correspondent Daniel Schorr this way: "Write your poisonous copy until everyone spits on you. . . . If I am struck on the right cheek, I will hit the ringleader so hard on his right cheek that his head won't remain on his shoulders."[42]

By the time he returned home on April 4, it was Khrushchev's head that was spinning. According to Adzhubei, the trip increased his "confidence in his own strength," giving him the "illusion he was rising brilliantly to the Olympus of world recognition," a "flushed-with-success syndrome that disturbed those of us in his inner circle."[43] But Khrushchev took the revolutionary step of *not* reporting to the people an hour after his plane landed, and when he addressed them the next day at the sports palace, he admitted he'd spent a restless night thinking about "how I represented my great country and whether I worthily expressed and defended the interests of the Soviet people."[44]

WHILE KHRUSHCHEV was away, the ground had shifted at home. Top military men were still seething over the January troop cuts, and discontent had spread into broader party and government circles. Reports came in that Adenauer had vetoed further Western concessions on Germany and that the Americans were again inclined to provide him with nuclear weapons. Ambassador Menshikov warned from Washington that the Western strategy was to stall endlessly; that came as no surprise to hardliners who had feared all along that Khrushchev's America-first priority would sow discord with China, while prompting dangerously pro-Western sentiment in the USSR. Even Khrushchev was worried about the prevailing mood. "Aren't we creating false hopes among all these people?" he once muttered to an aide. "What if we fail to make good on what they take as our promise to bring about a better international climate that will allow us to raise the standard of living significantly?"[45]

Members of the Presidium shared these doubts. Brezhnev reportedly questioned Khrushchev's January 1960 troop cuts.[46] Criticisms are said to have been directed at Khrushchev's policy when the Presidium met on April 7.[47] Given his colleagues' fear of him, their reservations were likely expressed as general concerns he shared. But such worries intensified after the April 9 U-2 flight, and in the light of two April warnings by Eisenhower administration spokesmen. Both Secretary Herter (on April 4) and his deputy Douglas Dillon (on April 20) reiterated the pre–Camp David line on Germany (the notion of turning West Berlin into a "free city" was absurd; West Berlin was already free), while warning that Khrushchev was "skating on very thin ice" and that the upcoming summit was unlikely to produce "dramatic achievements."[48] On top of all this, Mao chose April 22 to issue a philippic, "Long Live Leninism!," which denounced Moscow's courtship of Eisenhower as a betrayal of communism. In case Khrushchev hadn't noticed, the Chinese party newspaper *People's Daily* listed thirty-seven aggressive acts by the United States since Camp David, adding, "We see no substantive change in the imperialists' war policy or in Eisenhower himself."[49]

Khrushchev's tone changed on April 25. In a speech delivered in Baku, he suddenly stressed obstacles to summit agreements, uttering merely the faint hope that when the talks were over, "relations between the countries represented will be better than they were previously, rather than the reverse."[50] Troyanovsky later wrote, "Apparently the kind of mood change that was rather typical of Khrushchev had occurred, when euphoria gradually gave way to a more sober view of things."[51]

LOOKING BACK, the former Central Committee aide Fyodor Burlatsky, veteran Americanologist Georgy Arbatov, and Khrushchev "Press Group" consultant Melor Sturua believe Khrushchev seized on the May 1 U-2 flight to scuttle a summit that wouldn't live up to its advance billing. But those closer to Khrushchev insist he did not. When he telephoned Troyanovsky on the evening of May 1, Khrushchev still thought Eisenhower would save the summit by disclaiming any knowledge of the flight and blaming others. If the president went further and actually apologized, then instead of Khrushchev's going to Paris on the defensive (as whoever dispatched the U-2 presumably wanted), it was Eisenhower who would be at a disadvantage. Such an outcome was hardly guaranteed. In the meantime, according to his son, Khrushchev was "simply enjoying the game," gleefully preparing his trap for the White House, but with "no definite plan" for where it would lead.[52]

Washington's handling of the U-2 crisis made a bad situation worse. Instead of remaining silent or settling on a story and sticking with it, the Eisenhower administration started with a clumsy lie and then damagingly dribbled out the truth. When the CIA learned, as its deputy director Robert Amory put it in guarded language, that "one of our machines is down," NASA put out a prearranged cover story on May 3: One of its planes engaged in a high-altitude weather research mission over Turkey had gone down in the eastern part of the country.[53] Although the story was a transparent lie, Eisenhower thought it would allow Khrushchev to continue to ignore U-2 incursions. Even if the plane had been shot down, the president assumed its pilot had perished. Khrushchev had yet to reveal that the U-2 had been destroyed, but that same day in Moscow he stunned a visiting Egyptian delegation with the vehemence of his anti-American harangue.[54]

On Thursday morning, May 5, Khrushchev addressed thirteen hundred deputies of the Supreme Soviet in the Great Kremlin Palace. On the surface, all was calm. For some unknown reason Gromyko had specially invited Ambassador Thompson to attend and to sit in the first row of the diplomatic gallery; the American correspondent Priscilla Johnson was so overcome by the friendly presummit atmosphere that she crossed the gallery to sit with Eastern European Communist journalists. The first part of Khrushchev's speech proposed a domestic program that counted on reduced world tensions: increased priority for consumer goods; a shorter workweek; the abolition of certain taxes by 1965. Then, more than three hours into his speech, he suddenly revealed the U-2 flight and its fate (but not the fate of its pilot), which threw that very program into doubt.[55] American diplomat Vladimir Toumanoff, seated next to Thompson, remembered the moment: Although the day was dark and gloomy and the large hall unlit, making Khrushchev look dull and gray as he droned through the early portion of his speech, just as he dropped the U-2 bombshell, the clouds parted, and a shaft of brilliant sunlight reaching from roof to rostrum lit up his animated face.[56]

His revelation created near bedlam in the hall. To the accompaniment of hoots and catcalls, he hammered away at American treachery and intransigence. The Americans must have dispatched the U-2 to "pressure us," "to weaken our resolve," "to play on our nerves," "to bend our knees and our back."[57] But then he suggested how Eisenhower could save the summit: If "this aggressive act [had been] committed by Pentagon militarists without the President's knowledge," Khrushchev would go to Paris with "a pure heart and with good intentions" and would spare no effort to reach a "mutually satisfactory agreement." His voice, Priscilla Johnson noticed, was "hoarse, low-pitched, and tired."[58]

That same evening Deputy Foreign Minister Jakob Malik made a terrible gaffe at an Ethiopian diplomatic reception. Malik was asked by the Swedish ambassador under what article of the UN Charter the Soviets intended to raise the overflight incident. "I don't know for sure," Malik replied; "they're still questioning the pilot." Llewellyn Thompson, who overheard the remark, dashed back to his embassy and dispatched a MOST URGENT telegram to Washington. It arrived four minutes after a NASA spokesman had speculated publicly that the plane shot down over the USSR might be the NASA research plane that had been studying high-altitude meteorological conditions over Turkey and had been missing since Sunday morning. Since this statement not only lied but lied in detail, it provided a particularly juicy target when Khrushchev eventually sprang his trap. If Thompson's telegram had arrived a few minutes sooner, at least that extra embarrassment might have been averted.

Malik's faux pas forced Khrushchev's hand.[59] Once again the Supreme Soviet provided a forum. On Saturday afternoon, May 7, Khrushchev rehearsed in loving detail the American lies he was about to puncture. Then, with a smile and a chortle: "Comrades, I must tell you a secret. . . . I deliberately did not say that the pilot was alive and in good health and that we have parts of the airplane. [Laughter. Prolonged applause.] We did this intentionally, since if we had reported everything at once, the Americans would have made up another version [Laughter in the hall. Applause]."

With that, the irrepressible premier was off on a rollicking rampage. The U-2's reconnaissance photos, which the Soviets had developed, were excellent, but "I must say that our cameras take better pictures and are more accurate. . . . [Laughter in the hall]." The pilot, Powers, was supposed to have killed himself by pricking himself with a poison pin. "What barbarism! [Murmur in the hall. Shouts: 'Shame!' 'Shame!'] Here is this instrument—the latest achievement of the Americans for killing their own people [N. S. Khrushchev shows a photograph of the poisoned pin]." Powers had been given seventy-five hundred rubles. Did that mean that he had flown in to "exchange old rubles for [recently issued] new ones? [Outburst of laughter. Stormy applause.]" Besides his own watch, Powers had two other gold watches and seven women's rings. "What did he need all this for in the upper layers of the atmosphere? [Laughter in the hall. Applause.] Or perhaps the pilot was to have flown even higher—to Mars—and there intended to entice Martian ladies? [Laughter in the hall. Applause]."

Although this was great fun, it ensnared Khrushchev even as he ridiculed the Americans. He was still willing to grant that President Eisenhower "knew nothing about the incident." But by warning that the American military was giving its own orders, Khrushchev was goading the president into admitting his responsibility in order to prove he was in charge of the American government.[60] Yet it was the U-2 flight that provoked Khrushchev into provoking the president. As Troyanovsky put it later, "if [Khrushchev] hadn't reacted with sufficient harshness, the hawks in Moscow and Beijing would have used the [U-2] incident—and not without justification—to show that the Soviet leader was prepared to accept any insult from Washington."[61]

In an eyes-only telegram to the secretary of state dispatched on the evening of May 7, Ambassador Thompson warned against admitting that Eisenhower had known of the U-2 flights.[62] But the next day the president instructed aides to do just that, justifying the overflights as necessary to prevent surprise attack, denying only that he had specific knowledge of specific flights, including Powers's on May 1.[63]

If there was any chance Eisenhower might have changed his mind at the last minute, saving Khrushchev's face as well as his own, the Soviet leader's behavior on May 9 didn't enhance it. "It is impossible to admit it," he taunted the president at a Czechoslovak Embassy reception, "but also impossible to deny it. It is like the famous story about the spinster who isn't a spinster—she has a baby [Laughter, applause]." What kind of country was it "in which the military can do what the government opposes? . . . If one of our military allowed himself to behave like that, we would grab him by the ear, right here in the daylight [Amused stir]."[64] Yet in the same remarks Khrushchev revealed that he was considering further reductions in Soviet force levels (going beyond those announced in January 1960) and even poked fun at his own military's resistance to them. "I noticed Comrade Zhadov scratch his head at this—another reduction, he says. [Amused stir.] No, this won't happen now, Comrade General, but later. . . . [Amused stir, laughter]."

Soviet generals almost never talked to Ambassador Thompson, but they hinted to him during the U-2 crisis that Khrushchev was "being impetuous and running risks."[65] Khrushchev himself implied that the tensions he was stoking threatened his own standing as well as Eisenhower's. "I must talk with you," he whispered to Thompson. "This U-2 thing has put me in a terrible spot. You have to get me off it."[66]

Thompson promised to try, but it was too late. That same day the State Department press spokesman Lincoln White read the fourth U-2 statement in five days, this one admitting that the overall program had "Presidential authorization." To make matters worse, the statement did not forswear future missions. The president was saving that pledge to use if Khrushchev insisted on it as a condition for attending the summit.[67]

When Khrushchev read the latest American statement, according to his son, he "simply boiled over. If they had set out to drive him out of his wits, they had achieved precisely that result."[68] This was a "betrayal by General Eisenhower, a man who had referred to him as a friend, a man with whom he had only recently sat at the same table . . . , a betrayal that struck him in his very heart. He would never forgive Eisenhower for the U-2."[69]

Khrushchev put the situation this way: "Eisenhower's stand canceled any opportunity for us to get him out of the ticklish situation he was in. . . . It was no longer possible for us to spare the President. He had, so to speak, offered us his back end, and we obliged him by kicking it as hard as we could."[70] Yet even as his anger swelled, Khrushchev continued to prepare for the summit—partly to put the onus for canceling it on the West, partly because Paris would be a grand stage on which to humiliate his tormentor, but also because calling it off would mark the collapse of the policy he had been pursuing for several years.

His conflicting emotions were on display on May 10. The remains of Powers's plane, along with personal effects, including his gold watches, noiseless pistol, rubles for bribes, and unused poison pin, had been placed on display at Gorky Park. All morning crowds poured through the same pavilion where captured German equipment had been displayed during the war. At 4:00 P.M. the hall was cleared so that Khrushchev could inspect the exhibit. Then several hundred journalists, who had just been briefed by Foreign Minister Gromyko, were ushered in for "an impromptu" press conference at which Khrushchev stood on a wicker chair so as to be seen and heard by all.

Khrushchev was "horrified" to learn the president had approved the spy flights: "Impudence, sheer impudence!" It reminded him of criminals who had preyed on defenseless passersby in Yuzovka when he was a boy. "But we are not a defenseless passer-by. Our country is strong and powerful." More than "anger or ridicule," Priscilla Johnson thought, "disappointment at a friendship gone wrong appeared to be the leitmotif of his remarks." Asked if he would still welcome Eisenhower's visit to the Soviet Union, he hesitated a full thirty seconds. "What shall I say?" he finally replied. "Put yourself in my place and answer for me. . . . I am a man, and I have human feelings." Despite that, the summit and the visit were still on. Khrushchev guaranteed that "there will be no excesses during the president's stay." He was doing everything to ensure that "the international situation gets back on a normal track," and he asked the assembled journalists "not to write anything that might lead to greater tension and heat."[71] To Priscilla Johnson it seemed as if Khrushchev were "having a dialogue with himself", as if he were "trying to talk himself out of going to Paris."[72] The impression Khrushchev's remarks created, recalled Troyanovsky, was that "he couldn't make up his mind as to what to do."[73]

At a Presidium meeting on May 12, several members reportedly favored calling off the summit, but Khrushchev still hoped a last-minute gesture by Eisenhower would allow the meeting to proceed. He even told his son that he planned to get to Paris a day or two early so as to allow a peacemaking meeting with the president.[74] On the eve of his departure, during a long stroll at his dacha, Khrushchev reminisced about his visit to Eisenhower's Gettysburg farm. It would be important, he said, to invite the president to the dacha, to show him crops growing at neighboring collective farms, to take him for a motorboat ride on the Moscow River. Yet Khrushchev was "haunted" by what the Americans had done. His "doubts," he later said, "kept nagging at my brain. I became more and more convinced that our pride and dignity would be damaged if we went ahead with the conference as if nothing had happened."[75]

Khrushchev says he decided to wreck the summit while flying to Paris. In fact, the die was cast at Vnukovo-2 Airport. With the exception of Khrushchev, Gromyko, and Malinovsky, the Paris delegates had taken their seats on the plane. (All told, they included twenty-one advisers, five intelligence operatives, eight translators, five code personnel, ten stenographers, four communications specialists, four drivers, twenty-eight bodyguards, and assorted other personnel, such as finance specialists and physicians.) Presidium members gathered in the glass pavilion and then for a final exchange under the wing of the plane. Shortly after takeoff, Khrushchev informed his aides that he would demand that Eisenhower apologize, punish those directly responsible, and promise never to do it again; he thought it practically impossible that the president would agree, so the summit would almost certainly collapse. "This is really a pity," Khrushchev said, "but we have no choice. The U-2 flights are not only a flagrant violation of international law, they are a gross insult to the Soviet Union."

Troyanovsky listened in silence, disheartened at the thought of returning to the worst of the cold war. At the Soviet Embassy on the Rue de Grenelles in Paris, the usually emotionless Deputy Foreign Minister Valerian Zorin wandered the halls muttering, "What a situation! What a situation!" The only man who seemed pleased, according to Troyanovsky, was Defense Minister Malinovsky. Westerners concluded from his glowering visage that Malinovsky had been sent along to make sure Khrushchev didn't stray from the new hard line. Actually, recollected Troyanovsky, there was no danger of that. If anything, it was Khrushchev's anger that needed to be restrained. At one point in Paris, when Gromyko referred to U.S. Secretary of State Herter as a cripple on crutches, Khrushchev wondered aloud if "God has marked the scoundrel." Fearing he would say so to Herter himself, Gromyko and Troyanovsky objected in unison.[76]

WHEN HIS PLANE touched down at Orly Airport on May 14, Khrushchev was ready to erupt: "My anger was building up inside me like an electric force which could be discharged in a great flash at any moment. . . . Our delegation was like a powerful magnet which repels foreign bodies of opposite charge. Anything could happen."[77]

Although his extra day in Paris had been designed to allow for peacemaking, Khrushchev used it to vent his anger. After a night at a former royal hunting lodge now serving as a Soviet Embassy dacha and a morning stroll during which he "helped" a French farmer cut hay with a scythe, Khrushchev turned a courtesy call on de Gaulle into what the latter called "a veritable scene." Khrushchev handed the French president an ultimatum for Eisenhower. De Gaulle's reply, that the U-2 incident itself showed the need for the summit, provoked "a show of furious indignation." The Khrushchev now confronting de Gaulle was utterly unlike the man he had entertained in March, "a character so changed in identity and meaning as to belong to the realm of Russian fiction," the French president later remarked.[78]

Khrushchev was more "agreeable" when he met Macmillan later the same day, but his message was not. After reading from the same prepared statement he had left with de Gaulle, he "made a speech in violent terms, attacked the USA, President Eisenhower, the Pentagon, reactionary and imperialist forces generally." Along the way he remarked that the prime minister had "an aristocratic background," whereas he, Khrushchev, "had the background of a miner." In his youth he had "caught sparrows and the small birds had pecked at his hand," but the Soviet people were "not sparrows, they are strong enough to strike a crushing blow against anyone who would unleash a new war." Eisenhower had addressed Khrushchev as his "friend" at Camp David and even taught him the English word. Now, said Khrushchev, "his *friend* (bitterly repeated again and again), his friend Eisenhower had betrayed him."[79]

Western reactions to Khrushchev's histrionics differed. If Khrushchev wrecked the summit, "France would resign itself to the inevitable," de Gaulle said; it was not it "who had for so long been calling for such a conference." Although thoroughly riled, Eisenhower was still casting around for a way to save the summit. Macmillan, as always, was prepared to concede the most, even that "for Berlin to become a United Nations city was [not] such a terrible fate."[80]

On Monday, May 16, Khrushchev and his delegation arrived first at the Élysée Palace. De Gaulle ushered them up a broad marble staircase to a large, high-ceilinged, green room the windows of which overlooked gardens. In the middle of the room several tables formed a square. Several minutes later, after de Gaulle escorted in the British, Khrushchev and Macmillan shook hands. But when Eisenhower entered, he and Khrushchev did not.[81]

The four delegations seated themselves, with the French and Americans facing each other, the Soviets to the right of the Americans, and the British facing them. "We are gathered here for the Summit Conference," said de Gaulle, calling the meeting to order. "Yesterday I received a statement from one of the participants, Mr. Khrushchev, which I conveyed verbally to the other participants, President Eisenhower and Mr. Macmillan. Does anyone therefore wish to say anything?"

Mr. Khrushchev said he did. So did President Eisenhower. De Gaulle suggested Eisenhower, as chief of state as well as head of government, go first. Khrushchev angrily objected that all chiefs of delegation were equal and that he had been the first to request the floor. De Gaulle raised his eyebrows and looked at Eisenhower, who nodded grimly.

Khrushchev stood up again and, with what Macmillan later described as "a gesture reminiscent of Mr. Micawber," extracted "a large wad of folio typewritten papers out of his pocket" and began to "pulverize Ike (as Micawber did Heep) with a mixture of abuse, vitriolic and offensive, and legal argument."[82]

The Soviet leader took about forty-five minutes (including translation) to read his prepared remarks. "In a situation like this," he later recalled, "I knew I couldn't speak off the top of my head. Every word had to be exact, and every sentence had to be constructed in just the right way . . . leaving no room for any misinterpretation that might be used to the advantage of our adversaries."[83]

As he declaimed in a loud voice, pausing for an occasional drink of water, Khrushchev's left eyebrow twitched and his hands trembled.[84] Since President Eisenhower not only had failed to condemn the U-2 but had declared such flights would continue, the Soviet delegation could take no part in the conference and therefore proposed to postpone it for "approximately six to eight months," by which time, it went without saying, Eisenhower would no longer be president. Likewise, the president's visit to the USSR would be put off indefinitely.[85]

Khrushchev's voice rose even higher as he read. At one point de Gaulle interrupted: "The acoustics in this room are excellent. We can all hear the chairman. There is no need for him to raise his voice." Khrushchev glared over the top of his rimless glasses at de Gaulle but lowered his volume. To the American interpreter, Vernon Walters, it seemed the Soviet leader was "lashing himself into an ever greater frenzy." By the time he was through, Khrushchev later wrote, "I was all worked up, feeling combative and exhilarated. As my kind of simple folk would say, I was spoiling for a fight. I had caused quite a commotion, especially with the passage in which we warned we would rescind our invitation to Eisenhower if we didn't receive satisfaction from the other side."[86]

Eisenhower got madder and madder, his face and neck turning redder, as Khrushchev roared on. But his remarks, which followed Khrushchev's, were subdued. Although the United States would not "shirk its responsibility to safeguard against surprise attack," the U-2 flights "were suspended after the recent incident and are not to be resumed." The American delegation was prepared to continue with the conference. The president was also ready "to undertake bilateral conversations between the United States and the USSR while the main conference proceeds."[87]

Looking stricken, Macmillan begged his colleagues to recall the French proverb "What is postponed is lost." But de Gaulle, who had sat through the Khrushchev tirade appearing bored, again addressed the Soviet leader as one might an errant adolescent: "Before you left Moscow and after the U-2 was shot down, I sent my ambassador to see you to ask whether this meeting should be held or should be postponed. You knew everything then that you know now. You told my ambassador that this conference should be held and that it would be fruitful. . . . You have brought Mr. Macmillan here from London, General Eisenhower here from the United States, and have put me to serious inconvenience to organize and attend a meeting which your intransigence will make impossible. . . . "[88]

He also chided Khrushchev for making so much of airplane overflights when "yesterday that satellite you launched just before you left Moscow to impress us overflew the sky of France eighteen times without my permission. How do I know that you do not have cameras aboard which are taking pictures of my country?"

"As God sees me," replied the allegedly atheist Khrushchev, "my hands are clean."

"Well, then, how did you take those pictures of the far side of the moon which you showed us with such justifiable pride?"

"In that one I had cameras."

"Ah, in *that* one you had cameras."

Khrushchev's hands trembled even more after this exchange.[89] At another point he addressed Eisenhower directly: "I don't know whether I should use this expression—but we don't understand what the devil pushed you into doing this provocative act to us just before the conference. If there had been no incident we would have come here in friendship and in the best possible atmosphere. . . . God is my witness that I come here with clean hands and a pure soul."

Khrushchev allowed himself to express partial satisfaction with Eisenhower's ban on future flights. But when de Gaulle urged that statements made at the session not be made public, in order to preserve an atmosphere in which the conference might continue, he refused. If he did not release his statement, Soviet "public opinion" might think that "the United States has forced the Soviet Union to its knees" by negotiating "in the face of the threat." Since the threat and insult were known to all the world, the world must know that he had not come to Paris to ask NATO "for mercy."

De Gaulle saw no choice but to adjourn the meeting. When Macmillan tried to schedule a "second session," Khrushchev corrected him: "This is not the beginning of the summit conference. That has not started yet. We regard this meeting as a preliminary one."[90]

"I'm just fed up! I'm just fed up!" Eisenhower shouted after returning to the American ambassador's residence. Khrushchev was "a son of bitch" putting on a show to impress the Kremlin. When Macmillan came by later that evening, the president seemed "very much shaken." De Gaulle, on the other hand, was "in one of his rather cynical moods"; it was no surprise to him, he said, that "the whole thing was over." There were tears in Macmillan's eyes when he begged his Western colleagues to let him try to salvage the summit. Its breakup would mean "the collapse or near collapse" of the policy he had been pursuing for two years. "It is impossible to describe this day," Macmillan wrote in his diary that evening. It was "the most tragic day" of his life. When he called at the Soviet Embassy at 9:30 P.M., Khrushchev exulted about how he'd caught the United States red-handed, about how Eisenhower reigned but didn't govern. Khrushchev was "polite, but quite immovable"; Malinovsky, "hardly even blinking"; Gromyko, "also silent." Leaving the embassy, Macmillan grumbled, "The Soviets may know how to make Sputniks, but they certainly don't know how to make trousers."[91]

The Western leaders scheduled a second session—without any real hope, but to put the onus on Khrushchev for staying away. He meanwhile busied himself offstage. The next morning he and Malinovsky went for a drive in the French countryside, followed by a horde of journalists. The convoy stopped on its way to the Marne battlefield so that Khrushchev could "assist" a road crew in chopping up a tree that had fallen across the road, and later arrived at the village of Pleurs-sur-Marne, where Malinovsky had been billeted as a private during World War I. The news, as Macmillan put it, that Khrushchev had "held a series of meetings wherever he could collect a few villagers to listen to him" did not "improve the general temper of my colleagues." As they waited for the Soviet leader to respond to a written summons to a second session, de Gaulle fumed that Khrushchev "would probably go on sending telephone messages and making trips into the country [for] a week." Khrushchev's behavior "showed what a scoundrel he was," grumbled Eisenhower. The time had come "to cut the tail of the cat."[92]

Finally a Soviet aide brought word that Khrushchev refused to RSVP. "Tell him," harrumphed de Gaulle, "that it is the usage between civilized nations to reply to written communications by written communications."[93] A few minutes later the Soviet messenger announced that Khrushchev would answer in writing but would not attend unless the Americans accepted all his preconditions. Khrushchev may still have hoped that Eisenhower would relent. "Who should have taken the initiative?" he asked in a speech after returning to Moscow. "It is clear to all that it should have been the person who *broke* the good relations growing between our two countries. But you see, he expected *me* to ask for an audience!"[94]

Before leaving Paris, Khrushchev held a raucous two-and-a-half-hour press conference before nearly three thousand journalists in an overcrowded, overheated Palais de Chaillot. Standing between a gray-faced Gromyko and a scowling beetle-browed Malinovsky, Khrushchev "really lost it," as Troyanovsky put it. In response to hoots and hisses he thought were coming from West German newspeople, he shook his fists and shouted at "some of those fascist bastards we didn't finish off at Stalingrad. We hit them so hard that we put them ten feet underground right away. If you boo us and attack us again, *look out*! We will hit you so hard there won't be a squeal out of you." When that brought more catcalls (which *Pravda*'s account of the occasion registered as "stormy applause, shouts of 'Right!' 'Long live peace!'," plus "individual disapproving yells"), Khrushchev reminded his listeners whom they were dealing with: "I am a representative of the great Soviet people, who under the leadership of Lenin and the Communist party, accomplished the Great October Socialist Revolution, and. . . . " More shouts and catcalls. Khrushchev again: "I will not conceal my pleasure. I like coming to grips with the enemies of the working class and it is gratifying for me to hear the frenzy of these lackeys of imperialism.

"I remember my mother well," he suddenly added, "and my father, who worked in a mine. She rarely could afford to buy sour cream. But when we did have sour cream on the table the cat would sometimes lick the cream, and she would take the cat by the ears, give it a good shaking, shove its nose in what was left of the sour cream, then give it another shaking and shove its nose in again." Also, "if at the mine where I was raised, a cat was caught climbing into the pigeon coop, it would be grabbed by the tail and thrown to the ground. After that, the cat understood better the lesson he'd been taught."[95]

Khrushchev's performance wasn't a tantrum from start to finish. He struck at least one listener as "humorous and good natured" at times, and he ended not with a warning of war but with a plea for peace.[96] Actually, he had been on his best behavior, considering the circumstances; only later, at a meeting of Eastern European ambassadors, did all his hurt and rage show through.

At the request of Polish Ambassador to France Stanisław Gajewski, Khrushchev briefed Warsaw Pact envoys at the Soviet Embassy in a gilded, red-carpeted room bristling with chandeliers and heavy candelabra, leather sofas and easy chairs. He was animated and red-faced when he entered, accompanied by Gromyko and Malinovsky. After ordering a round of cognac for himself and his friends, Khrushchev told this story: At an isolated tsarist army garrison, officers coped with endless boredom with an unusual kind of concert. After they ate and drank themselves into a semistupor, the commanding general would kick a soldier, prompting him rhythmically to fart out the strains of "God Save the Tsar." But one day, at a command "performance" for guests from a neighboring garrison, the general's kick produced only silence, as did a curse for the silent soloist. Finally, Khrushchev continued, "the soldier could contain himself no longer: 'I tried so hard that I took a shit instead,' he said. That's what Eisenhower did. He tried so hard he took a shit instead. And that, dear Comrades, is what you can report to your governments."

Obsequious laughter all around, except from the sphinxlike Gromyko. Was it true, Khrushchev now asked his foreign minister, that at just this hour (eight o'clock in the evening) the English sat down to dine in their dinner jackets? Gromyko looked perplexed but nodded assent.

"So Macmillan must be dining right now in his tuxedo or dinner jacket," Khrushchev continued. "If so, let's invite him over right now."

How many minutes would it take the prime minster to get there? Khrushchev asked the Soviet ambassador to France Vladimir Vinogradov. About half an hour, Vinogradov replied.

"Then you go call him," said Khrushchev, "and say that I want to talk with him here, that the only possible time is tonight, and that he must be here in forty-minutes, no later. Stress the time. I want him to rush here, so that I can see him with omelette all over his dinner jacket."

Obviously embarrassed, Gromyko whispered something in his boss's ear. With his cheeks blazing and little eyes flashing, Khrushchev burst out laughing and announced loudly, "Andrei Andreyevich is reproaching me for mentioning such details in your presence. But I have no secrets from our allies."[97]

Perhaps Khrushchev changed his mind about summoning Macmillan. History does not record such a visit, with or without an egg-splattered dinner jacket. But as the saying goes, it's the thought that counts; in this case, the way an angry and humiliated Khrushchev tried to bring the elegant but vulnerable Macmillan down to his own boorish level.

Ambassador Gaevski was so appalled that he confessed to *New York Times* columnist C. L. Sulzberger that Khrushchev "was just a bit unbalanced emotionally," a sentiment it turned out West German Chancellor Adenauer shared. "Khrushchev has lost his mind," Adenauer told Sulzberger.[98] American Ambassador to Britain John Hay Whitney said Khrushchev acted in Paris "like a woman scorned."[99] The Chinese of course were pleased. Having warned that "US imperialism" couldn't be trusted, they now hoped (as they recalled in a 1963 letter to Moscow) that "the comrades who had so loudly sung the praises of the so-called spirit of Camp David would draw a lesson from these events. . . . "[100] The East Germans were expectant. When Khrushchev stopped in East Berlin on his way home from Paris, many of the ten thousand Communist faithful he addressed in Seelenbinder Hall expected the message of which the West lived in dread: that the USSR would at last sign that separate peace treaty with East Germany bringing an end to Western rights in Berlin. "The American President committed treachery!" Khrushchev shouted. "I repeat the word—treachery!" But he put off the treaty once again, saying, "We would like to believe that a summit conference will be held in six or eight months. Under the circumstances, it makes sense to wait a little longer. . . . It won't get away from us. We'll wait. It will ripen better."[101]

Khrushchev's Kremlin colleagues doubted his tactics, if not his sanity. "All I know," Shelepin recalled, "is that there have always been spies and always will be. So there must have been a way for him to find another time and place to tell off Eisenhower."[102] Many Soviet diplomats saw the summit's collapse as a disaster for a different reason. Instead of producing at least some progress on outstanding issues, Khrushchev had broken with Eisenhower, ruined Soviet–West German relations (at least for the time being), alienated East German intellectuals, who had hoped for improved ties with the West, and encouraged Walter Ulbricht to continue scheming to create a confrontation over Berlin.[103]

The mood in Khrushchev's plane as it flew back to Moscow was gloomy. This time he did not rush off to the Sports Palace to report to the Soviet people.

"THAT WAS no way to deal with Eisenhower," Mikoyan said many years later. "Because our antiaircraft missile finally accidentally shot down the U-2, Khrushchev engaged in inexcusable hysterics. . . . He simply spat on everyone. . . . He was guilty of delaying the onset of détente for fifteen years." Troyanovsky agreed: "Khrushchev had overdone it in bringing God's wrath down on Eisenhower." Troyanovsky wished he had tried tactfully to restrain his boss but admitted he hadn't dared. Nina Petrovna Khrushcheva later chided him and another aide for not doing so more frequently: "Why don't you correct him? If you don't point out his blunders, who in the world will?"[104]

Khrushchev himself wasn't entirely happy with his Paris performance; although his eyes twinkled when he recounted the commotion he had caused, Sergei Khrushchev remembered, they quickly "took on a guarded expression and turned from brown to almost black."[105] Perhaps that was why he still insisted in his memoirs that he'd handled the U-2 crisis just right: "There's an old Russian saying: once you let your foot get caught in a quagmire, your whole body will be sucked in. In other words, if we hadn't stood up to the Americans, they would have continued to send spies into our country."[106]

Bravado like that came naturally to Khrushchev. After all, the pursuit of détente was only part of his policy. So were competing against the capitalists, rebuffing Western threats, putting arrogant leaders in their place. Still, his discontent revealed itself in several ways that summer: in the especially frantic pace of his activities; in singularly sour references to Eisenhower; most serious of all, in precipitate actions against Mao Zedong that irretrievably damaged relations with the Chinese.

Khrushchev's summer schedule included ten days in Romania (June 18 through 27), nine in Austria (June 30 to July 8), and three in Finland (September 2 to 4) as well as an inspection trip to Astrakhan Province near the Caspian Sea and a return to his native Kalinovka (which he had somehow managed to skip in 1959). Everywhere he gloated about progress at home and abroad, but with a defensive undertone. He denied his high hopes for the summit had been excessive. He explained why he had gone to Paris at all ("to exercise self-restraint to the utmost"), why he hadn't met separately there with Eisenhower (the president's fault), why he hadn't warned the Americans about overflights before May 1 (because they would have gloated that the USSR couldn't shoot them down), and why he had not held the usual welcome home meeting with the public upon his return to Moscow (because he had just spoken in Berlin and because a gathering of Communist shock workers was soon to occur anyway).[107]

A press conference on June 3 included this diatribe: If Eisenhower needed a job when he left the White House, "we might hire him as the director of a kindergarten. (I'm sure he wouldn't mistreat the children.)" As for canceling Ike's visit to the USSR, "A man doesn't go to dinner in a place he has fouled." On the same occasion Khrushchev pledged to seek better relations with the United States after the American election, but also, if necessary, to sign the German peace treaty abrogating Western rights in Berlin. "Am I being clear?" he asked the four hundred or so assembled correspondents.

"*Shouts.*—Yes!

"*N. S. Khrushchev.*—I think it's clear, too. And if it isn't, we'll repeat it again. It will be even clearer after we conclude a peace treaty."[108]

On July 9 Khrushchev addressed a congress of schoolteachers in Moscow. Recollecting his recent trip to Austria and particularly the way the Catholic Church there had tried to mobilize the faithful against him, he stressed the first syllable of *pastva*, the Russian word for "congregation" and then asked his audience whether he had emphasized the correct syllable. "I must admit that I am trembling as I read because I know my shortcomings in pronunciation, and I know you are strict judges. . . . I don't want to pile the responsibility on my teachers. My teachers were good people, especially one woman whom I will never forget, Lydia Mikhailovna, whom I shall never forget as long as I live. She did everything she could, but apparently the environment in which I lived left its imprint on me. So what is it, *pástva* or *pastvá*?"[109]

Eager to please him, his aides managed to find his Kalinovka teacher and bring her to Moscow for a tender reunion with her former star pupil. Khrushchev must have gloried in having so exceeded even her lofty expectations. Yet the failure of the Paris summit continued to gnaw at him. In June, the KGB chief Shelepin recommended a long list of dirty tricks, including forged documents designed to discredit the CIA, its director, Allen Dulles, and President Eisenhower himself. It's not clear how many were actually carried out or whether Khrushchev requested the list in the first place. But if the aides who tracked down Lydia Mikhailovna could sense their boss's mood, so could Shelepin.[110]

Likewise, in spades, could Khrushchev's son-in-law, the *Izvestia* editor Adzhubei. One evening in Austria, Adzhubei drank too much and shouted at an American: "'You Americans are finished but you will not admit it. We are so strong we can crush you like this," at which point he broke off the neck of a wine bottle. When the American shot back that Adzhubei sounded like Hitler, Adzhubei grew so enraged that his compatriots tried to drag him out of the room. "No, no," he cried, "I want to tell this American just what I think of his government. It is composed of stupid and weak men who betray people."[111]

Mao and his men didn't look much better to Khrushchev. The collapse of the summit curtailed the Soviet courtship of Washington that so upset the Chinese. By moving closer to Beijing, Khrushchev could please those in Moscow who feared "losing China." But getting too close would encourage Chinese sympathizers in the Kremlin to push for a reconciliation on terms Khrushchev couldn't accept. To state these options is to imply Khrushchev coolly chose between them. In fact, he lashed out at Mao without thinking through the consequences.

The Third Congress of the Romanian Communist party was scheduled to open on June 20 in Bucharest. Until June 18 it shaped up as a routine conclave. On that day, however, Khrushchev suddenly announced his decision to attend, forcing leaders of other ruling Communist parties to do likewise, with the glaring exception of the Chinese and their budding allies the Albanians. When he arrived, he then surprised all the delegates with an anti-Chinese blitzkrieg.

Khrushchev's formal speech defended his pursuit of peaceful coexistence with the West despite the Paris setback. Meanwhile the Soviet delegation distributed an eighty-page "Letter of Information" that vigorously rebutted Chinese positions across the board. Peng Zhen, the head of the Chinese delegation, attacked the Soviet letter while circulating a private Soviet communication to the Chinese Communist party that was vituperative in the extreme, a letter described by a Westerner who saw it as "hectoring and bitter, [and] in construction loose and wide-ranging (like one of Khrushchev's own speeches)."[112]

If Khrushchev had been hoping to stun the Chinese, their release of this letter stunned him. At a final closed session of the congress, he threw away his prepared text and launched into a furious harangue. According to one account, he criticized Mao by name as "oblivious of any interests other than his own, spinning theories detached from the realities of the modern world." According to another, he referred to Mao as "a Buddha who gets his theory out of his nose" and as an old *galosh,* the word that means "scumbag" in both Russian and Chinese.[113]

Khrushchev's fiery performance, of a piece with his Paris press conference several weeks earlier, prompted a bitter reply from Peng, who mocked him for having no foreign policy except to blow hot and cold toward the West. Challenged, Khrushchev took his revenge: overnight he pulled all Soviet advisers out of China. According to the Chinese, Moscow withdrew 1,390 experts, tore up 343 contracts, and scrapped 257 cooperative projects in science and technology, "all within the short span of a month."[114] Besides the adverse economic impact (Sino-Soviet trade declined by more than half in 1961, and by 1962 Soviet exports to China were a mere quarter of what they had been in 1959),[115] Khrushchev's action deprived Moscow of the chance to gather invaluable intelligence from its advisers in China.

The Soviet ambassador in China at the time, Stepan Chervonenko, was "amazed" at news of the withdrawal and took steps to try to prevent it. "We sent a telegram to Moscow. We said the move would be a violation of international law. If our help to the Chinese must end, then at least let the advisers stay until their contracts were up. We hoped that in the meantime things would get patched up at the top."[116] Chervonenko attributed Moscow's mistake to Khrushchev's personal impulsiveness. So apparently did Leonid Brezhnev, whose former aide Aleksandrov-Agentov dated the start of the split between Khrushchev and his protégé to a series of "impulsive foreign policy measures that damaged our own state interests. All you have to remember is the unexpected pull-out from China not only of our military, but also economic advisers—all in spite of existing agreements and contracts."[117]

Former Central Committee official Lev Deliusin remembered how this fateful decision was made. Deliusin had heard that his bosses were thinking of pulling the advisers out, and he thought he had convinced Yuri Andropov, then in charge of relations with other Communist parties, that to do so would be a grave error. Andropov commissioned Deliusin to prepare a memorandum to that effect. But before he could start writing, said Deliusin, "we got a call from Khrushchev's Secretariat saying he had just signed an order withdrawing them. I consider this one of Khrushchev's most flagrant mistakes. Of course it led to a further worsening of relations. He thought it would improve them."[118]

In fact, Moscow and Beijing did move toward a truce that more or less held through the conference of eighty-one Communist parties held in Moscow in November 1960, a meeting that, despite some harsh exchanges, ended with a compromise declaration that both signed.[119] But as Mao's interpreter Yan Mingfu recalled, "it was a temporary armistice. In the long run, events were already out of control."[120]

AFTER PARIS, Khrushchev said he would wait six to eight months before resuming high-level East-West diplomacy. His notion that Eisenhower's successor would be prepared to parley following the November election or immediately after the January inauguration was wildly optimistic. In the meantime, early in June, he pondered attending the UN General Assembly in September. By the middle of July he had decided to go, but the official announcement followed only on August 10. His ostensible aim was to support his favorite causes, especially disarmament and decolonization. His more personal motive, remembered his son, was to "take revenge for what had happened in Paris," to take it by forcing Western leaders against their will to gather again at the highest level, by unmasking the United States and its president before the whole world, by proposing to move the UN out of the United States altogether. Most of all, according to Troyanovsky, his boss had "an irresistible urge to humiliate the Prince of Darkness by appearing uninvited at Eisenhower's own court."[121]

The cautious Gromyko worried that other world leaders would stay home, leaving Khrushchev embarrassingly isolated, except for Communist allies, in New York. So when other leaders followed his example, Khrushchev was "triumphant," his son recalled, and when the Americans decreed that Soviet delegation members wouldn't be allowed to leave Manhattan without official permission, he was "simply bursting to do battle."[122]

Khrushchev decided to travel to New York by ship. He dreamed of arriving there like the first American settlers he had read about in his youth (while avoiding the humiliation of having to stop for aircraft refueling since the Tu-114 he had flown nonstop to Washington the year before was undergoing repairs). Yet high anticipation seemed to alternate with moments of depression; increasingly, according to Sergei Khrushchev, "Father was preoccupied by thoughts of death." Ostensibly he worried that "NATO might try some sort of diversionary action against our ship,"[123] but he probably also feared his trip would prove a poor substitute for the diplomatic triumph that had eluded him in Paris.

Accompanied by the leaders of Hungary, Romania, and Bulgaria (and also Ukraine and Byelorussia, which Stalin had connived to get admitted to the UN as independent states in 1945), Khrushchev set sail from a Soviet naval base at Baltiisk (near the former East Prussian city of Konigsberg) on the evening of September 9. The good ship *Baltika* had been built in Amsterdam for the Germans in 1940, seized by the Soviets as reparations after the war, renamed the *Vyacheslav Molotov*, and then renamed again after the betrayal of the "anti-party group" in 1957.[124] Khrushchev's recollection of his first and only ocean crossing is one of concern giving way to exhilaration. His worry focused on the possibility of a hostile reception in New York. His exhilaration came from combining work (reading position papers and consulting with Eastern European leaders) with play (shuffleboard plus constant jokes at the expense of those who got seasick when he did not) and from the "new and rare feeling" he got from being "surrounded by water as far as the eye could see."[125]

A group of experts and assistants[126] took turns reading him intelligence reports on world events as they sat on deck chairs. One of the aides, Dmitri Goriunov, remembered Khrushchev as "very calm on the ship. There were no outbursts, although he was a very impulsive person."[127] But Gromyko was horrified when Khrushchev dictated notes sharpening speeches the Foreign Ministry had drafted for him in Moscow: "Remark more sharply on the one-sidedness of the UN actions. . . . It's worth thinking about moving UN headquarters to Switzerland, Australia or the USSR. . . . In reply to the US . . . smash them in the teeth and then say, 'Excuse me, I didn't mean to do it, but look at it from my point of view. I had to do it because you bared your teeth.' "[128]

As the long voyage dragged on, Khrushchev could often be found surrounded by sailors, regaling them with stories and jokes. While the Eastern European leaders played cards endlessly in the bar, he preferred to watch movies, but he joined them to watch amateur entertainment by the crew and for several drinking bouts, especially with his pal the Hungarian leader János Kádár. When his senior associates languished seasick in their cabins, and lower-level officials chased waitresses and typists, Khrushchev passed time with the likes of junior Soviet diplomat Arkady Shevchenko. Khrushchev lamented his unfamiliarity with Western literature but joked that rather than learn a foreign language, "it would be better for me to master Russian properly." As for how to handle the Western leaders, he looked forward to softening them up for later arms control talks with propaganda about general and complete disarmament. "Every vegetable has its season," he told Shevchenko genially.[129]

The *Baltika* lumbered into New York harbor on September 19. What a comedown from Khrushchev's triumphant arrival at Andrews Air Force Base the year before! The ship's decks had been painted en route and otherwise spruced up for arrival. But entering the harbor, it was "greeted" by International Longshoremen's Union demonstrators on a chartered sightseeing boat waving placards: ROSES ARE RED, VIOLETS ARE BLUE, STALIN DROPPED DEAD, HOW ABOUT YOU? and DEAR K! DROP DEAD YOU BUM!

"They were all dressed up in strange costumes," Khrushchev recollected, "waving posters in our direction, holding up scarecrows of some kind, and chanting slogans through megaphones. We all came out on deck pointing and laughing. As far as we were concerned, the demonstration was a masquerade staged by aggressive forces of the United States."[130]

If this "welcome" was unpleasant, Pier 73 was worse: a shabby, broken-down dock on the East River. *Pravda* correspondent Gennady Vasiliev filed his report on the arrival before it actually occurred: the morning bright and sunny; happy crowds lining the shore; bouquets of flowers in every hand. In fact, it was pouring as the *Baltika* eased in, and except for Soviet officials and their families, journalists, and police and security people, only Hungarian émigré demonstrators were there to "greet" the Communist leaders. With the longshoremen boycotting the *Baltika,* the ship's crew had to land in a lifeboat and then moor it to the dock, while diplomats lugged their own baggage. Meanwhile at least one sailor defected.

Shevchenko assumed that the Soviet ambassadors to the United States and the United Nations were to blame for the miserable arrival, that they had carried out too literally Moscow's instructions not to waste money on a fancy pier. In fact, Khrushchev himself had issued the order. He was "infuriated," Khrushchev later said; he was sure "Americans made fun of the Russians for arriving at such a decrepit pier," but he "didn't go looking for a scapegoat. I had only myself to blame," Khrushchev recalled in his memoirs.

Nonetheless, he managed to look jaunty as he stepped off the gangplank at 9:48 A.M., planted himself firmly on a rich oriental rug that soaked up the rain as if it were a vast sponge, and challenged President Eisenhower to join him in an impromptu UN summit. Vasiliev managed to remove the sunshine from his *Pravda* piece before it was published, but the happy crowds overflowing the pier remained.[131]

Khrushchev remained in New York until October 13, when he left for Moscow by plane. Altogether he was away from the Kremlin for more than a month. Even by his own peripatetic standard, this was a stunningly lengthy absence. Obviously he felt secure enough to leave others in charge at home. But he was so obsessed by his mission that he stayed on well past the time when he was an effective spokesman for his cause.

In New York Khrushchev was a whirling dervish. He gave several long speeches and took part vigorously in debate at the United Nations. He ad-libbed press conferences at all times of day and night in Manhattan and at the Soviet Mission's estate in Glen Cove, Long Island. He huddled with world leaders, orated at formal luncheons and dinners, appeared on David Susskind's TV show, and created chaos when, without informing police and security (so as to prove he had a right to move freely around the city), he took off for Harlem to see Fidel Castro, whom he embraced in a crowded hallway at the Hotel Theresa. Standing on a second-floor balcony at the Soviet Mission on Park Avenue and Sixty-eighth Street, he serenaded assembled journalists with a verse of "The Internationale." When a newsman warned that his white shirt against the red wall would make a tempting target, Khrushchev jutted out his jaw, puffed up his chest, made a fist with his right hand and swung it skyward in an uppercut.[132]

Of course the Soviet press depicted all this (well most of it anyway) as a triumph. And so did Khrushchev on his return. "He considered himself the victor," his son wrote, figuring that the UN session "compensated for the failure of the Paris summit."[133] But Khrushchev's behavior in New York was not just extravagant and erratic; it was bizarre. He pounded the top of his desk with his fist to protest a General Assembly speech by Secretary-General Dag Hammarskjöld, and continued doing so until joined (after some hesitation) by Gromyko, other members of the Soviet delegation, and finally all other Communist delegations. When British Prime Minister Macmillan publicly regretted the failure of the Paris summit, Khrushchev leaped to his feet to shout, "You sent your planes over our territory, you are guilty of aggression!" and again started waving his arms and pounding his fists on the table. Macmillan complained over his shoulder to the presiding Assembly president, Frederick H. Boland of Ireland, that if Mr. Khrushchev continued in the same vein, he would like a translation. Boland gaveled Khrushchev to order, and that day at least the Soviet leader refrained from further interruption.

Khrushchev was returning to his seat after addressing the Assembly on October 11 when he noticed that the Spaniards weren't applauding. Shaking his finger in the face of a young Spanish delegate, he unleashed a torrent of abuse in Russian and seemed ready to lunge at the offending diplomat. Only after UN and Soviet security men approached did the Soviet premier subside.

The most celebrated incident of all, the famous shoe banging, took place on Khrushchev's last full day in New York. A Philippine delegate turned the issue of decolonization against Moscow by charging that Eastern Europe had been "deprived of political and civil rights" and "swallowed up by the Soviet Union." After drumming on the table with both fists, the red-faced Soviet leader took off his right shoe (a loafer/sandal, according to his son, because he couldn't stand tying laces), waved it threateningly, and then banged it on the table, louder and louder, until everyone in the hall was watching and buzzing.[134] Gromyko, sitting next to Khrushchev, looked extremely pained. With a "grimace of determination" and the look of a man "about to plunge into a pool of icy water," the foreign minister removed his shoe and began tapping it gently on the desktop as if hoping his boss would notice but no one else would.[135]

Khrushchev was delighted with his own performance. Learning that Troyanovsky had missed it, he told him, "Oh, you really missed something! It was such fun! The UN is a sort of parliament, you know, where the minority has to make itself heard one way or another. We're in the minority for the time being, but not for long." Others were less impressed. Byelorussian Communist leader Kirill Mazurov found it "awkward." At the Soviet Mission after the session, according to Shevchenko, "everyone was embarrassed and upset." The usually strict and impeccable Gromyko was "white-lipped with agitation. But Khrushchev acted as if nothing at all had happened. He was laughing loudly and joking. He said it had been necessary to 'inject a little life into the stuffy atmosphere of the U.N.'"[136]

That evening, the Hungarian leader János Kádár, known for his wry humor, found a delicate way to convey his displeasure during dinner with Khrushchev: "Comrade Khrushchev, remember shortly after banging your shoe you went up to the rostrum to make a point of order? Well at that moment our foreign minister, Comrade Sik, turned to me and said, 'Do you think he had time to put his shoe on, or did he go barefoot?'" Troyanovsky wrote: "Many of those sitting at the table started snickering. I had the feeling that at that moment our leader realized that he may have gone too far."[137]

According to Khrushchev's son, the erratic behavior that appalled his own delegation, that was thrown in his face when he was ousted from power in 1964, and that many Russians still hold against him, was a calculated gesture, the sort that Khrushchev recollected from the prerevolutionary Russian Duma and assumed still occurred in Western legislatures.[138] But it was also petulant, reflecting his failure to get his way. He was gratified when the General Assembly agreed to debate decolonization but outraged when it voted overwhelmingly to refer his disarmament proposals to a smaller political committee. He nervously followed events in the Congo (where the Soviet-backed Patrice Lumumba was under siege from pro-Western Moise Tshombe and Joseph Mobutu) and was affronted at what he regarded as the UN's anti-Lumumba bias.[139] "I spit on the UN," he had snarled on the *Baltika* after Troyanovsky read him some bad news from the Congo. "It's not *our* organization. That good-for-nothing Ham [the Russian word for "boor" applied to Hammarsjköld] is sticking his nose in important affairs which are none of his business. . . . We'll really make it hot for him."[140]

Khrushchev demanded that the secretary-general be replaced by a three-member executive (a troika consisting of one Westerner, one representative of the Communist camp, and one from a neutral country) and that the UN be relocated in Europe—in Switzerland or Austria or perhaps even in the Soviet Union.[141] But these zany reforms would undermine the very UN forum in which Khrushchev had chosen to make his case, while contradicting the long-standing Soviet policy of opposing any revision of the UN Charter. They were not only opposed by the bulk of the UN membership, a fact American diplomacy promptly made the most of, but by members of Khrushchev's own delegation. "Suddenly Khrushchev began to insist on the troika," remembered Georgy Kornienko, who served in the Foreign Ministry at the time. "It was his own idea. The West would never accept it. In essence it was a nonstarter, an unrealistic idea, and that's how many of us saw it at the time. It was another of those things he kept coming up with, things that from the point of view of common sense were strange and incomprehensible."[142]

As the General Assembly session dragged on, Khrushchev found the debates "less and less interesting."[143] In private conversations with Macmillan, he seemed downbeat, still stewing about Eisenhower, whose stint in office proved, he said, that "the United States could do without any President at all."[144] At a September 26 luncheon with American businessmen, Khrushchev posed the questions he said others were asking: Why had he come? Was it worth coming? "I think it was worth it," was his answer.[145] Asked the same question at a UN press conference on October 7, he snapped, "He who believes that our efforts were made in vain does not know what is going on."[146] Back in Moscow on October 20 he began his "welcome home" speech by saying, "If anyone asks whether it was worth going to this session in New York, it can be said without any reservation that it was not only worthwhile but essential to go there." He added: "We strove to represent the Soviet Union's interests with honor and dignity. We didn't waste any time, understanding full well that we went to New York not for pancakes at our mother-in-law's but to work [Stir in the hall. Applause.]."[147]

Work, honor, dignity—well, there was no doubt about the work. The longer he stayed in New York, the more challenges to his honor he had to rebut. In response to condemnation of the 1956 Hungarian intervention and dismissal of his disarmament proposals: "We do not fear such issues. We routed the Whites [in the Russian civil war]. And you want to scare us with such disputes. Well, gentlemen, you haven't got the guts for that."[148] Although David Susskind was no intellectual heavyweight (he was a theatrical producer when not conducting his TV talk show), he interrupted and badgered his tired-looking guest. "Don't be in such a hurry," Khrushchev snapped. "Though you are a fiery young man and I am no longer young, I can still compete with you. . . . " When Susskind described Khrushchev as "baying at the moon," his guest retorted: " 'Baying'? Is that normal polite conversation in your country? We regard it as rude. After all, I'm old enough to be your father, and young man, it's unworthy of you to speak to me like this. I do not permit an attitude like that toward myself. I did not come here to 'bark.' I am the chairman of the Council of Ministers of the world's greatest socialist state. You will therefore please show respect for me. . . ."[149]

Unceasing attention, rather than respect, was what New York offered. "No matter who turned up at a party," said one observer, "few guests had eyes for anybody but Mr. K. He would bounce into the room, pudgy and smiling, leaning earnestly forward, to be swallowed up instantly by a pushing, shouldering mob of the curious."[150] All sorts of circumstances irritated and provoked him. In between UN sessions he went stir crazy inside the Soviet Mission. Denied his usual walks for security reasons, he "paced up and down like a tiger in a cage" and gulped fresh air on the small balcony.[151] At night there was "the nerve-wracking, unceasing roar" of the police motorcycles, especially as they changed shifts. "It would first sound like people clapping, then like gunfire, then like artillery shells exploding—and all right under my window. It was impossible to sleep. No matter how tired I was, I'd lie there awake, either listening to one shift leaving, or waiting for another to arrive."

Even the luxurious Glen Cove estate, a fake English castle called Kenilworth once owned by Harold Pratt and later bought by the Rockefeller family, provided little respite. The weather for much of the month was warm and clear, but even on the spacious lawns of the estate, "there was always the sound of people hooting and whistling and passing cars honking their horns," all expressing "their rage against our presence in America."[152]

Some of the tension building in Khrushchev came out in public, but more appeared behind closed doors. To Mohamed Heikal, the Egyptian journalist who knew him quite well, Khrushchev seemed "in a strange mood in New York." Nasser and Khrushchev met twice, once in Manhattan and once at Glen Cove, but "these were unsatisfactory meetings, much of the time being wasted on raking over old arguments."[153]

Nasser and other neutralist leaders were Khrushchev's natural constituency at the UN. Although he resented their failure to support him fully in the General Assembly, he had to contain his anger. Instead he directed it against his faithful, long-suffering foreign minister. One day at the Soviet Mission he found himself seated between Gromyko and the Soviet UN representative, Valerian Zorin. "Which one of you is the minister of foreign affairs?" Khrushchev demanded. "Andrei Andreyevich, of course," answered a puzzled Zorin. "No, he's not," growled Khrushchev. "He's not foreign minister; he's a piece of shit."[154]

So much for Gromyko's doglike devotion. All it earned him, that day at least, was having Khrushchev's contempt, for himself as well as for others, projected onto his foreign minister.

CHAPTER SEVENTEEN

Khrushchev and Kennedy: 1960–1961

When Khrushchev returned from New York in mid-October 1960, the U.S. presidential election was still a month away. Anxious as he was to start afresh with a new president, he had to wait upon the American electorate. In the meantime he faced an agricultural crisis at home.

Back in August he had reported to the Presidium on his Astrakhan Province inspection trip. Despite popular complaints about a lack of meat, which he attributed to the "criminal incompetence" of local party leaders, prospects for the harvest were good, as were those in Kalinovka, where he spent two days later in the month.[1] How different the tone of an October 29 memo conveying the bad news that awaited him upon his return from New York! The year was turning out to be the worst one for agriculture since Stalin's death. The Virgin Lands, in particular, which Khrushchev's assistant Andrei Shevchenko had toured while his boss was at the United Nations, were a bitter disappointment. Meat, milk, and butter were in short supply all over. The situation was so bad, Khrushchev wrote, that "if we don't take necessary measures, we could slide back to where we were in 1953." If that happened, after all the rising expectations he had encouraged, the result could be a political as well as an agricultural crisis. "I think all of us understand the significance of this problem," he told his colleagues. But the only remedy he could think of was the same package he'd been pushing for years: bureaucratic tinkering (such as reorganizing the party leadership of Virgin Lands), cultivating more corn (not to mention raising ducks of the sort he had seen in Indonesia and now recommended for the Volga River delta), pressing reluctant peasants to transfer their cows to collective farms, and, of course, emulating Kalinovka, the allegedly brilliant successes of which he cited only slightly defensively.[2]

October's agitated memo marked the start of a frenzied five-month campaign to energize agriculture. Khrushchev called a special Central Committee plenum for January and spent much of the fall dictating a lengthy report. After the plenum came a two-month trip, or series of trips, crisscrossing the country as if it were wartime, trying to mobilize Soviet farmers and the functionaries who supervised them.[3] Ukraine (January 28), Rostov (February 1), Tbilisi (February 7), Voronezh (February 11), Sverdlovsk (March 2), Novosibirsk (March 8), Akmolinsk (March 14), Tselinograd (March 18), Alma-Ata (March 31): At each stop his speeches expressed not only contempt for bumbling or corrupt functionaries but hints of doubt about himself.

From the January 1961 Central Committee plenum: The Ministry of Agriculture allowed "anyone to pretend to be an expert. If he's eaten some potatoes in the dining room, he feels he knows agriculture. . . . " Khrushchev's idea of a genuine agricultural expert? T. D. Lysenko, whose crackpot successes he cited at some length.[4] It wasn't Ukrainian corn that was "burning up," Khrushchev thundered in Kiev; it was "the poor excuses for leaders who are burning up on the stalk." Yet here sat Comrade Kalchenko, a member of the Central Committee and head of the Ukrainian government, "and it means nothing to him that he made a mistake—it's like water off a duck's back."[5] Suddenly, Khrushchev was referring to shepherds and swineherds who "used to be considered persons of a very low level. . . . I say this," he continued, apologizing and boasting at the same time, "because I . . . was a shepherd myself, and now the people and the party have made me first secretary of the party Central Committee, and chairman of the USSR Council of Ministers. Apparently, there are good men among shepherds, too. [Prolonged applause.] Understand me correctly, comrades, don't condemn me, don't say that I have begun to praise myself. [Animation, applause.] After all, I did not appoint myself, you elected me and you will not elect people unworthy of your trust. That is why I treat you with respect. If you elected me, I must be worth something."[6]

Khrushchev buttressed his self-esteem by comparing the 1960 Ukrainian harvest unfavorably with that of 1949; he didn't have to remind his audience who had led the republic in 1949. On his way to

Voronezh, Khrushchev and his suite were due to drive past about six hundred acres of corn that hadn't been harvested. Anticipating this, local officials had commandeered a seventy-five-foot rail from the local railroad, attached it to a tractor, and proceeded to knock down the corn so it would appear to have been gathered. "Well now, comrades," growled Khrushchev when he found out. "Something new in agricultural equipment! Maybe you should patent this invention, Comrade Khitrov [whose name means "one of the clever ones" in Russian]!"[7]

At a dinner in Kazakhstan, Khrushchev was brought a sheep's head and asked to pass pieces to other guests. "I cut off an ear and eye," Khrushchev told journalists at a reception at the American Embassy on July 4. He had given both to Kazakhstan leaders and then asked, "Who gets the brains?" When an academician offered to take them, Khrushchev had joked, "An academician needs brains, whereas as chairman of the Council of Ministers, I can get along without brains."[8]

"Why don't you applaud?" Khrushchev demanded at a meeting in Moscow that spring. "I don't ask you to applaud me. No, I am no longer at an age when my mood is defined solely by whether I'm applauded or not. In this case I would like to regard applause as agreement with the party Central Committee in criticizing . . . you yourselves for lowering grain output. . . . Now then"—after telling his audience how shortages were to be remedied—"do you agree with this? [Stormy applause.] Does that mean I consider your applause to be approval . . . ? [Stormy applause.]."[9]

By March 31, 1961, when he sent another memo to the Presidium, proposing a fifteen-point program to revivify agriculture, Khrushchev was sounding more optimistic. About the only thing not on his list was an attempt to analyze the structural flaws built into the whole collective farm system. Instead, he counted on more miracles and blamed others when they didn't turn up.

THE GERMAN QUESTION too preoccupied Khrushchev before and after the American elections. "I spent a great deal of time trying to think of a way out," he later recalled. According to his son, that was putting it mildly: "He had nightmares about it. The German problem gave him no peace; instead it kept slipping out of his hands."[10]

One of Khrushchev's initial aims had been to stabilize East Germany (along with Eastern Europe as a whole) by forcing the Western powers to recognize Ulbricht's regime. Instead, the crisis he provoked further destabilized the situation. The rising tension swelled the flow of East German refugees, creating a severe shortage of workers. Ulbricht's request to import Soviet workers reminded Khrushchev of Hitler's use of Slavic slave laborers. "He came home that day boiling with indignation," Sergei remembered. "'How could such an idea ever enter his [Ulbricht's] head?' he kept repeating."[11]

Almost as disturbing was the way prosperous West Germans bought up low-priced, Soviet-subsidized East German goods, thus aggravating both East German shortages and the huge debt Ulbricht owed Moscow. To make matters worse, instead of waiting for Khrushchev to carry out his Berlin threats, Ulbricht began to act unilaterally. In September and October 1960 the East Germans alarmed Moscow by trying to subject Western ambassadors to GDR passport controls. On November 30, at a meeting with Khrushchev, Ulbricht complained, "We can't repeat our campaign in favor of a peace treaty as we did before the Paris summit. We can only do this is if something is actually achieved this time." According to the East German leader, his people were already saying, "You only *talk* about a peace treaty, but you don't *do* anything about it."

"I thought that after Paris . . . you agreed with us that we shouldn't conclude a peace treaty," Khrushchev shot back. "We haven't lost the two years since our proposal was introduced; we've shaken up their position." However, he admitted it was "both our faults that we didn't think everything through sufficiently, and didn't work out economic measures."

Khrushchev got Ulbricht to confess that he didn't want a peace treaty in 1961 either, unless Moscow provided sufficient help to withstand the West German economic blockade that would likely ensue. But that was small consolation since the USSR couldn't afford much more aid anyway. Still, Khrushchev had to admit that "if we don't sign a peace treaty in 1961, then when will we? If we don't sign one in 1961, then our prestige will be dealt a blow, and the position of the West, and particularly of West Germany, will be strengthened."

Damned if he signed and damned if he didn't: that was the quandary into which Khrushchev's tactics had led him. "We must think through everything properly," he lectured Ulbricht, having failed to do so himself. The East Germans would have to support themselves economically. But while Khrushchev urged East German self-reliance, Ulbricht underlined Soviet irresolution: "If we don't succeed in concluding a peace treaty, but simply return to propaganda for a peace treaty, then we will discredit our policy and won't be able to reestablish our prestige for a year or two. We can't act as we did in 1960."[12]

This wasn't the last time the East German tail wagged the Soviet dog, or at least tried to do so. On January 18, 1961, Ulbricht griped again about how little had been accomplished since the 1958 ultimatum.[13] The next thing Khrushchev knew, an East German delegation unexpectedly turned up in Moscow on its way to talks with the Chinese, a meeting of which the Soviets had received no advance notice—this in the midst of Soviet–East German negotiations on next steps concerning Germany and Berlin.[14]

Confronted with East German carping, Khrushchev counted on the new American president. "We are now beginning to initiate a business-like discussion of these questions with Kennedy," he told Ulbricht on January 30. Initial diplomatic probes had shown that the new president needed time to work out his position. If, however, "we don't succeed in coming to an understanding with Kennedy," Khrushchev continued, "we will, as agreed, choose together with you the time for implementation" of measures, including a separate peace treaty.[15]

During the American election campaign Khrushchev had preserved a careful public neutrality: Asked whether he preferred Kennedy or Nixon, he answered, "Roosevelt!" In fact, he disliked Nixon intensely, regarding him as a McCarthyite cold warrior who had shown his true colors during his 1959 Soviet visit. Therefore, although he had met Kennedy only once, during their brief 1959 Senate encounter during which he told Kennedy he looked too young to be a senator, Khrushchev decided to "vote" Democratic. He did so first by discounting Henry Cabot Lodge's personal assurance (delivered in Moscow in February 1960) that Nixon would turn out less anti-Communist than his campaign speeches suggested and then by rebuffing a plea that American fliers forced down over the Soviet Union that summer be released before the election.[16]

Khrushchev was so delighted by Kennedy's victory on November 4, Sergei remembered, that he positively "beamed with satisfaction. He jokingly referred to Kennedy's triumph as a gift he had received for the anniversary of the revolution." Later he insisted he had "no cause for regret once Kennedy became president. It quickly became clear he understood better than Eisenhower that an improvement in relations was the only rational course."[17] Actually, however, Khrushchev's attitude toward Kennedy was never that simple, either politically or personally.

In August 1960, Gromyko sent his boss a profile prepared in the Foreign Ministry. It depicted JFK as a pragmatic politician who advocated talks with the Soviets and who, if he had been in power in May 1960, would have apologized for the U-2 flight. But the same Kennedy favored a military buildup and had adopted a "bellicose" stance on Berlin. Also, certain personal characteristics constituted an implicit challenge to Khrushchev: JFK's family was among "the seventy-five richest in the USA"; he had studied at Harvard, Princeton, Stanford, and the London School of Economics; he had "an acute, penetrating mind capable of quickly assimilating and analyzing. . . . "[18]

As time passed, Khrushchev received less flattering assessments from his ambassador in Washington and his son-in-law, Aleksei Adzhubei. It was an open secret in the Foreign Ministry that Adzhubei sneered at John and Robert Kennedy as "little boys in short pants." Ambassador Menshikov told Khrushchev that Kennedy was "an inexperienced upstart" who would never amount to a good president.[19] These dismissals added to Khrushchev's temptation to confront the president: Priding himself on his ability to out-argue Western leaders more educated and better mannered than he, he must have particularly relished the thought of trouncing a rich man's boy who was "younger than my own son."[20] Yet if Kennedy were in fact weak and inexperienced, he could also be dominated by American "ruling circles," including Wall Street and the military-industrial complex, which Khrushchev saw as sworn enemies of the USSR. Perhaps it was that thought that sparked the last-minute doubts Khrushchev expressed to Ambassador Thompson just before the election: "I wish Nixon would win because I'd know how to cope with him. Kennedy is an unknown quantity."[21]

For Kennedy, Khrushchev represented an equally vexing challenge. In the court of history, JFK would be judged by how well he dealt with the leader of the Communist world. In his own mind he would be up against a man who resembled his father. As a boy, Kennedy was often weak and sickly. Yet his father insisted that he excel and mocked him when he did not. John Kennedy eventually outdid his father, not only by becoming president, but as a carouser and womanizer. But the fact that he strained every fiber to become the sort of tough, macho leader his father wanted made it all the more important to stand up to Khrushchev, all the more traumatic when at first he failed to do so, all the more crucial to prevail, or at least to seem to do so, in the crises that followed.[22]

Immediately after the election Khrushchev began to besiege Kennedy with feelers and proposals. November 11: Khrushchev's friend and flatterer, the Ukrainian writer Aleksandr Korneichuk, told Averell Harriman that the Soviet leader wanted "to make a fresh start, forgetting the U-2 incident and all the subsequent gyrations."[23] Ambassador Menshikov to Harriman three days later: Khrushchev hoped he and Kennedy "could follow the line of relations that existed during President Roosevelt's time when Mr. Harriman was ambassador."[24] Menshikov to Adlai Stevenson on November 16: Khrushchev wanted "discussion off-the-record by letter and representatives" and polemic-free "informal talks," whether "there or here," that could lead to a nuclear test ban "in a short time" after the inauguration. Although Moscow could not get Beijing to accept that there were "two Chinas," when it came to Chinese "expansion" (*sic*) elsewhere, Moscow would be "glad to help."[25] Interesting as Harriman's views were, confided Menshikov on November 21, "the views of President Kennedy himself " would be even better. Alas, Harriman replied, the president-elect "would not authorize anyone to have talks until he had assumed office."[26]

"What can we do to help the new administration?" Deputy Foreign Minister Vasily Kuznetsov asked Kennedy advisers Walt Rostow and Jerome Wiesner, who were attending a meeting on disarmament in Moscow in late November. Rostow could foresee a possible New York summit if the American fliers downed during the summer were released, if a test ban accord were reached, and if this time Khrushchev came to Manhattan "wearing his shoes."[27] Menshikov invited Robert Kennedy to lunch on December 12. Two days later he pressed Harriman for secret informal talks "as soon as possible."[28] The *New York Times*'s former Moscow correspondent Harrison Salibury got the treatment on December 15. "No time should be lost," the ambassador repeated several times. Because "a year has already been lost," Khrushchev and Kennedy must meet "before those who would like not to see agreement have had a chance to act and prevent it."[29] Diplomat David K. E. Bruce got the same Menshikov message on January 5, followed by a hamper of vodka and caviar along with an invitation to meet again; the second conversation covered the same ground as the first.[30]

For someone allergic to seeming a supplicant, all this pleading was extraordinary. It revealed Khrushchev's congenital impatience, intensified by the two-year delay on Germany and Berlin and by the agricultural crisis at home. But his understanding of American politics went no deeper than his explanation of bad harvests. Obviously there could be no formal talks before the inauguration. Even afterward they would take more time to arrange and to consummate than he apparently had available.

THE DAY John Kennedy was sworn in, Khrushchev telephoned Ambassador Thompson at the American Embassy, the first time he had ever done so, and summoned him to the Kremlin. Sitting across from Thompson at the long, green baize–covered table in his second-floor office, the Soviet leader looked tired and sounded hoarse. But he had already read Kennedy's inaugural address, he saw "constructive things" in it, and he offered to release the downed fliers as a gesture toward the new president.[31]

Kennedy replied with several gestures of his own: halting U.S. Post Office censorship of Soviet publications, welcoming a resumption of civil aviation talks broken off in 1960, ordering military officials to tone down anti-Soviet rhetoric in their speeches, and lifting a ban on importation of Soviet crab meat. But each side's moves were overshadowed by more ominous signals (or, rather, what each side took to be signals) both before the inauguration and after it.

On January 6, Khrushchev reported to a closed meeting of Soviet ideologists and propagandists on the conference of eighty-one Communist parties held in Moscow the previous fall. Like the compromise declaration issued at the end of that conference, his talk was carefully balanced. On the one hand, an echo of the Chinese line: The world was going socialism's way; imperialism was growing weaker at home and abroad; the Third World was rising in revolution. On the other, an endorsement of Soviet-style coexistence: Contradicting Mao, Khrushchev insisted that nuclear war would be an "incalculable disaster" in which "millions would die." Nor could "local wars" be allowed to erupt since they could escalate into major ones. The only wars the Soviet Union supported, said Khrushchev in a bow to his own Marxist-Leninism as well as to Mao's, were "wars of national liberation." Such struggles, like that of the Algerian people against French colonialism, were both "inevitable" and "sacred."[32]

This speech was par for the Soviet course. Eisenhower saw it that way, privately noting that Khrushchev's tough talk was usually a substitute for, rather than a prelude to, tough action. But Kennedy did not. According to Arthur M. Schlesinger, Jr., "the bellicose confidence which surged through the rest of the speech [apart from the section rejecting nuclear war] and especially the declared faith in victory through rebellion, subversion, and guerrilla warfare alarmed Kennedy more than Moscow's amiable signals assuaged him." The new president took the speech as "an authoritative exposition of Soviet intentions," instructed top aides to "read, mark, learn and inwardly digest it," ignored a warning from Thompson that the speech expressed only one side of the complicated Khrushchev, and answered back in his State of the Union address on

January 30: "We must never be lulled into believing that either power [the Soviet Union or China] has yielded its ambitions for world domination—ambitions which they forcefully restated only a short time ago. On the contrary, our task is to convince them that aggression and subversion will not be profitable routes to pursue these ends."[33]

Two days later the United States test-launched its first Minuteman ICBM, the prelude, the press reported, to large-scale deployment by mid-1962. On February 6, Defense Secretary Robert S. McNamara revealed that the impression of a missile gap in the Soviet's favor, which Khrushchev had worked so hard to foster, was a myth.[34] Meanwhile, Khrushchev's plea for an early summit had still produced no formal response. None of these developments was designed directly to challenge Khrushchev, but he didn't know that.[35]

In private, Kennedy seemed less alarmed than his State of the Union speech suggested—so much so that after a February 11 meeting of advisers on Soviet affairs, Charles Bohlen worried that JFK underrated Khrushchev's determination to expand world communism. Or was it perhaps that Kennedy's alarm translated into what Secretary of State Dean Rusk regarded as overeagerness for an early meeting with Khrushchev? "Kennedy had the impression," Rusk recalled later, "that if he could just sit down with Khrushchev, maybe something worthwhile would come out of it—at least some closer meeting of minds on various questions." What Kennedy told his aide Kenneth O'Donnell was: "I have to show him that we can be just as tough as he is. I can't do that sending messages to him through other people. I'll have to sit down with him, and let him see who he's dealing with."[36]

After another conference with his Soviet advisers—Thompson, Harriman, Kennan, and Bohlen—on February 21, the president approved "an informal exchange of views" with Khrushchev, provided the international situation and their mutual schedules allowed it. Ambassador Thompson was to deliver a letter from Kennedy and to discuss details of a meeting when he returned to Moscow on February 27. In the meantime, however, according to Troyanovsky, Khrushchev's hopes for Kennedy had begun "quickly to evaporate," and instead he began playing a "waiting game," not "hurrying to reply" to the president's suggestion that they meet and exchange views.[37]

Developments in the Congo didn't help, where Prime Minister Patrice Lumumba's murder was revealed on February 13, a crime the Soviet leader blamed on Hammarskjold's UN-backed "Western colonialists." Meanwhile, Western stalling on Germany and Berlin continued. On

February 17 a Soviet memorandum to Bonn complained about Western leaders who had said: "'Wait a moment; this time isn't ripe. Preparations are under way for the presidential election in the U.S.A. We must wait until that is over.' After the election, they say, 'The president and the new U.S. government have just assumed their duties and have not yet mastered them.' . . . If matters are allowed to take this course, this can continue endlessely."[38]

Thompson returned to Moscow on February 27. Khrushchev left town the next morning, on the next leg of his agricultural barnstorming tour, without bothering to receive him. Thompson didn't deliver the president's letter until March 9, when he caught up with Khrushchev in Novosibirsk. The Soviet leader was staying at Akademgorodok, the college campus–like headquarters of the Siberian Academy of Sciences, which had recently been built at his command. Local academicians found the chairman in an angry mood. Thompson thought he looked "extremely tired, his appearance shocked even the Soviets who accompanied me," and Khrushchev's mood wasn't improved when he discovered Kennedy's message didn't even touch on Berlin.[39]

Kennedy had been trying to avoid that issue ever since his inauguration. Thompson warned in February that if there were "no progress" on Berlin and Germany, Khrushchev would "almost certainly proceed with [his] separate peace treaty," followed by a potential East German attempt at the "gradual strangulation" of Berlin. The way to avoid this was to produce "some activity on the German problem indicating that real progress could be made after the German elections."[40] But instead of holding out that prospect, the president instructed Thompson not to mention Berlin in Novosibirsk. If Khrushchev was able to contain himself in response, as Thompson's dry account suggests, that was because by now he had given up trying to squeeze milk from the American stone: " . . . Khrushchev noted that I had not mentioned the question of Germany which he wished to discuss. He said the USSR had put forth its position in an aide-memoire to Adenauer. . . . He said he had explained the Soviet position in great detail to President Eisenhower. . . . He said he would like very much that President Kennedy would regard with understanding the Soviet position on the German question."[41]

All Thompson could reply was that the president was "reviewing our German policy and would wish to discuss it with Adenauer and other Allies before reaching conclusions." But he could not foresee "much change" in the American stance. He cautioned Khrushchev that "if there is anything which will bring about a massive increase in U.S. arms expenditures of the type which took place at the time of the Korean War, it would be the conviction that the Soviets are indeed attempting to force us out of Berlin. . . ."[42]

Several days later Thompson warned his superiors: "All my diplomatic colleagues . . . consider that in the absence of negotiations, Khrushchev will sign a separate peace treaty with East Germany and precipitate a Berlin crisis this year."[43] He even imagined a Berlin wall that would "seal off the sector boundary in order to stop what they must consider the intolerable continuation of the refugee flow through Berlin." Both sides ignored his warnings. Concentrating on his own prestige, Khrushchev ignored the danger to Kennedy's. Kennedy thought that after three years of pressing for action, Khrushchev could accept a further, indefinite postponement.

In mid-April the American columnist Walter Lippmann and his wife, Helen, visited Khrushchev at his Pitsunda dacha. Managing to sandwich serious talks among a walking tour, a badminton match (in which the overweight but agile premier trounced the Lippmanns), and two lavish meals, Khrushchev portrayed a separate German peace treaty as a last resort. "I don't want the tension," he said several times. "I know it will create tension. I want to avoid it. But in the end, I've got to do it." When Lippmann raised the danger of war, Khrushchev declared, "There are no such stupid statesmen in the West who would unleash a war in which hundreds of millions would perish just because we sign a peace treaty with the GDR. . . . There are no such idiots or they have not yet been born." Prompted by Washington, Lippmann suggested a five-year moratorium on Berlin. His host stared at him as if he were insane.[44] A month later, when Thompson proposed leaving Berlin "as it is," Khrushchev swore that "the matter could not go beyond the fall or winter of this year. He reminded me that his original plan had been to act within six months. Thirty months have now passed."[45]

AFTER NOVOSIBIRSK, it seemed a Khrushchev-Kennedy summit would be delayed indefinitely, but less than two months later they met in Vienna. Two events in the meantime made it even less likely that they would see eye to eye. Yuri Gagarin's pioneering space flight and the failed invasion of Cuba at the Bay of Pigs increased Khrushchev's confidence that he could coerce from Kennedy what he had been unable to cajole.

Soviet rocket failures gave Khrushchev plenty of grief in the months before Gagarin blasted off on April 12. Back in October 1960, just after

Khrushchev had returned from New York, an R-16 rocket exploded at the Tyura-Tam test site, incinerating nearly a hundred, including the Rocket Forces commander Mitrofan Nedelin, of whom only a marshal's shoulder strap and half-melted keys to his office safe remained. Khrushchev was devastated, his son recalled.[46] Then Gagarin's feat stunned the world. *Sputnik* in 1957, the moon landing just before Khrushchev arrived in Washington, and now this on the eve of May Day 1961. According to Sergei Khrushchev, himself involved in the Soviet missile program, his father set no political target dates for dangerous launches, but no one associated with the Soviet space program had any doubt that they were in an all-out race with the United States.[47]

Gagarin's mission, called, *Vostok* (the East) to symbolize the triumph of communism, was announced only after the space pioneer had landed safely. Khrushchev paced nervously until the mission chief Sergei Korolyov called with the news. "Just tell me, is he alive?" Khrushchev shouted. As soon as Gagarin was on the ground, an ecstatic Khrushchev was on the phone with congratulations: "Let the whole world look and see what our country is capable of, what our great people, our Soviet science can do."[48]

When Sergei called that evening, his father was "in raptures." He had already raised Gagarin from senior lieutenant to major (skipping over the rank of captain that Defense Minister Malinovsky suggested), awarded him the nation's highest medal (Hero of the Soviet Union), declared a national holiday, decided to fly to Moscow to greet him, and ordered a huge Red Square rally and a grandiose Kremlin banquet to celebrate the occasion. Sergei worried about his father's health: "He was so tired after the preceding months, he had finally torn himself away for two weeks or so of rest, and here he was deciding to return to Moscow after only two or three days." But Khrushchev brooked no objection; he was "simply bursting to get to Moscow."[49]

When Gagarin, accompanied by an escort of four fighter planes, flew into Vnukovo Airport, Khrushchev was waiting with the entire party leadership, assorted ministers and marshals, and the cosmonaut's family. Gagarin strode across a long red carpet, uttered his formal "report" to Khrushchev ("mission accomplished," "excellent condition," "ready for any new assignment," etc.) and then disappeared into the party leader's enthusiastic embrace.[50] On the newsreel record of the event, Khrushchev can be seen wiping away his own tears with a white handkerchief. After his ouster from power, the same film, politically corrected, omitted Khrushchev, leaving Gagarin to direct his report into the ether.

Khrushchev initially decreed that Gagarin and his wife would ride down Leninsky Prospekt to Red Square alone at the head of the procession, but he couldn't resist joining them in a flower-bedecked open limousine. There were cheering crowds, sunny skies, windblown banners, and speeches from atop the Lenin Mausoleum, plus a gala diplomatic reception at which a beaming Khrushchev again embraced Gagarin and celebrated how far the country had come. We used to go "barefoot and without clothes," Khrushchev crowed. "Arrogant 'theoreticians'" predicted "bast-shoed Russians" would never become a great power. Yet "once-illiterate Russia," which many had regarded as "a barbaric country," had now pioneered the path into space.[51] "That's what you've done, Yurka!" Khrushchev exclaimed. "Let everyone who's sharpening their claws against us know, let them know that Yurka was in space, that he saw and knows everything. . . ."[52]

Four days later the United States botched the Bay of Pigs invasion. Fidel Castro's 1959 victory over the dictator Fulgencio Batista had not exactly galvanized Khrushchev's attention. Soviet intelligence knew nothing about the bearded revolutionary except what Cuban Communists told it, and they were denouncing Castro as an agent of the CIA. But after high-powered Soviet emissaries, including Mikoyan, decided that Fidel was a Marxist, Khrushchev became enchanted by the thought of a socialist outpost under Uncle Sam's nose. Even then Moscow proceeded cautiously, lest its support provoke the Americans. But by the end of 1960, Sergei Khrushchev recalled, not only had his father come to Castro's assistance, but "he was positively enamored" with Fidel Castro, whom he called "the bearded one."[53]

By March 1961 Soviet intelligence was reporting American preparations for intervention in Cuba. That was another reason, according to Troyanovsky, why Khrushchev delayed setting a date for a U. S.–Soviet summit,[54] while one reason Kennedy hesitated to launch the long-planned exile invasion was fear that Khrushchev might use it as an excuse to move against Berlin.[55] When the president finally gave the go-ahead, he refused to provide American air cover. The result was a debacle in which the invaders were wiped out.

Khrushchev's first public response, dispatched to Kennedy before the Cuban outcome was clear, had a ring of genuine alarm: "It is not yet too late to prevent what may be irreparable." Several days later, however, when the danger had passed, a second Khrushchev message lapsed into angry clichés: "Aggressive bandit actions cannot save your system. In the historic process . . . every people decides and will decide the fate of its country itself."[56] In private, Khrushchev lurched from dismay to delight. The fact that the invasion coincided with his birthday, April 17, at first seemed a particular slight. Moreover, he assumed the Americans would finish what they started by landing marines and bombing the island with their own planes. "I don't understand Kennedy," he muttered to his son after the president had failed to ensure an exile victory. "What's wrong with him? Can he really be that indecisive?"[57] Upon reflection, according to Troyanovsky, Khrushchev reached two conclusions: first, that there was absolutely no difference between Democratic and Republican presidents (something Marxism-Leninism should have taught him long before) and second, that now was the time to meet with a weakened Kennedy. By that same logic, Khrushchev expected Kennedy to avoid such a meeting. But the president surprised him.[58]

Immediately after the Cuban disaster, Kennedy went into a depression. According to his friend LeMoyne Billings, the president "constantly blamed himself for the Cuban fiasco." Another friend, Charles Spalding, commented: "It was the only thing on his mind, and we just had to let him talk himself out." Kennedy feared that his "Cuban mistake" would prompt the Communists to get "tougher and tougher," confronting him with "crises in all parts of the world."[59] He was particularly disturbed by reports that Khrushchev was cockier than ever after the Cuban defeat.[60] That's why, rather than shun a personal showdown with the Soviet leader, Kennedy felt compelled to undertake one. "Getting involved in a fight between Communists and anti-Communists in Cuba or Laos was one thing," he told O'Donnell. "But this is the time to let [Khrushchev] know that a showdown between the United States and Russia would be entirely something else again."[61]

On May 12, Khrushchev accepted Kennedy's long-standing invitation; the talks were set for June 3–4 in Vienna. Seeking to show strength before the summit, Kennedy gave a second State of the Union speech on May 25, requesting higher defense spending, including a threefold increase in funds for fallout shelters. Khrushchev of course behaved the same way, warning Ambassador Thompson that a German treaty couldn't wait very long.[62]

Once the summit was set, Kennedy pored over briefing books, read transcripts of previous summits, and consulted with people who had conversed with Khrushchev. "He's not dumb," JFK concluded. "He's smart. He's"—not finding the word, the president made a fist and shook it—

"he's tough!"[63] Harriman confirmed that, but advised Kennedy not to take Khrushchev's bluster too seriously: "Don't let him rattle you, he'll try to rattle you and frighten you, but don't pay any attention to that. . . . His style will be to attack and then see if he can get away with it. Laugh about it, don't get into a fight. . . . Have some fun."

De Gaulle reinforced Harriman's message when Kennedy and his entourage stopped in Paris en route to Vienna: If Khrushchev "had wanted war about Berlin he would have acted already." But the French leader also warned that Khrushchev would test Kennedy's manhood ("Your job, Mr. President, is to make sure Khrushchev believes you are a man who will fight. Stand fast. . . . Hold on, be firm, be strong") precisely because he had reason to doubt it: After the Bay of Pigs, de Gaulle himself had worried that Kennedy was "somewhat fumbling and overeager," that "the young man" might not stand up to Khrushchev on Berlin.[64]

Kennedy's advisers warned him to avoid ideological arguments with Khrushchev. All the advice he got, on top of the pressure he was placing on himself, added to the strain on the eve of the summit. To make matters worse, ailments that the president kept secret from the American public were acting up. Contrary to his carefully cultivated image of vigor and health, Kennedy had a low energy level that kept him in bed for nearly half of many days. In addition, he suffered from Addison's disease and from a bad back that often put him on crutches. He was on them on May 28 when he limped across his Hyannis Port lawn and settled himself in a lawn chair to read his Vienna briefing book. When he arrived in Vienna on June 3, he was taking cortisone, which bloated his face and made for mood oscillations, and the anesthetic procaine, for his back, plus a mystery mixture of amphetamines, vitamins, enzymes, and God knew what else, administered (as late as a few minutes before the first summit session) by the eccentric New York physician Max Jacobson, known among his celebrity patients as "Dr. Feelgood."[65]

Khrushchev had arrived in Vienna by train the day before. Among those greeting him was his old nemesis Molotov, now representing the USSR at the International Atomic Energy Agency. Molotov had nothing to do with the summit, of course, but his presence reminded Khrushchev it was past time to get concrete results. Kennedy and Khrushchev shook hands on the steps of the American ambassador's residence, where their first meeting was to be held, shortly after noon on June 3. Khrushchev's large head just about reached Kennedy's nose.

The two days of talks that followed were hair-raising. At least that was how Kennedy saw it. "Roughest thing in my life," he told the *New York Times* columnist James Reston immediately afterward. "I think he did it because of the Bay of Pigs. I think he thought that anyone who was so young and inexperienced as to get into that mess could be taken. And anyone who got into it and didn't see it through had no guts. So he just beat the hell out of me. . . . I've got a terrible problem. If he thinks I'm inexperienced and have no guts, until we remove those ideas we won't get anywhere with him. So we have to act."[66]

Afterward in London, where Kennedy talked privately and at length with Macmillan, the prime minister found him "completely overwhelmed by the ruthlessness and barbarity" of Khrushchev. It was, Macmillan wrote in his diary, "rather like somebody meeting Napoleon (at the height of his power) for the first time." It also reminded him "of Lord Halifax or Neville Chamberlain trying to hold a conversation with Herr Hitler."[67] Dean Rusk later put it this way: "Kennedy was very upset. He wasn't prepared for the brutality of Khrushchev's presentation. . . . " Harriman found the president "shattered." Scoffed Lyndon Johnson to friends: "Khrushchev scared the poor little fellow dead."[68]

Did Khrushchev really see Kennedy as JFK saw himself: under assault, fighting a rear-guard action, weak and open to intimidation? Sergei Khrushchev insisted not, that his father found Kennedy to be "a serious partner."[69] At first glance, Khrushchev's memoirs seem to confirm that. Kennedy "impressed me as a better statesman than Eisenhower," he wrote. Like his predecessor, Kennedy "feared war," but he was "a flexible President," who "seemed to have a better grasp of the idea of peaceful coexistence than Eisenhower did." Kennedy was "a reasonable man," Khrushchev continued. He was the sort of man who "wouldn't make any hasty decisions which might lead to military conflict."[70]

Reasonable, flexible, afraid of war, determined to avoid conflict. The trouble was that these same qualities suggested the lengths the president would go to avoid a confrontation, especially if Khrushchev seemed bent on one. The positive assessment in his memoirs reflects a view Khrushchev came to much later. Before Vienna, and even more afterward, he was convinced Kennedy could be pushed around. At a Presidium meeting ten days before the summit, Khrushchev said he was going to pressure Kennedy on Berlin. In response to Mikoyan's caution, Khrushchev insisted excitedly that the weakness Kennedy displayed at the Bay of Pigs must be exploited.[71] When he returned to the Soviet Embassy after his first session with Kennedy, Khrushchev was even more certain. "What can I tell you?" he said to Troyanovsky and others who were waiting. "This man is very inexperienced, even immature. Compared to him, Eisenhower was a man of intelligence and vision."[72]

THERE WERE moments, particularly toward the end of the second day of talks, when Kennedy went toe to toe with Khrushchev and got the best of it. Before that happened, the president doggedly and inexplicably pursued the very ideological argument he had been warned to avoid precisely because Khrushchev was likely to dominate it. What Kennedy didn't do at Vienna was to ignore the ideology, dismiss the bluster, propose a straightforward discussion of outstanding German issues, and, if Khrushchev refused, bid him a cool farewell with an invitation for practical negotiations when Khrushchev was ready for them.[73]

Khrushchev at first tried to avoid ideology. When Kennedy charged the Soviet Union with "seeking to eliminate free systems in areas that are associated with us," Khrushchev rebutted, but then added, "In any event this is not a matter for argument, much less for war." Yet instead of taking this cue, Kennedy plunged ahead, insisting Moscow supported pro-Communist minorities "which do not express the will of the people" because "the USSR believes that this is a historical inevitability." Khrushchev replied, "The United States wants to build a dam preventing the development of the human mind and conscience."[74]

Fruitless exchanges of this sort occupied almost the entire first session. After lunch (during which Khrushchev said that he envied the president because he was so young, but that even at age sixty-seven, he wasn't "renouncing the competition") and a stroll, and despite listing concrete issues (such as Laos, Germany, and nuclear tests) he wanted to discuss, Kennedy returned to the question of whether communism was destined to replace capitalism. This led to a sterile debate about whether communism had been imposed from the outside on a place like Cuba and whether the United States now intended to reimpose the old regime there.

This kind of colloquy wasn't devoid of practical significance. Kennedy was trying to show how dangerous ideological competition could be in the nuclear age. But his warning against any *further* extension of Soviet-sponsored communism seemed to imply American acceptance of communism wherever it already existed. When Soviet diplomat Georgy Kornienko read the transcript of the talks, he was amazed at the president's concession. Not only had JFK unaccountably allowed "the philosophical part" of the talks to drag on and on, but it sounded as if he had "agreed with Khrushchev's thesis that capitalism was on the way out while the future belonged to socialism." Kennedy's position was so surprising that Kornienko suspected the Soviet transcript had been doctored by underlings to make Khrushchev look good.[75]

Later in the talks Kennedy clarified his point: He wasn't opposed to any and all changes in the social status quo in other countries, only to those that altered the geopolitical balance of power by moving countries into the Soviet bloc. But Khrushchev could hardly accept that. Wasn't the American effort to crush Fidel Castro an attempt to alter the geopolitical status quo? Not to mention the fact that he himself was about to launch a new all-out push to remove West Berlin from the Western camp. Moreover, Kennedy phrased his concern in a way that Khrushchev found not just politically unacceptable but personally insulting.[76] The president warned that miscalculation by either side could have dire consequences. Khrushchev replied that miscalculation was "a very vague term." It looked to him as if the United States "wanted the USSR to sit like a schoolboy with its hands on its desk." But the Soviet Union would not be deterred from defending its interests.[77]

Strong as Khrushchev's response sounds, the diplomatic American note taker actually downplayed it. For as Kennedy recalled the scene that evening to Kenneth O'Donnell (while the president was warming his aching back in the ambassador's bathtub), "Khrushchev went berserk. He started yelling, 'Miscalculation! Miscalculation! Miscalculation! All I ever hear from your people and your news correspondents and your friends in Europe and everywhere else is that damned word, miscalculation! You ought to take that word and bury it in cold storage and never use it again! I'm sick of it!' "[78]

The Soviet leader's explosion revealed not just his country's supersensitivity but his own. What made the charge of miscalculation so painful was that it had been lodged against him by Molotov and that it was accurate. After all, what else was his own German policy based on? But when Khrushchev's tantrum bullied Kennedy into admitting American miscalculations (such as the failure to foresee Chinese intervention in the Korean War and even the Bay of Pigs invasion itself), Khrushchev took that for weakness, for that was how it would have felt to him to admit his own mistakes.

The fact that Kennedy was so highly educated made his being lectured like a "schoolboy" even harder to take. Lunch went better than the first session, but the postprandial stroll did not. Kennedy confessed his own domestic weakness (the product, he explained, of a narrow electoral victory and lack of support in Congress) and asked Khrushchev not to demand concessions that could undermine his position still further. Khrushchev replied with a diatribe on Berlin that showed both his tendency to bully and a presentiment that his German policy might be frustrated yet again by American reactionaries who had pushed Eisenhower away from détente and now would do the same with his successor.[79]

The afternoon session wasn't much better, but Khrushchev went away pleased. For Kennedy admitted that the United States regarded "the present balance of power between Sino-Soviet [*sic*] forces and the forces of the United States and Western Europe as being more or less in balance." Khrushchev took that to confirm what he had been insisting for so long: that the Soviet Union had achieved a rough equality in arms that made a new world war unthinkable.[80]

Kennedy saw Khrushchev to his limousine at 6:45 P.M. The president looked "dazed" to his friend, the *Sunday Times* correspondent Henry Brandon. "Is it always like this?" Kennedy asked Ambassador Thompson. "Par for the course," replied the diplomat, himself "very upset" because the president had ignored his advice to steer clear of ideology.

On the subject of advice, perhaps JFK should have taken some from his wife. After spending the evening with the Khrushchevs (including a state dinner in the massive Schönbrunn Palace, followed by opera and ballet), Jacqueline Kennedy concluded correctly that Mrs. Khrushchev was "hard and tough" and that although Adzhubei was said to have great influence on his father-in-law, "Khrushchev doesn't really like him" and was not "particularly close to him."[81] Sitting next to her at dinner, where his patter reminded her of Abbott and Costello, Khrushchev found Mrs. Kennedy "quick with her tongue." When he boasted that Ukraine had more teachers than before 1917, she snapped, "Oh, Mr. Chairman, don't bore me with statistics." Recalled Khrushchev: "She had no trouble finding the right word to cut you short if you weren't careful with her." Alas, that was more than could be said for Mrs. Kennedy's husband.[82]

On Sunday, June 4, the talks reconvened at 10:15 A.M. in the Soviet Embassy. Finally Kennedy got down to specifics. The two sides agreed on the need for a cease-fire in Laos and a neutral government there. But a Kennedy reference to American commitments in Asia and elsewhere triggered a Khrushchev outburst. The United States was "so rich and powerful that it believes that it has special rights and can afford not to recognize the rights of others." This was, if the president would excuse Khrushchev's bluntness, "megalomania" and "delusions of grandeur." The USSR couldn't accept being told, "Don't poke your nose" here, there, and everywhere, especially since the United States "has spread its forces all over." Westerners were "much better than Easterners at making threats in a refined way," but when the Americans talked about "commitments," that could mean they would "take over the Crimea since that would of course improve their position, too."[83]

An exchange on nuclear testing went nowhere. Khrushchev still preferred general and complete disarmament (on which, he said blithely, it should be possible to agree in just two years "given goodwill") to a test ban. On Berlin and Germany, he began politely but resolutely. What he intended to do would "affect relations between our two countries," especially "if the US were to misunderstand the Soviet position." He wanted to reach agreement with the president—he emphasized the words "with you"—but if the United States didn't reciprocate, the USSR would "sign a peace treaty" with East Germany, ending all occupation rights, including Western access to Berlin. Khrushchev repeated this pledge no fewer than ten times that day, as if trying to convince himself as well as Kennedy. "No force in the world" could stop him. How much longer did the United States want him to wait? Another sixteen years, another thirty years?

This time the president stood his ground, answering back coldly and effectively. Berlin was not Laos. It was "of the greatest concern to the US." The United States was not there on "someone's sufferance. We fought our way there. . . . West Europe is vital to our national security and we have supported it in two wars." Mr. Khrushchev had said that the president was "a young man," Kennedy continued, but "he had not assumed office to accept arrangements totally inimical to US interests."

In response to this tough talk, Khrushchev was at first petulant: Given Kennedy's expansive definition of national security, "the US might wish to go to Moscow because that, too, would of course, improve its position." Then he turned disingenuous, assuring Kennedy that "US prestige will not be involved, and everybody will understand this." Finally, he got nasty, declaring that if the United States wanted to start a war over Germany, then "let it begin now," rather than later, when even more horrible weapons had been devised. So frightening did these words seem that the Soviet note taker changed them to "then let the United States assume the entire responsibility for doing so," while his American counterpart replaced them with "then let it be so."[84]

Lunch was a lull before the next storm. Khrushchev promised not to resume nuclear testing unless the United States did (a pledge he broke before the summer was through), praised summits in which one could "listen to the position of the other side," and smilingly reassured Kennedy that although a peace treaty with East Germany might cause "great tensions," in the end "the clouds will dissipate, the sun will come out again and will shine brightly."

At 3:15 P.M., the two leaders reconvened for the final time, attended only by their interpreters. Kennedy warned against presenting the United States "with a situation so deeply involving our national interest." Khrushchev took that to mean "the US wants to humiliate the USSR and this cannot be accepted." He mentioned a possible interim agreement on Berlin that would protect the "prestige and interests of the two countries," but after that American rights would lapse. When Kennedy retorted that the USSR was offering a choice between a retreat and a confrontation, Khrushchev replied, "if the US wanted war, that was its problem." The Soviet decision to sign a peace treaty was "firm and irrevocable and the Soviet Union will sign it in December if the US refuses an interim agreement."

"If that's true," Kennedy said, ending the summit, "it's going to be a cold winter."[85]

"I NEVER MET a man like this," Kennedy told *Time* correspondent Hugh Sidey after returning from Vienna. "[I] talked about how a nuclear exchange would kill seventy million people in ten minutes and he just looked at me as if to say, 'So what?'" Robert Kennedy had never known his brother to be "so upset." The president read and reread transcripts of the summit, especially sections concerning Berlin.[86] Khrushchev had established a new six-month Berlin deadline in a memorandum given to the president at Vienna. Hoping it would not be publicized, Kennedy didn't mention it in his television report to the nation, saying that although he had just spent "a very sober two days," there had been "no threats or ultimatums by either side."[87]

Khrushchev published his memorandum on June 11 and repeated the six-month deadline in a TV report to the Soviet people on June 15. Several days later (dressed in his lieutenant general's uniform, no less) he delivered another tough speech at Kremlin ceremonies on the twentieth anniversary of the Nazi invasion. Western leaders who sought "a test of strength" on the German question would "share the fate of Hitler," he said, adding quickly, "Please do not take these words as a threat. This is an appeal for common sense."[88] A week later he blustered: "You can't bully us, gentlemen, a peace treaty will be signed."[89]

Kennedy offered no immediate response to Khrushchev's new ultimatum because he wasn't sure what to say. Asked for advice, former Secretary of State Dean Acheson urged a publicly announced nuclear and conventional arms buildup, the transfer of two or three divisions to West Germany, and the declaration of a national emergency. If Khrushchev didn't get that message and blockaded Berlin, Washington should break the blockade, demonstrating its determination to go nuclear if necessary. Other advisers, such as Ambassador Thompson, favored at most a quiet military buildup, preparing the ground for renewed diplomacy after West German elections scheduled for September.

The president decided to keep all options open; he ordered preparations for a nonnuclear defense of Berlin but didn't rule out negotiations. Robert Kennedy warned a back-channel Soviet interlocutor, Georgy Bolshakov, with whom he had been having secret discussions since May, that his brother preferred death to surrender, while Paul Nitze and Walt Rostow conveyed the same message to Menshikov. But the ambassador informed the Kremlin, in words he felt sure would appeal to Khrushchev, that the Kennedy brothers liked "to crow a lot," but when the time came to sign a treaty with East Germany, they would be "the first to drop a load in their pants."[90]

On July 19, Kennedy approved a $3.5 billion military buildup, but no national emergency. He asked Congress for authority to triple draft calls and call up the reserves and for funds to prepare and stock fallout shelters in case of nuclear war. Together with a somber address to the nation on July 25, these moves added up to more than Khrushchev had expected. He called British Ambassador Sir Frank Roberts to his box at a Bolshoi Ballet performance by Dame Margot Fonteyn and warned that his troops would outnumber Western troops dispatched to Germany by a hundredfold and that if nuclear war came, six hydrogen bombs would be "quite enough" for Britain and nine would do for France.[91]

John J. McCloy visited Khrushchev at his Black Sea dacha at the end of July. As Kennedy's chief disarmament negotiator McCloy had been in Moscow for talks when he and his wife and daughter were suddenly summoned to Pitsunda. Obviously, Khrushchev wanted to be able to reply immediately and directly to Kennedy's July 25 speech. Before reading it, he was in great good humor, inviting McCloy for a swim, lending him a spare, oversize bathing suit, posing for photos with his arm around the man known in New York as the chairman of the board of the eastern establishment, playing badminton with his guest, and joking that diplomatic sparring was like kicking a soccer ball back and forth.[92]

The next morning, however, after reading and digesting Kennedy's speech, Khrushchev was "really mad" and "used rough war-like language." Calling the speech a "preliminary declaration of war" because it presented him with "an ultimatum," Khrushchev repeated his by now familiar litany of threats: He would sign a peace treaty no matter what; Western access to Berlin would be cut off; if the West used force, a war was bound to be thermonuclear; though the United States and USSR might survive, America's European allies would be completely destroyed.[93] Khrushchev had so soured on Kennedy that Eisenhower looked good to him in comparison. During a break in the talks he praised the former president and hinted that he'd like to reinstate the invitation to visit the USSR that he had canceled so unceremoniously at the height of the U-2 crisis. "Of course, I'd never do it," Eisenhower told his son afterward, "but why Khrushchev would bring up such a thing sort of beats me."[94]

A week after seeing McCloy, Khrushchev recounted their conversation in a long, rambling speech to a secret Warsaw Pact summit conference in Moscow: "Please tell your president we accept his ultimatum and his terms and will respond in kind. . . . We will meet war with war." Khrushchev had said: "I am the commander in chief, and if war begins, I will give the order to the troops." If Kennedy started a war, he would be the "last president of the United States."[95]

Khrushchev's outburst to McCloy marked the peak of his campaign to intimidate Kennedy. It also conveyed his own unease. Kennedy's unexpectedly hard line hadn't shaken Khrushchev's view that JFK could be pushed around. On the contrary, he feared Kennedy was so weak he would let American reactionaries drag him into war. The United States was "barely governed," Khrushchev told his Warsaw Pact allies. Kennedy himself "exerts very little influence on the direction and development of American policies." The U.S. Senate resembled the medieval Veche of Novgorod, where the boyars "shouted, yelled, and pulled at each other's beards; that's how they decided who was right." Given the instability of American politics, "anything is possible, including war; they could unleash it." Although Dulles went to the brink, he was afraid of war. But "if Kennedy says that, he will be called a coward." Kennedy was such "an unknown quantity in politics" that Khrushchev "felt for him. . . . He is too much of a lightweight for both Republicans and Democrats, whereas the state is so big and so powerful that it poses certain dangers."[96]

The best way to restrain the American state, Khrushchev apparently thought, was to scare the daylights out of it. The way to do that was to break his promise not to resume nuclear testing unless the Americans did. Although the public announcement came at the end of August,

Khrushchev confided his intention to a secret Kremlin meeting in July. The assembled scientists weren't supposed to dissent, of course, but Andrei Sakharov dared to do so, first orally and then in a note to Khrushchev that said resuming tests would "only favor the USA" while "jeopardiz[ing] the test ban negotiations, the cause of disarmament, and world peace." Khrushchev forbore to reply until a gala dinner following the meeting. There, having raised his glass to the scientists, he launched into a half hour lecture—"calmly at first," Sakharov recalled, "but then with growing agitation, turning red in the face and raising his voice."

Sakharov had "moved beyond science into politics," Khrushchev said.

> Here he's poking his nose where it doesn't belong. . . . Politics is like the old joke about the two Jews traveling on a train. One asks the other: "So, where are you going?" "I'm going to Zhitomir." "What a sly fox," thinks the first Jew. "I know he's really going to Zhitomir, but he told me Zhitomir so I'll think he's going to Zhmerinka." Leave politics to us—we're the specialists. . . . We have to conduct our policies from a position of strength. . . . Our opponents don't understand any other language. Look, we helped elect Kennedy last year. Then we met with him in Vienna, a meeting that could have been a turning point. But what does he say? "Don't ask me for too much. Don't put me in a bind. If I make too many concessions, I'll be turned out of office." Quite a guy! He comes to a meeting but can't perform. What the hell do we need a guy like that for? Why waste time talking to him? Sakharov, don't try to tell us what to do or how to behave. We understand politics. I'd be a jellyfish and not Chairman of the Council of Ministers if I listened to people like Sakharov!

Khrushchev's tirade cast a pall. "The room was still," Sakharov remembered. "Everyone sat frozen, some averting their gaze, others maintaining set expressions."[97] The harangue also revealed Khrushchev's confusion. If he was so smart, why had he "helped" elect Kennedy? Given Khrushchev's assumption that sinister forces controlled American presidents, why had he counted on Kennedy in the first place?

If Khrushchev was alarmed at the direction events were taking, those charged with implementing his erratic course were even more dismayed. On May 19, Soviet Ambassador to East Germany Mikhail Pervukhin (he who had briefly supported Molotov, Malenkov, and Kaganovich against Khrushchev in 1957) dispatched a letter to Gromyko emphasizing the risks of signing a treaty with Ulbricht. To avoid a likely Western economic blockade, Pervukhin suggested an interim agreement that would *not* provide, upon expiration, for an automatic end to Western occupation rights—just the sort of terms that Khrushchev had dismissed out of hand at Vienna. On July 4, Pervukhin described "the most difficult issues which will arise after signing a peace treaty" (i.e., establishing GDR control over air and ground links between West Germany and West Berlin and over the border between West and East Berlin) in such a way as to imply that a treaty ought not be signed.[98]

According to Yuli Kvitsinsky, then a diplomatic attaché in East Germany, "we in the Embassy and in the Third European Department [of the Foreign Ministry] felt and repeated again and again to the Germans that we had to show more restraint. . . . " What worried Kornienko and others in Washington was that Khrushchev himself would not.[99]

The Soviet military high command wasn't any happier. If and when Khrushchev's bluff was called, they would have to back it up. Yet as a result of his rocket rattling, Western defense budgets were rising while the USSR's vaunted intercontinental missile capability amounted to virtually nothing. "With respect to ICBMs," Marshal Sergei Varentsov complained to Colonel Oleg Penkovsky, "we still don't have a damn thing. Everything is only on paper, and there is nothing in actual existence." To make matters worse, Penkovsky was an American secret agent who secretly told his handlers whatever Varentsov said. While Khrushchev was barnstorming the country in the winter of 1961, trying to get agriculture back on track, his marshals had met with Presidium members Mikoyan and Suslov to request more money for the military. "Stalin would just have banged on the table and that would have been that!" Varentsov later told Penkovsky. But this time no more funds were forthcoming.

On June 25, Varentsov invited a group of close friends to his dacha to celebrate his promotion to chief marshal. In private conversation with Penkovsky, he complained that the plan to back a GDR cutoff of main highways linking West Berlin and West Germany was risky. The whole scenario was based on the assumption that the West wouldn't fight or that if it did, a war could be limited. But as the marshals knew all too well, the Soviet Union wasn't prepared for a general war.[100]

Although none of the diplomatic and military grumbling constituted open opposition, some of it surely got back to Khrushchev. Combined with his own worries, others' doubts increased his impatience to resolve the Berlin question one way or another. At the end of July he cleared space for a vacation in the Crimea, which as usual turned into a round of beachfront meetings with rocket designers and assorted other lobbyists and functionaries. Much of their news was good: Projects such as an orbital bomb, a possible moon shot, and an atomic-powered plane were progressing. But, according to Sergei Khrushchev, "Father couldn't stop thinking about Germany. He'd made a last desperate attempt to pressure and frighten Kennedy at Vienna, but his threats had only spurred Kennedy to take counter-action."[101] Meantime his own blustering had accelerated the flow of East German refugees. More than a hundred thousand had fled during the first half of 1961, sixteen thousand more than during the first half of 1960. During June 1961 alone, almost twenty thousand crossed over into West Berlin, while twenty-six thousand had fled since Khrushchev had announced in July that he was raising the Soviet defense budget by one-third.[102]

As early as March 1961 Ulbricht had proposed building a wall across Berlin. Khrushchev vetoed the idea as too dangerous, then changed his mind. Several signals from Washington in the meantime (including Kennedy's repeated pledges to defend *West* Berlin, but not *East* Berlin, and a July 30 statement by Senator J. W. Fulbright seeming to accept a closed inter-German border) suggested the Americans wouldn't resist, but the Soviets couldn't be sure.[103] Khrushchev's nervousness manifested itself in the strict secrecy that surrounded preparations for construction; even highly classified Soviet transcripts of the Warsaw Pact summit, which record detailed discussions of the coming peace treaty and its consequences, include no discussion at all of the wall. Before signing off on the project, Khrushchev even paid an incognito visit to both East and West Berlin. "I never got out of the car," he recalled, "but I made a full tour and saw what the city was like."[104]

Khrushchev's agitation showed in public pronouncements that combined heightened belligerence with passionate calls for calm. "Our people will not falter in the face of trials," he declared in a televised speech on August 7. "They will answer force with force and will smash any aggressor." But the same speech appealed to Western leaders to "sit down as honest men around the negotiating table, let us not create a war psychosis, let us clear the atmosphere, let us rely on reason and not on the power of thermonuclear weapons." Four days later, at a Soviet-Romanian friendship meeting, Khrushchev warned that "hundreds of millions might perish" in a nuclear war. In Italy "not only the orange groves but also the people who created and who have extolled Italy's culture and arts" might die. So might "the Acropolis and other historical monuments of Greece." As for West Germany, "there will likely be no one and nothing in Germany to unite." Yet all hope was not lost: "Come to your senses, gentlemen! I appeal to those who have not lost the ability to think calmly and sensibly. . . . Let us not frighten each other, let us not seek out what divides us, let us not deepen the already deep differences. After all, we have common needs and interests since we have to live on the same planet."[105]

Sergei Khrushchev confirmed that his father was "far less resolute at home than he seemed on television." His August 7 speech sneeringly compared jittery Western statesmen with a wartime Soviet general who committed suicide before his very eyes. In conversation with his son, Khrushchev worried that "Kennedy's nerves wouldn't prove strong enough, that he might come unhinged."

As an extra precaution, Khrushchev decreed that the wall go up in stages; first, barbed wire, with concrete to follow only if the West acquiesced. Even so, the Soviets held their breaths on August 13, waiting to see how the Americans would react. There was a crisis atmosphere in the Foreign Ministry.[106] When it became clear that the wire wouldn't be torn down, Sergei Khrushchev later wrote, "Father sighed with relief. Things had turned out all right." Later, when Kennedy sent a convoy of fifteen hundred fully armed marines to West Berlin to make sure American access remained full and free, Khrushchev girded himself again. "His nervousness transmitted itself to me," wrote Sergei. As the two of them took their regular walk that evening, a bodyguard rushed toward them with a message, an unusual occurrence when the leader was supposed to be at ease. Khrushchev froze in his tracks. But it was a false alarm. In fact, Kennedy had acquiesced. After all, he had never promised to liberate East Germans, only to preserve the freedom of those in the West.

"Father was delighted," Sergei remembered. "By establishing control over its borders, he thought the GDR had achieved even more than it could have expected from a peace treaty."[107] But his foreign policy assistant Troyanovsky saw things differently. The wall "saved [Khrushchev's] face." It was "a silent recognition that he had not achieved his basic aim," which he had pursued with monomaniacal intensity for nearly three years, "to force the Western powers into a compromise favorable to East Germany."[108]

The fact that Kennedy accepted the wall had another effect: It convinced Khrushchev that he could pressure Kennedy again, thus setting the stage for the most explosive cold war crisis of all in Cuba.

CHAPTER EIGHTEEN

"*A Communist Society Will Be Just about Built by 1980*": 1961–1962

DURING THE SUMMER of 1961, when Khrushchev was jousting with Kennedy and then settling for a Berlin wall instead of a German treaty, the agricultural crisis that had so disturbed him the previous winter seemed to ease. In May he checked out the situation in the Caucasus. Late June found him in Kazakhstan. Everywhere he found local officials to criticize, but not as harshly as before, and he even laughed at his own expense. Treated to horsemeat by his Kazakh hosts, he complained it was fatty but added quickly, "True, it may only have seemed that way to me, since in judging how fat meat is, I take my own build into account."[1]

Prospects for the fall harvest looked good. "We live in a wonderful time," Khrushchev told a Kazakhstan audience. His July 20 memorandum to Presidium colleagues, reporting on visits to several other regions, contrasted sharply with the report he had sent them in March. Back then Ukraine had seemed headed for disaster; now a banner crop loomed, in part, crowed Khrushchev, because farms had increased acreage devoted to corn.[2] After two years of harvests "below our capabilities," he added on August 7, the current crop "will apparently be such as we have not had in all the years of the Soviet regime's existence." Data on industrial output, said to exceed targets for the first two years of the seven-year plan period, also delighted him, as did the country's latest scientific triumph, its second space flight, by cosmonaut German Titov.[3] On September 10, in

Stalingrad, a place redolent of wartime victory, Khrushchev celebrated the building of the giant new Volga hydroelectric station. "We are living, comrades, you and I," he told the assembled throng, "at a happy time, when the most cherished dreams of the finest sons of mankind are being realized."[4]

THE MOST cherished dream of all was of communism itself. Marx and Engels had reserved the term for the highest level of human development, the period when, as *The Communist Manifesto* puts it, "the free development of each is the condition for the free development of all,"[5] when abundance would be created by "each according to his ability," and distributed to "each according to his need." According to Lenin, communism would be preceded by an extended stage of socialism, during which a powerful state, the dictatorship of the proletariat, would prepare society for the realm of freedom to come. Stalin claimed to have built "the foundations" by 1936, but he was smart enough not to declare socialism fully and finally achieved, lest he be expected to conjure up communism itself in the near future. Yet that is precisely what Khrushchev was about to promise in a new party program.

The old program had been adopted in 1919. The notion of revising it had arisen as early as 1934; indeed the Seventeenth Party Congress had created a commission headed by Stalin to do so, but the Second World War intervened. The fact that an unpublished 1948 draft set the task of "building Communism in the USSR in the next twenty to thirty years" shows Khrushchev wasn't the only wild-eyed utopian around. But Stalin refused to commit himself to any concrete target date.

As early as the thirties Khrushchev talked eagerly of "constructing communism." In 1952 he described that as the party's main task, and at the Twentieth Party Congress in 1956 he boasted that the USSR had "climbed a mountain from whose heights one can see the broad path leading to the final goal—Communist society." At his prompting, the Twentieth Congress ordered a new program be prepared forthwith.[6]

Khrushchev was fired by enthusiasm that turned out to be misplaced, but that doesn't mean the preparation of a new program was entirely arbitrary. On the surface at least, it seemed careful and methodical. The year 1958 saw the formation of a high-powered drafting committee headed by the Central Committee's International Department chief Boris Ponomarev. The team asked scientific institutes, government departments, and other agencies for data on all spheres of Soviet life as well as on international developments. Two of the country's leading economic theorists, Eugen Varga and Stanislav Strumilin, drafted the major sections, paying particular attention to comparative economic prospects for the Soviet Union and United States over the next ten to fifteen years. Strumilin prefaced his contribution with a warning against "hasty attempts to resolve problems in the absence of necessary preconditions."

Supervised by Khrushchev himself, the commission completed an initial draft by the fall of 1958. That July he had instructed Ponomarev to make the program "clear, precise, and inspiring—like a poem, yet at the same time realistic, true-to-life, and broadly gauged." After reading the draft in October, Khrushchev ordered that excessive detail be deleted lest it deprive the program of its "profound, long-range character."

At the Twenty-first Party Congress in 1959 Khrushchev declared that the USSR had completed the "full and final construction of socialism." In other words, communism was next. In March he met at length with Ponomarev, and in July the Presidium ordered an even broader range of experts, institutes, and agencies to make more projections and predictions. In particular, the State Planning Commission and State Economic Council were asked for independent estimates. Both made the mistake of assuming that the boom years of the middle and late fifties would continue two decades into the future.[7]

Fyodor Burlatsky joined Ponomarev's group, which was living and working at a luxurious sanatorium in the woods outside Moscow, at the beginning of 1960. He recollected heated arguments about whether to include specific forecasts of Soviet and world economic performance in the program. When a top Khrushchev economic adviser, Aleksandr Zasyadko, proposed such a section, virtually all working group members, including both economists and noneconomists, rejected it as "superficial and unscientific." The proposed estimates of Soviet and American economic performance were "complete fabrications—pure wishful thinking," recalled Burlatsky. But when Zasyadko pulled out an eighty-page typed manuscript bound in blue and opened it to the first page, on which the words "to be included in the program" were followed by Khrushchev's familiar scrawled signature, that was that: Statistics "proving" that the USSR would catch up and overtake the United States went into the program. "Enthusiasm was running high," according to Burlatsky, "but as we used to say in the apparatus, you need ammunition as well as enthusiasm."[8]

Khrushchev himself edited the program text. On April 20 and 21, 1961, and again on July 18, he dictated forty-six pages of comments and corrections. Some of his suggestions (deleting a redundant adjective here; striking an anachronism there) were strictly editorial; he must have enjoyed proving himself a closer reader than the academicians he was correcting. Other "improvements" rendered the text even more utopian (if that was possible), such as when he insisted the USSR would surpass the United States in per capita production by 1970.

Several Khrushchev emendations actually hedged on specific pledges: Within the next two decades free housing for everyone would be achieved only "in the main"; although it would be wonderful to provide fully for the health of mothers and children, it was better not to specify "maternity wards, consultations, children's sanatoriums and hospitals, and summer schools, etc." without apparent limit. But it was just when he was at his most down-to-earth and realistic that his abiding unrealism was most apparent.

"From a means of existence," said the draft, work would become "genuine creativity," so that everyone would experience "an internal need to labor voluntarily for the public good." That meant, Khrushchev warned, that people might think they were free "to go to the beach" instead of to work . . . to say, 'Let others work; I won't work; I'll spend all my time lying around.'" Of course, he concluded, "the working day should be shorter, and vacations longer, but who will pay for all this, the Chinese?"[9] He was clear-eyed enough to see what real people were really like, but not that their nature precluded the paradise he was promising. He admitted that rising international tensions could "delay" realization of the program's promises, but not, of course, that his own policies heightened those strains.

Notwithstanding his frequent dismissal of empty theorizing and his preference for practical solutions, Khrushchev needed to make his ideological mark as the Soviet leader. Marx and Lenin had used the term "dictatorship of the proletariat" to describe how the victorious working class would expropriate capitalist expropriators; Stalin had insisted the proletarian dictatorship would endure despite Marx's promise that the state would "wither away." Khrushchev didn't so much suggest updating the founders' concept, as discarding it entirely and substituting a new term, "the all-people's state." He tried to use suitably highfalutin language—since "dictatorship means the predominance of one part, or one class, over another part," what that meant in a now-classless society was "not clear"—but his earthy common sense kept intruding. Ordinary people didn't understand (despite Lenin's insistence that a majority would dictate to a minority) how a dictatorship could be democratic. "If you ask me what this dictatorship consists of," Khrushchev strikingly confessed, "I won't be able to explain to you and you won't to me."[10]

The Presidium received the draft program on May 6 and approved it, with minimal changes, on May 24. Khrushchev presented the text to the Central Committee on June 19 in a speech that soared higher than the program itself. Within twenty years, he declared, "communism in our country will be just about built." During that time the USSR would "steadily win victory after victory" in economic competition with the United States. After two decades the Soviet Union would "rise to such a great height that, by comparison, the main capitalist countries will remain far below and way behind." The Soviet countryside would blossom with "such an array of appurtenances—apartment houses equipped with all modern conveniences, enterprises providing consumer services, cultural and medical facilities—that in the end the rural population will enjoy conditions of life comparable to those found in cities."[11]

Melor Sturua, a member of a group editing the program's text, tried to warn against promising too much. Knowing Khrushchev's temper, Sturua couched his reservations in convoluted ideological language, contending that Marxist stages of historical development, while succeeding one another in predictable progression, did not necessarily do so according to a preordained schedule. Thereupon Khrushchev stared at the dark-complexioned Georgian and said, "Listen, black one, little dilettantish tricks like that won't get you to the truth." So the timetable by which manna from heaven would rain down remained unchanged.[12]

Publication of the draft program on August 30, 1961, began what Soviet propagandists hailed as a mammoth national "discussion" in which 4.6 million people took part at party and nonparty meetings. All told, some three hundred thousand letters, articles, and notes were allegedly forwarded to twenty-two working groups, which analyzed fourteen thousand of them in particular detail and selected forty for inclusion in the final text.[13] It was this text that Khrushchev presented to the Twenty-second Party Congress on October 18, 1961. Within ten years, he boasted, the entire Soviet population would be "materially provided for." Sooner than that everyone would "enjoy a good diet of high quality." Consumer goods would soon be abundant, while the housing shortage would disappear "within this decade."[14]

The congress adopted the new program quickly and unanimously.

ACTUALLY, MIKOYAN later recalled, "Khrushchev didn't like statistics." When Mikoyan resisted including twenty-year projections of steel output in the new program, Khrushchev replied, "Nineteen-eighty won't arrive anytime soon," which Mikoyan took to mean that Khrushchev "didn't count on living until communism was fully constructed, so that it wasn't important to him whether the numbers were realistic or not." What he wanted, Mikoyan said, was to "impress the people. He didn't understand that the people would demand an explanation if the promises weren't fulfilled."[15]

Mikoyan didn't exhaust the list of Khrushchev's motives. Khrushchev probably hoped to light a fire under bureaucrats obliged to deliver on time. In the process he would look good. But he wasn't just burnishing his own image. He genuinely couldn't wait for the day when the Soviet people, who had sacrificed so much, would at last enjoy the good life.

Ironically, similar thinking may have prompted the all-out attack on religion that he authorized at about the same time. Of course, religion had always been anathema to the Bolsheviks, who had demolished churches, arrested priests, and persecuted believers from 1917 through the 1930s. It was Stalin, of all people, who reversed course during and just after World War II, if only to try to unite the populace for the war effort and to impress his Western allies. The number of Orthodox parishes registered by the state, of applications to open new churches, of monasteries, of christenings and church burial services, the rate of attendance at church services, and the number of applicants to seminaries: All these rose substantially until the late 1940s, after which growth leveled off until Khrushchev mounted his assault.[16]

That crackdown, which began in the late fifties and continued into the sixties, reached its peak in 1961: Antireligious propaganda was strengthened, taxes on religious activity increased, churches and monasteries closed—with the result that the number of Orthodox parishes dropped from more than fifteen thousand in 1951 to fewer than eight thousand in 1963.[17]

It isn't clear whether Khrushchev himself initiated the new offensive against religion, but he certainly approved it. It was a price he paid for de-Stalinization—in the sense that the crackdown was popular with Stalinist ideologues like Suslov—but he may have also seen it as a form of de-Stalinization in that it abandoned Stalin's compromise with religion and returned to Lenin's more militant approach. The fact that the new policy coincided with the preparation of the new party program wasn't accidental. What better time to rid the nation of "relics of the past" than when Khrushchev was firing up popular enthusiasm by outlining communism's shining future! If, however, as his close aide Andrei Shevchenko contended, Khrushchev himself retained residual religious convictions, his assault on religion must have deepened his sense of guilt, while increasing his need to assuage it with ever more public adulation.[18]

THE TWENTY-SECOND Congress convened on October 17, 1961, in the modernist marble and glass Palace of Congresses just completed on the Kremlin grounds. Work on the building had proceeded frantically until the very last moment. The fact that it was ready on time made the congress opening even more of an occasion. Besides nearly five thousand Soviet delegates, leaders of Communist parties from around the world were present. Five years had passed since the last regularly scheduled congress (the Twenty-first Congress in 1959 was an extraordinary one), and it was time to assess the state of the Soviet Union and of the world since 1956.

If the congress had had real power and authority, there would have been plenty to criticize: the agricultural slowdown; Khrushchev's German policy; his handling of relations with the Chinese and with his own intelligentsia. By 1961 people ranging from ordinary collective farmers to high-ranking generals certainly had doubts about his leadership. But this was the period of Khrushchev's sole stewardship, and the proceedings were an extended celebration of his achievements.

The munificent new program set the tone. Khrushchev delivered both the Central Committee's general report and an equally prolix explication of the party program; altogether the two speeches took more than ten hours. ("Is it really possible," Politburo member Dmitri Polyansky complained in October 1964, when Khrushchev was about to be ousted, "that a party with ten million members couldn't find one other person in its ranks to give one of these reports?"[19]) Before the congress closed, Leonid Brezhnev hailed Khrushchev's "indefatigable energy and revolutionary passion [that] inspire all of us to fighting deeds," while Nikolai Podgorny, who joined Brezhnev in the anti-Khrushchev conspiracy two years later, extolled Khrushchev's "indissoluble bond with the people, humanity and simplicity, his ability to learn constantly from the masses and to teach the masses. . . ."[20]

A close reading of congress speeches reveals varying degrees of rapture. Western Kremlinologists at the time took these to be signs of a secret struggle at the top.[21] However, if there had been any real opposition to

Khrushchev, the offending oligarchs wouldn't have lasted very long. Khrushchev's "real troubles" began later, recalled his colleague Pyotr Demichev; the Twenty-second Congress was his "time in the sun." Moscow city party boss Nikolai Yegorychev said later, "One had to be there to see how strongly Nikita Sergeyevich was supported."[22]

Yet the same congress had a strange countercurrent, a sudden renewal of the assault on Stalin that clashed with the generally celebratory tone. In keeping with the post-1957 muting of Khrushchev's anti-Stalin campaign, the new program mostly ignored the subject. Presidium member Otto Kuusinen had urged Khrushchev to include at least some criticism of the "cult of personality," if only because Mao was trying to recreate one in China, and Khrushchev accepted the suggestion. But Kuusinen's draft language, although much milder than Khrushchev's secret speech, never made it into the final version.[23] Although Khrushchev commended the Twentieth Congress line on Stalin, as well as the 1957 defeat of Molotov and the others, his language was hardly fiery. Yet his remarks released a flood of anti-Stalinist rhetoric that virtually drowned out the triumphalism of the congress.

When the congress convened, the tyrant's body still lay beside Lenin's in the mausoleum on Red Square, while Stalingrad, the "hero city" on the Volga, still bore his name, as did thousands of streets, squares, and enterprises across the land. Now, suddenly, a mud slide descended on Stalin's reputation, as well as on the names of Molotov, Malenkov, and Kaganovich. *Pravda* editor Pavel Satiukov blasted Molotov and company as "swamp creatures grown used to slime and dirt." According to Khrushchev, Molotov and the others opposed unmasking Stalin because they "feared that their own role as accomplices . . . would come to light." Recalling the execution of his friend General Yakir, Khrushchev reported that Molotov, Kaganovich, and Voroshilov had favored Yakir's rehabilitation in the 1950s. "But it was you who put these people to death," Khrushchev had told them. "So when were you acting according to your conscience, then or now?"[24]

He had leveled similar accusations in 1956 and 1957, but this was the first time they were heard in public. He even implied that Stalin had ordered the 1934 assassination of Sergei Kirov, and he called for a monument in Moscow to Stalin's victims. On its next to last day the congress voted to recognize as "unsuitable the continued retention in the mausoleum of the sarcophagus with J. V. Stalin's coffin," a resolution passed (unanimously, of course) after an old woman who had joined the party in 1902 cried out that she had "asked Ilyich [Lenin] for advice, and it was as if he stood before me alive and said, 'I do not like lying next to Stalin, who brought so much misfortune to our party.' "[25]

Stalin's body was removed from the mausoleum that very night. Under cover of darkness, and with Red Square cordoned off from prying eyes, his coffin was extracted from its place of honor, lugged out of the marble building, and dumped in a pit in the back. "They didn't carry it out horizontally," Shelepin recalled, "but at a 45-degree angle. I had the feeling he was going to open his eyes and say, 'What are you doing to me, you bastards?' " Instead of filling the pit with dirt, the authorities covered the coffin with several truckloads of cement.[26]

Besides communism's shining future and Stalinist mayhem, Khrushchev's version of term limits for Communist officials was also on the congress agenda. He wanted to limit leaders to two or three terms, with exception of those, like himself, who "by virtue of their recognized authority and their outstanding political, organizational, or other qualities," could serve for "longer periods."[27] But the question remains why Khrushchev let anti-Stalinist outbursts overshadow almost everything else. According to Sergei Khrushchev, his father "couldn't resist," and his impulsive outbursts prompted other speakers hurriedly to try to match him. Others insist Khrushchev knowingly forced his colleagues to join the anti-Stalinist chorus.[28] Both theories are plausible, but so is a classically Khrushchevian combination of doubt and confidence.

After all his domestic and foreign policy setbacks, Khrushchev had good reason to wonder how the congress would receive him. Before it began, Molotov dispatched another *j'accuse* to the Central Committee, this one attacking the new program as "scandalous for Communists." Whether he included his view (expressed later in conversations with friends) that Khrushchev was like a "bridleless horse who dictated the program with his left foot" is not clear.[29]

Molotov's letter provoked Khrushchev to attack the "antiparty group" at the congress; shortly afterwards its leading members were expelled from the party. That the traditionally obedient congress would support Khrushchev wasn't in doubt, but how much enthusiasm would it muster? When his new burst of anti-Stalinism produced an outpouring of support, on top of that for the new program, the coast seemed fully clear at last. With his main enemies finally crushed and with Stalin's reputation in tatters, Khrushchev now felt entirely in charge, far more so than in 1956, even more than in 1957.

His mood combined pleasure at his enhanced authority with bitterness that it had ever been in doubt. Both were visible when the new

Central Committee chosen by the congress convened to select its Presidium. The vast hall in which thousands of delegates and guests had just sat dwarfed the Central Committee's several hundred members. It was the job of party leader Khrushchev to begin the session, but for a long time he remained silent, as if to show that the plenum couldn't begin without him. "The floor is yours, Nikita Sergeyevich," someone called out. Feigning bewilderment, Khrushchev asked if anyone else wanted to talk. Finally, approaching the lectern, he fumbled through his pockets, extracted a tiny piece of paper, and joked, "If I'd lost this piece of paper, we'd have to do without a Presidium." The gesture showed that he had composed the list of nominees himself. In case anyone missed that, he added: "I sat over there with a pencil. . . . " With Central Committee members waiting nervously to see if they were still on his list, Khrushchev read out his nominations. When he neglected to include his own name, a chorus of voices had to prompt him again: "What about Khrushchev? . . . We nominate Khrushchev."[30]

THE TWENTY-SECOND Congress was another turning point. No longer constrained by Stalin, Molotov, or anyone else, and armed with new authority on top of all his old power, Khrushchev set out to attack the problems that had been vexing him.[31] Agriculture of course was one of them. Despite the good omens of summer, the 1961 harvest proved disappointing: Marketable output increased by only 0.7 percent, and meat production was less than in 1959 or 1960, while the Virgin Lands harvest was the smallest in five years. More devastating was the sharp contrast with the party program, which promised a "flourishing, fully developed, and highly productive agriculture," guaranteeing "an abundance of high-quality food products for the public and of raw materials for industry."[32]

The causes of the agricultural shortfall were many. Even when supplies grew, they were exceeded by demand, itself boosted by rising incomes. But in the face of food shortages, many blamed Khrushchev. On December 30 and 31 posters circulating in the city of Chita in Siberia included the slogans "Down with the Khrushchev dictatorship!" and "You're a blabbermouth, Khrushchev: Where's that abundance you promised?"[33]

Khrushchev's reaction to this latest crisis contrasts with his behavior before and after. In 1953 he had been certain that shortages would quickly yield to new reforms. In 1963 he practically despaired of finding a solution. In the winter of 1961–1962, however, no matter how frustrated and angry he was, he still thought he had answers.

His instinct, as usual, was to seek them in the fields instead of the office. Two weeks after the congress he met with cotton workers in Uzbekistan. From there he headed to the Virgin Lands and Siberia before returning to Moscow in mid-December. A week later he was in Kiev; in mid-January, in Minsk. The Central Committee took up agriculture in March. One can glimpse Khrushchev's gorge rising on all these occasions, even as he outlined his latest panaceas for the countryside.

Khrushchev's Tashkent audience got this response to a plea for more money: "What are we supposed to do now? Turn our pockets inside out and count our money? I could pull out my pockets for you and show you they are empty. . . . I don't have anything, and I have brought you nothing but good wishes."[34] To Kazakhstan's party leader, who admitted his republic had "reduced" its contribution to Virgin Lands output in 1961, Khrushchev shot back, "That's too mild an expression. You didn't reduce grain production, you disrupted it."[35] In Novosibirsk he condemned allowing up to a quarter of the nation's arable land to lie fallow or grow grasses, a practice developed in the thirties to make up for inadequate herbicides and fertilizers. Indiscriminate use of the grasslands approach was indeed deleterious, but so was the sort of wholesale junking of it, and its replacement by corn and other crops that required intensive cultivation, which Khrushchev now demanded.[36]

To the Moscow conference on December 14 Khrushchev brought "bitter words." Pro-grasslands agronomists "should be dragged out of the swamp by the ears, hauled into the bathhouse and washed." On some farms the misuse of the land was "absolutely criminal." When the assembled officials failed to respond properly to this harangue, Khrushchev complained, "You're not all applauding." All the more galling that when the nation faced a "shortage of meat in some cities," farm leaders "live the good life, are paid regularly, and even given bonuses. . . . No, this cannot go on."[37]

Khrushchev's Kiev speech was more upbeat, as if mellowed by his return to Ukraine, but in Minsk he lashed out again. After years of boasting about output gains, he suddenly refused to do so: "The population has increased, and the demand for food has risen a great deal. Therefore, it makes no sense merely to compare production with 1953. . . . I must speak the truth to your faces. Who will tell it to you if I do not?" Some of his obviously unhappy audience might say, " 'Khrushchev has come here to criticize and to blast us. 'What did you think I came for, to read Pushkin to you?' "[38]

The March 1962 plenum was attended by hundreds of officials who were not Central Committee members. The presence of such "guests," another "democratic" innovation introduced by Khrushchev, irritated the Central Committee. When he attacked party officials who expected peasants to "chop down corn with an axe while harvesting and silage combines stand idle because of poor repair work," the hall was silent. "Applaud, comrades," Khrushchev admonished his audience. "Why don't you applaud?" He also blasted peasants who "before sowing take their caps off, face east, cross themselves and then, after sowing, say, 'Now let God provide,'" not to mention agronomists who wrote such tomes as "Study of the Microclimate in the Cow Barns of the Estonian Republic," which included a section on "the chemical composition of the air." Khrushchev sneered: "Any person with a sense of smell who goes into a cow barn can tell you the composition of the air."

Opening the March plenum, Khrushchev called for increased investment, including funds for three new factories to manufacture agricultural machinery. Four days later he urged farmers to make do with what they had. So dramatic was this retreat that he had to deny that he had made it ("This does not mean I am going back in any way on the report . . ."), but its meaning was obvious: Grave as agriculture's predicament was, heavy industry and the military couldn't spare any resources.[39]

Instead of increased investment, Khrushchev proposed an awkward and unwieldy reorganization of agricultural administration. Ever since the 1920s the district party committee (called *raikom*) had been responsible for state and collective farms on their territory, as well as for rural life in general: education, health services, roads, etc. District party bosses (like Khrushchev himself in Petrovo-Marinsky in 1925 and 1926) had been celebrated in countless socialist realist stories. Now, however, he proposed replacing the fabled *raikom* with "territorial production administrations," whose writ would extend over two or three former districts, thus constituting yet another layer of bureaucracy between the countryside and the capital.[40]

In the meantime another wrenching decision awaited Khrushchev. On May 17, 1962, the Presidium approved a draft government decree, scheduled to take effect on June 1, raising retail prices by as much as 35 percent for meat and poultry products and by up to 25 percent for butter and milk. The increase made economic sense. Although state procurement prices for agricultural produce had increased several times since

1953, they still failed to cover the cost of production. As a result, the more output farms supplied to the state, the greater were their losses. Khrushchev's restrictions on private livestock, designed to increase collective farm herds, had made matters worse. Higher prices would allow the cash-starved treasury to pay more to farmers, thus stimulating production. But price rises broke with the popular expectation, encouraged since Stalin's time, that consumer prices would go steadily down, not up.[41]

To make matters worse, the price rise followed a move to raise factory output norms by requiring more work for the same pay or less pay for the same work. Khrushchev at first resisted the price hikes but gave in to arguments by Deputy Prime Minister Aleksei Kosygin. Even though agriculture wasn't his bailiwick, foreign policy aide Troyanovsky recalled urging Khrushchev to keep his distance from what would surely be an unpopular measure. But Khrushchev insisted on taking full responsibility.[42]

THE PRICE increases went into effect on June 1, 1962. Almost immediately handwritten leaflets and posters protesting them appeared around the country, calls for strikes sounded in Moscow, Kiev, Leningrad, Donetsk, and Chelyabinsk, and disturbances broke out in other cities.[43] The worst outbreak occurred at the huge Budenny Electric Locomotive Factory twelve miles outside the northern Caucasus city of Novocherkassk.[44] As the result of work-norm increases, take-home pay there had fallen by as much as 30 percent. Workers had also complained about poor working conditions (two hundred had fallen sick in one shop), the high cost of housing, and shortages and high prices at the market in town.[45] In response, a veteran director who was popular with the workers was replaced with a maladroit new one. When workers complained that they could no longer afford to eat pirozhki with meat at the factory cafeteria, the new director urged them, Marie Antoinette–like, to eat cabbage pirozhki instead. Once the strike broke out, "Pirozhki with Cabbage" became a sarcastic "slogan of the struggle."[46] Even the KGB admitted, in one of many reports prepared during the crisis, that Budenny factory workers had been greatly provoked, while local party leaders had failed to see the storm coming.[47]

At 7:30 A.M. on June 1, a group of steelworkers who had just arrived at the plant refused to work. Soon other laborers left their benches and moved to the factory yard, where angry workers from other shops followed. After failing to calm them, the factory director turned his back on the crowd and stalked back to his office. Later the workers marched to plant administration offices and then out into the street. By this time their number had grown to several hundred. Standing on a balcony, the province party boss defended the price rise, while the KGB tried to quiet the crowd by infiltrating veteran party members into it. The province party chief was drowned out by shouts of "Meat! Meat! Raise our pay!" and after several stones and at least one bottle had whizzed by his ear, he and other province officials retreated inside. That afternoon the crowd swarmed over the nearby railroad tracks, intercepted the Saratov–Rostov passenger train, and halted all movement on the line. Someone scribbled, "Cut up Khrushchev for meat!" on the locomotive with chalk; someone else sounded the train's whistle, summoning many more people from the factory and nearby houses.

By now all work at the plant had stopped, and the crowd had swelled to several thousand. According to a KGB report, "hooligans and drunks" began pulling down "certain portraits" from factory administration walls. Alert to leadership sensitivities, the KGB wasn't about to identify the subjects, even in a top-secret report, but eyewitnesses recalled that pictures of Khrushchev were ripped down, thrown in a heap, and then burned.[48] In the middle of the afternoon the captured train was briefly liberated by KGB and local police, only to be retaken by the angry crowd. Party officials trying to read the Central Committee's defense of the price rise were drowned out. "We've read it ourselves," someone shouted. "We're literate, you know. Tell us instead how we're supposed to live with pay lowered and prices raised!"[49]

About two hundred police arrived at the factory between 6:00 and 7:00 P.M. but were soon forced to flee. The same fate awaited soldiers who drove up in five cars and three armored personnel carriers. According to the KGB, several who tried to restore "law and order" were beaten by demonstrators.[50] Strike meetings continued through the night at the plant, workers arriving the next morning joined in, and at about 8:00 A.M. on June 2 the massive crowd headed for the city.

Long before this the Kremlin had of course been informed. A KGB report to Khrushchev and his colleagues also mentioned minor protests in other cities—Moscow, Tbilisi, Novosibirsk, Leningrad, Dnepropetrovsk, and Grozny—but assured the Presidium that measures were being taken to prevent any further "antisocial manifestations."[51] Measures in Novocherkassk included calling out Red Army troops and internal security troops to assist local militia. The commander of the North Caucasus Military District, General Issa A. Pliyev, who had been on maneuvers, reached Novocherkassk at 5:00 P.M. on June 1; more than a hundred special KGB agents had soon followed.[52] According to his son-in-law, Khrushchev was "bursting" to go to Novocherkassk to calm things down and was "barely dissuaded" from doing so.[53] He asked Mikoyan and Kozlov to go in his place, dismissing Mikoyan's objection that it would better for one man, not two, to be in charge. He also dispatched three other Presidium members—Kirilenko, Shelepin, and Polyansky—to Novocherkassk, along with the Central Committee secretary Leonid Ilychev and the deputy KGB chief Pyotr Ivashutin.[54]

The workers who marched toward Novocherkassk on June 2 were joined by others, including women and children. Those at the head of the column carried red flags and portraits of Lenin, Marx, and Engels. To Vadim Makarevsky, a military officer on Pliyev's staff, the scene recalled Bolshevik propaganda paintings of workers marching on the tsar's Winter Palace in 1917.[55] Others later compared it with the St. Petersburg workers carrying icons and portraits of the tsar who had died in a hail of fire on what became known as Bloody Sunday in January 1905. Like most of the previous day's protests, the June 2 march was peaceful, but party and police officials, who already faced reprimands for alienating ordinary workers, had an interest in depicting hooligans as in control.

To reach the city center, demonstrators had to cross the Tuzlov River; when tanks blocked the bridge, many marchers waded through the shallow water while others boldly climbed over and around the tanks. Soldiers standing nearby made no serious attempt to stop them. By now numbering nearly ten thousand, the crowd reached Lenin Square at 10:30 A.M. After calls for party leaders to answer to the people went unheeded, several protesters forced their way into the party headquarters and then appeared on the balcony, where they tore down red flags and a portrait of Lenin and urged the protesters to seize the police station and free demonstrators arrested the day before. Despite warning shots in the air, the crowd in the square refused to disperse. Suddenly more shots rang out. When the firing stopped, twenty-three people (most of them between the ages of eighteen and twenty-five) were dead, and eighty-seven wounded; three more died later. Of the dead, two were women and one was a schoolboy. The authorities were so determined to conceal the true toll that they repaved the street, which scrub brushes and fire hoses had proved unable to cleanse of blood, and buried the victims secretly in five separate cemeteries in widely dispersed parts of Rostov Province.[56]

Who, if anyone, gave the order to fire remains unclear. The KGB contended at the time that "military servicemen" did the shooting.

Makarevsky was told it started accidentally when demonstrators grabbed for soldiers' rifles. Military procurator investigators, reexamining the episode nearly three decades later, suspected KGB snipers. According to Mikoyan, Kozlov kept pressing Khrushchev for permission to use force and finally received it. Khrushchev, according to Mikoyan, was frightened that the turmoil would spread to other industrial areas, including the Donbas.[57]

The Lenin Square carnage, and the strict curfew that followed, broke the back of the protest, even though nearly five hundred people gathered the next morning, partly because of the hysterical shrieks of a woman whose son had been killed there the day before.[58] In response to this latest demonstration, authorities rolled out loudspeakers and replayed a speech Mikoyan had given on the radio the day before. That afternoon Kozlov in another radio address promised to rectify conditions that had prompted the strike. Although he defended the price rises, he insisted they were temporary and would lead to abundance within two years.[59] Meanwhile 116 demonstrators were arrested; 14 of them were subjected to a swift show trial, reminiscent of the 1930s. Seven, including at least one woman, were condemned to death, sentences greeted with shouts of "Give the dogs a dog's death!" and "Serve the vermin right!"; the others received ten to fifteen years in prison.[60]

The Novocherkassk demonstrations weren't the only ones to be put down by force: several died in Murom and Aleksandrovsk in Vladimir Province that same summer.[61] All the carnage didn't faze Khrushchev's deputy Kozlov; just after the Novocherkassk massacre, Makarevsky overheard him complaining on the phone to Suslov that he didn't have enough to eat: "This place is a fucking hole. Have some real grub sent down. And don't forget: I'm due for a vacation and I'm counting on you to support me." Khrushchev apparently took the bloodshed harder. He tried to justify the action, telling Kozlov that "since millions have already perished for the Soviet cause, we were correct to use force." He blamed everyone but himself: "workers who kicked up a row"; "local idiots [who] started shooting"; his Presidium colleagues in Novocherkassk. But Sergei Khrushchev insisted the Novocherkassk bloodshed "tormented Father to the end of his days. That was probably why he did not write about Novocherkassk in his memoirs." Nor, of course, did he order or permit any serious portmortem analysis, lest it reveal the deeper causes of the protests and his own role in provoking and crushing them.[62]

Speaking to an audience of Soviet and Cuban young people on June 2 (whether before or after news of the Novocherkassk denouement arrived is unclear), Khrushchev abandoned an upbeat text and compared the present with the darkest days of the civil war. The decision to raise prices hadn't been easy, he said. But "what were we supposed to do? What was the way out? We decided to tell the people and the party the truth." The truth included widespread shortages of meat and butter. But it was also true, he insisted, that within "a year or two," the price rise would have "a beneficial effect on the whole economy," while agriculture itself "will rise as if on yeast."[63]

Two days later the KGB chief Semichastny sent Khrushchev a secret report on popular reaction to his June 2 speech. Several intellectuals with recognizably Jewish names turned out to have loved it: "Now that was really a speech!"; "Other countries should envy us for having such a leader." (Surprise! Who would be more careful than they to praise their supreme leader to interlocutors who turned out to be KGB informers?) But Semichastny also reported "a few isolated unhealthy utterances," including several from military men. "The cult of personality remains just as it was," one officer had said. "No matter how bad Stalin was," said another, "he cut prices every year, but nowadays nothing's being done except raising prices." A third warned, "If the people were to revolt now, we wouldn't try to put them down."[64]

Khrushchev's March 1962 reorganization of the agricultural administration looked less like a panacea after Novocherkassk. In late June he complained about Kalinovka, to which he had recently returned yet again, about peasants' gathering hay with pitchforks and lolling about near a sleepy-eyed horse, just as they had in his childhood.[65] Later that summer and fall he sent the Presidium nine more memorandums on agriculture. On August 4 he boasted that the territorial production administrations introduced in March were "justifying themselves." But a month later he complained, "We still haven't found the proper system for directly managing agriculture."[66]

Later in August, while vacationing in the Crimea, Khrushchev had another brainstorm. Ever since Lenin, the party had jealously guarded its monopoly of power by centralizing its own ranks, especially its bureaucratic apparatus. Now Khrushchev proposed to split the party into two separate branches, one specializing in agriculture, the other in industry. Convinced that local officials shied away from rural problems, he was determined to force at least some of them to concentrate on feeding the people.[67]

Sergei Khrushchev was present when his father broached this scheme to Brezhnev, Podgorny, and Polyansky. After floating in the Black Sea, they were sitting under an awning on the beach. "Everyone supported his idea enthusiastically and all in one voice," Sergei recalled. "'What a wonderful idea! It must be done immediately!'"[68] In fact, however, Khrushchev's colleagues were appalled. Even before then Brezhnev had been "quietly indignant" over the liquidation of the rural *raikom*.[69] To Presidium agricultural specialist Gennady Voronov, the idea of splitting the party seemed "absurd." But no one in the top leadership objected.[70] "You have to remember the context for all this," Shelepin later recalled. "After Stalin came Khrushchev. He was the next boss. . . . No one had the courage to protest."

"It was all I could do to keep him from dividing the KGB," added the former police chief Semichastny. "Khrushchev pestered me to do it until I got so sick of it I told him a joke about how the Interior Ministry had been split, how policemen encountering drunks on the street and sniffing their breath adopted the following rule: If they smelled of home brew, they were sent to the agricultural sobering-up station; of cognac, to the industrial or urban one. I even added, 'How am I supposed to divide spies into rural and urban agents?'"[71] Semichastny was probably braver in retrospect than at the time. Yegorychev and his Moscow party committee colleagues "didn't understand this new undertaking. We considered it incorrect since the party had always stressed the unity of workers and peasants, and suddenly we were creating what essentially amounted to two parties." But "after the Twenty-second Congress, Khrushchev had a great deal of authority . . . and his political career was at its peak."[72]

In January 1963 Khrushchev confessed to Fidel Castro, who was visiting the USSR, that he had been uncertain about splitting the party when he first proposed the idea. Given his own doubts, he had been amazed when all reacted favorably. Only later had he begun to hear from those "who said we had broken up the unified party machine. You know, to this day I have doubts as to whether I was right or wrong about it."[73]

If Khrushchev was uncertain, you couldn't tell it from his September 10, 1962, memorandum proposing the party split, or his behavior afterward. By the time he left for a two-and-one-half-week tour of Central Asia in late September (during which he dashed off five more memos on agriculture in that region and elsewhere), the Presidium had apparently given its approval, but a Central Committee plenum to consider the question wasn't scheduled until November. Nonetheless, Khrushchev discussed the reform as if it were a done deal, just as he did another proposal (to create a single Central Asia Bureau of the Central Committee) that the Presidium had not yet had a chance to consider.[74] This too his colleagues were to throw in his face two years later, when they moved to oust him.

DURING 1962 the renewed anti-Stalin campaign gathered momentum. This couldn't have happened without Khrushchev's approval, but he apparently wasn't the driving force. It appears that liberal intellectuals, opposed strenuously by conservative cultural bureaucrats, but supported at key junctures by Khrushchev himself, took advantage of the opening given them by the Twenty-second Congress.

For Aleksandr Solzhenitsyn, the reclusive former political prisoner turned physics teacher, who was secretly writing books that soon stunned his nation and the world, there had seemed "nothing good to look forward to" during the period before the congress. "There was no way of foreseeing the sudden fury, the reckless eloquence of the attack on Stalin which Khrushchev would decide upon for the Twenty-second. Nor, try as we might, could we, the uninitiated, ever explain it! But there it was—and not even a secret attack, as at the Twentieth, but a public one! I could not remember when I had read anything as interesting as the speeches at the Twenty-second Congress."

Solzhenitsyn decided that "the long-awaited moment of terrible joy, the moment when my head must break water," had arrived. He submitted the manuscript of *Shch-854*, soon to be known as *One Day in the Life of Ivan Denisovich*, to Aleksandr Tvardovsky's *Novyi mir*. Tvardovsky too had given a bold speech at the congress, which had elected him a candidate member of the Central Committee. Yet he wasn't as encouraged by the congress as Solzhenitsyn was. "What speeches were given isn't important," Tvardovsky told editorial board colleagues. "What's important is what *Pravda* will say in its editorial a week later."[75]

Tvardovsky knew Khrushchev's mercurial nature all too well. Privy now to Central Committee materials, he saw things that alarmed him, like a secret directive guaranteeing Moscow and Leningrad regular supplies of meat. "If they're not making such provision for other cities," he said, "the situation must be very bad indeed." Within his inner circle Tvardovsky cursed Khrushchev for continually telling peasants what, where, when, and how to plant. Didn't the head of government have more important things to do? The June 1 price rise confirmed Tvardovsky's fears. He also knew that Khrushchev's top ideological aide, Leonid Ilychev, wasn't so much backing liberal writers against archconservatives as trying to get them to call off embarrassingly open warfare.[76]

Liberals scored a string of successes during the summer and fall of 1962, but conservatives were fighting back.[77] That explains why, although Tvardovsky considered *One Day* a masterpiece, he proceeded slowly and cautiously. Looking back years later, Solzhenitsyn wished Tvardovsky hadn't "held up publication for eleven months," for that had been precisely the time "when Nikita was still pelting and lambasting Stalin, looking around for more stones to cast at him. This tale by one of his victims would have come very conveniently to Nikita's hand! If it had been published right then, before the impetus of the Twenty-second Congress was spent, the anti-Stalinist hue and cry that greeted it later would have been even more easily raised, and I believe in the heat of the moment Nikita would have cheerfully splashed . . . chapters of *The First Circle* . . . over the pages of *Pravda*."[78]

Instead of trying to lobby Khrushchev directly for permission to publish *One Day*, Tvardovsky prepared the ground by collecting rave reviews from such eminent writers as Kornei Chukovsky and Samuel Marshak. In the meantime, grumbled Solzhenitsyn (who couldn't have gotten anywhere near Khrushchev without Tvardovsky's help), "the months went by, the excitement generated by the Twenty-second Congress cooled and was no more." And "the erratic Nikita, who was always even quicker to drop things than to take them up, and never in the same mood for long, now had to support Nasser, equip Castro with rockets, and discover the definitive (better than best!) scheme for saving Soviet agriculture and bringing it into full bloom, besides jollying along the space program and tightening up the camps, which had grown slack since Beria's fall."[79]

Actually, the window of opportunity didn't close quite that fast. Not only did Tvardovsky admire Solzhenitsyn's work but so did Khrushchev's aide Vladimir Lebedev, to whom Tvardovsky had shown the manuscript. Lebedev demanded certain changes, such as toning down the comic portrait of a former party member, Captain Buinovsky, so that he could emerge as a more positive hero; reducing the references to camp officers as "vermin"; and—this one amused Solzhenitsyn most—mentioning Stalin at least once as responsible for all woes. After some hesitation the author accepted most of the emendations. Meanwhile, Khrushchev had headed south to Pitsunda, where, on September 7, 1962, he met with the American poet Robert Frost, who was in the USSR on a cultural exchange program.[80] Sometime between September 9 and 14 Lebedev read portions of the manuscript aloud to Khrushchev.[81]

Khrushchev was smitten. The fact that the book depicts a Stalinist labor camp through the eyes of a simple peasant helped. Khrushchev and Mikoyan, whom he summoned to listen along with him, particularly liked a "labor" scene in which Ivan Denisovich carefully conserves mortar while laying bricks for a generating station under construction. The excitable Khrushchev wanted to invite Solzhenitsyn down to his dacha right then and there but thought better of it. He was also inclined to authorize publication on the spot but remembered he had colleagues to consult. Lebedev triumphantly called Tvardovsky on September 16, but five days later requested twenty-three copies of the manuscript, obviously for Presidium members to peruse.

Khrushchev left for Central Asia in late September. Sometime in early October the Presidium met twice to discuss Solzhenitsyn's manuscript. There was some grumbling about publication, but according to Khrushchev, "only one voice, Suslov's, squawked" in open opposition. "'How will the people perceive this? How will the people understand?' The people will understand correctly—that was my reply. The people will always distinguish good from bad."[82]

Tvardovsky was unofficially informed by Lebedev on October 15. He was received by Khrushchev on October 20. "The ice moved," Tvardovsky told his *Novyi mir* colleagues afterward. "I've never been greeted there so cordially." Khrushchev raved about *One Day* and, talking out of school, confided that not all his colleagues shared his view. He added that a special commission had prepared three volumes of materials on Stalin's crimes and that the investigation of Kirov's murder was proceeding apace. "We must tell the truth about that period," Khrushchev remarked. "Future generations will judge us, so let them know what conditions we had to work under, what sort of legacy we inherited."

Khrushchev regaled his guest with the story of the plot to oust Beria, admitted that his 1956 secret speech was personally risky ("You bet it was, I'll say it was"), and implied that the party apparat had opposed his campaign against the cult of personality. Tvardovsky made the case against censorship, asking why the chief editor of *Novyi mir*, a candidate member of the Central Committee, must have a petty bureaucrat standing over him, and Khrushchev seemed to agree. The censor would have cut *One*

Day to bits, Tvardovsky said. "They would have cut it to bits, cut it to bits," Khrushchev repeated with a broad grin on his face. "We must think this over. Perhaps you're right."[83]

The day after this remarkable conversation, without any explanation, *Pravda* printed "The Heirs of Stalin" by the young poet Yevgeny Yevtushenko, which had long been circulating privately without much hope of publication:

Mute was the marble.
Mutely glimmered the glass.
Mute stood the sentries,
bronzed by the breeze.
Thin wisps of smoke curled over the coffin.
And breath seeped through the chinks
as they bore him out the mausoleum doors.

Beginning with the removal of Stalin's coffin from the Lenin Mausoleum, the poem warns against still-entrenched Stalinists seeking to reverse the campaign against him:

While the heirs of Stalin walk this earth,
Stalin,
I fancy, still lurks in the Mausoleum.[84]

Together with the decision to publish *One Day*, the appearance of "The Heirs of Stalin" signaled the greatest triumph yet for the cause of reform. However, the cresting wave was about to crash, partly as the result of events nearly eight thousand miles away. The very next day, October 22, 1962, President Kennedy revealed to the world that Khrushchev had secretly sent missiles to Cuba.

CHAPTER NINETEEN

The Cuban Cure-all:
1962

ON OCTOBER 14, 1962, an American U-2 reconnaissance plane overflew Cuba. The photographs it brought back, taken from sixty-five thousand to seventy thousand feet but showing objects as small as two and one-half square feet, were analyzed that night at the CIA's National Photographic Interpretation Center in Washington. They showed that the Soviet Union was building launch sites for ballistic missiles capable of striking the United States. The national security adviser, McGeorge Bundy, was informed the next day, but since President Kennedy was out of town on a campaign trip and didn't return until 1:40 A.M. on October 16, Bundy didn't inform him until later that morning. Kennedy was sitting on the edge of his bed, still in a bathrobe and slippers, when Bundy gave him the bad news. The president looked at several photos of missile sites. "We're probably going to have to bomb them," he said.[1]

Kennedy and his advisers were stunned and mystified. Beginning in July, reports had come in of a massive Soviet military buildup in Cuba, but Kennedy, Bundy, Rusk, McNamara, and others had refused to believe it included rockets capable of reaching the United States. Only CIA Director John McCone had guessed, after Soviet surface-to-air missiles had been detected in Cuba in August, that Moscow was moving to deploy medium-range rockets. One reason Kennedy resisted the CIA head's conclusion was that partisan Republicans led by New York Senator Kenneth Keating insisted the Soviet buildup *was* offensive and charged the administration with lack of vigilance. More important, the White House couldn't imagine that Khrushchev would challenge the United States in its own "backyard," especially after having sworn numerous times that he would do no such thing. Robert Kennedy's not-so-statesmanlike reaction to the October 16 news was "Oh shit! Shit! Shit! Those sons of bitches Russians." Rusk wondered if Khrushchev was "entirely rational." President Kennedy told his advisers when they convened later that day, "He's playing God," but "Why is it—can any Russian expert tell us—why they. . . . " He added later: "Well, it's a goddamn mystery to me."[2]

Kennedy and his associates (who christened themselves the Executive Committee, or ExComm, of the National Security Council) met in secret for several days, urgently seeking to devise a response. Before announcing a blockade of Cuba on October 22, and during the next six days until the crisis ebbed on October 28, they kept trying to figure out Khrushchev's motives and what he would do next. One possibility was that he had sent missiles to Cuba to undo America's strategic nuclear superiority. This explanation appealed to the Joint Chiefs of Staff, who insisted the Cuban missiles could make a decisive difference in a nuclear conflict, but not to Defense Secretary McNamara, who thought Moscow would derive little military advantage from the move. Another hypothesis, advanced by the former ambassadors Bohlen and Thompson, was that Khrushchev wanted to counter, and then trade for, American missiles positioned near the USSR in Turkey.[3] Much more compelling, or so it seemed to Kennedy, was the notion that the Cuban missiles were linked to Berlin. Thompson, who had left his Moscow post only three months previously and knew Khrushchev better than any other American, thought Khrushchev wanted to strengthen his hand in upcoming negotiations, allowing him at last to extract the German settlement that had eluded him for four long years. "Mr. President," Thompson told Kennedy on October 22, "he made it quite clear in my last talk with him that he was squirming . . . that he couldn't back down from the position he had taken. He'd come so far . . . He gave an indication that time was running out. . . . " In Thompson's view, a "showdown on Berlin" was "the main thing" Khrushchev had in mind.[4]

President Kennedy saw other Berlin-Cuba connections. If the United States failed to get the missiles out of Cuba, the world would doubt Washington's will to protect Berlin. If America blockaded Cuba, the Soviets might blockade Berlin in return. If the United States launched air strikes or invaded Cuba, Moscow might seize Berlin, leaving the Europeans to blame the nervous, trigger-happy Americans who couldn't bear to live under the threat of nearby missiles, which the Europeans had long endured. JFK couldn't help "admiring Soviet strategy," he told his old friend British Ambassador David Ormsby-Gore on October 22. "They offered this deliberate and provocative challenge to the United States in the knowledge that if the Americans reacted violently to it, the Russians would be given an ideal opportunity to move against West Berlin. If, on the other hand, he [JFK] did nothing, the Latin Americans and the United States' other allies would feel that the Americans had no real will to resist the encroachments of Communism and would hedge their bets accordingly."[5]

Still another theory came from Rusk: that Khrushchev was no longer in charge, that instead "the hard-line boys have moved into the ascendancy."[6] The one explanation no one in the White House considered was what Russians then and since have insisted was their main motive: to protect Fidel Castro from an American invasion. But that, it turns out, wasn't the whole story either.

In addition to Khrushchev's strategy, Kennedy and company tried to divine his tactics. "We must assume," said the president on October 22, before publicly revealing the presence of Soviet rockets in Cuba, "that Khrushchev knows that we know of his missile deployments, and, therefore, he will be ready with a planned response." On October 26 Kennedy marveled at how Khrushchev turned his reputation as a bully into an advantage: "If you're a son of a bitch [like Khrushchev], then every time he looks at all agreeable, everybody falls down with pleasure."[7]

But if Khrushchev was so smart, why, as Rusk put it, did he "grossly misunderstand the importance of Cuba to this country"? Having installed surface-to-air missiles to protect against early detection by American U-2s, why hadn't he used them? Why had he left rockets and support equipment in open fields, where American planes were bound to detect them? "Maybe some Russian will explain to me someday," said Kennedy on October 25, "why they didn't camouflage them before. And why they do it now. And at what point they thought we were going to find out." Not to mention why Khrushchev proposed a way out of the crisis on October 26 and then upped the ante the very next day. "How can we negotiate with somebody who changes his deal before we even get a chance to reply," McNamara complained on October 27, "and announces the deal publicly before we even receive it?"[8]

The answer is that Khrushchev had not thought things through or prepared backup plans for various contingencies. He badly misjudged the American response, improvised madly when he was found out, and was fortunate the crisis ended as safely as it did. As for Kennedy, his threats to Cuba helped provoke a crisis that he had failed to foresee, and he pressed Khrushchev nearly to the wall despite a real risk of war. In the end, each man found the courage to pull back, leaving the other room to retreat, and the crisis ended peacefully, but not before the world came closer than it ever has to a nuclear conflagration.

That the two superpowers could be so wrong about each other speaks volumes about the precariousness of peace in the nuclear age. But it also underlines the questions of what Khrushchev *was* up to. Why *did* he send missiles to Cuba? What would he have done with them if they hadn't been detected? Why did the Soviets botch both the decision to deploy missiles and the process of doing so? Finally, where did Khrushchev find the courage to retreat before it was too late? Answers to these questions begin with Cuba itself. As Washington guessed, they also involve the overall nuclear balance and Berlin, but not in the way the Americans imagined. In addition, they reflect Khrushchev's domestic and personal position in 1962: besieged by troubles; increasingly irritated as setbacks mounted; determined to prove himself (to himself as well as to his colleagues); ready to lash out and take risks to regain the initiative. In that sense the Cuban missiles were a cure-all, a cure-all that cured nothing.

IN THE BEGINNING, Cuba couldn't have seemed less important to Moscow. Stalin viewed Latin America, along with the rest of the Third World, as a sideshow. Khrushchev welcomed revolutions that could bring the USSR new allies in the developing world, but when Fidel Castro's forces came sweeping out of the Sierra Madre and seized Havana in January 1959, Moscow had no clear idea of who they were and what they stood for. Even after learning that Castro's brother Raúl was a Communist and suspecting that Fidel himself might become one, the Kremlin hesitated to come to their aid. While Khrushchev was in the United States in September 1959, the Presidium, on the advice of the Foreign Ministry, decided not to provide military aid to Cuba, a decision prompted by fear of an adverse American reaction. However, when Khrushchev returned home, he made sure that the decision was reversed and that Warsaw Pact weapons were dispatched to Havana,[9] a pattern that repeated itself three years later: Khrushchev's advisers knew enough to be cautious, but he didn't.

As Moscow and Havana grew closer during 1960 and 1961, the Soviet stake in Cuba grew. Mikoyan reconnoitered the island in February 1960, was charmed by Castro, and came home convinced: "Yes, he is a revolutionary. Completely like us. I felt as though I had returned to my childhood."[10] Khrushchev felt the same way, especially after he embraced Castro in Harlem that same year. For him too Cuba had become "a beacon, a hopeful lighthouse for all the unfortunate, exploited peoples of Latin America."[11] Thus, as U.S.-Cuba relations soured and Castro began to fear an American attack, Khrushchev took another step toward the 1962 crisis to come: On June 9, 1960, before a gathering of Soviet schoolteachers, and with his own former teacher from Kalinovka present in the auditorium, he placed Cuba under Soviet nuclear protection: " . . . if need be, Soviet artillerymen can support the Cuban people with their rocket fire, should the aggressive forces in the Pentagon dare to start intervention against Cuba."[12]

At this point Khrushchev's threat was only rhetorical, but it seemed to pay off. It didn't actually prevent an attack, since the Americans weren't yet ready to launch one anyway; indeed, initial CIA moves, such as an airdrop of supplies to rebels in Oriente Province in September 1960, were embarrassingly feeble. But Castro was grateful and more willing than before to move toward the Soviet camp. In November he proclaimed (whether truthfully or not isn't clear) that he had been a Marxist ever since his student days. Shortly before Kennedy's January 1961 inauguration, another invasion scare proved unfounded. Once again Moscow and Havana expected the worst and, when it didn't happen, assumed Soviet nuclear threats had deterred it.[13]

When the Bay of Pigs invasion finally happened, it was no surprise. What *was* surprising was that Washington sent Cuban exiles instead of American marines and then failed to ensure their success. Although Castro prevailed, Khrushchev assumed Kennedy would strike again, next time using American troops. The fact that U.S. forces were already stationed at Guantánamo Naval Base would make it easy; all they had to do was claim the Cubans had attacked the base and strike back in "self-defense." When Khrushchev asked his defense minister how long it would take the United States to destroy Castro's armed forces, Malinovsky estimated only a few days.[14]

The Americans *were* planning assaults of all sorts. Following the Bay of Pigs, Washington launched political and economic warfare, staged threatening military maneuvers in the Caribbean, and prepared Operation Mongoose, a covert-action plan including sabotage raids, attempts to assassinate Castro, and, ultimately, American military intervention in October 1962. Of the Mongoose menu of options, the administration approved only operations "short of those reasonably calculated to inspire a revolt within the target area, or other developments which would require U.S. armed intervention." But that wasn't known to the Cuban and Soviet intelligence agents.[15] If Khrushchev had any doubt that the United States was determined to finish off Castro, it wasn't strengthened by something Kennedy told Aleksei Adzhubei, who interviewed the president in Washington on January 30, 1962. According to American minutes of the meeting, Kennedy said the United States was psychologically unprepared for a hostile neighbor so close at hand, noted that the "USSR would have the same reaction if a hostile group arose" in its vicinity, and, "in this connection, referred to the Soviet reaction to the Hungarian uprising." Adzhubei's version of the conversation, reported to Khrushchev in Moscow, was considerably more vivid: Kennedy recalled summoning Director of Intelligence Allen Dulles after the Bay of Pigs and dressing him down: "I told him: you should learn from the Russians. When they had difficulties in Hungary, they liquidated the conflict in three days. . . . But you, Dulles, have never been capable of doing that."[16] Adzhubei was capable of exaggerating Kennedy's words so as to underline the importance of his having heard them, but however Kennedy put it, Khrushchev expected the worst.

The Soviets approved expanded military aid to Cuba in February 1962. Then, when the KGB reported an American invasion wasn't imminent, a Defense Ministry recommendation to supply SA-2 ground-to-air missiles was shelved. Yet a mere two months later, Khrushchev raised the issue of sending medium-range rockets to Cuba. In the meantime the United States mounted the largest Atlantic-Caribbean military maneuvers ever conducted while, at about the same time, a split between Castro and the pro-Soviet Cuban Communist leader Anibal Escalante posed the danger that Fidel might move closer to Mao Zedong.[17] Both developments concentrated Khrushchev's mind wonderfully. To lose Cuba to the United States would "be a great blow to Marxist-Leninist teaching, would cast us away from Latin America, and would lower our prestige." Khrushchev saw Castro's defeat "as his own," Sergei Khrushchev wrote later. According to Troyanovsky, Khrushchev "constantly feared" that he would be forced to "retreat" and that "he would bear the responsibility when that happened." He kept recalling Stalin's warning that the imperialists would strangle his successors "like kittens." The taunts kept coming back to him, Troyanovsky assumed, because of constant Chinese accusations that Khrushchev "had capitulated to imperialism."[18]

IF KHRUSHCHEV wanted to protect Cuba, why didn't he use conventional weapons? Why not send Soviet troops without nuclear weapons to serve as a trip wire (like American forces in Europe), ensuring that any invasion would involve a Soviet-American clash? Loudly proclaimed warnings coupled with vague but ominous threats of Soviet retaliation were another favorite Soviet device, tried, if not always true, in past crises. Also, if Khrushchev simply *had* to "go nuclear," why not just tactical nuclear weapons incapable of reaching American soil but powerful enough to pulverize invading American forces? Washington was caught by surprise because the risks of strategic nuclear missiles seemed wildly disproportionate to any extra advantage they might provide. What the Kennedy administration failed to understand was the logic of nuclear deterrence as idiosyncratically understood by Khrushchev. Khrushchev later recalled:

> My thinking went like this. If we installed the missiles secretly, and then the United States discovered the missiles after they were poised and ready to strike, the Americans would think twice before trying to liquidate our installations by military means. I knew the United States could knock out some installations, but not all of them. If a quarter or even a tenth of our missiles survived—even if only one or two big ones were left—we could still hit New York, and there wouldn't be much of New York left. I don't mean to say everyone in New York would be killed—not everyone, of course, but an awful lot of people would be wiped out. I don't know how many. . . . But that's all beside the point. The main thing was that the installation of our missiles in Cuba would, I thought, restrain the United States from precipitous military action against Castro's government.[19]

This was vintage Khrushchev. The missiles were meant to frighten, not to be fired. Eisenhower's thinking hadn't been all that different, but Kennedy's was: Worried about how to make deterrence credible, he sought a nuclear superiority great enough to convince Moscow that he would actually risk nuclear war. Khrushchev's notion was simpler: As long as he had (or seemed to have) a minimum number of missiles and sounded prepared to use them, the Americans would be intimidated. As long as the Cuban missiles were operational before Washington discovered them, the Americans wouldn't do anything about them, or about Castro either.

Until 1962 Khrushchev had backed his diplomacy by boasting that the USSR was mass-producing intercontinental missiles capable of obliterating the United States. Despite U-2 reconnaissance photographs, American intelligence couldn't dismiss Khrushchev's bluff until the middle of 1961, at which point Corona spy satellites and information provided by turncoat Soviet Colonel Oleg Penkovsky demonstrated that the Soviets had only a handful of operational ICBMs. But by that time the Kennedy administration's own buildup was giving it an overwhelming strategic advantage.[20]

On October 30, 1961, the USSR tested a fifty-megaton bomb, with ten times the power of all weapons used during World War II, including the Hiroshima and Nagasaki A-bombs.[21] Even before that, however, Kennedy had decided to reveal to the world that Khrushchev was bluffing. On October 21 Deputy Secretary of Defense Roswell Gilpatric announced that the United States had "a second strike capability which is at least as extensive as the Soviets can deliver by striking first." In February 1962, McNamara told the Senate Foreign Relations Committee that the United States had "a clear military superiority for major nuclear conflict," and a month later the president discarded the doctrine "that the United States would never strike first with the nuclear weapon. . . . Khrushchev must *not* be certain that, where its vital interests are threatened, the United States will never strike first." He told columnist Stewart Alsop, "In some circumstances, we might have to take the initiative."[22]

The Soviet reaction to this reversal of fortune—angry denials that the United States had a strategic advantage, plus attacks on Kennedy for threatening to strike first—was allergic in the extreme. Given Khrushchev's assumption that even a seeming strategic superiority could be decisive, the actual American advantage was doubly damaging: not only had he lost the kind of atomic leverage he had been employing for four years, but the Americans had gained it.

The personal implications for Khrushchev were particularly pointed. It was he who had insisted on relying on intercontinental rockets, rather than conventional weapons, even when the Kremlin had practically none. Just as the potential loss of Cuba could be laid at his door, so could the loss of a seeming nuclear advantage. No wonder he described the American attempt to gain nuclear leverage as "particularly arrogant" in a conversation with Anatoly Dobrynin in March 1962, the same conversation in which, speaking of Washington's nuclear reach, he said, "It's high time their long arms were cut shorter."[23]

In February 1962, Khrushchev headed for Pitsunda for some rest and to prepare for an important meeting of the country's Defense Council. In attendance were the top military commanders, leading missile designers, and members of the Presidium. Presiding over the session in vacation attire (a green jacket and gray pants) that contrasted oddly with the formal dress of everyone else, Khrushchev listened as commanders confessed that existing Soviet ICBMs were in no shape to stand up to the Americans. The R-16 (known in the West as the SS-6) took several hours to prepare to fire, whereas American Minuteman missiles could be launched in several minutes. "Before we get it ready to launch," lamented Marshal Moskalenko, "there won't be even a wet spot left of any of us." Moreover, if the Americans didn't destroy the R-16, its own unstable liquid fuel might; to avoid an explosion, it had to be drained after thirty days, whereas the solid-fuel Minuteman could remain at the ready indefinitely. "Father looked around the room gloomily," Sergei Khrushchev said later. "The result he wanted had once again proved impossible to achieve. . . . He asked those present to think about what could be done to reduce to a minimum the amount of time it would take to catch up with the Americans."[24]

In contrast with intercontinental missiles, which the Soviets did not have in substantial numbers, Moscow possessed plenty of medium- and intermediate-range missiles. Placing them in Cuba would at least double the number of warheads capable of reaching such American cities as Washington, Atlanta, Dallas, and New Orleans.[25] Troyanovsky assumed these rockets were designed "to redress the nuclear balance in favor of the Soviet Union, a domain where the U.S. had an overwhelming superiority at the time." As Yuri Andropov, then in charge of relations with other socialist countries, put it to Khrushchev in a conversation Troyanovsky overheard, "Once this is done we'll be able to target them at the soft underbelly of the United States."[26] "In addition to protecting Cuba," Khrushchev confirmed in his memoirs, "our missiles would have equalized what the West likes to call 'the balance of power.' The Americans . . . would learn just what it feels like to have enemy missiles pointing at you; we'd be doing nothing more than giving them a little of their own medicine. . . . We Russians have suffered three wars over the last half century. . . . America has never had to fight a war on her own soil . . . and made a fortune as a result. America has [made] billions by bleeding the rest of the world."[27]

TROYANOVSKY, who should know, later wrote that Cuba wasn't linked to Berlin. Khrushchev's former aide contended that the Berlin wall in effect ended the Berlin crisis. To be sure, there were continuing "diplomatic exchanges, there were public statements from both sides, some tough, some reasonable, depending on the circumstances." But "these were the last receding waves of the storm. . . . At least that is how it looked from our side of the fence. Obviously, Khrushchev could not just switch off the West Berlin problem with the East German leaders looking over his shoulder and prodding him to take some further forceful action. But what he was doing was more shadow boxing than anything else."[28]

Certain Berlin developments fit Troyanovsky's interpretation. Khrushchev withdrew his latest Berlin ultimatum, proclaimed just after the Vienna summit, on October 17, 1961. The scary tank standoff in Berlin at Checkpoint Charlie, which occurred several days later, looked a lot worse than in fact it was.[29] When ongoing Berlin talks, first between Gromyko and Ambassador Thompson in Moscow and then in Washington between Rusk and Dobryin, went nowhere, Soviet negotiators seemed unperturbed. In January 1962 Thompson was "struck by the fact that [Gromyko] showed no disposition to be in a hurry, or interest in how long the present phase might continue." In February, said Rusk, Moscow seemed half prepared to "put the Berlin question on ice." Despite American intransigence, Gromyko neither threatened to break off the talks nor publicized the impasse. Instead, a surprised Rusk told a National Security Council meeting on February 28, the Soviets were "quite willing to play their long-playing record over and over again."[30]

Troyanovsky clinched his case against the Berlin connection by citing an episode that occurred after the crisis erupted. When Deputy Foreign Minister Vasily Kuznetsov proposed a Berlin blockade to counter Washington's Cuban quarantine, Khrushchev blew up: "We're just beginning to get ourselves out of one adventure, and you're suggesting we climb into another."[31] But Khrushchev's refusal to blockade Berlin in the midst of a white-hot crisis doesn't prove that the German question played no role in causing the crisis; plenty of evidence seems to suggest that it did.

Khrushchev and Kennedy engaged in a secret correspondence (dubbed the "Pen Pal Correspondence" by White House aides), beginning in September 1961 and continuing until after the Cuban showdown. Throughout this period Kennedy showed little, if any, give on Berlin, and his stance seemed to drive Khrushchev to distraction. On November 9, Khrushchev sounded desperate, especially in a passage that Kennedy advisers remembered once the Cuban crisis broke out: "You have to understand, I have no ground to retreat further, there is a precipice behind me."[32] When Kennedy's December 2 reply took no notice of Khrushchev's plight, the Soviet leader accused the United States of "megalomania" and swore, "We must conclude a German peace treaty and we will conclude it even if you do not agree."[33]

White House Press Secretary Pierre Salinger traveled to Moscow in mid-May 1962 to discuss information exchanges with Soviet officials. To his astonishment, he was whisked away to Khrushchev's dacha for two days with the Soviet leader himself. Both days were crammed with typical Khrushchev pastimes—eating, drinking, boating, target shooting, joking, and comparing himself with Stalin (Stalin "understood only Marxism-Leninism. But he didn't know how to apply it to agriculture and industry. He was no good at practical things. I wish he could see this farm [next to the dacha] now. Then he would know I was right")—but Khrushchev kept coming back to Berlin. If he and Kennedy couldn't agree, they would find themselves "on the verge of a very great test." Khrushchev seemed sure the United States would not "fight over West Berlin, which it needs like a dog needs five legs."[34]

On July 26 the Soviet leader bade farewell to Ambassador Thompson, who was returning to Washington. Again he warned he "could not wait indefinitely" for a German peace treaty; he seemed "deeply troubled."[35] That September, Khrushchev summoned U.S. Secretary of the Interior Stewart Udall, who was on a Russian tour, to Pitsunda. The German situation was "no longer tolerable," he warned. Since Kennedy didn't have the necessary "courage," Khrushchev would "help him solve the problem. We will give him a choice—go to war, or sign a peace treaty. . . . Do you need Berlin? Like hell you need it. . . . It's been a long time since you could spank us like a little boy. Now we can swat your ass."[36]

On October 16, Khrushchev told Thompson's successor, Foy Kohler, that he planned to attend the UN General Assembly session in New York in November, at which time he would like to agree on West Berlin with the president.[37] What better time to get what he wanted in Berlin than when the Americans would just be learning about Soviet rockets in Cuba!

By this time Moscow may have been using Berlin "to distract" the Americans' attention from Cuba, as Mikoyan later claimed to Castro.[38] But that doesn't prove that all of Khrushchev's sound and fury signified nothing. If, as Troyanovsky insisted, the Berlin crisis had been over since the Berlin wall went up, why did Khrushchev keep hammering so hard at the issue? Asked that question directly in 1999, Troyanovsky answered, "He had to hammer away at something. After all, there was a cold war going on."[39]

Believe it or not, that seems confirmed by what Khrushchev told his Eastern European allies. By concluding a German peace treaty, he told

Polish leader Władisław Gomułka in October 1961, the Soviet camp would "lose," for the West "might declare an economic boycott against the USSR and the socialist countries." Given that danger, "we should not exacerbate the situation," but "we must continue our game . . . we should keep applying pressure." Khrushchev asked Ulbricht in February 1962: "What is pushing us to a peace treaty? Nothing. Until August 13 [the day the Berlin wall went up], we were racking our brains over how to move forward. Now, the borders are closed."[40]

Nonetheless, when Dobrynin met Khrushchev in March 1962, on the eve of the new ambassador's departure for Washington, "it was clear that [Khrushchev] regarded the problems of Germany and Berlin as the principal issue in Soviet-American relations, and he wanted them solved along the lines he had laid out to Kennedy at their meeting in Vienna." According to Dobrynin, "Khrushchev believed he had a chance to shift the status quo in his favor in Berlin."[41]

Was Khrushchev's bluster merely designed to get Dobrynin to "play the game properly"? Or were Berlin and Cuba connected in some part of his mind to which Troyanovsky lacked access? Was Khrushchev continually changing his mind? Or didn't he know his own mind at all, an explanation for why no one else did either? Moscow party boss Nikolai Yegorychev had nothing to do with Berlin or Cuba, but a pattern he noticed in Moscow may help explain why Khrushchev kept pounding away at Berlin: "Even when Khrushchev made a mistake, even when he knew he'd done so, perhaps especially then, he couldn't bring himself to admit it. This was partly because he was party and government leader, but it was also part of his character."[42]

Whatever his thinking about Berlin, it was clear to Khrushchev that U.S.-Soviet relations were going nowhere in 1961 and 1962, while Sino-Soviet ties further deteriorated as well. Zhou Enlai politely but firmly set out the Chinese line at the Twenty-second Congress, then left town before Khrushchev could administer a not so friendly rebuke. Zhou paid tribute at Red Square not only to Lenin but to Stalin, while Khrushchev informed the Chinese that whereas "the voice of the Chinese Communist Party was then [in 1956] important to us," now "we shall go our own way."[43] Several attempts to mediate the rift were mounted during 1962, but instead the tension escalated. So the secret installation of missiles in Cuba, followed by the successful browbeating of Kennedy in New York, would pay dividends in Beijing as well, confirming Khrushchev's contention that firmness combined with flexibility could better advance Communist interests than China's rigid, dogmatic approach.

"Khrushchev possessed a rich imagination," Troyanovsky wrote in 1994, "and when some idea took hold of him, he was inclined to see in its implementation an easy solution to a particular problem, a sort of cure-all" for many problems. "In such instances, he could stretch even a sound idea to the point of absurdity."[44]

ACCORDING TO Khrushchev, the decision to send missiles to Cuba "was, from the outset, worked out in the collective leadership. It wasn't until after two or three lengthy discussions" that he and his colleagues decided "it was worth the risk." He was determined, he recalled, "that the initial, as well as the subsequent, decisions should not be forced down anyone's throat." He wanted his comrades "to accept and support the decision with a clear conscience and a full understanding" that the consequence might be war with the United States. "Every step we had taken had been carefully considered by the collective."[45]

In fact, it didn't happen that way at all. In April 1962 Malinovsky visited Khrushchev by the Black Sea. The defense minister's report on the strategic balance was depressing, as was his complaint that American Jupiter missiles had recently become operational in Turkey. Like other Soviet officials who lobbied Khrushchev, Malinovsky was probably preparing to ask him for money. What Khrushchev got out of the conversation was an idea: "Rodion Yakovlevich, what if we throw a hedgehog down Uncle Sam's pants?"[46]

Khrushchev had earlier broached the idea of Cuban missiles to Mikoyan, whose travel to Havana established him as an expert on Cuba. The two men conversed on the grounds of Khrushchev's Lenin Hills residence. Khrushchev's notion was to deploy the missiles "very speedily" by September or October and then inform Kennedy, possibly in person at the United Nations, after the congressional elections in November. He expected Washington to accept the news calmly, "as the Turkish missiles were received in the Soviet Union." Mikoyan doubted the missiles could really be transported and installed secretly, and feared they would trigger a crisis. Meanwhile, Fidel Castro would have to be consulted, and Mikoyan assumed he would object. Mikoyan's point was that the whole scheme would be dangerous, but, Khrushchev insisted, "I myself expressed the same view."[47]

If Khrushchev had taken Mikoyan's advice seriously, he might not have proceeded at all. At least he would have been prepared for what happened. It also would have helped to consult Dobrynin and Troyanovsky, who knew a lot about the United States, but he didn't do that either. Instead of soliciting and weighing counterarguments, he moved to marshal support for his scheme by convening a small group of advisers: Presidium members Mikoyan and Kozlov, Malinovsky, Gromyko, and the head of Soviet Strategic Rocket Forces, Sergei Biryuzov. After outlining his idea, Khrushchev asked Malinovsky a hypothetical question: "If there were an island 140 kilometers [eighty-seven miles] off our shore which we needed to invade and pacify no matter how desperately it was defended, and if you were given any and all means to do so except nuclear weapons, how much time would it take you to accomplish the job?" Malinovsky estimated three to five days, or a week at most. "You see," Khrushchev exclaimed, "what can we do [to help Cuba]? Not a thing. In any event, our help would be late in reaching the other side of the world. And once the fight is over, fists are useless." Case closed!

If Malinovsky had doubts, he didn't press them. Why should Biryuzov object if Khrushchev was about to give him medium-range rockets capable of reaching American soil? Mikoyan repeated his reservations, but Khrushchev brushed them aside: "Let Marshal Biryuzov and a couple of other specialists gauge the possibility of installing missiles without the Americans discovering them, and let them take a letter to Fidel asking Castro whether he'd accept the deployment." Mikoyan was sure Biryuzov's report would be negative on both counts.[48]

Tall, bespectacled Aleksandr Alekseyev, ostensibly a Soviet correspondent in Cuba, was actually an intelligence agent. First posted to Havana in October 1959, the Spanish-speaking Alekseyev quickly became closer to Castro and Ernesto ("Che") Guevara than was Soviet Ambassador Sergei Kudriavtsev, a stodgy diplomat who incurred Cuban contempt by demanding to be protected by a small army of bodyguards at all times. In early May, Alekseyev was summoned home to Moscow. Just before meeting Khrushchev on May 7, he was named to replace Kudriavtsev, thus increasing his stake in following Khrushchev's all-knowing lead. Khrushchev didn't mention missiles at their first meeting. Instead he peppered Alekseyev with general questions about Cuba and its leaders, picking up the phone several times to expedite assistance to the island. Alekseyev was impressed by Khrushchev's knowledge of Cuba and warm feelings for Castro and overwhelmed that he seemed "to understand what I was going to say before I could get the words out of my mouth."[49]

Several days later the small ad hoc group convened again, this time with the addition of Sharaf P. Rashidov, Presidium candidate member, Uzbekistan Communist chief, and frequent emissary to Third World countries likely to be impressed by Central Asia's progress under communism. As Alekseyev and Mikoyan offered their impressions of Cuba's situation, Khrushchev kept interrupting to underline the danger Castro faced. Suddenly he asked Alekseyev a question that "nearly turned me to ice": How would Castro react to a Soviet proposal to deploy nuclear missiles in Cuba?

Alekseyev blurted out that Castro wouldn't agree lest he alienate other Latin American countries. Malinovsky retorted that if republican Spain had accepted Soviet military aid against Franco in the 1930s, "how can the Cuban Revolution give up this opportunity?"

Instead of letting the debate be joined, Khrushchev launched into a lengthy defense of his idea. The Americans were planning a full-fledged invasion. The only way to deter them was with nuclear missiles. The operation had to be secret, particularly with the U.S. election campaign going on. Once the rockets were operational, the Soviet Union could truly speak to America as an equal. Nor would the pragmatic Americans take foolhardy risks—no more than the Soviets had when the United States had installed missiles in Italy and Turkey. Although the full Presidium had yet to discuss the issue, Khrushchev announced that Alekseyev, Biryuzov, and Rashidov would be going to Cuba "to explain to Fidel Castro our concerns."[50]

Meanwhile, Khrushchev and Gromyko spent a week in Bulgaria. While he was there, Khrushchev recalled, the thought of losing Cuba "kept hammering away at my brain."[51] In retrospect, his speeches (full of references to Turkish missiles, Western intractability, and the need to force Washington to treat Moscow as an equal) confirm that. He was preoccupied because he couldn't confide in the Bulgarian party leader Todor Zhivkov, and that showed too. The director of an agricultural institute in Bulgaria's bread basket, the Dobrudja Valley, was describing how science and technology could boost grain production when the Soviet leader cut him off and ordered an aide to tell the Bulgarians how to do it. When the Bulgarian speaker questioned Soviet advice to plant "peas, peas and only peas" instead of pumpkins, Khrushchev flapped his hands in the air, knocked over a bottle, spilling water all over his white straw hat, and abruptly ended the meeting.[52]

Khrushchev and his foreign minister discussed the Cuban missile scheme on the flight back to Moscow on May 20. Khrushchev insisted missile deployment was essential and only then asked Gromyko's opinion. Gromyko expected his boss to "fly into a rage" if he disagreed, itself a commentary on Khrushchev's incapacity for eliciting unpleasant truths from his entourage, but later insisted he dared to object: "Putting missiles in Cuba would cause a political explosion in the United States. I am absolutely certain of that. . . . " In fact, Khrushchev didn't explode, but he had "no intention of changing his position."[53]

The next day the Soviet Defense Council met. The country's highest civil-military body was headed by Khrushchev and included party secretaries Kozlov and Brezhnev, Presidium members Mikoyan and Kosygin (who was also first deputy premier), Malinovsky and his first deputy, Marshal Andrei Grechko, and Aleksei Yepishev, a political general who monitored the military for the party Central Committee. Also attending was Colonel General Semyon P. Ivanov, from the General Staff, who served as the council's secretary. Ostensibly, the meeting was to brief Khrushchev on developments during his trip to Bulgaria. But when Ivanov returned to the Defense Ministry afterward, he was "more agitated" than his deputy, General Anatoly Gribkov, had ever seen him. "Clutching a few sheets of paper in his left hand, he started speaking before he was fully through the door. 'Anatoly Ivanovich,' he said, waving the pages he held, 'this has to be written up immediately. In a clean copy. By hand. No typist.'"

What Ivanov's supersecret notes indicated, according to Gribkov, was that "our top policy-makers had decided to install medium- and intermediate-range missiles in Cuba. . . . " The decision still wasn't final; it would have to be approved again by the Defense Council and by the Presidium. But prior to a combined Defense Council–Presidium session on May 24, Gribkov was to prepare an initial operational plan, a preliminary blueprint for "the creation, transportation and supply of a military unit similar in its makeup and mission, if not its size, to [Soviet forces] stationed in eastern and central Europe."

For the next three days and nights Gribkov lived in his office, napping occasionally on a folding cot. On May 24, Malinovsky presented the plan, which Khrushchev immediately endorsed. Khrushchev's colleagues "either shared his assessment," Gribkov remembered, "or feared to voice their doubts." Although its vote was still "tentative," pending the delegation's trip to Cuba, the Defense Council ratified a resolution "to deploy a Group of Soviet forces on the island of Cuba consisting of all types of Armed Forces. . . . "[54]

Signs of unease did appear when General Ivanov made the rounds of Presidium members to get their signatures on the formal document. Tradition called for writing the word *za* (for) before signing. In this case, at least Mikoyan and perhaps others provided only signatures, while Central

Committee secretaries who were Presidium candidate members failed to sign at all. The latter practice was standard since candidate members lacked formal voting rights, but Khrushchev ordered Ivanov to "go round to their dachas, too. They'll sign." After a call from Khrushchev, even Mikoyan added his *za*.[55]

On Sunday, May 27, the Presidium met at Khrushchev's dacha to give the Cuba delegation its instructions. The spring day was flawless, and the leader's guests sat around sipping tea and eating pastries. In theory, Rashidov and Biryuzov were to solicit Castro's reaction to Khrushchev's idea, but their actual mission involved more telling than asking. "The only way to save Cuba is to put missiles there," Khrushchev declared. Being "intelligent," Kennedy would not "set off a nuclear war." Although long-range Soviet rockets were already aimed at the United States, "if missiles are deployed near the U.S. they will be even more afraid." Khrushchev added, "So try to explain it to Fidel."[56]

The delegation left for Cuba on a secret flight, traveling under assumed names (Marshal Biryuzov's fake passport rechristened him Engineer Petrov), carrying no documents, and sternly warned against communicating with Moscow, even by coded radio transmissions.[57] Castro understood immediately that something big was up. "For the first and only time in eight years," Alekseyev recalled, "I saw the Cubans writing things down." Castro was grateful for the offer but feared to damage his revolution's image in Latin America and aggravate already high tensions with the United States. He doubted missiles were needed since he assumed the Soviets already had hundreds of missiles capable of reaching the United States. But if the far more experienced Soviets wanted to "buttress the defensive power of the entire socialist camp," Cuba had "no right to base our decision on narrow self-interest."

Like his erstwhile enemies in the Kennedy administration, years later Castro still wondered about Khrushchev's motives. "Of course, it's true Nikita loved Cuba very much. He especially cherished Cuba. He had a weakness for Cuba you might say—emotionally and so on." But he was also "capable of talking about an issue in one set of terms while thinking about it in other terms." Even when Castro spent several weeks in the USSR in 1963, he was "never able to get to the bottom of that." He asked all the Presidium members he met one by one, "'How was this decision made? Which were the arguments used?' And I wasn't able to get a single word. They often simply didn't reply to my questions. And of course, you can't be impertinent and say, 'Hey, answer my question.'"[58]

While Castro wondered, Biryuzov was off roaming the island,

inspecting places where the missiles might be hidden from the CIA's prying eyes. Because he was a "can do" military man, his conclusion was naturally "Can do," especially since the missiles, presumably the most difficult of all installations to conceal, could be disguised as palm trees with the help of some palm fronds covering the warheads. Biryuzov "wasn't very bright," Mikoyan recalled. "I myself had seen those palms, and there was no way you were going to hide rocket launch sites under them."[59]

Upon returning to Moscow, the delegation briefed the political leadership on June 10. Both Rashidov's report on Castro's reaction and Biriuzov's on military feasibility were positive. By now Gribkov's May 24 plan was even more comprehensive. After Malinovsky read a Defense Ministry memorandum summarizing the plan, the Presidium voted unanimously to confirm the decision it had made three weeks earlier.

That was how the decision was made: Khrushchev led, and his colleagues obediently followed.[60] If Troyanovsky dared to voice reservations, that was because Khrushchev "practically never raised his voice at his immediate subordinates" but "preferred to vent his bad mood on somebody else."[61] Troyanovsky got his chance in late May, when fellow Khrushchev staffer Vladimir Lebedev told him, "Oleg Aleksandrovich, you better sit down. What I'm going to tell you will shock you. The issue of deploying missiles in Cuba is being discussed." Troyanovsky was indeed "flabbergasted." To an advocate of better relations with the United States, the move seemed "a nightmare." Carefully choosing a propitious moment, Troyanovsky expressed reservations to his boss. True to form, Khrushchev listened attentively and then replied that he wasn't doing anything that Americans hadn't already done by deploying nuclear weapons along Soviet borders. But "that totally ignored the mood in the United States and the possible U.S. reaction," according to Troyanovsky. "It is also totally beyond my comprehension how, taking into account the tremendous scale of the operation, anyone could seriously hope to keep it secret, whereas its success hinged entirely on springing a surprise."[62]

Sergei Khrushchev learned of the plan about the same time; his father told him as they strolled from their dacha to the Moscow River on a glorious spring day. Sergei had doubts and expressed them; indeed, he suspects his father confided in him precisely because he wanted to hear the sorts of objections that no colleague except Mikoyan dared make. But a son was no substitute for a cabinet, a council, or a presidium, for advisers who were fully informed, able to assess options, and courageous enough to tell the truth to power.[63]

A FLAWED decision-making process having produced a decision, an equally flawed process of implementing it began. Khrushchev wanted a small expeditionary force, large enough (by his lights) to deter the Americans from attacking the missile installations but small enough to be transported and deployed without being noticed. Instead the military put together a larger force much more likely to draw American attention. The core of the force was the missiles: thirty-six medium-range (twelve hundred nautical miles) rockets with their twenty-four launchers, plus twenty-four intermediate-range (twenty-two hundred nautical miles) missiles with their sixteen launchers. Nuclear warheads for the medium-range ballistic missiles (MRBMs) extended from two to seven hundred kilotons (ten to thirty-five times larger than the American bomb that leveled Hiroshima), while the intermediate-range ballistic missile (IRBM) warheads spanned from two to eight hundred kilotons. Each of five missile regiments had its own mobile technical support base, including vans to transport the warheads from underground storage bunkers to the rockets when orders came to prepare them for launch.

All sorts of other forces were to defend the missiles: three surface-to-air missile regiments of four launch complexes each for a total of 144 launchers; two cruise missile regiments with eighty missiles in all, each with a range of ninety miles and equipped with five-to-twelve kiloton atomic warheads; one regiment of thirty-three helicopters; a squadron of eleven Il-28 bombers equipped with conventional weapons and six more planes fitted for nuclear bombs; a transport and communications squadron with eleven planes; four motorized rifle regiments, each with twenty-five hundred men, thirty-four tanks, and other arms and equipment; a naval squadron of submarines, cruisers, and destroyers; and a brigade of missile-launching patrol boats.

The plan approved by Malinovsky on July 4 and by Khrushchev three days later called for transporting 50,874 men to Cuba, including personnel for field hospitals, bakeries, mechanical workshops, and other support units, along with a three-month supply of food and fuel. In September the number of troops was reduced to 45,234 men, 3,332 of whom turned back at sea during the crisis. That left a total of 41,902, whereas on October 26 American intelligence would estimate that at most there were 10,000 servicemen on the island.

Of all these forces, the rockets capable of reaching the American heartland were the most provocative. But since they weren't likely to be fired for fear of triggering all-out nuclear war, the most dangerous weapons were actually the short-range nuclear systems, both those originally assigned to the operation and additional tactical nuclear weapons dispatched in September, including twelve Luna missiles capable of dropping twelve two-kiloton warheads on invading American troops up to a range of twenty-five miles. Khrushchev's initial instructions allowed these weapons to be fired without checking with Moscow. That authorization, which was conveyed orally but not in writing, was rescinded on October 22, but in the fire of war who knew if they would be used? Khrushchev had no *physical* control over the nuclear weapons in Cuba. In the event of American invasion, General Gribkov asked himself years later, "would the attackers have found and neutralized the bunkers where the nuclear charges for the Lunas and the cruise missiles were stored? Or would a desperate group of Soviet defenders, with or without an order from above, have been able to arm and fire even one Luna warhead—with a yield one-tenth that of the bomb dropped on Hiroshima—or one of the more powerful [cruise missile] charges? If such a rocket had hit U.S. troops or ships, if thousands of Americans had died in the atomic blast, would that have been the last shot of the Cuban crisis or the first of global nuclear war?"[64]

This most dangerous expedition required a very special commander. Yet Khrushchev and Malinovsky passed over the General Staff's first choice, the Strategic Rocket Forces' Lieutenant General Pavel B. Dankevich, in favor of their old World War II comrade General Issa Pliyev, fresh from crushing the demonstrations in Novocherkassk. The elderly Pliyev had fought in the Russian civil war, commanded a division defending Moscow against the Nazis, served at Stalingrad, and then led offensives in Hungary and against the Imperial Japanese Army in Manchuria. North Caucasus Military District colleagues regarded him as "a calm, firm, intelligent, thoughtful man who was nonetheless prepared to take big risks." Khrushchev liked and trusted him, but Pliyev had yet another advantage: He reminded his boss of the Great Fatherland War. Back then Khrushchev had merely implemented Stalin's will. Now it was he who had conceived a daring operation, overseen its planning, and directed its deployment, just as Stalin had during the war. The grizzled Pliyev may have also reminded Khrushchev of the hero of the war against Napoleon, General Kutuzov, as portrayed in Tolstoy's *War and Peace.* But the old man proved brittle from the start (when he refused to adopt the pseudonym "Ivan Aleksandrovich Pavlov," which had been prepared for him), he quickly quarreled with aides, and during the crisis his lack of diplomacy made for "a temperamental mismatch between Castro and Pliyev [which] exacerbated the misunderstandings that arose between Castro and Khrushchev."[65]

If the design of the force, and the choice of its commander, boded ill, so did the plan for getting it to Cuba. Named after a far northeastern river that empties into the Bering Sea, Operation Anadyr was ostensibly to deposit troops and equipment near the Arctic Circle. That was why many units were outfitted with skis, felt boots, and fleece-lined parkas rather than shorts and summer shirts. The shortage of summer clothing didn't fatally compromise the operation, but the presence of winter togs didn't help much either.

The good ship *Maria Ulyanova* (named after Lenin's sister) set sail for the Cuban port of Cabañas in mid-July, the first of eighty-five passenger ships and freighters to make some 150 round trips over the next three months. Getting men and equipment to six Soviet ports, ranging from Sevastopol in the southern Crimea to Severomorsk near Murmansk, required assembling them secretly in special loading areas and moving them by night under special armed guard, with final destinations unannounced and mail and telegrams to troops banned. At embarkation points, troops were kept in barracks under special guards until time to depart and stripped of all party, Komsomol, and military identification until their return. Ships' crews were forbidden shore leaves or correspondence.

Once on board, troops became carpenters (building bunk beds on the lower decks and covering missile mounts with wooden planks to disguise them as parts of ship superstructures) and stevedores (loading tanks, antiaircraft guns, disassembled airplanes, and sixty-seven-foot-long missiles into oversize cargo holds). All recognizably military equipment was stored below, with missiles and launchers shielded with metal sheets from infrared photography; cars, trucks, tractors, and other agricultural equipment were displayed on deck.

To look the part of "agricultural advisers," troops were provided with civilian clothes, including standard plaid shirts that distinguished them from Cubans as clearly as if they had been wearing regulation Soviet military uniforms. Even so, they were allowed on deck (in groups of no more than five or six men) only at night (although the temperature belowdecks reached nearly ninety degrees during the day) once the ships approached the Bahamas, where U.S. air and sea surveillance began. By then the soldiers had at least learned their destination, contained in a small sealed envelope inside a larger sealed envelope tied with a brown ribbon, which the senior commander and ship's captain opened in the presence of a KGB officer at an assigned spot in the Atlantic Ocean. With sweat pouring off them, with rations issued mostly in darkness, and toilet use limited to a preset schedule on some of the ships, an eighteen- to twenty-day passage to the tropics, ordinarily a dream for winter-ravaged Russians, turned into a nightmare.

Nor did much fun begin when the ships arrived: the *Maria Ulyanova* on July 26, followed by nine more during the next four days. Since Moscow had forgotten to provide ships and local greeting parties with passwords to identify each other, some captains and commanders refused to be rerouted from originally assigned ports. Military equipment had to be unloaded at night, hidden in sheds, and trundled along back roads (the missiles in eighty-foot-long carriers that couldn't turn corners unless peasant shacks in the way were knocked down) from eleven ports to bases around the country. During this forced march, all commands were issued in Spanish while the exhausted troops, still dressed as civilians, maintained total radio silence to foil U.S. electronic eavesdropping devices. All communication between the field and Soviet headquarters in Havana was handled orally and in person by messengers, who scurried back and forth.

Upon reaching their bases, troops found conditions inhospitable to both them and their equipment. The combination of moist heat, swarming mosquitoes, and (in eastern Cuba) poisonous guayaco trees made life nearly unendurable. Instead of conventional trenches, which couldn't be dug without hitting underground water, the soldiers built earthen embankments topped with barbed wire, hard-laboring through ten- to twelve-hour shifts in alternating heat and rain. Huge reinforced concrete slabs had been hauled all the way from the USSR to undergird missile launching pads. When the rocky topsoil thwarted heavy earthmoving equipment, soldiers had to anchor the slabs in the ground by hand. The same army whose rockets could hit targets a thousand miles away, lamented General Gribkov, was still "shackled to the old soldier's proverb: 'One sapper, one axe, one day, one stump.'"

Nor of course did palm trees provide much camouflage. Even if there had been more of them, they couldn't have concealed "multiple command and support buildings, rows of fuel trucks and tanks, and hundreds of meters of thick cable—all surrounding the large concrete slabs that anchored the missile launchers. Once the heavy equipment had been moved in [according to General Gribkov], such an installation—but not the road built to it—could be hidden from ground-level view. From above, however, it could and did stick out like a sore thumb."

Medium-range Soviet missiles arrived in mid-September, their nuclear warheads, under special KGB guard, came on October 4. The ship carrying the IRBMs, which was still at sea when the crisis began, turned back, while the IRBM warheads, which had been sent separately, were kept stowed on a Soviet ship in a Cuban port throughout the confrontation. By October 14, when General Gribkov flew in for a General Staff inspection (on an Aeroflot flight that carried life jackets and other evacuation equipment in an inaccessible baggage compartment under the passenger cabin), eighty cruise missile warheads, six atomic bombs for Il-28 bombers, and twelve Luna warheads had also reached Cuba. These nuclear warheads were stored in specially guarded bunkers and depots near, but not too near, the missiles and planes with which they were to be mated in time of war.

All wasn't yet in readiness; General Pliyev, whose kidney illness probably contributed to the sour reception he gave his General Staff visitors, reported deployments running behind schedule. But there was worse news than that: The very day Gribkov arrived, an American U-2 overflew missile sites with impunity.[66]

U-2S HAD BEGUN photographing Cuba early in 1962, and the Soviets knew it. Yet Khrushchev, who had examined photos Francis Gary Powers took on May 1, 1960, and knew how good they were, put the danger out of his mind. When Moscow's chief military representative in Cuba, Major General Aleksei Dementyev, tried to raise the issue before the Presidium finally approved sending missiles, Defense Minister Malinovsky kicked him under the table to shut him up. In early July, Khrushchev ordered that surface-to-air missiles be deployed, but the SA-2s weren't used lest doing so precipitate a crisis prematurely.[67]

The surprise is not that Soviet rockets were discovered before they were ready but that it took so long for Khrushchev's scheme to unravel. In retrospect, Admiral Nikolai N. Amelko insisted a secret missile deployment was impossible: "The missiles were visible when they were brought down rivers to Odessa to be loaded on ships. Everybody in Odessa was talking about missiles being sent overseas. They were also visible when they were unloaded and transported to their Cuban bases." It was, in short, "a crackpot scheme."[68]

"Not a single specialist" whom veteran diplomat Georgy Kornienko later talked to "believed that this could be done secretly."[69] Added General Gribkov: "It is remarkable that the secret stayed a secret for a full month after the MRBM's reached Cuba."[70] Troyanovsky marveled: "It is beyond my comprehension how . . . one could seriously hope to keep it secret, while its success hinged entirely on springing a surprise."[71] Dobrynin said: "Frankly, I don't have the impression that everything was thought through to the last move, as in a game of chess. Undoubtedly, there was a conception, steps were taken, but there was improvisation as things unfolded."[72] According to Cuban Politburo member Jorge Risquet, "It seems to us that Comrade Khrushchev did not think of all the subsequent moves that the adversary would make and the moves that he would make. . . . "[73]

Not thinking things through was typical of Khrushchev, especially in his last years in power. But although he lacked a contingency plan, he did have a notion: If the Americans discovered Soviet missiles before they were fully operational, surely he could negotiate himself out of the situation. It was his "near certainty that Kennedy would not choose war," according to Adzhubei, that made it seem "relatively safe" to provoke the U.S. president.[74] What Khrushchev ignored was his own contention that Kennedy wasn't in control of his own government, that he lived in fear of reactionaries who might now cite Cuban missiles as an excuse to demand an all-out invasion. In that sense, Khrushchev's sin was failing to confront the contradiction at the heart of his own thinking about Kennedy.

Mikoyan and Troyanovsky weren't the only ones who raised warning flags. The Cubans were also worried. Raúl Castro spent two weeks in Moscow in early July negotiating a formal five-year treaty regulating the stationing of Soviet forces in Cuba. Delivered to Havana in August by the newly accredited Ambassador Alekseyev, the draft treaty was revised and returned to Moscow in late August by Che Guevara. Throughout these two months the Cubans kept urging that the agreement, minus details about specific weapons, be made public. When Raúl was in Moscow, Fidel recalled, "I wanted him to ask Khrushchev a single question: what would happen if the operation were discovered while it was in progress? That was the single question I wanted to ask him." Fidel remembers saying before Guevara departed, "If our conduct is legal, if what's more, it's correct, why should we do something that may give rise to a scandal? Why should it seem that we are doing something secretly, covertly, as if we were doing something wrong, to which we have no right?"[75]

It's possible of course that announcing the deployment would immediately have triggered a crisis. But according to Kennedy administration veterans, it was "much less likely that the U.S. government would have sought, or been able, to compel retraction of the Soviet decision and preclude deployment."[76] This makes Khrushchev's quick and disdainful dismissal of Cuban doubts all the more revealing. "You don't have to worry," he told Guevara "There will be no big reaction from the U.S. And if there is a problem, we will send the Baltic Fleet."

"He was totally serious," said Guevera aide Emilio Aragones. "When he said it, Che and I looked at each other with raised eyebrows. But you know, we were deferential to the Soviets' judgments, because, after all, they had a great deal of experience with the Americans, and their information was superior to what we had."[77]

Even hotheaded Cuban revolutionaries knew some old-style geopolitics; they weren't counting on the Baltic fleet, but on Moscow's will and determination, backed by its global missile strength. Nor was Polish Communist leader Gomułka filled with confidence when Khrushchev confided in him that summer. In response to Gomułka's uneasiness, Khrushchev offered not the Baltic fleet but this story: A poor Russian peasant brought his goat into his hut for the winter (just as Khrushchev's own family had done in Kalinovka); the goat smelled awful, but the peasant got used to the smell. Kennedy too would "learn to accept the smell of the missiles."[78]

Although the Cuban crisis was largely of Khrushchev's own making, he might have avoided it with Kennedy's help. On September 4 the president issued a warning: If evidence were to appear of "any organized combat force in Cuba from any Soviet bloc country . . . or of the presence of ground-to-ground missiles; or of other significant offensive capability either in Cuban hands or under Soviet direction and guidance . . . the gravest issues would arise."[79] If Kennedy had said that in April, Khrushchev might have stepped back.

In mid-August CIA aerial photographs showed Soviet ships riding unusually high in the water, suggesting that the huge crates on their decks carried cargo as lightweight as it was oversize. A refugee arriving in Miami described a long truck convoy he had encountered before dawn on August 5: "After about every third truck there was a long flatbed pulled by a tractor-like vehicle. On each vehicle there was a round object as tall as a palm tree and covered by a tarpaulin." If, as seemed likely, these were SA-2s, State Department and military intelligence assumed they were to protect Cuba from invasion. Only CIA head McCone, combining fierce anticommunism with a former businessman's sense of cost, figured the SA-2s were protecting an even more valuable investment—namely, ground-to-ground missiles capable of reaching the United States.[80] McCone's fears, along with stinging criticism from Senator Kenneth Keating (who Kennedy assumed was being briefed by disgruntled CIA types) led to the president's September 4 warning. But JFK "drew the line precisely where he thought the Soviets were not and would not be," Theodore Sorensen said many years later. "If we had known that the Soviets were putting forty missiles in Cuba, we might under this hypothesis have drawn the line at one hundred, and said with great fanfare that we would absolutely not tolerate the presence of more than one hundred missiles in Cuba." Added McGeorge Bundy: "We did it [issued the warning] because of the requirement of domestic politics, not because we seriously believed that the Soviets would do anything as crazy from our standpoint as placement of Soviet nuclear weapons in Cuba."[81]

For Khrushchev, however, Kennedy's September 4 statement meant trouble. As early as July he had begun to fear his secret might be discovered.[82] After Kennedy's September 4 admonition, exposure seemed all the more likely. In theory, Khrushchev could have halted the operation; as of September 5 no ground-to-ground missiles or warheads had arrived in Cuba. Instead he took several steps that made the crisis even more dangerous. One was to expedite delivery of weapons already under way, a second to dispatch additional tactical nuclear weapons, and a third to bombard the Americans with assurances, which looked all the more sinister when the truth became known, that he was doing no such thing.[83]

Expedited delivery hastened the arrival of medium-range missiles by two weeks. The extra tactical nuclear weapons, which he ordered sent on September 7, included six atomic bombs for the Il-28 bombers, plus twelve Luna short-range rockets with nuclear warheads. Khrushchev turned down a proposal to add even more nuclear-armed tactical missiles, and two weeks he later canceled submarines and surface ships previously scheduled for deployment. But adding any battlefield nuclear weapons at all, when he knew a confrontation was coming, was reckless in the extreme.

Khrushchev's last-minute assurances were just as desperate. On September 4, Dobrynin informed a "highly agitated" Robert Kennedy that there "would be no ground-to-ground or offensive weapons placed in Cuba" since "Khrushchev would do nothing to disrupt the relationship of our two countries during this period prior to the election." Chairman Khrushchev "liked President Kennedy and did not wish to embarrass him," Dobrynin said. When Robert Kennedy said the chairman had "a very strange way of showing his admiration," adding that "it would be of the gravest consequence if the Soviet Union placed missiles in Cuba," Dobrynin answered that this would "never happen." Uninformed about Khrushchev's plans, the ambassador spoke with conviction. "I never even imagined the idea of stationing our nuclear missiles in Cuba," he later recalled.[84] Two days later Dobryinin read Sorensen a personal message from Khrushchev to Kennedy: "Nothing will be undertaken before the American Congressional elections that could complicate the international situation or aggravate tension in the relations between our two countries."[85] On September 11, by which time Kennedy had asked Congress for standby authority to call some 150,000 reserve troops to active duty, the Soviet government declared, "There is no need for the Soviet Union to transfer its weapons for repulsing aggression, for inflicting a retaliatory blow, to another country–to Cuba, for instance." Arms currently being sent to Cuba were "solely for defensive purposes."[86]

Khrushchev may have thought Kennedy would believe this. More likely, he was encouraging him to do what he assumed the president wanted to do anyway—namely, look the other way so as to avoid a preelection crisis and pave the way for a postelection summit. Late in August, secret emissary Bolshakov met a president who looked "tired and a bit worried." Khrushchev had been complaining about American planes flying low over Cuba-bound Soviet ships. "Tell him [Khrushchev]," Kennedy told Bolshakov, "I've ordered these flyovers stopped." A concession like that implied that Kennedy was trying to avoid trouble. So did the rest of the president's message: "[T]he outlook for American-Soviet relations is good"; JFK hoped to see Khrushchev again "in the near future." Robert Kennedy, whom Bolshakov also saw, begged Khrushchev not to undermine his brother: "Goddamn it, Georgie, doesn't Premier Khrushchev realize the President's position? Doesn't the Premier know that the President has enemies as well as friends? Believe me, my brother really means what he says about American-Soviet relations. But every step he takes to meet Premier Khrushchev halfway costs him a lot of effort. If the Premier just took the trouble to be, for a moment at least, in the President's shoes, he would understand him."[87]

Was Kennedy trying "not to notice" Khrushchev's Cuban deployment? Is that why, in his September 6 conversation with Secretary Udall at Pitsunda, the Soviet leader tried to strengthen the president's backbone? Udall cited congressional pressure for an invasion of Cuba but assured Khrushchev that "the President makes the policy." Khrushchev replied that members of Congress "do not see with their eyes but with their asses. All they can see is what's behind them." He added what he described as Tolstoy's line to Gorky: "'Men are poorly designed. When they're young, they can satisfy their sexual desires. But as they grow old, the ability to reap this satisfaction disappears. The desires, however, do not.' So it is with your Congressmen. They do not have power, but they still have the same old desires."[88]

When Bolshakov arrived at Pitsunda several days later, a "sun-tanned and smiling" Khrushchev met him by the pool in a straw hat and an embroidered Ukrainian shirt open at the neck. Obviously "anxious about Cuba," the chairman asked if "the United States would go to the length of an armed confrontation" with Castro. Bolshakov thought it would, emphasizing that the president was under heavy pressure from "reactionary forces" eager to crush Castro. But Kennedy "knows it's no use trying," Khrushchev said. "Cuba is not what it used to be." If it were up to JFK himself, Bolshakov responded, he would probably seek some sort of compromise. But it wasn't. Told of Robert Kennedy's fear for his brother's position, Khrushchev retorted, "They can't mean it. Is he the President, or isn't he? If he is a strong President, he has no one to fear. He has full powers of government, and his brother is the Attorney General in the bargain." But Khrushchev wasn't so confident in Kennedy either. He ordered Bolshakov to observe and report his reactions in minute detail: "You've got to take note of everything—the tone, gestures, conversations. We in Moscow need to know everything, especially at a time like this."[89]

The tone wasn't good when Bolshakov saw Robert Kennedy on October 4 and 6. The attorney general was formal and edgy; he asked Bolshakov to repeat Khrushchev's oral assurance about Soviet weapons in Cuba being defensive, wrote it down himself, and asked his secretary to type it up. The next day the Washington journalist and close Kennedy friend Charles Bartlett invited Bolshakov to lunch and asked him to dictate the Khrushchev message all over again so that the president could have it in writing.

Two more U.S.-Soviet meetings occurred just before President Kennedy learned the truth. On October 15, Dobrynin denied to Ambassador-at-Large Chester Bowles that Il-28 bombers were being shipped to Cuba. The next day in Moscow, Khrushchev assured Ambassador Kohler that he was "most anxious not to do anything that will embarrass the President during the campaign."[90] Several days earlier Khrushchev had been in Tashkent, probably to disguise the rapt attention

Offering a toast at picnic with artists and writers outside Moscow about 1960. Left to right are Politburo members: Yekaterina Furtseva, Anastas Mikoyan, Leonid Brezhnev, Voroshilov, Mikhail Suslov, and Frol Kozlov. (Sergei Khrushchev collection)

Showing his skill at one of his favorite sports at the same picnic with the intelligentsia. Voroshilov is seated at left with Suslov standing to his left. (Sergei Khrushchev collection)

With liberal *Novyi mir* editor, Aleksandr Tvardovsky, Moscow, 1962. (Sergei Khrushchev collection)

With Soviet writer Mikhail Sholokhov on the Don River. (courtesy of MN Publishing House)

Castigating artists ("A donkey could smear better than that with his tail") at Manezh exhibit of modern art, Moscow, December 1962. Artist Boris Zhutovsky (center) bears the brunt of Khrushchev's explosion. Suslov stands at Khrushchev's left. (Sergei Khrushchev collection)

Shouting at poet Andrei Vosnesensky ("Your view of Soviet power is from the toilet . . . If you don't like it, you can go to hell.") during a meeting with the intelligentsia, Moscow, March 1963. (courtesy of MN Publishing House)

Tired and pensive at a concert during the Tchaikovsky piano competition in the Great Hall of the Conservatory, Moscow, late 1950s. (courtesy of MN Publishing House)

Inspecting grain in the Virgin Lands' Tselinograd Province, 1964. (Sergei Khrushchev collection)

Donning a miner's gas mask as his party deputy, Aleksei Kirichenko, and KGB bodyguard Leonid Litovchenko look on, Donbas, Ukraine, 1957. (Sergei Khrushchev collection)

Welcoming pioneering cosmonaut Yuri Gagarin and his wife, Valya, to the Kremlin after Gagarin's first space flight, April 14, 1961. (Sergei Khrushchev collection)

With Presidium colleagues Mikoyan (left) and Kirichenko, Red Square, Moscow, 1959. (Sergei Khrushchev collection)

With Presidium colleagues (Kozlov to the left of Khrushchev, Nikolai Ignatov and Suslov to the right) in the Kremlin about 1961. (Sergei Khrushchev collection)

Nina Petrovna Khrushcheva straightens her husband's tie, Moscow, 1959. (Walter Carron/SIPA)

Relaxing at resort of Zavidovo, 1960. (Sergei Khrushchev collection)

With grandson Nikita Khrushchev at dacha by the Black Sea in Pitsunda, Soviet Georgia, 1960. (Sergei Khrushchev collection)

With his son Sergei and grandsons Nikita and Aleksei Adzhubei at dacha outside Moscow, early 1960s. (courtesy of MN Publishing House)

The Khrushchev extended family, outside Moscow, 1963. Left to right: son-in-law Aleksei Adzhubei; daughter Yelena; daughter Rada Adzhubei; Nina Petrovna Khrushcheva; grandson Nikita Adzhubei; Nikita Khrushchev; his son Sergei Khrushchev; Sergei's wife, Galina Shumova; and (in front of them) grandsons Aleksei and Ivan Adzhubei, and Nikita Khrushchev. (courtesy of MN Publishing House)

With Mao Zedong in Beijing, 1954. Bulganin is at left.
(Sergei Khrushchev collection)

With Yugoslav leader Josef Broz Tito and his wife, Iovanka, at Belgrade airport before Khrushchev's peacemaking tour of the country in May 1955. (courtesy of MN Publishing House)

With Burmese leader U Nu in Rangoon, 1955. (courtesy of MN Publishing House)

With British Prime Minister Harold Macmillan, who had come to Moscow to try to defuse the Berlin crisis, February 1959. Interpreter Viktor Sukhodrev stands between them. (courtesy of MN Publishing House)

With Vice President Richard Nixon at American exhibition in Moscow, July 1959. (courtesy of MN Publishing House)

With President Dwight Eisenhower at Camp David, September 1959. (Ed Clark/TimePix)

En route from Los Angeles to San Francisco, September 1959. To right of Khrushchev are Soviet Ambassador to the United States Mikhail Menshikov and interpreter Viktor Sukhodrev. Opposite Khrushchev is Henry Cabot Lodge. (Ed Clark/TimePix)

With Roswell Garst (facing Khrushchev) at the Garst farm in Coon Rapids, Iowa, September 1959. (Sergei Khrushchev collection)

Joking with an American while touring the United States, September 1959. (AP/Wideworld Photos)

Celebrating the tenth anniversary of the People's Republic of China with Mao Zedong, Beijing, October 1, 1959. One of the few upbeat moments in an otherwise disastrous visit. (courtesy of MN Publishing House)

With Polish Communist leader Wladyslaw Gomulka, Poland, 1959. (Sergei Khrushchev collection)

With Indian Prime Minister Jawaharlal Nehru, and the latter's daughter, Indira Gandhi, New Dehli, February 1960. (Sergei Khrushchev collection)

With King Muhammed Zahir Shah, in Kabul, Afghanistan, 1960, the same king who returned to Afghanistan in 2002 after a lengthy exile in Rome. (courtesy of MN Publishing House)

With Indonesia President Sukarno, Jakarta, 1960. (Sergei Khrushchev collection)

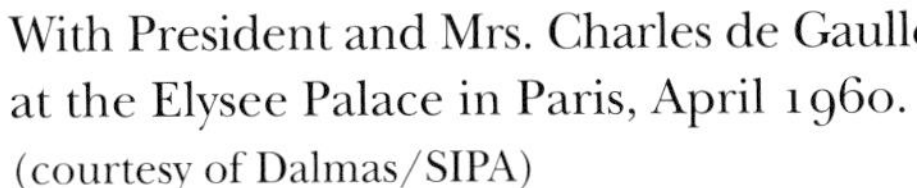

With President and Mrs. Charles de Gaulle at the Elysee Palace in Paris, April 1960. (courtesy of Dalmas/SIPA)

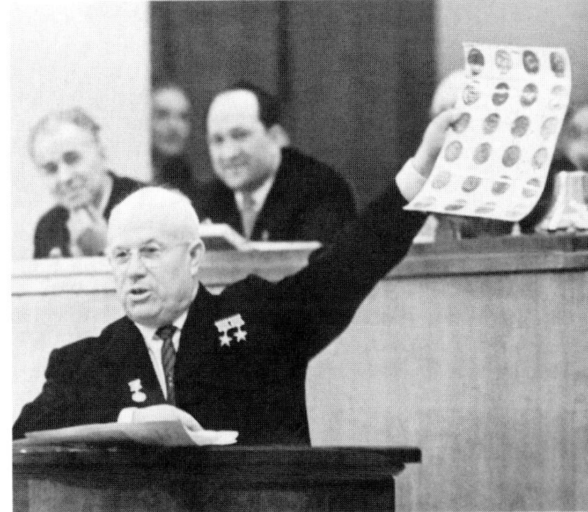

Revealing that the U.S. Government lied about its U-2 spy plane. At USSR Supreme Soviet session, May 7, 1960. (UPI/Bettmann Newsphotos)

After berating foreign journalists ("I like coming to grips with the enemies of the working class . . . to hear the frenzy of these lackeys of imperialism") at stormy press conference in Paris after summit collapsed owing to U-2 flight. Defense Minister Marshal Rodion Malinovsky at right. (UPI/Bettmann Newsphotos)

Playing shuffleboard en route to the United Nations in New York, September 1960. (Sergei Khrushchev collection)

At the United Nations in New York, September 1959. (courtesy of MN Publishing House)

Pounding his fists at the United Nations in September 1960. Whether his shoe was banged next is the subject of controversy described in a footnote to the Preface. (UPI/Bettmann Newsphotos)

With Egyptian President Gamal Abdel Nasser, Soviet estate, Glen Cove, Long Island, New York, September 1960. (Sergei Khrushchev collection)

With President John F. Kennedy at Vienna summit, June 1961. (The John F. Kennedy Library)

With East German Communist leader Walter Ulbricht, July 1963. (courtesy of MN Publishng House)

With Hungarian Communist leader Janos Kadar, Budapest, 1962. (Sergei Khrushchev collection)

Feasting with Cuban Communist leader Fidel Castro on the road to Lake Ritsa, Soviet Georgia, May 1963. (Sergei Khrushchev collection)

Rambling on too long at a party in honor of his birthday, April 17, 1964. Looking pained to right of Khrushchev are his wife, daughter Yelena, Mikoyan, and Leonid Brezhnev. (Sergei Khrushchev collection)

The dacha at Petrovo-Dalneye where Khrushchev lived from 1965 until his death in 1971. Picture taken in 1967. (Sergei Khrushchev collection)

A quiet moment in the woods near Petrovo Dalneye with his dog, Arbat, and a tame rook, Kava, summer of 1967. (Sergei Khrushchev collection)

At Petrovo-Dalneye, 1969. (Sergei Khrushchev collection)

Being hugged on his birthday by his daughter Rada, Petrovo-Dalneye, April 17,1969. (Sergei Khrushchev collection)

Khrushchev and wife, Nina Petrovna, on his birthday, Petrovo-Dalneye, April 17, 1971, the last before his death in September 1971. (Sergei Khrushchev collection)

Memorial headstone, designed and built by Ernst Neizvestny, at Novodevichy Cemetery, Moscow. (photo by author)

he was devoting to Cuba. He telephoned General Ivanov from Uzbekistan, wanting to know "how the shipment is going." Told that the Lunas and Il-28s were en route, he replied, "Everything is clear. Thanks."[91] About the same time, Troyanovsky had a final chat with Khrushchev about the missiles. All summer Troyanovsky had felt as if he were in a car that "had lost its steering." The two men were alone in Khrushchev's Kremlin office when the Soviet leader blurted out, "Soon the storm will break loose."

"Let's hope the boat will not capsize altogether," the ever-diplomatic Troyanovsky replied. "Khrushchev was lost in thought for a moment," Troyanovsky remembered. "'Now it's too late to change anything,'" he said.[92]

FROM THE MOMENT Kennedy and his advisers met at 11:50 A.M. on October 16 to consider how to respond to Khrushchev's challenge, they were determined the missiles must go. No matter what his motives were, if Khrushchev got away with this, he would inevitably try other adventures. Even if Berlin weren't the target this time, surely it would be next.

Domestic and personal considerations also entered in. "We've just elected [Homer] Capehart [Republican] in Indiana," Kennedy told Kenny O'Donnell after seeing the first U-2 photos, "and Ken Keating will probably be the next President of the United States." He was only partly kidding.[93] If Kennedy worried previously about Khrushchev's underestimating his resolve, how would the chairman view a president who tolerated the Cuban missiles or who tried and failed to remove them? The Bay of Pigs and Vienna summit had been bad enough. This time Khrushchev had deliberately deceived him, luring him into a false sense of security, which, to make matters worse, Kennedy had then tried to foist on his own country.

None of Kennedy's advisers favored accepting the status quo. Almost immediately the ExComm rejected trying to talk the missiles out of Cuba, lest Khrushchev stall the negotiations while accelerating installation of the rockets and mobilizing public opinion against Washington. In the meantime, Gromyko was slated to see the president on October 18. Would he spring the unpleasant surprise? If not, should the president tip his hand? Kennedy was determined to preserve complete secrecy until he had chosen a course of action. But how could the two men talk without mentioning the main thing on both their minds?

The meeting took place at 5:00 P.M. in the Oval Office. Gromyko noted that Kennedy and Rusk seemed tense and that the secretary of state looked red "like a crab." He also noticed a folder on the President's desk and later wondered whether the U-2 photos had been in it; actually, those pictures were in the middle drawer of Kennedy's desk. After the usual pleasantries, Gromyko raised non-Cuban issues: After the November elections, Moscow would be *compelled* (Gromyko repeated the word for emphasis) to sign a German peace treaty. So if Khrushchev came to New York in late November, "it would probably be useful" if he and the president talked about Berlin. Kennedy rejected official negotiations but seemingly agreed to informal talks. After Gromyko left, the president sent word (through Thompson to Dobrynin) that such a meeting would not be "appropriate."

Gromyko condemned American intimidation of Havana, adding that Soviet assistance to Castro presented no threat to anyone. "Were matters to be otherwise," the foreign minister continued, paraphrasing language from Kennedy's September 4 warning, "the Soviet government would never have been a party to rendering such aid."

In response, Kennedy read aloud his September 4 statement. According to Gromyko's minutes of the meeting, the president characterized the situation as "the most dangerous development since the end of the war" and remarked "where it would end he had no idea." Kennedy denied any intention to invade Cuba, adding he had been trying to restrain those who advocated such an attack.

The real issue hadn't been joined. But both men had come very close. Gromyko later contended that if Kennedy "had begun speaking openly about the missiles, I would have given him the reply that had been agreed upon back in Moscow: 'Mr. President, the Soviet Union has provided Cuba with a small quantity of missiles of a defensive nature. They will never threaten anyone!" According to Rusk, Kennedy gave Gromyko "every opportunity to confess knowledge of Soviet missiles in Cuba." JFK wished he could have mentioned the missiles, if only to puncture "more barefaced lies than I have ever heard in so short a time."[94]

Years later Khrushchev still relished his foreign minister's performance: "Gromyko answered like a gypsy who was caught stealing a horse: 'It's not me and it's not my horse. I don't know anything.'"[95] In fact, Gromyko ill served his master. He was in a tough spot, of course. His conversation with Kennedy was "perhaps the most difficult," he said later, of any he ever had with the nine Americans presidents he dealt with.[96] In addition, his difficulties didn't end with the meeting itself. Surely he sensed Kennedy was on to the missiles. If so, it would take courage to convey the bad news to Moscow. Moreover, how could he report fully on his fears without alerting embassy personnel to the secret of which they had been denied knowledge?

His apparent solution to the problem was to send two cables to Moscow. The first, on the day of the meeting, reported his Oval Office conversation in sufficient detail to alarm anyone, such as Khrushchev, who was fully aware of Soviet deployments and could read between the lines. But the second, dated October 19, was positively complacent: The White House meeting had "confirmed" that the Cuban situation was "entirely satisfactory"; rather than prepare a Cuban invasion, the United States was relying on the economic boycott; the reason for American restraint was Soviet "boldness" in aiding Castro; Washington's anti-Cuban campaign was actually subsiding; with Congress on its preelection break, a "military adventure against Cuba was "virtually out of the question."[97]

According to Sergei Khrushchev, his father was "more concerned than ever."[98] But thanks to Gromyko's caution, the full dimensions of the trap Khrushchev had set for himself still weren't clear.

WASHINGTON HAD still to decide on its course of action. For a while opinion oscillated between taking the missiles out with air strikes, perhaps accompanied by a full invasion, and blockading Cuba as a step toward removing them one way or another. On the evening of October 18, an ExComm straw vote favored a blockade by eleven to six. The next morning sentiment swung toward bombing. Carefully keeping to a visible public schedule, Kennedy departed on a campaign trip. In his absence, Robert Kennedy, reflecting his brother's preference, pushed for a "quarantine," which had the semantic advantage over "blockade" of not constituting an act of war. Former Secretary of State Dean Acheson argued for a showdown on the grounds of Khrushchev's character: "You must remember we are dealing with a madman." But if Khrushchev really had come unglued, then a massive air strike could trigger nuclear retaliation against the United States.[99]

On Saturday, October 20, the president returned to Washington, using a "cold" as an excuse to cut off campaigning. Meanwhile, in Moscow, Ambassador Kohler dined with Khrushchev's deputy, Frol Kozlov, who "sat with his elbows on the table, ate like a pig, and drank like a fish. He got thoroughly drunk—a nasty drunk. . . . Kozlov didn't put himself out one whit. . . . Kohler made every effort to engage him in conversation. His replies were curt."[100]

As Kennedy approached his decisive choice, both quarantine and air strikes were still on the table. The former would leave Khrushchev room to retreat. But after one last ExComm discussion on October 21, air strikes seemed the likely choice. To his credit, Kennedy opted for a quarantine, even after Air Force Chief of Staff Curtis LeMay had condemned a blockade as "almost as bad as the appeasement at Munich."[101] The next morning, JFK informed former President Eisenhower, and later the same day, congressional and allied leaders. With the president scheduled to address the nation on television at 7:00 P.M., Dobrynin, who had accompanied the departing Gromyko to Idlewild Airport in New York, was summoned to the State Department at 6:00 P.M. Dobrynin knew it was a crisis, but whether over Cuba or Berlin he wasn't sure. Rusk gave him a copy of the president's speech but refused to answer any questions or comment on the text. Rusk noticed that "Dobrynin seemed to age ten years while we were talking."[102]

In Moscow, meanwhile, Kohler received a cable from Rusk containing a letter from Kennedy to Khrushchev. In it, the president recalled his frequent warnings about miscalculation (while deliberately avoiding the word itself, to which Khrushchev had reacted so badly at Vienna). Despite those cautions, "the rapid development of long-range missile bases and other offensive weapons systems in Cuba has proceeded." Now, the president continued, "the United States is determined that this threat to the security of the hemisphere be removed."[103]

In the very early hours of Tuesday, October 23, American diplomat Richard Davies delivered this letter, together with a copy of the president's speech, to the Soviet Foreign Ministry. The speech spelled out the American case against the missiles in more detail, stressed Moscow's "deliberate deception" (including Gromyko's false statements as late as four days earlier), announced a "quarantine" of Cuba as Washington's "initial" course of action, and called upon Khrushchev to "halt and eliminate this clandestine, reckless and provocative threat to world peace and to stable relations between our two countries."[104]

IT WAS 7:00 P.M. Moscow time (noon in Washington) on October 22 when Pierre Salinger announced that President Kennedy would address the nation that evening. Khrushchev had just returned from a stroll around his residence and had yet to remove his coat when he was called to the phone. After hanging up, he stepped outside again. "They've probably discovered our rockets," he told his son. "Nothing else would explain it. Berlin is quiet. If they were about to invade Cuba, then they would be [quiet], too." What would happen next? Sergei wanted to know. "I wish I knew," Khrushchev answered. "The missiles aren't operational yet. They're defenseless; they can be wiped out from the air in one swipe."

If the Americans were going to do that, they wouldn't announce it in advance. Did that mean Kennedy wanted to negotiate? "You'll find out tomorrow morning," Khrushchev said to Sergei, adding, "Don't bother me. I've got to think." The two continued walking in silence. Then Khrushchev reentered the house and picked up his special Kremlin phone: "Call round to all [Presidium] members and tell them to gather at the Kremlin in an hour. What's it about? I'll tell them once we're there. Invite Malinovsky and [Vasily] Kuznetsov [Gromyko's deputy since the foreign minister was on his way back from Washington], too."

Khrushchev picked up another phone and ordered his car. "Don't wait up for me, I'll be back late," he said to Sergei.[105]

When the Presidium met, the only item on its formal agenda, "determining further measures in connection with Cuba and Berlin," was another sign of the potential link between the two in his mind. In addition to regular and candidate members, Central Committee secretaries and top Foreign and Defense Ministry officials attended. Khrushchev was "red-faced and very agitated" when he entered the room. After informing the group of Kennedy's upcoming talk and his assumption that it would concern Cuba, Khrushchev looked at Malinovsky. "You blew it," he grunted, adding with a wave of the hand when the bulky marshal started to rise to his own defense, "There's nothing to say. Stay in your seat."

Malinovsky tried to calm the boss. "I don't think they can undertake anything at once," he said. If the Americans were to invade Cuba, they would need "twenty-four hours more for final preparation." But Khrushchev couldn't calm down; he was already second-guessing himself: "The thing is we were not going to unleash war. We just wanted to intimidate them, to deter the anti-Cuban forces." He mentioned two "difficulties": "We didn't deploy everything we wanted to, and we didn't publish the [Soviet-Cuban] treaty." It was "tragic," he said. Instead of preventing war, his masterstroke might trigger one. "They can attack us," he blustered, "and we shall respond. This may end up in a big war." Grasping at straws, he said the Kremlin could announce that "all the equipment belongs to the Cubans, and the Cubans would announce that they will respond." Of course Castro wouldn't be allowed to threaten use of the medium-range missiles against the United States, but he could threaten to "use the tactical ones."[106]

The real issue was whether the Soviets were prepared to use atomic weapons. In fact, they weren't sure. While waiting for Kennedy to speak, the Presidium drew up an order to Pliyev designed to avoid accidental nuclear war: in the event of invasion, all Soviet and Cuban forces were to be used to "destroy the enemy, with the exception of equipment under the command of Statsenko and Beloborodov." Major General Igor Statsenko commanded the medium-range rockets; Colonel Nikolai Beloborodov was in charge of nuclear warheads. Then the Presidium reversed itself, authorizing Pliyev to use tactical nuclear weapons but not to strike the United States without a direct order from Moscow. Then it switched again, dispatching the first order and holding back the second.[107]

About an hour before Kennedy spoke (it was now 1:00 A.M. Moscow time), the Foreign Ministry relayed by phone the English text of his letter. Troyanovsky translated for the Presidium. Khrushchev's first reaction was "relief rather than anxiety," Troyanovsky remembered. The blockade seemed "like something intangible, all the more so since the President called it a 'quarantine' which created an illusion of still greater vagueness. In any case, it did not look like an ultimatum or a direct threat of an attack on Cuba." Instantaneously Khrushchev's mood swung from alarm to elation. "We've saved Cuba!" he exclaimed. Then he began composing a hot reply to a president who seemed to have blinked.[108]

As sent later that day, Khrushchev's letter labeled Kennedy's actions a "serious threat to peace and security" that constituted "naked interference" in the domestic affairs of Cuba and the USSR. He demanded that Kennedy "renounce actions pursued by you which could lead to catastrophic consequences for peace throughout the world." Khrushchev had dictated an initial draft in the dead of night, in the presence of his colleagues. The Foreign Ministry prepared a final version later that morning. Meantime, Khrushchev urged his associates to spend the rest of the night in their Kremlin offices, lest foreign correspondents or other prying eyes detect that a emergency meeting had occurred and conclude the Soviet leaders were nervous. No one objected, even though half the group lacked Kremlin offices. Khrushchev retired to a bed in his suite; those who usually worked in the Central Committee complex on Staraya Ploshchad' settled themselves in chairs in the Presidium meeting room.

When puffy-eyed participants reassembled at 10:00 A.M., aides read aloud the edited letter to Kennedy as well as a draft statement of the Council of Ministers. The statement was approved as drafted. The letter to Kennedy was further revised. Kuznetsov handed the letter to Kohler at 3:10 P.M. Fifty minutes later Radio Moscow broadcast the Soviet government statement, which informed the Soviet people of American actions (but not of the Soviet deployments to which they were a response), and announced military measures, including the cancellation of military leaves and discharges, and heightened combat readiness throughout the armed forces.[109]

Having countered Kennedy's initial thrust, Khrushchev went to the opera. He had been previously scheduled to escort a visiting Romanian delegation to an American production of *Boris Godunov* at the Bolshoi that evening. To conceal his anxiety, he kept the engagement, demonstratively greeting the American artists backstage afterward.[110] But during a short stop at home before the opera, he looked exhausted and sounded uncertain. Obviously the Americans had found out, he told Sergei, but how much did they know? Perhaps they were relying on rumors. On the other hand, would they have reacted so strongly unless they had been fully informed?

Sergei was stunned that his father had no plan for just this contingency. For the moment Khrushchev's response was to accelerate installation of the missiles. Only now, after they had been discovered, were missile sites camouflaged. Until October 22 Khrushchev had raved about General Pliyev's performance; after that the encomiums ceased. Khrushchev feared the two modest-looking freighters carrying nuclear warheads wouldn't get through before the blockade went into effect, and even after they did, he seethed at the thought of Soviet ships being stopped at sea. When Sergei asked on the twenty-third if war was a real possibility, Khrushchev answered: "It's one thing to threaten with nuclear weapons, it's another to use them." That was his creed, one he had counted on the Americans to share. But he couldn't be certain they would.[111]

Back in Washington, Kennedy wasn't more confident. He too was relieved the worst hadn't happened, but what next? If a U-2 were to be downed over Cuba, the United States would destroy the Soviet SAM site, but where would that lead? Meanwhile, the CIA reported a puzzling mixed picture on and around the island: Soviet ships were still steaming toward Cuba, and missile site construction was proceeding apace, but Soviet and Cuban military planes were parked in rows as if waiting to be destroyed in an American air strike.[112]

Khrushchev's letter to Kennedy arrived during the afternoon on October 23. Kennedy dispatched a curt two-paragraph reply that evening. It called for prudence on both sides and for Khrushchev to observe the quarantine that was scheduled to take effect the next morning.[113]

As of the evening of October 23, Ambassador Dobrynin hadn't

received any instructions from Moscow, another sign of disarray in the Kremlin. Only on the twenty-fourth did Soviet envoys in non-Communist countries receive the official Soviet version of what had happened. On the twenty-third, Dobrynin informed Moscow that the Americans were "getting nervous" and were "prepared to go quite far in a test of strength with the USSR." That same evening Robert Kennedy called on Dobrynin in the Soviet ambassador's third-floor embassy office. According to Dobrynin, the attorney general was "obviously agitated; he kept repeating himself and going off on tangents." Kennedy said his brother had "staked his political career" on Soviet assurances about Cuba. He pressed Dobrynin to admit that even he hadn't been informed of the missile deployment. The result, he said, was that key confidential channels between the two leaders were now undermined. As he was leaving, Kennedy asked how Soviet ship captains would respond to the quarantine. They were "not to obey anyone's unlawful order to stop and be searched on the high seas," answered Dobrynin.

"I don't know how this is going to end," Kennedy said, "since we are determined to stop your ships."

"But that would be an act of war," Dobrynin replied. Kennedy shook his head and departed.[114]

"After some hesitation," Dobrynin recalled, he reported this conversation to Moscow. "I conveyed all of Robert Kennedy's harsh statements word for word, including those that were not at all flattering to Khrushchev and Gromyko. I wanted to give Moscow an idea of the state of agitation in the president's inner circle . . . so that the Kremlin could visualize overall the nervous atmosphere in Washington." Dobrynin later learned that Gromyko conveyed his report to Khrushchev orally (possibly deleting Robert Kennedy's harsh words about Soviet lies) and denied it to other members of the leadership.[115] That the ambassador himself received no immediate reply from either Khrushchev or Gromyko may owe something to their personal irritation. But the deeper reason for Moscow's silence, conveyed to top embassy staffers by Kuznetsov, who arrived in New York on October 28, was Khrushchev's own abiding "confusion." Not knowing what to do, he had "covered" his bewilderment with "his tough statements of October 23 and 24."[116]

DOBRYNIN LATER called Wednesday, October 24, the most "memorable" day of his nearly three decades as ambassador to the United States.[117] That same morning, Robert Kennedy recalled, was "the time of greatest worry by the President." As the ExComm waited to see if Soviet ships would turn back, "[JFK's] hand went up to his face and covered his mouth, and he closed his fist. His eyes were tense, almost gray, and we just stared at each other across the table."[118]

At 10:00 A.M., Washington time, when the quarantine went into full effect, the U.S. Strategic Air Command moved from Defense Condition 3 to DEFCON 2, one level below that of general war. For the first time in history all American long-range missiles and bombers were now on alert, and scores of planes loaded with atomic bombs were aloft around the clock, refueled by aerial tankers, waiting over Greenland and northern Canada for the signal to proceed toward their assigned Soviet targets.[119] To make sure Moscow noticed, the SAC commander, General Thomas Power, took it upon himself to "announce" the move in uncoded messages to his men.[120]

Meanwhile, in Moscow, Richard Davies had delivered the official quarantine order to the Foreign Ministry at 6:00 A.M. As he was ushered toward the American Department on an upper floor of the ministry's Stalinist wedding cake–style skyscraper, he caught sight of a man wearing a gas mask, an old World War II canister type of contraption that looked as if it had been dug out of somebody's basement. Was the sighting designed to show Washington that the ministry was on a war footing? That same day, Davies recollected, Soviet officials he dealt with, "at best brusque and often rude," suddenly became "gushingly polite," continually telephoning him (itself unusual) and asking, "Mr. Davies, how is Mrs. Davies? How are the children? How are you feeling? Is everything all right? Are you happy in our country?' "[121]

If rusty gas masks were one Soviet answer to DEFCON 2, Khrushchev's own performance, blending threats and retreats, wasn't much more impressive.[122] The evening before, he had ordered Soviet ships to proceed (and Soviet submarines to fire if fired upon), but in the light of the Dobrynin–Robert Kennedy conversation, he wasn't so sure. At a morning Presidium meeting on the twenty-fourth, he suggested halting at least some of the ships; all necessary weapons had already reached Cuba, he said, even though intermediate-range rockets had not. Later that day he wavered over whether to let tankers, to which the military attached particular significance, proceed. Just before the American deadline the Soviet ships nearest the quarantine line stopped or turned back.[123]

Earlier that afternoon the president of the Westinghouse Electric International Company, William Knox, who was in Moscow to talk about patents, was summoned to see Khrushchev, whom he had met in New

York two years earlier. Khrushchev was "calm, friendly, and frank—without any histrionics," but looked "very tired." What he said suggested he was still torn between anger and fear, still unsure whether to reassure Kennedy or to rage on against him. About to order his ships to turn back, Khrushchev warned Knox that if U.S. ships tried to stop Soviet vessels, he would order Soviet subs to sink them. Having deceived Kennedy, he complained that the president had betrayed him. Even Eisenhower, Khrushchev said, would have handled the situation in a more mature fashion. "How can I deal with a man who is younger than my own son?" Khrushchev demanded.[124]

He had no good answer. Two days later Soviet Ambassador to the United Nations Zorin was still denying Soviet missiles were in Cuba. Yet Khrushchev assured Knox those missiles were under Soviet, not Cuban, control. Khrushchev insisted "he was not interested in the destruction of the world, but if we all wanted to meet in hell it was up to us." However, he practically begged for a meeting with the president, saying "that he would be glad to receive him in Moscow, that he would be glad to visit him in Washington, [that] they could both embark on naval vessels and rendezvous at sea, or that they could meet at some neutral place where, without fanfare, some of the major problems between our two great countries could be resolved."[125]

That same day Khrushchev dispatched another tough letter to Kennedy. "Who asked you to do this?" he demanded, as if the young president were incapable of acting on his own. Kennedy was "advancing an ultimatum" and trying "to intimidate us." But "in your heart you recognize that I am correct. I am convinced that in my place you would act the same way. . . . Try to put yourself in our situation and think how the USA would react to these conditions," urged a man whose failure of empathy was central to the crisis. The Soviet Union could never accept the American blockade, warned Khrushchev, only hours before he did just that. Yet at the same time all-out work on the missiles sites was still continuing.[126]

ON THURSDAY, OCTOBER 25, the middle of the morning brought a cold but calm reply from Kennedy. It wasn't he who had issued "the first challenge," the president insisted. He regretted the crisis had caused "a deterioration in our relations" and hoped Khrushchev would act so as "to permit a restoration of the earlier situation."[127] According to his son, Khrushchev was "touched" as well as impressed. Sergei says the letter helped convince his father to compromise. But DEFCON 2 didn't hurt either. According to Sergei, his father regarded the move as a "bluff" but still took it into account.[128]

When the Presidium met after lunch, Khrushchev rejected further "caustic" exchanges with Kennedy, favored having ships carrying missiles turn around, and indicated that he wanted to resolve the crisis. "We must dismantle the missiles to make Cuba into a zone of peace," he told his colleagues. He proposed saying to Kennedy, "Give us a pledge not to invade Cuba, and we will remove the missiles." He was even willing to allow the United Nations to inspect the sites. This was in fact the basis on which the crisis ultimately ended. But Khrushchev still wasn't quite ready for that. Before dismantling his missiles, he wanted to "look around," to make sure Kennedy wouldn't settle for less. As usual, Khrushchev's colleagues backed his new position, most of them expressing fulsome support, with Malinovsky and Gromyko seeming less enthusiastic.[129]

Later that evening at home, Khrushchev and his son took one of their regular walks. Sergei feared a compromise settlement would amount to "national humiliation." By reassuring him, Sergei thought, his father was trying to convince himself. Kennedy was under tremendous pressure to attack Cuba. If he did so, what should the Soviets do, attack the Americans in Berlin? That would be stupid and wouldn't solve anything. Once the shooting started there would be no stopping it.

In the past Khrushchev had rattled rockets to get out of tight spots. But his atomic bluster had always been bluff, and now that bluff had been called. Under similar circumstances another autocrat might have taken the world down in flames with him, as Hitler had, or collapsed, like Stalin in June 1941. But Khrushchev was no Hitler or Stalin. As one dream of glory came crashing down around him, he glimpsed another in the ruins. Not only would he save Cuba, but he would save the world, save it from the brink to which his own recklessness had brought it.

At the end of the evening Khrushchev drank his usual glass of tea with lemon, distractedly leafed through the day's papers (*Pravda*'s lead headline that morning had been THE AGGRESSIVE DESIGNS OF THE UNITED STATES IMPERIALISTS MUST BE FOILED. PEACE ON EARTH MUST BE DEFENDED AND STRENGTHENED! HANDS OFF CUBA!), and trudged slowly up the stairs to his bedroom.

ON FRIDAY, OCTOBER 26, the largest concentration of American forces since the Korean War was gathering in the southeastern United States.

The Joint Chiefs of Staff were pressing for air strikes and invasion. In Cuba, missile site construction was racing ahead, as was assembly of Il-28 bombers. Moscow had endured a painful defeat at the UN, where Adlai Stevenson trumped Soviet Ambassador Zorin's delaying tactics by displaying U-2 photos of Soviet missile installations. But UN Secretary General U Thant had played into Soviet hands by suggesting a two- to three-week moratorium on both the quarantine and the Soviet arms shipments.[130] Until Khrushchev opened the grayish blue folder filled with intelligence reports that awaited him on Friday morning, he was still "looking around" to see if Kennedy might fold before he did.

What he found in the folder was stunning: According to an American in a position to know, the Kennedy administration had decided to "finish with Castro." Its invasion plan was complete down to "the last detail," and "the attack could begin at any moment." Other information, such as a report that U.S. hospitals were preparing to receive casualties, seemingly provided confirmation. As Kuznetsov later told a colleague, when Khrushchev got this news, "he dropped a load in his pants." He was now ready to offer Kennedy the deal he had broached to his own colleagues the day before.[131]

In fact, this decisive intelligence report proved false. It was based on a conversation between two American journalists, overheard by an émigré Russian bartender at the National Press Club late Wednesday evening. Warren Rogers of the *New York Herald Tribune* was on a Pentagon list of correspondents scheduled to cover an invasion if and when it took place. The bartender, Johnny Prokov, thought Rogers said he was leaving that night since the attack was to start the next day. Prokov repeated the story to Anatoly Gorsky, a TASS correspondent who was actually a KGB officer, at 1:00 A.M. on Thursday. That day the Soviet Embassy went all out to confirm the news. One Russian connived to bump into Rogers in the Willard Hotel parking lot. Diplomat Georgy Kornienko arranged to lunch with Rogers. Both came away convinced an invasion was at hand. Both the Soviet Embassy and the KGB so informed Moscow on Thursday afternoon.[132]

When Khrushchev got the message, he started dictating a long emotional letter to Kennedy. Gone were his trademark nuclear threats. War, he insisted, would be a "calamity" for all peoples. "You can be calm in this regard, that we are of sound mind and understand perfectly well that if we attack you, you will respond the same way. But you too will receive the same that you hurl against us." If "war should break out, then it would not be in our power to stop it, for such is the logic of war." If both sides did not pull back, they would "clash, like blind moles, and then reciprocal extermination will begin." At all costs, "we and you ought not now pull on the ends of the rope in which you have tied the knot of war, because the more the two of us pull, the tighter that knot will be tied."

To loosen the knot, Khrushchev made a proposal. He did not formally propose a trade; he did not spell out all the conditions. Nor, he said, could he commit Fidel Castro (although forty-eight hours later he did do just that). But the basic outline of a settlement—missiles out, no Americans in—was clear.

Khrushchev dictated his letter without reconvening the Presidium. The copy delivered to the American Embassy that afternoon at four forty-two (bypassing the Foreign Ministry, which usually transmitted documents) contained corrections inserted in violet ink by the same hand that signed the letter "N. Khrushchev." In the meantime, Khrushchev aides sent around copies to Presidium members and Central Committee secretaries. Having approved the general approach the day before, they apparently didn't have to do so in person again.[133]

Embassy officers divided up Khrushchev's text for purposes of translating it and then cabled it to Washington. It began arriving after 6:00 P.M. Washington time, eight hours after the Embassy received it. As it gradually spilled out of the Teletype machine in four parts, the President's advisers could see it was encouraging. The ExComm would meet at 10:00 the next morning to consider it. Meantime, in Moscow, Khrushchev and other officials took in another concert, this time a Cuban performance. Afterward he spent the night in his office again.

ON SATURDAY, OCTOBER 27, Khrushchev awoke as Washington was going to bed. His mood had changed again overnight. The day before he had feared a Cuban invasion was imminent. Now he told the Presidium, "I think they won't venture to do this." If the Americans hadn't attacked so far, then "to my mind they are not ready to do it now." That meant the "measures we have taken were right." Still, he added, "there is no guarantee." To make sure, "we must not be obstinate." Khrushchev was in no mood to look back: "Did we make a mistake or not? It will be possible to determine this later." In the meantime he proposed a new letter to Kennedy, one that added another condition to the previous day's offer, a demand that the Americans pull their missiles out of Turkey.

In the presence of the Presidium, Khrushchev dictated the new letter. As polished up afterward by aides, it was much calmer and more formal than his missive of the twenty-sixth: "We are willing to remove from Cuba the means [weapons] you regard as offensive." The United States "will remove its analogous means from Turkey." The Soviet government "gives a solemn pledge . . . not to invade Turkey," while the U.S. government "will make a similar statement in the Security Council regarding Cuba." Both sides would send representatives to New York with "comprehensive instructions in order that an agreement may be reached more quickly."[134] Since previous letters had taken so long to reach Washington, this one would be broadcast over Radio Moscow.

Why this second letter? "If we could achieve additionally the liquidation of the bases in Turkey," he told the Presidium, "we would win," and he also thought the Americans had broached such a deal themselves. Two journalists with close Kennedy connections, Frank Holeman and Charles Bartlett, had seemed to raise Turkish missiles in conversations with Bolshakov on October 23, Walter Lippmann suggested a Cuban-Turkish swap in a column published on October 25, and another American newsman conveyed the same impression in conversations with KGB agents whose report reached Moscow by October 27.[135] Although Khrushchev had added a new condition, the fact that his letter was made public (complete with his first public admission that Moscow had sent missiles to Cuba) confirmed that he was seeking a settlement. According to Troyanovsky, Khrushchev thought the Americans would reject his October 26 letter as too vague. "It never occurred to anyone," Troyanovsky later wrote, "that publicizing the Turkish aspect of the deal would create additional difficulties for the White House."[136]

"Difficulties" is putting it mildly. When Khrushchev's latest missive arrived on Saturday morning, Kennedy and his advisers were stunned. Khrushchev's October 26 message hadn't been a real offer, McNamara complained. It was "12 pages of fluff. That's no contract. You couldn't sign that and say we know what we signed." But "before we get the damn thing read, the whole deal changed—*completely* changed."[137]

Again, Khrushchev had failed to anticipate the danger: that making the new offer public virtually guaranteed it would be rejected, that Washington would see it as evidence of bad faith, and might even take military action. Luckily for Khrushchev, while most members of the ExComm were outraged, the president was tempted. The Turkish missiles had never been a high priority for Washington in the first place, and Kennedy had thought of removing them himself.[138] "It seems to me," he now said, "we ought to—to be reasonable. . . . We're going to have to take our weapons out of Turkey."[139] Still, for the time being, he chose to ignore Khrushchev's second offer and to reply instead to his first: If the Soviets would remove "all weapons systems in Cuba capable of offensive use," then, after adequate UN verification, the United States would "remove promptly the quarantine measures now in effect" and "give assurances against an invasion of Cuba."[140]

The president's reply was dispatched at about 8:00 P.M. Saturday, and delivered to the Soviet Foreign Ministry around 10:30 on Sunday morning. By then three developments had altered Khrushchev's mood yet again. On the morning of the twenty-seventh, an Alaska-based U-2 on a "routine air-sampling mission" strayed into Soviet airspace over the Chukotka Peninsula, prompting both Soviet interceptors and American fighters to scramble toward the Bering Sea. Fortunately the plane managed to leave Soviet airspace without being fired on. The territory itself (which was the subject of Soviet ethnic jokes at the expense of the native peoples who inhabit it) was so strategically insignificant that even Khrushchev concluded the incursion was a mistake. Even so, the incident was unnerving.[141]

The second incident was more than that. Around noon on October 27 a U-2 was shot down over Cuba; its pilot, Major Rudolf Anderson, was killed. The previous day Castro had ordered his troops to fire at any plane entering Cuban airspace, but having no surface-to-air missiles and only limited radar, the Cubans failed to hit anything on the morning of the twenty-seventh. Lieutenant General Stepan Grechko, Soviet air defense commander on Cuba, knew General Pliyev had put Soviet surface-to-air missiles on full alert and had asked Moscow for permission to shoot down American planes threatening Soviet installations. Moscow had yet to reply when Major Anderson's U-2 appeared. Convinced that the battle was about to begin, Grechko or someone else in his command gave the order to fire.[142]

News of the shoot-down shocked both Washington and Moscow. Support for retaliation was strong at the White House, but Kennedy vetoed any for the time being. Khrushchev feared the same sort of scenario McNamara was sketching in Washington: "We're going to send surveillance aircraft in tomorrow. Those are going to be fired on without question. We're going to respond. You can't do this very long. . . . So we must be prepared to attack Cuba—quickly. . . . If we do this, and leave those missiles in Turkey, the Soviet Union may, and I think probably will, attack the Turkish missiles. . . . We cannot allow a Soviet attack on the Jupiter missiles in Turkey without a military response by NATO."[143]

It was at this moment, Khrushchev later told his son, that he knew "deep down" that the missiles had to be removed. If a military officer could decide to fire a surface-to-air missile, Troyanovsky remarked later, then "in a situation when everybody was at the end of his tether, one spark could trigger an explosion." The first explosion occurred when Malinovsky explained that lacking time to consult with their commanders, Soviet antiaircraft officers had decided to be guided by Fidel Castro's instructions to his troops. "Whose army is our general in?" Khrushchev bellowed. "The Soviet or the Cuban army? If he's in the Soviet army then why does he follow someone else's orders?"[144]

The event that shook Khrushchev most of all involved Fidel Castro himself. Until October 26, Castro hoped his just cause would prevail. That evening he became convinced an American invasion loomed within twenty-four to seventy-two hours. At about 2:00 A.M. on the twenty-seventh he arrived at Ambassador Alekseyev's apartment. After consuming a substantial amount of sausages and beer, Fidel spent the rest of the night drafting an urgent message to Khrushchev. He dictated at least ten versions to Alekseyev, who, although not a professional interpreter, translated the text himself. "I'd write it and dictate it, and then I'd revise it again," Castro later recalled. "I'd say, for example, 'Delete this word, add this, change that.' This was in the wee hours of the morning of the 27th. . . . You have to understand that on the night of the 26th we saw no possible solution. We couldn't see a way out."[145]

"At the beginning," Alekseyev recollected, "I couldn't understand what he meant by his complicated phrases." Was Castro really saying that the USSR should launch a preemptive nuclear strike against the United States? "No," Castro replied, "I don't want to say that directly, but under certain circumstances, we must not wait to experience the perfidy of the imperialists, letting them initiate the first strike and deciding that Cuba should be wiped off the face of the earth."[146]

What Castro wanted to get across to Khrushchev, he later explained, was that an American attack was coming. Soviet forces would presumably respond with nuclear weapons, triggering a U.S. nuclear retaliation in return. But Khrushchev should not let the Americans strike first the way Hitler had in 1941. "If [all] this happens," Castro wanted to say, "there shouldn't be any hesitation. We should not allow for a repetition of the events of the Second World War." That was why "I dared to write a letter to Nikita, a letter aimed at encouraging him. That was my intention. The aim was to strengthen him morally, because I knew that he had to be suffering greatly, intensely. I thought I knew him well."[147]

The message Castro finally sent read this way: "If . . . the imperialists invade Cuba with the goal of occupying it, the danger that aggressive policy poses for humanity is so great that following that event the Soviet Union must never allow circumstances in which the imperialists could launch the first nuclear strike against it." Instead that would be "the moment to eliminate such danger forever through an act of clear legitimate defense, however harsh and terrible the solution would be, for there is no other."[148]

Alekseyev broke away from Fidel long enough to alert Moscow that a Castro warning was coming; it arrived there at 1:10 A.M. on the twenty-eighth. Troyanovsky, who was spending his nights in the Central Committee building on Staraya Ploshchad', got the telegram, called Khrushchev at home, and read him Castro's text. Khrushchev interrupted him several times, asking him to repeat key passages.[149]

Instead of "encouraging" Khrushchev, Castro's letter appalled him. Khrushchev thought the Cuban leader was urging that "we immediately deliver a nuclear missile strike against the United States." This showed that "Fidel totally failed to understand our purpose," which was not to attack the United States "but to keep the United States from attacking Cuba."[150]

One last development set the stage for Sunday's climax: another long meeting between Robert Kennedy and Ambassador Dobrynin on Saturday evening. The president wanted to reinforce his latest letter to Khrushchev. His brother was to threaten military action if the missiles were not withdrawn and to offer to remove the Turkish missiles. There could be no public reference to Turkey (lest it seem to Ankara and the rest of NATO that the United States had sold out the Turks under pressure from Moscow), but the president would get the missiles out once the Cuban crisis was resolved.[151]

Dobrynin arrived at the Justice Department at 7:45 P.M. According to the cable he sent to Moscow later that night, the president's brother was "extremely agitated, the first time I had ever seen him in such a condition." (Later Khrushchev told his son that "we didn't look much better.") Bobby Kennedy skipped further recriminations and arguments. He stressed one theme: "Time is running out. We mustn't miss our chance."

The attorney general cited the downed U-2. The American military were demanding that reconnaissance flights continue, and the next time fire would be answered with fire. The U.S. government was prepared to bomb the missile sites too, but if so, a terrible chain reaction might end in nuclear war. The Americans didn't want that and assumed the Soviets didn't either. But there were "hotheads among the generals, and in other places as well, who were spoiling for a fight." The solution was an agreement based on Khrushchev's October 26 letter and Kennedy's reply. Although Dobrynin still hadn't seen the full text of Khrushchev's October 27 message and had no specific instruction to press the Turkish issue, he took it upon himself to ask, "What about Turkey?" If that were the only obstacle to an agreement, Bobby Kennedy replied, then the president was prepared to act. That would take some months to arrange, however, and the agreement must be kept strictly secret. Only two or three people in Washington besides the Kennedys would know about it.

Having held out this carrot, the attorney general waved a stick. He needed Khrushchev's answer the very next day. He was not issuing an ultimatum but a "request." The president "hoped that the head of the Soviet government would understand what he meant." Kennedy specifically asked that Khrushchev not send another long, rambling letter that "might drag this out." He gave Dobrynin his direct telephone number at the White House.[152]

ON SUNDAY, OCTOBER 28, Khrushchev awoke to learn about the downing of the U-2 over Cuba. Kennedy's October 27 letter also arrived overnight. The Presidium convened at noon at the same Novo-Ogaryovo dacha outside Moscow where almost three decades later Mikhail Gorbachev and leaders of Soviet republics tried to save the USSR by cobbling together a new federal treaty. Khrushchev occasionally used Novo-Ogaryovo to receive foreigners or for leisurely Presidium gatherings. But this day's atmosphere was "highly electric," Troyanovsky recalled. Sitting around a long table in the large dining hall, all present were "on edge from the outset." Khrushchev was virtually the only one who spoke, except for occasional remarks by Mikoyan and Gromyko. The others "preferred to remain silent," Troyanovsky remembered, "as if to say to Khrushchev, 'You got us into this, now you get us out.'"[153]

Khrushchev began by recalling one of Lenin's greatest retreats, the March 1918 Brest-Litovsk agreement in which the Bolsheviks abandoned their western borderlands and more as the price for peace with the Germans. "Our interests dictated that decision—we had to save Soviet power. Now we find ourselves face to face with the danger of war and of nuclear catastrophe. . . . In order to save the world we must retreat. I called you together to consult and debate whether you are in agreement with this kind of decision."[154]

Before considering (or, rather, adopting without really considering)

Khrushchev's proposal, the Presidium took up instructions to General Pliyev. The previous morning Pliyev had signaled his determination to "employ all available means of air defense" in the event of an American attack, and Malinovsky, and Khrushchev too, had at first approved. But later that day, about the same time Khrushchev's new message was read over Moscow Radio, Pliyev had been "forbidden" to mount nuclear warheads on tactical missiles or planes "without authorization from Moscow." Now, on the twenty-eighth, the Presidium decided to let Pliyev fight back if attacked, without altering the previous order not to use tactical atomic weapons.[155]

At this point Khrushchev asked Troyanovsky to read aloud Kennedy's letter of the twenty-seventh, copies of which were in folders on the white tablecloth in front of each Presidium member. The fact that Kennedy's name at the end wasn't preceded by the usual "Sincerely" seemed an ominous sign. When Troyanovsky finished, Khrushchev asked for reactions. Before there could be any, Troyanovsky was called to the phone; the Foreign Ministry was transmitting Dobrynin's report on his climactic meeting with Robert Kennedy. Troyanovsky summarized the conversation; when he finished, he was asked to repeat his account. "The entire tenor" of Robert Kennedy's words, Troyanovsky later wrote, made it clear that "the time of reckoning had arrived." After that "it didn't take long to decide to accept President Kennedy's conditions." One more piece of "intelligence" made it imperative to inform Kennedy of Khrushchev's concession as fast as possible. The president was apparently scheduled to give another televised speech at 5:00 P.M., Moscow time. The Presidium assumed he would announce an air strike or an invasion of Cuba. As it turned out, the program was a rerun of the president's October 22 speech.[156]

Once again Khrushchev summoned a stenographer: "Dear Mr. President: I have received your message of October 27. I express my satisfaction and thank you for the sense of proportion you have displayed. . . . " Khrushchev accepted Kennedy's terms (without mentioning Turkey, as requested). The Soviet government had "given a new order to dismantle the arms which you described as offensive, and to crate and return them to the USSR."[157]

After Khrushchev's dictation was "brought up to the mark" (as those who did the polishing put it), Mikhail Smirnovsky, head of the Foreign Ministry's American desk, was directed to deliver the letter to the American Embassy, while the Central Committee secretary Leonid Ilychev carried it to Moscow Radio before five o'clock. Smirnovsky's limousine was delayed by demonstrators blocking the embassy and shouting, "Hands off Cuba." Ilychev made it to Radio Moscow on time, but the announcer who was to read it over the air wanted time to rehearse. Ilychev ordered him to broadcast it immediately.[158]

Besides the public letter, Khrushchev sent a secret message to Robert Kennedy, alerting him that Moscow's positive response would soon be heard over the radio. Fidel Castro was also informed, in a way that was sure to enrage him, that the fate of his island had been decided without his advice or consent. There was no need to copy Khrushchev's latest letter to Havana because, he wrote to Castro, "you surely know the text which is now being broadcast over the radio." Instead Khrushchev urged his fiery Cuban friend "not to be carried away by sentiment." Only yesterday the Americans had tried to provoke Cuba with overflights and "you shot down one of these." Why Khrushchev insisted on blaming the Cubans for what he knew Soviet forces had done isn't clear.

Meanwhile, the Khrushchev family had driven from the Lenin Hills to their Moscow River dacha. The dacha was only ten minutes from Novo-Ogaryovo, but it seemed an eternity away. While the stoic Nina Petrovna watched television, Sergei wandered aimlessly around the large house. When the text of his father's message to Kennedy finally came over the radio, in the dulcet tones of Yuri Levitan, who had brought his countrymen news of every great event of his time going back to the war, it sounded to Sergei like a "shameful retreat."[159]

Back at Novo-Ogaryovo, Khrushchev and his colleagues listened to the Moscow Radio broadcast too. After that he suggested they all go to the theater. Troyanovsky checked the papers to see what was playing; Khrushchev chose a touring troupe from Bulgaria. He picked up his family at the dacha, drove back to the Lenin Hills, where he changed his shirt, and headed downtown. Afterward he had second thoughts about not mentioning Turkish missiles in his public letter to Kennedy. Late that night he prepared yet another secret message to the president, insisting that his earlier public letter assumed that "you had agreed to resolve the matter of your missile bases in Turkey, consistent with what I had said in my message of October 27 and what you stated through Robert Kennedy in his meeting with Ambassador Dobrynin on the same day."[160]

The Russian text of this latest message was dispatched to the Soviet Embassy in Washington at 5:15 A.M. on October 29. Khrushchev was trying to put the president's Turkish concessions on the record so as to be able to rebut charges of caving in to the imperialists. But when Dobrynin presented this new missive to Robert Kennedy, the president's brother confirmed the Turkish part of the deal orally but refused to accept the letter.[161]

SATURDAY NIGHT was the most tense yet in Washington. Unless Khrushchev yielded, an American attack on Cuba seemed imminent. "Black Saturday," the president's men called it, some wondering whether they'd still be alive a week hence. Dobrynin and his aides were equally anxious; according to their information, American bombing of Cuba was slated to begin on October 29 or 30 at the latest.[162]

The ExComm was scheduled to meet at 10:00 A.M. on Sunday. Kennedy was in bed reading the *New York Times* when word came that Radio Moscow would have an important announcement. At 9:00 A.M. Khrushchev's letter started coming over the air. "Dismantle . . . crate and return." By noon the president had drafted a reply welcoming Khrushchev's "important contribution to peace."[163]

The crisis was over. Difficult negotiations about implementing the settlement lay ahead, as did arguments about who had won and who lost. For the world at large this was all anticlimax. But not for Khrushchev. On October 28 he felt a sense of satisfaction. It took time for the whole truth to sink in and contribute to his final unraveling.

CHAPTER TWENTY

The Unraveling: 1962–1964

NO SOONER HAD Khrushchev agreed to pull Soviet missiles out of Cuba than Moscow hailed his retreat as a triumph. The Soviet government's "calm and wisdom" saved the world from a "nuclear catastrophe," boasted *Pravda* on October 30. Khrushchev hailed his own victory in a long, impassioned speech to the Supreme Soviet on December 12. It had proved possible "to prevent the invasion" and to "overcome a crisis that threatened general thermonuclear war." The United States had pledged "before the whole world" that it would not attack Cuba. The Soviet Union and the "forces of peace and socialism" had "imposed peace [Prolonged applause]." "Reason triumphed," and "the cause of peace and security of nations won [Stormy applause]."[1]

Fyodor Burlatsky helped edit Khrushchev's speech and watched him deliver it. "His face truly shone with happiness. It was not the face of a man who was suffering pangs of conscience or a feeling of guilt. . . . No, it was the face of . . . a man who had saved the world." But Burlatsky also recalled a section that Khrushchev originally dictated but then toned down, words that rebuffed Chinese charges that his Cuban policy amounted to "adventurism" followed by "capitulationism." Said Burlatsky: "It was clear that their criticism had cut him to the quick. He was indignant, insulted and irritated."[2]

If Khrushchev was so irritated when he dictated the speech, was he really so pleased when he delivered it? Although British Ambassador Sir

Frank Roberts found him looking "tired and preoccupied" on November 12, Khrushchev "warmed up into his usual good form" like a "battery recharging himself." But toward the end of a long, spirited conversation, he grumbled that "there were still idiots on both sides who did not understand" the Cuban compromise.[3] At a November 23 Central Committee plenum, his defensiveness was even more graphic: "It was not necessary to act [in Cuba] like the czarist officer who farted at the ball and then shot himself." All the Chinese had done for Cuba was to have their diplomats in Havana give blood—"What demagogic and cheap assistance!" declared Khrushchev—whereas Soviet "antiaircraft guns shot twice and brought down an American U-2 plane. What a shot! And in return we received a pledge not to invade Cuba. Not bad!"[4] Then at a Presidium meeting on December 3 he accused Castro of forcing him to yield too soon: "Fidel Castro openly advised us to use nuclear weapons, but now he retreats and smears us." Moreover, Colonel General Ivanov, who planned Operation Anadyr, was fired, while the Presidium ordered an investigation of military intelligence for its role in the crisis.[5]

According to Dobrynin, the Soviet leadership took the Cuban outcome as "a blow to its prestige bordering on humiliation."[6] Khrushchev did too, recalled his Kremlin colleague Pyotr Demichev. "He made a show of having been brave, but we could tell by his behavior, especially by his irritability, that he felt it had been a defeat."[7]

The problem wasn't just that Khrushchev had yielded; it was what happened afterward. Kennedy's insistence on keeping the Turkish missile deal secret meant Khrushchev couldn't point to an American concession matching his own. Nor did Kennedy ever formalize in writing his pledge not to invade Cuba, citing Castro's refusal to allow on-site inspections in Cuba as an excuse.[8] In addition, the Americans insisted that the obsolete Il-28 bombers be removed from Cuba along with Soviet missiles. To Khrushchev and Castro this looked like a last-minute upping of the ante, which in fact it was, but it was the price Khrushchev had to pay for refusing to call a missile a missile, for referring to them during the crisis as "those weapons you regard as offensive." Meanwhile, in Havana, Castro was in a rage: "Son of a bitch . . . bastard . . . asshole. . . . *No cojones* [balls]. *Maricón* [homosexual]." Thus Castro's opinion, expressed privately on October 28, of the man who had saved the world.[9]

Khrushchev's short telegram to Castro on the twenty-eighth, the one accusing the Cubans of shooting down the American U-2, didn't exactly mollify Havana. Nor did a much longer letter two days later. To the Cubans' charge that he had failed to consult them, Khrushchev countered that he had—in the process of weighing Castro's alarmist cable of the night of October 26–27.[10] But Fidel wasn't buying that. He denied that he had been consulted and that he had proposed a nuclear first strike. He also demanded five preconditions for a settlement (including a halt to the American economic blockade, to subversion of Cuba, and to all overflights and naval incursions, as well as U.S. departure from Guantánamo Bay) that far exceeded what Khrushchev had agreed to.[11]

The fact that Chinese and Cuban criticism coincided was particularly painful to Khrushchev. Although the Chinese were more important ideologically and geopolitically, Khrushchev had practically written them off as irredeemable adversaries, whereas he had regarded Castro as a ward of the revolution, even as a sort of surrogate son. However, now this "son" regarded him as "a traitor" (to use Sergei Khrushchev's term), an outcome hard to take given Khrushchev's difficult relations with his own father and first son. Castro's rejection, according to Sergei, "wounded Father to the depths of his soul."[12]

Khrushchev decided to send a special emissary to Havana. Mikoyan was the obvious choice, but his wife of forty years, Ashkhen, was dying. Although trained to put cause ahead of family, Mikoyan hesitated. Khrushchev insisted it was too late to help Mikoyan's wife and that Mikoyan was badly needed in Havana. "Anastas," said Khrushchev, "if the worst comes to pass, we'll take care of everything. You don't need to worry."[13]

The Cubans greeted Mikoyan coldly, both at the airport and when talks began on November 3. Before negotiations could get very far, Mrs. Mikoyan died. Khrushchev's telegram left it up to Mikoyan whether to return for the funeral. He opted to stay and sent his son, Sergo, who had accompanied him to Havana, home instead.[14] This extraordinary act deeply touched Castro, with the result that the talks went more easily than expected for a while, but it had a different effect on Khrushchev. According to Sergo Mikoyan, Khrushchev had promised to attend the funeral. When he didn't appear at the wake, the Mikoyan family turned to Nina Petrovna. She urged delaying the departure for the cemetery, but her husband didn't show up for the burial either. The next time Khrushchev saw Sergo, he remarked that he didn't like funerals. "After all," he added coolly, "it's not like going to a wedding, is it?"[15]

Whatever Khrushchev's reason, Troyanovsky recalled that the episode "left a bitter taste in the mouth." When Anastas Mikoyan returned to Moscow, Khrushchev praised his conduct of the Cuban negotiations. "Only his oxlike stubbornness could have succeeded," Khrushchev told Sergo. "If I'd been there, I would have soon slammed the door (on

Castro] and flown home." But Khrushchev later told Castro: "I trust [Mikoyan] least of all. He's a shrewd fox from the east; you can't count on him. In both 1953 when we arrested Beria, and in 1957 with the 'anti-party group,' I was more nervous about Mikoyan's position than anyone else's."[16] Mikoyan never reproached Khrushchev for not bidding farewell to his wife, but he never forgave him either.[17]

All told, Mikoyan spent twenty-two days in Cuba. Among other things he endured tirades from Fidel, several days cooling his heels in Havana while Castro claimed to be ill, and an anniversary of the Bolshevik Revolution dinner at which Soviet military men neglected to toast Castro and the head of Cuban military intelligence toasted Stalin. This last sin made Khrushchev so angry that he ordered Mikoyan to interrogate all Soviet officers who had been present at the dinner, and he considered ending all aid to Cuba, "Either they will cooperate," Khrushchev told the Presidium on November 16, "or we will recall our personnel." It took sixteen days to get Castro to agree to removing the Il-28s, and he never did accept UN inspection, with the result that American planes overflew missile-toting Soviet ships instead. The fact that Washington refused to talk directly to Havana until all the details were settled with the Soviets further sharpened Castro's wrath.[18]

American crowing didn't help either. Kennedy was careful not to claim victory in public, and more than a few, especially in the military, regarded the failure to liquidate Cuban communism as a defeat. But the media made up for the president's modesty (for example, in a two-hour CBS News special that labeled the outcome as "a humiliating defeat for Soviet policy"), and Kennedy and his men were more assertive in "private" conversations that, with a little White House help, inevitably leaked. In one such discussion with friends Kennedy referred to the same part of Khrushchev's anatomy that had come to Castro's mind on October 28. "I cut his balls off," said the president.[19]

KHRUSHCHEV'S LAST two years in power were a time of not so quiet desperation. After the collapse of his Cuban adventure, he tried to address other foreign problems the solutions to which had eluded him, but without the positive momentum that a Cuban triumph would have provided. His diplomacy produced some successes in the summer of 1963, but much of his energy and imagination were gone. Khrushchev had learned at last that bluff and bluster didn't pay, but they had been his main weapons, and without them, he was lost.[20]

Domestic issues also awaited action. Splitting the Communist party in two was Khrushchev's most radical attempt yet to jump-start Soviet agriculture, but the move outraged party officials without increasing the harvest. More than anything else, his failure to energize agriculture left Khrushchev puzzled, frustrated, and angry, still flailing about for solutions, looking for anyone but himself to blame.

An anti-Stalin offensive in culture also seemed about to begin in October 1962. Again Khrushchev retreated, taking out his wrath on liberal writers and artists and, in the process, wounding himself. His public meetings with intellectuals had always been tense and awkward. Now they were raucously tumultuous. On three occasions in the winter and spring of 1962–1963, he seemed to come apart at the seams. Later, after recovering his equilibrium, he made new gestures to Tvardovsky and other liberals, but he never fully embraced them. As a result, the liberal intelligentsia joined the ranks of those glad to see him go.

Khrushchev's reformist impulses weren't finished. Another commission to investigate Stalin's crimes, formed in 1961 under Presidium member Nikolai Shvernik, reported to the party leadership in February 1963, but its scathing conclusions (among them, that all leaders purged from the late 1930s on were entirely innocent) led to no further action.[21] Khrushchev flirted with radical economic reforms and prepared a new Soviet constitution that pointed toward the sorts of changes Gorbachev later adopted, but these projects stalled as well. With almost everyone against him, Khrushchev spent less and less time in Moscow, fleeing to the provinces and to the warm glow of admiration abroad. But his travels too were barren of results and sometimes, as in the case of his 1964 trip to Egypt, added to the case against him.

By 1962 the most influential of Khrushchev's colleagues were his own men, longtime associates he had promoted to high office, protégés who had rallied to his side in 1957. Yet as his miseries multiplied, he withdrew into an inner circle of personal aides and advisers, avoiding his colleagues, acting without informing them, and berating them in public and private for what they regarded as *his* sins.

KHRUSHCHEV TRIED to parlay the Cuban settlement into talks with the United States on a broad range of issues. His letters to Kennedy on October 27, 28, and 30 proposed talks on a nuclear test ban treaty, liquidating military bases, even "general and complete disarmament." "The German question," he suddenly assured the president, was practically solved.

Khrushchev urged a quick summit; an addendum to his October 30 letter pressed Kennedy "to pick up from the questions listed by me those which are ripe" and then "to meet, maybe at the U.N. or maybe at a specially arranged meeting."[22] Two days after approaching the brink, and several weeks before the crisis was fully settled, Khrushchev was at last ready for the relationship that Kennedy had offered at the Vienna summit but that he, Khrushchev, had spurned. According to Troyanovsky, his boss's doubts about the president's "will and intellect" had now "completely evaporated." Instead of "bullying" him, he would try to persuade him.[23]

On October 30, Khrushchev's speechwriter and adviser, *Pravda* foreign editor Yuri Zhukov, raced down to Washington from Andover, Massachusetts, where he had been attending a Ford Foundation session on U.S.-Soviet relations. In quick succession he talked with Thompson, Harriman, Salinger, and others known to be close to the president. To Thompson he proposed a summit within a month to discuss disarmament, a test ban, and a NATO–Warsaw Treaty nonaggression pact, a message Deputy Foreign Minister Kuznetsov repeated to Stevenson.[24] When Mikoyan stopped in Washington on his way home from Cuba, he told Kennedy that they "should proceed to a point-by-point negotiation of all outstanding questions" and that Moscow was awaiting "constructive proposals from the U.S." on Berlin.[25] According to Zhukov, Khrushchev needed to show the Chinese that Cuban concessions could lead to agreements with Washington. The Soviet leader virtually said so himself to *Saturday Review* editor Norman Cousins in December. "The Chinese say I was scared," admitted Khrushchev, whose elegant attire (dark blue suit, white silk shirt, gray tie with small jewel stickpin, and French cuffs with large gold links) was marred only by a flash of long-sleeved winter underwear showing through the break in his cuffs. "Of course I was scared. It would have been insane not to be scared." But now that being scared had "helped avert [the] insanity" of nuclear war, there was "one thing the President and I should do right away"—namely, conclude a test ban treaty and work on preventing nuclear proliferation.

Cousins, who had seen Kennedy before departing for Moscow, told Khrushchev that JFK was "genuinely seeking an agreement to end testing."[26] Khrushchev tested Kennedy's commitment five days later by meeting him partway on the key issue of on-site inspections. Until then the Soviets had rejected any inspections as espionage, while the Americans insisted on a dozen a year, or at a minimum eight to ten. According to Khrushchev, American negotiator Arthur Dean told Kuznetsov on October 30 that Washington would accept as few as three or four. If so, he was prepared to accept two or three inspections, in which case it should be possible to wrap up a treaty by the end of the year.[27]

This was the high point of Khrushchev's hope for a post-Cuban crisis détente, but it wasn't all that high, and it didn't last long. For the next two months Kennedy directed U.S. officials to "talk only about Cuba and the removal of offensive weapons," to make "no response" to broader Soviet overtures "until the Cuban situation has been resolved."[28] The president barely mentioned Khrushchev's broader agenda in his letters of November 3 and 6 and not at all on November 15. Only on December 14 did he return to the subject, but in a perfunctory way, not so innocently inquiring "what you think about the position of the people in Peking" on the test ban issue and quarreling with Khrushchev's view that a Berlin agreement was nearly at hand.[29] On December 28 the president quashed Khrushchev's test ban hopes by informing him that the United States continued to insist on eight to ten on-site inspections; Khrushchev's sense of the Dean-Kuznetsov conversation must have been based on a misunderstanding.[30]

Khrushchev was infuriated. He broke off the test ban talks in February, and he was still steaming in late March, when Dobrynin delivered a rude message to Robert Kennedy: Instead of addressing larger U.S-Soviet issues, the president was "putting pressure on us." Instead of standing up to "aggressive circles" in Washington, Kennedy demanded Soviet concessions to "suit the bad mood of a senator [Barry Goldwater] from . . . Arizona." During his first two years in office, when he was "learning the ropes," Kennedy couldn't decide key questions. Now "he cannot decide them because he might otherwise, we are told, lose the election campaign." Robert Kennedy rejected Khrushchev's message as insulting; he thought Dobrynin "was obviously embarrassed" to be delivering it.[31]

In mid-March, Khrushchev struck foreign diplomats as "essentially pro forma" in talks. At a reception for the visiting Finnish prime minister, he "displayed little of his normal vivacity" and read speeches in a "listless, monotonous voice." At a conference he appeared "dispirited," with "the air of a man overwhelmed by his burdens."[32]

Even Pitsunda didn't altogether revive him. When Norman Cousins visited there in April, pursuing his campaign for a test ban, he found his host "weighted down, even withdrawn." At times he appeared his usual hospitable self, greeting Cousins in the driveway wearing a green and tan cape and a large gray unblocked fedora, showing him around the grounds, challenging his guest to a energetic game of badminton, and demonstrating his "disappearing act" (in which he covered himself with a huge bear coat from which he suddenly reemerged with a loud "Boo!") for Cousins's young daughters. But later he recounted how he got his colleagues to accept three test ban inspections only to have the Americans disdain his concession. "Back came the American rejection," said Khrushchev. "They now wanted neither three inspections nor even six. They wanted eight. And so once again I was made to look foolish. But I can tell you this: it won't happen again."[33]

Of course Khrushchev's explanation was too simple. Even after the Cuban debacle his cowed colleagues didn't require much persuasion, and his anger at the Americans was meant to make them feel guilty. But his defensiveness was real. Speaking in East Germany in January, he admitted that "some may say that time seems to have been wasted, that the socialist countries have gained nothing by posing the question of a German peace treaty so sharply." Not to mention "some people who claim that Cuba and the Soviet Union suffered a defeat in the Caribbean conflict."[34] As usual, Khrushchev had answers, but the fact that he had to provide them at all is revealing. Later, when he addressed his "electoral constituents" in Moscow, he thanked them for "having gathered here, if I might put it this way, to strengthen my morale."[35]

In March 1963 the Defense Council met in expanded session outside Moscow to acquaint high-ranking military-industrial personnel with two intercontinental missile programs vying to become the backbone of Soviet deterrence forces.[36] As Khrushchev strolled through the exhibition halls, chatting with military commanders and rocket designers, he seemed obsessed with how far and how fast technology had developed under his leadership. It was as if "he couldn't stop talking," recalled his son. "Those present listened attentively, even though many had heard it all several times before."

For the assembled generals and engineers, this was a chance to lobby the boss. Marshal Grechko pushed for tactical nuclear weapons (the Americans had an abundance, he complained, but Soviet forces practically none), moving closer to Khrushchev to press his point. "Get back a couple of steps, will you?" growled Khrushchev, who didn't like having to look up at Grechko. "And don't try to convince me, because I have no money. We don't have enough under the mattress for everything." Malinovsky complained that since the birthrate had gone down during the war, and with draft deferments too readily available, the armed forces weren't getting enough soldiers. Grechko urged extending obligatory military service from two to three years in the army and three to four in the navy.

"Who's serving whom?" Khrushchev snapped, glaring at Malinovsky and Grechko. "The army, the people? Or the people, the army? Has it ever occurred to you how many useful things are produced by young men during the third year they *don't* spend in the army?" Under Tsar Nicholas I soldiers had served twenty-five years. Was that Marshal Grechko's ideal?

Grechko tried to smile. Malinovsky stared gloomily at the floor. "You just don't understand," Khrushchev barked at Grechko. "If you did, you wouldn't ask such a stupid question. It's not easy to think up something like that: We spend billions training needed specialists, and all you want to do is grab them away, and make them goosestep."

By this time sweat was pouring from Khrushchev's face. Grechko had complained that university reserve officer training programs were turning out inferior personnel and suggested drafting such students instead. If everyone were drafted, Khrushchev retorted, there would be no one left to defend. Drafting students who would otherwise become key economic specialists would be "impermissible squandering of state resources, sheer wasting of them." It would be—Khrushchev used the dreaded Stalinist accusation from the 1930's—"wrecking."

Having threatened his leading generals, Khrushchev now proceeded to appall them. As if thinking aloud, he remarked that the Soviet Union hardly needed a mass army anymore, just a few rockets, a small set of forces to guard them, and, beyond that, a people's militia, living at home, training from time to time, and serving only in a war that Khrushchev didn't expect anyway. These ideas weren't new, but never before had he put them all together and flung them in the face of the men who stood to lose most if his schemes were carried out. In the long run, Khrushchev may have been right; he was anticipating deep cuts in Russian armed forces carried out by Gorbachev and Yeltsin. But in March 1963 the cold war was still on. Either he didn't realize the effect of his words on a crucial audience, or he didn't care.[37]

KHRUSHCHEV'S PLAN for dividing the party was endorsed unanimously by the Central Committee in November 1962. Central Committee culture tsar Dmitri Polikarpov returned from the plenum in dismay because the division between industry and agriculture made no provision for ideology, education, and culture. "You know," a colleague complained bitterly, "if this is his level of competence, then you and I could run this economy no worse than Nikita does."[38] Prowling the corridors during the three days of the plenum, journalist Nikolai Barsukov heard "not one good word about the new reorganization, only bewilderment and outright rejection." Yet when the voting started, it was "adopted unanimously" and with "stormy applause."[39]

While most of Khrushchev's colleagues kept their doubts to themselves, Byelorussian party boss Kirill Mazurov cornered him at the Byelovezhsky Forest retreat, the same sanatorium at which the leaders of Russia, Ukraine, and Byelorussia were to agree to disband the USSR in 1991. When Mazurov reminded his guest that the great Lenin himself had insisted on party unity, Khrushchev "erupted." Actually, the great Lenin's views weren't a problem; before long *Pravda* unearthed a "newly discovered" Lenin article that placed a higher priority on economic management than on the party's political and ideological tasks.[40] But to have a colleague talk back was almost intolerable. "We quarreled so badly," Mazurov recalled, "that he called for his car, got into it, and left. The next morning Kozlov called me from Moscow and said, 'Listen, what the hell did you do? Nikita just called and told me to find someone else for your job.'"[41]

Mazurov was spared, but he could no longer be counted on, and neither could the province party bosses who had supported Khrushchev against the "antiparty group." The division of the party deprived them of sole control of areas the size of many nation-states. After Khrushchev's reform they would answer for only agriculture or industry and might lose their Central Committee seats at the next party congress. Instead of being judged and rewarded for political skill and ideological purity, at which they were specialists par excellence, their test would be economic efficiency, which all too often eluded them. Khrushchev's reform didn't exactly create a two-party system, but to many apparatchiks it seemed to move in that direction. No wonder the Central Committee Secretariat, which Khrushchev chaired, found ways to thwart his plan, with the result that a full one-third of province party committees never implemented it before his ouster.[42]

Was Khrushchev deliberately trying to undermine the existing party apparatus so as to build a new political base? Mikhail Gorbachev, who had mixed success of his own in this area, thinks so.[43] But surely Khrushchev's primary aim was to energize the economy, especially agriculture, by "professionalizing" the party functionaries who supervised it. The harvest in 1962 turned out better than in 1961,[44] but several months later he was again on the defensive, lashing out at so-called experts who "can't tell an ear from a snout."[45] The only positive result of splitting the party was to allow Khrushchev to blame party cadres all the more categorically, for now that the "ideal" system was supposedly in place, the continuing agricultural stagnation must be their fault.[46]

Nor was his obvious agitation confined to agriculture. Who *didn't* come in for a tongue-lashing in an April 1963 speech to industry and construction executives? Defense industry chief Dmitri Ustinov, whom Khrushchev had just replaced with a younger man "so we can shake him up as successfully as we shook up Comrade Ustinov" was lambasted, as were violators of public order and "swindlers, thieves, and all kinds of filth," who should be "squashed like bugs"; novelists and poets who "root around in the garbage can, dig out the garbage, and suck on it"; and writers, who "went abroad, saw panties for their wives in colors we do not have here, and started sighing: 'That's America for you, they make better panties than we do.' "

Khrushchev still believed in miracles, he told his April audience, like the way Yuzovka had resurrected its shattered coal mines after the First World War. All people needed was to be properly led. On this occasion, like several others in 1963, he hailed an East German documentary film titled *The Russian Miracle*: "You see barefoot people on the screen; even bast shoes are a luxury for them. They carry their rifles on a piece of rope; they have no uniforms. But our working class was marching . . . going into battle for the revolution. . . . And they won!"[47]

AS LATE AS November 1962 liberal writers and artists were still pushing the "thaw" forward. Their most spectacular gain was the publication that month of Solzhenitsyn's *One Day in the Life of Ivan Denisovich*. Khrushchev revealed his personal support for this step to the plenum that approved the party split.[48] But rather than start a sustained burst of glasnost, November marked a retreat. More "camp literature" poured into publishing houses, but conservatives, who had been waiting for an opportunity to turn Khrushchev against their intelligentsia foes, now pounced, cleverly exploiting his sour post-Cuba mood.

On Monday evening, November 26, 1962, an exhibit of avant-garde art opened in the Moscow studio of an art teacher named Eli Beliutin. Although formally closed to the public, it attracted several hundred invited guests, including Soviet cultural officials and Western correspondents, while hundreds more waited outside, hoping to get in. Three days later a similar exhibit was suddenly postponed before it could open in the

Yunost Hotel. Equally abruptly, the Beliutin studio exhibit was moved to the vast Manezh Exhibition Hall across from the Kremlin, where a large exhibit of traditional socialist realist works, marking "Thirty Years of Moscow Art," had been on view for nearly a month.[49]

Some unorthodox artists imagined their work was at last finding official approval. The painter Boris Zhutovsky and others worked through the night, hauling their canvases and sculpture to the Manezh gallery. The sculptor Ernst Neizvestny suspected a provocation since the works about to be prominently displayed had never enjoyed party approbation,[50] and in fact, the move to Manezh was a setup. The Artists' Union chief Vladimir Serov and Central Committee Secretary Leonid Ilychev supplied Khrushchev with mocking descriptions that unorthodox artists had allegedly used to ridicule him: "Ivan-the-fool on the throne," "corn-man," "loud mouth." Zhutovsky later overheard Serov crowing to a colleague, "How well we set it up! It all went perfectly!"[51]

Whatever they told Khrushchev, it convinced him to inspect the Manezh exhibit. Just before he arrived with a large suite, officials lined up the offending artists to greet him, placing people recognizable as Jews in the front row. As Khrushchev entered the hall and glanced at the paintings on the wall, his facial expression (captured on film) transmogrified from tired to tentative and unsure of himself to ill at ease to annoyed to enraged. The artists applauded Khrushchev, but among the first words he uttered were, "It's dog shit! . . . A donkey could smear better than this with his tail."[52] He shouted at a young artist, "You're a nice-looking lad, but how could you paint something like this? We should take down your pants and set you in a clump of nettles until you understand your mistakes. You should be ashamed. Are you a faggot [*pideras*] or a normal man? Do you want to go abroad? Go then; we'll take you as far as the border. . . . We have a right to send you out to cut trees until you've paid back the money the state has spent on you. The people and the government have taken a lot of trouble with you, and you pay them back with this shit."[53]

Khrushchev demanded, "Who's in charge here?" Beliutin was pushed forward, along with Neizvestny, a gruff, husky paratrooper before he turned sculptor. Neizvestny too must be a homosexual, Khrushchev shouted. "Nikita Sergeyevich," the burly sculptor shot back, after excusing himself to Minister of Culture Yekaterina Furtseva, "give me a girl right here and now and I'll show you what sort of homosexual I am."

That stopped even Khrushchev. At least for a moment. Until Neizvestny warned him that his aides were exploiting his own ignorance of art. "When I was a miner, they said I didn't understand," Khrushchev retorted. "When I was a political worker in the army, they said I didn't understand. When I was this and that, they said I didn't understand. Well, now I'm party leader and premier, and you mean to say I still don't understand? Who are you working for, anyway?"[54]

Fortunately for posterity (but not for Khrushchev's reputation), Manezh witnesses recorded his further artistic assessments as follows: "Dmitri Stepanovich Polyansky [fellow Presidium member] told me a couple of days ago that when his daughter got married, she was given a picture of what was supposed to be a lemon. It consisted of some messy yellow lines which looked, if you will excuse me, as though some child has done his business on the canvas when his mother was away and then spread it around with his hands.

"I don't like jazz. When I hear jazz, it's as if I had gas on the stomach. . . . Or take those new dances which are so fashionable now. Some of them are completely improper. You wiggle a certain section of the anatomy, if you'll pardon the expression. It's indecent. As Kogan once said to me, 'I've been married twenty years and never knew that this kind of activity is called the fox-trot. . . . '

"He can paint and sell these if he wants, but we don't need them. We are supposed to take these blotches with us into communism, are we?

"Who painted this picture? I want to talk with him. What's the good of a picture like this? To cover urinals with?

"The Dutch masters painted differently. You can look at their paintings through a magnifying glass and still admire them. But your painting just gives a person constipation, if you'll excuse the expression."[55]

AFTER KHRUSHCHEV'S Manezh tirade, several Stalinists were restored to prominent cultural posts, while conservatives demanded that all artists be herded into one monolithic union that would be easier for the authorities to police. But liberals fought back, with seventeen leading intellectuals (including two Nobel Prize scientists, the writers Ilya Ehrenburg, Kornei Chukovsky, and Konstantin Simonov, the composer Dmitri Shostakovich, and the film director Mikhail Romm) petitioning Khrushchev to "stop the swing in the representational arts to past methods which are alien to the whole spirit of our times."[56]

This was the situation on December 17, when four hundred guests arrived at the House of Receptions on the Lenin Hills not far from Khrushchev's residence. Liberal writers and artists hoped Khrushchev was reverting to his more benevolent self, and what they saw in the main corridor strengthened their hope. Alongside socialist realist canvases were abstract paintings of the sort damned at Manezh. Similar sculptures, including works by Neizvestny, stood in the main hall. The tables in the hall, attended by frock-coated waiters, were completely "covered"—that is, groaning with a cornucopia of food and drink.[57]

Khrushchev actually did want to smooth things over. On December 15 he ordered Chernoutsan to prepare two speeches for the occasion. One, which Ilychev would deliver, would "answer their foul language with some of our own"; the other, which Khrushchev would give, would mollify his guests and calm things down.[58] The fact that Khrushchev raised a toast on December 17 to Solzhenitsyn (who reluctantly attended the meeting in old clothes, much-mended shoes, and bad need of a haircut), going so far as to claim personal credit for the publication of *One Day,* confirms his benevolent intent.[59] So does the fact that Khrushchev conspicuously waited in line to use the men's room between banquet and speeches, sending those near him into spasms of uncertainty (punctuated by cries of "Go ahead, Nikita Sergeyevich, go ahead" and his own "Of course not, no need for you to wait, I'll stand") on whether 'tis nobler to yield to the premier or take one's legitimate place at the pissoir.[60]

However, Khrushchev's after-dinner speech didn't turn out to be conciliatory, if one assumes that "speech" is the word for what transpired. He spoke for two hours or so, then continually interrupted other speakers, and grabbed the microphone again at the end. He had a text in front of him, recalled Neizvestny, who had been seated prominently near the head table, where the entire Presidium was arrayed. But he put it aside and launched into a harangue that not only froze his audience but produced looks of horror on faces of some of his Presidium peers.[61]

Neizvestny, the recipient of an apparently friendly wave as Khrushchev entered the hall, turned out to be a prime target. "Is that a horse or a cow?" Khrushchev pointed to a Neizvestny sculpture. "Whatever it is, it makes an ugly mockery of a perfectly noble animal." Later: "If that's supposed to be a woman, then you're a faggot. And the sentence for them is ten years in prison."[62]

The irony, according to Mikhail Romm, who was sitting up close and observing intently, was that Khrushchev was actually trying to rise to the occasion: "It was obviously extraordinarily difficult for him. What struck me was the painstakingness with which he was talking about art, all the while knowing essentially nothing about it. There he was trying to explain what was beautiful and what wasn't, what would be comprehensible to the people and what would not, which artists aspired to reach communism and which were of no help to communism at all."[63]

Straining to offer aesthetic/political criticism, Khrushchev again ended up in the toilet. That was where, in a peroration with few parallels in the history of art, he insisted Neizvestny belonged: "Your art resembles this: It's as if a man climbed into a toilet, slid down under the seat, and from there, from under the toilet seat, looked up at what was above him, at someone sitting on the seat, looking up that particular part of the body from below, from under the seat. That's what your art is like. . . . That's your position, Comrade Neizvestny, you're sitting in the toilet."

You think I'm crude, Khrushchev was in effect saying, I'll show you how crude I am. You think you're smarter than I am, I'll make you feel uncomfortable. Thus, in a perverse way, did he make a virtue out of his vice. His penchant for profanity was ironically true to the working-class origins of the party (as anyone who has encountered its ubiquitousness on the Russian street can attest), yet the party, or at least its more cultured members, now shunned it. Given Khrushchev's own aspiration to culture, it must have been mortifying to personify the lack of it! In the very act of indicting Nizevestny, Khrushchev demonstrated why he himself deserved to be. Angry and defiant as he was, in some part of his soul the truth must have registered. In that sense his whole astounding performance amounted to self-flagellation in the guise of flagellating others, to wallowing in the very boorishness that he had long tried to transcend. Perhaps that was why at least one of his victims in the hall, the painter Zhutovsky, felt pity along with shock and dismay.

The fact that Khrushchev's subject was partly himself is confirmed by the way his nonspeech rambled over his whole life. His poetry-writing friend from the Yuzovka mines made an appearance. So did the issue of whether he was now or had ever been an anti-Semite. He talked at length about Stalin, pausing to reject a charge that liberals in the hall would never dare make: "I can see in their eyes that they are thinking to themselves: 'You, Khrushchev, are the number one Stalinist.' " Even Pinya, the hapless prisoner in the short story Khrushchev had read as a boy, showed up again, risking a bullet in the face by leading the escape attempt. " 'I'm the leader, so I'll go first.' That's what Pinya said, comrades. And I'm he, I'm Pinya!" What that reference implied was that the very policemen Pinya/Nikita was trying to escape included the intellectuals he was chastising.[64]

KHRUSHCHEV'S POGROM met some resistance. When he grumbled that "only the grave can cure the hunchback," poet Yevgeny Yevtushenko retorted, "Nikita Sergeyevich, we live in a time when not the grave but the living correct mistakes."[65] In addition, at least passive opposition continued after the meeting. When Ilychev summoned 140 writers and artists to the Central Committee, some found excuses not to attend. Mikhail Romm feigned illness and then wrote a letter restating views that had been judged heretical in the first place.[66]

The result of the resistance was another surreal session on March 7, 1963. The scene this time was the Kremlin's vast Sverdlovsk Hall with its snow white columns and high blue cupola. With upward of six hundred attending, artists and writers were outnumbered by party, Komsomol, and KGB functionaries, plus ideology and propaganda specialists from around the country. No banquet this time; instead the guests seated themselves in rows facing a raised platform on which Presidium members sat. In front of the Presidium was a podium from which various speakers addressed the audience, their backs, awkwardly, to the most powerful men in the land.[67]

The sharp contrast between Khrushchev and his Kremlin colleagues struck several in the hall, he seeming about to burst; Brezhnev, Suslov, and the others sitting stone-faced and immobile. Romm noticed Khrushchev's second-in-command, Frol Kozlov: "Not only didn't he move; he didn't even blink. With his limpid eyes, curly hair, and sleek face, and with the leaden gaze with which he slowly scanned the hall, it was as if he were chewing us up with his eyes; that's how icy they were."[68]

The proceedings lasted two full days. Again Khrushchev began by trying to be hospitable and balanced. He apologized for the lack of a banquet but promised food during breaks. "So, please, eat," he added. He castigated liberals but praised Solzhenitsyn and Tvardovsky. He denied that Stalinist writers were mere "varnishers" but criticized them for "embellishing" reality. "We believe even today that Stalin was devoted to communism," he said, but in the last years of his life Stalin was "a profoundly sick man who suffered from suspiciousness and a persecution mania."[69]

As in December, aides had prepared a moderate text, and once again Khrushchev "didn't use a word of it."[70] No sooner had he welcomed his guests than he suddenly declared, "All volunteer informers for foreign agencies—I ask you to please leave the hall." In the face of a puzzled silence, he identified his targets: "renegades" who had briefed Western reporters on the December meeting, thus accounting for highly unflattering accounts that had appeared in the Western press. "I know, you can't just get up now and give yourselves away, so during the break, when we're in the cafeteria, you just pretend to go to the toilet and then get lost. You understand?"[71]

At one point during the meeting Mikhail Romm tried to champion director Marlen Khutsiev's controversial film *Ilyich's Gate,* in which a young man sees his late father in a dream and asks him how to live. "How old are you?" asks the father, who died in the war. Told his son is twenty-two, the father says, "But I'm only twenty," and disappears. The meaning, Romm explained, was that the son must make up his own mind, just as his father had when he fought and died for Soviet power. "No, no, no," Khrushchev objected. "You're interpreting it incorrectly, Comrade Romm, incorrectly. The meaning is just the opposite. . . . Even a cat doesn't discard its kitten, but at a difficult moment, this father turns away from his son. That's what it means."

Was Khrushchev thinking of the way his father had doubted him or how he had recoiled from his own son? When Romm tried to defend his view, Khrushchev whined, "So what am I then? Not a human being. Am I not a person? Don't I get to have my say?"[72]

The next bizarre exchange began when Khrushchev's old friend Wanda Wasiliewska complained about two Soviet writers who had praised Boris Pasternak in an interview with a Polish newspaper. Wasiliewska didn't identify the offenders, but Khrushchev demanded their names: the poet Andrei Voznesensky and the young novelist Vasily Aksyonov. When the hall erupted with shouts of "Shame!" and demands that the traitors show their faces. Voznesensky approached the lectern. The slender dark-haired young poet started to quote Mayakovsky, but before he could complete a sentence, Khrushchev thundered, "Slander! . . . Slanderer! . . . Who do you think you are? . . . Your view of Soviet power is from inside a toilet! . . . If you don't like it here, you can go to hell. . . . We're not keeping you. . . . Get yourself a passport and I'll approve it in two minutes. Is Gromyko here? He is? Approve his passport and let him get the hell out!"[73]

With his back to the Presidium, Voznesensky wasn't sure who was shouting. When he turned around, he thought Khrushchev was "out of his mind." Swearing and cursing, with "his eyes rolling and saliva flying, he looked insane, hysterical, as if he were having a seizure."[74] Voznesensky tried to continue, but Khrushchev kept cutting him off. When the poet read his verse about Lenin, Khrushchev exploded again: "It's good for nothing. You can't write, and you don't know anything. Here's a question for you: How many people are born in the Soviet Union every year? Three and a half million. So you, Comrade Voznesensky, you're nothing, you're only one of three and a half million, one who won't amount to anything. You can carve it on your nose: You are nothing!"[75] He added: "The only thing that can help you is a little modesty. Success has gone to your head. You were born a prince. When I was twenty-nine years old, I was a responsible person. But you're irresponsible."[76]

Suddenly, in the middle of this harangue, Khrushchev pointed to the back of the hall. He thought he had spotted Aksyonov. "Hey, you! That agent over there [incorrectly accenting the first syllable of the word "agent"]! The jerk in the red sweater with the glasses. No, not you, him!"

It wasn't Aksyonov. Khrushchev was pointing instead at a painter named Ilarion Golitsyn, not an abstract artist but an old-style realist.

"So you're Aksyonov," roared Khrushchev. "I know what you're doing. You're taking revenge on us for the death of your father."

Khrushchev thought Aksyonov's father had perished in the purges; actually his parents had spent years in the camps, about which his mother, Yevgenia Ginzburg, wrote two moving memoirs upon her release.[77]

"But I'm not Aksyonov," replied Golitsyn.

"What do you mean, you're not?" grumbled Khrushchev. "Who are you?"

"I—I'm Golitsyn."

"Prince Golitsyn? [The Golitsyns were an ancient princely family of Russia.] So you're a prince, are you? Is that who you are? A prince?"

"No, no, I'm not a prince, I'm just an artist, a realist, Nikita Sergeyevich. If you like, I can show you a piece of my work."

"No, no. Not necessary. But say something!"

"What should I say?"

"You're asking me? You're the one who came up here to speak."

"I don't know what to say. I wasn't planning to speak."

"Don't you know why you were called up here?"

"No, I don't."

"Well, think about it."

"Was it because I applauded Voznesensky?"

"No," snapped Khrushchev.

"Then I don't know."

"Well, think about it," Khrushchev repeated.

"May I keep working?" whimpered Golitsyn.

"Yes, you may," replied the benevolent party boss.[78]

Wild laughter resounded through the hall, all the more hysterical after the almost unbearable tension. Muttering that people who didn't dress decently didn't applaud properly either, Khrushchev released the "false Aksyonov" and began another absurdist dialogue with the real one.

"So you don't like Soviet power?"

"It's not that," Aksyonov answered. "I just try to write the truth as I see it."

"You're taking revenge on us because of your father, right? That's why you're slandering us. Well, all right, he perished, we mourn for him."

"My father's alive."

"Alive? Alive, you say? How can that be?"

"My parents were repressed under Stalin, but they were rehabilitated after the Twentieth Congress. We associate that with your name."[79]

This raised the infernal question of Khrushchev's own role under Stalin. Soon he addressed that himself: "Did the leading cadres of the party know about, let us say, the arrests of people at the time? Yes, they knew. But were they aware that people who were innocent of any wrongdoing were arrested? No. This they did not know. . . . We learned about Stalin's abuses of power and arbitrary acts only after his death and the unmasking of Beria. . . ."[80] But having said this, Khrushchev contradicted himself by boasting that he had prevented witch-hunts in Ukraine and Moscow.

Ilya Ehrenburg had confessed in his memoirs that he knew that innocent people were arrested under Stalin, but he had been afraid to speak out. Khrushchev took that as a refutation of his claim not to have known. "So Comrade Ehrenburg writes that he knew and understood," he now declared. "So he understood, did he . . .? If he understood, why was he silent? He makes it seem everyone was silent. Not at all, Comrade Ehrenburg, not all were silent, many were not silent. . . . You think it was easy for us? Well, just between us, just between us, the man was insane in his last years, IN-SANE, I tell you. A madman on the throne. Can you imagine that? . . . And you think it was easy? Our nerves were strained to the limit, and we had to drink vodka all the time. And we always had to be on the alert."[81]

Ehrenburg had left the hall by this time. Khrushchev seemed out of control. Mikhail Romm thought the drinks that a silent aide placed beside him every ten minutes, and that Khrushchev gulped down, were doping him up. Khrushchev's erstwhile liberal allies were scared and appalled. Even conservatives, though pleased to have his support, were stunned.

DURING THE spring and summer of 1963 Khrushchev's morale improved. Of all things, a visit from Fidel Castro helped lift his spirits. Yet even in Castro's buoyant presence, his host was subject to sudden mood swings.

The Soviet leader wrote Castro a twenty-seven-page letter in January 1963, seeking to restore good relations with Havana. Invited to visit the USSR, Fidel wasn't quite ready to go, but once he arrived on April 25, he spent nearly a month and a half roaming from far northern Murmansk to Central Asia. According to Nikolai Leonov, the KGB officer who doubled as Castro's interpreter, formal negotiations were overshadowed by mass meetings, banquets, industrial and agricultural inspections, and informal talks. Khrushchev arranged a Red Square welcome and a mammoth friendship rally, and the two men huddled at Khrushchev's Lenin Hills residence and Moscow River dacha and at a resort in Zavidovo about sixty miles from the capital. Photographs from the visit include many of Castro posing with the Khrushchev family, as well as pictures he himself took of them.

Khrushchev spared no expense to ease tensions left over from the missile crisis. Would Castro like to inspect rocket bases off-limits even to foreign Communists? Missile-carrying submarines? Just step this way! How about a sacred Order of Lenin for his honored guest? During Pitsunda talks about military aid, Khrushchev benevolently instructed Marshal Biryuzov to "add one [of each weapons system] from me—as a sign of my personal respect for our guest." When the General Staff received the list in Moscow, it was at a loss to explain the seemingly random assortment of tanks, cannons, and other weapons.[82]

Castro reviewed the May Day parade with the entire Soviet leadership. Afterward the company repaired to a Kremlin palace for an elegant lunch around a large antique inlaid table. Suddenly, in the presence of horrified colleagues, Khrushchev engaged in a shouting match with Castro about who hadn't consulted whom during the Cuban crisis. In the middle of it, Leonov unintentionally dropped a bottle of cognac, spilling it on the ascetic Suslov. That allowed Khrushchev to break the tension by telling the Cuban leader, "In our country, a breaking glass can only mean happiness."

After hunting wild boar at Zavidovo, the two men sat in a secluded summer house on a river island, examining the entire Kennedy-Khrushchev correspondence from the recent crisis. "Read them aloud," Khrushchev told Leonov, the only other person present. "Translate for Fidel from beginning to end." After several hours Khrushchev asked

Castro, "Are you satisfied?" Castro said he was, and dropped the subject for good.[83]

Khrushchev favored Castro with wisdom on all sorts of subjects: the sources of Sino-Soviet tension ("unclear" even to Khrushchev), the Soviet-Albanian conflict (traceable to Stalin's "saying any stupidity in the last years of his life when he was in fact mentally ill"), even the infernal unreformability of Russia: "You'd think I, as first secretary, could change anything in this country. Like hell I can! No matter what changes I propose and carry out, everything stays the same. Russia's like a tub full of dough, you put your hand in it, down to the bottom, and think you're the master of the situation. When you first pull out your hand, a little hole remains, but then, before your very eyes, the dough expands into a spongy, puffy mass. That's what Russia is like!"[84]

To govern Russia one had to be ruthless. "Forty years after the October revolution," Khrushchev told Castro, "we had to use force" in Tbilisi and Novocherkassk. He counseled his pupil to "crush [antigovernmental activity] quickly, decisively," even "to open fire," if necessary, a lesson that also applied to exiled anti-Communists like the Ukrainian nationalists Khrushchev had faced: "There are times when security services should physically eliminate the leaders of the counter-revolution in exile." Doubtless, Khrushchev was referring to the KGB's assassination of two leading émigrés, one of them Stepan Bandera, the Ukrainian nationalist leader who had been Khrushchev's archfoe in western Ukraine and had been murdered in October 1959.[85]

The intelligentsia, on the other hand, had to be treated gently: "They're the hardest of all to deal with, the writers and artists. They think they can govern the state much better than the party can. So they keep trying to teach us what to do and how to do it; they'd like to be the spiritual leaders of society. But they're undisciplined. With people like that you have to be careful, to keep a sharp lookout, because they can always let you down."[86]

At Zavidovo, Marshal Grechko shot better than Khrushchev. In response, Khrushchev mocked Grechko as if he were the dumbest recruit in the army. When Brezhnev, as formal head of state, pinned a Hero of the Soviet Union medal on Castro's broad chest, Khrushchev demonstratively walked up, removed the medal, and affixed it to another spot a centimeter or so from where Brezhnev had placed it. During a skeet-shooting session at his dacha, when no one was hitting much of anything, Khrushchev yelled, "Call Lyonia [Brezhnev], he's no good at anything, but he can shoot skeets."[87]

Khrushchev's colleagues were "embarrassed" by his behavior, Leonov recalled. "They were upset. That was obvious. But they didn't object; they tried to hide behind each other's backs, to get out of his field of vision."[88]

As late as June 1963 Khrushchev was still trying to convince himself that the Cuban crisis had ended in victory. A week after Castro left, Khrushchev briefed the Presidium on his talks with the Cuban. "If we were cowards," he had told the Cuban leader, then "why did we deploy missiles in Cuba? Was this cowardice? No. Is this a retreat? No. It is a step forward." Of course "it would have been better not to have had to remove these missiles: even an idiot understands this." But "the Americans wanted to wipe you off the face of the earth. So who suffered defeat? Who did not get what he wanted? We attained our goal; so they lost, we won."[89]

AFTER KHRUSHCHEV'S March 7 assault on liberal writers and artists, conservatives intensified their offensive. The only way to stop them, Tvardovsky told friends, was to get to Khrushchev himself, but even that might not help. In April the Stalinist journal *Oktyabr* blasted Sozhenitsyn. "How could they dare to do that?" Tvardovsky aide Vladimir Lakshin asked himself. "Can it really be that easy to smash something [*One Day in the Life of Ivan Denisovich*] that Khrushchev and the Presidium have approved?"[90]

At a June Central Committee plenum on ideology and culture, more than two thousand "workers from the cultural sector" packed the Kremlin for a session that lasted several days. This time Khrushchev managed to strike a balance. He praised Tvardovsky, got in several swipes at Stalin, and sounded positively mellow about the state of the economy, but he also projected his embarrassment at his own boorishness onto others. "Just a minute," he said, pointing to two Central Committee members, one of them a Kazakh, who were whispering to each other. "Why are you smirking? What's so funny? You are attending a meeting of the Central Committee. Don't you know how to behave properly? . . . How dare you behave this way in the presence of the Central Committee of the party! This is an outrage!"[91]

Khrushchev's targets had no choice but to grovel, but the spectacle wasn't finished. Suslov and Ilychev were about to sum up the proceedings when Khrushchev grabbed center stage again, started to read a short speech, and then rambled on for two and half more hours on topics ranging from writers who should be excluded from the party to how Mao Zedong had tried to humiliate him by flaunting his superior swimming skills. All that remained after that was for Central Committee members unanimously to approve resolutions that had just been given to them. In a spasm of democratic magnanimity, Khrushchev invited the nearly two thousand guests to vote as well. Central Committee members were appalled, as was Mikhail Romm. "There we were," the filmmaker recalled, "voting as one to drop a paragraph we had never read from a document we had never seen. . . . That was Khrushchev for you."[92]

That July, after the jury at the Third International Film Festival (consisting of nine judges from Communist countries and six from Western or neutral nations) voted to award first prize to Federico Fellini's modernist, surrealistic *8½*, Ilychev thought of canceling the prize and disbanding the jury but feared to provoke an international scandal. The State Cinema Trust chairman Aleksei Romanov was also at a loss. "Get out of here," Khrushchev shouted at Romanov, "send the picture to me. I'll look at it myself since you don't understand anything about it."[93]

Khrushchev was watching *8½* at his dacha when his son tried to convince him that Fellini was a genius. According to Sergei, "Father flew into a rage: 'Get out of here and don't bother me. I'm not sitting here for the fun of it.'" Later he admitted to Sergei, "I don't understand a thing, but the international jury has awarded it a first prize. What am I supposed to do? They understand it better than I do; that's what they're there for. Why do they always palm these things off on me? I've already called Ilychev and told him not to intervene. Let the professionals decide."[94]

At least in this incident Khrushchev seemed to know his own limits. At times he didn't so much seize his role as chief culture critic as have it thrust upon him by one artistic camp battling another. Central Committee culture specialist Georgy Kunitsyn recollected an incident when Ukrainian party authorities fired several Kiev film officials for approving Kira and Aleksandr Muratovs' liberal-minded *Our Honest Bread.* Without telling anyone in Moscow what had happened in Kiev, Kunitsyn had the film shown to Khrushchev, who liked it. When Kiev got the news, it rescinded the ouster before Moscow even had a chance to approve it.[95] On the other hand, said Mikoyan, conservatives like Suslov and Ilychev readily exploited Khrushchev's "lack of education" to incite him against liberals. The net result, according to Mikoyan, was that Khrushchev had "an amazing facility for turning the intelligentsia against him."[96]

Sometime that same summer, with reports reaching the West that an ideological pogrom was under way in Moscow, Khrushchev's cultural advisers decided to prove it wasn't so. They seized on a conference on the modern novel to be attended by writers from both East and West in Leningrad in August under the auspices of UNESCO and the left-wing

Community of European Writers. As part of the show they invited Ilya Ehrenburg, the sophisticated veteran writer who had lived abroad and had extensive European ties. Khrushchev had trashed Ehrenburg at the March 7 meeting with the intelligentsia ("You eat our Russian bread, but you dream of French chestnuts. Maybe you belong there, not here"),[97] but when Ehrenburg at first declined to attend the Leningrad gathering, Khrushchev pleaded with him to do so.

Khrushchev couldn't have been nicer. Instead of dominating the Kremlin conversation between him and Ehrenburg, he actually listened and didn't even interrupt. Attributing past recriminations to misunderstandings or bad advice from his aides, he asked Ehrenburg not to "hold a grudge." When Ehrenburg defended Voznesensky and Yevtushenko, Khrushchev didn't disagree. He even offered Ehrenburg the right to censor himself: "You and I are oldsters, so what sort of censors do we need?" He chortled about how he had just put the Chinese in their place. He positively glowed when Ehrenburg told him he'd go down in history for eliminating Stalinist lawlessness.[98]

Khrushchev thought of going to Leningrad himself but instead invited a small group of writers (including Britons Angus Wilson and William Golding, and Alain Robbe-Grillet and Natalie Sarraute from France) to Pitsunda following the conference. August by the Black Sea couldn't have been more beautiful. The proud host showed off his swimming pool, retracting the glass walls that enclosed it with the press of a button. His idea of welcoming remarks, a rambling attack on imperialism, the Chinese, and even his Western guests themselves, went as follows: "You intellectuals of course support and serve your bourgeoisie, but we spat on all that. Here too not all writers wanted to join the revolution, but we called them to order. You may call us barbarians, but we're not about to make our policies to suit you. So keep that in mind and don't try to change our minds."[99]

French Communist leader Maurice Thorez had complained to Khrushchev (leaving him looking "dark and gloomy," recalled an aide) that no French Communist writer had been invited to Pitsunda. The effect was to cast a pall over an elaborate luncheon that was consumed in near silence. Khrushchev aides scurried about trying to implement his abrupt order that "none of the bourgeois" be present for the poetry reading following dessert, but the best they could do was to remove a Swedish writer named Lundquist, by arranging a special flight to take him home, where, he had previously informed them, a member of his family was sick. The poetry reading itself, lasting forty minutes with a break for smoking (which wasn't permitted in Khrushchev's presence), saved the day. Tvardovsky read a boldly anti-Stalinist poem that had failed to gain the censor's approval. In his "Tyorkin in the Other World," the simple soldier hero of the World War II epic finds the afterlife ruled by a *vozhd* who erects endless monuments to himself. Khrushchev listened carefully, frowned occasionally, but also chuckled and even guffawed, and afterwards pumped Tvardovsky's hand. Several days later Adzubei's *Izvestia* published the poem, but only after Khrushchev hesitated in the face of Stalinist objections. "Are you sure it isn't anti-Soviet?" Khrushchev asked Chernoutsan.

"Not at all, Nikita Sergeyevich," Chernoutsan answered, "although as a satirical piece it of course contains certain grotesques."

"Then you take out the grotesques," Khrushchev ordered.

Better relations with Washington also account for Khrushchev's more upbeat mood in mid-1963. In mid-June, President Kennedy gave a conciliatory speech at American University in Washington. He hailed "the Russian people for their many achievements," while recognizing that they had suffered more than any other nation during the world war, the equivalent of "the devastation of this country east of Chicago." Both the Soviet Union and the United States inhabited "this small planet. We all breathe the same air. We all cherish our children's future. And we are all mortal." Calling for a reexamination of American attitudes toward the USSR, Kennedy hoped for "a fresh start" in the form of a test ban treaty, and announced that high-level Soviet-American-British talks would soon begin in Moscow.[100]

Kennedy's speech was balm to Khrushchev, who later called it "the best speech by any president since Roosevelt." Aides like Troyanovsky pressed their boss to respond in kind.[101] Several days later the United States and the USSR signed an agreement establishing a hot line for communicating during crises. Also, during the last two weeks in July, Khrushchev, Averell Harriman, and the British negotiator Lord Hailsham successfully negotiated the most important arms control agreement since the start of the cold war, a treaty banning nuclear weapons testing in the air, underwater, and in outer space. Since on-site inspection wasn't required for verification, that poisonous issue was put aside.

The ten days it took to agree on the test ban gave Harriman a close look at Khrushchev. Back in April, Khrushchev had seemed "much older, less bouncy, and looked tired." He was more chipper in July, but Harriman also noticed the way he mocked his own generals, calling them "smart alecks" who wasted money when in office and wrote too many memoirs in retirement. At a lunch with Harriman and Hungarian leader János Kádár, Khrushchev taunted Grechko so aggressively (joking that he would be swapped for better American commanders) that the marshal couldn't conceal his consternation.

On July 23, Khrushchev unexpectedly showed up with Kádár and Brezhnev and their wives at Lenin Stadium, where Harriman was attending a Soviet-American track meet. As the two teams walked arm in arm around the stadium, Khrushchev had tears in his eyes. That evening he demonstratively ignored Kádár and regaled Harriman with stories that debunked Stalin but also suggested that Khrushchev "has a certain reverence for Stalin in spite of his public denunciations of him."

Throughout the talks Khrushchev pushed for steps beyond a test ban itself, especially for a NATO–Warsaw Pact nonaggression pact. So intense was his pressure that Harriman feared the talks would founder on this issue. As Khrushchev put it in a July 27 letter to Kennedy, a nonaggression pact "would be not only an important step toward normalization of the entire world situation, but could signify the beginning of a turning point in the history of contemporary international relations. . . ."[102] But the Western negotiators resisted on the grounds that a non-aggression pact alone would not prevent aggression. The most Harriman would promise was to raise the question again once the test ban treaty was signed.

Khrushchev reluctantly accepted the test ban without the nonaggression pact. He hoped Kennedy himself would come to Moscow to sign the new treaty, but instead he got Rusk (along with a bipartisan delegation of senators), whose instruction was to dangle the prospect of a nonaggression pact to "maintain the mood which Harriman's visit created" but otherwise to stall on the issue.[103]

An elaborate signing ceremony in the vaulted, white marble Catherine Hall of the Great Kremlin Palace eased Khrushchev's disappointment, as did a gala luncheon featuring brandy, speeches, and a Soviet orchestra playing Gershwin's "Love Walked In." Afterward the Soviet leader invited Rusk and his party to Pitsunda, where the U.S. secretary of state proved himself the consummate diplomat, managing both to lose to his much older host at badminton and to paddle around the pool so awkwardly in borrowed water wings as to leave Khrushchev feeling himself the superior swimmer. But when talk turned to Berlin, Rusk didn't give an inch.[104]

All in all, Khrushchev wasn't displeased. At a meeting on August 5, he struck British Foreign Secretary Lord Home as "jovial though tired." Home reported, "Even Gromyko has tried to look cheerful," and the overall atmosphere was "remarkably relaxed."[105] According to Sergei Khrushchev, his father wasn't just "extraordinarily satisfied"; he was positively "happy." That happiness reflected Khrushchev's conviction that better things lay ahead. Having reestablished a relationship with Kennedy, he had six more years (if the president was reelected) to build a real partnership.[106]

Khrushchev needed Kennedy and thought Kennedy needed him. In a long conversation with Dobrynin on August 26, the president seemed to favor measures to prevent surprise attacks and a prohibition of weapons of mass destruction in outer space. On November 15, Robert Kennedy foresaw another Khrushchev-Kennedy meeting in which the two leaders could "calmly sit and talk everything over" for two or three days. "If Kennedy had lived," according to Dobrynin, relations between the two countries would have improved, particularly since "Khrushchev did not want a repetition of the painful and damaging 1961 meeting in Vienna." He couldn't afford "two unsuccessful" summits; he "had to demonstrate some success to [Soviet] public opinion."[107]

Khrushchev had finished his evening reading on November 22 and was preparing to climb the stairs to his bedroom when the government phone rang. Nighttime calls were unusual; he almost never told his family what they were about. This time, however, he informed them that President Kennedy had reportedly been shot. With Nina Petrovna, Sergei, and Lena gathered around the dining room table, Khrushchev waited for Gromyko to call back. Khrushchev had instructed him to telephone the ambassador to check on the report, but Gromyko tried to reach Dobrynin in Washington instead of Kohler in Moscow. Once the error was corrected, the terrible news was confirmed: The president was dead.

In the hours following the assassination Khrushchev seemed in a state of shock. Troyanovsky could see that he took the news as "a personal blow." The next day at Spaso House, where Khrushchev went to sign an official condolence book, he appeared to have been weeping. Besides an official letter of sympathy, he added a personal note to the president's widow.[108]

Khrushchev ascertained from the KGB chief Semichastny that the president's alleged assassin, Lee Harvey Oswald, who had lived in the USSR for nearly three years, wasn't working for Soviet security services. Khrushchev suspected American reactionaries had killed the president to torpedo a U.S.-Soviet détente. The KGB reported that the new president, Lyndon Johnson, "supports conservative and reactionary views," and according to Soviet sources, a friend of the Kennedy family passed the word that Johnson was a "clever timeserver" who would be "incapable of realizing Kennedy's unfinished plans."[109] Actually, LBJ was tempted to mount a major effort to improve relations with Moscow, but he had other things (such as reelection and Vietnam) on his mind. Even if he didn't, the Soviets assumed he did. Khrushchev was prepared to take risks with Kennedy as a partner, he told his son, but with Johnson in power, "everything will be different."[110]

BY THE TIME Khrushchev's hopes for Soviet-American détente were finally dashed, so were any chances to patch things up with Mao. After an uneasy winter during which Moscow and Beijing traded accusations at other parties' congresses, they agreed to bilateral peace talks in Moscow beginning on July 5.[111] But the talks were part ritual dance, in which each side issued formal statements excoriating the other and then politely waited for the other's equally negative reply, and part verbal slugfest, in which Khrushchev's invective against Stalin was thrown back in his face. "Murderer," "criminal," "bandit," "fool," "shit," "idiot"—all these "curses and swear words," said Chinese delegate Kang Shen, "came from the mouth of Comrade N. S. Khrushchev." Did Khrushchev really mean to claim that a "fool" had developed Soviet nuclear weapons? Could Communists of all countries have considered "some sort of 'shit' " to be their commander? Was Khrushchev, who blamed Stalin for everything, "completely clean"?[112]

Deng Xiaoping, who led the Chinese delegation, was somewhat more restrained, directing his fire against Khrushchev's vain pursuit of détente: Whenever Khrushchev "grasped some kind of straw" handed to him by Eisenhower or Kennedy, he was "beside [himself] with joy and in all fury" against fraternal parties that failed to follow his lead. Yet, Deng commented, "when you suffer setbacks because of your erroneous policy, then you get enraged. . .and sacrifice the interests of the entire socialist camp in order to cater to the imperialists and reactionaries. . . ."[113]

On July 20 the Sino-Soviet talks broke down. Several days later the test ban treaty was agreed upon. Having warned many times against arms control agreements that might limit Chinese freedom to develop nuclear weapons, Beijing condemned the treaty as a "dirty fake," a "fraud," and a "sellout." The Soviets replied in kind. As propaganda barrage and counterbarrage followed each other, involving other Communist parties, extending into international organizations, even touching on potentially explosive Sino-Soviet border disputes, both Mao and Khrushchev came in for violent personal attacks.[114] Yet the rapidly escalating rift had two compensating advantages. With Sino-Soviet relations beyond repair, Khrushchev no longer needed to appease Beijing. As Troyanovsky put it, the impossibility of reconciliation with the Chinese "gave him much more room to seek an understanding with the United States and the other Western nations."[115] However, by the time Khrushchev realized this, it was too late for such an understanding.

A second "benefit" of the break was that with the Chinese in full cry, and Khrushchev himself under attack, his colleagues had to rally around, even though they attributed the split largely to him. In early 1963 Ambassador to China Chervonenko was "called on the carpet" for being too soft on China. Instead of administering a tongue-lashing himself, Khrushchev delegated the chore to Kozlov, who heard Chervonenko out politely, expressed no real criticism, and then reported to Khrushchev that he had given the ambassador "a good thrashing." The moral of the story, Chervonenko concluded, was that Kozlov and his colleagues "didn't share Khrushchev's positions on China. Why didn't they tell him so? That is another matter."[116]

Obviously they were afraid. But Khrushchev sensed their reservations. At a December 1963 plenum on the Sino-Soviet split, he explained why the Chinese were singling out "Khrushchev" (he used the third person to refer to himself) for special curses: "Probably, someone's [read Mao's] mama is to blame. If mama doesn't provide the brains, no one else can add them, not even school." Khrushchev conceded that "some comrades don't agree with me, but I don't want to get into an argument, I'm just expressing my opinion." The Chinese leaders hoped to "wake up one day and find that the plenum had ousted Khrushchev. Well, comrades, I'm already almost seventy years old. I'm not working for myself, but for the party and the people. It's up to you to decide whether I stay at my post or not." In the meantime, "as the saying goes, there's still powder in the powder keg [All stand. Stormy, prolonged applause]."[117]

Suslov went out of his way to defend Khrushchev: Although the Chinese were trying "to split Khrushchev off from the Central Committee," their "dirty design" was bound to fail.[118] Nine months later Suslov presided over the plenum that ratified Khrushchev's ouster.

CHEMICALS! Mineral fertilizer! Khrushchev came up with his latest panacea for agriculture in the summer of 1963. The Americans produced thirty-five million tons of fertilizer for 118 million hectares of land, whereas Soviet output for 218 million hectares was only twenty million tons. Moscow needed to quadruple fertilizer production in four years. Sixty new fertilizer plants, as well as more production from current facilities, would do the job. Sure, 6 billion rubles was a lot of money, but it took 5.3 billion to harness the Virgin Lands.[119] Several days after recommending a crash program to the Presidium, Khrushchev received U.S. Secretary of Agriculture Orville Freeman. Preempting the Presidium and the Central Committee, which had not yet considered the issue, Khrushchev mentioned a hundred million tons of fertilizer and upped the price tag to 10 billion rubles. Not only that, but, he blithely confided to his American guest, the Soviet defense budget would be further reduced.[120]

That autumn drought struck in central Russia, Siberia, Ukraine, Kazakhstan, and Transcaucasus. Two years after being promised milk and honey without limit, people found themselves standing in breadlines. Agitated letters began arriving at national newspapers, but Brezhnev and the others feared to show them to "the old man."[121] When Kosygin finally broached the truth at a Presidium lunch, Khrushchev kept eating in silence, but he exploded when the deputy premier recommended buying grain in the West. Only after his minister of agricultural procurement had reported that the country was essentially out of grain did Khrushchev agree to seek help abroad: 6.8 million tons from Canada, 1.8 million from Australia, almost 2 million from the United States, even 400,000 on loan from lowly Romania.[122]

Khrushchev's inner turmoil was visible throughout the autumn. On September 5 he fired off a memorandum fulminating against "our barbaric attitude toward fertilizers" and "our inefficiency, clumsiness, and ignorance when it comes to managing our own mineral resources."[123] What he saw several days later at the Volga-Don State Farm "did not make me happy." The trouble, he complained to local officials, was that "any ignoramus can work as he wants [and] even undertake to teach others, although he himself doesn't understand what he's doing."[124] Next stop, Krasnodar, where Soviet farmers wasted fertilizer in a way that would be "inconceivable to an American farmer," who "pays money for fertilizers and knows that if they aren't used correctly, he will, as they say, go broke."[125] Sometime later another memo with yet another reference that applied to himself: Too many heads of collective and state farms had "outlived themselves" but didn't know enough to retire, and no one removed them.[126]

All told, the 1963 grain harvest was disastrous: only 107.5 million tons compared with 134.7 in 1958. The Virgin Lands produced their smallest crop in years, although the sown area was now ten million hectares larger than in 1955. Things got so bad that the Kremlin seriously considered adopting rationing.[127] Yet all Khrushchev had to offer in February 1964 was an exhortation to match miracle workers like Trofim Lysenko and Roswell Garst and insults for "pumpkinheads" masquerading as ministers.[128]

"Father didn't understand what was wrong," Sergei Khrushchev wrote later. "He grew nervous, became angry, quarreled, looked for culprits and didn't find them. Deep inside, he began subconsciously to understand that the problem was not in the details. It was the system itself that didn't work, but he couldn't change his beliefs."[129]

Not every prospect looked bleak. Khrushchev toyed with notions of economic reform being developed by Yevsei Liberman, the Kharkov economist whose ideas suddenly started appearing in *Pravda*,[130] as well as with those of Ivan Khudenko, the Kazakhstan state farm chairman who put his farm on the contract system and increased output almost overnight.[131] Political reforms such as multicandidate elections for soviets and greater glasnost on governmental affairs also fascinated Khrushchev.[132] During a visit to Yugoslavia in late summer 1963 he displayed interest in Yugoslav "self-management" based on "workers' councils." But while Tito rhapsodized about Yugoslav reforms, Khrushchev, more interested in a toy he had just been given than what Tito was telling him about the Yugoslav economic model, kept pulling a small clock in the shape of a camera out of his pocket.[133] During an August 1963 session with Ukrainian party officials at Mezhgorie, his villa in the late thirties and forties, Khrushchev kept switching on a small portable radio, turning up the volume to hear foreign news, and then reporting what he'd heard to his dumbfounded interlocutors.[134]

That same summer, outside KremGES, a town serving the recently finished Kremenchug Hydroelectric Station, his motorcade passed a sign rechristening the city Khrushchev. A hallowed tradition under Stalin, the practice of naming cities after leaders had been a bête-noire of Khrushchev's. This time, as local officials poured on the flattery, he didn't object. Only at the last moment, when his steamer to Dnepropetrovsk was about to set sail, did he suddenly erupt: "Don't you read Central Committee resolutions? Or don't you think them obligatory? I insisted on a ban on naming cities after leaders. And what do I find here but my name!!! Do you realize what sort of situation you've put me in?"[135]

KremGES city fathers knew what they were doing. The toadying that had always tempted Khrushchev was now almost irresistible. When aides showed him a fawning film titled *Our Nikita Sergeyevich*, which depicts his life and career in outrageously hagiographic fashion, he sat through it in silence and didn't praise it, but he didn't ban it either.[136]

In early May 1964 Khrushchev left for Egypt to participate in dedicating the Aswan High Dam.[137] Prior to his departure, Nasser confidant/Cairo journalist Mohamed Heikal arrived in Moscow because "the big man" (as Adzhubei called his father-in-law) had a lot of questions about Egypt. Heikal spent a day with Khrushchev at his dacha and four more days on the boat to Alexandria. "I'll ask the questions, not you, " Khrushchev promised, but instead he talked nonstop about everything from his Suez triumph to Stalin's conduct of war. On the third morning at sea, he finally asked about Egyptian agriculture but cut off Heikal almost immediately: "This is all nonsense. You're wasting your time. Do you know what you ought to do? Chemical agriculture is the answer!" That and hydroponic cultivation of crops, which could substitute for reclaiming the desert: "You don't need to reclaim it. Fill your deserts with containers of water! Do you think President Nasser knows about this? I've got a report about it and a film. I'll send them to him. This could be better for you than the High Dam."

Told that the Egyptians were interested in desalination, Khrushchev knew an academician who could teach them that too. "But that's no good for you," he added. "It's much too expensive. Glass and plastic water containers will provide you with everything you need."[138] Only the last day at sea did Khrushchev finally ask the sorts of questions—about religion, language, customs, and politics—that Heikal had expected.

When Khrushchev wasn't lecturing Heikal, he was preparing for talks with Nasser. Other members of the delegation were dying to play dominoes but knew better than to do so in his presence. "Games of any kind were frowned on," recalled Sergei Khrushchev, who was on board. "The others were afraid of Father, who didn't like games and considered them a waste of time. He never had any time for soccer, dominoes or cards." Sergei remembered another voyage on which Brezhnev, Podgorny, Grechko, and others broke out the dominoes the moment Khrushchev headed for his cabin and quickly cleared them away when he was about to return.[139]

Considering past strains between Moscow and Cairo, Khrushchev feared his welcome would be low-key. So the grandiose reception when the *Armenia* docked brought tears to his eyes, as did crowds numbering in the millions who lined the long route to Cairo.[140] Talks with the Egyptians weren't so pleasant. But the disagreements (Nasser wanted more money and weapons than Moscow could afford; Khrushchev demanded Egypt practice "peaceful coexistence" with its neighbors) were overshadowed by the dam's dedication. Nasser and Khrushchev pressed the button; the Nile roared through the floodgates; the dignitaries present (including Presidents Abdur Rahman Aref, Abdullah as-Sallal, and Ahmed Ben Bella of Iraq, Yemen, and Algeria respectively) received commemorative gold medals. Khrushchev proudly accepted the Necklace of the Nile, the highest award of the United Arab Republic. In return he awarded Hero of the Soviet Union medals to both Nasser and Marshal Abdel Hakim Amer. In October 1964, Dmitri Polyansky condemned Khrushchev for decorating a president who "drove Communists into concentration camps" and who acted as if socialism's founder were Muhammad, not Marx.[141]

For at least part of the time Khrushchev seemed to enjoy himself. He loved playing the wise benefactor, distributing aid and advice to the grateful Egyptian people. He relished putting anti- Communist leaders like Iraq's Aref in their place. Some of the sights reminded him of heaven as he had imagined it as a child in the church school in Kalinovka. But the heat was almost unbearable, and so, he recalled later, was the view of the Nile from his plane: vibrant life along its green banks but surrounded by the desert, a vast "waterless expanse," representing "death."[142]

As the Aswan visit came to an end, Khrushchev seemed oddly out of sorts. Unhappy that Aref was coming on a Red Sea cruise, he told a story about a Russian naval commander during the Russo-Japanese War who was "an incompetent and a brute" but whose second-in-command was well liked by all. When their ship sank, there was rejoicing at the commander's death, but grief that his deputy died too. Then came news that the captain had been saved. "I'll tell you what the sailors said then," Khrushchev continued. "'Gold sinks, but shit floats.'" Suddenly realizing how his listeners were taking the story, Khrushchev lamely tried to retreat: "Of course, none of this applies to present company."[143]

The nearly three-week visit dragged on. Khrushchev spent several days in one of King Farouk's summer palaces in Alexandria. Suddenly, after being in particularly good form at lunch, he declared, "Nobody's talking! This is a dull party! Isn't there any music? . . . You make music!" he ordered Gromyko, handing him a plate and rapping it like a tambourine. Then to Grechko: "And marshal, you dance!" Gromyko accepted the plate with weak smile, while Grechko looked pained. The scene recalled Stalin's last years, when he had humiliated Khrushchev by making him dance.[144]

Something was eating at Khrushchev. Even before leaving Yalta, Heikal had been struck by his embarrassing "half-serious banter" toward his colleagues. When the Kiev party boss Pyotr Shelest fulsomely announced he would take care of everything in Ukraine, Khrushchev snapped, "Comrade, it seems to me you think I'm not going to come back from this trip. . . . But I am going to come back, and when I do, you will have to give me a full account. . . ."

Several times in Egypt Khrushchev praised himself as "still a peasant," as a simple, straightforward man who wasn't irreplaceable. He also ate and drank like a peasant, downing six large sweet cakes at one sitting even after his daughter Rada had begged him to stop, guzzling brandy, and pouring his soup into a saucer and then drinking it without a spoon. On the day the Soviet party left Egypt, Khrushchev confessed he was angry because Heikal had described him as a peasant in the press.

"But, Mr. Chairman," Heikal objected, "you've always spoken with such pride of being a peasant!"

"But you wrote I was like a peasant from a story by Dostoevsky—why didn't you say peasant from Tolstoy?"[145]

It is unlikely that Khrushchev's reproach reflected a close reading of the role of peasants in Tolstoy and Dostoevsky. At most he probably knew that Tolstoy idealized peasants, whereas Dostoevsky, with his religious mysticism, Russofilism, and scathing attacks on radical revolutionaries, did not.

HAVING RETURNED from Egypt on May 25, Khrushchev left for Scandinavia on June 16. He later admitted that the trip had no "particular political significance." The main reason he went was that a previously scheduled visit had been postponed and he was embarrassed by the long delay in rescheduling it. "Although the weather was sunny," Adzhubei remembered, "there was something sad about this trip." Ordinarily supersensitive about how he was greeted abroad, this time Khrushchev was strangely distracted. The punctilious Swedes hadn't planned a twenty-one-gun salute (formally Khrushchev wasn't a head of state), but Soviet protocol people insisted on it. When the guns' roar greeted the *Bashkiria* on its entrance to Stockholm Harbor, Khrushchev asked, "What are they firing at?" and, without waiting for the cannonade to end, walked off to his cabin.[146]

His speeches in Scandinavia lacked fire and energy. His ritual report to the Soviet people on his return reads like a travelogue. His memoirs highlighted Nina Petrovna's breaking the traditional bottle of champagne to launch a Danish ship, that the Danish king's daughter was "still just a girl, and she had a very nice appearance," and that the man who met him at the door of the Norwegian royal palace in a "khaki-colored uniform of some sort" and then showed him into a study and offered him a chair turned out to be the king. "He could easily have been mistaken for the gardener," Khrushchev recalled.[147]

Official minutes of Khrushchev's conversations are no more inspiring. To the Danish king, we are told, "N. S. Khrushchev recounted the remarkable conditions for hunting in various regions of the USSR." Queen Ingrid and Princess Margrethe, the heiress to the throne, were briefed by their high guest on the state of "Soviet theater, music and ballet."[148] Even important lessons he learned proved bittersweet. Years later Khrushchev closed his eyes and still saw the agricultural "miracles" little Denmark had wrought: "Yes, I understand they're miraculous for us," whereas "for other countries they're not miracles, just long-standing accomplishments." In Norway he learned why its Communist party was so unpopular. "Because," he was told, "many of our workers have their own homes, boats, and other property."[149]

KHRUSHCHEV THOUGHT of retiring; he talked of it often at home and in the Kremlin. "We're oldsters, we've done our bit," he would say to Presidium colleagues. "It's time to yield the road to others. We've got to give youth a chance to work." They assumed he was joking or testing their loyalty, as Stalin had done toward his end. In no mood to retire themselves, they knew what to say in response: "What are you talking about, Nikita Sergeyevich? You look terrific! You're a lot stronger than most younger men."

One thing that deterred Khrushchev was the issue of succession. The Soviet Union had no established procedure for transferring power. After Lenin and Stalin died, the battle to replace them shook the system. A fixed term for the leader and a regularized process for replacing him would help, but that would limit Khrushchev. He could try to handpick a successor, but an heir apparent could threaten his anointer. The way to reduce that danger was to appoint two conflicting contenders, but that would ensure a bigger contest later on.

Khrushchev's first top lieutenant, the particularly crude Aleksei Kirichenko, proved too aggressive. When he tried to transfer Shelepin from Moscow to Leningrad, Khrushchev blew up, beating on the desk with his fist and shouting into the phone: "Who the hell do you think you are? The Leningrad leadership can't be assigned without discussion, and it wasn't discussed. Leningrad is my bailiwick; I make the decisions about it!"[150]

After Kirichenko came Frol Kozlov. With his carefully coiffed white hair, impeccable business suits, and button-down shirts (the latter a rarity in the USSR at the time and long afterward), the former metallurgical engineer turned party bigwig was not "such a brute as we," Khrushchev told Harriman in 1959.[151] According to Shelepin, who was a potential rival, Kozlov was a "very limited man. His only strength was his vocal cords. . . . You'd come into his office and what would you see? A perfectly clean desk—not a single piece of paper or a pencil in sight. And this was the number two man in the party!" Mikoyan considered Kozlov an "unintelligent pro-Stalinist reactionary and careerist."[152]

Until the beginning of 1963 Kozlov hewed to the Khrushchev line, but then, according to Sergei Khrushchev, he "began to act a little independently." At that point, recalled Presidium candidate member Pyotr Demichev, other members gravitated to Kozlov as de facto second secretary of the party. None of this added up to organized opposition; on the contrary, Sergei wrote later, "Father liked Kozlov. . . . The fact that he occasionally objected and argued with Father elicited Father's respect rather than irritation."[153] However, Kozlov occasionally misstepped, for example, when he allowed the CPSU's ritual May Day 1963 greeting to other Communist parties to imply a change of line on Yugoslavia. Khrushchev was resting at Pitsunda when he noticed Yugoslavia described in the greeting as just "building socialism" rather than as having already completed the "foundations" thereof. A trivial distinction it would seem, but it implied a slap at Khrushchev's on and off policy of cultivating Tito.

Sergei was present when his father telephoned Kozlov, demanded a retraction, and instead got some backtalk. At this point "Father shouted at Kozlov, and accused him of being arbitrary. . . . "[154] Khrushchev's words were surely spicier than that. Shelepin remembered a hunt in the Byelovezhsky Forest, where Khrushchev and Kozlov shot simultaneously at a wild boar that "beaters" conveniently drove right in front of them. Both men claimed the kill. The quarrel continued until Khrushchev ordered an autopsy to determine whose bullet had done the job. When it turned out to be his, Khrushchev had it washed, kept it in his pocket, and deliberately pulled it out and played with it at Presidium meetings to annoy Kozlov.[155]

Whether it was the quarrel about the bullet (as Shelepin claimed), Khrushchev's May Day harangue (as other Central Committee rumors had it), or just a weakness in Kozlov's genetic makeup, he suffered a major stroke at just this time, meaning that another number two had to be found. Shelepin wasn't ready, Khrushchev confided to his son, the Ukrainian first secretary Nikolai Podgorny was "narrow," and Brezhnev "isn't suited either." He had the right sort of experience, both in the central party apparatus and in the field, but "before the war, when we appointed him Dnepropetrovsk province secretary, the boys nicknamed him 'the ballerina,'" because "anyone who wants to can turn him around."

Kremlin infighting was the most sacred of secrets. Khrushchev had never discussed Presidium personnel with his son before and never did afterward. "If he had to confide in me on a topic like this," wrote Sergei, "how hard it must have been for Father, how alone he was."

That same evening Khrushchev mentioned retirement again: "My strength isn't what it used to be, and it's time to make way for the young. I'll carry the torch till the Twenty-third Congress and then hand in my resignation. . . . I was forty-five when I joined the Politburo. That's the right age for matters of state; you have the strength and there's lots of time ahead of you. At age sixty you no longer think about the future. It's time to baby-sit for your grandchildren."[156]

He couldn't bring himself to do it. Instead, according to Mikoyan, Khrushchev "kept going on in everyone's presence about the need to expand the Presidium to bring in young people." All the talk reminded his colleagues of how Stalin had reshaped the Politburo in 1952; they feared the next step would be their ouster. "It was as if he were purposely creating enemies," Mikoyan added, "without even noticing that he was doing it."[157]

KHRUSHCHEV'S SEVENTIETH birthday marked a new peak in the Khrushchev cult: Congratulations from around the country and the world filled the airwaves; newspapers and magazines hailed "The Great Decade" since he took office; he was awarded the grand title of Hero of the Soviet Union for his many accomplishments.[158] Early on the morning of April 17, security men lugged a large new radio-television console into Khrushchev's Lenin Hills living room; it bore a metal plate with the inscription "From your comrades at work in the Central Committee and the Council of Ministers." The gift was a violation of Khrushchev's own rule. "No presents!" he had growled. "Don't waste the people's money!" Neither his family nor his colleagues paid any attention, knowing how disappointed he would have been if they had.

The guests began to arrive at nine o'clock: relatives, Presidium members, secretaries of the Central Committee. The rest of the day was to be devoted to public celebration; now was the time for colleagues to kowtow in private. Careful not to smoke, they waited until their leader appeared on the oaken staircase, elegantly attired in a dark suit with his three Hero of Socialist Labor stars arrayed on his chest. After everyone found seats around the dining room table, the speeches commenced. As chairman of the Supreme Soviet Presidium (and titular head of state) Brezhnev read a fulsome tribute: "Dear Nikita Sergeyevich! We, your close comrades in arms, members and candidate members of the Presidium and secretaries of the Central Committee, extend special greetings and fervently congratulate you, our closest personal friend and comrade, on your seventieth birthday."

Brushing away tears, Brezhnev hugged Khrushchev and presented him with a handsome case containing the just-read speech signed by all the guests. During the lengthy toasts Brezhnev and Suslov looked particularly nervous. Afterward Khrushchev's colleagues found an excuse—they didn't want to tire N. S.—to hurry away, even though, Pyotr Shelest recalled, "you could tell Khrushchev neither wanted nor expected a quick end to the occasion."[159]

By the end of the day, after congratulations at work and a grand reception and banquet in the Kremlin that evening, Khrushchev was worn out, both, one suspects, from craving the daylong acclaim and from being mortified by it. For him the two feelings were probably more or less in balance. For his wife and family, a photograph taken that morning suggests, embarrassment predominated: It shows Khrushchev on his feet with glass raised, resolutely addressing his colleagues. Brezhnev sits with eyes modestly lowered; Nina Petrovna, her daughter Elena, and Anastas Mikoyan look pained and grim-faced as Khrushchev plows on.[160]

BY THIS TIME Khrushchev's colleagues couldn't stand him. Even before his birthday, Brezhnev was conspiring against him. In early March he and Podgorny had begun approaching Presidium members about removing Khrushchev.[161] In June, Brezhnev briefly considered having him arrested as he returned from Scandinavia.[162] Instead he and other plotters spent the summer and early autumn secretly securing the support of Central Committee members so as to avoid the fate of Khrushchev's rivals in 1957.

Brezhnev and Khrushchev had a lot in common: humble backgrounds, an obvious lack of education and culture (Brezhnev's only reading, besides official documents, was the Soviet satirical journal *Krokodil*); likable, sociable styles. However, Brezhnev liked to put on airs, especially in his role as titular head of state. Khrushchev didn't like that, and word of his annoyance got back to Brezhnev. In July 1964 Khrushchev elevated Brezhnev to deputy party leader, while making Podgorny a rival heir apparent. But even after this Khrushchev continued to mock them, asking other Kremlin colleagues (who of course passed the word to Brezhnev and Podgorny), "You mean to say you regard those two as real leaders?" Brezhnev hid his resentment, going so far as to inscribe sycophantic entries into his desk calendar at work (e.g., "Met Nikita Sergeyevich—a joyous and pleasant meeting") just in case prying eyes noticed them.[163]

A Central Committee plenum in July 1964 brought Khrushchev's declining fortunes to a new low. So shameful was his behavior that neither he nor his successors ever publicized the plenum; instead it went down in Soviet oral history lore as "the plenum that never occurred."[164] He demanded that the Agricultural Academy be exiled from Moscow to the countryside.[165] He called for abolition of the Academy of Sciences, the illustrious history of which went back to the eighteenth century. Moscow party chief Nikolai Yegorychev was sitting next to the Academy of Sciences president Mikhail Keldysh. "I'll resign, I'll resign, I won't do it," Keldysh muttered bitterly. Yegorychev asked Suslov, with whom he traveled to Paris shortly after the plenum, if the leadership had already decided the issue. "What do you mean, Comrade Yegorychev?" the always formal Suslov replied. "What do you mean? Of course not. No, no, no."[166]

If the Academy of Sciences was anathema to Khrushchev, Lysenko was a hero. Convinced Lysenko had been involved in "some bad business" and that his science wasn't genuine either, Khrushchev had briefly turned against him after Stalin's death. But Lysenko had fought his way back into Khrushchev's good graces, aided by a competition between him and another academician, Nikolai Tsytsin, both of whom claimed their wheat produced higher yields. The competition took place at a collective farm near Khrushchev's dacha; he regularly rowed down the Moscow River and clambered up the bank to inspect the rival crops. Tsytsin took an early lead, but Lysenko's wheat ended up bigger and better.[167]

As a scientific "experiment" this made no sense (since no control plantings of any kind were made), but the "results" were less important than Khrushchev's need for miracles of the sort Lysenko was promising. In April 1963 two Lysenkoites received coveted Lenin Prizes after Khrushchev personally intervened to reverse the prize committee's negative vote. In June he tried to get three Lysenko followers elected to the Academy of Sciences. After legendary physicists Andrei Sakharov, Igor Tamm, and others indicted Lysenkoism as false science and accused one of the nominees of denouncing the great geneticist Nikolai Vavilov, who had been arrested and died in the gulag, that nominee was rejected.[168]

This was the background for Khrushchev's explosion at the July plenum. It also prompted Rada Adzhubei (a biologist by training as well as a graduate of Moscow University's journalism program) and Sergei Khrushchev to try to discuss Lysenko with their father one evening at the dacha. They were sitting on a terrace overlooking the Moscow River when Khrushchev grumbled to no one in particular about Lysenko's unfair treatment by "antiscientific Weismannist-Morganist idealists."[169] Khrushchev condemned biologists who experimented with mere fruit flies, whereas Lysenko worked with cows. Instead of retreating, Rada defended fruit fly research. She and Sergei rejected as absurd Lysenko's contention that no one had actually seen a gene. No one had seen an atom either, but that hadn't prevented the USSR from developing an atomic bomb. What happened next was described by Sergei: "The conversation really angered Father. He never shouted at his family, never cursed or raised his voice. . . . But this time he flared up and in a raised voice repeated his old arguments that unscrupulous people were using us for their own purposes, and that we, ignorant in this matter, were echoing their words. Finally, he lost his temper altogether and declared that he wouldn't tolerate carriers of an alien ideology in his own home, and that if we persisted, we'd better not darken his door again." According to Sergo Mikoyan, who was present, Khrushchev stomped his foot, pounded the table with his fist, and shouted, "Shut up!" at his daughter.[170]

ONE OF THE first rules for an autocrat on his last legs is not to leave rivals minding the capital. Yet Khrushchev was away from Moscow, either in the USSR or abroad, for some 170 days in 1963 and 150 during the first nine and half months of 1964 alone.[171] In mid-July 1964 he was in Warsaw for the twentieth anniversary of the Polish People's Republic. He spent half of August touring Soviet agricultural regions from Saratov Province to Central Asia. After a short breather in Moscow, he visited Czechoslovakia from August 27 through September 4.

To speechwriter Fyodor Burlatsky, with him in Czechoslovakia, Khrushchev looked "happy, contented, even inspired."[172] Andrei Shevchenko knew his boss better. One night during their August tour of the provinces, Moscow called to report that fighting had broken out on

Cyprus and to check a statement it was issuing with Khrushchev. The next day Khrushchev summoned Shevchenko before going to bed. "I'm tired, damned tired, and I'm going to bed. Even if war breaks out, don't wake me."[173]

In the past, visits to the Virgin Lands seemed to revitalize Khrushchev. This time, according to party official Fyodor Morgun, he was "angry, there were no jokes, and he avoided conversations. It was as if he were very worried about something."[174] During the same trip Khrushchev blew up at Shevchenko for the first time. That same summer, Shevchenko also witnessed Khrushchev explode at his wife, Nina Petrovna.[175]

Two other aides got the treatment on a Sunday in late August. Khrushchev dropped in on Moscow party boss Yegorychev and Vladimir Promyslov, the city's mayor, at a nearby sanatorium. He demanded to know what toilet seats in new apartments being built in Moscow were made of. Informed that they were made of wood, Khrushchev retorted, "You see. I knew it. You're spendthrifts! You've got to use plastic. I was recently in Poland. I lived in a villa. When you sit on a toilet seat like the one there, it doesn't feel cold. So you take a trip there, check it out, and do the same in Moscow." With that, he clambered back in his motor launch to return to his dacha. Recalled Yegorychev: "These were the last instructions we received from Khrushchev about how to do things in Moscow."[176]

In early September, Khrushchev traveled to a military base at Kubinka, thirty-seven miles west of Moscow, for a demonstration of tanks, artillery, and helicopters. After the assembled marshals had proudly briefed him on their plans, he berated them for wasting valuable resources. "Are we planning to conquer anyone?" Khrushchev asked, glaring at Defense Minister Malinovsky. "No." He answered his own question. "Then why do we need the weapons we saw today?" Since any war would go nuclear, but nuclear war itself was unimaginable, only a minimum of missiles was necessary; beyond that, excessive spending was a drain on the civilian economy. "Otherwise," he told his officer audience, "we'll all lose our pants because of you."

This joke, accompanied by a friendly poke in Malinovsky's ribs, was supposed to ease the tension in the room. But "the joke fell flat," according to Sergei Khrushchev. "Malinovsky forced a sour smile. No one said anything."[177]

After spending ten days at the Tyura-Tam missile range, Khrushchev stopped in Moscow, where he received Indonesian President Sukarno, and then headed south. Landing in Simferopol, he devoted a couple of days to inspecting the Crimea. The Ukrainian party boss Pyotr Shelest thought his guest looked pressured and anxious. Khrushchev complained about Suslov and dismissed Mikoyan as "a big mouth and a dandy."[178] Khrushchev had intended to vacation in the Crimea, but grousing that it was cold and gloomy there, he left for Pitsunda instead. Officially his vacation began on October 3. Although he didn't know it, he had ten days left as leader of his country.

CHAPTER TWENTY-ONE

After the Fall: 1964–1971

KHRUSHCHEV'S OUSTER WASN'T announced to the world until two days after it happened. Rumors began to circulate almost immediately, and references to him vanished overnight from the media, but official word appeared in *Pravda* only on October 16, followed the next day by an editorial, "Unshakable Leninist General Line of the CPSU," which didn't mention Khrushchev by name but condemned "subjectivism and drift in Communist construction, harebrained scheming, half-baked conclusions and hasty decisions and actions divorced from reality, bragging and bluster, attraction to rule by fiat, [and] unwillingness to take into a account what science and practical experience have already worked out."[1]

By the morning of the fifteenth, a new security detail had replaced the bodyguards who had worked for Khrushchev for many years. Of the multiple telephone lines in his Lenin Hills residence, including several city lines and special government phones, only one local line, plus the phone to the guardhouse, was still connected. Early that morning, a large black Chaika sedan pulled up to replace the even more mammoth black ZIL limousine to which only three people in the entire country were entitled: the party leader, the prime minister, and the chairman of the Supreme Soviet Presidium. Later the same day the Chaika itself gave way to an ordinary black Volga, thus reducing Khrushchev to the level of middle-level functionaries who had so resented it when he reduced their privileges.

Khrushchev's habit had been to be at his desk in the Kremlin or at the Central Committee promptly at nine. On October 15 he came down for breakfast about then. The night before he had taken a sedative prescribed by his physician, Dr. Vladimir Bezzubik, but he had hardly slept anyway. "His face seemed to have grown thinner and grayer," remembered Sergei Khrushchev, "and he moved more slowly."

After barely tasting his food, Khrushchev went out in the yard and walked slowly around the house. As he neared the gate, his new security chief, Sergei Melnikov, asked whether he would like to take a drive to his dacha.

"You've got quite a tedious job cut out for you," the former premier replied. "I'm a loafer now. I don't know what to do with myself. You'll waste away from boredom with me. But you may be right. Why sit around here? Let's go."

New guards were also stationed at the dacha when Khrushchev, his son, and Melnikov arrived. After hesitating by the door to the house, Khrushchev walked down the hill past a brook, and across a small bridge to a nearby state farm. During the summer the corn had been cultivated with particular care so as to impress the farm's important neighbor; now the field was bare except for cornstalk stumps sticking up from lumps of earth. As the three men circled the field on a narrow path, Khrushchev began to spout statistics and his favorite agricultural nostrums as if he were addressing local party leaders. Melnikov politely asked questions until, in the midst of the conversation, Khrushchev suddenly stopped.

"No one needs me now," he said in a muffled voice. "What am I going to do without work? How am I going to live?"[2]

NINA PETROVNA KHRUSHCHEVA was vacationing in Karlovy Vary, Czechoslovakia, on October 14, 1964, accompanied by Brezhnev's wife, Viktoria. Immediately after his ouster, Khrushchev asked anxiously how his wife could be informed. Earlier that day he would have picked up the government phone and asked the operator to get her for him. Now, insulated as they had been by the perquisites of power, no one in the family knew how reach her on an ordinary line. Khrushchev's security men finally contacted her and said Nikita Sergeyevich asked her to return home at once but didn't explain why. Instead she had got the news when the Soviet ambassador to Czechoslovakia, Mikhail Zimyanin, who had been fawning over her, mistakenly called her (while trying to reach Mrs. Brezhnev) and exulted about how Khrushchev had been ousted, about how he (Zimyanin) had blasted the old man at the Central Committee plenum from which he had just returned, about how wonderful it would be to have "dear Leonid Ilich" as party leader. Only when Nina Petrovna remained silent did Zimyanin realize his error and hang up in confusion.

Khrushchev worried about who would meet Nina Petrovna at the airport, but Melnikov arranged to do so. When at last her car drove up to the Lenin Hills residence on the evening of the fifteenth, she was still carrying flowers given to her at the Prague airport. Without skipping a beat, she took control of the household, as seemingly calm as she had been during the thirties, when a midnight knock at the door could have meant the end, and in the fifties, when she played first lady to her husband's first secretary. As Sergei Khrushchev recollected it, his mother "saw to it that everyone was fed, made sure that Father wore his habitual clean white shirt, put everything in its place. . . . She acted as if . . . the Central Committee had simply made another decision, in this case involving the dismissal of her husband, and she accepted it as she had so many others in her day. After all, she wasn't just his wife, but a party member, and . . . subordination . . . had become second nature."[3]

If it weren't for the terrible pain Khrushchev's ouster obviously caused him, Nina Petrovna might have been relieved. After his death she recalled her "suffering" and the "agonized nighttime monologues" she addressed to Brezhnev after her husband's fall. "Her torment was no less than ours," Sergei wrote, "but she concealed it better behind an exterior of calm cordiality."[4]

For the next several months, almost until summer, the man who had ruled the Soviet Union for a decade was profoundly depressed. His family tried everything to cheer him up, but he would be neither comforted nor consoled. While in power, Khrushchev regularly studied each day's newspapers; now he merely glanced distractedly at them. Previously he'd been too busy to read books; now "he would leaf mechanically through the pages, lay the book aside, and set off again on one of his interminable walks."[5] In an effort to distract him, Khrushchev's children showed films in a large room at the dacha. "But he never got caught up in them," Sergei recalled. Even *The Chairman*, a recent film glorifying a Khrushchev-style collective farm chairman, produced almost no response. "It was a good film" was all Khrushchev said.[6]

Visitors, of whom there were very few, were no help either. Former colleagues and subordinates had no reason to see him, and no desire either. Others feared unfortunate consequences, as well they might have since Khrushchev's security men kept track of all guests. Beyond that, a more troubling question must have arisen in Khrushchev's mind: did he in fact have any friends? The last people who had befriended him on anything like a basis of equality had done so in the Donbas in the twenties. A few old friends eventually reappeared during his retirement, but not in the beginning.

Early on the only visitors were friends of Khrushchev's children, invited, according to Sergei, to "distract Father, to dispel his gloomy thoughts." At first the device worked, particularly when the company entered a hydroponic greenhouse recently built at the dacha, and he began to hail hydroponics as if his listeners were heads of state. But "at the height of his peroration," Sergei reported, "Nikita Sergeyevich stopped short and fell silent; the light had gone out of his eyes. 'This is no longer any of my business. And you don't understand much about it anyway.' "[7]

In the autumn Khrushchev was ordered to vacate both his Lenin Hills residence and his dacha. His new dacha was to be in Petrovo-Dalneye on the other side of Moscow. His new apartment in town (where he was to spend practically no time) was at 19 Starokonyushenny Lane in a house built in the 1930s for Central Committee employees. With five rooms, a kitchen, and a spacious entrance hall, it was pretty grand by Soviet standards, but a far cry from his former residences. Nonetheless, he immediately agreed to take it. He "had little interest in how and where he was going to live," Sergei remembered, "and would have agreed to anything."[8]

With endless time on his hands, Khrushchev mostly walked—around and around the dacha grounds, sometimes with Sergei and security chief Melnikov, mostly alone, almost always in silence. "The silence oppressed us," wrote Sergei. "We tried . . . to strike up a conversation about more or less neutral news from Moscow, but he didn't react. Sometimes he himself broke the silence and repeated bitterly that his life was over, that life made sense as long as people needed him, but now, when nobody needed him, life was meaningless. Sometimes tears welled up in his eyes. We were worried, of course, but Vladimir Grigorievich told us not to be afraid. 'This is one of the consequences of shock,' he explained to us. Meanwhile, the endless walks continued, and Father remained withdrawn."[9]

Vladimir Grigorievich Bezzubik, Khrushchev's personal physician, didn't abandon his patient. Besides sitting and talking with him for hours at a time, he prescribed sleeping pills and tranquilizers. The family didn't fear suicide, as they did several years later. But when one of Khrushchev's grandsons was asked by his school headmaster what his grandfather did in retirement, the boy answered, "Grandfather cries."[10] Asked the same question many years later, the Khrushchev family cook had a similar recollection: "He sat and cried. He sat and cried."[11]

New Year's Eve 1965 found the Khrushchevs still in their old dacha, but with the move to Petrovo-Dalneye in the offing. Since the dacha's furniture was government issue and not moving with them, the big, dark dining room where the extended family assembled on December 31 looked the same as always: a long table for thirty to forty people in the center, uncomfortable black leather couches along the walls, an unusable gray marble fireplace at the end of the room. For the first time in years Khrushchev wasn't surrounded by thousands on New Year's Eve; even his extended family couldn't fill all the seats at the dining room table. The contrast with the past oppressed them all, but everyone except Khrushchev tried to look happy and cheerful. "Father sat there quietly taking no part in the festivities, just looking on," Sergei later wrote.[12]

Several people managed to telephone, but most of the calls were for Khrushchev's children. A few calls came from Donbas comrades or from veterans of the Moscow electric lamp factory where Nina Petrovna had worked in the thirties, but nobody asked to speak to Khrushchev. Finally, one brave caller did. After hesitating, Khrushchev rose slowly from the table and shuffled toward the phone in the next room. It was Mikoyan. Suddenly Khrushchev was listening intently and answering in a strong voice: "Thank you, Anastas. Happy New Year to you too. My best wishes to your family. Thank you. I'm trying to keep my spirits up. My business is now retirement. I'm learning how to take it easy."

Khrushchev looked revivified when he reappeared. Once he was seated at the table, Sergei recalled, "the new life in his eyes died out."

Mikoyan's call took courage; still hanging on in the leadership, he had plenty to lose. Soon after this phone call, which his son later learned was reported to the new team in the Kremlin, Mikoyan's stenographer/secretary began repeating "fool things" about Mikoyan that Khrushchev had allegedly told his chauffeur. These reports were fourth hand; the stenographer almost certainly worked for the KGB, but Mikoyan believed them. He had long been convinced that Khrushchev envied him, that the reason Khrushchev "often refused to agree with me was that he didn't want to admit I was right." Now, he believed, Khrushchev blamed him for not detecting the plot that had ousted him and stopping it—in other words, added Sergo Mikoyan, for not doing what Khrushchev couldn't or wouldn't do himself. Given their mutual sense of grievance, the fact that Mikoyan never telephoned Khrushchev again isn't surprising. The surprise is that he called this last time.[13]

Isolated and depressed, Khrushchev was no threat to anyone. But his former colleagues weren't taking any chances, especially after what had happened on October 23. That day the latest triumphant cosmonauts, whom Khrushchev had greeted in space via the phone from Pitsunda, got their heroes' welcome in Moscow. The festivities began with a morning ceremony at Vnukovo Airport; from there a motorcade drove down Leninsky Prospekt to a Red Square rally, followed by a gala reception. The Khrushchevs watched the airport arrival on live television in their Lenin Hills residence. After a few minutes Khrushchev got up, groused that he wasn't going to look, and went out.

Unable to calm down, he hailed his security chief and asked to drive to his dacha. The trouble was that their route at first took them toward Red Square. Brezhnev and company got word that he was coming and nearly panicked, but before they could figure out how to stop him, his car turned west toward his dacha. That evening Melnikov received new orders: Khrushchev was to move to his dacha the next morning and stay there until further notice. The rest of the family could continue to use the Lenin Hills residence for the time being. The next day the family moved to the dacha, where they remained until the Petrovo-Dalneye residence was ready in early 1965.[14]

The Petrovo-Dalneye house was more modest than Khrushchev's former manse. Only one-story high, built of logs instead of stone, and painted dark green, it stood atop the pine-covered bank of the Istra River not far from where it joins the Moscow River. Near the house the pines gave way to an apple orchard flanked by flower beds, with paths winding among the trees. Wooden stairs led down a steep incline to a wooden platform and dressing hut at the edge of the Istra. Near a tall fence that surrounded the property was a meadow; from a bench in the clearing, which became Khrushchev's favorite resting place, he could see the river and the fields of a state farm in the distance.

Inside, as Sergei Khrushchev remembered it, the house "seemed spacious and yet cozy."[15] There were separate bedrooms for Nikita Sergeyevich and Nina Petrovna; a room for Yelena Khrushcheva and her husband, Viktor Yevreinov, a young chemist; a small room for Nina Petrovna with a large desk; a kitchen; the former billiards room overlooking the orchard, which Nina Petrovna turned into a large dining room. There was also a veranda covered by translucent yellow plastic where Khrushchev liked to sit, a separate summer kitchen, and a heated bungalow by the gate in which Khrushchev's security detail with its eavesdropping equipment took up residence.[16]

Khrushchev's own room opened on to the veranda and the garden. Besides a bed, small tables, and his personal belongings (including a gift picture of a girl inlaid in ebony from Nehru, an English phonograph in a wooden box from Ghana's Nkrumah, and a yellowish red armchair from Finland's Kekkonen), it housed a large safe in which Khrushchev kept his secret documents—except that he no longer had any secret documents, and he kept even his treasured party card in his desk since he didn't have the strength to open the huge yellow and brown safe.

The move itself was Nina Petrovna's province, the latest (but not the last) of the many she had to superintend in the course of her peripatetic life. Mostly, said her son, these moves were "against her wishes. Sometimes she joked sadly that she could become a professional packer."[17] What made it worse this time was that her husband fell ill with what his doctor at first feared was pancreatic cancer. It turned out to be less serious, but the illness further delayed his recovery from the shock of his ouster and the depression that followed it.

After the move his family tried to distract him with new hobbies. He hadn't enjoyed fishing on the Dnieper near his Kiev dacha, but he agreed to try again. After reading several books on fishing, he trudged down to the Istra, attached lures once given to him by Walter Ulbricht to a rod provided by his son, and cast out his line. But he didn't catch anything at first, and he wasn't about to wait. "You sit there feeling like an absolute idiot!" he complained afterward. "You can even hear the fish laughing at you under the water. That's not for me."[18]

Khrushchev "used to call us good-for-nothings when he found us in front of the television," according to Sergei. Now he relied on TV, radio, and newspapers for news. Deprived of intelligence reports and briefings, he read *Pravda* every morning in the upholstered seat in front of his bedroom window, took a small portable radio with him on his walks, and unearthed a Zenith shortwave radio that the American businessman Eric Johnston had given him in the 1950s. He listened to music, but also to news, both from Moscow and on Western stations like Voice of America and BBC. But the news wasn't good; too many of his reforms were being reversed. Also, the party propaganda in which he had put such stock now struck him as heavy-handed and inept. "This is just garbage!" he muttered about *Pravda.* "How can they write like this? What kind of propaganda is this? Who will believe it?"[19]

His home was one of several in the village of Petrovo-Dalneye, all separated from one another by high green fences but sharing the same asphalt road. Other bigwigs living nearby included two deputy premiers, Mikhail Lesechko and Ignaty Novikov, and former Finance Minister Arseny Zverev. Not knowing what to say when they encountered Khrushchev, they informed him of their official activities as if he were still their boss. According to Sergei, "these meetings oppressed Father, and he tried to avoid contacts with former subordinates." So he also avoided a small club in the village that showed new movies twice a week.

He did venture into the fields of a nearby farm. Watching the workers gather a pitifully small harvest of barley and oats, he itched to order them to grow vegetables for the profitable Moscow market instead. At first he groused only to his family, but after a while he started monitoring the fieldwork through binoculars, and when someone in authority appeared, he hustled over to dispense advice. The fact that his neighbors didn't take it, citing orders from higher-ups that had to be fulfilled, made Khrushchev even angrier, but "Father never butted in with advice again, although he kept complaining to us about the scandalous management."[20]

Hunting had been Khrushchev's only hobby while in office; except between 1950 and 1953, when Stalin discouraged it, he had hunted regularly near Kiev and Moscow. He had also collected two dozen or so rifles and carbines, which he received as gifts from generals after the war and from Soviet and foreign guests. A Parabellum, a Walther, and another fancy pistol, seventieth birthday gifts from the KGB, lay in an elegant wooden box atop a mahogany-veneer wardrobe in his Petrovo-Dalneye room. Before his ouster, he had loved to take out his guns, examine them, and show them to guests. Afterward he never hunted and rarely looked at his collection. In 1968 he gave most of it away (to his son, older grandsons, his doctor, even guards who helped him with everyday chores), saying, "Let some good people have the guns—something to remember me by. Otherwise, they'll be stolen after I'm gone."[21]

Gradually, as Khrushchev regained his equilibrium in the spring and summer of 1965, other activities began to divert him. From the top of a rise near the house, which his grandchildren dubbed Grass Snake Hill in honor of the snakes that soaked up the sun there in the early spring, Khrushchev could see the whole neighborhood. Vacationers at a nearby lodge spotted him and were sufficiently low on the Soviet ladder that they didn't fear to approach. The first time they exchanged shouted greetings over the fence; later, after village authorities had agreed to cut a small gate in the fence, vacationers crowded around him, taking pictures of him and listening to his stories. Current Soviet politics was off-limits, but that didn't prevent "Khrushchev visits" from becoming a regular part of the lodge's "cultural program." Home movies taken by Sergei in the spring of 1969 show him coming alive on these occasions, grinning and gesticulating as of old, but they also show him exhausted afterward, subsiding into the portable canvas chair that he carried with him on his walks.

Letters from around the USSR and abroad provided another link to the past—at least until KGB chief Yuri Andropov, reflecting the Kremlin leadership's continuing anger at Khrushchev, cut most of them off in late 1970.[22] But perhaps because they reminded him too much of what he had lost, Khrushchev showed little interest in them. It was Nina Petrovna who sorted through the mail, read some of it aloud to her husband, typed up answers to some letters (but not those she thought were sent by autograph seekers), and gave them to him to sign. When he finally began to do more reading, he rejected war memoirs, saying the generals exaggerated their own heroics and ignored his contributions. He also avoided other memoirs his son suggested (by Churchill, de Gaulle, even those of nineteenth-century Russian statesmen), putting them aside after a few pages and muttering, "I'll read it later."

Khrushchev preferred fiction—Tolstoy, Turgenev, Leskov, Kuprin, and Saltykov-Shchedrin—as well as books about nature and technology.[23] When Sergei brought him a dog-eared, typewritten, samizdat copy of Pasternak's *Doctor Zhivago,* Khrushchev took a long time reading it and didn't talk about it except to say, "We shouldn't have banned it. I should have read it myself. There's nothing anti-Soviet in it."[24] This verdict reflected his increasingly jaundiced view of ideological orthodoxy. In addition, he must have found it satisfying to take on the poet's allusive novel and arrive at his own independent view of it.

Emboldened by his father's reaction to *Zhivago,* Sergei produced Solzhenitsyn's *First Circle* and *Cancer Ward* and George Orwell's *1984.* At these, however, Khrushchev drew the line; "he didn't like them," Sergei said.

Once it became clear Khrushchev was boycotting the dacha community club, Sergei dredged up a Yugoslav projector and a German screen, transformed a dacha corridor into a small screening room, and began showing movies that he rented or that friends brought back from abroad. Khrushchev liked escapist fare, including a Disney film about birds, and historical films, such as *July 6,* based on the play about 1918 by the anti-Stalinist playwright Mikhail Shatrov.

The Shatrov showing followed a rare outing to the Sovremennik Theater to see another Shatrov play titled *The Bolsheviks.* Khrushchev had difficulty hearing the actors, and "the fact that people stared at him made him uncomfortable, as though he were some kind of weird exhibit." Still, he went backstage during the intermission, and after the show he entertained the troupe with reminiscences about historical characters depicted in the play. Noting that Shatrov hadn't included Bukharin and Kamenev at a meeting of the Council of People's Commissars that they surely attended, Khrushchev said, "They were good men. We should have rehabilitated them. But we didn't have time."[25]

In time more visitors began coming to Petrovo-Dalneye. Some were old family friends like Vera Gostinskaya, who had lived with the Khrushchevs on Olginskaya Street in Kiev in 1928. Stella and Pyotr Yakir were children of Iona Yakir, the Red Army commander and friend of Khrushchev's from Kiev whom Stalin liquidated; later in the sixties Pyotr Yakir was arrested as a dissident. Sergei Khrushchev invited rocket engineers and weapons designers and their families. Yulia Khrushcheva (Leonid's daughter) brought Shatrov and Boris Zhutovsky, one of the artists Khrushchev had lambasted at the Manezh exhibit in December 1962. Soviet documentary film director Roman Karmen arrived with his wife, Maya (who later married Vasily Aksyonov, whom Khrushchev had chewed out in March 1963). In 1970 Yulia brought Yevgeny Yevtushenko, another target of Khrushchev's March 1963 wrath, and the nonconformist bard Vladimir Vysotsky. Khrushchev apologized for shouting at artists and writers in 1962 and 1963; the reason he had yelled, he admitted, was that they had been right. A home movie shows Khrushchev and Yevtushenko sitting on a bench, Khrushchev speaking animatedly and poking his listener on the arm, flashing the shy but sly grin of a man who thinks he's said something important but doesn't want to seem full of himself. Both the grin and gesture recall the 1930s newsreels, but they're labored now, almost in slow motion.[26]

Most of these guests arrived on weekends. The rest of the time Khrushchev and his wife were alone. He'd had a camera in the Donbas when he was young; before the war he'd used a Leica but left it in Kiev in 1941. He'd started taking pictures again in 1947 after his bout with pneumonia, and now he resumed again, going so far as to develop films in his bathroom, a practice virtually unheard of among Soviet amateur photographers in the 1960s and 1970s. Soon Khrushchev switched to slides, which he delighted in showing to his children, grandchildren, and guests. For a while he carried his camera (along with the portable radio) with him on walks, taking endless pictures of nature. In the long run, Sergei reported, "Father wasn't really interested. Photography was just a way to pass the time. After several years . . . he became utterly bored and put the camera away. . . ."[27]

Gardening was a more enduring preoccupation. When his daughter, Yelena, an inveterate gardener, brought him a book titled *Industrial Hydroponics*, Khrushchev studied it carefully, covering its pages with underlinings, checkmarks, and notes in the margins. Then he prepared a mixture to nurture plants, built troughs and placed them on the open terrace, and filled the cement vases flanking the stairs with the mixture as well. He also built a makeshift hothouse by stretching polyethylene plastic sheeting over a frame of used water pipes, which he bent into shape, painted, and pounded into the ground. When the hydroponic harvest proved disappointing, he concentrated on an old-fashioned garden, irrigating it with pipes he laid and planting dill, radishes, potatoes, pumpkins, sunflowers, and of course corn. Driving himself to near exhaustion, he recruited helpers among relatives, guests, and even the younger security men until they were barred from helping out. Each week Khrushchev planned his campaign for the coming weekend: When company arrived, he deployed all those who couldn't come up with a valid excuse or hadn't demonstrated their ineptitude (whether deliberately or not) by weeding cucumbers instead of weeds. His ten-year-old grandson Nikita, as awkward as he was eager, was among his most faithful lieutenants. The former metalworker particularly enjoyed "commanding" helpers with higher educations. "I'll show you how this has to be done," he would say, using a set of tools and oakum and flax to fit pipe sections together. "You call yourselves engineers but you can't even bend or twist a pipe."[28]

Khrushchev's favorite pastime was building open-air bonfires. "In any weather, even in rain," Sergei remembered, he donned a greenish beige cloak given to him by a capitalist he'd met in France in 1960, gathered brushwood, started a fire, and then would "stare at it for hours." During the week his sole company was his German shepherd, Arbat, and later a mixed-breed named Bel'ka, who took over when Arbat died. ("The mutt is smarter, more loyal and less capricious," Khrushchev remarked. "What do I need a blockhead with a pedigree for?")[29] On weekends he drafted family and friends to prepare the fire and then listen to him retell familiar stories about the Donbas and his dream of becoming an engineer who would build "clever" machines himself. "When the fire died out, the stories stopped," said Sergei. Khrushchev built fires in all seasons, but he liked spring best. "He didn't like autumn. In fact he dreaded it. The darkness and the howling wind weighed down on him, and the dark, gloomily swaying pines reminded him of death."[30]

KHRUSHCHEV WASN'T the first leader to fall into depression after being suddenly removed from office. So, for example, did Richard Nixon. Both men's declines reflected how much their political life meant to them, how bound up their self-images were with having and holding power.[31] Yet in another sense Khrushchev's exile provided a kind of comfort. Although the world didn't know it, because he seemed so bloody sure of himself, he was a severe critic of his own misdeeds. Only now, after a lifetime driven by ambition, was he free to confess and partially atone for them. He expressed regret for not having rehabilitated Bukharin and for browbeating intellectuals in 1962 and 1963. He condemned the 1966 arrest and imprisonment of two dissident writers, Andrei Sinyavsky and Yuli Daniel; warned against rehabilitating Stalin; and criticized the 1968 invasion of Czechoslovakia. Of a Soviet workers' paradise that locked up its borders, he had this to say: "Paradise is a place where people want to end up, not a place they run from! Yet in this country the doors are closed and locked. What kind of socialism is this? What kind of shit is it when you have to keep people in chains? What kind of social order? Some curse me for the times I opened the doors. If God had given me the chance to continue, I would have thrown the doors and windows wide open."[32]

He also became "gentler, more sincere and attentive" to his children. Until then he hardly ever talked with Yulia about her late father, Leonid, and her mother, Liuba. Now during a walk he suddenly said, "You can be proud of your father—he was a brave pilot. And your mother wasn't guilty of anything."[33] Khrushchev had always doted on his grandchildren, but now he had more time to express his affection. In a touching home movie scene young Nikita breaks off from weeding the garden, and spontaneously embraces his grandfather, who tenderly kisses and hugs him in return.

More than anything else, however, Khrushchev devoted himself to preparing his memoirs, a herculean effort that became the centerpiece of his last years. Family members began urging him to write up his recollections in 1966, when he was finally recovered from his pancreatic illness, and weekend guests invariably asked whether he was doing so. At first, he resisted; having himself rejected a KGB proposal to prevent Marshal Zhukov from working on his memoirs, he knew the furor his own could create. In the end, however, ambition and guilt prevailed again. What better way to justify his life and career than to tell his own story! Yet how could he do so if he provided a fully candid reckoning?

By August 1966 he was ready to start. Even before then he had reminisced to family and guests, especially about the war and Stalin's last years, but he had avoided matters in which his successors were involved, particularly the way they were reversing his reforms. It was these reversals, according to his son, and especially the prospect that Stalin would be rehabilitated that finally decided Khrushchev. That plus the charges that he had been "voluntarist" and "subjectivist" or, in plain language, virtually incompetent.[34]

One warm morning in August 1966, with his granddaughter Yulia's husband, journalist Lev Petrov, sitting across from him in the garden with a tape recorder, Khrushchev began dictating his memoirs. In the beginning, he retold stories he had recounted to visitors to his dacha. The first day, at Petrov's suggestion, he talked about the Cuban missile crisis, but soon he was dictating several hours a day, in the morning and after lunch, with or without someone to ask him questions and listen to his answers.

At the outset, he moved from subject to subject more or less at random. Later, with his son's help, he picked themes in advance and thought carefully about what he wanted to say before speaking. At one point, father and son drew up a list of subjects in order of importance and then tried to follow this "plan," crossing off issues as they were covered and adding new ones as they occurred to Khrushchev. Sergei could have collected published speeches and other materials, but Khrushchev was used to working with people rather than papers and preferred to trust to his still-prodigious memory. Of course he had no access to official records and documents that were buried deep in KGB-controlled archives.

Lev Petrov tried to transcribe and edit the tapes, but Khrushchev didn't like the results: too much Petrov, too little Khrushchev. Next, Nina Petrovna typed and edited, but she was too slow and unprofessional, complained her husband, annoyed that she used only four fingers to type.[35] Sergei urged him to ask the Central Committee for a secretary and typist, but Khrushchev rejected that out of hand: "I don't want to ask them for anything. If they offer assistance I won't reject it. But they won't offer, they don't need my memoirs, they'll only get in the way."[36]

Sergei found a typist at his rocket design bureau who agreed to transcribe the tapes at home. He himself began editing the pages she produced. Both jobs were difficult since Khrushchev's words poured forth (or dribbled out, depending on his mood) in a semistream of consciousness with subject and predicate often transposed and words sometimes omitted or spoken in the wrong order. Eventually the flow totaled about 250 hours of tape and thirty-five hundred pages of transcripts.

First of all, Khrushchev told Sergei, "I want to talk about Stalin, about his mistakes and his crimes, particularly since they want to clean the blood off him and place him on a pedestal again." Second, he said, "I want to tell the truth about the war. All that garbage they're cramming into people on radio and TV makes me sick. I have to tell the truth."[37] So he concentrated on the thirties as he had experienced them in Moscow and Ukraine, and then he turned to the war. After that came the postwar period down to Stalin's death and Beria's ouster, but then he stopped. He intended to omit his time in power, he said, to avoid offending his successors, who had been directly involved, but also, Sergei suspected, because his father "considered it immodest" to dwell upon his achievements.

Khrushchev managed to overcome his immodesty and eventually produced hundreds of pages on his domestic and foreign achievements, but several other areas remained mostly off limits—not only his childhood and his family but, until the very end, his stormy relationship with the artistic intelligentsia. This was the subject of the last section he dictated, which he then wanted to erase.[38]

DESPITE HIS efforts to avoid provoking his successors, trouble began in the summer of 1967, when an American filmmaker, Lucy Jarvis, perhaps assisted by Khrushchev family members, made a documentary film about him that was eventually shown on NBC TV. While mostly based on old footage, the film included shots of Khrushchev in retirement, sitting beside a bonfire in his green French cloak. His voice was covered over by a translation, but he could be heard saying something about the Cuban crisis. Outraged authorities removed Khrushchev's too-friendly security chief, Melnikov, and replaced him with another, who gave Khrushchev a much harder time.[39]

Defiant, Khrushchev intensified work on his memoirs. Whether because Brezhnev personally envied and hated him, as Sergei Khrushchev insisted, or for general reasons of regime self-protection, the Kremlin summoned Khrushchev to a dressing down by three of his former colleagues. Politburo member Andrei Kirilenko had been a Khrushchev underling in Ukraine and his deputy in the Central Committee Bureau for the Russian Federation. Arvid Pelshe, chief of the Party Control Commission, was responsible for disciplining errant party members. Pyotr Demichev, the former Moscow aide to Khrushchev, was now Moscow party boss.

Kirilenko began without a greeting: "The Central Committee has received information that you have been writing your memoirs for quite some time, and that they include many events of party and state history." However, interpreting party and state history was "the business of the Central Committee, and not of private individuals, let alone pensioners. The Politburo demands that you stop work on these memoirs and immediately turn over what you've already dictated to the Central Committee."

Khrushchev answered quietly: "I cannot understand, Comrade Kirilenko, what you and those who sent you want. A lot of people in the world write memoirs, and in our country, too. There's nothing wrong with it. Memoirs aren't history, they're just a person's view of the life he'd led."

Soon his voice was rising: "I consider your demand to be an act of force against a Soviet citizen, and as such a violation of the constitution, and therefore I refuse to obey you. You can put me in prison, or you can seize this material from me by force. You can do all this today if you wish, but I categorically protest."

Kirilenko tried to insist, but by now Khrushchev was shouting that he was being treated like Taras Shevchenko, the Ukrainian writer and artist whom Tsar Nicholas I had banished into the army for twenty-five years: "You can take everything away from me: my pension, the dacha, my apartment. That's all within your power, and it wouldn't surprise me if you did. So what—I can still make a living. I'll go to work as a metalworker—I still remember how it's done. If that doesn't work out, I'll take my knapsack and go begging. People will give me what I need. But no one would give you a crust of bread. You'd starve."

Pelshe reminded Khrushchev that Politburo decisions were binding on all party members and that "hostile forces" could exploit the situation by purloining the memoirs. Khrushchev retorted that the "American spies" could be easily foiled if the party provided him with a stenographer and a typist and kept a copy of the material in the Central Committee.

By this time he was calming down, but then he remembered another grievance: Instead of helping with his project, "you violated the constitution again when you stuck listening devices all over the dacha. Even in the bathroom—you spend the people's money to eavesdrop on my farts."

After a more elevated peroration ("I want what I write to be useful to the Soviet people, to our Soviet leaders, and to our nation. The events I have witnessed should serve as a lesson for the future"), the scandalous scene ended and Khrushchev departed. Kirilenko and his colleagues had failed, but Khrushchev was shaken.[40]

"He was very agitated and immediately went for a walk by the river," his wife later recalled. She went with him, but for a long time he refused to speak.[41] The next day, when Sergei arrived at the dacha, his father "looked tired, his face seemed grayer and older." Sergei found him sitting in the sun at the edge of the forest. Having been warned by Nina Petrovna, he didn't ask about the Central Committee encounter, but he didn't have to.

"Scoundrels!" snarled Khrushchev. "I told them what I think of them. Perhaps I went too far, but it serves them right. They thought I would crawl on my belly in front of them." As he recounted the conversation, his face turned red. For months afterward he rehearsed it over and over in his mind. Meantime, however, he stopped dictating regularly, and he didn't record much at all for the rest of 1968.[42]

From the beginning Khrushchev had worried about what would eventually happen to his manuscript. "It's all in vain," he had grumbled to Sergei. "Our efforts are useless. Everything's going to be lost. As soon as I die, they'll take it away and destroy it, or they'll bury it so deep there'll be no trace of it."

Sergei had made extra copies and hidden them in secure places, but even before the Central Committee showdown, they had discussed finding a safer place abroad. At first Khrushchev feared losing control of the manuscript and having it used against the USSR; after all, one should add, he and his men had hounded Boris Pasternak to death for just such a sin. But he eventually authorized Sergei to proceed and even to prepare for foreign publication in case the manuscript was seized in the Soviet Union. Since smuggling a manuscript out and publishing it abroad were illegal, in taking this step the former Soviet leader transformed himself from a near dissident into a potential criminal.

How the tapes and manuscripts got abroad, who arranged their passage, and who, if anyone, in high places looked the other way were a closely kept secret for almost thirty years.[43] According to Sergei, Lev Petrov, who was not just a journalist but an officer in Soviet military intelligence, introduced him to Viktor Louis, an even more complex, shadowy figure who had done time in labor camps in the late forties and early fifties, been released after the Twentieth Congress, and ended up working as Moscow correspondent for the *London Evening Standard*, carrying out assignments for the KGB, such as placing an abridged version of Stalin's daughter's memoir with a Western publisher so as to preempt the full edition scheduled for publication on the eve of the revolution's fiftieth anniversary. Louis, who was married to an Englishwoman, was a logical candidate to transmit Khrushchev's material. Nikita Khrushchev not only approved the transaction but urged that foreign publication be prepared, with the final go-ahead to await a signal from him. Louis reached an agreement with *Time* and Little, Brown publishers, apparently receiving substantial royalty rights in exchange for his considerable troubles. The last thing Khrushchev wanted was to be paid for his labors; to him, said Sergei, being "in the pay of the capitalists" was the worst charge that could be leveled against him.[44]

Everything went smoothly, at least for a while. When *Time* and Little, Brown sought assurance that the memoir material they were receiving was really Khrushchev's, they asked Viktor Louis to present him with a gift of two wide-brimmed hats, one red, the other black, purchased at Locke the Hatter on St. James Street in London. To verify that Khrushchev approved of the project, his American partners asked for photographs of him wearing the hats. Khrushchev received the hats at Petrovo-Dalneye, where his son, Sergei, explained the real reason for the gift. Nina Petrovna, who wasn't in on the trick, was shocked that her husband would even think of wearing such loud, garish headgear. Khrushchev, who relished the game, loudly asked to try the hats on to see if they fit. Sergei took pictures, which were sent back to *Time* and Little, Brown.

Meanwhile, back in Moscow, Louis had a friend in a very high place—none other than Yuri Andropov, who became head of the KGB in 1967. Louis told Sergei Khrushchev that he had briefed Andropov on his plans and even offered to show him the manuscript. Andropov declined with a smile to read it, but as a result of his good offices, elements of the foreign intelligence service apparently assisted Louis, while counter-intelligence didn't interfere, at least for the time being. This may sound unlikely, but Andropov too was a "complex" man who could dump dissidents in insane asylums and at the same time resist the re-Stalinization process on which some of his Politburo colleagues were itching to embark.[45]

WHILE KHRUSHCHEV devoted the summer of 1968 to his garden, party authorities whom Andropov couldn't or wouldn't control increased the pressure on Khrushchev family members. Aleksei Adzhubei had been Khrushchev's unofficial emissary to presidents and prime ministers and may even have dreamed of succeeding Gromyko as foreign minister.[46] Ousted along with his father-in-law, he had found refuge at the magazine *Sovetskii Soyuz* (Soviet Union), but now he was called in and urged to find a new job in the Soviet Far East. He refused to leave Moscow but advised his father-in-law to give up the memoir project. Sergei Khrushchev was forced out of Vladimir Chelomei's missile design bureau and found work at the Computer Control Institute. Nonetheless, Nikita Khrushchev resumed more frequent dictating in the fall of 1968 and picked up the pace even more in 1969. By the summer of that year he had covered not just the Stalin era but the Twentieth Party Congress, the Geneva summit, and Sino-Soviet relations. During the summer he reread the whole batch, decided he didn't like the way much of it had been edited, and got Sergei to find a professional writer, Vadim Trunin, scenarist of the well-known film *The Byelorussian Station*, to help out.

In the fall of 1969 it became clear that someone in authority had neither forgotten nor forgiven Khrushchev. When an American physician, A. McGehee Harvey, came to Moscow to examine Yelena Khrushchev, whose case of systemic lupus had taken a turn for the worse, the Khrushchevs invited him and his wife to their dacha. A few days later the Harveys and Sergei were sitting in a National Hotel room overlooking Manezh Square, waiting to watch the Anniversary of the Revolution parade, when KGB agents burst in and searched in vain for Khrushchev manuscript microfilms. Sergei Khrushchev suspected that Viktor Louis sicced the police on Harvey to remove suspicion from himself. In any case, Khrushchev devoted more time than ever to his memoirs in early 1970, even though it interfered with his gardening. Dr. Bezzubik warned that his patient had developed arteriosclerosis, and on May 29, after hoeing the garden on a very hot day, Khrushchev suffered a serious heart attack. For the next ten days his condition was critical, and he spent the better part of three months in the elite Kremlin hospital on Granovsky Street. But once he began to mend, he put up his usual bluff front, demanding to know why Sergei spent so much time visiting him. "Don't you have anything better to do? You're wasting your own time and bothering me. I'm pretty busy here. Either they're giving me drops or shots, or the doctors are examining me, or they're taking my temperature. No time to get bored."[47]

Following doctors' orders, Sergei conveyed only optimistic news about the memoirs. Actually he was now in trouble. Back in March, Andropov had alerted the Politburo that Khrushchev's memoirs contained state secrets, urged that KGB surveillance be heightened, and recommended that the former leader be called in and warned again.[48] Andropov may have been going through the motions, for he made no move to stop Viktor Louis. But counterintelligence agents now began shadowing Sergei everywhere. They raided his typist's apartment, questioned Yulia about Lev Petrov, who had died in the meantime, and finally called in Sergei and demanded the memoir manuscript. Out of fear, and because copies had been already hidden in the USSR and overseas, he turned over tapes and transcripts. But he also signaled Little, Brown to proceed with publication, which was soon scheduled for early in 1971.

When Khrushchev emerged from the hospital at the end of August 1970, he was pale and weak. After he had regained enough strength to walk to his favorite bench on Grass Snake Hill, Sergei told him what had happened. Khrushchev approved the decision to publish, but even in his weakened state, he gave Sergei a verbal thrashing for surrendering the manuscript to the KGB: "Never mind about saving the text; it's a matter of principle. They are violating the constitution. You had the gall to make decisions about something you had no right to decide in the first place. Contact the man immediately and express the strongest possible protest in my name. Demand that everything be returned!"[49] Then Khrushchev grabbed for his pills and took a tranquilizer.

Sergei tried to carry out his father's order, but when he demanded the manuscript, his KGB contact, who had promised to return the text upon Khrushchev's recovery, coolly declined to do so. The materials had been transferred to the Central Committee, he remarked, over which the KGB had no control.

"To hell with them!" raged Khrushchev when Sergei reported the news. "There's nothing more we can do. We won't get a thing out of them!!! Don't ever go back there!"[50]

BY THE AUTUMN of 1970 the imminent publication of *Khrushchev Remembers* had been announced in the West. Just after the anniversary of the revolution, Khrushchev received a call from Pelshe's office demanding that he appear that same day at the Party Control Commission. A Kremlin car was already on its way to pick him up.

The meeting that followed, this time with Pelshe and two aides, was extraordinary—not only because Khrushchev gave as good as he got in heated exchanges but because he revealed so much of his despair.[51] He conceded the minimum on the memoirs: He denied he had either transferred them to anyone overseas or authorized anyone else to do so ("At no time did I pass any memoirs to anyone, nor would I ever have allowed such a transfer to take place"), but he signed a statement in which the memoirs were labeled a "fabrication" and a "falsification."

Pelshe was partly satisfied with this, but not with the rest of the conversation.[52] Khrushchev compared current party leaders with Tsar Nicholas I, blasted them as Stalinists, and charged them with ruining his reforms and "pissing away" gains he had made in Egypt and the Middle

East.[53] Pelshe reminded Khrushchev he was in "a party house" and demanded that he "behave himself accordingly." When Khrushchev accused his successors of ruining the country, Pelshe retorted he was blaming others for his failures. When he charged Pelshe with interrupting him in "Stalinist fashion," the latter snapped, "You're the one in the habit of interrupting people." Khrushchev replied, "I too was infected by Stalin, but I also freed myself from him, whereas you did not."

Khrushchev's remarks were full of self-pity—"I'm completely isolated; in fact I'm under house arrest. . . . Help me in my suffering. . . . Being retired is like being tortured in hell"—but also of anti-Stalinism: "Murderers must be unmasked." He recalled a man who had been a good historian and another who had worked for the Comintern: "Stalin shot them both. . . . So many were put to death! So many of my friends were executed, all dedicated beyond doubt to the party! So many were killed by Mao in the Cultural Revolution! By Mao and Stalin, both!"

And by Khrushchev! He must have had his own complicity in mind too when he pleaded with Pelshe: "Arrest me, please, shoot me. I'm sick of living. I don't want to live. Today the radio reported de Gaulle died. I envy him. . . . Maybe your summoning me here will help me to die sooner. I want to die. . . . I want to die an honest man. . . . I'm seventy years old. I'm in my right mind, and I answer for all my words and deeds. . . . I'm prepared for any punishment up to and including the death penalty. . . . I'm ready to die on the cross. Bring on the nails and the hammer. That's not just a phrase. I want it. Russians say there's no avoiding begging and prison. I was always in a different position. Throughout my whole political career, I was never the one who was interrogated."

Is it fair to read so much guilt into the near ravings of a dying man? ("Every madman denies he's insane," said Khrushchev at another point in the meeting. "I don't consider myself mad. But perhaps you evaluate my condition differently.") Is it any fairer to note that by comparing himself with Jesus Christ, Khrushchev was staking yet another claim to a blessed place in history? In a conversation about this time with Mikhail Shatrov, the playwright asked what Khrushchev regretted about his life. "Most of all the blood," he replied. "My arms are up to the elbows in blood. That is the most terrible thing that lies in my soul."[54]

By the end of the meeting at the Party Control Commission he was exhausted. "I've done what you asked," he said quietly. "I signed. Now I want to go home. My chest hurts."

IF DEATH was his wish, Khrushchev's meeting at the Control Commission sped the day. Shortly afterward he suffered another heart attack, enough to return him to the hospital until just before the New Year. Less to protect him, probably, than to protect others from him, he was placed not in the heart patients' ward but in the neurological section, which had been emptied of other patients. It was there, shortly after he began to feel better, that the doctor in charge of his treatment, Praskovia Moshentseva, found him reading *Pravda.* When she hesitated to interrupt him, he laughingly insisted he was just reading about socialism, which he described as "only water." She tried to ignore that and concentrate on his intravenous tubes, but he told her a story about a party lecturer who consumed three glasses of water while rambling on endlessly to an indifferent audience of collective farmers. When the lecturer asked for questions, there were none until a short peasant in the back row stood up. "Respected lecturer," he said, "here you go and talk about socialism for three hours, you drink three glasses of water, and not once do you take a leak. How can that be?"

Dr. Moshentseva was mortified, but her patient shook with laughter. "Now you know what socialism is," he said. "It's water."

It's hard to believe Khrushchev meant it, after a life devoted to the service to the cause. But not impossible, since the same life had witnessed so much damage done, by himself among others, to the very ideals he had served.

Before he checked out of the hospital, Dr. Moshentseva caught Khrushchev at the nurses' station, entertaining them with jokes and stories while one of them stood guard by the door. "Ah, respected Praskovia Nikolaevna," he said with a grin, "I beg you not to punish anyone. I ordered them to do it. Keep in mind: It's my last order. Now I'm no one."[55] Back home he couldn't even walk to the meadow without stopping to rest. Despite his weakened condition, he started dictating again in early February, but he also lapsed back into depression. His seventy-seventh birthday came and went in April; on this occasion he dressed up in a white shirt and dark suit with two medals on his lapels, but with the usual portable radio incongruously hanging over his shoulder. He could no longer tend the garden, but he perked up somewhat during Sergei's July 2 birthday party, guiding the assembled guests around the garden, herding them into his room to listen to records—Ukrainian and Russian folk songs and operatic arias—on his phonograph, taking everyone's picture on his Hasselblad and being photographed by them in return, and sitting with them around a big bonfire. It was the last such gathering at Petrovo-Dalneye.

Afterward he complained bitterly about not being needed. "I'm just wandering around aimlessly. I could go hang myself and no one would even notice." When Khrushchev mentioned suicide several times, his doctor ordered that he not be left alone. Dr. Bezzubik attributed the depression to arteriosclerosis, but family members were sure it was more than that. Whatever it was, the darkest period seemed to pass as August gave way to September.

On Sunday September 5, the Khrushchevs visited the Adzhubeis at their dacha near Iksha northwest of Moscow, near the canal (built by murderous forced labor) that links the Moscow River with the Volga. Arriving just before noon, the Khrushchevs dined on soup that Rada prepared from a packet. It was the first time her father had tried such a thing, and he liked it. "Your mother deprived me of this pleasure," he said. "So many wonderful products I've never tried."[56]

After lunch the company set off on a walk. Before reaching the woods, Khrushchev stopped and asked his grandson Alyosha to run back for a folding chair. Nina Petrovna gave him a pill. Aleksei Adzhubei and a gardener who worked part time at the dacha stayed with Khrushchev while the others wandered away. The gardener gathered thirteen mushrooms, which he placed by Khrushchev's feet.

"Thirteen . . . ," grumbled Nikita Sergeyevich. "A devil's dozen, unlucky number."

After the gardener disappeared in search of a fourteenth mushroom, Khrushchev turned to Adzhubei. "When I leave this life, the hatred toward you will diminish. They're taking vengeance on the family because of me. Don't be sorry that you've lived in stormy times, or that you worked on the Central Committee with me. They're going to remember us."

Adzhubei remained silent. Khrushchev had never spoken to him so gently. It was then that he told Adzhubei the story, quoted in the beginning of this book, about meeting an old woman in a clearing in Kalinovka, an old woman who told him, "Little boy, a great future awaits you. . . ."

Shortly afterward the Khrushchevs returned to Petrovo-Dalneye. Nikita Sergeyevich took another pill, which seemed to help, but several nights later he had trouble breathing. Waking his wife, at four in the morning, he whispered, "Sit with me, I'm in pain."[57] After a nitroglycerin pill eased the pain, he ordered Nina Petrovna to go back to bed, but to leave the door to his bedroom open, as it had been for the last week and a half. "Perhaps he's now afraid of the dark," she thought, "but doesn't want to admit it."[58]

The next morning the doctor advised going to the hospital as a precaution but didn't insist. That afternoon, when Khrushchev had another attack, Bezzubik did insist, but he allowed him to go by car instead of summoning an ambulance. "I just don't like your ambulances," growled Khrushchev. "They make you feel like you're already dead." He seemed in good form as he lowered himself into Dr. Bezzubik's Volga, bidding farewell to the cook and gardener who worked at the dacha and joking with the driver. As the car crossed a bridge over the Moscow River, he complained heatedly that nearby corn was planted "the wrong way." He also noticed the chestnut trees on Kalinin Prospekt, boasting that they'd been planted in the thirties at his insistence, over the objections of other city officials.[59]

Khrushchev walked into the hospital without assistance, joking with nurses and orderlies whom he knew from his previous stays. He told Nina Petrovna to go home, and that evening he shooed Sergei away: "No sense wasting time. Don't you have anything to do? Don't bother me, can't you see I'm busy: it's time to swallow some pills, and have my temperature taken. They don't let you get bored here! When you come tomorrow, bring me something to read." That night Khrushchev had another massive heart attack.

On Wednesday the situation looked grave, but Khrushchev was still able to grump about the gladiolas Yelena brought him ("Why should I have them? Better you keep them!") and pretend to the nurse that the flowers were actually for her. Thursday was worse. No more jokes; Nina Petrovna was reduced to kissing the palm of his left hand and he to stroking her cheek. On Friday, Khrushchev seemed a bit better, and at nine o'clock Saturday morning, when Nina Petrovna and Rada arrived, better still. He asked for a sour pickle and a bottle of beer, complained that the beer was bad, traded jokes with his doctor, and waved as Nina Petrovna left to see her own doctor. When she returned twenty-five minutes later, he was near death. How bad was it? she asked the doctor who emerged from Khrushchev's room. "Bad," the doctor replied. "Worse than Thursday?" asked Nina Petrovna. "He's dead" was the answer.[60]

The usually stoic Nina Petrovna burst into tears. When Sergei was at last allowed in the room, his father's face "was quite different, unfamiliar: the nose seemed much sharper, aquiline; the lower jaw was bandaged; a sheet covered him up to the throat. Drops of blood streaked the wall, a sign of the resuscitators' efforts."[61]

WHEN NINA PETROVNA recovered, she assumed there would be some sort of funeral. Whether it would be official or private was up to the state to decide, and the state took its time doing so. All through Saturday the official word was "Wait."

Fearful that the Kremlin would bury the news of Khrushchev's death, Sergei Khrushchev telephoned Viktor Louis to get the word out. Meanwhile, at Petrovo-Dalneye, the KGB locked the house, posted a guard at the door, and barely deigned to let Nina Petrovna in. They also sealed Khrushchev's room and stationed another guard outside it. That evening two men from the Central Committee combed through Khrushchev's personal effects. After checking the safe in his room, they dumped all his recording tapes into a briefcase, including not just memoir material but a calisthenics tape that Nina Petrovna wanted to keep in which an instructor began with the words "Good morning, Nikita Sergeyevich! How did you sleep?"

Khrushchev's "papers" didn't take much time to collect since all his official ones had been left at the Central Committee and the memoirs had been previously confiscated. So the searchers moved on to books and records and to examining his wardrobe and the closet. Coming upon a typewritten copy of Osip Mandelshtam's poem about Stalin, the very verses that spelled doom for the great poet in the thirties, the Central Committee men confiscated that too. The poem was a gift from a nuclear physicist to Khrushchev. Yelena Khrushcheva was so incensed that she screamed at the intruders and then stormed out of the room. But they kept methodically about their business, making sure to impound the Presidium's florid congratulatory greeting to Khrushchev on his seventieth birthday in 1964, as well as award certificates signed in the thirties and forties by the then Soviet president, Mikhail Kalinin.

Finally, funeral arrangements were decided: There would be no Red Square funeral, of course, just a private burial at Novodevichy (the cemetery named after the sixteenth-century nunnery adjacent to it that is the last resting place of many famous Russians) at noon on Monday. The interment would be preceded by a wake at a suburban morgue in Kuntsevo at 10:00 the same morning. The Central Committee would pay all expenses. It would also announce Khrushchev's death at 10:00 A.M. on Monday, so that no one except those informed by the family would have time to attend either the wake or the funeral.

Family members half expected condolence calls from Khrushchev's former colleagues. None came. When word of Khrushchev's death was reported abroad that evening, it produced a flood of foreign consolation, from heads of state and leaders of Communist parties, which the authorities didn't know what to do with. Eventually, some but not all of these messages reached the family in filthy, torn envelopes.

The Khrushchev family rose early on Monday, September 13, so as to reach Kuntsevo by ten o'clock. The sky was overcast, and light rain fell. Relatives from outside Moscow had spent the night in the Khrushchevs' Moscow apartment and on cots and sofas at Petrovo-Dalneye. That morning's *Pravda* had no obituary, only a tiny notice at the bottom of the first page "regretfully" announcing the death of "former First Secretary of the Central Committee of the CPSU and Chairman of the Council of Ministers of the USSR, personal pensioner Nikita Sergeyevich Khrushchev, age 78."

The wake was held in a dreary little room in a unimposing red-brick building. Along the empty street outside and in the woods behind a fence were trucks loaded with soldiers carrying machine guns, their commanders communicating with one another through field radios. Despite the regime's best efforts, a few brave souls dared to attend. Aleksandr Tvardovsky's colleague at *Novyi mir,* Vladimir Lakshin, remembered being stopped by a police captain who demanded to know where he was going, but his orders were apparently only to intimidate since he let Lakshin and wife proceed. Around the open coffin were wreaths from relatives and friends, plus a modest one from the Central Committee and the Council of Ministers. Funeral music by Chopin and Beethoven emerged scrapingly from antiquated loudspeakers. Family members, along with several old comrades of Khrushchev's from the Donbas, stood around the body. A few foreign journalists and diplomats waited outside. Before departing for the cemetery, the immediate family was left alone: "the two sobbing Yulias, older and younger, Rada, stone-faced, and Mama in a state of near collapse."[62]

The cortege to the cemetery was as threadbare as the Kuntsevo hall. The coffin occupied the aisle of an old bus with family members in the seats beside it. Behind the bus and a truck with the wreaths came a car with a nurse and then several more cars, followed by a caravan of foreign journalists. The route the procession took at an unseemly high rate of speed was almost empty. Novodevichy Cemetery itself was surrounded by another ring of machine gun–toting troops and their tarpaulin-covered trucks. Within the outer circle of soldiers, were five inner rings of police, four of them in uniform, the fifth in plain clothes except for an occasional officer with blue KGB piping on his epaulets.

As the bus/hearse entered the grounds (violating the rule against vehicles so as further to conceal the proceedings from the public), it passed a sign saying CEMETERY CLOSED TODAY FOR CLEANING. The wooden speakers' platform had been removed. The burial plot was near the far wall of the cemetery, not easily approachable from the path. Would-be mourners who didn't arrive with the family had to run a daunting gauntlet. Passengers weren't allowed to disembark from trains at the nearest Metro stations, nor did buses and trolleys that passed Novodevichy run that day. Only the boldest of a small crowd outside the outermost police line were able to get through, being photographed as they did so, by insisting that they were relatives or close friends of the deceased.

Although the authorities didn't want speeches, Nina Petrovna couldn't imagine burying the former leader of his country without some ceremony. So Sergei Khrushchev recruited some speakers at the Kuntsevo morgue. He himself clambered up a mound of earth next to the open grave and talked about Khrushchev as a father and husband. Nadezhda Dimenshtein, a short, gray-haired woman who had known Khrushchev in the twenties and been arrested and imprisoned during the thirties, thanked him in the name of the millions he had released from the camps or rehabilitated. The third speaker was a coworker of Sergei's who hardly knew Khrushchev but whose father had died in the camps. He thanked Khrushchev for returning his father's good name and allowing his children to be proud of him.

When the speeches were over, plainclothesmen tried to prevent the two hundred or so onlookers from approaching the grave, but family members got them to relent. After the crowd retreated, relatives threw dirt on the coffin as it was lowered into the grave. The gravediggers were adding more earth, along with a layer of fresh flowers, when a man came running up with another wreath: "To Nikita Sergeyevich Khrushchev from Anastas Ivanovich Mikoyan." Mikoyan was the only well-wisher who remained in the Soviet empyrean that Nikita Khrushchev had paid such a high price to enter and in which he left such a mixed legacy.

EPILOGUE

It took four years after Khrushchev's death for his family to obtain permission to erect a monument at his grave. After innumerable delays and run-arounds, in which functionaries at various levels never said no but were apparently afraid to say yes, his widow telephoned Prime Minister Aleksei Kosygin and got him to approve a memorial.[1]

Designed by Ernst Neizvestny, the artist whom Khrushchev had excoriated in 1962 and 1963, the monument consists of intersecting slabs of white marble and black granite on one of which sits a bronze head of Khrushchev with what looks like a pained expression on his face. It sums up a man in whose character so many contrasts were so starkly intertwined: both true believer and cold-eyed realist, opportunistic yet principled in his own way, fearful of war while all too prone to risk it, the most unpretentious of men even as he pretended to power and glory exceeding his grasp, complicit in great evil yet also the author of much good.

Between his death in 1971 and the advent of perestroika and glasnost in the late 1980s, this colorful, contradictory, many-sided man became a "nonperson" in the USSR, his name suppressed by his Kremlin successors and ignored by most Soviet citizens. The technique of erasing disgraced leaders from Soviet history books was not new, having been perfected by Stalin and then applied by Khrushchev to Stalin himself. In addition, Brezhnev and his colleagues still nursed grievances against their former patron, even as they reversed many, but not all, of his domestic and foreign policies.[2] As late as 1984, at a meeting at which the Politburo considered whether to readmit Molotov into the Communist party, Khrushchev was the subject of a colloquy. Defense Minister Dmitri Ustinov: He committed "scandalous disgraces . . . in relation to Stalin. No other enemy brought us as much harm as Khrushchev did. . . ." Prime Minister Nikolai Tikhonov: "He soiled and stained us and our policies. . . ." Foreign Minister Andrei Gromyko: "He dealt an irreversible blow to the positive image of the Soviet Union in the eyes of the world."[3]

Ordinary citizens had no chance to come to Khrushchev's defense, either in October 1964 or afterward, but few of them would have wanted to in any case. Many did gratefully remember his contributions. As Roy Medvedev put it, "The fact that during the years of his rule, about 20 million people were rehabilitated—granted, many of them posthumously—this fact alone outweighs all of Khrushchev's faults and mistakes."[4] But many more, associating his name with everything from bread shortages to international crises and regarding his lack of culture as a stain on Russia's reputation, had been glad to see him go.

Mikhail Gorbachev's view was different. He reached political maturity during the Khrushchev era and remembered its openness and optimism with nostalgia. Although he rose rapidly under Khrushchev's successor (from a provincial party official in 1964 to Central Committee secretary and Presidium member in 1980), he regarded "Brezhnevism [as] nothing but a conservative reaction against Khrushchev's attempt at reforming. . . ." Gorbachev's own generation, he added, "considered itself 'children of the Twentieth Congress'" and regarded the task of renewing what Khrushchev had begun as "our obligation."[5]

In undertaking his own reforms, Gorbachev was guided by Khrushchev's experience. Khrushchev hadn't gone far enough, in either analysing the roots of Stalinism or attacking them; Gorbachev would go further. Khrushchev's attempt to ease the cold war had been contradictory and self-defeating; Gorbachev would be steadier and more convincing. "The apparatus broke Khrushchev's neck," Gorbachev secretly warned his colleagues when party functionaries began resisting change, and "the same thing will happen now." It was in 1987–1988, he later recalled, when his "reforms were threatened with the fate of the Twentieth Congress," that Gorbachev moved to radicalize them.[6] Until then he still hadn't mentioned Khrushchev in public. But in a speech on the eve of the seventieth anniversary of the revolution, in which he filled in at least some of what he called "blank spots" in Soviet history, Gorbachev in effect granted Khrushchev a political pardon: "It took more than a little courage for the party and its leadership, headed by N. S. Khrushchev, to criticize the personality cult and its consequences and to restore socialist legality."[7]

Gorbachev had important advantages compared with Khrushchev. He was far better educated, having graduated from Moscow State University's law school. After years of Brezhnevite stagnation, followed by the dispiriting interregnum under Yuri Andropov and Konstantin Chernenko, resistance to reform was much weaker, and support for it broader and deeper, than in Khrushchev's time. Gorbachev had crucial backing from fellow leaders like Aleksandr Yakovlev, who had begun working in the Central Committee apparatus in 1953, and Eduard Shevardnadze, who had joined the Georgian Central Committee in 1958. Boris Yeltsin, who eventually abandoned communism altogether and helped break up the USSR itself in December 1991, had become a Communist in 1961. Outside the Kremlin as well, Gorbachev drew on Khrushchev's legacy as it shaped the *shestidesiatniki,* men and women of the 1960s, who had long dreamed of recapturing the hope and idealism of their youth. Ludmilla Alexeyeva was almost twenty in 1956, when Khrushchev denounced Stalin at the Twentieth Congress. His speech, she later recalled, "put an end to our lonely questioning of the Soviet system. Young men and women began to lose their fear of sharing views, knowledge, beliefs, questions. Every night we gathered in cramped apartments to recite poetry, read 'unofficial' prose, and swap stories that, taken together, yielded a realistic picture of what was going on in our country. That was the time of our awakening."[8]

Some of Alexeyeva's generation later became open dissidents—not organized, few in number, but bravely pressing for human rights and democratization, which Gorbachev eventually championed. Others, who feared to mount overt resistance to the Brezhnev regime, secretly sympathized with protests circulating clandestinely in samizdat. The most famous dissenters, of course, were men like Andrei Sakharov and Aleksandr Solzhenitsyn, but Khrushchev's own memoirs too were a harbinger of glasnost to come. Seen from afar, Soviet society in the early 1980s still seemed atomized and demoralized. But beneath the surface Khrushchev's efforts at de-Stalinization, awkward and erratic though they had been, had allowed a nascent civil society to take shape where Stalinism had once created a desert.

The changes carried out by Gorbachev and Yeltsin far transcended Khrushchev's reforms, but they too failed to live up to their promise, partly because Gorbachev shared Khrushchev's naiveté about the extent of the Soviet people's commitment to communism, while Yeltsin echoed Khrushchev's blustering impulsiveness. As a founding father of reform Khrushchev experienced a "revival" as the 1980s gave way to the 1990s. Memoirs, including his own, and articles about him were at last published, exhibits were mounted, and documentary and feature films made. But almost as quickly as it revived, interest in him waned after the collapse of the USSR.

Engulfed in their post-Communist problems, most Russians had little time for history and less for a failed Communist reformer. Gorbachev's own foundation sponsored two conferences on Khrushchev in 1994 and 1996, the first on the hundredth anniversary of his birth, the second forty years after the Twentieth Congress.[9] From time to time, hot arguments about Khrushchev have flared up between odd adversaries. In 1996 the chief ideological spokesman of the still-orthodox Communist party condemned Khrushchev for his "secret speech," for "distracting" the party in 1956 by "dethroning" Stalin's authority with a "mostly nonobjective and slanderous attack." Thereupon a spokesman for Russian "patriotic forces," a nasty amalgam of nationalist and even semifascist groups, praised Khrushchev not just for confronting Russia's enemies in Hungary in 1956 and Cuba in 1962 but even for defending its honor by banging that infamous shoe at the United Nations.[10]

At the turn of the twenty-first century, the Russian public's view of Khrushchev is mixed. According to the dean of Russian pollsters, Yuri Levada, the only two periods of the twentieth century that Russians evaluate positively are those associated with the last tsar, Nicholas II, and Nikita Khrushchev.[11] In a May 1998 survey young adults between the ages of eighteen and twenty-nine were asked to evaluate twentieth-century Russian leaders. In their view, not only Lenin, Stalin, and Brezhnev but Gorbachev and Yelstin had done more harm than good. The only leader they assessed positively was Nicholas II. On Khrushchev, opinion was evenly divided.[12]

KHRUSHCHEV'S GREATEST rivals outlived him by a substantial margin. Molotov, who was indeed readmitted to the party in 1984, died two years later. Malenkov and Kaganovich lived on until 1988 and 1991, respectively. After Khrushchev's death, the Petrovo-Dalneye dacha in which he spent his last years was razed, lest it someday become a shrine to its last occupant. Khrushchev's wife, Nina Petrovna, lived in their Starokonyushenny Lane apartment and spent the last seven years of her life in a small wooden dacha in Zhukovka outside Moscow, where Molotov also resided. Although she loved to take walks and work in her garden, after she became ill and her legs failed her, she mostly sat alone in her house or on its veranda. She died on August 9, 1984.

Nikita and Nina Khrushchev's daughter Yelena died in 1972. Yulia Nikitichna Khrushcheva, Nikita Sergeyevich's daughter by his first wife, died in 1981. In 1991 Sergei Khrushchev moved to Providence, Rhode Island, where he has since been a fellow of the Thomas Watson Institute for International Affairs at Brown University, teaching occasional courses on international affairs and on current relations among post-Soviet states, lecturing on Russian affairs, and writing books about his father. Sergei and his wife, Valentina, obtained American citizenship in 1999, an act that outraged many Russians. Even those who aren't nostalgic for communism are chagrined at how empty Nikita Khrushchev's boasts turned out to be. Khrushchev crowed that grandchildren of Americans he met would live under communism. Instead his own son is living under capitalism.

The Khrushchevs' other daughter, Rada Adzhubei, has worked for many years for a fine Russian magazine called *Nauka i zhizn'* (Science and Life). Her husband, Aleksei Adzhubei, who took his father-in-law's fall especially hard because he himself fell almost as far, died in 1993. Yulia Leonidovna Khrushcheva, Leonid Khrushchev's daughter, who was adopted by her grandparents, has served as literary adviser at the famous Vakhtangov Theater in Moscow. Her daughter Ksenia, named after Nikita Khrushchev's mother, has two children, one of them called Nikita. Yulia's other daughter, Nina, received a Ph.D. from Princeton University in comparative literature and now lives and works in New York. Yulia's half brother, Yuri Khrushchev, recently retired as a test pilot, has devoted much of his time to trying to clarify the fate of their father, Leonid Khrushchev. Lyonia's widow, the remarkably irrepressible Liuba, lives on in Kiev. Her son, Tolya, who after his childhood homelessness graduated from the Kiev Polytechnical Institute, worked as an engineer, and had two daughters, died in 2000.

Nikita Khrushchev's grandson Nikita (also Nikita Sergeyevich since he is Sergei's son), besides working for *Moscow News*, carefully tracks contemporary coverage of his grandfather while helping his father gather materials for his books. Sergei's other son, Sergei, is a biologist. One of Rada and Aleksei Adzhubei's three sons, Nikita, is an economist, and Ivan and Aleksei Adzhubei are biologists. Aleksei lives and works in Western Europe.

ABBREVIATIONS

AAN, PZPR	Archiwum Akt Nowych, Polska Zjednoczona Partia Robotnicza
AWF	Ann Whitman File
CDSP	*Current Digest of the Soviet Press*
CWIHPB	*Cold War International History Project Bulletin*
d.	*delo* (file)
DADO	Derzhavnyi arkhiv Donetskoi oblasti
DALO	Derzhavnyi arkhiv L'vivskoi oblasti
DASBU	Derzhavnyi arkhiv sluzhby bezpeki Ukrainy
DDEL	Dwight D. Eisenhower Library
DSB	*United States Department of State Bulletin*
f.	*fond* (collection)
FBIS	Foreign Broadcast Information Service, *Daily Report: Foreign Radio Broadcasts*
FO	Foreign Office
FRUS	*Foreign Relations of the United States*
IA	*Istoricheskii arkhiv*
l.	*list* (page)
ll.	*listy* (pages)
LOC	Library of Congress
JFKL	John F. Kennedy Library
NA	United States National Archives
NiNI	*Novaia i noveishaia istoriia*

NK1	Nikita S. Khrushchev, *Khrushchev Remembers,* trans. and ed. Strobe Talbott (Boston: Little, Brown, 1970)
NK2	Nikita S. Khrushchev, *Khrushchev Remembers: The Last Testament,* trans. and ed. Strobe Talbott (Boston: Little, Brown, 1974)
NK3	Nikita S. Khrushchev, *Khrushchev Remembers: The Glasnost Tapes,* trans. and ed. Jerrold L. Schecter with Vyacheslav Luchkov (Boston: Little, Brown, 1990)
NK4	Nikita S. Khrushchev,"Memuary Nikity Sergeevicha Khrushcheva," *Voprosy istorii,* nos. 2-12, (1990); nos. 1–12 (1991); nos. 1–3, 6–9, 11–12 (1992); nos. 2–10 (1993); nos. 1–8, 10–12 (1994); nos. 2–6 (1995)
NK5	Nikita S. Khrushchev, *N. S. Khrushchev: vospominaniia—vremia, liudi, vlast'* (Moscow: Moskovskie novosti, 1999). 4 vols.
NK6	Nikita S. Khrushchev, Verbatim transcript of Khrushchev memoirs as delivered to the West in 1970 and preserved at the Russian Institute, and later at the Oral History Collection, of Columbia University
NSF	National Security Files
op.	*opis'* (inventory)
POF	President's Office Files
PREM	Prime Minister's Office Files
PRO	Public Record Office
RGANI	Rossiiskii gosudarstvennyi arkhiv noveisshei istorii
RGASPI	Rossiiskii gosudarstvennyi arkhiv sotsial'no-politicheskoi istorii
SK1	Sergei N. Khrushchev, *Pensioner soiuznogo znacheniia* (Moscow: Novosti, 1991)
SK2	Sergei N. Khrushchev, *Khrushchev on Khrushchev: An Inside Account of the Man and His Era,* trans. and ed. William Taubman (Boston: Little, Brown, 1990)
SK3	Sergei N. Khrushchev, *Nikita S. Khrushchev: krizisy i rakety* (Moscow: Novosti, 1991). 2 vols.
SK4	Sergei N. Khrushchev, *Nikita Khrushchev and the Cre-*

	ation of a Superpower (University Park: Penn State Press, 2000)
Stroi	Nikita S. Khrushchev, *Stroitel'stvo kommunizma v SSSR i razvitie sel'skogo khoziaistva* (Moscow: Gosudarstvennoe izdatel'stvo politicheskoi literatury, 1962–1964). 8 vols.
TsAMO	Tsentral'nyi arkhiv Ministerstva oborony
TsDAHOU	Tsentral'nyi derzhavnyi arkhiv hromads'kykh ob'ednan' Ukrainy
TsAODM	Tsentral'nyi arkhiv obshchestvennykh dvizhenii Moskvy
VI	*Voprosy istorii*

NOTES

PREFACE

1 Both the *New York Times* and the *Washington Post* reported on October 13, 1960, that Khrushchev banged his shoe on October 12, and other sources, who claim to have been there or to have talked to witnesses, confirm it. However, James Feron, a young reporter for the *Times*, who was in the hall but didn't file a story that day, later insisted, "I actually saw Khrushchev *not* bang his shoe [emphasis added]." According to Feron, Khrushchev "leaned over, took off a slip-on shoe, raised it, and then waved it pseudomenacingly and put it on his desk," but he "never banged his shoe." Moreover, efforts to find films of the incident have proved unavailing. There do exist still photos of Khrushchev brandishing a shoe and of the shoe resting on the desk, but it is difficult to establish beyond reasonable doubt that the shoe actually collided with the table. Moreover, a UN staff worker who said she was in the General Assembly that day claimed that Khrushchev didn't so much take off his shoe (indeed he "couldn't have," she added, because "the size of his stomach prevented him" from reaching under the table) as have it fall off when an overly zealous news correspondent stepped on his foot. The staff worker claimed that she passed the shoe back to him wrapped in a napkin, after which, she remembered, he did indeed bang it. Despite the conflicting accounts (others are cited in endnotes in Chapter 16), and with full historiographical humility, I have adopted the view that the shoe was not only brandished but banged. James Feron's recollection was reported by Donna Greene in "Westchester Q & A: James Feron, Turning Outpost into Career Milestone," *New York Times*, October 5, 1997, section 13WC, p. 3. Author's interview with Mr. Feron and his wife, Jeanne Feron. The unnamed UN staff worker was cited in N. A. Zenkovich, *Sobranie sochinenii: Tainy ushedshego veka: Vlast', raspri, podopleka* (Moscow: OLMA-PRESS, 2000), vol. 1, p. 283. The extent to which Khrushchev's shoe has become an iconic symbol connoting the power to compel attention is indicated by the publication of Roy Underhill, *Khrushchev's Shoe and Other Ways to Captivate an Audience of 1 to 1000* (Cambridge, Mass.: Perseus, 2000).

2 I described my year at MGU in *The View from Lenin Hills: Soviet Youth in Ferment* (New York: Coward-McCann, 1967). Students' feelings about Khrushchev are reported on p. 195.

3 *Stalin's American Policy: From Entente to Détente to Cold War* (New York: Norton, 1982).

4 *Stroitel'stvo kommunizma v SSSR i razvitie sel'skogo khoziaistva* (Moscow: Gosudarstvennoe izdatel'stvo politicheskoi literatury, 1962–1964), 8 vols. (hereafter Stroi).

5 *Khrushchev Remembers,* trans. and ed. Strobe Talbott (Boston: Little, Brown, 1970) (hereafter NK1); *Khrushchev Remembers: The Last Testament,* trans. and ed. Strobe Talbott (Boston: Little, Brown, 1974) (hereafter NK2).

6 Sergei Khrushchev, *Pensioner soiuznogo znacheniia* (Moscow: Novosti, 1991) (hereafter SK1); Aleksei Adzhubei, *Te desiat let* (Moscow: Sovetskaia Rossiia, 1989); *Khrushchev Remembers: The Glasnost Tapes,* trans. and ed. Jerrold L. Schecter with Vyacheslav Luchkov (Boston: Little, Brown, 1990) (hereafter NK3); "Memuary Nikity Sergeevicha Khrushcheva," *Voprosy istorii,* nos. 2–12 (1990); nos. 1–12 (1991); nos. 1–3, 6–9, 11–12 (1992); nos. 2–10 (1993); nos. 1–8, 10–12 (1994); nos. 2–6 (1995) (hereafter cited as NK4, with issue number and year).

7 Sergei Khrushchev, *Khrushchev on Khrushchev: An Inside Account of the Man and His Era,* trans. and ed. William Taubman (Boston: Little, Brown, 1990) (hereafter SK2). Although Adzhubei's book was never published in English, the additional material he provided in response to my queries was included in the Russian version, *Krushenie illiuzii* (Moscow: Interbuk, 1991).

8 Among main sources consulted are *The Standard Edition of the Complete Psychological Works of Sigmund Freud,* ed. James Strachey (London: Hogarth Press, 1953–1974); Alfred Adler, *The Individual Psychology of Alfred Adler* (New York: Basic Books, 1956); Karen Horney, *Neurosis and Human Growth: The Struggle toward Self-Realization* (New York: Norton, 1950); and Erik H. Erikson, *Childhood and Society* (New York: Norton, 1963).

9 The Russian edition of Khrushchev's memoirs from *Voprosy istorii* (hereafter VI) was later published, complete with alternative versions of sections that Khrushchev dictated more than once, helpful endnotes, and recently declassified documents from the Soviet archives in *N. S. Khrushchev: vospominania—vremia, liudi, vlast'* (Moscow: Moskovskie novosti, 1999), 4 vols. (hereafter NK5). Since, according to Sergei Khrushchev, the VI version was slightly abridged for reasons of space, this four-volume version is the fullest available. Throughout this book I have quoted from all available editions of Khrushchev's memoirs. I have cited the English-language volumes not only when they contain passages not found in Russian but also when they cover the same ground as the Russian versions in a felicitous translation, as well as to provide access to the memoirs to non-Russian readers.

10 Tapes and transcripts of Khrushchev's memoirs are available in the United States at the Oral History Collection of Columbia University and at the John Hay Library of Brown University. Similar materials are also preserved at Tsentral'nyi arkhiv obshchestvennykh dvizhenii Moskvy (Central Archive of Social Movements in Moscow, hereafter TsAODM) and Rossiiskii gosudarstvennyi arkhiv sotsial'no-politicheskoi istorii (Russian State Archive of Sociopolitical History, hereafter RGASPI) in Moscow.

INTRODUCTION

1 Walter Bedell Smith, American ambassador to the USSR from 1946 to 1949, describes diplomatic receptions during his time in *My Three Years in Moscow* (Philadelphia: Lippincott, 1950), pp. 98–101. On the 1950s see Max Frankel, *The Times of My Life and My Life with the Times* (New York: Random House, 1999), pp. 149–50, 157–58; and Daniel Schorr, *Staying Tuned: A Life in Journalism* (New York: Pocket Books, 2001), pp. 85, 88, 90–91, 98, 102, 107–08, 110. Marvin Kalb and Daniel Schorr also described diplomatic receptions attended by Khrushchev in interviews with the author.

2 According to Khrushchev speechwriter Fyodor Burlatsky, who heard his boss recount the same story on another occasion, Khrushchev identified it as one he had first encountered in a primer entitled "How to Read and Recite." Burlatsky, *Khrushchev: The Era of Khrushchev through the Eyes of His Advisor*, trans. Daphne Skillen (New York: Scribner's, 1991), p. 39.

3 "Khrushchev—A Personality Sketch," OCI, No. 2391/61, pp. 1–2, declassified, undated copy provided to the author by the History Staff, U.S. Central Intelligence Agency.

4 V. Vinnichenko, *Tvori*, vol. 9 (Kyiv-Viden': 1919). Informal Russian translation.

5 Dr. Bryant Wedge, "Khrushchev at a Distance: A Study of Public Personality," *Trans-action* (October 1968), pp. 24–28. The reason the CIA wasn't so keen to have this article published is that it prefers not to reveal how it goes about assessing the personalities of foreign leaders.

6 *Diagnostic and Statistical Manual of Mental Disorders*, 3rd ed. (Washington, D.C.: American Psychiatric Association, 1980), pp. 206–07.

7 Nancy McWilliams, *Psychoanalytic Diagnosis: Understanding Personality Structure in the Clinical Process* (New York: Guilford Press, 1994), p. 248. McWilliams quotes S. Akhtar, *Broken Structures: Severe Personality Disorders and Their Treatment* (Northvale, N.J.: Jason Aronson, 1992), p. 193.

8 Author's interview with Jane Thompson.

9 Ernst Neizvestnyi, "Moi dialog s Khrushchevym," *Vremia i my*, no. 4 (May 1979), p. 182.

10 Cited in the preface to NK5, vol. 1, p. 4.

CHAPTER 1. THE FALL: OCTOBER 1964

1 This description is taken from a variety of sources, including author's interviews with Khrushchev's son Sergei, home movies provided to the author by Sergei Khrushchev, Norman Cousins's memoir, *The Improbable Triumvirate: John F. Kennedy, Pope John XXIII, Nikita Khrushchev* (New York: Norton, 1972), an interview with Cousins's daughter, Andrea, who visited Pitsunda with her father in 1964, and a detailed account by Eric Johnston, who visited Pitsunda in October 1958 and described the scene in a report to the U.S. State Department. Johnston's report was obtained from Public Record Office, Kew, London, U.K. (hereafter PRO), Foreign Office (hereafter FO) 371/143419, pp. 2, 9–10.

2 Adzhubei, *Krushenie Illiuzii*, p. 288.

3 Recalled by former Khrushchev colleagues Aleksandr Shelepin and Vladimir Semichastny in an interview with Nikolai Barsukov, March 27 and May 22, 1989, and printed in "Beseda s Shelepinym A. N. i Semichastnym, V. E." *Neizvestnaia Rossiia: XX vek*, vol. 1 (Moscow: Istoricheskoe nasledie, 1992), p. 279.

4 Cousins, *Improbable Triumvirate*, pp. 85–86.

5 Recalled by Anastas Mikoyan in Mikoian, *Tak bylo: razmyshleniia o minuvshem* (Moscow: Vagrius, 1999), p, 614.

6 Accounts of this conversation differ. Sergei Khrushchev's account, for example, in SK2, pp. 133–34, has chief Kremlin ideologue Mikhail Suslov making the call instead of Brezhnev. But Pyotr Shelest and Vladimir Semichastny both confirm that Brezhnev did the telephoning. P. E. Shelest, . . . *Da ne sudimy budete: dnevnikovye zapiski, vospominaniia chlena Politburo KPSS* (Moscow: Edition q, 1995), p. 224. Author's interview with Semichastny.

7 Sergei Khrushchev, *Nikita Khrushchev: krizisy i rakety* (Moscow: Novosti, 1994), vol. 2, pp. 472–74 (hereafter SK3).

8 SK2, p. 108.

9 SK3, vol. 2, p. 498.

10 Ibid., pp. 490–91.

11 Semichastny recalled this and other examples of Brezhnev's near panic in an interview with V. A. Starkov, editor of the Soviet magazine *Argumenty i fakty*. The interview appeared as "Kak smeshchali Khrushcheva," *Argumenty i fakty* (May 20–26, 1989). The author has also consulted an unpublished full transcript of the interview. See also SK2, p. 135, and Shelest, . . . *Da ne sudimy*, p. 191.

12 Nikolai Egorychev, "Beseda s Egorychevym N.G.," interview by Nikolai Barsukov (September 19, 1990), in *Neizvestnaia Rossiia* (Moscow: Istoricheskoe nasledie, 1992), vol. 1, p. 291.

13 SK2, pp. 124–25.

14 Valerii Alekseev, "Chelovek iz teni," *Pravda*, March 18, 1993, p. 5.

15 See Shelepin and Semichastny in "Beseda s Shelepinym A. N. i Semichastnym, V. E," interview by Nikolai Barsukov.

16 Unpublished transcript of V. A. Starkov interview with Semichastny, p. 11. Author's interview with Semichastny.

17 SK2, p. 138.

18 Unpublished transcript of V. A. Starkov interview with Semichastny, p. 8.

19 Author's interview with Semichastny.

20 The following account draws on those of several participants in the Presidium meeting. Vladimir Malin, head of the Central Committee's General Department, secretly took notes, which, after being hidden for years in party archives, were published in "Zapiski V. Malina na zasedanii Prezidiuma TsK KPSS," *Istochnik*, no. 2 (1998), pp. 125–35. The notes summarize all speakers' remarks at the session but leave out many of the more colorful phrases. Presidium candidate member Leonid Efremov published a more vivid account in "Kak snimali Khrushcheva," *Dialog*, no. 7 (July 1993), pp. 47–55. Other recollections include Andrei Karaulov's June 15,

1989, interview with Pyotr Shelest in "Brezhnevu ia tak skazal," *Teatral'naia zhizn'*, no. 17 (1989), pp. 28–32, and V. A. Starkov's interview with Semichastny (both as published in *Argumenty i fakty* and in the unpublished transcript provided to the author). Also see Shelepin and Semichastny in "Beseda s Shelepinym A. N. i Semichastnym, V. E," interview by Nikolai Barsukov, pp. 281–84.

21 Efremov, "Kak snimali Khrushcheva," p. 51.

22 Ibid.

23 Unpublished transcript of Starkov interview with Semichastny, p. 9. Also see SK2, p. 150.

24 SK2, pp. 149–54.

25 Efremov, "Kak snimali Khrushcheva," p. 52.

26 See ibid., p. 53; and Andrei Aleksandrov-Agentov (Brezhnev's former foreign policy adviser), "Brezhnev i Khrushchev," in *Novoe vremia*, no. 22 (1993), p. 40.

27 No full transcript is available for this speech, and the available accounts listed above differ in details. The version quoted in the text includes quotations from all accounts on the theory that each stressed different elements.

28 A transcript of Suslov's speech, along with other documents from the October 14, 1964, plenum, is published in "Kak snimali N. S. Khrushcheva: materialy plenuma TsK KPSS, oktiabr' 1964 g.," *Istoricheskii arkhiv* (hereafter IA), no. 1, 1993, pp. 3–19. Central Committee member Aleksandr Lyashko described Khrushchev's body language in an interview with the author.

29 SK2, p. 160.

30 Russian commentators on Khrushchev's ouster have debated whether it was the result of an unlawful coup or of action authorized in party rules (which give the Central Committee the right to appoint members of the Presidium and to name the party leader) but prepared in secret so as to prevent Khrushchev from thwarting them. Besides being academic, the issue seems especially moot in a state that was itself not based on the rule of law.

31 Oleg Troianovskii, *Cherez gody i rasstoianiia* (Moscow: Vagrius, 1997), p. 263.

32 Harsh as Khrushchev's treatment was, it obviously compares favorably with the fates of those who were "forcibly retired" in Stalin's time.

33 SK2, pp. 161–62.

CHAPTER 2. KALINOVKA'S OWN: 1894–1908

1 During his life, Khrushchev celebrated his birthday as April 17, 1894. But the birth register of the Archangel Church in his village records the actual date as two days earlier. According to Russia's old-style prerevolutionary calendar, the dates were April 3 and 5. See the account by a Kursk Province archivist in NK5, vol. 1, p. 722.

2 SK2, p. 238.

3 According to Dmitri Shepilov, who worked closely with Khrushchev for many years before joining an abortive putsch against him in 1957, Khrushchev "didn't like talking about his peasant origin, and in fact carefully avoided" doing so. Shepilov's animus against his former patron is such that his testimony isn't always reliable, but in this case it rings true. See D. T. Shepilov, "Vospominaniia," VI, no. 4 (1998), pp. 18–19.

4 The author made this journey in 1991 accompanied by Khrushchev's son Sergei and his wife, Valentina Golenko.

5 Richard Pipes, *Russia under the Old Regime* (New York: Scribner, 1974), pp. 167–68.

6 S. Stepniak, *The Russian Peasantry: Their Agrarian Condition, Social Life and Religion* (Westport, Conn.: Hyperion, 1977), pp. 142–43.

7 Sir John Maynard, *Russia in Flux*, ed. and abr. S. Haden Guest (New York: Macmillan, 1948) p. 50.

8 *Pamiatnaia knizhka Kurskoi gubernii na 1892* (Kursk: Tipografiia Gubernskogo Pravleniia, 1892), p. 20.

9 *The Village of Viriatino: An Ethnographic Study of a Russian Village from before the Revolution to the Present*, trans. and ed. Sula Benet (Garden City, N.Y.: Anchor Books, 1970), pp. 58–62.

10 Stepniak, *Russian Peasantry*, p. 160.

11 *Village of Viriatino*, p. 122.

12 Remarks of August 31, 1959, in Stroi, vol. 4, p. 47. See also *Pravda*, May 19, 1962, p. 3.

13 Conversation with Roswell Garst and John Crystal in Stroi, vol. 8, p. 6.

14 NK1, p. 266. Although the English text refers to Khrushchev's time in Yuzovka, he almost certainly was talking about Kalinovka.

15 Stroi, vol. 4, p. 47.

16 *Village of Viriatino*, pp. 143–44.

17 Ibid., p. 151.

18 Overall, zemstvo schools had greater enrollments: 3.8 million pupils nationwide in 1907, compared with 2 million in church schools in 1906.

19 Khrushchev wasn't clear about exactly when he went to which school and for how long; most of his references range from two to four years. He did imply that he first attended the parochial school and later entered the state school in Kalinovka. See NK3, p. 5. Shepilov insists that Khrushchev told him that he attended school regularly for only one year, that the next winter he went irregularly, and that after that, he quit altogether. See Shepilov, "Vospominaniia," p. 19.

20 *Village of Viriatino*, p. 150.

21 Ibid., pp. 151–52.

22 Cited in Harold H. Martin, "Back to the Beginning of the Tumultuous Life of Nikita Khrushchev," *Saturday Evening Post* (November 7, 1964), p. 19.

23 NK3, p. 4.

24 Khrushchev speech in Kalinovka, July 28, 1962, in Foreign Broadcast Information Service, *Daily Report: Foreign Radio Broadcasts* (hereafter FBIS), August 3, 1962, p. CC7.

25 See NK5, vol. 1, pp. 722–23.

26 NK3, p. 4.

27 Christine D. Worobec, *Peasant Russia: Family and Community in the Post-Emancipation Period* (Princeton: Princeton University Press, 1991), p. 79.

28 NK3, pp. 4–5. Khrushchev indicated that he and his mother and sister accompanied his father to Yuzovka on one of his trips and spent about a year and half there before returning to Kalinovka.

29 Ibid., p. 6.

30 Author's interview with Nikita Khrushchev's daughter Rada Adzhubei.

31 Adzhubei, *Krushenie illiuzii,* p. 150.

32 *Village of Viriatino,* p. 22.

33 *Rasskaz o pochetnom shakhtere: N. S. Khrushchev v Donbasse* (Stalino: Knizhnoe izdatel'stvo, 1961), p. 11.

34 Martin, "Back to the Beginning," p. 19.

35 NK1, p. 269.

36 Author's interviews with Liuba Sizykh.

37 Author's interview with Nina Ivanovna Kukharchuk.

38 Conversation with the author.

39 Cited in George Paloczi-Horvath, *Khrushchev: The Making of a Dictator* (Boston: Little, Brown, 1960), p. 13.

40 NK3, pp. 8–9.

41 Author's interviews with Liuba Sizykh.

42 Adzhubei, *Krushenie illiuzii,* p. 151.

43 Ibid.

44 Author's interview with longtime Khrushchev aide Andrei Shevchenko.

45 Ernest Jones, *The Life and Work of Sigmund Freud* (New York: Basic Books, 1961), p. 6.

46 Harold Lasswell, *Power and Personality* (New York: Norton, 1948), p. 50.

47 According to Nancy McWilliams, boys like Khrushchev, who are intense, sociable, and eager to learn, particularly need an authoritative father who can teach them how the world works and how to modulate and organize their "aggressive drive and fantasy." In the absence of such a father, such boys are likely to look for "father figures." See Nancy McWilliams, "Mothering and Fathering Processes in the Psychoanalytic Art," *Psychoanalytic Review,* vol. 78, no. 4 (Winter 1991), pp. 527–30.

48 NK3, p. 5.

49 Ibid., p. 5.

50 Ibid., pp. 5–6.

51 Adzhubei, *Krushenie illiuzii,* p. 18.

52 NK1, p. 22.

53 Ibid.

54 Address to trade unionists, March 31, 1960, *Pravda,* April 2, 1960, p. 2.

55 Cited in Michael Beschloss, *The Crisis Years: Kennedy and Khrushchev, 1960–1963* (New York: HarperCollins, 1991), p. 82.

56 Khrushchev's stepped-up persecution of the religion is treated in Chapter 18.

57 Author's interview with Andrei Shevchenko.

58 Lewis Feuer, ed., *Marx and Engels: Basic Writing on Politics and Philosophy* (Garden City, N.Y.: Anchor Books, 1959), pp. 11, 18.

59 See N. N. Kozlova, *Gorizonty povsednevnosti Sovetskoi epokhi: golosa iz khora* (Moscow: Institut filosofii, 1996), pp. 131–34.

CHAPTER 3. MAKING IT AS A METALWORKER: 1908–1917

1 Khrushchev never clearly specified when he visited Yuzovka and for how long. For one reference to his having done so, see NK4, no. 6, 1990, p. 88.

2 See Lazar Pistrak, *The Grand Tactician: Khrushchev's Rise to Power* (New York: Praeger, 1961), p. 5; Mark Frankland, *Khrushchev* (New York: Stein and Day, 1967), p. 17.

3 NK1, p. 403.

4 Hiroaki Kuromiya, "Donbas Miners in War, Revolution and Civil War," in *Making Workers Soviet: Power, Class and Identity*, ed. Lewis H. Siegelbaum and Ronald Grigor Suny (Ithaca, N.Y.: Cornell University Press, 1994).

5 G. I. Petrovsky, as cited in Theodore H. Friedgut, *Yuzovka and Revolution*, vol. 1: *Life and Work in Russia's Donbass, 1869–1924* (Princeton: Princeton University Press, 1989), p. 73.

6 *Rasskaz o pochetnom shakhtere*, p. 12.

7 Khrushchev interview with *Le Figaro*, in *Pravda*, March 27, 1958, p. 2.

8 See William J. Tompson, *Khrushchev: A Political Life* (New York: St. Martin's, 1995), p. 6.

9 *Rasskaz o pochetnom shakhtere*, p. 22.

10 NK2, p. 88.

11 Friedgut, *Yuzovka and Revolution*, vol. 1, p. 274.

12 In 1958, in the midst of a campaign for a Big Four summit conference that Western leaders were resisting, Khrushchev compared them with Yuzovka mine owners who announced that wages would be paid at the end of the month. The catch, he recalled, was that they didn't say which month, and often several went by without pay. Khrushchev interview with the *Times* of London, in *Pravda*, February 16, 1958, p. 1.

13 Khrushchev compared cholera riot rumors with those that arose in 1952, when Kremlin doctors were falsely accused of poisoning Soviet leaders. "And now, in our own time, these same dark powers were rearing their heads again, and the persecution of intellectuals and doctors came back out into the open." NK1, p. 287.

14 Quoted in Friedgut, *Yuzovka and Revolution*, vol. 1, p. 73.

15 See George L. Mosse, *Fallen Soldiers: Reshaping the Memory of the World Wars* (New York: Oxford University Press, 1990), pp. 159–81.

16 Kuromiya, "Donbas Miners in War, Revolution and Civil War," pp. 142–43.

17 Friedgut, *Yuzovka and Revolution*, vol. 1, pp. 83, 93–94.

18 Kuromiya, "Donbas Miners in War, Revolution and Civil War," p. 141.

19 Friedgut, *Yuzovka and Revolution*, vol. 1, pp. 173, 333–34; Pistrak, *The Grand Tactician*, p. 5.

20 Friedgut, *Yuzovka and Revolution*, vol. 1, p. 330.

21 Ibid., pp. 256–57.

22 Edward Crankshaw, *Khrushchev: A Career* (New York: Viking Press, 1966), pp. 11–12.

23 On the importance of choosing a vocation and a spouse and on what such choices can reveal about personality, see Daniel J. Levinson, *The Seasons of a Man's Life* (New York: Knopf, 1970), especially pp. 22, 71–83, 90–93, 101–11.

24 A former Khrushchev coworker describes the scene in Martin, "Back to the Beginning," p. 23.

25 NK3, pp. 6–7.

26 Ibid.

27 Khrushchev speeches in *Pravda,* March 10, 1963, August 28, 1963, and August 31, 1963, p. 1.

28 Picture is in *Rabochaia biografiia: fotoal'bom o donetskom mashinostroitel'nom zavode imeni Leninskogo komsomola Ukrainy* (Kiev: Mystetsvo, 1989).

29 Victoria E. Bonnell, ed., *The Russian Worker: Life and Labor under the Tsarist Regime* (Berkeley: University of California Press, 1983), p. 10.

30 Ibid., pp. 45–46.

31 Ibid., p. 50.

32 Friedgut, *Yuzovka and Revolution,* vol. 1, p. 304.

33 NK2, p. 86.

34 Author's interviews with Olga Kosenko, Donetsk, June 1991 and July 1993.

35 Ibid.

36 The police report on the incident is in NK5, vol. 1, pp. 727–29.

37 Iu. I. Shapoval, *M. S. Khrushchov na Ukraini* (Kyiv: Tovaristvo "Znannia," 1990), p. 6; "Dovidkova Kartka" December 24, 1971, Tsentral'nyi derzhavnyi arkhiv hromads'kykh ob'ednan' Ukrainy (Central State Archive of Social Organizations of Ukraine, Kyiv, Ukraine, hereafter TsDAHOU), f. 39, op. 4, no. 223, ark. 28–29.

38 *Rasskaz o pochetnom shakhtere,* p. 22. Although this description is obviously phrased as positively as possible, its general point jibes with other accounts.

39 NK3, p. 8.

40 *Rasskaz o pochetnom shakhtere,* p. 22.

41 Author's interview with Nina Barmut, a niece of Khrushchev's first wife.

42 Even after Yefrosinia's death, Khrushchev and his second wife, Nina Petrovna Khrushcheva, kept in close touch with the Pisarev family. In 1929 the Khrushchevs invited Yefrosinia's sister Anna to live with them in Kiev and help care for her niece and nephew, Yulia and Leonid Khrushchev. The elder Khrushchevs helped out the Pisarevs in various ways over the years, especially by sending them books. Mrs. Khrushchev made a point of remembering their birthdays, and Nikita Khrushchev visited them at their home near Sochi—with the result that the road to their remote mountain cottage was paved and informally christened the Khrushchevka. Author's interview with Nina Barmut.

43 Adzhubei, *Krushenie illiuzii,* p. 152.

44 Beschloss, *Crisis Years,* p. 194.

45 Adzhubei, *Krushenie illiuzii,* p. 89.

46 NK2, p. 87.

47 Joseph E. Persico, *The Imperial Rockefeller: A Biography of Nelson Rockefeller* (New York: Simon and Schuster, 1982), p. 86.

48 *Rasskaz o pochetnom shakhtere,* p. 16.

49 Translated in Roy Medvedev, *Khrushchev,* trans. Brian Pearce (Garden City, N.Y.: Doubleday/Anchor, 1983), p. 5.

50 *Rasskaz o pochetnom shakhtere,* p. 16.

51 Author's interviews with Yuri (July 1993) and Sergei Khrushchev.

52 Author's interviews with Yulia Leonidovna Khrushcheva.

53 *Rasskaz o pochetnom shakhtere,* p. 25.

54 NK3, pp. 10–11.

55 *Rasskaz o pochetnom shakhtere,* p. 16.

56 Khrushchev's article in *Diktatura truda* is reprinted in NK5, vol. 1, pp. 732–33.

57 NK3, pp. 7–8.

58 The question was posed to Khrushchev in retirement by Soviet playwright Mikhail Shatrov. See *N. S. Khrushchev (1894–1971): Materialy nauchnoi konferentsii, posviashchennoi 100-letiiu so dnia rozhdeniia N. S. Khrushcheva* (Moscow: Rossiiskii gosudarstvennyi gumanitarnyi universitet, 1994), p. 39. As noted in the previous chapter, Khrushchev's inconsistency extended to his various accounts of which elementary schools he attended and for how long.

CHAPTER 4. TO BE OR NOT TO BE AN APPARATCHIK: 1918–1929

1 For a general treatment of the Donbas during the years covered in this chapter, see Hiroaki Kuromiya, *Freedom and Terror in the Donbas: A Ukrainian-Russian Borderland, 1870s–1990s* (Cambridge, U.K.: Cambridge University Press, 1998), pp. 71–150.

2 Khrushchev's interlocutor in retirement was the Soviet playwright Mikhail Shatrov. See Shatrov's recollections in *N. S. Khrushchev (1894–1971)*, p. 39.

3 In addition to Kuromiya, *Freedom and Terror in the Donbas*, the following account relies on Kuromiya, "Donbas Miners in War, Revolution and Civil War."

4 Kuromiya, "Donbas Miners in War, Revolution and Civil War," p. 151.

5 Khrushchev's posts are mentioned in *Rasskaz o pochetnom shakhtere*, pp. 34–39. A copy of the Protocol of the Rutchenkovo Soviet session of May 29, 1917, is in Derzhavnyi arkhiv Donetskoi oblasti (State Archive of Donetsk Province, Donetsk, Ukraine, hereafter DADO), f. R-42, op. 1, d. 1, ark. 39–40. For two May 17 and 19, 1917, documents signed by Khrushchev as chairman of the Rutchenkovo Soviet's executive committee, see NK5, vol. 1, pp. 729–30.

6 Feliks Chuev, *Sto sorok besed s Molotovym* (Moscow: Terra, 1991), p. 352.

7 NK3, p. 11.

8 Ibid., p. 9.

9 Kuromiya, "Donbas Miners in War, Revolution and Civil War," pp. 151–52.

10 *Rasskaz o pochetnom shakhtere*, pp. 42–43.

11 See Evan Mawdsley, *The Russian Civil War* (Boston: Allen & Unwin, 1987), p. 29.

12 From the very beginning, the Bolsheviks had condemned the war as an interimperialist conflict the only redeeming virtue of which would be to usher in proletarian revolutions in the warring states. Once in power, Lenin sought an immediate armistice but refused to accept harsh German terms that included occupation of Poland, Ukraine, Lithuania, and western Latvia. During the German-Soviet negotiations at Brest-Litovsk, People's Commissar of Foreign Affairs Leon Trotsky stunned his German counterparts by declaring a policy of "neither war nor peace." To this, the representative of the German High Command snorted, "*Unerhört* [unheard of]!," whereupon German troops resumed an offensive that left them occupying all Ukraine by April 1918.

13 Kuromiya, *Freedom and Terror in the Donbas*, pp. 99–103.

14 *Rasskaz o pochetnom shakhtere*, p. 44, says that Khrushchev was denounced to the Germans' Ukrainian collaborators, who mounted a manhunt for him, and that in a stirring Hollywood-style finale, he descended into a mine shaft, crawled through tunnels, emerged at the edge of the steppe, and escaped to the east. But Bolshevik documents of the time railed against workers and soldiers who deserted the front and the mines. Said one of them: "Recently, workers have been leaving the mines. We therefore declare that only people who have forgotten their conscience, only the blind, the ignorant, and those who have been deceived by provocateurs can flee at such a desperate moment. Only saboteurs and counterrevolutionaries are abandoning their work. Toilers! Every man at his post! To work!" See N. Goncharenko, *Oktiabr' v Donbasse* (Lugansk: Luganskoe oblastnoe izdatel'stvo, 1961), pp. 257–58. The fact that even Molotov didn't accuse Khrushchev of desertion suggests a more benign interpretation of his departure is probably accurate.

15 *Rasskaz o pochetnom shakhtere,* p. 45.

16 See Dorothy Atkinson, *The End of the Russian Land Commune, 1905–1930* (Stanford: Stanford University Press, 1983), pp. 165–85; and Richard Pipes, *The Russian Revolution* (New York: Knopf, 1990), p. 714.

17 Kuromiya, "Donbas Miners in War, Revolution and Civil War," pp. 154–55; Kuromiya, *Freedom and Terror in the Donbas,* pp. 103–14.

18 A. Kritskii, cited in Richard Pipes, *Russia under the Bolshevik Regime* (New York: Knopf, 1993), p. 86.

19 Mawdsley, *Russian Civil War,* p. 195.

20 Mark Von Hagen, *Soldiers in the Proletarian Dictatorship: The Red Army and the Soviet Socialist State, 1917–1939* (Ithaca, N.Y.: Cornell University Press, 1990), p. 92.

21 Quoted in Mawdsley, *Russian Civil War,* p. 62.

22 NK1, p. 15.

23 NK2, p. 88.

24 Ibid., pp. 83–84.

25 From a speech Khrushchev gave in Los Angeles in September 1959, cited in *Rasskaz o pochetnom shakhtere,* p. 50.

26 NK2, p. 88.

27 NK3, p. 12.

28 See Von Hagen, *Soldiers in the Proletarian Dictatorship,* pp. 129–30.

29 NK3, p. 12.

30 The exact date and circumstances of Yefrosinia's death are not documented.

31 "Maminy Tetradi," unpublished notes handwritten and then typed for her children and grandchildren by Nina Petrovna Khrushcheva. Provided to the author by Sergei N. Khrushchev.

32 Patrick A. Croghan, A. A., *The Peasant from Makeyevka: Biography of Bishop Piu Neveu, A.A.* (Worcester, Mass.: 1982), p. 56.

33 Sheila Fitzpatrick, *The Russian Revolution* (Oxford: Oxford University Press, 1982), p. 85.

34 Theodore H. Freidgut, *Yuzovka and Revolution,* vol 2: *Politics and Revolution in Russia's Donbas, 1869–1924* (Princeton: Princeton University Press, 1994), p. 430.

35 Croghan, *Peasant from Makeyevka,* p. 56. Flavius Josephus was a Jewish priest and historian who was in Jerusalem at the time of the Jewish revolt against the Romans. He settled in Rome A.D. 70 and wrote a history of the war.

36 N. M. Borodin, *One Man in His Time* (London: Constable, 1955), pp. 39–40.

37 Medvedev, *Khrushchev,* p. 9–10.

38 Friedgut, *Yuzovka and Revolution,* vol. 2, p. 398. In the Donbas as a whole Bolsheviks numbered only 3,198 in mid-1919. In Yuzovka's New Russia Factory, in 1920, out of nearly 6,000 workers, only 70 were Bolsheviks.

39 Kuromiya, "Donbas Miners in War, Revolution and Civil War," pp. 155–56.

40 In 1923 alone, more than sixty thousand miners took part in almost two hundred strikes. See Kuromiya, *Freedom and Terror in the Donbas,* pp. 119–37.

41 See Leonard Schapiro, *The Communist Party of the Soviet Union* (New York: Random House, 1960), pp. 278–79.

42 Friedgut, *Yuzovka and Revolution,* vol. 2, p. 456. There are stories (cited in *Komsomol'skaia pravda,* May 19, 1989), which are widely credited in Donetsk, that the city of Yuzovka itself was briefly renamed Trotsky in 1923 before being changed to Stalino in April 1924, but Friedgut reports that no record of such a renaming can be found in the Donetsk archives.

43 Quoted in Medvedev, *Khrushchev,* pp. 10–11.

44 *Rasskaz o pochetnom shakhtere,* pp. 63–64.

45 NK2, p. 87.

46 See NK4, no. 8, 1993, p. 82; Martin, "Back to the Beginning," p. 24.

47 NK3, p. 13.

48 See Sheila Fitzpatrick, *Everyday Stalinism: Ordinary Life in Extraordinary Times: Soviet Russia in the 1930s* (New York: Oxford University Press, 1999), pp. 16–18, 80–82, 88–92.

49 Cited in Yuri Shapoval, "The Ukrainian Years," in *Nikita Khrushchev,* ed. William Taubman, Sergei Khrushchev, and Abbott Gleason (New Haven: Yale University Press, 2000), p. 11.

50 Sheila Fitzpatrick, *Education and Social Mobility in the Soviet Union, 1921–1934* (Cambridge, U.K.: Cambridge University Press, 1979), p. 14. The discussion that follows draws on pp. 9–14. According to Fitzpatrick, Lenin tolerated the workers' training programs although he was generally against what he thought of as "caste schools." A highly educated man himself, a highbrow intellectual in comparison with most of his followers, he never apologized for his background. The notion of proletarian culture, highly popular at the time, struck him as unsatisfactory. The sooner the mass of Russian workers and peasants got themselves educated and cultured in the old-fashioned, bourgeois sense of those terms, the better off the revolution and the country would be. But in the beginning, compromises with "bourgeois" standards were necessary.

51 Quoted in Fitzpatrick, *Education and Social Mobility,* p. 49.

52 *Rasskaz o pochetnom shakhtere,* p. 81.

53 See the following interviews with Antonina Gladky: "Khrushchev Poor Pupil," *Hartford Courant,* July 18, 1959, p. 1; "Manchester Woman Once Taught Khrushchev," *Hartford Times,* August 22, 1962, p. 37; "Woman Becomes Citizen," *Hartford Courant,* June 15, 1963, p. 5; "Nikita Khrushchev's First Teacher," *High Point* [North Carolina] *Enterprise,* February 28, 1989.

54 Frankland, *Khrushchev,* p. 32; Pistrak, *Grand Tactician,* p. 17.

55 Interviews at the Donetsk Polytechnical Institute (the *tekhnikum*'s latter-day name) in June 1991. Also see Medvedev, *Khrushchev,* p.11.

56 *Rasskaz o pochetnom shakhtere*, p. 79.

57 When I visited Donetsk in 1991 and again in 1993, I saw a questionnaire Khrushchev filled out in connection with his attendance at a Stalino party conference in 1926. Under the heading "Education," he wrote, "Finished *rabfak*." But the museum archivist was skeptical. In the absence of documentary evidence she could not say for sure if Khrushchev actually completed his *rabfak* studies.

58 Various documents in the DADO, f. 9, o. 1, d. 40, ark. 213; f. 9, o. 1, d. 38, ark. 22; and f. 109, o. 1, d. 51, ark. 2.

59 In 1924 Stalin announced his doctrine of socialism in one country in contrast with Trotsky's (and Lenin's) expectation that the revolution could triumph only if it swept the world. Intellectually sophisticated followers of Trotsky found that slogan a contradiction in terms (by definition, socialism was international), and ludicrous to boot ("Why," the witty Karl Radek wondered, "did Stalin restrict himself to socialism in one country? What was wrong with socialism in one district or even one street?"). See review of Alex De Jonge, *Stalin and the Shaping of the Soviet Union* (New York: Morrow, 1986) by John Keep in the *Times Literary Supplement*, October 24, 1986.

60 NK4, no. 4, 1990, p. 77.

61 Friedgut, *Yuzovka and Revolution*, vol. 2, p. 456.

62 The story of Khrushchev's relationship with Marusia was told to the author in June 1991 by an old Khrushchev family friend, Olga Kosenko, herself the daughter of a childhood friend of Khrushchev's, who claimed to have talked to Marusia's cousin as well as to the doctor who treated Marusia's daughter. The story was confirmed to the author by Zakhar Glukhov, who, beginning in the late 1930s, served for thirty-five years as party secretary of a district near Yuzovka where Khrushchev served in 1925.

63 Nikita and Nina Khrushchevs' children trace the fact that their parents didn't officially register their marriage for four decades to their Communist disdain for "bourgeois morality." (Nor, it turns out, did Anastas Mikoyan and his wife ever register their marriage. See Mikoian, *Tak bylo*, p. 19.) But in many other ways, the elder Khrushchevs insisted on observing just such norms.

64 Author's interviews with Yulia Leonidovna Khrushcheva, Moscow.

65 This account is based on notes that Nina Khrushcheva dictated in her old age for her children and grandchildren. Excerpts are in her son-in-law's memoir, Adzhubei, *Krushenie illiuzii*, pp. 43–59; a fuller translation is in Sergei N. Khrushchev, *Nikita Khrushchev and the Creation of a Superpower* (University Park.: Penn State Press, 2000) (hereafter SK4), pp. 6–21; and information also came from Nina Petrovna Khrushcheva, "Maminy Tetradi."

66 Author's interview with Sergei Khrushchev, Kalinovka, June 1991.

67 Khrushcheva, "Maminy Tetradi."

68 Party membership numbers in Shapoval, *M. S. Khrushchov na Ukraini*, p. 9.

69 Martin, "Back to the Beginning," p. 25.

70 Recollection by S. Ya. Priazhdnikova in TsDAHOU, f. 1, o. 23, d. 727, ark. 12.

71 NK1, pp. 20–21.

72 Martin, "Back to the Beginning," p. 25. Peasants like these almost never showed up in Petrovka, where Khrushchev had his office. Yet he apparently spent as much of his time as possible in the industrialized part of the district. He did so, he said, because the miners wanted him around. But given his attitude toward rural life, there seems more to it than that. See Frankland, *Khrushchev,* p. 33.

73 Quoted in Crankshaw, *Khrushchev,* p. 37. In October 1925, Khrushchev wrote a letter to *Pravda* in Moscow that illustrates his activist/populist approach. In it he complained that since the paper arrived several days late by horse from a railroad station approximately thirty-three miles away (except in winter, when there was such "a fantastic amount of mud and dirt" that the paper reached Petrovka even later), circulation had dropped from 500 copies in December 1924 to 285 in October 1925. If, on the other hand, *Pravda* could be delivered on a direct train from Kharkov that stopped closer to Petrovka, he could guarantee not only 500 to 600 subscribers but "an end to the justified bitterness and indignation felt by the workers as the result of this foul way of delivering the paper." Khrushchev's letter is in TsDAHOU, f. 633, o. 1, d. 259, ark. 345.

74 NK5, vol. 1, p. 19. Nina Petrovna Khrushcheva recalls in "Maminy Tetradi" that her husband first traveled to Moscow in January 1924 for Lenin's funeral, but Khrushchev mentions no such trip in his memoirs.

75 Verbatim transcript of Khrushchev memoirs as delivered to the West in 1970 and preserved at the Russian Institute of Columbia University (hereafter cited as NK6), pp. 47–48.

76 NK5, vol. 1, pp. 735–37.

77 Lazar Pistrak makes this point in *Grand Tactician,* p. 31.

78 NK1, p. 31.

79 NK3, p. 10.

80 NK5, vol. 1, p. 34. Kaganovich confirms that he used the pseudonym Kosherovich. See Lazar' Kaganovich, *Pamiatnye zapiski* (Moscow: Vagrius, 1996), p. 96.

81 Khrushchev and Kaganovich remembered the date and content of their 1925 encounter somewhat differently. See NK3, p. 10; Kaganovich, *Pamiatnye zapiski,* p. 565.

82 Secret protocols of the bureau of the Stalino party committee include approval of death sentences on January 11, 1927, and July 30, 1927, in DADO, f. 9, o. 1, d. 381, ll. 1 and 42. The meeting that supported the move against Trotsky and Zinoviev is reported in *Rasskaz o pochetnom shakhtere,* p. 123.

83 Protocols 13 and 14 of the bureau of the Stalino party committee in DADO, f. 9, o. 1, d., 381, ll. 45, 49. An excerpt from the former is in NK5, vol. 1, p. 740.

84 Quoted in *Donbas,* no. 2 (1991), p. 191. Such corruption was endemic (a similar scandal in Smolensk produced a purge there in 1928), especially where local officials felt themselves isolated and under siege and learned to cover up for one another's sins. See article by Georgii Malenkov in *Partiinoe stroitel'stvo* (Party Construction), no. 2 (1930), cited by Crankshaw, *Khrushchev,* p. 43.

85 NK4, no. 2, 1990, p. 83.

86 Kaganovich, *Pamiatnye zapiski,* p. 565.

87 From Khrushchev's remarks at the Soviet Communist party's June 1957 plenum at which he was rescued from near ouster. See the transcript published as "Posledniaia 'antipartiinaia' gruppa: stenograficheskii otchet iiun'skogo plenuma (1957 g.) TsK KPSS," IA, nos. 3–6 (1993), nos. 1–2 (1994) (hereafter cited by abbreviated title, issue number, and year). Khrushchev's remarks are in no. 2 (1994), pp. 43–44.

88 Stroganov presumably perished during the terror of the 1930s. NK6, pp. 55–56.

89 Ibid., p. 60.

90 NK4, no. 2, 1990, pp. 90–91.

91 NK6, p. 60.

92 Kaganovich, *Pamiatnye zapiski,* p. 565.

93 NK4, no. 2, 1990, pp. 90–91.

94 NK6, pp. 61–62.

95 NK4, no. 2, 1990, p. 92.

96 See Bohdan Nahaylo and Victor Swoboda, *Soviet Disunion: A History of the Nationalities Problem in the USSR* (New York: Free Press, 1990), pp. 44–67.

97 See Kuromiya, *Freedom and Terror in the Donbas,* pp. 145–46. The name of the city, Shakhty, means "mine shafts" in Russian.

98 TsDAHOU, f. 39, o. 4, d. 223, l. 2.

99 NK6, p. 63.

100 Ibid.

101 Ibid.

102 Much of the following account is based on the author's interview with Vera Aleksandrovna Gostinskaya.

103 Author's interview with Rada Adzhubei. Also see Larissa Vasilieva, *Kremlin Wives,* trans. Cathy Porter (New York: Arcade Publishing, 1994), p. 197.

104 Gostinskaya maintained her faith even after being arrested and imprisoned in the USSR in 1937. After being released, she renewed her friendship with the Khrushchevs in the fifties, and she loyally stood by them after 1964, visiting them often when others didn't dare. In her late eighties in post-Communist Poland, she was still living modestly (rising early, doing her exercises, cleaning her apartment, and reading and rereading her books and documents, including those on Soviet-Polish relations which she edited and published), still devoted to the Communist cause.

CHAPTER 5. STALIN'S PET: 1929–1937

1 The educational level of the new students, most of whom were in their twenties or even thirties, was low. In 1927, just 8.7 percent of all Communists, and 4 percent of working-class party members, had completed secondary school. Party members in white-collar jobs had only four to five years of schooling on average. Fitzpatrick, *Education and Social Mobility,* p. 182.

2 Ibid., p. 305; A. N. Ponomarev, *N. S. Khrushchev: Put' k liderstvy* (Moscow: Znanie, 1990), p. 7.

3 Author's interview with Ada A. Federolf-Shkodina. Federolf-Shkodina went on to teach English at the Institute of Philosophy, Literature, and History in Moscow, where she was arrested in 1938. Later released, she was living in a hospital on the outskirts of the capital in 1991.

4 NK4, no. 2, 1990, p. 94.

5 Kaganovich, *Pamiatnye zapiski,* pp. 565–66. On the continuing authority in 1929 of rightist leaders like Bukharin, see O. V. Khlevniuk, *Politbiuro: Mekhanizmy politicheskoi vlasti v 1930-e gody* (Moscow: ROSPEN, 1996), p. 21.

6 In 1929 Moscow Province was amalgamated into a huge region composed of four former tsarist *gubernii* (Moscow, Ryazan, Tula, and Tver), plus 60 percent of a fifth, Kaluga. See Timothy Colton, *Moscow: Governing the Socialist Metropolis* (Cambridge, Mass.: Harvard University Press, 1995), p. 188.

7 Winston Churchill, *The Second World War,* vol. 4, *The Hinge of Fate* (Boston: Houghton Mifflin, 1950), pp. 447–48. Also see Robert C. Tucker, *Stalin in Power* (New York: Norton, 1990), p. 195; Dmitri Volkogonov, *Stalin: Triumph and Tragedy* (New York: Grove Weidenfeld, 1988), p. 166; and Khlevniuk, *Politbiuro,* pp. 53–60.

8 See Robert Conquest, *The Harvest of Sorrow: Soviet Collectivization and the Terror-Famine* (New York: Oxford University Press, 1986).

9 Estimates of the number who perished in the terror of the middle to late thirties range from several hundred thousand to many millions. Various Russian and Western estimates are in *Entsiklopedicheskii slovar' narodonaseleniia* (Moscow: Bolshaia Rossiiskaia entsiklopediia, 1994), pp. 342–45. Excerpts from the reports of two Soviet commissions that cite lower figures, one formed in 1961 and headed by N. Shvernik, the other established in 1987 under the direction of Aleksandr Yakovlev, are in "Massovye repressii opravdany byt' ne mogut," *Istochnik,* no. 1 (1995), pp. 117–24. Much higher totals are in Robert Conquest, *The Great Terror: A Reassessment* (New York: Oxford University Press, 1990), pp. 484–89, and Volkogonov, *Stalin,* pp. 307–08. Also see S. Maksudov, *Poteri naseleniia SSSR* (Benson, Vt.: Chalidze Publications, 1989); *Naselenie Sovetskogo Soiuza: 1921–1992* (Moscow: Nauka, 1993), pp. 37–50; and J. Arch Getty, Gabor T. Rittersporn, and Viktor N. Zemskov, "Victims of the Soviet Penal System in the Prewar Years: A First Approach on the Basis of Archival Evidence," *American Historical Review,* vol. 98, no. 4 (October 1993), pp. 1007–49.

10 Medvedev, *Khrushchev,* p. 19.

11 Anastas Mikoyan's memoir, edited and introduced by his son, historian Sergo Mikoyan, offers a somewhat fuller and more candid account of the terror and of Mikoyan's role in it. See Mikoian, *Tak bylo,* especially pp. 14–15, 352–75.

12 NK1, p. 44.

13 Khrushchev made this remark in conversation with Mikhail Shatrov. See *N. S. Khrushchev (1894–1971),* p. 38.

14 See Conquest, *Great Terror,* p. 118; and Tucker, *Stalin in Power,* p. 178.

15 See Khlevniuk, *Politbiuro,* pp. 18–20, 53–60; Tucker, *Stalin in Power,* pp. 178, 189; and Colton, *Moscow,* pp. 215–16.

16 NK4, no. 2, 1990, p. 96; no. 3, 1990. p. 61. Also see NK1, p. 72.

17 Text of speech at April 15, 1964, Soviet-Polish friendship rally in Moscow, recorded live and translated in FBIS, April 16, 1964, p. BB40.

18 NK1, pp. 73–74.

19 See R. W. Davies, *The Soviet Economy in Turmoil, 1928–1930* (Cambridge, Mass.: Harvard University Press, 1989) and Tompson, *Khrushchev,* p. 30.

20 Tucker, *Stalin in Power,* pp. 206–07.

21 Tucker (ibid., pp. 211–12) and Conquest, (*Great Terror,* pp. 24–25) credit reports of opposition by Kirov and Sergo Ordzhonikidze. Khlevniuk (*Politbiuro,* pp.

74–79) contends that such reports have not been confirmed by documents newly available in the Soviet archives. In any event, Riutin got ten years instead, but five years later Stalin got his man, as well as Riutin's wife and two sons; the only family members who lived on were Riutin's twenty-year-old daughter and her small child.

22 Conquest, *Great Terror,* p. 31.

23 Tucker, *Stalin in Power,* pp. 242–43.

24 See ibid., pp, 238–47. Khlevniuk disagrees with Tucker.

25 NK3, pp. 20–21. See also Tucker, *Stalin in Power,* p. 250.

26 NK3, p. 18.

27 Ibid., p. 20; see Tucker, *Stalin in Power,* p. 260.

28 From Khrushchev's "secret speech" to the twentieth Party Congress in 1956 in NK1, p. 573.

29 NK3, p. 20.

30 NK1, p. 39.

31 Ibid., p. 38.

32 Ibid., pp. 38–39.

33 Adzhubei, *Krushenie illiuzii,* p. 154.

34 Author's interview with Ada Federolf-Shkodina.

35 Author's interview with Viktor Yevreinov, widower of Khrushchev's daughter Yelena.

36 From Khrushcheva, "Maminy Tetradi."

37 NK1, p. 37.

38 Moscow party authorities made the same demand in a secret letter that Molotov insisted they write. See A. N. Ponomarev, "Khrushchev: Nachalo kar'ery," in *Neizvestnaia Rossiia: XX vek* (Moscow: Istoricheskoe nasledie, 1993), vol. 3, pp. 120–21.

39 Lars T. Lih, Oleg V. Naumov, and Oleg V. Khlevnuik, eds., *Stalin's Letters to Molotov, 1925–1936* (New Haven: Yale University Press, 1995), p. 182.

40 See "Nadezhde Sergeevne Alliluevoi lichno ot Stalina," *Istochnik,* no. 0 (1993), pp. 9–22.

41 NK4, no. 2, 1990, p. 95.

42 Quoted in Ponomarev, *N. S. Khrushchev,* p. 8.

43 NK1, p. 39.

44 Ibid., pp. 40–41. The article, which appeared in *Pravda* on May 26, 1930, is reprinted in NK5, vol. 1, pp. 748–50.

45 Ponomarev, "Nikita Khrushchev," pp. 121–22.

46 NK4, no. 5, 1990, p. 56.

47 Quoted in Ponomarev, *N. S. Khrushchev,* p. 13

48 Records of bureau meetings from June 9 to December 27, 1930, TsAODM, f. 160, o. 1, d. 10, l. 53.

49 Ibid., ll. 38–39; Ponomarev, *N. S. Khrushchev,* p. 13.

50 Cited in Ponomarev, *N. S. Khrushchev,* p. 14.

51 Cited in ibid., p. 16.

52 NK1, p. 42.

53 In an indication of how relatively relaxed security still was, Khrushchev shared his pass with friends.

54 For an account of their acquaintance, see NK4, no. 2, 1990, p. 98.

55 NK1, p. 43.

56 NK4, no. 2, 1990, pp. 99, 101.

57 NK1, pp. 43–44.

58 NK4, no. 2, 1990, p. 100.

59 The identity of the woman who was with Stalin is not clear. At one point in his memoirs (NK3, p. 16), Khrushchev identified her as the wife of a military man named Gusev. But there were at least three high-level military men named Gusev at the time. Khrushchev also expressed uncertainty (NK3, p. 16) on whether Alliluyeva killed herself or was killed by Stalin. Also see Volkogonov, *Stalin,* pp. 154–55; Roy Medvedev, *Let History Judge: The Origins and Consequences of Stalinism,* rev. and exp. ed., trans. George Shriver (New York: Columbia University Press, 1989), pp. 298–303; Svetlana Alliluyeva, *Twenty Letters to a Friend,* trans. Priscilla Johnson McMillan (New York: Harper & Row, 1967), pp. 106–10. Note also that Nadezhda Alliluyeva's grave in Moscow's Novodevichy Cemetery is not far from Khrushchev's.

60 Stalin's former secretary Boris Bazhanov imagined just such a turn of events in his memoirs. See his "Pobeg iz nochi," *Kontinent,* no. 9 (1976), p. 391. But Anastas Mikoyan agreed with Khrushchev that Alliluyeva probably praised him to Stalin. See Mikoian, *Tak bylo,* p. 614.

61 To be sure, Khrushchev's memoirs didn't obliterate his debt to his first Bolshevik mentor. But as Aleksei Adzhubei said, "at least in my presence, Nikita Sergeyevich didn't like to speak about Kaganovich." See Adzhubei, *Krushenie illiuzii,* p. 155.

62 NK4, no. 2, 1990, p. 101. Also see NK1, p. 43.

63 Ponomarev, *N. S. Khrushchev,* p. 18.

64 Minutes of the eleventh district party conference, January 1 to January 7, 1931, TsAODM, f.. 63, o. 1, d. 394, ll. 111–12; Ponomarev, *N. S. Khrushchev,* p. 17.

65 Tompson, *Khrushchev,* p. 36.

66 Quoted in Ponomarev, *N. S. Khrushchev,* p. 19.

67 Ibid., pp. 20–21.

68 Ibid., p. 20.

69 NK1, p. 48.

70 Anonymous official quoted in A. N. Ponomarev, "Intrigi i repressii—po pravilam igry," *Rossiiskaia gazeta,* July, 29, 1995, p. 10.

71 Colton, *Moscow,* pp. 210–45; Tompson, *Khrushchev,* p. 43. The Cathedral of Christ the Savior was rebuilt after the fall of the USSR by the Moscow city government headed by Mayor Yuri Luzhkov.

72 Oskar Maria Graf quoted in Medvedev, *Khrushchev,* p. 17.

73 NK1, pp. 58–61.

74 Ibid., p. 57.

75 Arnosht (Ernst) Kolman, *My ne dolzhny byli tak zhit'* (New York: Chalidze Publications, 1982), p. 192.

76 Records of meetings of the Moscow City Committee Secretariat, June 10 to August 21, 1933, TsAODM, f. 4, o. 3, d. 32, korobka 36.

77 NK1, pp. 63–64.

78 See Kolman, *My ne dolzhny,* pp. 191–94.

79 Tompson, *Khrushchev,* p. 47.

80 See NK1, pp. 68–70.

81 Ibid., p. 64.

82 Tompson, *Khrushchev,* pp. 45–46.

83 Quoted in Pistrak, *Grand Tactician,* p. 87.

84 NK2, p. 89.

85 Author's interview with Boris Agaev.

86 Ponomarev, *N. S. Khrushchev,* pp. 33–34.

87 "Bulganin and I began to work feverishly," Khrushchev wrote. "We personally inspected building and courtyards. We also booted the militia [the uniformed city police] off their behinds and got them to help. Later Stalin assigned us the task of installing clean, modern pay toilets." Khrushchev's conclusion: "This episode, trivial as it may seem, shows how Stalin, the leader of the world's working class, wasn't too busy to bother himself over as important a detail as city toilets." See NK1, pp. 62–63.

88 From the transcript of the February–March 1937 plenum, published in "Materialy fevral'skogo-martovskogo plenuma TsK, VKP(b) 1937 goda," VI, no. 6 (1993), p. 20.

89 Transcript of Fourth Moscow Conference, May 23-24, 1937, TsAODM, f. 4, o. 8, d. 1.

90 A. Iakovlev, *Tsel' zhizni: zapiski aviakonstruktora,* 4th rev. ed. (Moscow: Politizdat, 1974), pp. 180–82.

91 *XVII s"ezd kommunisticheskoi partii (b): stenographicheskii otchet* (Moscow: Partizdat, 1934), p. 145.

92 Kirov's assassination has often been attributed to Stalin. Khrushchev himself "had no doubt Stalin was behind the plot" (NK3, p. 24). But although Amy Knight finds plenty of circumstantial evidence linking the murder to Stalin, she can provide no proof that he ordered the killing. See Amy Knight, *Who Killed Kirov? The Kremlin's Greatest Mystery* (New York: Hill & Wang, 1999). Khlevniuk (*Politbiuro,* p. 141) agrees that Stalin's responsibility has so far not been proved.

93 Conquest, *Great Terror,* p. 41.

94 Medvedev, *Let History Judge,* p. 340.

95 Tucker, *Stalin in Power,* p. 305.

96 Many of those purged were charged with having failed to "master" the details of the party program. Once again, however, Khrushchev proved to be more Stalinist than Stalin. Since party rules required not mastery, but only acceptance, of the program, Moscow party authorities were later criticized and required to reinstate some four thousand party members excluded in the purge. See Ponomarev, *N. S. Khrushchev,* p. 33.

97 Conquest, *Great Terror,* pp. 87–105.

98 *Pravda,* June 10, 1936, p.2.

99 Cited in Pistrak, *Grand Tactician,* pp. 121–22.

100 In the dock this time were former "left oppositionists" Georgy Piatakov, whom Khrushchev had known in Ukraine and whom Lenin had thought enough of to evaluate as a future leader in his "Testament"; Grigory Sokolnikov, a former Politburo candidate member; Karl Radek, famous as a biting, sharp-tongued propagandist; and former Central Committee Secretary Leonid Serebryakov. The month before the trial began, Sergo Ordzhonikidze, one of Stalin's oldest and closest Politburo colleagues, visited Piatakov, who had been Ordzhonikidze's right-hand man at the People's Commissariat of Heavy Industry, in jail. Piatakov's arrest was apparently the last straw: Ordzhonikidze, affectionately known as Sergo by comrades, including Khrushchev, who said he looked on him as a kind of father figure, shot himself on February 18, 1937. Although the cause of death was announced as a heart attack, rumors about a suicide or murder circulated quickly and widely. Despite that, Khrushchev insisted he learned the truth only much later. At Ordzhonikidze's funeral, Khrushchev proclaimed that it was Piatakov who "struck a blow to thy noble heart" through treason that "hastened the death of our dear Sergo." See Conquest, *Great Terror*, pp. 167–73, and Tucker, *Stalin in Power*, pp. 258–65. Khrushchev's account in his memoirs characteristically described the incident in which he learned the truth as one in which he naively praised Sergo at a wartime dinner with Stalin, only to be chided afterward by Malenkov for not knowing the truth and thus causing an embarrassed silence at the table. See NK4, nos. 9–10, 1991, p. 74. In another later twist, Serebryakov's widow, Galina Serebryakova, returned from the camps nearly twenty years later still a committed Communist and determined to haunt the newly proclaimed anti-Stalinist Nikita Khrushchev.

101 As reported in *Pravda*, January 30, 1937, and quoted in Pistrak, *Grand Tactician*, p. 123.

102 According to Stalin's summary of the situation, some Central Committee members voted for a trial followed by a ten-year sentence, others backed a trial without preordaining the sentence, and still others favored sending the case to the NKVD for further investigation. What allowed this diversity was that Stalin had either not yet arrived at his own conclusion or was holding back to see what others would say. Once Stalin endorsed the last option (which would quickly lead to trial and execution anyway), it carried the day. Stalin's statement, in the plenum transcript, is in "Materialy fevral'skogo-martovskogo plenuma TsK, VKP(b) 1937 goda," vol. 6, no. 1 (1994), pp. 12–13. Excerpts from other speeches, including Bukharin's and Rykov's, are in J. Arch Getty and Oleg V. Naumov, *The Road to the Terror: Stalin and the Self-Destruction of the Bolsheviks* (New Haven: Yale University Press, 1999), pp. 364–419. Also see Volkogonov, *Stalin*, p. 287.

103 "Materialy fevral'skogo-martovskogo plenuma TsK, VKP(b) 1937 goda," vol. 6 (no. 6), 1993, pp. 18–21.

104 Ibid., vol. 6, no. 2 (1993), pp. 7–8, 17.

105 Khrushchev's vote is recorded in a commission protocol reproduced in Getty and Naumov, *Road to the Terror*, p. 144. No one besides Stalin, Yezhov, and their immediate circle could be sure the charges against Bukharin and Rykov were false. But Khrushchev must have had doubts. When he first encountered Bukharin, at a meeting of his unit's party cell during the civil war in 1919, Khrushchev was "absolutely spellbound": Bukharin had "an appealing personality and a strong democratic spirit." He was even more impressed when "simple progressive Communists from Moscow who were more or less at my level of political development told me Bukharin had lived with them in their dormitory, and eaten with them at the same table." But Khrushchev insisted in his memoirs that he learned the complete falsity of the charges against him only after Stalin's death. See NK1, pp. 29–30; NK3, p. 41.

106 Quoted in Pistrak, *Grand Tactician*, p. 117.

107 Conquest, *Great Terror*, p. 214.

108 Quoted in Ponomarev, *N. S. Khrushchev*, p. 41.

109 Transcript of the Fourth Moscow city party conference, in TsAODM, f. 4, o. 8, d. 1, l. 15.

110 Ponomarev, *N. S. Khrushchev*, p. 46.

111 See ibid.; Tompson, *Khrushchev*, p. 57; Colton, *Moscow*, pp. 288–89; Medvedev, *Let History Judge*, p. 410.

112 NK4, no. 4, 1990, pp. 65–66. Also see NK3, pp. 27–28.

113 Vladimir Naumov, "Repression and Rehabilitation," in *Nikita Khrushchev*, ed. Taubman, Khrushchev, and Gleason, pp. 88–91. See Khlevniuk, *Politbiuro*, pp. 189–90, and Conquest, *Great Terror*, p. 286, on the troika system. According to Natal'ia Gevorkian, ("Vstrechnye plany po unichtozheniiu sobstvennogo naroda," *Moskovskie novosti*, June 21, 1992, p. 18), Khrushchev would have served on the Moscow city and province troikas, and indeed he specifically asked to do so, but Stalin may have relieved him of that obligation, perhaps because he was aware that most troika members eventually followed their victims into NKVD execution cellars. Naumov reports, however, that it was only with regard to certain specific purge processes that Khrushchev was excused from the Moscow troika and that in general, Khrushchev, like other regional party bosses, must have signed death lists.

114 See Central Committee report, "Ob antikonstitutsionnoi praktike 30-40-kh i nachala 50-kh godov," December 25, 1988, in *Istochnik*, no. 1 (1995), p. 126; Naumov, "Repression and Rehabilitation," p. 90.

115 Conquest, *Great Terror*, p. 286; author's interviews with Arsenii Roginsky, a Moscow-based researcher who has had access to KGB archives; Gevorkian, "Vstrechnye plany," p. 18; and Colton, *Moscow*, p. 841.

116 Some victims, according to A. N. Ponomarev, "appealed to Khrushchev for help either before or after being arrested. But there was practically no instance in which the leader of Moscow's Bolsheviks stood up for his party comrades, vouched for them, or simply requested that the accusations be reexamined. Innocent Muscovites, who were repressed at the time, and then rehabilitated after the Twentieth Party Congress, testify unanimously to this fact." *N. S. Khrushchev*, p. 47.

117 Colton, *Moscow*, p. 289.

118 Kolman's wife was expelled from the Komsomol and fired from her job. But even though Kolman had committed the further sin of publishing a book on mathematics with a dedication to his now-discredited wife, and a rival academic raised a ruckus over the book and its dedication, "Khrushchev laughed the whole thing off in his typical goodhearted way," and a few days later Kolman was named an aide to the chairman of the recently formed All-Union Committee on Higher Schools. See Kolman, *My ne dolzhny*, pp. 196–97.

119 "Ob antikonstitutsionnoi praktike," p. 124.

120 On the basis of his extensive acquaintance with materials in the former Soviet archives, Vladimir Naumov, a former Central Committee official and later the executive secretary of a post-Soviet commission on Soviet-era repression, reports that "Khrushchev's signature of approval can generally be found on arrest orders for prominent Moscow functionaries." The Soviet general turned historian Dmitri Volkogonov asserts that in the 1950s "a whole series of lists [containing death sentences] bearing Khrushchev's signature was removed on Khrushchev's orders from the archives by I. A. Serov, then deputy minister of state security." But when challenged by Khrushchev's son Sergei to document rumors of a Khrushchev-sponsored purge of incriminating Moscow documents, Naumov replied that although he had "tried to clarify the circumstances in which a purge of the Moscow party archives took place, the matter turned out to be very complicated. There are various versions as to what happened. All of them involved N. S. Khrushchev in one way or another. But no one can produce documents proving any of these accounts." See Naumov, "Repression and Rehabilitation," p. 90; Volkogonov, *Stalin,* p. 308; SK1, manuscript of revised edition, p. 238/10.

121 Colton, *Moscow,* p. 286.

122 NK1, p. 82.

123 Ibid.

124 Ibid., pp. 78–79.

125 In the case of this resolution, Khrushchev claimed to have alerted Stalin to the danger that an excessively overwrought text might spark panic if, as usual, it became the model for others adopted around the country. Thereupon, he said, Stalin personally edited out the most inflammatory phrases, convincing Khrushchev that his boss "didn't want any unnecessary heightening of tensions, any unnecessary blood." See NK4, no. 4, 1990, pp. 78–79.

126 NK4, no. 3, 1990, pp. 70–71.

127 NK3, pp. 27–28.

128 V. Volkovinskii, "Iona Yakir," *Politika i vremia,* no. 5 (1991), p. 77.

129 Conquest, *Great Terror,* pp. 188–95.

130 Printed, with facsimile of document, in NK5, vol. 1, pp. 752–53.

131 NK4, no. 4, 1990, pp. 64–67. The Volkovinskii account contends that Yakir was arrested before he got to Moscow from Kiev. Yakir of course was condemned to death. His wife was also killed, as were his brother, his sister-in-law and her son, and other relatives, but not his son, who later became a dissident.

132 Ibid., p. 65. Also see Colton, *Moscow,* p. 289.

133 Author's interview with Yulia Leonidovna Khrushcheva. Korytny's daughter (Yakir's niece) spent many years in the camps, and committed suicide after her release. Vladimir Lakshin, *"Novyi mir" vo vremena Khrushcheva: Dnevnik i poputnoe (1953–1964)* (Moscow: Knizhnaia palata, 1991), p. 195.

134 NK4, no. 4, 1990, pp. 65–66.

135 Ibid., p. 68.

136 Crankshaw, *Khrushchev,* p. 97.

137 NK4, no. 4, pp. 77–78. Kaganovich claims that Khrushchev came to him "in tears" and that after they talked, he himself consulted with Stalin. See Feliks Chuev, *Tak govoril Kaganovich: Ispoved' Stalinskogo apostola* (Moscow: "Otechestvo," 1992), p. 99.

138 NK4, no. 4, 1990, pp. 65–73.

139 Chuev, *Sto sorok besed s Molotovym,* p. 364.

140 "Opis' stenogramm vystuplenii tov. N. S. Khrushcheva [1935–1949]," TsDA-HOU, f. 1, op. 31, spr. 3233a, ark 1–21.

141 Similar sartorial differences crop up again and again in photographs of the time. Each leader was cultivating a distinctive image; in Khrushchev's case education and urbanity (a dark suit) didn't entirely obscure his provincial roots (an embroidered Ukrainian shirt) or proletarian credentials (the jaunty workman's cap he wore when others affected military-style caps or, in Molotov's case, a fedora or homburg).

142 NK4, no. 3, 1990, p. 74.

143 NK1, p. 50.

144 Author's interview with Pyotr N. Demichev.

145 "Posetiteli kremlevskogo kabineta I. V. Stalina (1932–1933)," IA, no. 2 (1995), pp. 156, 187; "Posetiteli kremlevskogo kabineta I. V. Stalina (1934–1935)," IA, no. 3 (1995), pp. 127, 130, 162, 166.

146 NK1, p. 62; NK4, no. 2, 1990, p. 105.

147 NK1, p. 62.

148 As early as the summer of 1934 Khrushchev also got to share an elegant dacha in the Vorontsov Palace in the Crimea with Kaganovich, Molotov, and Voroshilov. See Chuev, *Tak govoril Kaganovich*, p. 62.

149 Volkogonov, *Stalin*, pp. 204–05.

150 According to the official medical examination of Stalin's body after his death, he was 170 centimeters tall. "Akt: patologo-anatomicheskogo issledovaniia tela Iosifa Vissarionovicha Stalina," March 6, 1953, in Dmitri Volkogonov Collection, Library of Congress (hereafter LOC), container 23, reel 16.

151 Conquest, *Great Terror*, p. 53.

152 Cited ibid., p. 61. For a description of Stalin's personal library and an analysis of the sorts of comments he wrote in the margins of his books, see Boris Ilizarov, "Stalin: Shtrikhi k portretу na fone ego biblioteki i arkhiva," *Novaia i noveishaia istoriia* (hereafter cited as NiNI), no. 3 (2000), pp. 182–208; no. 4 (2000), pp. 152–66.

153 NK1, p.34.

154 Ibid., pp. 94, 96, 98.

155 Ibid., p. 34. Although Khrushchev's praise of Yezhov seems particularly egregious, consider the following recollection by writer I. A. Sats: "When [Yezhov] worked in the provinces, he gave people the impression of a nervous but well-meaning and attentive person, free of arrogance and bureaucratic manners. Perhaps this was a mask. But it is more likely that he was turned into a butcher by the Stalinist system and the personal influence of Stalin himself." Cited in Medvedev, *Let History Judge*, p. 358.

156 NK1, p. 96.

157 Khrushchev's chauffeur during the thirties liked him best of all the bigwigs he drove. Revealing what Belov regarded as the simplicity of a real workingman, Khrushchev invited him to eat in the kitchen with the Khrushchev family. See Aleksandr I. Solzhenitsyn, *The Gulag Archipelago 1918–1956: An Experiment in Literary Investigation, I–II*, trans. Thomas P. Whitney (New York: Harper & Row, 1973, 1974), pp. 230–31.

158 Lidiia Shatunovskaia, *Zhizn' v Kremle* (New York: Chalidze Publications, 1982), p. 66.

159 Author's interview with Liuba Sizykh, who later married Lyonia Khrushchev, June 1993.

160 NK1, p. 57.

161 Ibid., p. 61.

162 Kolman, *My ne dolzhny,* p. 193.

163 NK4, no. 4, 1990, p. 64. Author's interview with Rada Adzhubei, July 1993.

164 Author's interview with Maria Sorokina.

165 Author's interview with Viktor Yevreinov, widower of Khrushchev's daughter Yelena.

166 From Khrushcheva's "Maminy Tetradi," with commentary by Sergei Khrushchev, in SK4, p. 16.

167 Quoted in Vasilieva, *Kremlin Wives,* pp. 197–98.

168 Author's interview with Maria Sorokina. Dima Sorokin regretfully studied literature instead and later became a film cameraman, but he managed to remain friends with Lyonia and the latter's wife, Liuba.

169 Author's interview with Yuri Khrushchev, June 1991. According to Sara Babyonysheva, who knew her ten years later, Ettinger was reduced to sewing dresses to support herself. Author's interview with Sara Babyonysheva, February 1996, Boston.

170 NK1, p. 83.

171 Roza's story is hard to pin down. Film critic Maya Turovskaya, who attended the film institute with her after the war, remembers that Roza used Khrushcheva as her last name and claimed to have a son by Lyonia. A Russian journalist reports that Roza actually had a child by a friend with whom she and Lyonia were staying. Lyonia's marriage to Roza is confirmed by a Soviet Defense Ministry certificate prepared after his death in 1943, which lists their marriage date, November 11, 1937. Undated "Spravka," signed "Danilov," photocopy provided to the author by Yuri L. Khrushchev. "Pervyi sekretar'," *Moskovskaia pravda,* April 9, 1989, p. 3.

172 Quoted in Larisa Vasil'eva, *Kremlevskie zheny* (Moscow: Vagrius, 1993), p. 438.

173 From Khrushcheva, "Maminy Tetradi."

174 Vasil'eva, *Kremlevskie zheny,* pp. 437–38.

175 Adzhubei, *Krushenie illiuzii,* p. 53.

CHAPTER 6. STALIN'S VICEROY: 1938–1941

1 NK1, pp. 105–06.

2 Author's interview with Vasily Kostenko, June 1991.

3 Author's interview with Zakhar N. Glukhov.

4 NK4, no. 6, 1990, p. 91. Also see Conquest, *Great Terror,* pp. 232–33.

5 The arrest figures for 1938–1940 are in a report to the Central Committee by a Politburo Commission headed by Aleksandr Yakovlev. The report is in "Massovye repressii," p.127; Chuev, *Sto sorok besed,* p. 433. The document Khrushchev signed is discussed further below.

6 See Orest Subtelny, *Ukraine: A History,* 2d ed. (Toronto: Toronto University Press, 1994).

7 Conquest, *Great Terror,* p. 228.

8 See Conquest, *Harvest of Sorrow.*

9 Postyshev was named deputy Ukrainian party leader in keeping with the practice of letting members of the local nationality occupy the first secretaryship in non-Russian republics while reserving real power to a Russian second secretary.

Until his Kiev assignment, Postyshev had been a secretary of the all-union Communist party in Moscow. His appointment, along with the purge of three members of the Ukrainian politburo and secretariat, was decreed by Moscow without consulting Kiev, as mandated by party rules.

10 Conquest, *Great Terror*, pp. 228–29.

11 Nikolayenko was a graduate student in the Institute of History of the All-Ukrainian Association of Marxist-Leninist Institutes when she began leveling her accusations. In 1936 she was expelled from the institute's party cell, which had been headed by Postyshev's wife. After a visit to Kiev by Kaganovich in January 1937, Nikolayenko was reinstated in the party. In an exchange at the June 1957 plenum, at which Khrushchev defeated a challenge to his power by Molotov, Malenkov, Kaganovich, and others, Khrushchev accused Kaganovich of siccing Nikolayenko on the then Ukrainian leaders, while Kaganovich insisted Stalin had sent him to Kiev to investigate her charges. See "Posledniaia 'antipartiinaia' gruppa," no. 5, 1993, pp. 43–44, 77. Also see Iu. I. Shapoval, *L. M. Kaganovich na Ukraine* (Kiev: 1993), p. 24; and Getty and Naumov, *Road to the Terror*, p. 359.

12 Demoted to party leader of Kuibyshev Province, Postyshev twisted slowly in the wind, while being attacked for failing to "correct his errors," until his arrest in Moscow on February 21, 1938. See Conquest, *Great Terror*, pp. 178, 247.

13 NK3, p. 32.

14 Conquest, *Great Terror*, pp. 232, 247, 419–20, 435–36.

15 Uspensky cited in Pistrak, *Grand Tactician*, p. 148. For a different view, see Roi Medvedev, *Khrushchev: politicheskaia biografia* (Benson, Vt.: Chalidze Publications, 1986), p. 30.

16 Naumov, "Repression and Rehabilitation," p. 91. Also see Tompson, *Khrushchev*, pp. 60–64. The arrest figures for 1939 and 1940 are from the Central Committee's 1988 report, "Ob antikonstitutsionnoi praktike," p. 127. Figures on the "renewal" of officers in the Kiev military district are in a March 26, 1938, document in NK5, vol. 1, pp. 762–63. Khrushchev's post-1937 contributions to the terror were not limited to Ukraine. He was apparently "massively complicit" in the purge of his successor as Moscow party chief, Aleksandr Ugarov, whom Stalin used as a scapegoat for food and other shortages. Called back to Moscow in November 1938, Khrushchev informed a secret joint plenum of the city and province party committees that Ugarov "has been arrested and has confessed that he is an old enemy, recruited by Trotskyites and Rightists," and had "carried out hostile work" in Leningrad and Moscow for years. Ugarov was shot in February 1939. See Colton, *Moscow*, p. 291.

17 Texts of some speeches survive as carbon copies in TsDAHOU. While Khrushchev's special storage of his speeches and their 1949 transfer to Moscow can be documented, it is not clear that his ultimate aim was their destruction. It is possible that these documents were retained in his personal files and are now preserved in the Presidential Archive, to which access has been strictly limited since the fall of the USSR. Between 1959 and 1963, still another cache of material, this time concerning the Ukrainian purges themselves, was reportedly removed to Moscow, but that claim has been disputed. See *M. S. Khrushchov i Ukraina* (Kyiv: National'na Akademia Nauk Ukraini, 1995), pp. 181–90.

18 Transcript in TsDAHOU, f. 1, o. 1, d. 548, ll. 4, 79.

19 "These monsters," Khrushchev continued, "these dregs of humanity cursed by the toilers of the Ukraine—the Polish and German fascists were counting on them. With the help of these enemies of the people, the fascists wanted to enslave the flowering Soviet Ukraine. But . . . anyone who encroaches on the land of the freedom-loving Ukrainian people . . . will be destroyed like mad dogs!" *XVIII s"ezd vsesoiuznoi kommunisticheskoi partii (b), 10–21 marta 1939 g., stenograficheskii otchet* (Moscow: Gosudarstvennoe izdatel'stvo politicheskoi literatury, 1939), p. 169.

20 Author's interview with Vasily S. Kostenko, August 1993.

21 NK4, no. 6, 1990, pp. 90–91.

22 Excerpts from Usenko's NKVD file, including a photocopy of the page with Khrushchev's order on it, are in NK5, vol. 1, pp. 757–61. I obtained the complete Usenko file from Derzhavnyi arkhiv sluzhby bezpeky Ukrainy (State Archive of the Security Service of Ukraine, Kyiv, Ukraine, hereafter DASBU). The fact that Khrushchev authorized the arrest several days after it occurred confirms that the NKVD did hold the initiative in such cases.

23 Author's interview with Olga I. Kosenko, August 1993.

24 Ibid., June 1991 and August 1993.

25 Kovalenko diary, cited in Iurii Shapoval, "Khrushchev i Ukraina: Vliianie ukrainskogo opyta na ego deiatel'nost' v 50-60-e gody" (Providence: Brown University, Khrushchev Centennial Conference, December 1994, paper prepared for delivery), pp. 16–17. Also see English version of this paper, "The Ukrainian Years," pp. 25–26.

26 Stalin replaced NKVD Chief Yezhov with Lavrenty Beria in December 1938, ushering in a relative lull in the terror.

27 NK4, no. 6, 1990, p. 84.

28 NK4, no. 5, 1990, p. 52.

29 NK4, no. 6, 1990, pp. 78–79.

30 NK1, p. 115.

31 NK4, no. 5, 1990, pp. 47, 63–64; NK1, pp. 96–97; Khlevniuk, *Politbiuro,* pp. 212–13. According to former NKVD intelligence official Pavel Sudoplatov, Uspensky tried to save himself by assuring interrogators that he and his family had been close friends of Khrushchev's and his. Sudoplatov said Khrushchev did indeed bring Uspensky to Ukraine to head the NKVD there. Sudoplatov's testimony is less than entirely reliable owing to his advanced age when he dictated his memoirs and to his grievance against Khrushchev for having had him arrested after Stalin's death. But Khrushchev himself admitted that he first met Uspensky in Moscow, where Uspensky was the NKVD representative for Moscow Province and later the commandant of the Kremlin. See Pavel Sudoplatov, with Anatoly Sudopatov and Jerrold L. and Leona P. Schecter, *Special Tasks* (Boston: Little, Brown, 1994), pp. 110–11.

32 NK1, p. 108. Also see NK4, no. 6, 1990, p. 80.

33 That this was indeed Khrushchev's strategy is suggested by his admiring account of how a certain Dr. Medved protected himself against a woman who got up at a party meeting, pointed her finger at him, and said, "'I don't know that man over there but I can tell from the look in his eyes that he's an enemy of the people.'" Khrushchev wrote: "Fortunately, Medved didn't lose control of himself. He retorted immediately, 'I don't know this woman who's just denounced me, but I can tell from the look in her eye that she's a prostitute'—only he used a more expressive word. Medved's quick comeback probably saved his life. If he'd let himself be put on the defensive and had started protesting that he wasn't an enemy of the people, he would have fallen all the more under suspicion, and the woman who denounced him would have been encouraged to press her charge against him. . . . " NK1, p. 114.

34 TsDAHOU, f. 1, op. 1, d. 548, l. 82.

35 TsDAHOU, f. 1, op. 1, d. 604, ll. 105–07.

36 Georgy Malenkov also defended his record by telling his son that he had tried to slow the terror by warning that those who denounced the innocent were themselves subverting the system. Author's interview with Andrei Malenkov.

37 NK1, pp. 109–10.

38 Ibid., p. 110; NK4, no. 5, p. 60. Ukraine was the breadbasket for a nation whose primary food was bread. Yet collectivization and famine had ruined Ukrainian agriculture. Between 1929 and 1934, Ukrainian peasants slaughtered half their horses, 40 percent of their cattle, half their pigs, and three-quarters of their sheep. Nor was Stalin willing to make up these and other losses through imports; even at the height of the famine he had insisted on exporting scarce grain. The bulk of funds for investment was still going into industry and more than ever, with war looming in Europe, into military spending. About all Khrushchev had to help Ukrainian farming with was his own energy and wit. The very month he arrived in Kiev (January 1938) wasn't too early to start worrying about spring sowing.

39 Author's interview with Andrei Shevchenko, August 1993.

40 T. Glotova, "Vstrechi v Mar'inke," *Vechernyi Donetsk*, July 1, 1991, p. 2.

41 Author's interview with Aleksandr P. Lyashko.

42 See, for example, Khrushchev's performance at a Central Committee plenum held October 28–30, 1940, the transcript of which is in TsDAHOU, f. 1, op. 1, d. 630. All party leaders of course were free to browbeat their underlings. But the ever more expansive Khrushchev particularly dominated these occasions.

43 Shapoval, *M. S. Khrushchov na Ukraini*, p. 27; Medvedev, *Khrushchev*, p. 28. A 13 percent gain in livestock reportedly included a 125 percent jump in the number of cattle, 176 percent in the number of pigs, and 156 percent in sheep and goats.

44 NK1, pp. 120–24; NK4, no. 7, 1990, pp. 77–80.

45 Pistrak, *Grand Tactician*, 179; Robert S. Sullivant, *Soviet Politics and the Ukraine* (New York: Columbia University Press, 1962), pp. 226–33.

46 From Khrushchev's speech at the Fourteenth Ukrainian Party Congress, TsDAHOU, f. 1, op. 1, d. 548, ll. 61–66.

47 Author's interview with Vasily S. Kostenko, June 1991.

48 George S. N. Luckyj, *Literary Politics in the Soviet Ukraine* (Durham: Duke University Press, 1990), pp. 33, 110, 166.

49 NK4, no. 5, 1990, p. 47. In the same account, Khrushchev recalled defending the same song's composer who was in prison in 1938 and stayed there until Khrushchev got him released by threatening to complain to Stalin about a miscarriage of justice. Khrushchev took Ryl'ski and his family under his wing. When the NKVD was about "to work over" the poet in 1939, Khrushchev saved him by criticizing the offending work himself. He urged Ryl'ski to write a poem titled, "I Am a Child of the Land of the Soviets." In time the poet and the first secretary became friends. Together they visited the grave of Taras Shevchenko, the nineteenth-century

Ukrainian poet, and Khrushchev took Ryl'ski's ten-year-old son to an air show as a reward for getting good grades in school. This account is based on a conversation with archivists at the Ryl'ski house/museum in Kiev. Ryl'ski noted on a copy of "I Am a Child of the Land of the Soviets" that he had read the poem to Khrushchev.

50 See Luckyj, *Literary Politics in the Soviet Ukraine.*

51 Author's interview with Nina V. Bazhan.

52 So wrote Stanislav Tel'niuk in a 1988 review of Ukrainian writers under Stalin cited in Luckyj, *Literary Politics in the Soviet Ukraine,* p. 255.

53 Marco Carynnyk, ed. and trans., *Alexander Dovzhenko: The Poet as Filmmaker* (Cambridge, Mass.: MIT Press, 1973), pp. xx, xxiii.

54 Ibid., pp. xxiii–iv. Also see excerpt from Dovzhenko's diary in Anatolii Latyshev, "I. V. Stalin: Ob antileninskikh oshibkakh i natsionalisticheskikh izvrashcheniiakh v kinopovesti Dovzhenko, 'Ukraina v ogne,'" *Iskusstvo kino,* no. 4 (1990), p. 85.

55 As the titular head of state Mikhail Kalinin pinned the medal on Dovzhenko in February 1935, Stalin remarked, "Now he must do a *Ukrainian Chapaev*"—that is, a film about a Ukrainian civil war hero on the model of the brothers Vasil'ev's famous movie about the Russian civil war commander, Chapaev. "I. V. Stalin: Ob antileninskikh oshibkakh i natsionalisticheskikh izvrashcheniiakh," p. 87.

56 Author's interviews with archivists at the Dovzhenko Museum in Kiev.

57 NK1, pp. 116–18.

58 David Joravsky, *The Lysenko Affair* (Cambridge, Mass.: Harvard University Press, 1970), pp. 58, 62, 85, 91.

59 Zhores Medvedev, *The Rise and Fall of T. D. Lysenko,* trans. I. Michael Lerner (New York: Columbia University Press, 1969), p. 17.

60 Joravsky, *Lysenko Affair,* p. 111; Pistrak, *Grand Tactician,* p. 230.

61 Cited in Iurii Shapoval, "Khrushchev i Ukraina," p. 21.

62 See Joravsky, *Lysenko Affair,* on how "even Vavilov" had praised Lysenko, pp. 93, 99, 101.

63 During his first years as Ukrainian party boss, Khrushchev dabbled at "inventing" agricultural implements: a "comb," as he called it, to lift stalks beaten down by rain so that the combine could harvest them; boll weevil–exterminating equipment; and a beet-cleaning machine that the Ukrainian press later reported was unsuccessful because "it was bulky, had a separate motor and many unnecessary parts," whereupon Khrushchev devised a new version built entirely of wood that collective farmers could make themselves. The former metal worker *not* turned engineer consulted with real engineers and drew up blueprints in his own hand. Pistrak, *Grand Tactician,* pp. 229–31.

64 Khrushchev recalled the Molotov invitation in NK4, no. 6, 1990, p. 78. He compared being in Kiev and Moscow in his report to the Fourteenth Ukrainian Party Congress, TsDAHOU, f. 1, op. 1, d. 548, ll. 96–97.

65 *Pravda Ukrainy,* January 28, 1938.

66 Ibid., June 21, 1938, p. 2.

67 Author's interview with Vasily Kostenko, Kiev, June 1991. Korotchenko ended his name with the Ukrainian *o* while stationed in Kiev, but added a *v* so as to sound Russian when serving with Khrushchev in Moscow.

68 These and other photos appeared in *Pravda Ukrainy* on the following dates, respectively: July 8, 1938, July 23, 1938, July 26, 1938, August 11, 1938, August 12, 1938, August 15, 1938, June 20, 1938.

69 The case has been made that the Nazi-Soviet Pact was necessary to allow Stalin to prepare his country for war, but if so, he failed to use that time effectively.

70 NK1, p. 127.

71 Ibid., pp. 127–28. Alas, neither Khrushchev nor any of the other marksmen have left a detailed account of the hunt. If it was anything like outings by later Communist leaders, Khrushchev's boasting bespeaks further self-delusion. In Gomułka's Poland, which took its cue from Moscow in almost everything, the hunt was prepared this way, according to the chief gamekeeper: "We have to make sure that the animals get used to finding food each day at a certain time and in a certain place. Then, when we have to organize a hunt, we know where to look for the game. And incidentally, they get very tame. After years of daily feeding the animals' mouths start to water when they hear the motor of the jeep that brings the food or smell its exhaust. When we arrive in the van we are surrounded by expectant animals. We really have to take care not to bump into them." On one hunt for "wild duck" which Gomułka interpreter Erwin Weit attended, a visiting East German potentate was taken to an island where the ducks were bred. As the boat approached the island, "the sky was black with flying ducks. All he had to do was raise his gun and shoot for a few birds to be hit and fall into the water." Afterward the proud marksman "handed out cigarettes that did not belong to him to all and sundry, and used the liberal supplies of alcohol in the villa to stand one round of drinks after another to the beaters." Erwin Weit, *Eyewitness: The Autobiography of Gomułka's Interpreter*, trans. Mary Schofield (London: Deutsch, 1973), p. 149.

72 The following account particularly relies on Jan T. Gross, *Revolution from Abroad: The Soviet Conquest of Poland's Western Ukraine and Western Belorussia* (Princeton: Princeton University Press, 1988).

73 Ibid., pp. 6, 29–30. The yellow and blue Ukrainian flag became a symbol of ultranationalism, rendering particularly ironic the fact that crowds carried red Soviet flags as well.

74 Ibid., p. 76.

75 Ibid., pp. 78, 89, 92.

76 Ibid., pp. xiii, 146, 155, 225, 185, 229; Shapoval, *M. S. Khrushchov na Ukraini*, p. 330; Shapoval, "Khrushchev i Zapadnaia Ukraina," *Svobodnaia mysl'*, no. 6 (1996), p. 78. A report prepared by the KGB in the late 1980s for a Politburo commission studying repression carried out between the 1930s and the early 1950s lists lower figures for those exiled from western Ukraine and Belorussia, respectively: in 1940, 121,996 and 73,521; in 1941, 41,645 and 31,754. See "Meropriiatiia po vyseleniiu iavlialis' chrezvychainoi meroi," *Istochnik*, no. 1 (1996), 128.

77 Gross, *Revolution from Abroad*, pp. 205–06, 230.

78 Ibid., p. 108.

79 *Pravda Ukrainy*, October 4, 1939, p. 1.

80 Ukrainian Politburo decrees in these areas are cited in Shapoval, "Khrushchev i Zapadnaia Ukraina," p. 79. A Ukrainian Politburo decree condemning "incorrect treatment" of former members of the Polish Communist party is in NK5, vol. 1, pp. 766–67.

81 Even anti-Communist Ukrainian nationalists, it must be admitted, have come to welcome the fact that eastern and western Ukraine are united (although not the way Stalin united them) in a state that became formally independent in 1991.

82 NK1, p. 142.

83 Ibid., p. 144.

84 Sudoplatov, *Special Tasks,* pp. 107–08. His account of this incident is particularly credible because he is reporting a conversation he himself overheard and took part in.

85 Excerpt from Serov's September 27, 1939, memorandum to Beria in NK5, vol. 1, pp. 764–66.

86 NK1, p. 145. Jozef Piłsudski was the first chief of state (1918–1922) of the newly independent Poland established in November 1918.

87 Ibid., pp. 145–46; NK4, no. 4, 1894, p. 66.

88 Mikoian, *Tak bylo,* p. 386.

89 NK4, no. 8, 1990, p. 55.

90 Ibid., p. 67.

91 NK1, p. 164.

92 Author's interview with Khrushchev's daughter-in-law, Liuba Sizykh, January 1993.

93 NK1, pp. 99–100.

94 Ibid., p. 159.

95 NK4, no. 8, 1990, p. 70.

96 NK1, p. 151.

97 Ibid., p. 155, NK3, p. 54.

98 Ibid., p. 154.

99 Ibid.; NK4, no. 8, 1990, pp. 57–62, 70–73.

100 Destroyed during the war and later rebuilt, the villa in 1991 housed the Ukrainian Foreign Ministry press center. The author visited the house in June 1991. Also see the description in SK4, pp. 4–5.

101 Author's interviews with Liuba Sizykh, January 1993, and Rada Adzhubei. Adzhubei, *Krushenie illiuzii,* p. 5. The author drove out to Mezhgorie in 1991 with Sergei Khrushchev and his wife, approaching it along one of those rare, perfectly paved roads that signal the approach to the some very important person's retreat. But a large gray gate blocked our way (and our view as well), and even the presence of the former Soviet leader's son couldn't persuade the KGB guard to let us in for a look. Rada Adzhubei remembered that the wives of the leaders became friendly and children of all three families played volleyball in the evening.

102 Khrushcheva, "Maminy Tetradi."

103 In Khrushchev's time a visiting Westerner would never have gotten past the guards at the gate. Even in 1991 the author was stopped by a guard on duty and managed to proceed farther only because he was accompanied by Nikita Sergeyevich Khrushchev, the grandson of the former resident. Once in the building, we climbed to the fifth floor, where the corner apartment was located. Alas, the nine-room apartment itself was not open for inspection, but Sergei Khrushchev later made a drawing of it.

104 At the time Soviet troops invaded western Ukraine, the world had no notion that Hitler and Stalin had agreed in advance how, when, and where to divide Poland. But Khrushchev phoned his wife from the front lines and told her that her native village of Vasiliev, where her parents were living, would be occupied by the Germans. Khrushchev's deputy Mikhail O. Burmistenko arranged for Nina Petrovna to travel to Lvov with two women party workers. He ordered the three to wear military uniforms and carry revolvers so that military patrols would be less likely to stop them on the way. Her husband was appalled at her outfit ("For decades the local people have been told we're oppressors, and now you and your revolvers confirm the slander," he said), but after changing clothes, she continued on her way. Neither the newly organized local authorities nor junior officers in Soviet military units stationed in the village were aware that it would soon be German territory. But, recollected Nina Petrovna, "Comrade Timoshenko had authorized me to reveal why I had come for my parents."

After spending a night in her father's hut, guarded by a Soviet tank standing in front of it, Nina Petrovna packed her parents and her brother and his family in a truck and took them to a rich landowner's estate near Lvov, where her husband was headquartered. When her father first turned on a water faucet, Nina Petrovna recalled, he shouted to his wife, "'Come see—water's coming out of this pipe!'" At first, Pyotr Kukharchuk took Timoshenko for his new son-in-law. But he "wasn't disappointed," Nina Petrovna concluded, "to learn it was N. S." Khrushcheva, "Maminy Tetradi."

105 Khrushcheva, "Maminy Tetradi;" SK4, pp. 21–22. Other Khrushchev family members who contracted TB included Nina Petrovna's parents and brother, all of whom died from it.

106 Recollections of Rada Adzhubei as recounted in Vasilieva, *Kremlin Wives*, pp. 196–97.

107 Author's interview with Liuba Sizykh, January 1993.

108 The author first met Lyonia's widow in 1991 in Kiev and later spent time with her both there and in Moscow. She is so sunny and cheerful that it is hard to believe her tragic tale. She is puzzled too by her own perennial optimism because, she says, she didn't have a happy childhood either. This account of Khrushchev family life between 1938 and 1941 is largely based on these interviews.

CHAPTER 7. KHRUSHCHEV AT WAR: 1941–1944

1 NK4, no. 9, 1990, p. 84.

2 See Volkogonov, *Stalin*, pp. 370–71; John Erickson, *The Road to Stalingrad* (New York: Harper & Row, 1975), p. 79.

3 Volkogonov, *Stalin*, p. 368; Walter Laqueur, *Stalin: The Glasnost Revelations* (New York: Scribner, 1990), pp. 213–14; Seweryn Bialer, ed., *Stalin and His Generals: Soviet Military Memoirs of World War II* (New York: Pegasus, 1969), pp. 59–62; speech prepared but not given by Marshal Georgy Zhukov in 1956, published as "Chego stoiat polkovodcheskie kachestva Stalina: Neproiznesennaia rech' marshala G. K. Zhukova," *Istochnik*, no. 2 (1995), pp. 144–45.

4 NK1, pp. 158–59.

5 Volkogonov, *Stalin,* p. 391; NK1, pp. 588–89; NK3, p. 56; Robert Conquest, *Stalin: Breaker of Nations* (New York: Viking, 1991), p. 235; "Chego stoiat polkovodcheskie kachestva," pp. 145–46. According to Mikoyan, Stalin didn't expect Hitler to attack until 1943 and thought Churchill was trying to pull the USSR into the war prematurely. Mikoian, *Tak bylo,* pp. 377, 382.

6 NK4, no. 9, 1990, p. 85; Volkogonov, *Stalin,* pp. 407–08; Medvedev, *Let History Judge,* p. 753.

7 G. Zhukov, *Reminiscences and Reflections* (Moscow: Progress Publishers, 1985), vol. 1, p. 286.

8 "Chego stoiat polkovodcheskie kachestva," p. 147; Edvard Radzinsky, *Stalin: The First In-Depth Biography Based on Explosive New Documents from Russia's Secret Archives,* trans. H. T. Willetts (New York: Doubleday, 1996), p. 408; Volkogonov, *Stalin,* pp. 408–10.

9 Volkogonov, *Stalin,* p. 505.

10 See Yelena Zubkova, *Obshchestvo i reformy: 1945–1964* (Moscow: Rossiia molodaia, 1993), pp. 16–25.

11 NK1, p. 593.

12 Konstantin M. Simonov cites Marshal Zhukov in *Glazami cheloveka moego pokoleniia: Razmyshleniia o I. V. Staline* (Moscow: "Kniga," 1990), p. 328. Also see Bialer, *Stalin and His Generals,* p. 34 ff.; Volkogonov, *Stalin,* pp. 415, 451, 456, 466, 474.

13 NK4, no. 12, 1990, p. 87.

14 On Zhdanov's tendency to panic and to drink, see Mikoian, *Tak bylo,* pp. 562–63. Also see Sergo Beria, *Beria, My Father: Inside Stalin's Kremlin* (London: Duckworth, 2001), p. 75. Sergo Beria is far from a reliable source about many things reported in his book, especially about his father, but some of his descriptions of Stalin's other associates, including this one of Zhdanov, seem well founded.

15 Volkogonov, *Stalin,* p. 415.

16 Quoted ibid., p. 419.

17 Author's interview with Andrei Shevchenko, August 1993. On Khrushchev's aversion to war films and memoirs, see SK2, p. 211.

18 Author's interview with Dmitri Volkogonov. The 1930 document "Attestatsiia za period s 21/VII/1930 po 1/IX/30 na Komissara zapasa /K-7/ Khrushcheva, Nikity Sergeevicha" was provided to the author by Ministry of Defense archivists.

19 NK1, p. 169.

20 Simonov, *Glazami cheloveka moego pokoleniia,* p. 317. Mikoyan confirms that, particularly during the war, Stalin accepted candid advice. Mikoian, *Tak bylo,* p. 464.

21 This account is based on many lengthy conversations with several Khrushchev family members: Khrushchev's children, Rada Adzhubei and Sergei Khrushchev; Leonid Khrushchev's widow, Liuba, and her children, Yulia, and Tolya Lezhnenko; Nina Khrushcheva's niece Nina; and others. It also draws on SK4, pp. 21–26.

22 Yulia Nikitichna Khrushcheva, Khrushchev's daughter by his first wife, spent wartime exile in Alma-Ata, Kazakhstan, with her husband, Viktor Gontar, who directed the Capella Dunka. Later he headed the Lesia Ukrainka Russian Drama Theater in Kiev and then the Kiev Opera and Ballet.

23 Ilya Ehrenburg, *The War: 1941–1945,* trans. Tatiana Shebunina (Cleveland: World Publishing, 1965), p. 18.

24 Vasily Grossman, *Life and Fate: A Novel*, trans. Robert Chandler (New York: Harper & Row, 1985), p. 121.

25 Sergei Khrushchev contradicts his cousin's account, insisting that Irina Sergeyevna often visited Nikita Khrushchev's dacha after the war and in fact died there on a sofa from a stroke. Other Khrushchev family members also warned me not to take Rona Kobiak seriously. My telephone conversation with her was indeed odd. She refused to see me and at first refused to talk on the phone. She said she was writing her own book about Khrushchev (in English, she added, because as a veteran translator she felt more comfortable writing in it than in her native Russian). But then she chattered on a great length, mixing self-advertisement ("Although I'm not trained in literature, I have a gift for it.") with nasty innuendoes about other Khrushchev family members. Part of her bitterness has to do, she said, with the family's cutting her off since the late sixties. (They say she dropped *them* shortly after Nikita Sergeyevich was deposed and then exaggerated a family enmity to justify her own behavior.) But the enmity goes all the way back to 1941 and before. Fortunately, Rona is not the only source on the tension between Irina Sergeyevna and her brother and sister-in-law.

26 Author's interview with Sara Babyonysheva.

27 "Leonid Nikitovich Khrushchev: Lichnoe delo," document from Ministry of Defense Archive given to the author by Yuri L. Khrushchev.

28 "Vypiska iz doneseniia nachal'niku shtaba VVS 22 armii,. No. 012/so ot 16.7.41," document from Ministry of Defense Archive given the author by Yuri L. Khrushchev.

29 "Boevaia kharakteristika na pilota 134 SBP Leitenanta Khrushcheva Leonida Nikitovicha," document from Ministry of Defense Archive, provided to the author by Yuri L. Khrushchev.

30 *Pravda*, July 26, 1941.

31 Nina Kukharchuk remembers hearing this mentioned in the Khrushchev family.

32 Stepan Mikoyan, speaking on the television program *Kak eto bylo*. Also see Evgenii Zhirnov, "Sovetskii prints," *Komsomol'skaia pravda*, November 25, December 2, December 9, 1994.

33 Memoirs of Stepan Mikoyan, as cited in SK4, p. 23. Liuba Sizykh's account is essentially the same. In retrospect she's amazed she didn't try to get Lyonia to give up the trick, but she herself was a daredevil who had parachuted off the wings of a plane and who loved high-speed motorcycle rides with her husband.

34 Stepan Mikoyan's recollection as cited in SK4, p. 23. Liuba Sizykh confirmed the account to the author.

35 Copy of letter in Tsentral'nyi arkhiv Ministerstva oborony (Ministry of Defense Archive, Podol'sk, Russia; hereafter TsAMO), f. 290, o. 32631s. d. 4, ll. 44–47.

36 NK1, p. 190.

37 Former KGB Major General Vadim Udilov in "Za chto Khrushchev otomstil Stalinu," *Nezavisimaia gazeta*, February 17, 1998. Also see A. Kolesnikov, "Letchik, L. N. Khrushchev," *Voenno-istoricheskii zhurnal*, no. 11 (1989), pp. 91–95; "Pogib? Propal bes vesti? Zhiv?" *Voenno-istoricheskii zhurnal*, no. 41 (1990), p. 79.

38 Chuev, *Sto sorok besed*, pp. 351–52.

39 In 1990 the conservative journal *Voenno-istoricheskii zhurnal* assigned two investigators to search the archives. Although they unearthed no documents supporting the theory that Khrushchev's son fell into German hands, they reported signs that others had previously checked through the same materials and that nearly two thousand pages were missing from German interrogation files. Author's interview with Major Yu. Starkov (one of the researchers). Also see "Pogib? Propal bes vesti" Zhiv?" p. 80.

40 Zamorin's admission, in a letter to the Brezhnev-era Soviet defense minister Dmitri Ustinov is reported in Sergei Ivanov, "Priznanie pered smer'tiu," *Novoe russkoe slovo,* April 4, 2000, p. 11. Wreckage of a plane found in 1994 near Briansk, some twenty-five miles from where Lyonia's plane was last sighted, is thought by some to contain his remains, but that seems unlikely if Zamorin's confession is correct. See "Syn N. S. Khrushcheva pogib na Brianshchine," *Brianskii rabochii,* January 20, 1995.

41 Interview with Sara Babyonysheva, Amherst, Massachusetts, February 1996.

42 Abakumov later served as the minister of state security from 1946 to 1951.

43 Actually, Yulia had already learned the truth from Marshal Budyonny's daughter Nina, who lived in the same apartment house as the Khrushchevs in Moscow. As soon as Liuba arrived in Moscow in 1954, KGB Chief Serov "invited" her to his Lubyanka office (not the same one in which Abakumov had interrogated her) and asked her not to see Yulia until she was older.

44 "Who do you want to be when you grow up?" Ksenia Ivanovna asked Tolya. "A general," he recalls answering. "Where will you serve, Tolya?" "In the Kremlin." "Well done, Tolya!" she cried. "What a fine boy you are!" Author's interview with Liuba Sizykh, July 1993.

45 Mikoyan (*Tak bylo,* pp. 390–91) reports Stalin's curse, his protracted absence from Moscow, and the frightened look on his face when his colleagues arrived. See also Volkogonov, *Stalin,* p. 410, and Radzinsky, *Stalin,* p. 468. In a letter written after his arrest in June 1953, Beria credited Molotov with spearheading the move to get Stalin back in action. See "Lavrentii Beriia: 'Cherez 2–3 goda ia krepko ispravlius' . . .'," *Istochnik,* no. 4 (1994), p. 7. Khrushchev's recollection of Stalin is in NK4, no. 10, 1990, p. 79. Radzinsky speculates that Stalin may have been faking a collapse to see how his underlings were reacting, but given the scope of the catastrophe and Stalin's responsibility for it, that seems unlikely.

46 Zhukov, *Reminiscences and Reflections,* vol. 1, pp. 377–79; Georgii Zhukov, *Vospominaniia i razmyshleniia,* llth ed. (Moscow: Novosti, 1992), vol. 2, pp. 126–27. Although these are the English and Russian versions of the same work, the eleventh Russian edition includes passages omitted from earlier editions, including the English translation.

47 Zhukov, *Reminiscences and Reflections,* vol. 1, pp. 388–89.

48 Quoted in Bialer, *Stalin and His Generals,* p. 386.

49 The order is quoted as Tupikov paraphrased it, prefacing his summary with the sarcastic phrase "That's a real decision." See ibid., pp. 394–99.

50 NK1, p. 171.

51 Vladimir Shamberg, whose father was the Central Committee official who conveyed the Politburo's view, recounts the episode in "Stalin's Last Inner Circle," *Harriman Review,* vol. 10, no. 1 (Spring 1997), p. 34.

52 Zhukov, *Vospominaniia i razmyshleniia,* vol. 2, pp. 133–37.

53 Erickson, *Road to Stalingrad,* pp. 251–98.

54 Zhukov, *Vospominaniia i razmyshleniia,* vol. 2, p. 287.

55 Bagramian sensed that Khrushchev's arguments were neither strictly military nor without sentimental resonance for a man, like Khrushchev, who had spent his early years in Ukraine. "We understood," Bagramian recalled, that "they were guided not only by purely military-strategic aims, but by the necessity to strengthen our military-industrial potential by recapturing the country's 'furnace'—the Donbas and a key industrial center like Kharkov." See I. Kh. Bagramian, *Tak shli k pobede* (Moscow: Voennoe izdatel'stvo, 1977), pp. 49, 51, 54. Also Viktor Gobarev, "Khrushchev i voennye: istoriko-psikhologicheskii analiz." Paper prepared for delivery. (Providence, R.I.: Brown University, Khrushchev Centennial Conference, December 1994), pp. 23–24.

56 Voroshilov, Zhukov, and Shaposhnikov also attended the meeting at which Khrushchev and his colleagues initially made their case. Shaposhnikov was particularly opposed. He remained skeptical after its advocates revised their plan, but others were silent except for Voroshilov, who praised it. See Zhukov, *Vospominaniia i razmyshleniia,* vol. 2, pp. 287–88. In earlier editions, Khrushchev's name was omitted from the list of those attending the meeting. Also see Bagramian, *Tak shli k pobede,* pp. 59–61; and A. M. Vasilevskii, *Delo vsei zhizni* (Moscow: Politizdat, 1974), pp. 190–91.

57 Erickson, *Road to Stalingrad,* p. 344; NK4, no. 11, 1990, p. 72.

58 Vasilevskii, *Delo vsei zhizni,* p. 191.

59 Erickson, *Road to Stalingrad,* p. 346.

60 Bagramian confirms this, saying he tried and failed to convince Timoshenko to call a halt on the evening of the seventeenth. See Bagramian, *Tak shli k pobede,* p. 116.

61 See Erickson, *Road to Stalingrad,* p. 346; Vasilevskii, *Delo vsei zhizni,* p. 192; "Uspeshnoe nastuplenie voisk iugo-zapadnogo fronta na Khar'kovskom napravlenii: nashi trofei," Letter to Comrade Stalin from S. Timoshenko and N. Khrushchev, May 17, 1942, TsAMO, f. 206, o. 258, d. 3, ll. 121–22.

62 "I still can't believe that Timoshenko told Stalin I had forced the decision down his throat," Khrushchev wrote in his memoirs. "I think Stalin was simply trying to force me off balance and undercut my argument." NK1, pp. 184–86.

63 Zhukov, *Vospominaniia i razmyshelniia,* vol. 2, pp. 291–92. Whether Zhukov's testimony corresponds to reality is itself open to question. For whereas Zhukov was certainly present at headquarters, where Stalin was when he spoke to Timoshenko on May 18, it is by no means certain that Zhukov, who wasn't a member of Stalin's inner circle, was at the dacha where Khrushchev tried to reach Stalin.

64 In a series of articles published from 1989 to 1990, the journal seemed determined to give the lie to Khrushchev's account; hence the title of its series, "*This* Is Where the Truth Lies, Nikita Sergeyevich." The articles read as if everything that became clear in hindsight should have been clear at the time, as if any failure to foresee disaster ahead resulted from a lack of "objective" or "strictly scientific analysis." See "Vot gde pravda, Nikita Sergeevich!," *Voenno-istoricheskii zhurnal,* no. 12 (1989), pp. 17–18; no. 1 (1990), pp. 16–18; no. 2 (1990), pp. 35–36 (hereafter cited by title, issue number, and year).

65 Bagramian, *Tak shli k pobede,* p. 117; Vasilevskii, *Delo vsei zhizni,* p. 192. Transcripts of two additional conversations between Khrushchev and Timoshenko, on one hand, and Vasilevskii, on the other, which took place on May 19, at 3:35 and 3:50 P.M. respectively, do not require altering the interpretation given in the text. See NK5, vol. 1, pp. 777–79.

66 Additional losses included 652 tanks, 3,278 mortars, 9,053 machine guns, 1,646 other guns, 143,226 rifles, and (a revealing indicator of the state of Soviet military technology as late as the spring of 1942) 57,626 horses. "Vot gde pravda, Nikita Sergeevich!," no. 2 (1990), p. 41.

67 Vasilevskii, *Delo vsei zhizni,* p. 193.

68 NK1, pp. 187–89. Also see NK4, no. 11, 1990, pp. 83–85.

69 According to Marshal Zhukov's daughter Margarita, this story was told to her by General Bagramian. Author's interview with Margarita Zhukova. In June 1942, Stalin stopped Vasilevsky after a 2:00 A.M. meeting and said, "Wait a minute. I want to say something about the Kharkov defeat again: Those who deserve it should be punished." In the name of the State Defense Committee, Stalin dictated a letter to the Southwest Command. Besides Bagramian's mistakes, he wrote, there was also "the question of errors committed by the Military Council, above all by Comrades Timoshenko and Khrushchev. If we were to tell the country the full scale of the catastrophe suffered and still being suffered by the front, with the loss of eighteen or twenty divisions, I am afraid people would deal with you very harshly." See Volkogonov, *Stalin,* pp. 432–33. Shortly after the war, when Mikoyan praised Khrushchev for trying to ward off the Kharkov disaster, Stalin looked ready to strangle him on the spot. Khrushchev recalled this incident in a speech to the October 1957 Central Committee plenum that ratified the firing of Marshal Zhukov. See the October 1957 plenum transcript in Rossiiskii gosudarstvennyi arkhiv noveishei istorii (Russian State Archive of Recent History, Moscow, Russia, hereafter RGANI), f. 2, op. 1, d. 271, l. 78.

70 Bagramian, *Tak shli k pobede,* p. 131.

71 NK4, no. 11, 1990, p. 80.

72 Author's interview with Rada Adzhubei, June 1991.

73 NK4, no. 11, 1990, pp. 79–80, 88.

74 In his memoirs Khrushchev conveniently said, "I forget who had taken the initiative for organizing the Kharkov operation in the first place. . . . I don't deny that I may have played a part in it," he continued, "but, as I asked Stalin, 'What about the commander, Timoshenko?'

"'No,' said Stalin. 'It was your idea and Timoshenko simply gave in to you.'

"'That's impossible,' I replied. "You must not know Timoshenko very well. He's very strong willed, and he would never have given his consent to the operation unless he thought it was a good idea.'

"As a matter of fact," Khrushchev added, "it was Comrade Bagramian who worked out the plan of attack for the Kharkov counteroffensive." NK1, p. 184.

75 Zhukov, *Reminiscences and Reflections,* vol. 2, p. 88.

76 Erickson, *Road to Stalingrad,* pp. 402, 436.

77 See NK4, no. 11, p. 93, and no. 1, 1991, pp. 69–75. Also see Tompson, *Khrushchev,* p. 81.

78 NK1, p. 190.

79 Ibid., p. 199.

80 Carrynyk, *Alexander Dovzhenko*, p. 89.

81 According to the same Malinovskaya, the main Stalingrad commanders, Yeremenko, Chuikov, and others, admired Khrushchev's personal bravery and indefatigable energy, even praising these qualities after his ouster when speaking well of him wasn't advisable. Cited in Gobarev, "Khrushchev i voennye," pp. 28, 30.

82 Transcript of October 1957 Central Committee plenum, in RGANI f. 2, op. 1, d. 271, l. 78.

83 NK4, no. 1, 1991, p. 80.

84 Ibid., p. 92; Transcript of October 1957 Central Committee plenum, in RGANI, f. 2, op. 1, d. 271, l. 78. Nor did Khrushchev disavow even more expansive claims for him that Yeremenko made in his memoirs, claims that John Erickson characterizes as "fanciful," "tendentious" and a "myth." See Erickson, *Road to Stalingrad*, pp. 429, 560–68.

85 Zhukov, *Reminiscences and Reflections*, vol. 2, p. 99. In an interview with the author, Dmitri Volkogonov contended that Zhukov's memoirs are more reliable than Khrushchev's. While the Stalingrad counterattack was in preparation, Vasilevskii remembered driving "from one army to another, from one set of units to another, and everywhere I went Khrushchev went with me in the same car. Never once did he travel in anyone else's car: everywhere I went, so did he. But then you read the official history [of the war written in the Khrushchev era] and it says, 'Comrade Khrushchev arrived at such-and-such unit,' 'Comrade Khrushchev visited the headquarters of such-and-such corps,' 'Comrade Khrushchev said this or that to so-and-so,' etc., etc. As to the whereabouts of the Chief of the General Staff, that remains unknown." Vasilevskii is cited in Simonov, *Glazami cheloveka moego pokoleniia*, p. 410.

86 Cited ibid., p. 418. Like Zhukov, Vasilevskii was later forced into unwanted retirement by Khrushchev. So he too had reason to seek revenge in his memoirs. Once again, the truth seems mixed—more so than Zhukov and Vasilevskii would have it or than Khrushchev too would allow.

87 NK1, p. 196.

88 Ibid., pp. 196–97.

89 NK4, no. 12, 1990, pp. 83–87.

90 Ibid., nos. 2–3, 1991, p. 74.

91 Ibid., p. 71.

92 Cover notes for these reports from Khrushchev to Stalin in TsAMO, f. 206, op. 258, d. 3, ll. 123–24.

93 NK4, no. 1, 1990, p. 89.

94 Zhukov, *Vospominaniia i razmyshleniia*, vol. 3, p. 10.

95 Volkogonov, *Stalin*, p. 467.

96 John Erickson, *The Road to Berlin* (Boulder, Colo.: Westview Press, 1983), p. 101. "Both commands watched this fiery escalation with grim, numbed fascination," writes Erickson. "German officers had never seen so many Soviet aircraft, while Soviet commanders—who had seen a lot—had never before seen such a formidable massing of German tanks, all blotched in their green and yellow camouflage." As the men and armor clashed, the battle "roared on hour after hour leaving ever-greater heaps of the dead and the dying, clumps of blazing or disabled armor, shattered personnel carriers and lorries, and thickening columns of smoke coiling over the steppe. With each hour also, the traffic in mangled, twisted men brought to steaming, blood-soaked forward dressing stations continued to swell."

97 For fuller, more objective accounts, see Erickson, *Road to Stalingrad*, p. 65, 93; *Road to Berlin*, pp. 65, 97.

98 "I have no idea why he was so cool and controlled on this occasion," Khrushchev added, "while on other occasions he flew completely off the handle. It was as though the devil himself held a string attached to Stalin's main nerve, and no one knew when the devil would give the string a jerk, sending Stalin into one of his fits of rage. Both Stalin's temper and his self-control were developed to an advanced degree." NK1, p. 210.

99 Ibid., pp. 209–11.

100 Author's interview with D. M. Sukhanov.

101 Reported by Ukrainian historian Yuri Shapoval. When Shapoval remarked on this in the presence of Khrushchev's son Sergei, the latter insisted that strong leaders' assistants are almost always mediocrities whose job is to carry out orders and not question them. Whether or not that holds as a general rule, it is still possible that Khrushchev chose mediocrities as assistants so that he could stand out in comparison.

102 Author's interviews with Vasily Kostenko in June 1991 and August 1993. Kostenko sighed when he recounted this story. This, above all, was the message he had sought me out to convey. "What a conversation like that showed," he said, "was that it wasn't at the Twentieth Congress that Khrushchev saw the light, but ten years before Stalin died. And this wasn't the only revealing moment like this; there were many of them."

103 Gapochka list dated October 31, 1943, and Savchenko reply of January 6, 1944, are in TsDAHOU, f. 1, op. 23, d. 699, ll. 1–9, 10–15. This episode is also recounted and analyzed in an unpublished article by Iurii Aksiutin, "Ukrainskii sinodik Nikity Khrushcheva."

104 For examples of letters and other appeals to Khrushchev and of his responses, see documents in NK5, vol. 1, pp. 769–75, 781–82, 790–91, 810–12, 817–18.

105 Shapoval, "M. S. Khrushchov na Ukraini," p. 30.

106 In 1941 Dovzhenko received a Stalin Prize for his civil war film *Shchors* (1939). On August 3, 1942, the day after a short story by the filmmaker appeared in the army newspaper, *Krasnaia zvezda* (Red Star), Dovzhenko got word that Stalin himself "thanked him for the story which told the army and the people what it was extremely necessary that they be told." See Latyshev, "I. V. Stalin: Ob antileninskikh oshibkakh," p. 88.

107 Excerpts (in English) from Dovzhenko's diary in Carynnyk, *Alexander Dovzhenko*, pp. 67–68. Excerpts in Russian in Latyshev, "I. V. Stalin: Ob antileninskikh oshibkakh," p. 89.

108 Ibid., pp. 93–94.

109 Dovzehnko diary excerpt, ibid., p. 88.

110 Ibid.

111 Reprinted, ibid., p. 89. In all, Stalin's jeremiad takes up almost six two-columned pages of extremely small print in Latyshev, "I. V. Stalin: Ob antileninskikh oshibkakh." Also see excerpts from Dovzhenko diary entries in Lev Ozerov, "Chelovek, zemlia i zvezdy," *Ogonek*, no. 43 (1987), pp. 3–6.

112 *Ukraine in Flames: A Film Scenario by Aleksandr Dovzhenko*, trans. and with intro. by Abigail Marceluk (Zhaba Productions, 1997), pp. xiv, xxiv. Carynnyk, *Alexander Dovzehnko*, p. 95.

113 Dovzhenko diary excerpt cited in Shapoval, "Ukrainian Years," pp. 29–30.

114 See the Ukrainian Politburo's resolution of February 12, 1944, in "Aleksandr Dovzhenko: 'Ia protiven vam i chem-to opasen,'" *Istochnik*, no. 0 (1993), p. 126. Khrushchev claims that resolution was deliberately made "as painless as possible." See NK4, no. 11, 1991, p. 53. The archivist at the Dovzhenko Film Studio in Kiev quotes the filmmaker's widow, Yulia Solntseva, as saying Dovzhenko got a certain minimum of protection from Khrushchev, while Sergei Khrushchev contends his father tried to control the situation by undertaking to chastise the sinner himself. Interviews with the author in Kiev, July 1991.

115 NK1, pp. 172–73. See also NK4, no. 11, 1991, pp. 52–53. Khrushchev also claimed to have been misled in his assessment of *Ukraine in Flames* by the facts that Stalin himself had been praising Dovzhenko's work and that Malenkov had liked the scenario.

116 Even after Dovzhenko's death in 1956, his widow, Solntseva, was allowed to complete the filming of *Poema o more*, which Khrushchev himself viewed at Mosfilm at her invitation.

117 NK1, p. 200.

118 Ibid., pp. 200–05.

119 Ibid., p. 215.

120 Ibid., p. 211.

121 Simonov, *Glazami cheloveka moego pokoleniia*, pp. 414–15, 418.

122 See Erickson, *Road to Berlin*, pp. 128, 141. Khrushchev's version differs. Although "it might have looked as though we deliberately arranged the liberation of Kiev as a celebration of the anniversary," Khrushchev said, "actually it was only a happy coincidence." See NK1, p. 216.

123 The command post for the operation was on a small rise. Nearby, across a field, was a series of dugouts including one occupied by Khrushchev. I visited the spot on a dark, rainy day in June 1991. A guide at the monument that stands there said that as late as 1985 there had been no pictures of Khrushchev among photos exhibited there and that guides were not allowed to mention his name.

124 NK1, pp. 216–17; Photograph is in ibid., p. 214. Author's interview with Vasily Kostenko, August 1993. P. T. Tron'ko, head of the Kiev Young Communist League, who was part of the caravan along with Kostenko, recalls Khrushchev's repeatedly wiping tears from his eyes with his handkerchief. Tron'ko, "Moi zustrichi z M. S. Khrushchovim," in *M. S. Khrushchov i Ukraina*, informal Russian translation.

125 Tron'ko, "Moi zustrichi," Russian translation.

126 NK4, no. 6, 1991, p. 50.

127 "When I learned that Germany had capitulated my joy was beyond belief. . . . "NK4, nos. 7–8, 1991, p. 100.

128 Khrushchev's message is a tour de force that blended deep emotion with enough references to what he himself had seen and heard to remind his boss that Khrushchev was as invaluable as he was tireless. Khrushchev's November 8, 1943, memorandum to Stalin is in NK5, vol. 1, pp. 793–95. His recollection of it is in NK4, no. 6, 1991, p. 59.

129 Stalin returned the favor by having Khrushchev's note printed in *Pravda* for all to see. But then he chided Khrushchev for sending in code what turned out to be publishable, although Khrushchev insists his note wasn't secret at all but rather was called in over an open phone line. See NK4, no. 7–8, 1991, p. 100.

CHAPTER 8. UKRAINIAN VICEROY AGAIN: 1944–1949

1 Voznesensky's report is paraphrased in Volkogonov, *Stalin*, p. 504.

2 Subtelny, *Ukraine*, pp. 479–80; David Marples, *Stalinism in Ukraine in the 1940's* (New York: St. Martin's, 1992), p. 62.

3 Pasternak and Sakharov cited in Conquest, *Stalin*, pp. 269–70. For a more general survey of the postwar mood, see Zubkova, *Obshchestvo i reformy*, pp. 25–44.

4 NK4, no. 11, 1991, p. 43.

5 Cited in Sullivant, *Soviet Politics and the Ukraine, 1917–1957*, p. 248.

6 Text in NK1, p. 596.

7 NK4, nos. 7–8, 1991, pp. 76, 98.

8 NK1, p. 218.

9 Marples, *Stalinism in Ukraine*, p. 59; John A. Armstrong, *Ukrainian Nationalism*, 3d ed. (Englewood, Colo.: Ukrainian Academic Press, 1990), pp. 175–76; NK1, p. 228.

10 NK1, p. 229.

11 NK4, nos. 7–8, p. 11.

12 Transcript of conference of province party secretaries for personnel, April 20–22, 1944, in TsDAHOU. f. 14, op. 44, d. 1649, l. 189.

13 Author's interview with Olga Kosenko, August 1993.

14 Khrushchev's report to Stalin dated July 26, 1944. Copy received from Yuri Shapoval.

15 Transcript of Ukrainian Central Committee plenum, December 12–14, 1945, in RGASPI, f. 17, 45, d. 1967, ll. 271–72, 290–96.

16 *Rasskaz o pochetnom shakhtere*, pp. 163–64.

17 Author's interview with Zakhar Glukhov. See also Glotova, "Vstrechi v Mar'inke," p. 2.

18 Author's interview with Andrei Shevchenko, August 1993.

19 Conversations with peasants during a visit to Kalinovka in the summer of 1991. The "tsarevich" was the tsar's son.

20 Author's interview with Andrei Shevchenko, August 1993. Also see Anatolii Strelianyi, "Poslednii romantik," in *Svet i teni velilkogo desiatiletiia: N. S. Khrushchev i ego vremia* (Leningrad: Lenizdat, 1989), pp. 238–39.

21 Author's interview with Andrei Shevchenko, October 1993.

22 Khrushchev memorandum to Stalin in NK5, vol. 1, pp. 819–20; NK4, nos. 7–8, 1991, p. 89; Shapoval, "Ukrainian Years," p. 27.

23 Khrushchev's letter to Stalin in Ukrainian Party Archive TsDAHOU, f. 1, op. 23, spr. 711, ark. 6–7; Shapoval, "Ukrainian Years," pp. 27–28.

24 P. Knyshevskii, "Shtrikhi k portretu kremlevskoi gallerei," *Novoe vremia*, no. 9

(1994), p. 54, quoted in Shapoval, "Ukrainian Years," pp. 28–29. For an account of Khrushchev's 1954 decision to transfer the Crimea to the Ukrainian Soviet Socialist Republic, see Dmitri Volkogonov, *Sem' vozhdei* (Moscow: Novosti, 1995), vol. 1, pp. 358–68. Also see Roman Laba, "The Russian-Ukrainian Conflict: State, Nation, Identity," *European Security*, vol. 4, no. 3 (Autumn 1995), pp. 463–68.

25 Medvedev, *Khrushchev*, p. 42; Shapoval, *N. S. Khrushchev na Ukraine*, p. 43.

26 *Pravda,* December 14, 1944, trans. in Pistrak, *Grand Tactician*, pp. 164–65.

27 *Velikomu Stalinu: Narodni pisni ta dumy* (Kiev: 1949), p. 325. Still another "Song about Khrushchev" (words by T. Masenka, music by P. Batiuk) includes this chorus:

Together with the people through battles he marched,
Leading our region to happiness.
Let our friend comrade Khrushchev be glorified,
Let the people strike up a song about him.

28 The reader will recall Maksym Ryl'ski, the neoclassical poet imprisoned in the early thirties whom Khrushchev befriended in 1938. Ryl'ski sang of Khrushchev in 1942 as "quiet and glowing strong as fire" and of his "silver-gray youthfulness," anticipating the blessed moment of victory when "We'll shake the firm hand of Nikita Khrushchev in the name of the people we so cherish and love." In 1944 Ryl'ski imagined a joyful reunion in which Khrushchev "will greet us with a tender smile." Both cited in Pistrak, *Grand Tactician*, p. 184. Ryl'ski's birthday tribute appeared in *Pravda Ukrainy*, April 17, 1944, p. 1.

29 Birthday greetings are collected in TsDAHOU, f. 1, op. 23, d. 724. Examples of fawning letters include Korotchenko's letter of May, 3, 1943 (f. 1, op. 23, d. 378), and General Bagramian's letter of June 28, 1942 (f. 1, op. 23, d. 72).

30 Author's interviews with Rada Adzhubei, with Nina Kukharchuk, and with Vasily Kostenko, June 1991.

31 This description of family life in Kiev is based on the author's interviews with Yulia Leonidovna Khrushcheva, Rada Adzhubei, Nina Kukharchuk, and Yuri Khrushchev and on SK4, pp. 26–28. The author visited Khrushchev's prewar and postwar residences in June 1991.

32 Vasilii Makovetskii, a former hunting lodge staffer, describes the lodge and Khrushchev's visits in "Dacha Khrushcheva," *Raduga* (Kiev) (1990), pp. 110–13.

33 Cousins, *The Improbable Triumvirate*, pp. 52–53.

34 According to Yuri Khrushchev, he visited the Khrushchevs once a year when they were in Kiev and once a week in Moscow. Another family member, who confirmed that Yuri reminded Nina Petrovna of Tolya, insisted Yuri visited Kiev only once and spent only rare holidays with Khrushchevs in Moscow. Yuri also reported that the Khrushchevs supported his mother when she was ill but did not take steps to see her.

35 Marshall MacDuffie, *The Red Carpet: 10,000 Miles through Russia on a Visa from Khrushchev* (New York: Norton, 1955), p. 200.

36 MacDuffie manuscript, "Russia after Stalin," p. 30/19, BAR/MacDuffie, Box 3, Rare Book and Manuscript Library, Columbia University.

37 Milovan Djilas, *Conversations with Stalin*, trans. Michael B. Petrovich (New York: Harcourt, Brace & World, 1962), pp. 120–24.

38 Marples, *Stalinism in Ukraine*, pp. 46–48, 75; Mikhail Heller and Aleksandr Nekrich, *Utopia in Power: History of the Soviet Union from 1917 to the Present* (New York: Summit Books, 1986), p. 453; Subtelny, *Ukraine*, p. 461.

39 Subtelny, *Ukraine*, p. 444; Marples, *Stalinism in Ukraine*, pp. 49–58.

40 The Uniate Church was first formed in 1596, when Orthodox bishops of Ukraine and Byelorussia (then part of the Polish-Lithuanian Commmonwealth) recognized the primacy of the Roman Catholic pope in return for papal guarantees that the Uniates would maintain their Byzantine-Slavonic rite, the Church-Slavonic language, and Eastern canon law, which provided for a married clergy. In those parts of Ukraine that were united with Russia in 1654, tsarist authorities moved to subordinate the Uniates to the Russian Orthodox Church. But in Austrian-annexed Galicia, the Greek Catholic Church grew ever stronger and, by the turn of the twentieth century, was the main defender of the idea of Ukrainian independence.

41 See Bohdan R. Bociurkiw, *The Ukrainian Greek Catholic Church and the Soviet State: 1939–1950* (Edmonton: Canadian Institute of Ukrainian Studies Press, 1996).

42 Marples, *Stalinism in Ukraine*, pp. 101, 112; Tompson, *Khrushchev*, p. 88.

43 Khrushchev's January 17 report to Stalin is in *M. S. Khrushchov i Ukraina*, pp. 159–64. His March 21 telegram is in NK5, vol. 1, pp. 802–03. His November 15 report is cited in Shapoval, "Nikita Khrushchev i zapadnaia Ukraina," p. 83. The 1945 Ukrainian Politburo resolutions are cited in V. I Sergeiichuk, "Mikita Khrushchov proti OUN-UPA," in *M. S. Khrushchov i Ukraina*, pp. 47–51.

44 Organized opposition largely ceased after UPA Commander P. Shukhevich was killed on March 5, 1950, but uncoordinated incidents continued until the mid-1950s. See Shapoval, "Nikita Khrushchev i zapadnaia Ukraina," p. 84.

45 Jeffrey Burds, "The Early Cold War in Soviet West Ukraine, 1944–1948," no. 1505, in *The Carl Beck Papers in Russian and East European Studies* (Pittsburgh: University of Pittsburgh Press, 2001), p. 8.

46 Shapoval, "Ukrainian Years," p. 38.

47 This account is based on Jeffrey Burds, "AGENTURA: Soviet Informants' Networks and the Ukrainian Rebel Underground in Galicia, 1944–1948," *East European Politics and Societies*, vol. 11, no. 1 (Winter 1997), pp. 89–130.

48 Vladimir Naumov says that he once saw a 1953 document in the archives, signed by Khrushchev, that specified about 600,000 victims. Author's interview with Vladimir Naumov, March 1998. According to Iurii Shapoval ("Nikita Khrushchev i zapadnaia Ukraina," p. 15), between 1939 and 1955 more than 2 million people, or roughly 20 percent of the population were exiled from western Ukraine. A KGB report from the 1980s listing the number exiled from the USSR's western provinces reports 77,751 exiled from Ukraine in 1947 and 8,984 as late as 1951. See "Meropriiatiia po vyseleniiu iavlialis' cherezvychainoi meroi," pp. 137–39.

49 These last two incidents were condemned by a Ministry of the Interior prosecutor in a February 1949 memorandum to Khrushchev, as were other incidents before then. See "Dokladnaya zapiska o faktakh grubogo narushenia sovetskoi zakonnosti i deiatel'nosti t. n. spetsgruppy MGB," February 15, 1949, memorandum from MVD military procurator in Ukraine, Kosharskii to N. S. Khrushchev, TsDAHOU, f. 1, op. 16, spr. 68, ark 10–17. Also see Burds, "AGENTURA," pp. 1,

5–6; Shapoval, "Nikita Khrushchev i zapadnaia Ukraina," p. 85; Memorandum from Ukrainian NKVD chief Riasnoi to N. S. Khrushchev, August 24, 1945, TsDAHOU, f. 1, op. 23, spr. 3905, ark. 1-7.

50 Marples, *Stalinism in Ukraine*, pp. 61, 78–79; Burds, "AGENTURA," pp. 22–23.

51 Letter cited in Shapoval, "Nikita Khrushchev i zapadnaia Ukraina," pp. 83–84. According to Shapoval, troikas weren't established, but public executions took place.

52 Transcript of Central Committee meeting, November 22–24, 1944, RGASPI, f. 17, op. 44, d. 1628, pp. 130, 158.

53 Transcript of conference of district party secretaries, district soviet chairmen, and heads of district NKVD and NKGB office, January 10, 1945, in Derzhavnyi arkhiv L'vivskoi oblasti (State Archive of L'viv Province, L'viv, Ukraine, hereafter cited as DALO), f. 3, op. 1, spr. 191, ll. 8–9. I am grateful to Mark Kramer for providing a full text.

54 Transcript of meeting of district party secretaries and district NKVD and NKBG chiefs, Lvov, May 15, 1945, DALO, f. 3, op. 1, d. 196, ark. 1, 3, 6–7, 19, 29–30. I am grateful to Jeffrey Burds for providing this document.

55 Extermination detachments consisted of twenty-eight thousand men supported by twenty-five hundred self-defense groups with twenty-nine thousand men. During this period troops were garrisoned in every district, with up to a hundred soldiers in every village. See Bociurkiw, *Ukrainian Greek Catholic Church*, p. 146.

56 Ibid., pp. 102–88.

57 Soviet authorities and the Russian Orthodox Church accused Ukrainian nationalists and "Vatican agents." But Father Kostel'nyk's widow recalls his complaining to the authorities and being warned to keep silent, as well as the withdrawal of his security men a short time before he was murdered. See ibid., pp. 205–06.

58 Ibid., pp. 221–22.

59 The source for Khrushchev's complicity is Pavel Sudoplatov, the former Soviet secret policeman who arranged assassinations at home and abroad and who wrote that he was in Uzhgorod, trying to track down Romzha's contacts with the Vatican, when the murder took place. As noted earlier, Sudoplatov's testimony isn't always reliable, but his version of Khrushchev's motive rings especially true. Khrushchev "knew that Romzha was infiltrating both government and party administrations but he didn't know how. Fearing exposure of his ineptitude, Khrushchev initiated Romzha's secret assassination." Sudoplatov, *Special Tasks*, pp. 252–53. Bociurkiw (*Ukrainian Greek Catholic Church*, p. 22) cites the Basilian sister Teofila, who said she witnessed the execution.

60 One of Khrushchev's few recollections concerns a tense visit to the city of Rovno in the winter of 1944. He went there to discuss nationalist resistance with Soviet forces that were liberating the area, and although the local commanders considered the region secure enough for him to spend the night, he didn't dare. Heading north along the old border with Poland, he stopped for a rest at a rear supply base where he noticed "a curiously large number of people loitering about. I wondered to myself how many of them were Banderites in disguise, eating our food, warming themselves in front of our fires, and spying on us. I was warned that the area was swarming with Banderites." Rather than spend the night at this supply base, Khrushchev pushed on to a safer site. NK1, p. 218.

61 On "solid evidence in Soviet archives [that] reveals not only that U.S. and British intelligence were supporting Ukrainian and Polish underground rebel actions against Soviet forces from as early as mid-1943 . . . but moreover that Stalin was deeply cognizant of this support," see Burds, "AGENTURA," pp. 29–30. For an even fuller account of Western support for nationalist operations and of what the Soviets knew about that support, see Burds, "Early Cold War in Soviet West Ukraine."

62 The fate of Nina Petrovna's relatives, including a nephew who was killed by what she called Polish bandits, as reported by Sergei Khrushchev. Khrushchev's speech at a memorial meeting for Vatutin in Kiev, which seems to contain a unusual amount of personal feeling, is in NK5, vol. 1, pp. 798–801.

63 See Burds, "AGENTURA," p. 30.

64 "On Deficiencies in Political Work among the Populace of the Western Provinces of the Ukrainian Soviet Socialist Republic," September 27, 1944, in Robert H. McNeal, *Resolutions and Decisions of the Communist Party of the Soviet Union*, Vol. 3, *The Stalin Years: 1929–1953* (Toronto: University of Toronto Press, 1974), pp. 226–32. Although Khrushchev's name wasn't mentioned, as Ukrainian party leader he was obviously to blame.

65 Sudoplatov, *Special Tasks*, p. 254.

66 See Taubman, *Stalin's American Policy*, pp. 73–165.

67 See Elena Zubkova, *Russia after the War: Hopes, Illusions and Disappointments, 1945–1957*, trans. and ed. Hugh Ragsdale (Armonk, N.Y.: M. E. Sharpe, 1998), pp. 35–39, 74–98.

68 See Medvedev, *Let History Judge*, pp. 786–87; Volkogonov, *Stalin*, p. 510; Sullivant, *Soviet Politics and the Ukraine*, p. 257.

69 Zhukov, *Reminiscences and Reflections*, vol. 2, p. 339.

70 Alliluyeva, *Twenty Letters to a Friend*, pp. 188–91.

71 Djilas, *Conversations with Stalin*, pp. 147–61.

72 Cited in Sullivant, *Soviet Politics and the Ukraine*, p. 252.

73 Cited in Pistrak, *Grand Tactician*, p. 228.

74 "Special" NKVD-NKGB reports, TsDAHOU f. 1, op. 23, d. 685.

75 *Pravda Ukrainy*, September 1, 5, 1946. See also Pistrak, *Grand Tactician*, pp. 181–83.

76 *Kommunist*, no. 12 (August 1957), p. 26, as cited in Pistrak, *Grand Tactician*, p. 183.

77 That this was Khrushchev's tactic was asserted by archivists at the Ryl'ski Museum in Kiev in an interview with the author. For a passage in Khrushchev's memoirs in which he indicates that the best way to soften a blow was to inflict it oneself, see NK4, no. 11, 1991, p. 53.

78 NK1, p. 229.

79 Tompson, *Khrushchev*, p. 91.

80 See O. M. Veselova, "M. S. Khrushchev i golod v Ukraini 1946–1947," in *M. S. Khrushchov i Ukraina*, informal Russian translation.

81 NK1, p. 232.

82 Throughout the year the Ukrainian Politburo met daily to monitor agriculture. In the autumn Khrushchev demanded province officials speed up the harvest.

Late deliveries were a criminal offense, and many collective farm chairmen were arrested and tried as "saboteurs" and "wreckers."

83 The housekeeper, Valechka, later recounted this episode to Stalin's daughter. "'It's a wonder they weren't ashamed,' wailed Valechka, the tears streaming down her face. 'To deceive your father of all people! And now they're blaming him for it, too.'" Alliluyeva, *Twenty Letters to a Friend,* pp. 189–90.

84 NK4, no. 11, 1991, p. 37.

85 Author's interview with Zakhar Glukhov.

86 NK1, pp. 232–35.

87 Adzhubei, *Krushenie illiuzii* p. 30; NK4, no. 11, 1991, p. 38.

88 See Veselova, "Khrushchev i golod," pp. 6–7; Khrushchev's letter to Stalin of about December 1, 1946, in TsDAHOU, f. 1, op. 23, spr. 3482, ark. 58–60; Khrushchev's letter to Stalin of December 17, 1946, cited in TsDAHOU, f. 1, op. 23, spr. 3488, ark. 34.

89 NK1, pp. 233–34; NK4, no. 11, 1991, p. 38.

90 Shapoval, *M. S. Khrushchov na Ukraini,* p. 36.

91 "Stalin said this in Malenkov's presence," Khrushchev wrote. "He was absolutely correct, but it was all the more astounding that Stalin had assigned Malenkov to handle agriculture if he knew that Malenkov was totally incompetent in this area. The paradox was interesting to me, and I have no ready explanation. But then, anything was possible with Stalin." NK1, p. 236.

92 NK1, pp. 236–40; NK4, no. 11, 1991, pp. 38–40.

93 Transcript of plenum of March 10–13, 1947, in TsDAHOU, f. 1, op. 1, spr. 740, ark. 2–76, especially 3–4. For an example of Khrushchev's interrupting, hectoring, and humiliating other speakers, see his speech at a Ukrainian Central Committee plenum, June 5–8, 1945, TsDAHOU, f. 17, op. 45, d. 1966, ll. 95–102.

94 Author's interview with Rada Adzhubei. See also Adzhubei, *Krushenie illiuzii,* p. 31.

95 SK4, p. 26.

96 While Kaganovich toured the countryside arranging famine relief, Khrushchev said, he remained in Kiev, "like a telephone dispatcher," trying "to rush seed consignments out by rail." NK1, pp. 240–41; NK4, no. 11, 1991, p. 40–41.

97 Interview with Rada Adzhubei. Kaganovich later contended that although Khrushchev was "distressed and perhaps insulted" to be demoted, "he greeted me happily, saying, 'I'm very pleased that it's you who've been appointed first secretary.'" Kaganovich, *Pamiatnye zapiski,* p. 566.

98 NK1, p. 243.

99 That Kaganovich pressed for action against Ryl'ski is clear from his comments on a thirty-three-page attack on Ryl'ski by F. Enevich and from a letter to Kaganovich in which Enevich described the manuscript as written in accordance with Kaganovich's instructions. Both are in TsDAHOU, f. 1, op. 23, spr. 4162. Also see a similar hatchet job sent to Kaganovich in August 1947 in *Komsomol'skoe znamia* (November 6, 1990), pp. 4–5.

100 Iurii Shapoval, "N. S. Khrushchev: nachalo biografii i kar'ery, gody v Ukraine, 1894–1949." Paper prepared for delivery. (Providence, R.I., Brown University, Khrushchev Centennial Conference, December 1994), pp. 38–39.

101 Glotova, "Vstrechi v Mar'inke," p. 2.

102 According to former Ukrainian Komsomol chief Vasily Kostenko, Stalin's son, Vasily, recounted this incident to him. Author's interview with Kostenko, August 1993.

103 NK1, pp. 243–44.

104 In 1961 then Ukrainian party leader Nikolai Podgorny described Kaganovich's 1947 behavior this way: "Kaganovich surrounded himself with a gang of unprincipled sycophants. He slaughtered cadres who were devoted to the party, and tormented and terrorized leading officials of the republic. Like a sadist, Kaganovich enjoyed taunting activists and members of the intelligentsia, degrading them, threatening them with arrest and imprisonment. It is no accident that even now many party and soviet workers refer to the period when Kaganovich was in the Ukraine as the 'black days' of the republic. . . . Comrade Khrushchev, relying on his immense prestige among the working people of the Ukraine and on their support, did everything he could to foil Kaganovich's provocations." *Pravda,* October 20, 1961, p. 3.

105 See Medvedev, *Khrushchev,* p. 46; Tompson, *Khrushchev,* pp. 95–97; Marples, *Stalinism in Ukraine in the 1940's,* pp. 112–26, 147. As described in the next chapter, several years later Khrushchev's championing of agro-cities got him into trouble with Stalin.

106 Khrushchev's address to a March 9–11, 1948, Central Committee plenum is in TsDAHOU, f. 1. op. 1, spr. 768. His Sixteenth Congress speech is in f.1, op. 1, spr. 814. Khrushchev's 1948 and 1949 letters to Stalin are in f. 1, op. 23, spr. 5601 and spr. 6257.

107 Adzhubei, *Krushenie illiuzii,* pp. 29–30.

108 NK1, p. 244; NK4, no. 11, 1991, p. 43.

109 Khrushchev's letter proposing the antiparasite decree is in TsDAHOU, f. 1, op. 1, spr. 5601. The decree itself is in f. 1, op. 23, spr. 5177. Khrushchev's later eighteen-page letter, dated April 17, 1948 (his fifty-fourth birthday) is in f. 1, op. 23, spr. 5177, ark. 27–44.

110 Shapoval, *M. S. Khrushchov na Ukraini,* p. 41.

111 Shapoval, "N. S. Khrushchev—nachalo biografii," p. 32.

CHAPTER 9. THE HEIR NONAPPARENT: 1949–1953

1 Svetlana Alliluyeva, *Only One Year* (New York: Harper & Row, 1969), p. 422. Not all who knew Adzhubei shared this high opinion, especially once he married Rada, parlayed his role as Khrushchev's son-in-law into political power, and began to throw his weight around in the USSR and abroad. In the beginning, however, the budding romance required admirable boldness from both Rada and Aleksei.

2 Adzhubei, *Krushenie illiuzii,* p. 16. In addition, the author draws on several interviews and an extended correspondence with Adzhubei between 1989 and 1991. Sergo Beria remembered Malenkov's wife as "an authoritarian woman who was always dressed to the nines" and recalled Lavrenty Beria's warning: "She's dangerous, a gendarme in skirts . . . with a much stronger will than her husband." Beria, *Beria, My Father,* p. 160.

3 Adzhubei, *Krushenie illiuzii,* p. 96.

4 Ibid., pp. 16, 77–78.

5 Ibid., p. 24.

6 In July 1944, when Khrushchev asked Korneichuk to give up his entirely honorary role as Ukraine's people's commissar for foreign affairs (honorary because the notion that Ukraine was independent enough to need a foreign minister was itself a figment of Soviet propaganda) and assume instead the chairmanship of the Ukrainian Committee on the Arts, the pampered Korneichuk "categorically refused to do so," with the result that in the midst of war, Khrushchev had to appeal to Stalin for a special dispensation that would increase Korneichuk's prerogatives as the Arts Committee chair. See two July 1944 letters from Khrushchev to Stalin in NK5, vol. 1, pp. 810–12.

7 Adzhubei, *Krushenie illiuzii,* pp. 24–25.

8 NK1, p. 248. NK4, no. 11, 1991, p. 44.

9 Adzhubei, *Krushenie illiuzii,* p. 29.

10 NK1, p. 246; NK2, p. 95.

11 NK4, no. 11, 1991, p. 44.

12 See Michael Parrish, *The Lesser Terror: Soviet State Security, 1939–1953* (Westport, Conn.: Praeger, 1996), p. 215.

13 NK1, p. 250.

14 NK4, no. 12, 1991, p. 55; NK1, p. 289.

15 Adzhubei speculated on Khrushchev's thinking this way: "I imagine him attentively observing not only the aging leader, whose stupid willfulness was becoming more and more evident, but also those who were readying themselves to inherit Stalin's autocratic cudgel. It was during the last years of Stalin's life, I'm convinced, that Khrushchev realized he was strong enough to toss all his colleague rivals aside." Adzhubei, *Krushenie illiuzii,* p. 159.

16 See Zubkova, *Obshchestvo i reformy,* pp. 90–102.

17 Conquest, *Stalin,* p. 269; Amy Knight, *Beria: Stalin's First Lieutenant* (Princeton: Princeton University Press, 1993), p. 144,

18 Alliluyeva, *Twenty Letters to a Friend,* pp. 193, 196–97.

19 According to Iu. N. Zhukov, the Politburo as a whole met only twice for meetings that were minuted during Stalin's last six years. See Zhukov, "Bor'ba za vlast' v rukovodstve SSSR v 1945–1952 godakh," VI, no. 1 (1995), p. 28.

20 Such scenes are graphically portrayed in *The Inner Circle,* a film by Andrei Konchalovsky.

21 NK1, p. 297.

22 *Testimony: The Memoirs of Dmitri Shostakovich,* related to and ed. Solomon Volkov, trans. Antonina W. Bouis (New York: Harper & Row, 1979), pp. 251–52.

23 NK1, pp. 298, 300; NK4, no. 1, 1992, p. 53.

24 Alliluyeva, *Twenty Letters to a Friend,* pp. 20–22, 205; Colton, *Moscow,* p. 323; Djilas, *Conversations with Stalin,* p. 75; Radzinsky, *Stalin,* pp. 545–46; Shepilov, "Vospominaniia," VI, no. 3 (1998), pp. 5–6.

25 Shepilov, "Vospominaniia," VI, no. 3 (1998), p. 5.

26 NK1, pp. 300–01.

27 Alliluyeva, *Only One Year,* p. 385.

28 Chuev, *Sto sorok besed,* p. 255.

29 Mikoian, *Tak bylo,* p. 353; NK1, p. 301.

30 NK4, no. 12, 1991, p. 52.

31 Ibid.

32 Beria, *Beria, My Father,* p. 141; Alliluyeva, *Only One Year,* pp. 385–86. The same Poskrebyshev once deftly lifted a dagger out of Foreign Minister Andrei Vyshinsky's full-dress diplomatic uniform at a Red Square parade and substituted a cucumber. Arkady Vaksberg, *The Prosecutor and the Prey: Vyshinsky and the 1930s Moscow Show Trials,* trans. Jan Butler (London: Weidenfeld & Nicolson, 1990), pp. 278–79.

33 Author's interview with a former Khrushchev associate who asked not to be identified, Moscow, August 1993.

34 Teresa Toranska, *Them: Stalin's Polish Puppets,* trans. Agnieszka Kolakowska (New York: Harper & Row, 1987) p. 305.

35 NK1, p. 301.

36 Ibid., pp. 302–03.

37 Ibid., pp. 304–05.

38 Ibid., p. 303.

39 Ibid.

40 NK4, no. 11, 1991, pp. 49, 54; no. 1, 1992, p. 55; nos. 2–3, 1992, p. 76.

41 Norbert Elias described a similar scene at Louis XIV's Versailles: "The affairs, intrigues and conflicts knew no end. Everyone depended on everyone else, and all on the king. Each could harm each. He who rode high today was cast down tomorrow. There was no security. Everyone had to seek alliances with others whose stock was high, avoid unnecessary enmities, fight unavoidable enemies with cold calculation, and scrupulously maintain toward all others the degree of distance befitting their status." Elias, *The Court Society,* trans. Edmund Jephcott (New York: Pantheon Books, 1983), p. 104.

42 In the thirties Molotov and Stalin had struck Khrushchev as "inseparable, the closest of friends; they always went on vacation together." NK4, no. 12, 1991, p. 65.

43 Chuev, *Sto sorok besed,* p. 415. Even after clashing furiously with Molotov and condemning him as an unrepentent Stalinist, Khrushchev offered this tribute: "I considered Molotov to be very experienced, especially in matters of foreign policy. He often talked about foreign policy matters in my presence, and he always expressed himself knowledgeably, logically and forcefully." NK1, p. 309.

44 Alliluyeva, *Only One Year,* pp. 406–07.

45 Vasilieva, *Kremlin Wives,* pp. 136–59; Sudoplatov, *Special Tasks,* p. 327.

46 Chuev, *Sto sorok besed,* p. 466. See also Vasilieva, *Kremlin Wives,* pp. 136–60. When Stalin informed the Politburo of the case against Zhemchuzhina, Molotov recalled, "my knees shook." (Chuev, *Sto sorok besed,* p. 473.) At first he abstained on a vote to exlude his wife from the party, but then he wrote to Stalin renouncing her. See A. Danilov, "Stalinskoe Politbiuro v poslevoennye gody," in *Politicheskie partii Rossii* (Moscow: Izdatel'stvo Moskovskogo universiteta, 2000), pp. 210–11. When Shmuel Mikunis, the former leader of the Israeli Communist party, encountered Molotov in the Kremlin Hospital in 1955, he "went up to him and asked, 'How could you, a member of the Politburo, let them arrest your wife?' He gave me a cold look and asked me who I thought I was. I replied, 'I am the General Secretary of the Israeli Communist Party, and that's why I'm asking you—and not only you: I'm going to ask the Central Committee too. Why did you let them arrest Polina Zhemchuzhina?' Without moving a muscle in his steely face, he replied, 'Because I am a member of the Politburo and I must obey Party discipline. . . .'" Cited in Roy Medvedev, *All Stalin's Men* (Garden City, N.Y.: Anchor, 1984), p. 99.

47 NK1, p. 309.

48 Quoted in Medvedev, *All Stalin's Men*, p. 19.

49 Alliluyeva, *Only One Year*, pp. 402–03.

50 NK1, p. 308. Khrushchev claimed that he and his colleagues answered, "He didn't worm his way in. You appointed him yourself." Whether they were actually brave enough, or drunk enough, to do so is unclear.

51 Alliluyeva, *Only One Year*, pp. 404–05.

52 Cited in Radzinsky, *Stalin*, pp. 549–50.

53 NK1, pp. 309–10. Mikoyan agreed that he and Molotov were destined for "physical annihilation." Mikoian, *Tak bylo*, p. 580.

54 That this factional division was the postwar lineup is the consensus of most observers, both Soviet and Western, ranging from Robert Conquest (see his *Stalin*, pp. 272–74) to Pavel Sudoplatov (see *Special Tasks*, p. 315). A notable dissenter is Malenkov's son, Andrei G. Malenkov, who insists that his father was actually Beria's enemy, even though he had to appear to be friendly (author's interview with Andrei Malenkov). As pointed out in the text, however, I assume that the logic of their situation required that all of Stalin's lieutenants be simultaneously both friends and enemies of one another.

55 Vladislav Zubok and Constantine Pleshakov, *Inside the Kremlin's Cold War: From Stalin to Khrushchev* (Cambridge, Mass.: Harvard University Press, 1996), pp. 140–43; Knight, *Beria*, p. xv; Medvedev, *All Stalin's Men*, pp. 140–47.

56 Chuev, *Sto sorok besed*, p. 336.

57 Alliluyeva, *Only One Year*, pp. 414, 420.

58 Ibid., p. 412. Like Andrei Malenkov, Sergo Beria was particularly protective of his father, portraying him as a fine family man and as a closet reformer who secretly hated Stalin and couldn't wait for him to die. See Beria, *Beria, My Father*, p. 237. The Russian edition of Sergo Beria's book is *Moi otets—Lavrentii Beria* (Moscow: Sovremennik, 1994).

59 Adzhubei, *Krushenie illiuzii*, pp. 107–08.

60 According to Adzhubei, one of the two hundred young women so "seduced" ended up as "an unofficial but permanent concubine," somehow coinhabiting the Kachalov Street house with Nina Teimurazovna. According to Adzhubei, the woman later insisted she loved Beria, who was "sweet, gentle, and kind" to her. See ibid., pp. 166–68.

61 Djilas, *Conversations with Stalin*, p. 108.

62 Alliluyeva, *Only One Year*, p. 376.

63 Khrushchev first noted Stalin's fear at a postwar dinner at which the dictator suddenly looked around at the people serving him and asked angrily, "Why am I surrounded by Georgians?" After Beria tried vainly to explain, Stalin demanded that they be removed immediately. "The Georgians—including the shashlik cook and the provisions officer—were immediately whisked away," Khrushchev later said, "and Beria shuffled out of the room like a man who has been beaten up." NK1, p. 311. According to Sergo Beria (*Beria, My Father*, p. 245), his father deliberately signaled Stalin that he was prepared "to declare open war upon him should Stalin decide on his liquidation."

64 Ibid., p. 313.

65 Zhdanov apparently unearthed irregularities in the dismantling of German industry, which Malenkov oversaw. Malenkov was dropped from the secretariat when the aviation industry chief A. I. Shakhurin was arrested. See "Lavrentii Beriia: 'Cherez 2–3 goda ia krepko ispravlius' . . . ," *Istochnik,* no. 4 (1994), footnote 17, pp. 11–12. Reportedly, Malenkov was even exiled to Uzbekistan, but Stalin's office log records Malenkov's frequent presence in the Kremlin during this period. See Danilov, "Stalinskoe Politbiuro," pp. 201–02.

66 Even though Beria continued to oversee police affairs as the deputy chairman of the Council of Ministers and also took control of Stalin's crash program to develop nuclear weapons, Abakumov, the man who took charge of the security police in 1946, wasn't close to Beria, at least not initially. Among those who see these changes as a setback for Beria are: Conquest, *Stalin,* p. 274; R. G. Pikhoya, "O vnutripoliticheskoi bor'be v sovetskom rukovodstve, 1945–1948," NiNI, no. 6 (noiabr'–dekabr' 1995), p. 5; and Sudoplatov, *Special Tasks,* p. 315. Amy Knight, to the contrary, described this as a "positive change" since, while not losing overall control of the police, Beria "gained the stature of an all-around statesman." See Knight, *Beria,* p. 140.

67 Cited in Radzinsky, *Stalin,* p. 528. Mikoyan described Voznesensky as "arrogant" and a Russian "chauvinist" and Kuznetsov as "less ambitious," "charming and sincere." *Tak bylo,* pp. 549, 564.

68 Beria claimed as much in a letter written to Malenkov from prison on July 1, 1953. See "Lavrentii Beriia: Cherez 2–3 goda," p. 6.

69 See Mikoian, *Tak bylo,* pp. 563–68; Pikhoya, "O vnutripoliticheskoi bor'be," p. 6; Parrish, *Lesser Terror,* pp. 215–21; Radzinsky, *Stalin,* pp. 528, 534–35; Knight, *Beria,* pp. 151–52; Volkogonov, *Stalin,* p. 522; Vaksberg, *Prosecutor and the Prey,* p. 355. With his father's blessing, Sergo proceeded to get married despite the threat to his bride's father. Both Andrei Malenkov and Sergo Beria have challenged the notions that their fathers played the role in the Leningrad affair I have described.

70 Cited in Conquest, *Stalin,* p. 310.

71 Chuev, *Sto sorok besed,* p. 326.

72 See Mikoian, *Tak bylo,* pp, 568, 579. Kaganovich later insisted that no such purge was in the offing. See Chuev, *Tak govoril Kaganovich,* pp. 175–76.

73 NK4, no. 11, 1991, pp. 46-51.

74 NK1, pp. 246–49. When Stalin raised the issue of Popov, Khrushchev wrote, "his eyes narrowed and bored into mine; then he tossed his nose into the air and snorted—it was one of his favorite mannerisms." But although "he cursed angrily, he let the matter drop."

75 NK4, no. 12, 1991, p. 72.

76 See Sudoplatov, *Special Tasks,* pp. 316, 326; A. Avtorkhanov, *Zagadka smerti Stalina: zagovor Beriia* (Frankfurt am Main: Posev, 1976), p. 75; Anton Antonov-Ovseenko, *The Time of Stalin: Portrait of a Tyranny* (New York: Harper & Row, 1981), p. 298; Chuev, *Sto sorok besed,* p. 323. Also see Werner G. Hahn, *Postwar Soviet Politics: The Fall of Zhdanov and the Defeat of Moderation, 1946–1953* (Ithaca, N.Y.: Cornell University Press, 1982), pp. 38, 48, 50.

77 Colton, *Moscow,* pp. 298–99.

78 On secret police appointments, see Knight, *Beria,* p. 158; Sudoplatov, *Special*

Tasks, p. 338. Andrei Malenkov cited his father in *O moem ottse Georgii Malenkove* (Moscow: Tekhnekos, 1992), p. 58. Khrushchev's claim to have been "stumped" by the composition of the expanded Presidium is in NK1, pp. 279–80. The veteran Western Kremlinologist T. H. Rigby suggested it was "improbable that [Stalin] failed to involve at least one of his senior lieutenants by either giving them a direct role in his moves or at least encouraging them to see themselves as direct beneficiaries of them." Rigby suspected "Khrushchev is the most likely candidate for such involvement, although it must be stressed that there is no more than circumstantial evidence for this view." See T. H. Rigby, "Khrushchev and the Rules of the Games,"*Khrushchev and the Communist World*, ed. R. F. Miller and F. Feher (London and Canberra: Croom Helm, 1984), p. 52. Knight (pp. 171, 173) speculated about a Khrushchev role in the doctors' plot but without adducing any evidence.

79 Adzhubei, *Krushenie illiuzii*, pp. 33–34.

80 Author's interview with Vasily Kostenko, August 1993.

81 NK1, pp. 313–14; SK4, p. 30; author's interview with Vladimir Shamberg (former son-in-law of Malenkov's).

82 Author's interview with Rada Adzhubei.

83 Author's interview with Andrei Malenkov.

84 NK1, p. 314.

85 Adzhubei, *Krushenie illiuzii*, p. 97.

86 Ibid., pp. 96–99; NK4, no. 1, 1992, p. 64.

87 Chuev, *Sto sorok besed*, pp. 255, 323, 332.

88 Adzhubei, *Krushenie illiuzii*, pp. 98, 159.

89 NK4, nos. 2–3, 1992, pp. 87, 89.

90 NK1, p. 311.

91 Cited in Adzhubei, *Krushenie illiuzii*, p. 106.

92 Volkogonov, *Stalin*, p. 517; Medvedev, *Khrushchev*, pp. 51–52; Ponomarev, *N. S. Khrushchev*, p. 53.

93 See NK2, pp. 96–98.

94 Ponomarev, *N. S. Khrushchev*, p. 53.

95 Medvedev, *Khrushchev*, p 52; Medvedev, *Let History Judge*, pp. 797–801.

96 Author's interview with Andrei Shevchenko, August 1993.

97 Writes Roy Medvedev: "It was a good thing such experiments were tried only on small plots." Medvedev, *Khrushchev*, pp. 52–53.

98 NK2, pp. 117–18

99 Ibid., p. 116.

100 Quoted in Ponomarev, *N. S. Khrushchev*, p. 56.

101 Transcript of a conference of secretaries of district committees, the Moscow city party committee, the Central Committee, and district soviet executive committee chairmen, April 5, 1950, in TsAODM, f. 3, op. 124, d. 188, ll. 48–62.

102 For an incisive discussion that places the collective farm amalgamation movement in the broader context of Stalin and post-Stalin agricultural policy and includes key documents as well, see "Vtoroi i vazhneishii etap," *Otechestvennaia istoriia*, no. 1 (1994), pp. 27–50.

103 Khrushchev's March 16 and March 31, 1950, speeches were combined and published in *Pravda* on April 25, 1950, and are translated in Thomas P. Whitney, ed., *Khrushchev Speaks* (Ann Arbor: University of Michigan Press, 1963), pp. 23–37. His Moscow party plenum speech is cited in Ponomarev, *N. S. Khrushchev,* p. 58. See also Pistrak, *Grand Tactician,* pp. 239–40; Medvedev, *Khrushchev,* pp. 52–53.

104 Whitney, *Khrushchev Speaks,* pp. 38–53.

105 Shevchenko, in an interview with the author in August 1993, mentioned Stalin's call.

106 Khrushchev's letter is reprinted in "Vtoroi i vazhneishii etap," p. 44.

107 "Ispytanie Stalinshchinoi," *Vecherniaia Moskva,* April 15, 1994, p. 4. Author's interview with Andrei Shevchenko, August 1993. Author's interview with Pyotr N. Demichev. Chuev, *Sto sorok besed,* p. 362; Pistrak, *Grand Tactician,* p. 242.

108 "I. A. Benediktov: O Staline i Khrushcheve," *Molodaia gvardiia,* no. 4 (1989), p. 58. Note that Benediktov's brother, Aleksei, charged that the *Molodaia gvardiia* interview is mostly a fabrication. See his letter in *Ogonek,* no. 37 (1989), p. 8.

109 Ponomarev, *N. S. Khrushchev,* 60; Chuev, *Sto sorok besed,* p. 362; author's interview with Anatolii Ponomarev.

110 The April 1, 1958, decree rescinding that of April 2, 1951, is in "Vtoroi i vazhneishii etap," pp. 49–50.

111 Author's interview with Aleksei Adzhubei.

112 NK1, pp. 277–78.

113 Ibid., pp. 285–86.

114 Adzhubei, *Krushenie illiuzii,* pp. 87–88.

115 NK4, no. 1, 1992, p. 53.

116 Adzhubei, *Krushenie illiuzii,* pp. 87–89.

117 Chuev, *Sto sorok besed,* pp. 268, 325, 347, 367, 428.

118 Adzhubei, *Krushenie illiuzii,* p. 86.

119 Ibid., pp. 40, 86–88; SK4, p. 31.

120 Author's interview with Rada Adzhubei. As far as Khrushchev's children were concerned, she added, "We didn't think about it, we closed our eyes to some things, weren't aware of others, and so enjoyed ourselves. Nowadays my older son says, 'Are you trying to tell me that you didn't know what was going on, didn't feel it? That can't be.' But the truth is that what was going on didn't register at home."

121 Adzhubei, *Krushenie illiuzii,* pp. 75, 86.

122 Author's interview with Rada Adzhubei; Adzhubei, *Krushenie illiuzii,* p. 76.

123 Adzhubei, *Krushenie illiuzii,* pp. 40–41. Having cut himself off from his own family, Stalin expected his colleagues to see little of theirs. Wives and children generally weren't welcomed at Kremlin receptions.

124 Ibid., pp. 87, 36.

125 Ibid., pp. 41, 88.

126 Ibid., p. 40.

127 Ibid., p. 41.

128 Ibid., p. 82.

129 Volkogonov, *Stalin,* p. 525.

130 Ibid., p. 42. Adzubei, *Krushenie illiuzii,* p. 42.

131 Whitney, *Khrushchev Speaks,* p. 20.

132 Author's interview with Dmitri Goriunov.

133 Adzhubei, *Krushenie illiuzii,* pp. 42–43; author's interview with Aleksei Adzhubei.

134 NK4, no. 12, 1991, p. 69.

135 NK1, pp. 289–90.

CHAPTER 10. ALMOST TRUMPHANT: 1953–1955

1 NK1, p. 316. Volkogonov (*Stalin*, p. 571), without citing his source, portrayed Stalin as angry with his men. A.T. Rybin, a former Stalin bodyguard, quoted a colleague of his as saying that only juice was served that night. See A.T. Rybin, "Riadom s Stalinym," *Sotsiologicheskoe issledovanie*, no. 3 (1988), p. 92.

2 Conquest, *Stalin*, p. 311; Volkogonov, *Stalin*, p. 572. NK1, p. 316, differs slightly on details. Also see Rybin, "Riadom so Stalinym," pp. 92–93.

3 Volkogonov, *Stalin*, p. 572; Radzinsky, *Stalin*, pp. 571–75.

4 Dmitrii Volkogonov, *Sem' vozhdei: Galereia liderov SSSR* (Moscow: Novosti, 1995), vol. 1, p. 315; Volkogonov, *Stalin*, 572; *Beriia: Konets kar'ery* (Moscow: Izdatel'stvo politicheskoi literatury, 1991), p. 130; Rybin, "Riadom so Stalinym," p. 93.

5 Khrushchev's account is in NK4, nos. 2–3, 1992, pp. 90–93. It is supported by his son's recollections in SK3, vol. 1, p. 25. For a guard's account, see Rybin, "Riadom so Stalinym," p. 93.

6 NK4, nos. 2–3, 1992, p. 91.

7 Volkogonov, *Sem' vozhdei*, p. 323.

8 *Molotov Remembers: Conversations with Feliks Chuev*, ed. Albert Resis (Chicago: Ivan R. Dee, 1993), pp. 233, 237, 326. If in fact Stalin was murdered, Molotov said, "Khrushchev would scarcely have had a hand in it."

9 Radzinsky, *Stalin*, pp. 567–68, 574.

10 Volkogonov, *Sem' vozhdei*, pp. 313, 324. In the fall of 1947, when Oleg Troyanovsky, a young Foreign Ministry translator, spent several days at Stalin's Black Sea compound, he was surprised to learn that there was no physician present, just a *fel'dsher* (nurse-practitioner) capable of administering only the most elementary medical assistance. See Troianovskii, *Cherez gody i rasstoianiia*, pp. 157–58.

11 For more far-reaching speculation, extending to the possibility that Beria poisoned Stalin or otherwise acted so as to trigger his stroke in the first place, see A. Avtorkhanov, *Zagadka smerti Stalina: Zagovor Beriia* (Frankfurt am Main: Posev, 1976).

12 See NK4, nos. 2–3, 1992, p. 91; Radzinsky, *Stalin*, p. 575; Volkogonov, *Sem' vozhdei*, p. 318; and Evgenii Aleksandrov, "Smert' tirana," *Nezavisimaia gazeta* (March 4, 1993), p. 5. The conclusions of the medical team that examined Stalin are in the Volkogonov Collection, LOC, reel 16.

13 See *Molotov Remembers*, p. 236; NK4, nos. 2–3, 1992; p. 92; Radzinsky, *Stalin*, p. 576.

14 NK1, p. 323.

15 Simonov, *Glazami cheloveka moego pokoleniia*, p. 228. Before proceeding with his nominations, Malenkov announced that Stalin continued to fight for life, but that even if he recovered his condition would remain grave. Since the country could not be without leadership, he went on, it was necessary to form a new government. See Radzinsky, *Stalin*, pp. 577–78.

16 Alliluyeva, *Twenty Letters to a Friend*, pp. 8, 10.

17 NK1, p. 322.

18 Ibid., pp. 318, 323; Alliluyeva, *Twenty Letters to a Friend*, pp. 6, 12; Volkogonov, *Stalin*, p. 574; Shepilov, "Vospominaniia," VI, vol. 6, no. 3 (1998), p. 23.

19 Simonov, *Glazami cheloveka moego pokoleniia*, p. 229.

20 See Shepilov, "Vospominaniia," VI, vol. 6, no. 3 (1998), p. 12.

21 *Pravda*, March 10, 1953, p. 2.

22 N. A. Barsukov, "Analiticheskaia zapiska: Positsiia poslestalinskogo rukovodstva v otnoshenii politicheskikh repressii 30-x—40-x i nachala 50-x godov," unpublished article, pp. 28–29.

23 Beria apparently destroyed key documents after Stalin's death, and his rivals reportedly continued this process after his arrest. See transcript of interrogation of the longtime Beria bodyguard Rafael Sarkisov, July 1, 1958, in Volkogonov Collection, LOC, reel no. 3. Also see Naumov, "Repression and Rehabilitation," p. 103. Naumov provides no concrete information about the destruction of documents, but several former officials claim to have been aware of, or involved in, such destruction. See "Poslednii Stalinskii rasstrel," *Vecherniaia Moskva* (September 26, 1994,) p. 3.

24 Barsukov, "Analiticheskaia zapiska," p. 72. Aleksandr Solzhenitsyn, *The Gulag Archipelago* (New York: Harper & Row, 1978), vol. 3, pp. 279–331.

25 NK2, p. 79.

26 Khrushchev's speech to the September 1953 Central Committee plenum as printed in *Pravda*, September 15, 1953, and translated in Whitney, *Khrushchev Speaks*, pp. 82, 91; Elena Zubkova, "The Rivalry with Malenkov" and Anatolii Strelianyi, "Khrushchev and the Countryside," in *Nikita Khrushchev*, ed. Taubman, Khrushchev, and Gleason, pp. 69, 113.

27 Oleg Troyanovsky, "The Making of Soviet Foreign Policy," in *Nikita Khrushchev*, ed. Taubman, Khrushchev, and Gleason, p. 209. On Stalin's foreign policy in the postwar period, see Taubman, *Stalin's American Policy* and John Gaddis, *We Now Know: Rethinking Cold War History* (New York: Oxford University Press, 1997).

28 NK2, pp. 39–40. Author's interview with Sergei Khrushchev. On the evolution of Soviet military strength and of the overall military balance, see Lawrence Freedman, *The Evolution of Nuclear Strategy* (New York: St. Martin's, 1981).

29 NK2, p. 46. Perhaps this is why Khrushchev was so pleased when his son Sergei set out to become a rocket scientist.

30 Ibid., pp. 35, 220. On U.S. overflights, see Gregory W. Pedlow and Donald E. Welzenbach, *The CIA and the U-2 Program, 1954–1974* (Washington, D.C.: Central Intelligence Agency, 1998), pp. 2–4; R. Cargill Hall, "The Truth about Overflights," *Quarterly Journal of Military History* (Spring 1997), pp. 25–39. I interviewed an American pilot who flew for the CIA in 1953; he confirmed that American superiority in nighttime and poor weather flying allowed him and his colleagues to violate Soviet airspace at will.

31 NK2, p. 194.

32 Khrushchev later said that 109 people had been killed in the crush outside the House of Unions. See his speech to the Sixth Plenum of the Polish Workers' Party in March 1956, in Archiwum Akt Nowych, Polska Zjednoczona Partia Robotnicza (Archive of Modern Records, Polish United Workers' Party, Warsaw, Poland, hereafter AAN, PZPR), Z634.

33 Simonov, *Glazami cheloveka moego pokoleniia*, pp. 236–37.

34 Beria's control over documents is discussed in Naumov, "Repression and Rehabilitation," pp. 103–04, and Barsukov, "Analiticheskaia zapiska," pp. 25–26. Beria's possession of incriminating material on Malenkov was alleged at the July 1957 Central Committee plenum at which Khrushchev finally defeated the so-called antiparty group. See the transcript published in "Posledniaia 'antipartiinaia' gruppa," no. 3 (1993), p. 22, and no. 1 (1994), p. 57. Malenkov was reportedly the subject of a 1938 denunciation by Yezhov and of "evidence" indicating his role in a planned assassination of Kaganovich.

35 Speaking at the July 1953 Central Committee plenum that indicted Beria, Khrushchev recalled (whether accurately or not isn't clear) how Beria had responded to a question from the Hungarian party leader Mátyás Rákosi a month before. Rákosi asked how policy making should be divided between the party Central Committee and the Council of Ministers. Beria replied: "What do you mean, the Central Committee? Let the Council decide everything, and let the Central Committee occupy itself with cadres and propaganda." See Boris Starkov, "Sto dnei Liubianskogo marshala," *Istochnik,* no. 4 (1993), p. 88. Also see Knight, *Beria,* p. 183.

36 Simonov in *Glazami cheloveka moego pokoleniia,* p. 247. Author's interview with Pyotr Demichev. Author's interview with Sergo Mikoyan, October 1987. According to Sergo Beria, his father regarded the party as "a superstructure that accomplished nothing concrete, yet controlled everything without being responsible for anything." *Beria, My Father,* p. 295.

37 Sergo Beria's summary of his father's reforms is in *Beria, My Father,* pp. 259–68. For a more objective account, see Knight, *Beria.*

38 Sudoplatov, *Special Tasks,* p. 314.

39 Beria also dropped the Mingrelian case, in which he himself had been Stalin's target, and, citing a deported Volga German's heartrending letter to the Presidium, began reexamining the status of Germans exiled by Stalin. Documents proposing almost all these moves are collected in "'Novyi kurs' L. P. Berii," IA, no. 4 (1996), pp. 132–64. Further information about the amnesty, the Mikhoels case, and the doctors' plot secret letter is in Barsukov, "Analiticheskaia zapiska," pp. 24, 30, 33–34. After the April amnesty, hundreds of thousands of petty criminals began pouring into Moscow and other cities. Beria's rivals and others later accused him of trying to form a mass following of former criminals, whose activities also required the presence of Ministry of the Interior troops in cities plagued by sudden crime waves. In retrospect, others doubt that was Beria's main purpose. See Roy A. Medvedev and Zhores A. Medvedev, *Khrushchev: The Years in Power* (New York: Columbia University Press, 1976), p. 9, and Barsukov, "Analiticheskaia zapiska," p. 30. The episode is also the subject of a film by Aleksandr Proshkin, *Cold Summer of 1953.*

40 Konstantin Simonov, "Strashnyi chelovek," in *Beria: konets kar'ery,* pp. 188–89.

41 Iu. Krotkov, "Ia vypolnial prikaz Berii," in *Beria: konets kar'ery,* p. 257.

42 Beria's June 8 memorandum to the Presidium about the ethnic composition of the Byelorussian MVD is in "'Novyi kurs' L. P. Berii," pp. 157–59. Further information about his nationality policy is in Starkov, "Sto dnei 'Lubianskogo marshala," pp. 87–88, and in "Lavrentii Beriia: 'Cherez 2–3 goda,'" p. 11. Beria's maneuvers in western Ukraine are summarized in Knight, *Beria,* pp. 188–89, and interpreted in Sudoplatov, *Special Tasks*, p. 357. His call to Strokach was cited by Malenkov at the July 1953 Central Committee plenum that took place after Beria's arrest; see the transcript in "Delo Berii: plenum TsK KPSS, iiul' 1953 goda—stenograficheskii otchet," *Izvestiia TsK KPSS*, no. 1 (1991), pp. 141–42. Incriminating information about Beria provided at this plenum is not always reliable, but Sudoplatov's account tends to confirm it in this case. Mark Kramer rejects the notion that Beria's memorandum posed a threat to Khrushchev. See Mark Kramer, "The Early Post-Stalin Succession Struggle and Upheavals in East-Central Europe: Internal-External Linkages in Soviet Policy-Making, Parts 1–3," *Journal of Cold War Studies*, vol. 1, no.1 (Winter 1999), pp. 3–55; no. 2 (Spring 1999), pp. 3–38; no. 3 (Fall 1999), pp. 3–66 (hereafter cited by abbreviated title and issue number). Kramer makes this argument in no. 2, pp. 20–21.

43 The text of the letter is in Starkov, "Sto dnei,"p. 86.

44 Transcript of Soviet-Hungarian talks, June 13, 1953, found in the Hungarian Central Archives, published by Gyorgy T. Varga in *Multunk*, nos. 2–3 (1992), pp. 234–69, trans. Monica Borbely for Christian F. Ostermann, ed., *Uprising in East Germany, 1953: The Cold War, the German Question and the First Major Upheaval Behind the Iron Curtain* (Budapest: Central European University Press, 2001), pp. 144–54.

45 In the absence of a transcript of the May 27 meeting, the memoirs of people who had reason to distance themselves from Beria are the basis for this account. Sudoplatov (*Special Tasks*, p. 364) reported Beria instructed him to prepare secret intelligence probes designed to test Western receptivity to his idea. Beria's comments at the May 27 meeting were cited by Molotov in Chuev, *Sto sorok besed*, p. 333, and by Andrei Gromyko, *Memoirs* (New York: Doubleday, 1989), p. 317; Mikoian, *Tak bylo*, p. 584; and Shepilov, "Vospominaniia," VI, no. 8 (1998), p. 13. Mark Kramer challenges this interpretation, insisting instead that Beria and his colleagues agreed on a significantly less radical stance toward East Germany. See Kramer, "The Early Post-Stalin Succession Struggle," no. 1, pp. 22–30, and no. 3, pp. 5–14. Hope M. Harrison contends that Beria's actual stance remains unclear in Harrison, "Soviet Policy toward Germany: March–August 1953," unpublished article, p. 24. For an account that details Molotov's preparation of draft reports in the days before May 27, see Vladislav Zubok, "Unacceptably Rude and Blatant on the German Question," paper prepared for delivery at conference on "The Crisis Year, 1953, and the Cold War," Potsdam, Germany, November 10–12, 1996, pp. 5–9. Zubok's paper was later published in Christoph Klessmann and Bernd Stoever, eds., *Krisenjahr des Kalten Krieges in Europa* (Cologne: Boehlau, 1999), pp. 29–48.

46 Beria's memorandum to Khrushchev is cited in Barsukov, "Khrushchev: Osnovnye vekhi eskalatsii vlasti." Paper prepared for delivery. (Providence, R.I.: Brown University, Khrushchev Centennial Conference, December 1994), p. 10. Sudoplatov (*Special Tasks*, p. 354) reports on Beria's phone conversations.

47 Transcript of July 1953 Central Committee plenum in "Delo Berii," *Izvestiia TsK KPSS*, no. 1 (1991), p. 150.

48 Chuev, *Sto sorok besed*, pp. 332, 436.

49 NK4, nos. 2–3, 1992, p. 94; NK1, p. 325.

50 July 1953 plenum transcript in "Delo Berii," *Izvestiia TsK KPSS*, no. 1 (1991), p. 158, and in D. M. Stickle, ed., *The Beria Affair: The Secret Transcripts of the Meetings Signaling the End of Stalinism* (New York: Nova Science Publishers, 1992), p. 23. For a full unedited transcript, see *Lavrentii Beriia—1953: Stenogramma iiul'skogo plenuma TsK KPSS i drugie dokumenty* (Moscow: Mezhdunarodnyi fond, "Demokratiia," 1999).

51 Krotkov, "Ia vypolnil prikaz," p. 256.

52 See Sudoplatov, *Special Tasks*, pp. 358–59, 372–73.

53 Khrushchev characterized Beria's position on Germany and on nationality policy at the July 1953 Central Committee plenum. See transcript in "Delo Berii," *Izvestiia TsK KPSS*, no. 1 (1991), pp. 153, 157. Khrushchev's memorandum "On the Situation in Latvia," along with a draft Central Committee resolution on the same subject, in RGANI, f. 5, op. 30, d. 6, ll. 20–29, is discussed in Zubkova, "The Rivalry with Malenkov." See also Kramer, "The Early Post-Stalin Succession Struggle," no. 3, p. 5, and Kaganovich, *Pamiatnye zapiski*, p. 500. The Komsomol episode is recounted by Aleksandr Shelepin in "Istoriia—uchitel' surovyi," *Trud*, March 14, 1991, p. 4. Simonov's recollection is in *Glazami cheloveka moego pokoleniia*, pp. 250–51.

54 Author's interview with Pyotr Demichev.

55 Malenkov took credit in later conversations with his son. Author's interview with Andrei Malenkov.

56 "Khrushchev took the initiative into his hands," recalled Molotov. "He was without doubt a good organizer, and he was an active and effective one in preparing the meeting that took care of Beria." Malenkov was "weak-willed, extremely so, in fact, whereas I considered then, and I still do, that Khrushchev rendered us a great service." Chuev, *Sto sorok besed*, pp. 343, 345. Mikoian, *Tak bylo*, p. 586.

57 NK1, p. 331.

58 Plenum transcript in "Delo Berii," *Izvestiia TsK KPSS*, no. 1 (1991), p. 155. Also see NK4, nos. 2–3, 1992, pp. 94–95. Beria's June 15, 1953, proposal to the Presidium, along with a draft Presidium resolution to give it effect, are in "'Novyi kurs' L. P. Berii," pp. 160–61.

59 For Khrushchev's account of the German confrontation see NK4, nos. 2–3, 1992, p. 94. Molotov's version, which credits Khrushchev with forcing Beria to yield, is in Chuev, *Sto sorok besed*, pp. 332–36. Malenkov's position is portrayed variously: Khrushchev insisted Malenkov sided with Beria; Andrei Gromyko said Malenkov backed Molotov; see Gromyko, *Memoirs*, pp. 317–18. Gromyko would appear to be the most objective observer, but in his animus against Khrushchev, he didn't even mention Khrushchev's presence at the meeting. Most likely, Malenkov took an ambiguous position that various participants interpreted differently. For a later account, see Zubok, "Unacceptably Rude and Blatant," pp. 2–9.

60 Molotov remembered being approached by Khrushchev only two days before Beria was arrested. See Chuev, *Sto sorok besed*, p. 343.

61 NK1, p. 331. It is possible that a massive uprising which broke out in East Germany between June 17 and 20, 1953, gave Khrushchev a chance by requiring Beria's presence in Berlin to put it down. For more about this uprising, see Chapter 12.

62 Author's interview with Andrei Malenkov. Also see Malenkov, *O moem ottse*, p. 66. Andrei Malenkov's testimony is not fully reliable, but this part of his account seems plausible.

63 NK1, p. 332.

64 Khrushchev's memoirs quote Malenkov on the conversation; see NK4, nos.

2–3, 1992, p. 99. Molotov said (Chuev, *Sto sorok besed,* p. 343) the phone covering occurred in Khrushchev's initial meeting with Voroshilov, but in view of the latter's reaction on that occasion, that seems unlikely.

65 NK1, p. 334.

66 See ibid., p. 333, and NK4, nos. 2–3, 1992, p. 98.

67 NK1, p. 337, contends that Mikoyan actually defended Beria, arguing that he could be useful if allowed to remain in the leadership. Mikoian, *Tak bylo,* pp. 586–87. Author's interview with Sergo Mikoyan, October 1987. SK4, pp. 35–36. Nikita Khrushchev also reported that recruiting Saburov for the coup wasn't difficult but that Pervukhin, the other junior member of the Presidium, was more cautious. The best Malenkov could get out of him was an ominous "I'll think it over." Khrushchev's crudeness proved more productive. "If Malenkov had put it to me as clearly as you have done," Pervukhin told Khrushchev, "there wouldn't have been any question in my mind. I agree with you entirely. There's no alternative."

68 July 1953 plenum transcript in "Delo Berii," *Izvestiia TsK KPSS,* no. 1 (1991), p. 158, and in Stickle, *The Beria Affair,* p. 23.

69 July 1953 plenum transcript in "Delo Berii," *Izvestiia TsK KPSS,* no. 1 (1991), p. 173.

70 See Knight, *Beria,* p. 196; Iurii Zhukov, "Bor'ba za vlast' v partiino-gosudarstvennykh verkhakh SSSR vesnoi 1953 goda," VI, nos. 5–6 (1996), p. 56; NK4, nos. 2–3 (1992), p. 99.

71 NK1, pp. 335–36.

72 This account is based on G. K. Zhukov, "Riskovannaia operatsia" and K. S. Moskalenko "Kak byl arestovan Beria," in *Beria: Konets kar'ery,* pp. 281–88; Valentin Moskolenko, "Iiun' 1953," *Zhurnalist,* no. 7 (1991), p. 64; Knight, *Beria,* pp. 196–97; Sudoplatov, *Special Tasks,* p. 370; NK4, nos. 2–3 (1992), pp. 99, 101. See also a long-unpublished chapter of Marshal Zhukov's memoirs, "Ia pishu kak bylo, ia nikogo ne shchazhu," IA, no. 3 (1999), pp. 45–46.

73 Mark Kramer cites draft remarks prepared by Malenkov, as well as the latter's marginal notations, but it is not clear from that document, still preserved in the archives, how many of these remarks Malenkov actually delivered. See Kramer, "The Early Post-Stalin Succession Struggle," no. 2, pp. 28–32.

74 NK1, pp. 336–37. Mikoian, *Tak bylo,* p. 588. Mikoyan and several others who had not been told that Beria would be arrested seemed shocked. See account of one of the arresting officers, Ivan Zub, in "Zadanie osobogo svoistva: istoriia i sud'by," *Krasnaia zvezda* (March 19, 1988), p. 6.

75 Kramer, "The Early Post-Stalin Succession Struggle," no. 2, pp. 34–35; Knight, *Beria,* pp. 198–99; SK4, p. 36.

76 See Malenkov, *O moem ottse,* pp. 66–67. Malenkov made a similar case in an interview with the author, as did Sukhanov in an another interview.

77 In an extraordinary exchange at the June 1957 Central Committee plenum that ratified Khrushchev's defeat of Malenkov, Molotov, and Kaganovich, Malenkov claimed that Beria's police had bugged his fourth-floor apartment on Granovsky Street, whereupon Khrushchev retorted that since the listening devices were placed over his own fifth-floor apartment, it was his place, not Malenkov's, that had been bugged. See "Posledniaia 'anti-partiinaia gruppa,' " no. 3 (1994), p. 25. Adzhubei cites a possible Serov role in *Krushenie illiuzii,* pp. 99, 101.

78 NK4, nos. 2–3, 1992, p. 99.

79 See Volkogonov, *Sem' vozhdei*, pp. 346–48, 353–54; Knight, *Beria*, pp. 201–03, 222; Chuev, *Sto sorok besed*, p. 340; NK4, nos. 2–3, 1992, p. 102. Three Beria letters to Malenkov and others are in "Lavrentii Beriia: 'Cherez 2–3 goda,' " pp. 3–14.

80 See Volkogonov, *Sem' vozhdei*, p. 353; Knight, *Beria*, pp. 217–19.

81 For a summary of the interrogation and trial, along with a list of documents about both that have been released, see Kramer, "The Early Post-Stalin Succession Struggle," no. 2, pp. 35–38. Also see A. Antonov-Ovseenko, "Put' naverkh," in *Beria: Konets kar'ery*, pp. 138–39; Radzinsky, *Stalin*, p. 580; Sudoplatov, *Special Tasks*, p. 428, footnote 9. Sergo Beria is convinced, although he has no evidence, that his father was in fact killed on June 26, 1953, and that a double of Beria was executed instead in December. See *Beria, My Father*, p. 271.

82 The plenum transcript is in *Izvestiia TsK KPSS*, no. 1 (1991), pp. 140–214, and no. 2 (1991), pp. 141–208, and in *Lavrenty Beria—1953*. The former text is translated in Stickle, *The Beria Affair*. Simonov, *Glazami cheloveka moego pokoleniia*, pp. 246–47.

83 Author's interview with Rada Adzhubei; SK4, pp. 38–41.

84 Adzhubei, *Krushenie illiuzii*, pp. 100, 117.

85 The Crimean anecdote was recounted by Igor Chernoutsan, who headed the Central Committee's Literature Section under Khrushchev, in an unpublished draft memoir, provided to the author by Chernoutsan's family. The 1960 incident was witnessed by Fyodor Burlatsky, who recounted it in *Khrushchev*, pp. 35–40. Burlatsky reported that Yuri Andropov, who was present, "considered it out of place to discuss such matters with a crowd around" and looked as if he felt "embarrassed for Khrushchev."

86 Author's interview with Sergo Mikoyan, October 1987. Benediktov, "O Staline i Khrushcheve," p. 52. According to Malenkov's former son-in-law Vladimir Shamberg, Malenkov was convinced by aides to agree to Khrushchev's promotion. See Shamberg, "Stalin's Last Inner Circle," pp. 40–41.

87 See SK4, pp. 60–63. The description of the villas and their courtyards (in later years occupied by the embassies of Thailand and the Republic of Guinea) draws on a visit by the author in 1993.

88 Shamberg, "Stalin's Last Inner Circle," p. 41. The possibility of a Khrushchev-Malenkov alliance, along with the question of why it didn't endure, is raised by Zubkova in "The Rivalry with Malenkov." Also see a different version of this article, E. Iu. Zubkova, "Malenkov i Khrushchev: Lichnyi faktor v politike poslestalinskogo rukovodstva," *Otechestvennaia istoriia*, no. 4 (1995), pp. 99–115.

89 See Tompson, *Khrushchev*, pp. 125, 130, and Shamberg, "Stalin's Last Inner Circle," p. 40.

90 Tompson, *Khrushchev*, p. 130.

91 Author's interview with Gennady Voronov. Benediktov, "O Staline i Khrushcheve," pp. 47, 52; Aleksandr Shelepin, "Istoriia—uchitel' surovyi," *Trud*, March 14, 1991.

92 Chuev, *Sto sorok besed*, p. 359. Nikolai Yegorychev, then a district party boss, was delighted with Khrushchev's "heroic" defeat of Beria and his later moves against "the old Stalinist guard." Author's interview with Nikolai Yegorychev, August

1993. Kirill Mazurov, appointed Byelorussian premier in November 1953, liked the way Khrushchev attacked agricultural "serfdom," under which peasants "barely eked out the most miserable sort of existence." Kirill Mazurov, "Ia govoriu ne tol'ko o sebe," *Sovetskaia Rossiia*, February 18, 1989. Kaganovich contended: "If only Khrushchev had preserved later on the style of work he showed during his first year as first secretary, the results would have been different." Kaganovich, *Pamiatnye zapiski*, p. 502.

93 See remarks exchanged at the June 1957 plenum as published in "Posledniaia 'antipartiinaia' gruppa," no. 3 (1993), p. 22; no. 1 (1994), p. 57.

94 Naumov, "Repression and Rehabilitation," p. 103.

95 See Zubkova, "The Rivalry with Malenkov," pp. 77–78.

96 Andrei Malenkov, *O moem ottse*, p. 73; Roy Medvedev, *All Stalin's Men*, p. 157.

97 Malenkov's remarks, dating from August 1953 and March 1954 respectively, are cited in Zubok and Pleshakov, *Inside the Kremlin's Cold War*, pp. 155, 166. Also see James G. Richter, *Khrushchev's Double Bind: International Pressures and Domestic Coalition Politics* (Baltimore: Johns Hopkins University Press, 1994).

98 Fyodor Burlatsky's description cited by Andrei Malenkov in *O moem ottse*, p. 71.

99 Chuyev, *Sto sorok besed*, p. 358. Mikoian, *Tak bylo*, pp. 599–600. In his memoirs, Khrushchev said that Malenkov pressed him to make the leadership's first statement on agriculture, that he declined because he wasn't ready with concrete proposals, but that he knew "how ill equipped [Malenkov] was to deal with agriculture," since "even Malenkov himself acknowledged his own limitations in this regard." NK2, p. 119. Khrushchev's main charge against Malenkov, who had been officially in charge of agriculture during Stalin's last years, was that he had declared the country's grain problem "solved" in 1952. But that was more Stalin's view than Malenkov's, and historian Yelena Zubkova considers that Malenkov was among the leaders best informed about the real state of agriculture in 1953. Zubkova traces the initial preparation of reform proposals by Malenkov's staff, the scheduling of an August 1953 Central Committee plenum at which Malenkov was to introduce them, the decision to delay the plenum until September with Khrushchev making the main speech, and Malenkov's outlining the plans anyway in an August speech to the USSR Supreme Soviet. See Zubkova, "The Rivalry with Malenkov," pp. 77–79.

100 Strelianyi, "Poslednii romantik," pp. 193–95.

101 Memorandum to Presidium, January 22, 1954, in Stroi, vol. 1, pp. 85–87. The eight volumes of this work contain Khrushchev's speeches and memorandums on agriculture.

102 Both Andrei Malenkov (in an interview with the author) and Yelena Zubkova ("The Rivalry with Malenkov," p. 81) cite Khrushchev's deeper collectivist prejudices to argue that Malenkov, not he, was the main author of agricultural innovations. But for the time being, with the countryside in desperate straits and at the height of a struggle for power, Khrushchev wasn't about to let his own convictions stand in his way.

103 Speeches in Saratov, March 18, 1955, and Leningrad, April 12, 1955, in Stroi, vol. 2, pp. 27, 126–27.

104 The following account is based mainly on the author's interviews with

Andrei Shevchenko, August and October 1993. Khrushchev referred to his clash with Kazakh party leaders in NK2, pp. 120–121.

105 One hectare equals 2.47 acres. Khrushchev mentioned in his memoirs that relatives in a village near Kalinovka were resettled in Siberia in 1908; see NK4, no. 12, 1994, p. 102.

106 Assuming an average harvest of 10–11 centners (100 kilograms or 220.46 pounds) per hectare, Khrushchev figured the new lands would yield 800–900 million extra poods (1 pood equals 36.113 pounds) of grain, including 70 million in 1954. Memorandum to Presidium, January 22, 1954, in Stroi, vol. 1, p. 89.

107 See Medvedev and Medvedev, *The Years in Power*, p. 59.

108 SK4, pp. 50–51; Adzhubei, *Krushenie illiuzii*, pp. 119–20.

109 Barsukov, "Analitichesakaia zapiska," pp. 60–63;

110 Volkogonov, *Sem' vozhdei*, p. 360; Barsukov, "The Rise to Power," in *Nikita Khrushchev*, ed. Taubman, Khrushchev, and Gleason, pp. 51–52; A. Openkin, *Ottepel': Kak eto bylo (1953–1955 gg.)* (Moscow: Izdatel'stvo "Znanie", 1991), pp. 53–56.

111 Openkin, *Ottepel'*, pp. 53–55; Barsukov, "Analiticheskaia zapiska," p. 78.

112 Enver Hoxha, *The Artful Albanian*, ed. Jon Halliday (London: Chatto and Windus, 1986), p. 153; Enver Hoxha, *The Khrushchevites: Memoirs* (Tirana: 8 Nenteri Publishing House, 1980), pp. 36–37.

113 SK4, pp. 62–63. Author's interview with Andrei Shevchenko, October 1993.

114 Draft resolution of the Central Committee plenum of January 25–31, 1955, in RGANI, f. 2, op. 1, d. 116. Excerpts from speeches at the plenum by Khrushchev, Molotov, and Kaganovich, in RGANI, f. 2, op. 1, d. 127.

115 According to his son, Malenkov was so deeply chagrined by Khrushchev's betrayal that he never again mentioned the January 1955 plenum. Andrei Malenkov, *O moem ottse*, pp. 75–76.

116 Most of the indictment wasn't made public when Malenkov stepped down and was superseded by Bulganin. The statement Malenkov read to the Supreme Soviet submissively asked to be replaced by "some other comrade who possesses greater experience in state affairs." See Openkin, *Ottepel'*, pp. 58–60. According to Seweryn Bialer, then a Polish Central Committee official, "we were indignant at the way in which Malenkov had been removed, rather like a schoolboy, and not like the Premier of a great country. . . ." Bialer and his friends also found the Kremlin's explanation, contained in a secret letter to foreign Communist leaders, "absurd." How could Malenkov be responsible for the farm crisis if Khrushchev had been party boss of "the granary of the Soviet Union"? If Malenkov knew so little about agriculture, how could Bulganin, who "never had anything to do with farming," know any more? As for rank-and-file Soviet Communists, one factory shop party organizer complained, "In my opinion, Comrade Malenkov took too much of the blame on himself. Surely he isn't the only one guilty of mistakes. All the workers in my shop reacted badly to his statement [to the Supreme Soviet]. People don't take seriously the argument about his lack of experience. It would have been better to base it on the state of his health." U.S. Congress, Senate, Committee on the Judiciary, Subcommittee to Investigate the Administration of the Internal Security Act and Other Internal Security Laws, *On the Scope of Soviet Activity in the United States: Hearing*, 84th Cong., 2d sess., June 8, 11, and 12, 1956, pt. 29, p. 1559.

117 So testified Oleg Troyanovsky, who at that time worked for Molotov but later became Khrushchev's foreign policy assistant. See Troianovskii, *Cherez gody i rasstoianiia*, p. 176.

118 So said both Khrushchev and Saburov at the July 1955 Central Committee plenum that subjected Molotov to withering criticism. Saburov's remarks in transcript of evening session on July 11, 1955, RGANI, f. 2, op. 1, d. 175, l, 179; Khrushchev's concluding speech in transcript of morning session on July 12, 1955, RGANI, f. 2, op. 1, d. 161., l. 292.

119 Khrushchev's concluding speech at July 1955 plenum, RGANI, f. 2, op. 1, d. 176, ll. 290–91.

120 Chuev, *Sto sorok besed*, p. 346.

121 NK2, p. 122.

122 Transcript of Khrushchev's concluding speech, RGANI, f. 2, op. 1, d. 176, ll. 290–91, 294.

123 Chuev, *Sto sorok besed*, pp. 346–47.

124 NK2, pp. 98–101.

125 NK1, pp. 377–78.

126 Ibid., pp. 377–79.

127 This visit, including Khrushchev's erratic conduct as delegation leader, is described in some detail in Chapter 13.

128 This Molotov-Khrushchev exchange occurred during Molotov's main speech at the evening session on July 9, 1955, RGANI, f. 2, op. 1, d. 172. Khrushchev's Korean revelation appears on p. 80 of a typed draft of minutes of the session.

129 The crossfire continued as others spoke. Bulganin: "Molotov kept constantly attacking us, saying we weren't Leninists, that we were opportunists, especially Comrade Khrushchev." Molotov: "I got soundly attacked too, of course." Khrushchev: "We have strong fists too, and we gave you no quarter."

130 Kaganovich's speech at evening session on July 11, 1955, RGANI, f. 2, op. 1, d. 175, l. 38.

131 Molotov's speech at morning session on July 12, 1955, RGANI, f. 2, op. 1, d. 161, l. 229.

132 Khrushchev's concluding speech, RGANI, f. 2, op. 1, d. 176, l. 295.

133 In the meantime, however, the plenum promoted Khrushchev's Ukrainian client, Kirichenko, to full member of the Presidium and replaced Malenkov's man on the Secretariat, Shatalin, with three seeming Khrushchevites, including *Pravda* editor Dmitri Shepilov. Within a year Shepilov replaced Molotov as foreign minister.

134 Khrushchev's concluding speech, RGANI, f. 2, op. 1, d. 176, l. 295.

CHAPTER 11. FROM THE SECRET SPEECH TO THE HUNGARIAN REVOLUTION: 1956

1 Robert Conquest, *Power and Policy: The Study of Soviet Dynastics* (New York: St. Martin's Press, 1961), p. 277.

2 *Pravda*, February 15, 1956, p. 1.

3 Vittorio Vidali, *Diary of the Twentieth Congress of the Communist Party of the Soviet Union*, trans. Nell Amter Cattonar and A. M. Elliot (Westport, Conn. Lawrence Hill and Co., 1974), p. 15.

4 Ibid., p. 20.

5 *Pravda,* February 18, 1956, p. 4.

6 Vidali, *Diary of the Twentieth Congress,* pp. 26, 39. Although there were no explicitly positive or adverse reactions in the hall to Khrushchev's and Mikoyan's anti-Stalinist hints, the congress received a telegram from a low-level Czechoslovak party official protesting Mikoyan's comment and two telegrams hailing it, one from the Fourth (Trotskyite) International in Paris and another from Trotsky's widow, Natalia Sedova-Trotskaya, in Mexico. A third telegram supporting the use of the term "cult of personality" reportedly came from none other than Stalin's wayward son, Vasily. See "Vasilii Stalin za ottsa otvechat' ne khotel," *Obshchaia gazeta,* February 15–21, 1996, p. 9.

7 "O kul'te lichnosti i ego posledstviiakh: doklad pervogo sekretaria TsK KPSS tov. Khrushcheva N. S. XX s"ezdu Kommunisticheskoi partii Sovetskogo Soiuza," in *Izvestiia TsK KPSS,* no 3 (1989), pp. 131, 133, 137, 145–46, 155. An earlier draft is in RGANI, f. 1, op. 2, d. 16, ll. 1–172.

8 "O kul'te lichnosti," pp. 149, 154, 159, 160.

9 For many years, a debate raged in the West on whether Stalin betrayed Lenin or in fact fulfilled his totalitarian legacy. For a statement of the latter position, see Martin Malia, *The Soviet Tragedy: A History of Socialism in Russia, 1917–1991* (New York: Free Press, 1994). For the former, see Stephen F. Cohen, *Rethinking the Soviet Experience: Politics and History since 1917* (New York: Oxford University Press, 1985). A similar public debate, which began in the USSR during the Gorbachev years and has continued in the post-Soviet era, has more or less been resolved, except for Communists, against Khrushchev's point of view.

10 "O kul'te lichnosti," pp. 162–64.

11 Ibid., p. 165.

12 Semichastny's recollections appear in "Taina zakrytogo doklada," *Sovershenno sekretno,* no. 1, 1996, p. 4. Author's interview with Zakhar Glukhov. Author's interview with Dmitri Goriunov. Yakovlev quoted in Iurii V. Aksiutin's presentation to a Gorbachev Foundation conference on the Twentieth Congress in "Replika," *XX s"ezd: materialy konferentsii k 40-letiiu XX s"ezda KPSS* (Moscow: "Aprel'-85," 1996), p. 127. Author's interview with Aleksandr N. Yakovlev.

13 Chernoutsan, unpublished draft memoir, pp. 8–9. The official version of this passage is in "O kul'te lichnosti," p. 149.

14 Aleksei Adzhubei cited Nurridin Mukhitdinov, appointed a Presidium candidate member at the Twentieth Congress, as the source for this. Adzhubei, *Krushenie illiuzii,* p.159. Also see Nuriddin Mukhitdinov, *Gody provedennye v Kremle* (Tashkent: Izdatel'stvo narodnogo naslediia imeni Abdully Kadyri, 1994), pp. 169–76. Yakovlev remembered that Khrushchev's colleagues looked "depressed." Author's interview with Yakovlev.

15 Chernoutsan, unpublished draft memoir, pp. 8–9.

16 Ibid., p. 10.

17 Burlatsky, *Khrushchev,* pp. 35–35, 39–40, 63–64.

18 Conquest, *Power and Policy,* p. 279.

19 See Vladimir P. Naumov, "K istorii sekretnogo doklada N. S. Khrushcheva," in *XX s"ezd: materialy konferentsii,* pp. 12–13.

20 Data on numbers released and still held, as well as on information provided to relatives, in Barsukov, "Analiticheskaia zapiska," pt. I, pp. 24, 85. The incident involving K. B. Bogomolova-Gamarnik is cited in Naumov, "Repression and Rehabilitation," pp. 98–99.

21 Noted in Barsukov, "Analiticheskaia zapiska," pt. II, pp. 2, 5.

22 Adzhubei recalled this in *Krushenie illiuzii,* p. 167.

23 NK1, pp. 344–45.

24 Mikoyan, who also claimed not to have "fully comprehended" the extent of "unlawful arrests," said he was particularly shocked by personal accounts of torture. See Mikoian, *Tak bylo,* p. 589.

25 NK4, nos. 6–7, 1992, pp. 80–87.

26 Presidium and Central Committee documents containing the decision to call the Twentieth Congress are in RGANI, f. 1, op. 2, d. 1, ll. 4–5, 6–8, 19–12. On the pace of state security reexamination of cases, see Naumov, "Repression and Rehabilitation," p. 99. On the Khrushchev-Rudenko exchange, see Nikolai Barsukov, "XX s"ezd v retrospektive Khrushcheva," *Otechestvennaiia istoriia,* no. 4 (1996), p. 172. In another article ("Utverdit' dokladchikom tovarishcha Khrushcheva," *Moskovskie novosti,* no. 5 [4–11 February 1996], p. 34), Naumov speculates that one reason Khrushchev felt free to denounce Stalin in 1956 was that by then he had arranged the destruction of most documents that incriminated him in Stalin's crimes. Naumov cites Dmitri Volkogonov's claim that Khrushchev destroyed "eleven paper bags full of documents" from Beria's files and had Serov carry out a "great purge of the archives." But neither man cites conclusive proof, either that the key documents were destroyed by 1956 or that this influenced the timing and content of Khrushchev's speech. Sergei Khrushchev insisted that his father didn't have the power before 1956 to destroy such sensitive documents and that the KGB chief Ivan Serov, close though he was to Khrushchev, wouldn't have dared do so without authorization from the entire Presidium. Letter to author from Sergei Khrushchev, March 6, 1996.

27 Snegov's story is summarized in SK2, pp. 11–13, and recounted in more detail in Adzhubei, *Krushenie illiuzii,* pp. 161–67. Mikoyan emphasized the key roles of Snegov and Olga Shatunovskaya, another former prisoner, in *Tak bylo,* pp. 589–93. The material Snegov sent Khrushchev on February 1, 1956, is mentioned in "Vasilii Stalin ne otvechaet." Sergo Mikoyan refers to Olga Shatunovskaya, who had worked in the Moscow party organization in the thirties, in *XX s"ezd: materialy konferentsii,* p. 41, and Z. L. Serebriakova, a camp returnee, recalled how she and her son were banished from Moscow in the summer of 1955, in *XX s"ezd: materialy konferentsii,* p. 91.

28 Mikoian, *Tak bylo,* pp. 590–91. Sergo Mikoyan insisted his father and Khrushchev worked together—to the point of using the anti-Stalinist hint in Mikoyan's congress speech as a kind of trial balloon. See Sergo Mikoyan's recollection in *XX s"ezd: materialy konferentsii,* p. 42.

29 See Vladimir P. Naumov, "Bor'ba N. S. Khrushcheva za edinolichnuiu vlast'," NiNI, no. 2 (1996), p. 14, and Volkogonov, *Sem' vozhdei,* p. 369.

30 See Naumov, "Utverdit' dokladchikom tovarishcha Khrushcheva"; Volkogonov, *Sem' vozhdei,* pp. 369–70; NK3, p. 42; Nikolai Barsukov, "Zapiska Pospelova i doklad Khrushcheva," in *XX s"ezd: materialy konferentsii,* p. 50. Other members of the Pospelov commission were the Central Committee secretary Averki Aristov, the trade union chief Nikolai Shvernik, and Pyotr Komarov, vice-chairman of the Party Control Committee. Mikoyan (*Tak bylo,* pp. 591–92) recalled recommending that he himself sit on the commission along with Molotov and Voroshilov, but Khrushchev thought commissioners should not include Presidium members who had been particularly close to Stalin.

31 See Volkogonov, *Sem' vozhdei,* pp. 370–71; "O kul'te lichnosti," p. 145; Naumov, "K istorii sekretnogo doklada," p. 19. Later in 1956 Rodos was sentenced by the Military Collegium of the USSR Supreme Court to be shot.

32 Naumov, "Utverdit' dokladchikom tovarishcha Khrushcheva."

33 See transcript of June 1957 plenum in "Posledniaia 'anti-partiinaia gruppa," no. 4 (1993), p. 81, footnote 93; Naumov, "Utverdit' dokladchikom tovarishcha Khrushcheva"; Naumov, "Bor'ba N. S. Khrushcheva," p. 15; Mikoian, *Tak bylo,* p. 592.

34 Naumov, "Utverdit' dokladchikom tovarishcha Khrushcheva" and "K istorii sekretnogo doklada," p. 21.

35 See Naumov, "Utverdit' dokladchikom tovarishcha Khrushcheva" and "Bor'ba N. S. Khrushcheva," p. 15. Khrushchev's remarks to the Central Committee are in a verbatim stenographic report of the plenum on February 13, 1996, which the author has seen. The edited version of the same transcript is in RGANI, f. 2, op. 1, d. 181, ll. 2, 4–5. In his memoirs (NK4, nos. 6–7, 1992, p. 85) Khrushchev recalled suggesting that Pospelov give the speech but that other Presidium members insisted he himself do so. Mikoyan claimed to have proposed Pospelov, adding that it was Khrushchev who disagreed, saying, "If instead of giving the report himself, someone else does, it will be thought the Central Committee [first] secretary is evading his responsibility." Looking back long afterward, Mikoyan said Khrushchev "turned out to be right." *Tak bylo,* p. 594.

36 The chronology recounted here, established on the basis of documents and memoirs of participants, raises doubts about accounts by Khrushchev and Kaganovich; according to their memoirs, authorization for the speech came moments before it was actually delivered. Khrushchev recalled threatening to address the congress with or without Presidium approval (taking advantage of the party rule that once a congress was under way and the general Central Committee report had been given, party members were free to present their own views) and only thus obtained his colleagues' approval. Kaganovich remembered a last-minute scene in a crowded Presidium lounge where, with delegates already waiting in their seats, Khrushchev suddenly passed around a red-covered copy of his attack on Stalin and demanded immediate endorsement. In fact, the last-minute clash mentioned by both men concerned not the decision to authorize the speech, which was taken on February 13, but the text itself. See NK4, nos. 6–7, 1992, p. 84, and Kaganovich, *Pamiatnye zapiski,* pp. 508–09. For Yuri Aksiutin's different view—that the struggle over the speech occurred in the open rather than underground—see his article "Novye issledovanniia o XX s"ezde KPSS," reprinted in NK5, vol. 2, p. 780.

37 Naumov, "K istorii sekretnogo doklada," p. 21; Pospelov draft in RGASPI, f. 629, op. 1, d. 54, l. 107.

38 Text of Khrushchev's dictations, along with the Pospelov-Aristov draft, in "O kul'te lichnosti i ego posledstviiakh," *Istochnik,* no. 6 (2000), pp. 83–108. Also see Naumov, "K istorii sekretnogo doklada," p. 26; Barsukov, "XX s"ezd," p. 174; Volkogonov, *Sem' vozhdei,* pp. 373–74. According to Naumov, who has seen other dictations that did not get into the speech itself, one of them concerned a meeting at which Khrushchev sat opposite Stalin with a tall pile of papers between them. "What are you doing, hiding?" Stalin joked. "Don't worry, we're not going to arrest you now."

39 D. T. Shepilov, "'Ia byl prichasten k dokladu o kul'te lichnosti . . .': beseda s D. T. Shepilovym," interview by Nikolai Barsukov (February 23, 1989), *Ogonek,* no. 7 (February 1996), p. 66. Also see *I primknuvshii k nim Shepilov: pravda o cheloveke, uchenom, voine, politike* (Moscow: "Zvonnitsa-MG," 1998), p. 27.

40 The text of the February 23, 1956, version is in RGANI, f. 1, op. 2, d. 16, ll. 1–80. Pages with handwritten marks and corrections, which are not always fully visible, are in f. 1, op. 2, d. 16, ll. 84, 99, 100, 104, 110, 113, 123, 130, 133, 160–61, 164–72. Also see "Vasily Stalin za ottsa otvechat' ne khotel"; Iurii V. Aksiutin, "Novye dokumenty byvshego arkhiva TsK," in *XX s"ezd: materialy konferentsii,* p. 125.

41 Aksiutin, "Novye dokumenty," pp. 124–25.

42 Author's interview with Pyotr Demichev.

43 *XX s"ezd: materialy konferentsii,* p. 6.

44 See NK4, nos. 6–7, 1992, p. 84; SK4, p. 93.

45 Of full members of the Central Committee elected in 1956, 79 were carried over from the cohort selected as full or candidate members in 1952, while 41 were newly elected. Of candidate members chosen in 1956, 71 new faces joined 122 left over from the Nineteenth Congress. See Conquest, *Power and Policy,* pp. 398, 413, 423, and Tompson, *Khrushchev,* p. 161.

46 Chuev, *Sto sorok besed,* pp. 349–50.

47 Andrei Sakharov, "Vospominaniia," in *Znamia,* no. 11 (1990), p. 147. According to Sakharov, his fellow physicist Igor Tamm agreed, but not entirely: "Yes, I like Khrushchev; he is not Stalin. But it would be better if he differed from Stalin even more."

48 According to Sergei Khrushchev, when Malenkov first proposed building a series of Lenin Hills residences, Khrushchev "hesitated—wasn't it too expensive?—but then agreed." See SK2, p. 53.

49 Initially the Khrushchevs lived in the central residence on the Lenin Hills. Three years later they moved to the one on the far left facing downtown Moscow. It was the latter house that I subsequently visited and describe. But since all the residences resembled one another, with even the state-assigned furniture identical, a description of the second apparently applies to the first as well.

50 Khrushchev wanted the secret kept until he had spoken, and it was. Few knew the speech was coming, and no one who did would say it was, if for no other reason than in the end it might not actually be delivered. So Khrushchev told Aleksei Adzhubei. See *Krushenie illiuzii,* p. 145.

51 SK4, p. 99.

52 The editing reportedly shows which lines in the speech had been off Khrushchev's cuff and which were considered too strong even though they had been on paper all along. The former included the charge that Stalin had planned war operations on a globe, an exaggeration that was later held against Khrushchev by many generals, and his conversation with Bulganin about not knowing whether a visit to Stalin would end at home or in prison. The latter included Khrushchev's saying that

Stalin's war leadership had cost "millions of lives." The editors had also strengthened the warning at the end by adding the line about not "providing ammunition to enemies" by "baring our injuries." See "Vasily Stalini za ottsa otvechat' ne khotel" and Naumov, "K istorii sekretnogo doklada," pp. 30–31.

53 The Presidium decree is in "O kul'te lichnosti," p. 166.

54 Interview with a former Soviet high school teacher.

55 See Christian F. Ostermann, "East Germany and the Hungarian Revolution" (Budapest: "Hungary and the World, 1956: The New Archival Evidence," September 26–29, 1996, paper prepared for delivery), pp. 3–6.

56 See Leszek W. Gluchowski, "The Struggle against 'Great-Power Chauvinism': CPSU-PUWP Relations and the Roots of the Sino-Polish Initiative of September–October 1956" (Hong Kong: "New Evidence on the Cold War in Asia," January 1996), paper prepared for delivery.

57 Exactly how the Israelis got hold of the speech is unclear. The most fetching account has it that a thirty-one-year old Polish journalist of Jewish origin caught sight of a copy on the desk of his girlfriend, also secretly Jewish, who worked at Polish Communist headquarters, that he borrowed it for a while, and managed to get it copied and transferred to the Israeli Embassy. See Abraham Rabinovich, "The Man Who Touched History," *Jerusalem Post* (International Edition), December 9, 1995, pp. 20–21, and Yossi Melman and Dan Raviv, "The Leak of the Century," *Washington Post* (Outlook Section), March 27, 1994. For other accounts, see Leszek W. Gluchowski and Edward Jan Nalepa, "The Soviet-Polish Confrontation of October 1956: The Situation in the Polish Internal Security Corps," Working Paper no. 17, Cold War International History Project, Woodrow Wilson International Center for Scholars, April 1997; Ian Black and Benny Morris, *Israel's Secret Wars: A History of Israel's Intelligence Services* (New York: Grove, Weidenfeld, 1991), pp. 168–71; John Ranelagh, *The Agency: The Rise and Decline of the CIA* (New York: Simon & Schuster, 1987), p. 286; Allen Dulles, *The Craft of Intelligence* (New York: Harper & Row, 1963), pp. 81–82; Peter Grose, *Gentleman Spy: The Life of Allen Dulles* (Boston: Houghton Mifflin, 1994), p. 189; Toranska, *Them,* pp. 173–74.

58 NK1, p. 351.

59 Veljko Mićunović, *Moscow Diary,* trans. David Floyd (Garden City, N.Y.: Doubleday, 1980), pp. 18, 22, 26, 36.

60 Author's interview with Rada Adzhubei.

61 Adzhubei, *Krushenie illiuzii,* p. 145.

62 L. K. Chukovskaia, *Zapiski ob Anne Akhmatovoi,* vol. 2, *1952–1962* (Paris: YMCA Press, 1980), p. 137.

63 A partial listing of incidents, including the Thermo-Technical Laboratory meeting, is provided in Yuri Aksiutin, "Popular Responses to Khrushchev," in *Nikita Khrushchev,* ed. Taubman, Khrushchev, and Gleason, pp. 182–92. The Moscow University incident is described in Raisa Berg, *Sukhovei: vospominaniia genetika* (New York: Chalidze Publications, 1983), pp. 175–76. The Kabardinian episode is mentioned in Nikolai Barsukov, "The Reverse Side of the Thaw" (Moscow: "New Evidence on Cold War History," January 1993, pp. 8–9, paper prepared for delivery). A Russian version of the article is "Oborotnaia storona 'ottepeli' (Istoriko-dokumental'nyi ocherk)," *Kentavr,* no. 4 (July–August 1993), pp. 129–43. On the Siberian confusion, see N. S. Zlobin, "Khoroshikh diktatur ne byvaet," in *XX s"ezd: materialy konferentsii,* p. 99.

64 The KGB report is cited in "'Vasilii Stallin za ottsa otvechat' ne khotel." Mikhail Gorbachev, "Vstupitel'noe slovo," *XX s"ezd: materialy konferentsii,* p. 4; Gorbachev, *Memoirs* (New York: Doubleday, 1995), pp. 61–63. The pattern of ordinary citizens' praising purges of local officials who had lorded it over them had been established during the 1930s. See Sheila Fitzpatrick, "How the Mice Buried the Cat: Scenes from the Great Purges of 1937 in the Russian Provinces," *Russian Review,* vol. 52, no. 3 (July 1993), pp. 299–320.

65 See "'Ne dopustili kritiki Stalina,'" *Istochnik,* no. 6 (1995), pp. 62–68; SK4, p. 163; Mićunović, *Moscow Diary,* pp. 29–30, 33–34. The signs and shouts are noted in *Ottepel' 1953–1956: Stranitsy russkoi sovetskoi literatury* (Moscow: Moskovskii rabochii, 1989), p. 463. Casualties are cited in V. A. Kozlov, *Massovye besporiadki v SSSR pri Khrushcheve i Brezhneve (1953–nachalo 1980)* (Novosibirsk: Sibirskii khronograf, 1999), p. 160.

66 Although not published, the resolution was sent to all party organizations around country, along with strict instructions to prevent similar outbreaks. See Naumov, "Bor'ba N. S. Khrushcheva," p. 16.

67 The June 30 Central Committee resolution is translated in *The Anti-Stalin Campaign and International Communism,* edited by the Russian Institute of Columbia University (New York: Columbia University Press, 1956), pp. 275–306. In July the Central Committee ordered all party organizations to act against those who "incorrectly" understood what had occurred at the Twentieth Congress. See Naumov, "Bor'ba N. S. Khrushcheva," p. 16.

68 See Barsukov, "Zapiska Pospelova i doklad Khrushcheva," pp. 52–53, and Barsukov, "Analiticheskaia zapiska," pt. 2, p. 12. Mikoyan, who headed the Central Rehabilitation Commission, proposed the traveling troikas, which had the task of liberating people, not condemning them, at Snegov's suggestion. See *Tak bylo,* pp. 595–96.

69 Besides Molotov, Kaganovich, and Voroshilov, the commission included the Khrushchevites Aristov, Furtseva, and Rudenko. See Barsukov, "Analiticheskaia zapiska," pt. 2, pp. 26–27.

70 See NK1, p. 353.

71 Mićunović, *Moscow Diary,* pp. 38, 43–45. On the eve of the May Day holiday, the Yugoslav Embassy heard numerous criticisms of Khrushchev's crude personal style: "It is being said that he is coarse, unbalanced, too direct and impolite, and that such a person cannot be the leader of a great country like the Soviet Union." To judge by an informal "poll" the Yugoslavs had taken, Russians "still prefer people like Molotov and Malenkov, who appear bigger to Soviet people insofar as they are more remote from them . . . unlike Khrushchev, whom they all know well and who is just like them."

72 Ibid., pp. 59–75.

73 Mark Kramer, "New Evidence on Soviet Decision-making and the 1956 Polish and Hungarian Crises," *Cold War International History Project Bulletin* (hereafter CWIHPB), nos. 8–9 (Winter 1996–1997), p. 360; Gluchowski, "Struggle against 'Great Power Chauvinism,' " p. 44.

74 Charles Gati, *Hungary and the Soviet Bloc* (Durham, N.C.: Duke University Press, 1986), pp. 133–36.

75 See interview with Staszewski in Toranska, *Them,* pp. 155–56.

76 Quoted ibid., p. 164.

77 See NK4, no. 5, 1994, p. 73. For a summary of Polish leaders' reactions, see Gluchowski, "Struggle against 'Great-Power Chauvinism,'" pp. 6–11. Ochab is quoted in Toranska, *Them,* p. 55. Broader Polish reactions are examined in Tony Kemp-Welch, "Khrushchev's 'Secret Speech' and Polish Politics: The Spring of 1956," *Europe-Asia Studies,* vol. 48, no. 2 (1996), pp. 181–206.

78 On these Hungarian developments and Soviet reactions to them, see Kramer, "New Evidence on Soviet Decision-Making," pp. 363.

79 Notes taken of Soviet party Presidium meetings on July 9 and 12, 1956, by Vladimir N. Malin, head of the Central Committee's General Department, are in "Kak reshalis' 'voprosy Vengrii': Rabochie zapiski Prezidiuma TsK KPSS, iiul'-noiabr' 1956 g.," IA, no. 2 (1996), p. 77 (this article extends over two issues; hereafter it will be cited by abbreviated title and issue number).

80 A verbatim Russian transcript of Khrushchev's speech of March 20, 1956, is in AAN, PZPR, 2631, k. 14–87. An English translation of excerpts from the speech, along with an introduction by Leszek W. Gluchowski, is in "Khrushchev's Second Secret Speech," CWIHPB, no. 10 (March 1988), pp. 44–49.

81 Toranska, *Them,* pp. 169–72.

82 NK4, no. 4, 1994, p. 74; NK2, p. 200.

83 NK2, p. 200. Mikoyan recalled Khrushchev's request to him in an account of the trip that he dictated on May 28, 1960. Sergo Mikoyan elaborated on the account (part of which is in the Volkogonov Collection, LOC, reel 20) in a draft chapter of a memoir tentatively titled *Diplomatiia Mikoiana.* Ochab's recollection in Toranska, *Them,* pp. 75–76. Gomułka's report in Leszek W. Gluchowski, "Khrushchev, Gomułka and the 'Polish October,' " CWIHPB, no. 5 (Spring 1995), p. 40.

84 Gomułka's description of the Belvedere talks is in documents translated in Gluchowski, "Khrushchev, Gomułka and the 'Polish October,' " p. 40.

85 On Soviet and Polish troops mobilization, see Gluchowski and Nalepa, "The Soviet-Polish Confrontation of October 1956." Khrushchev's description of Gomułka, and the latter's words as recalled by Khrushchev, are in NK4, no. 4, 1994, pp. 75–76.

86 Mikoyan's May 28, 1960, account describes the flight home and the Presidium's rump session. Khrushchev's comments at October 21 and 22 Presidium meetings are in Malin's notes in "SSSR i Pol'she: oktiabr' 1956-go: Postanovleniia i rabochie zapisi zasedanii Prezidiuma TsK KPSS," IA, nos. 5–6 (1996), pp. 182–83. Khrushchev's remarks at the October 24 meeting are in Czech minutes of that meeting as translated by Mark Kramer in "Hungary and Poland, 1956: Khrushchev's CPSU CC Presidium Meeting on East European Crises, 24 October 1956." CWIHPB, no. 5 (Spring 1995), pp. 53–54.

87 This account of the Hungarian crisis relies heavily on Kramer, "New Evidence on Soviet Decision-Making and the 1956 Polish and Hungarian Crises."

88 Malin's notes of October 23, 1956, Presidium meeting in "Kak reshalis' 'voprosy Vengrii,'" no. 2, pp. 82–83.

89 See Kramer, "New Evidence on Soviet Decision-Making in the 1956 Polish and Hungarian Crises," p. 367.

90 See Malin's notes in "Kak reshalis' 'voprosy Vengrii,' " no. 2, pp. 88–95, and Mark Kramer's translation in "The 'Malin Notes' on the Crises in Hungary and

Poland, 1956," CWIHPB, nos. 8–9 (Winter 1996–1997), pp. 389–92.

91 Malin's notes in "Kak reshalis' 'voprosy Vengrii,' " no. 2, pp. 97–102, and in Kramer translation in "The 'Malin Notes,'" pp. 392–93.

92 SK4, pp. 185, 188.

93 Mićunović, *Moscow Diary,* pp. 133–34.

94 Khrushchev said he and his colleagues decided to intervene before Mao recommended doing so; see NK1, pp. 418–19. Yan Mingfu, who later served as Mao's interpreter in talks with Khrushchev, insisted, in remarks at a conference on "Sino-Soviet Relations and the Cold War," Beijing, October 1997, that the Chinese urged intervention before Khrushchev changed his mind. Also see Kramer, "New Evidence on Soviet Decision-Making," p. 373; and Chen Jian, "Beijing and the Hungarian Crisis of 1956" (Budapest: "Hungary and the World, 1956: The New Archival Evidence," September 26–29, 1996, paper prepared for delivery).

95 Malin's notes in "Kak reshalis' 'voprosy Vengrii,'" no. 3, p. 87.

96 See Kramer, "New Evidence on Soviet Decision-Making," pp. 369–70; Malin's notes in "Kak reshalis' 'voprosy Vengrii,' " no. 2, p. 92.

97 See NK4, no. 5, 1994, p. 80, and SK4, pp. 195–97.

98 Mikoian, *Tak bylo,* p. 598. See Malin's notes in "Kak reshalis' 'voprosy Vengrii,'" no. 3, pp. 94–108, and in Mark Kramer, "'Malin Notes,'" pp. 394–95.

99 NK1, pp. 420–21.

100 Mićunović, *Moscow Diary,* pp. 131, 141, 144.

CHAPTER 12. THE JAWS OF VICTORY: 1956–1957

1 Mićunović, *Moscow Diary,* p. 148.

2 Malin's notes in "Kak reshalis' 'voprosy Vengrii,' " no. 3, pp. 111–12, 117, and in Kramer, "'Malin Notes,'" pp. 398, 400.

3 Mićunović, *Moscow Diary,* pp. 159, 177–78, 205.

4 Ibid., pp. 187, 196.

5 Speech at a meeting of young people in Moscow in Stroi, vol. 1, p. 273.

6 *Pravda,* December 1, 1956, p. 1.

7 See Aksiutin, "Popular Responses to Khrushchev," pp. 192–93; Wolfgang Leonhard, *The Kremlin since Stalin,* trans. Elizabeth Wiskemann and Marian Jackson (New York: Praeger, 1962), p. 231; Vladimir Bukovsky, *To Build a Castle: My Life as a Dissenter,* trans. Michael Scammell (New York: Viking, 1979), p. 110.

8 See Aksiutin, "Popular Responses to Khrushchev," p. 193.

9 Undated report to N. S. Khrushchev from F. Kozlov, and February 12, 1957, report to the Central Committee from V. Churaev, head of the Central Committee's department of RSFSR party organs, in RGANI, f. 89, dokument 4, l. 4; dokument, 6, l. 1.

10 Other members included KGB chief Serov and chief procurator Rudenko as well as Malenkov and two other Central Committee secretaries.

11 Cited in Naumov, "Bor'ba N. S. Khrushcheva," p. 17.

12 Naumov, "Repression and Rehabilitation," p. 109. Barsukov, "Analiticheskaia zapiska," pp. 41–45; and Barsukov, "Reverse Side of the Thaw," pp. 19–22, 32–36.

13 The harvest saved the country from a major grain shortage caused by a drought in the western lands, the development of which Molotov had championed as an alternative to the crash program for the Virgin Lands.

14 Tompson, *Khrushchev,* pp. 172–74.

15 Mićunović, *Moscow Diary,* pp. 192–93.

16 This account draws on Tompson, *Khrushchev,* pp. 174–78; William J. Tompson, "Nikita Khrushchev and the Territorial Apparatus, 1953–1964," Ph.D. dissertation, University of Oxford, 1991, pp. 148–66; and William J. Tompson, "Industrial Management and Economic Reform under Khrushchev," in *Nikita Khrushchev,* ed. Taubman, Khrushchev, and Gleason, pp. 140–46.

17 Author's interview with Pyotr N. Demichev, who in 1957 was Moscow Province party leader.

18 Molotov is quoted in Chuev, *Sto sorok besed,* p. 347. See Kaganovich, *Pamiatnye zapiski,* p. 512. Khrushchev did indeed claim total credit for the reform in a later conversation with Mićunović; see *Moscow Diary,* p. 239. Speaking after the attempted coup against him had failed, Khrushchev accused Pervukhin and Shepilov of opposing him on economic regionalization. See "Posledniaia 'antipartiinaia' gruppa," no. 2 (1994), p. 20.

19 Transcript (undated) of Kozlov's talk, RGASPI, f. 556, op. 2, d. 664, ll. 111–17.

20 Mićunović, *Moscow Diary,* p. 241.

21 "Ia byl prichasten k dokladu o kul'te lichnosti," p. 67.

22 Anatolii Strelianyi provides general background for Khrushchev's speech in "Khrushchev and the Countryside," pp. 113–15. Citations from the speech are taken from a radio broadcast of it as translated into English in FBIS, May 24, 1957, pp. CC6–13.

23 Kaganovich, *Pamiatnye zapiski,* pp. 513–14.

24 Transcript (undated) of meeting of Moscow party activists, obtained by the author in Moscow, p. 43.

25 Interview as transcribed and translated in FBIS, June 4, 1957, p. BB4.

26 Author's interview with Maya Turovskaya.

27 See Leonhard, *Kremlin since Stalin,* pp. 77–79

28 See ibid., pp. 213–17; Harold Swayze, *Political Control of Literature in the USSR, 1946–1959* (Cambridge, Mass.: Harvard University Press, 1962), pp. 165–79; Dina Spechler, *Permitted Dissent in the USSR: Novy Mir and the Soviet Regime* (New York: Praeger, 1982), p. 66.

29 Swayze, *Political Control,* p. 189.

30 V. Kaverin, "Literaturnaia Moskva," in *Voprosy literatury,* no. 5 (1989), pp. 209–12.

31 Adzhubei, *Krushenie illiuzii,* p. 204.

32 The same Korneichuk was present when Chernoutsan delivered some draft remarks on Dudintsev's novel that Shepilov had ordered prepared for Khrushchev. Chernoutsan had been careful to keep them balanced and judicious, and having read them through, Shepilov approved. Yet the next day Khrushchev delivered "a loud and abusive speech reviling Dudintsev forwards and backwards and accusing him of all sorts of sins." When Chernoutsan asked Shepilov what had happened, the latter "brushed me off in irritation and annoyance."

33 Chernoutsan, unpublished draft memoir.

34 Adzhubei, *Krushenie illiuzii,* p. 205.

35 Chernoutsan, unpublished draft memoir; Vladimir Tendriakov, "Na blazhennom ostrove kommunizma," in *Svet i teni 'velikogo desiatiletiia,'* pp. 293–95; Sara Babenysheva, "Tsena prozreniia," in *SSSR: Vnutrennie protivorechiia,* no. 2, pp. 276–77; Chukovskaia, *Zapiski ob Anne Akhmatovoi,* vol. 2, p. 571. Note that although Tendryakov says the scene he describes occurred in July 1960, the authoritative documentary collection *Ottepel' 1957–1959: Stranitsy russkoi sovetskoi literatury* (Moscow: Moskovskii rabochii, 1990), pp. 380–81, confirms that Tendryakov's account actually depicts the May 19, 1957, meeting.

36 See Molotov's remark at the June 1957 Central Committee plenum in "Posledniaia 'antipartiinaia' gruppa," no. 3 (1993), p. 73, plus his recollection in Chuev, *Sto sorok besed,* p. 347.

37 According to Kaganovich, Khrushchev's chiding of Molotov confirmed the old saying "What the sober man has in his mind, the drunkard has on his tongue." Kaganovich, *Pamiatnye zapiski,* pp. 514–15.

38 Cited in Nikolai Barsukov, "Personal'noe delo 'anti-partiinoi gruppy,'" unpublished article, pp. 58–59.

39 See "Posledniaia 'antipartiinaia' gruppa," no. 3 (1993), p. 72, and no. 2 (1994), p. 9.

40 Cited in Nikolai Barsukov, *XX s"ezd KPSS i ego istoricheskie real'nosti* (Moscow: Izdatel'stvo politicheskoi literatury, 1991), p. 47.

41 See "Posledniaia 'antipartiinaia' gruppa," no. 3 (1993), p. 57. Author's interview with Andrei Malenkov.

42 "I agree with Klimenti Yefremovich in essence," Khrushchev commented, "but to talk this way to the Iranian ambassador, to say that they are merely courtiers—that's just not suitable." See "Posledniaia 'antipartiinaia gruppa," no. 5 (1993), p. 74.

43 Ibid., p. 57. "Ia byl prichasten k dokladu," p. 67.

44 Mićunović, *Moscow Diary,* p. 272.

45 Galina Vishnevskaya, *Galina: A Russian Story* (New York: Harcourt Brace Jovanovich, 1984), pp. 139, 145–48, 161–70.

46 "Posledniaia 'antipartiinaia' gruppa," no. 2 (1994), p. 39.

47 Ibid., no. 1 (1994), p. 35.

48 Ibid., no. 3 (1993), p. 63, no. 1, 1994, p. 50.

49 Ibid., no. 3 (1993), pp. 57–58, 60.

50 Chernoutsan, unpublished draft memoir.

51 Shepilov, "Vospominaniia," VI, no. 5 (1998), p. 18.

52 Mićunović, *Moscow Diary,* p. 210.

53 "Posledniaia 'antipartiinaia' gruppa," no. 2 (1994), p. 10.

54 Ibid., no. 4 (1993), p. 69.

55 Transcript of meeting of Leningrad Province party activitists, July 2, 1957, in RGASPI, f. 556, op. 2, d. 664, l. 141.

56 Mohamed Heikal, *The Sphinx and the Commissar: The Rise and Fall of Soviet Influence in the Middle East* (New York: Harper & Row, 1978), p. 92.

57 "Posledniaia 'antipartiinaia' gruppa," no. 1, 1994, p. 47.

58 Cited by Shepilov's grandson Dmitri Kosyrev in *I primknuvshii k nim Shepilov,* p. 29.

59 "Ia byl prichasten k dokladu o kul'te lichnosti," p. 67.

60 Charles Bohlen, *Witness to History, 1929–1969* (New York: Norton, 1973), p. 497.

61 On Malenkov's approach, see Zhukov, "Ia pishu kak bylo," p. 50. Bulganin is quoted in "Posledniaia 'antipartiinaia' gruppa," no. 3 (1993), pp. 29, 36, 48–49.

62 "Ia byl prichasten k dokladu o kul'te lichnosti," p. 67. According to Shepilov, Zhukov never forgave Khrushchev for ridiculing Stalin's wartime leadership, even though he had been cast down by Stalin. Although this claim seems odd, it may well be the case, as Timothy J. Colton has argued, that "the following words in Vasilevsky's memoirs could have been written equally well by Zhukov: 'I had good relations with Khrushchev in the first postwar years. But they changed sharply when I was unable to support his claims that Stalin did not know the particulars of operational and strategic matters and was incompetent as Supreme Commander-in-Chief. To this day, I cannot understand how he could say this. . . . Khrushchev must have known how great was the authority of Stavka and Stalin on questions of military leadership." See Colton, *Commissars, Commanders and Civilian Authority: The Structure of Soviet Military Politics* (Cambridge, Mass.: Harvard University Press, 1979), p. 1887.

63 See "Posledniaia 'antipartiinaia' gruppa," no. 3 (1993), p. 65.

64 Ibid., no. 5 (1993), p. 50.

65 Mićunović, *Moscow Diary*, pp. 278–79.

66 Mikoian, *Tak bylo*, pp. 597–98. Sergo Mikoyan remains outraged at Khrushchev's notion that his father was on the brink of betrayal: "How can he say that? It was my father who saved his neck!"

67 See "Posledniaia 'antipartiinaia' gruppa," no. 4 (1993), pp. 28–29; no. 1 (1994), p. 64.

68 Although the 250th anniversary of the founding of the city occurred in 1953, celebration of it had been delayed and was now scheduled for June 1957.

69 Barsukov, "Personal'noe delo," p. 33.

70 SK4, pp. 231–32. Zhukov, "Ia pishu kak bylo," p. 49.

71 Author's interview with Pyotr N. Demichev.

72 No transcripts were kept of this meeting or of the party Presidium sessions that followed it. This account is based mainly on descriptions given by speakers at the Central Committee plenum that began on June 22. Such descriptions are of course biased. This is especially true of those coming from the triumphant Khrushchev camp as well as from accounts contained in the Khrushchev, Kaganovich, and Molotov memoirs. Furthermore, such historians as Naumov and Barsukov rely on participant accounts. Nonetheless, I have tried to exclude testimony that seems particularly tendentious and include that which seems compatible with what is otherwise known about the situation and the participants. On the calling of the June 18 meeting and its attendance, see "Posledniaia 'antipartiinaia' gruppa," no. 3 (1993), pp. 14, 55; no. 4 (1993), pp. 29–31; no. 5 (1993), pp. 4, 8. Also see Nikolai Barsukov, "Proval 'antipartiinoi gruppy,'" *Kommunist*, no. 6 (1990), p. 100.

73 Chuev, *Sto sorok besed*, p. 354.

74 See Kaganovich, *Pamiatnye zapiski*, pp. 518–21.

75 Reported in Naumov, "Bor'ba N. S. Khrushcheva," p. 21.

76 Author's interview with Andrei Shevchenko, August 1993.

77 Author's interviews with Vladimir Naumov (September 1997) and Sergo Mikoyan (May 2000). The latter remembered seeing Khrushchev at the Mikoyan dacha early in the crisis.

78 Zhukov, "Ia pishu kak bylo," p. 53.

79 Mikoian, *Tak bylo*, p. 599.

80 See "Posledniaia 'antipartiinaia' gruppa," no. 1 (1994), p. 31; no. 3 (1993), pp. 55, 60.

81 Andrei Malenkov, who overheard his father talking to Bulganin on the phone, described the conversation in *O moem otse*, p. 77.

82 See "Posledniaia 'antipartiinaia' gruppa," no. 3 (1993), p. 7; no. 4 (1993), pp. 56–57; SK4, p. 237.

83 Mićunović, *Moscow Diary*, pp. 252, 260.

84 "Posledniaia 'antipartiinaia' gruppa," no. 4 (1993), p. 32; no. 1 (1994), p. 50. Author's interview with Andrei S. Shevchenko, August 1993. SK4, pp. 239–43. Author's interview with Gennady Voronov. Nurridin Mukhitdinov, "12 let s Khrushchevym: beseda s N. A. Mukhitdinovym," interview in *Argumenty i fakty*, no. 44 (1989), p. 6. Kaganovich, *Pamiatnye zapiski*, p. 52.

85 See Barsukov, "Proval 'antipartiinoi gruppy,' " p. 102; "Posledniaia 'antipartiinaia' gruppa," no. 3 (1993), pp. 12, 14–15; no. 4 (1993), pp. 43, 60; no. 5 (1993), pp. 32, 72; no. 6 (1993), p. 26; no. 2 (1994), p. 81.

86 Naumov, "Bor'ba N. S. Khrushcheva," p. 22.

87 Author's interview with Vladimir Naumov, March 1998.

88 "Posledniaia 'antipartiinaia' gruppa," no. 3 (1993), pp. 13–20.

89 Kaganovich insisted that he too had believed the charges, even though, he added, he himself had been falsely accused of being Yakir's partner in crime. Ibid., pp. 25, 43–44.

90 Ibid., pp. 74–87.

91 "Posledniaia 'antipartiinaia' gruppa," no. 4 (1993), p. 19; Mićunović, *Moscow Diary*, p. 273.

92 "Posledniaia 'antipartiinaia' gruppa," no. 4 (1993), pp. 23, 35, 43, 63, 74, 81.

93 Khrushchev's final speech, ibid., no. 2 (1994), pp. 8–59. For remarks by Malenkov, Molotov, and Kaganovich, see ibid., no. 3 (1993), pp. 26, 42, 85.

94 Recalled by Oleg Troyanovsky in "The Making of Soviet Foreign Policy," p. 215.

95 See Chuev, *Sto sorok besed*, p. 357.

96 "Ia byl prichasten k dokladu o kul'te lichnosti," p. 68.

97 Mićunović, *Moscow Diary*, p. 280.

CHAPTER 13. THE WIDER WORLD: 1917–1957

1 I owe this phrase to the late Earl Latham, formerly professor of political science at Amherst College. According to Anastas Mikoyan, Khrushchev "became captivated by foreign policy after Stalin's death." *Tak bylo*, p. 604.

2 NK2, p. 148.

3 Ibid. NK3, p. 128. He liked the Czechs so much he invited them home for tea and jam, in return for which they tutored him in technical drawing, something

"I needed as a metalworker, something I had dreamed of learning to do." NK4, no. 6, 1994, p. 105.

4 NK4, no. 11–12, 1992, p. 71.

5 NK2, p. 190.

6 Ibid., p. 150. Ukrainian colleagues were surely more alert to Kossior's nationality than Khrushchev was, especially by the beginning of the thirties, when Stalin began moving against "Ukrainian nationalism."

7 NK3, pp. 128–29.

8 NK2, p. 237.

9 NK4, no. 6, 1994, p. 121; no. 8, 1993, pp. 84–85.

10 NK2, pp. 154–56.

11 Ibid., pp. 162–63.

12 Ibid., p. 158.

13 Ibid., p. 169.

14 NK3, pp. 130–31; NK1, p. 362.

15 NK2, pp. 185, 188–89; NK3, pp. 145–46; NK1, p. 481.

16 Charles de Gaulle, *The Complete War Memoirs of Charles de Gaulle* (New York: Da Capo Press, 1984), p. 756.

17 NK2, pp. 347–49.

18 NK1, p. 361.

19 His situation reminded Khrushchev of "a joke I used to hear from miners in my youth. A priest gets up at a pulpit and shows a huge book to the congregation. 'Have you read this book?' he asks. Everyone is silent. 'Good,' he says. 'Then I don't have to read it either.' " NK2, pp. 351–52.

20 NK4, no. 6, 1994, p. 115; no. 8, 1993, pp. 74–75; nos. 8–9, 1992, p. 90; no. 8, 1994, p. 76; no. 2, 1995, p. 78. Also see NK3, p. 133; NK2, p. 28; NK1, pp. 372–73.

21 NK2, pp. 165, 174.

22 Ibid., pp. 184, 186.

23 NK3, pp. 99–100.

24 NK1, pp. 223–24; NK2, pp. 191, 352–53.

25 NK2, pp. 355–56.

26 NK1, pp. 220–22. Stalin had several reasons to like Ike. When many in the Anglo-American camp wanted him to race the Russians to Berlin, Eisenhower refused. When the same colleagues urged him stay on in areas designated as the Soviet zone of occupation, Eisenhower pulled out. Eisenhower had military, political, and even legal reasons for these moves, which were later held against him by cold war critics: to save the lives of his troops; to live up to wartime agreements; perhaps most important of all, to demonstrate trust in the Russians so as to elicit their trust and goodwill in return. See Stephen Ambrose, *Eisenhower* (New York: Simon & Schuster, 1983–1984), vol. 1, pp. 391–97, 428–29.

27 An entry from the diary of A. G. Soloviev, as published in "Tetradi krasnogo professora," *Neizvestnaia Rossiia: XX Vek*, vol. 4 (1993), p. 204.

28 NK4, no. 2, 1995, p. 78.

29 Ibid., p. 76.

30 Of course, the Chinese eventually saved the day by intervening against the Americans. See NK1, pp. 368–70; NK3, p. 146–47; NK4, no. 2, 1995, p. 77. For key excerpts from the documentary record, including Soviet contacts with North Koreans and Chinese, plus interpretative articles about the documents, see CWIHPBB, no. 6 (winter 1995–1996), pp. 30–122. These documents confirm Khrushchev's depiction of Stalin's readiness to lose the war before the Chinese intervened. But once the war stabilized in a kind of standoff, Stalin preferred to keep it going indefinitely rather than negotiate the armistice that his successors encouraged in 1953.

31 See Boris N. Slavinsky, "The Soviet Occupation of the Kurile Islands and the Plans for the Capture of Northern Hokkaido," *Japan Forum*, vol. 5, no. 1 (April 1993), pp. 97–98.

32 NK2, pp. 11, 35, 58; NK1, p. 362; NK3, p, 100; NK4, no. 2, 1995, p. 77. Speaking at a conference on "Stalin and the Cold War," at Yale University in September 1999, Vladimir Naumov, who had unparalleled access to the long-secret Stalin Fond in the Soviet archives, contended that Stalin undertook a massive military buildup opposite Alaska, possibly in preparation for a nuclear attack against the United States. Naumov's evidence was inconclusive, particularly since he was unable to cite his archival sources directly. If the buildup did take place, and even if it reflected more than contingency planning, it may have been undertaken just because Stalin was so fearful of an American attack. The latter interpretation was shared by Lev Petrov, Yulia Leonidovna Khrushcheva's late husband, who served in the area among some one hundred thousand troops being mobilized there. Author's interview with Sergei Khrushchev.

33 For a discerning sketch of both Beria and Malenkov and their approaches to foreign policy, see Zubok and Pleshakov, *Inside the Kremlin's Cold War*, pp. 138–73.

34 A. M. Aleksandrov-Agentov, *Ot Kollontai do Gorbacheva* (Moscow: Mezhdunarodnye otnosheniia, 1994), p. 55.

35 See Bohlen, *Witness to History*, pp. 377–79; Troianovskii, *Cherez gody*, pp. 138, 170; Gromyko, *Memoirs*, pp. 315, 377.

36 Troianovskii, *Cherez gody*, p. 177. C. D. Jackson, Notes on Molotov Dinner (Friday, January 29, 1954), J. P. File—Berlin, C. D. Jackson Papers, Dwight D. Eisenhower Library (Abilene, Kansas, hereafter DDEL).

37 According to Bohlen (*Witness to History*, p. 362), the lip-reading proved useless.

38 See Richter, *Khrushchev's Double Bind*, pp. 30–81. Also see Jack Snyder, *Myths of Empire: Domestic Politics and International Ambition* (Ithaca, N.Y.: Cornell University Press, 1991), pp. 230–33.

39 Author's interview with Georgy Kornienko.

40 MacDuffie, *Red Carpet*, pp. 202–12.

41 Although the Laborites preferred Malenkov to Khrushchev, the delegation wasn't exactly ecstatic about any of the Russians. Asked which one he would like to talk to, a tired Clement Attlee answered, "None of them." Trying to encourage conversation between Attlee and Malenkov, Parrott elicited the fact that fishing was Mr. Malenkov's favorite sport, along with Malenkov's question "Is Mr. Attlee a fisherman?" Attlee replied, "No, I don't fish." What did Mr. Attlee do when on holiday? asked Malenkov after a long, painful pause. "Went on a motoring tour." Malenkov continued, "Ah, then, Mr. Attlee likes driving?" Atlee: "No, my wife does," followed by another long silence.

The Labor delegation's meetings with Soviet leaders were described in a report by Thomas Brimelow (sent by Hayter to Sir Ivone Kirkpatrick on August 14) and Harry Hohler (in an internal Northern Department minute of August 27). These are in the PRO, FO 371/111765. Also see Sir William Hayter, *The Kremlin and the Embassy* (New York: Macmillan, 1966), pp. 37–39, and 106–08; and Cecil Parrott, *The Serpent and the Nightingale* (London: Faber and Faber, 1977), pp. 63–65.

42 Bohlen, *Witness to History,* pp. 369–70, and in a diplomatic report on a Soviet reception honoring the anniversary of the revolution on November 7, 1954, in *Foreign Relations of the United States, 1952–1954,* vol. 8, *Eastern Europe; Soviet Union; Eastern Mediterranean* (Washington, D.C.: Government Printing Office, 1988), p. 1255. (Hereafter, volumes of this series will be cited as FRUS, with years covered, volume number, and part number [where applicable]. Full citations, including titles, are listed in the bibliography.)

43 In return for Soviet entry into the war against Japan, Chiang had acquiesced in the loss of Outer Mongolia, agreed to share the port of Dairen and to give Moscow the Port Arthur naval base, and ceded part ownership of the Manchurian Railway. Stalin now gave Mao a greater voice in the railway but did not return it. In return for Soviet credits he insisted on the creation of Sino-Soviet joint stock companies to exploit Chinese mineral resources. Given "the threat from the United States and Japan," Mao did not seek the return of Dairen and Port Arthur. Mao's aggrieved account of this visit, which is confirmed by Khrushchev's and Gromyko's memoirs, was to some extent challenged by his Soviet interpreter during the stay, Nikolai Federenko, whose version was in turn contradicted by that of General Ivan Kovalev, who was Stalin's personal envoy in China from 1948 until the early 1950s. Mao's later version, as well as an article by Mark Kramer analyzing the divergent versions, is in "The USSR Foreign Ministry's Appraisal of Sino-Soviet Relations on the Eve of the Split, September 1959," CWIHPB, nos. 6–7 (Winter 1995–1996), pp. 156–85.

44 See Aleksandr Y. Mansourov, "Stalin, Mao, Kim and China's Decision to Enter the Korean War, September 16–October 15, 1950: New Evidence from the Russian Archives," CWIHPB, nos. 6–7 (winter 1995–1996), pp. 94–107; Gaddis, *We Know Now,* pp. 79–80.

45 NK4, nos. 11–12, 1992, pp. 73–74.

46 Steven M. Goldstein, "The Sino-Soviet Alliance, 1937–1962: Ideology and Unity," unpublished article, pp. 24–26; Chen Jian and Yang Kuisong, "Chinese Politics and the Collapse of the Sino-Soviet Alliance," in *Brothers in Arms: The Rise and Fall of the Sino-Soviet Alliance, 1945–1963,* ed. Odd Arne Westad, (Washington, D.C.: Woodrow Wilson Center Press, 1998), pp. 257–59; Deborah A. Kaple, "Soviet Advisers in China," in *Brothers in Arms,* ed. Westad, pp. 117–40; M. Iu. Prozumenshchikov and I. N. Shevchuk, "Soviet-Chinese Relations" (Moscow: "New Evidence on Cold War History," January 1993, paper prepared for delivery), p. 6.

47 See Goldstein, "The Sino-Soviet Alliance," pp. 31, 40; Zubok and Pleshakov, *Inside the Kremlin's Cold War,* pp. 216–17.

48 Kirby and Yan Mingfu spoke at an International Symposium on Sino-Soviet Relations and the Cold War in Beijing in October 1997.

49 NK1, p. 466; NK2, p. 247; NK4, nos. 11–12, 1992, p. 70.

50 K. I. Koval', "Peregovory I. V. Stalina s Zhou Enlaiem v 1953 g. v Moskve, i N. S. Khrushcheva s Mao Tze Dunom v 1954 g. v Pekine," NiNI, no. 5 (1989), pp.

107–13. The way the Presidium voted is itself instructive. With just a few hours left before the delegation's departure, Khrushchev and Mikoyan voted yes and then dispatched Koval to visit other members at home. All quickly assented except for Voroshilov, who greeted Koval in his pajamas, took an hour to read the documents, and then registered his objection. That forced Khrushchev to call an emergency Presidium meeting the next morning.

51 Chinese interpreter Shi Zhe described the Cantonese dish incident, as cited in Zubok and Pleshakov, *Inside the Kremlin's Cold War,* p. 218. The tea torture is recounted in NK4, nos. 11–12, 1992, p. 79.

52 Mao listed his grievances against Stalin in a March 31, 1956, conversation with Soviet Ambassador Yudin; see translation of transcript in CWIHPB, nos. 6–7 (Winter 1995–1996), pp. 164–67. Dr. Li Zhisui's recollections are in his memoir, *The Private Life of Chairman Mao,* trans. Tai Hung-Chao (New York: Random House, 1994), pp. 115–18. Remarks by Li Yueren and Yan Mingfu were made at the International Symposium on Sino-Soviet Relations and the Cold War in Beijing, October 22–25, 1997.

53 See Chen and Yang, "Chinese Politics," pp. 259–66; Gaddis, *We Now Know,* pp. 211–13; Prozumenshchikov and Shevchuk, "Soviet-Chinese Relations," pp. 10–11.

54 The nature and timing of Chinese advice have been discussed in Chapter 11. Also see Mark Kramer, "USSR Foreign Ministry's Appraisal of Sino-Soviet Relations," p. 173. Former Mao interpreter Yan Mingfu contended in an interview with the author that Chinese advice to intervene preceded Khrushchev's change of mind. See also David Wolff, "In Memorium: Deng Xiaoping and the Cold War," CWIHPB, no. 10 (March 1998), pp. 149–50; Goldstein, "The Sino-Soviet Alliance," p. 34.

55 Goldstein cites Mao's 1956 speech in "The Sino-Soviet Alliance," pp. 37–38. Mao's January 27, 1957, text is in CWIHPB, nos. 6–7 (Winter 1995–1996), pp. 152–53.

56 Deliusin recounted the scene at the Beijing symposium on "Sino-Soviet Relations and the Cold War," October, 1997.

57 An excerpt from Zhou's January 24, 1957, report is in CWIHPB, nos. 6–7 (Winter 1995–1996), pp. 153–54.

58 Voroshilov's visit and Peng Dehuai's remarks were described by Yan Mingfu at the Beijing conference in October 1997.

59 Michael Schoenhals, "Document: Mao Zedong: Speeches at the 1957 'Moscow Conference,'" *Journal of Communist Studies,* vol. 2, no. 2 (June 1986), p. 123.

60 Mićunović, *Moscow Diary,* p. 322.

61 Cited in Schoenhals, "Document: Mao Zedong," pp. 121–22.

62 Ibid., p. 119; NK4, nos. 11–12, 1992, p. 67; NK2, pp. 256–57.

63 See Li Zhisui, *The Private Life of Chairman Mao,* pp. 218–25. Other details were recalled by Yan Mingfu, Wang Jingxian, Mao's former chief bodyguard, and Lev Deliusin at the Beijing Symposium on "Sino-Soviet Relations and the Cold War."

64 See Zbigniew Brzezinski, *The Soviet Bloc: Unity and Conflict* (Cambridge, Mass.: Harvard University Press, 1967), pp. 168–80.

65 NK3, pp. 112, 138.

66 NK1, p. 379; Mićunović, *Moscow Diary,* p. 3; Adzhubei, *Krushenie illiuzii,* p. 126.

67 NK4, no. 7, 1994, pp. 81–82; SK4 p. 80, 103; Crankshaw, *Khrushchev,* pp. 15–16.

68 Crankshaw, *Khrushchev,* p. 16; Galina Vishnevskaya, the Soviet opera singer who was at the dinner table, describes the scene in *Galina,* p. 147.

69 Crankshaw, *Khrushchev,* pp. 19–20.

70 Mićunović, *Moscow Diary,* pp. 59–60, 66–79.

71 Ibid., pp. 72–74.

72 Ibid., pp. 81–82.

73 Ibid., pp. 93, 97, 113, 125.

74 Highlights of Tito's Pula speech: The Twentieth Congress hadn't gone nearly far enough in condemning Stalinism; it wasn't Stalin who was primarily to blame but the Stalinist system, which survived him; the Soviets themselves had brought on the Hungarian revolt by sticking so long with Rákosi and then replacing him with Gero; and the second and decisive Soviet intervention in Hungary, which the Yugoslavs had reluctantly approved, was necessary because of the mistaken intervention a few days earlier. See Mićunović, *Moscow Diary,* p. 159. Also see Leonid Gibianskii, "Soviet-Yugoslav Relations and the Hungarian Revolution of 1956," CWIHPB, no. 10 (March 1998), pp. 139–49.

75 Mićunović, *Moscow Diary,* pp. 164–65, 177–81, 205, 211.

76 Tito's retreat was visible at the November 1957 Moscow conference that Mao attended but he did not. Since the conference had been called to rebuild the bloc, it confronted Belgrade with a painful choice: If the Yugoslavs rejoined the camp "headed" by the USSR, they would lose their cherished independence; if they didn't, they would again be isolated. Having met in a narrow, unlit Yugoslav Embassy passageway, the one place in the building where they had not found "bugs" hidden in ceilings and under the parquet floors, the Yugoslav delegation refused to agree to the official conference declaration, but it did sign its Peace Manifesto, which endorsed Soviet policy in the Middle East and elsewhere. Shortly before the conference Belgrade even acceded to the long-standing Soviet request that it recognize East Germany. See Mićunović, *Moscow Diary,* p. 320, and Brzezinski, *Soviet Bloc,* p. 317.

77 SK4, p. 53. Aleksandrov-Agentov, *Ot Kollontai do Gorbacheva,* p. 56. On Khrushchev's preference for more activism and innovation, also see Troianovskii, *Cherez gody,* p. 182; Adzhubei, *Krushenie illiuzii,* p 124.

78 Stalin's awareness of the decisiveness of nuclear weapons has been obscured by his failure to integrate strategies and tactics for using them into Soviet defense doctrine and his insistence instead on "permanently operating factors" of war. But the crash program he pushed for developing such weapons speaks for itself. He took his policy of publicly downplaying the importance of the bomb (so as not to reveal his fear of the American arsenal) to the extreme of not publicizing the fact that the Soviets had broken the American atomic monopoly in 1949 and certainly not gloating over that feat. See David Holloway, *Stalin and the Bomb: The Soviet Union and Atomic Energy, 1939–1956* (New Haven: Yale University Press, 1994), pp. 224–72.

79 Holloway, ibid., p. 322, cites a November 1952 bomb estimate and himself estimates the actual number possessed by the Soviets in 1953. The actual 1953 figure is in Iu. B. Khariton and A. A. Brish, "Iadernoe vooruzhenie," in *Sovetskaia voennaia moshch' ot Stalina do Gorbacheva,* ed. A. V. Minaev (Moscow: "Voennyi parad," 1999), p. 167. A U.S. National Security Council subcommittee estimate is in FRUS, 1952–1954, vol. 2, pt. 1, p. 335. Soviet bombers' inability to reach the United States and return in 1956 is reported in Sergei Khrushchev, "The Military-Industrial Complex," in *Nikita Khrushchev,* ed. Taubman, Khrushchev, and Gleason, pp. 255–57.

80 Quoted in Heikal, *Sphinx and the Commissar,* p. 129. Also see Sergei Khrushchev, "Military-Industrial Complex," p. 247.

81 SK4, p. 108; Sergei Khrushchev, "Military-Industrial Complex," pp. 257–58; Holloway, *Stalin and the Bomb,* p. 324.

82 Troianovskii, *Cherez gody,* p. 200; Troyanovsky, "Making of Soviet Foreign Policy," p. 214.

83 See Parrott, *Serpent and the Nightingale,* pp. 65–74; Hayter, *Kremlin and the Embassy,* pp. 36, 42, 46. Zhukov's negative reaction to Khrushchev's post–air show performance was described in Chapter 12.

84 NK4, no. 8, 1993, pp. 76–78.

85 Ibid., pp. 80–81.

86 On Dulles, see John Lewis Gaddis, *The United States and the End of the Cold War: Implications, Reconsiderations, Provocations* (New York: Oxford University Press, 1992), pp. 65–86. Also see Fred I. Greenstein, *The Hidden-Hand Presidency: Eisenhower as Leader* (New York: Basic Books, 1982) pp. 26–31.

87 As noted by C. D. Jackson on July 11, 1955. See FRUS, 1955–1957, vol. 5, pp. 301–02. Robert Bowie, then head of the State Department Policy Planning Staff, doubts that Dulles would have expressed such sharp doubts to Jackson. Author's interview with Robert Bowie.

88 According to Anatoly Dobrynin, Khrushchev nonetheless favored accepting the Open Skies proposal for tactical reasons. Assuming that Eisenhower was bluffing and that, even if he wasn't, the U.S. Congress wouldn't allow Soviet planes to overfly American territory, Khrushchev calculated that Washington would eventually have to back away from its own scheme. But, wrote Dobrynin, the Presidium rejected Khrushchev's tactic. See Anatoly Dobrynin, *In Confidence: Moscow's Ambassador to America's Six Cold War Presidents* (New York: Times Books, 1995), pp. 37–38.

89 Bohlen, *Witness to History,* p. 386; Hayter, *Kremlin and the Embassy,* p. 118; Dobrynin, *In Confidence,* p. 38. In fact, Molotov had gallantly proposed Soviet adherence to NATO at the Berlin foreign ministers' conference. On the Soviet offer to join NATO, along with Anthony Eden's understated reply that Moscow's membership would not in itself be sufficient assurance of its good intentions toward NATO's members, see *Documents on International Affairs, 1954,* ed. Denise Folliot (London: Oxford University Press, 1957), pp. 42–43, and Coral Bell, *Survey of International Affairs, 1954* (London: Oxford University Press, 1957), p. 154.

90 NK1, p. 393. Khrushchev's July 4 remarks are in FRUS, 1955–1957, vol. 5, pp. 258–59. See SK4, pp. 82.

91 NK1, p. 394.

92 NK4, nos. 8–9, 1992, p. 71; NK1, p. 395.

93 The scene is described by Livingston T. Merchant, assistant secretary of state for European affairs, in a private account written for members of the American delegation, "Recollections of the Summit Conference: Geneva 1955," November 1957, pp. 26–27, Box 2, Livingston T. Merchant Papers, Seeley Mudd Library, Princeton University, Princeton, New Jersey.

94 NK1, p. 399.

95 Merchant, "Recollections of the Summit," p. 32.

96 FRUS, 1955–1957, vol. 5, pp. 369, 398; Bohlen, *Witness to History*, p. 383; Merchant, "Recollections of the Summit," p. 39; Memorandum of conversation by Livingston T. Merchant, July 18, 1955, Box 2, Livingston T. Merchant Papers, Seeley Mudd Library, Princeton University. Whether Khrushchev believed what he said or was just pulling Western legs is not clear.

97 Harold Macmillan, *Tides of Fortune, 1945–1955* (New York: Harper & Row, 1969), p. 622; Pinay is cited in Michael Beschloss, *Mayday: Eisenhower, Khrushchev and the U-2 Affair* (New York: Harper & Row, 1986) p. 104. Considering the rapid turnover in French Fourth Republic governments, Khrushchev saw "no point in paying serious attention to the French delegation." Nonetheless, he would have been hurt to learn that Edgar Faure, whom he "nicknamed Edgar Fyodorovich" and regarded as a "very prepossessing man who went out of his way to be friendly and hospitable toward us," was in fact so unimpressed in return. See NK1, p. 399.

98 Report by Macmillan to Conservative party Parliamentary Foreign Affairs Committee, July 26, 1955, Conservative Party Archives, Bodleian Library, Oxford University, U.K., CRD2/34/1.

99 FRUS, 1955–1957, vol. 5, p. 376; Merchant, "Recollection of the Summit," p. 58; NK1, p. 400. According to Robert Bowie, Eisenhower did not expect a breakthrough at Geneva, but did want to give détente, for which the British as well as the Soviets were pushing, a try. Although Dulles worried that the very atmosphere of a summit would "lull" the West, Eisenhower believed that the way to maintain uncertain support for a long cold war struggle was to show that he had tried to find an alternative to it. Eisenhower also sought to make sure Soviet leaders understood that use of nuclear weapons would be suicidal. Author's interview with Robert Bowie.

100 NK4, nos. 8–9, 1992, p. 73; Dobrynin, *In Confidence*, p. 38.

101 SK4 p. 86.

102 Adzhubei, *Krushenie illiuzii*, p. 127; NK4, nos. 8–9, 1992, p. 75.

103 Beschloss, *Mayday*, p. 105.

104 Dulles's radio and television address of November 18, 1955, in U.S. Department of State Bulletin (hereafter DSB), vol. 33, no. 857, pp. 870–71; Khrushchev's speeches of November 24 and 26, 1955, in *Pravda*, November 26, 1955, p. 2, and November 28, 1955, p. 1.

105 NK4, no. 9, 1993, p. 77. Although Adenauer privately accepted the existence of two Germanys as a long-term prospect, in public he was committed to German reunification.

106 NK4, no. 8, 1994, p. 75; Heikal, *Sphinx and the Commissar*, p. 92.

107 Khrushchev describes the tour in his memoirs, NK4, no. 8, 1994, pp. 75–92, and no. 10, pp. 77–83. Also see British diplomatic reports in PRO, Prime Minister's Office Files (hereafter PREM), 11/1606.

108 On the disarmament proposals, see Holloway, *Stalin and the Bomb*, pp.

340–41. Also see Matthew Evangelista, "'Why Keep Such an Army?' Khrushchev's Troop Reductions," Working Paper no. 19, Cold War International History Project, December 1997. Khrushchev says Molotov opposed the return to Finland of the Porkkala base; see NK2, pp. 222–25.

109 Bohlen, *Witness to History*, p. 390.

110 Eden invited Khrushchev and Bulganin to Britain for "thorough discussions at our leisure on the many problems that troubled the world" and "to give our visitors a chance to see something of the country." Nor did the prime minister retract the invitation in response to Khrushchev's angry anticolonialist speeches in Asia and upon his return to Moscow. "The violence of Mr. Khrushchev's speech," Eden later explained, "showed the depth of his ignorance of our country and I did not think this a reason to deny him the chance of informing himself." See Anthony Eden, *Full Circle: The Memoirs of Anthony Eden* (Boston: Houghton Mifflin, 1960), pp. 307, 355.

111 NK4, nos. 8–9, 1992, p. 77.

112 SK4 pp. 112–16; NK1, pp. 406-07. Despite Malenkov's respectful reception, the Soviet KGB chief Ivan Serov, who also preceded Khrushchev and Bulganin to England, was met by pickets and protests. Although British Ambassador Hayter found the Tu-104's exterior "splendidly smooth and modern," he thought the inside "was furnished, as Miss Nancy Mitford said of another Soviet plane, like a cottage, with a good deal of red plush and china figurines in glass cases." Hayter, *Kremlin and the Embassy*, p. 135.

113 SK4, pp. 121–22; Peter Wright, *Spycatcher: The Candid Autobiography of a Senior Intelligence Officer* (New York: Viking, 1987), p. 72.

114 Note on "Bulganin and Khrushchev," by Mr. T. Brimelow and Mr. W. Barker, April 28, 1956, PRO, PREM, 11/1625. NK4, nos. 8–9, 1992, p. 81.

115 Note by Brimelow and Barker; Troianovskii, *Cherez gody*, pp. 198–99.

116 NK1, pp. 405–07.

117 Hayter, *Kremlin and the Embassy*, p. 136.

118 Hugh Gaitskell, *The Diary of Hugh Gaitskell, 1945–1956*, ed. Philip M. Williams (London: Jonathan Cape, 1983) pp. 497, 508.

119 Eden, *Full Circle*, p. 360.

120 Ibid., pp. 357, 360–61; Harold Macmillan, *Riding the Storm, 1956–1959* (London: Macmillan, 1971), p. 95; Troianovskii, *Cherez gody*, p. 196.

121 Mićunović, *Moscow Diary*, pp. 76–77, 86, 127, 133.

122 Television and radio address to the nation, October 31, 1956, in DSB, vol. 35, no. 907 (November 12, 1956), pp. 743–44.

123 William E. Griffith, "RFE and the Hungarian Revolution and the Polish October" and Paul B. Heinze, "Recollections of Radio Free Europe" (Budapest: "Hungary and the World, 1956: The New Archival Evidence," September 26–29, 1996, papers prepared for delivery).

124 William Bragg Ewald, *Eisenhower the President: Crucial Days, 1951–1960* (Englewood Cliffs, N.J.: Prentice-Hall, 1981), p. 121.

125 Mićunović, *Moscow Diary*, p. 156.

126 Heikal, *Sphinx and the Commissar*, pp. 69–71.

127 NK1, p. 435. Sergei Khrushchev reported his father's jealousy of Bulganin in SK4, p. 209.

128 Mićunović, *Moscow Diary*, p. 148; SK4, p. 211.

129 On the timing of Soviet and American warnings, see Edward Crankshaw's comments in NK1, p. 436. Heikal, *Sphinx and the Commissar*, pp. 73, 82, 98, 128.

CHAPTER 14. ALONE AT THE TOP: 1957–1960

1 NK4, no. 3, 1995, p. 69.

2 Roman Kolkowicz, *The Soviet Military and the Communist Party* (Princeton, N.J.: Princeton University Press, 1967), p. 130.

3 Mićunović, *Moscow Diary*, pp. 310–11.

4 SK4, p. 249.

5 Quoted by Khrushchev in his speech to the fourth session of a Central Committee plenum held on October 28–29, 1957, RGANI, f. 2, op. 1, d. 269, l. 17.

6 Author's interview with Vladimir Naumov, who has seen classified documents relating to the Zhukov affair, March 1998. Also V. P. Naumov, "'Delo' marshala G. K. Zhukova, 1957, g.," NiNI, no. 5 (2000), pp. 87–108; no. 6 (2000), pp. 71–91.

7 Vladimir Naumov, who has seen the unedited transcript of the October 1957 Central Committee plenum that ousted Zhukov, cited this line of Khrushchev's in an interview with the author, March 1998.

8 NK4, no. 3, 1995, p. 72.

9 Furtseva's speech to Moscow city party organization *aktiv*, October 31, 1957, RGASPI, f. 2, d. 774, ll. 13, 216. SK3, vol. 1, pp. 330–31. According to Khrushchev, the secret brigade had twenty-five hundred commandos.

10 Adzhubei, *Krushenie illiuzii*, p.196.

11 Transcript of the third session of the Central Committee plenum of October 29, 1957, RGANI, f. 2, op. 1, d. 268, ll. 56, 72.

12 The three marshals' remarks were made at an October 31, 1957, meeting of the Moscow party *aktiv* after the plenum. RGASPI, f. 2, d. 774, ll. 161, 209, 244.

13 The resentment of Zhukov's colleagues went back to wartime infighting between Supreme Headquarters in Moscow, which Zhukov often represented, and the fronts his fellow generals commanded. It was compounded by his attempts to portray himself as *the* military hero of the war.

14 Mikoyan and Marshal Zakharov reported this incident to the third session of the Central Committee plenum on October 28. RGANI, f. 3, op. 1, d. 268, ll. 58, 77. Khrushchev confided the same story to Yugoslav ambassador Mićunović. See Mićunović, *Moscow Diary*, p. 305. Zhukov's version is in Zhukov, "Ia pishu kak bylo," p. 60.

15 Uncorrected verbatim transcript of Khrushchev speech at the fourth session of the October 28–29, 1957, plenum in RGANI, f. 2, op. 1, d. 269, l. 18.

16 See Chapter 12, above. Shepilov is also quoted as incriminating Zhukov in *I primknuvshii k nim Shepilov*, p. 38. For Bulganin's charge that Zhukov had the idea of ousting Khrushchev and replacing the post of party first secretary with secretary for general questions, see the unedited verbatim transcript of the June 1957 plenum in *Molotov, Malenkov, Kaganovich, 1957: Stenogramma iiun'skogo plenuma TsK KPSS i drugie dokumenty* (Moscow: Mezhdunarodnyi fond "Demokratiia," 1998), pp. 26, 75. For Saburov's remarks, which referred to Zhukov's threat to "bring down" Serov if he tried to denounce those who were criticizing Khrushchev, see edited transcript of June 1957 plenum in "Posledniaia 'antipartiinaia' gruppa," no. 3 (1993), p. 58. Vladimir Naumov, who has seen a broad range of documents concerning the Zhukov affair, believes that Zhukov "actively pushed for eliminating the post of party first secretary."

17 On Khrushchev's approval and its disappearance from the edited transcript, see *Molotov, Malenkov, Kaganovich, 1957*, p. 20. Mikoyan's remark at the October plenum's third session is in RGANI, f. 2, op. 1, d. 268, l. 64. Even the edited plenum transcript wasn't published until 1993, after the USSR had collapsed.

18 Zhukov had served as chairman of a Central Committee commission on the rehabilitation of Soviet prisoners of war; his role is described in "Nezakonchennoe srazhenie marshala Zhukova," IA, no. 2 (1995), pp. 108–10.

19 Zhukov, "Ia pishu kak bylo," pp. 55–56; Adzhubei, *Krushenie illiuzii*, pp. 195–96.

20 Uncorrected verbatim transcript of Khrushchev's speech, RGANI, f. 2, op. 1, d. 269, ll. 12–17, 24–27, 33, 37, 54. Zhukov "never finished a single military academy," Bagramian remarked after the October 1957 plenum, "and I don't even think he finished high school. There's no harm in that since not everyone had a chance to get an education, but the way he treats our military academies and our military scholars is boorish beyond belief." Meeting of Moscow party activists in October 1957, RGASPI, f. 2, d. 774, l. 249.

21 *Pravda*, January 30, 1959, p. 5; February 1, 1959, p. 4; February 5, 1959, p. 8.

22 Author's interview with Nikolai Yegorychev, June 2000.

23 Tompson, *Khrushchev*, p. 198.

24 See Evangelista, "'Why Keep such an Army?,'" pp. 17–18.

25 G. I. Voronov, "Nemnogo vospominanii," *Druzhba narodov*, no. 1 (1989), pp. 194, 200.

26 Benediktov, "O Staline i Khrushcheve," p. 47; Shelepin, "Istoriia—uchitel' surovyi"; Mikoian, *Tak bylo*, pp. 601–02. Two other former associates dated Khrushchev's transformation to 1961 rather than 1957, but that may be because they saw less of him until then than did the others. Nikolai Yegorychev: "Until the Twenty-second Party congress [in October 1961] there was one Khrushchev, and after the congress he became another man altogether." Until the end of 1961 "one could discuss and resolve matters with him," whereas after the congress renewed his mandate with an overwhelming show of support, "he overestimated himself, developed an inflated sense of himself as if he knew it all, considered his opinion beyond any reproach; it was if someone else had taken his place." See Nikolai Yegorychev, "Napravlen poslom," interview by Leonid Pleshakov, *Ogonek*, no. 6 (1989), p. 7. Kirill Mazurov, former Byelorussian party leader, remembered two Khrushchevs: "One was a reformer in the good sense of that word." But after the Twenty-second congress "it was as if someone had replaced him." See Mazurov, "Ia govoriu ne tol'ko o sebe."

27 Author's interview with Georgy Kornienko.

28 Author's interview with Oleg Troyanovsky, June 1991.

29 Author's interview with Rada Adzhubei, June 1991.

30 Troianovskii, *Cherez gody*, pp. 205–06; Adzhubei, *Krushenie illiuzii*, pp. 189; SK4, p. 710. Two agencies in particular, the party Central Committee's General Department and the Administrative Department of the Council of Ministers, were theoretically at Khrushchev's personal service, but they were also beholden to the larger party and government apparatuses.

31 SK4, pp. 246–47.

32 Mićunović, *Moscow Diary*, p. 405.

33 NK2, p. 18.

34 Andrei Malenkov, *O moem otse*, pp. 82–88.

35 "Ia prichasten k dokladu o kul'te lichnosti," p. 68.

36 Chuev, *Sto sorok besed*, p. 518.

37 "This is no way to behave with a country about which Lenin himself often spoke," Molotov recalled saying. "We've got to patch things up with China." Ibid., p. 450,

38 A copy of Molotov's May 21, 1959, letter is in RGANI, f. KPK, d. 13/76, t. 1, ll. 122–23.

39 Chuev, *Sto sorok besed*, p. 467. Molotov also continued to disparage Khrushchev's talk of "peaceful coexistence" with the West as "naive." As he put it much later, "It was as if we said, 'Please, give us peace!' But of course, they gave us no such peace." Chuev, *Sto sorok besed*, pp. 496, 498.

40 The Control Commission's report on the matter is in RGANI, f. KPK, d. 13/76, t. 1, ll. 43–60.

41 Mićunović, *Moscow Diary*, p. 355.

42 Ibid., pp. 355–56.

43 Molotov was sent to live out his days at a dacha outside Moscow.

44 Andrei Malenkov, *O moem ottse*, pp. 82–88. Author's interview with Andrei Malenkov.

45 Kaganovich is quoted by Khrushchev at the Twenty-second Party Congress. See *XXII s"ezd: Stengraficheskii otchet* (Moscow: 1961), vol. 2, p. 588. Sergo Mikoyan reported his father's version of Khrushchev's taunt in an interview with the author, May 2000.

46 See *I primknuvshii k nim Shepilov*, pp. 203, 238, 240–50. Stalin's provision of books reported in author's interview with Sergei Khrushchev.

47 Barsukov, "Personal'noe delo 'antipartiinoi gruppy,' " pp. 71–72.

48 Sergo Mikoyan, "The Red Emperors: A Kremlin Insider's View," unpublished draft family memoir, provided to the author by Mr. Mikoyan; Mikoian, *Tak bylo*, p. 607. Adzhubei, *Krushenie illiuzii*, p. 198. Also See Nikolai Petrov, "Pervyi predsedatel' KGB General Ivan Serov," *Otechestvennaia istoriia*, no. 5 (1997), pp. 23–43.

49 Speech to all-Union conference of state farm workers, February 5, 1954, in Stroi, vol. 1, p. 170.

50 *Pravda*, February 15, 1956, p. 7.

51 Whitney, *Khrushchev Speaks*, p. 101.

52 Speeches at Ukrainian Central Committee plenum, December 26, 1957, and to Byelorussian agricultural shock workers, January 22, 1958, in Stroi, vol. 2, pp. 498, 526.

53 See Zubkova, "The Rivalry with Malenkov," pp. 80–81; Strelianyi, "Poslednii romantik," p. 242.

54 SK4, pp. 335–36.

55 Harold Lee, *Roswell Garst: A Biography* (Ames: Iowa State University Press, 1984), pp. 167, 179, 182.

56 Strelianyi, "Poslednii romantik," pp. 198–99.

57 Lee, *Roswell Garst*, pp. ix, 188–90, 222.

58 NK4, no. 12, 1994, p. 111.

59 NK2, pp. 132–33.

60 Speech to agricultural workers, Leningrad, April 12, 1955, in Stroi, vol. 2, p. 119.

61 Speech to Urals agricultural workers, June 20, 1956, ibid., p. 239.

62 Speech on August 13, 1958, in Stroi, vol. 3, p. 272.

63 Speech on June 11, 1959, in Stroi, vol. 4, p. 19.

64 Speech to agricultural workers, Saratov, March 18, 1955, in Stroi, vol. 2, p. 28.

65 From speech at Twentieth Party Congress, in *Pravda*, February 15, 1956, p. 6.

66 Speech to black earth zone agricultural workers, Moscow, March 30, 1957, in Stroi, vol. 2, p. 439.

67 Speech in Voronezh, March 30, 1957, ibid., p. 57.

68 Speech in February 1960, in Stroi, vol. 4, p. 112.

69 Stroi, vol. 3, p. 8.

70 Toranska, *Them*, pp. 155–58.

71 Speech of May 11, 1959, in Stroi, vol. 3, p. 520.

72 Speech in Voronezh, April 3, 1957, in Stroi, vol. 2, p. 380.

73 Speech to agricultural shock workers, February 15, 1954, in Stroi, vol. 1, pp. 192–93.

74 Speech of March 30, 1957, in Stroi, vol. 2, p. 376.

75 Speech to agricultural workers, April 8, 1957, ibid., p. 405.

76 Speech to district party secretaries, Gorky, April 9, 1957, ibid., p. 425.

77 Speech to agricultural workers, Moscow, April 7, 1955, ibid., p. 75.

78 NK2, p. 126.

79 Speech at Ukrainian Central Committee plenum, December 26, 1957, in Stroi, vol. 2, p. 500, and on March 27, 1958, in Stroi, vol. 3, p. 132.

80 Less than a year after Khrushchev formally broached the reform, just 385 of 8,000 machine tractor stations remained, with only 34 by the end of 1959. Zhores A. Medvedev, *Soviet Agriculture* (New York: Norton, 1987), p. 178.

81 Roy Medvedev, *Khrushchev*, p. 161.

82 Medvedev and Medvedev, *Khrushchev*, p. 96.

83 Author's interview with Andrei Shevchenko, October 1993.

84 Medvedev and Medvedev, *Khrushchev*, pp. 96–97. Khrushchev speech to Central Committee Plenum, December 25, 1959, in *Pravda*, December 29, 1959, p. 1.

85 Speech in Ryazan, February 13, 1959, in Stroi, vol. 3, pp. 490–91.

86 *Pravda*, October 17, 1959, p. 1.

87 Remarks of November 14, 1959 in *Pravda*, November 18, 1959, p. 1.

88 *Plenum Tsentral'nogo Komiteta Kommunisticheskoi Partii Sovetskogo Soiuza, 22–25 dekabria 1959 goda: Stenograficheskii otchet* (Moscow: Gosudarstvennoe izdatel'stvo politicheskoi literatury, 1960), pp. 39, 92, 172. *Pravda*, December 23, 1959, p. 4; *Pravda*, December 24, 1959, p. 1. The translation of the phrase "show you the beetle's mother," one of the more puzzling and colorful of Khrushchev's many colloquial expressions, is in *Current Digest of the Soviet Press* (hereafter CDSP), vol. 11, no. 52 (January 27, 1960), p. 10.

89 This account relies on Medvedev and Medvedev, *Khrushchev*, pp. 96–101. See also N. Shundik, "Chudo kotorogo ne bylo," *Trud*, December 18, 1988.

90 Speech to voters of Kalinin electoral district, Moscow, March 14, 1958, in Nikita S. Khrushchev, *For Victory in Peaceful Competition with Capitalism* (New York: Dutton, 1960), pp. 157–58.

91 See Ed A. Hewett, *Reforming the Soviet Economy: Equality vs. Efficiency* (Washington, D. C.: Brookings Institution, 1988), pp. 31–55. One factor among many that distorted official economic statistics was the pressure to exaggerate plan fulfillment.

92 SK4, p. 260.

93 Remarks of January 4, 1958, and of April 9, 1958, in Khrushchev, *For Victory*, pp. 23, 309.

94 Mićunović, *Moscow Diary*, pp. 301, 311, 340–41; SK4, pp. 264–65.

95 "Text of Khrushchev Interview on Wide Range of Issues between East and West," *New York Times*, October 10, 1957, p. 10.

96 NK2, p. 48; Sergei Khrushchev, "Military-Industrial Complex," p. 258; SK3, vol. 1, p. 384.

97 For a detailed account of Khrushchev's cuts in Soviet armed forces and their causes, see Evangelista, "'Why Keep Such an Army?'"

98 Khrushchev's remark of July 26, 1959, is in the American memorandum of conversation in FRUS, 1958–1960, vol. 9, p. 38.

99 NK2, pp. 31–33.

100 Evangelista, "'Why Keep Such an Army?'" pp. 4–5.

101 Arkady P. Shevchenko, *Breaking with Moscow* (New York: Knopf, 1985), p. 93.

102 SK3, vol. 1, p. 409.

103 Ibid., pp. 401–02.

104 NK2, p. 49.

105 SK3, vol. 1, pp. 388–92, 405–07, 468. The system did not become operational until 1963–1964.

106 Ibid., p. 407.

107 Ibid., pp. 408–09.

108 The famous physicist and future dissident Andrei Sakharov got a glimpse of Khrushchev's growing arrogance at a 1959 conference on defense issues in the Kremlin's Oval Hall. Targets of Khrushchev's wrath on this occasion were Dmitri Ustinov, the deputy prime minister in charge of arms production, and the aircraft designers Aleksandr Yakovlev and Andrei Tupolev. Having observed Khrushchev at a similar session in 1955, Sakharov noted a change. This time his manner was "much more assertive." He now took center stage "with evident pleasure, asking the speakers pointed questions, interrupting and making it clear that he had the last word." He impressed Sakharov as "an intelligent man and a leader of stature, though also as brash, susceptible to flattery (true this is easier to see in hindsight), and uncultivated (this, too, I probably became conscious of only later)." Andrei Sakharov, *Memoirs*, trans. Richard Lourie (New York: Knopf, 1990) pp. 210–11.

109 This description of housing reform draws on Donald Filtzer, *Soviet Workers and De-Stalinization: The Consolidation of the Modern System of Soviet Production Relations, 1953–1964* (Cambridge, U.K.: Cambridge University Press, 1992), pp. 51–52;

and Filtzer, *The Khrushchev Era: De-Stalinization and the Limits of Reform in the USSR, 1953–1964* (London: Macmillan, 1993), pp. 33–34.

110 Filtzer, *Khrushchev Era,* pp. 33–37; Medvedev and Medvedev, *Khrushchev,* p. 144; N. S. Khrushchev, *O kommunisticheskom vospitanii* (Moscow: Izdaltel'stvo politicheskoi literatury, 1964), p. 47.

111 See Adzhubei, *Krushenie illiuzii,* pp. 186–87. Vladislav Zubok pointed out the ironic mix of impressions at a seminar at George Washington University, March 2000.

112 This account draws particularly on Richard Stites, *Russian Popular Culture: Entertainment and Society since 1900* (Cambridge, U.K.: Cambridge University Press, 1992), pp. 123–47.

113 See Adzhubei, *Krushenie illiuzii,* pp. 207–98.

114 See Lazar Fleishman, *Boris Pasternak: The Poet and His Politics* (Cambridge, Mass.: Harvard University Press, 1990), p. 281.

115 Vladimir Ia. Lakshin, *"Novyi mir" vo vremia Khrushcheva: dnevnik i poputnoe (1953–1964)* (Moscow: Izdatel'stvo "Knizhnaia palata," 1991), p. 24.

116 A. Tvardovskii, "Iz rabochikh tetradei (1953–1960)," *Znamia,* no. 8, July 1989, pp. 135–40.

117 The following account draws on Fleishman, *Boris Pasternak,* pp. 247–314.

118 See Robert Conquest, *Courage of Genius: The Pasternak Affair* (London: Collins and Harvill Press, 1961), pp. 127–36, 176–78.

119 SK2, pp. 208–09; NK2, p. 77.

120 NK2, pp. 76–77. According to Adzhubei, when Khrushchev read the book in retirement, he "found it boring. The narration was too complicated, the heroes alien in their lives and spirit; too many things, as he put it, seemed unimportant, not part of his circle of aspirations. But at the same time he regretted the novel hadn't been published, and with some sadness he admitted, 'Nothing bad would have happened.'" *Krushenie illiuzii,* pp. 212–13.

121 Vladimir Semichastnyi, "Ia by spravilsia s liuboi rabotoi," interview by K. Svetitskii and S. Sokolov, *Ogonek,* no. 24 (1989), p. 24. Sergei Khrushchev can't imagine his father "slyly inserting paragraphs into someone else's speech."

122 *Pravda,* May 24, 1959, p. 2.

123 Author's interview with Sara Babyonysheva, Amherst, Massachusetts, February 1996.

124 Chernoutsan, unpublished draft memoir.

125 *Pravda,* May 24, 1959, p. 3.

126 Lakshin, *"Novyi mir" vo vremia Khrushcheva,* p. 33.

127 A. Tvardovskii, "Iz rabochikh tetradei (1953–1960)," *Znamia,* no. 9 (September 1989), pp. 173, 182, 183.

128 Ibid., p. 183.

129 See *Ottepel' 1953–1956,* p. 120.

130 Mićunović, *Moscow Diary,* pp. 423–38.

131 See Goldstein, "Sino-Soviet Alliance," p, 38; Vladislav Zubok, "Sovetsko-kitaiskie peregovory na vysshem urovne 31 iiulia–3 avgusta 1958 g. i oktiabria 1959 goda," unpublished article. According to Sergei Khrushchev, his father gave R-12 missile blueprints to the Chinese and had them sent prototypes of P-15 and shore defense Comet cruise missiles, both to be produced at factories being built with Soviet help. See SK4, p. 266. Also see Mikhail Pervov, *Raketnoe oruzhie raketnykh voisk strategicheskogo znacheniia* (Moscow: "Violanta," 1999), p. 73.

132 Yan Mingfu, one of Mao's interpreters in his talks with Khrushchev, confirmed this turning point in remarks at the October 1997 Symposium on Sino-Soviet Relations and the Cold War held in Beijing.

133 NK2, p. 258. On the two Soviet proposals, see Chen and Yang, "Mao's 'Continuous Revolution,'" pp. 37–38.

134 Chinese minutes of conversation between Mao Zedong and Ambassador Yudin on July 22, 1958, are translated in CWIHPB, nos. 6–7 (winter 1995–1996), pp. 155–59. Also see Vladislav Zubok, "Deng Xiaoping and the Sino-Soviet Split, 1956–1963," CWIHPB, no. 10 (March 1998), p. 155.

135 Quan Yanchi, *Mao Zedong yu Xeluxiaofu* (Mao Zedong and Khrushchev) (Ne mongu: Nei monggu Renmin chubanshe, 1998), informal English translation of the Chinese text prepared for the author.

136 NK1, p. 465.

137 Quan, *Mao Zedong yu Xeluxiaofu,* Eng. trans.

138 SK3, vol. 1, p. 349.

139 Quan, *Mao Zedong yu Xeluxiaofu,* Eng. trans.

140 Russian minutes of the Khrushchev-Mao talks on July 31 and August 3 are in the Volkogonov Collection, LOC, reel 17. Excerpts from both sets of minutes are in David Wolff, "One Finger's Worth of Historical Events: New Russian and Chinese Evidence on the Sino-Soviet Alliance and Split, 1948–1959," Working Paper no. 30, Cold War International History Project, Woodrow Wilson International Center for Scholars, August 2000, pp. 51–59. For an account that includes sharper phrases that were apparently softened or omitted entirely in the official minutes, as well as descriptions of gestures, see Quan, *Mao Zedong yu Xeluxiaofu,* Eng. trans.

141 Quan, *Mao Zedong yu Xeluxiaofu,* Eng. trans. Mao Zedong, "Anna Louise Strong: Three Interviews with Chairman Mao," interview by Anna Louise Strong, compiled by Tracy B. Strong and Helene Keyssar, *China Quarterly,* no. 103 (September 1985), p. 503.

142 Quan, *Mao Zedong yu Xeluxiaofu,* Eng. trans.

143 Ibid., p. 26. His account was confirmed by Yan Mingfu at the October 1997 Beijing Conference on Sino-Soviet Relations and the Cold War.

144 Li, *Private Life,* p. 261.

145 NK2, p. 259.

146 Quoted by Mikhail Romm, leading Soviet film director who was in Khrushchev's audience, in Mikhail Romm, *Ustnye rasskazy* (Moscow: Kinotsentr, 1991), p. 154.

147 On the lack of advance warning, see M. A. Suslov, "O poezdke sovetskoi partiino-pravitel'stvennoi delegatsii v Kitaiskuiu narodnuiu respubliku," draft speech to CPSU Central Committee plenum, December 22–26, 1959, included in "Materialy k protokolu no. 15 zasedaniia plenuma TsK KPSS, " RGANI, f. 2, op. 1, d. 447, l. 22. Chen and Yang, "Chinese Politics," p. 271; Zubok and Pleshakov, *Inside the Kremlin's Cold War,* pp. 220–27. For further analysis along with Chinese documents and recollections relating to the Taiwan crisis, see "Mao Zedong's Handling of the Taiwan Straits Crisis of 1958: Chinese Recollections and Documents" and "Khrushchev's Nuclear Promise to Beijing during the 1958 Crisis," in CWIHPB, no. 6 (winter 1995–1996), pp. 208–27.

148 See Gordon H. Chang, *Friends and Enemies: The United States, China and the Soviet Union, 1948–1972* (Stanford, Calif.: Stanford University Press, 1990), pp. 186–88.

149 Gromyko, *Memoirs*, p. 252.

150 Li, *Private Life*, p. 261.

151 Mao may have been chastened by the troubles of the Great Leap, as well as by opposition from his fellow oligarch and longtime champion of Sino-Soviet military cooperation, Marshal Peng Dehuai. Khrushchev was hoping to reestablish the warm ties with Beijing that had once been the cornerstone of his bloc leadership. In early 1959, the Chinese asked for more Soviet advice and assistance in the area of economic planning. In February the two capitals announced Moscow would provide five billion rubles' worth of Soviet goods and services, largely in heavy industry, over the next seven years. That same spring the Soviets were still sharing their nuclear secrets with China. See Goldstein, "Sino-Soviet Alliance," p. 43; Prozumenshchikov and Shevchuk, "Soviet-Chinese Relations," p. 26; Adam Ulam, *Expansion and Coexistence: Soviet Foreign Policy, 1917–73* (New York: Praeger, 1974), p. 621; Zubok and Pleshakov, *Inside the Kremlin's Cold War*, pp. 227–28.

152 Goldstein, "Sino-Soviet Alliance," p. 43; Zubok and Pleshakov, *Inside the Kremlin's Cold War*, p. 228; Chen and Yang, "Chinese Politics," p. 45.

153 Author's interview with the former Soviet ambassador to China Stepan V. Chervonenko. Khrushchev's speech in Nikita S. Khrushchev, *Mir bez oruzhiia–mir bez voin: Vystupleniia po voprosam vneshnei politiki SSSR i mezhdunarodnogo polozheniia, interviu i besedy s inostrannymi deiateliami* (Moscow: Gosudarstvennoe izdatel'stvo politicheksoi literatury, 1960), vol. 2, p. 312.

154 Russian minutes of the Khrushchev-Mao talks on October 2, 1959, are in the Volkogonov Collection, LOC, reel 17, and are cited in Volkogonov, *Sem' vozhdei*, pp. 423–15. English excerpts are in Wolff, "One Finger's Worth," pp. 64–66. This account is also based on recollections by Li Yueran and Yan Mingfu at the 1996 Beijing Symposium on Sino-Soviet Relations and the Cold War.

155 A week after Chinese forces crushed an uprising in Lhasa in March 1959, the Dalai Lama managed to escape across the Indian border.

156 Author's interview with Stepan V. Chervonenko.

157 Zubok and Pleshakov, *Inside the Kremlin's Cold War*, p. 230. Khrushchev's use of the term "old galoshes" was recalled at the 1997 Beijing Symposium by Mao's former interpreters at the 1959 talks.

158 Deliusin recalled Khrushchev's exclamation at the 1997 Beijing Symposium.

159 Recollections reported at the 1997 Beijing Symposium on Sino-Soviet Relations and the Cold War.

160 Chervonenko recalled Khrushchev's appearance upon departing Beijing in an interview with the author. Author's interview with former naval officer Nikolai A. Govorushko. Also see Govorushko's two-part memoir, "Pochetnyi posetitel'," *Boevaia vakhta* (February 28, 1990, and March 1, 1990).

CHAPTER 15. THE BERLIN CRISIS AND THE AMERICAN TRIP: 1958–1959

1 Khrushchev, *For Victory*, p. 738.

2 Thompson cables to Washington of November 11 and 14, 1958, in FRUS, 1958–1960, vol. 8, pp. 47–48, 62. Eisenhower-Herter phone conversation of November 28, ibid., p. 114.

3 The scene is described in Oleg Grinevskii, "Berlinskii krizis 1958–1959 gg.," *Zvezda*, No. 2, 1996, p. 127. Priscilla Johnson McMillan recalled Khrushchev's demeanor in an interview with the author. Also see Beschloss, *Mayday*, p. 162.

4 Beschloss, *Mayday*, pp. 162–63. FRUS, 1958–1960, vol. 8, pp. 143, 173.

5 Khrushchev's former foreign policy assistant Oleg Troyanovsky analyzed his boss's Berlin reasoning in *Cherez gody*, pp. 209–13. Also see Zubok and Pleshakov, *Inside the Kremlin's Cold War*, pp. 195–200. All three writers credit Khrushchev's concerns about West German nuclearization. But Oleg Grinevsky cites a meeting at which Khrushchev expressed skepticism that Adenauer would want weapons that, if he were to obtain them, would alarm not only the Soviets but other West Europeans too. See Grinevskii, *Tysiacha i odin den' Nikity Sergeevicha* (Moscow: Vagrius, 1998), pp. 26–28. For a detailed diplomatic history that portrays Soviet policy as rooted in concerns about German nuclear aspirations, see Marc Trachtenberg, *A Constructed Peace: The Making of the European Settlement, 1945–1963* (Princeton, N.J.: Princeton University Press, 1999).

6 Humphrey's report to Ambassador Thompson in Thompson's telegram no. 1208 to secretary of state, December 3, 1958, Box 126, President's Office Files (hereafter POF), John F. Kennedy Library, Boston, Massachusetts (hereafter JFKL). Mikoyan (*Tak bylo*, pp. 604–05) added that Khrushchev "manifested an amazing misunderstanding of the whole complex of problems" concerning Berlin. Anatoly Dobrynin characterized Gromyko's relationship with Khrushchev in *In Confidence*, p. 32. Also see Aleksandrov-Agentov, *Ot Kollontai do Gorbacheva*, p. 71. Aleksandrov-Agentov later served as foreign policy aide to all Soviet leaders from Brezhnev to Gorbachev. V. M. Falin recalled that at one point that autumn the Central Committee's Information Department was asked to brief Khrushchev on prospects for Germany, that G. M. Pushkin dared express skepticism about Khrushchev's plan, and that when he did so, Khrushchev labeled his views "nonsense" and lost interest in the Information Department altogether. See Falin, *Bez skidok i obstoiatel'stva: Politicheskie vospominaniia* (Moscow: "Respublika": "Sovremennik," 1999), pp. 22, 79–80.

7 Troianovskii, *Cherez gody*, pp. 211–13.

8 SK3, vol. 1, p. 416. The Polish leader Gomułka apparently also saw a draft of Khrushchev's November 10 speech just before it was delivered and was shocked. See Douglas Selvage, "New Evidence on the Berlin Crisis, 1958–1962," in CWIHPB, no. 11, (Winter 1998), p. 200.

9 Department of State telegram no. 1773, March 9, 1959, 4:00 P.M., from Thompson, Moscow, to Secretary of State, Document no. 922, in William Burr, ed., *The Berlin Crisis* (Washington, D.C.: National Security Archive/Chadwyck-Healey, 1991).

10 DSB, vol. 37, no. 940 (July 1, 1957), p. 15; no. 964 (December 16, 1957), p. 989.

11 FBIS, May 14, 1957, pp. BB1, 4, 6–7, 10.

12 *Pravda*, November 19, 1957, p. 2.

13 Author's interview with Jane Thompson.

14 "Extract of Report by Mr. John Carrey of conversation with Yuri Gvozdev on January 22, 1958," Box 46, Papers of Dwight D. Eisenhower as President (Ann Whitman File) (hereafter AWF), International Series, DDEL. Eisenhower's initials can be found at the top of the personal and confidential memorandum reporting this conversation, indicating that he was well aware of Khrushchev's views. Also see Beschloss, *Crisis Years*, pp. 153–54.

15 DSB, vol. 37, no. 970 (January 27, 1958), pp. 122–27; no. 974 (February 24, 1958), p. 291.

16 Several days later Mićunović warned that Westerners opposed to talks would use Khrushchev's "violent attack" in Minsk to "spoil the atmosphere further." But Khrushchev was sure the "sharp words used on both sides would soon be forgotten." See Mićunović, *Moscow Diary*, pp. 337–38.

17 Khrushchev's interview with Polish correspondents, March 10, 1958, in *Pravda*, March 12, 1958, p. 2. On March 3, Soviet Ambassador Menshikov told Eisenhower and Dulles that his government "would not oppose the holding of a meeting of Heads of Government in the United States at a city to be selected by the United States." See FRUS, 1958–1960, vol. 10, pt. 1, p. 152.

18 Although five months had passed since the USSR proposed a formal four-power summit, Khrushchev continued, the Western powers had "still not replied" to questions about the organization of the conference or its agenda. From speech to Warsaw Pact Political Consultative Commission conference, *Pravda*, May 27, 1958, p. 3.

19 The American Embassy was informed in advance that although "spontaneous" demonstrations would be held, "everything would be all right." But after "demonstrators" smashed windows at the West German Embassy, Ambassador Kroll, who prided himself on friendly relations with Khrushchev, was found sitting morosely near a pile of broken glass, bricks, and other rubble. The political atmosphere reminded Mićunović of November 1956 after the Soviet intervention in Hungary, but Khrushchev informed him that this too would pass. See Mićunović, *Moscow Diary*, p. 401.

20 SK3, vol. 1, p. 396; Heikal, *Sphinx and the Commissar*, pp. 97–99.

21 Transcript of August 5, 1958, conversation between Khrushchev and Adlai Stevenson, pp. 8–9, Adlai E. Stevenson Papers, Seeley Mudd Library, Princeton University.

22 When Mićunović paid his farewell call on October 8, Khrushchev crowed over a string of victories, including the coming withdrawal of the Americans and British from Lebanon and Jordan. The latter, Khrushchev said, amounted to their "having been driven out by force." This proved that "capitalism was getting steadily weaker," especially in the Third World. Khrushchev and his colleagues were "very satisfied with the development of the situation both internally and externally." See Mićunović, *Moscow Diary*, p. 432.

23 Excerpts from reports by Eric Johnston on his conversation with Khrushchev are in FRUS, 1958–1960, vol. 10, pt. 1, pp. 189–205. The quote from Khrushchev is on p. 199.

24 Troianovskii, *Cherez gody*, pp. 208–13; Troyanovsky, "Making of Soviet Foreign Policy," pp. 216–17.

25 Grinevskii, *Tysiacha odin den'*, p. 23.

26 In August 1958 Macmillan inquired of his Moscow embassy about Khrushchev's "megalomania," asking in particular, "Could Khrushchev do foolish things as Hitler did? . . ." British Ambassador Reilly replied on August 25: "I do not think Khrushchev's incipient megalomania is as yet nearly as dangerous as Hitler's, and I think the odds are against it becoming so. First, Khrushchev is a normal human being, with a normal family life. (Moreover he lost a son in the war.) Secondly, there is no Khrushchev *mystique* here." See PRO, PREM 11/5115.

27 Eisenhower diary entry for January 23, 1956, Dwight D. Eisenhower Diary Series, DDEL.

28 Transcript of Eisenhower telephone call to Allen Dulles, July 8, 1957, 3:13 P.M., Eisenhower-Dulles telephone conversations, Box 12, John Foster Dulles Papers, Seeley Mudd Library, Princeton University.

29 Eisenhower-Dulles telephone conversation, February 9, 1958, 4:00 P.M., in Eisenhower Library-John Foster Dulles Papers, Seeley Mudd Library, Princeton University.

30 On this point in particular, but on Soviet-East German relations in general, see Hope M. Harrison, "Ulbricht and the Concrete 'Rose': New Archival Evidence on the Dynamics of Soviet-East German Relations and the Berlin Crisis, 1958–1961," Working Paper no. 5, Cold War International History Project, Woodrow Wilson International Centers for Scholars, May 1993, pp. 6–7.

31 His tactics were even odder. He insisted that his threats of war were a breakthrough toward peace. Although his proposals were patently unacceptable to the West, he presented them in his November 27 note as a kind of concession: By rights, all Berlin ought to belong to East Germany, but he would generously agree to treat West Berlin as a "free city." Although his ultimatum could only overheat the already supercharged atmosphere, he said his six-month deadline was designed to avoid "haste and friction." If the Western powers turned down his concessions, they would have have resorted to "brute force, threats and intimidation." In that case, since "only madmen" could want a war, Khrushchev would have to provide "straitjackets." See Soviet government note to U.S. government of November 27, 1958, in DSB, vol. 40, no. 1020 (January 12, 1959), pp. 81–89.

32 William Burr, "Avoiding the Slippery Slope: The Eisenhower Administration and the Berlin Crisis, November 1958–January 1959," *Diplomatic History*, vol. 18, no. 1 (Winter 1994), pp. 9–10, 21.

33 This account of Humphrey's visit and of his impressions is drawn from notes he took during his conversation with Khrushchev and dictated afterward, as well as from a transcript of a Humphrey interview with *Life*, and from his later debriefing by State Department officials. See "Trip Files: Russia," in Senatorial Files, 1949–1964, Box 703, Hubert Horatio Humphrey Papers, Minnesota Historical Society, Minneapolis, Minnesota. Also see Ambassador Thompson's telegrams, no. 1208, December 3, 1958, and no. 1216, December 4, 1958, and a memorandum of conversation between Humphrey and Acting Secretary of State Christian Herter, December 8, 1958, in Box 126, POF, JFKL, and State Department reports on Humphrey-Khrushchev conversation in FRUS, 1958–1960, vol. 8, pp. 149–53.

34 See C. L. Sulzberger, *The Last of the Giants* (New York: Macmillan, 1970), p. 860.

35 Beschloss, *Crisis Years,* p. 154.

36 SK4, p. 306. Troianovskii, *Cherez gody,* pp. 214–15.

37 See SK4, p. 307; Troianovskii, *Cherez gody,* p. 215; Mikoian, *Tak bylo,* p. 605.

38 Troianovskii, *Cherez gody,* p. 216.

39 Mikoyan did get into a heated exchange about Berlin with Dulles, but he confided to Eisenhower that if Khrushchev had been able to vote in the 1956 American election he would have "voted for the President." See transcripts of Mikoyan's conversations in FRUS, 1958–1960, vol. 8, pp. 233–39, 270–81; FRUS, 1958–1960, vol. 10, pt. 1, pp. 207–58.

40 SK4, p. 307.

41 John P. S. Gearson, "Macmillan and Berlin, 1958–1961" (Washington, D.C.: Nuclear History Project Berlin Study Conference, May 1993, paper prepared for delivery), p. 10. Also see Gearson, *Harold Macmillan and the Berlin Wall Crisis, 1958–1962: The Limits of Interest and Force* (New York: St. Martin's, 1998), p. 57. Macmillan insisted he wasn't "coming to negotiate." Instead, he wrote in his diary, he would "try to discover something of what is in the mind of the Soviet leaders." See Macmillan, *Riding the Storm,* p. 585.

42 Beschloss, *Mayday,* p. 173.

43 Macmillan, *Riding the Storm,* p. 598.

44 Ibid., p. 603.

45 Alistair Horne, *Macmillan* (London: Macmillan, 1988), vol. 2, p. 125.

46 SK4, p. 308; Macmillan, *Riding the Storm,* p. 619; Gearson, "Macmillan and Berlin," p. 14.

47 Macmillan, *Riding the Storm,* pp. 610–11.

48 "Visit of the Prime Minister and the Foreign Secretary to the Soviet Union, February 21–March 5, 1959," top secret, PRO, PREM 11/2690, p. 31.

49 See two dispatches by D. P. Reilly to Selwyn Lloyd of March 9 and March 16, 1959, PRO, FO 371/143439, and PREM 11/2690.

50 Cited by a knowledgeable source who prefers not to be identified.

51 SK4, p. 308.

52 *Pravda,* May 12, 1959, p. 4.

53 SK3, vol. 1, p. 422.

54 *Pravda,* June 20, 1959, p. 3.

55 This account is based on "Diary of Gov. Harriman's Soviet Trip: May 12–June 26, 1959," and a transcript of "Conversation of Gov. Harriman with Mr. Khrushchev, June 23, 1959," in W. Averell Harriman Collection, Washington, D.C.

56 *Public Papers of the Presidents of the United States: Dwight D. Eisenhower, 1959* (Washington, D.C.: Government Printing Office, 1960), p. 507.

57 FRUS, 1958–1860, vol. 8, p. 521; FRUS, 1958–1960, vol. 10, pt. 1, p. 264.

58 *Public Papers: Eisenhower, 1959,* pp. 172–73, 209.

59 Ibid., p. 27.

60 This account is based on documents in FRUS, 1958–1960, vol. 8, pp. 971–77, 1027–43, and FRUS, 1958–1960, vol. 10, pt. 1, pp. 309–25; and also accounts in Dwight D. Eisenhower, *Waging the Peace 1956–1961* (New York: Doubleday, 1965), pp. 405–07, and Beschloss, *Mayday,* pp. 177–78.

61 See Campbell Craig, *Destroying the Village: Eisenhower and Thermonuclear War* (New York: Columbia University Press, 1998), p. 105; Gearson, *Harold Macmillan and the Berlin Wall Crisis,* p. 105.

62 *Public Papers: Eisenhower, 1959,* p. 153.

63 SK3, vol. 1, p. 442.

64 NK2, p. 369.

65 SK3, vol. 1, pp. 442–43; Troianovskii, *Cherez gody,* p. 208.

66 Richard M. Nixon, *Six Crises* (Garden City, N.Y.: Doubleday, 1962), pp. 244–45.

67 Richard N. Nixon, *Leaders* (New York: Warner Books, 1982), p. 182.

68 See Nixon, *Six Crises,* pp. 264–66. The American memorandum of this conversation is in FRUS, 1958–1960, vol. 8, pp. 336–45.

69 For a description and analysis of the exhibition, including attempts to gauge Soviet public reaction, see Walter Hixson, *Parting the Curtain: Propaganda, Culture and the Cold War* (New York: St. Martin's, 1996), pp. 174–80.

70 Granting that the USSR might be ahead of the United States in certain areas such as rockets, Nixon stiffly allowed as how "there may be some areas," like color television, "where we are ahead of you." At that point Khrushchev interrupted, saying, "Nyet, nyet, nyet," and shaking his head vigorously. "No, we're ahead of you in that technology, too." Later, after repeating several times his agreement with an innocuous point Nixon had made, Khrushchev suddenly stopped, did a double take, flashed a grin at the audience (including Mikoyan, Kozlov, and Furtseva as well as journalists and others), and said, "Wait, I want to get clear on what it was I just agreed with." Later still, after Nixon agreed that the two men's exchange should be shown on American television, with Khrushchev's remarks translated into English, Khrushchev raised his hand high and slapped Nixon's to seal the deal. Film of the exchange, United States National Archives (hereafter NA), RG 64, pt. 15.

71 For an account of the "kitchen debate," see Stephen E. Ambrose, *Nixon: The Education of a Politician, 1913–1962* (New York: Simon and Schuster, 1987), pp. 524–25.

72 Nixon recounts his trip in *Six Crises,* pp. 235–91, and in *Leaders,* pp. 177–200.

73 Cited in Beschloss, *Mayday,* p. 184.

74 *Public Papers: Eisenhower, 1959,* p. 560; DSB, vol. 61, no. 1057 (September 28, 1959), p. 437.

75 *Public Papers: Eisenhower, 1959,* p. 592.

76 Adzhubei, *Krushenie illiuzii,* p. 215; SK2, p. 356.

77 SK4, pp. 326–27.

78 SK3, vol. 1, 446; Adzhubei, *Krushenie illiuzii,* p. 216, 220. This brain trust included personal aides Shuisky, Lebedev, and Troyanovsky, Central Committee Propaganda Department head Leonid Ilychev, Foreign Ministry press chief Leonid Zamyatin, Adzhubei, and the brilliant young interpreter, Viktor Sukhodrev.

79 SK3, p. 446.

80 Chalmers Roberts, *First Rough Draft: A Journalist's Journal of Our Times* (New York: Praeger, 1973), p. 158.

81 NK4, no. 4, 1993, p. 36.

82 SK4, p. 327.

83 NK4, no. 4, 1993, p. 37.

84 NK2, p. 371.

85 SK4, p. 329. Another reason for the plane's height was the giant propellers. Author's interview with Sergei Khrushchev.

86 NK2, p. 373.

87 Ibid.

88 *Pravda,* August 4, 1959, in CDSP, vol. 11, no. 31 (September 2, 1959), pp. 3–7.

89 SK4, p. 329.

90 Ibid., p. 330.

91 Khrushchev wouldn't be "completely on my own," for veteran Foreign Minister Gromyko was to be at his side. But Khrushchev was damned if he'd "start whispering questions back and forth with him in the middle of my talks with Eisenhower," the way Eisenhower let Dulles "shove notes in front of him all through our negotiations at Geneva."

92 NK4, no. 4, 1993, pp. 38–39; NK2, pp. 373–75.

93 M. Kharlamov, ed., *Face to Face with America: The Story of N. S. Khrushchev's Visit to the U.S.A, September 15–27, 1959* (Moscow, 1960), pp. 52–53.

94 NK2, p. 377; NK4, no. 4, 1993, p. 40.

95 Troianovskii, *Cherez gody,* p. 210; Beschloss, *Mayday,* p. 190; John S. D. Eisenhower, *Strictly Personal* (Garden City, N.Y.: Doubleday, 1974), p. 257.

96 Beschloss, *Mayday,* pp. 189–90.

97 *Face to Face with America,* pp. 446.

98 Adzhubei, *Krushenie illiuzii,* p. 220.

99 Author's interview with Oleg Troyanovsky, February 1993.

100 Author's interview with Richard T. Davies.

101 Adzhubei, *Krushenie illiuzii,* pp. 220–21.

102 Author's interview with Jane Thompson.

103 Adzhubei, *Krushenie illiuzii,* p. 220.

104 DSB, vol. 41, no. 1058 (October 5, 1959), p. 478; Beschloss, *Mayday,* pp. 193–94.

105 *Face to Face with America,* pp. 89-92.

106 Nikita S. Khrushchev, *Khrushchev in America: Full Texts of the Speeches Made by N. S. Khrushchev on His Tour of the United States, September 15–27, 1959* (New York: Crosscurrents Press, 1960), p. 18.

107 Ibid., p. 26. See also Beschloss, *Mayday,* p. 194.

108 *Times* (London), November 19, 1956, p. 8. Not surprisingly, the Russian text of Khrushchev's remarks in *Pravda* omits this remark. Earlier the same evening, at a Kremlin reception, Khrushchev had used the words "fascist," and "bandits" to refer to Britain, France, and Israel, prompting ambassadors from NATO countries to walk out.

109 *Khrushchev in America,* p. 31.

110 Ibid., p. 28.

111 NK2, p. 381.

112 *Face to Face with America,* p. 157.

113 *Khrushchev in America,* p. 48.

114 John Kenneth Galbraith, "The Day Khrushchev Visited the Establishment," *Harper's Magazine*, February 1971, p. 73.

115 NK2, pp. 382–83.

116 *Khrushchev in America*, p. 65; Beschloss, *Mayday*, p. 198.

117 Memorandum of Conversation between Khrushchev and Henry Cabot Lodge, September 18, 1959, in FRUS, 1958–1960, vol. 10, pt. 1, p. 417.

118 NK4, no. 4, 1993, p. 43; NK2, p. 385; FRUS, 1958–1960, vol. 8, p. 433.

119 *Face to Face with America*, p. 223; Beschloss, *Mayday*, p. 199.

120 Richard T. Davies, unpublished transcript of oral history, provided to the author by Mr. Davies, p. 4/154.

121 *Face to Face with America*, p. 224; Henry Cabot Lodge, *The Storm Has Many Eyes: A Personal Narrative* (New York: Norton, 1973), p. 163.

122 It was on this occasion that Khrushchev told the story I have already quoted about his being billeted during the civil war with an aristocratic family that at first looked down their noses at him and then came to respect his commitment to bringing culture to the masses.

123 NK2, p. 385. *Khrushchev in America*, pp. 104–13. Also see Lodge, *Storm Has Many Eyes*, pp. 163–64, and Daryl F. Gates, *Chief: My Life in the LAPD* (New York: Bantam, 1992), p. 73. Richard T. Davies, transcript of oral history, pp. 3/152–53 added that Soviet advancemen had previously opposed a Disneyland visit; Davies suspected Khrushchev deliberately asked to go, knowing his request would be denied. It occurred to Khrushchev that "if I did go and if there were disorders against me, this man whose father had lost his factories in Rostov might be pleased for me to get just such a reception." Therefore, "I decided not to insist." Sinatra cited in Beschloss, *Mayday*, p. 199.

124 *Face to Face with America*, p. 228. The author viewed KTLA kinescopes of the scene at the Museum of Television and Radio in New York City. The dancers refused to raise their skirts. When President Eisenhower heard about that, he told Lodge he would write them a letter of thanks. See Lodge, *Storm Has Many Eyes*, p. 165.

125 From transcript of Khrushchev meeting with labor leaders, September 20, 1959, in Whitney, *Khrushchev Speaks*, pp. 342–43.

126 NK2, p. 386.

127 Author's interview with Alexander Akalovsky.

128 *Face to Face with America*, p. 232; Lodge, *Storm Has Many Eyes*, p. 166.

129 Khrushchev also boasted that the KGB used double agents to intercept CIA messages and to send back disinformation and even requests for additional funds. See Lodge, *Storm Has Many Eyes*, pp. 165–66; Sanche de Gramont, *The Secret War: The Story of International Espionage Since World War II* (New York: Putnam 1962), p. 149; Beschloss, *Mayday*, pp. 198–99; FRUS, 1958–1960, vol. 10, pt. 1, pp. 426–27. For confirmation that Western embassies were regularly bugged and broken into, see Christopher Andrew and Oleg Gordievsky, *KGB: the Inside Story of Its Foreign Operations from Lenin to Gorbachev* (New York: HarperCollins, 1990), pp. 450–55.

130 NK2, p. 388.

131 *Face to Face with America*, p. 233.

132 NK2, p. 388; Lodge, *Storm Has Many Eyes*, p. 167. Even Lodge, who had seen an advance copy of the speech, tried to get Paulson to desist, saying Khrushchev would surely think the U.S. government was behind it.

133 *Khrushchev in America,* pp. 119–21.

134 SK2, p. 358; Lodge *Storm Has Many Eyes,* p. 167; Roberts, *First Rough Draft,* p. 159.

135 NK2, p. 389.

136 SK2, p. 358; NK2, p. 389; Rada Adzhubei insisted her father's explosion was "entirely deliberate." Author's interview with Rada Adzhubei, June 1991.

137 Adzhubei, *Krushenie illiuzii,* p. 222.

138 Lodge, *Storm Has Many Eyes,* pp. 169–70; *Face to Face with America,* p. 242.

139 Roberts, *First Rough Draft,* p. 160.

140 Christopher remembers breaking the ice at the San Francisco train station by joking that the "big bosses" of the Soviet delegation and the San Francisco welcoming committee were, in fact, Mrs. Khrushchev and Mrs. Christopher, a remark to which Khrushchev responded, "I like you. You are different." Letter with attachment from George Christopher to Sergei Khrushchev, July 9, 1999.

141 SK4, p. 334. Upon returning to Moscow, Khrushchev ordered that food service be organized on the IBM model and that self-service supermarkets of the sort he saw in San Jose be adopted as well. Also see Harrison E. Salibury, *Heroes of My Time* (New York: Walker, 1993), pp. 86–87; Thomas J. Watson, *Father, Son and Co.: My Life at IBM and Beyond* (New York: Bantam, 1990), pp. 329–31.

142 "Summary of Meeting of Labor Leaders with Prime Minister Nikita Khrushchev of the USSR, Mark Hopkins Hotel, San Francisco, September 20, 1959," Office of the President, Folder 6, Box 318, Walter P. Reuther Collection, Archive of Labor History and Urban Affairs, Wayne State University, Detroit, Michigan.

143 NK2, pp. 394–95.

144 The following account draws broadly on FRUS, 1958–1960, vol. 9, pp. 35–53; FRUS, 1958–1960, vol. 10, pt. 1, pp. 459–85; and Beschloss, *Mayday.*

145 See FRUS, 1958–1960, vol. 9, pp. 35–41.

146 FRUS, 1958–1960, vol. 10, pt. 1, 467–68.

147 George B. Kistiakowsky, *A Scientist at the White House: The Private Diary of President Eisenhower's Special Assistant for Science and Technology* (Cambridge: Harvard University Press, 1976), p. 90.

148 Ibid., p. 93.

149 Ibid., pp. 91, 93.

150 Ibid., p. 92.

151 Ibid., p. 93.

152 FRUS, 1958–1960, vol. 10, pt. 1, pp. 470–76 See also Beschloss, *Mayday,* p. 209.

153 FRUS, 1958–1960, vol. 10, pt. 1, p. 479.

154 FRUS, 1958–1960, vol. 9, p. 42. Eisenhower's commitment may actually have gone further. Several months later, when the Western powers continued to hew to a position on Berlin that they had first adopted in the summer of 1959, U.S. Ambassador Thompson cabled from Moscow that this meant "the United States would in fact go back on its Camp David commitment that it would secure the agreement of its allies for a solution of the specific problem of Berlin." Cited in Gearson, "Macmillan and Berlin," p. 19.

155 What, Khrushchev wanted to know, did the president mean by duress? Eisenhower replied that duress was "a situation where one party intended to take unilateral actions without regard to other countries concerned." Khrushchev disavowed any such intention on the part of his government which he said had "never intended to create a situation of duress." FRUS, 1958–1960, vol. 9, p. 44.

156 Ibid., p. 47.

157 Dwight D. Eisenhower, *Waging Peace, 1956–1961: The White House Years* (Garden City, N.Y.: Doubleday, 1965), p. 447. Khrushchev would have blown up if he'd heard the president's interpretation of another draft sentence: "It was further agreed that these [Berlin] negotiations should not be prolonged indefinitely. . . ." No problem with that, Eisenhower told his aides, since clearly the United States did not "contemplate fifty years of occupation there." Forty-nine years wouldn't have exactly satisfied Khrushchev. See FRUS, 1958–1960, vol. 9, p. 46.

158 NK2, p. 412. When Khrushchev first arrived in Washington, Eisenhower made a personal appeal to him in a one-on-one conversation in the White House. He said his guest could become "the greatest political figure in history" because Khrushchev "had tremendous power in a complex of states with great might." However, since the Western allies "have their own ways of doing things and have their own independent approaches," an American president had power "only as far as one nation—the U.S.—is concerned." After Eisenhower left office in sixteen months, he would "still love people—all people, including the Russian people," just as he loved all of them now, but it was Khrushchev who "could be the man to do a great deal to secure peace in the world."

This was Eisenhower's way of playing to Khrushchev's ego. But it failed. Khrushchev may have been flattered. But he must have also been suspicious (since he knew no one was more powerful than the president of the United States), as well as all the more determined to play on Eisenhower's commitment to peace to get him to make concessions on Germany and agree to a full four-power summit. See FRUS, 1958–1960, vol. 10, pt. 1, pp. 409–10.

159 With the benefit of hindsight, Troyanovsky later described the results as "mixed." Bitter over his treatment by Khrushchev, Gromyko remembered "no real improvement." Khrushchev himself changed his view in his memoirs, claiming he too had been "upset" with the outcome, though not as much as Eisenhower because "I hadn't come to the United States with any illusions, and I had known all along that it was premature to expect an agreement." See Troianovskii, *Cherez gody*, p. 218; A. A. Gromyko, *Pamiatnoe* (Moscow: Politizdat, 1988), vol. 1, p. 379; NK2, p. 412.

160 Adzhubei, *Krushenie illiuzii*, p. 223.

161 *Khrushchev in America*. p. 216.

162 SK4, p. 346.

163 *Pravda*, February 5, 1960, p. 1.

164 Beschloss, *Mayday*, pp. 228–29; SK3, vol. 1, pp. 477–78.

165 Author's interviews with Vladimir I. Toumanoff, November 1986 and June 2000.

166 SK3, vol. 1, pp. 476–78.

CHAPTER 16. FROM THE U-2 TO THE UN SHOE: APRIL–SEPTEMBER 1960

1 SK3, vol. 2, pp. 12–13; SK4, pp. 369–70.

2 For a brief history of pre-U-2 overflights plus related aerial reconnaissance flights that operated near Soviet territory but without overflight authorization (and which lost 170 U.S, Air Force and Navy aircrew members between 1946 and 1991), see Hall, "The Truth about Overflights," pp. 25–39.

3 Cited by Richard Bissell, Jr., the manager of the U-2 program within the Central Intelligence Agency, in his memoir, *Reflections of a Cold Warrior: From Yalta to the Bay of Pigs* (New Haven: Yale University Press, 1996), p. 123.

4 SK3, vol. 1, p. 484.

5 SK4, pp. 365–67; G.A. Mikhailov and A. S. Orlov, "Tainy 'zakrytogo neba,'" NiNI, no. 6 (1992), p. 105.

6 Khrushchev later characterized imperialist thinking this way in a speech to the USSR Supreme Soviet on May 5, 1960. *Pravda,* May 6, 1960, p. 5.

7 SK3, vol. 2, pp. 8–10; Mikhailov and Orlov, "Tainy 'zakrytogo neba,'" p. 106.

8 Beschloss, *Mayday,* pp. 241–42; Bissell, *Reflections,* p. 125–26.

9 Orlov and Mikhailov, "Tainy 'zakrytogo neba,'", p. 107. SK4, pp. 372–73.

10 Orlov and Mikhailov, "Tainy 'zakrytogo neba,'" p. 107; SK3, vol. 2, pp. 20–21, 27. Sergei Khrushchev discussed the cover-up and misleading announcement of honors that followed. A few days after Nikita Khrushchev revealed the U-2 flight, a U.S. Embassy officer traveling by train was told by a Soviet Air Force fellow passenger that a missile aimed at the U-2 had downed a Soviet plane instead. Author's interview with Vladimir Toumanoff, June 2000.

11 Orlov and Mikhailov, "Tainy 'zakrytogo neba,'" p. 108. Grinevsky reports Yulia Leonidovna Khrushcheva's recollection of the scene in *Tysiacha i odin den',* p. 211.

12 SK3, vol. 2, p. 23.

13 Ibid.

14 Dr. A. McGehee Harvey, "A 1969 Conversation with Khrushchev: The Beginning of His Fall from Power," *Life* (December 18, 1970), p. 48B.

15 Telegram from the embassy in the Soviet Union to the Department of State, January 2, 1960, in FRUS, 1958–1960, vol. 9, p. 162.

16 De Gaulle press conference of November 10, 1959, in *Documents on International Affairs, 1959,* ed. Gillian King (London: Oxford University Press, 1963), p. 463.

17 FRUS, 1958–1960, vol. 9, pp. 218–19. Also see William Burr, "Eisenhower and the Diplomacy of the Berlin Crisis, 1958–1960," (Washington, D.C.: Cold War International History Project/Nuclear History Project, Conference on the Berlin Crisis, 1993, paper prepared for delivery), pp. 42–43.

18 Harold Macmillan, *Pointing the Way: 1959–1961* (New York: Harper & Row, 1972), pp. 94–95.

19 From "Record of a Conversation in the Palais d'Elysées on December 21, 1959," in PRO, PREM 11/2991. As the conversation continued, Macmillan remarked that Khrushchev was "a man of no education or training and therefore very sensitive." De Gaulle replied that "of course Mr. Khrushchev had a miserable life. He had been humiliated and insulted and generally badly treated, and until now had never been in a good position."

20 Macmillan, *Pointing the Way,* pp. 179, 191, 195.

21 De Gaulle, *Memoirs,* p. 243.

22 Grinveskii, *Tysiacha i odin den'*, pp. 102, 113.

23 Khrushchev's December 8, 1959, memorandum, as translated and analyzed by Vladislav M. Zubok, is in "Khrushchev's 1960 Troop Cut: New Russian Evidence," CWIHPB, nos. 8–9 (Winter 1996–1997), pp. 416–20.

24 FRUS, 1958–1960, vol. 10, pt. 1, p. 499.

25 For Thompson's account of the New Year's Eve festivities and his political analysis of Khrushchev's remarks see FRUS, 1958–1960, vol. 9, pp. 159–61, 162–65. Grinevskii describes the scene in *Tysiacha i oden den'*, pp. 118–19.

26 Author's interview with Boris Klosson. See also Grinevskii, *Tysiacha i odin den'*, pp. 119–22.

27 FRUS, 1958–1960, vol. 10, pp. 507–09.

28 SK3, vol. 1, p. 478.

29 Khrushchev complained in his memoirs that Indonesian President Sukarno's "theatrical streak" led him to overdo such jubilees, but that didn't prevent him from enjoying them. NK2, pp. 304–05, 313–14.

30 Nikita S. Khrushchev, *O vneshnei politike Sovetskogo Soiuza, 1960 god* (Moscow: Gosudarstvennoe izdatel'stvo politicheskoi literatury, 1960), vol. 1, p. 102. Kalinovka peasants' behavior, including that of Khrushchev's cousins, is described in Chapter 8.

31 NK2, pp. 313–18.

32 Khrushchev, *O vneshnei politike*, vol. 1, p. 173.

33 Airplane antics as seen in a home movie provided to the author by Sergei Khrushchev. Khrushchev's son insists that sending the foul-smelling fruit was not meant as a joke since his father didn't taste them himself until after they had been dispatched. Author's interview with Sergei Khrushchev.

34 See Aleksandrov-Agentov, *Ot Kollontai do Gorbacheva*, p. 105.

35 Adzhubei, *Krushenie illiuzii*, p. 230.

36 NK2, pp. 439–42.

37 PRO, PREM 11/2978, Record of a conversation between President de Gaulle and the Prime Minister at Buckingham Palace, at 6:00 P.M. on Tuesday, April 5, 1960, p. 1; Record of a meeting held at Buckingham Palace at 9:45 A.M. on Wednesday, April 6, 1960.

38 Soviet transcripts of the Khrushchev-de Gaulle talks are in "N. S. Khrushchev–Sharl' de Goll: Vstrechi v Parizhe, 1960 g.," IA, no. 1 (1996), pp. 27–40; and no. 2 (1996), pp. 105–32.

39 NK2, p. 429.

40 Ibid., p. 428.

41 *Pravda*, March 29, 1960, p. 1.

42 Ibid., p. 2.

43 Adzhubei, *Krushenie illiuzii*, p. 229.

44 FBIS, April 5, 1960, p. BB5.

45 Troianovskii, *Cherez gody*, pp. 220–22. Also see Grinevskii, *Tysiacha i odin den'*, pp. 123–29, 144–58.

46 Aleksandrov-Agentov, "Brezhnev i Khrushchev," p. 39.

47 See Grinevskii, *Tysiacha i odin den'*, pp. 162–63. Also see Richard Ned Lebow and Janice Gross Stein, *We All Lost the Cold War* (Princeton: Princeton University Press, 1994), pp. 55–56.

48 DSB, vol. 42, no. 1087 (April 25, 1960), pp. 635–40; no. 1089 (May 9, 1960), pp. 723–29.

49 Beschloss, *Mayday*, p. 240.

50 *Pravda*, April 26, 1960, p. 5.

51 Troianovskii, *Cherez gody*, p. 221.

52 Burlatsky, *Khrushchev*, pp. 156–57; Georgy Arbatov, *The System: An Insider's Life in Soviet Politics* (New York: Times Books, 1992), p. 96. Sturua spoke at the Khrushchev Centennial Conference at Brown University in December 1994. Also see SK4, pp. 381–82.

53 Beschloss, *Mayday*, p. 39.

54 Heikal, *Sphinx and the Commissar*, pp. 112–13. At a May 4 Central Committee meeting, two Khrushchev protégés (Kirichenko and Beliaev) were dropped from the Presidium and three more (Aristov, Furtseva, and Ignatov) from the Secretariat, while those who replaced them included the considerably more independent Aleksei Kosygin and Frol Kozlov. Some speculate that Khrushchev critics were already using the U-2 against him. But Khrushchev himself was dissatisfied with his own proteges: Kirichenko was even cruder than Khrushchev and not nearly as smart; when Khrushchev tried to talk business, Aristov kept changing the subject to fishing; and Ignatov and Furtseva lacked sufficient weight, especially on international matters. According to Sergei Khrushchev, "Father's struggle was not with some sort of opposition, but with himself. . . . " SK3, vol. 2, p. 30.

55 Khrushchev half admitted the contradiction: "Some comrades" might ask, "Are we not hasty in abolishing taxes and increasing investments in consumers' goods? Will this not weaken . . . the country's defense?"

56 Author's interview with Vladimir I. Toumanoff, June 2000.

57 Priscilla Johnson McMillan recalled the scene in remarks to the Khrushchev Centennial Conference at Brown University in December 1994. Khrushchev's speech is in *Pravda*, May 6, 1960, p. 5. Yet another Khrushchev grievance was that President Eisenhower had insisted he could spend at most a week at the summit in Paris, an announcement Khrushchev took as personally "insulting and humiliating," said his son, especially since Ike cited a previous appointment in Portugal with the anti-Communist dictator Salazar. SK3, vol. 2, p. 24.

58 Author's interview with Priscilla Johnson McMillan. This account is also based on McMillan's draft recollection, Priscilla Johnson, "How They Took the Bad News," provided to the author by Mrs. McMillan.

59 Khrushchev was "angry and upset," but after at first ordering Malik dismissed from his post and expelled from the party, he settled for a public confession in an overflowing Foreign Ministry conference hall where the repentant sinner bleated, "Comrades, I have never before revealed state secrets," and his colleagues tried unsuccessfully to muffle their laughter. Sergei Khrushchev characterized his father's reaction in SK3, vol. 2, p. 25. Malik's fate is described by Arkady N. Shevchenko, *Breaking with Moscow* (New York: Knopf, 1985), p. 94. Also see Troianovskii, *Cherez gody*, pp. 223–24; and Grinevskii, *Tysiacha i odin den'*, pp. 217–22.

60 *Pravda*, May 8, 1960, p. 2; Bohlen, *Witness to History*, p. 466.

61 Troianovskii, *Cherez gody*, p. 225.

62 FRUS, 1958–1960, vol. 10, p. 515.

63 Ibid., pp. 252–53.

64 *Pravda,* May 10, 1960, p. 1.

65 Thompson later revealed these contacts at a meeting of the National Security Council's Executive Committee during the Cuban missile crisis. The Soviet military hint took the form of trying to calm Thompson down, thus implying that Khrushchev ought to do likewise. See Ernest R. May and Philip Zelikow, eds., *The Kennedy Tapes: Inside the White House during the Cuban Missile Crisis* (Cambridge, Mass.: Harvard University Press, 1997), p. 151.

66 FRUS, 1958–1960, vol. 10, pp. 519–20, doesn't mention the last quote, which is cited in Harrison E. Salisbury, *A Journey for Our Times: A Memoir* (New York: Harper & Row, 1983), pp. 489–90.

67 Beschloss, *Mayday,* pp. 257–58.

68 SK3, vol. 2, p. 26.

69 SK3, vol. 2, p. 36.

70 NK2, p. 448.

71 *Pravda,* May 13, 1960, pp. 1–2; Johnson, "How They Took the Bad News," p. 18. Khrushchev was so worried that his own comments might increase tension that journalists phoning their reports to the West were cut off for twenty-four hours by Soviet censors, after which the official transcript of the press conference eliminated Khrushchev's comment that he had been "horrified" by the president's approval of the U-2 flight and had changed his view of Eisenhower. See Beschloss, *Mayday,* pp. 261–63.

72 Author's interview with Priscilla Johnson McMillan; Johnson, "How They Took the Bad News," pp. 17–19.

73 Troianovskii, *Cherez gody,* p. 225. Not surprisingly, the Americans were also unsure whether Khrushchev wanted the Paris summit to proceed. The CIA's Office of Current Intelligence thought he did. Ambassador Thompson thought he did not. See FRUS, 1958–1960, vol. 9, p. 391; and Beschloss, *Mayday,* p. 266.

74 SK3, vol. 2, p. 32.

75 NK2, p. 451.

76 Troianovskii, *Cherez gody,* pp. 225–26; Grinveskii, *Tysiacha i odin den',* p. 250.

77 NK2, p. 452.

78 See FRUS, 1958–1960, vol. 9, p. 422; de Gaulle, *Memoirs,* p. 248; Beschloss, *Mayday,* p. 277. Also Genêt, "Letter from Paris," *New Yorker* (June 4, 1960), p. 150.

79 "Record of a conversation between the Prime Minister and Mr. Khrushchev at the British Embassy at 4:30 P.M. on May 15," in "Conference of Heads of State and Government of France, the United Kingdom, the Soviet Union, and the United States of America together with Records of other Related Meetings: Paris, May 14–19, 1960," PRO, PREM 11/2992, p. 15. Also see Macmillan, *Pointing the Way,* p. 202.

80 De Gaulle, *Memoirs,* p. 248; FRUS, 1958–1960, vol. 9, pp. 417–22, 433, 435.

81 American interpreter Vernon A. Walters, *Silent Missions* (Garden City, N.Y.: Doubleday, 1978), p. 342, describes the room, but also see Beschloss, *Mayday,* p. 263. For differing recollections on whether it was Eisenhower or Khrushchev who refused to shake hands, see Walters, *Silent Missions,* p. 343; NK2, p. 454; and Gromyko, *Pamiatnoe,* vol. 1, p. 380.

82 Macmillan, *Pointing the Way,* p. 205.

83 NK2, p. 454.

84 Walters, *Silent Missions,* p. 344. See also Grinevskii, *Tysiacha i odin den',* p. 270.

85 FRUS, 1958–1960, vol. 9, pp. 439–44.

86 Walters, *Silent Missions,* p. 344; NK2, p. 455.

87 FRUS, 1958–1960, vol. 9, pp. 444–45.

88 Ibid., p. 445. Beschloss, *Mayday,* p. 287 differs from FRUS, 1958–1960, vol. 9, p. 446.

89 Walters, *Silent Missions,* p. 344; Beschloss, *Mayday,* p. 288. The willingness of all sides to accept reconnaissance satellites as a means to collect the same intelligence spy planes had gathered marked a crucial shift in the cold war. Not only did it avoid future spy flight scandals, but it provided information that had the effect of reassuring both East and West that they knew the other side's military capabilities.

90 FRUS, 1958–1960, vol. 9, pp. 448–52.

91 Beschloss, *Mayday,* pp. 290, 292, 295; "Conference of Heads of State and Government," PRO, PREM 11/2992, p. 34; FRUS, 1958–1960, vol. 9, pp. 470, 475; Horne, *Macmillan,* vol. 2, p. 228; Gearson, "Macmillan and Berlin," pp. 25–26.

92 Macmillan, *Pointing the Way,* p. 210. "Conference of Heads of State and Government," PRO, PREM 11/2992, pp. 41–46.

93 Walters, *Silent Missions,* p. 347.

94 Beschloss, *Mayday,* p. 306. Khrushchev's ability to gauge his fellow leaders left something to be desired. He got Macmillan right, but utterly misread de Gaulle, sensing the French president "was more bitterly disappointed than Macmillan with the collapse of the conference. It could be that he had greater hopes and expectations. I can't be sure. I'm basing this opinion only on the impression I got from my reading of the expressions on their faces." NK2, p. 460.

95 *Pravda,* May 19, 1960, p. 2. See also Beschloss, *Mayday,* p. 299.

96 Sulzberger, *Last of the Giants,* p. 669.

97 Stanisław Gaevski, "Kak Nikita Sergeyevich vstrechy v verkhakh sorval," *Kievskie novosti,* no. 1 (1993). "If Khrushchev had simply not come to Paris," Gaevski recalled, "everything would have been clear." But when he came and dropped his "bomb," "I, like my fellow diplomats, was bewildered."

98 Sulzberger, *Last of the Giants,* pp. 672–73.

99 Cited in John S. D. Eisenhower, *Strictly Personal,* p. 294.

100 David Floyd, *Mao against Khrushchev: A Short History of the Sino-Soviet Conflict* (New York: Praeger, 1964), pp. 82–83.

101 *Pravda,* May 21, 1960, pp. 1–2.

102 Shelepin, "Istoriia—uchitel' surovyi"; Aleksandr Shelepin and Vladimir Semichastny, interviews by Nikolai Barsukov (March 27 and May 22, 1989), in *Neizvestnaia Rossiia: XX vek,* p. 282.

103 Author's interview with Oleg Troyanovsky, February 1993.

104 Mikoian, *Tak bylo,* p. 605; Troianovskii, *Cherez gody,* p. 228.

105 SK4, p. 391.

106 NK2, p. 461.

107 Speech to Moscow workers, May 28, 1960, *Pravda,* May 29, 1960, pp. 1–2.

108 *Pravda,* June 4, 1960, p. 2. Although Khrushchev hedged a bit in other portions of his remarks, he still seemed to commit himself to sign a German peace treaty.

109 Khrushchev, *O vneshnei politike*, p. 181; FBIS, July 11, 1960, p. CC6. Pástva is the correct pronunciation.

110 June 7, 1960, memorandum from A. N. Shelepin, translated and analyzed by Vladislav M. Zubok, "Spy vs. Spy: The KGB vs. the CIA, 1960–1962," CWIHPB, no. 4 (Fall 1994), pp. 22–33.

111 July 26, 1960, CIA memorandum from Richard Helms to Hugh S. Cummings, Jr., on "Reactions of Aleksei I. Adzhubei" (sanitized version), Folder no. 14, Box 126, POF, JFKL.

112 Edward Crankshaw, *The New Cold War: Moscow v. Pekin* (Harmondsworth, U.K.: Penguin Books, 1963), p. 105.

113 Crankshaw reports the relatively more polite reference, ibid., p. 107. The less polite phrases were recounted at the Beijing Symposium on Sino-Soviet Relations and the Cold War, October 1997.

114 From Chinese Communist party Central Committee letter of February 29, 1964, to Soviet Central Committee, excerpted in John Gittings, ed., *Survey of the Sino-Soviet Dispute: A Commentary and Extracts from Recent Polemics, 1963–1967* (London: Oxford University Press, 1968), p. 139.

115 Ibid., pp. 130–31; Goldstein, "Sino-Soviet Alliance,: pp. 54–55.

116 Author's interview with Stepan V. Chervonenko.

117 Aleksandrov-Agentov, "Brezhnev and Khrushchev," p. 39.

118 Deliusin recalled this at the October 1997 Beijing Symposium on Sino-Soviet Relations and the Cold War.

119 During preparations for the November conference, Khrushchev and Deng Xiaoping engaged in a shouting match. During the conference itself Khrushchev attacked Mao without mentioning his name directly, and Deng counterattacked by charging that Khrushchev had evidently been "talking without knowing what he was saying, as he did all too frequently." At another point Deng observed contemptuously that in keeping the peace, Communists should rely on their own camp, the world Communist movement, and the peoples of developing countries, instead of on "a few bourgeois statesmen." See Crankshaw, *The New Cold War*, pp. 117, 133. Also see "The Sino-Soviet Dispute and Its Significance," Report of CIA Sino-Soviet Task Force, April 1, 1961, appendix, p. 21, "USSR General," Box 76–9, National Security Files (hereafter NSF), JFKL.

120 Remarks at October 1997 Beijing Symposium on Sino-Soviet Relations and the Cold War.

121 SK3, vol. 2, p. 56; Troianovskii, *Cherez gody*, p. 229.

122 SK3, vol. 2, pp. 62–64.

123 NK2, p. 463; SK4, p. 409.

124 Grinevskii, *Tysiacha i odin den'*, pp. 326–27.

125 NK2, p. 464.

126 These aides included Adzhubei and Troyanovsky, along with *Pravda* editor Satyukov and personal aides Shuisky and Lebedev.

127 Author's interview with Dmitri Goriunov.

128 Volkogonov, *Sem' vozhdei*, vol. 1, pp. 404–05.

129 Grinevsky cites the secretary of the Soviet delegation, N. I. Moliakov, in *Tysiacha i odin den'*, pp. 331–32. Shevchenko, *Breaking with Moscow*, pp. 96–101.

130 NK2, p. 466.

131 Gennadii Vasil'ev, "Samaia gromkaia sessiia," *Pravda,* December 6, 1990, p. 5; Adzhubei, *Krushenie illiuzii,* p. 234; Shevchenko, *Breaking with Moscow,* p. 105; NK2, p. 466.

132 See Adzhubei, *Krushenie illiuzii,* p. 235.

133 SK3, vol. 2, p. 73.

134 This account of Khrushchev's exploits draws particularly on reports in the *New York Times,* September 9–October 15, 1960. Former KGB General Nikolai Zakharov, who was present at the UN, recalled the shoe incident in "Kak Khrushchev Ameriku pokorial," *Argumenty i fakty,* no. 52 (2000), p. 12.

135 Sergei Khrushchev quoted a diplomat or, rather, "a man who may have had a different name at the time, and who had been assigned by his agency to observe everything that happened, Georgy M. Zhivotovsky, in SK3, vol. 2, pp. 71–72. According to the *New York Times* (October 13, 1960), Khrushchev removed his shoe a second time but did not bang it on the table, during a speech by U.S. Assistant Secretary of State Francis O. Wilcox.

136 Mazurov, "Ia govoriu tol'ko o sebe;" Shevchenko, *Breaking with Moscow,* p. 108; Troianovskii, *Cherez gody,* p. 231.

137 Troianovskii, *Cherez gody,* p. 231.

138 In the speech he prepared for the October 1964 Central Committee plenum that ratified Khrushchev's removal, Dmitri Polyansky referred to the UN shoe-banging incident as "a shameful episode that he still presents as an act of valour." See "Takovy, tovarishchi, fakty," *Vestnik,* no. 2 (1998), p. 117.

139 SK3, vol. 2, pp. 57–58.

140 Shevchenko, *Breaking with Moscow,* p. 102.

141 *Khrushchev in New York: A Documentary Record of Nikita S. Khrushchev's Trip to New York, September 19 to October 13*th, *1960* (New York: Crosscurrents Press, 1960), p. 53.

142 Author's interview with Georgy Kornienko. Years later Khrushchev recalled the naysayers and his own reaction to them: "Some people who thought they were pretty smart kept trying to convince me that my idea wasn't possible; even some who were friendly toward us insisted that having three heads of the UN would paralyze the organization. But I was convinced I was right and promoted the idea enthusiastically." NK2, p. 483.

143 Ibid., p. 479.

144 The Khrushchev-Macmillan conversations took place on September 29 and October 4, 1960. See "Visit of the Prime Minister and Foreign Secretary to Washington and New York; September-October 1960. Volume II: Conversations with Mr. Khrushchev and Mr. Gromyko," pp. 5, 15. PRO, PREM 11/2981.

145 *Khrushchev in New York,* p. 110.

146 Ibid., p. 153.

147 *Pravda,* October 21, 1960, pp. 2, 4.

148 *Khrushchev in New York,* p. 196.

149 The text of the interview is in *Khrushchev in New York,* pp. 165–84. The author viewed a tape of the show at the Museum of Television and Radio in New York City. Viktor Sukhodrev, Khrushchev's brilliant interpreter, thought afterward that he should have translated Susskind's remark, which followed a series of routine propaganda claims by Khrushchev, as "breaking down an open door." But under the pressure of live television, he rendered it literally, thus provoking his boss. See V. M. Sukhodrev, *Iazyk moi–drug moi: ot Khrushcheva do Gorbacheva* (Moscow: AST, 1999), pp. 52–53. Susskind apologized for his comment, and so at the end did Khrushchev, who expressed the hope he had not "offended" his host.

150 John Gunther, *Procession* (New York: Harper & Row, 1965), p. 487.

151 Sukhodrev, *Iazyk moi*, p. 49.

152 NK2, pp. 469, 477.

153 Heikal, *Sphinx and the Commissar*, p. 114.

154 The Soviet source who witnessed this exchange and recounted it to the author did not wish to be quoted by name.

CHAPTER 17. KHRUSHCHEV AND KENNEDY: 1960–1961

1 Memorandum to Presidium, August 5, 1960, and remarks in Kalinovka, August 27, 1960, in Stroi, vol. 4, pp. 137–50; 151–61.

2 Memorandum to Presidium, October 29, 1960, ibid., pp. 160–84.

3 See Strelianyi, "Poslednii romantik," p. 213.

4 *Pravda*, January 21, 1961, p. 2.

5 Ibid., p. 4.

6 Ibid., p. 2.

7 *Pravda*, February 19, 1961, p. 3.

8 The Kazakhstan episode is recounted by Volkogonov in *Sem' vozhdei*, p. 402. The July 4 exchange was recounted in a TASS correspondent's memorandum, Volkogonov Collection, LOC, reel 16.

9 *Pravda*, March 1, 1961, p. 2.

10 NK1, p. 454; SK3, vol. 2, p. 92.

11 SK3, vol. 2, p. 92.

12 The Soviet transcript of the Khrushchev-Ulbricht talks is translated in Harrison, "Ulbricht and the Concrete 'Rose,'" Appendix A. See also Hope M. Harrison, "Driving the Soviets up the Wall: A Super-Ally, a Superpower, the Building of the Berlin Wall," *Cold War History*, vol. 1, no. 1 (August 2000), pp. 53–74.

13 ". . . two years have flowed by. . . . The possibilities for eliminating at least a part of the remnants of war in West Berlin are thus favorable since the Adenauer government is not interested in a worsening of the situation in the period of the Bundestag election campaign, and President Kennedy, in the first year of his presidency, also does not want any exacerbation of the situation." Quoted in Harrison, "Ulbricht and the Concrete 'Rose,'" Appendix B.

14 Ibid., p. 32.

15 Ibid., p. 32, Appendix C.

16 Beschloss, *Mayday*, p. 340; Beschloss, *Crisis Years*, pp. 33–35; NK2, pp. 489–91.

17 SK3, vol. 2, p. 88; NK2, p. 491.

18 Actually, the profile prefaces its praise of Kennedy's intellect by saying that "while not a mediocrity," Kennedy was "unlikely to possess the qualities of an outstanding person." The memorandum is translated in "'A Typical Pragmatist': The Soviet Embassy Profiles John F. Kennedy, 1960," CWIHPB, no. 4 (Fall 1994), pp. 65–67.

19 Georgy Kornienko described the views of Adzhubei and Menshikov in an interview with the author. On Menshikov's comment, see Lebow and Stein, *We All Lost the Cold War*, p. 72.

20 Beschloss, *Crisis Years*, p. 34.

21 Ibid., p. 37.

22 See Nigel Hamilton, *JFK: Restless Youth* (New York: Random House, 1992), pp. 42–158; Seymour Hersh, *The Dark Side of Camelot* (Boston: Little, Brown, 1997), pp. 13–60.

23 Letter from Harriman to President-elect Kennedy, Box 125, November 12, 1960, Box 125, POF, JFKL.

24 Letter from Harriman to President-elect Kennedy, November 15, 1960, Box 125, POF, JFKL.

25 Letter from Stevenson to President-elect Kennedy, November 22, 1960, Box 125, POF, JFKL.

26 Memorandum of conversation with Ambassador Menshikov, November 21, 1960, POF, JFKL.

27 Beschloss, *Crisis Years*, p. 41.

28 "Conversation with Ambassador Menshikov," December 14, 1960, POF, JFKL; Beschloss, *Crisis Years*, p. 42.

29 According to Menshikov, there was "more to be gained by one solid day spent in private and informal talk between Khrushchev and Kennedy than all the meetings of underlings taken together." When Salisbury joked, "Maybe Khrushchev would like to spend a vacation at Palm Beach," where the president-elect was staying, the ambassador replied seriously, "Yes, but it takes two to make that possible. There must be an invitation as well as an acceptance." Memorandum of conversation with Ambassdor Menshikov, cited in *New York Times* telegram from E. Freedman to Blair, December 16, 1960, Box 125, POF, JFKL.

30 FRUS, 1961–1963, vol. 5, pp. 9–12.

31 Beschloss, *Crisis Years*, pp. 49, 54.

32 *Kommunist*, no. 1 (January 1961), in CDSP, vol. 8, no. 3 (February 15, 1961), pp. 16–19; no. 4 (February 22, 1961), pp. 8–15, 24.

33 Arthur M. Schlesinger, Jr., *A Thousand Days: John F. Kennedy in the White House* (Boston: Houghton Mifflin, 1965), pp, 302–03; Beschloss, *Crisis Years*, pp. 60–61.

34 Two days later the president tried to take that back, telling a press conference, "It would be premature to reach a judgment as to whether there is a gap or not a gap." The administration didn't officially recognize that no missile gap existed until Deputy Secretary of Defense Roswell Gilpatric declared as much in October 1961. It should be added that Democratic party spokesmen, including Senator John F. Kennedy, had fostered the notion that a gap existed in the Soviet favor in the first place.

35 See Beschloss, *Crisis Years*, pp. 65–66.

36 Kenneth P. O'Donnell and David Powers, *"Johnny We Hardly Knew Ye": Memories of John Fitzgerald Kennedy* (Boston: Little, Brown, 1972), p. 286. See also Beschloss, *Crisis Years*, pp. 70, 77.

37 Troianovskii, *Cherez gody*, pp. 233–34.

38 *Pravda*, March 4, 1961, p. 3

39 FRUS, 1961–1963, vol. 5, p. 94. Also see Beschloss, *Crisis Years*, pp. 80–81.

40 FRUS, 1961–1963, vol. 14, p. 7.

41 Ibid, p. 18.

42 Beschloss, *Crisis Years,* p. 175.

43 FRUS, 1961–1963, vol. 14, p. 30.

44 Ronald Steel, *Walter Lippmann and the American Century* (Boston: Little, Brown, 1980), pp. 526–28; *Conversations with Walter Lippmann* (Boston: Little, Brown, 1965), p. 51: Beschloss, *Crisis Years,* pp. 110–12, 176. The Soviet transcript is in the Walter Lippmann Papers, Sterling Memorial Library, Yale University, New Haven, Connecticut, Group 326, Series VII, Box 239, Folder 30, Yale University Library.

45 FRUS, 1961–1963, vol. 14, p. 68.

46 SK4, pp, 416–25. See also Volkogonov, *Sem' vozhdei,* vol. 1, pp. 389–90.

47 Beschloss, *Crisis Years,* pp. 112–13.

48 *Pravda,* April 13, 1961, p. 2.

49 SK3, vol. 2, pp. 100–01.

50 According to Adzhubei, Gagarin realized his shoes were untied as he walked along the red carpet, leaving him and watching journalists worried that he would trip and fall before he reached the reviewing stand. Adzhubei, *Krushenie illiuzii,* p. 275.

51 *Pravda,* April 15, 1961, p. 2.

52 Cited in Volkogonov, *Sem' vozhdei,* vol. 1, p. 396.

53 SK3, vol. 2, pp. 58–61. Also see Aleksandr Fursenko and Timothy Naftali, *"One Hell of a Gamble": Khrushchev, Castro and Kennedy, 1958–1964* (New York: Norton, 1997), pp. 10–18, 20–34, 36–40, 42–55, 60–73.

54 Troianovskii, *Cherez gody,* p. 233.

55 Beschloss, *Crisis Years,* p. 121.

56 *Pravda,* April 19, 1961, p. 1, and April 23, 1961, p. 3.

57 SK3, vol. 2, pp. 102–06.

58 Troianovskii, *Cherez gody,* pp. 233–34.

59 Quoted in Beschloss, *Crisis Years,* pp. 143–44.

60 Richard Reeves, *President Kennedy: Profile of Power* (New York: Simon & Schuster, 1993), p. 99.

61 Quoted ibid., p. 286.

62 See Beschloss, *Crisis Years,* p. 180; Reeves, *President Kennedy,* p. 136; FRUS, 1961–1963, vol. 14, p. 68.

63 Hugh Sidey quoted in Reeves, *President Kennedy,* p. 136.

64 FRUS, 1961–1963, vol. 14, p. 81; Reeves, *President Kennedy,* p. 142; Beschloss, *Crisis Years,* p. 183.

65 See Beschloss, *Crisis Years,* pp. 178–91; Reeves, *President Kennedy,* pp. 42–44, 158–59; Hersh, *Dark Side of Camelot,* p. 236.

66 See Beshcloss, *Crisis Years,* pp. 224–25; James Reston, *Deadline: A Memoir* (New York: Random House, 1991), pp. 290–91.

67 Macmillan, *Pointing the Way,* pp. 356–57. Also cited in Ernest R. May and Philip D. Zelikow, eds., *The Kennedy Tapes: Inside the White House during the Cuban Missile Crisis* (Cambridge, Mass.: Harvard University Press, 1997), p. 30.

68 Beschloss, *Crisis Years,* p. 234.

69 SK3, vol. 2, p. 112.

70 NK1, p. 458; NK2, pp. 491–98.

71 Dobrynin, *In Confidence*, p. 44.

72 Troianovskii, *Cherez gody*, p. 234. Although Troyanovsky is the best source on Khrushchev's reaction to Kennedy, because he heard it immediately afterward and directly from Khrushchev's lips, others got the same impression. According to Leonid Zamyatin, deputy head of the Foreign Ministry's American Department, as reported by Arkady Shevchenko, Khrushchev concluded Kennedy was a mere "boy," and he was therefore thinking about "what we can do in our interest and at the same time subject Kennedy to a test of strength." Shevchenko himself said he attended a meeting later in 1961 at which Khrushchev lectured his aides about Kennedy's "wishy-washy" behavior, ending up by saying, "I know for certain that Kennedy doesn't have a strong backbone, nor, generally speaking, does he have the courage to stand up to a serious challenge." See Shevchenko, *Breaking with Moscow*, pp. 110, 117. Georgy Bolshakov, a KGB operative who became a secret back-channel contact with Robert Kennedy even before the summit, told an American friend that the Soviets were "amazed" that the president seemed so "affected and scared" by Khrushchev in Vienna. "When you have your hand up a girl's dress, you expect her to scream, but you don't expect her to be scared," said Bolshakov. See Beschloss, *Crisis Years*, p. 234. Mikoyan later remarked that "Gagarin's flight and the strengthening of our positions in Africa and Asia so went to Khrushchev's head that he decided to overwhelm the young president, instead of using the opportunity to develop détente." Mikoian, *Tak bylo*, p. 606.

73 The author acknowledges insight into the summit offered by former American diplomat, Vladimir Toumanoff in a June 2000 interview.

74 FRUS, 1961–1963, vol. 5, pp. 174–75.

75 Georgii Kornienko, *Kholodnaia voina: svidetel'stvo ee uchastnika* (Moscow: "Mezhdunarodnye otnosheniia," 1994), p. 58.

76 Aleksandrov-Agentov comments on this in *Ot Kollontai do Gorbacheva*, p. 108.

77 FRUS, 1961–1963, vol. 5, p. 177.

78 O'Donnell and Powers, *"Johnny,"* p. 195; Beschloss, *Crisis Years*, p. 196.

79 Beschloss, *Crisis Years*, p. 199.

80 FRUS, 1961–1963, vol. 5, p. 187. See also Beschloss, *Crisis Years*, p. 202.

81 Actually, it was de Gaulle who warned Mrs. Kennedy, when the presidential party stopped in Paris, that Mrs. Khrushchev was "wilier" than her husband, an impression confirmed in Vienna when the two women went out on a balcony to respond to crowds. Mrs. Khrushchev, "with little pig eyes," Mrs. Kennedy later recalled, "grabbed my hand and held it aloft before I could stop her." See Katharine Graham, *Personal History* (New York: Knopf, 1997), p. 287.

82 NK2, pp. 498–99. Also see Beschloss, *Crisis Years*, pp. 205–09. Other Khrushchev impressions of Jacqueline Kennedy: "Journalists kept referring to her as a beauty who cast a spell over men, but she didn't produce an impression like that on me. Yes, she was young, energetic and pleasant, but without any special brilliance." As for her sharpness of tongue, "that didn't concern me at all as head of the Soviet delegation; that was her husband's concern. If he liked her, then good health to him and to her!" See NK4, no. 10, 1993, p. 65.

83 FRUS, 1961–1963, vol. 5, pp. 208–09.

84 Kornienko, *Kholodnaia voina*, p. 63; FRUS, 1961–1963, vol. 5, p. 223.

85 FRUS, 1961–1963, vol. 5, pp. 229–30.

86 Kennedy's conversations with Sidey and Robert Kennedy are cited in Hersh, *Dark Side of Camelot*, pp. 253–54. Also see Reston, *Deadline*, pp. 291–92, and Bohlen, *Witness to History*, p. 483.

87 Beschloss, *Crisis Years*, pp. 230–31. Also see Reeves, *President Kennedy*, pp. 181–83.

88 *Pravda*, June 22, 1961, p. 4.

89 *Pravda*, June 29, 1961, p. 2.

90 Kornienko, *Kholodnaia voina*, p. 66. See Beschloss, *Crisis Years*, p. 225. Bolshakov was a Soviet military intelligence colonel, who was operating undercover as head of the Washington bureau of TASS. Yet Robert Kennedy seemed convinced that the friendship between him and Bolshakov was authentic. See Christopher Andrew and Vasili Mitrokhin, *The Sword and Shield: The Mitrokhin Archive and the Secret History of the KGB* (New York: Basic Books, 1999), p. 181.

91 Beschloss, *Crisis Years*, p. 244.

92 Kai Bird, *The Chairman: John J. McCloy and the Making of the American Establishment* (New York: Simon and Schuster, 1992), p. 508; Beschloss, *Crisis Years*, p. 262.

93 Telegram from McCloy to the secretary of state, July 29, 1961, Box 125A, POF, JFKL.

94 John Eisenhower, *Strictly Personal*, pp. 293–94, 390–91.

95 Transcript of conference of first secretaries of Central Committees of Communist and Workers' parties of socialist countries for an exchange of views on questions related to preparation and conclusion of a German peace treaty, August 3–5, 1961. Miscellaneous documents of the of the International Department of the CPSU Central Committee, RGANI. Portions are translated by Vladislav Zubok in "Khrushchev's Secret Speech on the Berlin Crisis, August 1961," CWIHPB, no. 3 (Fall 1993), pp. 58–61. Full text is in "Kak prinimalos' reshenie o vozvedenii Berlinskoi steny," NiNI, no. 2 (March–April 1999), pp. 63–75.

96 Ibid.

97 Sakharov, *Memoirs*, pp. 215–17.

98 Harrison, "Ulbricht and the Concrete 'Rose,'" Appendices D and F.

99 Since arguing with Menshikov was out of the question, Kornienko, the number two man in the USSR's Washington embassy, decided to go around him. In a July 5 meeting with Kennedy aide Arthur M. Schlesinger, Jr., who was reputed to be opposed to Acheson's hard line, Kornienko suggested that if the Americans didn't credit Soviet pledges that a "free city" of Berlin would truly be free, they ought to propose guarantees of their own. Kornienko meant to strengthen the hand of those in Washington who favored negotiations, and he did. Although nothing he said indicated renewed talks would lead to agreement, Schlesinger later recalled, "it looked as if the Russians might want to get off a collision course." That led Schlesinger and others in the White House to propose exploring alternatives that involved negotiations once again. See Kornienko, *Kholodnaia voina*, pp. 66–77; Schlesinger, *A Thousand Days*, pp. 385–90.

100 Jerrold L. Schecter and Peter A. Deriabin, *The Spy Who Saved the World: How a Soviet Colonel Changed the Course of the Cold War* (New York: Scribner, 1992), pp. 80, 113,126, 186, 205, 210.

101 SK3, vol. 2, pp. 122–28.

102 Honoré M. Catudal, *Kennedy and the Berlin Wall Crisis: A Case Study in U.S. Decision Making* (Berlin: Berlin Verlag, 1980), p. 164; Beschloss, *Crisis Years*, p. 264.

103 See May and Zelikow, eds., *The Kennedy Tapes*, p. 31; Beschloss, *Crisis Years*, pp. 264–68; Peter Wyden, *Wall: The Inside Story of Divided Berlin* (New York: Simon and Schuster, 1989), pp. 84–88; McGeorge Bundy, *Danger and Survival: Choices about the Bomb in the First Fifty Years* (New York: Random House, 1988), pp. 367–71; Hersh, *Dark Side of Camelot*, p. 259.

104 NK2, p. 506.

105 *Pravda*, August 8, 1961, p. 2, and August 12, 1961, pp. 2–3. Also see Bundy, *Danger and Survival*, p. 365.

106 Shevchenko, *Breaking with Moscow*, p. 112.

107 SK3, vol. 2, pp. 132–35.

108 Troianovskii, *Cherez gody*, p. 236.

CHAPTER 18. "A COMMUNIST SOCIETY WILL BE JUST ABOUT BUILT BY 1980": 1961–1962

1 *Pravda*, June 25, 1961, p. 4.

2 Stroi, vol. 5, pp. 419–20.

3 *Pravda*, August 8, 1961, p. 1.

4 *Pravda*, September 11, 1961, p. 3.

5 Feuer, ed., *Marx and Engels: Basic Writing on Politics and Philosophy*, p. 29.

6 This account—of the pre-history of the new program, of preparations for the new program, and of the program itself, draws extensively on two unpublished studies done by the Communist party historian Nikolai Barsukov: "Kommunisticheskie illiuzii Khrushcheva: O razrabotke tret'ei programmy partii" and "Mysli vslukh: Zamechaniia N. S. Khrushcheva na proekt tret'ei programmy KPSS."

7 Barsukov, "Kommunisticheskie illiuzii," pp. 11, 34–35.

8 Burlatsky, *Khrushchev*, p. 130.

9 Cited in Barsukov, "Mysli vslukh," pp. 13–16, 51–53, 64–65.

10 Ibid., pp. 37–42.

11 Ibid., pp. 75–77.

12 Sturua told this story at the Khrushchev Centennial Conference at Brown University, in Providence, Rhode Island, in December 1994.

13 Barsukov, "Kommunisticheskie illiuzii," pp, 13–14.

14 *Pravda*, October 19, 1961, pp. 5–6.

15 Mikoian, *Tak bylo*, p. 613.

16 See V. A. Alekseev, *Illiuzii i dogmy* (Moscow: Izdatel'stvo politicheskoi literatury, 1991), pp. 364–65.

17 Ibid., pp. 368–75. Author's interview with Anatoly Krasikov.

18 Shevchenko's claim is cited in Chapter 2, above.

19 Text of Polyansky's speech prepared for the October 1964 Central Committee plenum but not actually delivered there, as published in "Takovy, tovarishchi, fakty," *Istochnik*, no. 2 (1998), p. 121.

20 *Pravda*, October 20, 1961, p. 2; October 21, 1961, p. 2.

21 See, for example, Michel Tatu, *Power in the Kremlin: From Khrushchev to Kosygin*, trans. by Helen Katel (New York: Viking Press, 1969), pp. 151–64.

22 Author's interview with Pyotr N. Demichev. Yegorychev spoke at the Khrushchev Centennial Conference at Brown University in December 1994.

23 Barsukov, "Mysli vslukh," pp. 6, 69–72, includes Kuusinen's letter and proposed text as well as Khrushchev's instruction that they be accepted.

24 *Pravda,* October 27, 1961, p. 7, and October 29, 1961, pp. 1, 3.

25 Ibid., October 31, 1961, pp. 1–2.

26 Cited in Roy Medvedev, *Khrushchev,* p. 211.

27 Changes in party rules that would have established "systematic renewal of cadres" went through ten drafts in advance of the congress, prompted in part by protests from younger party officials, who feared terms limits would deprive them of long stints at the top. In the end the new rules were so watered down that they had almost no effect at higher levels of the party. See Tompson, *Khrushchev,* pp. 242–43; Burlatsky, *Khrushchev,* pp. 129–30; Tatu, *Power in the Kremlin,* pp. 181–84.

28 Compare SK4, p. 463, and Burlatsky, *Khrushchev,* p. 133.

29 As summarized by Satiukov at the congress, Molotov's latest missive attacked the program as "antirevolutionary," "pacifist," and revisionist"; insisted that Lenin had never believed in the "peaceful coexistence"; and called upon the party to step up its support for "the revolutionary struggle of the working class." With Khrushchev not looking on (he thought it would be unseemly to occupy his usual place during his son-in-law's speech), Adzhubei attacked Molotov for "slanderous chatter about 'concessions'" to capitalists. See *Pravda,* October 27, 1961, p. 7, and October 28, 1961, p. 5. Molotov's later conversations with friends are reported in Chuev, *Sto sorok besed,* pp. 355, 501. See also Adzhubei, *Krushenie illiuzii,* p. 247.

30 Adzhubei described the scene in *Krushenie illiuzii,* pp, 248–49.

31 Even certain surprises on Khrushchev's list of Presidium members fit this pattern. The removal of three of his protégés, Kirilenko, Mukhitidinov, and Furtseva, rather than meaning that his position was under attack, almost certainly indicated that he felt sufficiently secure to dispense with supporters who for one reason or another had displeased him. According to Adzhubei, Furtseva fled the hall in tears. ("What sort of party position is that?" the ascetic ideologist Suslov was heard to sneer. "The party isn't a school for daughters of the nobility.") Adzhubei reported that Furtseva contemplated suicide but regained her equilibrium when Khrushchev appointed her minister of culture. *Krushenie illiuzii,* pp, 248–49. Mikoyan adds that Furtseva had a heart attack. *Tak bylo,* p. 600.

32 To achieve the program's aims, total agricultural output was supposed to grow by 150 percent in ten years and 250 percent in twenty years, gross grain output was to double in a decade, and meat production roughly to triple in the first decade and almost quadruple in twenty years. See *Pravda,* November 2, 1961, pp. 5–6.

33 Roy Medvedev, *Khrushchev,* p. 166. "'Ob"ediniaites' vokrug Khrista': Bolsheviki povysili tseny': Otnoshenie naseleniia SSSR k povysheniiu tsen na produkty pitaniia v 1962 g.," *Neizvestnaia Rossiia: XX vek,* vol. 3 (1993), p. 145. Also see Beschloss, *Crisis Years,* p. 356.

34 *Pravda,* November 19, 1961, p. 1.

35 *Izvestiia,* November 22, 1961, in CDSP, vol. 13, no. 47 (December 20, 1961), p. 24.

36 *Pravda,* November 29, 1961, pp. 1–3. Also see Roy Medvedev, *Khrushchev,* pp. 167–68.

37 *Pravda,* December 16, 1961, pp. 1–3.

38 *Pravda,* January 16, 1962, pp. 1–3.

39 See Tompson, *Khrushchev,* p. 244; G. A. E. Smith, "Agriculture," in *Khrushchev and Khrushchevism,* ed. Martin McCauley (Bloomington: Indiana University Press, 1987), p. 107; Tatu, *Power in the Kremlin,* pp. 215–16.

40 The best agronomists in each area would be assigned to the new agencies, as would high-powered party organizers sent down from the province center or from Moscow itself. Although the new cadres would be expected to perform miracles, with new and old agencies duplicating each other, miracles were less likely than ever. Once territorial production administrations were set up, the old *raikom* had no clear raison d'etre. Indeed, Khrushchev soon arranged to enlarge them so as to coincide with the larger production administrations themselves. Khrushchev's September 10, 1962, memorandum proposing enlargement is in Stroi, vol. 7, pp. 163–77. Also see Roy Medvedev, *Khrushchev,* 169–70.

41 See Smith, "Agriculture," pp. 107–10; Filtzer, *Khrushchev Era,* pp. 51–52; Medvedev, *Khrushchev,* pp. 170–71; *Neizvestnaia Rossiia: XX vek,* no. 3 (1993), pp. 145–46; Volkogonov, *Sem' vozhdei,* p. 386; Kozlov, *Massovye besporiadki,* p. 231.

42 Adzhubei, *Krushenie illiuzii* p. 278. Author's interview with Oleg Troyanovsky, February 1993.

43 See Volkogonov, *Sem' vozhdei,* pp. 386–87; "'Ob"ediniaites' vokrug Khrista,'" p. 146; "Novocherkasskaia tragediia, 1962," IA, no. 1 (1993), p. 110; Memorandum from V. Semichastnyi, chairman of the Committee on State Security, June 12, 1962, p. 2, RGANI, f. 89, perechen' 6, dokument 17, l. 2.

44 The fullest Russian account of the Novocherkassk turmoil is in Kozlov, *Massovye besporiadki,* pp. 301–83. For a detailed history that covers the aftermath as well, see Samuel H. Baron, *Bloody Saturday in the Soviet Union: Novocherkassk 1962* (Stanford, Calif.: Stanford University Press, 2001).

45 Memorandum to the CC CPSU from vice chairman of the Committee on State Security, P. Ivashutin, June 7, 1962, RGANI, f. 89, per. 6, dok. 16, l. 2; Also see *Ottepel' 1960–1962* (Moscow: Moskovskii rabochii, 1990), pp. 503–04.

46 Letter to the author from Vadim Makarevsky, who served with the troops that eventually put down Novocherkassk demonstrations, November 16, 1992. *Ottepel' 1960–1962,* p. 503, offers a slightly different version of what happened. Kozlov, *Massovye besporiadki,* p. 309, cites "pirozhki with liver" as the director's recommendation.

47 Memorandum to the CPSU Central Committee from P. Ivashutin, KGB vice chairman, Novocherkassk, June 7, 1962, RGANI, f. 89, per. no. 6, dok. 16, l. 2.

48 Ibid., p. 3. *Ottepel' 1960–1962,* p. 504, quotes one of demonstrators later sentenced to twelve years. Makarevsky's letter to author of November 16, 1992, cites slogan, "Khrushchev *na myaso.*"

49 Memorandum to the CPSU Central Committee from P. Ivashutin, KGB vice chairman, Novocherkassk, June 7, 1962, RGANI, f. 89, per. 6, dok. 16, ll. 4–5.

50 Ibid., p. 7.

51 Memorandum to CPSU Central Committee from P. Ivashutin, June 1, 1962, RGANI, f. 89, per. 6, dok. 4, l. 3.

52 Iurii Bagraev (senior assistant to Russia's chief military prosecutor) and Vladislav Pavliutkin, "Novocherkassk, 1962: tragediia na ploshchadi," *Krasnaia zvezda*

(October 7, 1995), p. 7. This article, said to be based entirely on findings of a 1990–1991 investigation by the chief military procurator, provides a detailed account both of strike-related activities and efforts by the military to contain them.

53 Adzhubei, *Krushenie illiuzii*, p. 285.

54 Mikoian, *Tak bylo*, p. 610.

55 Author's interview with Vadim Makarevsky.

56 See Bagraev and Pavliutkin, "Novocherkassk, 1962" and Iurii Bespalov and Valerii Konovalov, "Novocherkassk, 1962," *Komsomol'skaia pravda* (June 2, 1989), p. 4. Also see Volkogonov, *Sem' vozhdei*, p. 388; "Novocherkasskaia tragediia, 1962," pp. 110–11; June 7, 1962, Report to Central Committee by P. Ivashutin, RGANI, f. 89, per. 6, dok. 16; June 12 Report to Central Committee by V. Semichastnyi, RGANI, f. 89, per. 6, dok. 17; June 14 Report to N. S. Khrushchev by V. Semichastnyi, RGANI, f. 89, per. 6, dok. 18.

57 Author's interview with Vadim Makarevsky; June 7, 1962, Report to Central Committee by P. Ivashutin, RGANI, f. 89, per. 6, dok. 16, l. 9; Bagraev and Pavliutkin, "Novocherkassk, 1962"; Mikoian, *Tak bylo*, pp. 610–11. Pliyev's first deputy, Lieutenant General M. K. Shaposhnikov, remembered that Pliyev ordered him to stop the march, and when Shaposhnikov replied he lacked the troops to do so, Pliyev retorted, "I'm sending you tanks. Use them! Attack!" Attack civilians, including women and children, with tanks? Shaposhnikov couldn't believe his ears until Pliyev repeated his order and confirmed it in writing: "Employ weapons!" See *Ottepel': 1960–1962*, p. 504.

58 June 7, 1962, Report to the Central Committee by P. Ivashutin, p. 9, in RGANI.

59 Text of Kozlov's radio address of June 3, 1962, RGANI, f. 89, per. 6, dok. 15.

60 Volkogonov, *Sem' vozhdei*, p. 388. The Budenny factory director who failed to prevent the strike was replaced. The KGB used the tragedy to lobby for more resources to prevent or, if necessary, put down similar uprisings. See June 12, 1962, Report to Central Committee by V. Semichastnyi, RGANI, f. 89, per. 6, dok. 17; June 13, 1962, Report to Central Committee by Colonel Shchebetenko (senior KGB investigator for specially important matters). RGANI, f. 89, per 6, dok. 19.

61 See Kozlov, *Masssovye besporiadki*, pp. 258–87; "O massovykh besporiadkakh s 1957 goda. . . .", *Istochnik*, no. 6 (1995), pp. 146–53.

62 Kozlov quoted Khrushchev to General Pliyev, as reported by Vadim Makarevsky in an interview with the author. SK4, p. 501; Adzhubei, *Krushenie illiuzii*, pp. 285–86.

63 *Pravda*, June 3, 1962, p. 2.

64 Memorandum to Khrushchev from V. E. Semichastny, KGB chairman, June 4, 1962, in "Ob"ediniaites' vokrug Khrista," pp. 166–69.

65 Speech of July 28, 1962, Kalinovka, in Stroi, vol., 7, pp. 111–12.

66 Memorandums of August 4 and September 5, 1961, ibid., pp. 126, 151.

67 This is the way Khrushchev explained his reasons for splitting the party to Fidel Castro when the Cuban leader visited the Soviet Union in January 1963. Interview with Nikolai Leonov, who interpreted in conversations between the two leaders, Moscow, August 1993.

68 SK2, p. 20.

69 Aleksandrov-Agentov, "Brezhnev i Khrushchev," p. 39.

70 Voronov, "Nemnogo vospominanii," p. 199.

71 Shelepin and Semichastnyi, "Beseda s Shelepinym A. S. i Semichastnym V. E.," interview by Nikolai Barsukov, pp. 276–77.

72 Egorychev, "Beseda s Egorychevym N. G.," interview by Nikolai Barsukov, p. 298.

73 Interview with Nikolai Leonov, Moscow, August 1993.

74 Speeches in Ashkhabad, Turkmenistan, October 1, 1962, and in Tashkent, October 3, 1962, in Stroi, vol. 7, pp. 215, 220, 232.

75 Aleksandr Solzhenitsyn, *The Oak and the Calf: Sketches of Literary Life in the Soviet Union,* trans. by Harry Willets (New York: Harper & Row, 1980), pp. 13–14; Lakshin, *"Novyi mir" vo vremena Khrushcheva,* p. 49.

76 Lakshin, *"Novyi mir" vo vremena Khrushcheva,* pp. 54, 57–58.

77 See Priscilla Johnson McMillan, *Khrushchev and the Arts: The Politics of Soviet Culture, 1962–1964* (Cambridge, Mass.: M.I.T. Press, 1965), pp. 2–4.

78 Solzhenitsyn, *Oak and the Calf,* p. 32.

79 Ibid., p. 34.

80 For an account of Frost's trip, including Khrushchev's visit to a guesthouse where the octogenarian Frost had fallen ill, as a result of which he couldn't visit the Soviet leader at Pitsunda itself, see F. D. Reeve, *Robert Frost in Russia* (Boston: Little, Brown, 1963).

81 See Lakshin, *"Novyi mir" vo vremena Khrushcheva,* p. 63; Solzhenitsyn, *Oak and the Calf,* pp. 39–40; Michael Scammell, *Solzhenitsyn: A Biography* (New York: Norton, 1984), p. 433.

82 NK3, p. 198; Solzhenitsyn, *Oak and the Calf,* pp. 39–41, Scammell, *Solzhenitsyn,* pp. 433–35.

83 Lakshin, *"Novyi mir" vo vremena Khrushcheva,* pp. 75–76. But Solzhenitsyn thought Tvardovsky heard Khrushchev say what he wanted him to say. See Scammell, *Solzhenitsyn,* p. 436.

84 Patricia Blake and Max Hayward, eds., *Half-way to the Moon: New Writing from Russia* (New York: Holt, Rinehart and Winston, 1963), pp. 219–21. The story of how Aleksei Adzhubei convinced Khrushchev to authorize publication of Yevtushenko's poem is told in SK4, p. 709.

CHAPTER 19. THE CUBAN CURE-ALL: 1962

1 See Dino A. Brugoni, *Eyeball to Eyeball: The Inside Story of the Cuban Missile Crisis* (New York: Random House, 1991), pp. 182–220; FRUS, 1961–1963, vol. 11, pp. 29–30; May and Zelikow, *The Kennedy Tapes,* pp. 45–46; Reeves, *President Kennedy,* pp. 368–70.

2 Brugoni, *Eyeball to Eyeball,* p. 223; May and Zelikov, *The Kennedy Tapes,* 60, 88, 99, 107.

3 FRUS, 1961–1963, vol. 11, p. 97; May and Zelikow, *The Kennedy Tapes,* p. 138.

4 May and Zelikow, *The Kennedy Tapes,* pp. 236, 254.

5 Ibid., p. 207.

6 Ibid., p. 255.

7 Ibid., pp. 211, 480.

8 Ibid., pp. 61, 400, 509.

9 Fursenko and Naftali, *"One Hell of a Gamble,"* pp. 23–24.

10 Quoted ibid., p. 39.

11 NK4, no. 7, 1993, p. 93.

12 Quoted in Fursenko and Naftali, *"One Hell of a Gamble,"* p. 52.

13 See ibid., pp. 71, 85.

14 See NK4, no. 7, 1993, pp. 91–94.

15 U.S. guidelines for Mongoose are cited in Raymond L. Garthoff, *Reflections on the Cuban Missile Crisis,* rev. ed. (Washington, D.C.: Brookings Institution, 1989), pp. 6–9. Also see James G. Blight, Bruce J. Allyn, and David A. Welch, *Cuba on the Brink: Castro, the Missile Crisis, and the Soviet Collapse* (New York: Pantheon Books, 1993), pp. 16–18; *Cuba between the Superpowers,* transcript of meetings on Antigua, January 3–7, 1991, ed. James G. Blight, David Lewis, and David Welch, 1991, pp. 1–12; James G. Hershberg, "Before the Missiles of October: Did Kennedy Plan a Military Strike against Cuba?," *Diplomatic History,* vol. 14, no. 2 (Spring 1990), pp. 163–98.

16 See FRUS, 1961–1963, vol. 5, p. 357; Fursenko and Naftali, *"One Hell of a Gamble,"* p. 153.

17 See Fursenko and Naftali, *"One Hell of a Gamble,"* pp. 160–69.

18 NK4, no. 7, 1993, p. 95; SK4, p. 482; Troianovskii, *Cherez gody,* pp. 239–40.

19 NK1, p. 494.

20 See May and Zelikow, *The Kennedy Tapes,* pp. 32–33; Lebow and Stein, *We All Lost the Cold War,* pp. 32–42; Garthoff, *Reflections on the Cuban Missile Crisis,* rev. ed., pp. 21–26; Desmond Ball, *Politics and Force Levels The Strategic Missile Program of the Kennedy Administration* (Berkeley: University of California Press, 1980), pp. 88–104; Schecter and Deriabin, *The Spy Who Saved the World,* pp. 271–99.

21 See Viktor Adamsky and Yuri Smirnov, "Moscow's Biggest Bomb: The 50-Megaton Test of October 1961," CWIHPB, no. 4 (Fall 1994), pp. 3, 19–21.

22 Meanwhile, McNamara was developing a "counterforce nuclear strategy" (according to which military sites, not cities, would be targeted) that would allow the United States to fight and try actually to win a nuclear war. See Lebow and Stein, *We All Lost the Cold War,* pp. 36–38; Brugoni, *Eyeball to Eyeball,* p. 81; Beschloss, *Crisis Years,* pp. 370–71, 407.

23 Dobrynin, *In Confidence,* p. 52.

24 SK3, vol. 2, pp. 158–59, 164.

25 Gaddis, *We Now Know,* p. 268; James G. Blight and David A Welch, *On the Brink: Americans and Soviets Reexamine the Cuban Missile Crisis,* 2d ed. (New York: The Noonday Press, 1990), p. 328; author's interview with Sergei Khrushchev.

26 Troianovskii, *Cherez gody,* p. 240.

27 NK1, p. 494.

28 Troyanovsky, "The Making of Soviet Foreign Policy," p. 233.

29 The Checkpoint Charlie incident began when an American diplomat and his wife were prevented from routinely entering East Berlin on their way to the theater. After the envoy was escorted through by four tanks, and after President Kennedy's special representative, General Lucius Clay, stationed ten tanks near Checkpoint Charlie, the Russians countered with ten of their own. When the Soviet tanks withdrew on October 28, followed by the American tanks thirty minutes later, it looked as if the Soviets had blinked. In fact, both movements were preceded by secret Kennedy assurances that if Khrushchev's tanks moved back, his own would do likewise, a promise that itself looked like a forced concession given the Soviet interpretation of what General Clay was up to in the first place.

Unknown to the president, Clay had been practicing ways to breach the Berlin wall. The Soviets had observed Clay's secret maneuvers, which consisted of building a section of the wall and testing special bulldozer tanks against it, and interpreted the Checkpoint Charlie standoff as Clay's next move. Since a U.S. breach of the wall would have threatened Moscow's biggest dividend yet from the Berlin crisis, Moscow was genuinely alarmed. All the more striking, then, that Kennedy seemed to retreat from his aggressive design (which in fact he had never adopted in the first place) when confronted with the possibility of a real clash. See Raymond L. Garthoff, "Berlin 1961: The Record Corrected," *Foreign Policy*, no. 81 (Fall 1991), pp. 142–56.

30 See FRUS, 1961–1963, vol. 14, pp. 725, 808; vol. 15, pp. 72, 91, 114.

31 Troianovskii, *Cherez gody*, p. 247.

32 Ambassador Thompson regarded this letter as "the toughest statement to date" of Khrushchev's position, one that "certainly destroys any hope . . . that a broad settlement of the Berlin-German problems is possible at this time." FRUS, 1961–1963, vol. 6, pp. 45–57.

33 After receiving Khrushchev's message, Kennedy waited two full months to reply, only to urge Khrushchev to take the long view and "patiently expect the negotiations . . . to extend over a considerable period of time," to remember that "world conditions will look very differently to us three to five or seven years from now, as the result of evolutionary changes, or progress in disarmament or other areas." What that meant, Khrushchev replied irritably on March 10, was that "after so many meetings of our representatives and in spite of our confidential communication, the negotiations on the questions relating to the German peaceful settlement do not make any progress, to put it mildly." FRUS, 1961–1963, vol. 14, pp. 634–35; vol. 6, pp. 69–78; 92–95; 118–26.

34 Pierre Salinger, *With Kennedy* (Garden City, N.Y.: Doubleday, 1966), pp. 230–35.

35 FRUS, 1961–1963, vol. 14, pp. 253–54.

36 FRUS, 1961–1963, vol. 15, pp. 309–10.

37 Ibid., pp. 361, 371–72.

38 Cuban record of conversation between Mikoyan and Castro, November 4, 1962, translated in "The Mikoyan-Castro Talks, 4–5 November 1962: The Cuban Version," CWIHPB, nos. 8–9 (Winter 1996–1997), p. 340.

39 Author's telephone interview with Oleg Troyanovsky, February 1999.

40 Transcripts of Khrushchev's conversations, obtained in Polish and East German archives and translated by Douglas Selvage in "The End of the Berlin Crisis, 1961–1962: New Evidence from the Polish and East German Archives," CWIHPB, no. 11 (Winter 1998), pp. 222–29.

41 Dobrynin, *In Confidence*, pp. 51–52, 64.

42 Author's interview with Nikolai Yegorychev, June 2000.

43 John Gittings, *Survey of the Sino-Soviet Dispute: A Commentary and Extracts From the Recent Polemics 1963–1967* (London: Oxford University Press, 1968), pp. 156–57; Floyd, *Mao Against Khrushchev*, pp. 143–47.

44 Oleg Troyanovsky, "Nikita Khrushchev and the Making of Soviet Foreign Policy." Paper prepared for delivery. (Providence, Rhode Island: Brown University, Khrushchev Centennial Conference, December 1994), p. 39.

45 NK1, p. 499. One doubts that Khrushchev's caution to his colleagues was quite so blunt. What he almost surely did instead was assume that placing missiles in Cuba did *not* risk war.

46 See Volkogonov, *Sem' vozhdei,* p. 420; Fursenko and Naftali, *"One Hell of a Gamble,"* p. 171. Also see Garthoff, *Reflections on the Cuban Missile Crisis,* rev. ed., p. 12; Anatoli I. Gribkov and William Y. Smith, *Operation Anadyr: U.S. and Soviet Generals Recount the Cuban Missile Crisis,* ed. Alfred Friendly, Jr. (Chicago: edition q, inc., 1994), p. 12.

47 Sergo Mikoyan recalled his father's conversation with Khrushchev in Blight and Welch, *On the Brink,* p. 238. Anastas Mikoyan's own account is in *Tak bylo,* p. 606. Khrushchev's recollection is in NK4, no. 7, 1993, p. 97. Also see Blight and Welch, *On the Brink,* p. 331, and Garthoff, *Reflections on the Cuban Missile Crisis,* rev. ed., p. 13.

48 Malinovsky's and Biryuzov's views are characterized by Georgii Kornienko in *Kholodnaia voina,* p. 85. Also Blight and Welch, *On the Brink,* p. 239. Author's interview with Sergo Mikoyan, May 2000.

49 Aleksandr Alekseev, "Karibskii krizis," *Ekho planety,* no. 33 (November 12–18, 1988), p. 27. Bruce Allyn, James G. Blight, and David Welch, eds., *Back to the Brink: Proceedings of the Moscow Conference on the Cuba Missile Crisis, January 27–28, 1989,* CSIA Occasional Paper no. 9 (Lanham, Md.: University Press of America, 1992), p. 150; Fursenko and Naftali, *"One Hell of a Gamble,"* pp. 173–75.

50 Alekseev, "Karibskii krizis," p. 28; Blight, Allyn, and Welch, *Cuba on the Brink,* p. 78; Allyn, Blight, and Welch, *Back to the Brink,* p. 150; Fursenko and Naftali, *"One Hell of a Gamble,"* pp. 179–80; May and Zelikow, *The Kennedy Tapes,* pp. 675–76, footnote 38, on p. 711. Note that Alekseyev dated this meeting to May 11, whereas Fursenko and Naftali, partly on the basis of interviewing Alekseyev, dated it to May 20, putting it after Khrushchev's seven-day trip to Bulgaria.

51 NK1, p. 493.

52 Stefan Poptonev, "Khrushchov krai General Tosheva . . ." *Dossier* (April 1991), p. 12.

53 At meetings that followed, Gromyko recalled, Khrushchev showed "no sign of hesitation whatever," from which the foreign minister concluded that his boss "had reached agreement on the matter beforehand with at least the country's military leadership. Judging from the way Marshal Malinovsky . . . conducted himself at the session, one got the impression that he supported Khrushchev's proposal unconditionally." Andrei A. Gromyko, "Karibskii krizis: o glasnosti teper' i skrytnosti togda," *Izvestiia,* April 15, 1989, p. 5. For further discussion on whether Gromyko would have dared to object to Khrushchev's scheme, see Lebow and Stein, *We All Lost the Cold* War, p. 413, n. 59.

54 Gribkov and Smith, *Operation Anadyr,* pp. 7–10. For a translation of the Ministry of Defense plan adopted on May 24 and of Ivanov's untitled notes on the meeting, see Raymond L. Garthoff, "New Evidence on the Cuban Missile Crisis: Khrushchev, Nuclear Weapons and the Cuban Missile Crisis," CWIHPB, no. 11 (Winter 1998), pp. 254–57.

55 Gribkov and Smith, *Operation Anadyr,* p. 14, and SK3, vol. 2, pp. 178–79, agree in general if not on all details.

56 Fursenko and Naftali, *"One Hell of a Gamble,"* pp. 181–82; Allyn, Blight, and Welch, *Back to the Brink,* p. 150.

57 SK3, vol. 2, p. 184.

58 Blight, Allen, and Welch, *Cuba on the Brink,* pp. 197–204.

59 SK3, vol. 2, pp. 185–87. Mikoian, *Tak bylo,* p. 606.

60 Only in policy areas for which they were specifically responsible, and sometimes not even there, did other Presidium members have a voice in Kremlin policy making. The Presidium decided tens, if not hundreds, of issues at its weekly sessions, and the only way it could get through its agenda was to rubber-stamp decisions prepared by party and government agencies. Add to this the old Bolshevik fear of leadership factionalism, and it's clear why vigorous opposition to the Cuban decision wasn't wanted. Still, Khrushchev's allergy to personal criticism also played a role.

61 Troyanovsky, "The Making of Soviet Foreign Policy," p. 235.

62 Ibid. Author's interview with Oleg Troyanovsky, Moscow, April 1993; Troyanovsky, "The Caribbean Crisis: A View from the Kremlin," *International Affairs* (April–May 1992), p. 147.

63 SK3, vol. 2, pp. 179–80.

64 Gribkov and Smith, *Operation Anadyr,* pp. 5–7, 24, 26–29. Other summaries of Soviet deployments are in Fursenko and Naftali, *"One Hell of a Gamble,"* pp. 188–89, and May and Zelikow, *The Kennedy Tapes,* pp. 676–77. For discussion of the tactical nuclear weapons—which ones were actually deployed, and when—see Aleksandr Fursenko and Timothy Naftali, "The Pitsunda Decision: Khrushchev and Nuclear Weapons," CWIHPB, no. 10 (March 1998), pp. 222–26, and Raymond L. Garthoff, "Khrushchev, Nuclear Weapons and the Cuban Missile Crisis," CWIHPB, no. 11 (Winter 1998) pp. 251–54. For a detailed account of which Soviet missiles arrived and when, and of what the Americans knew about them and when they knew it, see Raymond L. Garthoff, "U.S. Intelligence in the Cuban Missile Crisis," *Intelligence and National Security,* vol. 13, no. 3 (Autumn 1998), pp. 18–63.

65 Gribkov and Smith, *Operation Anadyr,* pp. 25–26; Fursenko and Naftali, *"One Hell of a Gamble,"* pp. 193, 267, 272; NK4, no. 7, 1993, p. 98. Volkogonov suggests, in *Sem' vozhdei,* p. 423, that Khrushchev's role in Cuban deployment must have reminded him of Stalin's in World War II. North Caucasus Military District colleagues' impression of Pliyev is reported in a letter to the author by Vadim Makarevsky.

66 This account of deployments is based mainly on Gribkov and Smith, *Operation Anadyr,* pp. 26–57; Fursenko and Naftali, *"One Hell of a Gamble,"* pp. 191–93; N. C. Leonov, *Likholet'e* (Moscow: "Terra," 1997), p. 58; and the author's interview with Raymond L. Garthoff. The quotes from Gribkov are in *Operation Anadyr,* pp. 40, 55.

67 See Fursenko and Naftali, *"One Hell of a Gamble,"* pp. 190–93.

68 Unpublished interview with Admiral Nikolai N. Amelko by Richard Ned Lebow, Moscow, December 1991. Provided to the author by Mr. Lebow.

69 *Cuba between the Superpowers,* Antigua conference transcript, p. 65.

70 Gribkov and Smith, *Operation Anadyr,* p. 52.

71 Troyanovsky, "Caribbean Crisis," p. 150.

72 Allyn, Blight, and Welch, *Back to the Brink,* p. 84.

73 Ibid., p. 70.

74 Author's interview with Aleksei Adzhubei.

75 Blight, Allyn, and Welch, *Cuba on the Brink,* pp. 83–85.

76 Garthoff, *Reflections on the Cuban Missile Crisis,* rev. ed., p. 24.

77 Blight and Welch, *On the Brink,* p. 334.

78 Lebow and Stein, *We All Lost the Cold War,* p. 77.

79 Cited in Reeves, *President Kennedy,* p. 347.

80 See Beschloss, *Crisis Years,* p. 413; Reeves, *President Kennedy,* p. 339.

81 Cited in Beschloss, *Crisis Years,* p. 420.

82 "So it is impossible to move these forces to Cuba secretly," Khrushchev reportedly said to several military advisers on July 7. Cited in Fursenko and Naftali, *"One Hell of a Gamble,"* p. 192.

83 See ibid., pp. 192, 196, 206. My discussion of the dispatch of additional tactical nuclear weapons relies on Fursenko and Naftali, "The Pitsunda Decisions," and Garthoff, "Khrushchev, Nuclear Weapons and the Cuban Missile Crisis."

84 Robert F. Kennedy, *Thirteen Days: A Memoir of the Cuban Missile Crisis* (New York: Norton, 1969), pp. 25–26; Dobrynin, *In Confidence,* pp. 68–69.

85 Theodore C. Sorensen, *Kennedy* (New York: Bantam, 1966), pp. 667–68.

86 *Pravda,* September 12, 1962, p. 2.

87 Georgy Bolshakov, "The Hot Line: The Secret Communication Channel between John Kennedy and Nikita Khrushchev," *New Times,* no. 5 (1989), pp. 3–4.

88 FRUS, 1961–1963, vol. 10, p. 1048.

89 Bolshakov, "Hot Line," p. 4. According to what Mikoyan later told Castro, by mid-September Moscow had good reason to believe the Americans knew of Soviet missile deployment. That may explain the intense anxiety Khrushchev showed in his conversation with Bolshakov. See Fursenko and Naftali, *"One Hell of a Gamble,"* p. 294.

90 Beschloss, *Crisis Years,* pp. 429, 438–39; Garthoff, *Reflections on the Cuban Missile Crisis,* p. 28.

91 Telephone conversation reported by Volkogonov, *Sem' vozhdei,* p. 424, and translated in Garthoff, "New Evidence on the Cuban Missile Crisis," p. 261.

92 Troianovskii, *Cherez gody,* pp. 243–44.

93 Lebow and Stein, *We All Lost the Cold War,* p. 97.

94 The American minutes of the Kennedy-Gromyko talks are in FRUS, 1961–1963, vol. 5, pp. 533–34; vol. 7, pp. 589–91; vol. 11, pp. 110–14, and vol. 15, pp. 370–76. Gromyko's minutes are in a telegram of October 18, 1962, Russian excerpts of which the author has had access to and which are translated in "Russian Documents on the Cuban Missile Crisis," CWIHPB, nos. 8–9 (Winter 1996–1997), pp. 279–82. Also see Beschloss, *Crisis Years,* pp. 455–58; Reeves, *President Kennedy,* pp. 381–82; Dean Rusk, *As I Saw It,* as told to Richard Rusk and ed. Daniel S. Papp (New York: Norton, 1990), p. 223; Allyn, Blight, and Welch, *Back to the Brink,* p. 54.

95 NK3, p. 175.

96 Gromyko, *Memoirs,* p. 179.

97 Gromyko's October 19 telegram, which the author has read in Russian, is translated in "Russian Foreign Ministry Documents on the Cuban Missile Crisis," CWIHPB, no. 5 (Spring 1995), pp. 66–77.

98 SK3, vol. 2, p. 264.

99 Reeves, *President Kennedy*, p. 386.

100 Cited in Beschloss, *Crisis Years*, p. 461.

101 May and Zelikow, *Kennedy Tapes*, p. 178.

102 Beschloss, *Crisis Years*, p. 481.

103 FRUS, 1961–1963, vol. 6, pp. 165–66.

104 Cited in Beschloss, *Crisis Years*, pp. 483–85.

105 SK3, vol. 2, pp. 265–66.

106 Fursenko and Naftali cite notes on the session secretly taken by Vladimir Malin, head of the Central Committee's General Department, in *"One Hell of a Gamble,"* pp. 240–42. Also see SK3, vol. 2, p. 271.

107 Fursenko and Naftali, *"One Hell of a Gamble,"* pp. 242–43.

108 Troianovskii, *Cherez gody*, pp. 244–45.

109 SK3, vol. 2, pp. 273–74.

110 See Beschloss, *Crisis Years*, p. 489.

111 SK3, vol. 2, p. 279.

112 Beschloss, *Crisis Years*, pp. 489–90; Reeves, *President Kennedy*, pp. 397–400.

113 FRUS, 1961–1963, vol. 6, p. 168.

114 The author has had access to Dobrynin telegrams of October 23 and 24, 1962. See also Fursenko and Naftali, *"One Hell of a Gamble,"* pp. 252–53; Dobrynin, *In Confidence*, pp. 81–82.

115 Gromyko never returned Dobrynin's text to his assistants (as would have been the usual procedure), nor could Dobrynin find it in the archives many years later. See Dobrynin, *In Confidence*, p. 82. Also see Anatolii Dobrynin, "Karibskii krizis: svidetel'stvo uchastnika," *Mezdunarodnaia zhizn'*, no. 7 (July 1992), p. 60.

116 Kornienko, *Kholodnaia voina*, p. 91.

117 Dobrynin, *In Confidence*, p. 83.

118 Quoted in Arthur M. Schlesinger, Jr., *Robert Kennedy and His Times* (New York: Random House, 1978), p. 514.

119 May and Zelikow, *Kennedy Tapes*, p. 347.

120 Laurence Chang and Peter Kornbluh, eds., *The Cuban Missile Crisis, 1962: A National Security Archive Documents Reader* (New York, New Press, 1992), p. 371.

121 Richard T. Davies, unpublished transcript of oral history.

122 Of course the main Soviet counter to the American state of alert was the USSR's own heightened state of readiness. But although Soviet forces were officially on full alert, U.S. intelligence detected "no significant deployments." See Fursenko and Naftali, *"One Hell of a Gamble,"* p. 266.

123 SK3, vol. 2, pp. 282–88; Beschloss, *Crisis Years*, p. 498.

124 Khrushchev was obviously referring to his late son, Leonid, who, like Kennedy, had been born in 1917.

125 William Knox, "Close Up of Khrushchev during a Crisis," *New York Times Magazine*, November 18, 1962, pp. 32, 128–29.

126 Khrushchev letter is in FRUS, 1961–1963, vol. 6, pp. 169–70.

127 Ibid., p. 171.

128 SK3, vol. 2, pp. 297–98.

129 Malin's notes on Presidium session, as cited in Fursenko and Naftali, *"One Hell of a Gamble,"* pp. 259–60.

130 See May and Zelikow, *Kennedy Tapes*, pp. 440–41; Fursenko and Naftali, *"One Hell of a Gamble,"* p. 266.

131 Fursenko and Naftali quote from the copy of the intelligence report distributed to Khrushchev in *"One Hell of a Gamble,"* p. 261. Kornienko reports Kuznetsov's comment in *Kholodnaia voina*, p. 96.

132 Dobrynin's October 25, 1962, telegram about the Press Club encounter is in the Volkogonov Collection, LOC, reel 17. Also see Fursenko and Naftali, *"One Hell of a Gamble,"* pp. 257–61. Compare with Kornienko account, *Kholodnaia voina*, pp. 87–88, which claims he saw through the report, but too late.

133 The text of Khrushchev's October 26 letter, in the unofficial American Embassy translation that Washington decision makers actually read and relied on, is in May and Zelikow, *Kennedy Tapes*, pp. 485–91. The description of the letter as received at the embassy is in Beschloss, *Crisis Years*, p. 516. Naftali and Fursenko describe the writing of the letter in *"One Hell of a Gamble,"* pp. 262–63. Sergei Khrushchev's rather different account has Khrushchev dictating the text in the presence of the Presidium. But Fursenko and Naftali could find no evidence of a formal Presidium session on October 26. See *"One Hell of a Gamble,"* footnote 28, p. 392.

134 FRUS, 1961–1963, vol. 6, pp. 178–81.

135 See Fursenko and Naftali, *"One Hell of a Gamble,"* pp. 249–50, 274–75, footnote 66 on pp. 393–94.

136 Troianovskii, *Cherez gody*, pp. 248–49.

137 May and Zekilow, *Kennedy Tapes*, pp. 509, 585.

138 See Philip Nash, *The Other Missiles of October: Eisenhower, Kennedy and the Jupiters, 1957–1963* (Chapel Hill: University of North Carolina Press, 1997), pp. 110–12.

139 May and Zelikow, *Kennedy Tapes*, p. 554.

140 FRUS, 1961–1963, vol. 6, pp. 181–82. On the way Khrushchev failed to foresee possible dangers, see May and Zelikow, *Kennedy Tapes*, p. 687.

141 SK3, vol. 2, pp. 335–36.

142 Gribkov and Smith, *Operation Anadyr*, pp. 65–67.

143 Reeves, *President Kennedy*, pp. 418–19.

144 See SK3, vol. 2, pp. 334–35, and Troyanovsky, "Caribbean Crisis," p. 153. How exactly Khrushchev reacted to the U-2 shoot-down is the subject of some dispute. The next day, in a message to Castro, Khrushchev said, "You shot down" the U.S. overflight. But both Sergei Khrushchev and General Gribkov reported that Khrushchev knew the truth. On Khrushchev's letter to Castro, see May and Zelikow, *Kennedy Tapes*, footnote 91, p. 714. Also see SK3, vol. 2, pp. 334–36; Gribkov and Smith, *Operation Anadyr*, p. 67; *Cuba between the Superpowers*, Antigua conference transcript, pp. 133–34.

145 Blight, Allyn, and Welch, *Cuba on the Brink*, pp. 108–11.

146 Alekseyev's November 2 report to the Soviet Ministry of Foreign Affairs, cited in Fursenko and Naftali, *"One Hell of a Gamble,"* pp. 272–73.

147 Blight, Allyn, and Welch, *Cuba on the Brink*, pp. 108–11.

148 Ibid., p. 481. Castro's letter is more understandable if he believed the Soviet Union possessed a huge nuclear superiority over the United States. He might even have imagined that a massive Soviet first strike, followed by a puny U.S. response, would have allowed Cuba to escape destruction.

149 *Cuba between the Superpowers,* Antigua conference transcript, p. 97; Troianovskii, *Cherez gody,* pp. 249–50.

150 NK3, p. 177. See SK3, vol. 2, pp.356–57.

151 See Bundy, *Danger and Survival,* pp. 432–33.

152 The author has had access to an edited version of Dobrynin's October 27, 1962, telegram. Fursenko and Naftali cite the same telegram in *"One Hell of a Gamble,"* pp. 281–83. See also Dobrynin, *In Confidence,* p. 87.

153 Troianovskii, *Cherez gody,* p. 250, and "Caribbean Crisis," pp. 153–54.

154 From the Malin notes as cited in Fursenko and Naftali, *"One Hell of a Gamble,"* p. 284.

155 See ibid., pp. 271–72, 276, 285.

156 Troianovskii, *Cherez gody,* pp. 251–52.

157 FRUS, 1961–1963, vol. 6, pp. 183–87.

158 Troyanovsky, "Caribbean Crisis," p. 155. Unpublished inteviews by Richard Ned Lebow with Oleg Grinevsky (Vienna, October 1991) and Leonid Zamyatin (Moscow, December 1991), provided to the author by Mr. Lebow.

159 SK3, vol. 2, p. 367.

160 FRUS, 1961–1963, vol. 6, pp. 189–90.

161 The timing and fate of the letter are described, and the Russian text is printed in "Back from the Brink: Cuban Missile Correspondence between John F. Kennedy and Nikita S. Khrushchev, October 22 through December 4, 1962," in *Problems of Communism,* vol. 46, Special Issue—Spring 1992, pp. 60–62.

162 Robert McNamara recalled wondering whether he would still be alive the next weekend; see the CNN documentary series on the cold war, program on the Cuban Missile Crisis. Dobrynin, "Karibskii krizis," p. 66.

163 FRUS, 1961–1963, vol. 6, pp. 187–88.

CHAPTER 20. THE UNRAVELING: 1962–1964

1 *Pravda,* December 13, 1962, p. 2.

2 Burlatsky, *Khrushchev,* pp. 179–80. Chinese charges are in Alexander Dallin, ed., *Diversity in International Communism: A Documentary Record, 1961–1963* (New York: Columbia University Press, 1963), pp. 656–59.

3 Roberts telegram to Foreign Office, No. 2251 of November 12, p. 5, PRO, PREM 11/3996.

4 Cited in Fursenko and Naftali, *"One Hell of a Gamble,"* pp. 324–25.

5 Ibid., pp. 314–15.

6 Dobrynin, *In Confidence,* p. 93.

7 Author's interview with Pyotr N. Demichev.

8 Dobrynin in particular cites these two American positions as allowing Kennedy to appear to be "the big winner in the crisis," adding that if the full truth had been known, the terms of the final settlement might have seemed "neither a great defeat nor a great victory for Kennedy or Khrushchev." *In Confidence,* p. 91.

9 Cited in Beschloss, *Crisis Years,* p. 543. Early that morning Cuban President Osvaldo Dorticos called Soviet Ambassador Alekseyev about radio reports that Moscow had decided to withdraw its missiles. Alekseyev remembered answering that American radio was capable of anything. When Dorticos added that the radio in question was Moscow Radio, Alekseyev wrote, "I immediately imagined Fidel's reaction to the same news, and felt myself the most unhappy person on the face of the earth." See Alekseev, "Karibskii krizes," p. 33.

10 That cable itself, Khrushchev implied, with its "proposal that we be the first to launch a nuclear strike against the enemy," had prompted him to yield. For "we are not struggling against imperialism in order to die," but rather to "achieve the victory of communism," and "now, as a result of the measures we have taken, we have reached the goal sought when we agreed with you to send missiles to Cuba." Translated in Blight, Allyn, and Welch, *Cuba on the Brink*, pp. 485–88.

11 Castro also told Khrushchev (on October 31) that "countless eyes of Cuban and Soviet men who were willing to die with supreme dignity shed tears upon learning about the surprising, sudden and practically unconditional decision to withdraw the weapons." Ibid., pp. 490–91.

12 SK3, vol. 2, p. 378.

13 SK4, p. 643.

14 Mikoyan's sole request was that he be informed "immediately, by all possible means, of the day and hour of the funeral of his wife." See Naftali and Fursenko, *"One Hell of a Gamble,"* p. 295.

15 Sergo Mikoyan recounted this episode in his "Introduction" to his father's *Tak bylo*, p. 13, and in a May 2000 interview with the author.

16 Sergo Mikoyan's "Introduction" to *Tak bylo*, p. 17. Author's interview with Nikolai Leonov, Khrushchev's interpreter during his talks with Castro in April 1963.

17 SK3, vol. 2, p. 390.

18 Fursenko and Naftali, *"One Hell of a Gamble,"* pp. 295–306; Garthoff, *Reflections on the Cuban Missile Crisis*, pp. 114, 124–28; Alekseev, "Karibskii krizis," pp. 36–37.

19 See Beschloss, *Crisis Years*, pp. 544, 549. With the perspective of time, one can argue that Khrushchev could indeed take pride in certain accomplishments: avoiding war with the United States, extracting a public assurance that the United States would not attack Cuba, the withdrawal of Jupiter missiles from Turkey, and the abandonment of American demands for on-site inspection in Cuba. Although the nuclear imbalance in Washington's favor was not rectified, Moscow itself proceeded to do so by building more ICBMs. All this is not to say, however, that Khrushchev actually thought he had been so successful.

20 SK3, vol. 2, p. 397.

21 See excerpts from the Shvernik Commission report in "Massovye repressii opravdany byt' ne mogut," pp. 117–22.

22 FRUS, 1961–1963, vol. 6, pp. 190–98. The addendum is included in the text of coded telegram, special no. 1224-1235, Ministry of Foreign Affairs, October 30, 1962, which the author has seen.

23 Originally, of course, Khrushchev had wanted broader negotiations to follow a great Cuban victory. Now he would have to work with defeat. At one point in November, Deputy Foreign Minister Kuznetsov warned John McCloy, "You Americans will never be able to do this to us again," hinting at the strategic military buildup that would eventually bring the USSR to rough nuclear parity with the United States. In the meantime, Soviet strategic strength lagged far behind America's, while Soviet conventional weaponry was being drastically cut back by none other than Khrushchev himself. Cited in Beschloss, *Crisis Years*, p. 563. Also see Garthoff, *Reflections on the Cuban Missile Crisis*, p. 134.

24 Memorandum of conversation among Yuri Zhukov, Georgy Bolshakov, and Ambassador Thompson, October 31, 1962, W. Averell Harriman Collection. Memorandum to the Secretary of State from Llewellyn E. Thompson, October 31, 1962, W. Averell Harriman Collection. Excerpts from November 1, 1962, telegram from Zhukov to Ministry of Foreign Affairs, provided to the author. Kuznetsov-Stevenson conversation reported in Beschloss, *Crisis Years*, p. 553.

25 Cited in Beschloss, *Crisis Years*, p. 570.

26 Cousins, *Improbable Triumvirate*, pp. 46, 54, 56.

27 Ibid., p. 76; Glenn T. Seaborg, *Kennedy, Khrushchev and the Test Ban* (Berkeley: University of California Press, 1981), pp. 178–81.

28 Summary record of meeting of the Executive Committee of the National Security Council, October 31, 1962, in FRUS, 1961–1963, vol. 11, p. 333.

29 FRUS, 1961–1963, vol. 6, p. 233.

30 Ibid., pp. 238–40.

31 Ibid., pp. 250–65.

32 American Ambassador Foy Kohler reported these impressions in a telegram on March 16, 1963. See FRUS, 1961–1963, vol. 5, pp. 642–44.

33 Cousins, *Improbable Triumvirate*, pp. 83–97. Author's interview with Andrea Cousins.

34 *Pravda*, January 17, 1963, p. 2.

35 *Pravda*, February 28, 1963, p. 3.

36 At this point the Soviet Union still lacked the equivalent of the American Minuteman missile, whose stable solid-fuel technology allowed it to stand guard indefinitely, prepared for launch at short notice. Not until 1966 was a Soviet counterpart of the Minuteman, the SS-11, ready for deployment. See Ball, *Politics and Force Levels*, pp. 57–58.

37 SK3, vol. 2, pp. 417–29; SK4, pp. 666–77.

38 Chernoutsan, unpublished draft memoir.

39 Barsukov, "Rise to Power," p. 62.

40 *Pravda*, September 28, 1962.

41 Mazurov, "Ia govoriu ne tol'ko o sebe." Khrushchev thought better of his threat—until he quarreled again with Mazurov at the same resort fifteen months later. Something Mazurov said about Byelorussia's economic problems annoyed him, and when he arrived in Moscow he announced, "I didn't like the way Mazurov behaved at all. We had a long talk. His proposals won't stand up to criticism. We'll have to think about replacing him." See SK2, pp. 49–50.

42 Author's interview with Aleksandr N. Yakovlev. Also see Tompson, *Khrushchev*, pp. 253–54. In the indictment prepared for the October 1964 plenum that ratified Khrushchev's ouster, Polyansky characterized the result of dividing the party as "the worst confusion our Soviet state has known since it was created." "Takovy, tovarishchi, fakty," p. 111.

43 Gorbachev speculated as much at a conference in Moscow (at the International Foundation for Socio-Economic and Political Research) on the centennial of Khrushchev's birth, April 18, 1994. See *N. S. Khrushchev (1894–1971)*, p. 4.

44 "Setbacks in Soviet Agriculture," Current Support Brief, CIA Office of Research and Reports, January 4, 1963, Box 180–83, POF, USSR General, JFKL.

45 *Pravda,* March 14, 1963, p. 3.

46 In March 1963 Khrushchev fired off two more memos to the Presidium, one advocating new dairy and vegetable farms around major cities, the other on animal husbandry in Byelorussia, the Baltic republics, and the Russian northwest. Once again he was micromanaging, recommending the potato chips that he recalled from his American trip ("We'd all be sitting in a plane, talking and enjoying factory-prepared potato chips. Companies sell them in special packages and they keep very well, since they're dry. This food is cheap . . . "), and urging that potatoes be fertilized with manure and that the manure in winter fields be stacked in "covered heaps." *Pravda,* March 17, 1963, p. 1.

47 *Pravda,* April 26, 1963, pp. 1, 3, 5.

48 McMillan, *Khrushchev and the Arts,* pp. 5–6.

49 Ibid., pp. 7–8.

50 Author's interview with Boris Zhutovsky; Neizvestnyi "Moi dialog," p, 174.

51 Allegedly Ilychev was seeking to ingratiate himself with his boss, gain leverage against his Kremlin rival Suslov, and end up a full member of the Presidium. Author's interview with Georgy I. Kunitsyn, who worked in the Central Committee Ideological Department beginning in 1961. Author's interview with Boris Zhutovsky. Mockery quoted by Burlatsky, *Khrushchev,* p. 140.

52 Neizvestnyi, "Moi dialog," p. 176.

53 McMillan, *Khrushchev and the Arts,* p. 103. The word *pideras* without the letter *t* became ironic Russian slang for homosexual after Khrushchev's mispronunciation.

54 Neizvestnyi, "Moi dialog," p. 177.

55 McMillan, *Khrushchev and the Arts,* pp. 101–05. For an account by Beliutin, himself, see his "Khrushchev i Manezh," *Druzhba narodov,* no. 1, 1990, pp. 136–61.

56 McMillan, *Khrushchev and the Arts,* p 9.

57 Romm, *Ustnye rasskazy,* pp. 125–28, Boris Zhutovskii, "Gruppovoi portret v kazennom inter'ere," *Literaturnaia gazeta* (July 5, 1989), p. 8.

58 Chernoutsan, unpublished draft memoir.

59 Solzhenitsyn, *Calf Butted the Oak,* p. 61. Zhutovskii, "Gruppovoi portret"; Romm, *Ustnye rasskazy,* p. 128.

60 Romm, *Ustney rasskazy,* p. 127.

61 Neizvestnyi, "Moi dialog," p. 186.

62 Chernoutsan, unpublished draft memoir.

63 Romm, *Ustnye rasskazy,* p. 129.

64 Neizvestny, "Moi dialog," pp. 185–86, Romm, *Ustnye rasskazy,* pp. 129–31.

65 Chernoutsan, unpublished draft memoir.

66 Romm, *Ustnye rasskazy,* p. 132.

67 Ibid. Vasilii Aksenov, "Zima trevogi nashei ili kak marksist Nikita uchil pisatelei partiinoi pravde," *Literaturnyi kur'er,* no. 12 (1986–1987), pp. 10–11. Andrei Voznesenskii, "N. S. Khrushchev: 'V voprosakh iskusstva ia Stalinist,'" in *Nikita Sergeevich Khrushchev: Materialy k biografii* (Moscow: Izdatel'stvo politicheckoi literatury, 1989), p. 128. Interview with Boris Zhutovsky, Moscow, April 1988.

68 Romm, *Ustnye rasskazy,* p. 137.

69 *Pravda,* March 10, 1963, p. 2.

70 Author's interview with Georgy Kunitsyn.

71 Romm, *Ustnye rasskazy,* p. 133.

72 Ibid., pp. 137–38.

73 "Dve vstrechi N. S. Khrushcheva s predstaviteliami tvorcheskoi intelligentsii (dekabr' 1962 g. i mart 1963 g.)," in *SSSR: vnutrennie protivorechiia,* no. 6, pp. 198–99, Romm, *Ustnye rasskazy,* pp. 141–42. See also Voznesenskii, "N. S. Khrushchev: 'V voprosakh iskusstva ia Stalinist,'" pp. 128–31.

74 Author's interview with Andrei Voznesensky.

75 Romm, *Ustnye rasskazy,* p. 142.

76 "Dve vstrechi," p. 199.

77 See Evgenia Semenovna Ginzburg, *Into the Whirlwind,* trans. by Paul Stevenson and Manya Harari (London: Collins, Harvill, 1967), and *Within the Whirlwind,* trans. by Ian Boland (New York: Harcourt Brace Jovanovich, 1981).

78 Romm, *Ustnye rasskazy,* p. 144. Interview with Andrei Voznesensky, Moscow. Aksenov, "Zima trevogi," p. 16.

79 Aksenov, "Zima trevogi," p. 16; "Dve vstrechi," p. 200; Romm, *Ustnye rasskazy,* p. 145.

80 *Pravda,* March 10, 1963, p. 2.

81 Romm, *Ustnye rasskazy,* pp. 147–49. For an account of how Ehrenburg's claim was used against him and Khrushchev by conservatives, see Tatu, *Power in the Kremlin,* pp. 298–311.

82 Leonov, *Likholet'e,* pp. 72–73. Author's interview with Leonov. As the title of his book, "Epoch of Disturbances and Disasters," suggests, Leonov is not well disposed toward Khrushchev.

83 Leonov, *Likholet'e,* p. 71. Author's interview with Leonov.

84 Leonov, *Likholet'e,* p. 73.

85 Soviet notes of Khrushchev-Castro conversation cited in Fursenko and Naftali, *"One Hell of a Gamble,"* pp. 332–34. On the two KGB assassinations, the other of a leader of the National Labor Alliance (NTS) in October 1957, see Andrew and Mitrokhin, *Sword and the Shield,* pp. 361–62. In the light of Khrushchev's comments, one wonders about the "heartache" he allegedly felt after the Novocherkassk massacre. Even if it were real, it yielded to realpolitik, especially when instructing a protégé. As for liquidating genuine class enemies, Khrushchev never had qualms about that.

86 Author's interview with Nikolai Leonov.

87 As endless lines of citizens poured through Red Square on May Day, Voroshilov urged speeding up proceedings lest he stand on the Lenin Mausoleum all day. "You know where you can go, Klim!" growled Khrushchev. "You can damn well stand here and review the parade. When I was party secretary of the Industrial Academy, we got up at six in the morning on May Day, and it took us hours to get here on foot. Once we got here, we wanted to stay a while, to get a look at our dear leader, Stalin. But instead the Chekists [security police] kept shouting at us to move faster. All these people here want to have a look at us, so that they can tell about it afterward. I'm not going to speed up anyone. So take a chair over there, Klim, sit down and shut up!" Author's interview with Nikolai Leonov.

88 Leonov, *Likholet'e,* p. 71. Author's interview with Nikolai Leonov. Leonov particularly remembered "Grechko's reaction when Khrushchev was mocking him; he was standing next to Malinovsky, and they both looked disturbed."

89 Presidium notes cited in Fursenko and Naftali, *"One Hell of a Gamble,"* p. 335.

90 Lakshin, *"Novyi mir" vo vremena Khrushcheva,* p. 124.

91 Romm, *Ustnye rasskazy,* p. 152.

92 Ibid., pp. 154–55.

93 Chernoutsan, unpublished draft memoir.

94 SK2, pp. 210–11.

95 Author's interview with Georgy Kunitsyn.

96 Mikoian, *Tak bylo,* p. 628.

97 Chernoutsan, unpublished draft memoir.

98 N. Oklianskii, *Roman s tiranom* (Moscow: Moskovskii rabochii, 1994), pp. 123–24; Lakshin, *"Novyi mir" vo vremena Khrushcheva,* pp. 145–48, 215–16; Chernoutsan, unpublished draft memoir.

99 Chernoutsan, unpublished draft memoir.

100 Cited in Beschloss, *Crisis Years,* pp. 598–99.

101 Troianovskii, *Cherez gody,* pp. 256–57.

102 FRUS, 1961–1963, vol. 6, pp. 301–02.

103 FRUS, 1961–1963, vol. 5, p. 726. The Americans stalled on the nonaggression pact because they suspected it was a Soviet propaganda device that would add little to European security.

104 Frustrated, Khrushchev responded, "I've never understood why you Americans are so stubborn about Berlin. De Gaulle doesn't want a war over Berlin, and Macmillan certainly doesn't. Why is it only the Americans?" Rusk replied, "Well, Mr. Chairman, you had better believe that we Americans are just damn fool enough to do it." Beschloss, *Crisis Years,* p. 631, Thomas J. Schoenbaum, *Waging Peace and War: Dean Rusk in the Truman, Kennedy and Johnson Years* (New York: Simon & Schuster, 1988), pp. 364–65.

105 Telegram to Prime Minister, No. 1767, August 7, 1963, in PRO, PREM 11/5123.

106 SK3, vol. 2, pp. 458–59.

107 Dobrynin, *In Confidence,* pp. 106–07, 111–12; Fursenko and Naftali, *"One Hell of a Gamble,"* p. 339.

108 SK3, vol. 2, pp. 463–65; SK2, p. 51; Author's interview with Oleg Troyanovsky, February 1993; Beschloss, *Crisis Years,* p. 679.

109 On KGB reporting, see Andrew and Mitrokhin, *Sword and the Shield,* pp. 225–26. On Khrushchev's suspicions, see Dobrynin, *In Confidence,* p. 111. Journalist turned abstract painter William Walton allegedly conveyed word that the Kennedys believed that the president was killed not by a single assassin but by right-wing conspirators. See Fursenko and Naftali, *"One Hell of a Gamble,"* pp. 343–53.

110 SK3, vol. 2, p. 465.

111 See Gittings, *Survey of the Sino-Soviet Dispute,* pp. 184–86.

112 Cited in Zubok, "Deng Xiaoping," p. 158. Also see M. S. Kapitsa, *Na raznykh paralleliakh: Zapiski diplomata* (Moscow: Kniga i biznes, 1996), p. 74.

113 Zubok, "Deng Xiaoping," pp. 158–59. While these pleasantries were being exchanged in one part of Moscow, Khrushchev was huddling with Harriman and

Lord Hailsham in another. Kennedy had instructed Harriman to "elicit K's view of the means of limiting or preventing Chinese nuclear development and his willingness either to take Soviet action or to accept U.S. action aimed in this direction." But Harriman's efforts to do so ran into a Soviet stone wall. Things were bad enough in the international Communist movement without word leaking out that Khrushchev was conspiring with Washington against China's nuclear program! For an account of Soviet-American contacts concerning the Chinese threat, see Craig deLaurier, "The Ultimate Enemy: Kennedy, Johnson and the Chinese Nuclear Threat, 1961–1964," (senior essay, Department of History, Yale University, April 2000).

114 See William Griffith, *The Sino-Soviet Rift* (Cambridge: MIT Press, 1964), p. 169.

115 Troyanovsky, "Making of Soviet Foreign Policy," p. 238.

116 Author's interview with Stepan V. Chervonenko.

117 Excerpts from Khrushchev's concluding speech to the plenum, December 13, 1963, in materials appended to transcript, RGANI, f. 2, op.1, ll. 52–53.

118 Suslov's speech to the plenum, "Bor'ba KPSS za splochennost' mirovogo kommunisticheskogo dvizheniia," December 14, 1963, RGANI, f. 2, op. 1.

119 Khrushchev's memorandum to Presidium, July 12, 1963, in Stroi, vol. 8, pp. 22–39.

120 Transcript of Khrushchev-Freeman conversation, ibid., pp. 44–61. Freeman politely warned that fertilizers alone wouldn't do the job, especially in the absence of expanded irrigation, a warning that was confirmed when drought struck that fall.

121 Adzhubei, *Krushenie illiuzii*, p. 279.

122 Author's interview with Leonid Yefremov. Grain import amounts, not including from the United States, mentioned in Khrushchev's speech of September 26, 1963, *Pravda*, October 2, 1963, p. 2. Also see Beschloss, *Crisis Years*, pp. 644–45; Theodore C. Sorenson, *Kennedy* (New York: Harper and Row, 1965), p. 741.

123 Stroi, vol. 8, pp. 105–24.

124 *Pravda*, September 18, 1963, p. 1.

125 *Pravda*, October 2, 1963, p. 1.

126 Stroi, vol. 8, p. 245.

127 See Tompson, *Khrushchev*, p. 264.

128 Speech to agricultural conference, February 28, 1964, *Pravda*, March 7, 1964, p. 1.

129 SK4, pp. 700–01.

130 See Tompson, "Industrial Management and Economic Reform," pp. 139–40; 151–53; 155–59.

131 SK2, pp. 18–19. Also see Alexander Yanov, *The Drama of the Soviet 1960's: A Lost Reform* (Berkeley: Institute of International Studies, University of California, 1984).

132 G. L. Smirnov, "Malen'kie sekrety bol'shogo doma," *Neizvestnaia Rossiia: XX vek*, vol. 3 (1993), pp. 378–79; SK2, p. 23. Also see Mikoian, *Tak bylo*, pp. 617–18.

133 Burlatsky, *Khrushchev*, p. 122.

134 Author's interview with Aleksandr P. Lyashko.

135 SK2, p. 48.

136 Ibid., pp. 47–48.

137 Although Moscow's relations with Cairo were uneven, and the Soviets were particularly outraged at Nasser's penchant for imprisoning and torturing Egyptian Communists, Khrushchev prided himself on his Suez crisis success and on his support for construction of the Aswan Dam. When Moscow indicated it was prepared to send "a high-ranking delegation" to the dam's dedication, Nasser got the hint. Heikal, *Sphinx and the Commissar,* pp. 122–23; SK2, pp. 56–58.

138 Heikal, *Sphinx and the Commissar,* pp. 124–32.

139 SK2, p. 59.

140 A. E. Egorin, "N. S. Khrushchev—G. A. Nasser: istoriia otnoshenii," *Obozrevatel',* no. 16 (1993), p. 100; Heikal, *Sphinx and the Commissar,* p. 135.

141 Polyansky claimed that Khrushchev ordered the medals in imperious telegrams from Cairo. Sergei Khrushchev insists that his father's Kremlin colleagues approved. See SK2, pp. 61–63; Polyansky in "Takovy, tovarishchi, fakty," pp. 117–18.

142 NK4, no. 1, 1994, pp. 75–97.

143 Heikal, *Sphinx and the Commissar,* pp. 20–22.

144 Ibid., pp. 136–37.

145 Ibid., pp. 127, 131, 137.

146 Adzhubei, *Krushenie illiuzii,* p. 287.

147 NK2, pp. 515–27.

148 Memorandums of conversations between Khrushchev and Danish interlocutors in "O vizite v Daniiu na vysshem urovne v 1964 godu," *Diplomaticheskii vestnik,* nos. 7–8 (April 1994), p. 71.

149 NK4, no. 2, 1994, pp. 77–90.

150 Shelepin and Semichastnyi, "Beseda s Shelepinym A. N. i Semichastnym, V. E.," interview by Nikolai Barsukov, p. 287. According to Mikoyan, Kirichenko wasn't any worse than Brezhnev or other possible pretenders, yet Khrushchev cast him aside after they had worked together for twenty years. Mikoian, *Tak bylo,* p. 600.

151 Memorandum of conversation between Khrushchev and Harriman, June 23, 1959, p. 17, W. Averell Harriman Collection. Also see Beschloss, *Crisis Years,* pp. 583–84.

152 Shelepin and Semichastnyi, "Beseda s Shelepinym A. N. i Semichastnym, V. E.," interview by Nikolai Barsukov, pp. 287–88. Mikoian, *Tak bylo,* p. 609.

153 SK4, p. 678. Author's interview with Pyotr Demichev. Western Kremlinologists likewise deduced that Kozlov was more conservative than Khrushchev; see Tatu, *Power in the Kremlin,* p. 207.

154 SK4, p. 680.

155 Shelepin and Semichastnyi, "Beseda s Shelepinym A. N. i Semichastnym, V. E.," interview by Nikolai Barsukov, p. 287.

156 SK2, pp. 30–32.

157 Mikoian, *Tak bylo,* p. 602.

158 Tompson, *Khrushchev,* pp. 267–68.

159 Shelest, . . . *Da ne sudimy budete,* p. 194.

160 Tompson, *Khrushchev,* pp. 52–56; photo follows, p. 114.

161 Shelest recounts a series of hints and contacts in . . . *Da ne sudimy budete,* pp. 173–93.

162 Author's interview with Vladimir Semichastny. Also see William J. Tompson, "The Fall of Nikita Khrushchev," *Soviet Studies,* vol. 43, no. 6 (1991), p. 1106.

163 Shelest recalls Khrushchev's berating Brezhnev on the phone for incompetence. See . . . *Da ne sudimy budete,* p. 186. According to Brezhnev's former aide, his boss and Podgorny didn't like Khrushchev's handling of the 1960 and 1961 summit conferences, the withdrawal of Soviet advisers from China, Khrushchev's military budget cuts, and the way the new party program was prepared, but they kept their reservations to themselves. Aleksandrov-Agentov, *Ot Kollontai do Gorbacheva,* pp. 115–30.

164 Shelepin and Semichastnyi, "Beseda s Shelepinym A. N. i Semichastnym, V. E.," interview by Nikolai Barsukov, p. 277.

165 Voronov, "Nemnogo vospominanii," pp. 198–99; Nikolai Egorychev, "Napravlen poslom," interview by Leonid Pleshakov.

166 Egorychev, "Beseda s Egorychevym N.G.," interview by Nikolai Barsukov, pp. 292–93.

167 SK2, p. 36; Valery N. Soyfer, *Lysenko and the Tragedy of Soviet Science,* trans. by Leo Gruliow and Rebecca Gruliow (New Brunswick, N. J.: Rutgers University Press, 1994), pp. 231–55.

168 Soyfer, *Lysenko,* pp. 255–80, Zhores Medvedev, *Rise and Fall of T. D. Lysenko,* pp. 197–220.

169 When Lysenko and his associates rejected genetics, they damned it with eponymic labels such as "Weismannism-Morganism," after the turn-of-the-century cell biologist August Weismann and the early Mendelian geneticist T. H. Morgan.

170 SK2, pp. 44–45. Author's interview with Sergo Mikoyan, May 2000.

171 See Polyansky in "Takovy, tovarishchi, fakty," p. 116.

172 Burlatsky, *Khrushchev,* pp. 201–02.

173 Strelyanyi, "Poslednii romantik," p. 262. It was during this inspection trip that Khrushchev came up with his last cure-all for the USSR's agricultural ills, his proposal (mentioned in Chapter 1) to create nine centralized agencies in Moscow specializing on particular crops nationwide, each agency to be responsible for guaranteeing the nation sufficient supplies of grain, meat, sunflower oil, sugar, etc. Before leaving Moscow for a Black Sea vacation, Khrushchev asked Brezhnev to circulate his memo to all members of the Central Committee. Brezhnev showed it only to fellow members of the Presidium. See Shelepin and Semichastnyi, "Beseda s Shelepinym A. N. i Semichastnym, V. E.," interview by Nikolai Barsukov, p. 279

174 Author's interview with Fyodor T. Morgun.

175 Author's interview with Andrei Shevchenko, August 1993. Other signs of Khrushchev's agitation during his last months in office: When someone dared question a proposal of his at a Presidium session, recalled a colleague, Khrushchev "lost his temper and unleashed a torrent of curses, producing a terrible impression on everyone present." Another time, at an informal Presidium luncheon to which Khrushchev invited two elderly pensioners from his Donbas days, he held forth endlessly about his life in the mines. Afterward, on the way back to the Kremlin, Brezhnev, Podgorny, and Kirilenko complained bitterly about Khrushchev's latest "caprice," saying that "the old man is falling back into his childhood." See Efremov, "Kak snimali Khrushcheva," pp. 47–48.

176 Egorychev, "Beseda s Egorychevym N. G.," interview by Nikolai Barsukov, pp. 299–300.

177 SK4, pp. 719–20.

178 Shelest, . . . *Da ne sudimy budete,* p. 219.

CHAPTER 21. AFTER THE FALL: 1964–1971

1 *Pravda,* October 17, 1964, in CDSP, vol. 16, no. 40 (October 28, 1964), p. 6.

2 SK2, pp. 168–69.

3 Ibid., p. 186.

4 Ibid., p. 187.

5 Ibid., p. 186.

6 Ibid., p. 169.

7 Ibid., p. 188.

8 Ibid., p. 190.

9 Ibid., p. 195.

10 Roy Medvedev, *Khrushchev,* p. 249.

11 Author's interview with A. G. Deshkant.

12 SK2, p. 197.

13 Mikoian, *Tak bylo,* pp. 12, 603. Author's interview with Sergo Mikoyan, May 2000.

14 According to Sergei Khrushchev, his parents were the only ones to live permanently in their dachas. Their children, who had their own apartments in the city, stayed with them from time to time, and the grandchildren often spent longer periods of time with their grandparents.

15 SK2, p. 192.

16 Sergei Khrushchev described how he learned of the eavesdropping equipment, ibid., p. 193.

17 Ibid.

18 Ibid., p. 200.

19 Ibid.

20 Ibid., p. 203.

21 Ibid., pp. 215–17.

22 Andropov's memorandum to the Central Committee, proposing to "limit" Khrushchev's "foreign correspondence," is in NK5, vol. 3, pp. 632–33.

23 SK2, pp. 206–07.

24 Ibid., p. 208.

25 Ibid., p. 220; Mikhail Kozakov, *Akterskaia kniga* (Moscow: Vagrius, 1997), pp. 187–88. Author's interview with Galina Volchek (Sovremennik Theater).

26 Author's interview with Yevgeny Yevtushenko. Home movie provided to author by Sergei Khrushchev.

27 SK2, pp. 228–29.

28 Ibid., pp. 230–31.

29 Ibid., pp. 229, 306.

30 Ibid., pp. 229–30.

31 See Robert Sam Anson, *Exile: The Unique Oblivion of Richard M. Nixon* (New York: Simon & Schuster, 1984), pp. 26–38.

32 NK3, p. 203.

33 Adzhubei, draft manuscript for *Krushenie illiuzii.*

34 Sergei Khrushchev, draft manuscript for a revised version of SK1.

35 From Nina Petrovna Khrushcheva's account, cited by Adzhubei, *Krushenie illiuzii,* p. 320.

36 SK2, p. 235.

37 Ibid., pp. 238–39.

38 Ibid., p. 240.

39 Sergei Khrushchev, draft manuscript for revised version of SK1.

40 SK2, pp. 245–48.

41 Adzhubei, *Krushenie illiuzii*, p. 320.

42 SK2, pp. 245–48.

43 The following account is based on Sergei Khrushchev, draft manuscript for revised edition of SK1, and on author's interviews with Sergei Khrushchev and Jerrold Schecter.

44 Author's interview with Sergei Khrushchev.

45 See Roy Medvedev, *Neizvestnyi Andropov: politicheskaia biografiia Iuriia Andropova* (Moscow: Prava cheloveka, 1999).

46 Although Adzhubei had been close to key anti-Khrushchev conspirators like Shelepin and Semichastny, it is unlikely that he was part of the plot itself. For a devastating portrait of Adzhubei by his brother-in-law, see SK4, pp. 706–13.

47 SK2, p. 274.

48 KGB memorandum of March 25, 1970, no. 745-A/ov (from Presidential Archive), in Volkogonov Collection, LOC, reel 16.

49 SK2, p. 300.

50 Ibid., p. 301.

51 An official transcript of the conversation was published in "'Gotov na krest, berite gvozdi i molotok': beseda s Khrushchevym na Komitete Partiinogo Kontrolia," *Istochnik*, no. 4 (1994), pp. 64–75. Sergei Khrushchev provided an account, based on what his father told him afterward, in a draft manuscript for a revised edition of SK1.

52 Khrushchev's September 13, 1970, statement, along with Pelshe's memorandum of the same date, which describes Khrushchev's behavior at the session as "insincere and incorrect," are in the Volkogonov Collection, LOC, reel 16.

53 SK2, p. 304.

54 *N. S. Khrushchev (1894–1971)*, p. 39. The reader will recall from Chapter 3 that the second thing Khrushchev told Shatrov that he regretted was having had too little education and culture.

55 P. Moshentseva, *Tainy kremlevskoi bol'nitsy* (Moscow: Kollektsia "Sovershenno sekretno," 1998), pp. 190–96.

56 Adzhubei, draft manuscript for *Krushenie illiuzii*.

57 SK2, p. 328.

58 From Khrushcheva, "Maminy Tetradi."

59 Ibid.

60 Ibid.

61 SK2, p. 331.

62 Ibid., p. 349. Author's interview with Vladimir Lakshin.

EPILOGUE

1 SK2, pp. 361–98.

2 See Ronald Grigor Suny, *The Soviet Experiment: Russia, the USSR, and the Suc-*

cessor States (New York: Oxford University Press, 1998), pp. 421–46; and George Breslauer, *Khrushchev and Brezhnev as Leaders: Building Authority in Soviet Politics* (Boston: Allen and Unwin, 1982).

3 Minutes of Politburo meeting of July 12, 1984, translated in CWIHPB, no. 4 (Fall 1994), p. 81.

4 Roi Medvedev, *Khrushchev: Politicheskaia biografiia,* p. 303.

5 Gorbachev, *Memoirs,* p. 138; *N. S. Khrushchev (1894–1971)* p. 6.

6 Gorbachev, *Memoirs,* p. 188; *N. S. Khrushchev (1894–1971)* p. 6.

7 *Pravda,* November 3, 1987, p. 3.

8 Ludmilla Alexeyeva and Paul Goldberg, *The Thaw Genration: Coming of Age in the Post-Stalin Era* (Pittsburgh: University of Pittsburgh Press), p. 4.

9 *N. S. Khrushchev (1894–1971); XX s"ezd: Materialy konferentsii.*

10 The Communist point of view is in R. Kosolapov, "Ottepel' dala rasputitsu: XX s"ezd KPSS–vzgliad cherez 40 let," *Pravda,* February 15, 1996, p. 3. The "patriotic" praise is cited in Iurii Aksiutin in an unpublished article, "Otnoshenie k XX s"ezdu KPSS i Khrushchevu." Neither Khrushchev nor Gorbachev is among Communist "heroes," but neither are Molotov, Malenkov, and Kaganovich. Among those honored by busts in the space between the Lenin Mausoleum and the Kremlin wall on Red Square are Stalin, Voroshilov, Zhdanov, Brezhnev, Andropov, and Konstantin Chernenko.

11 Author's interview with Yuri Levada.

12 Richard B. Dobson, "Young Russians' Lives and Views: Results of a May 1998 USIA Survey," Office of Research and Media Reaction, USIA, September 1998, p. 16.

BIBLIOGRAPHY

ARCHIVAL SOURCES

Amherst Center for Russian Culture, Amherst College, Amherst, Massachusetts
Archive of Labor History and Urban Affairs, Wayne State University, Detroit, Michigan, Walter P. Reuther Collection
Archiwum Akt Nowych, Polska Zjednoczona Partia Robotnicza (Archive of Modern Records, Polish United Workers' Party), Warsaw, Poland
Bodleian Library, Oxford University, U.K.
Derzhavnyi arkhiv Donetskoi oblasti (State Archive of Donetsk Province), Donetsk, Ukraine
Derzhavnyi arkhiv L'vivskoi oblasti (State Archive of L'viv Province), L'viv, Ukraine
Derzhavnyi arkhiv Sluzhby bezpeki Ukrainy (State Archive of the Security Service of Ukraine), Kyiv, Ukraine.
Dwight D. Eisenhower Library, Abilene, Kansas
    Papers of Dwight D. Eisenhower as President (Ann Whitman File)
    Ann Whitman Diary Series
    C. D. Jackson Papers
    Dwight D. Eisenhower Diary Series
Gosudarstvennyi arkhiv Rossiiskoi Federatsii (State Archive of Russian Federation)
W. Averell Harriman Collection, Washington, D.C.
John Hay Library, Brown University, Providence, Rhode Island
Library of Congress, Washington, D.C.
    Dmitri Volkogonov Collection
John F. Kennedy Library, Boston, Massachusetts
    National Security Files
    Presidential Office Files

Seeley Mudd Library, Princeton University, Princeton, New Jersey
John Foster Dulles Papers
Adlai E. Stevenson Papers
Livingston T. Merchant Papers
Minnesota Historical Society, Minneapolis, Minnesota
Hubert Horatio Humphrey Papers
Museum of Television and Radio, New York, New York
National Security Archive, Washington, D.C.
Oral History Collection, Columbia University, New York, New York
Public Record Office, Kew, London, U.K.
Foreign Office; Political Correspondence
Prime Minister's Office File
Rare Book and Manuscript Library, Columbia University, New York, New York
Rossiiskii gosudarstvennyi arkhiv noveishei istorii (Russian State Archive of Recent History), Moscow, Russia
Rossiiskii gosudarstvennyi arkhiv sotsial'no-politicheskoi istorii (Russian State Archive of Socio-Political History) Moscow, Russia
Sterling Memorial Library, Yale University, New Haven, Connecticut
Walter Lippmann Papers
Tsentral'nyi arkhiv Ministerstva oborony (Ministry of Defense Archive), Podol'sk, Russia
Tsentral'nyi derzhavnyi arkhiv hromads'kykh ob'ednan' Ukrainy (Central State Archive of Social Organizations of Ukraine), Kyív, Ukraine
Tsentral'nyi arkhiv obshchestvennykh dvizhenii Moskvy (Central Archive of Social Movements in Moscow)
United States National Archives, Washington, D.C.

PERIODICALS

American Historical Review
Argumenty i fakty
Boevaia vakhta
Brianskii rabochii
Carl Beck Papers in Russian and East European Studies
China Quarterly
Cold War History
Cold War International History Project Bulletin
Current Digest of the Soviet Press
Dialog
Diktatura truda
Diplomatic History
Diplomaticheskii vestnik
Donbass
Dossier
Druzhba narodov
East European Politics and Societies
Ekho planety

Europe-Asia Studies
European Security
Foreign Broadcast Information Service, *Daily Report: Foreign Radio Broadcasts*
Foreign Policy
Harper's Magazine
Harriman Review
Hartford Courant
Hartford Times
High Point (North Carolina) *Enterprise*
Intelligence and National Security
International Affairs
Iskusstvo kino
Istochnik
Istoricheskii arkhiv
Izvestiia
Izvestiia TsK KPSS
Japan Forum
Jerusalem Post
Journal of Cold War Studies
Journal of Communist Studies
Kentavr
Kievskie novosti
Kommunist
Komsomol'skaia pravda
Komsomol'skoe znamia
Kontinent
Krasnaia zvezda
Life
Literaturnaia gazeta
Literaturnyi kur'er
Mezdunarodnaia zhizn'
Molodaia gvardiia
Moskovskaia pravda
Moskovskie novosti
New Times
New York Times
New York Times Magazine
New Yorker
Neizvestnaia Rossiia: XX vek
Nezavisimaia gazeta
Novaia i noveishaia istoriia
Novoe russkoe slovo
Novoe vremia
Obozrevatel'
Obshchaia gazeta
Ogonek
Otechestvennaia istoriia

Politika i vremia
Pravda
Pravda Ukrainy
Problems of Communism
Psychoanalytic Review
Quarterly Journal of Military History
Raduga (Kiev)
Rossiiskaia gazeta
Russian Review
Saturday Evening Post
Sotsiologicheskoe issledovanie
Sovershenno sekretno
Sovetskaia Rossiia
Soviet Studies
SSSR: Vnutrennie protivorechiia
Svobodnaia mysl'
Teatral'naia zhizn'
Times Literary Supplement
Times (London)
Trans-action
Trud
Vecherniaia Moskva
Vechernyi Donetsk
Vestnik
Voenno-istoricheskii zhurnal
Voprosy istorii
Voprosy literatury
Vremia i my
Washington Post
Zhurnalist
Znamia
Zvezda

PUBLISHED DOCUMENTS AND PUBLISHED COLLECTIONS OF DOCUMENTS

NOTE: These are alphabetized variously by author, compiler/editor, or title, depending on the individual case.

"Aleksandr Dovzhenko: 'Ia protiven vam i chem-to opasen.'" *Istochnik*, no. 0 (1993).

The Anti-Stalin Campaign and International Communism, ed. Russian Institute of Columbia University. New York: Columbia University Press, 1956.

Back from the Brink: Cuban Missile Correspondence between John F. Kennedy and Nikita S. Khrushchev, October 22 through December 4, 1962." *Problems of Communism*, vol. 41 (Special Issue—Spring 1992).

Chang, Laurence, and Peter Kornbluh, eds. *The Cuban Missile Crisis, 1962: A National Security Archive Documents Reader.* New York: New Press, 1992.

"Chego stoiat polkovodcheskie kachestva Stalina: Neproiznesennaia rech' marshala G. K. Zhukova." *Istochnik*, no. 2 (1995).

Dallin, Alexander, ed. *Diversity in International Communism: A Documentary Record, 1961–1963*. New York: Columbia University Press, 1963.

"Delo Berii: Plenum TsK KPSS, iiul' 1953 goda—stenograficheskii otchet," *Izvestiia TsK KPSS*, no. 1 (1991).

Dobson, Richard B. "Young Russians' Lives and Views: Results of a May 1998 USIA Survey." Office of Research and Media Reaction, U.S. Information Agency, September 1998.

Documents on International Affairs, 1954, ed. Denise Folliot. London: Oxford University Press, 1957.

Documents on International Affairs, 1959, ed. Gillian King. London: Oxford University Press, 1963.

Dovzhenko, Aleksandr. *Ukraine in Flames: A Film Scenario by Aleksandr Dovzhenko*, trans. and with introduction by Abigail Marceluk. Zhaba Productions, 1997.

"Dve vstrechi N. S. Khrushcheva s predstaviteliami tvorcheskoi intelligentsii (dekabr' 1962 g. i mart 1963 g.)" *SSSR: Vnutrennie protivorechiia*, no. 6.

Foreign Relations of the United States, 1952–1954, vol. 2, pt. 1, *National Security Affairs*. Washington, D.C.: U. S. Government Printing Office, 1984.

———, *1952–1954*, vol. 8, *Eastern Europe; Soviet Union; Eastern Mediterranean.* Washington, D.C.: U. S. Government Printing Office, 1988.

———, *1955–1957*, vol. 5, *Austrian State Treaty; Summit and Foreign Ministers Meetings, 1955*. Washington, D.C.: U. S. Government Printing Office, 1988.

———, *1958–1960*, vol. 8, *The Berlin Crisis 1958–1959*. Washington, D.C.: U. S. Government Printing Office, 1993.

———, *1958–1960*, vol. 9, *Berlin Crisis, 1959–1960; Germany; Austria*. Washington, D.C.: U. S. Government Printing Office, 1993.

———, *1958–1960*, vol. 10, pt. 1, *Eastern Europe Region; Soviet Union; Cyprus*. Washington, D.C.: U. S. Government Printing Office, 1993.

———, *1961–1963*, vol. 5, *Soviet Union*. Washington, D.C.: U. S. Government Printing Office, 1998.

———, *1961–1963*, vol. 6, *Kennedy-Khrushchev Exchanges*. Washington, D.C.: U. S. Government Printing Office, 1996.

———, *1961–1963*, vol. 10, *Cuba 1961–1962*. Washington, D.C.: U. S. Government Printing Office, 1993.

———, *1961–1963*, vol. 11, *Cuban Missile Crisis and Aftermath*. Washington, D.C.: U. S. Government Printing Office, 1996.

———, *1961–1963*, vol. 14, *The Berlin Crisis 1961–1962*. Washington, D.C.: U. S. Government Printing Office, 1993.

———, *1961–1963*, vol. 15, *Berlin Crisis 1962–1963*. Washington, D.C.: U. S. Government Printing Office, 1994.

Garthoff, Raymond L. "New Evidence on the Cuban Missile Crisis: Khrushchev, Nuclear Weapons and the Cuban Missile Crisis." CWIHPB, no. 11 (Winter 1998).

Gittings, John, ed. *Survey of the Sino-Soviet Dispute: A Commentary and Extracts from Recent Polemics, 1963–1967*. London: Oxford University Press, 1968.

Gluchowski, Leszek W. "Khrushchev's Second Secret Speech." CWIHPB, no. 10 (March 1988).

"'Gotov na krest, berite gvozdi i molotok': Beseda s Khrushchevym na Komitete Partiinogo Kontrolia." *Istochnik,* no. 4 (1994).

"Kak prinimalos' reshenie o vozvedenii Berlinskoi steny." NiNI, no. 2 (March–April 1999).

"Kak reshalis' 'voprosy Vengrii': Rabochie zapisi Prezidiuma TsK KPSS, iiul'-noiabr' 1956 g." IA, nos. 2–3 (1996).

"Kak snimali N. S. Khrushcheva: Materialy plenuma TsK KPSS, oktiabr' 1964 g." IA, no. 1 (1993).

Khrushchev in New York: A Documentary Record of Nikita S. Khrushchev's Trip to New York, September 19 to October 13th, 1960. New York: Crosscurrents Press, 1960.

Khrushchev, Nikita S. *For Victory in Peaceful Competition with Capitalism.* New York: Dutton, 1960.

———. Nikita S. *Khrushchev in America: Full Texts of the Speeches Made by N. S. Khrushchev on His Tour of the United States, September 15–27, 1959.* New York: Crosscurrents Press, 1960.

———. *Mir bez oruzhiia–mir bez voin: Vystupleniia po voprosam vneshnei politiki SSSR i mezhdunarodnogo polozheniia, interviu i besedy s inostrannymy deiateliami.* Moscow: Gosudarstvennoe izdatel'stvo politicheksoi literatury, 1960. Vol. 2.

———. *O kommunisticheskom vospitanii.* Moscow: Izdaltel'stvo politicheskoi literatury, 1964.

———. *O vneshnei politike Sovetskogo Soiuza, 1960 god.* Moscow: Gosudarstvennoe izdatel'stvo politicheskoi literatury, 1960. Vol. 1.

———. *Stroitel'stvo kommunizma v SSSR i razvitie sel'skogo khoziaistva.* Moscow: Gosudarstvennoe izdatel'stvo politicheskoi literatury, 1962–1964. 8 vols.

"Khrushchev's Nuclear Promise to Beijing during the 1958 Crisis." CWIHPB, no. 6 (Winter 1995–1996).

Kramer, Mark. "Hungary and Poland, 1956: Khrushchev's CPSU CC Presidium Meeting on East European Crises, 24 October 1956." CWIHPB, no. 5 (Spring 1995).

———. "The 'Malin Notes' on the Crises in Hungary and Poland, 1956." CWIHPB, nos. 8–9 (Winter 1996–1997).

Lavrentii Beriia—1953: Stenogramma iul'skogo plenuma TsK KPSS i drugie dokumenty. Moscow: Mezhdunarodnyi fond, "Demokratiia," 1999.

"Lavrentii Beriia: 'Cherez 2-3 goda ia krepko ispravlius' . . . '." *Istochnik,* no. 4 (1994).

Lih, Lars T., Oleg V. Naumov, and Oleg V. Khlevnuik, eds. *Stalin's Letters to Molotov, 1925–1936.* New Haven: Yale University Press, 1995.

Latyshev, Anatolii. "I. V. Stalin: Ob antileninskikh oshibkakh i natsionalisticheskikh izvrashcheniiakh v kinopovesti Dovzhenko, 'Ukraina v ogne.'" *Iskusstvo kino,* no. 4 (1990).

"Mao Zedong's Handling of the Taiwan Straits Crisis of 1958: Chinese Recollections and Documents." CWIHPB, no. 6 (Winter 1995–1996).

"Massovye repressii opravdany byt' ne mogut." *Istochnik,* no. 1 (1995).

"Materialy fevral'skogo-martovskogo plenuma TsK, VKP(b) 1937 goda." VI, nos. 2 and 6 (1993); no. 1 (1994).

May, Ernest R., and Philip Zelikow, eds. *The Kennedy Tapes: Inside the White House during the Cuban Missile Crisis.* Cambridge, Mass.: Harvard University Press, 1997.

McNeal, Robert H. *Resolutions and Decisions of the Communist Party of the Soviet Union:* vol. 3, *The Stalin Years: 1929–1953.* Toronto: University of Toronto Press, 1974.

"Meropriiatiia po vyseleniiu iavlialis' chrezvychainoi meroi." *Istochnik,* no. 1 (1996).

"The Mikoyan-Castro Talks, 4–5 November 1962: The Cuban Version." CWIHPB, nos. 8–9, (Winter 1996–1997).

Molotov, Malenkov, Kaganovich, 1957: Stenogramma iiun'skogo plenuma TsK KPSS i drugie dokumenty. Moscow: Mezhdunarodnyi fond "Demokratiia," 1998.

"N. S. Khrushchev—Sharl' de Goll': vstrechi v Parizhe, 1960 g." IA, nos. 1–2 (1996).

"'Ne dopustili kritiki Stalina.'" *Istochnik,* no. 6 (1995).

"Nezakonchennoe srazhenie marshala Zhukova." IA, no. 2 (1995).

"Novocherkasskaia tragediia, 1962." IA, no. 1 (1993).

"'Novyi kurs' L.P. Berii." IA, no. 4 (1996).

"O kul'te lichnosti i ego posledstviiakh." *Istochnik,* no. 6 (2000).

"'O kul'te lichnosti i ego posledstviiakh': Doklad pervogo sekretaria TsK KPSS tov. Khrushcheva N. S. XX s"ezdu Kommunisticheskoi partii Sovetskogo Soiuza." *Izvestiia TsK KPSS,* no. 3 (1989).

"O massovykh besporiadkakh s 1957 goda. . . . " *Istochnik,* no. 6 (1995).

"O vizite v Daniiu na vysshem urovne v 1964 godu." *Diplomaticheskii vestnik,* nos. 7–8 (April 1994).

"Ob antikonstitutsionnoi praktike 30-40-kh i nachala 50-kh godov." *Istochnik,* no. 1 (1995).

"'Ob"ediniaites' vokrug Khrista': Bol'sheviki povysili tseny': otnoshenie naseleniia SSSR k povysheniiu tsen na produkty pitaniia v 1962 g." In *Neizvestnaia Rossiia: XX vek.* Moscow: Istoricheskoe nasledie, 1993. Vol. 3.

Ostermann, Christian F. ed. *Uprising in East Germany, 1953: The Cold War, the German Question, Upheaval behind the Iron Curtain.* Budapest: Central European University Press, 2001.

Pamiatnaia knizhka Kurskoi gubernii na 1892. Kursk: Tipografiia Gubernskogo Pravleniia, 1892.

Plenum Tsentral'nogo Komiteta Kommunisticheskoi Partii Sovetskogo Soiuza, 22-25 dekabria 1959 goda: Stenograficheskii otchet. Moscow: Gosudarstvennoe izdatel'stvo politicheskoi literatury, 1960.

"Posetiteli kremlevskogo kabineta I. V. Stalina (1932–1933)." IA, no. 2 (1995).

"Posetiteli kremlevskogo kabineta I. V. Stalina (1934–1935)." IA, no. 3 (1995).

"Posledniaia 'antipartiinaia' gruppa: Stenograficheskii otchet iiun'skogo plenuma (1957 g.) TsK KPSS." IA, nos. 3–6, 1993; nos. 1–2, 1994.

Public Papers of the Presidents of the United States: Dwight D. Eisenhower, 1959. Washington, D.C.: U.S. Government Printing Office, 1960.

"Russian Documents on the Cuban Missile Crisis." CWIHPB, nos. 8–9 (Winter 1996–1997).

"Russian Foreign Ministry Documents on the Cuban Missile Crisis." CWIHPB, no. 5 (Spring 1995).

Schoenhals, Michael. "Document: Mao Zedong: Speeches at the 1957 'Moscow Conference.'" *Journal of Communist Studies,* vol. 2, no. 2 (June 1986).

Selvage, Douglas. "The End of the Berlin Crisis, 1961–1962: New Evidence from the Polish and East German Archives." CWIHPB, no. 11 (Winter 1998).

Solov'ev, A. G. "Tetradi krasnogo professora." In *Neizvestnaia Rossiia: XX vek.* Moscow: Istoricheskoe nasledie, 1993. Vol. 4.

"SSSR i Pol'sha: Oktiabr' 1956-go: Postanovleniia i rabochie zapisi zasedanii Prezidiuma TsK KPSS." IA, nos. 5–6 (1996).

Stickle, D. M., ed. *The Beria Affair: The Secret Transcripts of the Meetings Signaling the End of Stalinism.* New York: Nova Science Publishers, Inc., 1992.

"Takovy, tovarishchi, fakty." *Istochnik,* no. 2 (1998).

Tvardovskii, A. "Iz rabochikh tetradei (1953–1960)." *Znamia,* no. 8 (July 1989); no. 9, (September 1989).

"'A Typical Pragmatist': The Soviet Embassy Profiles John F. Kennedy, 1960." CWIHPB, no. 4 (Fall 1994).

U.S. Department of State. *United States Department of State Bulletin.*

U.S. Congress. Senate. Committee on the Judiciary. Subcommittee to Investigate the Administration of the Internal Security Act and Other Internal Security Laws. *On the Scope of Soviet Activity in the United States: Hearing.* 84th Cong., 2d sess., June 8, 11, and 12, 1956.

Whitney, Thomas F., ed. *Khrushchev Speaks.* Ann Arbor: University of Michigan Press, 1963.

XVII s"ezd kommunisticheskoi partii (b): Stenographicheskii otchet. Moscow: Partizdat, 1934.

XVIII s"ezd vsesoiuznoi kommunisticheskoi partii (b), 10–21 marta 1939 g., stenograficheskii otchet. Moscow: Gosudarstvennoe izdatel'stvo politicheskoi literatury, 1939.

XXII s"ezd: stenograficheskii otchet. Moscow: 1961.

"Zapiski V. Malina na zasedanii Prezidiuma TsK KPSS." *Istochnik,* no. 2 (1998).

Zubok, Vladislav M. "Khrushchev's 1960 Troop Cut: New Russian Evidence." CWIHPB, nos. 8–9 (Winter 1996–1997).

———. "Khrushchev's Secret Speech on the Berlin Crisis, August 1961." CWIHPB, no. 3 (Fall 1993).

———. "Spy vs. Spy: The KGB vs. the CIA, 1960–1962." CWIHPB, no. 4 (Fall 1994).

UNPUBLISHED DOCUMENTS

"Attestatsiia za period s 21/VII/1930 po 1/IX/30 na Komissara zapasa /K-7/ Khrushcheva, Nikity Sergeevicha." Provided to the author by Ministry of Defense archivists.

"Boevaia kharakteristika na pilota 134 SBP Leitenanta Khrushcheva Leonida Nikitovicha." Document from Ministry of Defense Archive. Provided to the author by Yuri L. Khrushchev.

Coded telegram (declassified) from Foreign Minister Gromyko about his meeting with President Kennedy, October 18, 1962.

Coded telegram (declassified) from Foreign Minister Gromyko to CPSU Central Committee, October 19, 1962.

Coded telegrams (declassified) from Ambassador Dobrynin to Soviet Foreign Ministry, October 23 and October 24, 1962.

Coded telegram (declassified) from Ambassador Dobrynin to Soviet Foreign Ministry, October 27, 1962.
Coded telegram (declassified) special no. 1224-1235, Ministry of Foreign Affairs, October 30, 1962.
Coded telegram (declassified) from Zhukov to Ministry of Foreign Affairs, November 1, 1962.
Khrushchev report to Stalin dated July 26, 1944. Provided to the author by Yuri Shapoval.
"Leonid Nikitovich Khrushchev: Lichnoe delo." Document from Soviet Ministry of Defense Archive. Given to the author by Yuri L. Khrushchev.
"Spravka." Undated Soviet Defense Ministry certificate, signed "Danilov." Photocopy provided to the author by Yuri L. Khrushchev.
Transcript (undated) of meeting of Moscow party activists. Obtained by the author in Moscow.
United States. Central Intelligence Agency. "Khrushchev—A Personality Sketch." OCI, No. 2391/61. Declassified, undated copy provided to the author by the History Staff.
"Vypiska iz doneseniia nachal'niku shtaba VVS 22 armii, iskh. No. 012/so ot 16.7.41." Document from Ministry of Defense Archive. Given the author by Yuri L. Khrushchev.

MEMOIRS

Adzhubei, Aleksei. *Krushenie illiuzii.* Moscow: Interbuk, 1991.
———. *Te desiat' let.* Moscow: Sovetskaia Rossiia, 1989.
Aksenov, Vasilii. "Zima trevogi nashei ili kak marksist Nikita uchil pisatelei partiinoi pravde." *Literaturnyi kur'er,* no. 12 (1986–1987).
Aleksandrov-Agentov, Andrei M. "Brezhnev i Khrushchev." *Novoe vremia,* no. 22 (1993).
———. *Ot Kollontai do Gorbacheva.* Moscow: Mezhdunarodnye otnosheniia, 1994.
Alexeyeva, Ludmilla, and Paul Goldberg. *The Thaw Generation: Coming of Age in the Post-Stalin Era.* Pittsburgh: University of Pittsburgh Press, 1993.
Alliluyeva, Svetlana. *Only One Year.* New York: Harper & Row, 1969.
———. *Twenty Letters to a Friend,* trans. Priscilla Johnson McMillan. New York Harper & Row, 1967.
Arbatov, Georgy. *The System: An Insider's Life in Soviet Politics.* New York: Times Books, 1992.
Babenysheva, Sara. "Tsena prozreniia." *SSSR: Vnutrennie protivorechiia,* no. 2.
Bagramian, I. Kh. *Tak shli k pobede.* Moscow: Voennoe izdatel'stvo, 1977.
Bazhanov, Boris. "Pobeg iz nochi." *Kontinent,* no. 9 (1976).
Beliutin, Eli. "Khrushchev i Manezh." *Druzhba narodov,* no. 1 (1990).
Berg, Raisa. *Sukhovei: Vospominaniia genetika.* New York: Chalidze Publications, 1983.
Beria, Sergo. *Beria, My Father: Inside Stalin's Kremlin.* London: Duckworth, 2001.
Beriia, Sergo. *Moi otets—Lavrentii Beriia.* Moscow: Sovremennik, 1994.
Bissell, Richard Jr. *Reflections of a Cold Warrior: From Yalta to the Bay of Pigs.* New Haven: Yale University Press, 1996.

Bohlen, Charles. *Witness to History, 1929–1969.* New York: Norton, 1973.

Bolshakov, Georgy. "The Hot Line: The Secret Communication Channel between John Kennedy and Nikita Khrushchev." *New Times,* no. 5 (1989).

Borodin, N. M. *One Man in His Time.* London: Constable, 1955.

Bukovsky, Vladimir. *To Build a Castle: My Life as a Dissenter,* trans. Michael Scammell. New York: Viking, 1979.

Burlatsky, Fyodor. *Khrushchev: The Era of Khrushchev through the Eyes of His Advisor,* trans. Daphne Skillen. New York: Scribner, 1991.

Chuev, Feliks. *Sto sorok besed s Molotovym.* Moscow: Terra, 1991.

———. *Tak govoril Kaganovich: Ispoved' Stalinskogo apostola.* Moscow: "Otechestvo," 1992.

Chukovskaia, L. K. *Zapiski ob Anne Akhmatovoi.* Paris: YMCA Press, 1980. Vol. 2, 1952–1962.

Churchill, Winston. *The Second World War,* vol. 4, *The Hinge of Fate.* Boston: Houghton Mifflin, 1950.

Cousins, Norman. *The Improbable Triumvirate: John F. Kennedy, Pope John XXIII, Nikita Khrushchev.* New York: Norton, 1972.

de Gaulle, Charles. *The Complete War Memoirs of Charles de Gaulle.* New York: Da Capo Press, 1984.

Djilas, Milovan. *Conversations with Stalin,* trans. Michael B. Petrovich. New York: Harcourt, Brace & World, 1962.

Dobrynin, Anatolii. "Karibskii krizis: svidetel'stvo uchastnika." *Mezdunarodnaia zhizn',* no. 7 (July 1992).

Dobrynin, Anatoly. *In Confidence: Moscow's Ambassador to America's Six Cold War Presidents.* New York: Times Books, 1995.

Eden, Anthony. *Full Circle: The Memoirs of Anthony Eden.* Boston: Houghton Mifflin, 1960.

Efremov, Leonid. "Kak snimali Khrushcheva." *Dialog,* no. 7 (July 1993).

Ehrenburg, Ilya. *The War: 1941–1945,* trans. Tatiana Shebunina. Cleveland: World Publishing, 1965.

Eisenhower, Dwight D. *Waging the Peace 1956–1961.* New York: Doubleday, 1965.

Eisenhower, John S. D. *Strictly Personal.* Garden City, N.Y.: Doubleday, 1974.

Falin, V. M. *Bez skidok na obstoiatel'stva: Politicheskie vospominaniia.* Moscow: "Respublika": "Sovremennik," 1999.

Frankel, Max. *The Times of My Life and My Life with the Times.* New York: Random House, 1999.

Gaitskell, Hugh. *The Diary of Hugh Gaitskell, 1945–1956,* ed. Philip M. Williams. London: Jonathan Cape, 1983.

Gaevski, Stanislaw. "Kak Nikita Sergeyevich vstrechy v verkhakh sorval." *Kievskie novosti,* no. 1 (1993).

Gates, Daryl F. *Chief: My Life in the LAPD.* New York: Bantam, 1992.

Ginzburg, Evgenia Semenovna. *Into the Whirlwind,* trans. Paul Stevenson and Manya Harari. London: Collins, Harvill, 1967.

———. *Within the Whirlwind,* trans. Ian Boland. New York: Harcourt Brace Jovanovich, 1981.

Gorbachev, Mikhail. *Memoirs.* New York: Doubleday, 1995.

Govorushko, Nikolai A. "Pochetnyi posetitel'." *Boevaia vakhta* (February 28, 1990, and March 1, 1990).

Gribkov, Anatoli I., and William Y. Smith. *Operation Anadyr: U.S. and Soviet Generals Recount the Cuban Missile Crisis,* ed. Alfred Friendly, Jr. Chicago: edition q, inc., 1994.

Gromyko, Andrei. *Memoirs.* New York: Doubleday, 1989.

———. "Karibskii krizis: O glasnosti teper' i skrytnosti togda." *Izvestiia,* April 15, 1989.

———. *Pamiatnoe.* Moscow: Politizdat, 1988. Vol. 1.

Harvey, A. McGehee. "A 1969 Conversation with Khrushchev: The Beginning of His Fall from Power." *Life* (December 18, 1970).

Hayter, Sir William. *The Kremlin and the Embassy.* New York: Macmillan, 1966.

Heikal, Mohamed. *The Sphinx and the Commissar: The Rise and Fall of Soviet Influence in the Middle East.* New York: Harper & Row, 1978.

Hoxha, Enver. *The Artful Albanian,* ed. Jon Halliday. London: Chatto and Windus, 1986.

———. *The Khrushchevites: Memoirs.* Tirana, Albania: 8 Nenteri Publishing House, 1980.

I primknuvshii k nim Shepilov: Pravda o cheloveke, uchenom, voine, politike. Moscow: "Zvonnitsa-MG," 1998.

Iakovlev, A. *Tsel' zhizni: Zapiski aviakonstrutkora,* 4th rev. ed. Moscow: Politizdat, 1974.

Kaganovich, Lazar. *Pamiatnye zapiski.* Moscow: Vagrius, 1996.

Kapitsa, M. S. *Na raznykh paralleliakh: Zapiski diplomata.* Moscow: Kniga i biznes, 1996.

Kennedy, Robert F. *Thirteen Days: A Memoir of the Cuban Missile Crisis.* New York: Norton, 1969.

Kharlamov, M., ed. *Face to Face with America: The Story of N. S. Khrushchev's Visit to the U.S.A, September 15–27, 1959.* Moscow: 1960.

Khrushchev, Nikita S. *Khrushchev Remembers,* trans. and ed. Strobe Talbott. Boston: Little, Brown, 1970.

———. *Khrushchev Remembers: The Glasnost Tapes,* trans. and ed. Jerrold L. Schecter with Vyacheslav Luchkov. Boston: Little, Brown, 1990.

———. *Khrushchev Remembers: The Last Testament,* trans. and ed. Strobe Talbott. Boston: Little, Brown, 1974.

———. "Memuary Nikity Sergeevicha Khrushcheva." VI, nos. 2–12 (1990); nos. 1–12 (1991); nos. 1–3, 6–9, 11–12 (1992); nos. 2–10 (1993); nos. 1–8, 10–12 (1994); nos. 2–6 (1995).

———. *N. S. Khrushchev: Vospominaniia—vremia, liudi, vlast'.* Moscow: Moskovskie novosti, 1999. 4 vols.

Khrushchev, Sergei N. *Khrushchev on Khrushchev: An Inside Account of the Man and His Era,* trans. and ed. William Taubman. Boston: Little, Brown, 1990.

———. *Nikita Khrushchev and the Creation of a Superpower.* University Park: Penn State Press, 2000.

———. *Nikita S. Khrushchev: Krizisy i rakety.* Moscow: Novosti, 1994. 2 vols.

———. *Pensioner soiuznogo znacheniia.* Moscow: Novosti, 1991.

Kistiakowsky, George B. *A Scientist at the White House: The Private Diary of President Eisenhower's Special Assistant for Science and Technology.* Cambridge, Mass.: Harvard University Press, 1976.

Kolman, Arnosht. *My ne dolzhny byli tak zhit'.* New York: Chalidze Publications, 1982.

Kornienko, Georgii. *Kholodnaia voina: Svidetel'stvo ee uchastnika.* Moscow: "Mezhdunarodnye otnosheniia," 1994.

Kozakov, Mikhail. *Akterskaia kniga.* Moscow: Vagrius, 1997.

Krotkov, Iu. "Ia vypolnial prikaz Berii." In *Beriia: Konets kar'ery.* Moscow: Izdatel'stvo politicheskoi literatury, 1991.

Lakshin, Vladimir Ia. *"Novyi mir" vo vremia Khrushcheva: Dnevnik i poputnoe (1953–1964).* Moscow: Izdatel'stvo "Knizhnaia palata," 1991.

Leonov, N. C. *Likholet'e.* Moscow: "Terra," 1997.

Lippmann, Walter. *Conversations with Walter Lippmann.* Boston: Little, Brown, 1965.

Lodge, Henry Cabot. *The Storm Has Many Eyes: A Personal Narrative.* New York: Norton, 1973.

MacDuffie, Marshall. *The Red Carpet: 10,000 Miles through Russia on a Visa from Khrushchev.* New York: Norton, 1955.

Macmillan, Harold. *Pointing the Way: 1959–1961.* New York: Harper & Row, 1972.

———. *Riding the Storm, 1956–1959.* London: Macmillan, 1971.

———. *Tides of Fortune, 1945–1955.* New York: Harper & Row, 1969.

Malenkov, Andrei. *O moem ottse Georgii Malenkove.* Moscow: Tekhnekos, 1992.

Mazurov, Kirill. "Ia govoriu ne tol'ko o sebe." *Sovetskaia Rossiia,* February 18, 1989.

Mićunović, Veljko. *Moscow Diary,* trans. David Floyd. Garden City, N.Y.: Doubleday, 1980.

Mikoian, Anastas. *Tak bylo: Razmyshleniia o minuvshem.* Moscow: Vagrius, 1999.

Molotov, Vyacheslav. *Molotov Remembers: Conversations with Feliks Chuev,* ed. Albert Resis. Chicago: Ivan R. Dee, 1993.

Moshentseva, P. *Tainy kremlevskoi bol'nitsy.* Moscow: Kollektsia "Sovershenno sekretno", 1998.

Moskalenko, K. S. "Kak byl arestovan Beria." In *Beriia: Konets kar'ery.* Moscow: Izdatel'stvo politicheskoi literatury, 1991.

Moskolenko, Valentin. "Iiun' 1953." *Zhurnalist,* no. 7 (1991).

Mukhitdinov, Nuriddin. *Gody provedennye v Kremle.* Tashkent: Izdatel'stvo narodnogo naslediia imeni Abdully Kadyri, 1994.

Neizvestnyi, Ernst. "Moi dialog s Khrushchevym." *Vremia i my,* no. 4 (May 1979).

Nixon, Richard M. *Leaders.* New York: Warner Books, 1982.

———. *Six Crises.* Garden City, N.Y.: Doubleday, 1962.

O'Donnell Kenneth P., and David Powers. *"Johnny We Hardly Knew Ye": Memories of John Fitzgerald Kennedy.* Boston: Little, Brown, 1972.

Parrott, Cecil. *The Serpent and the Nightingale.* London: Faber & Faber, 1977.

Quan Yanchi. *Mao Zedong yu Xeluxiaofu* (Mao Zedong and Khrushchev). Jilin: Jilin remin chuban she. Informal English translation of the Chinese text prepared for the author.

Reston, James. *Deadline: A Memoir.* New York: Random House, 1991.

Roberts, Chalmers. *First Rough Draft: A Journalist's Journal of Our Times.* New York: Praeger, 1973.

Romm, Mikhail. *Ustnye rasskazy.* Moscow: Kinotsentr, 1991.
Rusk, Dean. *As I Saw It,* as told to Richard Rusk and ed. Daniel S. Papp. New York: Norton, 1990.
Rybin, A. T. "Riadom so Stalinym." *Sotsiologicheskoe issledovanie,* no. 3 (1988).
Sakharov, Andrei. *Memoirs,* trans. Richard Lourie. New York: Knopf, 1990.
———. "Vospominaniia" *Znamia,* no. 11 (1990).
Salinger, Pierre. *With Kennedy.* Garden City, N.Y.: Doubleday, 1966.
Salisbury, Harrison E. *Heroes of My Time.* New York: Walker, 1993.
———. *A Journey for Our Times: A Memoir.* New York: Harper & Row, 1983.
Schorr, Daniel. *Staying Tuned: A Life in Journalism.* New York: Pocket Books, 2001.
Semichastnyi, Vladimir. "Taina zakrytogo doklada." *Sovershenno sekretno,* no. 1 (1996).
Shamberg, Vladimir. "Stalin's Last Inner Circle." *Harriman Review,* vol. 10, no. 1 (Spring 1997).
Shatunovskaia, Lidiia. *Zhizn' v Kremle.* New York: Chalidze Publications, 1982.
Shelepin, Aleksandr. "Istoriia—uchitel' surovyi." *Trud,* March 14, 1991.
Shelest, P. E. . . . *Da ne sudimy budete: Dnevnikovye zapiski, vospominaniia chlena Politbiuro KPSS.* Moscow: Edition q, 1995.
Shepilov, D. T. "Vospominaniia." *VI* nos. 3–12, 1998.
Shevchenko, Arkady N. *Breaking with Moscow.* New York: Knopf, 1985.
Shostakovich, Dmitri. *Testimony: The Memoirs of Dmitri Shostakovich,* related to and ed. Solomon Volkov, trans. Antonina W. Bouis. New York: Harper & Row, 1979.
Simonov, Konstantin. "Strashnyi chelovek." In *Beriia: Konets kar'ery.* Moscow: Izdatel'stvo politicheskoi literatury, 1991.
Smirnov, G. L. "Malen'kie sekrety bol'shogo doma." In *Neizvestnaia Rossiia: XX vek.* Moscow: Istoricheskoe nasledie, 1993. Vol. 3.
Smith, Walter Bedell. *My Three Years in Moscow.* Philadelphia: Lippincott, 1950.
Solzhenitsyn, Aleksandr I. *The Gulag Archipelago 1918–1956: An Experiment in Literary Investigation, I–II,* trans. Thomas P. Whitney. New York: Harper & Row, 1973, 1974.
———. *The Gulag Archipelago.* New York: Harper & Row, 1978. Vol. 3.
———. *The Oak and the Calf: Sketches of Literary Life in the Soviet Union,* trans. Harry Willets. New York: Harper & Row, 1980.
Sorensen, Theodore C. *Kennedy.* New York: Bantam, 1966.
Sudoplatov, Pavel, with Anatoly Sudoplatov and Jerrold L. and Leona P. Schecter. *Special Tasks.* Boston: Little, Brown, 1994.
Sukhodrev, V. M. *Iazyk moi—drug moi: Ot Khrushcheva do Gorbacheva.* Moscow: AST, 1999.
Sulzberger, C. L. *The Last of the Giants.* New York: Macmillan, 1970.
Taubman, William.. *The View from Lenin Hills: Soviet Youth in Ferment.* New York: Coward-McCann, 1967.
Tendriakov, Vladimir. "Na blazhennom ostrove kommunizma," in *Svet i teni ' velikogo desiatiletiia': N.S. Khrushchev i ego vremia.* Leningrad: Lenizdat, 1989.
Toranska, Teresa. *Them: Stalin's Polish Puppets,* trans. Agnieszka Kolakowska. New York: Harper & Row, 1987.
Troianovskii, Oleg. *Cherez gody i rasstoianiia.* Moscow: Vagrius, 1997.

Vasiliev, Gennadii. "Samaia gromkaia sessiia." *Pravda,* December 6, 1990.

Vasilevskii, A. M. *Delo vsei zhizni.* Moscow: Politizdat, 1974.

Vidali, Vittorio. *Diary of the Twentieth Congress of the Communist Party of the Soviet Union,* trans. Nell Amter Cattonar and A. M.. Elliot. Westport, Conn.: Lawrence Hill and Co., 1974.

Vishnevskaya, Galina. *Galina: A Russian Story.* New York: Harcourt Brace Jovanovich, 1984.

Voronov, G. I. "Nemnogo vospominanii." *Druzhba narodov,* no. 1 (1989).

Voznesenskii, Andrei. "N. S. Khrushchev: 'V voprosakh iskusstva ia Stalinist.'" in *Nikita Sergeevich Khrushchev: Materialy k biografii.* Moscow: Izdatel'stvo politicheckoi literatury, 1989.

Walters, Vernon A. *Silent Missions.* Garden City, N.Y.: Doubleday, 1978.

Watson, Thomas J. *Father, Son and Co.: My Life at IBM and Beyond.* New York: Bantam, 1990.

Weit, Erwin. *Eyewitness: The Autobiography of Gomułka's Interpreter,* trans. Mary Schofield. London: Deutsch, 1973.

Wright, Peter. *Spycatcher: The Candid Autobiography of a Senior Intelligence Officer.* New York: Viking, 1987.

Zakharov, Nikolai. "Kak Khrushchev Ameriku pokorial." *Argumenty i fakty,* no. 52 (2000).

Zhisui, Dr. Li. *The Private Life of Chairman Mao,* trans. Tai Hung-Chao. New York: Random House, 1994.

Zhukov, Georgii K. "Ia pishu kak bylo, ia nikogo ne shchazhu." IA, no. 3 (1999).

———. "Riskovannaia operatsia." In *Beriia: Konets kar'ery.* Moscow: Izdatel'stvo politicheskoi literatury, 1991.

———. *Vospominaniia i razmyshleniia,* llth ed. Moscow: Novosti, 1992. 3 vols.

Zhukov, Georgy. *Reminiscences and Reflections.* Moscow: Progress Publishers, 1985. 2 vols.

Zhutovskii, Boris. "Gruppovoi portret v kazennom inter'iere." *Literaturnaia gazeta* (July 5, 1989).

Zub, Ivan. "Zadanie osobogo svoistva: Istoriia i sud'by." *Krasnaia zvezda,* March 19, 1988.

UNPUBLISHED MEMOIRS

Chernoutsan, Igor. Unpublished draft memoir. Provided to the author by Chernoutsan's family.

Davies, Richard T. Unpublished transcript of oral history. Provided to the author by Mr. Davies.

Khrushchev, Nikita S. Verbatim transcript of Khrushchev memoirs as delivered to the West in 1970 and preserved at the Russian Institute, and later the Oral History Collection, Columbia University.

Khrushchev, Sergei N. Draft manuscript for revised edition of SK1. Provided to the author by Mr. Khrushchev.

Khrushcheva, Nina Petrovna. "Maminy Tetradi." Unpublished diary, draft memoir, and notes handwritten for her children and grandchildren. Provided to the author by Sergei N. Khrushchev.

MacDuffie, Marshall. "Russia after Stalin." Unpublished draft memoir.

Makarevsky, Vadim. Letter to the author, November 16, 1992.

McMillan, Priscilla Johnson. "How They Took the Bad News." Unpublished draft memoir. Provided to the author by Mrs. McMillan.

Mikoian, Sergo."Diplomatiia Mikoiana." Tentative title of an unpublished draft memoir. Chapters provided to the author by Mr. Mikoyan.

Mikoyan, Sergo. "The Red Emperors: A Kremlin Insider's View." Unpublished draft family memoir. Provided to the author by Mr. Mikoyan.

AUTHOR'S INTERVIEWS

NOTE: In cases when I have interviewed a subject more than once, I list the date of the interview in the notes, except in the cases of subjects whom I interviewed multiple times in multiple places. Otherwise, dates and places of my interviews are listed only here.

Adzhubei, Aleksei. Multiple interviews (Moscow) and extended correspondence between 1989 and 1991.

Adzhubei, Rada. Multiple interviews between 1989 and 2000. Moscow.

Akalovsky, Alexander. March 1983, Washington, D.C.

Archivists, Dovzhenko Museum. May 1991, Kiev.

Archivists, Ryl'ski Museum. May 1991, Kiev.

Babyonysheva, Sara. February 1996, Boston, Amherst, Massachusetts.

Barmut, Nina. May 1991, Kiev.

Bazhan, Nina V. May 1991, Kiev.

Bowie, Robert. June 2000, Washington, D.C.

Chervonenko, Stepan V. January 1994, Moscow.

Cousins, Andrea. May 1998, Northampton, Massachusetts.

Davies, Richard T. March 1983, Washington, D.C.

Demichev, Pyotr N. August 1993, Moscow.

Deshkant, A. G. June 1991, Moscow.

Federolf-Shkodina, Ada A. June 1991, Moscow.

Feron, James and Jeanne. January 2002, Hightstown, New Jersey.

Garthoff, Raymond L. May 2000, Washington, D.C.

Glukhov, Zakhar N. August 1993, Petrovo-Marinsky, Ukraine.

Goriunov, Dmitri. June 1991, Moscow.

Govorushko, Nikolai A. August 1993, Kiev.

Gostinskaya, Vera Aleksandrovna. August 1993, Warsaw, Poland.

Kalb, Marvin. December 1992, Cambridge, Massachusetts.

Khrushchev, Sergei. Multiple interviews from 1989 to 2001, Moscow, Kalinovka, Donetsk, Providence, Amherst, Massachusetts.

Khrushchev, Yuri. June 1991 and July 1993, Moscow.

Khrushcheva, Yulia Leonidovna. Multiple interviews from 1988 to 2000, Moscow.

Klosson, Boris. May 1983, Washington, D.C.

Kobiak, Rona. June 1991, Moscow by telephone.

Kornienko, Georgy. November 1990, Moscow.

Kosenko, Olga. May 1991, July 1993, and August 1993, Donetsk.

Kostenko, Vasily. May 1991 and August 1993, Kiev.

Krasikov, Anatoly. April 2000. Washington, D.C.
Kukharchuk, Nina Ivanovna. June 1991, Kiev.
Kunitsyn, Georgy I. August 1993, Moscow.
Lakshin, Vladimir. July 1991, Moscow.
Leonov, Nikolai. August 1993, Moscow.
Levada, Yuri. April 2000, Washington, D.C.
Lezhnenko, Anatoly. August 1993, Kiev.
Lyashko, Aleksandr. July 1993, Kiev.
McMillan, Priscilla Johnson. December 1998, Cambridge, Massachusetts.
Makarevsky, Vadim. August 1993, Moscow.
Malenkov, Andrei. January 1993, Moscow.
Mikoyan, Sergo. October 1987, New York and May 2000, Washington, D.C.
Morgun, Fyodor T. April 1994, Moscow.
Naumov, Vladimir. September 1997 and March 1998, Moscow.
Ponomarev, Anatoly. July 1993. Moscow.
Roginsky, Arsenii. September 1992 and September 1993, Moscow.
Schecter, Jerrold. April 2000, Washington, D.C.
Schorr, Daniel. May 1993, Washington, D.C.
Semichastny, Vladimir. June 2000, Moscow.
Shamberg, Vladimir. April 1997, Amherst, Massachusetts.
Shevchenko, Andrei. August 1993 and October 1993 (this interview carried out for the author by Yuri Krutogorov), Moscow.
Sizykh, Liuba. May 1991, Kiev; January 1993, Moscow; July 1993, Kyiv.
Sorokina, Maria. June 1991, Moscow.
Starkov, Yu. August 1993, Moscow.
Sukhanov, D. M. June 1991, Moscow.
Thompson, Jane. March 1983, Washington, D.C.
Toumanoff, Vladimir I. November 1986 and June 2000, Washington, D.C.
Troyanovsky, Oleg. June 1991, Moscow; February 1993, Washington, D.C.; April 1993, Moscow; February 1999, by telephone.
Turovskaya, Maya. March 1995, Amherst, Massachusetts.
Volchek, Galina. January 1993, Moscow.
Volkogonov, Dmitri. December 1991, Washington, D.C.
Voronov, Gennady. June 1991, Moscow.
Voznesensky, Andrei. April 1988, Moscow.
Yakovlev, Aleksandr N. March 1998, Moscow.
Yan Mingfu. October 1997, Beijing.
Yefremov, Leonid. August 1993, Moscow. This interview carried out for the author by Valery Alekseyev.
Yegorychev, Nikolai. August 1993 and June 2000, Moscow.
Yevreinov, Viktor. June 1991, Moscow.
Yevtushenko, Yevgeny. May 1988, Peredelkino, Russia.
Zhukova, Margarita. August 1993, Moscow.
Zhutovsky, Boris. April 1988, Moscow.

OTHER INTERVIEWS

Amelko, Nikolai N. Unpublished interview by Richard Ned Lebow (Moscow, December 1991). Provided to the author by Mr. Lebow.

Benediktov, I. A. "I. A. Benediktov: O Staline i Khrushcheve." *Molodaia gvardiia*, no. 4 (1989).

Egorychev, Nikolai. "Napravlen poslom." Interview by Leonid Pleshakov. *Ogonek*, no. 6 (1989).

———. "Beseda s Egorychevym N.G." Interview by Nikolai Barsukov (September 19, 1990). In *Neizvestnaia Rossiia: XX vek.* Moscow: Istoricheskoe nasledie, 1992. Vol. 1.

Gladky, Antonina. "Khrushchev Poor Pupil." *Hartford Courant*, July 18, 1959.

———. "Manchester Woman Once Taught Khrushchev." *Hartford Times*, August 22, 1962.

———. "Nikita Khrushchev's First Teacher," *High Point* (North Carolina) *Enterprise*, February 28, 1989.

———. "Woman Becomes Citizen." *Hartford Courant*, June 15, 1963.

Grinevsky, Oleg. Unpublished interview by Richard Ned Lebow (Vienna, October 1991). Provided to the author by Mr. Lebow.

Khrushchev, Nikita S. Interview with *Le Figaro.* In *Pravda*, March 27, 1958, trans. CDSP, vol. 10, no. 13 (March 28, 1958).

———. Interview with the *Times* (London). In *Pravda*, February 16, 1958, trans. CDSP, vol. 10, no. 10 (March 28, 1958).

———. Interview with Polish correspondents (March 10, 1958). In *Pravda*, March 12, 1958, in CDSP, vol. 9, no. 10 (April 16, 1958).

———. Interview by James Reston. *New York Times*, October 10, 1957.

Mukhitdinov, Nurridin. "12 let s Khrushchevym: beseda s N. A. Mukhitdinovym." Interview in *Argumenty i fakty*, no. 44 (1989).

Semichastnyi, Vladimir. "Ia by spravilsia s liuboi rabotoi." Interview by K. Svetitskii and S. Sokolov. *Ogonek*, no. 24 (1989).

———. "Kak smeshchali Khrushcheva." Interview by V.A. Starkov. *Argumenty i fakty* (May 20–26, 1989).

———. Interview by V. A. Starkov. Unpublished full transcript of the interview later published in part as "Kak smeshchali Khrushcheva." *Argumenty i fakty* (May 20–26, 1989).

Shelepin, Aleksandr, and Vladimir Semichastnyi. "Beseda s Shelepinym A. N. i Semichastnym, V. E." Interviews by Nikolai Barsukov (March 27 and May 22, 1989). In *Neizvestnaia Rossiia: XX vek.* Moscow: Istoricheskoe nasledie, 1992. Vol. 1.

Shelest, Petr. "Brezhnevu ia tak skazal." Interview by Andrei Karaulov (June 15, 1989). *Teatral'naia zhizn'*, no. 17 (1989).

Shepilov, D. T. "'Ia byl prichasten k dokladu o kul'te lichnosti . . . ': beseda s D. T. Shepilovym." Interview by Nikolai Barsukov (February 23, 1989). *Ogonek*, no. 7, February 1996.

Zamyatin, Leonid. Unpublished interview by Richard Ned Lebow (Moscow, December 1991). Provided to the author by Mr. Lebow.

Zedong, Mao. "Anna Louise Strong: Three Interviews with Chairman Mao." Interview by Anna Louise Strong, comp. Tracy B. Strong and Helene Keyssar. *China Quarterly*, no. 103 (September 1985).

BOOKS

Adler, Alfred. *The Individual Psychology of Alfred Adler.* New York: Basic Books, 1956.

Akhtar, S. *Broken Structures: Severe Personality Distorders and Their Treatment.* Northvale, N.J.: Jason Aronson, 1992.

Alekseev, V. A. *Illiuzii i dogmy.* Moscow: Izdatel'stvo politicheskoi literatury, 1991.

Allyn, Bruce, James G. Blight, and David Welch, eds. *Back to the Brink: Proceedings of the Moscow Conference on the Cuba Missile Crisis, January 27–28, 1989.* CSIA Occasional Paper no. 9. Lanham, Md.: University Press of America, 1992.

Andrew, Christopher, and Oleg Gordievsky . *KGB: The Inside Story of Its Foreign Operations from Lenin to Gorbachev.* New York: HarperCollins, 1990.

Andrew, Christopher, and Vasili Mitrokhin, *The Sword and the Shield: The Mitrokhin Archive and the Secret History of the KGB.* New York: Basic Books, 1999.

Anson, Robert Sam. *Exile: The Unique Oblivion of Richard M. Nixon.* New York: Simon & Schuster, 1984.

Ambrose, Stephen. *Eisenhower.* New York: Simon & Schuster, 1983–1984. Vol. 1.

Antonov-Ovseenko, Anton. *The Time of Stalin: Portrait of a Tyranny.* New York: Harper & Row, 1981.

Armstrong, John A. *Ukrainian Nationalism.* 3d ed. Englewood, Colo.: Ukrainian Academic Press, 1990.

Atkinson, Dorothy. *The End of the Russian Land Commune, 1905–1930.* Stanford, Calif.: Stanford University Press, 1983.

Avtorkhanov, A. *Zagadka smerti Stalina: zagovor Beriia.* Frankfurt am Main: Posev, 1976.

Ball, Desmond. *Politics and Force Levels: The Strategic Missile Program of the Kennedy Administration.* Berkeley: University of California Press, 1980.

Baron, Samuel. *Bloody Saturday in the Soviet Union: Novocherkaask 1962.* Stanford, Calif.: Stanford University Press, 2001.

Barsukov, Nikolai. *XX s"ezd KPSS i ego istoricheskie real'nosti.* Moscow: Izdatel'stvo politicheskoi literatury, 1991.

Bell, Coral. *Survey of International Affairs, 1954.* London: Oxford University Press, 1957.

Beriia: Konets kar'ery. Moscow: Idatel'stvo politicheskoi literatury, 1991.

Beschloss, Michael. *The Crisis Years: Kennedy and Khrushchev, 1960–1963.* New York: HarperCollins, 1991.

———. *Mayday: Eisenhower, Khrushchev and the U-2 Affair.* New York: Harper & Row, 1986.

Bialer, Seweryn, ed. *Stalin and His Generals: Soviet Military Memoirs of World War II.* New York: Pegasus, 1969.

Bird, Kai *The Chairman: John J. McCloy and the Making of the American Establishment.* New York: Simon & Schuster, 1992.

Black, Ian, and Benny Morris. *Israel's Secret Wars: A History of Israel's Intelligence Services.* New York: Grove Weidenfeld, 1991.

Blake, Patricia, and Max Hayward, eds. *Half-way to the Moon: New Writing from Russia.* New York: Holt, Rinehart and Winston, 1963.

Blight, James G., Bruce J. Allyn, and David A. Welch. *Cuba on the Brink: Castro, the Missile Crisis, and the Soviet Collapse.* New York: Pantheon, 1993.

Blight, James G., and David A. Welch. *On the Brink: Americans and Soviets Reexamine the Cuban Missile Crisis,* 2d ed. New York: Noonday Press, 1990.

Bociurkiw, Bohdan R. *The Ukrainian Greek Catholic Church and the Soviet State: 1939–1950.* Edmonton: Canadian Institute of Ukrainian Studies Press, 1996.

Bonnell, Victoria E., ed. *The Russian Worker: Life and Labor under the Tsarist Regime.* Berkeley: University of California Press, 1983.

Breslauer, George. *Khrushchev and Brezhnev as Leaders: Building Authority in Soviet Politics.* Boston: Allen & Unwin, 1982.

Brugoni, Dino A. *Eyeball to Eyeball: The Inside Story of the Cuban Missile Crisis.* New York: Random House, 1991.

Brzezinski, Zbigniew. *The Soviet Bloc: Unity and Conflict.* Cambridge, Mass.: Harvard University Press, 1967.

Bundy, McGeorge. *Danger and Survival: Choices about the Bomb in the First Fifty Years.* New York: Random House, 1988.

Carynnyk, Marco, ed. and trans. *Alexander Dovzhenko: The Poet as Filmmaker.* Cambridge, Mass.: MIT Press, 1973.

Catudal, Honoré M. *Kennedy and the Berlin Wall Crisis: A Case Study in U.S. Decision Making.* Berlin: Berlin Verlag, 1980.

Chang, Gordon H. *Friends and Enemies: The United States, China and the Soviet Union, 1948–1972.* Stanford, Calif.: Stanford University Press, 1990.

Cohen, Stephen F. *Rethinking the Soviet Experience: Politics and History since 1917.* New York: Oxford University Press, 1985.

Colton, Timothy J. *Commissars, Commanders and Civilian Authority: The Structure of Soviet Military Politics.* Cambridge, Mass.: Harvard University Press, 1979.

———. *Moscow: Governing the Socialist Metropolis.* Cambridge, Mass.: Harvard University Press, 1995.

Conquest, Robert. *Courage of Genius: The Pasternak Affair.* London: Collins and Harvill Press, 1961.

———. *The Great Terror: A Reassessment.* New York: Oxford University Press, 1990.

———. *The Harvest of Sorrow: Soviet Collectivization and the Terror-Famine.* New York: Oxford University Press, 1986.

———. *Power and Policy: The Study of Soviet Dynastics.* New York: St. Martin's, 1961.

———. *Stalin: Breaker of Nations.* New York: Viking, 1991.

Craig, Campbell. *Destroying the Village: Eisenhower and Thermonuclear War.* New York: Columbia University Press, 1998.

Crankshaw, Edward. *Khrushchev: A Career.* New York: Viking, 1966.

———. *The New Cold War: Moscow v. Pekin.* Harmondsworth, U.K.: Penguin Books, 1963.

Croghan, Patrick A. A. *The Peasant from Makeyevka: Biography of Bishop Piu Neveu, A.A.* Worcester, Mass., 1982.

Davies, R. W. *The Soviet Economy in Turmoil, 1928–1930.* Cambridge, Mass.: Harvard University Press, 1989.

de Gramont, Sanche. *The Secret War: The Story of International Espionage since World War II.* New York: Putnam, 1962.

Diagnostic and Statistical Manual of Mental Disorders, 3d ed. Washington: American Psychiatric Association, 1980.

Dulles, Allen. *The Craft of Intelligence.* New York: Harper & Row, 1963.

Elias, Norbert. *The Court Society,* trans. Edmund Jephcott. New York: Pantheon, 1983.

Entsiklopedicheskii slovar' narodonaseleniia. Moscow: Bolshaia Rossiiskaia entsiklopediia, 1994.

Erickson, John. *The Road to Berlin.* Boulder, Colo.: Westview Press, 1983.

———. *The Road to Stalingrad.* New York: Harper & Row, 1975.

Erikson, Erik H. *Childhood and Society.* New York: Norton, 1963.

Ewald, William Bragg. *Eisenhower the President: Crucial Days, 1951–1960.* Englewood Cliffs, N.J.: Prentice-Hall, 1981.

Feuer, Lewis, ed. *Marx and Engels: Basic Writing on Politics and Philosophy.* Garden City, N. Y.: Anchor Books, 1959.

Filtzer, Donald. *The Khrushchev Era: De-Stalinization and the Limits of Reform in the USSR, 1953–1964.* London: Macmillan, 1993.

———. *Soviet Workers and De-Stalinization: The Consolidation of the Modern System of Soviet Production Relations, 1953–1964.* Cambridge, U.K.: Cambridge University Press, 1992.

Fitzpatrick, Sheila. *Education and Social Mobility in the Soviet Union, 1921–1934.* Cambridge, U.K.: Cambridge University Press, 1979.

———. *Everyday Stalinism: Ordinary Life in Extraordinary Times: Soviet Russia in the 1930s.* New York: Oxford University Press, 1999.

———. *The Russian Revolution.* Oxford, U.K.: Oxford University Press, 1982.

Fleishman, Lazar. *Boris Pasternak: The Poet and His Politics.* Cambridge, Mass.: Harvard University Press, 1990.

Floyd, David. *Mao against Khrushchev: A Short History of the Sino-Soviet Conflict.* New York: Praeger, 1964.

Frankland, Mark. *Khrushchev.* New York: Stein and Day, 1967.

Freedman, Lawrence. *The Evolution of Nuclear Strategy.* New York: St. Martin's, 1981.

Freud, Sigmund. *The Standard Edition of the Complete Psychological Works of Sigmund Freud,* ed. James Strachey. London: Hogarth Press, 1953–1974.

Friedgut, Theodore H. *Yuzovka and Revolution,* vol. 1, *Life and Work in Russia's Donbass, 1869–1924.* Princeton, N.J.: Princeton University Press, 1989.

———. *Yuzovka and Revolution,* vol 2: *Politics and Revolution in Russia's Donbass, 1869–1924.* Princeton, N.J.: Princeton University Press, 1994.

Fursenko, Aleksandr, and Timothy Naftali. *"One Hell of a Gamble": Khrushchev, Castro and Kennedy, 1958–1964.* New York: Norton, 1997.

Gaddis, John Lewis. *The United States and the End of the Cold War: Implications, Reconsiderations, Provocations.* New York: Oxford University Press, 1992.

———. *We Now Know: Rethinking Cold War History.* New York: Oxford University Press, 1997.

Garthoff, Raymond L. *Reflections on the Cuban Missile Crisis,* rev. ed. Washington, D.C.: Brookings Institution, 1989.

Gati, Charles. *Hungary and the Soviet Bloc.* Durham, N.C.: Duke University Press, 1986.

Gearson, John P. S. *Harold Macmillan and the Berlin Wall Crisis, 1958–1962: The Limits of Interest and Force.* New York: St. Martin's, 1998.

Getty, J. Arch, and Oleg V. Naumov. *The Road to the Terror: Stalin and the Self-Destruction of the Bolsheviks.* New Haven: Yale University Press, 1999.

Gittings, John. *Survey of the Sino-Soviet Dispute: A Commentary and Extracts from the Recent Polemics 1963–1967.* London: Oxford University Press, 1968.

Goncharenko, N. *Oktiabr' v Donbasse.* Lugansk: Luganskoe oblastnoe izdatel'stvo, 1961.

Greenstein, Fred I. *The Hidden-Hand Presidency: Eisenhower as Leader.* New York: Basic Books, 1982.

Griffith, William. *The Sino-Soviet Rift.* Cambridge, Mass.: MIT Press, 1964.

Grinevskii, Oleg. *Tysiacha i odin den' Nikity Sergeevicha.* Moscow: Vagrius, 1998.

Grose, Peter. *Gentleman Spy: The Life of Allen Dulles.* Boston: Houghton Mifflin, 1994.

Gross, Jan T. *Revolution from Abroad: The Soviet Conquest of Poland's Western Ukraine and Western Belorussia.* Princeton, N.J.: Princeton University Press, 1988.

Grossman, Vasily. *Life and Fate: A Novel,* trans. Robert Chandler. New York: Harper & Row, 1985.

Gunther, John. *Procession.* New York: Harper & Row, 1965.

Hahn, Werner G. *Postwar Soviet Politics: The Fall of Zhdanov and the Defeat of Moderation, 1946–1953.* Ithaca, N.Y.: Cornell University Press, 1982.

Hamilton, Nigel. *JFK: Restless Youth.* New York: Random House, 1992.

Heller, Mikhail, and Aleksandr Nekrich. *Utopia in Power: History of the Soviet Union from 1917 to the Present.* New York: Summit Books, 1986.

Hersh, Seymour. *The Dark Side of Camelot.* Boston: Little, Brown, 1997.

Hewett, Ed A. *Reforming the Soviet Economy: Equality vs. Efficiency.* Washington, D.C.: Brookings Institution, 1988.

Hixson, Walter. *Parting the Curtain: Propaganda, Culture and the Cold War.* New York: St. Martin's, 1996.

Holloway, David. *Stalin and the Bomb: The Soviet Union and Atomic Energy, 1939–1956.* New Haven: Yale University Press, 1994.

Horney, Karen. *Neurosis and Human Growth: The Struggle toward Self-Realization.* New York: Norton, 1950.

Jones, Ernest. *The Life and Work of Sigmund Freud.* New York: Basic Books, 1961.

Joravsky, David. *The Lysenko Affair.* Cambridge, Mass.: Harvard University Press, 1970.

Khlevniuk, O. V. *Politbiuro: Mekhanizmy politicheskoi vlasti v 1930-e gody.* Moscow: ROSPEN, 1996.

Klessmann, Christoph, and Bernd Stover. *1953 Krisenjahr des Kalten Krieges in Europa.* Cologne: Boehlau, 1999.

Knight, Amy. *Beria: Stalin's First Lieutenant.* Princeton, N.J.: Princeton University Press, 1993.

———. *Who Killed Kirov? The Kremlin's Greatest Mystery.* New York: Hill and Wang, 1999.

Kolkowicz, Roman. *The Soviet Military and the Communist Party.* Princeton, N.J.: Princeton University Press, 1967.

Kozlov, V. A. *Massovye besporiadki v SSSR pri Khrushcheve i Brezhneve (1953–nachalo 1980).* Novosibirsk: Sibirskii khronograf, 1999.

Kozlova, N. N. *Gorizonty povsednevnosti Sovetskoi epokhi: Golosa iz khora.* Moscow: Institut filosofii, 1996.

Kuromiya, Hiroaki. *Freedom and Terror in the Donbas: A Ukrainian-Russian Borderland, 1870s–1990s.* Cambridge, U.K.: Cambridge University Press, 1998.

Laqueur, Walter. *Stalin: The Glasnost Revelations.* New York: Scribner, 1990.

Lasswell, Harold. *Power and Personality.* New York: Norton, 1948.

Lebow, Richard Ned, and Janice Gross Stein. *We All Lost the Cold War.* Princeton, N.J.: Princeton University Press, 1994.

Lee, Harold. *Roswell Garst: A Biography.* Ames: Iowa State University Press, 1984.

Leonhard, Wolfgang. *The Kremlin since Stalin,* trans. Elizabeth Wiskemann and Marian Jackson. New York: Praeger, 1962.

Levinson, Daniel J. *The Seasons of a Man's Life.* New York: Knopf, 1970.

Luckyj, George S. N. *Literary Politics in the Soviet Ukraine.* Durham, N.C.: Duke University Press, 1990.

Maksudov, S. *Poteri naseleniia SSSR.* Benson, Vt.: Chalidze Publications, 1989.

Malia, Martin. *The Soviet Tragedy: A History of Socialism in Russia, 1917–1991.* New York: Free Press, 1994.

Marples, David. *Stalinism in Ukraine in the 1940's.* New York: St. Martin's, 1992.

Mawdsley, Evan. *The Russian Civil War.* Boston: Allen & Unwin, 1987.

Maynard, Sir John. *Russia in Flux.* ed. and abr. S. Haden Guest. New York: Macmillan, 1948.

McCauley, Martin, ed. *Khrushchev and Khrushchevism.* Bloomington: Indiana University Press, 1987.

McMillan, Priscilla Johnson. *Khrushchev and the Arts: The Politics of Soviet Culture, 1962–1964.* Cambridge, Mass.: MIT Press, 1965.

McWilliams, Nancy. *Psychoanalytic Diagnosis: Understanding Personality Structure in the Clinical Process.* New York: Guilford Press, 1994.

Medvedev, Roi. *Khrushchev: Politicheskaia biografia.* Benson, Vt.: Chalidze Publications, 1986.

———. *Neizvestnyi Andropov: Politicheskaia biografiia Iuriia Andropova.* Moscow: Prava cheloveka, 1999.

Medvedev, Roy. *All Stalin's Men.* Garden City, N.Y.: Anchor, 1984.

———. *Khrushchev,* trans. Brian Pearce. Garden City, N.Y.: Doubleday/Anchor, 1983.

———. *Let History Judge: The Origins and Consequences of Stalinism,* rev. and expanded ed. trans. George Shriver. New York: Columbia University Press, 1989.

Medvedev, Roy, and Zhores A. Medvedev. *Khrushchev: The Years in Power.* New York: Columbia University Press, 1976.

Medvedev, Zhores A. *The Rise and Fall of T. D. Lysenko,* trans. I. Michael Lerner. New York: Columbia University Press, 1969.

———. *Soviet Agriculture.* New York: Norton, 1987.

Miller, R. F., and F. Feher, eds. *Khrushchev and the Communist World.* London and Canberra: Croom Helm, 1984.

Mosse, George L. *Fallen Soldiers: Reshaping the Memory of the World Wars.* New York: Oxford University Press, 1990.

M. S. Khrushchov i Ukraina. Kyiv: Natsional'na Akademia Nauk Ukraini, 1995.

Nahaylo, Bohdan, and Victor Swoboda. *Soviet Disunion: A History of the Nationalities Problem in the USSR.* New York: Free Press, 1990.

Naselenie Sovetskogo Soiuza: 1921–1992. Moscow: Nauka, 1993.

Nash, Philip. *The Other Missiles of October: Eisenhower, Kennedy and the Jupiters, 1957–1963.* Chapel Hill: University of North Carolina Press, 1997.

Nikita Sergeevich Khrushchev: Materialy k biografii. Moscow: Izdatel'stvo politicheskoi literatury, 1989.

N. S. Khrushchev (1894–1971): Materialy nauchnoi konferentsii posviashchennoi 100-letiu so dnia rozhdeniia N. S. Khrushcheva. Moscow: Rossiiskii gosudarstvennyi gumanitarnyi universitet, 1994.

Oklianskii, N. *Roman s tiranom.* Moscow: Moskovskii rabochii, 1994.

Openkin, A. *Ottepel': Kak eto bylo (1953–1955 gg.).* Moscow: Izdatel'stvo Znanie, 1991.

Ottepel' 1953–1956: Stranitsy russkoi sovetskoi literatury. Moscow: Moskovskii rabochii, 1989.

Ottepel' 1957–1959: Stranitsy russkoi sovetskoi literatury. Moscow: Moskovskii rabochii, 1990.

Ottepel' 1960–1962. Moscow: Moskovskii rabochii, 1990.

Paloczi-Horvath, George. *Khrushchev: The Making of a Dictator.* Boston: Little, Brown, 1960.

Parrish, Michael. *The Lesser Terror: Soviet State Security, 1939–1953.* Westport, Conn.: Praeger, 1996.

Pedlow, Gregory W., and Donald E. Welzenbach. *The CIA and the U-2 Program, 1954–1974.* Washington, D.C.: Central Intelligence Agency, 1998.

Persico, Joseph E. *The Imperial Rockefeller: A Biography of Nelson Rockefeller.* New York: Simon & Schuster, 1982.

Pervov, Mikhail. *Raketnoe oruzhie raketnykh voisk strategicheskogo znacheniia.* Moscow: "VIOLANTA," 1999.

Pipes, Richard. *Russia under the Bolshevik Regime.* New York: Knopf, 1993.

———. *Russia under the Old Regime.* New York: Scribner, 1974.

———. *The Russian Revolution.* New York: Knopf, 1990.

Pistrak, Lazar. *The Grand Tactician: Khrushchev's Rise to Power.* New York: Praeger, 1961.

Politicheskie partii Rossii. Moscow: Izdatel'stvo Moskovskogo universiteta, 2000.

Ponomarev, A. N. *N. S. Khrushchev: Put' k liderstvy.* Moscow: Znanie, 1990.

Rabochaia biografiia: Fotoal'bom o donetskom mashinostroitel'nom zavode imeni Leninskogo komsomola Ukrainy. Kiev: Mystetsvo, 1989.

Radzinsky, Edvard. *Stalin: The First In-Depth Biography Based on Explosive New Documents from Russia's Secret Archives,* trans. H. T. Willetts. New York: Doubleday, 1996.

Ranelagh, John. *The Agency: The Rise and Decline of the CIA.* New York: Simon & Schuster, 1987.

Rasskaz o pochetnom shakhtere: N. S. Khrushchev v Donbasse. Stalino: Knizhnoe izdatel'stvo, 1961.

Reeve, F. D. *Robert Frost in Russia.* Boston: Little, Brown, 1963.

Reeves, Richard. *President Kennedy: Profile of Power.* New York: Simon & Schuster, 1993.

Richter, James G. *Khrushchev's Double Bind: International Pressures and Domestic Coalition Politics.* Baltimore: Johns Hopkins University Press, 1994.

Scammell, Michael. *Solzhenitsyn: A Biography.* New York: Norton, 1984.

Schapiro, Leonard. *The Communist Party of the Soviet Union.* New York: Random House, 1960.

Seaborg, Glenn T. *Kennedy, Khrushchev and the Test Ban.* Berkeley: University of California Press, 1981.

Shapoval, Iu. I. *L. M. Kaganovich na Ukraine.* Kiev, 1993.

———. *M. S. Khrushchov na Ukraini.* Kyiv: Tovaristvo "Znannia," 1990.

Schecter, Jerrold L., and Peter A. Deriabin. *The Spy Who Saved the World: How a Soviet Colonel Changed the Course of the Cold War.* New York: Scribner, 1992.

Schlesinger, Arthur M., Jr. *Robert Kennedy and His Times.* New York: Random House, 1978.

———. *A Thousand Days: John F. Kennedy in the White House.* Boston: Houghton Mifflin, 1965.

Schoenbaum, Thomas J. *Waging Peace and War: Dean Rusk in the Truman, Kennedy and Johnson Years.* New York: Simon & Schuster, 1988.

Siegelbaum, Lewis H. and Ronald Grigor Suny, eds. *Making Workers Soviet: Power, Class and Identity.* Ithaca, N.Y.: Cornell University Press, 1994.

Simonov, Konstantin M.. *Glazami cheloveka moego pokoleniia: razmyshleniia o I. V. Staline.* Moscow: "Kniga," 1990.

Snyder, Jack. *Myths of Empire: Domestic Politics and International Ambition.* Ithaca, N.Y.: Cornell University Press, 1991.

Soyfer, Valery N. *Lysenko and the Tragedy of Soviet Science,* trans. Leo Gruliow and Rebecca Gruliow. New Brunswick, N.J.: Rutgers University Press,1994.

Spechler, Dina. *Permitted Dissent in the USSR: Novy Mir and the Soviet Regime.* New York: Praeger, 1982.

Steel, Ronald. *Walter Lippmann and the American Century.* Boston: Little, Brown, 1980.

Stepniak, S. *The Russian Peasantry: Their Agrarian Condition, Social Life and Religion.* Westport, Conn.: Hyperion, 1977.

Stites, Richard. *Russian Popular Culture: Entertainment and Society since 1900.* Cambridge, U.K.: Cambridge University Press, 1992.

Subtelny, Orest. *Ukraine: A History,* 2d ed. Toronto: Toronto University Press, 1994.

Sullivant, Robert S. *Soviet Politics and the Ukraine.* New York: Columbia University Press, 1962.

Suny, Ronald Grigor. *The Soviet Experiment: Russia, the USSR, and the Successor States.* New York: Oxford University Press, 1998.

Svet i teni velilkogo desiatiletiia: N. S. Khrushchev i ego vremia. Leningrad: Lenizdat, 1989.

Swayze, Harold. *Political Control of Literature in the USSR, 1946–1959.* Cambridge, Mass.: Harvard University Press, 1962.

Tatu, Michel. *Power in the Kremlin: From Khrushchev to Kosygin,* trans. Helen Katel. New York: Viking, 1969.

Taubman, William. *Stalin's American Policy: From Entente to Détente to Cold War.* New York: Norton, 1982.

Taubman, William, Sergei Khrushchev, and Abbott Gleason, eds. *Nikita Khrushchev.* New Haven: Yale University Press, 2000.

Tompson, William J. *Khrushchev: A Political Life.* New York: St. Martin's, 1995.

Trachtenberg, Marc. *A Constructed Peace: The Making of the European Settlement, 1945–1963.* Princeton, N.J.: Princeton University Press, 1999.

Tucker, Robert C. *Stalin in Power.* New York: Norton, 1990.

Ulam, Adam. *Expansion and Coexistence: Soviet Foreign Policy, 1917–73.* New York: Praeger, 1974.

Underhill, Roy. *Khrushchev's Shoe and Other Ways to Captivate an Audience of 1 to 1000.* Cambridge, Mass.: Perseus, 2000.

Vaksberg, Arkady. *The Prosecutor and the Prey: Vyshinsky and the 1930s Moscow Show Trials,* trans. Jan Butler. London: Weidenfeld & Nicolson, 1990.

Vasil'eva, Larisa. *Kremlevskie zheny.* Moscow: Vagrius, 1993.

Vasilieva, Larissa. *Kremlin Wives,* trans. Cathy Porter. New York: Arcade Publishing, 1994.

Velikomu Stalinu: Narodni pisni ta dumy. Kiev, 1949.

The Village of Viriatino: An Ethnographic Study of a Russian Village from Before the Revolution to the Present, trans. and ed. Sula Benet. Garden City, N.Y.: Anchor, 1970.

Vinnichenko, V. *Tvori.* Kyiv-Viden', 1919. Vol. 9.

Volkogonov, Dmitri. *Stalin: Triumph and Tragedy.* New York: Grove Weidenfeld, 1988.

Volkogonov, Dmitrii. *Sem' vozhdei: Galereia liderov SSSR.* Moscow: Novosti, 1995. Vol. 1.

Von Hagen, Mark. *Soldiers in the Proletarian Dictatorship: The Red Army and the Soviet Socialist State, 1917–1939.* Ithaca, N.Y.: Cornell University Press, 1990.

Westad, Odd Arne, ed. *Brothers in Arms: The Rise and Fall of the Sino-Soviet Alliance, 1945–1963.* Washington, D.C.: Woodrow Wilson Center Press, 1998.

Worobec, Christine D. *Peasant Russia: Family and Community in the Post-Emancipation Period.* Princeton, N.J.: Princeton University Press, 1991.

Wyden, Peter. *Wall: The Inside Story of Divided Berlin.* New York: Simon & Schuster, 1989.

XX s"ezd: Materialy konferentsii k 40-letiiu XX s"ezda KPSS. Moscow: "Aprel'-85," 1996.

Yanov, Alexander. *The Drama of the Soviet 1960's: A Lost Reform.* Berkeley: Institute of International Studies, University of California, 1984.

Zenkovich, N. A. *Sobronie sochinenii: Tainy ushdshego veka: vlast', raspri, podopleka.* Moscow; OLMA-Press, 2000. Vol. 1.

Zubkova, Elena. *Obshchestvo i reformy: 1945–1964.* Moscow: Rossiia molodaia, 1993.

———. *Russia after the War: Hopes, Illusions and Disappointments, 1945–1957,* trans. and ed. Hugh Ragsdale. Armonk, N.Y.: M. E. Sharpe, 1998.

Zubok, Vladislav, and Constantine Pleshakov. *Inside the Kremlin's Cold War: From Stalin to Khrushchev.* Cambridge, Mass.: Harvard University Press, 1996.

ARTICLES

Adamsky, Viktor, and Yuri Smirnov. "Moscow's Biggest Bomb: The 50-Megaton Test of October 1961." CWIHPB, no. 4 (Fall 1994).

Aleksandrov, Evgenii. "Smert' tirana." *Nezavisimaia gazeta* (March 4, 1993).

Alekseev, Aleksandr. "Karibskii krizis." *Ekho planety,* no. 33 (November 12–18, 1988).

Alekseev, Valerii. "Chelovek iz teni," *Pravda,* March 18, 1993.

Aksiutin, Iurii V. "Novye dokumenty byvshego arkhiva TsK." In *XX s"ezd: Materialy konferentsii k 40-letiiu XX s"ezda KPSS.* Moscow: "Aprel'-85," 1996.

———. "Novye issledovanniia o XX s"ezde KPSS." Reprinted in NK5, vol. 2.

———. "Replika." *XX s"ezd: Materialy konferentsii k 40-letiiu XX s"ezda KPSS.* Moscow: "Aprel'-85," 1996.

Aksiutin, Yuri. "Popular Responses to Khrushchev." In *Nikita Khrushchev,* ed. William Taubman, Sergei Khrushchev, and Abbott Gleason. New Haven: Yale University Press, 2000.

Antonov-Ovseenko, A. "Put' naverkh." In *Beriia: Konets kar'ery.* Moscow: Izdatel'stvo politicheskoi literatury, 1991.

Bagraev, Iurii, and Vladislav Pavliutkin. "Novocherkassk, 1962: Tragediia na ploshchadi." *Krasnaia zvezda,* October 7, 1995.

Barsukov, Nikolai. "Oborotnaia storona 'ottepel' (Istoriko-dokumental'nyi ocherk)." *Kentavr,* no. 4 (July–August 1993).

———. "Proval 'antipartiinoi gruppy.'" *Kommunist,* no. 6 (1990).

———. "The Rise to Power." In *Nikita Khrushchev,* ed. William Taubman, Sergei Khrushchev, and Abbott Gleason. New Haven: Yale University Press, 2000.

———. "XX s"ezd v retrospektive Khrushcheva." *Otechestvennaia istoriia,* no. 4 (1996), p. 172.

———. "Zapiska Pospelova i doklad Khrushcheva." In *XX s"ezd: Materialy konferentsii k 40-letiiu XX s"ezda KPSS.* Moscow: "Aprel'-85," 1996.

Bespalov, Iurii, and Valerii Konovalov. "Novocherkassk, 1962." *Komsomol'skaia pravda,* June 2, 1989.

Burds, Jeffrey. "The Early Cold War in Soviet West Ukraine, 1944–1948." No. 1505 in *Carl Beck Papers in Russian and East European Studies.* Pittsburgh: University of Pittsburgh Press, 2001.

———. "Agentura: Soviet Informants' Networks and the Ukrainian Rebel Underground in Galicia, 1944–1948." *East European Politics and Societies,* vol. 11, no. 1 (Winter 1997).

Burr, William. "Avoiding the Slippery Slope: The Eisenhower Administration and the Berlin Crisis, November 1958–January 1959." *Diplomatic History,* vol. 18, no. 1 (Winter 1994).

Chen, Jian, and Yang Kuisong. "Chinese Politics and the Collapse of the Sino-Soviet Alliance." In *Brothers in Arms: The Rise and Fall of the Sino-Soviet Alliance, 1945–1963,* ed. Odd Arne Westad. Washington, D.C.: Woodrow Wilson Center Press, 1998.

Danilov, A. "Stalinskoe Politbiuro v poslevoennye gody." In *Politicheskie partii Rossii.* Moscow: Izdatel'stvo Moskovskogo universiteta, 2000.

Egorin, A. E. "N. S. Khrushchev—G. A. Nasser: Istoriia otnoshenii." *Obozrevatel',* no. 16 (1993).

Evangelista, Matthew. "'Why Keep Such an Army?' Khrushchev's Troop Reductions." Working Paper No. 19, Cold War International History Project, December 1997.

Fitzpatrick, Sheila. "How the Mice Buried the Cat: Scenes from the Great Purges of 1937 in the Russian Provinces." *Russian Review,* vol. 52, no. 3 (July 1993).

Fursenko, Aleksandr, and Timothy Naftali. "The Pitsunda Decision: Khrushchev and Nuclear Weapons." CWIHPB, no. 10 (March 1998).

Galbraith, John Kenneth. "The Day Khrushchev Visited the Establishment." *Harper's Magazine* (February 1971).

Garthoff, Raymond L. "Berlin 1961: The Record Corrected." *Foreign Policy*, no. 81 (Fall 1991).

———. "Khrushchev, Nuclear Weapons and the Cuban Missile Crisis." CWIHPB, no. 11 (Winter 1998).

———. "U.S. Intelligence in the Cuban Missile Crisis." *Intelligence and National Security*, vol. 13, no. 3 (Autumn 1998).

Genêt. "Letter from Paris." *New Yorker* (June 4, 1960).

Getty, J. Arch, Gabor T. Rittersporn, and Viktor N. Zemskov. "Victims of the Soviet Penal System in the Prewar Years: A First Approach on the Basis of Archival Evidence." *American Historical Review*, vol. 98, no. 4 (October 1993).

Gevorkian, Natal'ia. "Vstrechnye plany po unichtozheniiu sobstvennogo naroda." *Moskovskie novosti*, June 21, 1992.

Gibianskii, Leonid. "Soviet-Yugoslav Relations and the Hungarian Revolution of 1956." CWIHPB, no. 10 (March 1998).

Glotova, T. "Vstrechi v Mar'inke." *Vechernyi Donetsk*, July 1, 1991.

Gluchowski, Leszek W. "Khrushchev, Gomulka and the 'Polish October." CWIHPB, no. 5 (Spring 1995).

Gluchowski, Leszek W., and Edward Jan Nalepa. "The Soviet-Polish Confrontation of October 1956: The Situation in the Polish Internal Security Corps." Working Paper no. 17, Cold War International History Project, Woodrow Wilson International Center for Scholars, April 1997.

Gorbachev, Mikhail. "Vstupitel'noe slovo." *XX s"ezd: Materialy konferentsii k 40-letiiu XX s"ezda KPSS.* Moscow: "Aprel'-85," 1996.

Grinevskii, Oleg. "Berlinskii krizis 1958–1959 gg." *Zvezda*, no. 2 (1996).

Hall, R. Cargill. "The Truth about Overflights." *Quarterly Journal of Military History* (Spring 1997).

Harrison, Hope M. "Driving the Soviets Up the Wall: A Super-Ally, a Superpower, and the Building of the Berlin Wall, 1958–1961." *Cold War History*, vol. 1, no. 1 (August 2000).

———. "Ulbricht and the Concrete 'Rose': New Archival Evidence on the Dynamics of Soviet-East German Relations and the Berlin Crisis, 1958–1961." Working Paper no. 5, Cold War International History Project, Woodrow Wilson International Center for Scholars, May 1993.

Hershberg, James G. "Before the Missiles of October: Did Kennedy Plan a Military Strike against Cuba?" *Diplomatic History*, vol. 14, no. 2 (Spring 1990).

Ilizarov, Boris. "Stalin: shtrikhi k portrety na fone ego biblioteki i arkhiva." NiNI, no. 3 (2000); no. 4 (2000).

"Ispytanie Stalinshchinoi." *Vecherniaia Moskva*, April 15, 1994.

Ivanov, Sergei. "Priznanie pered smert'iu." *Novoe russkoe slovo*, April 4, 2000.

Kaple, Deborah A. "Soviet Advisers in China." In *Brothers in Arms: The Rise and Fall of the Sino-Soviet Alliance, 1945–1963*, ed. Odd Arne Westad. Washington, D.C.: Woodrow Wilson Center Press, 1998.

Kaverin, V. "Literaturnaia Moskva." *Voprosy literatury,* no. 5 (1989).

Keep, John. Review of *Stalin and the Shaping of the Soviet Union,* by Alex De Jonge. *Times Literary Supplement,* October 24, 1986.

Kemp-Welch, Tony. "Khrushchev's 'Secret Speech' and Polish Politics: The Spring of 1956." *Europe-Asia Studies,* vol. 48, no. 2 (1996).

Khariton, Iu. B., and A. A. Brish. "Iadernoe vooruzhenie." In *Sovetskaia voennaia moshch' ot Stalina do Gorbacheva,* ed. A. A. Minaev. Moscow: "Voennyi parad," 1999.

Khrushchev, Sergei N. "The Military-Industrial Complex." In *Nikita Khrushchev,* ed. William Taubman, Sergei Khrushchev, and Abbott Gleason. New Haven: Yale University Press, 2000.

Knox, William. "Close Up of Khrushchev during a Crisis." *New York Times Magazine,* November 18, 1962.

Kolesnikov, A. "Letchik, L. N. Khrushchev." *Voenno-istoricheskii zhurnal,* no. 11 (1989).

Kosolapov, R. "Ottepel' dala rasputitsu: XX s"ezd KPSS—vzgliad cherez 40 let." *Pravda,* February 15, 1996.

Koval', K. I. "Peregovory I. V. Stalina s Zhou Enlaiem v 1953 g. v Moskve, i N. S. Khrushcheva s Mao Tze Dunom v 1954 g. v Pekine." NiNI, no. 5 (1989).

Kramer, Mark. "The Early Post-Stalin Succession Struggle and Upheavals in East-Central Europe: Internal-External Linkages in Soviet Policy-Making, Parts 1–3," *Journal of Cold War Studies,* vol. 1, no.1 (Winter 1999); no. 2 (Spring 1999); no. 3 (Fall 1999).

———. "New Evidence on Soviet Decision-Making and the 1956 Polish and Hungarian Crises." CWIHPB, nos. 8–9 (Winter 1996–1997).

———. "The USSR Foreign Ministry's Appraisal of Sino-Soviet Relations on the Eve of the Split, September 1959." CWIHPB, nos. 6–7 (Winter 1995–1996).

Kuromiya, Hiroaki. "Donbas Miners in War, Revolution and Civil War." In *Making Workers Soviet: Power, Class and Identity,* ed. Lewis H. Siegelbaum and Ronald Grigor Suny. Ithaca, N.Y.: Cornell University Press, 1994.

Laba, Roman. "The Russian-Ukrainian Conflict: State, Nation, and Identity." *European Security,* vol. 4, no. 3 (August 1995).

Makovetskii, Vasilii. "Dacha Khrushcheva." *Raduga* (Kiev) (1990).

Mansourov, Aleksandr Y. "Stalin, Mao, Kim and China's Decision to Enter the Korean War, September 16–October 15, 1950: New Evidence from the Russian Archives." CWIHPB, nos. 6–7 (Winter 1995–1996).

Martin, Harold H. "Back to the Beginning of the Tumultuous Life of Nikita Khrushchev." *Saturday Evening Post* (November 7, 1964).

McWilliams, Nancy. "Mothering and Fathering Processes in the Psychoanalytic Art." *Psychoanalytic Review,* vol. 78, no. 4 (Winter 1991).

Melman, Yossi, and Dan Raviv. "The Leak of the Century." *Washington Post* (Outlook Section), March 27, 1994.

Mikhailov, G.A., and A. S. Orlov. "Tainy 'zakrytogo neba.'" IA, no. 6 (1992).

Moskalenko, Valentin. "Iiun' 1953." *Zhurnalist,* no. 7 (1991).

Naumov, Vladimir P. "Bor'ba N. S. Khrushcheva za edinolichnuiu vlast'." NiNI, no. 2 (1996),

———. "Delo Marshala G. K. Zhukova, 1957, g." NiNI, nos. 5, 6 (2000).

———. "K istorii sekretnogo doklada N. S. Khrushcheva." In *XX s"ezd: materialy konferentsii k 40-letiiu XX s"ezda KPSS.* Moscow: "Aprel'-85," 1996.

———. "Repression and Rehabilitation." In *Nikita Khrushchev,* ed. William Taubman, Sergei Khrushchev, and Abbott Gleason. New Haven: Yale University Press, 2000.

Ozerov, Lev. "Chelovek, zemlia i zvezdy." *Ogonek,* no. 43 (1987).

"Pervyi sekretar'." *Moskovskaia Pravda,* April 9, 1989.

Petrov, Nikolai. "Pervyi predsedatel' KGB General Ivan Serov." *Otechestvennaia istoriia,* no. 5 (1997).

Pikhoya, R. G. "O vnutripoliticheskoi bor'be v sovetskom rukovodstve, 1945–1948." NiNI, no. 6 (noiabr'–dekabr' 1995).

"Pogib? Propal bes vesti? Zhiv?" *Voenno-istoricheskii zhurnal,* no. 4 (1990).

Ponomarev, A. N. "Intrigi i repressii—po pravilam igry." *Rossiiskaia gazeta,* July 29, 1995.

———. "Khrushchev: Nachalo kar'ery." in *Neizvestnaia Rossiia: XX vek.* Moscow: Istoricheskoe nasledie, 1993. Vol. 3

Poptonev, Stefan. "Khrushchov krai General Tosheva. . . . " *Dossier,* April 1991.

"Poslednii Stalinskii rasstrel." *Vecherniaia Moskva,* September 26, 1994.

Rabinovich, Abraham. "The Man Who Touched History." *Jerusalem Post* (International Edition), December 9, 1995.

Rigby, T. H. "Khrushchev and the Rules of the Games." In *Khrushchev and the Communist World,* ed. R. F. Miller and Feher. London and Canberra: Croom Helm, 1984.

Selvage, Douglas. "New Evidence on the Berlin Crisis, 1958–1962." CWIHPB, no. 11 (Winter 1998).

Shapoval, Iurii. "Khrushchev i Zapadnaia Ukraina." *Svobodnaia mysl',* no. 6, 1996.

Shapoval, Yuri. "The Ukrainian Years." In *Nikita Khrushchev,* ed. William Taubman, Sergei Khrushchev, and Abbott Gleason. New Haven: Yale University Press, 2000.

Shundik, N. "Chudo, kotorogo ne bylo." *Trud,* December 18, 1988.

Slavinsky, Boris N. "The Soviet Occupation of the Kurile Islands and the Plans for the Capture of Northern Hokkaido." *Japan Forum,* vol. 5, no. 1, April 1993.

Smith, G. A. E. "Agriculture." In *Khrushchev and Khrushchevism,* ed. Martin McCauley. Bloomington: Indiana University Press, 1987.

Starkov, Boris. "Sto dnei Liubianskogo marshala." *Istochnik,* no. 4 (1993).

Strelianyi, Anatolii. "Khrushchev and the Countryside." In *Nikita Khrushchev,* ed. William Taubman, Sergei Khrushchev, and Abbott Gleason. New Haven: Yale University Press, 2000.

———. "Poslednii romantik." In *Svet i teni velilkogo desiatiletiia: N. S. Khrushchev i ego vremia.* Leningrad: Lenizdat, 1989.

"Syn N. S. Khrushcheva pogib na Brianshchine." *Brianskii rabochii,* January 20, 1995.

Tompson, William J. "The Fall of Nikita Khrushchev." *Soviet Studies,* vol. 43, no. 6 (1991).

———. "Industrial Management and Economic Reform under Khrushchev." In *Nikita Khrushchev,* ed. William Taubman, Sergei Khrushchev, and Abbott Gleason. New Haven: Yale University Press, 2000.

Troyanovsky, Oleg. "The Caribbean Crisis: A View from the Kremlin." *International Affairs* (April–May 1992).

———. "The Making of Soviet Foreign Policy." In *Nikita Khrushchev,* ed. William Taubman, Sergei Khrushchev, and Abbott Gleason. New Haven: Yale University Press, 2000.

Udilov, Vadim. "Za chto Khrushchev otomstil Stalinu." *Nezavisimaia gazeta,* February 17, 1998.

"Utverdit' dokladchikom tovarishcha Khrushcheva." *Moskovskie novosti,* no. 5 (4–11 February 1996).

"Vasilii Stalin za ottsa otvechat' ne khotel." *Obshchaia gazeta,* February 15–21, 1996.

Volkovinskii, V. "Iona Yakir." *Politika i vremia,* no. 5 (1991).

"Vot gde pravda, Nikita Sergeevich!" *Voenno-istoricheskii zhurnal,* no. 12 (1989); no. 1 (1990); no. 2 (1990).

"Vtoroi i vazhneishii etap." *Otechestvennaia istoriia,* no. 1 (1994).

Wedge, Bryant. "Khrushchev at a Distance: A Study of Public Personality." *Transaction* (October 1968).

Wolff, David. "In Memorium: Deng Xiaoping and the Cold War." CWIHPB, no. 10 (March 1998).

———. "One Finger's Worth of Historical Events: New Russian and Chinese Evidence on the Sino-Soviet Alliance and Split, 1948–1959," Working Paper no. 30, Cold War International History Project, Woodrow Wilson International Center for Scholars, August 2000.

Zhirnov, Evgenii. "Sovetskii prints." *Komsomol'skaia pravda,* November 25, December 2, December 9, 1994.

Zhukov, Iurii N. "Bor'ba za vlast' v partiino-gosudarstvennykh verkhakh SSSR vesnoi 1953 goda." VI, nos. 5–6 (1996).

———. "Bor'ba za vlast' v rukovodstve SSSR v 1945–1952 godakh." VI, no. 1 (1995).

Zlobin, N. S. "Khoroshikh diktatur ne byvaet." In *XX s"ezd: materialy konferentsii k 40-letiiu XX s"ezda KPSS.* Moscow: "Aprel'-85," 1996.

Zubkova, Yelena. "Malenkov i Khrushchev: Lichnyi faktor v politike poslestalinskogo rukovodstva." *Otechestvennaia istoriia,* no. 4 (1995).

———. "The Rivalry with Malenkov." In *Nikita Khrushchev,* ed. William Taubman, Sergei Khrushchev, and Abbott Gleason. New Haven: Yale University Press, 2000.

Zubok, Vladislav. "Deng Xiaoping and the Sino-Soviet Split, 1956–1963." CWIHPB, no. 10 (March 1998).

UNPUBLISHED MANUSCRIPTS AND ARTICLES

Aksiutin, Iurii. "Otnoshenie k XX s"ezdu KPSS i Khrushchevu."

———. "Ukrainskii sinodik Nikity Khrushcheva."

Barsukov, Nikolai A. "Analiticheskaia zapiska: pozitsiia poslestalinskogo rukovodstva v otnoshenii politicheskikh repressii 30-x—40-x i nachala 50-x godov."

———. "Kommunisticheskie illiuzii Khrushcheva: o razrabotke tret'ei programmy partii."

———. "Personal'noe delo 'anti-partiinoi gruppy.' "
———. "Mysli vslukh: zamechaniia N.S. Khrushcheva na proekt tret'ei programmy KPSS."
deLaurier, Craig. "The Ultimate Enemy: Kennedy, Johnson and the Chinese Nuclear Threat, 1961–1964." Senior essay, Department of History, Yale University, April 2000.
Goldstein, Steven M. "The Sino-Soviet Alliance, 1937–1962: Ideology and Unity."
Harrison, Hope M. "Soviet Policy toward Germany: March–August 1953."
Johnson, Priscilla. "How They Took the Bad News."
Tompson, William J. "Nikita Khrushchev and the Territorial Apparatus, 1953–1964." Ph.D. dissertation, University of Oxford, 1991.
Zubok, Vladislav. "Sovetsko-kitaiskie peregovory na vysshem urovne 31 iiulia–3 avgusta 1958 g. i oktiabria 1959 goda."

UNPUBLISHED PROCEEDINGS OF CONFERENCES

Barsukov, Nikolai. "The Reverse Side of the Thaw." Moscow: "New Evidence on Cold War History," January 1993.
Burr, William. "Eisenhower and the Diplomacy of the Berlin Crisis, 1958–1960." Washington, D.C.: Cold War International History Project/Nuclear History Project, Conference on the Berlin Crisis, 1993.
Chen, Jian. "Beijing and the Hungarian Crisis of 1956." Budapest: "Hungary and the World, 1956: The New Archival Evidence," September 26–29, 1996.
Cuba between the Superpowers. Transcript of meetings on Antigua, January 3–7, 1991, ed. James G. Blight, David Lewis, and David Welch, 1991.
Gearson, John P. S. "Macmillan and Berlin, 1958–1961." Washington, D.C.: Nuclear History Project, Berlin Study Conference, May 1993.
Gluchowski, Leszek W. "The Struggle Against 'Great-Power Chauvinism': CPSU-PUWP Relations and the Roots of the Sino-Polish Initiative of September–October 1956." Hong Kong: "New Evidence on the Cold War in Asia," January 1996.
Gobarev, Viktor. "Khrushchev i voennye: Istoriko-psikhologicheskii analiz." Paper prepared for delivery. Providence, R.I.: Brown University, Khrushchev Centennial Conference, December 1994.
Griffith, William E. "RFE and the Hungarian Revolution and the Polish October." Budapest: "Hungary and the World, 1956: The New Archival Evidence," September 26–29, 1996.
Heinze, Paul B. "Recollections of Radio Free Europe." Budapest: "Hungary and the World, 1956: The New Archival Evidence," September 26–29, 1996.
Ostermann, Christian F. "East Germany and the Hungarian Revolution." Budapest: "Hungary and the World, 1956," September 26–29, 1996.
Prozumenshchikov, M. Iu., and I. N. Shevchuk. "Soviet-Chinese Relations." Moscow: "New Evidence on Cold War History," January 1993.
Shapoval, Iurii. "Khrushchev i Ukraina: Vliianie ukrainskogo opyta na ego deiatel'nost' v 50-60-e gody." Paper prepared for delivery. Providence, R.I.: Brown University, Khrushchev Centennial Conference, December 1994.

———. "N. S. Khrushchev: Nachalo biografii, kar'ery, gody raboty v Ukraine (1894–1949). Providence, R.I.: Khrushchev Centennial Conference, December 1994.

Troyanovsky, Oleg. "Nikita Khrushchev and the Making of Soviet Foreign Policy." Paper prepared for delivery. Providence, R.I.: Brown University, Khrushchev Centennial Conference, December 1994.

Zubok, Vladislav. "Unacceptably Rude and Blatant on the German Question." Potsdam: "The Crisis Year 1953 and the Cold War in Europe," November 10–12, 1996.

GLOSSARY

Central Committee: The body within the Communist party that, in theory, directed the party between party congresses. The term also referred to the committee's extensive apparatus, which oversaw the work of government agencies and enterprises and social organizations throughout the USSR.

Congress: The national party congress, supposed to be held at regular intervals but not necessarily convened on schedule, was theoretically the ultimate authority within the Communist party. In fact, real power initially devolved to the Central Committee in the years after 1917 and then to the Politburo.

Council of Ministers: The directing agency of the Soviet government, in effect, its cabinet, consisting of the heads of its leading ministries.

Council of People's Commissars: Predecessor to the Council of Ministers, consisting of the heads of its leading People's Commissariats.

Collective farm: Theoretically an agricultural cooperative—i.e., a voluntary union of free peasants—but actually a regimented, state-controlled entity into which peasants were forcibly herded.

Dacha: Summer and holiday residence outside a city.

KGB: Abbreviation of Komitet Gosudarstvennoi bezopasnosti, or Committee of State Security, the official name for the Soviet security police in the years after 1953.

Kolkhoz: Collective farm (see above).

Komsomol: Abbreviation of Kommunisticheskii Soiuz Molodezhi, or Young Communist League (officially: All-Union Leninist Communist League of Youth).

KPSS: Abbreviation of Kommunisticheskaia Partiia Sovetskogo Soiuza, Communist party of the Soviet Union. Equivalent in English is CPSU.

Kulak: Well-off peasant.

Local party committee: The main party body at local levels, such as district, city, and province, headed by the local party secretary.

MVD: Abbreviation for Ministerstvo Vnutrennikh Del, Ministry of Internal Affairs.

NKVD: Abbreviation for Narodnyi Kommissariat Vnutrennikh Del, People's Commissariat of Internal Affairs, name of the Soviet security police from 1934 to 1946.

Politburo: The Political Bureau of the Central Committee of the Communist party, the party's main policy-making body, theoretically only between sessions of the Central Committee, but actually in general.

Presidium: Term by which the Politburo was known from 1952 to 1966. Note, however, that the Council of Ministers also had its own Presidium, whose membership partly overlapped with the party Presidium.

Secretariat: Administrative organ of the Central Committee, headed by Central Committee secretaries charged with supervising main areas of Soviet life. Membership largely overlapped with that of the Politburo.

Soviet: Literally "council," the basic governmental entity of the Soviet system.

Supreme Soviet: The highest legislative organ of government in the USSR, nominally the Soviet Parliament.

ACKNOWLEDGMENTS

A LONG BOOK, written over the course of many years, requires much assistance. Members of Nikita Khrushchev's family have aided me immeasurably: his children Sergei Khrushchev and Rada Adzhubei; his grandchildren, Yulia Leonidovna Khrushcheva, Yuri Khrushchev, and Nikita Khrushchev, Jr.; his great-granddaughter, Nina Khrushcheva; and his daughter-in-law, Liuba Sizykh.

Others in the former Soviet Union helped me gain access to archives and interviews and interpret what I learned from those sources. They include Yuri Aksiutin, Nikolai Barsukov, Aleksandr Chubarian, Sofia Gitis, Viktor Gobarev, Mikhail Narinsky, Vladimir Naumov, Yuri Shapoval, Oleg Troyanovsky, and Yelena Zubkova. For putting me up and making me feel at home while I worked in Moscow, I am grateful to old friends Yuri Krutogorov and Inna Babyonysheva and Viktor, Lena, and Olga Yakubovich.

Among psychologists and psychiatrists on whom I have tried out ideas about Khrushchev's character are Amy Demorest, my colleague in Amherst's Psychology Department, with whom I co-teach a colloquium on Personality and Politics, and Nancy McWilliams, who guest-lectured in our seminar, as well as Jerrold M. Post, Eugene Goldwater, Andrew Looker, Tamsin Looker, and Yuri Freidin. In addition, two political scientists who have written about the role of personality in politics, Alexander George and Fred I. Greenstein, were particularly helpful when I was beginning this project.

Those to whom I turned for insight on Soviet, Eastern European, Chinese, and American history include Aleksandr Babyonyshev, Jeffrey Burds,

William Burr, Chen Jian, John Lewis Gaddis, Abbott Gleason, Leszek Gluchowski, Steven M. Goldstein, Hope M. Harrison, Mark Kramer, Lan Hua, Christian Ostermann, Peter Reddaway, Constantine Pleshakov, Mikhail Nikolayev and Vladislav Zubok. Special thanks to Burds, Kramer, Gluchkowski, Goldstein, Harrison, and Zubok for providing me with documents obtained from Communist archives.

Yuri Aksiutin helped me with research in Russia, as did Yuri Shapoval in Ukraine, Dan Somogyi in Great Britain, and Irina Porokhova, Viktoria Ivleva, Svetlana Novikova, Ilya Somin, Olga Ryzhkova, Mark Richman, and Constantine Rusanov in the United States. Tatyana Babyonysheva did the painstaking, yeoman work of transcribing Russian-language interviews, Tatyana Chebotareva deciphered a complicated Russian text written in nearly illegible handwriting, and Chih-Ping Chen translated excerpts from Chinese memoirs. Maria Sharikova helped check the verbatim text of Khrushchev's memoirs, Stacy Kitsis helped prepare the manuscript, and Sam Charap, in addition to providing invaluable research assistance, created the Bibliography. Thanks also to Leona P. Schecter, who was my literary agent.

My obligation to institutions is also far-reaching. Archives where I have worked and to which I am grateful are listed in the Bibliography. Of archive directors and their deputies, I should single out Natalia Tomilina, Kirill Anderson, Sergei Mironenko, Ruslan Pyrih, Igor Lebedev, Oleg Naumov, and Vitaly Afiani. In addition, I appreciate the help I received from the Cold War International History Project (especially its directors, James G. Hershberg, David Wolff, and Christian Ostermann) at the Woodrow Wilson Center for Scholars, the Davis Center for Russian Studies at Harvard University, the National Security Archive in Washington, the Watson Institute for International Studies at Brown University, and the Institute on General History of the Russian Academy of Sciences in Moscow.

Along the way I have received financial support for which I am indebted: a Rockefeller Humanities Fellowship, a Kennan Institute for Advanced Russian Studies Visiting Grant, a National Council for Soviet and East European Research Contract, a Karl Loewenstein Fellowship from Amherst College, a Senior Fellowship at the Harriman Institute at Columbia University, a Fulbright-Hays Faculty Research Fellowship, a place on the ACLS-Soviet Academy of Sciences Exchange Program administered by the International Research and Exchanges Board, a National Humanities Endowment Fellowship, and a Woodrow Wilson International Center for Scholars Fellowship. In addition, Amherst College has generously supported me and my work with two Faculty Research Awards and several small grants. At Amherst I particularly appreciate the steadfast support of Presidents Peter Pouncey and Tom Gerety and Dean of the Faculty Lisa Raskin.

I am especially grateful to friends who read and commented on my manuscript. Robert Bowie, Peter Czap, Jr., N. Gordon Levin, Jr., Thomas Looker, Nancy McWilliams, Sergo Mikoyan, Vera Shevzov, Kathleen E. Smith, Vladimir Toumanoff, and Vladislav Zubok read parts of it. Those who braved the whole text are Amy Demorest, John Lewis Gaddis, Abbott Gleason, Marina Goldovskaya, Sergei Khrushchev, Constantine Pleshakov, Stephen S. Rosenfeld, Strobe Talbott, Lori Williams, my stepmother, and Milton Williams. I particularly thank my patient, supportive editor at W. W. Norton, James Mairs, and his assistant, Catherine Osborne.

My greatest gratitude, as always, is to my wife, Jane, for supporting and sustaining me both before and especially after she gave an early draft of this book a particularly clear-eyed, critical reading. Thanks also to my children, Alex and Phoebe, and to my brother Phil and his family, for their steady moral support.

INDEX